COUNSELING CHILDREN AND ADOLESCENTS

Victoria E. Kress
Youngstown State University

Matthew J. Paylo
Youngstown State University

Nicole A. Stargell
The University of North Carolina at Pembroke

 Pearson

330 Hudson Street, NY, NY 10013

Director and Publisher: Kevin M. Davis
Portfolio Manager: Rebecca Fox-Gieg
Content Producer: Pamela D. Bennett
Portfolio Management Assistant: Casey Coriell
Executive Field Marketing Manager: Krista Clark
Executive Product Marketing Manager: Christopher Barry
Media Project Manager: Lauren Carlson
Procurement Specialist: Deidra Smith
Cover Designer: Melissa Welch, Studio Montage
Cover Photo: Carlos Sanchez Pereyra/Getty Images
Full-Service Project Management: Sudip Sinha, iEnergizer Aptara®, Ltd.
Composition: iEnergizer Aptara®, Ltd.
Printer/Binder: LSC Communications
Cover Printer: LSC Communications
Text Font: TimesLTPro

Library of Congress Cataloging-in-Publication Data
Names: Kress, Victoria E., author. | Paylo, Matthew J., author. | Stargell,
   Nicole A., author.
Title: Counseling children and adolescents / Victoria E. Kress, Youngstown
   State University, Matthew J. Paylo, Youngstown State University, Nicole A.
   Stargell, The University of North Carolina at Pembroke.
Description: First edition. | Boston : Pearson, [2019] | Includes
   bibliographical references and index.
Identifiers: LCCN 2017042454| ISBN 9780134745138 | ISBN 0134745132
Subjects: LCSH: Children—Counseling of. | Teenagers—Counseling of. |
   Counseling psychology.
Classification: LCC BF636.6 .K74 2019 | DDC 158.3083—dc23 LC record available
at https://lccn.loc.gov/2017042454

77 2024

ISBN 10:   0-13-474513-2
ISBN 13: 978-0-13-474513-8

To my children, Isaac and Ava. Daily, you inspire in me unconditional love and gratitude. I'm so glad that of all the people in this world I got you two!

And to the kiddos who were the backdrop of this text: Rachel, Gracie, Becky, Hayden, Hope, and Max. Thank you for enriching my life.

And finally, to all of my young clients who have taught me more about counseling than any book ever could. Thank you!   ~VEK

To my five wonderful children, without whom this book would have been done sooner; yet, I would have lacked a real understanding of childhood development that only experience teaches!   ~MJP

To the strong women in my life—my role models, my teachers, my advocates. Mom, you tirelessly love me, and I love you! Margaret and Lori, I cherish your friendship and mentorship. Victoria Kress, there is no way to measure the effect you have had on my life. You are my friend, my mentor, my open door, and my inspiration. Thank you for this opportunity.

To my husband, Keith. You make me a better person.

To all the people who have dedicated their life's work to helping others. This is a tough, rewarding job, and I thank you for your compassion and desire to make the future brighter.   ~NAS

PREFACE

When we were students in graduate school, we did not learn much about counseling youth and their families per se. Our education focused primarily on counseling adults; it was assumed that most of our clients would, in fact, be adults. Many counseling textbook writers gear their books' content toward work with adults. As such, we were excited to construct a textbook—the textbook we wish we had in graduate school—to place a spotlight on counseling young people.

In graduate school, we were presented with and absorbed a great deal of foundational counseling information, such as various counseling theories and basic techniques for use with clients. However, when faced with our first counseling sessions, we struggled with how to proceed. When most counselors start out, they feel flooded with information that they need to digest and determine how to apply. New counselors are challenged to apply academic information, to conceptualize their clients, and to determine how to proceed in helping them to make the changes they desire; however, applying this information and moving forward as a counselor is no easy task. Our aim in writing this text was to develop a practical resource that would help counselors to feel empowered to thoughtfully and deliberately assist their clients in tackling their complex issues and difficulties.

Counselors have a strength-based, humanistic orientation; they believe in the power of their clients' strengths, and they aim to empower their clients. Of fundamental importance to us in developing this text was our desire to create a book that highlighted our value of such an approach. Our conceptual framework (i.e., the I CAN START model) involves a way of thinking about clients' concerns that is strength-based and contextually sensitive. This conceptual model is detailed in Chapter 9 and is applied to each case study in subsequent chapters.

Our clients deserve the most effective treatments available. We have seen too many circumstances where well-meaning counselors have neglected and sometimes even harmed their young clients. This text provides readers with information on evidence-based approaches that can be used to address numerous issues young people navigate. There is a paucity of research on addressing some problems in living described in this text. In these situations, we have made every attempt to provide the reader with the most comprehensive, rigorous assimilation of the current literature, along with a summary of any important emerging approaches or counseling considerations.

There are multiple interventions that are associated with the counseling theories and approaches discussed in this text. There are also hundreds of ways these interventions can be applied, illustrated, and woven into the fabric of counseling. We frequently hear our students and supervisees comment that they want to better understand what it "looks like" to apply various theories and/or interventions. Students often say to us, "But how do you *do* or apply this intervention?" To illustrate the varied ways counseling methods can be applied, each chapter includes examples of creative applications of counseling interventions. These creative interventions are intended to illustrate the vehicles that can be used to apply interventions (e.g., art, play, movement).

Throughout the text readers will find boldfaced words. These words highlight concepts that are important and that readers should take note of. Various features are also included in the text. At least two creative toolbox features are included in most chapters (Chapters 5–19); these features are clinical activities that have a creative flavor. The creative toolbox activities are intended to highlight applied, creative ways that counselors can engage young people. Various clinical toolbox activities are also included, which etext readers can access. The clinical toolbox activities include various clinically focused, practical resources such as clinical interventions, worksheets, and additional information counselors can use to inform their counseling practice.

ORGANIZATION OF THE TEXT

This book is organized in three parts: Part 1: Developmental and Systematic Foundations of Youth Counseling (Chapters 1–2); Part 2: Foundations of Youth Counseling: Theory and Practice (Chapters 3–9); and Part 3: Common Presenting Concerns and Counseling Interventions (Chapters 10–19).

Chapter 1 introduces human development and the developmental foundations of youth counseling. We assume that our readers have some basic knowledge of human development, or that they will at some point in their training complete a human development course. Therefore, only basic human development information that is relevant in the context of counseling youth is provided. In addition, youth development and individual risk and protective factors are discussed in Chapter 1.

Chapter 2 addresses the contextual and systemic risk and protective factors that affect youth. More specifically, family, school, and community risk and protective factors are presented so counselors can account for these when counseling youth. The chapter highlights the importance of considering youth's holistic context in relation to their mental health.

Chapter 3, we delve into the structure of youth counseling, and we discuss the basic foundations central to all youth counseling. The chapter begins with a discussion of the qualities, characteristics, and behaviors that effective counselors possess. Then, it discusses the preliminary—or initial—counseling tasks that lay the foundation for individual counseling with young clients. Next, the chapter discusses the working and termination stages of youth counseling. Emphasis is placed on practical matters associated with youth counseling.

Ethics should always be counselors' top priority. Above all, counselors should do no harm. When counseling youth, ethical matters are especially complicated because parents/caregivers and other children are often involved in counselors' decision making. Chapter 4 focuses on the common ethics-related struggles youth counselors traverse, along with practical suggestions for how counselors can make ethical decisions.

In Chapters 5, 6, and 7, we address common theories that are useful in youth counseling. The theories selected are the ones most commonly discussed in the popular and research literature (e.g., cognitive behavioral theory, person-centered, therapy, reality therapy), as well as those evidenced to have the greatest clinical use with youth. As with Chapter 1, we assume that readers have—or will soon have—some advanced training on specific counseling theories. Our aim was to discuss these theories in the context of counseling youth and to illuminate the theories' major components with an eye to young people's—and their families'—unique counseling needs. Because effective youth counselors work with their clients' families, Chapter 7 focuses exclusively on family and systems counseling perspectives.

Chapter 8 addresses play and expressive arts counseling. Both play and expressive arts theories and methods are developmentally appropriate and thus important in counseling young people. Chapter 8 provides an overview of how these approaches can be used as part of an overarching theoretical philosophy or as inherently therapeutic counseling methods with youth.

Chapter 9 presents the I CAN START case conceptualization and counseling/treatment planning model. The I CAN START model is a comprehensive case conceptualization model that integrates a strength-based and contextually sensitive way of thinking about clients and their presenting struggles. Chapter 9 discusses the components of this model and introduces readers to a case application of the model. Subsequent chapters begin with a brief case and end with a counseling application using the I CAN START counseling/treatment model.

Chapter 10 focuses on select safety-related clinical issues that must be a priority in counseling youth. An emphasis is placed on practical steps counselors can take to promote and support young people's safety. The clinical issues selected are those that counselors encounter with the greatest frequency and those that invite the most serious potential for risk to clients, counselors, and/or members of the community, including suicide, homicide, and self-injury.

Family-related transitions and struggles can have a positive or negative impact on young people's development, wellness, and mental health. Chapter 11 addresses family-related transitions and struggles, including parental divorce or separation, blended families, kinship caregiving relationships, adoption, parental substance abuse, and youth grief and loss. The chapter discusses how counselors can address and counsel youth who are navigating these family-related transitions. In addition, the chapter explores protective factors that families and counselors may cultivate and strengthen to increase children's resiliencies.

Most youth experience academic, career, or social-emotional struggles at some point. Chapter 12 discusses common struggles that counselors help youth to navigate and offers approaches that can be used to help youth. Topics include study skill deficits and test anxiety, intimacy and dating, bullying and relational aggression, making and retaining friends, struggles associated with changing schools, and managing school attendance problems.

Chapter 13 discusses the diagnosis, assessment, and counseling approaches that are useful when working with youth who have neurodevelopmental and intellectual impairments. The chapter addresses the disorders that counselors most frequently encounter, including attention-deficit/hyperactivity disorder (ADHD), autism spectrum disorder, intellectual disabilities, and learning disorders.

Counselors in any setting commonly see youth, especially adolescents, who engage in disruptive behaviors. Teachers and caregivers, and even the legal system, reach out to counselors to mediate and manage these behaviors. Chapter 14 provides a discussion of the characteristics, symptoms, and types of disruptive behavior problems in youth, including conduct disorder and oppositional defiant disorder. The chapter discusses counseling interventions that are effective with youth who display disruptive behaviors.

Many youth experience traumatic events—whether acute or ongoing—that affect their mental health. Counselors play an important role in helping young people and their families adapt to traumatic experiences. In the United States, child abuse is the most common cause of childhood trauma. As such, Chapter 15 discusses trauma with a special focus on child maltreatment. It provides the diagnostic criteria, assessment, and counseling approaches that are useful and effective when working with youth who have experienced abuse and traumatic events. Adverse effects and difficulties associated with trauma may, in some cases, develop into mental health disorders, including reactive attachment disorder, posttraumatic stress disorder, and complex trauma reactions.

Substance use among young people is a serious community problem, and it creates problems not just for young people, but also for their parents, school personnel, and members of the community. Because young people are still growing and developing biologically, psychologically, and socially, the use of substances presents challenges beyond those faced by adults. Chapter 16 provides information on the risks, prevalence, assessment, and counseling and treatment options for young people who are misusing alcohol or other substances.

Anxiety is one of the most frequently diagnosed psychiatric disorders in youth, with a lifetime anxiety prevalence rate of 15–20%. Chapter 17 discusses separation anxiety disorder, generalized anxiety disorder, phobias, panic disorders, and obsessive-compulsive disorder, along with associated intervention approaches.

With prevalence rates for adolescent depression hovering around 11%, counselors must be versed in addressing youth depression. Chapter 18 addresses depressive and bipolar disorders, along with the ways counselors can support youth who have these disorders.

Chapter 19 discusses challenges youth face relative to physical health–related problems. More specifically, two categories of disorders—eating disorders and elimination disorders—are explored as well as counseling considerations for youth who have a chronic physical illness or health-related disability.

ACKNOWLEDGMENTS

We would also like to thank our publishing team at Pearson. Kevin Davis, you have truly been an AMAZING mentor! Thank you for believing in us and for your wisdom, support, patience, and of course, your sense of humor. Rebecca Fox-Gieg, thank you for your warmth and support during the later stages of this project!

Thank you to our contributors—Denise Ben-Porath, Kelly Bhatnagar, Stephanie Sedall, and Amy Williams—who added their voices and expertise to this text.

Matthew Walker, Lisa Bullock, and Stephanie Sedall, thank you for your assistance in multiple aspects of this text's development. Brooke Shorrab, Kim Duong, David Cleveringa, and Maggie Noday, thank you for your assistance in the early stages of the text's development. You were all wonderful to work with and extremely helpful.

We would also like to thank the following people who offered useful suggestions, which helped us in developing this text: Thomas Sweeney, Elizabeth Graham, and Lucy Lewis Purgason.

Thank you, too, to our Pearson book reviewers, who provided us with invaluable feedback that served to make this text better: Charles Crews, Texas Tech University; Steve Johnson, Liberty University; Jodi Sindlinger, Slippery Rock University of Pennsylvania; Debra Tokach, Shepherd University; and Lee Wetherbee, Ashland University.

SPECIAL ACKNOWLEDGMENTS

First, I want to acknowledge those who have taught me the most about counseling youth—the children and adolescents with whom I have worked. Over the past 20 years, I have counseled many young people, and I remember every young person I have counseled; all have touched my head and my heart in some unique way. It has been a privilege to connect with these youth—and their families—in such a deeply personal way. Many are children who have been the victims of years of sexual and physical abuse and neglect. These youth have taught me about the resilience inherent in the human spirit; it is literally amazing that children can survive what they do. Their ability to not only endure but to thrive even in the face of adversity, barriers, and injustices has forever changed me and how I see the world. No book can teach what these children have taught me, but I hope that some of the strength-based perspectives and wisdom I have gained through my work can shine through and permeate parts of this text.

Writing a book necessarily requires sacrifice, not only from the authors, but also from the people who surround them. My profound thanks go out to my husband, Rob, and my children, Ava and Isaac, who did without my presence more than I would have liked while we constructed this text.

Matt and Nicole, thank you for being such gracious, patient coauthors and for working so very hard on this text. You are my professional rocks, and the fact that we can have fun together on these projects is the proverbial cherry on the cake. Kate, Hudson, Kennedy, Weston, Genevieve, and Blaise, thank you for sharing Matt with us! Keith, Raki, and Bow, the same—thank you!

~Victoria E. Kress

First, I want to thank my two coauthors, Vicki and Nicole, for your support, tireless work, and dedication to this project. Vicki, I thank you for your leadership, patience, guidance, and mentorship. I would gladly take this journey with you both again!

I want to thank my five children, Hudson, Kennedy, Weston, Genevieve, and Blaise for tolerating all those mornings and nights when I was less than available. You are my joy! Know you are loved!

I want to thank my family, who were instrumental in supporting my wife and children throughout this time-consuming process. Mom, Robert, and Leigh, thank you for your love, time, and support.

Last, I want to thank my wife. Katie, all of this would never have been possible without your unfailing faith in me. You have always believed in me, even when I found it hard to believe in myself. You challenged me to envision even bigger dreams than I thought were possible! I love you, and I am thankful for you every day!

~Matthew J. Paylo

Growing up above my dad's veterinary office, I learned from an early age how to extend compassion and kindness to all. Thanks, Mom and Dad, for supporting me always.

Thank you to my family and friends, who have encouraged me through this process. Grandma, Mikey and Alyssa, Lauren and Rushad, Angie and Kevin, I love you! Thanks Mom and Dad S. for always checking in, supporting me, and sharing your love. Amy, Courtney, Emily, Kelli, Kristina, Natalie, and Shenika, I wouldn't know what to do without you.

I extend my warmest thanks to the UNC Pembroke community for their support throughout this entire project. Thank you Dean Bryant, Associate Dean McDonald, and The University.

Thank you to my coauthors, Vicki and Matt, and their families for the countless hours of sacrifice and work. Also, thank you to Kevin and Rebecca for your wisdom and guidance!

Thank you to the youth who have been so important to my personal and professional development. Krystial, you are doing great things! Dee and Evie, you will always be missed. Gavin, "it's hard work workin'," and I'm gonna keep doing what I can to make this world a better place!

~Nicole A. Stargell

ABOUT THE AUTHORS

Victoria E. Kress, Ph.D./LPCC-S (OH), NCC, CCMHC, is a Professor, a Counseling Clinic Director, and the Director of the Clinical Mental Health and Addictions Counseling Programs at Youngstown State University. She also works as the Director of Advocacy for the National Board of Certified Counselors. She has over 20 years of clinical experience working in various settings, including community mental health centers, hospitals, residential treatment facilities, private practices, and college counseling centers. She has published over 120 refereed articles and book chapters, and she has coauthored three books on diagnosing/assessing and counseling youth and adults. She has been cited as a top contributing author to the *Journal of Mental Health Counseling* as well as the *Journal of College Counseling,* and she served as the Associate Editor of the Theory and Practice Sections of the *Journal of Mental Health Counseling.* Dr. Kress served two terms as a governor-appointed member of the Ohio Counselor, Social Worker, and Marriage and Family Therapist Board and served as the Chair of the Counselor Professional Standards Committee. She also served as the ethics liaison for Ohio's state regulatory board and presently serves as a consultant/expert witness for counselor ethics cases. CACREP honored her with the *Martin Ritchie Award for Excellence in Advocacy.* She also received the following American Counseling Association (ACA) awards: the *Gilbert and Kathleen Wrenn Award for a Humanitarian and Caring Person,* the *Distinguished Mentor Award,* the *Counselor Educator Advocacy Award,* and the *Government Relations Award.* She has been the recipient of the following Association for Counselor Education and Supervision (ACES) awards: the *Outstanding Mentor Award,* the *Robert Stripling Award for Excellence in Standards,* and the *Leadership Award.* She has also received numerous Youngstown State University awards (e.g., *Distinguished Scholar, Distinguished Public Service*) as well as various Ohio Counseling Association awards, including the *Research and Writing Award,* the *Legislative Advocacy Award,* the *Leadership Award,* and the *Counselor of the Year Award.* She is a past President of Chi Sigma Iota International and the Ohio Counseling Association, and she is a past ACA Region Chair.

Matthew J. Paylo, Ph.D./LPCC-S (OH), is an Associate Professor, Coordinator of the Student Affairs and College Counseling Program, and Program Director of the Counseling Program at Youngstown State University. He has over 13 years of clinical experience in various settings, including community mental health centers, prisons, hospitals, adolescent residential treatment facilities, and college counseling centers. Dr. Paylo is passionate about implementing evidence-based interventions in therapeutic relationships that highlight empathy, unconditional positive regard, and genuineness. He has presented and published extensively in the areas of diagnosing and treating mental and emotional disorders. Dr. Paylo recently coauthored a book on assessing, diagnosing, and treating mental and emotional disorders from a strength-based perspective. In addition, he has published numerous journal articles and book chapters on trauma, evidence-based treatments, offender treatments, counseling adolescents, social justice counseling, and the implementation of the *Diagnostic and Statistical Manual of Mental Disorders.* Dr. Paylo has received numerous teaching and research awards, including the *Distinguished Professor of Teaching* at Youngstown State University and the *Research and Writing Award* from the Ohio Counseling Association (OCA). In addition, Dr. Paylo is on his second term as a governor-appointed member of the Ohio Counselor, Social Worker, and Marriage and Family Therapist Board and currently is serving as the Board Chair.

Nicole A. Stargell, Ph.D., LPCA, LSC, NCC, is an Assistant Professor at The University of North Carolina at Pembroke (UNCP) and serves as the Field Placement and Testing Coordinator for the Clinical Mental Health Counseling and School Counseling Programs. She also serves as the CFA of the Phi Sigma Chapter of Chi Sigma Iota (CSI) and is a member of the UNCP Institutional Review Board. Dr. Stargell earned her dual master's degree in clinical mental health counseling and school counseling from the CACREP-accredited Youngstown State University in Ohio. She earned her doctoral degree in counseling and counselor education

 from The University of North Carolina at Greensboro. Dr. Stargell is a member of the American Counseling Association Practice Brief Advisory Group, an Editorial Review Board Member for the *Counseling Outcome Research & Evaluation Journal*, and a Music Section Reviewer for the CSI International Counselors' Bookshelf. She is chair of the Emerging Leaders committee for the Association for Assessment and Research in Counseling and Co-chair of the Leadership Development Taskforce for the Association for Counselor Education and Supervision. She is a member of the CSI International Counselor Community Engagement Committee, and she serves as an annual reviewer for the CSI International Research Grant Competition and International Award Competition. Dr. Stargell was the recipient of the 2013 American Counseling Association *Courtland C. Lee Multicultural Excellence Scholarship Award*, and she received the *CSI International Outstanding Student Award* at both the entry and doctoral levels. She has authored or coauthored 18 peer-reviewed articles, 6 book chapters, and 19 newsletter articles. Dr. Stargell has delivered 35 national/international, 8 regional, 19 state, and 30 local counseling presentations. Her areas of counseling competence include diagnosis and treatment planning, multiculturalism, issues of grief and loss, and counseling children and adolescents. She has served as a counselor in the school setting (as both a clinical mental health counselor and school counselor intern), outpatient/intensive outpatient setting, home-based setting, and in a hospital/cancer center. Dr. Stargell is passionate about delivering quality mental health services to consumers and educating others about the most effective ways to support clients' desired mental health goals.

ABOUT THE CONTRIBUTORS

Denise D. Ben-Porath, Ph.D., is a Professor in the Department of Psychology at John Carroll University. She has extensive experience working with difficult-to-treat, multidiagnostic individuals. She has worked and consulted in various clinical settings, including university counseling centers, community mental health centers, adolescent residential treatment programs, correctional settings, and private practices. Dr. Ben-Porath has consulted at mental health agencies throughout the United States in the treatment of borderline personality disorder, eating disorders, and the implementation of dialectical behavior therapy programs. Her research interests include eating disorders, borderline personality disorder, and dialectical behavior therapy. She has published numerous articles in these areas and currently maintains a private practice at Cleveland Center for Eating Disorders, where she treats individuals who have eating disorders.

Kelly Bhatnagar, Ph.D., is the Director of Research-Practice Integration at The Emily Program. In her role, she oversees quality improvement/program development projects and research protocols for the organization. Dr. Bhatnagar holds clinical expertise in the treatment of child and adolescent eating disorders and is certified by the Training Institute for Child & Adolescent Eating Disorders to deliver family-based treatment (FBT; "The Maudsley Approach"). Dr. Bhatnagar also holds the appointment of Adjunct Assistant Professor in the Department of Psychological Sciences at Case Western Reserve University. She has worked and trained in various settings across the nation, including pediatric hospitals, academic institutions, community mental health centers, private practices, and college counseling centers. She has published numerous journal articles and book chapters and has presented nationally and internationally on the topics of eating disorders and body image.

Stephanie Sedall, MA, is a Research Assistant at Youngstown State University. She has researched emotion regulation, depression, and emotion recognition. She has published research on bipolar disorder in youth and adults, and she has presented at many national conferences on topics such as emotion regulation and self-injury.

Amy E. Williams, Ph.D., is an Assistant Professor in the Department of Counseling, Special Education, and School Psychology at Youngstown State University. Her research focuses on substance use disorders (SUDs) and their treatment, SUDs and family systems, and SUD counselor training and supervision. Dr. Williams also engages in research related to assessment development for problematic substance use patterns. Her clinical experience includes individual, group, couple, and family counseling in residential and outpatient settings, with a focus on substance-related concerns and SUDs.

BRIEF CONTENTS

PART 1 **Developmental and Systematic Foundations of Youth Counseling**

Chapter 1   Developmentally Informed Youth Counseling   1

Chapter 2   Systemically Informed Youth Counseling   35

PART 2 **Foundations of Youth Counseling: Theory and Practice**

Chapter 3   Individual Counseling Foundations   57

Chapter 4   Ethical and Legal Foundations   94

Chapter 5   Counseling Theories That Focus on Thought and Behavior Change and Action   121

Chapter 6   Counseling Theories That Focus on Background Experiences and Relationships   171

Chapter 7   Counseling Theories That Focus on Family Change Processes   209

Chapter 8   The Use of Play and Creative Arts in Counseling   228

Chapter 9   Conceptualizing Young Clients' Situations and Directing Counseling   253

PART 3 **Common Presenting Concerns and Counseling Interventions**

Chapter 10   Youth Suicide, Self-Injury, and Homicide   279

Chapter 11   Family-Related Transitions and Struggles   299

Chapter 12   Academic and Social–Emotional Transitions and Struggles   324

Chapter 13   Neurodevelopmental and Intellectual Impairments   348

Chapter 14   Disruptive Behavior Problems   375

Chapter 15   Abuse and Trauma   397

Chapter 16   Substance Abuse   430

Chapter 17   Anxiety, Obsessive-Compulsive, and Related Disorders   455

Chapter 18   Depressive and Bipolar Disorders   482

Chapter 19   Physical Health-Related Counseling Issues: Eating Disorders, Elimination Disorders, and Chronic Illness/Disability Counseling   506

CONTENTS

Part 1   Developmental and Systematic Foundations of Youth Counseling

Chapter 1 DEVELOPMENTALLY INFORMED YOUTH COUNSELING   1

Aspects of Youth Development   4

Physical Development   5

Cognitive Development   5

Self-Development   7

Psychosocial Development   7

Emotional Development   8

Early Childhood   9

Early Childhood Developmental Characteristics   9

Early Childhood Counseling Considerations   12

Middle Childhood   15

Middle Childhood Developmental Characteristics   15

Middle Childhood Counseling Considerations   20

Early Adolescence   23

Early Adolescence Developmental Characteristics   23

Early Adolescence Counseling Considerations   27

Late Adolescence   29

Late Adolescence Developmental Characteristics   29

Late Adolescence Counseling Considerations   31

Summary   33

Chapter 2 SYSTEMICALLY INFORMED YOUTH COUNSELING   35

Context and Culture   35

Strength-Based Philosophy   36

The Family System: Risk and Protective Factors   39

Family Structure and Boundaries   40

Family Communication   42

Family Involvement and Support   42

Child Maltreatment   43

Violence in the Home   45

The School System: Risk and Protective Factors   47

Family Influences on Academic Development   47

School Climate   48

Peer Relationships   49

Bullying and School Violence   50

The Community: Risk and Protective Factors   51

Community and Neighborhood Norms   52

Neighborhood Violence and Crime   53

Technology   54

   Summary   *55*

Part 2   Foundations of Youth Counseling: Theory and Practice

Chapter 3 INDIVIDUAL COUNSELING FOUNDATIONS   57

Foundations of the Counseling Process   58

Preliminary Counseling Considerations   60

   Creating a Comfortable Counseling Experience   60

   Intake and Assessment   62

   Building a Working Alliance with Young Clients and Their Families   68

Working Stage Counseling Considerations   71

   Communication Approaches   71

   Motivation and Counseling   75

   Technology and Counseling   80

Termination   81

   Natural Termination   82

   Premature Termination   90

   Termination and Referral   92

   Summary   *93*

Chapter 4 ETHICAL AND LEGAL FOUNDATIONS   94

Defining Ethical and Legal Matters   95

Competence   97

Minors' Rights and Legal Consent to Counseling   97

Informed Consent/Assent   98

Confidentiality   99

Informed Consent/Assent and Confidentiality in School Settings   102

Child Maltreatment Reporting   103

   Counselors' Personal Reactions to Reporting   104

   Statutory Requirements and Reporting   105

   Assessing the Situation: Should a Report Be Made?   106

   Making a Report   106

   The Aftermath of Filing a Report   107

Confidentiality of Documents and Federal Laws   108

   Health Insurance Portability and Accountability Act   108

   Family Educational Rights and Privacy Act   108

   Comprehensive Alcohol Abuse and Alcoholism Prevention, Treatment, and Rehabilitation Act   109

The Schools and Disability: IDEA and Section 504   110

   IDEA   110

   Section 504   110

Child Custody   111
   Consent for Treatment   111
   Custody Proceedings   112
Multiple Relationships   113
Ethical Decision Making: Practical Suggestions   115
   Be Thorough and Thoughtful   115
   Be Sensitive and Aware of Self and Others   116
   Be Transparent and Communicative   116
   Be Educated   117
   Be Support Seeking   117
An Ethical Decision-Making Model   118
   Summary   120

Chapter 5 COUNSELING THEORIES THAT FOCUS ON THOUGHT AND BEHAVIOR CHANGE AND ACTION   121
Behavior Therapy   123
   Core Concepts and Goals of Counseling   124
   Role of the Counselor in Behavior Therapy   126
   Counseling Process and Procedures   128
   Family Interventions and Involvement   136
Cognitive Behavioral Therapy   138
   Core Concepts and Goals of Counseling   140
   Role of the Counselor in Cognitive Behavioral Therapy   146
   Counseling Process and Procedures   147
   Family Interventions and Involvement   158
Reality Therapy and Choice Theory   160
   Core Concepts and Goals of Counseling   161
   Role of the Counselor in Reality Therapy   163
   Counseling Process and Procedures   164
   Family Interventions and Involvement   167
   Summary   168

Chapter 6 COUNSELING THEORIES THAT FOCUS ON BACKGROUND EXPERIENCES AND RELATIONSHIPS   171
Psychodynamic Therapy   172
   Core Concepts and Goals of Counseling   173
   Role of the Counselor in Psychodynamic Therapy   182
   The Psychodynamic Counseling Process   182
   Family Interventions and Involvement   189
Adlerian Therapy: Individual Psychology   190
   Core Concepts and Goals of Counseling   191
   Role of the Counselor in Adlerian Therapy   194

The Adlerian Therapy Counseling Process   194

Family Interventions and Involvement   198

Person-Centered Therapy   200

Core Concepts and Goals of Counseling   201

Role of the Counselor in Person-Centered Therapy   202

Person-Centered Therapy Counseling Process   203

Family Interventions and Involvement   205

Summary   206

**Chapter 7   COUNSELING THEORIES THAT FOCUS ON FAMILY CHANGE
PROCESSES   209**

Family Therapy   209

Core Concepts   210

Role of the Counselor in Family Therapy   213

Counseling Process   214

Family-Based Interventions   216

Summary   227

Chapter 8   THE USE OF PLAY AND CREATIVE ARTS IN COUNSELING   228

Specialized Certification and Registration   230

Play Therapy and the Use of Play in Counseling   230

Play Therapy: The Setting   232

Foundations of Play Therapy   232

Techniques and Interventions   235

Creative Arts in Counseling   245

Foundations of Creative Arts in Counseling   246

Creative Techniques and Interventions   246

Summary   252

**Chapter 9   CONCEPTUALIZING YOUNG CLIENTS' SITUATIONS AND
DIRECTING COUNSELING   253**

**Where to Begin: Suggestions for Directing Counseling and Developing a
Treatment Plan   253**

Take a Relational, Collaborative, and Strength-Based Approach with Clients   254

Focus on Evidence-Based Counseling Approaches and Interventions   255

Consider Context and Culture   255

Follow the Golden Thread   257

Be Flexible: Treatment Plans Are Not Static   258

**A Conceptual Framework for Case Conceptualization and Treatment
Planning   258**

Components of the Conceptual Framework   259

Summary   278

Part 3   Common Presenting Concerns and Counseling Interventions

Chapter 10 YOUTH SUICIDE, SELF-INJURY, AND HOMICIDE   279
Suicide   279
Counselor Considerations   280
Client Characteristics   280
Assessment   281
Intervention   283
Nonsuicidal Self-Injury   287
Counselor Considerations   287
Client Characteristics   288
Assessment   288
Intervention   289
Homicide   292
Counselor Considerations   292
Client Characteristics   293
Assessment   294
Intervention   295
Summary   296

Chapter 11 FAMILY-RELATED TRANSITIONS AND STRUGGLES   299
The Nature of Family-Related Transitions and Struggles in Youth   300
Types of Family-Related Transitions and Struggles   300
Family-Structure Transitions   300
Parental Substance Abuse   313
Grief, Loss, and Bereavement   315
Summary   323

Chapter 12 ACADEMIC AND SOCIAL–EMOTIONAL TRANSITIONS AND STRUGGLES   324
Academic Struggles   324
Time Management Difficulties   325
Study Skills Deficits   327
Test Anxiety   329
School Attendance Problems   330
Changing Schools   331
Social–Emotional Transitions and Struggles   335
Difficulty Making and Maintaining Friendships   335
Bullying   336
Sexual Orientation Struggles   339
Intimacy and Dating   342
Intimate Partner Violence   343
Summary   347

**Chapter 13 NEURODEVELOPMENTAL AND INTELLECTUAL
IMPAIRMENTS   348**

    Attention-Deficit/Hyperactivity Disorder (ADHD)   349

        Counselor Considerations   350

        Assessment of ADHD   352

        Counseling Interventions   354

    Autism Spectrum Disorder   360

        Counselor Considerations   361

        Assessment of Autism Spectrum Disorder   362

        Counseling Interventions   363

    Intellectual Disabilities   366

        Counselor Considerations   367

        Assessment of Intellectual Disabilities   368

        Counseling Interventions   369

    Specific Learning Disorders   370

        Counselor Considerations   370

        Assessment of Learning Disorders   371

        Counseling Interventions   372

          Summary   374

Chapter 14 DISRUPTIVE BEHAVIOR PROBLEMS   375

    The Nature of Disruptive Behavior Problems in Youth   376

        Description of Disruptive Behavior Problems   378

        DSM-5 Disorders Associated with Disruptive Behavior Problems   379

        Differential Diagnoses   381

    Assessment of Disruptive Behavior Problems   382

        Diagnostic Interview   382

        Standardized Assessments   382

    **Integrated Treatment Components for Youth Who Have Disruptive Behavior
Problems   384**

        Behavioral Interventions   384

        Mindfulness-Based Skills   386

        Cognitive Restructuring Abilities   387

        Problem-Solving Skills   390

        Dialectical Behavior Therapy   391

        Integrating Family   392

        Psychopharmacotherapy   394

          Summary   396

Chapter 15 ABUSE AND TRAUMA   397

    The Nature of Abuse and Trauma-Related Difficulties in Youth   398

    Types of Abuse and Trauma-Related Difficulties   401

        Youth Maltreatment   401

Adult Partner Violence in the Home (or Intimate Partner Violence)   405

Mass Violence, Terror, or Disaster   406

Trauma-Related Disorders   408

Assessment of Abuse and Trauma-Related Difficulties   410

Counseling Interventions   413

Promoting Safety   413

Incorporating Psychoeducation   414

Enhancing Distress Reduction and Affect Regulation Skills   414

Facilitating Emotional Processing   416

Implementing Cognitive Interventions   419

Enhancing Identity   420

Increasing Family Involvement   422

Specific Trauma-Focused and Disaster Intervention Approaches   423

Trauma-Focused Cognitive Behavioral Therapy (TF-CBT)   423

Cognitive Behavioral Intervention for Trauma in Schools (CBITS)   425

Combined Parent-Child Cognitive Behavioral Therapy (CPC-CBT)   425

Eye Movement Desensitization and Reprocessing (EMDR)   425

Trauma-Focused Integrated Play Therapy (TFIPT)   426

Psychological First Aid: One Crisis Intervention Model   427

Psychopharmacotherapy   427

Summary   429

Chapter 16 SUBSTANCE ABUSE   430

The Nature of Substance Use Disorders in Youth   431

Risk Factors   431

Etiology   432

Developmental Considerations   433

Development of Substance Use Disorders   435

Long-Term Effects of Substance Misuse   436

Classification of Substance Use Disorders   437

Assessment of Substance Use Disorders   440

Assessment Measures   441

Assessing Comorbidity   441

Assessing Needed Levels of Care   442

Counseling Interventions   443

Legal and Ethical Considerations   443

Developmental Considerations   443

Family Involvement and Support   444

Prognosis   444

Integrated Treatment Components   444

Detoxification   444

Individual and Group Counseling   445

Integrating Family into Treatment   449

Community-Based Interventions   450

Psychopharmacotherapy   451

Summary   454

Chapter 17 ANXIETY, OBSESSIVE-COMPULSIVE, AND RELATED DISORDERS   455

The Nature of Anxiety and Obsessive-Compulsive Disorders in Youth   455

Symptoms of Anxiety-Related Problems   456

Types of Anxiety Disorders   457

Assessment of Anxiety Disorders   459

Symptoms of Obsessive-Compulsive and Related Disorders   460

Types of Obsessive-Compulsive Disorders   462

Assessment of Obsessive-Compulsive and Related Disorders   463

Counseling Interventions   464

Integrated Treatment Components: Anxiety and Obsessive-Compulsive Disorders   465

Relaxation Training   465

Affective Education   466

Social Skills Training (SST)   469

Cognitive Skills Training   470

Problem Solving   473

Contingent Reinforcement   474

Habit Reversal Training   476

Exposure-Based Procedures   477

Integrating Family   478

Psychopharmacotherapy   478

Summary   481

Chapter 18 DEPRESSIVE AND BIPOLAR DISORDERS   482

The Nature of Depressive and Bipolar Disorders in Youth   482

Symptoms of Depression   483

Types of Depressive Disorders   486

Assessment of Depressive Disorders   487

Symptoms of Bipolar Disorders   489

Types of Bipolar Disorders   491

Assessment of Bipolar Disorders   492

Counseling Interventions   494

Integrated Treatment Components with Youth Who Have Depressive and Bipolar Disorders   495

Psychoeducation (Affective Education)   496

Cognitive Restructuring   497

Problem-Solving Approaches   499

Activity Scheduling   501

Family Involvement   502

Psychopharmacotherapy   502
   Summary   505

Chapter 19   PHYSICAL HEALTH-RELATED COUNSELING ISSUES: EATING DISORDERS, ELIMINATION DISORDERS, AND CHRONIC ILLNESS/ DISABILITY COUNSELING   506

Eating Disorders Overview   506

Anorexia: Symptoms and Counselor Considerations   509

Bulimia: Symptoms and Counselor Considerations   510

Counseling Interventions and Treatment for Youth Who Have Eating Disorders   513

Anorexia Nervosa: Treatment Models and Interventions   513

Bulimia Nervosa: Treatment Models and Interventions   516

Elimination Disorders   518

Enuresis: Symptoms and Counselor Considerations   519

Encopresis: Symptoms and Counselor Considerations   520

Counseling Interventions and Treatment for Youth Who Have Elimination Disorders   521

Enuresis Interventions and Treatment   522

Encopresis Interventions and Treatment   523

Chronic Illness/Disability Counseling   525

Physical and Health-Related Conditions   525

Adjustment to Chronic Illness/Disability   526

Management of Stress   527

Counseling Interventions   528
   Summary   533

References   534

Name Index   562

Subject Index   571

CHAPTER 1

Developmentally Informed Youth Counseling

Counseling is a professional relationship through which diverse clients are supported toward achievement of their unique goals (Kaplan, Tarvydas, & Gladding, 2014). Counselors aim to help clients to address various problems in living, achieve optimal development, receive early intervention, and prevent problems from developing (Vereen, Hill, Sosa, & Kress, 2014). To understand youth counseling, counselors must understand youth development. In this chapter, youth development and what counselors need to know about development relative to youth counseling are discussed.

Children and adolescents have many needs that counselors can help to address. Approximately 20% of youth in their teenage years have a diagnosable mental health difficulty, and about 50% of mental health disorders develop before the age of 14; if left unaddressed, these disorders can last a lifetime (Merikangas et al., 2010). Early intervention is one way counselors can stop problems from escalating. In addition, counselors play an important role in the prevention of problems. There is a strong need for effective and intentional mental health interventions with youth, and throughout this text the ways counselors can help with prevention and intervention are discussed. Counselors cannot counsel youth unless they have a good understanding of young people's normal developmental characteristics.

Development can be defined as a process of growth and maturity that is noticed physically, cognitively, personally, socially, and emotionally (Broderick & Blewitt, 2014). Although developmental changes occur across the life span, change is especially swift and remarkable in the early years, and development informs the ways youth understand and interact with the world. When working with young people, counselors' conceptualizations, approaches, and methods must be grounded in a firm understanding of youth development.

Youth develop at different rates, and many youth experience delayed—or sometimes accelerated—development. A 14-year-old boy who was abused, traumatized, and abandoned by his parents as a child, for example, may not experience the same developmental milestones as his peers because he has not been able to progress out of earlier stages of change (Simpson, Collins, & Salvatore, 2011; Zilberstein, 2014). Such examples highlight that it is impossible to understand young people's developmental struggles without understanding their unique lived experiences and contexts. It is also important that counselors understand typical developmental milestones so instances of delayed or accelerated development can be considered and addressed as needed. According to the *ACA Code of Ethics* (American Counseling Association [ACA], 2014), professional counselors should encourage the growth and development of their clients (Section A.1b) and provide interventions that are effective and appropriate to clients' developmental levels. In Table 1.1, an overview of common youth developmental milestones is provided.

As a profession, counselors value a developmental focus, and we believe many young people's problems in living are rooted in disruptions in typical developmental processes, the unblocking of which can foster healthy transitions (Vereen et al., 2014). For example, an 8-year-old girl whose parents were just divorced might struggle with feelings of sadness and loss secondary to this transition. If considering this girl's situation from a developmental perspective, loss and sadness would be a normal reaction, and the

Table 1.1	Common Developmental Milestones in Youth
Age Level	**Common Milestones**
Early childhood (3–5)	• Gross and fine motor skills are developing. • Use of symbols in communication, play, and problem solving develops. • Preacademic skills develop (e.g., alphabet, counting). • Attachment bonds are strengthened and extended to nonparental figures. • Youth begin to determine their sense of self in relation to others. • Self-concept, self-esteem, and self-regulation begin to develop.
Middle childhood (6–12)	• Gross and fine motor skills solidify. • Problem-solving skills emerge. • Concrete problem-solving skills emerge. • Sense of self and self-understanding expand. • Self-concept, self-esteem, and self-regulation skills expand. • Social skills and an ability to secure and maintain friendships develop. • Awareness of feelings and an ability to communicate feelings develop.
Early adolescence (10–14)	• Puberty and the development of secondary sex characteristics begin. • Abstract thinking (formal operational) emerges. • Self-focused/egocentric cognitions develop. • Ability to self-evaluate emerges. • Friendship networks expand.
Later adolescence (15–18)	• Sexual maturation is achieved. • Insight and the ability to verbalize emotions/feelings expand. • Abstract thinking (formal operational thinking) solidifies. • Friendships based on interests and shared experiences develop. • Intimate/romantic relationships begin. • Independence and autonomy develop. • Identity development (through experimentation) begins to solidify.

resolution of this struggle would provide an opportunity for her to build her sense of resiliency. Mental health difficulties can also develop in response to normal developmental transitions (e.g., puberty). All youth require some form of support and guidance to develop a strong mental health foundation.

Factors that inhibit healthy growth and development are called **risk factors**, and factors that lead to healthy, desirable development are commonly referred to as **protective** or **resiliency factors** (Kelly, Matthews, & Bartone, 2014). Risk and protective factors play an important role in youth development. In Table 1.2, an overview of common youth individual risk factors is provided, and in Table 1.3, common youth individual protective factors are provided.

All risk and resiliency factors work synergistically with one another; in other words, they connect and affect each other and youth in unique ways. Young people's intricate webs of risk and protective factors are continually interacting—across all stages of development; they are intertwined and connected with and are influenced by all lived experiences (Simpson et al., 2011; Skinner & Zimmer-Gembeck, 2016).

In this chapter, factors that contribute to physical, cognitive, self-, psychosocial, and emotional development in youth—at the individual level—are explored with an eye to risk and protective factors. In Chapter 2, the systemic and contextual risk and protective factors (i.e., the family, school, and community) that affect youth are discussed in more detail.

Table 1.2	Youth Developmental Risk Factors
Development Type	Common Youth Individual Risk Factors
Physical development	• Genetic/biological vulnerabilities • Low birth weight • Understimulating environment • Poor physical health • Malnourishment/neglect • Mental and emotional disorders
Cognitive development	• Neurodevelopmental delays or disorders • Low intelligence • Attention issues • Negative thinking styles • Poor problem-solving skills • Irrational thoughts about self, others, and/or the world
Self-development	• Undefined sense of self • Low self-esteem • Sensation seeking • Impulsivity • Rebelliousness • Positive attitudes toward problematic behaviors • Lack of hobbies and interests • External locus of control • Attribution of difficulties to personal qualities rather than external circumstances
Psychosocial development	• Poverty • Poor living situation (e.g., homeless, overcrowding) • Trauma, neglect, and abuse • Poor attachment models • Poor communication skills • Poor social boundaries • Marked lack of empathy • Criminal involvement (e.g., violence, gang activity) • High childhood stress • Perceived lack of social support (e.g., family, peers, extended family) • Family members/peers who engage in antisocial behaviors • Family members' substance-related issues • Family members' mental health–related issues • Family conflict, disruption, and divorce
Emotional development	• Unhelpful models of emotional expression and regulation (e.g., avoidance, screaming, hitting) • Poor fit with cultural norms of emotional expression • Lack of empathy • Inability to regulate emotions

Table 1.3	Youth Developmental Protective Factors
Development Type	**Common Youth Individual Protective Factors**
Physical development	• Good physical health • Minimal genetic/biological vulnerabilities • Stimulating environments that support learning and play
Cognitive development	• Moderate to high intelligence • Mental flexibility (e.g., ability to take different perspectives) • Problem-solving skills • Stimulating exposure to preacademic skills • School engagement
Self-development	• Easygoing temperament • Behavioral, emotional, and self-regulation • Spirituality/religiousness • Humor • Sense of hope (e.g., optimism) • Autonomy and self-reliance • Sense of purpose (e.g., meaning, future oriented) • Perseverance • Gratitude • Internal locus of control (e.g., can take steps to control difficult situations) • Motivation for personal success • Hobbies and interests • Attribution of difficulties to external circumstances instead of personal qualities
Psychosocial development	• Financial stability and resources within family/community • Minimal life stressors • Secure attachment models • Perceived social support (e.g., family, peers, extended family) • Volunteering in the community • Mentorship opportunities • Social skills • Communication skills • Positive peer relationships • Positive family relationships • Reasonable, positive parental and caregiver expectations • Lack of family conflict and disruption
Emotional development	• Healthy models of emotional expression and regulation • Emotional intelligence • Empathy • Ability to identify and support others' emotional experiences • Ability to identify and express emotions nonjudgmentally • Ability to regulate emotions

ASPECTS OF YOUTH DEVELOPMENT

The aspects of development discussed in this chapter are not intended to be exhaustive, but it is hoped they provide a brief overview of the important developmental factors relevant to how counselors consider and work with youth. More specifically, the developmental factors included here can be used to gain a baseline of the thoughts, feelings, and behaviors that youth are expected to experience at different stages of their development. Counselors can use this information to determine if a youth's subjective experience is developmentally appropriate and to assess the ways more helpful developmental trajectories can be supported. Specific ways in which developmental disruptions can be observed in youth (e.g., behavior problems, anxiety) are discussed later in the text.

Physical Development

Physical development directly relates to cognitive, personal, self-, psychosocial, and emotional development. Young people's thoughts, beliefs, emotions, and interpersonal relationships are intertwined with their physical development. Physical growth allows youth to complete physical tasks that support self-efficacy, self-esteem, and peer relationships, and neurodevelopmental growth supports cognitive abilities and attachment bonds (Niepel, Brunner, & Preckel, 2014; Raz, Newman, DeBastos, Peters, & Batton, 2014; Steeger, Gondoli, & Gibson, 2015; Zilberstein, 2014).

Some aspects of physical development are visibly noticeable (e.g., a youth's height in relation to peers), whereas others occur internally as neural pathways form within the brain and organs strengthen and develop over time. Visible physical growth occurs rapidly in newborns and slows as youth progress through childhood. The rate of physical growth again picks up in adolescence—with the onset of puberty—and then slows as youth reach full physical development in late adolescence or early adulthood (Raz et al., 2014; Steeger et al., 2015). Even when youth are not outwardly growing at a fast pace, their bodies are experiencing marked neurodevelopmental growth for gross motor skills (e.g., throwing, jumping, climbing) and fine motor skills (e.g., writing with a pencil; Decker, Englund, Carboni, & Brooks, 2011; Raz et al., 2014).

Risk factors for healthy physical development in youth include genetic variations and birth defects (e.g., brain injuries, spina bifida), understimulation in the environment, child maltreatment, and malnourishment (Decker et al., 2011; Groark, McCall, McCarthy, Eichner, & Gee, 2013; Osofsky & Leiberman, 2011; Raz et al., 2014; Steeger et al., 2015). In youth, these risk factors can lead to academic difficulties, aggression toward peers, difficulty regulating emotions, and an incomplete or negative sense of personal identity. Protective factors for healthy physical development in young children include a small (e.g., 3-to-1) child–caregiver ratio (whether that is in the home, daycare setting, or preschool/kindergarten setting), opportunities to learn and practice helpful emotional regulation skills, safe and secure relationships with caregivers and peers, and stimulating environments that encourage learning through play (Groark et al., 2013; Osofsky & Leiberman, 2011).

As youth progress into adolescence, physical risk factors include those that were present in childhood (e.g., biology, genetics, malnourishment, limited development of neural pathways), as well as risks sometimes associated with puberty and the development of primary and secondary sex characteristics (e.g., increased sexual activity; Moore, Harden, & Mendle, 2014). The hormonal changes and growth spurts that are characteristic of puberty can also place youth at an increased risk for depression and other mental health difficulties (Mendle, Harden, Brooks-Gunn, & Graber, 2012). Physical development in puberty can be uncomfortable and frightening, and counselors can take care to explore and normalize such feelings while supporting positive relationships among youth, parents, and their peers (Mendle et al., 2012; Moore et al., 2014).

Cognitive Development

Cognitive development can be defined as the continual formation of thought that supports information processing, problem solving, reasoning, memory, and communication (Broderick & Blewitt, 2014; Raz et al., 2014). Cognitive development goes hand in hand with neural development; as youth experience enhanced neurodevelopment, they are able to grasp new concepts and skills that can be used for further learning and growth (Decker et al., 2011; Skinner & Zimmer-Gembeck, 2016).

Jean Piaget (1928/2002) proposed a **stage theory** that explained the typical course of cognitive development from birth through adolescence. His model outlines four stages that explain how youth attain and integrate new information into their existing cognitive schemas. The four stages include sensorimotor (ages 0–2), preoperational (ages 2–7), concrete operational (ages 7–11), and formal operational (ages 11–16 and beyond; Piaget, 1928/2002; Sigelman & Rider, 2012). Counselors should be aware of the general facets of this stage model when accounting for individual risk and protective factors that might amplify or slow down a youth's cognitive development.

In the first 2 years of life, youth are typically in the **sensorimotor** stage of cognitive development. In this stage, babies and toddlers use their five senses of touch, taste, smell, sight, and hearing to explore the world. When first born, babies primarily act on innate instincts (e.g., closing the hand when their palm is touched; Broderick & Blewitt, 2014). These instinctual responses gradually become more intentional as babies become toddlers and begin to explore the world and their role in it (Skinner & Zimmer-Gembeck, 2016). As an example, a toddler who finds his way to a mirror will discover his own reflection using the sense of sight. He might integrate the sense of touch by reaching out and placing his hand on the reflection; he might even place his mouth and nose to the mirror to integrate his taste and smell senses. Toddlers explore their environments with as many senses as possible to gain a better understanding of themselves, others, and the world.

Next, from ages 2 to 7, youth are in the **preoperational stage** in which they develop language skills, an understanding of symbolic representations, and concrete problem-solving abilities (Broderick & Blewitt, 2014). Youth ages 2 through 7 do not have abstract reasoning abilities or highly developed problem-solving skills (Prout & Fedewa, 2015). At this age, youth tend to express themselves and explore their world through play. Counselors should take note that children's play in early childhood can be interpreted to indicate real-life struggles. The toys that youth select are often symbolic of people and objects in their actual lives, and play scenarios often represent their real-life dilemmas. Through play, youth will often devise concrete solutions to such problems, and counselors can work with parents, teachers, and other significant individuals to support more sophisticated and complex versions of these resolutions in real life (Menassa, 2009).

It is also developmentally appropriate for youth in the preoperational stage to be egocentric, which means they lack insight into others' perspectives and are not worried about how others perceive or understand them (Piaget, 1928/2002). In the preoperational stage, youth are most focused on satisfying their own needs, which can sometimes lead to selfish play behaviors and potential social difficulties. Counselors can work to educate parents, teachers, and caregivers about how cognitive development manifests at this age and help them to implement rules that promote prosocial behaviors.

Youth ages 7 through 11 are typically in the **concrete operational stage** in which egocentrism dissipates, cognitions become logical, and concrete problems can be solved. Youth at this age are not able to understand hypothetical situations or multiple perspectives on a problem, but they are able to connect behaviors with consequences. For example, a youth in the concrete operational stage will be motivated to regain harmony with a peer after an altercation, and he or she will understand that an apology is an effective method for conflict resolution. However, abstract reasoning is not fully developed; the youth would have trouble gaining insight into the peer's perspective of the altercation and would struggle to identify hypothetical situations that might arise if the youth chooses not to apologize, not to apologize immediately, or to wait until later to apologize (Prout & Fedewa, 2015; Sigelman & Rider, 2012). When working with youth in the concrete operational stage, counselors can continue to facilitate empathy and encourage prosocial skills to support young people's movement into the final stage of development.

In the last stage of Piaget's model, youth ages 11 through 16 reach the **formal operational stage** of development. As they approach puberty, youth are typically better able to gain insight into others' perspectives and consider the long-term consequences of their current behaviors (Sigelman & Rider, 2012). At the formal operational stage, traditional talk therapy approaches might become more appropriate, but counselors may still want to integrate some creative activities or play as these are developmentally appropriate (Capuzzi & Stauffer, 2016; Choudhury, Blakemore, & Charman, 2006). Youth at this stage are less likely to draw or color if handed a blank sheet of paper, but youth can be given a specific prompt or asked to color in the outline of a mandala (a circular graphic), which can be a soothing—yet structured—way to meld creativity with self-expression in counseling. When counselors and caregivers can genuinely connect with youth of various ages, protective factors such as positive parental/teacher/adult expectations, peer support, and social and emotional regulation skills can be harnessed and promoted effectively (Chronis-Tuscano et al., 2015; Hopson & Weldon, 2013; Mendle et al., 2012; Osofsky & Leiberman, 2011).

Self-Development

The concept of the self is formed through the **attachment bonds** infants and toddlers develop with their parents (Broderick & Blewitt, 2014; Zilberstein, 2014). When parents nurture their children and meet children's needs, healthy bonds and attachments are formed. For example, babies cry when they need something, whether it is feeding, a diaper change, or affection and soothing. If a baby boy cries and a caregiver promptly attends to his needs, the baby will learn that the world is a safe place and that he can trust others to meet his emotional and physical needs. When children's needs are met, they are soothed and feel important and worthwhile. Unhealthy attachments are formed when parents do not consistently meet a youth's needs. If a baby boy lies in his crib crying with no response from a caregiver, he may come to believe that others are not reliable or safe, he may struggle to learn how to self-regulate and sooth uncomfortable feelings, and he may come to believe that the world is an unpredictable or unsafe place (Zilberstein, 2014).

By the age of 2, youth are able to recognize themselves in a mirror and know that they are autonomous people who have unique thoughts, feelings, and behaviors (Broderick & Blewitt, 2014). With this realization, youth move to building an understanding of themselves via their interpersonal relationships, and they develop a self-concept and self-esteem. **Self-concept** is a mental representation of one's abilities and characteristics (Niepel et al., 2014). **Self-esteem** is informed by the self-concept and encompasses one's sense of his or her overall worth and value (Brummelman et al., 2014; Niepel et al., 2014). Youth have multiple self-concepts in relation to academics, social relationships, family relationships, and even leisure activities or hobbies (e.g., the self as a boy scout or an athlete).

Clinical Toolbox 1.1

In the Pearson eText, click here to review an activity that can help youth to identify and develop their self-concept.

Especially in childhood, parents and other caregivers have a significant influence on a child's sense of self (Broderick & Blewitt, 2014). The ways parents react to their children's endeavors (e.g., supportive or punitive) influence the ways youth view their abilities and characteristics. As youth age, peer relationships become increasingly important and can have an even greater impact on their self-development than parents' influence (Lereya, Copeland, Costello, & Wolke, 2015; Moore et al., 2014). Counselors can help youth of all ages foster positive self-concepts in relation to their peers through social skills training, the use of activities that foster positive interpersonal emotions, addressing and reframing unhelpful cognitions, helping youth to identify and apply their character strengths, and increasing young people's sense of gratitude and mindfulness (Broderick & Blewitt, 2014; Suldo et al., 2015).

Psychosocial Development

Psychosocial development is characterized by the thoughts, feelings, and experiences a youth has as the result of relational contexts and interactions (Broderick & Blewitt, 2014). Young people's sense of self-worth is based—in large part—on the ways in which significant others respond to them and the ways in which they respond to others. A model of psychosocial development was created by Erik Erikson (1968) to explain the various struggles, or crises, that humans experience throughout all stages of life. From birth through adolescence, young people are constantly attempting to determine if they can trust others, if they can trust themselves, and what their roles are and will be in the world (Broderick & Blewitt, 2014). Youth who successfully navigate **Erikson's psychosocial crises** will learn to trust others, gain a positive sense of self, and identify the special role they will play in relation to others.

Previously, attachment was discussed as an important factor that influences self-development. The concept of attachment overlaps with the concept of psychosocial development that begins at birth when babies are dependent on their parents for survival and basic needs (Erikson, 1968). In general, if parents provide youth with a safe environment in which their needs are consistently met, young people form a sense of trust in others and the world. If youth's needs are not consistently met early in life, they will learn to distrust others and devalue themselves (Broderick & Blewitt, 2014; Erikson, 1968; Zilberstein, 2014). Young people's ability to trust—or not—directly affects their ability to understand themselves in relation to others.

As psychosocial development progresses, youth practice behaviors that are autonomous, and they begin to show personal initiative. Positive responses from caregivers and peers create a sense of independence and identity, whereas scornful or displeased responses from others can create a sense of self-doubt and role confusion. For example, imagine that a 7-year-old boy finds that he is interested in and talented at tap dancing. The boy is disinterested in sports. If his parents show support of his behaviors verbally (e.g., praise, excited comments) and behaviorally (e.g., attending recitals, taking him to practice), the young boy will learn that his talents are special, and he will more likely form a positive self-concept and feel as though he has a purpose in the world (Broderick & Blewitt, 2014; Brummelman et al., 2014; Suldo et al., 2015). However, imagine that the boy's parents really want him to play football, rather than dance, and they consistently make negative comments about (e.g., "football is better") or even ban him from tap dancing. This could lead to the youth feeling rejected and judged, which could diminish his self-concept and lead to unpleasant emotions.

Interpersonal relationships play an integral role in youth development from birth through adolescence, and even throughout adulthood (Broderick & Blewitt, 2014; Mendle et al., 2012). Counselors should take care to assess children's attachment relationships with their caregivers to identify and address any insecurities or attachment injuries. Counselors can foster adaptive social skills and positive peer interactions when working with youth, and the pivotal role that social interactions play in their psychological development should be consistently considered and integrated into counseling.

Emotional Development

Emotional development involves youth learning to understand, fully experience, and regulate their feelings. Key emotional development skills include identification of feelings in one's self and others, emotional expression, and emotional regulation. It is important to note that emotional expression is highly dependent on one's culture. Emotional development is also intertwined with physical, cognitive, self-concept, and psychosocial factors. Youth who experience difficulty identifying, expressing, and regulating emotions early in life can experience long-term consequences such as interpersonal difficulties, antisocial behaviors, academic struggles, and substance use problems (Girio-Herrera, Dvorsky, & Owens, 2015; Gulley, Oppenheimer, & Hankin, 2014). Conversely, youth can learn that positive and negative emotions are an expected part of life and use verbal expression of feelings and emotional regulation techniques to work toward healthy emotional development across the life span (Suldo et al., 2015).

Young people initially learn about their emotions and emotional expression by observing their parents, family members, and those around them (Gulley et al., 2014). As an example, imagine an 8-year-old girl who recently lost her mother. She will observe her father's coping mechanisms and will unconsciously absorb ideas about the ways that she should cope with and manage her emotional experiences. Her father might respond to the loss with increased anger and agitation, which is a common male response to loss and expression of sadness and/or depression (American Psychiatric Association [APA], 2013a). In this instance, the young girl may learn to deal with uncomfortable emotions with anger reactions. Conversely, her father might avoid all expression of emotion, and the girl could learn to internalize negative emotions. Finally, her father could express his thoughts and feelings and practice healthy coping skills (e.g., reminiscing) to work through the loss. In this later scenario, the young girl would learn that both positive and negative emotions are an inevitable part of life, difficult experiences can be tolerated and managed, and uncomfortable feelings can be fully experienced as one moves forward.

The most common physical, cognitive, self-, psychosocial, and emotional developmental concerns presented by youth at each age level are presented in this chapter, beginning with early childhood and moving through adolescence. The interplay between risk and protective factors is also explored in the context of each developmental level. Just as certain risk and protective factors are more salient based on individual circumstances, some are also more relevant at different developmental stages.

EARLY CHILDHOOD

In this discussion, the term *early childhood* is used to describe youth who are 3 to 5 years old. Children younger than 3 or 4 years are not able to intentionally identify their thoughts, feelings, and behaviors, so mental health intervention for children younger than 3 years is typically focused on behavioral modifications related to neurodevelopmental disorders (e.g., autism spectrum disorder) and/or parent training (Skinner & Zimmer-Gembeck, 2016; Zeanah, 2009). Neurodevelopmental disorders are discussed in Chapter 13, and counseling considerations that relate to supporting positive parenting practices are discussed throughout the text. There is an important and growing area related to infant mental health, but due to space limitations this topic is not addressed in this text. Readers are encouraged to review others sources for information on this important area of study (e.g., Shulman, 2016).

When counseling young children, parents should be an integral part of the process as children are highly dependent on their parents or caregivers at this age (Prout & Fedewa, 2015). Parents might initiate counseling for their young children, or youth might be referred by personnel at preschools, kindergartens, or social services. Counselors might also encounter young children in the counseling setting if their older siblings are also receiving services and a systemic approach is employed with the entire family.

Early Childhood Developmental Characteristics

PHYSICAL DEVELOPMENT

In early childhood, youth form important pathways between neurons in the body, which support communication between the brain and all other organs (Skinner & Zimmer-Gembeck, 2016; Steeger et al., 2015). Every time a connection between the brain and a body part is used (e.g., the hand when writing with a pencil), the pathway strengthens. Counselors can encourage parents and caregivers to stimulate strong neural development in children through active engagement that supports growth and development (e.g., play time and story time). Youth who receive ample stimulation and support in early childhood experience marked physical, behavioral, and cognitive benefits (Groark et al., 2013; White, Kim, Kingston, & Foster, 2014).

In early childhood, youth grow, and their muscles develop and become stronger and more effective. By the age of 3 years, youth have experienced significant growth in their gross motor skills (e.g., waving an arm, walking) and fine motor skills (e.g., tying a knot, writing with a pencil; Skinner & Zimmer-Gembeck, 2016). Even with adequate stimulation and engagement with parents and peers, physical growth in childhood can be limited by a number of genetic and environmental factors. For example, Down syndrome is a common genetic disorder in which youth experience physical, cognitive, and interpersonal deficiencies throughout the life span (de Santana, de Souza, & Feitosa, 2014). Babies born to mothers older than the age of 35 are at a greater risk for Down syndrome, but there is limited additional information about risk and protective factors for this (and many other types of) genetic disorders (Centers for Disease Control and Prevention [CDC], 2014b). In the absence of a marked genetic or neurodevelopmental disorder, environmental factors such as lead in the paint of older homes can contribute to reduced physical growth of the nervous system in early childhood (Morsy & Rothstein, 2015). Although lead has been removed from currently manufactured products, remnants still exist in window frames, pipes, and the ground, and counselors should keep this, and other similar considerations, in mind.

Youth who are exposed to chronic stress and depression in the household during their early developmental years often have higher levels of cortisol (a stress hormone), which can lead to a more difficult temperament (e.g., generally negative affect, greater emotionality) and higher levels of stress and depression throughout the life span (Mackrell et al., 2014). Counselors should take note of the affect a youth's environment can have on long-term physical development and work to secure support systems for youth and their families (Skinner & Zimmer-Gembeck, 2016). Youth who experience supportive, happy home environments in early childhood are protected from neurodevelopmental and other physical difficulties throughout the life span.

COGNITIVE DEVELOPMENT

At least 50% of the brain develops after birth, and the most rapid brain development occurs in the first 2 years of life (Zeanah, 2009). According to Piaget's theory of cognitive development, humans are in the

sensorimotor stage of cognitive development during the first few years of life (Sigelman & Rider, 2012). At this age, the parts of the brain that control emotions, physiological arousal, and emotional regulation are primarily used (Schore, 2012).

Youth need stimulation from others and the environment for the right side of the brain to mature as effectively as possible. Environmental stimulation includes things to touch, see, hear, smell, and taste, and caregivers should intentionally provide new and exciting sources of stimulation for youth of all ages. As youth mature in the early years, the left side of the brain, which controls decision making and communication, is used more and more.

According to Piaget's model, at age 2 or 3 years, youth are in the **preoperational stage** of cognitive development (Sigelman & Rider, 2012). In early childhood, youth are able to understand symbols that appear in communication, playful interactions, and problem-solving scenarios. For example, young children are typically able to understand that the word *dog* is used as a symbol to represent the cuddly, furry creature that lives in many homes. When playing, youth are able to use dolls or toys to represent objects in their real lives (Prout & Fedewa, 2015; Sigelman & Rider, 2012). A counselor could ask a 4-year-old child to identify a doll or toy that represents the youth's mother, and the child would be able to choose an object and explain why or how it represents her mother. However, the child's representations would typically be concrete (e.g., this doll is a girl, and my mom is a girl).

Cognitive development in early childhood also includes the formation of preacademic cognitive skills (e.g., counting and reciting the alphabet). Youth at this age also begin to understand the relationship between mental representations (also called *symbols*) and actual objects or words. Protective factors for healthy academic development include positive messages from parents regarding preacademic skills and parental dedication to teaching and practicing the alphabet and counting with their children (Hopson & Weldon, 2013; Search Institute, 2015). Even at this early age, messages from parents, caregivers, and teachers about academic success can have long-term protective or harmful effects.

Cognitive deficits that occur early in life can have long-lasting effects on academic achievement (Prout & Fedewa, 2015; Search Institute, 2015). For example, youth in impoverished homes often do not have access to reading materials over summer break, so they enter the next school year after forgetting some material. Other students, in contrast, may have gained a bit of reading skill—or at least remained stable— over the summer break by practicing at home (White et al., 2014).

SELF-DEVELOPMENT

In early childhood, youth are able to recognize themselves as unique and distinct from others, and self-development at this stage is characterized by the formation of self-concept and self-esteem (Broderick & Blewitt, 2014). By age 3 years, a child begins to form multiple **self-concepts**, which are cognitive maps of the youth's perceived physical abilities, academic aptitudes, interpersonal skills, and emotional experiences. **Self-esteem** is a reflection of these multiple areas of self-concept and serves as a youth's holistic representation of the self in relation to others (Broderick & Blewitt, 2014; Brummelman et al., 2014; Niepel et al., 2014).

A child's inherent temperament plays a significant role in his or her sense of self. **Temperament** refers to a youth's inherent, biologically based tendency for reactivity and self-regulation in relation to environmental stimuli (Dyson et al., 2015; Prout & Fedewa, 2015). Temperament has recently been defined in terms of five dimensions, including positive affect, sociability, dysphoria, fear/inhibition, and impulsivity versus constraint (Dyson et al., 2015). A child might inherently be more prone to positive or negative **affect** (emotional expression), which can have an impact on a youth's mood, feelings, cognitions, and overall self-concept. Temperament can have a profound effect on one's emotional, social, and cognitive development.

Some youth are inherently more adept at performing tasks that they'd rather not do (e.g., cleaning up toys), but the role of a supportive and warm caregiver can serve as a protective factor when practicing such tasks (Chronis-Tuscano et al., 2015; Skinner & Zimmer-Gembeck, 2016). Parents serve as models of behavior and emotional regulation for youth, and parents should maintain a calm demeanor even when feeling frustrated or angry. It is also very helpful for parents to verbalize their feelings and teach youth that both positive and negative emotions are a normal part of life.

Overall, a youth's self-development in early childhood sets the stage for a positive self-concept and healthy self-esteem across the life span. Self-development in early childhood can affect cognitive, emotional, and behavioral development later in life. A youth's self-development is heavily influenced by others (e.g., peers, caregivers), and a strong connection exists between self- and psychosocial development.

PSYCHOSOCIAL DEVELOPMENT

Psychosocial development refers to a youth's sense of self in relation to others, which is first guided by his or her attachment to parents and is later expanded on by social interactions in childhood (Prout & Fedewa, 2015). When youth are in the first 2 years of life, eye contact with a caregiver helps the right brain (i.e., the emotional part of the brain) develop, and youth are able to regulate their emotions and gain a sense of safety in the world as a result (Zeanah, 2009). Youth learn that they can turn to their caregivers for comfort, and this is known as an **attachment bond**.

Attachment bonds formed with caregivers early in life inform a child's working model of attachment (Zilberstein, 2014). Secure attachment bonds are formed when an infant's needs are met consistently in a caring and loving manner; this leads to a healthy working model of attachment in which youth feel as though they are worthy of receiving love and attention from others and believe that others are well-intentioned and approachable. Insecure attachments form when an infant's needs are not consistently met, and thus the youth is left feeling unwanted, unloved, and unsafe with others (Sigelman & Rider, 2012; Zilberstein, 2014).

During the first year of life, youth must overcome Erikson's stage of **trust versus mistrust**, whereby they determine whether others can be trusted (Erikson, 1963). Youth who form secure attachment bonds in the first year of life are able to successfully navigate this stage and progress to the struggle of **autonomy versus shame and doubt**. In this stage, youth need to learn that they are able to separate from their attachment figures periodically and return back to the safety of the caregiver when needed/desired (Erikson, 1963). For example, when it is safe, youth might be allowed to play in the sandbox while a parent sits on park bench. In this stage, caregivers should help youth continue to build emotional regulation skills to prevent autonomy that is unsafe (e.g., running into the street), while encouraging a sense of independence in youth when possible.

In early childhood, youth navigate Erikson's psychosocial stage of **initiative versus guilt** (Erikson, 1963; Sigelman & Rider, 2012). Youth experience healthy psychosocial development when they are able to initiate creative projects (e.g., building a house out of blocks, choosing an outfit) that meet their personal goals and support positive social engagement in the process. Youth can experience psychosocial difficulties if their initiatives are not well received by their peers, parents, or other adults. For example, imagine a 4-year-old girl who wants to build a neighborhood of houses with her peers using blocks, but she repeatedly takes the best blocks from her playmates for her own house. Although this might satisfy an internal need within herself (to build the best house), the neighborhood will never get built, and her peers might stop playing with her because of her unfair behavior. Ideally, the girl would learn to focus on having fun (as opposed to building the best house) and playing fairly, thus building strong social relationships. Specific techniques and interventions for facilitating this growth process are provided later in the text.

Numerous risk factors can affect a child's psychosocial development. For example, youth who experience low-quality childcare (i.e., high child-to-caregiver ratio, unhealthy interpersonal modeling, inconsistent rules) outside the home might display more externalized behavior problems (e.g., hitting, throwing objects) when interacting with their peers and often have poor self-control (Huston, Bobbitt, & Bentley, 2015). Behavior problems and poor self-control can affect peer relationships because other youth might elect to play with children who are more easygoing and less temperamental (Mackrell et al., 2014).

The behavioral difficulties experienced in early childhood can be compounded when youth are from economically disadvantaged families (Huston et al., 2015). Counselors should ensure that youth have access to basic resources such as food and clean clothing. According to **Maslow's hierarchy of needs**, it will be difficult for youth to work on counseling goals if their basic needs are not met (Sigelman & Rider, 2012). Counselors can also work to support stimulating home environments by securing resources (e.g., books, educational games) for youth who would not otherwise have access to these materials at home (White et al., 2014). Next, counselors should work to identify a youth's strengths, teach healthy coping skills, and praise positive social behaviors to help the youth experience strong psychosocial development (Broderick & Blewitt, 2014; Brummelman et al., 2014; Niepel et al., 2014; Search Institute, 2015).

EMOTIONAL DEVELOPMENT

Young children experience a range of emotions, including happiness, surprise, disgust, sadness, anger, and fear (de Santana et al., 2014). The extent to which children are able to experience and regulate their emotions in healthy, helpful ways affects their self-esteem and ability to form interpersonal relationships (Broderick & Blewitt, 2014; Wagner et al., 2015). At this stage, children understand basic feelings (e.g., mad, sad, happy), yet they have a weak awareness of their own or others' feelings.

Nonverbal recognition of others' emotions is a key component of empathic, healthy interpersonal relationships (Broderick & Blewitt, 2014; de Santana et al., 2014; Klaus, Algorta, Young, & Fristad, 2015; Wagner et al., 2015). Children initially learn to recognize facial expressions and the corresponding emotions by observing and interacting with parents and peers. When youth observe modeling of inappropriate responses to others' emotions (e.g., degrading an individual despite a look of sadness on the face), they can form similar, unhelpful responses to others' needs (Klaus et al., 2015). Although unhelpful modeling is one risk factor related to emotion recognition in early childhood, some youth are born with developmental difficulties (e.g., autism spectrum disorder), which also inhibit **emotion identification** and **emotional regulation** (APA, 2013; de Santana et al., 2014).

Healthy emotional regulation, expression, and recognition are key contributors to positive self-esteem and successful interpersonal relationships in early childhood. Counselors should work with parents to encourage helpful modeling of emotional regulation and expression. Counselors should also assess youth's inherent abilities to recognize others' emotions and provide social skills training for children who display deficits in this area (Chronis-Tuscano et al., 2015). Helpful emotional regulation and empathy can allow youth to gain a positive sense of self in relation to others and focus on healthy physical and cognitive development.

Early Childhood Counseling Considerations

COMMON PROBLEMS IN EARLY CHILDHOOD

Youth in early childhood can experience various mental health difficulties, and these are often unique from those seen in youth at other developmental stages. Children manifest their struggles through their behavior—not necessarily their words—and as such, behavioral problems are one of the most common problem that bring young children to counseling (Chronis-Tuscano et al., 2015; Mackrell et al., 2014). For example, children might throw frequent temper tantrums, use physical aggression with peers or siblings, or disobey developmentally appropriate rules. There are multiple reasons why youth might display behavioral problems at day care, school, or home. Often, behavior problems manifest during significant transitions (e.g., loss of a loved one, attending a new day care). Behavior problems in young children can also suggest exposure to traumatic experiences (e.g., various types of abuse or neglect). Youth have unique reactions to trauma, including lowered self-esteem/self-concept, anger, depression, anxiety, and social difficulties (APA, 2013; Centers for Disease Control and Prevention [CDC], 2015b). Other mental health concerns can develop as the result of developmental difficulties in early childhood.

Youth might also develop maladaptive behaviors secondary to ineffective environmental reinforcers that need to be modified (Barkley, 2013a; Chronis-Tuscano et al., 2015). For example, children might learn that when playing quietly, their parents ignore them and attend to other siblings or household tasks. However, parents pay attention (even if it is negative) to children who are throwing tantrums or acting out. In a youth's eyes, negative attention is often better than no attention at all (Barkley, 2013a). Counselors can work with the adults in a child's life to help them develop strategies for managing young children's behaviors.

COUNSELING APPLICATIONS

Youth in early childhood are unique individuals with independent thoughts, feelings, and preferences that should be acknowledged and celebrated by parents, caregivers, and counselors. At the same time, the physical differences between children and adults can serve as a visible reminder of the internal cognitive, emotional, and psychosocial development that is yet to occur. As such, counselors should approach children differently than they would approach adolescents or adults in the counseling relationship. Specifically, counselors working with youth in early childhood should:

- be mindful of the child's basic needs, especially with young children; counseling will be less effective when a child is tired, hungry, or uncomfortable;
- assess the child's comfort with being away from his or her parents and allow parents to be present, if necessary/possible, until the therapeutic relationship has formed;
- remember that children are highly dependent on parents, and integrate the family system into counseling interventions whenever possible;
- as appropriate, use varied animated or soothing voice intonations to make children feel excited and at ease, respectively;
- provide eye contact that conveys genuine interest and compassion for the child;
- use open posture and exaggerated gestures to convey safety and openness to the child;
- position your body closer to the ground to join the child on his or her level;
- remember that children have a limited attention span, so pace and plan sessions accordingly;
- allow children to take an active role in directing counseling to promote their autonomy;
- provide stimulating environments and activities that are developmentally appropriate and allow children to develop fine and gross motor skills;
- integrate toys, games, and characters from children's favorite books or television shows into the counseling process;
- validate and support children's exploration of self through simple counseling interventions, such as games, playing with toys, singing, and art;
- interpret children's use of symbolism in play to understand important risk factors that can be addressed and protective factors that can be harnessed;
- acknowledge children's egocentric cognitions, and work to foster insight and empathy when possible;
- remember that children are literal in thought, so use concrete language to communicate with them;
- remember that children have a limited vocabulary, so avoid the use of advanced words or language they might not understand;
- model healthy interpersonal behaviors and emotional expression; and
- integrate the family system into counseling whenever possible.

Group counseling might be particularly relevant for young children who have social skills deficits or are experiencing high levels of stress or anxiety (Chronis-Tuscano et al., 2015; Huston et al., 2015). It might seem as though youth in early childhood are too young to engage in group counseling, but that is not always the case. It is common for babies to engage in parallel play in which they do not interact with their peers even when physically close to one another. By age 2 or 3 years, youth engage with one another and begin to build their social skills. Youth in early childhood are influenced by one another, and group interactions with other children can be helpful (Weisz & Kazdin, 2010). In Table 1.4, group interventions that can be used with youth in early childhood are provided. In terms of group counseling with younger children, special considerations and activities a counselor might apply include:

- selecting and screening group members intentionally based on the purpose of the proposed counseling group;
- keeping group sessions brief in length and appropriate to the developmental level and focus of the group;
- ensuring group sessions have a specific focus or purpose;
- integrating play and other creative outlets for youth to use in self-expression (Zilberstein, 2014);
- allowing children to interact with their peers in ways that are developmentally appropriate and comfortable;
- encouraging children to interact with one another by encouraging, validating, and praising desirable social interactions (Chronis-Tuscano et al., 2015);
- explaining to parents how and why group counseling is effective or appropriate for youth;
- telling children how and why group counseling can be helpful; and
- using group interactions as a rich source of ongoing assessment information.

Table 1.4	Group Interventions Appropriate for Younger Children	
Goal	Activity	Brief Description
To help youth to understand their own emotions	Angry Monster	Provide each youth with a sheet of paper and coloring supplies. Help youth to think of the most recent time they were especially angry. Have group members explain how it feels in their bodies when they are angry, and compare and contrast their answers while validating each one. Next, have youth draw their Angry Monsters and share them with the group. Process any underlying or primary emotions such as sadness, jealousy, or anxiousness when possible.
To help youth to regulate their emotions	Triangle Jump	Place three pieces of paper on the ground. One should be labeled "Thought," one labeled "Feeling," and one labeled "Behavior." Begin with a story in which the character behaves inappropriately. Trace the character's thought, feeling, and behavior on the floor by walking on each paper and identifying the thought that led to the feeling and behavior. Work with the group to identify healthier thoughts and behaviors. Ask a volunteer to come up and trace one of his or her own recent behaviors and have the group help to reframe the thoughts and identify healthier ways to express the feelings.
To help youth to regulate their behaviors	Gimme Five	The materials for this activity should be prepared in advance. Counselors will need to print and cut out 1-inch pictures of an eye, ear, mouth, hand, and foot for each youth. Counselors should fold an 8 × 10 piece of paper in half four times, and then cut on the lines. Fold each slip of paper in half, and staple it on the open end to create tubes that can slide over a youth's finger. Each youth will need five paper tubes. Allow youth to color their eye, ear, mouth, hand, and foot icons, and tape them onto a slip of paper. Place each slip of paper over a different finger. Read scenarios to the group and have youth hold up the icon that should be controlled. For example, "Johnny hit his sister." The youth should hold up their hand icons.
To help youth to interact with peers in healthy and satisfying ways	The Interview	Place youth into pairs and have them ask their peers two questions: "What is your name?" and "What is your favorite food?" Have each pair come to the front of the group and introduce each other. Have youth welcome each other and ask if anyone else shares the same favorite foods.

When first engaging with young children, take care to remember their internal processes and needs. Remember that many children have limited experience with individuals other than their parents, and a brief separation can be difficult even if they have strong and secure attachments. As such, counselors can allow parents to stay in sessions until a strong therapeutic relationship has formed and the child feels safe with the counselor. Children are dependent on their parents and spend the majority of their time with them, so it is vitally important to integrate family into counseling whenever appropriate or necessary.

To join with a child and build a therapeutic relationship, counselors should be mindful of their nonverbal behaviors. Counselors should assume a nonthreatening posture, which means allowing plenty of personal space for the child and joining the youth on the floor or in low chairs so the child does not feel threatened. Counselors should allow children to take control in sessions to maintain interest and engagement, and counselors should use soothing or excited voice tones when providing direction to children so young people are attentive and engaged. Counselors should maintain eye contact to display genuine interest and approval for the child, but not so much that it seems as though the child is being watched or judged.

Counselors who work with young children should take care to ensure their methods and counseling goals are developmentally appropriate. Family-based interventions are especially relevant when working with children who are highly dependent on their caregivers. Play-based interventions and creative arts are especially effective with young people. Individual and even group counseling can be helpful, and counselors should strive to learn about a child's favorite characters or games and integrate these into counseling so as to hold the child's attention as best as possible. Children respond well to a counselor expressing interest in their preferences as this conveys that the counselor truly cares about and supports them.

MIDDLE CHILDHOOD

In this discussion, the term *middle childhood* is used to describe youth who are 6 to 12 years old. Middle childhood is the stage that bridges early childhood to adolescence. As youth age and move through this stage, they become less childlike; some of their spontaneity and playfulness fades away and is replaced with a new-found self-consciousness and independence. During this developmental period, children begin to have increasingly active social relations with people outside the home. Friendships become more prominent, and school involvement provides these youth with opportunities to test out new behaviors and learn more about themselves in a social context. As they begin to explore new places, people, and things, they develop their social skills and their sense of self. Gradually, these youth become more independent and confident in their abilities, thus preparing them for the next stage of development: early adolescence. In this section, the developmental characteristics and the counseling considerations that relate to middle childhood are discussed.

Middle Childhood Developmental Characteristics

PHYSICAL DEVELOPMENT

During middle childhood, children physically grow and change in ways that influence all aspects of their psychological development (Broderick & Blewitt, 2014). From birth until about age 6 years, children grow at approximately the same rate as their peers; there are some unique differences, but overall the range of development is fairly narrow. However, in middle childhood, growth differences become more dramatic, and there is greater variability in terms of physical presentation (e.g., height, weight; Broderick & Blewitt, 2014). Most often, girls' physical growth (e.g., height, muscle, and fine motor skills) occurs earlier than boys; however, it is not uncommon to see early and late maturation in both genders. Related to the idea of variable growth, some children at this stage may seem more mature—both physically and mentally—than others of the same age.

Like younger children, children at this age are often very physically active. Muscle coordination and control are still developing in the early stages of middle childhood, but children become almost as coordinated as adults by the end of this period. Small muscles often develop rapidly, and this allows these youth to better manage activities that require the development of fine motor skills (e.g., playing musical instruments, precise drawing). Gross motor skills, which assist with tasks completed by larger muscle groups, also develop during this time. Gross motor skills enable everyday functions (e.g., walking, running, standing upright), as well as hand–eye coordination skills (e.g., throwing or catching a ball). Because of their activity levels and active growth, children at this stage require about 10 hours of sleep each night, and deficiencies in sleep can affect mental functioning and growth (Broderick & Blewitt, 2014).

As youth—especially girls—approach adolescence and puberty, many experience growth spurts. In the later stages of middle childhood, bodily changes occur (e.g., hips widen, breasts buds and testes develop, pubic hair appears, acne breaks out) and signal that **puberty** is fast approaching. As children adjust to the changes of their body, feelings of awkwardness and clumsiness will occur. The production of estrogen and testosterone are activated, which are accompanied by the development of secondary sex characteristics such as enlargement of breasts and testes development (Berk, 2003). As children begin to experience the physical changes associated with puberty and as their physical differences become more pronounced, so do their insecurities about their bodies (Sweeney, 2009). Affirming there are many body types and types of beauty can help children to deal with the differences in growth they experience in comparison with their peers, as well as any puberty-related body changes. Their awareness of gender roles, sexual awareness, and attractions to their peers will also increase at this stage. Another facet contributing to physical growth is food intake. Physically, youth may require extra calories and nutrients such as calcium, iron, and protein to maintain sufficient growth.

COGNITIVE DEVELOPMENT

The brain develops rapidly during middle childhood, and these changes usher in many exciting cognitive developments. Children at this age (by age 8) are in Piaget's (1928/2002) **concrete operational stage** of cognitive development. The prefrontal lobe of the brain develops dramatically during middle childhood, and this cognitive development leads to new ways of thinking and interacting with one's world. The prefrontal lobe controls planning and problem solving, and as such, children at this stage begin to show significant advances in their reasoning and planning abilities, and their thinking becomes more organized and rational (Piaget, 1928/2002). For example, they can begin to think through their actions and trace events back to explain situations (e.g., they can consider why they forgot to turn in their homework). The prefrontal lobe continues to develop into adulthood, and children's abilities to problem solve, plan, and control their own behavior continues to improve. The onset of puberty can also influence brain development and play a role in both white and gray matter development as the frontal lobe and cerebral cortex further develop (Zembar & Blume, 2009). As children experience and explore their environments, significant connections are made throughout their brains. Significant synaptic pruning (e.g., getting rid of unwanted or unused connections) occurs during this stage, and this enhances their capacity to learn new information. Thus, youth experience dramatic improvements in areas such as memory, reasoning, planning, and categorizing. The processes of myelination (growth of tissue around neurons) and selective pruning help to crystallize certain behaviors that, in turn, assist in shaping children's environmental reactions and allow them to respond in a progressively more reasoned manner (Zembar & Blume, 2009). Advanced cognitive abilities enable these children to begin to think about their own behavior, see the consequences of their actions, and make meaningful predictions about the outcomes of future actions.

Even though they become more logical and better at problem solving, youth still have room to grow cognitively and are limited in terms of the solutions they can generate; they struggle to think in abstract terms (e.g., they make assumptions or jump to conclusions; Piaget, 1928/2002). As an example, if someone sits in a child's usual seat, the child might think the person did this on purpose—maybe to "steal" the seat—and not consider alternative explanations (e.g., maybe the person mistakenly sat in the seat). Even though abstract thinking is not fully developed, children do start to develop an awareness of other perspectives and incorporate these into their interpretation of the environment. Children begin to see themselves connected to social groups as they start to form friendships and work cohesively on tasks. They become aware of their surroundings but have not yet mastered the capacity to fully empathize with others.

In middle childhood, youth develop the requisite skills needed to engage in academic pursuits. In the early part of this stage, youth can group like things together (e.g., teachers, school busses, and principals are all part of a school). They also begin to think about multiple aspects of a problem (Piaget, 1928/2002). However, these children are still not able to understand abstract concepts, and they tend to focus on multiple parts of a situation rather than the whole. As children near adolescence, they master sequencing and ordering, skills needed for academic success. As youth engage in school, they have an opportunity to apply their developing cognitive skills. Cognitive delays or disorders that affect neurocognitive functioning (e.g., attention-deficit/hyperactivity disorder [ADHD], oppositional defiant disorder [ODD], learning disabilities) will often begin to manifest as children interact with their schools and navigate academic expectations. Family transitions such as divorce, remarriage, and death also affect children's academic expectations. Parenting issues are most complicated if the parents divorce, remarry, or change partners. In a divorce situation, these children may place the blame on themselves as they do not fully understand the real reasons or the complexities associated with the changed family dynamic (Pedro-Carroll, 2010). Confusion and emotional reactions (e.g., anger, feeling unloved, sadness) may fester in the child, and these can manifest at later developmental stages.

Children at this stage learn best if they are active and engaged in the learning process. They should be provided with opportunities to ask questions, explore concepts, and practice as a way to learn (e.g., the use of role-play in counseling). As an example, when teaching young clients about feelings, it is not enough for the counselor to tell them about different emotions or even to show them a feeling chart. Children will learn more about feelings if they engage with the feeling concepts and draw the pictures they see, draw pictures of times when they have experienced certain emotions, act out the emotions, or engage in any other engaging activity that brings the concept to life (Broderick & Blewitt, 2014).

During middle childhood, young people also develop and make enormous advances in social cognition—the ability to understand people and to think about their social relations—which affects their self- and emotional development. Young people learn that they can infer others' thoughts and that they, in turn, can infer their thoughts. Because of this development, youth begin to think about how other people may react to their behavior. In other words, youth become better able to engage in role or perspective taking. Role-taking abilities may include the capacity to understand what another person sees (perceptual role taking), how another person feels (affective role taking), and what another person thinks (cognitive role taking). This role-taking ability lays the foundation for youth developing important social, decision-making, and problem-solving skills.

SELF-DEVELOPMENT

Youth in middle childhood often define themselves by their activities (e.g., I am a dancer), their possessions (e.g., I have a dog), or their appearance (e.g., I have freckles), and they can identify numerous ways of defining themselves (Broderick & Blewitt, 2014). They also begin to identify justifications for their perceived characteristics. For example, a girl might believe she is good at gymnastics because she received a gymnastics trophy.

At this stage, youth increasingly develop a sense of identity as separate from their families, and whereas up until now they have likely idealized their parents, they may begin to judge parents and question them and their ideas, especially as they approach adolescence (Broderick & Blewitt, 2014). Youth begin to view themselves as more independent; however, they still continue to seek affirmation from their parents. Youth may begin to ask their parents questions that are difficult to answer (e.g., Why did you and Dad get a divorce?), and they begin to expect more thoughtful responses as they make sense of their worlds. Some parents may struggle at this stage with how to support their child's emerging independence.

Youth in middle childhood acquire the freedom to, in many ways, take care of themselves. Their emerging independence allows them to develop a better sense of their capacities and how they are similar or unique to others. It is in this relational context that youth begin to define who they are and who they are not. Children start to develop a self-concept as they are better able to reflect on perceptions, abilities, and competencies. They become better aware of their real selves relative to their ideal selves, and they begin to understand how they are influenced by their environment (Harter, 2006). Because of their expanding experiences, many factors can alter and develop children's self-perceptions and affect how they perceive themselves and their place in the world. As these youth experience new situations outside the home, they will experience stress, and they will need to adapt and adjust to these new experiences. If they struggle to manage these new experiences or have negative interactions with their world, then their sense of self can be adversely affected.

During middle childhood, children start to better understand and think through the consequences of their actions, an ability related to both their capacity to take the perspectives of others and the increasing value friendships play in their lives. In addition, the nature of their friendships evolves as long-term friendships become more common. The settings in which children interact with their peers also expand and become more diverse. By the end of middle childhood, they understand that their social standing with friends and peer groups depends on their ability to behave in ways similar to their peers, follow rules, achieve success in certain activities (e.g., sports, school), and treat others kindly. At home, they strive to comply with house rules and complete chores and homework because of the pride and accomplishment they experience when they do these things well. They feel good about themselves, and they develop a healthy self-identity when they can say "I did this" or when they are successful in various ways.

As they develop an awareness of others and themselves, children begin to compare themselves to others to evaluate their own skills, and this informs their identity development. They also develop an increased ability to consider other people's perspectives as their ability is influenced by the environments in which they socialize (e.g., school, home). A child might ask himself "Am I as good as my neighbor at sports?" If so, he might come to see himself as being good at sports. By the time these youth enter early adolescence, they start to integrate this understanding of their skills into their sense of identity. So, for example, "I am good at sports" transitions into "I'm a sports person." Ideally, youth are provided with multiple opportunities to connect with activities that can help them to develop a healthy identity and a sense of being competent and industrious.

As some children compare themselves to others, they may believe they fall short, which can result in them becoming self-critical and insecure (Broderick & Blewitt, 2014). The messages youth receive in the home can play an important role in how they perceive themselves in relation to other children. A child who receives positive messages about himself from his parents will not be as sensitive to being the last person picked for a team in gym class as a child who receives critical messages from his parents. Youth who feel insecure and self-critical are less likely to try new activities or to take risks in their academic and social relationships, and they may be quicker to misperceive their interactions with others, thus resulting in strained peer relationships.

As children begin to explore other aspects of their identity, they start to reflect on how they fit in with their social circles. Youth begin to engage in social comparison and judgment and have new concerns about being "popular." In addition, children develop a greater awareness of their ethnic and racial identity, their socioeconomic status, and how similar and different they are from others.

By experimenting with different roles, youth begin to develop and expand their identity by testing limits and engaging in back talk and mild forms of rebellion with authority figures. This behavior allows youth to establish a sense of the boundaries of their worlds and themselves. It is important that authority figures express clear, consistent boundaries so these youth have a predictable experience in which they can get to know and define themselves. Parenting becomes very important at this age, and parents may find they need to adapt their parenting style to match their child's evolving needs. The primary parenting styles are often conceptualized as being authoritarian, permissive, and authoritative (Santrock, 2011). Authoritarian parents set high demands and expectations for their children but provide little nurturance and feedback. This type of parenting is a more restrictive, punishment-heavy parenting style, and these parents are generally less likely to provide explanations or feedback to the children about the reasons behind their rules and expectations (Santrock, 2011). Permissive parents are reluctant to set rules; they do not exert control because they believe children can best regulate themselves (Santrock, 2011). Authoritative parents are nurturing, yet also rightfully demanding; they set clear limits, and there is a sense of boundaries (Santrock, 2011). These parents set and communicate clear standards for their children, monitor the limits they set, and allow children to develop autonomy (Santrock, 2011). The authoritative parenting style is believed to promote the most positive development, encouraging strong relationships and improving youth's self-regulation skills (DeVore & Ginsburg, 2005). It is essential that parents take a prominent and responsible role in helping their child to develop while maintaining a strong level of support, and counselors can help parents to this end.

PSYCHOSOCIAL DEVELOPMENT
During middle childhood, children are at Erikson's (1968) stage of **industry versus inferiority**. During this stage, children ideally begin to build a self-image as industrious and productive. If children struggled with demonstrating power during the initiative versus guilt stage, they may appear shy or withdrawn and may require help with exhibiting their abilities (Erikson, 1968). Therefore, if encouraged, an identity as a productive worker can translate into positive career choices and career development. With encouragement, children gain increased self-confidence in their ability to achieve goals and succeed. Along with increased competence, children at this stage should develop an internal locus of control. This internal locus of control involves children feeling as though they are responsible for their own situations and have some control over their lives. Successful navigation of this psychosocial stage helps children to develop a sense of competence or a belief in their ability to handle various life tasks.

Social relationships become increasingly important in middle childhood (Erikson, 1968). At this stage, friends often live in the same neighborhood, and they are most commonly of the same gender. Children at this age generally have a small group of friends (e.g., 5), and they often have a perceived "enemy" as well. These children may be nurturing or commanding with younger children but follow and depend on older children. They are typically more selective about their peers and who they associate with than they were in early childhood. As children age, they are also more inclined to yield to peer pressure, and they may choose to follow their friends and do what they do.

Children in this stage develop moral reasoning, and the desire to be a "good person" and to please others becomes more prominent. Youth often want to engage in caring behaviors and are aware of the consequences of negative behaviors. Children also show increased forgiveness because they may believe it is expected of them or they feel pressured to forgive.

Children also demonstrate increasingly effective communication skills as their vocabulary increases tremendously from about 10,000 to approximately 40,000 words (Berk, 2003). As their vocabulary increases, so does their understanding of humor and semantics, which increases their ability to relate to others. The development of humor and semantics can result in their appreciation of "gross out" or "bathroom" humor, which is used as a way to connect with peers (Finnan, 2008).

Teachers and school counselors often set the conditions for social interactions that occur in schools. As they progress through elementary school, academic performance and achievement play an ever-increasing role in self-identity and self-esteem and how youth are received by their peers. Children who meet school expectations feel good about themselves, make friends with classmates who also get good grades, and may even have better social skills (Erikson, 1968).

Children at this age may become attached to adults other than their parents (e.g., teachers, club leaders), and they may idealize these adults and try to please them to gain attention. These youth may "tattle" on other kids as a way to attract adult attention in the early years of middle childhood. Children who are encouraged and commended by parents and other adults develop a feeling of competence and belief in their skills and a sense of self-worth. Those who receive little or no encouragement from parents, teachers, or peers may question their ability to be successful.

EMOTIONAL DEVELOPMENT

In middle childhood, an increased ability to problem solve leads to greater self-control. As their problem-solving and self-control skills develop, youth are better able to self-soothe and regulate their strong emotions (Sigelman & Rider, 2012). As such, they experience fewer angry outbursts, and they are better able to endure frustration when they do not immediately get what they want. However, 6- and 7-year-olds may still have the occasional tantrum when they are upset. These youth generally rely on their parents to help them calm down. However, the frequency and intensity of emotional distress typically decreases as youth develop and learn emotional coping skills (e.g., walking away from difficult situations, figuring out solutions instead of getting caught up in the problem). An enhanced ability to self-regulate is motivated in part by the growing realization that their peers do not want to be friends with children who have outbursts that interfere with play, hurt their feelings, or make them feel uncomfortable.

Clinical Toolbox 1.2

In the Pearson eText, click here to review a counseling activity that can facilitate young people's emotional regulation.

Emotionally, youth in middle childhood often feel self-conscious, and they believe that everyone notices even small differences (e.g., a new haircut, a hug in public from a parent; Sigelman & Rider, 2012). These children also start to become aware of more **complex emotions**. For example, they can come to understand embarrassment, and they can articulate a series of events that led to feeling embarrassed. Because of their increased sensitivity to and awareness of emotions and their ability to have perspective, this is a time when we first see children control—and even hide—their feelings.

Friendships in middle childhood are defined by loyalty and involve supportive behaviors, and this provides a new source of emotional support for youth (Sigelman & Rider, 2012). As they start to realize they can rely on their friends, their friends become more important to them. Middle childhood is a time when youth first begin to have "best friends" and enemies, and these relationships provide an important outlet for learning and practicing new social and emotional regulation skills.

In terms of fears, earlier in middle childhood (i.e., around ages 6–8), children may still be afraid of monsters and the dark. As they move through middle childhood, these fears are replaced by ones related to school performance, various disasters (e.g., tornadoes), social relationships, death, the unknown, failure, family problems, and/or rejection (Sigelman & Rider, 2012).

For these youth, winning, leading, or being first is valued (Sigelman & Rider, 2012). As youth learn to navigate the realities of their social standings and various social situations, they may struggle and be sensitive, and they will need support from caring adults. Children's feelings may get hurt easily as they learn how to deal with perceived failures.

Middle Childhood Counseling Considerations

COMMON PROBLEMS IN MIDDLE CHILDHOOD

Because middle childhood is a time of transition, it is not uncommon for youth to struggle with these transitions. At this age, any disruption to their "normal" can upset them, and naturally, frequent transitions and changes can be experienced as stressful. How youth manage their life transitions depends on their experiences at home, at school, and with their friends, and these can fluctuate daily.

Some children may also require counseling to provide support related to demonstrating and managing their increased independence. This independence manifests itself in three main areas: family and home, school, and social relationships.

Common family-related struggles that may emerge include changes within the family structure (e.g., parental separation or divorce), conflicts with siblings, or difficulties meeting their evolving family responsibilities (e.g., completing chores or homework). It is not uncommon for children and their parents to experience some degree of stress and emotional unrest in the wake of all these changes, and some young people may struggle to manage these transitions and thus may require supports (Masarik & Conger, 2017). Many youth have to manage serious family problems such as substance abuse, violence between parents, or poverty, and children's ability to recognize, define, and understand these problems becomes more pronounced in middle childhood. When working with children at this stage—or any other stage—it is important to consider how their unique developmental factors influence how they deal with family issues.

Youth may benefit from counseling as a means of helping them to move into school and navigate complex social relationships. For example, children may be afraid of new situations (e.g., attending a Girl Scout meeting where she does not know anyone), or they may struggle to manage the pressure to fit in (e.g., my friends are mean to the new girl at school, but I like her). The effects of bullying during this stage are enhanced as bullying may involve physical, social, and psychological dimensions (Jimerson, Swearer, & Espelage, 2010). With this as an issue, it is important that professionals implement strategies to address bullying and encourage a safe and positive environment. Young people may also require support in learning how to make and keep friends. Counselors can play a role in social skills training, providing information about healthy friendships, and problem solving how to manage difficult situations.

As youth progress in their schooling, they may also struggle academically (e.g., a decline in school performance or failure to perform at an appropriate level of functioning), and this may lead to counseling referrals. Counselors can play a role in identifying and assessing various neurological disorders that may be affecting a child's school success (e.g., ADHD, autism spectrum disorder) or any other life stressors that may be at play (e.g., parental divorce, traumatic experiences).

Related to schooling, behavior problems may manifest in this setting, and this can also lead to counseling referrals. Certain youth behaviors may not be an issue at home, yet they may present as concerning at school. For example, aggressive behaviors may be commonplace in a youth's home, but these same behaviors are not acceptable in a school setting. Thus, they become defined as problematic by an important system in the child's life.

COUNSELING APPLICATIONS

Counselors should be aware that youth ages 6 through 8 years can rarely sit for longer than 15 to 20 minutes for an activity. However, young people's attention spans get progressively longer as they approach adolescence. Counselors should structure sessions and select counseling activities with an eye to the attention span of their young clients.

Youth at this age prize the attention of adults and counselors. This can be used to facilitate the development of the counseling relationship and as a resource in motivating clients to reach their goals and make changes. Positive feedback for successes will be especially well received by these youth. Counselors should also encourage parents to provide their children with positive feedback and to spend quality time with them (Centers for Disease Control [CDC], 2016; Mitchell & Ziegler, 2012).

Clinical Toolbox 1.3

In the Pearson eText, click to review information counselors can share with parents to improve their ability to support their children.

Children at this stage are increasingly able to talk through and solve problems, and this has implications for how counselors can approach this population. Counselors can talk about concepts and teach children skills related to good decision making. It is also important that adults support and build children's confidence in their ability to make decisions while not expecting them to do more than they may be ready to do. Counselors should have an understanding of the challenges commonly experienced by children during this stage of development (e.g., bullying, peer pressure).

As they develop cognitively, children of this age can benefit from being involved in setting counseling goals and working toward those goals. Young people's ability to develop and meet goals provides an exciting opportunity to integrate goal setting into counseling (Wong, Hall, Justice, & Hernandez, 2015). Goal setting allows clients to be active participants in directing and focusing their counseling. Similarly, they appreciate helping to establish boundaries and rules, and counselors can engage them in conversations around the structure and limits of counseling (e.g., talking with parents about different topics, how to pull parents into the counseling process). Young clients garner a sense of control and ownership in counseling when they can contribute to its structure and focus.

Clinical Toolbox 1.4

In the Pearson eText, click here to review an example of a goal worksheet that can be used to help youth set goals.

Despite their increased ability to set and work toward goals, cognitively these youth are concrete. They need support in organizing their thinking and in developing and applying their decision-making and problem-solving processes. Counselors can help to facilitate young people's thought processes by:

- being curious and asking them "what if . . ." questions (e.g., "I wonder what would happen if you tried to do with your friend what you did with your brother last week when you got angry?");
- encouraging their basic problem-solving skills (e.g., "How could you make sure you get to play kickball at recess, too?"); and
- asking if you can help them to think about ways they can solve different problems.

Counselors should approach and develop interventions for youth in middle childhood with an eye to their achievement of developmental milestones. Generally, counselors might:

- plan more structured activities (than with younger children) while keeping in mind that youth at this age do not likely have the attention span to stay focused on an hour-long task;

- understand that as youth at this age gain more independence from their parents, they can be encouraged to take ownership of and assume an active role in their counseling sessions;
- identify activities appropriate to youth's increasing development of fine and gross motor skills;
- integrate family system approaches into counseling because family-related struggles are common for this age group, and these youth are increasingly able to influence and participate in these approaches;
- use developmentally appropriate language because youth are continuing to acquire more complex vocabulary;
- provide support for emotion identification as youth continue to develop appropriate empathetic response and understanding of complex emotions;
- support youth's need for creative self-expression through writing, drawing, reading, and role-play activities; and
- consider the matters that are important to youth at this age and how they may be affecting their mental health (e.g., physical changes, more important friendships resulting in increased peer pressure and the need to fit in).

As young people's self-control and ability to solve problems develop, they are better able to develop their social skills, an important life skill frequently addressed in counseling (Skinner & Zimmer-Gembeck, 2016; Wong et al., 2015). The importance of being patient, sharing, and respecting others' rights are concepts that these youth can, at this stage, understand, and these are the foundations of social skills training with young clients.

Youth at this age are better able to recognize and express their feelings than they could when they were younger (Skinner & Zimmer-Gembeck, 2016). These youth have not yet developed the emotional defenses that typically come with age, and they are very transparent about their feelings. Although they may not be able to identify and express their feelings with ease, they are often very open and verbal about their experiences and with their expressions, and it is typically easy for counselors to glean their associated feelings. These youth can benefit from affective education, which involves helping youth to understand their own and others' emotional and social behavior and enabling them to make any necessary changes to this behavior. As a part of affective education, young people learn about feelings, what they mean, and how to regulate and manage these feelings.

One of the common reasons this population comes to counseling is behavioral problems. At this age, children's behavior can be managed with verbal reasoning, positive reinforcement, deprivation of privileges, appeals to their sense of humor, or reminders of the consequences of their actions. Counselors can use this information to set boundaries within counseling, and this information can also be used to support parents in managing their children's behavior.

Children begin to read and write early in middle childhood and should be proficient in these skills by the end of this developmental stage. As such, counselors may be able to integrate interventions that pull on these abilities. Youth in the later stages of middle childhood, in particular, may be able to benefit from between-session activities such as journaling or otherwise documenting their behavior or experiences or reading (Malchiodi, 2013).

Youth at this stage become better candidates for group counseling, and developmentally appropriate activities a counselor might engage in or encourage with young people in middle childhood include (Jacobs, Schimmel, Masson, & Harvill, 2015; Prout & Fedewa, 2015; Senn, 2004):

- receiving validation and support from others in a safe environment, along with the development of supportive, intimate relationships and an increased understanding that others have similar problems;
- focusing on facilitating empathy, emotion identification, and emotional regulation;
- addressing matters traversed by youth at this age (e.g., identity formation, social skill development, self-concept development, friendships, family transitions, social and family conflict resolution);
- focusing on setting short- and long-term goals and problem solving (e.g., goal charts, planning, reward/reinforcement) via teamwork and team building activities;
- taking into account youth developing and increasingly complex vocabulary (e.g., emotion bingo, creating and revising self-stories, and coping skill identification games); and
- using games, role-play, and art to facilitate both normal developmental tasks and problems common to this age group.

Clinical Toolbox 1.5

In the Pearson eText, click here to review an activity that can be used to enhance young people's empathy capacities.

EARLY ADOLESCENCE

In this discussion, the term *early adolescence* is used to describe youth who are 10 to 14 years old. Early adolescence is full of developmental transitions and changes. As youth increasingly explore relationships outside their families, they begin to identify—and sometimes even solidify—their personal interests, values, and attitudes. Adolescence can be a confusing, exciting, and difficult time for youth. As children transition from a state of dependence to independence, numerous challenges and opportunities emerge that both youth and their parents must navigate. In the next section, the developmental characteristics and the counseling considerations that relate to early adolescence are discussed.

Early Adolescence Developmental Characteristics

PHYSICAL DEVELOPMENT

The hallmark of early adolescence is rapid physical growth (Broderick & Blewitt, 2014). Individual variations exist with the timing of these physical changes, and growth occurs at different rates and times (e.g., arms may grow before the torso, weight may increase before height), which may lead to some youth appearing awkward or even clumsy. Regular exercise (e.g., sports, dance, bike riding) can improve coordination, boost mood, facilitate emotional regulation, and develop lifelong healthy habits (Jenson & Bender, 2014). Physical growth, characterized by an increase in height and weight, parallels the onset of puberty.

Simplistically, puberty is the process of sexual maturation that enables an individual to be fertile and sexually reproduce. More specifically, puberty is when the hypothalamus begins to produce gonadotropin-releasing hormone (Wong et al., 2015), luteinizing hormone, and follicle-stimulating hormone; these hormones serve as catalysts for the increased production of estrogen and androgens (e.g., testosterone), which alter and change different parts of the human body (e.g., genitalia, breasts, menstruation, pubic hair) and prepare an individual for sexual reproduction (Wong et al., 2015).

Genetic and environmental factors can affect the onset of puberty, and the timing of puberty varies for girls (between the ages of 8 and 13) and boys (between the ages of 9 and 15; Broderick & Blewitt, 2014). Girls generally develop physically before boys, and this discrepancy can influence the way girls and boys interact and relate to each other. Recent trends reveal an even more dramatic gap between the timing of puberty for boys and girls, with a downward shift in the average age of girls' first menstruation (Greenspan & Deardorff, 2014), which usually occurs just before girls turn 13 (Broderick & Blewitt, 2014). Increased anxiety, concerns with body image and weight, and higher-risk behaviors (e.g., use and abuse of alcohol, sexual promiscuity, relationships with older peers) are all risks associated with early sexual maturation (Downing & Bellis, 2009). Conversely, those adolescents (especially boys) who mature later than others are more susceptible to higher rates of anxiety, depression, and other adjustment-related issues (Broderick & Blewitt, 2014; Wong et al., 2015).

Adolescents not only begin to go through physical changes but also experience sexual changes such as increased sexual arousal, desire, curiosity, and urges. As their **sexual drive** escalates, adolescents are confronted with their own sexuality and begin to consider their sexual identity. One's sense of his or her **sexual identity** and **sexual orientation** becomes more pronounced during early adolescence and continues into adulthood (Broderick & Blewitt, 2014). Sexual transitions and changes can be uncomfortable and influence adolescents' intimate and peer relationships. Youth may begin to have sexual fantasies, masturbate, and engage in sexual activity during this stage (Wong et al., 2015). Adults can encourage resilience in adolescents by providing accurate and appropriate sexual-related information, which can aid youth in progressing through these physical and sexual changes (Jenson & Fraser, 2015). In addition, adults should attempt to create a supportive, open environment by providing adolescents with a safe space to discuss these physical and sexual changes.

In addition, adolescents' brain development—primarily in the cerebellum and the frontal lobes (e.g., prefrontal cortex)—continues to develop throughout early adolescence (Dixon, Rice, & Rumsey, 2017). The cerebellum is the region of the brain responsible for muscle tone, motor movement coordination, and balance (Broderick & Blewitt, 2014). Conversely, the frontal lobes are the executive functioning area of the brain, aiding young people in engaging in complex cognitive behaviors (e.g., decision making, planning), personality expression, and impulse control; the frontal lobes are often the last parts of the brains to fully develop (Johnson, Blum, & Giedd, 2009). Although adolescents may appear impulsive and reckless, they may actually be selecting risky behaviors due to a lack of foresight and an inability to anticipate long-term consequences. During this time period, adolescents attempt to gain mastery and control over their movements, executive functioning, and high-order cognitive behaviors. Adults should attempt to understand how young people's behaviors continue to develop and should aid youth in navigating these years by promoting the use of more adaptive, positive behaviors (Dixon et al., 2017).

COGNITIVE DEVELOPMENT

In early adolescence, youth move from concrete to **formal operational thinking** (Piaget, 1970). Although the complete transition to formal operational thinking often occurs in later adolescence (ages 15–18), youth in early adolescence gradually begin to think more abstractly about ideas, hypothesize about cause-and-effect relationships, and consider and create alternatives (Broderick & Blewitt, 2014). For example, a youth at the concrete operational stage may find it difficult to consider multiple ways of dealing with a bully at school, whereas an adolescent progressing through the formal operational stage will most likely be able to formulate multiple alternative behaviors for this situation and present the associated consequence for each action; in other words, adolescents are able to increasingly think abstractly.

Cognitive development is a process that evolves over time. Early adolescents may still have difficulty connecting their thinking, feelings, and situations, but they are moving toward an increased ability to predict the consequences of their behaviors. Formal operational thinking is characterized by adolescents' ability to detect inconsistencies, process information, think about the future in relation to the present, see potential possibilities, and foresee the logical sequence of events (Bergin & Bergin, 2015). Cognitive changes (e.g., from concrete to formal operational) are one of the more dramatic shifts that people experience over their life span. Adults need to demonstrate patience with early adolescents as they develop and mature in their cognitive abilities. These youth struggle with being consistent in their thinking (e.g., they may apply abstract thinking to a homework assignment but not to personal/social dilemma), and this can be confusing for them, their parents, and those around them (Bergin & Bergin, 2015). In addition, adults may help to facilitate adolescents' social and problem-solving skills, which may inversely decrease their risk-taking behaviors, impulsivity, and sensation-seeking choices (Jenson & Fraser, 2015).

Clinical Toolbox 1.6

In the Pearson eText, click here to review an example of a weekly assignment planner that youth can use to support their school organizational skills.

SELF-DEVELOPMENT

Adolescence is characterized by youth moving toward a greater sense of competency, independence, and identity. These young people wrestle with not only their sense of mastery and competency (i.e., industry vs. inferiority) but also who they are in relation to others (i.e., **identity versus identity role confusion**; Erikson, 1968). This process of identity formation should be understood as a process of development that is unique to each youth, consisting of times of **crisis**—or the reevaluation and exploration of one's values and beliefs—often leading to a **commitment** or personal investment in a belief or identity (Marcia, 1967). Although identity formation begins in early adolescence, it is a process that continues into later adolescence (i.e., 15–18) and even into early adulthood (Paladino & DeLorenzi, 2017). In Table 1.5, a summary of the categories in adolescent identity development is provided.

Table 1.5	Categories of Identity Development	
Categories	Category Overview	Example Applied to Religious/Spiritual Identity Examples
Identity foreclosure	Identity foreclosure is characterized by a commitment to traditional, cultural, and/or family values and beliefs rather than exploring and determining one's own beliefs or values. Youth may appear to be overly conforming and accommodating. *Commitment without crisis.*	*My parents do not believe in God. My grandparents do not believe in God. So, I do not believe in God. I trust them; they must be right.*
Identity diffusion	Identity diffusion is characterized by a lack of commitment or adherence to certain ideals, along with a lack of desire for exploration. Youth may seem avoidant, uninterested, or even disorganized. *No commitment and no crisis.*	*I am not interested in thinking about whether there is a God. I really don't care, nor do I care to find out. I would rather talk about something else.*
Identity moratorium	Identity moratorium is characterized by exploration without any commitment to values, beliefs, and/or goals. These young people may appear to be inconsistent, reactionary, and opportunistic. *Crisis without commitment.*	*I am not sure if there is a God. More important, how would I even know if there was a God? What does it mean to have faith in something I can't see? Should I explore other perspectives on whether God exists? Could there be a God or other? I am not sure this is even important.*
Identity achievement	Identity achievement is characterized by the resolution of a crisis by committing to a set of values, beliefs, and/or goals after a period of extensive exploration. These young people may appear more self-assured, confident, and self-reliant. *Commitment after a crisis.*	*After researching and evaluating multiple perspectives (i.e., Judaism, Islam, Christianity, Hinduism), I believe that God exists. I believe that God made me and loves me. Now, I have decided to become involved in church, the Catholic Church.*

Note. Adapted from "Ego identity status: Relationship to change in self-esteem, 'general maladjustment,' and authoritarianism," by J. E. Marcia, 1967, *Journal of Personality, 35*, pp. 118–133. doi:10.1111/j.1467-6494.1967.tb01419.x

Frequently, early adolescents will rely on and use their peer groups when forming their sense of beliefs, values, and identity. This process of identity exploration is essential as youth attempt to understand how they fit into the world around them. During childhood, these children may have identified with their parents and families, yet during early adolescence they frequently try to detach, differentiate, and rebel from the family system that often results in parent–child conflicts. Serious parent–child conflicts can increase the risk of substance abuse, risk-taking behaviors, aggression, and school-related problems (e.g., truancy, poor grades; Jenson & Bender, 2014).

Adolescents' drive toward **autonomy** (i.e., acting or existing separately from others) requires some degree of separation from parents and family members. The separation from parents can often be turbulent because these youth lack maturity, and they do not have their own real-world experiences to lean into for guidance. Adults should be supportive and consistent while they monitor youth and avoid personalizing the distancing from adults that comes with their push for independence and autonomy (Jenson & Bender, 2014). Even as youth become more reliant on their peer groups, the adults in their lives should remain involved and connected with their schooling, activities, and peer relationships. These adults should understand that peer groups will hold a significant position of influence and affect young people's interests, dress, and behaviors. In ethnic minority early adolescents, ethnicity and culture also begin to play an increasingly important role in young people's sense of self and how they fit into their world (Smith & Silva, 2011). More specifically, adolescent youth must negotiate if they will assimilate with the dominate culture, coalesce with their culture of origin, or manage bicultural/multicultural identities (Dixon et al., 2017).

Clinical Toolbox 1.7

In the Pearson eText, click here to review tips that adults can use to facilitate adolescent autonomy.

In addition to the desire of early adolescents to differentiate their identity from parents and family, they often become increasingly more egocentric (e.g., self-centered, thinking primarily of oneself; Broderick & Blewitt, 2014); they value themselves highly, and they think no one experiences the things they do or could ever understand them. Because of their adherence to an *imaginary audience* (i.e., everyone is listening and watching them intently), **egocentric** youth are especially vulnerable to the criticism of others, particularly concerning their appearance and performance (Broderick & Blewitt, 2014). The sensitivity of adolescents to criticism may appear to be more pronounced in females (Kirkcaldy, Siefen, & Merrick, 2007).

Youth in early adolescence are often contradictory; they desire uniqueness, yet they also want to fit in (e.g., in terms of how they look and think) with those around them. With their increased need for independence and autonomy, and an egocentric focus, early adolescents tend to paradoxically increase their dependency on others. In stressful situations, some youth can even revert back to childish behaviors (e.g., temper tantrums, intrusive touching and hugging). Self-development in early adolescence can be a confusing time for youth and their parents. Although most youth in early adolescence may attempt to spend time away from the family, parents must be supportive, patient, empathic, and understanding to aid their children in developing a strong sense of self (Jenson & Fraser, 2015).

PSYCHOSOCIAL DEVELOPMENT

In early adolescence, many changes occur with adolescents' relationships. Peers begin to play a more prominent role in a youth's socialization, experimentation, and decision making. Adolescents seek their parents' guidance less and become more attached to peers' opinions and thoughts.

Group norms emerge (e.g., how to dress and act), and youth begin to rely more heavily on peers for support. Early adolescents seek more freedom and activities outside parental supervision. Adults need to balance their responsibilities when monitoring, supervising, and providing youth with opportunities to have positive relationships with their peers. A greater focus on peer relationships exposes adolescents to new experiences, which in turn invites vulnerability (Jenson & Bender, 2014). Adolescents become more susceptible to being embarrassed or hurt by others; therefore, peer relationships become not only a source of pleasure but also a source of increased angst and stress (Wong et al., 2015).

Peer-related social concerns such as bullying and relational aggression, popularity, and peer pressure can dominate early adolescence. Early adolescence is a time when these relationships become increasingly more complex, yet youth often lack the skills to know how to handle these situations. Enhancing adolescents' ability to engage in emotional self-regulation, problem-solving, and conflict management skills can help them to navigate the aforementioned struggles (Jenson & Bender, 2014). In addition, youth at this stage wrestle with trying to figure out what they are *good at* as compared to others (i.e., industry vs. inferiority; Erikson, 1968). The development of one's sense of what they are good *at* and how that pertains to their peers begins to pave the way for a sense of self within the context of one's social world (i.e., ego identity vs. ego diffusion; Erikson, 1968). As early adolescents struggle with popularity and peer pressure, adults may need to assist them in discovering what they do well and how it fits into their social world because this can increase their overall sense of well-being (Bergin & Bergin, 2015; Broderick & Blewitt, 2014).

EMOTIONAL DEVELOPMENT

Emotions during early adolescence can be understood, metaphorically, as an emotional rollercoaster—feelings are fleeting, and their meaning may seem elusive. Emotions in early adolescence are often capricious and intense. Times of happiness often turn into euphoria, whereas times of frustration and anxiety spiral into shame, guilt, and despair. Because these negative emotions can overwhelm youth, outbursts of anger, indifference, and even aggression may mask feelings of vulnerability (Geldard & Geldard, 2010). These complicated feelings and reactions, as well as the difficulty youth experience in recognizing underlying emotions, inevitably distance them from others, especially parents and people in positions of authority (e.g., teachers, coaches).

Although some adolescents can think abstractly, others remain more concrete in their thinking and may feel stuck in situations (e.g., unable to generate alternative solutions). Adolescents' difficulties with identifying alternatives, in conjunction with an increase in anxiety, may lead them to feel guilt and shame (Geldard & Geldard, 2010). In addition, youth in early adolescence are more susceptible to anxiety and depression than they were in their younger years (Merikangas et al., 2010). Some children may also carry the effects of childhood trauma (e.g., abuse [physical, emotional, sexual, neglect]), family substance addiction, mentally ill family members, and incarcerated parents with them into adolescence, and this can serve to confound their emotional development (Vandell, Belskey, Burchinal, Vangergrift, & Steinburg, 2010).

Youth in early adolescence are emotionally vulnerable, so adults need to be measured in their responses to youth and not overreact or react insensitively (Jenson & Bender, 2014). Adults can facilitate adolescents' emotional development by helping them to (a) recognize and manage emotions, (b) develop more empathy for others, (c) learn to resolve conflict constructively, (d) increase a sense of belonging, and (e) attempt to consider others' perspectives (Ugoani & Ewuzie, 2013). The development of interpersonal skills can make adolescents more resilient to associated risks (e.g., substance abuse, delinquency, aggression, school-related issues) during adolescence.

Early Adolescence Counseling Considerations

COMMON PROBLEMS IN EARLY ADOLESCENCE

Common problems this population presents in counseling are behavior problems related to the regulation of emotions, identity, and peer and family struggles. In terms of mental health disorders, anxiety (e.g., separation anxiety disorder, specific phobias), behavioral (e.g., ODD, ADHD), and depressive disorders (e.g., major depressive disorder) are those most frequently diagnosed in the early adolescent population (Merikangas et al., 2010). In addition, preoccupation with eating or restriction of eating and disordered eating behaviors can also present during this stage (Micali, Ploubidis, De Stavola, Simonoff, & Treasure, 2014).

Adolescents are often overwhelmed by the intensity of their feelings and emotions, and these emotions may manifest through acting-out behaviors (e.g., risk taking, self-injury, substance use). Adults often misunderstand these acting out behaviors and view them as intentional, and this mind-set can create additional problems such as youth defiance and/or withdrawal (Geldard & Geldard, 2010).

Because of their egocentric perception of self and their preoccupation with their appearance, acceptance, and sexuality, adolescents often have conflicts in their interpersonal relationships with parents, siblings, and peers. In addition, their emerging desire for independence can stress the family structure as a whole, including sibling and parent–child relationships. For example, a youth may seek affection from her parents one minute and then react with hostility the next minute when a casual request is denied.

Youth in early adolescence often explore and change friend groups in an attempt to find a clear sense of self (e.g., identity), and they often overreact in their relationships with these friends (e.g., they are sensitive to criticism concerning their appearance and performance; Bergin & Bergin, 2015; Broderick & Blewitt, 2014). In addition, they may begin to seek out sexual relationships and sexual risk taking (e.g., sexual promiscuity, unprotected sex), and this can invite consequences such as sexually transmitted diseases or pregnancy (Wong et al., 2015). As social relationships become more important, the risk of peer pressure also increases, and issues associated with substance use/abuse may manifest. Although only 1 in 10 adolescents report regularly abusing alcohol, the normal median age of first consumption is 13 years old (Swendsen et al., 2012), and counselors should be aware of these pressures.

COUNSELING APPLICATIONS

Early adolescence is often associated with a move from dependence to independence, experimentation, risk taking, and relational conflicts. Counselors should remember that youth are attempting to figure out what they are *good at* and *who they are* in this world (Erikson, 1968). Counselors will need to select counseling applications and approaches that take into consideration these two developmental tasks. Specifically, counselors working with youth in early adolescence should consider (Cook-Cottone, Kane, & Anderson, 2015; Dixon et al., 2017; Kuther, 2017):

- constructing sessions to maximize the youth's attention span (e.g., change activities frequently if the client appears to have a shorter attention span);
- remembering that parents continue to play a role in early adolescence and should be integrated into counseling whenever possible;
- using peer-based interventions (e.g., peer mentoring and/or peer tutoring programs that could be supervised by a school counselor);
- acknowledging resistance to change and avoiding power struggles;
- integrating things the client seems interested in and possesses some expertise in such as skills, hobbies, and/or talents;
- identifying and cultivating an awareness of personal strengths and limitations;
- using developmentally appropriate language (e.g., be concrete), and check in often with the client to evaluate the appropriateness of questions, statements, and activities;
- doing something active: allowing the client to occupy his or her hands during sessions (e.g., squeeze balls) and incorporating activities that are focused on *doing* (e.g., engaging in activities and interactions);
- acknowledging his or her egocentric (e.g., self-involved) cognitions and aiming to increase his or her insight and empathy for others;
- allowing the client to offer challenges to perspectives concerning an issue or situation; and
- incorporating popular culture (e.g., media, music) into counseling activities.

Although most early adolescents begin to transition into formal operational thinking (which can aid in their decision-making, problem-solving, and perspective-taking skills), they are often inconsistent in their thinking and egocentric in their perspective, and they mask their feelings and emotions through withdrawal (from adults), indifference, and even angry responses (Broderick & Blewitt, 2014; Geldard & Geldard, 2010). Ultimately, many of this population's difficulties and problems reside with their thinking and reasoning. Concrete strategies may still be needed to help youth connect their emotions, thinking, and behaviors. In addition, because of their physical development, many adults may inadvertently assume that young adolescents have more advanced emotional and cognitive abilities than is often the case. Counselors can provide education to parents related to young people's cognitive development. Counselors can also help youth and parents to learn and practice strategies that can facilitate social, emotional, and cognitive growth (e.g., social skills training, emotional regulation, problem solving; Jenson & Bender, 2014).

In addition, counseling often involves educating parents and youth on puberty, emotions, decision-making skills, anger management, and conflict resolution, as well as increasing positive peer interactions (Jenson & Bender, 2014; Wong et al., 2015). Counselors should be engaging, experiential, and collaborative when working with early adolescents (Geldard & Geldard, 2010).

Finally, group counseling can be a powerful and effective modality when counseling youth in early adolescence (Dixon et al., 2017). Counseling groups with this population can meet for longer periods of time (i.e., 40–75 minutes), have diverse numbers of group participants, and cover more diverse topics (e.g., interpersonal, grief/bereavement) than do groups used with younger populations (Falco & Bauman, 2014). Group counseling can help adolescents in (Dixon et al., 2017; Kuther, 2017):

- forming social and emotional bonds with other adolescents, and aiding in the development of who they are and how they relate to others in the world;
- normalizing their experiences, while concurrently building empathy to and validation of others' lived experiences;
- formulating and cultivating social skills and conflict management skills;
- experimentation with personal identity within a controlled environment;
- receiving and often incorporating feedback more from peers (rather than from adults); and
- connecting and reaching more youth, especially within the schools, than can be achieved through individual counseling.

Counselors should consider establishing a counseling group as structured or semistructured. To increase group counseling's effectiveness, counselors should allow youth to be engaged, creative, active group participants. Groups that are focused on one issue and/or treatment-focused goal (e.g., social skills, grief, anger management, decision-making skills) can be helpful with some youth, particularly those who may not do well in unstructured environments (Dixon et al., 2017).

LATE ADOLESCENCE

In this discussion, the term *late adolescence* is used to describe youth who are 15 to 18 years old. As compared to early adolescents, those in late adolescence often feel less vulnerable, express their emotions and feelings more effectively, and engage in thoughtful discussions. Although not the case for all youth in late adolescence, this time period tends to be more developmentally stable than early adolescence. In the following sections, the developmental characteristics and the counseling considerations associated with counseling late adolescents are discussed.

Late Adolescence Developmental Characteristics

PHYSICAL DEVELOPMENT

During late adolescence, youth usually experience a slowing of physical growth, depending on when puberty started for them. However, continued growth spurts are common in boys, who often begin to catch up physically with girls of their chronological age during this time period. Before or during late adolescence, females develop breasts, begin menstruation, and grow pubic hair, whereas boys experience growth of testes, penis, and pubic hair and undergo voice changes (Broderick & Blewitt, 2014). These changes indirectly alter adolescents' social relationships (e.g., emerging sexual and intimate relationships), as discussed in the previous section on early adolescents.

Secondary to these ongoing physical changes, sexual urges become stronger during late adolescence. In addition, sexual exploration and curiosity will continue to increase during late adolescence and manifest as increased sexual fantasizing, masturbation, and sexual experimentation (Broderick & Blewitt, 2014). Although sexual activity is often unplanned, the risk of sexually transmitted diseases and pregnancy is real because of adolescents' sense of invincibility. For example, an adolescent may engage in unprotected sex because he has the mentality that sexually transmitted diseases or pregnancy "will not happen to me." Because adolescents often view themselves as immune to natural consequences, they can benefit from developing their problem-solving skills in relation to sex (Jenson & Bender, 2014).

Sexual orientation becomes increasingly manifested during late adolescence (Broderick & Blewitt, 2014). The formation of **sexual identity** can be difficult and anxiety producing for lesbian, gay, and bisexual youth, who often experience elevated distress and depression secondary to a lack of support and fear of stigma (Rosario et al., 2014). Adults should strive to provide these adolescents with an open, supportive environment where their experiences and emerging identities can be validated (Jenson & Fraser, 2015).

Over the past few decades, the connection between brain development in adolescence and impulsivity (e.g., risk-taking behaviors) has received considerable attention (Romer, 2010). In particular, sensation seeking (a form of impulsivity) appears to increase in adolescence with this population engaging in more frequent drug use, unprotected sexual activity, and unintended accidents (Broderick & Blewitt, 2014). Although brain development may influence adolescents' ability to control themselves, some contend that a lack of experience with these adult-oriented activities (e.g., sex, driving, substance use) is more to blame for self-control than brain maturation (Romer, 2010). Therefore, adults may mitigate developmental risk by providing adolescents with adequate supervision and alternative prosocial activities and by helping them develop adequate problem-solving and decision-making skills (Jenson & Fraser, 2015).

COGNITIVE DEVELOPMENT

The movement from concrete operational to formal operational thinking continues into late adolescence (Piaget, 1970). As **formal operational thinking** evolves, enhanced cognitive capabilities allow these youth to think and behave differently. For example, a youth who historically thought in an *either–or* mind-set may now begin to generate alternative behaviors based on the situation and predict future consequences. These adolescents are more flexible and abstract in their thinking and can hypothesize about cause-and-effect interactions (Bergin & Bergin, 2015). This type of thinking opens the adolescent to the realm of potential possibilities, often leading to new opinions about moral, social, and political issues.

Although this transition in thinking is generally positive, some adolescents still remain inconsistent in their thinking. They may be able to construct creative alternatives but lack the experience and self-understanding required to make appropriate choices. For example, a boy may be able to think creatively concerning a conflicted relationship, yet be unable to decide which alternative will improve the situation. Adults can help adolescents to increase their ability to systematically work through difficulties by guiding them in generating alternative options and implementing the best alternative. As adolescents develop problem-solving skills, their impulsivity and risk-taking behaviors may decrease (Jenson & Fraser, 2015; Romer, 2010).

SELF-DEVELOPMENT

In late adolescence, youth are often unconsciously preoccupied with establishing their identity and seeking independence. As part of their **identities**, adolescents want to form vocational, political, social, sexual, moral, and religious values and beliefs (Erickson, 1968; Marcia, 1967). It is during late adolescence when youth try out various roles and responsibilities. For example, an adolescent may attempt to expand or alter his perceived identity as "just an athlete" by trying out for the debate team. During late adolescence, youth will often engage in opinionated discussions, observe others' behaviors, dream big dreams, experiment, and explore (e.g., different music, dress, religions, political views; Bergin & Bergin, 2015; Geldard & Geldard, 2010). In addition, ethnic and cultural identity may contribute significantly to adolescents' self-development. Those from ethnic minority populations who are confident with their ethnic and cultural identity tend to experience more positive, overall well-being (Smith & Silva, 2011).

An important aspect of late adolescence is young people's desire to be unique. As self-confidence grows, these adolescents often try to distinguish themselves from others by not being, dressing, or behaving like everyone else around them. For example, an adolescent may dress in contrast to those around him as a way to stand out and be unique. Adolescents' desires for uniqueness can increase their ability to resist **peer pressure**. Because of their emerging sense of self-confidence and ability to consider long-term consequences, late adolescents are often better than younger adolescents at resisting peer pressure (Jenson & Bender, 2014). Unfortunately, this is not always the case for all adolescents, many of whom experience and struggle to manage intense peer pressure and bullying during middle school (Wong et al., 2015). School, extracurricular, and prosocial activities (e.g., dance, exercise, and/or running clubs) within the community may insulate youth from negative peer influences (Jenson & Fraser, 2015).

Clinical Toolbox 1.8

In the Pearson eText, click here to review an activity that can be used to teach youth how to resist peer pressure.

PSYCHOSOCIAL DEVELOPMENT

As in early adolescence, peer relationships are very important to late adolescents. Adolescents learn to tolerate individual differences and prepare themselves for more intimate friendships and partner relationships through exploration of their relationships at this stage. In conjunction with formal operational thinking, youth also begin to select friendships more intentionally. Although children typically choose friendships based on proximity (e.g., those who live close to them or who are in their classroom at school), in late adolescence youth increasingly begin to select friends based on shared interests and experiences, as well as need (e.g., "I like to laugh, and you're really funny"). In addition, adolescents more frequently explore and experiment with their intimate relationships.

During late adolescence, youth wrestle with *who they are* or their sense of self within the context of their social world (Erikson, 1968). Essentially, **personal identity** is the means by which adolescents differentiate themselves from others (Geldard & Geldard, 2010). More specifically, this population often faces intense social pressure to (a) define their views, beliefs, and values; (b) make meaning of their existence; (c) find and form romantic relationships; and (d) discover a focus or mission in their lives (e.g., a vocational pursuit; Paladino & DeLorenzi, 2017). Adults can aid these youth in discovering not only what they do well but also how what they do relates to their sense of self and their identity (Bergin & Bergin, 2015; Broderick & Blewitt, 2014).

EMOTIONAL DEVELOPMENT

Late adolescence is characterized by fewer mood fluctuations (than in early adolescence) because youth are often less overwhelmed and have greater insight into their emotions. In turn, these adolescents are often less defensive and better able to express their emotions and feelings to others. Possessing the ability to articulate thoughts, feelings, and emotions can significantly reduce conflict with parents, siblings, and peers, thus producing more resilient youth. However, the rate of depressive disorders gradually increases in adolescence, and this can diminish young people's ability to manage their feelings and emotions (Merikangas et al., 2010).

Although significant variations exist during adolescence in terms of emotional development, youth often become more empathetic and less impulsive, manage emotionally charged situations more effectively, and display less erratic behavior (Bergin & Bergin, 2015; Broderick & Blewitt, 2014). With the rapid transitions that occur during this stage, some youth can grow apart from their previously established support groups, become apprehensive about their future, and begin to experience self-doubt (e.g., become more insecure, feel inferior). Adults can insulate youth by facilitating positive interpersonal interactions through participation in family activities and by providing youth with empathetic reactions (Jenson & Fraser, 2015).

Late Adolescence Counseling Considerations

COMMON PROBLEMS IN LATE ADOLESCENCE

The problems that present in late adolescence are similar to those experienced in early adolescence; these include identity development and vocational considerations, risk-taking behaviors, and relationship and family conflicts. The mental disorders diagnosed and addressed in counseling are also similar (e.g., anxiety, depression, disruptive behavioral disorders; Merikangas et al., 2010).

Risk-taking behaviors (e.g., drug and alcohol use/abuse, truancy, fighting, illegal activity) frequently result in this population entering into counseling (Eaton et al., 2012). Risk factors that influence an adolescent to increase engagement in risk-taking behaviors include poor family communication, parent–child conflict, a lack of family support, and peer pressure (Dunn, Kitts, Lewis, Goodrow, & Scherzer, 2011; Jenson & Bender, 2014). Counselors can support risk-taking adolescents by enhancing their decision-making and problem-solving skills.

An example of a high-risk behavior that may lead youth to counseling is substance use/abuse. The use of alcohol and drugs is common during adolescence, and substance use rates gradually increase throughout this period, with alcohol and cannabis being the most commonly used substances (Swendsen et al., 2012). Although males and females usually have equal alcohol use rates, males often demonstrate higher abuse rates (Swendsen et al., 2012).

Peer relationships and family dynamics are often strained during late adolescence as youth push for more autonomy and desire to do more activities with peers independent of parental supervision. These activities include driving, socializing with friends, and dating. With the increase in sexual and intimate relationships, some adolescents may struggle with their sexual identity and sense of belonging and with feeling accepted by others. In addition, today's adolescents connect and nurture social relationships predominantly through the use of technological gadgets such as smartphones and tablets; they spend a great deal of time immersed in social media, and this may even be the predominant form of communication with their peers (Paladino & DeLorenzi, 2017). These changes in daily interactions and lifestyle can present adolescents with the following challenges: decreased face-to-face interactions, increased possibility of isolation and loneliness, increased sedentary lifestyle, slowed social skills development, cyberbullying, and potentially higher rates of depression and anxiety (Selfhout, Branje, Delsing, ter Bogt, & Meeu, 2009). Counselors need to understand how adolescents connect socially with their peers in an ever-changing technological landscape.

Bullying/cyberbullying and peer pressure within late adolescence are still areas of concern for many adolescents. Although many adolescents develop strong peer support systems, some continue to struggle with these relationships and are vulnerable to bullying. In addition to bullying, the risks of violence and rape increase significantly for later adolescents (Paladino & DeLorenzi, 2017). These adolescents thus have increased risks of suicidal ideation and suicide attempts (Skapinakis et al., 2011). Counselors need to continually assess for safety, violence, bullying, and peer pressure.

Finally, vocational identity and postsecondary plans (e.g., work, college, career) are another consideration for counselors working with late adolescents. Career counseling with adolescence can revolve around career planning (e.g., education, training, employment), potential career satisfaction, and personal characteristics (e.g., values, skills, interest).

COUNSELING APPLICATIONS

Although late adolescence is often associated with greater experimentation and risk taking, counselors need to remember that youth are ultimately attempting to define *who they are* in the world (i.e., ego identity vs. role confusion; Erikson, 1968); therefore, this experimentation serves a purpose. As such, counselors need to select counseling applications and approaches with these developmental tasks in mind. Specifically, counselors working with youth in late adolescence should consider (Cook-Cottone et al., 2015; Kuther, 2017; Paladino & DeLorenzi, 2017):

- focusing on the client and allowing him or her to be the expert on his or her lived experiences;
- exploring the development, management, and maintenance of peer and intimate relationships;
- identifying and praising the client's positive characteristics, resilience, and strengths;
- being genuine and authentic because adolescents quickly detect phony or inauthentic behaviors;
- incorporating current media, art, and music into sessions;
- using self-exploration activities such as bibliotherapy, journaling, watching movies depicting adolescents' difficulties, and/or accessing interactive websites aimed at increasing awareness of self and the external world;
- using activities that are engaging, creative, and experiential;
- modeling humor that is lighthearted and appropriate;
- avoiding the expert role, using labels, and asserting power within the relationship;
- exploring relevant developmental issues such as independence, autonomy, and identity; and
- allowing the client to choose from a host of ideas or strategies to address perceived problems.

Although much of how a counselor intervenes depends on the nature of the problem and the cognitive development and personality traits of the adolescent, interactive interventions work well with this population (e.g., group work, role-play, unstructured journaling, imagery exercises). In Figure 1.1, examples of writing prompts that counselors can use with adolescents are provided.

Finally, group counseling can be an effective modality when working with youth in late adolescence. Although older adolescents can often tolerate longer session times (e.g., 40–75 minutes) than younger youth, the number of group members should not exceed 12 (Falco & Bauman, 2014). In addition, segregation according to gender should be considered by topic (e.g., sexual trauma/assault); however, considering the use of mixed-gender groups provides adolescents with an opportunity to increase their interpersonal skills with all peers (Falco & Bauman, 2014).

As previously stated, youth in late adolescence are more verbal, express emotions and thoughts more clearly, and engage in thoughtful discussions; therefore, group counseling can be an effective modality to address most challenges and difficulties that late adolescents experience (Paladino & DeLorenzi, 2017). Counselors can assume a less directive role when working with older adolescents than with younger children (Paladino & DeLorenzi, 2017). Examples of age-appropriate groups for older adolescents include substance abuse, anxiety, depression, trauma, or eating disorder groups; groups focused on enhancing interpersonal effectiveness and social skills; process-oriented groups in which youth receive emotional support from others; grief and bereavement groups; family transition issues (e.g., divorce); anger management; and decision-making groups (Falco & Bauman, 2014).

Write about what you consider to be important experiences in your life (you can also ask the client to write about both positive or negative experiences per se, including traumatic experiences, ones where the client demonstrated strength, etc.).

Where do you see yourself a year from now? How do you think you will be the same and/or different? What do you need to do to be successful in getting where you want to be?

Write about a safe place and what your safe place means to you. What does the safe place look, smell, and feel like? How can you, in your head, connect with this safe place when you need to?

What are some hard feelings you experience (e.g., anger, sadness), and how do you cope with these feelings?

What are some challenges you have overcome in your life? How have you been able to overcome these challenges? What helped you overcome them? Who were your support people?

Draw a self-portrait, and describe what you see in writing. Who are you as a person? How do you see yourself as similar and different from those around you? What are your important personal qualities?

Draw and describe your perfect day, or draw and describe a typical day.

Have your older wiser you write you a letter in the present. What advice would your older self give to your current self?

What are some things that occur around you that upset you? How do you deal with these upsetting experiences?

What do you wish for or want for yourself?

If you could have three wishes, what would they be?

In the movie *The Wizard of Oz*, the characters wanted new or strengthened personal qualities that they did not believe they possessed, though they did. What is a personal quality you wish you had more of? What personal quality do you suspect you may have despite originally thinking you may *not* have it?

What is one thing you want to do differently this week? How will you do that one thing?

Who is important to you? What are your values? How do you uphold those values?

Who can you count on during times of worry and stress? Who else in your life might you lean on for support when you need it? How would you reach out for this support?

FIGURE 1.1 Examples of Journal Writing Prompts That Counselors Can Use with Adolescents

Summary

Counselors believe all clients, regardless of their internal and external barriers and challenges, are able to make meaningful changes. Inherent to a counseling philosophy is the idea that youth possess an innate ability to grow, change, and move forward in their development. Development is an important aspect of young people's change processes, and although developmental shifts can usher in problems of living, counselors can help clients to overcome their struggles. Because of the importance of understanding development when counseling youth, this chapter provided an overview of development, common concerns, and developmentally informed strategies for approaching this age group in counseling.

More specifically, physical, cognitive, self-, psychosocial, and emotional development were described in relation to various youth developmental stages. These developmental considerations interact with each other, so they cannot be considered in isolation. Although counselors are not generally qualified to assess physical development per se, they should maintain an awareness of young clients' physical development and refer them for physical health assessments and consultations as appropriate. Cognitive development is linked with physical development (i.e., neurodevelopment), and as youth develop they are better able to grasp new concepts and skills. Self-development relates to the bonds developed between youth and their parents and involves young people's development of a self-concept and self-esteem, among other things. Early attachment bonds are exceptionally important and can inform counselors' understanding of youth development. Psychosocial development is closely related to self-development and involves young people's interactions with their environment and the ways these interactions affect their own development. Finally, emotional development—which again is related to the other aspects of development—relates to how fully youth can understand, experience, and regulate their feelings. Early interactions with others can play an important role in young people's affective development. Culture plays an important role in all development, especially emotional development, so counselors must be culturally aware and sensitive to their clients' culture and context as they strive to understand young people's emotional development.

In addition, the important risk and protective factors that affect youth development were discussed in this chapter. When counseling young people, it is important that counselors understand these factors and influence them as possible and appropriate. Risk and protective factors do not exist independently; rather, they interact in a synergistic way and affect each youth in a unique way.

This chapter also laid the foundation for understanding youth development and individual-level risk and protective factors. Chapter 2 examines the systemic factors that influence youth development. More specifically, it discusses family, school, and community factors; the risk factors that adversely influence development and problems in living; and the protective factors that counselors can encourage and support. It is important to be aware that the individual- and systemic-level risk and protective factors discussed in this chapter and in Chapter 2 are not necessarily discrete; they can, and do, influence each other in meaningful ways. Consider, for example, one of the most significant youth development risk factors: poverty. Poverty can affect every aspect of young clients' development, including systemic factors such as their family dynamics and stability, the quality of their schools, and the risks inherent in their communities and individual-level factors such as physical and psychosocial development.

MyLab Counseling: Counseling Children and Adolescents

Try the Topic 1 Assignments: *Developmentally-Informed Youth Counseling.*

CHAPTER | **2**

Systemically Informed Youth Counseling

In Chapter 1, youth development and individual risk and protective factors are discussed. This chapter addresses the contextual and systemic risk and protective factors that affect youth. More specifically, family, school, and community risk and protective factors are discussed in the context of counseling youth. Before addressing the ways that family, school, and community risk and protective factors influence youth development, the importance of context, culture, and a strength-based counseling philosophy is explored.

CONTEXT AND CULTURE

Counselors practice from a holistic perspective, which means they believe all aspects of their clients' lives are interconnected (Kaplan, Tarvydas, & Gladding, 2014). The interrelated aspects of youth's lives are part of their **context**. An important aspect of counselors' professional identities is sensitivity to contextual and cultural considerations. A focus on, and sensitivity to, context relates to what is known from counseling outcome research: Young clients need to be understood in the context of their unique situations if counseling is to be effective (Norcross & Wampold, 2011b).

Context refers to the interrelated conditions in which clients' experiences and behaviors occur, or any factors that surround them and shine light on their situations. Many traditional understandings of the human experience focus on a pathology- and deficit-based perspective of clients' problems. When considering young clients' situations from a contextual perspective, culture, gender, and various developmental factors are just a few of the important factors that should be considered.

Culture, and as part of this, gender and ethnicity, are exceptionally important contextual considerations; culture defines, expresses, and interprets the beliefs, values, customs, and gender role expectations of a social group (Kalra & Bhugra, 2010). Multicultural considerations can have a significant impact on counselors' decision-making and intervention processes, and essentially all counseling can be referred to as multicultural counseling. The *ACA Code of Ethics* (American Counseling Association [ACA], 2014) emphasizes that culture influences the way clients' problems are understood, and this must be considered throughout counseling and treatment. Related to this, the *ACA Code of Ethics* indicates that counselors should recognize social prejudices that lead to overpathologizing clients from certain populations. Counselors are also encouraged to consider the roles they might unintentionally play in perpetuating these prejudices through their conceptualizations of clients and counseling practices (ACA, 2014).

Professional counselors place a premium on understanding culture and its influence on clients' situations because it is impossible to understand young clients and how to best help them without making cultural considerations. More specifically, counselors should consider cultural explanations of problems in living, cultural experiences and help-seeking behaviors, the cultural framework of clients' identities, cultural meanings of healthy functioning, and cultural aspects that relate to the counselor–client relationship (Eriksen & Kress, 2005).

Wide variations exist among people from different cultures in terms of their perspectives of appropriate or "normal" behaviors. For example, young clients' parents often bring their children to counseling because of perceived misbehavior and familial conflicts (Zeanah, 2009). Expectations of appropriate child behavior and the ways interpersonal relationships are navigated are largely based on cultural norms and expectations. Culture may influence what behaviors are acceptable and how children—and parents— are permitted to express frustration and suffering, as well as manage distress. Culture determines how one's friends, family, and community respond to distress or problematic behaviors, and it dictates the type and severity of the problem that must be evident before counseling intervention is deemed necessary. Culture also determines acceptable help-seeking behaviors and interventions and who may—and may not—intervene.

Socioeconomic status and social position influence how youth manifest and respond to their perceived problems both within and across cultures. Counselors must consider the complex relationship and interaction of culture, race, ethnicity, gender, and socioeconomic status with experiences of oppression and social position (Kress, Dixon, & Shannonhouse, 2018). Although non-White individuals in the United States are currently referred to as racial/ethnic minorities, it is predicted that this group will make up more of the American population by the year 2044 than White individuals (U.S. Census Bureau, 2015). Counselors work to understand the experiences of individuals who belong to a racial/ethnic minority group while also recognizing that non-White individuals are gaining power and majority status in the United States. Counselors should broach the topics of race, socioeconomic status, gender, and other multicultural factors when appropriate, and assumptions should be avoided by gathering a holistic understanding of each unique client's experiences.

Young people may experience **microaggressions**, or racially biased oppression, on a daily basis, and individuals belonging to a minority race or ethnicity can be marginalized and invalidated in various overt and covert ways (Sue & Sue, 2013). Some microaggressions might be subtle and covert, such as a classroom teacher giving special classroom duties to White students instead of Black students or a non-White student being sent to the principal's office for the same behavior for which a White peer previously received a verbal warning. White individuals, as the current racial majority in America, have a great deal of power in society, and racially biased behaviors can be detrimental to the well-being and growth of individuals belonging to a racial minority.

Culturally sensitive counselors are aware that those with less power in society experience a greater quantity of life's difficulties and are more likely to be vulnerable to mental health struggles, economic difficulties, and problems in living than are those from the dominant race, ethnicity, age, sexual orientation, or gender (Kress et al., 2018). They also realize that those from nondominant cultural groups garner fewer of society's resources, and thus often acquire interventions and supports later in their problem cycles. Because those with less power are less likely to seek help, they may come to the attention of counselors only when the problems have reached a greater intensity.

Overall, culture influences clients in multiple ways, including their experiences of problems, their internal senses of distress, their interpretations of problems, and their presentations of complaints (Eriksen & Kress, 2008). Culture also influences counselors' perceptions of clients' problems, their styles of interviewing, and their choices of theoretical perspectives and counseling approaches.

STRENGTH-BASED PHILOSOPHY

In addition to being sensitive to culture and context, counselors also value a **strength-based perspective** (Vereen, Hill, Sosa, & Kress, 2014). Young clients' strengths and resiliencies are essential resources in supporting their development. A strength-based approach is holistic in that it assumes young people cannot be understood apart from what is happening in their families or in their broader social contexts.

A strength-based philosophy is grounded in the assumption that the development and amplification of strengths and assets within and around young clients provides them with a greater sense of resiliency against future difficulties (Smith, 2006). In this sense, a strength-based approach is preventative in that it develops and identifies strengths and can be used not only to address current struggles but also to insulate clients from developing additional problems.

When counselors work from a strength-based perspective, they actively engage in enhancing, developing, and highlighting clients' resources, strengths, and times of resiliency, as well as their abilities to cope and persevere, thus enhancing their self-esteem by increasing their senses of self-determination, mastery of life, and internal fortitude (Smith, 2006). To be more concrete, counselors can work from a strength-based perspective by identifying the unique strengths a young person or his or her family has, or has access to, and amplifying those strengths.

Clinical Toolbox 2.1

In the Pearson eText, click here to take an assessment that can help counselors to identify the extent to which they have a strength-based orientation.

A strength-based lens is a paradigm shift away from focusing on clients' problems and toward a focus on clients' strengths, capacities, and resources, and how these can be used to support clients. A strength-based approach is firmly situated in the assumption that counselors should not only explore problems and weaknesses but also invest equal time and energy into exploring a young client's assets and strengths, thus providing a more holistic and balanced approach to treating each individual. Working from this perspective, counselors aim to instill hope by enhancing clients' awareness of their personal competencies, and they facilitate growth by building on strengths while addressing aspects of young clients' situations that may be perceived as problematic (Smith, 2006).

When counseling youth, counselors might focus on activities or engagements that enhance positive subjective experiences and positive individual character traits. Counselors can intervene early with youth by providing prevention programs that teach cognitive and coping skills to decrease the risk of various problems that youth face, including depression, anxiety, and exposure to violence. Counselors might also promote the virtues and character strengths of clients that are known to promote resiliency, and these consist of responsibility, gratitude, nurturance, altruism, civility, moderation, tolerance, and a solid work ethic (Seligman, 2012).

Clinical Toolbox 2.2

In the Pearson eText, click here for an activity that can be used to promote youth's gratitude.

As mentioned, **resilience**, or the ability to resist against difficulties, is an essential consideration when working from a strength-based approach. Counselors can attempt to foster resiliency in their young clients by enhancing their individual competencies in the following areas: (a) social competence, (b) problem solving, (c) autonomy, and (d) sense of purpose (Benard, 2004). Counselors should not only highlight these strengths but also seek to amplify these strengths throughout the counseling process in an attempt to build a client's resilience against illness and future difficulties.

In this text, a strength-based philosophy is integrated into our treatment planning model (in Chapter 9), and a strong emphasis is placed on the importance of connecting with clients' strengths and using these strengths to help them to overcome their struggles. Examples of specific character strengths and resiliencies in youth that can be identified and integrated into counseling are provided in Figure 2.1.

Clinical Toolbox 2.3

In the Pearson eText, click here to review categories of youth resiliency and protective factors.

It is important to consider that young people are inherently resilient (Sanders, Munford, Thimasarn-Anwar, Liebenberg, & Ungar, 2015; Search Institute, 2007). Youth can—and do—surmount adversity, but the ways they do so are unique; there is no "one size fits all" model for overcoming life's challenges. Counselors can validate, acknowledge—and when possible—address young clients' risk factors while

• Accepting	• Generous	• Playful
• Adventurous	• Gentle	• Positive
• Affectionate	• Graceful	• Powerful
• Alert	• Grateful	• Practical
• Altruistic	• Hardworking	• Problem solver
• Ambitious	• Helpful	• Prudent
• Appreciative	• Honest	• Punctual
• Aspiring	• Hopeful	• Purposeful
• Aware	• Humble	• Rational
• Brave	• Humorous	• Regulated
• Calm	• Hygienic	• Relaxed
• Capable	• Imaginative	• Reliable
• Caring	• Independent	• Religious
• Cheerful	• Industrious	• Resilient
• Committed	• Innovative	• Respectful
• Compassionate	• Insightful	• Responsible
• Confident	• Inspirational	• Restrained
• Conscientious	• Intelligent	• Self-confident
• Considerate	• Interested	• Self-esteemed
• Cooperative	• Intuitive	• Self-regulated
• Courageous	• Knowledgeable	• Selfless
• Creative	• Leader	• Sensitive
• Curious	• Logical	• Sincere
• Determined	• Loving	• Skilled
• Disciplined	• Loyal	• Social
• Educated	• Master	• Spiritual
• Empathetic	• Modest	• Spontaneous
• Empowering	• Moral	• Strong-willed
• Encouraging	• Motivated	• Successful
• Energetic	• Nonviolent	• Supportive
• Engaged	• Nurturing	• Sympathetic
• Enthusiastic	• Observant	• Tactful
• Ethical	• Open-minded	• Talented
• Expressive	• Optimistic	• Tenacious
• Fair	• Organized	• Thoughtful
• Fit	• Patient	• Thrifty
• Flexible	• Peaceful	• Tolerant
• Focused	• Persistent	• Trusting
• Forgiving	• Personable	• Trustworthy
• Friendly	• Physically fit	• Work-oriented

FIGURE 2.1   Examples of Character Strengths and Resiliencies in Youth

encouraging resiliency factors that support youth and facilitate their development (American Psychiatric Association [APA], 2013a; Sanders et al., 2015).

Throughout this chapter, the systems that influence youth—family, school, and community—and the risk and protective factors associated with each are discussed in the context of youth development. A summary of family, school, and community youth risk factors is provided in Table 2.1, and a summary of family, school, and community youth protective factors is provided in Table 2.2. Although the material in this chapter points to factors that are important in understanding and supporting youth development, the factors that contribute to a young person's normal—and abnormal development—are complex; youth respond in unique ways to various risk and resiliency factors. An understanding of young clients' contextual risk and resiliency factors can support counselors' abilities to thoughtfully conceptualize their clients' situations and ultimately determine the best courses of intervention.

Table 2.1 Family, School, and Community Youth Risk Factors		
Family Risk Factors	**School Risk Factors**	**Community Risk Factors**
• Emotional, physical, or sexual abuse and/or neglect • Overindulgence in childhood • Ineffective/harsh communication • Intergenerational trauma • Intimate partner/domestic violence • Lack of financial resources • Limited parental involvement or support • Parents with physical, mental, or emotional difficulties • Siblings or extended family members with physical, mental, or emotional difficulties • Shifts in family structure • Triangulation or enmeshment • Unclear or rigid boundaries	• Bullying • Delinquent peer influences • Ineffective classroom management • Lack of resources (e.g., desks, books, technology) • Mental health disorders that affect schooling (e.g., attention-deficit/hyperactivity disorder) • Negative expectations from teachers or school personnel • Past experiences of academic difficulty/learning disabilities • Racism/other prejudices • School violence	• Devaluation of education • Community violence • Drug and weapon availability • High residential mobility • High violence and crime • Immigrating from another country or culture • Lack of supportive institutions (e.g., religious organizations, community groups, afterschool programs) • Lack of nonparent adult role models • Moving from low-poverty to high-poverty neighborhoods • Poverty • Racism/prejudice • Unfair social policies (e.g., school funding)

Table 2.2 Family, School, and Community Youth Protective Factors		
Family Protective Factors	**School Protective Factors**	**Community Protective Factors**
• Clearly defined family expectations and rules • Clearly defined, yet flexible, family subsystems and boundaries • Consistent and reasonable discipline • Expression of warmth and love • Financial resources • High levels of involvement and support from parents and family members • Strong cultural identity and religious values • Youth living with one or both parents	• Effective classroom management • Experiences of academic success and competency • Positive expectations from teachers or school personnel • Positive peer influences • Provision of resources (e.g., desks, books, technology) • School personnel monitoring and advocacy • Trusting friendships and feelings of social connectedness • Youth motivation for achievement	• Advocacy initiatives • Afterschool programs • Collaborative partnerships between government agencies and community leaders • Community engagement and education • Community social and sports clubs • Discouragement of drugs and violence • Limited access to guns and violence • Value of education • Youth leadership and volunteer opportunities

THE FAMILY SYSTEM: RISK AND PROTECTIVE FACTORS

Risk and protective factors specific to the family system are discussed in this section. The family system is an integral part of young people's social and emotional development, and the home is where youth—especially younger children—spend the majority of their time (Center for Community Health and Development (CCHD), 2017; Laughlin, 2014; Search Institute, 2007). In this section, family structure and boundaries are explored, along with a discussion of the ways that these factors influence family relationships and affect young people's emotional and social well-being. Families' values, cultural expectations, degrees of involvement, communication patterns, and financial resources can all serve as both protective and risk factors, and as such, these considerations are also addressed. Physical and emotional difficulties that can occur within the family context are examined, and the role that emotional, physical, and sexual abuse can play on young people's development is discussed.

Family Structure and Boundaries

When discussing the role of the family, it is first important to define what exactly is meant by the term *family*. **Family** is a basic social unit that usually, but not always, includes parents and their children who typically live together. A youth's family can include various biological, step-, or adoptive parents; biological, step-, or adopted siblings; aunts, uncles, and cousins; grandparents; and even friends or neighbors (Bosch, Segrin, & Curran, 2012; Council on Foundations, n.d.). Family structure and family boundaries can provide valuable information for a counselor about a youth's life and the people who may serve as supportive resources.

The people who are included in a particular family create one's basic **family structure** (Lindahl, Bregman, & Malik, 2012). Some youth identify all people who live in their households as part of their families, others might include only certain people who live in their homes as family members, and still others might include people who live in their homes, as well as individuals who live outside their homes, as part of their family structures. When working with young clients, counselors should focus on their subjective definitions of family and pay special attention to family members who young people might intentionally exclude because this could indicate a potential source of risk (e.g., ongoing abuse, attachment injuries). Counselors might also identify sources of resiliency in family members who are included in a youth's subjective definition of family, such as a special grandparent or a neighborhood mentor.

Clinical Toolbox 2.4

In the Pearson eText, click here to review an activity that counselors can use to gain a better understanding of a youth's family structure.

Ethnic identity and traditions within a family play a significant role in how youth define and understand their family structures (Council on Foundations, n.d.). Some families might value the nuclear family in which parents and their children are most important and considered the core family. In nuclear family cultures, extended family members (e.g., cousins, grandparents) who live in other households and close friends are not considered part of the immediate family. However, some cultures might promote a more widespread definition of family in which all individuals who play an important role in a youth's life are collectively considered family, even if they live in separate households or are not biologically related (Council on Foundations, n.d.).

Counselors should note that family structure will inherently change over time. Shifts in the family structure can occur when:

- new members are added to the family (e.g., the birth of a younger sibling, exchange students or adopted siblings join the household, grandparents move into the home);
- existing members leave the household (e.g., an older sibling goes away to college or gets married, a parent moves out of the house because of divorce or separation, a parent or sibling deploys in the armed services, a family member dies);
- various friends and family members stay in the youth's home while working to overcome financial difficulties; and/or
- a family has high geographic mobility and frequently moves away from family and friends (Leventhal, Fauth, & Brooks-Gunn, 2005; Roy, McCoy, & Raver, 2014; Taylor & de la Sablonnière, 2013).

Some structural shifts in the family may be cause for celebration (e.g., the birth of a new sibling or an older sibling going away to college), but the outcome is still a change that can potentially lead to feelings of grief and contribute to interpersonal struggles and/or academic problems if left unresolved (Shapiro, 2012; Shaw, Bright, & Sharpe, 2015).

After any structural shift, youth must learn new ways of understanding their roles in the family and having their needs met. Counselors who understand the structure and dynamics of a youth's family can better identify the people who are significant to the young person and understand the losses a youth has experienced. Counselors can also work to understand the roles that family members play in supporting the youth's healthy growth and development by providing warmth and love, setting high expectations for the young person, and serving as a source for guidance and support (Froiland & Davison, 2014; Search Institute, 2007).

After assessing and working to understand the structure of a youth's family, counselors can next work to understand the **family boundaries**, which are the rules and norms that inform daily interactions between family members (Lindahl et al., 2012). Clearly communicated, consistent family rules and boundaries can serve as a youth protective factor (Barkley, 2013; Lindahl et al., 2012). Poorly enforced rules, expectations, and boundaries in the home setting can serve as risk factors for academic and social difficulties (Barkley, 2013; Bosch et al., 2012; Lindahl et al., 2012; Search Institute, 2007). Youth who are not taught to abide by rules and boundaries might not develop the self-control and emotional regulation skills needed to succeed in the neighborhood, school, and community settings.

There are many ways in which family boundaries, rules, and routines can shift in unhelpful ways. Olson (2011) developed a model for explaining the most healthy and unproductive patterns of family dynamics. Specifically, Olson's (2011) Circumplex model can be used to explain that family roles and rules should be predictable, yet flexible. In addition, family members should be connected to one another and intimately invested in each other's lives, but each family member should also maintain a unique identity within the family structure. Included in Table 2.3 is an overview of the ways that roles and cohesion between and among family members can manifest in healthy and unhelpful ways.

In addition to general patterns of family cohesion and flexibility, cross-generational boundary problems can occur when one parent and child are especially close, which causes jealousy from the other

Table 2.3	Overview of the Olson Circumplex Model
Family Dynamics	
Healthy	*Flexible*—Shared leadership in the home with parents who use democratic methods of discipline. Shared roles within the household with shifts in structure and rules when needed. Household is dynamic and supportive.
Healthy	*Structured*—Parents sometimes share leadership roles and decisions regarding discipline within the household. Roles in the household remain consistent unless specifically required, which creates stability with some flexibility.
Unhelpful	*Rigid*—Parents use strict discipline and don't share roles within the household. Change seldom occurs, and the household becomes stagnant/oppressive.
Unhelpful	*Chaotic*—Lacking a designated leader or set of leaders, inconsistent and/or harsh punishment, and significant and frequent changes in family roles leading to an unstable and unpredictable environment.
Family Relationships	
Healthy	*Connected*—High levels of loyalty and dependence, but some individuality.
Healthy	*Separated*—Moderate levels of loyalty and independence.
Unhelpful	*Disengaged*—High levels of independence and limited interaction between family members. Low amounts of support and loyalty.
Unhelpful	*Enmeshed*—Family members require constant support from one another, limiting one's ability to make independent choices.

Note: Adapted from "FACES IV and the Circumplex Model: Validation study," by D. Olson, 2011, *Journal of Marital and Family Therapy, 37*(1), pp. 64–80. doi:10.1111/j.1752-0606.2009.00175.x

2

parent or sibling(s). Triangulation occurs when two people are in conflict and pull in a third person to diffuse the tension and distract from the problem at hand. This often occurs between a youth and two parents in strife. The youth might be pulled into the triangle by one parent who vents in private to the young person about the other parent. Or the youth might be overtly pulled into the mix with one parent asking the youth to take sides (e.g., "Don't you agree that I'm right about . . ."). In either scenario, the youth is not given the freedom to focus on his or her own life challenges while being met with a safe and supportive parental subsystem.

Young people who live in stable, predictable environments and have healthy family boundaries are better able to spend their time and energy exploring their worlds with safety and building relationships with others (Barkley, 2013; Bosch et al., 2012; Lindahl et al., 2012; Search Institute, 2007; Shapiro, 2012). Counselors should remember, though, that parenting is challenging, and many factors can inhibit healthy family structures and boundaries. As such, counselors should work to harness as many protective factors as possible for youth and praise parents and family members for all efforts made toward facilitating more helpful family interactions.

Family Communication

Family boundaries, values, expectations, and approvals are conveyed through **communication**. Limited, ineffective, or harmful communication in the family is a risk factor that can lead to various developmental problems for youth (Bosch et al., 2012; Search Institute, 2007). Hostile or aggressive communication (e.g., yelling, harsh tones, shaming, blaming, bringing up past incidents, using threats) can lead to compromised emotional and/or behavioral development in youth (CCHD, 2017; Froiland, Peterson, & Davison, 2013; Search Institute, 2007).

Parents' family-of-origin dynamics, culture, and life experiences influence how love and support are conveyed to their children. Unproductive or harmful communication patterns are often passed down intergenerationally, and they often escalate when family members are experiencing additional transient stressors (e.g., loss of a job, divorce/separation) and/or more persistent stressors such as poverty or mental illness (APA, 2013; Hopson & Lee, 2011). When youth are exposed to hostile situations or unhelpful communication patterns (e.g., fighting, yelling), they can experience feelings of loss and internalized feelings of guilt, anger, and sadness that can contribute to social difficulties, academic troubles, and substance use (APA, 2013; Arkes, 2013; Search Institute, 2007; Shapiro, 2012; Sigal, Wolchik, Tein, & Sandler, 2012). In some families, there is a lack of communication about uncomfortable subjects (e.g., grief, divorce, sexual abuse), and this can be equally detrimental to a youth (Hopson & Lee, 2011; Search Institute, 2007). Counselors should strive to assess and facilitate healthy family communication patterns, especially around topics that may be difficult for the family to discuss.

One way that counselors can assess for family communication styles is via the use of incomplete sentence activities. To do so, counselors can create a list of simple sentence stems and allow the youth to complete them (e.g., When my mom gets mad she . . . ; When I get mad I . . . ; My parents often say to each other . . . ; My dad yells when . . . ; I express love by . . .). A similar activity can be used with parents as well, and these types of activities can be modified and made into a game that can be used in counseling.

Once counselors have an understanding of family communication patterns, they can support families in learning and using effective communication skills. Parents and youth can be taught to convey love and warmth by carefully choosing their words and the ways they deliver messages (Bosch et al., 2012; Search Institute, 2007; Shapiro, 2012). Nonverbal behaviors that convey warmth and acceptance include standing or sitting close to one another; physical expressions of affection; appropriate eye contact; and a calm, supportive tone. Family members learn best if they have opportunities to practice, or role-play, skills in a controlled setting with a counselor.

Family Involvement and Support

Family involvement and support of youth are defined as the ways in which parents—and other important people within the family unit—ensure their children's academic, interpersonal, and emotional needs are met. Family involvement and support are influenced by many factors, including family expectations, cultural values, boundaries, and communication styles. Positive family involvement does not mean that parents always give youth what they want; rather, it means that parents and loved ones encourage youth to meet developmental milestones and provide support and empathy when disappointments or difficulties occur. When family members are actively aware of the events in each other's lives, they can intentionally step in to offer support when it is most needed.

All youth need support around their education and schooling. When youth experience difficulties at school and parents do not employ positive support and appropriate expectations, young people are likely to experience a reduction of value on education, lower personal expectations, academic struggles, and limited belief that they can have satisfying careers (Search Institute, 2007; Zhu, Tse, Cheung, & Oyserman, 2014).

When parents are not actively involved in their children's lives, they are less able to monitor and influence their development and ensure youth stay on a desirable path. Youth with less support at home are more likely to experience negative or unhappy emotions, which can further separate youth from their academic and career focuses and reinforce unhelpful peer relationships (e.g., gangs, peers who also have limited family support) that do offer the support and sense of belonging that youth seek (Goel, Amatya, Jones, & Ollendick, 2014).

Youth might not receive the support they need to successfully navigate life's challenges for various reasons. Single parents or parents who both work outside the house can find it difficult to spend quality time with their children simply due to time and energy constraints. In addition, communication patterns in families of low socioeconomic status are often focused on "present moment" problem solving (e.g., securing food, paying bills) rather than supporting young people's growth and long-term goals (Centers for Disease Control and Prevention [CDC], National Center for Injury Prevention and Control, Division of Violence Prevention, 2014a; Leventhal et al., 2005; Roy et al., 2014; Taylor & de la Sablonnière, 2013). It is important for counselors to understand the cultural values held by a youth's family, identify the youth's subjective desires and goals, and find relevant skills and strengths that can support positive development for the young person.

There are many more life factors that can inhibit youth from receiving the parental support they need. Sometimes parents might serve as caregivers for elderly grandparents, which may take time and energy away from parents' abilities to support their children (Lundberg, 2014). Conversely, many grandparents serve as the primary caregivers for youth. Grandparents who are raising youth experience high levels of stress, health issues associated with aging, social isolation, and anxiety, and this may affect their ability to best meet young people's needs (Doley, Bell, Watt, & Simpson, 2015).

Youth who have siblings with mental health or physical disabilities might experience a lack of parental support because their siblings' special needs require extra attention and care (Bitsika, Sharpley, & Mailli, 2015; Ma, Roberts, Winefield, & Furber, 2015). Parental mental illness can also inhibit positive support of youth and even contribute to aggressive or neglectful parenting (discussed more in the next section).

Overindulged youth can be at risk for mental health problems as well (Schultz & Schultz, 2017). Parents who indulge their children's every desire teach them to expect instant gratification. These youth often come to expect others to attend to them in the same manner that their parents do; however, this is not a realistic expectation.

Counselors should take care to understand family dynamics and the ways they shift or pull based on the mental and physical health of each member. Key concepts for counselors to address with youth include recognizing and reframing distorted thinking that can occur when living with family members who have disorders and enhancing youth's emotional regulation skills (Bitsika et al., 2015). Counselors can also work to increase healthy support and stability within the home by reminding parents of a youth's need for rules, support, and positive communication (APA, 2013; Osypuk et al., 2012; Search Institute, 2007; Simpson et al., 2014). Counselors can help parents to determine strategies for more intentional provision of these needs within the family and identify additional sources of support from school personnel, other adults in the community, and positive peer influences (APA, 2013; Crean, 2012; Search Institute, 2007).

Child Maltreatment

Child maltreatment is an important topic because, depending on the work setting, counselors may find that many of their clients have experienced maltreatment. Although child maltreatment is explored more thoroughly in Chapter 15, this topic also deserves attention in this discussion of systemic risk and protective factors because of its prevalence and importance.

There are two primary types of child maltreatment: abuse and neglect. **Child abuse** includes physical, emotional, or sexual aggression; **child neglect** involves the failure of caregivers to provide the adequate emotional and physical resources needed by a child (Centers for Disease Control and Prevention [CDC], 2015b). The U.S. Department of Health and Human Services (USDHHS; 2015) reported that of the 3.5 million cases of reported and alleged child abuse and neglect, 80% of the reports involved allegations of neglect. As such, it is important that counselors regularly assess for neglect, not just for child abuse.

The effects of child maltreatment are exceptionally diverse and depend on numerous factors, including the:

- type(s) of maltreatment (e.g., physical abuse, emotional abuse, sexual abuse, neglect);
- resources available to the youth (e.g., counselors, peer supports, positive family communication);
- preexisting protective factors (e.g., support from family members, engagement in academics, after-school activities, mentoring relationships);
- duration, frequency, and severity of the abuse;
- nature of the child's relationship with the perpetrator (e.g., someone who was highly trusted versus a stranger);
- use of force by the perpetrator(s); and
- number of perpetrators (Briere & Lanktree, 2011; CDC, 2015b; Search Institute, 2007; USDHHS, 2015).

Possible reactions to child maltreatment may include:

- disruption to the child's emotional well-being (e.g., lowered self-esteem, poor self-concept);
- difficulty making and sustaining healthy attachments;
- anger, depression, and anxiety, which can be manifested in behavioral problems;
- academic struggles;
- social difficulties;
- hypersexualization; and
- decreased emotional regulation capacities (APA, 2013; CDC, 2015b; National Coalition for Child Protection Reform, 2009; Shaw et al., 2015; USDHHS, 2015).

Posttraumatic stress disorder has also been recognized as a common effect of child abuse, and this subject is discussed more in Chapter 15.

Secondary to maltreatment, feelings of helplessness often emerge, and youth may consequently have limited emotional resources and not feel safe enough to take risks, learn what they like and dislike, and form a sense of self in relation to others (Deblinger, Runyon, & Steer, 2014; Edwards, Probst, Rodenhizer-Stämpfli, Gidycz, & Tansill, 2014; Nasvytiené, Lazdauskas, & Leonavičiené, 2012; Sanders et al., 2015; Stein-Steele, 2013). The loss of identity and frustration experienced by many youth who are maltreated can lead to unhealthy choices and maladaptive coping skills (e.g., use of drugs, violence against others; Centers for Disease Control and Prevention [CDC], 2014b, 2014c, 2015a).

If abuse or neglect of a youth comes to the attention of authorities, maltreated children are often removed from the home and placed in foster care (Shaw et al., 2015). Although these moves contribute to the young person's immediate safety, the long-term effects of separation from the family can be serious and damaging, serving as a significant youth risk factor (National Coalition for Child Protection Reform, 2009). Young people who are removed from the home due to maltreatment might be at an additional risk for mental health difficulties as they work to adjust to a new setting and grieve the separation from their families.

Despite the negative effects that child maltreatment can invite, it is important for counselors to understand that most children do not develop ongoing traumatic reactions secondary to maltreatment; they can and do adapt and live healthy, productive lives (Deblinger et al., 2014; Sanders et al., 2015; USDHHS, 2015). Secondary to their maltreatment experiences, children can even experience posttraumatic growth and develop strengths such as advanced survival skills, a greater self-knowledge and self-appreciation, increased empathy for others, and a broader and more complex view of the world. It is important that counselors believe that maltreated children with whom they work can heal and thrive (Deblinger et al., 2014; London, Lilly, & Pittman, 2015; Martin, Gardner, & Brooks-Gunn, 2012).

Certain resiliencies and protective factors appear to insulate children from the long-term potentially deleterious effects of maltreatment, and these factors should be considered when counseling this population. These factors include:

- having at least one supportive relationship with a parent and/or another adult;
- positive personal attributes such as high self-regard, a healthy sense of spirituality, external blame (e.g., "the abuse was his fault, not mine"), a positive outlook on life, social competence, and emotional regulation skills;
- community activities that raise awareness of child abuse/maltreatment and promote safe, nurturing family relationships;
- collaboration between direct service agencies and local, state, and national health departments to create a culture of support and empathy;
- community programs that share parenting tips and information about youth development;
- resiliency and protective factors for parents (e.g., support networks, childcare resources); and
- data-driven programs and policies that create measurable changes in cultural norms of abuse/neglect (He, Fulginiti, & Finno-Velasquez, 2015; National Alliance of Children's Trust and Prevention Funds, 2014; Sanders et al., 2015; Search Institute, 2007).

Counselors can support youth in developing and connecting with these aforementioned resiliency factors through direct interventions and advocacy. Capitalizing and building on social connections is one way young people can gain or regain a sense of identity and reframe maladaptive self- and other cognitions (Edwards et al., 2014; He et al., 2015; Sanders et al., 2015; Stein-Steele, 2013). Youth who have been maltreated should connect with activities they enjoy and find skills that provide them with a sense of mastery and self-efficacy because these can give them a sense of control over their lives (Deblinger et al., 2014; Edwards et al., 2014; Nasvytiené et al., 2012; Sanders et al., 2015; Stein-Steele, 2013). As much as possible, individual protective factors should be identified, developed, and amplified in clients via counseling.

At the systemic level, it is important that the public is educated about the long-term mental and physical health effects of abuse and neglect on youth (National Alliance of Children's Trust and Prevention Funds, 2014). Ample research supports the notion that child abuse and neglect are detrimental to youth development, and they can create unhelpful, long-term consequences (APA, 2013; Hopson & Lee, 2011; National Coalition for Child Protection Reform, 2009; Shaw et al., 2015). An increased knowledge base about these types of youth risk factors can help to bring awareness to the topic and increase the availability of resources that can be used to prevent child maltreatment.

Violence in the Home

Violence between adults in the home, also known as **intimate partner violence**, can have serious negative impacts on youth development (Breiding, Basile, Smith, Black, & Mahendra, 2015; Franzese, Covey, Tucker, McCoy, & Menard, 2014; Tailor, Stewart-Tufescu, & Piotrowski, 2015). It is important for counselors to recognize that men can be the victims of violence as well as women, and same-sex couples are also at risk for intimate partner violence (Breiding et al., 2015). Counselors should continuously assess for violence between the adults in a youth's life in addition to child maltreatment.

Several factors influence the severity and consequences of intimate partner violence in the home. These risk factors include:

- type(s) of intimate partner violence (e.g., physical, sexual, verbal, stalking);
- number of episodes (more episodes are associated with increased risk);
- most recent episode (increased risk if within the past 12 months);
- intention of the violence (e.g., manipulation, sexual favors, financial gain);
- extent of the abuse (e.g., use of weapons);
- alcohol/substance use by perpetrator and/or victim;

- if the victim is pregnant during the abuse;
- if the victim and perpetrator are currently cohabitating;
- police involvement;
- advocate involvement;
- relationship of child to perpetrator and victim;
- health care received by victim;
- mental health care received by victim and perpetrator;
- substance abuse treatment for victim and perpetrator; and
- legal consequences for perpetrator (Breiding et al., 2015).

More recent episodes of intimate partner violence contribute to the likelihood that the frequency and intensity of intimate partner violence may increase over time (Breiding et al., 2015). Many negative consequences are associated with youth witnessing intimate partner violence in the home, including:

- long- and short-term mental health struggles (e.g., anger, helplessness, depression);
- increased risk for victimization by parents or peers (e.g., bullying, maltreatment);
- psychological and physical effects on caregivers;
- significant life disruptions (e.g., caring for caregiver, moving from home);
- financial difficulties in the family;
- death of caregiver(s); and
- incarceration of perpetrator or victim (Breiding et al., 2015).

Although youth who witness intimate partner violence in the home are not always directly affected in a physical way, the emotional consequences can be significant. Youth who witness violence between the adults in their lives experience physical and mental health difficulties, such as helplessness, anger, upset stomachs, headaches, and anxiety (Franzese et al., 2014). To offset feelings of helplessness and anger, youth might turn to bullying behaviors toward siblings or peers, believing their behaviors are justified because they have witnessed this behavior in the home (Voisin & Hong, 2012). Youth who witness violence at home but who choose not to re-create violent behaviors by bullying others are at greater risk for becoming victims of bullying; their feelings of helplessness and anxiety can make it difficult for them to protect themselves, and this can indicate to their peers that they are easy targets who will not stand up for themselves (Voisin & Hong, 2012).

Several protective factors exist for youth who are exposed to intimate partner violence in their homes. Mental health interventions can be focused on helping youth and their families to learn about healthy ways to cope with such situations and with the anxiety, helplessness, and stress that come as a result of intimate partner violence (Breiding et al., 2015; Tailor et al., 2015; Voisin & Hong, 2012). Mental health interventions specifically for substance use (if relevant) can help caregivers to identify optimally effective ways of coping with life's challenges, and rehabilitation programs specifically for intimate partner violence—for both perpetrators and victims—can allow youth and their families to identify new methods for healthy living (Breiding et al., 2015).

Youth protective factors from intimate partner violence can also come as the result of police or advocate involvement in the home (Breiding et al., 2015). This is especially important for victims who do not have many financial resources or access to an escape plan (e.g., a car packed with a change of clothes, identification, and money). Youth who have siblings are somewhat protected from the effects of violence in the home, especially when they can turn to each other for support. Finally, youth who avoid blaming themselves for the violence are at decreased risk for feelings of stress and depression (Tailor et al., 2015).

When working with youth who have witnessed violence in the home, counselors can try to combat the short- and long-term consequences by helping youth express and process their emotions. Counselors should also work to identify irrational or unhelpful thoughts and help youth to reconstruct more realistic views of themselves and the world. In addition, family counseling might be helpful, and some goal and intervention examples for family counseling are included in Table 2.4. In addition, counselors can help youth to connect their negative feelings with any experiences of somatic symptoms (e.g., headaches, stomachaches) and employ mindfulness techniques to create a sense of safety and well-being in the world.

Table 2.4	Example Goals and Interventions for Family Counseling
Goal	**Intervention**
To improve parent–child relationships	Give each family member a piece of paper. Have each individual write his or her name at the top and pass their paper to the right. Direct each family member to write one nice thing about the individual whose name is at the top and continue passing until each family member receives his or her own paper. Process how each individual feels to learn the positive things family members wrote about them. Ask individuals how they can use their specific talents to continue building positive relationships with other family members.
To increase understanding of expectations in the home	Work with parents and youth to develop a succinct list of concrete, positively worded rules to encompass the main behaviors that should be exemplified in the home. Make sure no rules overlap, and create only as many as are needed to cover the basic requirements. For example, (a) complete chores on a daily basis, (b) attend to parental requests the first time, (c) keep hands, feet, and objects to yourself, and (d) speak in a calm tone at all times.
To improve disciplinary practices in the home	Create a list of succinct, positively worded family rules. Ask youth to brainstorm a list of reinforcements that parents could offer to motivate desired behaviors. Ensure praise and thanks are included in the list. Also, make sure small rewards that don't cost much (e.g., trinkets, tokens) and don't involve food are included. Ask youth to create a list of punishments that can be used when rules are broken (not including corporal punishment). Encourage parents to provide plenty of reinforcements, especially praise, when youth behave as desired. Provide tokens on a 1:1 schedule at first and gradually reduce the frequency to a variable rate. Exchange a set amount of tokens for some larger reinforcers. Use punishment only as a last resort.
To improve communication between and among family members	Fill a jar or box with sentence stems and ask each family member to take a turn selecting a sentence stem and completing it aloud. Process each sentence, determine if any family members agree or disagree, and identify ways that the answers could be shifted for more healthy communication habits. Some sentence stems might include "I feel most sad when __" or "I know mom is mad when __."
To enhance relationships between and among family members	Challenge each family member to compliment every other family member at least once per day.
To enhance a natural support system for the family	Ask family members to list the family, friends, neighbors, and other community members with whom they commonly associate. Identify one inexpensive way the family can show gratitude toward each of these people (e.g., telling them "thank you," making them cookies).

THE SCHOOL SYSTEM: RISK AND PROTECTIVE FACTORS

School is an important system that influences young people's academic, career, and personal–social development (American School Counselor Association [ASCA], 2012). Although the primary purpose of school is to educate youth, the school setting also serves as a microcosm for youth to learn about themselves, others, and the world. This section discusses the risk and protective factors for youth development in the school setting. Specifically, the interaction between academic abilities, family influences, school climate, and peer relationships are explored in a counseling context.

Family Influences on Academic Development

Young people spend a significant amount of time in school, and their behaviors at school are intimately linked to their home environments and vice versa. Youth might experience academic or personal–social challenges as a result of difficulties that originate in the school and/or the home, such as negative family values regarding education, inconsistent rules at home, violence/maltreatment in the home, or a lack of resources. Young people with more helpful familial influences are more likely to succeed in school and are better able to adapt to the unique challenges of the school setting (Becker, 2013; Hamm, Farmer, Lambert, & Gravelle, 2014; Search Institute, 2007; Sorhagen, 2013).

The structure and boundaries of the family system influence not only religious, career, and interpersonal relationship beliefs but also youth's academic beliefs and values (Panasenko, 2013). High family expectations are a strong indicator of academic success in youth (Froiland & Davison, 2014; Hopson & Weldon, 2013; Search Institute, 2007). Parents convey their beliefs about school in the ways they refer to school, how they interact with school personnel, and in their school-related attitudes and behaviors. Parents can teach their children how to behave in the classroom by enforcing consistent and reasonable rules in the household. Parents can also set high expectations for school performance, ensure their children's homework is completed every night, and support youth in acquiring the resources they need to be academically successful.

A family value of education is important to a young person's academic development (Panasenko, 2013). Ideally, parents communicate to youth that school is important and explain that hard work and a commitment to schooling will lead to success in a youth's career later in life. However, some parents do not value formal education. Perhaps the parents were never exposed to the opportunities that a high school or college degree can invite, or perhaps they were exposed to disheartening institutional racism or gender discrimination that prevented them from securing well-paying jobs or advancing within their companies even after earning a degree. Or perhaps the parents have found alternate methods for making a living (legal or illegal) that circumvent the need for education.

Especially in low-income families, education is not always a top priority (CDC, 2014a; Leventhal et al., 2005; Roy et al., 2014; Taylor & de la Sablonnière, 2013; Vigo et al., 2014). Instead, youth may be encouraged to focus on ways they can bring money into the household in the present moment, and education—which necessarily requires delayed gratification—may be devalued (Vigo et al., 2014). Although a youth's decision to forego an education and instead work might satisfy an immediate need within the family, the long-term implications include insufficient education, limited career opportunities, and possibly underdeveloped personal–social skills (ASCA, 2012; Search Institute, 2007). Youth who do not exceed academically and socially might also experience diminished self-esteem and unclear identities. As appropriate, counselors might emphasize the multiple long-term benefits of an education to youth and their families and work to help youth form positive views of the school system and academic pursuits.

School Climate

The school climate is created through the interaction of various factors, including teacher and staff attitudes and behaviors, student attitudes and behaviors, interpersonal relationships, academic resources, classroom management, and safety in the school (O'Malley, Voight, Renshaw, & Eklund, 2015; Zullig et al., 2015). A poor school climate can serve as a risk factor for social, behavioral, and academic difficulties (O'Malley et al., 2015; Search Institute, 2007; Zullig et al., 2015). A lack of academic resources (paper, books, desks, and, increasingly, electronic devices) can feed into a negative tone and also limit youth from achieving their full academic potentials. In addition to academic resources, basic needs such as food and clothing are required for youth to comfortably focus on academics, build peer relationships, and behave in socially appropriate ways.

Poor teacher expectations and negative attitudes from school staff have an important impact on youth, who often come to believe unhelpful teacher/staff beliefs and create a self-fulfilling prophecy (Sorhagen, 2013). Poor teacher communication and a lack of **classroom management**, or a consistent set of classroom rules, can leave students feeling unsafe and uncertain about their roles in the school setting, which could lead to a sense of instability and eventual behavior problems (Barkley, 2013). Rules that are unclear or framed negatively (e.g., no talking) leave youth questioning what they should be doing and what is expected of them. Rules that are only enforced some of the time can potentially be broken with no consequences, and youth will not have the motivation to behave as asked in the school setting. Dysregulation of behavior can interfere with academic concentration, and a lack of predictability in the classroom can cause youth to focus their energies on testing boundaries or speculating about the day's events rather than focusing on personal, academic, and interpersonal growth.

Teachers, school staff, and school counselors can serve as protective factors in the school. Teachers who expect their students to do well communicate a positive message that encourages students to work hard and succeed. By implementing consistent classroom rules, helping youth learn to overcome challenges, and identifying young people's strengths, teachers can give youth the confidence and resources required to achieve maximum gains in the educational environment (Becker, 2013; Search Institute, 2007; Sorhagen, 2013).

Youth who perceive that school is a caring and encouraging environment can find a safe space to learn and grow (CCHD, 2017; Search Institute, 2007). School counselors can work to improve the school climate by providing emotional support and educating school personnel and parents about the importance of positive attitudes from students, parents, and school personnel. **Classroom resources** can also serve as protective factors for youth that support academic and personal/social growth (O'Malley et al., 2015; Zullig et al., 2015). Counselors can work with other professionals to submit grant proposals to fund their schools or collaborate with local businesses to bring extra revenue and materials into the school systems. Counselors can also provide referrals to local organizations that can help support their school climate initiatives.

Even if youth have tumultuous home lives, school can serve as a respite that supports healthy growth and development. It is important for young people to have at least one safe space in which they feel competent and can focus on their own well-being. Counselors can work with school staff, parents, and the community to make the school climate inviting and supportive for all young people.

Peer Relationships

Psychosocial development during the school-age years allows youth to identify who they are in relation to others and can be the source of important risk and protective factors for youth in the school setting. Youth learn about their personalities, values, career aspirations, favorite pastimes, style preferences, and self-efficacy as a result of interactions with other youth who are developmentally similar. Peer groups are, in a sense, more important to youth than parents or adults because youth can easily relate to one another and gauge their abilities and growth in relation to their peers (Hamm et al., 2014; Lereya, Copeland, Costello, & Wolke, 2015; Simpson et al., 2014). Youth need their parents to serve as nurturing, nonjudgmental supporters in their lives, but young people also need to feel connected to and supported by their peers (Search Institute, 2007; Sharkey et al., 2015; Wigderson & Lynch, 2013). Feeling understood and similar to peers can serve as a protective factor for various youth concerns, including:

- academic difficulties;
- self-esteem troubles;
- test anxiety;
- family discord;
- depression;
- self-injury;
- substance use and addictions;
- risk-taking behaviors;
- eating disorders; and
- violence and victimization (Anyon, Ong, & Whitaker, 2014; Gladding, 2012; National Eating Disorders Association, n.d.; Shlafer, McMorris, Sieving, & Gower, 2013).

Youth who feel connected and accepted by their peers are able to form a strong **self-concept** and **self-esteem**. When their best friends are positive role models, youth are more likely to display positive and prosocial behaviors such as helping others, working hard in school, and engaging in productive hobbies (Hamm et al., 2014; Sanderson, 2011). Young people who are confident in their social relationships are also more able to resist peer pressure and avoid dangerous situations such as alcohol or drug use, sexual behavior, and fighting (Search Institute, 2007).

Peer relationships can also serve as risk factors for youth and become problematic when a young person has difficulty making friends, is exposed to unhelpful peer influences, experiences bullying, or otherwise feels unsafe in the school setting (Hamm et al., 2014; Lereya et al., 2015; Wigderson & Lynch, 2013).

It can be difficult for some children to find a peer group that fits their personalities and interests and serves as a positive support system. Peer rejection can lead to various mental health concerns, including:

- aggression;
- antisocial behaviors;
- risk-taking behaviors;
- school violence; and
- bullying (Dodge et al., 2003; CDC, 2015a; Sharkey et al., 2015; Wigderson & Lynch, 2013).

Peer relationships are a strong indicator of social and interpersonal adjustment, and counselors should take care to assess peer relationships in youth when working in any setting. Counselors and teachers should take appropriate steps to foster caring, supportive relationships through social–emotional interventions in the school and by providing community referrals. Bullying and school violence relate to peer relationships and are discussed in the next section.

Bullying and School Violence

Bullying can leave young people at risk and feeling unsafe in the school or spillover settings (e.g., the bus stop, at home; Search Institute, 2007; Sharkey et al., 2015; Wigderson & Lynch, 2013). Bullying can occur in person or online, and it involves one young person attacking or putting down another. These attacks might be physical (e.g., hitting, shoving) or emotional, in which a bully spreads rumors or criticizes another youth's character, which can result in the loss of social support and feelings of depression, frustration, anger, and helplessness.

Youth bully one another for various reasons. Risk factors that might contribute to bullying behaviors include:

- history of victimization at home or by other bullies;
- attention-deficit/hyperactivity disorder;
- learning disorders or low IQ;
- substance use;
- lack of emotional regulation or behavioral control; and
- antisocial values (Centers for Disease Control and Prevention [CDC], 2015c; Dickerson Mayes et al., 2014; Voisin & Hong, 2012).

It is not uncommon for youth who are victims of bullying to bully others (CDC, 2015c; Voisin & Hong, 2012). Often, youth feel helpless and angry when they are bullied, and they work to counteract these feelings by asserting themselves onto others. Long-term consequences of bully victimization include overall mental health problems, anxiety, and depression (Lereya et al., 2015). Youth who attempt to overcome their feelings of helplessness by bullying others are especially vulnerable to suicidal ideation (Dickerson Mayes et al., 2014). The long-term mental health consequences for youth who are bullied are actually more complex and detrimental than the effects of childhood maltreatment from parents (Lereya et al., 2015).

Warning signs that a youth is being bullied include damaged belongings, a change in grades, self-deprecating thoughts or behaviors, difficulty sleeping, and somatic symptoms (e.g., headaches, feeling sick), which can result from feelings of anxiety or can be feigned to avoid going to school or other settings in which a bully might be present (Dickerson Mayes et al., 2014; Voisin & Hong, 2012). Counselors should educate parents and caregivers about these signs and intervene as appropriate and necessary.

It is important for counselors to remember the importance of social relationships for youth and to conduct ongoing assessment for bullying. Counselors should also work to harness various protective factors that prevent youth from participating in bullying behaviors, which include:

- positive peer relationships;
- personal values of altruism and low tolerance for antisocial behaviors;
- high intelligence;
- strong social skills;
- problem-solving skills;
- religious/spiritual beliefs;

- connection to family and other adults;
- positive parental expectations;
- commitment to academic achievement;
- consistent home routines;
- involvement in prosocial activities (e.g., volunteerism); and
- positive school climate (Anyon et al., 2014; Barkley, 2013; CDC, 2015c; Hamm et al., 2014; Search Institute, 2007).

In addition to ongoing bullying, **school violence** includes physical fights between youth, gang activity, and use of deadly weapons (e.g., guns, knives) against peers and/or school personnel (CDC, 2015a). Risk factors associated with school violence include previous aggressive behaviors, substance use, delinquent peer group association, unhelpful family boundaries and communication, academic struggles, and poverty in the home/neighborhood (CDC, 2015a). Counselors should work to identify youth who are at risk for conducting acts of school violence and should educate school personnel about these factors as well.

Safety at school is of paramount concern so youth can focus on academic, career, and personal–social goals. Counselors should make sure to validate the importance of peer relationships in adolescents and attend to any issues of bullying or school violence in a skilled, timely manner. The main goals of counseling interventions should include increased coping skills so youth can resist violence, improved social skills, enhanced relationships between youth and adults in the school and community, increased safety and connectedness in the community, and promotion of societal values that highlight safety and healthy behaviors in the schools (CDC, 2015a).

School counselors can offer guidance in classrooms and small group settings on character education and other social considerations such as bullying, identity development, friendship, and self-esteem. When youth are supported through the difficulties of making and keeping friends, they are more likely to fall into a healthy, supportive peer group with friends who model responsible, helpful behavior (Hamm et al., 2014; Search Institute, 2007). Although the school system cannot be solely responsible for a youth's well-being, the support and positive expectations of school counselors and personnel can help facilitate young people's positive, prosocial development.

Clinical Toolbox 2.5

In the Pearson eText, click here for a group counseling lesson plan for supporting female identity and relationship development.

The school setting can serve as a respite for youth who experience difficulties at home or in the community. Resiliency factors for youth in the school setting include positive role models, strong peer relationships, and a supportive school climate (Elliot et al., 2006; Hohl, 2013; Hopson & Lee, 2011; Search Institute, 2007; Sorhagen, 2013). Risk factors that affect a young person's school-based development include negative or unsupportive family influences, cognitive difficulties, a lack of resources (e.g., books, computers, notebooks), unhelpful teacher expectations, ineffective classroom management, negative peer influences, bullying, and school violence. It is important for counselors and parents to help young people to develop the self-confidence and personal identities needed to have healthy, successful interpersonal interactions. The healthy social skills learned in school can then be extended back into the home and community settings.

THE COMMUNITY: RISK AND PROTECTIVE FACTORS

Community is a broad term that refers to a shared environment and/or the people within it. Youth have unique community experiences that depend on where they live, available resources, and the organizations with which their families are connected. Young people's dependence on their caregivers for community exposure highlights the interplay between the home and the community; until children are old enough to independently navigate the world, the community is largely influenced by their parents' choices and geographic location. This section explores community-based risk and protective factors that are most salient to counseling youth, including neighborhood and community rules, norms, resources, violence, and crime.

When considering community and neighborhood factors, counselors should assume a holistic and multicultural perspective. It is especially important to note that youth who belong to racial, ethnic, sexual, or socioeconomic minority groups in the neighborhood or community might be at an increased risk for emotional, social, and developmental difficulties (Kress et al., 2018; Sue & Sue, 2013). Often, youth might find respite in their neighborhoods or other community outlets that are populated by individuals who belong to a similar minority group (e.g., an apartment complex that houses a high immigrant population; a bar designed specifically for members of the lesbian, gay, bisexual, transgender, and queer/questioning community). A holistic conceptualization of youth risk and protective factors within the neighborhood and community can help counselors to understand and address their mental health needs.

Community and Neighborhood Norms

Every community has a set of **norms**, which are mutually agreed-on behavioral standards that inform social organization and interaction (Rossano, 2012). Community norms are not only partially influenced by the standards and beliefs of the overarching society but also uniquely capture the values and standards of the smaller community (CDC, 2014a). Neighborhoods exist within a given community, and neighborhood norms convey the values and beliefs of an even more specific group of people.

It can be especially difficult for youth who emigrated from another country to adapt to the norms of their new communities and neighborhoods; this process of adaptation and integration is known as **acculturation** (Sue & Sue, 2013). Some immigrant youth might reject the norms of the dominant culture to maintain the values and norms of their cultures of origin. This might make it difficult for youth to form supportive social relationships with youth from other cultures and might leave them feeling quite out of place in many social settings (Katsiaficas, Suárez-Orozco, Sirin, & Gupta, 2013).

Some immigrant youth might fully accept the norms of their new cultures while leaving behind the values of their cultures of origin, and this can lead to emotional difficulties if they begin to believe that their cultures of origin are somehow inferior to the dominant culture (Sue & Sue, 2013). In addition, parents of immigrants might still ascribe to many of the values of their home countries, which might create struggle and tension between youth and their parents. A healthy method of acculturation includes youth intentionally adopting some values from their new cultures while maintaining some of the most important values from their cultures of origin (Sue & Sue, 2013). Counselors can work with youth to help them to navigate this complex and intensely personal process while paying special attention to protective factors that can support healthy development.

Protective factors within a neighborhood and community include a strong value for education, respect for human life, safe and stable interpersonal relationships, positive academic growth, and promotion of strong individual identities and self-esteem (ASCA, 2012; CDC, 2014a; Taylor & de la Sablonnière, 2013). Youth who live in communities that place a premium on human life, education, and cooperation are likely to find greater value in themselves and excel in their personal development (CDC, 2014a; Rossano, 2012; Taylor & de la Sablonnière, 2013). Young people can find satisfaction and autonomy by volunteering in the community, which provides them with social support and a genuine feeling of purpose (Hill & den Dulk, 2013; Search Institute, 2007).

Sports programs are often valued in communities, and these can be offered through the schools, community organizations, or unofficially organized by neighborhood members. Sports teach young people about teamwork, self-discipline, and healthy coping skills; young people who participate in sports often experience healthier overall development (CCHD, 2017; Search Institute, 2007). The athletic arena also provides an opportunity for young people to expel excess energy and form healthy connections between their minds and bodies. In addition, coaches can be a tremendous asset to young people as they provide information, show youth how to apply it, and typically praise them for their hard work and efforts (Sheridan, Coffee, & Lavallee, 2014).

Many communities have a strong sense of identity in which its community members join with one another for support. However, some communities are negatively affected by economic difficulties and oppression, and this creates risk factors for youth (Taylor & de la Sablonnière, 2013). Racism, sexism, and discrimination are everyday realities in many young people's lives, especially those living in economically disadvantaged communities (Diemer, Kauffman, Koenig, Trahan, & Hsieh, 2006). As the result of oppression, limited access to resources, and difficulty enduring delayed gratification, many economically disadvantaged communities do not value education (CDC, 2014a; Diemer et al., 2006; Taylor & de la Sablonnière, 2013). Long-term negative effects of living in depressed or dysfunctional communities include:

- a poor sense of identity;
- a lack of connection with others/minimal value placed on others;
- low self-esteem;
- poor self-control;
- feelings of helplessness and anger;
- limited access to resources;
- poor nutrition;
- poor academic achievement/school dropouts;
- substance abuse;
- violence/crime;
- gambling/risk-taking behaviors; and
- physical health issues (Diemer et al., 2006; Taylor & de la Sablonnière, 2013).

It is important for counselors to understand a youth's community context to address potential risk factors that youth might need to overcome. Counselors should openly discuss issues of diversity, encourage emotional expression from youth, reframe any irrational thoughts, and brainstorm concrete solutions for overt or covert discrimination (Zárate, Quezada, Shenberger, & Lupo, 2014). Counselors can work with parents and teachers to enhance youth's values of education and practice self-control for the delayed gratification that comes with school completion.

Even if a youth lives in a particularly difficult neighborhood, a community typically includes resources that counselors and parents can use to promote youth development. Parents can choose from various churches, parks, sporting events, afterschool programs, and community events to provide young people with additional outlets for personal and social development. Afterschool programs can serve a dual purpose of exposing youth to a supportive social culture and providing childcare/supervision for parents who work into the evening. Counselors should assess for activities in the community that youth might enjoy and consider suggesting to parents that their children participate in community roles that allow youth to feel valued and form helpful connections with others (Search Institute, 2007).

Neighborhood Violence and Crime

Neighborhood violence is common, and up to 75% of America's youth have been exposed to some form of neighborhood violence, ranging from fighting to murder (Aizer, 2008). Most severe forms of neighborhood violence are found in areas of high poverty in which youth have limited access to resources and family/social support. The negative effects associated with young people's exposures to neighborhood violence include:

- diminished emotional development;
- increased aggression;
- unhelpful social or academic behaviors;
- substance use;
- bullying;
- school violence;
- gang membership;
- committing crimes (e.g., assault, robbery/burglary, vehicle theft, larceny); and
- firearm use (Aizer, 2008; CDC, 2015a, 2015c; National Gang Center, n.d.).

There are many potential protective factors that can support youth who are exposed to neighborhood violence and crime. When neighborhood resources are limited and violence is high, safety within the home is a key source of support for youth (Elliot et al., 2006; Martin et al., 2012; Sanderson, 2011; Search Institute, 2007). In addition to supportive family members, enhanced relationships with positive peers and adults in the school and community can serve as factors that protect youth from neighborhood violence and/or a lack of resources (APA, 2013; Hohl, 2013; London et al., 2015; Sanderson, 2011). These relational connections serve multiple purposes; youth can build their identities and form strong peer relationships, and supportive adults can provide unique insights and additional encouragement for young people in need of social connectedness. Positive social networks meet youth's psychosocial needs without having to engage in gang membership or associating with violent peers. In addition, youth can share resources (e.g., food, sports equipment) and knowledge (e.g., neighborhood stories, help with homework) with their positive peers and mentors to further create a functional, supportive neighborhood community.

The identification of positive role models is a key consideration for counselors working with at-risk youth. Young people who have positive relationships with older adult neighbors tend to have a greater value for education, and they learn how to be responsible, helpful members of their communities (Gottfried, 2014; Search Institute, 2007). Youth mentorship can naturally occur or can be supported by referrals to community resources such as Big Brothers/Big Sisters of America, Girl Scouts/Boy Scouts of America, the YMCA/YWCA, or other community programs provided by trusted sponsors.

In addition to positive relationships with family, peers, and mentors, youth can increase their protective factors by assuming leadership positions, volunteering to help others, and connecting with spiritual resources in the neighborhood and community (Hohl, 2013; Holdsworth & Brewis, 2014; Search Institute, 2007). When youth give of themselves and connect to a higher power, they learn about the value of human life, their well-being improves, and their self-efficacy increases (Search Institute, 2007). Counselors should work to inform parents and family members about the interpersonal needs of youth; the risks associated with dangerous neighborhoods; and ways that family, friends, community resources, and mentors can provide security and a safe platform for youth to grow and develop.

Technology

Increasingly, youth are exposed to technology, and technology use continues to rise among youth and provide a new platform for interacting with the worldwide community (Tandoc, Ferrucci, & Duffy, 2015). Technology outlets such as the Internet can be helpful in offering academic support and career exploration tools, and social media can facilitate peer connection in a neutral environment that is not bound by issues of class, gender, or race. However, both risk and protective factors are associated with the games, social media, live chat programs, blogs, articles, and emails that youth access every day through computers, handheld devices, and smartphones.

It is undeniable that technology is an integral part of child and adolescent development, and it is important for parents and counselors to understand the risks and benefits of its use and how to help children to navigate technology. Excessive time spent on the Internet can be isolating for youth, who might not get the family and peer interactions they require if too much time is spent with technology and social media and not with others (Tandoc et al., 2015; Twenge, 2014). The Internet also provides ample access to pornography and violence. It is possible that exposure to pornography at a young age can lead to long-term problems, such as increased/early sexualization, behavioral problems, trauma-related symptoms, or even sexual assault perpetrated by the exposed youth (Leibowitz, Burton, & Howard, 2012). Counselors might work to support youth and their families in using the Internet or other forms of technology in helpful ways that allow them to lead full lives in their homes, schools, and communities.

The Internet is an excellent resource for learning and engaging with peers, but counselors should be aware of the unhelpful development that can result from inappropriate technology use and intervene with the support of parents or teachers when necessary. Youth need a well-balanced variety of resources and settings to achieve optimal development (Search Institute, 2007). Counselors can take extra steps to educate youth about the dangers of technology; ensure youth are exposed to *in vivo* stimulation in the home, school, and community; and promote the use of technology to foster knowledge, creativity, and social connection.

It is increasingly important for counselors to understand the ways in which community and neighborhood norms influence youth development and how issues of prejudice, discrimination, and oppression affect youth. Counselors should especially be aware of the key role that poverty plays in a youth's overall well-being, as well as the multiple risk factors that stem from limited access to resources. It is ideal to harness as many community resources as possible (e.g., neighborhood sports clubs, community organizations) and work to highlight additional protective factors from the youth's family and school contexts to provide holistic, wellness-based interventions that acknowledge and celebrate each youth's unique sense of self.

Clinical Toolbox 2.6

In the Pearson eText, click here to review process questions that counselor trainees might use to reflect on their childhood experiences and how they relate to counseling youth.

Summary

It is important that counselors conceptualize youth in the context of family, school, and community. Counselors who understand the complex interaction of contextual factors that influence youth will be able to identify and build on clients' strengths and resiliencies while also addressing, when possible, relevant risk factors. To aid counselors in identifying the strengths of young clients, detailed interview questions that can be used to assess young clients' strengths, capacities, and resources in relation to family, community, spirituality, and culture are provided in Table 2.5. As part of a strength-based approach, counselors should address barriers to healthy development and intervene with their young clients to harness as many internal and external assets as possible and pull these into counseling.

Table 2.5 Interview Questions to Assess Clients' Strengths, Capacities, and Resources

Family of Origin Strengths	Community/Cultural Strengths	Spiritual Strengths
• Who are you most similar to in your family? • When you grow up, who in your family do you want to be like? • Who is the kindest person in your family? • Who is the smartest person in your family? • Tell me about your grandparents. • Which family members are you closest to? • How often do you share quality time with your family? • Tell me about your family values. • Who are the most special people in your life? • What is one good thing about each of your family members? • What makes your family unique? • In what ways do your family members support you and your life? • What lessons have you learned from your family? • Which family member would you ask for help in school? • Which family member would you ask for help with friends? • What special traditions does your family share?	• What roles do you play in the community? • How does your culture fit into the culture of the whole community? • What are the best parts of your community? • What are some unique aspects of your culture? • What are your favorite parts of your culture? • What are your favorite parts of your community? • How do you help other people in your community? • In your community, who do you admire the most? • What community resources can you use to achieve your goals? • How have people in your community helped you to learn and grow? • How can you connect with more people in the community? • Can you think of any ways that you can use your talents, abilities, or traits to help others in the community? • What is your age, race, ethnicity, culture, socioeconomic status, and sexual orientation?	• Is religion or spirituality important to you? • How do you make meaning of your life? • What does religion mean to you? • What are your religious or spiritual values? • What does it mean for you to live your life to the fullest? • In what ways do religion or spirituality comfort you in times of difficulty? • How can spirituality or religion help you to achieve your goals? • Is there anyone in your religious community you feel can help to support or guide you in times of need? • How have members of your religious community helped you or your family in the past? • How are your spiritual/religious beliefs unique?

(Continued)

Table 2.5 Interview Questions to Assess Clients' Strengths, Capacities, and Resources (*Continued*)

Family of Origin Strengths	Community/Cultural Strengths	Spiritual Strengths
• Which family member do you trust the most? • On a scale of 1 (very little) and 5 (very much), how well do you fit in with your family? • How does your family deal with problems or disagreements? • When was the last time you and your family worked together on a project? • What is one way your family could be more helpful in your life? • What was the biggest challenge your family has overcome? • What do you contribute or add to your family? • How have you made your family proud? • Which family members are you proud of? • What activities do you do for fun with your family?	• What gendered pronoun (e.g., him, her, they) do you prefer? • Where were your parents born? Where were you born? • Where is your home? • What languages do you speak at home? • What do you miss most about your last home? • What are the key parts of your cultural identity? • How would you describe your community? • Do you belong to any groups or organizations? • Have you ever been discriminated against because of your culture? Where/how did it occur? • Have you ever been discriminated against due to your race, gender, or sexuality?	• How are your spiritual/religious beliefs similar to those of your peers or family? • Do you ever meditate or pray? When do you most often do so? • How do your religious or spiritual values affect your schooling or peer relationships? • How do your beliefs affect your interactions with others?

On a larger scale, counselors can become active advocates for youth by disseminating research information to the community about risk and protective factors. Counselors can help inform lobbyists and their national, state, and local legislators about the importance of drug and alcohol laws, equitable school funding, and mental health awareness initiatives. Large-scale collaborations between government entities, state and local health departments, mental health professionals, the school, and the community can lead to awareness of important counseling issues (e.g., family communication, abuse/neglect, importance of afterschool programs) and development of infrastructure to support healthy youth development.

MyLab Counseling: Counseling Children and Adolescents

In the Topic 2 Assignments: *Systemically-Informed Youth Counseling*, try Application Exercise 2.1: *Identifying Client Strengths and Using Strengths in Counseling* and Licensure Quiz 2.1: *Holistic Case Conceptualization and Intervention.*

Then try Application Exercise 2.2: *Risk and Protective Factors in the Family, School, and Community*, Licensure Quiz 2.2: *The Family System* and Licensure Quiz 2.3: *School and Community Risk Factors.*

CHAPTER 3

Individual Counseling Foundations

This chapter discusses the basic foundations central to all child and adolescent *individual* counseling. The American Counseling Association (ACA, 2015, para. 3) defines counseling as "a professional relationship that empowers diverse individuals, families, and groups to accomplish mental health, wellness, education, and career goals." At the most basic level, counseling involves two or more people coming together so one person (the counselor) can help the other person—or people in the case of families—make desired changes.

Counselors generally work with youth who self-identify as having a problem or have been perceived by others as having a problem (Bohart & Wade, 2013; Chronis-Tuscano et al., 2015). Identified problems may be related to psychopathology and mental disorders (e.g., depression, anxiety, anorexia nervosa), developmental transitions (e.g., adjusting to puberty), and/or environmental stressors (e.g., parents divorcing, adjusting to a new school).

Counselors may also work to prevent new problems from developing (Jenson & Bender, 2014). For example, when counseling a client who has conduct problems, a counselor may provide education and prevention related to substance abuse because it is known these two problems frequently co-occur. Another example of counseling serving as a type of prevention is a situation in which a counselor works with a child whose parents are divorcing so as to prevent problems from arising secondary to the parental separation.

Helping a client to live more optimally, even if he or she does not have an expressed problem, is another potential counseling goal (ACA, 2014). For example, consider a mother who brings her daughter into counseling to discuss ways they can strengthen their relationship, even though no specific problem is identified. A child entering individual counseling without an identified problem is rare but does sometimes occur. Realistically, most clients seek individual counseling because of an identified problem, not to prevent problems or to enrich their lives. Counselors in the school setting might focus on developmental matters; however, it is more typical in clinical settings for parents or an external force (e.g., school, local child protective services agency) to suggest and/or initiate counseling as a means of helping the child and changing youth behaviors seen as problematic.

Over the years, counselors have developed a better understanding of what makes for helpful counseling. The foundational ingredients of effective counseling are similar for both youth and adult populations (e.g., building the therapeutic relationship, harnessing client strengths; Norcross & Wampold, 2011a; Suldo et al., 2015a; Suldo, et al., 2015b. Increasing elementary school student's subjective well-being through a classwide positive psychology intervention: Results of a pilot study. Contemporary School Psychology, 19(4), 300-311.). However, multiple developmental considerations need to be taken into account when counseling youth, and these include young people's physical and cognitive abilities, social experiences, and emotional development factors. When counseling youth, it is important that counselors do not simply apply strategies specific to counseling adults; youth counseling requires unique, individually tailored skills and knowledge (Broderick & Blewitt, 2014).

Regardless of the theoretical approach, individual counseling evolves in a fairly predictable way, with a beginning, middle, and end. Although each counseling theory touched on in Chapters 5, 6, and 7 in this text has a different focus in terms of philosophy, approach, goals, methods, and techniques, all counseling shares a predictable structure and has similar helpful ingredients. The individual counseling foundations and considerations that cut across all counseling approaches are discussed in this chapter. Because a strong counseling relationship is the best predictor of positive counseling outcomes (Norcross & Wampold, 2011a), a heavy emphasis is placed on the counseling relationship in the context of the topics addressed.

This chapter begins by discussing the qualities, characteristics, and behaviors that effective counselors possess. Regardless of a counselor's theoretical orientation, the characteristics that are described are essential to all "good" counseling. The topics and material presented in this chapter are grounded or informed by these important counseling ingredients.

The chapter then moves on to discuss the preliminary—or initial—counseling tasks that lay the foundation for individual counseling with young clients. During the initial counseling phase, it is imperative that counselors establish a productive therapeutic alliance with clients. Because the therapeutic alliance is so important, key essential counselor qualities and behaviors in the early stages of counseling are reviewed. Counselors must consider the importance of creating a comfortable counseling environment or space and conducting a thoughtful intake process. They must also be prepared to review counselor and client expectations in a clear, concise manner, and as such, these topics are addressed.

Next, the working stage of counseling and considerations unique to individual counseling with youth are discussed. The chapter explores ways young clients' family members can be involved to maximize the benefit of the counseling process. The working stage section also covers age-appropriate communication styles and challenges, as well as interventions for difficult situations counselors may encounter during the working stage of counseling.

In addition, termination strategies that are effective when working with youth are presented. Termination is a topic that receives sparse attention in counselor training, yet it is an important aspect of the counseling process. Termination marks the end of the counseling experience, and counselors are responsible for facilitating a smooth transition. Counselors want clients' last session(s) to resonate and be memorable; thus, termination should be a thoughtful, deliberate process. Examples of specific activities that can facilitate termination with youth are provided.

FOUNDATIONS OF THE COUNSELING PROCESS

Before exploring the individual counseling process and its foundations, it is important to evaluate whether counseling is effective, and if so, what makes it effective. We know that counseling is effective, and meta-analyses of child and adolescent counseling suggest that counseling is just as effective with youth as it is with adults (Weisz & Kazdin, 2010). Youth who receive counseling also fair better than those who do not receive counseling, and change can sometimes occur rather quickly (Norcross & Wampold, 2011a). We also know that, in general, no one theoretical approach is superior to any other, and counseling outcomes are not based on the education or degree/license of the person providing services (Norcross & Wampold, 2011a).

To understand the individual counseling process, it is important to review what counseling ingredients are effective. We know that the counseling relationship is the single most important aspect of the individual counseling process and that certain counselor behaviors facilitate strong counseling relationships (Norcross & Wampold, 2011a; Wampold, 2010). What follows is a brief overview—based on more than 50 years of research—of the counselor qualities and behaviors that predict successful counseling outcomes (i.e., client satisfaction with counseling, clients reaching their goals) regardless of factors such as age or presenting issues (Norcross & Wampold, 2011a; Wampold, 2010):

- Effective youth counselors have advanced *interpersonal skills*, including the ability to convey sincerity and empathy and to understand and focus on what is important to young clients and their families. These interpersonal skills help to establish a warm connection and a positive therapeutic relationship. This relationship enables clients and families to feel understood, invites trust, and gives clients confidence in their counselors' ability to facilitate change.
- Effective youth counselors are able to form a *working alliance* with a diverse array of clients. This working alliance involves the previously mentioned therapeutic relationship, as well as agreement on the goals of counseling and how these goals will be achieved (the tasks of counseling). A strong working alliance suggests that the counselor and client are working in a deliberate, focused manner toward mutually agreed-on counseling goals. When working with youth, counselors must develop and

maintain a strong working alliance with clients and their families. They also need to consistently assess and monitor these working alliances for changes, disruptions, or ruptures. Examples of alliance ruptures include families questioning the usefulness of counseling or young clients disengaging or shifting away from counseling and avoiding important topics.

- Effective youth counselors provide an *explanation for the client's problems* or struggles that is acceptable (i.e., the explanation fits within the client's comfort level based on his or her socioeconomic status [SES], culture, and self-perceptions), adaptive (i.e., the explanation suggests a means of overcoming the struggle in a productive manner), and culturally sensitive (i.e., the explanation fits with the client's attitudes, values, culture, and worldview). Effective counselors are extremely sensitive to the client's viewpoint and understanding of problems and consider these factors before sharing explanations for the client's struggles. These explanations are cohesive with both the client's and the family's comprehension of the problem.

- Effective youth counselors provide a *counseling or treatment plan consistent with the explanation for the problem* that was provided to—or co-constructed with—the client. If the explanation of and plan to address the problem are mutually agreed on, clients will be more compliant and remain engaged in counseling. It is critical for clients to be aware of the goals and objectives of the plan, understand how counseling will be helpful, and believe in the plan. As such, an effective counselor must be persuasive and facilitate client buy-in with regard to the counseling plan. If clients have faith in their counseling plan, then they will be hopeful, have expectations for success, and feel motivated to action. Parents and youth may have different ideas about counseling goals and treatment plans. As much as possible, counselors should acknowledge and accommodate all family members' perspectives.

- Effective youth counselors *monitor clients' progress.* Monitoring does not need to include the use of assessment instruments. It might simply involve checking in with clients on their progress and reactions to the counseling experience. It is important for counselors to communicate that they authentically care about the client and his or her family and their progress and that they genuinely value their input. Monitoring helps counselors to identify potential problems before they arise, and it serves as an excellent tool to help to process clients' reactions to specific counseling interventions and counseling in general.

- Effective youth counselors are *flexible,* and they adjust their approach if the client is not responding and/or motivated to change. They alter their methods accordingly—that is, they use a different theoretical approach, refer to another provider, and/or integrate adjunctive services (e.g., psychiatric referrals, family therapy).

- Effective youth counselors can *address difficult counseling material* and topics. They know when to approach and when to avoid such material, and they are comfortable and skilled enough to directly address such material. Sometimes the difficulties may be related to clients' experiences (e.g., a fear of approaching painful material) or to aspects of the relationship between the clients and the counselor (e.g., client dissatisfaction with counseling). When the difficult material involves the relationship between the client and the counselor, an effective counselor is able to address the situation in a productive, therapeutic way.

- Effective youth counselors *communicate hope, enthusiasm, and optimism.* This communication is not unrealistic or flippant optimism but rather a genuine belief that hurdles can be overcome and solutions found. Related to this, effective counselors can recognize clients' strengths, capacities, and resources, as well as communicate these and the role they can play in helping clients to master their problems.

- Effective youth counselors *display sensitivity to clients' personal characteristics* (e.g., culture, race, ethnicity, spirituality, sexual orientation, age, physical health, motivation for change) and context (e.g., SES, family and support networks, community resources and services). Sensitivity to these factors helps counselors to coordinate client care with other psychiatric, psychological, medical, or social service providers. Effective counselors are also aware of their own personal characteristics (e.g., culture, gender, personality, background, lived experiences), and they understand how clients perceive these characteristics and interact with them.

- Effective youth counselors are *self-aware*—that is, they are mindful of their own psychological processes and dynamics, and they keep these out of the counseling process unless it is therapeutic to introduce them. The effective counselor reflects on his or her own reactions to clients (i.e., countertransference) and monitors these reactions.

- Practice appropriate and helpful ***interpersonal skills.***
- Form a ***working alliance*** with a diverse array of clients.
- Provide an ***explanation for the client's problems*** or struggles that is acceptable, adaptive, and culturally sensitive.
- Provide a ***counseling or treatment plan consistent with the explanation for the problem*** provided to the client.
- ***Monitor clients' progress.***
- Adjust their approaches as needed and remain ***flexible.***
- ***Address difficult counseling material*** and topics.
- ***Communicate hope, enthusiasm, and optimism.***
- ***Display sensitivity to clients' personal characteristics.***
- Self-monitor and become increasingly ***self-aware.***
- Seek to ***continually improve*** as a counselor.
- Maintain knowledge and stay ***aware of the research*** and evidence-based approaches.

FIGURE 3.1   Foundational Skills of Effective Youth Counselors

- Effective youth counselors seek to *continually improve*. They recognize that the development of a skill requires intensive training and practice as well as consultation and supervision. They seek continuing education and peer guidance and advice, with the aim to continually grow and improve.
- Effective youth counselors are *aware of the research* related to clients' presenting issues, and they pull on this literature base to select their approaches.

Figure 3.1 provides an overview of the foundational counseling skills that help to facilitate good counseling.

The idea that counselors pull on the research literature is especially important. Our young clients deserve to have counselors who integrate evidence-based practices into their work. Because the presented ingredients are universally accepted and well established as important and evidence based, the material provided in the rest of this chapter is—in large part—founded on these concepts.

PRELIMINARY COUNSELING CONSIDERATIONS

This section highlights the preliminary counseling tasks that lay the foundation for individual counseling with young people. The counseling considerations are relevant to all counseling, regardless of the counselor's theoretical orientation. More specifically, the physical setting of counseling, informed consent, development of a therapeutic relationship, and assessment of the client's presenting concern are addressed. Techniques for building a relationship with the client's family are also discussed. Generally, the preliminary counseling tasks described in this section occur over one to three sessions; however, some counselors, due to the nature of their setting (e.g., school counselors), may only have one or two sessions with a young client. Once preliminary counseling tasks are complete, counselors can move to the working stage of counseling.

Creating a Comfortable Counseling Experience

Counselors are responsible for creating a comfortable, age-appropriate counseling space for young clients. Factors that contribute to an adaptive counseling space include characteristics of the physical setting such as the room and seating structure; availability of toys and games, snacks, and incentives (when appropriate); and a predictable, stable session structure and counseling experience.

THE PHYSICAL SETTING

Young clients are especially sensitive to their environment, so counselors should provide an age-appropriate setting in which clients and their family members can feel comfortable. The physical setting should be suitable to the age level of the clients with whom the counselor works (e.g., if working with young children, lamps, breakable décor, or items that might be overturned should not be used as decorations). It is helpful to avoid dramatic décor, maintain consistency with regard to the structure of the room, and provide appropriate lighting (not too dim or too bright) in the counseling room (Vernon, 2009).

It is generally suggested that counselors sit at the client's eye level and avoid a seating arrangement that contributes to the client feeling too low and thus disempowered (e.g., feet dangling because a chair is too high, sinking into a couch; Broderick & Blewitt, 2014; Dowell & Berman, 2013; Frank & Frank, 1993). Couches placed against a wall may make clients feel safer and less vulnerable because they know what is behind them. It is also generally suggested that counselors avoid sitting behind a desk because this creates a barrier between them and the client that can be intimidating because it highlights the power differential inherent in the relationship. Also, for youth, it may feel too similar to a teacher–student relationship, a dynamic that counselors may want to avoid. Young clients usually do not prefer direct eye contact, so they often do best when engaged in an activity. As such, it is helpful to have a table that can be used to play games or create art and as a place to set down toys or any other media the counselor uses.

Counselors should also make sure their counseling space is free of distracting interruptions such as ringing phones, loud intercom speakers, or outside traffic. White noise machines can help to minimize distracting outside noises, and a sign on the door can communicate that the counselor is in a session and thus can help prevent colleagues from knocking on the door during sessions.

MEDIA

Counselors should be aware of clients' developmental levels and use media that are appropriate. Care should be taken to ensure the counseling room is not too distracting; too many games or toys and loud decorations can pull away from the intended focus. Some counselors who work with younger children may exclusively use a play therapy room for their sessions and/or may sit on the floor with the child.

It is important to provide access to toys or items that are age appropriate to the counseling populations (Ray et al., 2013). Toys that promote exploration and expression (e.g., dress-up clothes, doll houses, sand trays) are excellent choices.

Both child and adolescent clients often enjoy using fidget toys in their sessions. These toys come in different shapes, sizes, and textures and can include stress balls, tangles, Silly Putty, Play-Doh, and Squigglets. Fidget toys help clients to self-regulate energy and anxiety; they can facilitate a sense of calmness; aid in alertness, focus, and concentration; and provide youth with an outlet for their energy (Adamson & Kress, 2011; Stalvey & Brasell, 2006). Because of the ability of fidget toys to facilitate clients' ability to pay attention, they may also encourage learning (Stalvey & Brasell, 2006) and are especially helpful with anxious or energetic clients. Various online retailers sell fiddle or fidget toy packs and kits. Energetic youth, in particular, may enjoy tossing a stress ball back and forth with the counselor in sessions.

It is also helpful to have someplace where you and/or your clients can write or draw (e.g., easel, whiteboard, chalkboard, table) and easy access to paper, pencils, and markers or crayons. Availability of a craft box that contains various writing and art utensils may prove useful.

Finally, it may a good idea to have a basket with toys, games, and/or reading material applicable to youth in the waiting area. Waiting room toys may be useful in distracting siblings or other children parents may bring along to counseling sessions.

SNACKS AND INCENTIVES

Counselors should also determine whether they will have snacks available for clients if they are requested. It is not uncommon for young clients to come to a session and announce they are thirsty or hungry, and it may be difficult for them to focus if their basic needs are not met. Counselors should communicate with parents about their use of snacks and ensure parental consent prior to providing any food items.

The matter of providing clients with treats at the end of counseling sessions (e.g., allowing them to pick from a chest of small, inexpensive items such as stickers) is controversial. Some (e.g., Vernon, 2009) suggest that providing such gifts may distort boundaries, foster manipulations (by the counselor or client), or distort the intention of counseling. However, providing a small item at the end of sessions is developmentally appropriate, culturally supported, and fairly common among practicing counselors. Small items can be motivating to young clients and engage them in the counseling process (Barkley, 2013). If incentives are used, their availability should not be contingent on the child's behavior or participation in counseling.

PREDICTABLE STRUCTURE

Counselors should aim to create a counseling experience that feels comfortable, relaxed, and safe. All clients—regardless of their age—find security in a predictable, consistent counseling experience. As such, it is important that counselors begin and end their sessions on time and that the counselor prestructures each session so the young client and his or her family know what to expect. The importance of structuring sessions is discussed later in this chapter.

Related to predictability, communicating limits and boundaries provides young clients with a sense of safety (Barkley, 2013). Clients look to the counselor to understand these limits, and counselors should be clear in communicating these expectations early on. Some basic expectations related to the physical setting that counselors might communicate are cleaning up and putting away items before leaving a session, not taking items home, and using items for their intended purposes (e.g., sand is to be used in the sand tray, not on the floor).

Intake and Assessment

The initial one to two sessions are generally referred to as the client intake. Legally, guardians—who are usually but not always parents—must provide consent for minors to engage in counseling, and they should attend the initial intake session. The intake process involves a review of informed consent considerations and an assessment of the client's situation and counseling needs. Especially during the intake process, it is important that counselors employ active listening and communicate basic facilitative conditions with the young client and his or her family. Many clients fail to return to counseling after an intake, thus highlighting the importance of initial engagement (Baruch, Vrouva, & Fearon, 2009).

Before meeting with a young client for a first session, counselors typically have some sense of the presenting concern. The client may have already gone through an agency's intake process, which resulted in his or her referral to the counselor, or the client may have been referred by another agency (e.g., a hospital, child protective services). In these situations, the counselor typically has access to information that can aid in the development of hypotheses regarding the client's situation. Most counselors, however, conduct a preliminary intake assessment having little prior information apart from a brief phone conversation with a parent or a basic referral explanation listed on a form. As such, counselors are required, as part of the intake process, to gather and synthesize a great deal of information, while reviewing legal and ethical matters, setting counseling expectations, and focusing on therapeutic counseling.

Clinical Toolbox 3.1

In the Pearson eText, click here to view an example of an intake checklist that counselors can use to guide their intake process.

Informed consent procedures should be thorough. Young clients' parents are required to sign informed consent paperwork, but they typically have a limited understanding of what the information means. As such, parents and young clients (if age appropriate) should both be engaged in a discussion of informed consent–related considerations.

When working with young clients, informed consent considerations have important implications for the counseling process. A more detailed discussion of informed consent is provided in Chapter 4, so the following section only addresses informed consent considerations that relate to the establishment and maintenance of counseling relationships and the individual counseling process. The section begins with a discussion of informed consent with a focus on confidentiality considerations. Next, because counselor and client expectations of counseling are an important part of the intake process, the counselor's role in assessing and navigating these expectations is addressed. The process of identifying and assessing client's presenting problems are also discussed. Ways that counselors can structure counseling early on—in the initial sessions—to maximize success are then addressed. Finally, strategies for optimizing the therapeutic alliance when counseling youth and their families are discussed.

CONFIDENTIALITY

As part of the informed consent process, it is important that counselors review confidentiality expectations and requirements with the child and family. Legally—in most states—young clients have no confidentiality rights; parents have access to all their child's records and any information shared in counseling (Vernon, 2009). However, many young clients—especially adolescents—do not want their parents to be privy to all their personal experiences. It is helpful to talk with the family about how important a degree of confidentiality is in building a sense of trust and safety in the therapeutic relationship. Without trust, it is impossible to develop a positive therapeutic relationship, which is the foundation of individual counseling and critical to the success of counseling. See Chapter 4 for a more detailed discussion of the complex considerations associated with youth counseling and confidentiality.

ASSESSMENT

Assessment of a young client's situation and counseling needs is an important aspect of the intake process. Counselors typically have only one or two sessions or meetings to develop a conceptualization of the young client's situation. That said, assessment is not a one-time event; rather, it is an ongoing aspect of counseling, and counselors continually reassess and reconceptualize clients as more information and data are gathered.

In Chapter 9, a model for use in conceptualizing clients' situations and developing counseling/treatment plans—the I CAN START model—is discussed. The I CAN START model places a heavy emphasis on assessing clients' situations (e.g., strengths, context, culture, dynamics of the presenting problem). This section touches on the *process* or the "how to" of assessing young clients' presenting issues. It also provides a brief overview of individual counseling assessment considerations that includes a discussion of how counselors can evaluate and help young clients and their families in an effort to define the presenting problem.

An initial prompt that can help you get to know—and assess—young clients follows: "Tell me about a usual day for you. Start with the time you get up and take me through your day." Another prompt that gets at important information about a child's situation is "Tell me about your idea of a perfect day. Start with the time you get up and take me through your ideal day." These types of questions have the added value of providing the counselor with insights as to what counseling approaches and methods may best fit with the client's interests. For example, if a counselor learns a child likes to play with dollhouses, this can be integrated into counseling, or if an adolescent likes music, counselors can pull on this as a vehicle for crafting interventions.

One of the most important first aspects of assessing a client's situation is determining the client's, parents', and any other stakeholders' (e.g., school staff, the legal system) perspectives on the nature of the problem. Although assessing the problem might seem straightforward, it is not uncommon for the client, family, and others to have very different ideas about the identified problem.

It is helpful to directly ask young clients, at the initial session, their thoughts on why they believe they are meeting with a counselor. Counselors might say, "Tell me about what brought you here. I want to understand how you think about things. . . ." Another helpful statement is "Tell me about the reasons you think your parents brought you here. . . ." Young clients' responses to these two prompts can provide important information about their degree of insight, family dynamics, and their self- and other perceptions.

Counselors might use various media, including puppets, art, writing, free play, storytelling, incomplete sentence prompts (e.g., "I am happy when _____," "A good child _____," or "A good mom _____"), dollhouse or dress-up play, or role-playing activities, to assess young clients' perception of the problem (Vernon, 2009). For example, counselors can have a storytelling basket available in which they have finger puppets of people of different ages; animals; and small inanimate objects such as houses, cars, and household items, and clients can be asked to create a story—related to their problem—using the items in the basket.

In defining and understanding the problem, it is also helpful to inquire about clients', parents', and stakeholders' previous attempts to solve the problem. Counselors might say, "Talk about something you have each done to try and tackle this problem/situation . . . Now tell me one other thing you've tried. . . ." The counselor can inquire until it appears the list of attempts to solve the problem is exhausted. Such an inquiry can provide valuable information that can inform the counselor's conceptualization of the problem and how it might be addressed; it provides data on the dynamics of the problem, what additional important factors are contributing to the situation, and what fuels and helps to manage the problem.

As counselors work to understand young people's problems, another good question to ask them is what they wish could be different in their lives. Solution-focused brief therapy (de Shazer & Dolan, 2007) questioning may be helpful in understanding perceptions of problems, as well as possible solutions. Following are examples of these types of questions:

- Pretend that while you were sleeping last night a miracle happened—the problem disappeared. How would you know that a miracle had happened? What would be different?
- Imagine that you discover you have a unique superpower—with the mere snap of your fingers, you are able to make your problem vanish. Tell me about the first time you would use your superpower. Describe the situation leading up to the snap, and tell me all about what changes after you snap your fingers.
- Suppose you find a magic wand, and whenever you wave your wand, this problem would no longer exist. When would you wave your magic wand? How would you know the magic was working?
- Let's think about this same time next year. Imagine you run into your counselor at your favorite place. It's a beautiful day, and you are excited to tell your counselor all about the positive changes that have brought about happiness in your life. Describe what would have changed? What does that happiness feel like? What are you doing differently?
- What if you wanted to surprise your family by doing something super special for them . . . something to show how well you are doing. What would you have to do to not only surprise them but also convince them that promising changes are taking place?

The exact phrasing of questions will need to be adapted to meet the young client's age, developmental level, personality, needs, and/or interests. For example, a very young client may not have a clear understanding of a miracle. Solution-focused questioning can also be used to assess family members' perceptions of the problem and solutions.

A thorough mental status examination can facilitate the assessment process, especially for youth who have mental disorders. When assessing young clients and families, counselors should consider numerous factors that include physical presentation (e.g., grooming, energy level), cognitive development (e.g., sense of reality, ability to process consequences of actions), strengths and resources, culture and context (e.g., religion, SES), social development (e.g., friendships), important life experiences (e.g., traumatic events, losses), developmental history, and thoughts about a better future (Kress & Paylo, 2015).

In addition to assessing young clients in sessions, it may be useful to observe the child in his or her natural setting while interacting with family members and/or peers (Barkley, 2013). School counselors might pull on social observation opportunities, and those providing in-home therapy will readily have opportunities to observe the child in the home environment. Counselors might also seek collateral reports (e.g., from school staff or other family members) regarding the client's behavior and functioning across different settings.

Formal, informal, and *Diagnostic and Statistical Manual of Mental Disorders, Fifth Edition* (American Psychiatric Association [APA], 2013a) assessments are described later in this text in relation to the various problems young clients present in counseling. In the early stages of counseling, counselors should consider that tests, surveys, and various scales related to a young client's behavior, values, attitudes, interests, personality, school-related factors (e.g., aptitude, achievement, and intelligence tests), and psychopathology may be helpful—or even necessary—to gather a clear picture of his or her situation. It can also be helpful to request and review a young client's school records because these often contain information related to assessments and/or any school behavior problems.

REVIEW OF COUNSELOR AND CLIENT EXPECTATIONS

During intake and assessment, it is important that counselors listen for young clients' expectations of what they want from counseling and work with these as much as is realistic. It is also essential for clients to understand what counseling can—and cannot—do and for clients and parents to know what will be required of them as counseling participants. In general, education about counselor, client, and family roles in the counseling process can help to clear up misconceptions about and set the stage for the counseling experience (Constantino, Arnkoff, Glass, Ametrano, & Smith, 2011). Counselors should explain their counseling approach, beliefs around how they help young clients to make changes, and the methods they use to facilitate change.

Client and family expectations related to counseling duration and the frequency of meetings should also be assessed early in counseling. Some parents may expect that change will occur faster than what is realistic. Counselors should consider that clients generally prefer to meet the minimum number of sessions required to have the presenting problem dissipate, with most expecting to attend only 7 to 10 sessions (de Haan, Boon, de Jong, Geluk, & Vermeiren, 2014; Lambert, 2013). That said, although most clients will show improvements within approximately 7 to 8 counseling sessions, significant changes tend to occur with additional sessions (Lambert, 2013). Clients may also only be afforded a limited number of sessions (by third-party payers or external forces), and this is something else that should be factored into the conversation about the duration of counseling.

Client expectations about the effectiveness of counseling are very important, and in fact they play an important role in predicting counseling outcomes: If clients expect positive changes, then they are hopeful and thus open to possibilities, likely to commit to the work of counseling, and feeling trust in their counselors (Constantino et al., 2011). Clients' confidence in counseling as an effective vehicle for change and their belief in their counselor as someone who can help are critical to positive counseling outcomes (Frank & Frank, 1993). Counselors need to consider young clients' and parents' expectations of counseling, as well as their expectations about the process, nature, and course of counseling (Constantino et al., 2011). It is also essential for counselors to communicate information about counseling and expectations in a way that is appropriate to young clients' cognitive and developmental levels.

It is equally important that counselors' expectations of parents are addressed at the onset of counseling. To assess expectations, counselors can ask parents questions such as follows: "What do you know about counseling?"; "What do you hope to get out of counseling?"; and "If counseling was successful, what would be different?" One common misconception parents have is that the counselor will take responsibility for "fixing" their child or the problem and that they will have minimal involvement in counseling. Counselors should thus explain what they require of parents, and this may include reliably and punctually attending counseling sessions; helping the child to apply different skills at home; following through on agreed-on, between-session assignments (e.g., the parent and child spending 3 hours of quality time together each week); attending sessions with the child (in an agreed-on fashion) so they can be engaged and participative; being patient with the counseling process and committing to attend for an appropriate length of time; trusting the counselor; following through on counselor recommendations; and modeling healthy behaviors that relate to the child's counseling and/or affect the child. If parental and child misconceptions are not addressed early in counseling, then they may lead to premature termination (Deakin, Gastaud, & Nunes, 2012; de Haan et al., 2014).

Younger children often feel scared or uncertain about counseling, so it is important to address their fears (de Santana, de Souza, & Feitosa, 2014; Dyson et al., 2015). Because children go to see health care providers when they are sick, injured, or require immunizations, their thoughts of what goes on in a counseling office may not be positive. Also, because they have little understanding of the counseling process, they may fear they will do or say something wrong that could create additional problems. One 6-year-old child the authors worked with was very afraid to attend counseling. On exploration, it was learned that she had heard counselors referred to as "head shrinks," and she feared she would be forced to sit in a chair and have her head shrunk. It is important that counselors demonstrate empathy and help clients to identify their fears and worries so any questions they have can be answered.

It is also important to address what young clients believe their participation in counseling communicates to themselves and others. Following are some of the mistaken self-reference assumptions about counseling that the authors have heard young clients express and that counselors thus need to address:

- I did something wrong, and I am being punished.
- Something is wrong with me—I am sick or bad.
- I must be broken, and I need to be fixed.
- I am unlovable, and no one really likes me.
- If I was better, I wouldn't be in counseling.
- Other kids don't go to counseling—I'm the only one.

Providing young clients with information about counseling can help to defuse the power of these harmful misconceptions.

Clinical Toolbox 3.2

In the Pearson eText, click here to view common questions children ask about counseling.

It is our experience that some parents struggle to understand the use of play and creativity in counseling, so parents may need education on how and why these approaches are useful with young clients. One parent told us that she removed her 5-year-old daughter from previous counseling because all the counselor and client did together was "play." The counselor had not explained how she was using play as a vehicle for change and did not update the mother on progress or developments, so the mother was left to make sense out of the experience in her own way. It may also be helpful to explain to the family that it can take some time to establish a relationship with young clients, and although it may appear from the outside that the counselor and client are "just talking," they are really working to establish a necessary relationship connection. Particularly with adolescents, it can take time to develop a relationship, and counselors will need to discuss the topics that are important to the adolescent and that he or she is comfortable sharing (Norcross & Wampold, 2011a).

Counselors might explain counseling to adolescents and their families using excerpts from the following language (your exact language and approach will vary depending on the child's age and developmental level):

> When we meet we are going to talk about you. Your thoughts, feelings, things that are bothering you that you may want to get off your chest, things you want help with, things that are going well. My role is to help you make sense of things and to help you reach your counseling goals. Sometimes that will involve me being a good listener, sometimes it may involve me helping you understand yourself and your relationships with others, sometimes that will look like me teaching you different skills or providing you with information, sometimes I will be more of a coach and that may mean I ask you to think about things in a new way. What is most important is that you understand I am here to help you reach your goals. In order for me to help you, I need you to be honest with me and talk to me about what is on your mind. I also need you to tell me how you think things are going in counseling and what I can do to better help you. This is your counseling, and I want to make sure that you are having a good experience.

When meeting with younger children, a more simplistic explanation will suffice. Examples of how counselors might explain counseling to this age group are provided:

- Counseling can help kids to get "unstuck" when they are in sticky situations.
- Counselors can help kids to make sense of confusing situations,
- When kids get off track, counselors can help them to get back on the rails.
- Counselors help kids to make changes.

STRUCTURING COUNSELING

As counselors develop hypotheses about their clients' situations and their counseling needs, this information will inform how frequently you meet, the duration of counseling sessions, the length of time you expect clients to be in counseling, the frequency with which you will provide individual versus family counseling sessions, and how often you will engage parents in counseling. Information regarding the structure of counseling should be communicated to the child and the family.

As previously mentioned, a predictable session structure provides the child and the family with a sense of safety and comfort. Although it is important to detail the session structure early on, it is equally important to build flexibility into this structure.

Many counselors struggle with how often they should meet with parents. Should counselors meet with parents at the beginning or end of sessions or not at all? Should counselors meet with the parents with or without the child? There are no "right" answers to these questions, and how you approach this will depend on the nature of the setting in which you work, the child's developmental level, the child's presenting struggles and needs, and your philosophical and theoretical approach. What is important is that counselors recognize that young people are socially embedded (Vernon, 2009). As such, their parents—or caregivers—generally need to be engaged in some capacity if the child is to experience meaningful change.

The authors generally suggest that counselors initially—at the first session—meet with young clients' parents alone for part of the session because parents are sometimes more forthcoming with information when the child is not present. In addition, parents almost always need to share relevant information that is not appropriate for their children to hear, and the counselor will need to ask questions that may not be appropriate to ask in front of the child. Meeting with the parents alone also models appropriate boundaries, an issue with which some families struggle. With younger children who cannot be left alone in the waiting or play area, counselors can give them something to color or play with while they gather information.

After meeting with the parents alone, it is helpful to meet with the child and parents at the same time. This time together typically provides rich information about the child's and family's perceptions of the problem—that is, it provides the counselor with an opportunity to observe family system dynamics and get a glimpse into the young client's world (Orton, 1997). For younger children, first meeting the counselor with the family in the room may facilitate a sense of safety, thus alleviating some of their anxiety about counseling and/or the counselor.

Next, the authors suggest that the counselor meets with the young client alone for part of the session. Particularly with adolescents, this initial time together can provide important information that will help the counselor to better conceptualize the client's situation and determine counseling needs. It also provides an opportunity for the young client and the counselor to begin to build their relationship.

When determining how long a counseling session should last, it is important that the child's developmental level be taken into consideration. Younger clients may not be able to engage in a full-length session, and these developmental considerations should factor into how counselors structure sessions.

In terms of structuring sessions, it is helpful to start each session with a review of the prior session. With older youth, it is helpful to prestructure at the start of the session and review what will be focused on in relation to their counseling goals, emphasizing that the session plan is flexible. With adolescents, it is import that counselors not place too much emphasis on the structure of counseling (i.e., roles, tasks, relevance) at the exclusion of developing the counseling relationship because doing so can interfere with the development of the counseling relationship (Norcross & Wampold, 2011a).

At the end of sessions, counselors might ask clients to reflect on what was most important about the session for them. Questions such as "When you think about our time together today, what stands out for you?" or "What are you going to take away from our time together today?" are helpful. Counselors might also ask "How are you feeling about our work together today?" or "What is one thing we could have done to have made this session more helpful for you?" These questions communicate to the client that he or she is an active participant in counseling, keep the client engaged in the counseling process, and reinforce that counselors care about what the client thinks and how he or she feels.

One approach to ending sessions that may be helpful in enhancing the counseling relationship and preventing premature termination is the use of a brief assessment tool to gauge client and parental satisfaction—or dissatisfaction—with the therapeutic process. Tools such as these can be completed by the child or the parent at the beginning or end of each counseling session. By regularly seeking feedback, counselors send a strong message that they value the family's feedback and that their input matters. Feedback may also allow counselors to troubleshoot any misperceptions, miscommunications, or dissatisfaction before it escalates. When working with young clients, counselors may need to use visual charts or scales that allow children to rank their experience. For example, emoticons with expressions ranging from upset to happy may be used to gauge their reaction to the session or certain interventions. In Figure 3.2, two examples of counseling session evaluations that may be useful when working with young clients and their families are provided.

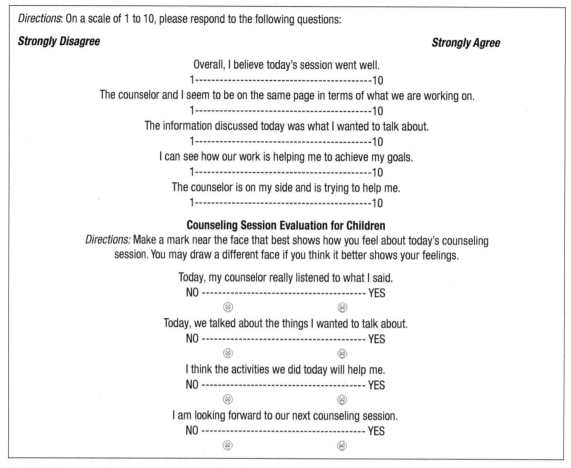

Directions: On a scale of 1 to 10, please respond to the following questions:

Strongly Disagree   ***Strongly Agree***

Overall, I believe today's session went well.
1---10
The counselor and I seem to be on the same page in terms of what we are working on.
1---10
The information discussed today was what I wanted to talk about.
1---10
I can see how our work is helping me to achieve my goals.
1---10
The counselor is on my side and is trying to help me.
1---10

Counseling Session Evaluation for Children
Directions: Make a mark near the face that best shows how you feel about today's counseling session. You may draw a different face if you think it better shows your feelings.

Today, my counselor really listened to what I said.
NO -------------------------------------- YES

Today, we talked about the things I wanted to talk about.
NO -------------------------------------- YES

I think the activities we did today will help me.
NO -------------------------------------- YES

I am looking forward to our next counseling session.
NO -------------------------------------- YES

FIGURE 3.2 Counseling Session Evaluation for Parents and/or Adolescents

Building a Working Alliance with Young Clients and Their Families

THE WORKING ALLIANCE

One of the most important preliminary individual counseling tasks is the development of the counseling relationship. In healthy counseling relationships, young clients perceive the counselor as honest, genuine, direct, helpful, and empathic, and they experience the relationship as a positive, warm, nonjudgmental place where they can share their experiences (Norcross & Wampold, 2011a). Young clients will feel safe in such an environment. A sense of safety allows clients to trust the counselor enough that they can be open and forthcoming about personal thoughts, feelings, and behaviors.

As discussed previously in this chapter, research supports the idea that for counseling to be optimally effective, a strong therapeutic relationship is necessary (Norcross & Wampold, 2011a). The first few counseling sessions generally set the tone of counseling, and as such they are critical to the long-term success of counseling (Norcross & Wampold, 2011a). A strong therapeutic relationship affects clients' satisfaction with counseling services, their level of disclosure, their optimism about counseling, and their sense of hope that their situation can change (Norcross & Wampold, 2011a).

A warm counseling relationship lays the foundation for the development of the therapeutic working alliance. A strong counseling relationship is one aspect of the therapeutic working alliance that involves three parts: a relational *bond* (a strong counseling relationship), agreement on counseling *goals*, and agreement on the *tasks* (or what needs to be done to reach the counseling goals; Bordin, 1979). A collaborative relationship in which counselors and clients agree on the direction they are headed and how they will meet their counseling goals inspires client trust and instills a sense of hope and optimism in the process and utility of counseling. Collaborative counseling relationships promote better counseling outcomes and predict clients' ability to eventually make the changes they desire (Bohart & Wade, 2013; Norcross & Wampold, 2011a).

Reinforcing the importance of the therapeutic working alliance, research suggests that highly successful counselors consistently ask young clients—and their families—for feedback on the direction, focus, approach, and interventions used in counseling (Hawley & Garland, 2008; Norcross & Wampold, 2011a). A collaborative approach communicates to clients and their families that the counselor cares about their ideas, and it encourages their participation and autonomy in counseling. The therapeutic working alliance is highly correlated with counseling outcomes across all theoretical treatment approaches (i.e., behavioral, psychodynamic, cognitive behavioral, humanistic) and modalities (i.e., individual, group, family; Norcross & Wampold, 2011a). In fact, the working alliance is the most influential factor in predicting clients' perceptions of counseling success (Lambert, 2013; Zuroff, Kelly, Leybman, Blatt, & Wampold, 2010).

CHALLENGES TO THE WORKING ALLIANCE

Although a strong counseling relationship is important when counseling all clients, it is especially important when counseling youth who are generally required—by others—to attend counseling (Norcross & Wampold, 2011a). There are many other obstacles that could get in the way of developing a positive relationship with young clients, and these include limited problem recognition and/or awareness of a problem, a tendency to perceive that their problems are rooted in outside sources, minimal motivation to make changes, and a lack of understanding of how counseling works and why it matters (Castro-Blanco & Karver, 2010).

It can be especially difficult to develop a working alliance with adolescents. Adolescents' developmental push toward autonomy, their lack of faith in adults' ability to understand them, and their primary value of peer relationships (as opposed to adult relationships) may make it difficult to establish a working alliance (Norcross & Wampold, 2011a). These factors can contribute to some adolescents approaching the counseling relationship with a sense of distrust.

In addition, there are certain situations in which young people are forced to come to counseling because of an outside influence (e.g., school requirement, legal mandate), and in these situations, parents may be distrustful of counselors and counseling in general. As such, young clients may be hesitant to engage in counseling because they fear that doing so will upset their parents. In mandated counseling situations, it is especially important to build a solid working alliance with the parents.

It is also important to recognize that although a therapeutic connection can be established after only a few sessions, some young clients may take months to trust a counselor. Youth who have been abused, neglected, traumatized, or experienced losses may be especially slow to warm to a counselor (Brier & Scott, 2014). One of our clients was in a residential treatment facility secondary to symptoms associated with having been sexually abused by her mother's boyfriend throughout her childhood, and even though she knew the authors knew about the sexual abuse, it took her 6 months to admit this and to begin to open up. Patience and a belief that eventually young clients will begin to trust you if you are authentic and open hearted and if you provide the right conditions are essential when building a working alliance.

Counseling is founded on speech as a primary form of communication. Counseling requires some degree of verbal participation on the part of clients. As such, one struggle that counselors may face when attempting to establish a working alliance with some young clients is the clients' lack of interest or ability to express themselves verbally. Some clients may have psychopathology that precludes their ability to be verbal (e.g., autism spectrum disorder); some may be defensive or guarded and may not want to talk; very young clients may be less verbal because of their developmental level; clients with certain personality characteristics (e.g., shyness, introversion) may not be as talkative; and some clients may have an intellectual disability or various organic disorders that may physically limit verbal communication (Kress & Paylo, 2015). Counselors should complete an inventory of each client's situation to assess the origins of the verbal communication difficulties to determine what is realistic or reasonable to expect from the client. Counselors' clinical approach must be tailored to clients' needs, capabilities, and preferred methods of communication.

With less verbal clients, it is helpful to pull on nonverbal forms of communication and to come to sessions prepared with approaches that do not rely on verbal interactions. Expressive arts activities, writing, play, music, physical activities, and the use of structured therapy games can all serve as relationship building forms of communication. Activities that require active participation (e.g., role-play) can also facilitate communication.

RELATIONSHIP BUILDING STRATEGIES

Counselors should be mindful of conveying relationship building characteristics such as empathy, congruence, positive regard, and affirmation (Norcross & Wampold, 2011a). Young clients need to perceive that they are understood by their counselor and that their counselor feels genuine compassion for them and their situation. In addition, it is important that clients perceive their counselors as being congruent, authentic, honest, and genuine because this contributes to the development of the counseling relationship. Assuming a nonjudgmental stance, viewing clients in a positive light and focusing on their strengths creates a sense of equality in an otherwise unequal relationship in which the counselor possesses a great deal of power (Norcross & Wampold, 2011a).

Counselors must be aware of how clients perceive them and how their approach affects the counseling relationship. Because some counselors' personal characteristics weaken the therapeutic alliance and influence counseling outcomes, counselors need to monitor their personal reactions and traits. Counselors who over- or understructure sessions; who are defensive, critical, and demanding; who push their agenda; or who maintain an unsupportive stance will obviously be perceived as less helpful (Sharpless, Muran, & Barber, 2010). Conversely, when counselors are warm, empathetic, interested, open minded, and confident and display flexibility in practice, they are perceived more favorably by their clients and experience better counseling outcomes (Sharpless et al., 2010).

Time spent getting to know clients facilitates relationship building and aids counselors in understanding clients' situations and contexts. Acknowledging and connecting with young clients' lived experiences and attending to clients' expressed emotion are especially important to the development of a warm relationship, especially with adolescents (Norcross & Wampold, 2011a). Interestingly, some research suggests that if counselors provide less structure in early counseling sessions, clients have greater compliance with counseling tasks in later sessions (Jungbluth & Shirk, 2009). It is not suggested that counselors be inactive in early sessions; rather, it is suggested that counselors spend time connecting with young clients' experiences and attend to relationship building factors in early counseling sessions (Jungbluth & Shirk, 2009). That said, counselors need to strike a balance between focusing on clients' presenting problems and focusing on relationship development and enhancement; too little of a focus on problems can amount to supporting avoidance, and too much of a focus on problems can affect the counseling relationship (Norcross & Wampold, 2011a). Flexible pacing is important in achieving a balance between nurturing the relationship and addressing counseling goals per se (Norcross & Wampold, 2011a).

When getting to know young clients, it is helpful to inquire about their personal interests and day-to-day lives. Casual inquiries provide a nonthreatening means of facilitating connection. Any of the following topics are generally of interest to young people: friends, potential romantic interests (with adolescents), teachers who they like and dislike, classes/school subjects they like and dislike, pets, siblings, relationships with immediate and extended family, hobbies, music (especially with adolescents), television shows, video games, favorite foods and restaurants, recreation activities (e.g., with young children, what do they like to play), and preferred games. There are many games that can also be used as a tool to get to know clients (e.g., the youth version of The Ungame), and a quick Internet search provides hundreds of youth-friendly questions that can be printed, cut out, and made into an interactive discussion game. We find that the information that most informs our understanding of young clients is typically provided in casual exchanges with clients and not necessarily during structured questioning.

Pushing clients to discuss difficult or uncomfortable material can be damaging to the counseling relationship (Norcross & Wampold, 2011a). Counselors might try scaffolding young clients' emotional disclosures by first discussing less emotionally intense material, and as the client appears to be more comfortable, move toward addressing weightier material (Norcross & Wampold, 2011a). It is important that the counselor accurately read a client's comfort level and gently guide the client toward increased sharing. Again, it is important that counselors trust that the counseling process works and that clients will share if counselors provide the right conditions for them to do so.

As stated, adolescents in particular may have ambivalence about attending counseling, and this can make it especially difficult for them to engage and develop a working relationship with the counselor (Norcross & Wampold, 2011a). It can be helpful to acknowledge this "elephant in the room" because doing so conveys an understanding of the client's ambivalence. When counseling adolescents—and as appropriate—counselors might even use humor to address this ambivalence. Empathizing with young clients' feelings around being forced to come to counseling and simply acknowledging this experience may also be helpful. Counselors might say "It sounds like you don't want to be here. I get it: None of us likes being told to do things we don't want to do. I just want you to know that this is your time and we can focus on things you want to talk about." Adolescents who attend counseling because of oppositional or externalizing behaviors (e.g., aggressive and disruptive behaviors) typically expect to be received by adults in a confrontational way, so a strong counseling relationship is especially important in breaking down their barriers (Norcross & Wampold, 2011a).

Once the preliminary counseling tasks have been addressed and counselors have laid the foundation for a productive working alliance that includes a focus on counseling goals and how these will be reached, counselors can begin to use their counseling skills and interventions to support clients in meeting their goals. In the next section, counseling considerations that relate to the working stages of counseling are addressed. More specifically, developmentally appropriate strategies for approaching young clients are provided. Challenges to the working stage of counseling and ways counselors can overcome these changes are also discussed.

WORKING STAGE COUNSELING CONSIDERATIONS

For this discussion, the working stage of counseling includes the counseling that occurs after the preliminary counseling tasks are addressed (the first one to three sessions) and a therapeutic relationship is established, yet before termination. In other words, the bulk of the individual counseling process can be conceptualized as the working stage of counseling. Because the working stage is where clients experience the most growth and change (Gladding, 2012), the bulk of the material presented in this text focuses on this topic.

Although preliminary counseling tasks are generally similar across counseling situations, the working stage of counseling is much more variable and can look very different depending on numerous factors. Some of the factors that influence the working stages of counseling include clients' presenting issues and developmental levels, degree of family involvement, counselors' theoretical approach, counseling setting, and session limits. However, some considerations can cut across all counseling, and these are addressed in this section. More specifically, the section discusses helpful communication styles, modalities and techniques that facilitate counseling, client motivation to change, and ways counselors can enhance this motivation.

Communication Approaches

Counselor communication has to do with how counselors use words, sounds, signs, or behaviors to provide or exchange information or to express their ideas, thoughts, or feelings to their clients in counseling (Broderick & Blewitt, 2014; Frank & Frank, 1993). Nonverbal communication includes eye contact, posture, distance between counselor and client, minimal encouragers (e.g., "mm-hmm"), voice tone, pace of conversation, and many other factors that convey meaning without using actual words (Dowell & Berman, 2013; Frank & Frank, 1993). It is important for counselors to use nonverbal behaviors artistically and intuitively; some behaviors (e.g., increased eye contact, leaning forward) are associated with improved therapeutic relationship (Dowell & Berman, 2013), but not every client will respond the same to given behaviors. For example, an adolescent whose culture does not favor direct eye contact may feel uncomfortable if a counselor uses this type of communication. Counselors should be sensitive to these cultural variances and modify their communication styles accordingly.

Play is a natural form of communication for young children; it is the main way children interact with and get to know their worlds. Regardless of a counselor's theoretical approach to counseling, he or she will need to integrate play as a method to provide developmentally appropriate forms of communication and intervention when counseling young children.

Clinical Toolbox 3.3

In the Pearson eText, click here to review the benefits of play therapy.

Because children are not comfortable using verbal communication as their primary communication strategy, they often use other behaviors to communicate their problems, fears, and needs. Most children's unhelpful behaviors (e.g., crying, screaming, hitting, disobeying) can be explained as nonverbal communication in pursuit of attention; in seeking a sense of control or dominance; or as an expression of hurt, frustration, or anger (Broderick & Blewitt, 2014).

Although nonverbal communication is a key consideration when working with youth, all counseling relies on verbal communication. Even when a young child is engaged in play therapy, counselors narrate and make meaning of the child's behaviors (Headley, Kautzman-East, Pusateri, & Kress, 2015; Ray et al., 2013). Children also use short words and sentences such as "She's a mean girl!" to express themselves during play. As a child develops, verbal communication becomes a central focus in counseling, and a child's vocabulary increases by thousands of words each year. A 6-year-old might understand 10,000 words as compared to a 10-year-old who understands an average of 40,000 words (Davies, 2011). Counselors should always use clear and succinct communication; however, it is especially important when working with youth to use phrases and language the client can understand and to avoid long or complex sentences or questions.

Counselors should listen to young client's language and mimic the style and words they use. This lets youth know the counselor understands them, and it contributes to building trust in the relationship. Counselors should also show that the communication used in counseling is unique from other social relationships. Rather than reciprocating conversations, counseling is focused on the thoughts, feelings, and beliefs of the client (Constantino et al., 2011; Wampold, 2010). Counselors should foster active participation of youth by engaging in developmentally appropriate conversation while fostering increased levels of youth disclosure.

Counselors can use various skills and techniques to help youth explore and express themselves. Questions are one way to spark conversation. Closed-ended questions produce a one-word answer and can be used to gather factual information (e.g., "How old are you?"). Open-ended questions invite longer client responses and can produce richer counseling material (e.g., "Talk about some of your best friends . . ."). Young clients are not generally accustomed to interacting with adults who give their focused attention and listen. As such, it may take some young clients time to learn how to respond to a counselor's open-ended inquiries.

Although the use of questions in counseling is valuable, counselors should take care to avoid overusing questions. Question stacking—asking question after question—can confuse clients, contribute to them possibly feeling interrogated, increase defensiveness, or even shut down conversation. As is true with all counseling, the use of "why questions" should be avoided. Young clients frequently hear their caregivers ask why questions in a negative context (e.g., "Why didn't you clean your room?"). Also, youth do not typically have insight as to why they behave a certain way, so asking them why questions may not be productive. The use of could, can, how, and what questions can be used to help counselors clarify what their young clients are communicating:

- "What happens when you . . . ?"
- "What is it like for you when . . . ?"
- "How is it for you when . . . ?"
- "Could you tell me more about your dad . . . ?"
- "Can you tell me about a time when you felt . . . ?"

In general, when interviewing youth, the skills of listening, paraphrasing, and reflecting are more important and effective than questioning (Vernon, 2009). Paraphrasing the content of a client's statement (e.g., "Your parents fight a lot") demonstrates the counselor is interested and the client has been heard. Reflecting the underlying meaning of a client's message (e.g., "You don't like it when your parents fight") makes the client feel understood, and reflecting the client's feelings (e.g., "It sounds like that makes you feel sad") facilitates insight and therapeutic expression (Vernon, 2009). Reflections and paraphrasing allow youth to be the focus of attention and foster exploration and insight in an effective, nonthreatening way. In Figure 3.3, a list of communication strategies are provided that may be particularly useful when counseling youth in early childhood, middle childhood, and adolescence.

Communicating with Youth in Early Childhood

- Interact with parents before interacting with the child.
- Stay at eye level with the child.
- Turn off televisions, cell phones, or other distracting devices.
- Use transition objects (e.g., a doll, toys) to initiate conversation with the child.
- Use brief sentences.
- Use the child's language.
- Use simple words and language.
- Use short sentences (slightly longer than the child uses).
- Avoid interrupting the child.
- Praise the child for adaptive positive behaviors.
- Rephrase, do not repeat, questions a child does not understand.
- Avoid using analogies and metaphors (young children are very literal and concrete).
- Respond to gestures and facial expressions as forms of nonverbal communication.
- Use visual aids to clarify information.
- Integrate the child's favorite toys, games, or TV shows into conversation.
- Rephrase the child's statements to demonstrate interest and understanding.
- Highlight the child's strengths, resources, and capacities.
- Make clear and simple requests (e.g., get your coat from the coat hook).
- Ask the child to repeat what you have asked or said.
- Use open-ended questions more often than closed-ended questions.
- Narrate the young child's behaviors and add meaning (e.g., you wanted to make a big fort so you kept adding blocks).
- Stay focused on the child's experience, not the experiences of those around him or her.

Communicating with Youth in Middle Childhood

- Stay at eye level with the child rather than towering over him or her.
- Integrate the child's interests into conversation.
- Avoid question stacking.
- Avoid using sarcasm.
- Be succinct.
- Highlight the child's strengths, resources, and capacities.
- Avoid double negatives in speech (e.g., "You don't deny it, do you?").
- Use visual aids to clarify information.
- Be clear and direct in your communication.
- Make requests one at a time (e.g., if engaged in a creative art activity, give one step of the directions at a time).
- State facts clearly—do not confuse the child with big words or unfamiliar phrases.
- Keep information logically organized.
- Speak at the same pace as the child to avoid confusing him or her.
- Eliminate distractions (e.g., telephone calls, loud music) when communicating with the child.
- Use minimal encouragers (e.g., "Mm-hmm") to show interest and encourage the child to continue talking.
- Repeat the child's words to ensure accurate interpretation.
- Add emotion words to help the child connect thoughts, feelings, and behaviors.
- Avoid becoming frustrated, angry, or defensive with the child.
- Model positive, helpful communication skills.
- Allow communication to be reciprocal rather than lecture style whenever possible.
- Validate the child's values, points of view, and concerns.
- Admit when you are wrong or do not know something.
- Address one problem at a time.
- Avoid arguing or power struggles; acknowledge both points of view.

FIGURE 3.3 Communicating with Youth at Different Ages

Communicating with Adolescents

- Be clear and direct.
- Do not try to protect the adolescent by keeping him or her in the dark; as appropriate, share information regarding the child's situation.
- Accept and normalize the adolescent's emotions.
- Be sensitive to the adolescent's lived experiences and struggles.
- Provide creative opportunities for the adolescent to talk and share.
- Listen without regularly interrupting.
- Be concise and avoid confusing the adolescent with too many facts.
- Avoid assuming a lecturing role.
- Use appropriate humor.
- Keep questions brief and focused.
- Remain oriented in the present when speaking to the adolescent.
- Do not assume the adolescent has developed adult narrative abilities.
- Pay attention to body language and nonverbal cues.
- Highlight the adolescent's strengths, resources, and capacities.
- Take an interest in the adolescent's activities, friends, hobbies, and school.
- Gradually move from less to more serious topics.
- Explore the issues that concern the adolescent (not only parents' concerns).
- Allow the adolescent (as appropriate) to have control over certain aspects of counseling.
- Take the adolescent's ideas and views seriously.

FIGURE 3.3 Communicating with Youth at Different Ages (*continued*)

At the beginning of the counseling relationship, youth may not be comfortable fully expressing their emotions and reactions, and many do not possess the skill required to do so. In Creative Toolbox 3.1, activities counselors may use with youth to help guide them toward emotional expression are provided.

Creative Toolbox 3.1   Emotion Expression Activities

Activities	Description
My *Inside Out* Feelings	This activity involves clients learning how to better recognize their feelings via the use of the characters from the movie *Inside Out*. Materials needed for this activity include markers, colored paper or poster board, cutouts of the *Inside Out* movie characters (made prior to the session by the counselor), and tape. Counselors instruct youth to identify with each character from *Inside Out*. There are five characters that represent each emotion: joy, sadness, anger, disgust, and fear. After youth have identified with each character, they are to come up with five different emotional words that are related to the character. For example, for sadness, youth may come up with tearful, lonely, and unhappy. These words may be personal based on how clients feel when they experience the emotion (e.g., sadness). Next, counselors instruct youth to write these words on colored pieces of paper that correspond with the emotion (e.g., sadness on blue paper). Youth decorate the papers and glue the characters onto the paper with their words. Next, youth think about how they know when they are feeling this emotion or what the cues are, and they write these down. For example, for anger, a child may write, "I squeeze my fists really hard" or "I sit alone in my room to calm down." The goal of this activity is for youth to identify with each feeling and recognize their experiences of the five emotions.
Calming Cards	With this activity, clients develop calming cards they can use to recognize and cope with strong negative emotions. Materials needed are note cards, a hole puncher, string or binder rings, markers, stickers, and pens. Counselors instruct youth to name five emotions that they often feel, and each emotion is given its own card. Youth may decorate the card

Creative Toolbox 3.1 (*Continued*)

Activities	Description
	in a fashion appropriate to the feeling and/or draw a picture that represents the word (e.g., a frustrated emoji). After this task is completed, youth are given more cards, and they write down ways they can cope with the emotion. For example, youth may write, "I take my dog for a walk," "I bake cookies with my sister," or "I take ten deep breaths." The cards can be dived into two booklets—one with the emotions and one with the coping skills. Counselors can discuss with the client how different skills can be used to manage different emotions.
Emotion Charades	In this activity, counselors play emotion charades with clients to help them to better understand emotions. Game cards can be made prior to the session or with the clients. The game cards should include an array of feeling words. Counselors and clients act out whatever feeling word they select. While acting out the words, counselors can ask clients questions to assess times they have experienced the emotions and how they cope with or handle the emotions.
My Emotional Buddy	Appropriate for younger children, this activity involves clients creating an '"emotional buddy"' that they teach to self-soothe, with the idea being the skills will transfer to them. Materials needed for the activity include socks, pillow stuffing, rubber bands, markers, and chenille bendable sticks. The counselor helps children to create a sock person or animal. After the clients create their buddy, counselors tell them that the buddy is very emotional and that they need to help the buddy manage its strong emotions. The counselor might say "Your emotional buddy is feeling angry, let's try to help your buddy calm down." Counselors may go through different feelings such as sadness, anger, and fear to help children to practice regulation skills using the buddy. A variation of this activity is to instruct children how to use the buddy when they feel those same emotions and how the feeling buddy can help. Counselors may say "When you are feeling angry, your buddy wants to help you calm down by practicing deep breathing." The goal of this activity is to help clients practice their emotion regulation skills both on the buddy and on themselves.
Emotion Thermometer	This activity involves clients creating a thermometer that is symbolic of a range of feelings and that they can use to better understand their own feelings. Materials needed for this activity include a poster board, markers, and pens. Counselors help youth to draw a large thermometer on the poster board. After the thermometer is drawn, counselors help youth color in each section of the thermometer starting from the bottom and moving up. Each section represents a different emotion. For example, the thermometer may read sad at the bottom, colored in as blue, and then fear, colored in as green, and then calm, colored in as orange, and then happy, colored in as yellow, and then anger, colored in as red. The thermometer may read whatever feeling the clients want to include in whatever color and order chosen. What matters is their interpretation of the colors. After the thermometer is made, counselors may ask clients the following questions: • How does the color/feeling feel? • How do you know when you are in that color/feeling? • What things put you in that color/feeling space? The goal of this exercise is to have youth create a visual representation of emotions and to recognize what they do and how they feel when those emotions are present.

Motivation and Counseling

A lack of client and/or family motivation to make changes is a common occurrence and a barrier to therapeutic progress. This section addresses some of the reasons young clients may lack motivation to engage in counseling and/or make changes. In addition, the section discusses strategies for identifying and enhancing young clients' motivation to change.

MOTIVATION AND CHANGE

All counselors chose counseling as a profession because—on some level—they want to assist others in making the changes they need to be at their best. At its essence, counseling is about helping people to make changes (ACA, 2015). When clients are motivated and ready to change, counseling progresses more effectively (Breda & Riemer, 2012). A common assumption though is that our young clients—or at least their families—want our assistance. However, counselors see many clients who are mandated or otherwise required to attend counseling. Young clients and/or their families might be mandated by the courts to receive counseling, or youth may be required by their parents to attend counseling. Regardless of the context, counselors should be aware that young people who are required to attend counseling may have minimal motivation to change, thus they may have little to no interest in counseling. A lack of interest in counseling can contribute to noncompliance in attending sessions and/or preclude active participation in the counseling process (Breda & Riemer, 2012).

All counselors struggle to engage clients who lack motivation to change. *Resistance* is a term commonly used to describe clients who have low motivation, especially adolescents (Lambert, 2013). The authors tend to not think of clients as being resistant to change. Instead, they think of clients as having misplaced their motivation to change. Or perhaps the clients are not yet entirely ready to change. It is the counselor's job to help young clients find their motivation to change, and techniques for doing so are discussed in the next section.

Adolescents in particular are notorious for being disinterested in counseling (Breda & Riemer, 2012). It is important to be patient when working with clients who have low motivation to attend counseling (Cohen, Berliner, & Mannarino, 2010). When working with this population, counselors may need to spend much of their time building trust with clients, and the relationship building techniques discussed previously in this chapter can help to that end. Some clients may require multiple sessions with the counselor before they begin to trust and open up, and it is important that counselors honor that process. If counselors begin to feel frustrated, clients will sense this and potentially become even more resistant to counseling.

Most counseling approaches are founded on the assumption that clients are motivated to want to change. Thus, all clients' motivation to make changes and engage in counseling should be considered, and their motivation should be enhanced as needed. As an example, before teaching the client how to use cognitive behavioral therapy (CBT) techniques to stop self-injuring, the client's motivation to want to stop self-injuring needs to be assessed; the client will most likely not follow through on using the CBT skills learned in counseling if he or she does not want to stop this behavior.

Sometimes clients' fear, disinterest, and/or opposition to counseling are rooted in a lack of understanding about what counseling is and is not. As previously stated, conveying clear expectations about the nature of counseling is important, and it may also help to minimize resistance. Another approach is to talk to the client about his or her resistance and attack the issue head on. Counselors might use the following prompts:

- I'm not about forcing you to talk about things you don't want to discuss. We can talk about whatever it is you are most interested in discussing.
- Help me understand what is going on for you right now as you think about how to respond to this question.
- Talk about the worst part of being here.
- What are the worries you have about counseling?

The use of these types of questions conveys to clients that you care about their perspectives, and it suggests that counseling is going to be a collaborative process. Many young people have never been in a relationship in which their views and opinions were solicited and honored, so communicating that their ideas are valued can go a long way toward enhancing their motivation and interest in counseling.

ENHANCING MOTIVATION TO CHANGE

A client's readiness or motivation to change is one of the most important client variables that affects counseling outcomes (Miller & Rollnick, 2012). Counselors need to be aware of young clients' levels of motivation to change and continually assess their readiness for change; low motivation to change may arise at any point in the counseling process. Clients will also have varied levels of motivation to change depending on the behavior and the context. For example, a 10-year-old boy might be motivated to learn new ways of inter-acting and relating to his peers but less interested in identifying and learning ways he can better relate to his sister.

For clients to change, they must be aware of a problem, open to the idea of change, and willing to make the changes necessary to alter their situation. When considering clients' levels of motivation, counse-lors must evaluate whether clients are preparing to change, contemplating change, or precontemplating change (Miller & Rollnick, 2012). To enhance clients' motivation to change, it is important to address their ambivalence around change (i.e., the part of the client that does not want to change) and aid them by incor-porating and increasing the language of change (i.e., discussing the change as though it will soon happen—"*when* you are getting on better with your sister . . ."), while seeking agreement on what problem they want to change.

Miller and Rollnick's (2012) approach, motivational interviewing (MI)—a motivational enhancement approach—highlights the importance of *not* attempting to define clients' problems and *not* persuading them that they should change. The Stages of Change model (Prochaska, DiClemente, & Norcross, 1992; see Chapter 16 for a discussion of the use of motivational interviewing with substance use disorders) is often discussed in relation to MI. Prochaska et al.'s (1992) Stages of Change model is a developmental stage the-ory that focuses on a client's readiness for change. The associated stages are precontemplation, contempla-tion, preparation, action, maintenance, and termination:

- In the **precontemplation stage**, a client is not aware a problem exists and typically has little motiva-tion to change any aspect of his or her current situation. *Example:* A client who self-injures may say "I don't have a problem . . . my parents are the ones with the problem . . . it is no one's business if I want to self-injure." Many young clients enter counseling at the request of adults in their lives, and as such, they are often at this precontemplation stage.
- In the **contemplation stage**, a client is able to acknowledge a problem exists but is apprehensive about making changes. The client feels he or she is at a crossroads because pros and cons of the behaviors are evident. *Example:* A client who self-injures may say "I really know I should stop self-injuring. I know it is really hurting my relationship with my parents and I hate the scarring, but it makes me feel better. . ."
- In the **preparation stage**, a client is getting ready to change. More ownership of personal responsibil-ity is evident in his or her speech. *Example:* A client who self-injures might say "I've really got to do something about this self-injury . . . this is serious . . . something has to change. I am sick of these scars, and the kids at school think I am nuts."
- In the **action stage**, a client begins to change his or her behaviors. The client believes change is pos-sible and acts on this belief. *Example:* A client who self-injures might say "I am ready to change. This self-injury is a problem. I am going to stop. When I want to self-injure, I am going to use my distrac-tion skills, and if those don't work, I will use my relaxation skills or call a friend." The client then follows through on using these preventative skills and is better able to control and thus prevent the behavior.
- In the **maintenance stage**, a client continues to maintain productive behavioral changes. During this stage, a client must avoid the temptation to slip back into the old habits and prior ways of being. A client in this stage needs to continually remind him- or herself how much change has occurred and how the change has been positive. A client at this stage must learn and use new skills to avoid relaps-ing. *Example:* A client who self-injures might say "I have made these changes, and I am better manag-ing the self-injury But I know I need to keep using what I learned in counseling or I might begin to self-injure again."
- The **termination (or relapse) stage** occurs when the client returns to older behaviors and abandons the new changes. In this situation, the client is encouraged to pick up where he or she left off. Ideally, if a client relapses, he or she will be back at the preparation or action stage again and not the precon-templation stage.

Motivational interviewing emphasizes the importance of a supportive, nonjudgmental, directive envi-ronment in which clients can explore their motivations, readiness, and confidence levels for change as well as ambivalence about change (Miller & Rollnick, 2012). When using MI, counselors consider ways they can gently help move clients forward in the stages of change, thus facilitating better counseling outcomes. Motivational interviewing allows counselors to address the issues that brought clients into counseling via a humanizing, collaborative, respectful, and empowering means. The use of MI restores responsibility to clients, thus theoretically increasing their level of engagement in the counseling process. Using MI, counselors do not necessarily need to directly confront resistance but instead can roll with the resistance and aid clients in understanding their ambivalence (Miller & Rollnick, 2012). This approach allows clients' ambivalence to be the focus of counseling and helps to prevent unproductive power struggles.

Clinical Toolbox 3.4

In the Pearson eText, click here to read a counseling application of motivational interviewing and enhancement with an adolescent who self-injures.

The foundations of MI include three main elements: (a) collaboration, (b) evocation, and (c) autonomy (Miller & Rollnick, 2012). The concept of **collaboration** highlights the importance of an egalitarian therapeutic relationship, which honors the experiences and perspectives of the client. **Evocation** refers to developing the client's inherent resources and intrinsic motivation for change. The final concept, **autonomy**, refers to a value of the client's right and capacity for self-direction and informed consent within the counseling process. Table 3.1 provides a review of the counselor tasks that can be used to promote client movement at the different change stages.

Table 3.1 Stages of Change and Associated Counseling Goals and Tasks

Stage of Change	Overview and Counseling Goal(s)	Counselor Tasks	Examples of Possible Questions
Precontemplation	*Overview:* Youth in this stage are unaware or unwilling to make changes to their behaviors. *Goal:* They will consider the possibility that they might have an issue, difficulty, and/or problem.	Assess overall health and well-being. Establish rapport through empathy. Address safety issues. Enhance awareness of self, the problem, and patterns of behaviors. Actively listen to concerns and reflect change talk language. Enhance awareness of the advantages of changing. Highlight client doubts about problematic behaviors. Provide education on the risks of behavior. Assess strengths, skills, and any cultural issues.	About your issue/problem/behavior, do you or others see it as a reason for concern? In what ways has this been a problem for you? Why would you want to make this change? What makes you think you need to change? In what ways do you think you or others have been harmed by this problem/behavior? What difficulties have you had in relation to this problem/behavior? Any issues at school, with friends, or with your parents? What are some of the things you don't like about your problem/behavior? On a scale of 1 to 10, how much does your problem/behavior concern you (e.g., 1 [not at all] and 10 [extremely])? Does your problem/behavior ever get in your way? Has it ever stopped you from doing something you wanted to do?

Table 3.1	(Continued)		
Stage of Change	**Overview and Counseling Goal(s)**	**Counselor Tasks**	**Examples of Possible Questions**
Contemplation	*Overview:* Youth in this stage are becoming aware that an issue, difficulty, or problem exists but have not made a commitment to change or take action. *Goal:* They will increase their own awareness of their problem (e.g., impact, observation [frequency, duration, intensity]).	Emphasize free choice and responsibility (e.g., introduce the idea that they are capable of changing). Assess cultural issues. Acknowledge strengths, skills, and values. Validate lack of readiness. Normalize the change process. Encourage a discussion of pros/cons of behavior. Elicit client's self-motivational statements. Provide specific feedback (e.g., risk factors, educational information).	What makes you think you can change? Have you ever changed? What might work for you, if you decided it was time to change? What do you think will happen if you decided not to change? Let's write these down. What are two reasons why you shouldn't change? What are two reasons you should? Can you think of any more reasons (for or against)? I can see you're feeling stuck here. What needs to change so you can make a decision (i.e., change or not)?
Preparation	*Overview:* Youth in this stage are intending to make a change or to take action, but have only made small steps toward addressing their issue, difficulty, or problem. *Goal:* They will begin to make a commitment to change through small steps with a large amount of supportive encouragement.	Identify options and barriers to change. Discuss previously utilized options and resources. Assist in establishing realistic expectations. Empower and aid a client to construct manageable goals or action. Brainstorm small steps to help a client begin to make changes (e.g., develop treatment plan). Provide additional information and ideas on possible strategies. Introduce coping strategies and skills. Identify a network of social support.	What is one thing you can do right now to make things better for yourself? Concerning this problem/behavior, what have you tried before? How helpful was that? Did it work some of the time? Can you name some other things/steps you'll need to do to make this change? What are some of the things you do when you need to make a hard decision? Do you go through any steps? Name some people who listen and care about you? Who could help you as you prepare for this? Can you share any of these first steps with them?
Action	*Overview:* Youth in this stage are making changes and taking action in their behavior, experience, and/or environment to address their issue, difficulty, or problem. *Goal:* They will create and implement an action plan with the use of support and reinforcements (e.g., internal and external).	Develop an action plan with a time line. Keep steps incremental and achievable. Practice and review coping strategies and skills. Reinforce any efforts or any "small success" (e.g., verbal praise). Affirm strengths and skills. Reiterate long-term benefits. Enlist help (increase social support).	How will you make this change? Why are you making this change again? What are you going to do instead of the (behavior)? What might work for you? I will write this down for you. If you were making a step-by-step list, what steps do you need to do to make this change? When will you try to do this (each step) by? Is this doable for you? How will you reward yourself for all your work? Who should we ask to be part of your plan (to help you out with this plan)? How will you keep this plan moving? What might make this difficult? What can you do to keep momentum?

(Continued)

Table 3.1	Stages of Change and Associated Counseling Goals and Tasks (*Continued*)		
Stage of Change	Overview and Counseling Goal(s)	Counselor Tasks	Examples of Possible Questions
Maintenance	*Overview:* Youth in this stage are working to maintain their change/action and prevent relapse. *Goal:* They will review counseling gains and plan for potential difficulties.	Review progress of goals, along with overall health and well-being. Review coping strategies and skills. Plan for follow-up support (e.g., referrals, recommendations). Reinforce internal rewards. Continue to identify supports (e.g., friends, family, community). Discuss and plan for the future (e.g., reviewing warning signs of relapse).	Is there a chance you might go back to the problem/behavior. If so, why? How can we plan so you'll be ready for that situation? What might get in your way in the future? How will you know if you need to come back to counseling? What would need to happen?

Note: Norcross, Krebs, & Prochaska, 2011.

Technology and Counseling

Counselors have increased access to multiple technology resources that can be used—in and out of session—to help clients make changes during the working state of counseling. Counselors can use tablets, computers, or other electronics in session. Therapy games, resources, and educational tools can be accessed and used to facilitate counseling goals and objectives. Electronics are a medium with which most youth are quite comfortable, and their use can deepen young people's understanding of various therapy concepts and how these concepts apply to their change processes.

Various electronic applications may be used with parents and youth. In Table 3.2, youth-, parent-, and counselor-friendly electronic applications that can be incorporated into counseling and/or used by counselors to facilitate their work are provided.

The application examples provided demonstrate the wide age range with which applications can be used; both young children and adolescents can benefit from the use of electronic applications. Because electronics have a universal appeal, their use may facilitate engagement and practice between counseling sessions. Most of the skills discussed later in the text have accompanying applications that may also be useful.

Table 3.2	Technology Resources That Can Be Used in Counseling
Application Name	Description of Application
Emotions Collection	This application is a collection of six short stories about feelings, including anger, happiness, sadness, fear, and worry. Youth can practice identifying emotions with each story. Appropriate for youth ages 2–8.
iTouchiLearn Feelings for Preschool Kids	This application helps youth to practice identifying, interpreting, and communicating emotions while using words, games, puzzles, and drawings. Appropriate for youth ages 5 and younger.
Montessori Family and Feelings	This application helps youth to practice emotion identification. It provides two games with which users can interact: a memory game that uses matching cards and a puzzle game. Appropriate for youth ages 1–4.
Puppet Pals 2	This application allows youth to create social stories using interactive puppets and characters. It is useful for storyboarding, character writing, speaking, and listening.

Application Name	Description of Application
Virtual Hope Box	This application helps youth with coping, relaxation, distraction, and positive thinking as a companion to counseling. It also provides activity planning, distraction tools, relaxation exercises, and guided meditation.
Breathe2Relax	This application assists clients with using diaphragmatic breathing exercises to facilitate stress management. It also provides clients with information on the effects stress has on the body.
Stop, Breathe & Think	This application helps clients to practice mindfulness, meditation, and compassion building. It has guided meditations and yoga videos that can help with stress, depression, and anxiety. Clients also have access to a tracker for mood and meditation progress.
MoodTools	This application provides tools for depression/mood symptoms, causes, and treatments. Clients have access to a thought diary, a personal safety plan, mood support activities, and mood assessments. Self-help guidelines and directives and videos on meditation are provided.
SoberTool	This application is used to track sober days and provide locations of 12-step meetings and information on the 12-step practice. It also provides community forums with questions and answers.
AA Big Book	This application resembles the AA big book. It has 12-step prayers, personal addiction stories, podcasts, and a meeting finder for any AA chapter in the United States.
Clinical Scales	This application provides an array of clinical assessments for mental health and health care professionals. Assessments for depression, anxiety, ADHD, bipolar, autism, and general scales such as the Mini-Mental Status Exam are all available for use and print.
Suicide Safe	This application is a suicide prevention learning tool based on the nationally recognized SAFE-T practice guidelines. It provides case studies, communication and language tips for suicide assessment, resources, and SAMHSA's Behavioral Health Treatment Services locator for referrals.
Teen Hotlines	This application provides a list of hotlines, help lines, and websites organized by subject, including depression, eating disorders, and suicide. Adolescents can identify state and local services in their community.
3D Brain	This application provides 29 interactive brain structures, how each brain region functions, what happens when the brain is injured, and how it is involved in mental illness. Each structure provides information on functions, disorders, brain damage, case studies, and links to modern research. This application can be useful in communicating to youth how a mental disorder may be biologically and physically situated.

Table 3.2 (Continued)

Application Name | Description of Application

Note: ADHD, attention-deficit/hyperactivity disorder; SAFE-T, Suicide Assessment Five-Step Evaluation and Triage; SAMHSA, Substance Abuse and Mental Health Services Administration.

TERMINATION

The goal of all counseling with young clients is for them to get to a point where they can thrive and function apart from the counseling relationship. As such, saying goodbye is an inevitable part of the counseling process. In this section, counseling termination is discussed, and readers are provided with information on how final sessions can be crafted to facilitate goodbyes.

The word **termination** is the term most commonly used to describe the process of finalizing or ending a counseling experience. Because the word *termination* conjures images of abrupt endings or even death, the authors wish that a better word could be used to describe counseling endings and transitions. Perhaps the words *finale* or *commencement*, or even the euphemism *new beginnings*, would better describe our perceptions of the termination process; however, for the purposes of this text, the traditional *termination* language is used.

Counseling termination can be planned and occur naturally—as the client progresses—or it can be premature and abrupt. **Natural termination** typically occurs when the family, child, and counselor all agree that the goals of counseling have been achieved. **Premature termination** occurs when counseling is forced to stop before the client's goals have been achieved. Counseling termination occurs for various reasons, and these may include the client reaching his or her goals or the counselor needing to leave the relationship due to factors such as administrative changes, changes to caseload, escalating client needs that are beyond the counselor's personal scope of practice, counselor or client relocation, or change in client insurance.

Termination is a topic that receives little attention in counselor training or in the professional literature, yet it is an integral part of the counseling process; the final counseling sessions are just as important as the initial sessions. Healthy terminations are especially important with younger children who cannot comprehend the prescribed boundaries of the professional counseling relationship and often struggle to understand why they may not be able to continue to have contact with their counselor posttermination. Because of these complexities, care and attention should be given to the termination process.

The authors often hear people make mention of the "termination session"; however, counseling termination is not a single, isolated event. Rather, termination is best described as a process or an evolution. Counselors are charged by their professional code of ethics to terminate the relationship "when it becomes reasonably apparent that the client no longer needs assistance, is not likely to benefit, or is harmed by continued counseling" (American Counseling Association [ACA], 2014, p. 6). It is also emphasized in the code of ethics that "counselors provide pretermination counseling and recommend other service providers when necessary" (ACA, 2014, p. 6). The language used in the ACA ethics code confirms the notion that termination is a process and that counselors are charged with carefully considering the changing status of the therapeutic relationship and clients' best interests. The ethics code also reminds us that there are ethical and legal ramifications that may occur if counselors mishandle the termination process.

Termination must be approached in a thoughtful, thorough fashion wherein counselors are mindful of the therapeutic relationship and outcomes of the counseling process. The following sections focus on the various aspects of the termination process. The sections initially address natural termination and considerations related to assessing for termination readiness, planning for termination, and termination activities. Next, the sections discuss premature termination, the common reasons it occurs, and the ways it can be avoided and managed.

Natural Termination

This section discusses how a counselor can assess readiness for natural termination, termination preparation and procedural considerations, as well as the importance of integrating activities into the client termination process when working with young clients. Concrete examples of creative activities that can be used when terminating counseling with youth are provided.

REASONS FOR NATURAL TERMINATION

Natural terminations are those that occur when counseling has progressed in a positive direction, culminating in clients reaching their goals and thus no longer needing counseling services (Joyce, Piper, Ogrodniczuk, & Klein, 2007). In an ideal world, all counseling would move forward, and then wind down in a predictable sequence with clients reaching their goals. The family or the counselor may initiate termination, but it is important that the process be collaborative and that young clients play a role in the decision to end counseling.

Natural termination can also occur when clients may not be functioning optimally but have achieved short-term goals appropriate to the nature of the counseling. For example, a counselor who works with clients in an acute setting (e.g., a hospital unit or a crisis stabilization facility) may only meet with clients for a brief period (e.g., 1–14 days). As such, termination planning will begin immediately, resulting in a referral to other providers once the child is "stepped down" to a lower level of care. To illuminate this example, consider an adolescent who is admitted into a residential intensive treatment center because of suicide risk. The immediate aim of counseling is to keep the adolescent safe by stabilizing suicidal behaviors and risk and for the adolescent to have zero suicidal gestures so he or she can be released back into the community (with, of course, appropriate wraparound services such as medication management, weekly individual counseling, and a crisis plan in place). In these situations, natural termination with the counselor will occur—albeit very quickly—even though the child will still require multiple services to be successful.

The authors would be remiss to suggest that the termination process is as linear and easily defined as it is being presented in this chapter. The reality is that many young clients seen by counselors have a choppy counseling experience that involves many sudden starts and stops, and young clients—along with their families—are often in and out of various mental health–related programs and services (e.g., case management, counseling, parenting classes) and levels of care (e.g., individual counseling, in-home family therapy, residential treatment).

Because youth experience so many developmental transitions and because those who enter counseling may be more vulnerable to returning to counseling, it is most realistic to expect that even a natural termination may not mean the end of a young person's counseling (Many, 2009). Counselors should convey to their clients that they are available should they want to return to counseling because this allows the client and the family permission to reach out for assistance should prior struggles reemerge or if new problems arise.

INTRODUCING THE IDEA OF TERMINATION

At the onset of counseling, it is important that counselors invite clients and their families to communicate a desire to terminate counseling for whatever reason (Harrison, 2009; Rappleyea, Harris, White, & Simon, 2009). A discussion of termination can be couched in the context of informed consent, the goals the client wants to work toward, and how long it might take to achieve these goals. The conversations about the length of counseling, including clients' expectations, as well as third-party payer restrictions, are important and help to frame the counseling experience.

Early termination discussions allow young clients and their families to understand that termination is a natural, desirable aspect of the counseling process, and it reinforces that they have the right to cease counseling at any point. Some clients fear hurting counselors' feelings or offending them by initiating termination, so an open invitation to terminate helps to empower them to make that decision when they are ready to do so.

Introducing the concept of termination early on may also motivate clients to set goals and commit to counseling, and it may keep them focused on the direction they are headed. Particularly with mandated clients or those who have low motivation to attend counseling, a focus on counseling completion may empower them to see the process as temporary—something they can handle—rather than uncertain, lengthy, and intimidating.

SIGNS OF TERMINATION READINESS

Counselors should attend to signs that termination may be approaching. The most obvious sign of termination readiness is that clients and/or their families may self-report successes—reaching their goals—and suggest readiness to terminate. Counselors may also notice positive changes in their clients' behavior—changes in accordance with their counseling goals. Being keenly aware of clients' behavior—and being sensitive to even the subtlest of changes—can help to facilitate counselors' openness to and awareness of the natural termination process. As counseling progresses and clients begin to meet their goals, counselors can plant the seeds of termination. For example, a counselor may plant a "seed" by saying "I can hear that this accomplishment was really exciting for you. You have been reaching many of the goals you set for yourself. It seems like in some ways you are starting to outgrow counseling. How would you know if you outgrew the need for counseling?" Clients' reactions to a question such as this can help counselors to gauge their clients' termination readiness.

A decrease in the intensity of counseling is another sign that natural termination may soon be approaching. A decrease in intensity might look like the client appearing less interested in discussing counseling topics. The client might also begin to talk more about things that are happening with the people around them and describe their day-to-day happenings (sometimes counselors call this "storytelling"), or they may shift to presenting more surface-level topics that do not relate to clinical matters. In Figure 3.4, signs or indicators that a client may be ready for termination are provided.

- Misses sessions
- Tardy to sessions or leaves early
- Is less focused on previous concerns and talks more about matters unrelated to counseling
- Fewer reports of problems (from client/family)
- Better relationships with peers and/or parents
- Greater openness and cognitive flexibility (open to different ways of thinking and new ideas)
- Increased independence and autonomy
- Better able to use and apply adaptive coping skills
- Increased ability to identify, tolerate, and manage intense emotions
- Mastery of the problems that brought them to counseling (e.g., control over impulsive behaviors)
- Displays functional independence from counselor and counseling process
- Interest expressed by client/family in reaching termination

FIGURE 3.4 Signs of Termination Readiness

TERMINATION READINESS COMPLEXITIES

Because counselors have an obligation to continually determine if their clients are benefiting or being harmed by counseling, assessment of progress—in the context of termination—is an important part of the counseling process (ACA, 2014). However, assessing clients' progress and their termination readiness is not as easy as it may appear. The number of sessions a young person needs before the cessation of counseling varies. Some clients only need a session or two to resolve a presenting issue (e.g., a communication problem within the family), whereas other clients may need more extensive counseling (e.g., treatment to resolve trauma reactions secondary to years of sexual abuse). Further complicating counselors' assessment of readiness for termination is the fact that even clients with the same presenting issue often need a different number of sessions to reach their unique needs and goals.

Another termination assessment complexity relates to the evolving nature of clients' struggles—that is, even when clients have met their goals, new struggles and goals may emerge (Joyce et al., 2007). Also, once clients have met their goals, the focus of counseling may shift to preventative counseling that is aimed at discouraging new problems from emerging.

As termination approaches, it is not uncommon for young clients to experience or report an increase in either new problems or an exacerbation of the struggles initially reported at the start of counseling. It is our experience that most young people struggle—on some level—with the ending of relationships, even those relationships that were not especially valued (e.g., a teacher the client did not like). Typically, children associate the end of a relationship with past painful memories such as a death, a parent leaving, or a friend moving away. Young people who have experienced losses, are struggling with grief, or have experienced trauma and abandonment issues may be especially vulnerable to termination (Many, 2009).

Termination can be viewed as an event that, because of its inherent focus on loss (i.e., the loss of the therapeutic relationship), can trigger grief reactions (Many, 2009). For many young people, counseling may have been one of the only times in their lives—and maybe the only time—that they felt cared for, important, and safe and that they had the undivided attention and support of an adult. It is especially difficult for some young people to distinguish between the feelings of grief and loss associated with the end of the counseling relationship and negative feelings that are rooted in past painful experiences. For some youth, the end of the counseling experience may trigger past loss experiences and cause them to either regress and lean into past maladaptive behaviors or act out to maintain a connection with the counselor. Some suggest that this escalation in struggles may be due to a fear or anxiety of functioning without the safety net that counseling can provide (Many, 2009).

Counselors are charged with ferreting out how much of any escalation of client problems is due to termination anxiety, a genuine increase in previously addressed struggles, and/or an occurrence of new struggles. Counselors need to observe and recognize clients' defensive reactions, work with them to understand the real cause of these reactions, and help them to use the skills they have learned to manage these reactions (Harrison, 2009). A well-managed natural counseling termination provides an opportunity for clients to learn to navigate and tolerate strong emotions such as grief and loss in a controlled, nurturing setting

(Many, 2009). A positive termination experience can provide youth who have had painful losses with a corrective experience and a template they can take into future situations in which they experience an ending. The counseling termination experience provides clients with an opportunity to learn to effectively separate from others and say goodbye.

There is a paradox inherent to the natural termination process: Even though termination marks the end of one road, it punctuates the beginning of another. The way a counselor frames termination is important, but a positive frame cannot be forced on a client. This idea that a natural counseling termination is a sign that a client has developed and moved to a place of independence is important, but counselors should be careful to not minimize a client's negative feelings related to termination; these feelings must be appropriately acknowledged, honored, and addressed.

Counselors should also be aware of their own personal reactions as they consider clients' readiness for termination. Because young clients are typically more vulnerable than adult clients, counselors may have strong personal reactions to termination, and these reactions can affect counselors' decision making related to termination. Commonly, children will request continued contact with a counselor after termination. Counselors should consider how to respond to these requests. For example, counselors might say "It can be sad to end counseling. Part of me feels sad about this ending, and I am really going to miss seeing you. But you have done wonderful work in counseling, and so part of me is really excited to see how you do on your own. I feel so lucky to have been able to have watched you make such great changes. As we talked about when we developed your action plan, you know what signs to look for that might tell you counseling is needed again."

Counselors must be aware of any potential feelings of responsibility, guilt, or shame that are triggered by client requests for continued contact or client responses to the termination process in general. It behooves counselors to consider their personal reactions to the termination because it may provide clues to important dynamics—especially in the case of premature terminations—and such an awareness can help counselors to grow

THE TERMINATION PROCESS

Natural terminations are exciting because they reflect the fact that the client has progressed and no longer needs counseling services (Schaeffer & Kaiser, 2013). Health, wellness, stability, independence, and client empowerment are the goals of all counseling, regardless of the theoretical approach used. However, as previously stated, termination sessions are just as important as initial counseling sessions, and they need to be approached in a deliberate fashion. During the termination process, clients should be empowered and their therapeutic gains highlighted (Joyce et al., 2007). The termination process is also a time to reinforce clients' hard work and identify aspirational goals for the future and ways clients can meet those goals.

Clinical Toolbox 3.5

In the Pearson eText, click here to view examples of prompts that can be used with youth during the termination process to help them in processing termination.

There are various strategies that can be used to plan and prepare for termination. One termination planning strategy is to schedule appointments further apart to see how clients do with less frequent contact with the counselor. As an example, a counselor might say something like this to assess the client/family's readiness to have fewer sessions:

We've met and talked about your fear of going to school for twelve weeks now. Over the past twelve weeks, you have made some BIG changes! You have learned what to do so you don't feel so scared and afraid to go to school. Over the past month, you haven't missed a single day of school, and it looks like you really have that problem on the run! You've really taken charge of your situation and shown that problem who the boss is. Talk to me about what you would think about maybe not meeting for two weeks . . . what comes up for you when I throw that idea out?

Another strategy for assessing readiness to terminate is to ask the youth and his or her parents *when* they want to have their next session and to not assume they want to meet at the current meeting pace. Often, clients and their families may begin to feel they are ready to wean off sessions or terminate but may fear disappointing their counselors (Headley et al., 2015; Rappleyea et al., 2009). It is important that counselors give clients permission to tell us as they become ready to terminate. Failure to do so may result in clients missing appointments or simply not returning, and this deprives the client of the opportunity to have a productive termination experience.

Counselors should be aware that on exiting counseling, all clients are vulnerable to reexperiencing the struggles that initially led them to counseling, especially as stressful life circumstances emerge. As such, counselors may work with clients to develop a plan that can be used to facilitate clients' ability to stay on track (Joyce et al., 2007). These plans are sometimes referred to as *maintenance, action, discharge*, or *prevention plans*. Clients who are being released from secure, acute care settings (e.g., hospitals, residential treatment) are at greater risk—because of the severity of their symptoms—to experience posttermination problems. As such, they need to have a thorough *discharge plan* (the term most frequently used in hospitals) in place, and counselors should ensure connections have been established with the new providers and appointments are scheduled as close as possible to the discharge date. It is important to engage parents in the planning process, especially with younger children, because they are often not as aware—because of their developmental levels—of triggers and red flags that could suggest an escalation of struggles.

Termination plans may contain potential behaviors that may be cause for concern, strategies that were previously identified as successful in addressing these behaviors, and a plan for seeking support should attempts to manage the behavior be unsuccessful (Headley et al., 2015; Joyce et al., 2007; Many, 2009). For example, anorexia nervosa is a potentially life-threatening eating disorder. When working with those who have anorexia nervosa, care should be taken to ensure a detailed prevention plan is in place. The plan might include a review of the stressful situations (e.g., fights with parents, examinations at school) and events (e.g., occasions that involve wearing a bathing suit, birthday parties with a lot of food) that trigger disordered eating patterns; a review of the signals or cues that suggest the client is engaging in disordered eating (e.g., weighing, counting calories, restricting food intake, excessive exercise); past behaviors that were successful in eliminating the behaviors (e.g., reaching out for support and talking to friends, walking the dog); identified behaviors or signals that indicate help is needed (e.g., weight falling below a certain threshold, skipping meals); and a plan for seeking help and support (e.g., reentering counseling, talking with a school counselor about concerns). In Figure 3.5, tips for preparing youth for counseling termination are provided.

In some natural termination situations, counselors may have an opportunity to stay connected with their clients. For example, school counselors will frequently have some casual contact with students who they have counseled. The counselor may want to talk with the client and discuss the nature and boundaries of their relationship as they move away from individual sessions. It can also be helpful to young clients in the school to know they have an opportunity to check back in with their counselor in the future.

- Introduce the idea of termination during the intake session; communicate that the client/family play an important role in determining the length and duration of counseling and that they have a right to terminate counseling at any time.
- Empower the client/family by offering them scheduling input (e.g., allowing them to schedule less frequent sessions).
- Regularly assess and communicate clients' progress toward reaching their goals so you and the client/family are oriented to where the client is at in relation to termination.
- Be sure to set aside adequate time over the course of several sessions to conduct termination activities.
- Consider positive, strength-based termination activities for use with the client and/or family.
- Work with the client/family to develop a postcounseling maintenance plan.
- Identify client supports outside counseling.
- If necessary, offer referrals or information about community resources.

FIGURE 3.5 Tips for Preparing Youth for Counseling Termination

COUNSELING TERMINATION ACTIVITIES

Termination activities are a wonderful way to punctuate clients' successes and accomplishments in counseling and to make their final sessions memorable. Activities involve a creative aspect that allows both the counselor and the client to achieve closure as counseling comes to an end. Creativity can facilitate a meaningful connection to what was learned in counseling, and for some clients it may be easier to express their feelings and experiences via the use of creative means (Headley et al., 2015). Creative interventions are also developmentally appropriate and accessible to youth. More specifically, the use of art, writing, transitional objects, and rituals can be a powerful medium when working with young clients (Paylo, Darby, Kinch, & Kress, 2014); their use during termination can provide a meaningful way to structure the termination process.

Counselors can pull on clients' interests when selecting a termination activity. For example, if a client has an interest in painting or drawing, a counselor might ask the client to paint a picture that represents something he or she learned in counseling. There are also many Internet resources that can be used to identify creative ideas for termination.

As clients meet their goals and begin to manage their problems more efficiently, the pace of sessions may slow down, and there will be less to focus on in sessions. The use of creative activities may not only ease the transition into termination but also inject new life into the counseling process as it comes to an end (Headley et al., 2015).

One example of a creative approach that can be integrated into client termination is the use of transitional objects. Transitional objects are symbolic items that are used to facilitate a sense of psychological comfort as clients transition out of the counseling relationship. These objects allow clients to take a piece of the counseling experience with them as they move forward. The object can be something that reminds the client of aspects of counseling or reminders of lessons learned or skills he or she wants to remember. For example, one of our 10-year-old clients who had a trauma history was enamored of a small desktop water fountain in the counseling office. As a part of her relaxation training, she used the fountain as a focal point. On termination, the counselor provided her with a pebble from the fountain that she could use as a reminder of the relaxation skills she had learned.

The use of creativity and art can be used with transitional objects to deepen their impact (Adamson & Kress, 2011). For example, consider a child who experiences severe nightmares and trauma symptoms secondary to ongoing sexual abuse. The counselor and the client might make a dream pillow, which involves using fabric paint to draw safe thoughts, images from the client's "'safe place'" relaxation scenario, and any other images or symbols that the client connects with a sense of safety on the pillow case. When the client goes to sleep at night, she can use the pillow to connect with her feelings of safety.

Rituals are another example of a creative approach that can be used when ending counseling. Essentially, a ritual is a set of actions or steps performed by an individual or group that are performed in such a way as to represent thoughts, feelings, or behaviors. Counselors create a termination ritual based on some important aspect of counseling or the client's experience. For example, consider a young client who shares that she thinks she will feel as if a weight has been lifted off her as she approaches the end of her time in counseling. As she achieves her goals and begins to exhibit signs of readiness for termination, she frequently mentions how much "lighter" she feels. At your final session, you may bring a balloon for her to release as a symbol of her being light enough to fly freely. The ritual—letting go of a balloon—represents the client's experience of completing counseling.

A ritual can aid young clients in a symbolic representation of their process of moving forward without the therapeutic relationship. Much like how the bar/bat mitzvah or the Catholic confirmation process might be used in a religious context to symbolize maturity and transition, rituals allow a client to tangibly connect with an internal experience; rituals provide external representations of an internal process. Creative termination rituals can provide clients with a sense of closure; a sense of ownership, accomplishment, and empowerment; and a culminating termination experience, which summarizes and punctuates the work of counseling. Rituals may also call to mind different tools the client has gained through counseling, and it may help a client to apply those tools to situations that occur after counseling is terminated.

Creative Toolbox 3.2 contains examples of activities that can be used as part of the termination process. These activities can easily be adapted to accommodate clients of different ages, and they are applicable to individual, family, or group counseling.

Creative Toolbox 3.2 Creative Termination Activities

Activity	Description
Aloha Lei	In this activity, the Hawaiian *aloha lei* is used as a metaphor for saying goodbye. Explain to the client that the word *aloha* means hello and goodbye because when something ends, a new beginning follows. Invite the client to consider that change is constant and that each new beginning will eventually come to an end. Present the client with a string and cut-out paper flowers with a hole punched through the middle. On each flower, the client is invited to write down coping skills, insights, or important counseling experiences. Other flowers may represent future goals or people who can be turned to for support. As the client places each flower on the string, he or she can share what each flower means. When finished, the counselor can take the string, tie the ends together, and place it around the client's neck as a parting gift. This activity may be expanded to include family members, who can create their own flowers for the lei.
Building Blocks	This activity is both physically and mentally engaging, and it is especially useful with younger children. At the final counseling session, lay out a set of blocks. Invite the client to build a tower. Explain that each block placed in the tower represents something learned in counseling. For example, the first block placed as the foundation might represent honesty or trust—one of the basic principles of the counseling relationship. The counselor can participate as well, either by helping to place blocks as the tower grows taller or by reminding the client of lessons learned or goals achieved. Each block represents a new skill or strength, and as the tower grows, the client sees his or her accomplishments and, ideally, feels empowered. As the client places the blocks, the tower may grow too tall, which is exciting and challenging for the client. Explain that it is okay if the tower eventually falls because all the pieces are still there and can be put back together. In other words, the client may experience some setbacks, but he or she has the essential foundations needed to be successful.
Goodbye Letter	Counselors can use a preformatted letter or have clients write an original letter to help them to recall and integrate their memories of counseling. The letter may be written to the client from the counselor, to the counselor from the client, from the client to the client, and/or any other variation that fits the client's situation. Counselors may include or provide prompts such as "I remember a time we . . . ," "One skill I learned is . . . ," or "The thing I am most taking away from counseling is. . . ." Try to choose phrases or sentence starters that will help clients narrow down the most important parts of counseling and, as with all termination activities, keep the conversation strength based.
The Survivor Tree	In this activity, the client draws a tree that represents his or her strengths, capacities, and resources. Remind the client that trees are strong and perseverant, just like the client. Trees also change in different seasons, and their leaves fall off and then come back, but they are always growing and maturing. Each branch of the tree can represent a different "branch" of counseling—skills learned, goals achieved, identified strengths, supports garnered, etc. Clients add leaves to the branches to represent what they have learned. They may place leaves on the ground to represent problems or struggles they have eliminated or overcome. If age appropriate, the counselor might share the story of the Survivor Tree located in New York City. After enduring the September 11, 2001, terror attacks at the World Trade Center, the tree stands as a living reminder of resilience, survival, and rebirth. This activity can be adapted to meet different levels of artistic ability. For example, counselors may use a preformatted tracing of a tree (readily found online), work with clients to draw a tree, or allow clients to create their own tree using different mediums if they have more advanced fine motor and artistic skills.

Creative Toolbox 3.2 (Continued)

Activity	Description
Making a Case for Counseling	A case is a box or receptacle that holds something. People also use a case to transport or take relevant items with them. In this activity, clients create a case in which they hold the important aspects of counseling; those they want to take as they move forward. One of the strengths of this activity is its flexibility. The type of case can be adapted to suit the client's needs or interests and might include a suitcase, a purse, a treasure chest, a toolbox, or even a toy boat. Cases can be created using simple tutorials found online, and recycled materials (e.g., cereal boxes, yogurt cups, jars) are free, accessible mediums that can be helpful for this application (see Adamson & Kress, 2011). If working with younger clients, counselors may want to prepare the case prior to meeting. Older clients may enjoy building their own case. Work with clients to decide what they will fill their case with—encourage them to delve into their counseling experience for memories, skills, or goals. Be creative in designing the item that will be placed in the case (e.g., tools for the toolbox, colorful pieces of paper for the treasure chest, oars or lifejackets for the boat). Review the meaning of each item before inserting it in the case. Family members can be encouraged to contribute items as well.
Memory Book	This activity can occur over several termination sessions. In this activity, counselors work with clients to create a memory book of their counseling experience. Counselors may help facilitate the content of the book or allow the client to choose what he or she wants to include. Counselors desiring to provide more structure may have pages in the book labeled or identified (e.g., skills learned, takeaway points, action plan). Clients may draw images or pictures, or if older they may write down their reflections. Clients may also complete pages between several sessions as termination approaches. Counselors may also want to tuck a brief goodbye note in the front cover or include a thoughtful inscription. At the final session, clients' family member(s) may be invited to contribute their reflections, words of encouragement, or observations.
The Big Picture	To clearly communicate the counseling process—including eventual termination—with clients, counselors can keep a chart that visually tracks each session. This activity is especially useful with younger children. Invite clients to color a tiny picture or choose a sticker to place on the chart at the end of each session. During each visit, clients will then have a visual reminder of how many times they have visited as well as how many sessions they have left. Although the number of sessions may be uncertain early in counseling, as termination approaches, the counselor can highlight the anticipated final session so the child can see that the final session is approaching. As the young client completes the chart activity, the counselor can review what was done in the session or in past sessions. At the final session, counselors may want to give the completed chart to the client so he or she can keep it as a review of counseling.
Wish Upon a Star	In this activity, clients reflect on their goals, hopes, and dreams for the future; clients are oriented to a brighter future. Encourage clients to consider what they wish for their future selves. Discuss the ways these wishes may come true or be realized using goal setting and other skills learned during counseling. Clients can write the words on the stars—or draw pictures if they are younger—to represent their goals, hopes, and dreams for the future. Review the content on the stars as the client places them in a constellation shape on a larger piece of paper. Clients may also elect to save the stars in an envelope instead, or they may even stick them to a space of their choosing (e.g., their ceiling, over their bed, on a bathroom mirror).

Premature Termination

Although it is ideal to have a planned, natural termination, it is more typical that counseling ends prematurely. In fact, it is estimated that between 40% and 60% of counseling ends before clients have met their treatment goals (Baruch et al., 2009; Deakin et al., 2012; Schaeffer & Kaiser, 2013). Some research suggests that younger clients are at an even greater risk for premature termination than are adults (Swift & Greenberg, 2015). The nature of clients' presenting problems can also play a role in premature termination. Young clients who have disruptive behavior symptoms (e.g., aggressive behaviors, antisocial behaviors, problems at school), for example, are more likely to stop attending counseling (Deakin et al., 2012). Counselors should possess an understanding of the factors that contribute to premature termination and work to prevent its occurrence.

Premature termination can be initiated by the counselor, client, or parents, or it may occur for reasons out of the counselor's or client's control. Premature termination may also involve a client simply not returning to counseling. Some clients and their families may think that they should stop attending counseling because things are improving; they may not understand why it is important to bring counseling to a formal end. Common reasons for premature termination include:

- family transportation problems;
- a weak working alliance and a belief that counseling is not helpful;
- a mistaken belief that counseling is complete;
- child/family illness;
- family geographic relocation;
- changes to insurance;
- provided session limits (through third-party payers) are met;
- incompatible counselor/family hours;
- change in school schedule (i.e., school ends for summer break);
- various cultural and poverty-related barriers; and
- counselor-initiated reasons (e.g., relocation, illness, change in position, referral due to inability to meet client's needs).

Termination can be particularly challenging when it occurs suddenly and with little warning. Youth who experience premature termination will express their reactions in different ways. As occurs even with natural terminations, some may experience a resurgence of the symptoms or behaviors that initially brought them to counseling, and others may act out their strong emotions in negative ways. When one of the authors was leaving a position as a residential treatment center counselor to go to another agency, one of her adolescent clients ran away from the facility and repeatedly self-injured in an attempt to continue the relationship. The client had severe attachment issues secondary to a lifetime of sexual and physical abuse and neglect, and the end of the counseling relationship triggered her abandonment fears and anger, causing her to act out in an attempt to maintain the therapeutic relationship. In these situations, awareness, supervision, and consultation help to ensure the transition is handled in an optimal way. Whatever the reason for termination—and if possible—it is always better to have at least several sessions to process counseling coming to an end.

FAMILY EXPECTATIONS AND PREMATURE TERMINATION

Families that have unclear or mistaken expectations about a counselor's role and the counseling process may be less engaged and thus at risk for premature termination. Not surprisingly, if a young client's parents do not perceive counseling as helpful and if they do not see the value in counseling, they are more likely to prematurely remove their child from counseling (Deakin et al., 2012). Parents who do not understand counseling and its requirements (e.g., the expectation of between-session homework) may be limited in their ability to support their children in applying the skills they are learning. Parents who do not expect counseling to be helpful are also more likely to miss sessions and be tardy (Deakin et al., 2012). When parents are not engaged in counseling, it is less likely the child will be successful, thus reinforcing a system dynamic in which the child is viewed as "the problem."

Conversely, parents who expect counseling to be helpful are more likely to engage in counseling, attend sessions, and follow through on applying counseling concepts outside counseling sessions. Some of the predictors of family engagement in counseling are a two-parent household, stable financial resources, a steady insurance provider, and support from the community (e.g., supportive interactions with school systems, physicians, and/or social services agencies; Deakin et al., 2012). In addition, some research suggests that female youth tend to stay engaged in counseling longer than male youth, and clients who have been in counseling services for longer periods of time are also more likely to see counseling through and have a natural termination (Deakin et al., 2012).

To prevent premature termination, it is imperative, as discussed previously in this chapter, that counselors have an honest and open discussion about counselor, child, and parental counseling expectations early in counseling. Parents' expectations should be explored, and they should be educated about counseling and what will be required of them during the counseling process. Accurate expectations facilitate a productive counseling relationship. Many parents expect that all the work of counseling will occur between the counselor and the child, and they may resent any requests to participate in the counseling process. Some other parents may also genuinely overestimate counselors' ability to facilitate change apart from family involvement. A periodic review with parents of how the child is progressing and how many more sessions the counselor believes the child will need may help to orient families to the counseling trajectory and reduce premature termination.

CULTURE AND PREMATURE TERMINATION

There are also cultural considerations that may affect a young client's and his or her parents' expectations about counseling. Some research suggests that up to 69% of ethnic minority youth leave counseling prematurely, and as such, extra efforts should be made to engage this population (de Haan et al., 2014). Another premature termination risk factor is low SES (Deakin et al., 2012). Clients who come from low-income, ethnic minority, single-parent households with lower educational attainment, poor academic performance, a family history of mental illness, and government financial or housing support are more likely to drop out of counseling (Deakin et al., 2012).

Aspects of different cultures may contribute to distrust of those outside the family, and many cultures place a premium on secrets or "family business" being kept within the family unit. For example, in the Appalachian culture, there is a strong mistrust of counselors, and family secrets are fiercely guarded. Although the idea of sharing family secrets with an outsider feels alien to people in some cultures, this sharing is central to the counseling process. Knowing that their child may be revealing personal family information to a counselor can cause some families to feel anger, discomfort, or embarrassment, or it may incite feelings of shame and guilt. Counselors have an obligation to attempt to prevent unnecessary premature terminations, and they should be especially sensitive to cultural factors that contribute to mistrust of counselors and counseling in general.

STRATEGIES FOR AVOIDING PREMATURE TERMINATION

Unplanned and/or undesired terminations are often the most difficult for both clients and counselors. Premature terminations most often occur secondary to outside circumstances apart from the counselor, but measures can be taken to minimize the risk of premature termination and thus prevent its occurrence. The development of a strong therapeutic relationship early on with clients and their families, an exploration of the benefits of counseling, a description of how counseling works, and clear expectations of all involved parties may help to prevent early termination when working with people from diverse backgrounds (Deakin et al., 2012). Termination situations that involve parents having unrealistic expectations are usually avoidable, and these can be corrected by imparting information about counseling and educating families. As previously discussed, the use of a brief assessment tool to gauge client and parental satisfaction with counseling may also open the lines of communication and prevent termination.

The most basic way to prevent termination is through the development of the working alliance. It is just as important to establish and maintain a good working alliance with parents as it is with the child. It can be challenging to connect with some parents, especially those who abuse or neglect their children or those who are mandated to counseling and/or have little investment in counseling. It is important though that both the child and the family feel equally connected to the counselor because a relationship imbalance may threaten continuation in counseling secondary to triangulation (i.e., between the counselor and child or between the counselor and parents).

Neophyte counselors may question their competence and feel particularly nervous about working with parents and communicating and enforcing expectations about their role in counseling. However, it is in young clients' best interest for counselors to work through reactions to parents (via personal counseling, consultation, and/or supervision) and develop a strong working alliance with the entire family (Rappleyea et al., 2009). When parents feel alienated from the counseling process or do not understand or agree with the goals and aims of counseling and when they are not kept abreast of the child's progress or asked for their input, they may be more likely to prematurely terminate (Swift & Greenberg, 2015). An example of this is a parent who removes her child from counseling and then reports, "All they did was color in counseling." Education about the methods used to help children to reach their goals, seeking out weekly reports and feedback from parents, and providing parents with regular reports of progress are just several ways that parents can be engaged and thus prevent premature termination. The authors suggest that counselors meet with parents either alone, or together with the child, for at least 5 to 10 minutes of each session to ensure there is strong communication, an opportunity to receive updates and review progress, and to ensure the working alliance is constantly tended to. In summary, strategies for reducing the potential for premature termination risk include:

- ensuring counselor/client/family expectations are communicated;
- forming a strong working alliance with clients and their families;
- regularly checking in with clients/families regarding their satisfaction with the counseling process;
- avoiding triangulation with the parents or the child;
- keeping open lines of communication with the family and maintaining regular contact;
- working to understand the cultural preferences and cultural needs of clients/families;
- clearly communicating session limits with clients/families early on;
- reminding clients/families of upcoming appointment dates and times;
- establishing a supportive, predictable, and comfortable counseling environment; and
- working collaboratively with schools, physicians, social services, and other resource people available to clients/families.

Termination and Referral

Regardless of the reason for termination, as part of the termination process, counselors must provide clients with a referral to another provider if they have a need for continued services (ACA, 2014). Client referral may be due to the client needing a different level of care (e.g., a step up to a more restrictive setting such as residential treatment or a step down from in-home therapy to counseling based in an agency), or it may be required because the counselor believes he or she does not have the resources needed to help the client.

Counselors must be aware of their unique personal scope of practice and know when clients would benefit from a referral to another provider (ACA, 2014). Particularly with younger children who may be less verbal, it can be difficult to determine and assess whether clients are making progress at an appropriate pace. In situations in which counselors are concerned, consultation and supervision are helpful resources. If the client is not progressing, referral to another counselor may be warranted. In situations where a counselor must refer a client because of an inability to meet the client's needs, a client's initial reactions might include feelings of sadness, hurt, anger, betrayal, or even anger (Harrison, 2009; Headley et al., 2015). It is important that counselors allow young clients to express these emotions. It is also helpful for the family to be involved in referral discussions because they can reinforce the reasons the child is being referred to a new provider. Even in referral situations, counselors should initiate a meaningful termination using the strategies discussed in this termination discussion to give the counseling experience some finality.

Counselors who work within an agency setting generally have ample professionals to whom they can refer. Counselors in settings where there are no other providers, or those in, say, rural areas, may need to dig deep and do research to find the proper referral sources. Many providers have long waiting lists, and it is important that counselors provide a referral as soon as they become aware that one is required.

As the end of the school year approaches, school counselors must consider termination, and they should begin to make plans for students who they counsel to transition into work with a community provider. School counselors may want to incorporate a summer-themed termination activity. For example, a young client can draw a sand bucket and various sand shoveling tools/toys. The client might write or talk about how each of the tools represents different skills that he or she will use during the summer. The picture can serve as a reminder and a cue for what was learned in counseling.

Summary

This chapter provided an overview of the individual counseling process and the important foundations of youth counseling with an eye to the early, middle, and later stages of counseling. The essential ingredients of good youth counseling were reviewed, and effective communication techniques were provided by developmental level.

Initially, considerations specific to the early stages of counseling were explored. These considerations included a discussion of the importance of creating a comfortable counseling environment with an appropriate office setting in which young people feel relaxed and welcome. The intake process—gaining informed consent, discussing confidentiality, performing assessments, ensuring client and counselor expectations are clear and realistic, structuring counseling sessions, and building a working alliance with clients and families—were

also discussed as being important in the early stages of counseling.

Next, important considerations and aspects of the working stage of counseling were reviewed. Optimal counselor communication and interviewing styles were discussed, as were the ways that counselors can facilitate clients' desires to make changes using motivational interviewing and motivational enhancement strategies.

Finally, the later part of this chapter focused on counseling termination. The unique considerations that relate to terminating counseling with young people were reviewed. Termination readiness, reasons for natural and premature termination, counselor strategies for avoiding premature termination, and creative ideas to facilitate successful and fulfilling termination experiences with young clients were discussed.

MyLab Counseling: Counseling Children and Adolescents

In the Topic 3 Assignments: *Youth Counseling Foundations*, try Application Exercise 3.2: *The Structure and Process of Youth Counseling* and Licensure Quiz 3.2: *Foundations of the Counseling Process.*

Then try Application Exercise 3.3: *The Therapeutic Relationship* and Licensure Quiz 3.3: *Considerations for Counseling Youth.*

CHAPTER 4

Ethical and Legal Foundations

Children have the right to:

> Privacy and confidentiality and to understand confidentiality limits
>
> Be involved in decision making and goal setting
>
> To be protected from abuse and neglect
>
> Be respected and told the truth
>
> To understand counseling methods and tasks and understand why they are being used
>
> To leave counseling if it is not helping or otherwise successful

— From the Convention on the Rights of the Child (United Nations, 1989)

When counseling youth, children's rights should always be a counselor's top priority. People often remark that "these days" things are worse than ever for children. However, there has never been a time in history when children in the United States have had so many rights or such broad access to supportive resources. In the late 20th century, laws were enacted that protect young people and place an increased emphasis on their rights apart from their families' rights. As an example, consider that it was not until 1976 that all states implemented laws requiring all professionals to report cases of child sexual abuse.

Young people's rights are expanding, and counselors play an important role in safeguarding their rights. As children's rights expand, counselors are required to understand and consider additional laws. Legal and ethical considerations can be intimidating and confusing to counselors. When counseling youth, these frustrations can be especially pronounced because counselors frequently experience conflicts between their ethical obligations and legally dictated requirements (Salo, 2015). From both ethical and legal perspectives, young people's rights can be unclear as counselors must—in addition to considering young people's unique developmental circumstances—consider parental and guardian rights. School counselors have an added level of complexity in that they have a school administration and other children in the school to consider. Further complicating counselor decision making is the fact that the laws related to minors' rights change with some frequency, and navigating these changes can feel like "walking through shifting sands" (W. Hegarty, personal communication, February 23, 2017).

Counselors face legal and ethical considerations in nearly every encounter they have with young clients and their parents, and these matters should always be at the forefront of counselors' minds. Consider the following examples that highlight the considerations counselors regularly navigate:

- A 6-year-old child tells his school counselor that his mother spanked him with a belt. Does the counselor need to report this to child protective services?
- A counselor's 16-year-old client mentions she has been engaging in nonsuicidal self-injury, but her parents do not know this. Does the counselor need to tell her parents?
- A school counselor gets a call from a 7-year-old child's father who asks the teacher for extra time on exams because the child was recently diagnosed with generalized anxiety disorder and has test anxiety. How should the school counselor proceed?

- A mother brings a child in for counseling and states that the child needs counseling secondary to ongoing abuse they both experienced by the child's father. She explains she is in the process of divorcing the child's father and she'd like you to testify to the psychological impacts of the abuse on the child so she can gain custody. Can the counselor testify in court regarding the effects of the abuse on the child? Can the counselor make a custody recommendation to the courts?

In counseling, both minors and guardians have important rights that should be honored and respected. When counseling minor clients, the *ACA Code of Ethics* (American Counseling Association [ACA], 2014) suggests that it is important for counselors to respect the rights and responsibilities of parents and include them in the counseling process. As suggested throughout this text, parents can be important collaborators; they play a critical role in supporting their children and should be included in counseling, as appropriate. Some even suggest that many counseling-related conflicts can be avoided if counselors approach parents as partners, not as adversaries, in the counseling process, especially around minor privacy concerns (Remley & Herlihy, 2016). Parents play an important role in counseling success, and for youth to bridge the skills they learn in counseling to other environments, parental involvement is paramount.

The ACA also states that counselors should balance the rights of minors with the rights of parents. Parents have many rights and these include:

- participating in counseling and helping to make decisions and set goals for their child;
- making decisions that they think are in their child's best interest;
- having access to information that pertains to their child's welfare;
- seeking and giving consent for their child to enter counseling; and
- releasing confidential information about their child.

In terms of minors' rights, counselors have an ethical obligation to provide information to youth that will help them to be active participants in counseling (ACA, 2014; Corey, Corey, Corey, & Callanan, 2015). When working with youth, the ACA (2014) advises counselors to seek the assent of their clients and include them in decision making, as appropriate. As discussed elsewhere in this text, a collaborative, cooperative approach can help to engage young clients in counseling, especially when they are required by the adults in their lives to attend counseling.

Minor is the legal term commonly used to describe young people who are not considered legally capable of taking care of themselves or are not legally responsible for themselves. Although most consider a minor to be one who is younger than 18 years, the age requirement for minors varies from state to state with the upper range being 18 to 21 years of age and other states indicating 16-year-olds are at the age of consent in certain circumstances (Corey et al., 2015). When legal matters are discussed in this chapter, the term *minor* is generally used to refer to children and adolescents, and either the legal terms **guardian** or *parents* (with the assumption that the parents are the guardians) are generally used to refer to young people's legal caregivers.

This chapter explores the prominent ethical and legal issues associated with youth counseling. More specifically, readers are provided with information related to basic ethical and legal concepts, confidentiality and informed consent/assent, counselor competence, child maltreatment reporting and management, custody considerations, and multiple relationships. Practical recommendations for how counselors might prevent ethics problems and navigate ethical and legal matters are also provided.

DEFINING ETHICAL AND LEGAL MATTERS

Before reviewing common legal and ethical matters, it is important to understand the difference between ethics and the law. Counseling ethics relates to counselor actions that are in the best interest of their clients. **Ethics**, in the context of counseling, involves counselors behaving in moral, virtuous, or principled ways and taking professional actions that support clients' well-being. As a profession, counselors have come to a consensus and developed guidelines regarding the ethical behaviors that should guide their decision making, and these behaviors are outlined in the profession's various codes of ethics. The ethics code counselors use will depend on their professional background and license/certification. These ethics codes may include those of the National Board for Certified Counselors (2012), American School Counselor Association (ASCA; 2010), American Association for Marriage and Family Therapy (2012), ACA (2014), American Psychological Association (2010), National Association of Social Workers (2008), American Art Therapy Association (2013b), and American Association of Pastoral Counselors (2012), among others.

The ethical codes provide *general* information counselors can use to inform their decision making, and all address similar ethics topics such as confidentiality, competence, and multiple relationships. Codes of ethics provide guidance on how counselors should behave professionally, lay out a standard of practice to which counselors can aspire, and encourage client care, all of which facilitates a favorable impression of professional counselors and the services they provide (Herlihy & Corey, 2015).

Association and certification boards interpret codes of ethics and make judgments regarding counselors' violations of such ethics. Ethics codes are aspirational in that they encourage practices that are sometimes difficult to quantify yet are ideal (e.g., being culturally sensitive in applying diagnoses to clients). The ethical codes that guide counselors' practice may, at times, conflict with their personal values, but because clients' needs must always come first, counselors must avoid imparting their values onto clients (Remley & Herlihy, 2016).

The **law** is different from ethics in that laws are created by the legislature (elected officials), enforced by law enforcement officers, and interpreted by officials within the legal system, not members or associations of one's profession. Laws indicate the minimum standards of behavior that society will tolerate before legal involvement will be required. The violation of laws can result in civil (i.e., the system of law concerned with private relations between members of a community) or criminal (i.e., system of law concerned with the punishment of those who commit crimes) penalties. Licensure boards are government agencies charged with enforcing the laws that govern counselor practice, and board members make judgments regarding counselors' violations of such laws. Many states adopt a profession's ethics code as part of their laws and rules that govern counselor practice, but states also have separate laws and rules that may conflict with professional ethics codes. Further complicating matters is that there are federal laws that may affect how counselors approach different situations.

When counseling youth, conflicts between ethical and legal issues sometimes arise. As an example of how ethics and the law can collide, as of this writing, the state of Tennessee had passed legislation that would allow counselors to use *personally held principles* as a reason to refuse to counsel clients. An application of this to youth is that a counselor might refuse to counsel an adolescent who wants to explore her identity as a lesbian. Section C.5 of the *ACA Code of Ethics* (ACA, 2014) explicitly prohibits licensed professional counselors from discriminating against those who seek their care. Further, Section A.11.b states, "Counselors refrain from referring prospective and current clients based solely on the counselor's personally held values, attitudes, beliefs, and behaviors." Because Tennessee law allows counselors to *not* see a client based on his or her personal beliefs, there is a conflict between the *ACA Code of Ethics* and the law. Conflicts between ethics and law can be confusing, and again, these matters are especially pronounced in matters related to youth counseling.

The professional literature provides little guidance to counselors on their decision making related to youth counseling, and the *ACA Code of Ethics* (ACA, 2014) only touches on youth-specific matters. A thoughtful review of the ethics considerations associated with youth counseling can invite many more questions than answers, and in this way ethics can be a frustrating topic for beginning counselors. This chapter reviews the youth-specific ethical and legal issues that counselors most frequently encounter in their practice.

THE CASE OF JESSICA

A counselor at a community agency is meeting with a new client, Jessica, who is a 15-year-old female. Jessica's parents did not present for counseling with her. Instead, her mom dropped her off at the center entrance and left to run errands.

What are some of the legal matters the counselor should be considering?

What are some of the ethics matters the counselor should be considering?

Discussion of the Case

After reading this chapter, you will have the information you need to know how to best respond to this situation. The *ACA Code of Ethics* (ACA, 2014) suggests that parents should be included in the counseling process as appropriate. The counselor will need to talk to the parent(s) and Jessica and review informed consent information related to confidentiality, consent to enter counseling, and payment information (e.g., the release of diagnostic information required to obtain third-party reimbursement), among other matters. The law in the state where the counselor lives will also be an important factor because some states require guardian consent to counseling, whereas other states do not require guardian consent if the client is seeking support for certain matters (e.g., pregnancy counseling). Still, some other states allow a client to be seen for counseling for a predetermined number of sessions before formal guardian consent is required.

COMPETENCE

Competence is having the knowledge, skills, and diligence required to effectively function and meet professional expectations and standards (Remley & Herlihy, 2016). Competence is not something one has and retains; rather, it is part of an ongoing process, and counselors who work with youth must commit to being lifelong learners (Corey et al., 2015).

It is not unusual for counseling programs—and programs in other professional disciplines—to require or offer perhaps only one class on counseling youth. As of this writing, the Council for Accreditation of Counseling and Related Educational Programs, the counseling profession's accreditation body, offers specialties in addiction counseling; clinical mental health counseling; clinical rehabilitation counseling; career counseling; college and student affairs counseling; school counseling; and marriage, couples, and family counseling, but it does not have a specialty in child and adolescent counseling. Despite this lack of youth-specific training, it is common for counselors, over the course of their careers, to counsel youth and their families. It is often assumed that coursework with a primary focus on adults can be generalized to youth. For many counseling students, this text and the associated class may be the only committed exposure they have to the topic of counseling youth, and this exposure will likely put many readers ahead of the curve in terms of understanding how to work with youth.

To counsel youth, counselors must possess adequate professional education, training, and supervised practice. The primary reason for having ethical and legal standards related to competence is to ensure the safety and welfare of clients. Competence can also prevent malpractice and harm to clients. Particularly important to working with children and adolescents is having strong knowledge of the ethical standards and state laws that relate to youth because helping professionals who work with this population are more likely to incur circumstances in which ethical and legal competency is imperative.

As mentioned, the professional ethics codes are generic and do not provide much guidance specific to working with youth. In addition, no professional competencies that delineate the knowledge, skills, and abilities required to be a youth counselor have been developed. Finally, the empirical literature on evidence-based practices for use with youth is relatively limited. Taken together, counselors are left with a lack of resources and guidance to use to support their practices when counseling youth.

The material provided in this text provides a starting place for understanding what is needed to effectively help youth. Education on youth development, theories that guide practice with youth, evidence-based approaches and techniques that can help address youth-specific problems in living, and a comprehensive model for structuring youth counseling can all help counselors in establishing their competence. However, staying current with developing best practices and updated information about youth counseling is essential to ensuring ongoing competence (ACA, 2014).

MINORS' RIGHTS AND LEGAL CONSENT TO COUNSELING

Counselors who counsel youth must be aware of their guardians' legal rights while also balancing their ethical obligations to their young clients (Hussey, 2008; Remley & Herlihy, 2016). As stated, at times, these legal and ethical considerations conflict. One of the issues that highlights the complexity of legal and ethical considerations is the ability of minors to begin counseling without parental consent. In most states, minors cannot consent to treatment; a guardian must consent on the minor's behalf. This protection is in place because it is believed that young people, because of their limited reasoning capacity and developmental level, may not be able to make decisions that are in their best interests (Remley & Herlihy, 2016). It is reasoned that, ideally, guardians can best make the decision for youth to enter counseling and safeguard youth's interests during the counseling process (Hussey, 2008). Age of consent is also important when counseling those who have intellectual or developmental delays or any diagnoses that may make them more vulnerable to exploitation or harm. In these cases, states may have exceptions written into their laws related to the age of consent for counseling, with ages of consent being older for those who have certain disabilities.

There are, however, some exceptions to minors agreeing to treatment consent. Some states allow minors who are deemed as mature (e.g., those who are married or in the armed services) to consent to counseling, and in some states minors may be legally able to consent to treatment for specific problems (e.g., counseling related to sexually transmitted diseases, substance abuse, or pregnancy and/or birth control). The rationale for allowing youth to have access to counseling without guardian consent is that they may not otherwise seek or receive needed counseling services, and this guarantee of privacy may empower them to seek help (Corey et al., 2015). Emancipated youth who are younger than 18 years or those who have been legally departed from their guardians and are now living independently also generally hold the legal rights to provide self-consent for counseling services.

There are few exceptions though, and generally the law deems individuals under a certain age (generally 18) not sufficiently mature to make the decision to begin counseling. In some states (e.g., California), however, youth are able to consent for their own mental health treatment when they are old enough to cognitively understand the limits of confidentiality, which is typically early adolescence (National Center for Youth Law, 2010). Counselors should be aware of the laws related to treatment consent age in the state in which they practice because they are all different.

INFORMED CONSENT/ASSENT

Counselors are required, as part of the intake process, to ensure clients understand the nature of counseling and make an informed decision around whether they want to continue in counseling. Clients have a basic right to understand the limitations and advantages of counseling and how the counseling process will unfold (Remley & Herlihy, 2016). The formal action of consenting to counseling—with a full awareness of all that is involved—is referred to as **informed consent**, and this consent serves as an agreement between all parties involved that they understand what will happen as the counseling experience moves forward (Remley & Herlihy, 2016). An important aspect of informed consent is voluntary consent, and one must be competent to give such consent.

Section A.2 of the *ACA Code of Ethics* (ACA, 2014) addresses informed consent and indicates that counselors should provide clients with adequate information about the counseling process. In Section A.2.d, it is stated that:

> counselors seek the assent of clients to services and include them in decision making as appropriate. Counselors recognize the need to balance the ethical rights of clients to make choices, their capacity to give consent or assent to receive services, and parental or familial legal rights and responsibilities to protect these clients and make decisions on their behalf.

Section B.4.b, when referencing couples and family counseling, states that counselors clearly define who is considered "the client" and that the expectations and limitations of confidentiality are discussed relative to these roles.

Informed consent procedures should be thorough. Young clients' parents are required to sign informed consent paperwork but typically have a limited understanding of what the information actually means. As such, parents and young clients (as appropriate to their developmental level) should both be engaged in a discussion of informed consent–related considerations. The ethics code also suggests the importance of young clients playing a role in **assent**—or generally agreeing to—counseling, even though they may not be able to legally consent to participation in counseling. Client assent is something that occurs in addition to a guardian's legal consent.

Because formal informed consent forms are often wordy and difficult to comprehend, it may be helpful to have a simple consent form that is appropriate to the child's age and developmental level. Having young clients sign this form and discussing it with them is one way to punctuate the importance of these matters and to communicate to youth that their voice matters in the counseling process. Counseling informed consent generally addresses certain elements, and these include:

- limits of confidentiality;
- the counselor's theoretical approach and commonly used techniques and methods;
- information about the counselor's license and credentials and the government agency or organization that oversees these (e.g., a state licensing board, National Board for Certified Counselors);
- child maltreatment reporting mandates;
- notice of privacy practices and clients' rights;
- any coordination of treatment;
- procedures related to emergency situations;
- procedures related to missed appointments; and
- procedures related to payments and missed payments.

Clinical Toolbox 4.1

In the Pearson eText, click here to review an example of youth counseling informed consent form language.

At the onset of counseling, counselors should clarify the relationship they will have with the youth and each person involved in the youth's counseling. Counselors should also review how they will share information, and all parties involved should understand what information will be shared with whom and under what circumstances.

Issues of consent can become especially complicated when parents are divorced. Some suggest that, ideally, in a divorce situation, both parents should provide consent to counsel the child (Welfel, 2010). Counselors should also be aware of the rights of noncustodial parents because they may have a requirement to be involved in counseling informed consent decision making (Welfel, 2010).

Counselors should be sensitive to the fact that as young clients age or develop, the ways they interact with the parents may shift, and thus informed consent related to the type and frequency of contact will need to be reviewed. Consider an adolescent who on entering into counseling engages in high-risk behaviors. The counselor may have weekly contact with the parents regarding the child's day-to-day behaviors and actions. Ideally, over time, the youth will develop more adaptive behaviors, and this may result in counselors needing less frequent communication and contact with the parents regarding the youth's behaviors.

Another important consideration is that as youth grow and develop psychologically, counselors should revisit discussions related to informed consent; consent is not a static event but a fluid process. Particularly with age, youth may develop an increased capacity for autonomy and independence, and this may require an increased emphasis on the child's need for privacy. As such, ethical practice will require that counselors revisit earlier informed consent–related discussions and renegotiate boundaries as appropriate.

All discussion of informed consent must occur in a developmentally appropriate fashion. When explaining informed consent matters, counselors should be thorough, and clients should be provided with examples of different concepts and have opportunities to ask questions. It is helpful to review informed consent information with youth and their guardians at different times.

CONFIDENTIALITY

Privacy is a broad term that refers to the rights of people to decide what information about them will be shared or withheld from others (Remley & Herlihy, 2016). **Confidentiality** is an ethical concept that is founded on the idea of privacy as applied in the context of professional relationships. In other words, it is basically the idea that counselors have an obligation to protect clients' privacy and the promise they made to them to keep the information they share in counseling private (Remley & Herlihy, 2016). **Privileged communication** is a legal concept that refers to laws that protect clients from having their confidential counseling information shared in courts of law without their express permission (Remley & Herlihy, 2016).

No place is the push and pull between ethical and legal issues more apparent than when considering minors' confidentiality rights. Parents who consent for their children to receive counseling generally have the right to be made aware of all information relayed in counseling. As such, counselors are placed in a bind; legally, parents have well-defined rights, but counselors generally perceive that their primary ethical obligation is to their young clients (Remley & Herlihy, 2016).

Almost all counselors would suggest that young people should have the right to some degree of privacy related to their counseling experience. Confidentiality helps clients to feel safe and secure in the counseling relationship and facilitates the development of a trusting relationship that is required for counseling to be successful. Ideally, counseling should facilitate young people's autonomy. In addition, counseling fosters a youth's autonomy and emerging independence, and to do this a young person needs some degree of privacy. However, minors' legal rights to confidentiality are very limited. Counselors can be placed in a bind in that they want to support their clients' emerging autonomy and independence, yet the law may not allow for this. Counselors have an ethical obligation to safeguard minors' privacy and a legal obligation to facilitate youth safety and protect parents' or guardians' privacy rights (Remley & Herlihy, 2016).

Counselors should consider the youth's developmental level when considering confidentiality. Younger children may not understand the concept of privacy. When counseling younger children, issues associated with confidentiality rarely arise; however, when counseling adolescents, counselors may struggle to manage the balance between a client's privacy and legal requirements to share information with parents or guardians.

Counselors should let young clients guide their thinking around privacy and understand that some youth may not mind their parents being privy to information that counselors may see as private. Counselors should also be aware that sometimes youth share information with the intent that the information will be communicated to their parents.

As part of the informed consent process, it is important that counselors review confidentiality expectations and requirements with the child and family. Legally—in most states—young clients have no confidentiality rights; parents have access to their child's records and any information shared in counseling (Vernon, 2009). However, as stated, many young clients—particularly adolescents—do not want their parents to be made aware of the personal experiences they share in counseling. It is helpful to talk with the family about how important confidentiality is in building trust and a sense of safety in the therapeutic relationship. Without trust, it is impossible to develop a positive therapeutic relationship, and the relationship is the foundation of and necessary to the success of individual counseling.

Parents should be made aware if their child is engaging in behaviors that are harmful or potentially harmful (e.g., suicidal or homicidal thoughts or intentions). There are, however, many muddy topics around which reporting is less clear; the boundary between what to share with parents and what *not* to share with them can be thin, particularly for adolescents. For example, consider consensual adolescent sexual activity. Is sexual activity between young people harmful or potentially harmful? Sexual activity could result in pregnancy or the contraction of a sexually transmitted disease. Is sexual activity then something that a counselor should share with parents? The answer to this question is much less clear. Seeing sexual activity as normal and private, some parents do not want to know about their adolescents' sexual activity; yet, other parents, for various personal, cultural, or religions reasons, may want to be made aware of their children's sexual activity. There are innumerable scenarios counselors must navigate and make judgments around in terms of youth confidentiality.

With regard to confidentiality, what is most important is that young clients and parents are aware of what information will be kept confidential between the client and the counselor. An awareness of the boundaries of confidentiality provides young clients with an opportunity to make informed decisions about what they share with their counselors and to feel safe within the counseling relationship. When working with adolescents, one approach to confidentiality is to speak with the client and the parents about the complex issues that most frequently present in counseling and to discuss and assess their disclosure preferences. If parents are separated, divorced, or not living together, counselors should attempt to—if appropriate—meet

- Suicidal ideation/intent
- Homicidal ideation/intent
- Sexual abuse or assault
- Physical abuse
- Neglect
- Nonsuicidal self-injury
- Reports of abuse of a minor (other than the client) or a protected population (e.g., someone who is intellectually disabled or an older adult)
- Plans/intent to run away
- Drug and alcohol use
- Sneaking out of the house
- Sexual activity
- Pregnancy
- Bullying/relational aggression
- Violence in romantic relationships
- Maladaptive eating behaviors that can be physically harmful (e.g., anorexia nervosa, bulimia)
- Criminal activity
- School truancy

FIGURE 4.1   Harmful Youth Behaviors That Counselors May Need to Report to Parents

with them together to facilitate consistency in expectations related to counselor disclosure and confidentiality. It is also helpful to document the agreed-on expectations and have the parents and child sign an agreement indicating that they consent to these expectations. Figure 4.1 shows a list of harmful—or potentially harmful—behaviors that counselors frequently encounter and that may be discussed in the context of counselor–client confidentiality.

When considering the complex issues associated with youth confidentiality and counseling, it can be helpful to consider the practical, legal, and ethics aspects of each unique situation. Counselors sometimes struggle with how much information they should share with parents, but they must remember that if they choose to withhold information that a client discloses, they are assuming full legal responsibility should some implicating circumstance occur (e.g., the counselor knew a child was using drugs, did not inform the parents, and the child overdoses). A parent who consents on the minor's behalf generally has the right to know the content of the child's treatment, and thus it may be better to be conservative around what information is shared. In other words, if a counselor is not sure, it may be better to share the information with the parents. It is also important for counselors to talk to adolescents before, during, and after a disclosure.

Youth need to be able to trust that not everything they say in counseling will be relayed back to their parents, and counselors must ensure that youth confidentiality is upheld while sufficiently informing caregivers of the youth's needs and progress (Remley & Herlihy, 2016). Counselors might choose to involve guardians in various ways when it comes to client disclosure and progress updates. Some counselors might choose to have guardians attend the first few minutes or last few minutes of a session with their child. The length of time the parent spends in session could be dictated by client need and degree of parental involvement in counseling. Time spent with parents might be therapeutic (e.g., working to increase positive communication practices between parent and child) and/or informative (e.g., the guardian is given an update on client's progress) in nature. Counselors might choose to provide information to the consenting parent with the child in the room or in private. In addition, it might be therapeutic to allow the youth to provide a progress update to the parent with the support and guidance of the counselor present. Counselors are challenged to continually assess and reassess how they will handle client confidentiality. Active discussion and regular communication with youth and parents about confidentiality practices is an effective way to ensure all parties are satisfied with how confidentiality is being handled.

THE CASE OF TREVON

A counselor at a community child and family agency has been working with Trevon on and off for the past 4 years. In early adolescence, when Trevon's father died, Trevon engaged in illegal and disruptive behaviors. These behaviors remitted; however, more recently, Trevon has experienced a renewed escalation in disruptive behaviors. At present, Trevon is 17 years old.

What are some of the parent–child confidentiality-related matters the counselor should be considering?

Discussion of the Case

When Trevon was 13 years old and right after he was released from the juvenile justice system, the counselor and Trevon's mother would regularly speak about Trevon's behavior. Trevon made positive progress. At the age of 14, Trevon asked that the counselor not speak with his mother or share information about their sessions with her. The counselor reviewed confidentiality considerations with Trevon, and they reached a compromise: The counselor would speak to Trevon's mother only when he was present. However, matters became more complicated over time as Trevon began to again demonstrate disruptive behaviors. The counselor came to believe that Trevon's mother needed to be privy to some of this behavior, but Trevon did not want to share such information. The counselor presented his struggles to Trevon, and despite processing this information and his concerns, Trevon still refused to allow him to share the information. After discussion, they agreed that Trevon would share this information with his mother and that the counselor would follow up with a phone call to his mother. This case demonstrates how confidentiality with youth—and how it is handled—can be an evolving and fluctuating process. It also demonstrates the importance of ongoing discussion with the youth and parents on how confidentiality matters will be handled.

INFORMED CONSENT/ASSENT AND CONFIDENTIALITY IN SCHOOL SETTINGS

As indicated, professional counseling ethics codes and laws require parental consent for youth to engage in counseling. As part of the consent process, counseling goals are clearly detailed and explained, as are the limits of confidentiality and how clients can voluntarily participate or exit the services. School counselors, however, do *not* generally have a legal obligation to obtain parental consent for counseling unless indicated in their state's laws and rules (Corey et al., 2015). Schools often have a student handbook in which they describe the services—such as counseling—that are made available to students, and parents generally have a right to request the child *not* receive specified services (Stone, 2014).

Section A.2 of the *Ethical Standards for School Counselors* (ASCA, 2010) suggests that informed consent to enter counseling is generally difficult and sometimes even impossible for school counselors to attain. To truly consent to counseling, students must have knowledge of all components of informed consent, voluntarily engage in the counseling services being provided, and be competent to understand the implications of engaging in counseling. However, because of their developmental levels, most young people do not hit all these targets, and they are unable to appreciate the full consequences of entering into counseling (Stone, 2014). Following are some strategies school counselors might use when pursuing youth informed consent (Stone, 2014):

- Understand that informed consent—from youth and parents—is aspirational but nearly impossible to obtain in a school setting.
- Do not provide counseling services if the potential risks outweigh the benefits.
- Try to obtain consent, but understand that true informed consent—when working with youth—is elusive.
- Provide multiple opportunities for students to ask questions and ask them questions to make sure they understand informed consent information.
- If a student is pushed to counseling (e.g., by an educator or guardian), avoid coercing the student or trying to persuade him or her to talk with you.

- Be persistent in attempting to obtain written or oral permission from a parent or guardian for counseling services.
- Be sensitive to the role that culture (e.g., language, cultural expectations related to counseling) plays in the informed consent process.
- Understand that consent to enter into and consent to stay in counseling—or informed consent—is not a static ritual but a process that is repeated as needed and appropriate.

In terms of confidentiality, school counselors must balance the interests of students, the school system, and youth guardians, and as such, confidentiality is a struggle for all school counselors (Corey et al., 2015). The *Ethical Standards for School Counselors* states that counselors "recognize their primary ethical obligation for confidentiality is to the students but balance that obligation with an understanding of parents'/guardians' legal and inherent rights to be the guiding voice in their children's lives" (ASCA 2010, Section A.2.d). School counselors have an obligation to protect minors' confidentiality to the extent possible, while also being aware of parental rights to information. Historically, the extension of privacy rights has belonged to the parent (even in cases when the child requests confidentiality; Hermann, Remley, & Huey, 2010), and judicial decisions have protected parental rights to information (Isaacs & Stone, 1999).

School counselors should be clear with students about the limits of confidentiality, as well as the situations or presented material that would need to be shared with an outside party or the student's guardian. With regard to parents, ASCA (2010) states that school counselors should make parents aware of the "confidential nature of the counseling relationship between the counselor and the student" (Section B.2.a). Even when school counselors need to share information with school personnel or parents, they should do so in the least intrusive manner possible and only share necessary information (Corey et al., 2015).

CHILD MALTREATMENT REPORTING

When counseling youth, their safety should always be a counselor's first priority (Kress, Adamson, Paylo, DeMarco, & Bradley, 2012). In the United States, all states have mandated reporting laws that require counselors—as mandated reporters—to report any incidences of suspected child maltreatment, which includes abuse and neglect, to a governmental agency. **Child abuse** includes physical, emotional, or sexual abuse (Centers for Disease Control and Prevention [CDC], 2017a). **Neglect** involves the failure of caregivers to provide adequate emotional and physical care for a child (CDC, 2017b). Child abuse typically receives more attention than neglect, which is unfortunate due to the well-documented higher rates of neglect. The most recent report from the U.S. Department of Health and Human Services (USDHHS; 2016) on child maltreatment rates suggests that of the 3.2 million cases of reported and alleged child abuse and neglect that occur each year, 75% of the reports involved allegations of neglect, 17% physical abuse, and 8% percent sexual abuse. In the United States in 2014, estimates indicate that 1,580 children died of abuse and neglect at a rate of 2.13 per 100,000 children in the national population (USDHHS, 2016).

It is important to recognize that child maltreatment may be initiated by another youth and that youth-initiated child abuse generally needs to be reported (depending on the jurisdiction) as with adult-initiated abuse. In other words, laws do *not* specify or suggest that abuse of a child by a child is exempt from reporting. According to the National Child Traumatic Stress Network (2009), about one third of all cases of child sexual abuse involve a youth perpetrator, usually someone known to the child and often a close relative such as a sibling or cousin. Because the child perpetrator is generally known to the parents and is often another child in the family, a relative, or a child in the neighborhood, child-to-child abuse is likely underreported (National Center for Victims of Crime, n.d.; USDHHS, 2016).

One consideration related to child abuse reporting is culture. It is important to recognize that norms regarding acceptable discipline and child punishment vary across cultures (Lansford, 2010). In general, Americans approve of the use of corporal punishment (e.g., washing children's mouths out with soap, spanking or hitting children with some type of an instrument; Aronson-Fontes, 2005). It is often reported that Blacks of African and Caribbean descent are more likely to use physical punishment in general and to use an instrument as part of corporal punishment (e.g., a belt or a switch; Aronson-Fontes, 2005). Also of note is that the use of corporal punishment is related to parents' religion, economic status, current stress, and educational levels, and not surprisingly, those who adhere to conservative religious beliefs, live in stressful environments and/or poverty, have lower levels of education, and reside in the South are more likely to use corporal punishment; thus, these findings should be considered in this larger context (Aronson-Fontes, 2005). Regardless of cultural norms and practices, acts of child maltreatment—as defined by one's jurisdiction—must be legally reported, and it is not a counselor's responsibility to determine how a child protective services agency might respond to cultural considerations.

Counselors' Personal Reactions to Reporting

It can be uncomfortable for counselors to report suspected child maltreatment, and counselors must be aware of their personal reactions and how these feelings could affect their judgment related to reporting. Most commonly, counselors may not report because of a fear of breaking confidentiality and the legal ramifications of such a breach (Corey et al., 2015). Counselors may believe their clients or their families will stop trusting them if they report, and related to this, they may fear retaliation from the family. Counselors may make excuses for why the abuse or neglect occurred (e.g., the parent is under a lot of stress, it was an accident, the client's culture condones physical discipline and punishment), and this may get in the way of counselors' willingness to report. Also, more seasoned counselors may be cynical and assume that the child protective services agency will not do anything or intervene, and this may influence their willingness to report. Related to this idea, some counselors may perceive that they can do a better job intervening to keep the child safe than will a social services agency (Remley & Herlihy, 2016). Figure 4.2 provides tips to help counselors with the process of mandated reporting.

Although some of the previously mentioned concerns counselors have about reporting may be valid, a child's safety must always take precedence. Counselors should be aware of their role when considering suspected child maltreatment situations—that is, counselors are mandated to report *suspected* maltreatment; they are not the investigators, they do not look for "proof" of maltreatment, and they do not make rulings or final judgments in these situations. Counselors do not have the burden of providing proof that abuse or neglect has occurred, and they should not let their fears of reporting unsubstantiated maltreatment guide their decision making. In fact, counselors can be sued by injured youth and/or their parents and be seriously reprimanded by a licensure board if they fail to make a legally mandated report of suspected abuse (Remley & Herlihy, 2016).

Counselors should be aware that reporting statutes protect mandated reporters from lawsuits that might be filed against them for reporting (Remley & Herlihy, 2016). Protective clauses are written into state laws to cover counselors who make reports in *good faith*, sincerely believing that child maltreatment has occurred or is occurring (Remley & Herlihy, 2016). Because of these statutory protections, young clients' parents or family members who sue counselors for defamation of character would likely not be successful, even if the abuse or neglect is not substantiated (Remley & Herlihy, 2016). Consulting with a colleague and documenting one's rationale for reporting is one way to offer support to a counselor's decision to report, especially in the case of a suspected perpetrator alleging a counselor made a report in bad faith (Remley & Herlihy, 2016).

- *Obtain consultation from others:* Reach out to and consult with coworkers, licensure board staff, supervisors, and attorneys as necessary.
- *Document everything:* It is very important to thoroughly document and provide as much data as possible to the child protective services agency. Doing so also protects the counselor.
- *Prepare for the consequences:* When reporting, a child and/or the parent(s) may not return to counseling (e.g., especially if the parent[s] or a family member is directly involved in the child maltreatment). Be prepared to handle parent reactions.
- *Practice self-care and wellness:* Take care of mental, physical, and emotional needs during the reporting process because a healthy wellness routine will help prevent the burnout and stress that the reporting process may bring.

FIGURE 4.2 Tips for Handling Mandated Reporting

Statutory Requirements and Reporting

The circumstances under which a mandated reporter must make a report vary by state. Typically, a report must be made when the counselor suspects or has reason to believe that a young client has been abused or neglected. In some states, counselors are even required to report situations in which the counselor has knowledge of, or observes a child being subjected to, conditions that would *reasonably* result in harm to the youth. It is important that counselors are familiar with the laws related to reporting in the state in which they practice. On their website at https://www.childwelfare.gov/pubPDFs/manda.pdf#page=5&view=Summaries of State laws Change?, the USDHHS (n.d.) provides a list of the most up-to-date information related to each state and U.S. territory's child maltreatment reporting laws.

States differ in terms of their child maltreatment reporting requirements, and counselors must read and understand their state's statutes and how they relate to their practices. More specifically, each state differs in term of (USDHHS, 2016):

- what professionals are required to report (e.g., some professionals such as clergy or court-appointed special advocates may not be required to report in some states);
- policies for taking reports from nonprofessionals (i.e., some states require that any person who suspects child abuse or neglect is required to report);
- responsibility of institutions to make reports (i.e., the role that the counselor's employing institution is required to take in terms of involvement in reporting);
- whether the counselor is legally required to report directly or if it is enough to tell the supervisor who is then legally required to report;
- standards for making a report (i.e., the standards under which one is mandated to report);
- requirement to include reporter's name in the report;
- if one can provide an oral report or if he or she is also required to provide a written report;
- whether past abuse experiences must be reported (e.g., a 17-year-old reports she was sexually abused by her grandfather when she was 13 years old);
- the time frame within which a report is required to be made (e.g., immediately, 24 hours, 48 hours);
- whether certain categories of suspected perpetrators must be reported (e.g., parents and/or guardians), whereas other categories of suspected perpetrators (e.g., neighbors or extended family) are not *required* to be reported but *may* be reported; and
- disclosure of the reporter's identity to the parties involved (the reporter's identity is protected in most states but not all).

In terms of child maltreatment, knowing what and when to report can be confusing for counselors, especially when it comes to neglect. One of the more confusing issues counselors who work with youth experience is whether past child abuse experiences should be reported if the youth is no longer in danger. A review of state statutes shows varied mandates in terms of when the abuse occurred, with some states indicating that past abuse must be reported, other states suggesting only current abuse needs to be reported, and still other states not speaking to the issue (Remley & Herlihy, 2016). A lack of clarity around these matters leaves counselors to interpret how to handle these difficult situations (Remley & Herlihy, 2016).

Another confusing issue is that some states only require the counselor to report parents or guardians suspected of child maltreatment but not others (e.g., siblings, peers, neighbors, extended family). Similarly, in some other states, counselors are permitted—but not required—to report suspected nonfamilial perpetrators (Remley & Herlihy, 2016). In such situations, counselors are left to wonder if they are justified in breaking confidentiality to report if the suspected perpetrator is *not* a guardian, and they may worry about whether the legal protections that are in place related to reporting guardians will protect them if they report other suspected perpetrators.

If new suspicions or reports of abuse or neglect emerge, counselors will need to report these as well. As complaints build, they can provide the child protective services agency with data they can use to inform their decision-making process.

Assessing the Situation: Should a Report Be Made?

Counselors are called on to use their clinical judgment in determining whether child maltreatment is suspected (Remley & Herlihy, 2016). Rarely do youth directly report maltreatment to their counselors, and it is more likely a counselor will establish suspicions over time as clients casually provide information in sessions. Although it is well established that counselors are required to report child maltreatment, determining and establishing maltreatment are not always easy, and in fact can be quite difficult. For instance, what qualifies as abuse or neglect is not always clear. For example, if a parent breaks a child's bone, this obviously qualifies as physical abuse, but what if a parent spanks a child with a belt? As another example, punching a child and giving him a black eye, again, obviously qualifies as physical abuse. However, what if a parent smacks a child on the face and the child's head bounces off the wall but no mark is left—is this abuse? Although physical and sexual abuse are easier to classify, emotional abuse is much harder to define, as is neglect, because both are highly variable depending on the observer's culture, life experiences, and personal values.

Next, when identifying child maltreatment, counselors may struggle with the nature or extent of the evidence they have of suspected maltreatment—that is, they may only be suspicious but feel uncertain they have enough information or evidence to report. Counselor suspicions of abuse may arise from observed signs or symptoms of abuse (e.g., a young child excessively masturbating or being physically aggressive with others). Counselors might also hear reports from children that raise suspicions of abuse (e.g., they are being hit with objects such as belts, repeated spankings), but they may struggle to understand whether these behaviors qualify as abuse in their jurisdiction.

In situations where counselors are uncertain if a child is being maltreated, they can continue to assess the situation and collect data. As the counseling relationship progresses, clients may be more forthcoming with information or the counselor may otherwise get more information that can be used to better assess the situation. Consulting with others may be a helpful way to generate ideas on how to further assess for maltreatment and to support one's decision making if there is ambiguity over the need to report. In addition, if counselors are unclear about their need to report, they should remember that they can call their local child protective services agency and consult about the need to make a report. These intake workers manage the complexities of child maltreatment cases on a daily basis, and they can offer insights related to the need to report and what additional information might be gathered to help counselors assess a need to make a report.

Making a Report

When reporting child maltreatment, counselors are required to report the facts and circumstances that led them to suspect that a young person has been abused or neglected. Counselors must report the abuse to officials in the jurisdiction where the abuse actually occurred, and this may be a different location from where the child lives or where the counselor practices. When calling in a report of child maltreatment, child protective services' agency workers will typically ask for:

- name and date of birth (or approximate age) of the parents/guardians, alleged perpetrator, and any children involved;
- addresses or other means to locate the subjects of the report;
- what school the child attends;
- the relationship of the alleged perpetrator to the child;
- when and where the alleged incident occurred;
- the details of the situation that prompted the report (e.g., If the child was hit, were marks left? Was the child hit with an object?); and
- any witnesses to the abuse/neglect.

Often, counselors do not have access to all the information, but what is important is that the report is made; the workers can gather the information they need if they choose to investigate. Because counselors are mandated reporters, it also helps to provide evidence that they have followed through on their legal obligation to report. Counselors should, in their progress notes, document the time and date they called, a written summary of their report, and the name of and any noteworthy interactions with the person with whom they spoke. Also, even though many states allow anonymous reports, counselors should consider providing their name and contact information should the investigators need to follow up and gather more information.

Counselors are typically required to follow certain reporting procedures with the institution where they work. Some schools or agencies may require the counselor to alert the principal, supervisor, or an agency child rights' advocate before or after reporting, and some employers will require that a counselor provide a written report to the institution. Some suggest that counselors notify their supervisors before or after a report is made, even if not mandated by institutional policy (Remley & Herlihy, 2016).

When counseling youth, their safety should always be a counselor's first priority (Kress et al., 2012). As mandated reporters, counselors are frequently called on to break confidentiality and report suspected abuse and/or neglect to their local child protective services agency. Mandated reporting situations can—and do— have an impact on the counseling relationship, especially if the counselor has to report the parent(s) or another family member (e.g., sibling, uncle). Poorly handled reports to a social services agency can result in relationship ruptures with both young clients and their families, and these ruptures may result in a parent removing his or her child from counseling. As such, it is important that these reporting situations are well managed.

If a counselor is reporting any type of child maltreatment to authorities, there is an obvious expressed concern about a child's welfare. As such, counselors have an obligation to consider and address immediate safety-related issues. If a young client is living in an abusive situation—whether it be exposure to others' violence or to personal maltreatment—counselors have an obligation to facilitate safety. The use of a safety plan is the most effective way counselors can do this (Kress et al., 2012). A safety plan can be applied in any situation, but three common applications include guardian interpersonal partner violence, youth interpersonal partner violence or a physical threat by another youth, and youth who live in violent homes and are at risk of abuse. See Chapter 15 for directions on how to go about helping a young person develop a safety plan.

The Aftermath of Filing a Report

As mandated reporters, counselors are called on to break confidentiality and report suspected maltreatment to their local child protective services agency or some other designated governmental agency. Obviously, mandated reporting situations can affect the counseling relationship, especially if the counselor has to report the parent(s) or another family member (e.g., sibling, aunt). Poorly handled reports can result in relationship ruptures with the young client and the family, and these ruptures may result in the parent(s) removing the child from counseling. As such, it is important that these reporting situations are handled with care. Counselors have an ethical obligation to communicate empathy in reporting situations and offer the client support as they move forward and manage the investigation process and its aftermath (Remley & Herlihy, 2016).

It is helpful to explain to the young client and the family the procedures you typically adhere to in reporting. Counselors need to use their judgment in determining whether to tell the child, family, and/or alleged perpetrator about the report. Some counselors let the family know that if they do have to make a report, they will typically alert them to this fact. Some counselors—if feasible and appropriate—may call in reports with the family. Family members might also be invited to make the report with the counselor in certain situations. A collaborative spirit in reporting situations helps promote trust and demystifies the reporting process. However, there may be circumstances when it would put the child in danger if a counselor reports with the parents or lets them know about the report in advance. Counselors should monitor these complex situations and use their clinical judgment as they balance the safety of the child with maintaining a strong working alliance with the family.

Many of the families with whom counselors work will have, or have had, anonymous reports made on them to child protective services, and families are often quick to assume reports came from the counselor. The collaborative approach mentioned previously provides reassurance that if a report is filed, the family will know whether it came from the counselor. An emphasis on a collaborative approach to reporting builds trust.

Procedurally, child protective service agencies will, if they believe it is warranted, conduct an investigation and apply a finding in the case or a case disposition. These dispositions are usually something along the lines of the child maltreatment being indicated, founded, or unfounded. The agency will, as legally mandated, report to local law enforcement, who will, if appropriate, move forward with legal proceedings. Throughout this process, the child protective services agency works with legal authorities and may contact the counselor to garner additional information. Remley and Herlihy (2016) suggested that counselors not speak with unverified investigators on the phone and that they cooperate—after confirming one's credentials and authority—and share information. Remley and Herlihy also suggested that school counselors should cooperate with investigators who want to interview youth at school, and they indicated that counselors should be aware of their state laws that govern law enforcement interviews with children in school settings.

CONFIDENTIALITY OF DOCUMENTS AND FEDERAL LAWS

There are many federal laws aimed at protecting the privacy of clients and students. The three federal laws that most affect counselors' practice are the Health Insurance Portability and Accountability Act of 1997 (HIPAA), Family Educational Rights and Privacy Act of 1974 (FERPA), and Comprehensive Alcohol Abuse and Alcoholism Prevention, Treatment, and Rehabilitation Act of 1972.

Health Insurance Portability and Accountability Act

The most important federal law that relates to mental health records is HIPAA (1996), which protects the privacy of medical patients' health records (U.S. Department of Health and Human Services [USDHHS] n.d.). Counselors who work in clinical settings are most likely to need to navigate HIPAA regulations.

HIPAA applies to organizations or individual providers who transmit health care information electronically as part of a health care–related transition, which is basically most counselors (Remley & Herlihy, 2016). According to HIPAA requirements, counselors must provide clients with information related to how they retain, use, and disclose health care–related information. Clients are also required to have access to their records, and a process to amend their records must be in place. Counseling offices must also designate a privacy officer to oversee the handling and management of confidential records. According to HIPAA, counselors must provide information on records disclosure policies and have a policy detailing who has access to information, how this information is used within the counseling office, and when the information will be disclosed to others (Remley & Herlihy, 2016).

Guardians make health care decisions for their minor children, and they can exercise the minors' rights with respect to protected health information; however, there are circumstances in which minors can keep their health records private from their guardians, such as when the minor can demonstrate that releasing records to a caregiver would place them at risk (HIPAA, 1996, 45 CFR § 160.103). In these situations, guardians do not control their minors' health care decisions, and thus they do not control the protected health information related to their care. Three exceptional circumstances when a guardian is not the minor's personal representative are:

- when state laws—or other law—does not require the consent of a guardian before a minor can obtain a particular health care service and the minor consents to the health care service (e.g., a state law allows for an adolescent to obtain counseling without the consent of her parent, and the adolescent consents to counseling without her parent's consent);
- when someone other than the guardian is authorized by law to consent to the provision of a particular health service to a minor and provides such consent (e.g., a court grants authority to a 16-year-old boy who has been emancipated to make health care decisions for himself); or
- when a parent agrees to a confidential relationship between a minor and a health care provider (e.g., a counselor asks the parent of a 15-year-old girl if she can talk confidentially with the girl about certain matters and the parent agrees).

Additional information on HIPAA and how it affects professionals can be found at http://www.hhs.gov/hipaa/for-professionals/faq.

Family Educational Rights and Privacy Act

All counselors who work in federally funded school settings (e.g., public K–12 schools, colleges/universities) will need to navigate FERPA regulations. FERPA (1974; 34 CFR Part 99) is intended to safeguard the privacy and confidentiality of students' educational records, and all schools who receive federal funds are required to adhere to the act's regulations. FERPA regulations apply to all special education records and any records of services provided to students under the Individuals with Disabilities Education Act (IDEA; 2004) as well. The term *educational records* includes records that directly relate to a student and are maintained by an educational agency or institution or by a party acting for the institution (FERPA, 1974, 34 CFR § 99.3). The regulations require that guardians must consent—in writing—for the release of records to third parties. FERPA regulations also provide legal guardians with the right to view their unemancipated children's educational records and to request a change to the records' content if they perceive information provided in the records is misleading or inaccurate (34 CFR Part 99).

Schools must have written permission from the parent or qualifying student to release information from a student's education record. FERPA (1974) does, however, allow schools to disclose those records—without consent—under certain conditions to (34 CFR § 99.31):

- school officials who have legitimate educational interest (described as follows);
- officials who are auditing or evaluating a school or program;
- officials associated with health and safety emergencies;
- schools to which a student is transferring;
- state and local authorities who are involved with the juvenile justice system;
- parties associated with student financial aid;
- organizations conducting certain studies for or on behalf of the school;
- as a part of a school's accreditation process; and
- in compliance with a judicial order or a subpoena.

FERPA (1974) guidelines also detail who in the school has legitimate educational interest and can access educational records. **Legitimate educational interest** relates to a need to know information about the student for the purpose of:

- completing a task related to a student's education;
- completing appropriate tasks within one's job description;
- performing a task related to student discipline; or
- providing a service or benefit related to the student or the student's family such as counseling, health care, or job placement.

Once students turn 18, they have the legal right to protect their own educational records; however, guardians may be given access to their records without their consent if the students are considered to be dependent (Remley & Herlihy, 2016). Dependent students are children—or stepchildren—who received most of their financial support in the previous tax year from their guardian (FERPA, 1974, 26 U.S.C.A. § 152). Most educational institutions grant access to student records to guardians who can provide evidence they claimed their child as a dependent on their previous year's taxes (Remley & Herlihy, 2016).

Educational records do not include records that are "in the sole possession of the maker" and are thus exempt from review (FERPA, 1974, 20 U.S.C.A. § 1232g(a)(B)(i)152). For the school counselors' records to qualify under this exemption, the records must serve solely as a memory aid and include only the counselors' observations and professional opinions; also, counselors must keep their notes separate from students' educational files, not allow anyone else to have access to the notes, and not discuss the content of the notes with anyone (Remley & Herlihy, 2016; Stone, 2003). If case notes do not meet the aforementioned criteria, then they are part of students' educational records and school counselors are legally required to provide them to the requesting parent (Stone, 2003). Stone cautioned that it is difficult to only record observations and professional opinions in case notes. This caution should make school counselors pause and consider consulting with their school attorney regarding their personal notes and how they manage these.

Comprehensive Alcohol Abuse and Alcoholism Prevention, Treatment, and Rehabilitation Act

Most substance abuse treatment agencies and centers have at least some type of federal funding they use to support their programming, and any program that receives federal funding is required to abide by all federal laws that relate to substance abuse treatment. As such, youth who are in substance abuse counseling in federally funded substance abuse treatment programs are provided with additional federal privacy protections via a federal statute known as the **Comprehensive Alcohol Abuse and Alcoholism Prevention, Treatment and Rehabilitation Act** (1972, 1997, 42 U.S.C.A. § 290dd-2). This regulation is often colloquially referred to as *42 CFR*.

The privacy provisions in 42 CFR were motivated by the idea that stigma and fear of legal prosecution might dissuade persons with substance use problems from seeking treatment, and 42 CFR requires strict adherence to privacy standards. These regulations outline under what circumstances information about a patient's treatment may be disclosed. The release of a young person's substance abuse treatment records requires a court order or the signed authorization of his or her guardian. A program providing substance abuse services may not identify any of its clients to a person outside the program or disclose any information identifying a client as having an alcohol or drug abuse problem unless the client's guardian consents in writing or the disclosure is forced by a court order, made to medical personnel in a medical emergency, or made to specified personnel for research, audit, or program evaluation purposes.

Importantly, under these regulations, records cannot be used in a legal investigation or in relation to criminal charges in the Comprehensive Alcohol Abuse and Alcoholism Prevention, Treatment and Rehabilitation Act—use of records in criminal proceedings (2003, 42 U.S.C.A. § 290dd-2(c)). Ideally, these regulations help to create a climate where young clients can feel safe to honestly share their experiences; this openness and safety are essential if counselors are to provide effective substance abuse treatment. So, to facilitate a sense of safety and security, counselors should take care to explain to clients what their rights are related to disclosure and confidentiality relative to 42 CFR.

THE SCHOOLS AND DISABILITY: IDEA AND SECTION 504

There are two more federal laws—IDEA and Section 504—of which school counselors must be aware. Although these laws primarily apply to school counselors, all youth counselors should be aware of them because they relate to children's rights.

IDEA

The **Individuals with Disabilities Education Act (IDEA; 2004)** was originally enacted by Congress in 1975 to ensure children with disabilities can receive a free public education that meets their unique learning needs. The law requires public schools (or any school that receives federal funding) to accommodate children who have a *physical* or *mental disability* (e.g., intellectual disabilities; emotional disturbances; specific learning disabilities; autism; hearing, visual, or speech disabilities) that limits one or more of their life activities. Over the years, IDEA has been revised many times.

School counselors are often the designated school personnel who facilitate the development of **Individualized Education Plans (IEPs)**. IEPs are documents developed for youth who have a disability and need special education provisions. IEPs are created through a team effort and must be periodically reviewed and updated. They spell out each accommodation that will be put into place to help a child be successful in school.

These provisions are intended to provide access to educational services and accommodations that minimize the impact of the disability and level the child's playing field as compared to other children. Accommodations may be related to a child's physical or mental disability and include scheduling accommodations (e.g., extra time to take an exam), setting accommodations (e.g., taking an exam in a private room), response accommodations (e.g., dictate answers to a scribe), presentation accommodations (e.g., hear instructions orally), and/or organizational skills accommodations (e.g., have help coordinating assignments in a book or planner).

Section 504

Section 504 of the Rehabilitation Act of 1973 requires that public schools provide a free and appropriate education to students who have a *physical* or *mental impairment* that limits one or more of their life activities. In the scenario mentioned earlier in this chapter—the one in which the child was recently diagnosed with an anxiety disorder—the counselor would want to convene a meeting to determine if the child qualified to have a 504 Plan, which might involve accommodations such as extra time to take exams and/or opportunity to take exams in a more private room.

As with IEPs, generally, school counselors are actively involved in developing 504 Plans. A team of people, which includes teachers, collaboratively develops and implements these plans.

It is common for IEPs or 504 Plans to include the provision of counseling services. As an example, counselors who work with students who self-injure might have these counseling-related 504 Plan goals: (a) develop an awareness of self-injury triggers, cues, and reducers and (b) use self-injury reducers in the school setting 100% of the time.

Although clinical counselors are generally not directly involved with the development and administration of IEPs or 504 Plans, they should be familiar with these plans because so many of the youth they counsel will need or may already have such plans. Clinical counselors can help to support the goals of youth's IEPs or 504 Plans through the work they do in community counseling.

CHILD CUSTODY

The divorce rate in the United States is significant, and divorce situations can require counselors to make complex decisions related to treatment consent and custody matters. One of the most common areas where counselors make mistakes is in navigating the complex waters associated with child custody situations (W. Hegarty, personal communication, September 23, 2016). Emotions run high when parents perceive their children are at risk, and this emotional intensity can lead parents to be especially guarded around any matters related to their children and their children's well-being and/or their ability to see their children (W. Hegarty, personal communication, September 23, 2016). It is easy for well-meaning counselors to overstep and take an advocacy role when this is not an appropriate role to assume.

As previously mentioned, when working with minors, it is important to maintain an awareness of who has legal custody of the youth and what the rights are of the noncustodial guardian. Custody issues can show up in the counseling relationship in two areas. First, counselors must ensure they have proper consent for treatment when working with any individual younger than 18 years. Second, counselors might be asked by caregivers to become involved in legal proceedings to determine who should receive or maintain custody of a youth. Both scenarios and how to respond require an understanding of one's state laws, and counselors should consult with an attorney who knows the specific laws in their state. Some general guidelines for managing these often contentious, complex situations follow.

Consent for Treatment

As previously discussed, counselors are responsible for knowing who is able to consent to a youth's treatment, and this depends on each state's unique laws. In general, the parent who has legal custody of the youth is able to consent for treatment; the noncustodial parent typically has a legal right to treatment records, and he or she may even have a right to be involved in the child's treatment process. Because family relationships are complex, counselors who work with young children should consider asking up front about any legal or custody arrangements between the youth, the parents, and any other caregivers who are involved (Smith-Adcock & Tucker, 2017). If the parents report that there is a separation or divorce, counselors should consider asking for a copy of the records that name the legal guardian and the legal documents to substantiate the custody claims. Increasingly, counselors routinely require that a copy of these court records are brought to the initial session and retained in the client's files.

Typically, both biological parents have legal custody of a child unless specified by a court ruling (Remley & Herlihy, 2016). It is important to note that parents who have not been granted legal custody of a youth might still have periodic physical custody (i.e., visitation). When parents have shared custody of a youth, both adults have the right to consent to treatment, and counselors should receive informed consent from both parents whenever possible. When one parent has legal custody of a youth, it is sufficient to get informed consent from just that parent. However, even parents who do not have legal custody are sometimes able to consent to treatment when they have physical custody of the youth (Remley & Herlihy, 2016).

Counselors can use the process of determining who is able to consent to a youth's treatment as an assessment tool to learn more about the family dynamics a youth must navigate on a daily basis. Counselors can also use the informed consent process as a therapeutic tool because the youth's parents are required to agree on the same goal and show support for the youth's progress in counseling.

In addition to determining who is able to consent to treatment for a youth, counselors must balance any competing demands between confidentiality for the youth and a desire for disclosure of session content from a parent (Remley & Herlihy, 2016). Counselors should be aware that noncustodial parents may have a right to a young client's treatment records, and when writing progress notes, counselors should assume that the noncustodial parent will, at some point, review the youth's records.

Custody Proceedings

It is not uncommon for counselors to find themselves in the midst of child custody battles. Noncustodial parents have the same rights as custodial parents, in most cases, unless legally mandated otherwise. Also, sometimes one parent might believe that he or she deserves more rights or privileges than the other parent. These disputes can occur as parents separate and divorce, or they may even occur after a divorce if a parent decides he or she would like to change the custody arrangement. Counseling can become one of the battlegrounds where such disputes play out. Counselors have an obligation to their clients to handle such situations well and to ensure the tensions do not affect their work with the youth.

Sometimes a guardian may have a child meet with a counselor with the intent of having the counselor make a custody recommendation. Child custody disputes are among the most contentious and difficult situations counselors traverse, and counselors should be cautious when they find themselves in such situations. From the outset of counseling—or at any point a counselor becomes aware that the child's parents are divorcing or there is a risk of a legal custody situation—counselors should consider communicating that it is not a counselor's role to make custody recommendations unless they have specifically contracted to do so.

Some counselors might have expertise in conducting child custody evaluations, and armed with appropriate training and competency, they are well prepared to provide such evaluations. Typically, such evaluations are contracted by the court and assigned to its agreed-on providers. Some counselors do work privately and contract to provide such evaluations. However, most counselors do not specialize in offering legal opinions, and unless they have specialized training, they should refrain from making custody-related recommendations. The counselors who do offer legal opinions regarding custody disputes typically perform extensive testing and evaluation of all involved parties, and this information better enables the counselors to provide objective recommendations.

Counselors who do specialize in practicing within the legal system should not have dual relationships with clients as evaluators and counselors. These relationships should remain separate because the evaluative role assumed by a counselor with a legal specialization can clash with the egalitarian approach typically assumed in a clinical/therapeutic role, and this can cause significant problems (Ordway).

Informed consent related to counselors' roles in legal proceedings may help to troubleshoot and prevent them from being subpoenaed to testify on custody matters (Koocher, 2008). Although state laws differ regarding custody-related matters, counselors should view evaluations as a formal service, requiring specialized training and competencies, and they should only provide such a service if contracted to do so and in accordance with the laws of their state.

Counselors who do not specialize in or who prefer not to be involved in custody disputes may consider adding a statement to their informed consent forms indicating they will not give testimony in custody cases. When children know that what they say in counseling will not be used against their parents, they may feel more secure in the counseling relationship. Children do not want to imagine that what they say will be revealed to their parent(s) and that that information could be used against one or the other in court or custody cases. The use of information against a parent could be harmful to youth and diminish their trust in counseling. Providing informed consent that the counselor will *not* testify in a court case (unless that is his or her role) also prevents one parent's efforts to eliminate the presence of the other parent from the child's life. There are situations when a child, unknowingly, has had things they said in counseling used against a parent in court, and this can be psychology harmful to the child. Counselors should make every effort to troubleshoot and prevent such occurrences.

Despite the precautions, counselors may still be called on to testify in court relative to a custody situation. Sometimes judges will sign a court order, which is different from and holds more weight than a subpoena from a lawyer. In such a situation, counselors will need to verify with their state to determine the specific limits of confidentiality. As the result of a court order or a subpoena, counselors' records can be requested and/or counselors may be asked to testify or make custody recommendations. If a counselor is asked by a judge to make custody recommendations, he or she should receive legal consultation from a qualified attorney. Sometimes, when the counselor lets an attorney or judge know it is not within his or her scope of practice to provide custody recommendations, the attorney or judge may withdraw the subpoena or court order.

Counselors should remember that judges, lawyers, and guardian *ad litems* are not at all concerned about a counselor's legal scope of practice, legal liability, or any repercussions that follow because the counselor overstepped his or her legal obligation to share. Laws regarding a counselor's role in custody hearings and other legal proceedings are different in every state, and only an attorney—who specializes in the counselor's state—will be able to speak authoritatively about how to handle these cases. In addition, if requested to make recommendations, a counselor might ask the judge to appoint a guardian *ad litem* who can speak to the child's interests and rights and advocate for the child (Koocher, 2008).

Ohio law is a good example of an application of many of the concepts discussed in this section, and it may serve as a guide to counselors whose state laws do not speak to the matter. The 2014 Ohio Revised Code (4757-6-01) states the following:

> Licensees with a client involved in a custody, visitation and/or guardianship case, if asked by a client and/or their lawyer or the guardian *ad litem* to make a recommendation as to custody, visitation and/or guardianship, shall cite their role as the primary therapist for their client. This section does not apply to a licensee hired to make a custody, visitation and/or guardianship recommendation for the court. Licensees shall inform the requestor that they have not performed a custody, visitation and/or guardianship evaluation and it would be unethical for them to make any recommendation outside of their role as a treating therapist.

If counselors do find themselves in a situation in which they are required to testify and contribute to court proceedings, they should be clear in stating the facts of the situation and withhold their personal opinions (Remley & Herlihy, 2016)—that is, counselors might reference the number of sessions a client has attended, the nature of the sessions, treatment goals, client's reports of matters, and possibly the client's progress in counseling. To best support the youth in future counseling sessions, the counselor needs to maintain a strong working relationship with both parents while meeting any legal requirements placed on them.

MULTIPLE RELATIONSHIPS

A **multiple relationship** (or *dual relationship*) is a type of relationship characterized by the counselor fulfilling multiple roles with a client and his or her family. Although a counselor will normally only maintain a professional (or counseling) role with a client, multiple relationships include any additional roles such as personal, familial, business, or financial. When counselors blend these other roles with their professional role, ethical considerations must be examined while always keeping the welfare and best interests of the youth and family in mind (Corey et al., 2015).

It goes without saying that multiple relationships should be avoided (ACA, 2014; American School Counselor Association [ASCA] 2016); however, pragmatically, many counselors are forced by environment or circumstance to manage these complicated relationships. For example, school counselors frequently need to manage multiple relationships with their students (e.g., counseling, advising, disciplinary, classroom guidance), while maintaining professionalism with their school colleagues. School counselors are often required to monitor the lunch room, engage in classroom guidance, or even oversee an extracurricular activity in which the youth participates. The school environment is wrought with multiple relationship dilemmas related to school counselors' interactions with students, parents, and other faculty and administration.

Clinical counselors often face unusual multiple relationship challenges as well. As an example, consider that counselors are frequently asked by the courts, as part of a family reunification plan, to provide counseling services for abuse victims and the victim's perpetrator. These multiple roles and responsibilities can be complicated, and they can invite a counselor's strong personal reactions. Counselors face a unique challenge as they balance position duties and requirements with their personal reactions to best support the well-being of their clients (ACA, 2014).

Another circumstance related to multiple relationships is working in areas where there are few providers. More specifically, the risk of multiple relationships increases in rural and sometimes in socioeconomically depressed areas or in certain target populations in an area (e.g., if there is only one Spanish-speaking counselor in an area; Pugh, 2007). Because a limited number of providers are often practicing in these areas, counselors can run the risk of already knowing about the potential client because of a relative, friend, or colleague who has had a previous relationship with the client.

Counselors must be aware of the power differential that exists within counseling and understand that complicating that differential with a dual relationship can potentially jeopardize clients' well-being and their best interests (Corey et al., 2015). For example, if a counselor already knows a family who attends her church, but due to limited providers in the area agrees to engage in a counseling relationship with the family, this counselor may need to manage a host of ethical constraints (e.g., breaking confidentiality in the church environment, bringing into counseling information known from the church environment, other church members' inquiries).

Clinical Toolbox 4.2

In the Pearson eText, click here to read about examples of boundary situations and examples.

Managing multiple relationships with clients (especially youth and families) can be stressful for counselors and can leave new and seasoned counselors feeling emotionally conflicted (Corey et al., 2015). Seeking supervision and consultation and documenting their decision making is the first way counselors can aid themselves in managing these conflicting roles, especially when working within a school environment.

Another way to diminish the threat of engaging in multiple relationships is for counselors to ask themselves several questions before entering into such a relationship (Corey et al., 2015):

- Do I have a choice in entering into this relationship, and is entering into it necessary?
- Is there potential to provide harm to the youth or the family if I decide to enter into this dual relationship or, conversely, if I decide not to enter into this relationship?
- Will this relationship disrupt the established therapeutic relationship?
- Am I able to remain professional, ethical, and objective in this relationship?

By addressing these questions, counselors can assess their personal risk associated with entering into such a relationship, as well as consider the risks, interests, and well-being of the client.

Clinical Toolbox 4.3

In the Pearson eText, click here to review a decision-making worksheet that can be used in different boundary-related situations.

Counselors should be mindful that a lack of awareness or inability to manage these multiple relationships may jeopardize the status of their license, as well as expose them to ethical inquiries and potential board violations, especially if client harm was avoidable. In summary, counselors should talk with youth and families when multiple relationships may arise, outlining the potential risk and adverse effects of this relationship. Making clients aware of how the counselor will respond and maintain appropriate boundaries is essential to ethical practice (Corey et al., 2015). Counselors must maintain healthy boundaries, inform youth and families of potential risks and problems, and seek supervision concerning multiple relationships.

ETHICAL DECISION MAKING: PRACTICAL SUGGESTIONS

Although ethical and legal considerations can feel intimidating to new counselors, there are many resources counselors can use to support their decision making. In this section, concrete suggestions for how counselors can handle the various ethics issues identified in this chapter are provided. It has been suggested that counselors ask themselves the following questions when working with young people (Smith-Adcock & Tucker, 2017):

- What is your legal and ethical obligation to the client?
- How do your life experiences influence the decisions you need to make relative to the client?
- How do your responses look if you consider them from the perspective of the client, parents, court system, or any relevant others?
- If you consider the situation and your possible responses from competing perspectives, how do these possible solutions appear?

Counselors who counsel young people are advised to be through and thoughtful, sensitive and aware of self and others, transparent and communicative, educated, and support seeking (Corey et al., 2015; Herlihy & Corey, 2015; Remley & Herlihy, 2016; Welfel, 2013). The following sections address these practical suggestions for ethical decision making.

Be Thorough and Thoughtful

CAREFULLY CONSIDER AND DEFINE THE PROBLEM

Determine whether the matter involves ethics, legal, or clinical issues (Remley & Herlihy, 2016). Ask yourself if this is a matter that requires you to gather factual information. If you need legal information, consult with an attorney or someone at your licensing or credentialing board who specializes in ethics and gather the factual information you need to make a decision. If the matter relates to clinical decision making, consult with a supervisor or colleague. If the matter involves ethics, you will likely need to gather information and supports from multiple sources because ethics matters are typically complex. It is important to be patient, consider the problem from multiple perspectives, and avoid settling on overly simplistic solutions (Remley & Herlihy, 2016). Understand that just because you previously responded a certain way to a situation does not mean you always need to respond in kind to the same or similar situations; each new situation has a unique context and considerations.

CONSIDER ETHICAL PRINCIPLES AND VIRTUES

Determine how the previously discussed moral principles apply to the problem, and identify ways in which these principles may bump into each other. Also consider how "bigger picture" ethics might apply to the situation; instead of focusing on what you need to *do* in the situation, ask yourself who you want to *be* and how your actions might affect or reflect on your sense of self (Remley & Herlihy, 2016).

IDENTIFY THE DESIRED OUTCOME(S) AND CONSIDER ALL POSSIBLE WAYS TO ACHIEVE THESE OUTCOMES

In any given ethical dilemma, there are usually multiple optimal outcomes. Counselors can brainstorm all ideal outcomes and actions that can be taken to achieve these outcomes. Remley and Herlihy (2016) suggested listing desired outcomes on one side of a paper and listing all actions that might facilitate the achievement of these outcomes on the other side. They also suggested pondering the implications and consequences of each option, not just for the client but also for others who will be affected and for the counselor.

DOCUMENT COMMUNICATIONS

Maintain thorough records of counseling matters and consultations by documenting them.

Be Sensitive and Aware of Self and Others

BE AWARE OF YOUR PERSONAL ATTITUDES, VALUES, AND BELIEFS

It is important to be comfortable with the ambiguity associated with ethical matters because it is rare that any ethics situation is black and white. Counselors should avoid quickly foreclosing and making snap decisions because of their discomfort with the uncertain. Instead, make decisions on ethical matters only after all sides of the situation have been examined. Also, get comfortable with the idea that ethics matters do not typically progress in a linear way, and in fact, as you gain more context and information, your decision making will shift. When necessary, refer a client to another provider when your personal characteristics may hinder your ability to help him or her.

PAY ATTENTION TO YOUR FEELINGS

When evaluating an ethics situation, consider your emotional reactions to the situation and to the ways you might respond to the situation. Poor ethical decision making is often rooted in situations where our prejudices, emotional needs, or values affect our ability to see a situation objectively (Corey et al., 2015). Consider how you are being influenced by fear, hurt, self-doubt, insecurity, and/or a sense of personal responsibility (Remley & Herlihy, 2016).

WORK TO UNDERSTAND CLIENTS' CONTEXTS AND THEIR DIVERSE CULTURAL BACKGROUNDS

Understand that any ethical dilemma will be colored by your own life experiences and worldview. Develop an awareness of how your context and cultural background may affect your values and beliefs and how they relate to a given dilemma. Also, be cognizant of how these same factors may have an impact on a client's values and beliefs. Consider how a given course of action might affect not just the client but also his or her family and community.

MAKE DECISIONS IN THE BEST INTERESTS OF YOUR CLIENTS

Make decisions that are in good faith and have no malicious intent. Be sure to check yourself and your intentions. Ask yourself if a certain course of action will be in your client's best interest, or yours.

PRACTICE WITHIN YOUR PERSONAL SCOPE OF PRACTICE

Each person has his or her own unique scope of practice. Understand your professional limitations, and practice only within the boundaries of your personal competence. Be aware of what you are—and are not—capable of managing as a counselor and the populations or presenting issues you may need to refer to other providers. Ask yourself if you have the education, training, and supervised experience required to work with a youth and his or her family around a particular issue or in a given situation.

Be Transparent and Communicative

INFORM CLIENTS AND THEIR GUARDIANS OF THE LIMITATIONS OF COUNSELING

Communicate an accurate portrayal of what counseling can and cannot do. Make clients and their guardians aware of any potentially negative repercussions of the counseling experience prior to starting counseling.

ENCOURAGE FAMILY INVOLVEMENT IN THE COUNSELING PROCESS

Make an effort to connect with families, whenever possible and appropriate, and attempt to actively engage them in the counseling process.

DEVELOP A WELL-ARTICULATED EXPLANATION OF WHAT YOU DO AS A COUNSELOR

Be confident in your methods and counseling practices. Know who you are, what you believe to be true as a professional, and how this information may conflict with alternative ideas and practices. Be able to articulate the methods you use to help youth to change. Be sure you have a theoretical rationale that guides your counseling approach.

INVOLVE YOUR CLIENTS AND THEIR GUARDIANS IN DECISION MAKING

All young clients and their guardians should be involved in decisions that affect the counseling care they receive. Demystifying the process and asking for client and family input is important to facilitating good communication.

OBTAIN THOROUGH INFORMED CONSENT

At the onset of counseling, be sure to outline all possible matters youth and their families may need to be aware of relative to your approaches and the limits of the practice or setting in which you work. Get all consent matters in writing. Make sure informed consent information has been communicated in a developmentally appropriate way and that all parties have an opportunity to ask clarifying questions. Be especially clear about how confidentiality will be handled. Understand that consent is not a one-time event but rather an ongoing process.

Be Educated

ENGAGE WITH PROFESSIONAL COUNSELING ASSOCIATIONS

Attend conferences, take advantage of continuing education opportunities, and read association publications to ensure you understand contemporary ethical and legal developments.

BE AWARE OF AND PRACTICE TO THE ETHICAL STANDARDS OF YOUR PROFESSION

These standards are outlined in the various codes of ethics and in the professional literature.

BE AWARE OF THE LAWS IN THE STATE IN WHICH YOU PRACTICE

Stay on top of current court rulings, especially those related to minors. When counseling youth who are involved in legal situations (e.g., a custody battle, mandated treatment), counselors must be aware of the state laws that govern their practice.

Be Support Seeking

HAVE A GROUP OF PEOPLE WITH WHOM YOU CAN CONSULT

Because difficult ethics situations will always be emerging, you need to have reliable, thoughtful colleagues with whom you can consult. Decisions made in isolation are rarely as good as decisions made in consultation with others (Remley & Herlihy, 2016). Your support group might include former or current supervisors, colleagues, former professors, a professional association ethics committee, or a representative of your state licensing board. In legal or court-related contexts, consultation and documentation of such consultation can serve to support your decision making.

MAINTAIN PROFESSIONAL LIABILITY INSURANCE AND CONSULT WITH AN ATTORNEY

Access to an attorney is a resource provided through your liability insurance, so be sure to secure and maintain liability insurance. Keep in mind that most people who have complaints filed against them with licensing boards are not charged. No one is exempt from having charges filed against them, not even those who engage in ethical practices. In questionable cases, seek legal advice prior to initiating action. The time invested in sorting through complex issues in *advance* of action is time well spent.

ENGAGE IN SELF-SUPPORT AND SELF-CARE

Navigating ethical decisions can be stressful for counselors, and it can even contribute to counselor burnout. Education and consultation are helpful in preventing burnout (Remley & Herlihy, 2016), but counselor self-care is also important. In Table 4.1, self-care exercises counselors can use to prevent burnout are provided.

Table 4.1	Self-Care Exercises for Counselors
Exercise	**Description**
My Self-Care Assessment	Counselors can benefit from conducting an informal assessment to monitor their self-care. They begin by making a list of about 15 values that are most important to them (e.g., my friends, my family, my physical health, my emotional health, relaxation, organization). After the list of topics is developed, counselors rate their satisfaction level on a scale of 1 to 10, with 1 being the least satisfied and 10 being the most satisfied. After each value is rated, they identify ways their values can be increased. For example, if physical health is rated a 3, then drinking more water and increasing exercise might be ways to increase that value. Counselors should revisit this list, at least monthly, to rescore and assess their self-care.
Reminder Jar	Counselors can use a reminder jar to remind themselves of the positive incentives, rewards, and motivations associated with being a counselor. On small pieces of paper, counselors write down rewarding counseling experiences, thoughts, or inspirational quotes that can serve as positive reminders of why what they do is important. These reminders are then put in a jar to be kept on a bed stand or a kitchen counter. Each day, counselors open the jar and read a personalized message for a constant, positive reminder.
Self-Care Action Plan	Counselors may be unaware of the signs of stress and burnout. By creating a personalized action plan, counselors become more aware of their needs and how these needs can be handled. Counselors might respond to the following questions: 1. Signs I am getting burned out: 2. Emotions during times of stress: 3. Sources of personal support: 4. Sources of professional support (e.g., colleagues, supervisor): 5. Places I go to calm myself down: 6. Activities I enjoy when under stress: Counselors may also add more to their plan based on different self-care needs. After the questions are completed, the plan may be saved for future reference and guidance during times of stress.
Self-Care Calendar	The use of a self-care calendar may help with routine and self-care consistency. Each day, at least one or more self-care goals can be listed on the calendar. For example, Monday may say "Wake up and exercise for 30 minutes" and Tuesday may say "Take a 60-minute yoga class." The activities may change week by week or day by day, but what is important is that they are acknowledged and scheduled.

Clinical Toolbox 4.4

In the Pearson eText, click here to view a counselor self-care checklist.

AN ETHICAL DECISION-MAKING MODEL

All counselors encounter complex ethical dilemmas. As previously stated, counselors should evaluate an ethics matter from many angles and gather as much information as possible before deciding what to do. That said, counselors often do not have the luxury of time and need to quickly make ethics-related decisions. For example, if a parent invites a counselor to a child's birthday party, the counselor will need to respond in that moment. How a counselor will respond to a situation will depend on the counselor's style, values, and principles and the nature of the ethical issue. Most ethical dilemmas have no one right response, and when determining the steps to take in addressing such a dilemma, many factors must be considered. These factors include matters related to the counseling setting, state laws, ethics codes, and the risk(s) to the counselor and the client.

There are numerous decision-making models that can serve to inform counselors on their ethical decision making, and these models have overlapping components. Decision-making models can be used to protect the counselor and the client, and such models are aimed at helping counselors think through complex situations. The use of a specific framework that can easily be remembered via an acronym can help counselors to remember important ethical decision-making steps. The original model presented in this text is a composite of other researchers' models (e.g., Corey et al., 2015; Welfel, 2010) and is represented by the acronym DIRECTION. Figure 4.3 provides an overview of the DIRECTION model.

What follows is an overview of the different aspects of the proposed decision-making model:

(D) With any situation, it is important to *develop ethical sensitivity and awareness*—the **D** aspect of the model—that is, a sense of what may or may not pose an ethical dilemma. Counselors who are not sensitive to ethics matters may not recognize when potential ethical problems exist, and this is addressed in the next step of the model. Ongoing training and education are ways counselors can develop an awareness of ethics-related situations.

(I) First, counselors should *identify when there is a problem*—the **I** aspect of the model—and gather and clarify all pertinent facts. A thoughtful, measured, and deliberate approach to information gathering is important. Here again, looping back to the I aspect of the model, counselors should be aware of the types of information they will need to fully inform the decision-making process. Developing a sensitivity and awareness is critical to identifying when an issue may need to be considered an ethics-related matter. Some ethics matters may involve only certain people (e.g., client, counselor, family members), thus an awareness of how various matters affect all parties is important.

(R) After identifying the ethical issue, counselors should *review and apply ethics codes and standards, legal considerations, and the professional literature*—the **R** aspect of the model—in considering which actions to take. Relevant ethics codes should always be considered. Counselors need to examine the laws and regulations pertaining to the state where the ethics matter is taking place or has occurred. States have unique laws and regulations pertaining to counseling. It is also important to reference the literature that relates to the matter.

(E) An important part of the decision-making process is considering—at all stages of the decision-making process—how one's personal reactions may be affecting the process. As such, *examine personal values, reactions, and context*—the **E** aspect of the model—is included in this model. Counselors are themselves their most important counseling tool. Yet, all counselors have values and biases that influence their decision making. There are countless examples of how the personality of the counselor might affect the ethical decision-making process. For example, if a counselor begins to feel too close to a child client who has been abused by her father, the counselor might be compelled to make a custody recommendation in favor of the mother. In this case, personal feelings would have an impact on decision making and may result in a legal offense. Even seemingly subtler contextual issues can influence counselors' decision making. Consider that a counselor is overextended at work and is running late for an intake appointment and skips over the informed consent process. In this situation, the counselor's personal context will affect his or her clinical practices. Counselors should be vigilant and constantly monitor their personal reactions and experiences and how they affect clients.

(C) *Consult with and obtain guidance from supervisors, colleagues, and other professionals*—the **C** aspect of the model—will prove to be great support as many counselors navigate an ethical dilemma. All ethical decision-making models highlight the importance of consulting with others. Colleagues have unique insights, may have even experienced similar situations, and can often provide valuable insights.

D – Develop ethical sensitivity and awareness;
I – Identify when there is a problem;
R – Review and apply ethics codes and standards, legal considerations, and the professional literature;
E – Examine personal values, reactions, and context;
C – Consult with and obtain guidance from supervisors, colleagues, and other professionals;
T – Take possible courses of action into consideration;
I – Interpret the various consequences of each action;
O – Obtain the best course of action based on the research and information gathered; and
N – Note the outcomes of their decisions and reflect on their actions.

FIGURE 4.3 DIRECTION: An Ethical Decision-Making Model

(T) After careful resource and information gathering, consulting, and identifying one's personal influences in the context of an ethics matter, counselors can ***take possible courses of action into consideration***—the **T** aspect of the model. It is important for counselors to brainstorm the various options they can take because this will help to identify different options and ways that dilemmas can be handled.

(I) Once the courses of action are weighed out, counselors should ***interpret the various consequences of each action***—the **I** aspect of the model. This is where the advantages and disadvantages of the various courses of action can be evaluated. The more options identified by counselors—from the previous step—the more they will have to work with at this point.

(O) After the various options and consequences of each course of action are determined, ***obtain the best course of action based on the research and information gathered***—the **O** aspect of the model. Obtaining a course of action is the final step in the decision-making process.

(N) Counselors should ***note the outcomes of their decisions and reflect on their actions***—the **N** aspect of the model. They should honor the decisions they have made and recognize that they made the best decision they could at that time with the information available. That said, counselors will continually develop perceptions of their ethics judgments as they witness how their action play out. These reflections can be exceptionally helpful as they move forward and encounter new ethical situations.

It is important to recognize that although the steps of this model are presented in a linear fashion, there is nothing linear about ethical decision making. In reality, it is a very circular process. After a person has identified a potential ethics issue, he or she will move back and forth between different steps in the model.

Clinical Toolbox 4.5

In the Pearson eText, click here to see an example of the DIRECTION model applied to an ethical dilemma.

Summary

Conflicts between legal and ethical considerations can present serious challenges to counselors who work with youth. The lack of clear guidance related to youth counseling forces counselors, for the most part, to rely on their professional judgment when dealing with ethical dilemmas (Remley & Herlihy, 2016).

As counselors wrestle with ethics-related decision making, they might ask themselves whether they would be comfortable if their actions or decisions were posted on the front page of the local newspaper. Counselors might also ask themselves if they would behave a certain way or take a certain action if their supervisors were sitting in the room with them. Finally, they might ask themselves how they would handle a situation if it was their own child. Such questions can help counselors to drill down to the heart of

an ethics-related matter and understand who they want to be and how they need to behave in different situations.

Counselors are also advised to be aware of their personal feelings and reactions in a given ethics-related situation. When counselors find themselves wanting to avoid dealing with an ethics decision, they should run—not walk—to consult with a colleague or supervisor. Avoidance of ethics situations, and certainly distorting or hiding information, is a sign that a counselor is having a strong personal reaction that may be affecting his or her judgment. It is also important for counselors to recognize that everyone makes mistakes and that attempts to avoid, hide, or cover up mistakes often make things much worse. Again, counselors are advised to document and consult when they find themselves in such situations.

MyLab Counseling: Counseling Children and Adolescents

In the Topic 3 Assignments: *Youth Counseling Foundations,* try Application Exercise 3.1: *Informed Consent as an Ongoing Process* and Licensure Quiz 3.1: *Ethical and Legal Foundations of Counseling Youth.*

Then try Application Exercise 3.4: *Confidentiality.*

CHAPTER 5

Counseling Theories That Focus on Thought and Behavior Change and Action

A t its core, counseling is about helping people grow and change. When clients present for counseling, it can be difficult to know what information needs to be gathered and how to proceed in helping clients and their families make the changes they desire. Counselors use theories to organize and simplify the vast amount of information that clients present. These theories serve as road maps in finding the best ways to help youth change. Theories also enable counselors to determine how to use the presenting strengths to assist clients.

Of the hundreds of counseling theories, many have been developed specifically for use with youth. Each counseling theory is grounded in unique ideas regarding counseling goals, concepts of counseling and counseling procedures, the role of the counselor, and the role that parents and family should play in a young person's change process. At the most basic level, theories help counselors to:

- sift through a vast amount of presenting information and understand and recognize what client information needs to be identified, gathered, and organized;
- conceptualize young people's situations and identify what is supporting their problems in living; and
- identify ways of approaching clients that can help them to make changes.

Some theories are more appropriate and more commonly used with youth than others. In this chapter, we address the dominant counseling theories that focus on thought and behavior change. More specifically, behavior, cognitive behavioral, and reality therapies are discussed in the context of youth counseling.

Simplistically, behavior therapy focuses on behavior change or behavior modification. Behaviors that need to be discouraged or encouraged are identified, and the young person and parents work to change the environmental factors that contribute to supporting these behaviors. Parents are also encouraged and supported in providing appropriate consequences for desirable and undesirable behaviors.

Because behaviors are concrete and observable (as opposed to feelings and internal change processes), behavior therapy is a highly relevant theoretical approach that can inform youth counselors' practices. Its focus on reducing behavior problems and promoting the development of healthy, adaptive skills is easily understandable and appealing to many clients (Fall, Holden, & Marquis, 2010). Because it is a targeted intervention, it is—theoretically—also less time-intensive than nondirective approaches that may require more time spent in counseling sessions.

Behavior therapy is a technique-heavy approach, and many associated interventions can be used to help youth and their families to create change. Its focus on learning new behaviors and skills and ceasing unproductive or disruptive behaviors is also attractive to many parents. The intervention activities vary and depend on the young person's developmental levels, presenting struggles, and unique needs. As an example, some techniques are aimed at discouraging destructive behaviors, whereas others are aimed at encouraging self-sufficiency. Praise, positive reinforcement, and the use of small rewards can encourage a child to learn the skills he or she needs to manage not only a presenting problem but also the complex situations the child encounters as he or she grows and develops. In this way, behavior therapy teaches youth how to respond to the increasing demands of their worlds in prosocial, productive ways and can thus prevent new problems from emerging. Over time, behavioral changes can become intrinsically motivated as youth consistently reap the rewards of prosocial behaviors.

Behavior therapy focuses on helping clients to make action-oriented, behavioral changes, which is often what parents and youth want to get out of counseling (Fall et al., 2010). Behavior therapy involves unlearning maladaptive, dysfunctional behaviors and replacing these behaviors with adaptive behaviors or skills that enhance functioning (Spiegler & Guevremont, 2016). Behavior therapy is a highly structured, active counseling approach that requires lively youth and family participation. It has demonstrated effectiveness with an array of youth problems in living, and along with cognitive behavioral therapies (CBTs), it is the approach of choice for treating many specific youth mental disorders (Butler, Chapman, Forman, & A. T. Beck, 2006). An extensive body of literature suggests that this approach can be useful not only with youth but also with the people who support them (e.g., caregivers, teachers; Butler et al., 2006).

It can be helpful to address client behaviors while also attending to clients' thoughts. As such, cognitive behavioral therapy is also addressed in this chapter. Using CBT approaches, youth are taught how their thoughts can affect their emotions, moods, and behaviors. They learn how to identify negative or distorted thought patterns and how to change these thought patterns so they feel better emotionally and behave more desirably. This type of therapy is especially helpful in addressing anxiety and depressive disorders, two of the most commonly diagnosed categories of mental disorders (Kress & Paylo, 2015).

CBT interventions are especially relevant for working with youth, who are just beginning to learn about their complex bodies and brains, and early interventions can have a lasting effect on youth's abilities to regulate thoughts, feelings, and behaviors. CBTs focus on altering faulty thinking patterns and developing coping skills corresponds with youth's developmental growth and learning processes. Thus, CBT approaches can prevent existing problems from worsening and new problems from developing.

CBT approaches hold that thoughts—or cognitions—influence young people's behaviors and emotions and that through an awareness and subsequent modification of unhelpful thoughts or thinking patterns, youth can change their behaviors and ultimately feel better. CBT focuses on the meaning that clients give to, and how they think about, their experiences—not how they feel about the experiences specifically (Seligman & Reichenberg, 2014). CBT approaches are founded on the idea that counseling should be focused on identifying and altering clients' automatic thoughts and the ingrained beliefs, assumptions, and schemas; as a result, clients' should consequently experience associated behavioral changes (Seligman & Reichenberg, 2014).

In a nutshell, the goal of CBT approaches is to help clients to recognize and respond adaptively to difficult thoughts and feelings and engage in healthy, functional, and adaptive behaviors. As an example, if a 5-year-old girl believes it is her fault that her father left her family, she will feel bad and perhaps behave in unhelpful ways. As such, a CBT counselor would work with the girl to alter how she thinks about her father's exit so she can feel better. As discussed later in this chapter, there are various developmentally appropriate ways counselors can go about helping clients to reach these goals.

As with behavior therapy, CBT has an extensive evidence base for use with youth (Butler et al., 2006). It is widely considered to be an effective approach for many issues with which youth struggle, and third-party payers often place a premium on behavior therapy and CBT approaches (Butler et al., 2006). CBT is an evidence-based approach for treating youth depression, disruptive behavior disorders, suicidal ideation, anxiety, eating disorders, and difficulties adjusting to life changes (Nezu & Nezu, 2016; Ng & Weisz, 2016).

Finally, reality therapy is addressed in this chapter. Reality therapy has a strong problem-solving focus. It addresses the here-and-now actions of the client and focuses on how the client can make behavioral choices that help him or her to achieve desired goals. Reality therapy was originally developed specifically for use with youth; thus, its tenants and associated methods are developmentally appropriate for this population. This approach emphasizes making decisions, being responsible for one's decisions, taking action, and, ultimately, assuming control of one's life. Reality therapy is founded on the idea that clients seek to discover what they want and need, and they benefit from engaging in behaviors that bring them nearer to these wants and needs and their personal goals. Reality therapy does not have the same evidence base to suggest its effectiveness as do behavior therapy and CBT, yet its focus on youth makes it a useful theoretical approach for this group.

All theories discussed in this chapter are helpful with youth, specifically in that the theories provide youth with new ways of thinking and behaving, and these learned skills can be transferred to many situations now and in the future. The same is true for parents—that is, when they learn the skills to help their child in a given situation, these skills will theoretically transfer to other situations or even to their own lives. In this way, the action-oriented theoretical approaches may prevent other problems from emerging.

In this chapter and Chapters 6 and 7, readers have an opportunity to explore numerous prominent theories. Most students who read this text will complete an entire course on counseling theories. As such, it is not our intention to provide an exhaustive review of counseling theories. Rather, we provide a brief overview of select theories in the context of counseling youth and their families. Once an overview of each theory has been provided, the theory is addressed in terms of its core concepts and goals, role of the counselor, counseling process and procedures, and family interventions and involvement.

BEHAVIOR THERAPY

During the first half of the 20th century, Freudian psychoanalysis and other related psychoanalytic therapeutic modalities were the dominant counseling theories. The late 1950s and early 1960s gave rise to a new force of counseling approaches that together forged the **behavior therapy** movement. Founded on the pioneering research of John Watson, Ivan Pavlov, and B. F. Skinner, behavior-focused counseling approaches applied the scientific method and learning principles of classical and operant conditioning to produce observable behavioral change in individuals (Antony & Roemer, 2011). Behavior therapy emphasizes:

- the individual assessment and evaluation of objective, operationally defined behaviors;
- identification of specific **target behaviors**, or those behaviors interfering most significantly with the current daily functioning of youth (i.e., those that are often the initial focus of counseling);
- identification of the functions of behaviors or why they occur, the consequences that follow specific behaviors, and how youth respond to these consequences;
- selection of interventions aimed at systematically extinguishing undesirable behaviors while reinforcing desired behaviors and teaching youth to implement interventions independently;
- ongoing assessment and monitoring of behavior to determine the effectiveness of interventions and modifying treatment plans and interventions as needed throughout the counseling process; and
- conducting follow-up assessments after treatment goals are met to determine the overall effectiveness of counseling as evidenced by the maintenance of adaptive behaviors and elimination of maladaptive behaviors.

Because of the deliberate, targeted, and methodical nature of behavior therapy, counseling processes are highly structured, active, and, most notably, learning oriented. In the broadest sense, behavioral counseling is essentially a process of unlearning maladaptive behaviors and replacing them with new, relearned behaviors or skills that enhance adaptive functioning (Spiegler & Guevremont, 2016). As an example, consider a 4-year-old boy whose father brings him to counseling for hitting his younger brother and children at his day care. A counselor working from a behavioral therapy perspective would focus on carefully defining the problematic behavior (e.g., the boy hits children at school) and teaching the boy how to respond when angry or frustrated (e.g., the use of a relaxation exercise such as imagining he has a balloon in his belly that he blows up when he inhales and a candle he blows out on the exhale). Then, a counselor would also remove the behavioral reinforcers by teaching the adults around the child to respond in a way that extinguishes the negative behavior (e.g., limiting verbal attention given to the youth and quietly placing the boy in a time-out when he hits).

Early in its development, traditional behavior therapy focused exclusively on learning principles (Kazdin, 1978), but newer behavior therapy models have placed a greater emphasis on the effects on behavior of cognitions, emotions, and biological factors. Consequently, counselors who use behavior therapy principles with youth are likely to integrate other evidence-based interventions (e.g., CBT) and place some emphasis on factors beyond just learning principles.

Because of the diverse range of associated interventions that can be implemented to address a broad range of presenting problems, behavior therapy is highly applicable to counseling youth. In addition, behavior therapy is supported for use in addressing struggles that youth face (Fall et al., 2010). In order to modify young people's undesired behaviors, facilitate youth (or parent) skill development, or target symptoms of distress, youth counselors may pull from any of the following selected interventions:

prompting, modeling, shaping, chaining, homework assignments, response cost strategies, token economy systems, behavioral rehearsal or role-playing, social skills and assertiveness training, progressive
muscle relaxation, reciprocal inhibition, systematic desensitization, exposure-based interventions, hyp-
nosis, biofeedback, self-management, and mindfulness strategies. These strategies are further addressed
later in this section.

Behavioral intervention techniques have been shown to address presenting concerns related, but not
limited to, communication skills, attention-deficit/hyperactivity disorder (ADHD), autism spectrum disorder, enuresis, parenting skills, childhood obesity, anxiety, phobias, posttraumatic stress disorder (PTSD),
depression, addiction, and eating disorders (Spiegler & Guevremont, 2016).

Core Concepts and Goals of Counseling

From a behaviorist's perspective, children are essentially born as a blank slate; they are neither good nor bad
but simply products of their environment. All behavior is presumed to be acquired through processes of
learning and conditioning, in which behavior occurs in response to environmental stimuli—that is, the
behavior of youth is influenced by their lived experiences and how they react to events or conditions in their
environments (Skinner, 1971). With repeated exposure, youth begin to develop predictable patterns of
behavior in response to certain events or environmental conditions. Behaviorists believe behavior patterns
can be subsequently modified with appropriate intervention. Importantly, enhancing insight, exploring
underlying internal conflicts, and demonstrating unconditional positive regard to foster self-actualization
are not of interest to behaviorists. Behavior therapy focuses on action—that is, youth and/or their parents are
expected to practice and use the new skills and strategies they learned in counseling to assist them with
changing their behaviors and achieving their counseling goals (Wagner, 2008).

Behaviorists believe all behavior is learned, and thus problem behaviors can be unlearned and replaced
with those that are more desired. From this lens, the etiology of maladaptive behavior is not attributed to the
individual or considered to be a personally held disturbance or impairment. In this way, a behavioral approach
is an inherently empowering approach.

Behavior therapy is founded on the core concepts of classical and operant conditioning. These concepts help to explain how behavior is acquired and maintained, and they help to inform treatment interventions that are widely recognized as best practice approaches for treating specific mental health disorders.

CLASSICAL CONDITIONING

Classical conditioning, also referred to as **respondent conditioning**, is a stimulus–response pairing process
in which the repeated presentation of a certain stimulus can, over time, cause a given response. Thus, the
stimulus and response become associated with one another, or paired, and every time the stimulus is presented, the associated response occurs—hence, the term *respondent conditioning*. As an example, if a child
is verbally reprimanded by his or her teacher every day during carpet reading time and experiences an
anxiety-related response, the child may eventually begin to experience anxiety during reading time, even
without the teacher's reprimand (stimulus)—that is, the neutral activity of reading may become paired with
the child's anxiety. Wolpe (1958, 1969, 1990) used the principles of classical conditioning to develop an
intervention known as **systematic desensitization** that can eliminate young people's anxiety and fears. Systematic desensitization involves assisting clients to rank aspects of their fears from least to greatest and
teaching them various behavioral relaxation techniques. Once youth have exhibited the ability to use relaxation skills, they imagine the least distressing aspect of the fear while applying relaxation techniques. The
fears of youth are eventually extinguished because they are gradually and repeatedly paired with a relaxation
response as opposed to anxiety or fear.

OPERANT CONDITIONING

Operant conditioning, also called **instrumental conditioning**, is applicable in counseling youth because many
behavioral treatment interventions pull on operant conditioning principles. Operant conditioning is based on
consequences and reinforcement, whereby behavior is influenced by the positive or negative association
of the consequence that follows a behavior. When followed by a positive consequence such as a reward,

the behavior is reinforced and is subsequently more likely to occur. The opposite is true for behavior followed by a negative consequence such as punishment. The absence of reinforcement or the presentation of an undesired consequence makes the behavior less likely to occur (Miltenberger, 2012). Counselors frequently use behavior modification interventions such as **positive reinforcement**, **negative reinforcement**, **punishment**, and **extinction techniques** to increase the frequency of youth's positive behaviors and decrease or eliminate undesired behaviors. It is important for counselors to be aware that positive reinforcement is the most effective operant conditioning technique. As a result, if possible, positive reinforcement should always be used over punishment or other undesired consequences. Although reinforcement strategies are most typically tailored to modify a certain behavior in a specific setting, the repeated reinforcement of a behavior may lead to **generalization** or the demonstration of that behavior in different settings.

SOCIAL LEARNING

Originally referred to as **social cognitive theory** (Bandura, 1986), social learning differs slightly from the aforementioned classical and operant conditioning methods that solely focus on behavior and the environment. Social learning differs in that it includes an additional focus on one's worldview, beliefs, perspectives, and other cognitive processes because internal appraisals or interpretations of events are assumed to significantly influence one's behavior. As it pertains to traditional behavior therapy, social learning informs how behavior can be learned through observation or by watching the behavior of others (Bandura, 1977). Observational learning is particularly relevant when counseling younger populations because they easily pick up or model the language and behaviors of those around them. Modeling is a commonly used social learning intervention that involves providing youth with a positive model or observable examples of desired behaviors they might imitate. An example of modeling is the use of peer models in a social skills training program for youth who have autism spectrum disorder. Table 5.1 provides a summary of behavior therapy's core concepts.

Table 5.1 Core Concepts of Behavior Therapy

Concept	Description	Example	Intervention Example
Classical conditioning	• A stimulus–response pairing process. • The repeated presentation of a certain stimulus can, over time, cause a given response.	• If a child is constantly laughed at by his or her classmates while giving a speech, the child may eventually develop anxiety around public speaking.	• Systematic desensitization
Operant conditioning	• Based on consequences and reinforcement. • Behavior is influenced by the positive or negative association of the consequence that follows a behavior.	• Every time the child cleans his or her room without being asked, the child gets an extra 15 minutes to play outside. • The child may leave the dinner table after he or she eats four more bites of his or her vegetables. • The parents take the child's favorite toy away after he or she throws a tantrum. • The parents ignore the child's tantrum after not getting candy at the store.	• Positive reinforcement • Negative reinforcement • Punishment • Extinction
Social learning	• Focus is on one's worldview, beliefs, perspectives, and other cognitive processes. • Internal appraisals or interpretations of events are assumed to significantly influence one's behavior.	• The child sees her mom brush her hair each morning, so the child imitates her mom by brushing her own hair each morning.	• Modeling

Role of the Counselor in Behavior Therapy

Counselors who use a behavioral approach with youth serve as consultants, teachers, architects, and/or problem solvers. Behavioral counselors conduct sessions in a directive, planned, and instructional manner, and they value the systematic, objective, observable, and rigorous elements of research-based therapeutic procedures and practices (Miltenberger, 2012; Spiegler & Guevremont, 2016). Despite this linear, scientific approach, behavioral counselors believe relational factors can influence treatment processes, and counselors who practice contemporary behavior therapy recognize the importance of establishing a strong therapeutic alliance when working with youth. Because learned behaviors are relatively enduring, behavioral change can be difficult. As such, behavioral counselors understand they must attribute the same degree of time and effort toward the therapeutic relationship as they do with assessment, evaluation, and implementation of behavioral interventions if they are to promote change and the accomplishment of goals. Without the trust of clients and their family members, even the most evidence-based interventions will be ineffective. Moreover, because behavior therapy requires that youth—and sometimes their families—take an active role in learning, monitoring, practicing, and using various skills, counselors' support, encouragement, and empathic understanding will reinforce, motivate, and encourage clients' efforts. Counselors can foster a positive therapeutic relationship by learning about the strengths, interests, and unique personal qualities of youth, and they can integrate such themes into youth's individually tailored interventions. For example, the counselor can create a token economy system using pictures of cars, dinosaurs, television characters, animals, or other themes that match the youth's interests.

In addition to forming a trusting therapeutic alliance, counselors who use a behavioral approach typically follow a set of systematic procedures known as **applied behavior analysis (ABA)**, which is the application of behavioral assessment and treatment strategies to change the undesired behaviors of youth. The applied aspect of ABA represents the literal application of research methods to modify human behavior. ABA also involves **functional behavior assessment (FBA)**, or **functional analysis**, evaluation procedures. Counselors use FBAs to systematically identify the contributing and maintaining factors of problem behaviors and the function or purpose these behaviors serve (Harvey, Luiselli, & Wong, 2009). Following the completion of assessment processes, counselors analyze obtained data and shift their roles toward (a) developing initial individualized treatment goals and objectives that target specific, observable behaviors, (b) identifying evidence-based behavioral interventions and teaching youth how they can be used, generalized across settings, and independently maintained, (c) continually monitoring behavior, assessing the effectiveness of interventions, and modifying treatment goals and objectives as needed throughout counseling, and (d) completing follow-up assessments to determine treatment effectiveness and the maintenance of positive behavioral change.

Behavior therapy inherently emphasizes individualized treatment practices that consider specific settings, environmental circumstances, people, and other factors associated with youth behavior. They also emphasize that counselors should individually tailor assessment processes and intervention techniques in a manner that is developmentally, intellectually, and contextually sensitive to the needs of each client. For example, counselors working with younger clients can design treatment plans that look similar to coloring books or children's stories, create rating scales with smiley faces as opposed to numbers to track self-report data, or use role-playing as a creative avenue for children to verbally express the new competencies they have learned throughout counseling or to demonstrate before-and-after examples of the behavioral changes they have made. Figure 5.1 provides an activity that can be used in sessions with youth.

Clinical Toolbox 5.1

In the Pearson eText, click here to view a self-reporting rating scale for use with younger children.

Activity Overview

In applying this activity, youth are invited to adopt the role of a teacher. At the end of counseling sessions, clients are asked to display their knowledge and understanding of new concepts, terms, rules or expectations, interventions, skills, or any other associated content introduced during the session. Counselors provide clients with materials and props and join with parents, guardians, and/or family members to create an audience of students for clients to teach.

Counseling Goals Addressed

This intervention creates an opportunity for children to demonstrate their understanding of new topics introduced during counseling sessions and evidence mastery of previously discussed concepts. Through interactive experiences such as teaching "lessons" to counselors and family members, clients learn to use effective communication skills; work through problems; identify rules, expectations, and positive behaviors at school, at home, and in the community; and apply therapeutic concepts in increasingly dynamic and complex ways.

Directions

1. Introduce and explain to the client how role-plays, "acting," or "pretending" can be used as a fun way to learn, practice, and master topics discussed in counseling (e.g., coping skills, relaxation techniques, social skills, other prosocial behaviors).
2. Ask the client if he or she has a favorite teacher or class subject, and process teaching strategies, classroom activities, and lessons that have helped the client to learn. Explain, model, and process how teachers verbally discuss learning material; provide examples to students; use worksheets, pictures, lists, or drawings to visually display information; or use activities and games to help students to learn. Counselors should modify content as needed to ensure developmental appropriateness.
3. Ask the client to adopt the role of his or her favorite teacher and provide an example of previously discussed teaching strategies. Counselors can also ask the client to explain and provide examples of classroom expectations; rules; positive behaviors in the school setting; and how teachers recognize, praise, or reward students.
4. Affirm and praise the client for his or her knowledge and understanding of discussed topics, and make connections to the competencies and skills the client has learned in counseling. Ask the client if he or she is willing to act as a teacher at the end of counseling sessions, and explain how the counselor, parents, caregivers, and/or family members will serve as students.
5. Review and process a current or previously learned therapeutic topic during counseling sessions. Provide concrete examples, model, and practice role-playing a "lesson" with the client as the teacher to build confidence and promote mastery of the behavior.
6. Provide the client with props and materials to enhance the experiential nature of the activity. Props might include a large finger pointer, fake glasses, a necktie or sports coat, teacher supply bag or briefcase, textbooks, folders, a chalk or Dry-Erase board, etc. Counselors should prepare concrete materials related to the client's "teaching" topic, such as worksheets or pictures that list or visually display information in a manner that is easily comprehensible for the client.
7. Explain the activity to parents, caregivers, and/or family members, and join family members as a student of the client's classroom. Counselors can invite the client to use their desks and computer chair as supplements to other props if desired. Depending on the developmental and intellectual functioning of the client, counselors may need to serve as a "coteacher" to facilitate the activity.
8. On completion of the role-play, celebrate the client's success; identify strengths, skills and competencies; praise the client; and process positive behavioral changes with the client and his or her family members. Counselors may also want to assign "homework" in which clients are instructed to teach family members or caregivers additional lessons based on their positive behaviors displayed in certain environments throughout the week.

Process Questions

1. Tell me what it was like to be a teacher and help us to learn.
2. What skills did you use while teaching us?
3. Tell me what you liked most about this activity, and why?
4. What was challenging for you? How did you overcome those challenges?
5. Where else will you show these positive behaviors? How can you teach your friends?

FIGURE 5.1 Teacher Role-Play Activity

Counseling Process and Procedures

ASSESSMENT

Behavioral counselors gather initial information related to youth's presenting concerns through various assessment approaches, including indirect, descriptive, and experimental methods (Flynn & Lo, 2016). To understand a child's behavior, a counselor might ask a parent to thoroughly explain a typical instance of the problem behavior. It is important for the parent to provide details because it is within these details that the counselor can identify what may be maintaining the problem. Counselors working from a behavioral approach are interested in the answers to three questions:

- What does the problem look like in concrete, specific, behavioral terms?
- What happens before the problem occurs?
- What happens after the problem occurs?

Counselors are thus able to help parents or others understand the problem in new terms.

For example, a childcare worker might report that a youth is "attention seeking," yet the actual behavior in question may involve a set of specific behaviors that can become the target of intervention. In these situations, a counselor might say to a childcare worker:

"I want you to walk me through what exactly happens in a situation where Ella 'goes off' as you say, or has an aggressive outburst. If I were a fly on the wall, what would I see start to happen five minutes before she became aggressive . . . what would I see right before she became aggressive. . . what would happen during the time she was aggressive. . . .?"

It is not uncommon for a parent to describe a child's behavior simply as "bad." A counselor might dig in to determine what "bad" looks like. On further exploration, it may be revealed that the child is being what the mother calls "difficult." Questioning related to the child being "difficult" follows:

- What exactly is the child doing when he or she is being "difficult"?
- Tell me about the frequency of the "difficult" behaviors. How frequently do they occur?
- Tell me about situations in which the child is less difficult.
- Is the child sometimes not "difficult"? If so, when? How often?
- What helps the child to be less "difficult"?

Indirect assessment approaches (e.g., clinical interviews, questionnaires, rating scales) and descriptive assessment approaches (e.g., direct observation of the frequency, intensity, and duration of behavior) allow counselors to collect valuable data that can inform case conceptualization and treatment planning processes, but FBAs have become one of the most frequently used, dynamic assessment methods among behavioral counselors. Similar to other ABA assessment methods, FBAs are intended to objectively identify youth problem behaviors, and determine the individual and environmental determinants that trigger and maintain behavior (Leaf et al., 2016; Oliver, Pratt, & Normand, 2015). The systematic procedures of FBAs are recognized as a particularly advantageous behavioral assessment because they enable helping professionals to obtain a comprehensive and precise understanding of the *cause–effect correlations* between specific behaviors and environmental circumstances that help to determine the underlying function of youth behavior (Shriver, Anderson, & Proctor, 2001)—that is, by making connections between the behavior and factors—such as the setting, time, around whom, and what happens before and after—FBAs allow counselors to identify what purpose behaviors serve for youth or what they are getting from engaging in a behavior.

FBAs are conducted using the **ABC model**, in which counselors observe and gather data on antecedents, observed behaviors, and the consequences of behaviors. Counselors first seek to identify the **antecedent events** or cues that occur before a certain behavior is displayed, or in other words, to determine what factors or aspects of a client's environment are responsible for eliciting the behavioral response. These responses in turn serve as the target behaviors around which counselors orient FBA processes. For example, while observing a child in the classroom to identify antecedents of target behaviors, counselors aim to answer questions about target behaviors similar to the following: In what setting do they occur? What are the physical characteristics of the setting, or how is the setting uniquely arranged? What time of day do behaviors occur? What is typically occurring in the environment before behaviors are displayed? Is the child experiencing academic difficulties? Who is around? Are there peer influences? Antecedents provide counselors with an understanding of the contributing determinants, or beforehand factors, prompting youth to demonstrate a certain behavioral response. Others' responses or events that follow a behavior are known as **consequences**, and not only do they keep youth's behaviors maintained, but they also explain the function of behavior. Behaviorists generally categorize behavior functions, or the purposes a behavior serves, into five domains:

- *Attention:* Gaining either positive or negative attention from others (e.g., earning positive attention from a parent for completing chores, gaining negative attention from a caregiver by breaking household items).
- *Escape:* Escape from or avoidance of a task, event, or undesired situation (e.g., an adolescent intentionally starts a fight with a peer to avoid a reading quiz).
- *Sensory:* Behaviors occur as a form of self-stimulation (e.g., an adolescent leaves his or her classroom to walk the hallways due to hypervigilance).
- *Physical:* Youth are feeling ill, pain, or other physical discomfort (e.g., a child refuses to do homework after eating dinner due to a stomachache).
- *Tangible:* Attempts to obtain a desired item (e.g., a child walks the dog every day to receive allowance).

Once antecedents and consequences have been identified, counselors form hypotheses about the function of behavior based on their conceptualization of how environmental determinants are influencing the expression and maintenance of target behaviors. Counselors then test their hypotheses by staging brief experiments in which youth are systematically presented with a series of events or situations that are expected to elicit target behavior responses—that is, counselors intentionally introduce previously identified antecedents to determine if youth exhibit target behaviors. Alternatively, counselors may also stage different events related to specific functional behavior domains (e.g., attention, escape, tangible) and track which set of circumstances most frequently elicits target behavior responses. Maladaptive functional relationships—those in which environmental determinants lead to youth's engagement in undesired target behaviors—are used as a foundation to establish treatment goals and objectives aimed at extinguishing such relationships and assisting youth to develop more adaptive behaviors.

Although FBAs take some effort to complete, they are very pragmatic and hold great utility for counselors working with youth. As FBAs reduce complex behaviors into isolated components or smaller parts, counselors can provide youth and their families with concrete, logical interpretations of problems. Reducing behaviors into smaller specific components can help in formulating realistic and attainable goals. Such behavioral approaches are particularly applicable in the school environment because many youth who experience behavioral problems in the classroom also encounter academic difficulties. Establishing small goals that youth are able to accomplish in a short time period can engender an advantageous sense of success and self-efficacy. Fostering young people's personal agency can act to increase therapeutic momentum because goal achievement naturally serves as reinforcement.

OPERANT CONDITIONING INTERVENTIONS

Subsequent to the completion of an individualized FBA and the establishment of clear, measurable, and observable goals, counselors identify empirically validated interventions that support the desired counseling outcomes. As previously noted, behavioral treatment strategies fall into intervention domains founded on the principles of classical and operant conditioning; however, when working with youth, most intervention techniques are likely to be operant in nature because reinforcement strategies can be readily implemented across different settings and applied by many different individuals in youth's lives. As such, counselors can provide psychoeducation about behavioral interventions and collaborate with parents, caregivers, teachers, and other school personnel to optimize the generalization of youth behaviors across environmental domains. In Table 5.2, operant conditioning methods that are commonly used with youth are provided.

Contingency Management.   Contingency management is essentially a positive reinforcement technique that requires youth to complete a less desirable or undesirable task prior to engaging in a preferred activity.

Table 5.2	Operant Conditioning Interventions	
Intervention	Application	Example
Positive reinforcement	• The addition of a positive stimulus as a consequence of behavior. • Behavior is increased.	• A teacher gives her student a sticker for following directions. • A mother praises her son for receiving good grades.
Negative reinforcement	• The removal of an aversive stimulus as a consequence of behavior. • Behavior is increased.	• A student can leave detention after completing a late assignment. • A child shares a toy to stop her younger sister's nagging.
Punishment	• *Positive punishment* is the addition of an aversive stimulus as a consequence of behavior. • *Negative punishment*, or *response cost*, is the removal of a reinforcing stimulus as a consequence of behavior. • Behavior is decreased.	• A father puts his son in time-out for hitting his younger brother (positive punishment). • Parents take away the car keys of an adolescent for staying out past curfew (negative punishment).
Extinction	• Behavior stops or extinguishes due to a lack of reinforcement. • Behavior is decreased.	• A teacher ignores a child's tantrum. • A father refrains from giving candy to his son each time he cries.
Prompting	• A verbal, visual, or physical cue is used to cause a behavior. • Behavior is likely to occur, and with reinforcement will increase.	• A teacher raises her hand to remind students who are speaking out. • An adolescent points at his teacher to redirect a friend who is talking in class.
Shaping	• Reinforcing *successive approximations*, or displayed behaviors that are similar to the target behavior, until it occurs. • Gradually increases similar behaviors until the target behavior is learned.	• Praising a shy adolescent for short interactions until he openly talks to peers. • Providing a child with a reward for completing small sections of her homework until the entire assignment is complete.
Chaining	• Reinforcing step-by-step or "chained" behaviors that lead to the learning of a complex behavior. • Gradually increases each step-by-step behavior until the more complex behavior is achieved.	• A child receives a gold star for each letter of the alphabet that is learned. • A child is praised for mastering each step required to tie her shoes.

Because the preferred activity is highly desired, it is more likely to occur. When a preferred activity is made contingent on the completion of an undesired task, which is less probable to occur, youth are motivated to first complete the undesired task to receive the ensuing reward. For example, if a child wants to play outside, he or she might first be required to complete assigned homework. Contingency contracts use preferred activities as positive reinforcements to increase youth's engagement in less desired tasks such as completing chores, eating vegetables, or completing homework.

      Token Economy Systems. A form of contingency management, token economy systems are operant reinforcement programs that can be applied to individuals or groups of youth, and they are often implemented by parents and teachers as home and classroom management strategies. Similar to all behavioral counseling processes, a target behavior or set of behaviors initially must be identified and defined. **Behavior contracts**

are used to document the terms or conditions of the token economy system, including specific behavioral expectations and schedules of reinforcement. Creating behavior contracts and using other visual aids makes token economies more concrete and understandable when working with youth who have developmental or intellectual delays. Youth begin earning tokens, points, tickets, or other small tangible items for demonstrating desired target behaviors. Tokens are provided *each time* the behavior occurs and are typically stored in a visible jar or container. Once a predetermined quantity is earned, the tokens can be traded in for a reward.

Clinical Toolbox 5.2

In the Pearson eText, click here to view an example of a behavior contract.

Token economies can be easily adapted to match the needs of youth. For instance, token economies can also include **response cost** conditions in which the youth is required to remove a token from the jar as a consequence of undesired behavior. The inclusion of this condition is not uncommon; however, because positive reinforcement is more effective than negative punishment in modifying behavior, counselors and other individuals who use token economies need to ensure they are designing and implementing reward systems that favor youth's success. A token economy should be set up so the young person can be successful and receive the desired reward. Consider a young child presenting with hyperactivity and impulsivity. If the child is earning tokens for raising his or her hand but is required to remove a token each time he or she speaks out, the child could hypothetically never reach the threshold quantity of tokens to earn a reward. Not only would this type of system be ineffective for reinforcing the target behavior, but it may result in the opposite effect and cause the child to experience increased levels of frustration, anger, or disappointment. Token economies that use response cost are more appropriate for youth who have evidenced a degree of behavioral improvement sufficient for progression toward more advanced reinforcement systems. For younger children and youth in the early stages of the counseling process, token economies solely based on positive reinforcement, and those that hold realistic, attainable reward thresholds, are likely the most appropriate option to foster their achievement of target behaviors.

It is imperative for counselors and other individuals using token economies—or any of the behavior modification operant interventions previously delineated—to remain mindful of the developmental and intellectual functioning of youth. It may be beneficial for counselors and those involved in counseling and intervention processes to reflect on their expectations of youth or the demands they are placing on them. It is important not to demand too much from them or administer punishment because they do not promptly change all their undesired habits simply after receiving a small reward. Counseling is a process, and youth must be met on their levels. Thus, counselors may initially need to use a high degree of prompting, shaping, chaining, and reinforcement to assist a child with remaining seated throughout a class period, but they can reduce the frequency of such interventions as the child masters the target behavior and begins to develop new skills. Temporarily and appropriately decreasing the amount of demands placed on youth during the initial phase of counseling and gradually increasing expectations as counseling progresses may prove advantageous because youth will be afforded opportunities to experience the gratification and pride that achievement provides, while also making the small changes needed to begin working toward more complex positive behavioral goals.

Clinical Toolbox 5.3

In the Pearson eText, click here to view an example of a daily behavior chart.

CLASSICAL CONDITIONING INTERVENTIONS

Interventions founded on the principles of classical conditioning are most applicable to youth who experience distress related to anxiety, panic, fear, or trauma—all of which share common features of heightened body responses such as increased heart rate, rapid breathing, or shaking, along with distressing thoughts about the feared object, event, or situation. Accordingly, classical conditioning interventions not only use behavioral learning principles to target the physiological responses characteristic of stress-related presenting concerns (e.g., separation anxiety, specific phobia disorder, social anxiety disorder, agoraphobia, panic disorder, posttraumatic stress disorder) but also include supplemental cognitive-oriented exercises to address thought-based symptoms (e.g., worrying about getting lost, being embarrassed in front of others, anticipation that harm, injury, or death will occur). Because many anxiety distresses or instances of trauma often manifest or occur during childhood, interventions such as progressive muscle relaxation, systematic desensitization, and exposure-based strategies are commonly used with youth. These treatment techniques have the empirical evidence to validate their effectiveness. Still another technique is eye movement desensitization and reprocessing (EMDR), an exposure-based therapy that has received significant attention due to the growing body of literature supporting its clinical utility for treating trauma-related distress.

Classical conditioning interventions, especially EMDR, are advanced treatment approaches that require specific training and practice. Novice counselors and other helping professionals early in their careers must ensure they have the competency, training, and clinical supervision necessary to use these interventions without harming youth, and they must be sensitive that they practice in an effective and ethical manner.

Progressive Muscle Relaxation.   Anxiety or other stress-related presenting concerns involve various physical symptoms, including muscle tension, heart palpitations, dizziness, fatigue, or sleep disturbance. **Progressive muscle relaxation** (PMR; Jacobson, 1938; Lopata, 2003) is one intervention behavioral counselors use to assist youth with calming their bodies and relaxing when they are feeling anxious or worried. Youth are encouraged to breathe deeply as they find a comfortable seated or lying position with their eyes closed. Counselors systematically guide youth to tense the muscles of a certain body area for approximately 5 seconds, release or let go of the muscle tension, and notice the state of relaxation that ensues. A progression through the major muscle areas of the body from head to toe is typically used. The most critical component of PMR involves youth's discrimination between sensations of tension and relaxation. Youth begin to recognize how their bodies respond to anxiety, and with continued practice they learn to relax their muscles on cue when presented with an anxiety-provoking stimulus. However, as with all conditioning interventions, repetition is imperative to yield the desired effect. Figure 5.2 provides an example of a script that counselors might use with younger children to teach PMR.

PMR processes can be modified for younger children by using metaphors or imagery techniques. Counselors can ask children to pretend or visualize scenarios associated with the tensing and releasing of different muscle regions. The following examples can be used with young children:

- "Pretend you're an owl looking for your friend. Keep your eyes closed, but raise your eyebrows *real* high! Keep looking for your friend . . . there he is! You can relax your eyebrows now."
- "Pretend you're a bunny smelling flowers. Oh, no! This flower smells bad! Scrunch your nose like a bunny . . . okay, now the smell is gone. Doesn't it feel nice to relax your nose?"
- "Pretend you're the Hulk and starting to turn green. Squeeze your fists *really* hard . . . keep squeezing! You're not mad anymore; now you can let go. Do you notice a difference from when you were turning green?"

Systematic Desensitization.   Developed by Joseph Wolpe (1958, 1969, 1990), systematic desensitization is an intervention that uses **reciprocal inhibition** and **counterconditioning** to extinguish phobias and anxieties. Using this approach, counselors first teach youth deep breathing and relaxation strategies and subsequently construct an **anxiety hierarchy**, or some prefer the term **subjective units of distress (SUDs)**, a scale that successively builds from the least anxiety-provoking situation to the most. Youth are then instructed to imagine the lowest level of their anxiety hierarchy while intentionally engaging in relaxation practices to prevent or extinguish manifestations of anxiety, thus representing reciprocal inhibition, which is the pairing of a stimulus with an incompatible response. When the imagined anxiety-provoking situation, event, or cue is repeatedly paired with the incompatible response of relaxation, anxiety or fear becomes **desensitized** or weakened. This process of unlearning is known as **counterconditioning**. Counselors use systematic desensitization to gradually work with youth to relax throughout each step of their hierarchies as a means to extinguish phobic or anxious responses. Similar to PMR, systemic desensitization requires daily practice to yield desired results.

What follows is a relaxation activity that can be used to teach younger children how to engage in progressive muscle relaxation:

"We are going to do an exercise to show you how good it feels to be relaxed and to teach you how you can help your body become relaxed. We are going to focus on different parts of the body, and when I tell you, you are going to tense them up as much as you can. If you feel comfortable, close your eyes and listen to the sound of my voice. Let's start with your face. Pretend you just ate a very sour piece of lemon. Scrunch your eyes and lips as much as you can. Now relax your lips and eyes. It feels good to relax, doesn't it? Relax your lips so much that maybe they even open a little bit.

Now scrunch your nose and your forehead. See how tense you can make them. Picture your eyebrows getting so high that they almost touch your hair. Now relax your muscles. Let your muscles slide back into place.

Next we will move to relaxing the lower part of your face. Pretend you have a big jawbreaker in your mouth with a piece of bubble gum inside. You really want to get to that bubble gum, but you are going to have to bite down hard to break it open. Now gently bite down and try to crack open the jawbreaker. It is really tough! Take a break and let your muscles relax. Give me one more good bite and the jawbreaker will break. Ready? Go! Good. Now relax and let your neck and jaw muscles release. Maybe even let your mouth hang open a little bit. It sure feels good to relax after biting down so hard, doesn't it?

Next, bring your attention to your neck and shoulders. You already used your neck muscles a little bit to break the jawbreaker, and we are going to use them again. Tense your back and shoulders up so much that your shoulders are close to your ears. Maybe try to make your shoulders touch your ears like earrings. Squeeze your muscles and make them as tight as you can. See if you can get your shoulders just a little bit higher. Tuck your chin to your chest and keep pushing your shoulders higher. Now let go. Pay attention to how good it feels to let your muscles relax and go back to their natural places. Doesn't it feel much better to relax?

Let's move to your belly. Pretend you are trying to suck your bellybutton in so hard that it is going to touch your back. Good. Now hold it in even tighter, like you are going to squeeze sideways through a tiny door. Make yourself as tiny as you can be. Now let your muscles relax and take a deep breath to fill up your tummy. That feels good, doesn't it?

Bring your attention to your legs and feet. Stand up and pretend you are on a sandy beach and you are pushing your feet into wet sand. Spread your toes down into the sand as the waves from the ocean are rolling by your waist. The waves are big and you need to really make your legs strong and spread your toes into the sand so you don't get swept onto shore. You have to stand really strong. Flex your leg muscles as strong as you can, a really big wave is coming! You don't want to get washed onto shore! Good job. Now relax your muscles again.

Think of how good it feels to relax your muscles after they have been tightened up. It feels much better to relax than to be tense, doesn't it? You can practice this exercise anytime to help you relax. Maybe you would like to practice this at bedtime to help you to relax before sleep. You can do these exercises anywhere, whenever you feel stressed or your muscles feel tense. You did a great job today! Keep practicing, and you will be an expert relaxer!"

FIGURE 5.2   Relaxation Script for Younger Children

Clinical Toolbox 5.4

In the Pearson eText, click here to view an example of an anxiety hierarchy.

Exposure-Based Interventions.   Whereas systematic desensitization requires youth to *imagine* anxiety-provoking stimuli, exposure-based interventions require youth to experience a real-world, or in vivo, encounter with such stimuli. The processes of ***in vivo* exposure** mirror those of systematic desensitization because counselors work with youth to develop a hierarchy that ascends from situations of least to greatest distress. While using relaxation strategies as coping mechanisms, youth are gradually exposed to higher levels of the feared or anxiety-provoking stimuli until they eventually exhibit the ability to encounter the stimuli without avoidance.

Similar exposure-based interventions, **implosion** and **flooding**, use the opposite procedure of systematic desensitization—that is, rather than gradually working from the least distressing stimuli to greatest, implosion and flooding strategies involve initial and repeated exposure to stimuli that are most distressing to youth. Implosion refers to the aforementioned process used solely during counselor-guided visualization exercises. Flooding involves the repeated real-life exposure to fears or distressing stimuli.

With direct exposure, youth encounter the stimulus for a prolonged period of time, and the body's stress response eventually becomes exhausted. When this process is conducted repeatedly within a short time frame, youth are able to learn that the aversive consequences they previously anticipated do not occur. Flooding may appear extreme, but the intervention most typically reduces anxiety or extinguishes fears quickly. However, as previously noted, it is imperative for counselors and other mental health professionals to implement interventions such as *in vivo* exposure, implosion, and flooding with a high degree of caution. Although parents give informed consent on behalf of youth, if counselors plan to use any exposure-based strategies, they should fully disclose the processes that are involved and also obtain assent from youth.

Eye Movement Desensitization and Reprocessing.   Developed by Francine Shapiro (2001), EMDR has gained popularity primarily as a treatment approach for individuals who have experienced traumatic stress (Kemp, Drummond, & McDermott, 2009; Rodenburg, Benjamin, de Roos, Meijer, & Stams, 2009). EMDR is an integration of rhythmic bilateral stimulation, imagined exposure, relaxation, and cognitive restructuring therapeutic techniques. Rapid eye movements are most typically used as the bilateral component that is purported to facilitate the reprocessing of traumatic experiences and associated maladaptive thoughts and body sensations, but other bilateral stimuli such as tones, lights, or tapping have also been used. The underlying premise of EMDR is that past traumatic experiences are stored in the sensory and motor areas of the brain (right hemisphere) rather than the area of the brain that stores everyday learning and memory (left hemisphere). Following the assessment and preparation stages of EMDR, in which the event or series of events are identified and relaxation skills are taught, counselors collaboratively work with clients to identify subjective units of distress (SUDs) associated with the event, and specific negative thoughts, emotions, and body areas where physical sensations are experienced. Positive replacement thoughts are then developed, and youth are requested to simultaneously think about the traumatic experience and the *positive* replacement thought (e.g., "I am safe.") while the counselor initiates the rapid lateral eye movement for approximately 15 to 30 seconds and relaxation techniques are subsequently employed. Administering these steps repeatedly is believed to essentially reprocess the memory in association with relaxation and the positive replacement thought (Field & Cottrell, 2011; Greyber, Dulmus, & Cristalli, 2012). In Table 5.3, an overview of classical conditioning interventions is provided.

Table 5.3   Classical Conditioning Interventions

Intervention	Description	Core Concepts	Example
Progressive muscle relaxation	• Calming the body through relaxation techniques • Used with youth during times of worry and anxiety • Relaxation techniques used to target core muscle groups	• Management of anxiety • Guided visual imagery • Relaxation using metaphors and imagery	• Every time the child has a fight with his older brother, he feels a sense of worry and anxiety. During the time of worry, the child feels tense in his fingers the most. Using PMR, the counselor asks the child to pretend he is holding a lime and asks him to squeeze it hard. Then the counselor tells the child to squeeze all the juice out, feeling the tightness in his arms and fingers as he squeezes. The boy is instructed to drop the lime and relax before repeating the process with the other hand.
Systematic desensitization	• Unlearning to extinguish phobias and anxieties • Used with youth to relax throughout each step of an anxiety hierarchy to extinguish phobic or anxious responses	• Counterconditioning • Anxiety hierarchy, also known as subjective units of distress (SUDS) • Reciprocal inhibition • Guided visual imagery	• The child has a fear of dogs, and each time the child sees or encounters one, the child screams and runs. With the counselor, the child creates an anxiety hierarchy of dogs with the least fear-provoking situation at the bottom and the most fear-provoking situation at the top. Using visual imagery, the child works his or her way up from the bottom of the hierarchy to the top and goes through the situations repeatedly until the fear situations exhibit no anxiety.

Table 5.3 (Continued)			
Intervention	**Description**	**Core Concepts**	**Example**
Exposure	• Requires youth to experience a real-world encounter with anxiety-provoking stimuli • Gradually exposed to higher levels of the feared or anxiety-provoking stimuli until youth exhibit the ability to encounter the stimuli without avoidance	• In vivo exposure • Coping strategies • Anxiety hierarchy, SUDS	• The child has a fear of spiders, and every time the child encounters one, it provokes worry, fear, and crying. The counselor gradually exposes the child to pictures of a spider and later to a spider crawling in a cage, and eventually he has the child hold a spider until the fear of spiders is eliminated.
Implosion	• Intensive visual review of anxiety-producing stimuli or events • Always done through imagery	• Recollection of most distressing stimuli • Adaptive response • Guided visual imagery	• The child is asked to visualize the most distressing fear situation when encountering a spider. The counselor and the child develop more adaptive ways to handle those situations.
Flooding	• Repeated real-life exposure to fears or distressing stimuli • Direct exposure until the body's stress response eventually becomes exhausted	• In vivo exposure • Direct exposure • Repeated exposure	• The child is repeatedly exposed to the greatest fear-provoking situation, which is holding a real spider, until the child's fear response of encountering a spider is exhausted and eliminated.
Eye movement desensitization and reprocessing (EMDR)	• Facilitates the reprocessing of traumatic experiences and associated maladaptive thoughts and body sensations with bilateral stimuli such as tones, lights, or tapping • Integration of rhythmic bilateral stimulation, imagined exposure, relaxation, and cognitive restructuring	• Rapid eye movement • Guided visual imagery • Bilateral stimulation • Cognitive restructuring • Anxiety hierarchy, SUDS • Relaxation • Positive replacement • Emotion regulation	• The child is brought to a counselor after experiencing one incident of molestation by her neighbor about 3 months ago. Nightmares, flashbacks, and sleep problems keep resurfacing. The counselor begins to ask the girl to visualize a safe place. The counselor installs the image by using EMDR, making her eyes follow a light back and forth. The counselor then asks her to tell the story of her molestation, asking the girl to give a hand signal whenever she needs to stop or go to her safe place. Using EMDR, the child works through the pain of the molestation.

ADDITIONAL BEHAVIOR THERAPY INTERVENTIONS

Social Skills Training.   Social skills training pulls on various behavioral techniques to assist youth in enhancing their interpersonal communication skills and thus their relationships with others. Social skills training can be used in both individual and group counseling, and it is often the focus of therapeutic summer programs for youth or school groups aimed at promoting positive peer connections. Groups are particularly advantageous due to their innate social orientation, and they can be easily adapted to match developmental levels ranging from young children to older adolescents. As youth gradually learn language and the social nuances of interacting with peers and adults throughout development, social skills training can provide youth with additional competencies to better communicate their needs, wants, thoughts, and feelings in an age-appropriate and effective manner.

Social skills training is both didactic and experiential. Counselors provide psychoeducation to youth about various topics associated with interacting with others and use interventions such as **modeling, role-playing**, and **homework assignments** to assist youth with learning, practicing, and applying these new skills in their natural environments. It is reasonable to assume that most counselors and other mental health professionals enjoy and are competent with their social interactions; however, any helpers need to allow youth to learn and explore at their own paces when practicing and implementing new skills because they may experience a lot of anxiety, fear, discomfort, or distress when presented with social situations. Counselors can use modeling to provide positive examples of different social skills, and when youth are ready, **behavioral rehearsal** or role-playing can be useful as a developmentally appropriate youth counseling technique. It is helpful for counselors to provide praise and gentle, constructive feedback while practicing. When teaching a new skill, counselors may want to model the behavior so youth can develop an idea of how the behavior might present. In groups, youth can role-play examples with one another or present a role-play to the group to reinforce positive peer modeling. Once youth have mastered the skills or at least feel comfortable enough to try them in their natural environments, counselors can assign homework in which youth are prompted to complete various tasks throughout the week, such as introducing themselves to three new people or asking one question in each of their academic classes. The overall goal of social skills training is for youth to transfer their new skills across daily living settings to effectively interact with others and establish and maintain meaningful interpersonal relationships.

Counselors working with younger children focus on the most basic foundations of communication. They can develop fun, creative, and concrete ways to teach youth about nonverbal communication, body language, eye contact, facial expressions, personal space, verbal communication, tone of voice, and volume of speech. Counselors can also teach youth how to identify emotions, use manners, and/or introduce themselves or ask a question. When working with adolescents, counselors introduce and process more complex and nuanced aspects of communicating and building relationships with others that often include some form of self-reflection or perspective taking. Topics for adolescents might include self-esteem, confidence, personal biases, assertiveness, dating culture, intimacy, conflict resolution, emotion regulation, and empathy.

Biofeedback. Biofeedback aims to assist youth with monitoring their physiological activities and learning to control how their bodies respond through the use of equipment that measures and monitors brain wave patterns, heart rate, blood pressure, body temperature, or muscle tension. Biofeedback has demonstrated success with youth who have autism spectrum disorder (Thompson, Thompson, & Reid, 2010), ADHD (Williams, 2010), enuresis and encopresis, anxiety, depression (Knox et al., 2011), and other diagnoses (Myers & Young, 2012). Biofeedback directly measures youth's physiology and uses sounds or visual images on a computer that responds accordingly to either inhibit or encourage brain wave activity. The sounds or visual images used in biofeedback function as a reward system. They are designed to stop when youth lose focus or stop relaxing and start again when youth begin to focus or relax. With extensive use, permanent changes in physiology are reported to occur (Culbert & Banez, 2016).

Family Interventions and Involvement

Because behavior therapy places a central focus on the principles of learning to shape, modify, replace, or extinguish the problem behaviors of youth or their symptoms of distress, factors such as psychoeducation, the implementation and practice of therapeutic interventions, modeling, and consistency of reinforcement are critical to counseling processes (Miltenberger, 2012). Just as youth are called to actively engage in counseling, behavioral counselors similarly expect parents, caregivers, and other family members to adopt highly involved, committed, and collaborative roles because such participation can significantly influence the course and outcomes of treatment. Consequently, not only must counselors hold competency in the assessment, treatment planning, intervention, and general ethical practice pertinent to behavior therapy implementation, but they should also have the knowledge and skills necessary to work with family members of youth and other interdisciplinary therapeutic support professionals who may be involved in counseling processes (e.g., teachers, other school faculty and staff, community support workers).

PSYCHOEDUCATION

Regardless of whether youth's presenting concerns are limited to one environment or manifest across numerous settings, parents and/or caregivers play a critical role in managing this behavior. As a result, they need to be educated on how to apply the interventions used with their children. However, because of the systematic and methodological nature of behavior therapy, clients' family members are likely to perceive psychoeducational information surrounding assessment procedures—making and understanding diagnoses, implementing behavior management strategies, monitoring or tracking behaviors, and reporting the effectiveness of treatment interventions—as complex or difficult to comprehend. Counselors need to remain mindful that even the most dynamic behavioral interventions will not be successful if parents cannot comprehend and apply the concepts. Counselors should strive to provide psychoeducation in an intellectually appropriate and culturally sensitive manner. Although interventions will vary and depend on the unique individual needs and environmental circumstances of each client, counselors may want to use the ABC model (i.e., *antecedents*, observed *behaviors*, and *consequences* of behaviors) when providing psychoeducation to parents for the following reasons:

- Counselors can readily adapt their language and description of the previously discussed ABC model to explain complex behavioral principles in an easily comprehensible fashion.
- Parents can understand how behaviors are learned and maintained.
- The ABC model naturally guides counseling processes toward treatment planning and discussions surrounding target behaviors, intervention strategies, generalization of behaviors across environments, and multidisciplinary treatment implications (e.g., collaboration with teachers and school staff, community support workers, and psychiatrists).
- Counselors can explicate the importance of using interventions appropriately and consistently to reinforce the development of youth's adaptive behaviors (Shriver et al., 2001).

Psychoeducation not only provides family members with the didactic experiences and pragmatic skills necessary to correctly and effectively use behavioral interventions to shape the behaviors of their children throughout counseling processes, but it also indirectly reinforces prevention, wellness, and optimal development of themselves and their children—that is, because psychoeducation fosters learning and use of intervention strategies, parents can begin to serve as behavioral counselors for their children when they demonstrate competency and mastery of behavioral treatment techniques. As a result, the development of newly learned skills will enable youth and their caregivers to better cope with and independently manage problematic behaviors.

PARENT MANAGEMENT TRAINING

Comprehensive and intentionally directed psychoeducation may be a sufficient means to facilitate parents' understanding and implementation of interventions aimed at reinforcing their children's adaptive behavioral changes. However, for the parents of youth who engage in disruptive, noncompliant, disrespectful, aggressive, destructive, or other problem behaviors that significantly impede daily functioning, a higher level of support and training is often required. Indeed, **parent management training (PMT)** is one of the most widely researched and frequently used treatment approaches for working with youth who have oppositional defiant disorder and conduct disorder diagnoses (Erford, Paul, Oncken, Kress, & Erford, 2014; Kazdin, 2005). Parent management training is an evidence-based, flexible approach that can be modified by counselors for use in group formats, during sessions with parents and youth, or when meeting with parents independently. Behavioral interventions used in PMT mirror those typically implemented in individual counseling processes. Such behavioral interventions include the use of social skills strategies and techniques such as shaping, chaining, prompting, redirecting, and reinforcement aimed at engendering positive parent–child interactions. The theoretical basis, psychoeducational content, and intervention strategies of PMT programs are not limited to behavioral perspectives, however, because cognitive-oriented components can be integrated to promote parents' insights into the manner in which their thoughts may be influencing how they respond to their child.

PMT approaches can be helpful in that they foster constructive changes in parents' and children's behaviors. In fact, the majority of interventions are focused on changing parents' behaviors, and they aim to assist parents with altering their own behaviors to promote positive behavioral changes in their children. Depending on the individual needs or wants of parents, counselors may focus sessions on addressing maladaptive parent–child interactions or communication patterns, resolving conflicts in a positive manner, outlining clear parental expectations, discussing appropriate compromise and limit setting, determining age-appropriate discipline practices, managing youth's school-related behaviors, coaching parents while they use techniques during sessions with youth, and providing feedback. For example, counselors can inform parents about the basic tenets of social learning theory, explain modeling processes, prompt parents to reflect on youth's behaviors that may have been learned as a result of their modeling, and subsequently explore and process any parenting practices, communication styles, or personal behaviors they might desire to change. Counselors should explore the expectations that parents have about making their own behavioral changes or their abilities to implement new parenting strategies and remind parents that meeting these expectations may not be easy. Discussing any difficulties that parents experience while making their own changes provides a natural bridge for discussions about parents' expectations of their children and may enhance their insight as to whether they are placing realistic and developmentally appropriate demands on their children.

It is similarly important for counselors and other mental health professionals to provide additional training to teachers, administrators, and other school staff working with youth who experience behavior difficulties in academic settings. Teacher management training or other school-based psychoeducational and behavior modification programs can assist educators to implement evidence-based, safe, and effective classroom management interventions to promote the academic success of youth. Moreover, such training initiatives also serve to promote interdisciplinary collaboration, encourage parent–teacher communication, and reveal valuable opportunities for counselor advocacy.

COGNITIVE BEHAVIORAL THERAPY

In the 1960s and 1970s, the dominance of traditional behavior therapy shifted, and theorists began to focus on the role cognitions play in behavior change. The focus on cognitions had a tremendous impact on counseling theories and approaches, eventually leading to a new, unified approach—**cognitive behavioral therapy (CBT)**. Cognitive behavioral therapy is a theoretical orientation that constitutes many different counseling approaches that use behavioral and cognitive-based interventions as a means to facilitate client change. Because CBT does not represent a single counseling theory, the approach does not have one sole founder or pioneering individual responsible for its theoretical underpinnings and intervention strategies. However, **rational emotive behavior therapy (REBT**; Ellis, 1962, 2004) and **cognitive therapy (CT**; A. T. Beck, 1963, 1964, 2005) are recognized as the most prominent early CBT frameworks. They are credited for establishing a basis for which many contemporary, alternative, and integrative cognitive behavioral modalities have been founded. Some of these contemporary theoretical approaches include **mindfulness-based therapies** such as **dialectical behavior therapy** (DBT; Linehan, 1993), **acceptance and commitment therapy** (ACT; Hayes, Strosahl, & Wilson, 1999), **mindfulness-based cognitive therapy** (MBCT; Segal, Williams, & Teasdale, 2002), and **mindfulness-based stress reduction** (MBSR; Kabat-Zinn, 1990), and all share some therapeutic components consistent with traditional core CBT principles. The theories and counseling approaches described in this section are organized and presented in correspondence with the historical development and progression of CBTs. Table 5.4 provides an overview of the first, second, and third "waves" or generations of behavior therapy from which CBT approaches evolved (Hayes, 2004).

Merging the rigor, objectivity, and systematic approach of behaviorism with the thought-based change mechanisms of cognitive therapy, CBT approaches emphasize the importance of changing beliefs, perceptions, and thinking patterns to produce positive affective and behavioral changes. Although the CBTs have theoretical differences, they are all based on the idea that there is an interactive relationship between cognitions, emotions, and behaviors and that changing any of these aspects will significantly influence the other aspects. It is important to note, however, most CBTs emphasize the role of cognitions because they are assumed to be the primary vehicle for change and those most readily controlled by clients. CBTs are action oriented, collaborative, didactic, present focused, and intended to be time limited.

Table 5.4	Development and Progression of Three Generations of Behavior Therapy		
Classification	Theories and Principles	Core Characteristics	Counseling Applications
First Generation			
Radical behaviorism (1950s–1960s)	• Scientific method • Learning theory • Classical conditioning • Operant conditioning • Social cognitive theory	• Experimental • Observable behavior change • Environmental determinants • Stimulus–response • Reinforcement • Modeling	• Behavior therapy • Systematic desensitization • PMR • *In vivo* exposure • ABA • Social skills training
Second Generation			
• Cognitive and CBT approaches (1960s–1990s)	• Cognitive theories (e.g., A. T. Beck's model) • Integration of cognitive and behavioral change strategies	• Irrational beliefs and cognitive distortions • Cognitive, affective, and behavioral relationships • Cognitive change strategies • Problem solving • Coping skills	• Rational emotive behavior therapy • Cognitive therapy • Cognitive behavior modification • CBT-play therapy • Self-management programs
Third Generation			
Mindfulness-based therapies (1990s–present)	• Buddhism • Mindfulness • Acceptance • Metacognition • Behavioral and cognitive change strategies	• Meditation • Awareness of present experience • Nonjudgment • Emotion regulation • Distress tolerance • Interpersonal effectiveness	• Dialectical behavior therapy • Acceptance and commitment therapy • Mindfulness-based cognitive therapy • Mindfulness-based stress reduction

Note: ABA = applied behavioral analysis; CBT = cognitive behavioral therapy; PMR = progressive muscle relaxation.

Because CBT has been extensively researched and empirically validated as an effective treatment for a multitude of presenting problems—and a best practice, evidenced-based approach for many issues with which youth struggle—it is widely accepted among third-party payers and managed care organizations and frequently used by counselors who work with youth (Butler et al., 2006). CBT has demonstrated effectiveness with youth who experience distresses related to depression, bipolar disorder, emotion regulation, anger and aggression, oppositional defiant disorder, substance use, attention-deficit/hyperactivity disorder, suicide, anxiety, panic, phobias, obsessive-compulsive disorder, anorexia nervosa and bulimia nervosa, adjustment-related problems, trauma, general stress management, and obesity, as well as distress related to medical conditions (Butler et al., 2006; Nezu & Nezu, 2016; Ng & Weisz, 2016).

CBT's broad focus on altering faulty thinking patterns, developing coping skills, and enhancing problem solving abilities and positive decision making promote competencies that correspond with youth's natural developmental growth and learning processes. As such, CBT approaches can serve an important function in helping youth to grow in ways that prevent future problems from developing. For example, consider a 7-year-old girl who participates in a CBT group to learn skills she can use to manage her ADHD symptoms in the classroom. These skills will be useful not only in the classroom setting but also in other settings for many years to come, and the use of these skills may prevent future problems from emerging.

Despite the breadth of empirical literature supporting the effectiveness of CBTs across a range of clinical diagnoses and presenting concerns, CBT-based approaches and intervention techniques are not productive unless they are tailored to match the intellectual, developmental, and contextual needs of individual clients and their families. Because CBT approaches emphasize the exploration, identification, and alteration of cognitive processes, it is particularly important for counselors to pay close attention to the appropriateness of interventions when working with younger children and adolescents who have intellectual or developmental delays or disabilities. For young clients who are in Piaget's (1952, 1954) preoperational (i.e., symbolic thought, cannot think logically) or concrete operational (i.e., logical reasoning but only in relation to concrete circumstances) stages of cognitive development, the awareness of their own thought processes or notions of internal self-talk, belief systems, or perceptions is too abstract for some to comprehend. Thus, it is critical that counselors provide concrete examples and use easy-to-understand language when communicating information to youth and family members regarding counseling processes, intervention strategies, and especially content related to cognitions.

Core Concepts and Goals of Counseling

As previously noted, each CBT approach has a unique foundation, but all share several core premises. The unifying assumptions of CBT are:

- cognitive processes such as thoughts, beliefs, perceptions, and schemas or worldviews hold the capacity to influence behavior and emotions;
- cognitive activity can be monitored, assessed, measured, and changed; and
- desired behavioral and affective change can be achieved by altering cognitions.

From a CBT approach, the etiology of clients' presenting distresses or behavior problems are not attributed to external environmental factors or unique life circumstances but, rather, are influenced by their internal cognitive processes—that is, errors in thinking, unrealistic beliefs, misattributions or erroneous appraisals of events, and the general ways in which youth understand themselves and their environments are largely held responsible for experiences of distress. Accordingly, cognitive behavioral counselors aim to assist youth in identifying, monitoring, replacing, modifying, or correcting maladaptive cognitive processes to promote new, more accurate and positive ways of thinking. Changes in thinking are believed to facilitate positive and productive behavioral and affective changes.

In addition to focusing on cognitive change, behavioral interventions are also applied to encourage the development of new skills and behavioral strategies that can help young people effectively get their needs met. For example, if a child thinks "My parents won't love me as much after my baby brother is born," he or she may experience feelings of inadequacy or low self-worth that may lead to an increase in unhealthy behaviors intended to grab their parents' attention. In this situation, cognitive behavioral counselors would assist the child with identifying his or her thoughts, recognizing any thought patterns that contribute to the bad feelings, developing more realistic ways of thinking, and learning to earn attention from his or her parents in a positive manner. CBTs essentially use changes in thinking to bring about changes in youth's doing and feeling.

RATIONAL EMOTIVE BEHAVIOR THERAPY

REBT (Ellis, 2001) was the first of the CBT approaches to be developed. This approach is based on the presumptions that all individuals are born with the innate capacity to think both rationally and irrationally and that all individuals hold inherent predispositions for self-preservation, growth, self-actualization, and happiness (Ellis, 2001). Paradoxically, youth are also inclined to engage in irrational thinking and behavior, self-destruction, avoidance of actualization, self-blame, perfectionism, and repetition of past mistakes. The psychological distress and problem behaviors of youth stem from the inflexible, extreme, or self-defeating beliefs, misinterpreted events, and poor emotional reactions that they learn through lived experiences. From Ellis's perspective, young people's emotions are primarily influenced by their beliefs, and thus, youth are considered to be the sources of their own distress. In particular, REBT most strongly emphasizes the role of blame and absolute **should, must, ought, always, never** demands or statements that youth desire for themselves, from others, or in the world around them. Demands of personal success, love and acceptance from others, and favorable life circumstances or experiences are the three primary irrational beliefs that occur most frequently, and although highly desirable, they are not necessary according to Ellis. When the "shoulds," "musts," and "oughts" of youth are not fulfilled as expected, they develop and internalize rigid irrational beliefs or use **self-talk** such as "I should have done better," "All teachers are mean and will always yell at me," or "I'm never going to be safe, no matter where I go."

REBT is an active, directive, educational, problem-focused, and highly cognitive-focused counseling approach. This therapy approach involves explaining REBT theory to youth and then teaching them how to apply related strategies in their daily lives so they can experience greater self-acceptance, acceptance of others, and, ultimately, an increased degree of happiness—that is, counselors teach youth the manner in which maladaptive beliefs, appraisals, and attitudes can influence emotions and behaviors, and then counselors help youth to identify examples related to their presenting distresses. Youth are expected to take responsibility for their problems and mistakes and realize they have the personal choice to make constructive changes. Counselors assist youth with identifying and minimizing irrational beliefs by disputing and replacing them with more logical, accurate, and affirming thoughts and attitudes, an intervention known as **cognitive restructuring**. Youth practice cognitive restructuring in collaboration with counselors during session. They also complete homework exercises to build insight into their unhelpful thought patterns and examine how their new thought patterns are affecting their emotions, behaviors, and associated consequences. The process of disputing youth's irrational beliefs and replacing them with more effective interpretations is the cornerstone of REBT change procedures, and this is referred to as the **A-B-C model**. The A-B-C model is the primary technique associated with REBT, and it is discussed within the REBT interventions subsection of this chapter.

Clinical Toolbox 5.5

In the Pearson eText, click here to view examples of cognitive restructuring.

COGNITIVE THERAPY

The **cognitive therapy** model (A. T. Beck, 1963) is one of CBT's most comprehensive theories. Cognitive therapy and REBT share several commonalities. Both modalities are highly active, structured, and problem focused, and both hold maladaptive thoughts or beliefs as the origin from which problems arise. However, whereas counselors using REBT confront youth about their irrational beliefs and use disputing processes to assist them with developing more effective ways of thinking, cognitive therapists rely on open-ended questions and collaborative dialogue to allow youth to engage in a self-guided exploration about the accuracy of their faulty cognitions or biased interpretations of events. Thus, rather than detecting and disputing the irrational beliefs of youth and instructing them through thought change processes, counselors who use cognitive therapy presume that it is necessary for youth to make such discoveries independently or with supportive counselor guidance (A. T. Beck, 2005).

Cognitive theory also maintains differing presuppositions from REBT concerning cognitive processes and the development of distress. Most notably, cognitive theory asserts that there are four primary domains of cognition that all play a significant role in the thinking processes of youth. The **hierarchical structural organization model** (A. T. Beck, Freeman, & Davis, 2004) can be used to explain the four domains of cognition:

- *Automatic Thoughts:* Spontaneously occurring involuntary thoughts about oneself, others, situations, or events that carry personal meaning and lead to emotional experiences. Automatic thoughts are internal conversations, or self-talk, that are completely normal to experience. However, they are often biased, faulty, or extreme.
- *Intermediate Beliefs:* Underlying attitudes, perspectives, assumptions, standards, or rules for living that guide behavior and influence automatic thinking and appraisal processes. Intermediate beliefs connect core beliefs to automatic thoughts.

- *Core Beliefs:* Fundamental ideas and views about the self, the world, and the future that are globally attributed. Core beliefs begin to develop during childhood and are shaped by lived experiences; they serve as the foundation from which intermediate beliefs and automatic thoughts are formed.
- *Schemas:* Overarching systems or information processing filters that function to interpret, integrate, organize, store, and ascribe meaning to lived experiences. Youth have cognitive, affective, behavioral, physiological, and motivational schemas. As an integrated network of systems, when youth experience cognitive distortions or misinterpreted information, all schema structures are influenced and respond.

A. T. Beck (1963, 1967) developed a **cognitive model of depression**, which supposes that individuals frequently interpret events in a negative, biased, or inaccurate manner. These "logical errors," or misperceptions, faulty assumptions, unrealistic beliefs, or general maladaptive thinking patterns, are known as **cognitive distortions** and typically occur about oneself, the world or environment, or the future. A. T. Beck referred to the aforementioned domains in which negative thoughts occur (i.e., views about one's self, the world or environment, or the future) as the **cognitive triad**. The principal goal of cognitive therapy is to help youth to identify automatic thoughts, exploring for evidence to support or negate cognitions, challenging maladaptive thoughts with evidence and positive self-talk, and developing more plausible, affirming, and self-enhancing ways of thinking, feeling, and behaving. What follows is a list of cognitive distortions commonly associated with cognitive therapy:

- *Dichotomous Thinking:* Perceiving things as absolute (all positive or all negative) or thinking in extremes without compromise or middle ground. This cognitive distortion is also referred to as all-or-nothing, black-and-white, or polarized thinking (e.g., "If I don't get all As, I'm never going to get a scholarship!").
- *Arbitrary Inference:* Jumping to conclusions without facts or evidence to support beliefs. This includes **mind reading**, or knowing what others are thinking (e.g., "I know she was trying to make me mad on purpose!"), and **fortune telling**, or making unfounded predictions about the future (e.g., "I knew he was going to start a fight with me, so I punched him first.").
- *Selective Abstractions:* Forming conclusions based on an isolated event or detail and ignoring other important contextual information. This type of thinking is also referred to as **mental filtering** because all information but a single aspect is filtered out (e.g., "My presentation went horrible because I mispronounced a word.").
- *Overgeneralization:* Similar to selective abstraction, overgeneralization involves making conclusions based on a single situation and associating them broadly or making conclusions based on dissimilar situations (e.g., "All girls love to gossip," "My parents gossip about me, too.").
- *Emotional Reasoning:* Assuming that feelings indicate the truth or the reality of a situation (e.g., "I wouldn't have been so angry if my mom wasn't being unfair," "I feel like a loser, so I must be one.").
- *Magnification and Minimization:* Overemphasizing or exaggerating the importance of insignificant details or negative aspects of a situation and dismissing or discounting the positives (e.g., "Look at these split ends! I'm so ugly," "I just got lucky on my math test. I'm really not very smart.").
- *Catastrophizing:* Expecting the worst or predicting that something catastrophic will happen (e.g., "Aden will hate me forever when I tell him I lost his calculator.").
- *Personalization:* Assuming that external or unrelated events, or the actions of others, are somehow related to oneself without any plausible reason to believe so (e.g., "Justine slammed her locker just to scare me," "Jayvon didn't come to my birthday, so he must not want to be my friend anymore.").
- *Labeling or Mislabeling:* Defining the identity of oneself or others based on imperfections or past behavior or mistakes (e.g., "I'm bad because I have trouble sitting still in class," "My mom is neglectful because she forgot to pick me up from school last week.").

MINDFULNESS-BASED THERAPIES

Since the early 1990s, there has been a proliferation of professional literature focused on mindfulness-based interventions (MBIs) and acceptance and mindfulness-oriented counseling approaches that have become known as the third wave of behavior therapies. Mindfulness-based therapies retain traditional CBT perspectives concerning the importance of cognitions, emotions, and information processing, and they also integrate additional core tenets and practices of awareness, acceptance, attention to the present moment, nonjudgment, mindfulness meditation (MM), and nonreactivity (Herbert & Forman, 2011). Mindfulness can be classified most broadly into two categorical domains of practice: (a) **focused attention**, or concentrative practices, and (b) open monitoring, or **bare attention** practices (Ainsworth, Eddershaw, Meron, Baldwin, & Garner, 2013). Both concentrative and bare attention mindfulness practices are used as intervention strategies to promote the mindfulness of youth; however, it is imperative to note that mindfulness is not something to be achieved or an end goal of the third-wave therapies. Rather, it is the application of mindfulness—youth's *practice* of being mindful throughout their daily lived experiences—that serves to enhance their inner awareness and nonjudgmental acceptance of both pleasure and distress, and, ultimately, to cultivate an enriched experience of living and well-being. Similarly, mindfulness also emphasizes themes of **self-compassion**, **nonstriving**, **letting go**, and **equanimity** or a stable balance of mind and an ability to remain calm even in difficult situations.

Various mindfulness-based therapies have emerged over the past 30 years, including dialectical behavior therapy (DBT; Linehan, 1993), acceptance and commitment therapy (ACT; Hayes et al., 1999), mindfulness-based cognitive therapy (MBCT; Segal et al., 2002), mindfulness-based stress reduction (MBSR; Kabat-Zinn, 1990), metacognitive therapy, and emotional schema therapy. Research on third-generation therapies has demonstrated the effectiveness of mindfulness-based approaches and MBIs, with studies suggesting their effectiveness for alleviating symptoms of major depressive disorder, generalized anxiety, panic disorder, posttraumatic stress disorder, addictions, and eating disorders (Brown, Marquis, & Guiffrida, 2013). In addition, mindfulness-oriented modalities and interventions have also been associated with increased self-compassion, spiritual experiences, metacognitive awareness, general well-being, and favorable counseling outcomes.

Although the investigation of acceptance and mindfulness applications to children and adolescents is still in its infancy, preliminary research has revealed positive affects for youth experiencing distresses related to body image concerns and eating disorders, anxiety, maladaptive behaviors associated with borderline personality disorder, externalizing disorders, and pediatric pain (Greco & Hayes, 2008). The most frequently used mindfulness-based therapies with youth are DBT, ACT, MBCT, and MBSR. These approaches are reviewed following a brief delineation of several important constructs that relate to their application: mindfulness and acceptance.

Mindfulness. Mindfulness is a practice that emerged from ancient Eastern spiritual teachings that date back more than 2,500 years and can be defined as "paying attention in a particular way: on purpose, in the present moment, and nonjudgmentally" (Kabat-Zinn, 1994, p. 4). As a tradition associated with Zen Buddhism, not only do mindfulness principles and practices represent a marked deviation from the objective and systematic nature of radical behaviorism (i.e., first generation of behavior therapy), but they also differ drastically from the Western and Eurocentric values from which the vast majority of traditional counseling and psychotherapy treatment modalities were founded. Most significantly, mindfulness-based approaches do not emphasize the use of cognitive change strategies to modify maladaptive thoughts and distressing emotions or attempt to change such experiences at all. In fact, not only are deliberate efforts to change thoughts and feelings discouraged, but such practices are also fundamentally contrary to the guiding philosophies of mindfulness practices. Counselors who use mindfulness-based therapies aim to assist youth with learning how to intentionally observe, become aware of, and nonjudgmentally accept distressing cognitions and emotions without attachment or reactivity (Greco & Hayes, 2008). By simply observing, youth can allow their negative thoughts and feelings to pass and come to recognize the impermanent or fleeting nature of distress.

What follows are five commonly held tenets of mindfulness that are believed to help people decrease distress and feel better (Baer, Smith, Hopkins, Krietemeyer, & Toney, 2006):

- *Observing Inner Experiences:* Attending to one's inner experience or observing internal and external sensations, cognitions, emotions, and perceptions.
- *Acting with Awareness:* Paying attention to the present moment and one's behavior.
- *Nonjudgment of Inner Experience:* Remaining nonjudgmental of one's inner experience.
- *Describing or Labeling Inner Experience:* Using words to express oneself or describe inner experiences, sensations, cognitions, emotions, and perceptions.
- *Nonreactivity:* Remaining nonreactive to inner experiences or noticing distressing cognitions, emotions, or sensations without reacting.

The constructs of decentering and metacognition are conceptually similar and closely related to mindfulness. **Decentering**, also known as **diffusion**, is the process of maintaining a degree of separation from inner experiences—thoughts, feelings, or perceptions—and recognizing such experiences as mental processes rather than facts or truth—that is, decentering and diffusion essentially mirror the mindfulness tenet of observing inner experiences, which enables youth to simply notice their thoughts, to pass without believing they must reveal truth about themselves or their environment, and to respond to distress in a desirable and adaptive manner. **Metacognition**, or **metacognitive awareness**, is a concept also used among traditional CBT approaches, and it refers to youth's awareness of their own thinking processes. Mindfulness, decentering, and metacognitive awareness all help youth distance themselves from their thoughts, thus influencing their emotions and behaviors in positive ways (Herbert & Forman, 2011).

Acceptance.   The construct of **acceptance**, another integral component of mindfulness-based therapies, can be understood as a willingness to experience psychological events (i.e., thoughts, feelings, memories) without having to avoid them or let them unduly influence behavior (Butler & Ciarrochi, 2007). The concept of acceptance is generally discussed in the context of youth's distressing or unpleasant feelings. However, acceptance also pertains to accepting and being aware of enjoyable or pleasurable experiences. The prolonged holding or excessive prizing of positive experiences without letting go has the potential to result in distressing thoughts, feelings, or maladaptive behaviors because people to try to hold onto things that they crave or desire, but these things are often fleeting. MBSR and ACT are two approaches that place a heavy emphasis on the concept of acceptance.

DIALECTICAL BEHAVIOR THERAPY

Dialectical behavior therapy (DBT) was originally developed by Linehan (1993) as an integrative and comprehensive treatment approach to assist individuals experiencing distresses related to borderline personality disorder. Because individuals who have borderline personality disorder commonly experience significant difficulties with emotion dysregulation, DBT places a heavy emphasis on emotion regulation and effective problem solving. DBT combines CBT perspectives and interventions, **dialectical philosophy**, **biosocial theory**, and mindfulness concepts. Unlike other mindfulness-based therapies such as ACT or MBSR that encourage the acceptance of all inner experiences, DBT uses both traditional CBT intentional change techniques and mindfulness interventions to promote acceptance. Although such strategies are fundamentally contrary to one another, they represent dialectical philosophies' notions of wholeness and polarity—that is, the idea that a whole comprises two opposite extremes or opposing forces. Because dialectical philosophy also presupposes that change is constant, life can essentially be conceptualized as the ongoing management of opposite extremes, such as experiences of suffering and pleasure, validation and invalidation, or stability and instability. The dialectic of balancing acceptance and change is the defining feature of DBT, and youth are encouraged to cultivate a "**wise mind**," an integration of the reasonable and emotional mind to manage distress.

Due to the abstract nature of the DBT framework and the complexity of intervention strategies, DBT is not an appropriate approach to implement when working with younger children or adolescents who have developmental or intellectual delays. However, Miller, Rathus, and Linehan (2007) developed a manualized DBT program for adolescents that pulls in the parents of youth as part of the counseling processes. Miller et al. explain the development of problems using **biosocial theory**, which asserts that both genetic neuropsychological and environmental factors play a significant role in the emotion regulation, distress tolerance, and interpersonal skills of youth. When adolescents endure repeated invalidating experiences, inconsistent parental demands and responses, or instability in the home throughout early life developmental phases, their degree of vulnerability to internalize this invalidation and experience pervasive physiological hyperarousal and heightened reactivity to distress becomes increased. Youth who hold genetic predispositions to emotional dysregulation are at an even higher risk of developing maladaptive emotional and behavioral responses when the aforementioned environmental circumstances are present. Thus, the inclusion of adolescents' parents or caregivers in DBT counseling processes is important because parental validation and self-validation are significant components of counseling (Harvey & Penzo, 2009).

ACCEPTANCE AND COMMITMENT THERAPY

Acceptance and commitment therapy (ACT; Hayes et al., 1999; Hayes, Strosahl, & Wilson, 2011) is a mindfulness-based approach that aims to promote youth's discovery of meaningful values and goals, commitment to engage in associated purposeful and fulfilling activities, and *total acceptance* of all lived experiences—those that are undesired *and* those that are welcomed or pleasurable. Unlike DBT, ACT does not espouse the use of cognitive change techniques or youth's avoidance of distressing thoughts, emotions, interactions, or events. Although these interventions may indeed help children and adolescents to cope with difficult experiences, they are ultimately escape oriented and hold limited clinical utility because they solely provide youth with temporary alleviation from distress. In fact, from an ACT perspective, the etiology of suffering and maladjustment are attributed to **experiential avoidance** because such avoidance allows youth's current sources of distress to continue to serve as barriers throughout development. When youth embrace acceptance of their experiences, however, distress can no longer maintain the aforementioned inhibitory function, and youth are enabled to pursue and engage in meaningful life activities.

ACT counselors initially focus on cultivating youth's acceptance of distress through the use of psycho-education and creative metaphors pertaining to the mindfulness practices of openly observing one's inner experiences; remaining in the present moment without judgment; and engaging in cognitive diffusion, which is the distancing of oneself from "private events" (e.g., thoughts, evaluations, emotions, mental images, memories, sensations) without reactivity. In addition, counselors promote youth's development of acceptance by facilitating exercises in which youth are prompted to mindfully attend to their distressing private events or inner experiences and verbally process them without avoidance.

Acceptance and commitment therapy's theoretical foundations in behaviorism and **relational frame theory** make this approach different from other mindfulness-based therapies—namely, with regard to its verbal processing and nonavoidance concepts. First, youth's nonavoidance of distressing thoughts and emotions can help them to adapt to the experiences, and thus their negative impact is diminished, similar to the concept of repeated exposure in exposure-based therapies. In other words, as youth repeatedly observe and process distressing thoughts and experiences without attempting to change or control these inner experiences, their distress becomes desensitized, making it easier for youth to practice acceptance. Second, relational frame theory asserts that language and verbal communication are important in supporting peoples' maladjustment in that the mind generates thoughts based on past experiences rather than one's present situation. As a result, thoughts are often out of context and do not necessarily have the same meaning or hold valid truth. According to Hayes (2004), this process is problematic because individuals tend to avoid distressing thoughts and emotions even if they are out of context, which subsequently leads to the avoidance of events associated with the uncomfortable experiences. Thus, mindfully attending, verbally processing, and consciously accepting distressing thoughts and feelings removes their power to prevent youth from engaging in meaningful events. Once youth develop the psychological flexibility to recognize and accept their private events as out of their control, counseling processes then shift toward the **values** and **committed actions** of youth—that is, counselors collaboratively assist youth with exploring and committing to valued, enriched ways of living. Due to the complexity of ACT's underlying theoretical basis and abstract nature of acceptance, it is important for counselors to select psychoeducational content based on the developmental and intellectual functioning of youth and to convey such material in an easily comprehensible manner.

MINDFULNESS-BASED GROUP PROGRAMS

Mindfulness-Based Stress Reduction. Mindfulness-based stress reduction (MBSR; Kabat-Zinn, 1990) was developed as a treatment program for individuals experiencing distress- and stress-related physiological symptoms associated with chronic medical conditions and diseases, including cancer, fibromyalgia, and high blood pressure. Emphasizing mind–body integration, MBSR is a long-standing, group-based treatment program aimed at promoting clients' physical, psychological, emotional, and spiritual health and well-being. MBSR differs from the aforementioned third-generation therapeutic modalities, however, because the approach does not incorporate cognitive-oriented interventions. Instead, it relies on the traditional Eastern healing practices of mindfulness meditation and yoga to engender enhanced awareness, balance, and appreciation of life in the present moment.

Mindfulness-Based Cognitive Therapy.   Mindfulness-based cognitive therapy (MBCT; Segal et al., 2002) was specifically developed to prevent the relapse of major depression in adults who experienced recurrent depressive episodes, and it is based on Kabat-Zinn's (1990) MBSR approach. Mindfulness-based cognitive therapy is a manualized, 8-week group program that uses cognitive- and mindfulness-oriented interventions to assist clients with detaching themselves from negative thoughts and developing skills to prevent relapse. More specifically, MBCT is based on the underlying premise that relapse of depression occurs as a result of maladaptive rumination patterns. Accordingly, MBCT aims to disrupt clients' automatic negative thought processes to prevent rumination and subsequent relapse into a depressive episode. The MBCT program curriculum includes psychoeducation, experiential learning activities, weekly group sessions, in-session practice, homework assignments, and various formal and informal mindfulness-based practices such as guided meditation, breathing exercises, body scan, and yoga. Both MBCT and MBSR have been adapted and implemented with clinical and nonclinical populations experiencing different presenting concerns. For example, MBCT and MBSR programs have been modified for use with children and adolescents who experience distress related to anxiety, eating disorders, ADHD, externalizing behaviors (e.g., acting out, aggressive behaviors), conduct disorder, substance use, and sleep disorders. For example, **mindfulness-based cognitive therapy for children** (**MBCT-C**; Semple, Reid, & Miller, 2005) was designed as an anxiety treatment program for youth. Table 5.5 provides an overview of the MBCT-C program, and the ways the MBCT approach was adapted to meet the developmental needs of youth is indicated.

Role of the Counselor in Cognitive Behavioral Therapy

The previously reviewed counseling approaches have unique theoretical foundations and presuppositions about the therapeutic change processes that influence the implementation, goals and objectives, intervention techniques, and conceptualization of client progress and desired outcomes. However, the most significant role of counselors, regardless of theoretical approach, pertains to the cultivation of a warm, accepting therapeutic relationship and a safe, affirming counseling atmosphere. Establishing and maintaining a trusting therapeutic alliance is particularly important for counselors who use CBT and mindfulness-based therapies because associated counseling processes may involve a degree of confrontation or challenging the thoughts of youth, or it may involve encouraging their exposure and acceptance of inner distresses. If youth and their parents are not well informed about the purpose or function of these interventions, they may feel invalidated or question the

Table 5.5   Overview of MBCT and MBCT-C Programs

Program Domain	Mindfulness-Based Cognitive Therapy (MBCT)	Mindfulness-Based Cognitive Therapy for Children (MBCT-C)
Program Structure Program length Session length Counselor–client ratio Intervention length	• 8 weeks • 2-hour sessions • Typically 1:12 • 20- to 40-minute meditations or activities	• 12 weeks • 90-minute sessions • Typically 1:4 • 3- to 10-minute activities, and activities are offered more frequently • Inclusion of family members at times
Curriculum Goals and objectives Mindfulness-based interventions Delivery modality	• Relapse prevention for depression • Promote decentering • Reduce rumination on negative automatic thoughts • Breath meditation, yoga, and body scan • Predominantly verbal communication and experiential activities	• Reduce anxiety, problems with attention, and behavior problems • Promote decentering • Increase emotion regulation • Sensory exercises aimed at promoting nonjudgmental awareness • Experiential activities, movement, and games with less verbal communication

intent or disposition of counselors. As such, it may be necessary for counselors to allocate time to discuss psychoeducational content to ensure youth's understandings of how interventions are designed to help them achieve their desired goals. Not only do comprehensive psychoeducation practices promote youth's initial comprehension and eventual mastery of intervention strategies, but they also provide youth with an additional sense of predictability with regard to the direction or aim of in-session activities and exercises.

Counselors using traditional cognitive behavioral approaches facilitate active, present-focused, educational, and structured counseling processes aimed at assisting youth with modifying their maladaptive or faulty thinking patterns as a means to bring about desired affective and behavioral changes. Rational emotive behavior therapy is generally associated with a more directive and confrontational counselor style due to the approach's key emphasis on disputing the irrational beliefs of youth. In fact, Ellis (1962) asserted that a warm therapeutic relationship *was not* a necessary component of REBT practices and could be disadvantageous to the counseling processes. Despite Ellis's personally held beliefs, as previously mentioned, establishing a strong therapeutic alliance *is* indeed critical; thus, counselors should tailor their disputing styles to the developmental, intellectual, and clinical factors that influence the individual needs of clients.

Counselors who use cognitive therapy take a collaborative approach and explore the thoughts of youth through a process based on **collaborative empiricism** or **guided discovery**—that is, they appraise the validity of youth's thoughts by searching for evidence or practical examples. Counselors' degree of guidance throughout cognitive exploration processes should be individually adapted to the unique needs of youth.

In addition to interventions oriented toward cognitive restructuring, counselors who use traditional CBT therapies take on a teacher role and frequently attempt to assist youth with learning effective coping strategies and positive decision-making or problem-solving skills. Because many youth experience distresses or behavioral problems across various environments, the integration of skills-building and emotion-regulation interventions function as valuable protective factors for youth, providing them with knowledge and pragmatic competencies that foster their self-management subsequent to termination.

Counselors who use acceptance and mindfulness-based therapies have roles and responsibilities that differ slightly from those who use the more traditional CBT modalities, primarily due to opposing philosophical presuppositions surrounding the etiology of suffering and how constructive client change occurs. Although the collaborative, psychoeducational skills building and guidance roles characteristic of CBT are maintained, the associated cognitive change strategies are contrary to the constructs of acceptance and mindfulness that counselors using third-generation therapies pull on. Counselors who use third-generation therapies do not provide a highly structured counseling experience oriented toward modifying the faulty cognitions of youth. Rather, these counselors aim to sustain a moment-to-moment presence and full experience with youth, along with a conscious awareness of their own internal experiences throughout counseling.

Interestingly, the practice of using mindfulness approaches, and even using mindfulness in sessions with clients, can be advantageous for counselors. Benefits to applying and personally using mindfulness techniques in sessions include increased relational skills, enhanced therapeutic relationships, focused attention, empathy, mindful attunement, self-awareness, social connectedness, emotional intelligence, congruence, unconditional positive regard, multicultural awareness and knowledge, and reduced experiences of compassion, fatigue, and burnout (Brown et al., 2013; Fulton & Cashwell, 2015; Ivers, Johnson, Clarke, Newsome, & Berry, 2016; Schomaker & Ricard, 2015).

Counseling Process and Procedures

CBT offers counselors a breadth of therapeutic strategies that can be easily tailored to assist youth with making constructive changes to their ways of thinking, feeling, and behaving so they can achieve their desired counseling goals. Because behavior therapy and its principles have already been discussed in this chapter, they are not emphasized in this section. However, the counseling interventions discussed in the Behavior Therapy section do indeed hold valuable clinical utility when appropriately paired with cognitive or acceptance and mindfulness-based counseling approaches. For example, cognitive behavioral counselors may integrate some of the following behavioral intervention strategies when working with children and adolescents: positive and negative reinforcement, positive and negative punishment, extinction, prompting, shaping, chaining, token economy systems, modeling; or role-playing.

ASSESSMENT

Cognitive behavioral counselors continually monitor and assess young people's cognitive processes and how they influence their individual experiences of distress. As such, standardized assessment measures designed to evaluate specific presenting problems of youth can be administered and used to assess young people's thoughts and behaviors. Beck developed various inventories that are frequently used by counselors. As an example, the **Beck Youth Inventories—Second Edition** (BYI-II; J. S. Beck, A. T. Beck, Jolly, & Steer, 2005) consists of five 20-question inventories that can be administered to children and adolescents ages 7 to 18 and are designed to assess symptoms of depression, anxiety, self-concept, disruptive behavior, and anger. The BYI-II assessments are a valuable tool that can be used to assist counselors with case conceptualization and determining the severity and presence of youth's symptoms. Moreover, these inventories are highly applicable for use with youth because they only take approximately 5 minutes for youth to complete and because they are representative of the U.S. population for ethnicity, socioeconomic status, gender, and age (J. S. Beck et al., 2005).

Assessment plays a role in most CBT approaches, but what is assessed will depend on the specific school of thought. As an example, J. S. Beck's (2005) *cognitive triad* can assist counselors using cognitive therapy with assessment, case conceptualization, and treatment processes because the negative thinking patterns youth disclose about themselves, their environment, and the future can provide insight into their deeply held beliefs and schemas. For example, an adolescent with depression may report the following automatic thoughts: "I hate myself" (self belief), "I let everyone down" (environmental belief), or "I'll never succeed" (future belief). Such automatic thoughts may reflect the adolescent's intermediate beliefs about not meeting some type of self, other, or societal standard; a core belief of "I'm a failure" that is based on prior life experiences; and a cognitive schema oriented toward ascribing negative meanings to neutral experiences or filtering information, interactions, situations, or events in a pessimistic fashion. This type of cognitive schema may be associated with additional symptoms of depression experienced by the adolescent, including feelings of shame, guilt, or despair (emotional schema); social withdrawal (behavioral schema); anhedonia (motivational schema); and increased sleeping patterns (physiological). Refer to Figure 5.3 for an example of J. S. Beck's cognitive triad.

TRADITIONAL CBT INTERVENTIONS

Prior to reviewing the most commonly used CBT interventions, it is first necessary to identify how CBT counseling sessions are generally structured because there are several noteworthy implications related to youth's development and generalization of skills. The following five steps provide an overview of a typical CBT counseling session (Wright, Brown, Thase, & Basco, 2017):

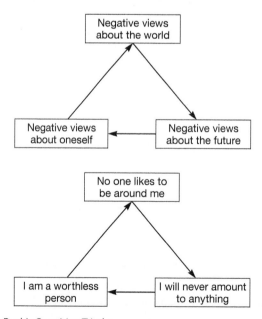

FIGURE 5.3   Examples of J. S. Beck's Cognitive Triad

1. Plan for the session and set an agenda with youth.
2. Review previously learned content and skills, and process weekly homework assignments. Counselors may want to bridge these discussions to the counseling goals of youth or even establish goals for the session.
3. Introduce new material, psychoeducation, and the practicing of techniques or skills.
4. Collaborative processing and feedback of the session are to be provided by counselor and youth.
5. Assign homework based on session content and new skills for youth to complete throughout the week.

When using this session structure, the counseling process essentially resembles the previously discussed behavioral practices of chaining, shaping, prompting, and fading. Counselors gradually promote youth's learning of concepts and skills acquisition in a sequential or progressive manner that enables them to build new competencies based on previously learned foundations. Counselors process the homework of youth to provide them with an opportunity to demonstrate their mastery of concepts and implementation of techniques outside counseling, which not only serves to inform counselors whether counseling processes are advancing at a pace that is most appropriate for each client but also promotes the generalization of skills and relapse prevention—that is, when youth demonstrate the ability to implement intervention techniques across multiple settings or when skills are mastered and become generalized, youth hold new capacities that serve as protective factors from subsequent experiences of maladjustment. For homework to serve as an effective intervention, however, counselors must ensure developmental appropriateness. Counselors may want to incorporate the interests or strengths of youth to create individually tailored worksheets, social stories, or other homework assignments. Although many CBT interventions are not recommended for children younger than 8 years, counselors can create charts or worksheets with basic, concrete information to begin introducing CBT concepts to younger children.

A-B-C Model.   The A-B-C model, also referred to as the **ABCDEF model**, is the defining element of REBT—the model functions to inform REBT's theoretical conceptualizations of the etiology of distress and how therapeutic change occurs (Ellis, 2001). As REBT presupposes that irrational beliefs are at the core of youth's problems, counselors use the A-B-C model to explain the manner in which unrealistic beliefs can influence emotion and behavior and as a cognitive restructuring intervention to assist youth with developing more rational ways of thinking. Figure 5.4 provides an overview of the A-B-C model.

Disputing youth's irrational beliefs—considered to be the key to therapeutic change—is the primary role of REBT counselors. Counselors listen for self-defeating statements, beliefs about blame, or words such

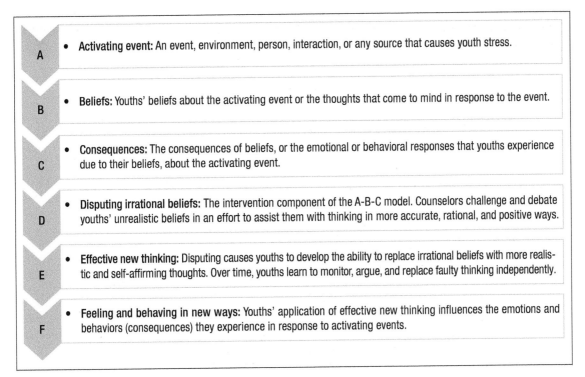

FIGURE 5.4 Rational Emotive Behavior Therapy's A-B-C Model

as *should*, *must*, *ought*, *always*, or never and then challenge and assist youth with differentiating negative and positive thoughts. Disputing processes help youth to recognize that activating events are *not* what cause them to experience distress or respond with maladaptive behaviors, but rather their *beliefs about* the activating event are what is problematic. Once youth begin replacing unrealistic and self-deprecating beliefs with those that are accurate and self-affirming, emotional and behavioral consequences change as well—that is, youth's new realistic and positive ways of thinking cause them to engage in more adaptive and constructive behaviors while experiencing associated positive emotions.

Socratic Questioning and Guided Discovery.   Whereas counselors working from an REBT framework aim to change the beliefs of youth by disputing and challenging, cognitive therapists approach thought change processes more gently and openly through **Socratic questioning** or **Socratic dialogue**. Socratic questioning is a fundamental CBT technique and a component of **guided discovery** that allows youth to explore and identify the ways in which their faulty perceptions and automatic thoughts affect their behavior or emotions. Counselors adopt a "not knowing" stance and curiously pose questions that guide youth in a direction that enables them to arrive at their conclusions. Socratic questioning and guided discovery are particularly advantageous for counselors working with children and adolescents for numerous reasons. Guided discovery processes inherently minimize power differentials that exist within the counseling relationship due to the nondirective and explorative nature of the techniques. For youth presenting with symptoms of anxiety, trauma, or depression who might be apprehensive about counseling processes or experiencing feelings of worthlessness, a less directive and nonconfrontational counseling approach that allows youth to process their distresses at an individually desired pace can provide them with a valuable sense of control, safety, and stability. Similarly, for youth who experience difficulties with emotion regulation or disruptive behavior engagement, counselors' use of guidance and collaboration, as opposed to explicitly disputing or challenging, can serve to foster trust, build rapport, and prevent responses of opposition or reluctance. Regardless of the presenting concerns of youth, allowing them time to contemplate and work through their thoughts during collaborative exploration activities promotes their development of problem-solving skills, reflexivity, and metacognitive awareness. The discovery process that naturally follows exploration also creates empowering experiences for youth because arriving at their own conclusions provides evidence of their competency, self-efficacy, and ultimately, their ability to implement such practices independently. The excitement, pride, and gratification associated with "Aha!" moments of self-discovery can further serve to reinforce youth's implementation of cognitive strategies outside counseling as well.

Clinical Toolbox 5.6

In the Pearson eText, click here to read a dialogue that involves Socratic questioning.

Thought Testing.   Once youth demonstrate the ability to identify their faulty automatic thoughts, appraisals, perceptions, or negative self-talk, counselors teach youth **thought testing**, which is an intervention designed to evaluate the validity of thoughts. Counselors and youth collaboratively engage in thought testing processes by searching for realistic evidence to either confirm or refute their cognitions. Counselors frequently assign homework to youth based on thought testing in an effort to promote their efficacy in monitoring, identifying, testing, and modifying or replacing cognitions in an independent manner and across various ecological living domains. From a cognitive perspective, youth's mastery of the aforementioned skills and processes essentially allows them to begin functioning as their own counselor.

Behavioral Experiments.   Although thought testing is a very practical CBT intervention strategy for assisting youth with determining the validity of their thoughts, many of them, especially younger children, may require the implementation of interventions that provide evidence that is more concrete and directly observable. As such, counselors can conduct **behavioral experiments**—during sessions or as homework—that require youth to engage in an activity or behavior designed to validate or refute their beliefs. For example, a child might ask different groups of peers to play at recess to test a thought such as "No one ever wants to play with me." Counselors can provide youth with worksheets or charts to document thought testing and behavioral experiment outcomes, and they can process their findings during sessions. Both thought testing and behavioral experiments are effective ways to assist youth with recognizing the ways in which their thoughts can influence emotions and behavior. Figure 5.5 provides an example of a simplified behavioral experiment worksheet for younger children.

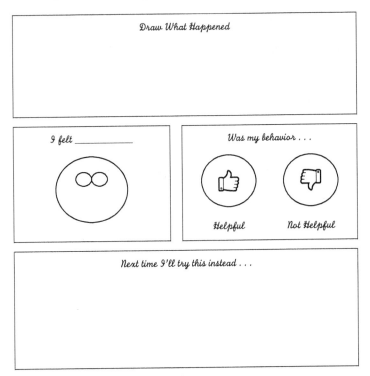

FIGURE 5.5 Behavioral Experiment Homework Chart for Children

DIALECTICAL BEHAVIOR THERAPY–BASED INTERVENTIONS

Dialectical behavior therapy interventions can be categorized into four domains, including a focus on emotion regulation, distress tolerance, mindfulness, and interpersonal effectiveness, and it is helpful for youth to develop these skills. Counselors implement these DBT interventions to assist youth with progressing through different stages of treatment, each holding specific "targets" or goals based on safety concerns and the severity of the youth's behavior. Table 5.6 provides a brief overview of the stages and targets of DBT. Readers interested in obtaining a comprehensive and detailed understanding of DBT stages and goals, treatment modules, and intervention techniques should reference Linehan's (2014) *DBT Skills Training Manual.*

Emotion Regulation.   Although mindfulness practices are at the core of DBT's underlying philosophy, facilitating youth's development of emotion regulation skills will be the first and most critical task of counselors because client safety is always the most important factor in treatment. Emotion regulation skills aim to promote youth's ability to understand and identify distressing emotions to prevent life-threatening behaviors, such as suicide attempts or self-injury. When focusing on reducing youth's life-threatening behaviors, not only is it important for counselors to implement affect-oriented interventions but also those that address the cognitive, physiological, and behavioral aspects of distress. It is imperative for youth to develop awareness of how their thoughts and physical body sensations are associated with their self-destructive behaviors and how such behavior engagement can prevent them from experiencing a higher quality of life. Thus, emotion regulation interventions may emphasize identifying, processing, and ultimately reducing youth's vulnerability to the following aspects of distress: negative perceptions or automatic thinking patterns, communication styles that lead to highly reactive emotional responses, how the body feels when strong emotions are experienced, and behaviors that serve to contribute to, rather than prevent, life-threatening behaviors such as poor sleeping or eating patterns, alcohol or drug use, or lack of exercise. Maintaining a dialectical framework, the aforementioned targets associated with youth's identification of distress-related treatment factors are paradoxically met with emotion regulation targets oriented toward engaging in pleasant activities, using effective problem-solving skills, and increasing positive emotions. Once youth are feeling stable and life-threatening behaviors are no longer an imminent concern, they can begin to learn and use mindfulness practices in ways that will enhance their emotion regulation even further.

Table 5.6	Stages and Goals of Dialectical Behavior Therapy
Stage	**Targets or Goals**
Stage 1: *"Moving from being out of control of one's behavior to being in control"*	Reduce and then eliminate: • Behaviors that are life threatening • Behaviors that serve as barriers to counseling • Behaviors that reduce one's quality of life • Stage 1 also focuses on developing emotion regulation skills to promote the preceding targets.
Stage 2: *"Moving from being emotionally shut down to experiencing emotions fully"*	Experience emotions: • Without allowing them to take over • Without experiencing symptoms associated with posttraumatic stress disorder (e.g., dissociation, derealization) • Without avoiding them or shutting down
Stage 3: *"Building an ordinary life, solving ordinary problems"*	Work to accomplish goals surrounding: • Ordinary problems of living (e.g., at school or in the home; with peers, teachers, and family members) • Continue using and engaging in treatment services.
Stage 4: *"Moving from incompleteness to completeness and connection"*	Discover and engage ways to feel complete: • Meaningful interests and/or activities • Meaningful groups that share interests • Relationships with others

That is, youth's subsequent development of mindful attending and observing skills will enable them to better sense, identify, and understand more of the ways they experience distress. Ideally, over the course of counseling, youth will develop their emotion regulation skills. Counselors may find it helpful to use worksheets or other visual means to assist youth with identifying and understanding their cognitive, affective, physiological, and behavioral manifestations of distress, how they interact and influence one another, and preexisting strategies they have used to cope with distress in the past. In Figure 5.6, an example of an emotion regulation exercise that can be used with youth is provided.

Mindfulness. Mindfulness is a fundamental component of youth's emotion regulation skills training, and, notably, mindfulness components are integrated into DBT treatment modules intended to promote

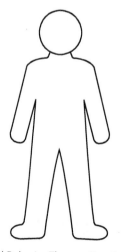

Where do you experience emotions in your body?

• Choose colors to represent different emotions, and draw where you experience them in your body.

• What thoughts might be associated with certain colors?

• What colors are associated with certain behaviors?

• Which colors are the most difficult to tolerate? Which colors are the easiest to tolerate?

• What strategies can you use to help tolerate each color?

FIGURE 5.6 Dialectical Behavior Therapy Emotion Regulation Exercise

distress tolerance and **interpersonal effectiveness**. Because of DBT's dialectical underpinnings, however, mindfulness practices are implemented into counseling and conceptualized from a slightly different lens than other third-generation modalities. The wise mind essentially represents the DBT treatment approach as a whole, integrating philosophical foundations of dialectics, CBT, and mindfulness through three different mind states that are used to explain behavior from cognitive, affective, and balanced ways of responding to distress (Linehan, 2014):

- *Rational Mind:* The rational mind pertains to logic, reason, planning, and youth's ability to use information and skills to problem solve and manage distressing situations in a safe, calm, and appropriate manner. The rational mind becomes difficult to use without adequate and healthy quantities of sleep, food, and exercise, or when youth are engaging in substance use or abuse.
- *Emotional Mind:* The emotional mind is associated with mood and sensations, impulsivity, reactivity, and feelings of high intensity and passion. When a distressing event occurs, the emotional mind can take over and distort the thinking of youth or make them feel out of control. Such experiences prevent youth from using aspects of the rational mind when faced with distress.
- *Wise Mind:* The wise mind is the integration of the rational and emotional minds. When youth are living balanced and mindful lives, they can respond to distress in intuitive ways or in ways they know and feel are right.

Because the wise mind represents the fusion of dialectically opposing rational and emotional forces, counselors can use a Venn diagram to easily explain the wise mind to youth or to explore the ways in which youth have responded to situations using aspects of their rational, emotional, and wise minds. For example, counselors can ask youth to label such experiences in the respective mind domain of a Venn diagram (see Figure 5.7). Counselors can then ask youth to subsequently process behaviors that were logical but still did not feel right (i.e., excess use of rational mind), times when behaviors felt right but were not rational (i.e., excess use of emotional mind), or instances in which they responded intuitively, knowing and feeling as though they made the best decision.

Counselors who use DBT aim to cultivate young people's wise minds through the implementation of core mindfulness practices such as deep breathing, attending to the present moment, observing inner experiences, letting go of distress, and radical acceptance (i.e., complete and total acceptance of something or some situation). Mindfulness practices are intended to function as an independent means to promote the distress tolerance of youth and serve to enhance their awareness of when additional strategies may be necessary to use. Counselors can use the acronym **IMPROVE** to provide youth with a foundation of distress tolerance skills that can be practiced and developed over the course of counseling (Linehan, 2014).

IMPROVE your current experience with:

- Imagery: Imagine your happy place or relaxing nature scenes such as a beach, mountains, a meadow, or a field of flowers.
- Meaning: Identify the meaningful things in your life. Thinking dialectically, what meaning might this difficult experience bring, or how might it cause you to grow in meaningful ways?

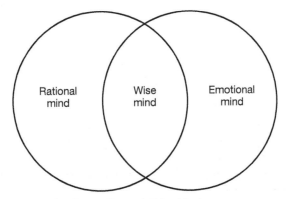

FIGURE 5.7 Components of Dialectical Behavior Therapy's Wise Mind

- **P**rayer: Engage in prayer, meditation, contemplation, introspection, or other spiritual practices to help to ease emotional pain or uncertainty.
- **R**elaxation: Engage in activities that are relaxing, such as taking a warm bath, yoga, stretching, lying down, deep breathing, or brushing your hair.
- **O**ne thing at a time: Focus your attention on the present moment. Simply observe and practice non-judgment, radical acceptance, and loving-kindness.
- **V**acation: Take a break from the stresses of daily life and disconnect from social media, email, texting, or electronics for a day; take a nap; or reconnect with an old friend for a special event at the park or your favorite restaurant.
- **E**ncouragement: Use positive affirmations or scripts to encourage yourself and foster self-compassion.

Distress Tolerance. DBT distress tolerance skills can be categorized into two primary domains: (a) self-soothing skills and (b) distraction skills. Self-soothing skills are intended to combat intense emotions and physiological sensations and help youth to let go of distress. DBT integrates cognitive behavioral distraction–based techniques that can be implemented by youth when they are unable to practice radical acceptance (i.e., accept something or a situation as it is) or when letting go of intense emotions does not seem possible. Essentially, distraction strategies are quick, easy to use, and useful in preventing crisis situations or high-risk behaviors. Counselors can cultivate mindfulness and introduce both self-soothing and distraction-oriented distress tolerance interventions to youth through the use of scripts or acronyms. Youth can repeat scripts, mantras, slogans, positive affirmations, or other preferred statements to assist them with tolerating distress or to remind themselves of additional coping strategies. For example, counselors can teach youth to use the **wise mind ACCEPTS** acronym as a script to help them to work through distressing situations (Linehan, 2014):

When Experiencing Distress, the Wise Mind ACCEPTS

- **A**ctivities: Engage in pleasurable self-soothing and distraction activities such as listening to music, going for a walk, exercising, painting, drawing, coloring, writing, reading, talking to a friend, or watching a positive movie or television show.
- **C**ontributing: Enhance feelings of generosity and find ways to contribute to your school, neighborhood, community, the environment, or to the well-being of others. Write a friend a gratitude letter to make him or her smile, clean up a dirty sidewalk, or volunteer at a local pet rescue shelter.
- **C**omparisons: Don't forget about the positives! Compare your current situation to all of the positive aspects of your life that you enjoy and that are going well.
- **E**motions: Remember that your current emotions are *not permanent—they will pass!* Accept the present moment as only the present moment. Let go of distressing emotions, and do things to replace these emotions with positive or calming feelings.
- **P**ushing away: If you are unable to accept or let go, it is okay—intentionally push away your current distress and solve the problem when you're feeling better.
- **T**houghts: Are my thoughts controlling me or am I controlling my thoughts? Am I using my wise mind—a balanced integration of emotional *and rational* minds? Don't forget to use logical thinking and problem solving when responding to distress.
- **S**ensations: Do something to cool down, self-soothe, or relax. Have a glass of juice or eat a cookie.

Interpersonal Effectiveness. The final skills-building training module of DBT targets interpersonal effectiveness because some youth—especially those presenting with features of borderline personality disorder or other severe mental health distresses—experience difficulties with maintaining stable relationships with others. Moreover, some youth experience chronic exposure to invalidating and/or traumatic experiences throughout development, and they may need to learn assertiveness skills and the ability to set age-appropriate and healthy relational boundaries. Many young people, as part of their developmental process, struggle with interpersonal boundaries, and thus these skills are very important for youth, especially as they navigate through the complexities of adolescent relationships. When applying DBT, counselors use interpersonal effectiveness interventions to promote youth's skills building in three core domains: (a) objective effectiveness, (b) relationship effectiveness, and (c) self-respect effectiveness. In summary, these interventions aim to provide youth with the skills necessary to help them to make requests or convey what they want from others, manage and resolve conflicts, establish and maintain positive relationships with others, and maintain and enhance self-respect when interacting with others. Although DBT's interpersonal effectiveness targets are indeed comprehensive and require youth to learn and practice various nuanced social skills, counselors can simplify such processes with the acronym **DEAR MAN GIVE FAST** (Linehan, 2014):

- **D**escribe: Describe what you want by stating information or facts.
- **E**xpress: Express your feelings, and explain why you want what you are requesting.
- **A**ssert: Be assertive and specifically ask for exactly what you want. When others say no, use skills to help you to cope with feelings and maintain self-respect.
- **R**einforce: Provide evidence of past experiences that further support your request.
- **M**indful: Remain focused on what you want, and don't allow small details to distract you.
- **A**ppear confident: Look at others, and convey your message in a clear, direct manner.
- **N**egotiate: Remain willing to discuss alternative options or to compromise to get what you want.
- **G**entle: Maintain a nonjudgmental stance, and do not make threats or attack others for having their own opinions.
- **I**nterested: Be open when listening to others, and take their perspective into account.
- **V**alidate: Validate others by reflecting their feelings and/or statements to let them know you are listening.
- **E**asy manner: Convey kindness, smile, keep the conversation lighthearted, be friendly, and use appropriate humor.
- **F**air: Work to maintain fairness for yourself and others throughout the discussion.
- **A**pology free: Do not apologize for asking what you want.
- **S**tick to your values: Remember your values and maintain integrity when compromising or negotiating.
- **T**ruthfulness: Be honest and refrain from exaggerating the truth to get what you want.

DEVELOPMENTALLY APPROPRIATE MINDFULNESS-BASED INTERVENTIONS

Although the third-generation therapies use mindfulness-based interventions to promote enhanced awareness, acceptance, attention to the present moment, nonjudgment, nonreactivity, self-compassion, equanimity, and loving-kindness, traditional mindfulness-based practices such as meditation, body scan, or yoga, for example, are too advanced or require too much time being still for many young people. Indeed, many mindfulness-based programs designed for youth, such as MBCT-C (Semple et al., 2005) and MSRB for school-age children (Saltzman & Goldin, 2008), support adaptations to the length, type, structure, and style of delivery for mindfulness exercises to suit the different needs of younger learners. Accordingly, the following sections introduce mindfulness-based practices that are developmentally appropriate for young people who present with a diversity of intellectual or functional individual needs. Counselors can implement these mindfulness strategies across various settings, or they can provide psychoeducation and associated materials to teachers and parents of youth to facilitate mindfulness practices in the school and home environments. As a general guideline, the age of clients can be used to determine the approximate length of mindfulness-based interventions, with consideration to other clinical or developmental factors that may influence youth's ability to sustain focused attention or remain in a still position.

Belly-Breathing Friend.   Counselors can introduce deep breathing exercises and help youth to cultivate daily breathing practices using the belly-breathing friend activities (Goleman, 2013). Counselors should offer an assortment of stuffed animals for children to choose from and provide a mat or have a soft surface that is comfortable for lying down. Counselors instruct youth to lie down on the mat, place their belly-breathing friend on their stomach area, and focus their attention on their breath. Noticing the up-and-down movement of their belly-breathing friend, youth can visually observe the rise and fall of their stomach and chest as they breathe. As a concentrative practice, counselors may want to provide brief statements throughout the exercise to gently remind youth to guide their attention back to their breath, simply noticing the passing of air and movement of their stomach. Counselors can also provide greater structure to the activity by directing children to breathe in and out using a mental 1-2-3 count. Following the activity, counselors can ask youth questions related to their focus on breathing, things they noticed, experiences with body sensations, or potential difficulties with sustaining focused attention or remaining in the present moment. When working with older children or adolescents who may not hold interest in stuffed animals, counselors can direct clients to use a pillow or their hands while focusing on the different sensations of air going through the nose, down the throat, filling the lungs, and so on.

Animal Parade.   The animal parade is intended for group formats but can also be used with individual children. This activity aims to increase children's mindful attention to the present moment, awareness of movement and the body, and observation of thoughts or emotions. Children select different animals and pretend to walk, hop, slither, or glide along a path that is predetermined by the counselor. For example, a child may choose to gallop like a horse; take long, stretched steps like an ostrich; swing like a monkey; fly like a bird; or waddle like a duck. Counselors should instruct children to mindfully attend to how the weight of their body shifts with different animals or how the movement of their feet varies with different animals. At different times throughout the exercise, children should be instructed to stop moving and bring their awareness to their breath, the pace of their heart, their body temperature, and other physiological sensations. Children should also indicate whether certain thoughts or emotions arose while pretending to be different animals.

Mystery Bag.   The mystery bag activity is intended to heighten youth's awareness and observation of sensory experiences with different sources of tactile stimulation. Counselors place objects that vary in size, texture, shape, and weight into nontransparent mystery bags and instruct youth to each put one hand into the mystery bag without looking and while focusing his or her attention on how different objects feel. Objects might include a golf ball, bar of dry soap, rocks, a spatula, candles, textured towels, silk ribbon, bubble wrap, or jelly beans. Counselors may use the mystery bag activity with groups or involve the family members of youth during individual sessions, allowing the client to describe what he or she feels while others make guesses about the object. Because youth are requested to reach into a "mysterious" bag, counselors can introduce and process themes of nonjudgment, trust, and letting go of thoughts or emotions, as well as bridge conversations to other experiences in which youth demonstrated similar abilities.

Vacation Destination.   The vacation destination exercise is designed to enhance youth's mindful attention to the present moment, auditory awareness and observation, visualization, and nonjudgmental attitude. Prior to the exercise, counselors need to prepare several short audio clips that correspond to different vacation destinations or general locations (e.g., waves on a beach, the crackle of a fire, a windy snowstorm or light rain, kids laughing and playing, roller coasters, safari animals); materials that make sounds characteristic of specific locations can also be created by counselors to facilitate the activity. Once youth are seated or lying down in a comfortable position, counselors present one sound at a time and ask youth to visualize the vacation destination or location of the sound. Counselors should allow moments of quietness between the presentation of each sound and may want to incorporate questions about what landscapes come to mind, temperature, wind, smells, time of day, or where they are standing. To foster acceptance and nonjudgment, counselors can include neutral audio or sounds that resemble boring or undesired locations (but not anxiety provoking) and subsequently process what it was like for youth to imagine such settings.

Letting Go.   To foster the acceptance of thoughts and emotions, nonjudgmental attitude, and understanding of the transient nature of inner experiences, counselors can facilitate letting-go guided imagery exercises using clouds in the sky, leaves drifting down a stream, hot air balloons floating into the distance, or any other preferred images that suit the preferences of youth. As opposed to concentrative meditation practices, letting-go guided imagery exercises are intended to promote youth's open monitoring of thoughts, feelings, sensations, and other inner experiences. To allow youth to clear their minds of any preexisting stress or worries, counselors should take the first several moments to encourage them to focus on the present moment and the rise and fall of their breath. As counselors begin to verbally portray the landscape, sounds, and pleasant, calming nature of the atmosphere selected for the guided meditation, they can begin to describe the passing of objects (e.g., leaves, clouds) and instruct youth to mentally place any thoughts or emotions that arise on the passing objects. Counselors can emphasize that youth do not need to intentionally generate thoughts but that whatever comes to mind—whether positive or negative—should be imagined as peacefully drifting or floating away into the distance, without judgment or attachment because all experiences are transient. Youth can then bring their awareness back to their breath and process the guided meditation after its completion.

Everyday Mindfulness Activities.   Similar to all CBT interventions, it is necessary for youth to regularly practice mindfulness to gain optimal benefits. As such, counselors can cultivate the enhanced awareness, acceptance, nonjudgment, self-compassion, loving-kindness, and equanimity of children and adolescents through mindfulness-based homework assignments. Counselors may desire to simply ask youth to practice mindfulness during specific activities of everyday life or select certain times throughout the day when they can mindfully attend to their current experiences. For example, youth can be assigned homework to practice mindfulness while brushing their teeth, stretching, showering, eating, walking, riding the school bus, washing their hands, eating lunch in the school cafeteria, playing outside at recess, taking a test, drinking water, or listening to music. Alternatively, youth might prefer to set a daily alarm for 5:00 p.m., take a 10-minute break to sit or lie down, and breathe in the present moment. Table 5.7 provides additional mindfulness exercises to use with youth.

Table 5.7 Mindfulness Exercises	
Exercise	Description
The Listening Dance	Counselors select music that may include nature sounds, ocean waves, or even words. During this exercise, youth are asked to stand still until the music starts. Once the music starts, youth are told to listen to the sounds and move to how they feel. Youth may use fast or slow dance moves using their arms, legs, and feet. After 1 minute, youth are instructed to stop and think about how they feel and what they heard. After each set of music and moves, youth are then asked to discuss what they heard and how it affected how they felt. Mindfulness and awareness can be discussed in the context of this activity.
Connecting the Smell	This activity involves youth using their sense of smell and different scents to promote awareness and relaxation. Counselors may use calming scents and/or scent-related objects such as an orange peel, a flower, a bar of lavender soap, a chamomile tea bag, or any other pleasant smells. Youth are instructed to close their eyes and touch and smell each object to connect with the fragrances. Youth are then asked to share what they smelled, how it smelled, and what it was like to focus their attention on the different scents of the object. Ways youth can use their senses of smell and scents to deepen their mindfulness practices can be discussed.
My Colorful Emotions	In this exercise, youth are initially guided into a state of relaxation. Counselors then instruct youth to think about where they feel a certain uncomfortable emotion (e.g., anger) and visually imagine that area on their bodies (e.g., jaw). Counselors ask youth to imagine that the area has a color. Is the color warm or cold? How big is the area when youth feel the emotion, and what shape does it take? Counselors ask youth to then visualize a new magic color that has the power to change the original color and size of the emotion (e.g., cold blue to warm yellow). Direct the youth to visualize the area with the new color for a minute, and invite them to reflect on how it feels. As the exercise continues, the goal is for youth to gain control of their feelings and understand they have the power to control how they manage pain and emotion using awareness and visual imagery.
My Pretend Image	In this exercise, visual imagery is used to achieve relaxation and mindfulness. Counselors instruct youth to sit calmly with their eyes closed and focus on their breath. For a few minutes, youth are asked to visualize themselves. They are invited to be aware of their physical and psychological features and to pay attention to them with no judgment or criticism. Next, youth are asked to visualize their biggest worry for about 30 seconds. Clients are then invited to visualize what resources or power they have that can be used to overcome this worry. Counselors instruct youth to again visualize their images, but this time they allow the resources or power to wash over the worry. This exercise can be used to help youth visualize themselves with the ability to conquer their biggest worry.

Family Interventions and Involvement

The involvement of parents, caregivers, and family members throughout counseling processes is particularly important for counselors using cognitive behavioral therapies because their active engagement not only greatly serves to reinforce the concepts and skills learned by youth but also enables parents and family members to obtain a better understanding of why certain behaviors occur and how to manage them. Although there is a great deal of empirical literature validating the effectiveness of CBT for a range of presenting concerns, the degree to which CBT counseling can help clients will be influenced by clients' application and utilization of CBT strategies in their daily lives. Because traditional CBT approaches are action oriented and didactic in nature and because they focus predominantly on the significant impact cognitions have on emotions and behaviors, youth's independent and regular practice of thought change strategies and completion of weekly homework assignments are critical treatment factors that promote their mastery of new skills and progress toward achieving their goals.

When providing initial CBT psychoeducation to youth, counselors can include parents and family members in session to familiarize them with key concepts and basic intervention techniques, how interventions are intended to work, and the ways in which family members can work to support youth and bridge skills from the counseling environment to the home setting. Parental involvement during introductory psychoeducation sessions and throughout counseling processes equips parents with the knowledge and skills necessary to recognize when youth are using techniques so they can monitor and identify which interventions appear to be most effective and under what circumstances. This information can be highly valuable to counselors during progress review processes because such feedback promotes individually tailored treatment plans and interventions or additional therapeutic techniques should be integrated because they are needed to target specific areas. Furthermore, holding a basic understanding of CBT interventions allows parents to have discussions with their children about cognitive distortions, overgeneralizations, acceptance, or other related practices, essentially serving as a counselor in the home environment until youth acquire the competency and skills to do so themselves—that is, parents and family members are enabled to catch youth when they are making irrational statements, suggest more positive and realistic ways of thinking, process youth's thoughts and feelings, and praise them for their hard work and progress toward achieving their goals. Regardless of the ways parents choose to engage their children about their experiences in counseling, how they are feeling, or ways they are implementing interventions, parental involvement throughout counseling processes will likely foster parent–child interactions at home about counseling. Counselors can facilitate such interactions by directly requesting parents to ask their children questions about counseling or homework assignments.

Parental and family participation allows counselors to address systemic familial factors that may be contributing to the distress or problem behaviors of youth, including undesired parenting or conflict resolution styles, maladaptive interaction patterns, poor modeling, or lack of supervision, reinforcement, or consequences. Counselors can work with parents to enhance their understanding of how their actions are influencing their children's behavior, assist parents with identifying and committing to making their own constructive behavioral changes, and provide parents with additional behavior modification training to promote positive parenting practices. At times, however, the need for systemic or parent interventions may be too significant for counselors to simply integrate the aforementioned components into the individual counseling sessions of youth. As such, counselors may choose to hold separate sessions with parents or suggest that parents complete an evidence-based parent management training (PMT; see Behavior Therapy section) group. If parents are experiencing clinically significant distress of their own, counselors can refer them to begin receiving individual counseling themselves.

PARENT AND FAMILY INTEGRATED CBT APPROACHES

Although the vast majority of CBT modalities were originally developed as treatments for individual clients, several approaches have been modified to include youth and parents, or families, in counseling processes. Indeed, both traditional and third-generation CBT modalities have made such modifications, suggesting that the inclusion of parents or family members in youth's counseling will provide additional therapeutic benefits to the individual CBT practices already recognized as evidence-based practices for various presenting concerns. Several cognitive behavioral treatments that include parents have been recognized as evidence-based practices, including DBT (Harvey & Rathbone, 2015; Linehan, 1993, 2014), **Coping Cat** (Kendall & Hedtke, 2006a) for childhood anxiety, **trauma-focused cognitive behavioral therapy** (TF-CBT; Cohen, Mannarino, Kliethermes, & Murray, 2012), and **alternatives for families: a cognitive behavioral therapy** (AF-CBT; Kolko, Simonich, & Loiterstein, 2014). Several other promising parent and family integrative CBT approaches that are still under investigation and may be helpful are **family CBT** (Wood, McLeod, Piacentini, & Sigman, 2009), **MBCT-C** (Semple et al., 2005), and **MBSR for School-Age Children** (Saltzman & Goldin, 2008).

Dialectical Behavior Therapy.   As previously mentioned, DBT is a biosocial theory that asserts that environmental factors, such as parenting, play a significant role in youth's development of emotional dysregulation, physiological hyperarousal, heightened reactivity, and maladaptive behavioral responses to distress (Miller et al., 2007). More specifically, the exposure of youth to chronic experiences of invalidation from their parents is particularly detrimental from DBT perspectives (Harvey & Rathbone, 2015). Accordingly, including parents in DBT counseling processes is critical because continued experiences of invalidation, inconsistent parental demands, or instability in the home environment can trigger youth and be harmful. Ben-Porath (2010) suggested using DBT skills-training modules with the parents of youth in counseling to teach them how to respond to their children. The use of DBT skills with parents may be especially helpful with parents who experience difficulties with regulating their own emotions. Moreover, as some parents may have clinically significant mental health struggles, not only can DBT skills training help caregivers improve their parenting styles and interactions with youth, but it may also provide them with additional emotion regulation strategies they can use to improve their overall adaptive functioning (Ben-Porath, 2010).

Coping Cat.   Coping Cat is a popular 16-week manualized CBT treatment for children ages 7 to 13 with diagnoses of separation anxiety disorder, generalized anxiety disorder, or social anxiety disorder (Kendall, Choudhury, Hudson, & Webb, 2002; Kendall & Hedtke, 2006a). As an evidence-based practice, the Coping Cat program helps youth to identify and understand the affective and physiological components associated with their reactions to anxiety-provoking stimuli, clarify their cognitions and emotions, develop coping skills to manage their anxiety, and learn to reward themselves for overcoming anxiety (Kendall & Hedtke, 2006b). Counselors facilitating Coping Cat programs use psychoeducation, relaxation training, cognitive restructuring based on a FEAR plan, problem-solving interventions, and exposure-based tasks in an effort to help youth to achieve the aforementioned goals.

Parents can play several critical roles during their child's participation in the Coping Cat program (Podell, Mychailyszyn, Edmunds, Puleo, & Kendall, 2010): (a) consultants, (b) collaborators, or (c) co-clients. Parents are conceptualized as consultants and collaborators because they provide counselors with pertinent information used to determine diagnoses and treatment outcomes and because they provide youth with support throughout the program. However, when parents accommodate or enable their children to avoid anxiety-provoking situations or are anxious about their children engaging in exposure tasks, they are serving to maintain their children's anxiety-related distress. When parents are involved in treatment processes, counselors can readily address parenting factors that may be impeding therapeutic processes (Podell et al., 2010).

Trauma-Focused Cognitive Behavioral Therapy.   TF-CBT is recognized as the most effective treatment approach for youth who have experienced trauma or abuse (Cohen et al., 2012). TF-CBT is a conjoint child and parent treatment approach that helps children, adolescents, and family members to address emotional and behavioral distresses associated with traumatic life events. The model integrates trauma-sensitive interventions with cognitive behavioral strategies, humanistic principles, and family involvement to decrease trauma symptomology. TF-CBT teaches children and parents new skills that can assist them with processing their thoughts and feelings related to traumatic life events; managing distressing emotions, thoughts, or behaviors stemming from trauma; and developing an enhanced sense of safety, personal growth, parenting skills, and improved family communication (Cohen et al., 2012). A free 10-hour certificate training program on TF-CBT can be completed through the TF-CBT website (Medical University of South Carolina, 2005). This training program is an excellent resource for developing a more comprehensive understanding of trauma treatment processes, and it can be completed by any helping professional or student currently enrolled in a graduate training program in a mental health discipline.

Alternatives for Families: A Cognitive Behavioral Approach.   Similar to TF-CBT, AF-CBT is a treatment approach that is specifically oriented toward children who have been physically abused by their parents or exposed to threats, excessive physical force, or aggressive conflicts (Kolko et al., 2014). AF-CBT is unique, however, because the approach aims to enhance relationships between children and caregivers and provide both parents and children with the skills necessary to manage their anger, aggressive behaviors, opposition, or poor social skills. Counselors facilitating AF-CBT programs use psychoeducation, individual skills-building family interventions to cultivate family safety, foster healthy and nonaggressive family interaction patterns, reduce arguments and conflicts, and ultimately promote the well-being of youth (Kolko et al., 2014).

MINDFULNESS-BASED THERAPIES

MBCT-C (Semple et al., 2005) and MBSR (Saltzman & Goldin, 2008), previously discussed approaches, rely on parental involvement. Because these approaches are centrally founded in mindfulness, practicing skills outside counseling is critical to young people's success. As part of these approaches, parents are engaged not only to promote the youth's completion of homework and engagement in mindfulness practices in the home environment but also to cultivate the mindfulness of parents themselves. It is assumed that if parents cultivate these skills, they serve as models for youth and can practice mindfulness strategies together. Although additional research is needed, preliminary studies suggest that MBCT-C is effective in reducing youth's symptoms of anxiety, attention problems, and behavior problems (Semple et al., 2005). Moreover, the MBSR for School-Age Children has demonstrated success in reducing youth's emotional reactivity as well as symptoms of depression and anxiety (Saltzman & Goldin, 2008).

REALITY THERAPY AND CHOICE THEORY

Originally developed by American psychiatrist, William Glasser (1965, 1972, 1976, 1998, 2000, 2011), **reality therapy** is a didactic, collaborative, and action-oriented therapeutic modality. Reality therapy is based on **choice theory** and aims to assist clients with changing their maladaptive behaviors so they can more effectively meet their individual needs and experience more satisfying relationships. During his psychiatric residency in the 1950s, Glasser began to renounce the then commonly used Freudian psychoanalytic approach because he observed that many clients failed to make positive decisions and constructive life changes despite their attainment of enhanced unconscious insight. W. Glasser's (1961, 1965, 2003) experiences working with youth in corrections and substance abuse treatment led him to further denounce the deterministic nature of psychoanalysis, and he also rejected the medical model used by psychiatrists that involved diagnosis, treatment, and use of pharmacological intervention.

W. Glasser (1969, 2001, 2003, 2005) developed his own treatment approach—*reality therapy*—in which he asserted that maladaptive behaviors and client unhappiness were the result of unsatisfying relationships or an absence of meaningful interpersonal connections, and not evidence of mental illness. Rather than attributing client's symptoms and behaviors to tensions of neurotic anxiety or imbalances in psychic energy associated with the unconscious forces previously believed to drive behavior, W. Glasser (1969, 2001, 2003, 2005) emphasized the role of choice and the power clients *do have* over their actions. Reality therapy's relational focus and nondeterministic conceptualization of behavior are well suited for counseling youth. His theory has a focus on foundational factors that support youth: fostering and maintaining social support systems, illuminating the possibilities of change, and promoting opportunities for youth to make positive choices so they can obtain their wants and needs. The aforementioned factors, along with others such as providing young people with a sense of safety, support, emotional attachment, hope, and control, are critical in supporting young people's development.

The central foci of reality therapy are choice and behavior: What are clients doing, and is what they are doing getting them what they want? Are their behaviors working to meet their needs, and are these behaviors helping them in ways that matter to them? How can clients choose to behave in ways that best help them obtain their wants? Reality therapy emphasizes the importance of counselors and clients being present focused; a strong therapeutic alliance; a focus on satisfying clients' basic needs through the use of adaptive behavioral choices; personal responsibility for choices; and self-evaluation (Wubbolding, 2000, 2011).

Core Concepts and Goals of Counseling

Choice theory is the theoretical foundation for reality therapy, serving to inform how our minds operate and develop, explain our innate needs and motivations, and provide a basis for understanding human behavior. According to W. Glasser's (1998, 2001, 2003) theory, our behavior is driven by five genetically encoded basic needs, including:

- *survival*, or a need for self-preservation;
- *love and belonging*, or a need for involvement, friendship, and caring;
- *power* or inner control, or a need for recognition and achievement;
- *freedom* or autonomy, or a need for personal choice and independence; and
- *fun*, or a need for pleasure, enjoyment, and laughter.

Although these five basic needs are presumed to be universal, the degree of satisfaction and intensity of each need varies by the moment and depends on individuals' unique life circumstances and perceptions of reality. W. Glasser (1998, 2001, 2005) believed that our need for belonging and love, both given and received, is the most essential basic need. However, because this need requires the cooperation of others and one's needs can often conflict with the needs of others, it is also the most difficult need to satisfy. It is important to explore the degree to which young people's need for belonging and love are being met because this speaks to the strength of youth's social support systems. Counselors may want to investigate what person, people, or groups are providing youth with meaningful relationships; in what environments; the consistency of need fulfillment; and how love and belonging might be influencing youth's behavioral choices.

When considering the relational dynamics of young people's lives, it is important for counselors to remain mindful of contextual and developmental factors that are unique to each individual client—such contingencies may distinguish unsatisfied needs from preferences that youth have intentionally chosen. For example, high levels of affection and parental interaction are needs of high priority for children, but adolescents are likely to desire higher amounts of separation from their parents or caregivers as they mature and, instead, ascribe greater meaning to the sense of belonging offered by peers or romantic partners. The primary goal of reality therapy is to assist youth with satisfying their basic needs by developing or reestablishing meaningful relationships with others.

According to Glasser's (1961) theory, humans' five basic needs drive all behavior. When our basic needs are unfulfilled, we experience unhappiness, pain, or loneliness (Wubbolding, 2000). In an effort to mitigate such distress, individuals choose behaviors that are sometimes maladaptive to satisfy their unmet needs. All behavior, even maladaptive behavior, is considered to be a reflection of individuals' current degree of knowledge and ability to best fulfill their needs. Accordingly, Glasser (1961, 2003) was vehemently opposed to the notion of mental illness and ascribing diagnoses to youth because he believed such practices pathologized young people's best efforts to gain a sense of control in their lives. Adopting this lens, consider the following diagnostic nomenclature commonly used to describe youth's presenting problems: *dysregulation*, *disturbance*, *oppositional*, *dysfunction*, *disorder*, *impairment*, *disruption*, or *defiant*. These terms suggest youth have deficits, and some suggest the youth may be intentionally acting out (e.g., *oppositional* is defined as "opposing" or "resisting"). When applying reality theory, counselors can provide parents or caregivers, families, and school personnel with psychoeducation about mental health stigma and associated adverse effects and refrain from using such language themselves in an effort to prevent youth from internalizing a negative identity that may critically affect their self-esteem, beliefs about their ability to fulfill their wants and needs, and/or expectations of the future.

Educating clients to make better choices to better meet their unsatisfied needs is central to reality therapy. Choice theory explains that we do not satisfy our needs directly (Wubbolding, 2000). Rather, beginning at birth, our brains begin to store information about what feels or is perceived to be good, thus developing what Wubbolding referred to as our **quality world**. Unlike the five basic needs that are universal to all humans, the quality world is unique to each individual and contains a **picture album** of personal wants or subjective perceptions of one's ideal reality (Glasser, 2000). The quality world picture album is an accumulation of specific mental images of people, events, life circumstances, and possessions that represent our own personal utopia or most preferred life experience. These wants are associated with our five basic needs and serve as inner forces that motivate our behavior. Counselors and other helping professionals can engage in collaborative exploration processes with youth aimed to identify the behavioral choices they make in an effort to fulfill their basic needs and achieve the wants of their quality world (Wubbolding, 2000, 2011). Due to developmental variations surrounding the comprehension of abstract concepts and use of verbal language to communicate, counselors working with younger children should consider infusing creative ways to explore young clients' wants and needs. Children might be invited to draw quality world pictures associated with each of the five basic needs by using crayons, markers, or paint or to display their quality world in a sand tray while sharing details about their creation. Not only are these techniques developmentally appropriate for children, but they may also reveal which basic wants and needs are most satisfied or lacking in fulfillment. Counselors can use this information to inform treatment planning and counseling processes, form hypotheses about the wants that might be motivating children's behavior and how their choices are functioning to meet unsatisfied needs, and aim to identify or create increased opportunities for children to make choices that will bolster presently unfulfilled wants and need domains.

TOTAL BEHAVIOR

Choice theory is based on the idea that all human experience can be described as behavior, and behavior consists of four discrete but interconnected components known as **total behavior** (Glasser, 1985, 1998):

- Acting
- Thinking
- Feeling
- Physiology

According to reality therapy, young people's behaviors are directed toward resolving discrepancies between their quality world and perceived world—that is, what they want and what they are getting. Although peoples' behavior is driven by basic needs and inner wants, behavior is presupposed to be a choice because it comes from within and functions to serve a purpose. As examples, children may demonstrate tantrum behaviors to obtain increased attention from a parent or teacher, a child might bully another child to satisfy needs related to power, or adolescents may steal or fight because of unmet survival needs.

Glasser (1984) refrained from describing youth as depressed, anxious, or angry and instead used the verb forms of these words—*depressing, anxietying,* and *angering*—to reinforce the notion that youth choose their behaviors and thus have the ability to change them. Counselors can demonstrate this notion in a manner that is more comprehensible to youth by asking them to safely act out different **paining behaviors**: "Show me what *depressing* looks like" or "Act out *angering* for me." Following enactments, counselors can process how youth chose to perform the behavior and how they control their behavioral choices during all other lived experiences as examples in session. This conception may seem harsh to young clients—they are being told they are choosing to experience distress, misery, or suffering—but counselors can teach youth that paining behaviors such as depressing, anxietying, or angering comprise only two components of their total behavior (i.e., acting and thinking) and that associated experiences of distress or misery are indirect manifestations of the other two components of their total behavior (i.e., feeling and physiology) that are not chosen. Consistent with cognitive behavioral explanations of behavior, if we choose to alter our behavior, other elements of our total behavior—our thinking, feeling, and physiology—will also begin to change.

Because youth are expected to listen to their teachers, adhere to school rules, and comply with the directives of their parents or caregivers on a daily basis, they often perceive that they do not have many choices, and thus they may not experience a sense of control over their lives. However, youth *can* control their behaviors. What they *cannot* control is the behavior of others, and according to Glasser (1998; Glasser & Glasser, 2000, 2007), attempts to do so result in frustration, interpersonal alienation, and difficulties in establishing or maintaining meaningful relationships with others. Thus, reality therapists teach young clients that they can only control *their own* behaviors. These therapists also emphasize personal responsibility and accountability and explain how behavioral choices affect the quality and disposition of their relationships with others. This focus on what young people can and cannot control can be helpful in supporting them. For example, as some behavioral problems begin to manifest when children experience difficulties adapting to new environments (e.g., transitions into preschool or kindergarten), they may struggle with following directions, separating from parents or guardians, sharing with others, keeping their hands to themselves, waiting their turn, sitting still, worrying, or engaging in temper tantrums. Reality therapy's structured orientation, which emphasizes personal responsibility, adult expectations, and behavioral consequences, is particularly well framed to address many of the problems with which young people struggle. Youth can be taught to make positive behavioral choices and learn new skills related to impulse control, emotional regulation, and positive decision-making and social skills.

Glasser (1992, 2000) posited seven deadly habits and seven caring habits to explain the interaction between behavioral choices and interpersonal relationships. The seven deadly habits include criticizing, blaming, complaining, nagging, threatening, punishing, and bribing or controlling with rewards. Because choice theory postulates that the majority of problems and unhappiness stem from unsatisfying relationship dynamics and experiences, youth are encouraged to replace deadly habits with caring habits. The seven caring habits are caring, listening, supporting, contributing, encouraging, trusting, and negotiating differences. For example, rather than complaining about others, counselors can encourage youth to identify ways they can fix their relationship problems by being flexible and compromising. Because adolescents have more advanced cognitive abilities than children, they are better able to understand the more complex facets of relationships and the multidimensional nature of the seven caring habits. When working with younger children, counselors can appropriately adapt their language. For example, they might replace the term *encouragement* with *warm fuzzies talk* or *negotiation* with *sharing muscles*.

The behavioral choices of youth can be gently challenged simply by posing the question "Are your behaviors helping you get what you want?" Dissonance between the wants and behavioral choices of youth can be used to engender commitment and willingness to change. Counselors subsequently engage in collaborative goal-setting and planning processes focused on youth's desired behavioral changes and help them to develop new skills that enable them to make more responsible behavioral choices to satisfy their wants and needs.

Glasser (1998) asserted 10 essential axioms, or principles, that serve as a foundation for choice theory. These axioms provide an overview of choice theory's conceptualization of human nature and inform the practice of reality therapy:

The 10 Axioms of Choice Theory

1. The only person whose behavior we can control is our own.
2. The best a counselor or another person can do is give information to a client.
3. All long-lasting psychological disturbances are rooted in relationship problems.
4. A person's relationship problem is always part of his or her present life.
5. Although the past may affect what we are today, we can only satisfy our basic needs in the present and plan to continue satisfying then in the future.
6. We can only satisfy our needs by satisfying the pictures in our quality world.
7. All we do can best be described as behaving.
8. All behavior is total behavior and comprises four components: acting, thinking, feeling, and physiology.
9. All total behavior is chosen, but we only have direct control over the acting and thinking components. We control our feelings and physiology indirectly through how we choose to act and think.
10. All total behavior is named by verbs and named by the most recognizable part.

Role of the Counselor in Reality Therapy

ESTABLISHING RAPPORT

Developing and maintaining a strong therapeutic alliance with clients is not only a fundamental task for counselors, but it is also, within the framework of reality therapy, considered to be a prerequisite to client change (Wubbolding, 2000; Wubbolding, Robey, & Brickell, 2010). Children and adolescents who have difficulties with making positive decisions to satisfy their wants and needs typically receive critical feedback about their behavior from parents, peers, teachers, other school personnel, or community members. Consequently, clients may begin to internalize these disapproving messages and adopt a failure identity, believing they are "bad" or unable to succeed. For treatment to be effective, counselors *must* establish a trusting relationship and work to become part of the client's quality world. Counselors need to create a safe, warm, affirming, and nonjudgmental therapeutic atmosphere, while befriending clients as an ally and making efforts to convey concern, empathy, positive regard, and genuine involvement explicitly known to the client. Wubbolding (2007), another pioneer of reality therapy, offered the ABCDEFG approach that can be used to guide counselors' interactions with youth:

- **AB:** Always be . . .
- **C**ourteous
- **D**etermined
- **E**nthusiastic
- **F**irm
- **G**enuine

PROMOTING RESPONSIBILITY AND COMMITMENT

Although counselors must demonstrate acceptance, interest, and support to foster trusting therapeutic relationships, responsibility and choice are maintained as core foci throughout counseling. Therefore, counselors also hold clients accountable for their behavioral choices, expect commitment, and do not accept excuses when plans are not followed through (Glasser, 1992, 1998). Reality therapy supposes that tolerating excuses enables clients to avoid accepting responsibility for their behavior and committing to plans of action. However, this premise does not imply that children and adolescents should be punished, blamed, or criticized for making excuses or failing to follow through with actions plans. Rather, counselors refrain from asserting judgment and redirect excuses toward identifying new plans that clients can more effectively commit and adhere to.

TEACHING AND ADVOCATING

Counselors practicing reality therapy assume the roles of teacher and advocate. Over the course of treatment, youth are educated about personal responsibility, choices, and the importance of meaningful relationships. Youth learn to engage in self-evaluation to determine the effectiveness of their behaviors in relation to fulfilling their wants and needs, how their behavioral choices influence their relationships with others, and what types of productive actions can accomplish their goals.

Despite reality therapy's emphasis on personal responsibility and the assumption that all behavior is internally, and thus individually, motivated, it is critical for counselors to communicate to youth that behavioral change is often very difficult and they are not engaging in such processes alone—that is, counselors also need to adopt roles (e.g., supporter, encourager, coach, advocate) that align them with youth and provide evidence for the collaborative nature of treatment and change procedures in an effort to instill hope (Glasser, 2011; Wubbolding, 2000). Counselors can engender hope by remaining optimistic and conveying a sense of anticipation for imminent change or by presupposing client success. When youth do begin to demonstrate desired changes, the affirming messages and efforts of counselors are reinforced, and youth learn that they do have control and are capable of making more positive behavioral choices. Integrating activities designed to concretely identify and display the personal strengths, resources, and capabilities of youth early in the counseling process may serve as an additional means to engender hope, build self-efficacy, or increase motivation.

Counseling Process and Procedures

The practice of reality therapy is, in essence, the application or operationalization of choice theory. Wubbolding's (1989, 1991, 2000, 2011) WDEP system is the prominent delivery method of choice theory that delineates counseling processes in a pragmatic and procedural manner. However, prior to implementing the WDEP system, counselors must create an environment and therapeutic relationship that are conducive to change. This integration of environment, relationship, and interventions comprise reality therapy's **cycle of counseling**.

CHANGE ENVIRONMENTS AND RELATIONSHIPS

The initial phase of reality therapy's cycle of counseling includes establishing open, friendly, and trusting therapeutic relationships with youth, along with creating a safe, warm, and nonjudgmental counseling environment. These primary components serve as a foundation for all subsequent therapeutic activity and are also considered to be prerequisites for client change. Choice theory contends that the vast majority of all problems are the result of unsatisfying relationships. Therefore, for counselors to assist youth with changing their behaviors to better fulfill unmet needs, youth must perceive their relationships with counselors as satisfying. Counselors practicing reality therapy aim to develop a strong therapeutic alliance and create a supportive and challenging environment to foster change processes. Wubbolding (2000, 2011) offered various interventions to promote change-facilitating environments and relationships, and these can be found in Table 5.8.

WDEP SYSTEM

Wubbolding's (2000, 2011) **WDEP system** focuses on the wants, behaviors, self-evaluation, and planning of youth. The WDEP system is clear, concrete, and uses straightforward language that is comprehensible to youth (Wubbolding, 1991, 2007). These characteristics increase the likelihood of favorable responses to interventions, and they also provide young people with a realistic opportunity to learn to implement the procedures themselves and to continue to do so throughout their development. Such learning opportunities promote empowering experiences for children and may provide them with a greater sense of mastery, enhanced self-efficacy, or pride in their new successes and accomplishments.

It is important to note that WDEP procedures may appear to be simplistic or easy to implement because of the use of concrete language; however, when considering the continuous flux and interplay between one's quality world, inner pictures, and total behavior, paired with the relational dynamics and contextual differences that exist within the counseling relationship, employing WDEP procedures while effectively navigating the counseling cycle may prove to be a complex task. Table 5.9 provides an overview of the WDEP system.

Table 5.8	Interventions That Promote Change Environments and Relationships
Intervention	**Description**
Suspend Judgment	Monitor your judgments, and convey this suspended judgment to youth.
Do the Unexpected	Reframe undesired youth behaviors to identify and emphasize strengths (e.g., tantrum behaviors = emotionally expressive).
Use Humor	Be fun and laugh with clients while maintaining boundaries.
Set Boundaries	Set clear and concrete limits with clients.
Self-Disclose	Foster trust with appropriate sharing of your experiences.
Listen for Metaphors	Metaphors offer additional insight into youth's wants and needs.
Listen for Inner Control Talk	Identify and celebrate youth's acceptance of responsibility and control over their behavioral choices.
Listen for Themes	Emphasize themes related to wants, needs, and choices.
Summarize & Focus	Let youth know they are being heard, and keep the focus on them rather than external forces they cannot control.
Allow or Impose Consequences	Consequences need to be within reason and should emphasize responsibility rather than punishment.
Silence	Allow youth time to process and self-evaluate.
Create Anticipation & Communicate Hope	Be curious and optimistic for adaptive behavioral changes, and create a sense of imminent success.

Note: Wubbolding (2000, 2011).

Table 5.9	**WDEP System**	
	Questions	Objectives
W	What do you want?	Explore Wants, needs, and perceptions
D	What are you doing?	Direction and Doing (total behavior)
E	Is what you are doing helping you?	*Self*-Evaluation = cornerstone
P	What is your plan?	Plan to replace ineffective behaviors

Wants, Needs, and Perceptions.   The first step of the WDEP system is designed to assist youth with obtaining a more comprehensive understanding of their wants, needs, and perceptions. Counselors often pose the question "What do you want?" and engage in collaborative exploration processes with youth to process and identify their wants from family, friends, the counselor and counseling process, their external environment, and themselves. Counselors continue to use skillful questioning to gain access to the quality world picture albums of their clients. As we indirectly satisfy our five basic needs through wants and behave in ways to bring our perceived (external) world closer to our quality world of inner wants, clients' responses provide insight to their unsatisfied needs and assist in the identification of treatment goals.

As an example, consider how quality world information can be used to assist adolescents experiencing difficulties with substance use behaviors. Regardless of the type of associated problems adolescents might be experiencing, nothing can *cause* them to engage in substance use behaviors, they can only make choices to do so. Counselors can assist adolescents with identifying quality world wants and how they might be choosing to use substances in an effort to fulfill their unsatisfied needs.

Counselors also seek to explore youth's perceptions of control and their degree of commitment to counseling. Youth presenting with a strong sense of external control, or perceptions that others and their environment are controlling their lives, may experience greater difficulties recognizing they do have choices, accepting responsibility for their actions, and committing to changing their behaviors. Counselors can use this information to modify their approaches and interventions in a strategic fashion to best meet the needs of each client and effectively work through reluctance to change. Counselors can determine youth's degree of reluctance by referencing Wubbolding's (1988, 1991, 2000, 2011) proposed five levels of commitment, which are described by the following statements:

- "I don't want to be here."
- "I want the outcome, but not the effort."
- "I'll try," "I might," or "I could."
- "I will do my best."
- "I will do whatever it takes."

Direction and Doing.   After the exploration and identification of youth's quality world wants, needs, and perceptions, counselors transition discussions with youth toward their total behavior, asking "What are you doing?" Although actions, thoughts, feelings, and physiology are all respective components of our total behavior, reality therapy avoids focusing on symptoms and how our problems may be related to the past because such foci are presumed to inhibit youth from acknowledging the source of their problems—the total behavior they are currently choosing. In addition to identifying youth's present behavioral choices, counselors also process the overall direction of youth's lives to assist them with anticipating the potential outcomes of their behaviors. Counselors might ask "Where are you headed?" or "Where are your behaviors taking you?" or "How do see yourself in the future?"

Self-Evaluation.   Self-evaluation is the key element of reality therapy. Choice theory posits that youth will not change until they decide that their behavioral choices are ineffective and they perceive change to be a more favorable option. Thus, counselors ask questions such as "Is what you are doing working for you?" or "Are your behaviors helping or hurting you?" or "Is what you are doing now leading you to where you want to be later in life?" Counselors teach youth to evaluate each aspect of their total behavior and then assist them in determining whether their current behavioral choices are helping them to satisfy their wants and the direction in which their behaviors are leading them. Effective self-evaluation processes will motivate youth to accept responsibility, plan to make new behavioral choices, and fully commit to counseling processes in an effort to better meet their wants and needs (Wubbolding, 2000, 2011).

Because most young children do not have the cognitive capacity to independently self-evaluate, it is critical for counselors to communicate and teach the self-evaluation process in a way that is developmentally appropriate for youth. Counselors may want to create "if–then" worksheets (i.e., If I do this, then this will happen— Is that what I want?) or use graphics of a weights and measures balance or a seesaw to allow children to visually connect with and evaluate their behaviors in a way they can understand.

The WDEP system's emphasis on self-evaluation makes this intervention highly applicable to adolescents because they are often egocentric and highly focused on themselves, experiencing biological changes that influence emotional reactivity; have difficulties delaying gratification and impulses to engage in risky behavior; and may have poor planning and decision-making skills. By asking adolescents to determine if their behaviors are helping them and where their behaviors are leading them, counselors can help adolescents to take a more realistic look at the future and develop better planning processes.

Planning.   Once youth decide that their actions are not working for them and they desire to change, they can begin planning to engage in more responsible behaviors. In a similar manner to the antecedent procedures, counselors collaboratively assist youth in exploring new behavioral options, allow youth to identify which choices they believe will best help them gain control over their lives, and develop an action plan for implementation. Although counselors aim to empower their clients and instill hope, it is important for them to communicate that not all action plans work and that planning processes are allowed to be revisited until youth identify a set of behaviors that satisfies their unique personal wants and needs. Moreover, for any action plan to be effective, youth need to demonstrate commitment. Wubbolding (1988, 2000) delineated characteristics of quality action plans by using the acronym **SAMIC**:

- **S**imple, or clear, to the point, and easy to understand.
- **A**ttainable, or realistic for youth to complete in small steps (i.e., developmentally/intellectually appropriate).
- **M**easurable, or concrete and specific. Is the plan working?
- **I**mmediate, or easy for youth to readily implement.
- **C**ontrolled, or created by youth and can be completed *without* others.
- **C**ommitted, or consistent with what youth are willing to do.
- **C**ontinuous, or repetitive and open to revision.

Although youth are encouraged to develop their own action plans and independently identify positive behaviors to achieve desired wants, children will again likely require assistance throughout the planning processes. Counselors can refer back to previously used lists or concrete materials to stimulate children's "planning muscles."

Family Interventions and Involvement

Family interventions and involvement can play an important role in youth's counseling experiences. Specifically, parents or guardians, siblings, and other family members can significantly influence youth's perceived satisfaction of their five basic needs, especially belonging and love, as well as their experiences throughout development that become encoded to inform their quality world picture albums (Glasser, 2000). Thus, it can be assumed that youth's relationships with their families will certainly play a role in the course of treatment and that favorable counseling outcomes will likely yield enhanced connections and relationships between youth and their families. These positive relationships satisfy the quality world wants and needs of youth and provide them with strong social support systems that function as critical protective factors against experiences of distress throughout development and later in life.

An example of an application of reality therapy to family counseling is the Parent Involvement Program (PIP), a six-session program that educates parents about reality therapy and provides them with different avenues to address youth's behaviors in a manner that is consistent with the ideals of reality therapy (McGuiness, 1977). The ultimate goal of PIP is to foster increased parent involvement and strengthen parent–youth relationships.

Although reality therapy focuses on youth's individual-level behavioral choices, the concepts can be integrated into family therapy and family approaches to change (Graham, Sauerheber, & Britzman, 2013). In applying the WDEP system, for example, the counseling process mirrors how the intervention is used with young clients independently and incorporates the addition of what the family wants, how the family is functioning to satisfy wants, and self-evaluation about how individual wants may be conflicting with those of the family (Graham et al., 2013). In a family application of the WDEP system, the final step of the model—the plan—could be aimed at enhancing, sustaining, and nurturing relationships among family members.

Summary

The theoretical approaches discussed in this chapter have, as their focus, helping youth to change their thoughts and behaviors. These approaches have broad applicability to various presenting youth concerns (e.g., ADHD, communication problems). There are many advantages to using these approaches with young people. These approaches and their accompanying concepts can be taught to parents who can reinforce the use of the concepts out of the counseling setting. For youth who may feel stigmatized, disliked, or singled out as a result of their presenting concerns, framing problems as learned behavior or thoughts that can be changed rather than personal attributes may engender a profound sense of hope, encourage a sense of control, and thus foster a sense of empowerment. Moreover, because the approaches discussed in this chapter are concrete in nature, counselors can explain the counseling processes and intervention strategies in a developmentally appropriate manner that many clients and their parents understand.

The use of active, directive, concrete approaches can also demystify the counseling process and facilitate client understanding, autonomy, and youth buy-in of counseling. It may also allow young clients to perceive behavioral change as a nonthreatening, realistic, and achievable task. As such, these action-oriented approaches are highly culturally appropriate because many clients prefer this concrete, clear, directive approach to counseling (Seligman & Reichenberg, 2014). In Table 5.10, an overview of the theories discussed in this chapter is provided. This table summarizes the three theories discussed in this chapter, and the following components are addressed: basic philosophy, key concepts, goals of counseling, therapeutic relationship, counseling techniques, applications/approaches, multicultural considerations, and youth-specific approaches associated with the theory.

Table 5.10 Summary of Counseling Theories

Behavioral Theory

Basic philosophy	All behaviors are either adaptive or maladaptive, and they are learned and can be unlearned. All maladaptive behaviors can be modified and relearned, and needed behaviors can be learned. The key to helping young people to change is teaching them new skills or helping them to unlearn and replace targeted, problematic behaviors or reactions.
Key concepts	Identification and classification of problematic or necessary behaviors lead to the identification of behaviors that need to be changed, altered, or added. Counseling focuses on the development of measurable counseling goals focused on changing specific behaviors and replacing them with more adaptive behaviors.
Goals of counseling	The use of learning theories to unlearn maladaptive behaviors and replace them with new, more adaptive behaviors. The main goal is for the youth and/or parents to take the skills and strategies learned in counseling and apply them in real-world settings to change their behaviors and accomplish preidentified and operationalized goals.
Therapeutic relationship	Although it is an objective, systematic, scientific, directive, instructional counseling approach, this approach emphasizes a strong therapeutic relationship because this is important in engaging the client/family in the development and implementation of skills and the new behaviors needed to achieve behavioral change.
Counseling techniques	Behavior therapy is a technique-heavy approach that involves a multitude of different techniques that all focus on changing behaviors and learning more adaptive behaviors. A premium is placed on learning new skills. These skills may include reinforcement (positive or negative), role-playing, functional behavioral assessments, or behavior contracts.

Table 5.10	(Continued)
Application/ approaches	Behavioral techniques are rooted in the scientific method and lend themselves well to assessment, evaluation, and verification. As such, these techniques have a strong evidence base for use with various issues. This approach is effective in addressing numerous issues, such as problematic school and home behaviors, stuttering, enuresis, phobias, and depressive and anxiety disorders.
Multicultural counseling	Behavior therapy models are largely applicable cross-culturally due to their focus on behavioral change, a focus that many seeking help desire. The techniques can be modified to fit cultural constraints without jeopardizing the validity of the interventions.
Limitations for multicultural counseling	Western ideas of empiricism and linear progression of behavior are not universal cultural values; many other cultures prefer a more holistic form of counseling that examines and cherishes the wholeness of experience.
Youth-specific approaches	Given the history and close connection to experimental and scientific methodology, behavior therapy enjoys a solid basis for accountability in practice. Also, the emphasis on a strong counseling relationship makes for a system that provides individually tailored and empirically valid interventions.

Cognitive Behavioral Theory

Basic philosophy	Cognitions, or how young people think, is foundational to how they feel. Clients experience change when they change how and what they think and how they behave. Psychoeducation and an increased understanding of one's thoughts and engaging in adaptive behaviors can create a new, more adaptive perspective that helps a young person to optimally feel and function.
Key concepts	New, more adaptive thoughts and behaviors can be learned. Distorted thinking reinforces preexisting thoughts, which then affects feelings and behaviors. Change occurs when faulty beliefs are replaced with effective beliefs and when maladaptive behaviors are replaced with adaptive behaviors. Over time, these new ways of thinking will be less forced and will become automatic ways of thinking.
Goals of counseling	Aid the young person in identifying distorted, faulty, or irrational beliefs and automatic thoughts, and replace these with new ways of thinking. Once identified, those thoughts and beliefs are challenged with contradictory evidence. CBT counselors also focus on behavioral change and emphasize the importance of engaging in new behaviors as well as new thinking.
Therapeutic relationship	CBT approaches emphasize the importance of a warm therapeutic connection. In some CBT modalities, the counselor acts as a teacher and behaves in an active, directive manner, whereas in others the counselor works collaboratively via a Socratic dialogue to aid the client in recognizing and changing his or her cognitions.
Counseling techniques	CBT approaches involve various techniques that focus on helping clients to alter their thinking and behaviors. Techniques from behavioral theory are sometimes used along with perspective- and thought-changing techniques. These include the ABCDEF model from REBT, Socratic questioning and dialogue, and mindfulness-based techniques.
Application/ approaches	CBT is one of the most widely-used theoretical perspectives due to its strong toolbox of techniques and its evidence base being helpful with many different problems youth face. This type of therapy is also helpful with youth and families who require more active, directive, concrete approaches to counseling.
Multicultural counseling	Collaborative and educational in nature, CBT focuses on how thoughts influence feelings and behaviors, which is an idea generally well received across diverse populations. Because a large portion of CBT involves psychoeducation, it is readily tailored to youth of different cultural or social backgrounds. CBT is generally brief in duration, with an emphasis on goal completion, and this brevity appeals to those from many cultures.
Limitations for multicultural counseling	It is impossible to keep culture out of discussions about what is and is not dysfunctional thinking; cultural appropriateness should always be factored into discussions about cognitions. Collectivistic cultures emphasize social harmony, deference to experts, and respect of elders, which will influence thoughts. Symptomology differs cross-culturally, with some demonstrating physical symptoms more than psychological or emotional ones, and this should be considered when applying the model that focuses on emotions.

(Continued)

Table 5.10	Summary of Counseling Theories (*Continued*)
Youth-specific approaches	As the development of new problem-solving skills and coping mechanisms takes shape, the involvement of the child's parents and broader social circle becomes relevant. Ideally, this immediate social influence provides the young person with reinforcement of adaptive thoughts and behavior and modeling of adaptive behaviors and coping mechanisms; however, it may do the opposite and disrupt system homeostasis. Youth at different developmental levels may not have the capacity to engage in abstract thought; therefore, concrete terms and methods are best. The inclusion of expressive arts and play activities may best communicate these concepts.

Reality Theory

Basic philosophy	Youth require quality relationships with others, which help to fulfill their basic needs of survival, love and belonging, power, freedom, and fun. Problems arise when those basic needs are not being met, and youth go about trying to meet these needs in unproductive ways.
Key concepts	The focus is on what clients are doing and helping them to evaluate if what they are doing is working for them. Places the responsibility of choices firmly on clients and whether they are currently making choices that are effective. Theory does not involve any focus on past events and how those influence current behavior.
Goals of counseling	Aid clients in understanding how their choices affect their quality world and the reality in which they live; promote self-responsibility, healthy choices, and the development of relationships that fulfill their needs in adaptive ways.
Therapeutic relationship	The relationship requires a didactic and directive approach, as well as a strong working alliance because counseling involves collaboratively evaluating youth's choices. If clients are not engaged, they may not be open to sharing what they want and how effective they are at getting their needs met. Provide support and advocacy during the formation of new choices and relationships.
Counseling techniques	Counselors find out what it is clients want, invite them to evaluate their present choices and behaviors, help them to make plans for behavioral changes moving forward, and assist them in committing to these changes. The WDEP (Wants, Direction and Doing, Evaluation, and Planning) system functions as a primary method of therapeutic work with youth. This system aids youth in defining their quality world and how their choices and relationships affect their lives.
Application/ approaches	Applicable to individual, school, group counseling, and other diverse fields. Youth benefit from the focus on responsibility, choice, and positive relationships. Provides a logical structure for progress, which youth can readily understand and implement during and after counseling.
Multicultural counseling	Focuses on personal choice influencing clients' lives and its insistence on young people's self-evaluation. Youth can benefit from the focus on personal responsibility that embodies choice theory and the formation of positive relationships.
Limitations for multicultural counseling	Counselors should avoid confusing their personal vision of a quality world with, those of clients. Western-centric ideals of individualism as well as the active, directive, and sometimes challenging approach of direct questions, may be inappropriate in some collectivistic cultures.
Youth-specific approaches	A systematic and direct approach to confronting young people's problems and formulating new adaptive choices and relationships. It is concrete and readily understandable to youth. The acronyms used to communicate the theory's concepts (e.g., WDEP) are tools youth can carry forward after counseling.

MyLab Counseling: Counseling Children and Adolescents

In the Topic 4 Assignments: *Theoretical Foundations for Counseling Youth*, try Application Exercise 4.1: *Identifying Thoughts, Feelings, and Behaviors* and Licensure Quiz 4.1: *Behavior Therapy*.

Then try Application Exercise 4.3: *Addressing Behavior Problems in Youth*.

CHAPTER 6

Counseling Theories That Focus on Background Experiences and Relationships

In Chapter 5, approaches that focus on targeted client action, thought, and behavior change are addressed. In this chapter, theories that focus on the roles that clients' past experiences play in their development are addressed, along with theories that focus on the counseling relationship. More specifically, psychodynamic theory, Adler's individual psychology, and person-centered theory are discussed in the context of youth counseling. Additional theories that are important but are not directly addressed in this chapter include Gestalt theory, existential theory, and transactional analysis.

Psychodynamic theory focuses heavily on early life experiences and how they influence personality and behaviors. This approach places a premium on the idea that early relationships have long-term impacts on one's development, and thus these relationships affect all aspects of a person's life. An emphasis on early life experiences is especially relevant when counseling youth. Psychodynamic theory also emphasizes defense mechanisms, and it holds that people experience internal and often unconscious conflicts. Young people's interpersonal experiences, especially with parents, can heavily influence a youth's defense mechanisms and internal conflicts, and these then affect future relationships. The counselor's role is to facilitate insight into one's inner world and help unconscious conflicts become conscious. Many play therapy approaches are rooted in psychodynamic theory, with an emphasis on the idea that the counseling relationship can serve to facilitate healing experiences and growth.

Alfred Adler's theory is also discussed in this chapter. Adler's theory—individual psychology—is a strength-based approach that promotes the idea that youth are constantly striving to become better versions of themselves. Sometimes Adler is referred to as a neo-Freudian, which would indicate that he branched off from psychodynamic theory with some of his own assumptions; however, Adler developed individual psychology with the intention of it being separate from Freud's theory. Although Freud and Adler have some overlap in their thinking, the two theories have quite different underlying assumptions.

Individual psychology is an approach to mental health that celebrates the inherent resiliency of individuals and embraces the holistic nature of mental health. Adler (1958) believed all parts of an individual are intimately connected—that is, one's mind, body, thoughts, feelings, experiences, relationships, hopes, and support resources come together to create each unique individual. The term *individual psychology* does not place each youth in isolation of his or her context; rather, individual psychology demonstrates the uniqueness of each youth within his or her specific situation.

In accordance with the relational focus of this chapter, Adlerian theory focuses on past relationships, personal experiences, birth order of siblings, lifestyle preferences, and individual qualities because these influence future feelings, behaviors, and thoughts. Individual psychology focuses on development and experience and how they shape and contribute to social relationships, self-concept, and self-worth. In addition, Adler (1958) posited that encouragement was a key focus in the therapeutic process. In individual psychology, it is important to understand youth holistically so key assets and resources (internal and external) can be harnessed and used for improved mental health.

Finally, person-centered theory is discussed in this chapter. Sometimes called client-centered therapy, the central tenets of person-centered theory are that youth have a natural capacity to resolve their own problems and, with the right conditions, they will move toward achieving their full potentials. The therapeutic relationship is the essential vehicle used to facilitate this change.

Person-centered therapy holds an optimistic view of human nature and honors young people's unique, individual perspectives. It is also based on the idea that an egalitarian counseling relationship, one in which the counselor does not direct or guide, facilitates the growth of young people. In this way, a person-centered approach is a humanistic, strength-based counseling approach that is consistent with the tenets of professional counseling.

The person-centered approach does not place an emphasis on insight, elimination of specific behavioral problems, or application of evidence-based techniques. Instead, person-centered counselors place a premium on establishing a trusting therapeutic relationship, one in which the client can guide the counseling experience. This supportive orientation is highly applicable to youth counseling. Young people are constantly developing and learning more about themselves, their identities, and their places in the world, and the nondirective nature of a person-centered approach provides them with the space and latitude they require to discover who they are and who they are becoming. This approach is also inherently empowering, and thus it facilitates young people's autonomy and helps them to develop a sense of personal efficacy as they begin to increasingly explore their worlds.

Many adolescents with whom counselors work are hesitant about counseling and what it has to offer. As part of the normal developmental process, many youth also struggle with self-doubt and insecurities. Thus, the warm, empathic, and supportive counseling relationship that a person-centered approach offers can be particularly advantageous to adolescents, especially those who may question the need for counseling. Motivational interviewing (Miller & Rollnick, 2012)—an expansion of person-centered therapy—is an approach that aims to enhance clients' intrinsic motivation to want to make changes. Its focus on facilitating clients' motivation to change can also be especially helpful when counseling adolescents.

Person-centered counseling has served as a foundation for various youth-specific therapeutic modalities, including child-centered play therapy (Axline, 1947a) and person-centered expressive arts therapy (Rogers, 1993, 2011), two approaches that are commonly used by counselors today. Both approaches emphasize counselors' ways of being, the therapeutic relationship, and young people's self-directed growth toward enhanced self-understanding, autonomy, and creativity.

This chapter provides readers with a brief overview of these theories in the context of counseling youth and their families. Each theory is addressed in terms of its core concepts and goals of counseling, the role of the counselor, the counseling process and procedures, and family interventions and involvement.

PSYCHODYNAMIC THERAPY

Psychodynamic theory is grounded in the idea that an analysis of youth's early life experiences is critical to understanding their personalities and behaviors. Early life experiences shape young people's deepest understandings of themselves and their external worlds. This theory emphasizes early relationships and places a premium on early caregiver attachments— that is, if youth are able to experience healthy, trusting attachments with caregivers early in their lives, then they are better able to explore their worlds with self-confidence and less apprehension and fear.

Sigmund Freud (1856–1939) is considered the founder of psychodynamic theory, and Anna Freud, Melanie Klein, and Erik Erikson are among those who substantiated that the psychodynamic approach could be directly and effectively used with children and adolescents (Kegerreis & Midgley, 2015). Although these historic giants diverged on different aspects of psychodynamic theory, they all contributed—in unique ways—to the theory's development and held in common a value of enhancing young people's insights into their *inner worlds* and using a therapeutic relationship to enhance young people's growth (Kegerreis & Midgley, 2015).

Clinical Toolbox 6.1

In the Pearson eText, click here to review an activity that helps youth to explore and explain their inner worlds.

Counselors who use a psychodynamic approach attempt to enhance young people's understandings of what influences, motivates, and affects their behaviors, thoughts, and feelings. Psychodynamic counseling processes intend to reveal behavior patterns, as well as generate insight into defenses and responses to internal conflicts that are held in youth's unconscious minds. The major assumption in psychodynamic counseling is that symptomology or problematic experiences diminish as youth become more aware of their internal conflicts and as these conflicts move from the unconscious to the conscious.

Psychodynamic theories are diverse, and their applications vary. Although variability exists among psychodynamic counseling approaches when working with youth, these approaches have the following components and aspects in common (Delgado, 2008):

- Development of a strong therapeutic alliance and counseling as a means of providing corrective experiences
- Central role of bringing the unconscious to the conscious
- Importance placed on early life experiences
- Belief in the existence of internalized unconscious conflicts (e.g., anger, anxiety, depression)
- Belief that thoughts, motives, emotional responses, and behaviors are not random but are the product of biological and psychological processes
- Belief that symptoms have meaning (e.g., behavior can be seen as problem solving or an attempt to cope)
- Belief that transference-based thoughts, emotions, and behaviors are essential to facilitating counseling

Quantitative research exploring the effectiveness of the psychodynamic approach is limited (Wagner, 2008), yet a significant amount of qualitative, practice-based psychodynamic research exists (Kegerreis & Midgley, 2015). This practice-based research covers various ages (e.g., 3–18), emotional and behavioral disorders (e.g., anxiety, depression, eating disorders), and settings (e.g., outpatient, residential, school based), thus suggesting the clinical potential and relevance of psychodynamic approaches in counseling youth (Kegerreis & Midgley, 2015).

Core Concepts and Goals of Counseling

Psychodynamic theory is multifaceted and has an evolving set of core concepts. Psychodynamic tenets can be organized into four primary areas of focus: (a) drives, (b) ego, (c) objects, and (d) self. Although most psychodynamic practitioners would agree that early life experiences are paramount to personality development, many may disagree on the degree or role of instinctual and sociocultural influences on this development (Wagner, 2008). In the following sections, we briefly outline and highlight each concept and goal of the psychodynamic counseling process.

DRIVE THEORY

According to Sigmund Freud's (1943) theory, humans have innate drives, or internal energies, that stem from one of two sources: sex/life and aggression/death. Freud theorized that these two energies ultimately *drive* humans' behaviors, and without an understanding of these often-unconscious forces, a person cannot be balanced or reconcile their instincts with social forces. Freud contended that much of what happens in our minds and bodies is below our levels of consciousness. Furthermore, mental difficulties and illness symptomology are the manifestations of these drives and the conflicts they create between the conscious and unconscious personality structures (i.e., the id, ego, and superego), which are meant to manage these impulses, drives, and energies. These internal conflicts are highlighted by desires for gratification, or satisfaction of a desire, and attempts to balance the drives to adhere to societal expectations. For example, consider a young boy who loves playing soccer but who at the strong encouragement of his parents tries out for a travel baseball team. During tryouts, he is unsettled and performs poorly; ultimately, he does not make the baseball team. Although he may have struggled with performing his best—because of his desire to do something else—he also did not possess the ability to be aware and verbalize his desire because he wanted to *both* please his parents and find a way to express his disinterest in baseball.

According to a psychodynamic perspective, human nature is deterministic. Essentially, determinism means that human behavior is believed to be the sum product of unconscious forces, irrational motivations,

Table 6.1	Structural Model of Personality	
Aspects of the Personality	Overview	Definition
Id	"Instincts"	The id, which is present from birth, comprises the basic instincts and drives of humans. These basic instincts are often irrational and impulsive, and they are firmly rooted in the unconscious. Ruled by the pleasure principle, the id seeks immediate gratification.
Ego	"Executive mediating"	The ego is the executor of the mind and the only part of personality that is in direct contact with reality. As the child begins to grow and develop, the ego emerges as a means of mediating the impulses of the id and the inhibitions of the superego. The ego resides in the conscious mind and can be thought of as the logical mind; it works to appease the id in a socially acceptable way.
Superego	"Conscience"	The judge of the mind, the superego, is the part of one's personality that internalizes values and houses one's moral code. In young children, the superego has not totally formed, but in older children and adolescents, it is firmly at work judging and pushing against id impulses.

and instinctual drives, and thus it is difficult to alter or change. Yet, according to the theory, individuals also have a conscious mind. It is this intersection between the conscious mind and unconscious urges and drives that produces a conflict between the three aspects of the personality—the **id**, **ego**, and **superego**—or the structure of personality (Freud, 1943). Table 6.1 provides a brief summary of the structural model of personality.

The components of personality form and progress through the **psychosexual stages of development** (Freud, 1922/1953). These stages of development are as follows:

- *ORAL STAGE* (BIRTH TO 18 MONTHS)—pleasure is associated with the mouth (e.g., sucking, biting, breastfeeding).
- *ANAL STAGE* (18 MONTHS TO 3 YEARS)—pleasure is associated with the anus (e.g., defecating); youth become better aware of their individuality and their abilities to self-control.
- *PHALLIC STAGE* (3 TO 6 YEARS)—pleasure is concentrated on genitals (e.g., rubbing and/or masturbation), and the increased awareness of sex differences can create internal conflict such as jealousy, rivalry, and/or fear (e.g., Oedipus complex or Electra complex).
- *LATENCY STAGE* (6 TO 12 YEARS)—the libido becomes dormant or even hidden during this time, and youth focus on acquisition of skills, hobbies/play, and new areas of knowledge.
- *GENITAL STAGE* (12 YEARS THROUGH ADULTHOOD)—the focus is on the process of sexual experimentation and successful establishment of a loving, monogamous relationship.

Freud contended that if a young person's pleasure-seeking needs and behaviors are exacerbated or frustrated during one of these psychosexual stages, fixation could occur, thus making a youth potentially susceptible to difficulties later in life due to libidinal repression (Freud, 1922/1953). For example, if sustained parent–youth conflict occurs during the anal phase (e.g., the phase aiming to produce a mastery of bowel control and toilet training), in the future youth may potentially regress during times of frustration to one of these polarities: (a) becoming *anal retentive*, which is fixating on order and/or cleanliness, or (b) becoming *anal explosive*, which is exhibiting destructive behaviors such as emotional outbursts, rebelliousness, or cruelty to self or others.

Another central tenet of the psychodynamic theory is the importance of awareness of self and the world or **consciousness**. Freud (1943) observed that individuals often act without really knowing why, and when questioned they frequently construct explanations that may have nothing to do with the real reason behind their behaviors. Freud's observations led him to suggest that the majority of an individual's awareness is unconscious, and he proposed that individuals have three levels of awareness:

- *Conscious*, or the thoughts, memories, and feelings the youth is aware of and can reason about; these become more logical and rational over time as a child grows and develops.
- *Preconscious*, or information that a youth holds that is not part of his or her current awareness but can be accessed if something triggers it (e.g., seeing someone at the park, reexperiencing something traumatic by sensory stimuli).
- *Unconscious*, or the reservoir of memories, drives, feelings, and impulses that are outside a youth's level of awareness and frequently consist of unpleasant or unacceptable feelings of anxiety, pain, or conflict.

Unconscious processes determine and affect young people's behaviors and conscious ideation. Therefore, psychodynamic counselors help youth to access these unconscious memories, impulses, recollections, and drives so these impulses do not emerge into the consciousness as either distorted, symbolic dreams or mental illness symptomology. Freud believed counselors could access a youth's unconscious mind through the use of dream analysis, free association, and play (which are covered in more detail in the 'Counseling Interventions' section).

Essentially, this conflict between these structures of personality combined with the irrational and unconscious motivations and instinctual drives is what creates internal conflict or anxiety. Although older children and adolescents have developed and formed a superego, younger children need assistance from adults (e.g., parents, counselors, teachers) to balance innate impulses and drives.

From a psychodynamic perspective, counselors assist youth in managing their internal conflicts, which, simplistically stated, involves helping them to balance what they want and what they believe to be right. For example, a 5-year-old may want to physically hit a girl who takes one of his toy cars (which just so happens to be his favorite car); yet, he may elect to not hit the girl because he does not want (a) the teacher to yell at him and (b) because he is friends with the girl and does not want to hurt her. Because of the interplay of these forces, the boy considers his options, which may result in him offering the girl another one of his cars so he can again play with his favorite one.

EGO PSYCHOLOGY

Propelled by key figures such as Anna Freud, Heinz Hartman, Ernest Kris, Erik Erikson, and David Rapaport, **ego psychology** grew out of Freud's drive theory (Elliott, 2015). Ego psychology theories have in common a focus on the ego, and they place less of an emphasis on the id or the unconscious.

Taking on a more relational and less deterministic focus than traditional psychodynamic approaches, Anna Freud explored the functioning of the ego (Freud, 1954). **Ego functioning** is the relationship between the id, ego, superego, and external world, which often involves reality testing, impulsivity, object relations, defense mechanisms, emotional regulation, and self-reflective functioning (Delgado, 2008). The central focus of ego psychology is building healthy ego functioning—or increasing a youth's ego adaptive capacities—which is the ability to mediate one's internal demands (e.g., instincts of the id; punitive, moral demands of the superego) and external demands (e.g., demands of others), while limiting the overuse of repressive, regressive, and tactical defenses that can become maladaptive.

Defenses of the ego can be emotional, cognitive, and interpersonal in nature; ultimately, **defense mechanisms** keep youth from dealing or thinking about anxiety-producing thoughts and feelings. Of the many defense mechanisms that exist, they all have two things in common: they distort or deny reality, or they are performed unconsciously. More specifically, repressive and regressive defenses are mostly internal processes that happen within youth, whereas tactical defenses are the maneuvers youth engage in interpersonally to dissuade others from getting close to them (Della Selva, 2004). Table 6.2 provides a summary of repressive, regressive, and tactical defenses.

Table 6.2	Repressive, Regressive, and Tactical Defenses	
Defenses	Overview	Examples and Definition
Repressive defenses	A group of defenses characterized by unconscious *forgetting* that prevents unacceptable thoughts, feelings, and impulses from emerging to a conscious level of awareness.	*Rationalization*—making rational excuses to justify irrational emotions and behaviors *Minimization*—not taking important matters and situations seriously *Intellectualization*—to block feelings and emotions with reasoning *Displacement*—to direct feelings onto an unthreatening object (e.g., other person, animal, possession) *Reaction formation*—to feel and/or behave in direct opposition of truth (e.g., to express fond affection for someone who person strongly dislikes)
Regressive defenses	A group of defenses characterized by reverting to early stages of development to prevent unacceptable thoughts, feelings, and impulses from emerging to their conscious levels of awareness. Regressive defenses are the most immature of all defense groupings.	*Projection*—to transfer one's own feelings onto someone else or the outside world *Denial*—to avoid or reject unpleasant truths *Antisocial acting out*—attempts to avoid managing the feelings associated with a thought and/or experience with impulsive acts (e.g., aggression, substance use) or attention-seeking behaviors (e.g., tantrums) *Dissociation*—to compartmentalize or separate oneself from an emotion or feeling *Somatization*—to turn mental conflict or pain into physical pain
Tactical defenses (verbal)	A group of verbal interpersonal defenses used to deflect or prevent meaningful emotional contact with others.	*Argumentative*—to become verbally combative toward another person or position *Rumination*—excessive worrying or perseverating on a thought, emotion, behavior, or experience *Vagueness*—unarticulated or undefined feelings, thoughts, and/or ideas *Sarcasm*—to mock or be verbally harsh and/or make cutting remarks *Diversification*—continually jumping from one topic to another
Tactical defenses (nonverbal)	A group of nonverbal interpersonal defenses used to deflect or prevent meaningful emotional contact with others.	Avoiding eye contact Smiling/laughing at inappropriate times/subject material Defensive body language (e.g., crossed arms/legs) Excessive crying Temper tantrums

Younger children, who developmentally have immature ego structures, often struggle to process early traumatic life experiences that typically have emotionally charged components. Due to their immature ego structures, youth often repress these uncomfortable thoughts, emotions, and situations into the unconscious mind. Defense mechanisms bolster a youth's ego, and when under pressure the ego is forced to relieve anxiety or conflict by defending and protecting the youth's ego. As the youth's ego grows and develops (e.g., maturing ego functioning), counseling or making the unconscious conscious allows young people to more adaptively deal with their repressed thoughts, emotions, and situations in the present.

Erik Erikson (1950), a student of Anna Freud, placed an emphasis on the conscious aspects of human development, and he expanded on Sigmund Freud's psychosexual stages primarily through the integration of the psychosocial aspect of ego functioning and development (Sharf, 2012). His psychosocial theory of human development outlined eight tasks or crises that each individual will attempt to address to grow and develop in the context of his or her external world. Emphasizing the resolution of social crises, Erikson's stage theory contended that individuals' egos develop through the management of competing internal and social forces. Table 6.3 provides a summary of Erik Erikson's psychosocial life stages.

According to Erikson's theory of psychosocial stages of development, young people may not resolve—and thus be stuck in—early stages of development, and failure to resolve developmental stages and move forward can affect their functioning in the present. Erikson's contribution to ego psychology emphasized ego defenses, interactions with others, development across the life span, and a focus on the conscious rather than the unconscious (Sharf, 2012).

OBJECT RELATIONS THEORY

Another theory associated with ego psychology is **object relations theory**, a theory—with many offshoots—that focuses on one's early self-concept development in the context of other people, especially mothers or

Table 6.3 Erikson's Stages of Psychosocial Development Connected with Youth

Stages	Age Group	Aims	Potential Outcomes
Trust vs. mistrust	Birth to 1 year old (Infancy)	*To be secure (Hope):* Development of trust through parent's adequate, reliable, and caring affection	Children develop a sense of trust when parents are dependable and caring in providing affection and meeting their needs. Mistrust or suspicion and fear of future encounters and events can occur when care and attention are lacking, thus leading to withdrawing behaviors or depression later in life.
Autonomy vs. shame and doubt	1 to 3 years old (Early Childhood)	*To be independent (Will):* Development of personal control over physical skills and sense of independence	Children develop a sense of independence and control over their physical skills, which results in feelings of autonomy. Feelings of shame and doubt can result when a child is unable to develop a sense of control and independence, thus leading to overcautious behaviors and inhibited independence.
Initiative vs. guilt	3 to 6 years old (Preschool)	*To be powerful (Purpose and Direction):* Development of control and power over the environment leading to a sense of purpose	Children develop a sense of control over their external worlds. If exploration is stifled, children can feel inadequate to be left on their own, thus leading to a sense of guilt and a decreased motivation to engage in and initiate activities.
Industry vs. inferiority	6 to 11 years old (School Age)	*To be good (Competence):* Development of competency by meeting new social and academic demands	Children build a sense of competency by adequately coping with a new set of social and academic demands (e.g., starting school). Inadequately navigating these new demands and challenges can create doubt, discouragement, and a sense of inferiority.
Identity vs. role confusion	12 to 18 years old (Adolescence)	*Who am I? (An Integrated Image):* Development of sense of self and personal identity	Adolescents attempt to build a cohesive sense of self. Confusion over who they are can cause them to lack a sense of identity, personal uniqueness, and inherent value, thus leading to a disintegrated, confused, and/or weak sense of self.

caregivers (Klein, 1921/1959). Simplistically, object relations consist of an object (e.g., others) and the self, as well as the relationship between these two entities or components. The relational aspect of object relations theory is comprised of the internal images or schemas of the self in relation to others in the present or based on one's past experiences with others.

As an example, a younger child may feel loved, accepted, and valued because her father is consistently thoughtful, compassionate, and caring toward her. She considers her relationship with her dad to be one that is predictable, warm, and affectionate, and this in turn influences her relationship expectations with others. Conversely, another child may feel unimportant or even forgettable because his father is scattered, busy, and frequently concerned with his other duties and responsibilities (e.g., work, spouse, other siblings). The child may feel that his relationship with his father is lonely, cold, and sad, and ultimately, this affects his expectations of his relationships with others. According to object relations theory, relationships and relationship expectations and perceptions are complex because they are a compilation of past experiences and internalized subjective interpretations of these experiences. These relations have the potential to color and structure what a youth will expect, desire, and fear from any interpersonal interaction. People's perceptions of these relationships, their roles, and the other person's role in these relationships can be thought of as similar to one's beliefs or schemas in cognitive therapy (Shapiro, 2015).

Object relations theory has many implications for understanding young people's behaviors. For example, if a child believes he is unlovable, inconsequential, and forgettable to his mother, he may do whatever he thinks is necessary to be relevant and known, hoping to receive recognition from her by acting out through disruptive behaviors, disengaging, or even isolating. There are countless ways that counselors can use object relations theory to understand and address youth needs on an individual basis.

ATTACHMENT THEORY

Attachment theory, developed by Bowlby (1907–1990), is based on the idea that the style of attachment experienced between youth and their parents predicts young people's personal characteristics and patterns of relating to others (Ainsworth & Bell, 1970). In essence, youth come into the world biologically programmed to form attachments, and through this attachment they attempt to explore the world around them (Bowlby, 1988). These early attachment relationships then determine how they experience their relationships with others. Attachment is primarily the responsibility of the caregiver, and if a caregiver responds promptly, appropriately, and consistently to an infant's needs, then the infant is more likely to form a secure attachment to that caregiver. If that same infant is treated in a distant or aloof manner by a caregiver, then it is likely that the attachment style between that infant and caregiver will be avoidant, ambivalent, or disorganized.

Essentially, there are four types of attachment that an infant or child may display (a) the *secure* pattern, (b) the *avoidant* pattern, (c) the *ambivalent/resistant* pattern, and (d) the *disorganized* pattern (Ainsworth, Blehar, Waters, & Wall, 2014; Bowlby, 1988). Children experience a *secure* attachment, the desired type of attachment, when their caregivers provide a secure base and they can freely explore their worlds. Children who have a secure attachment to their caregivers feel safe enough to accept and interact with nonprimary caregivers. Children experience an *avoidant* attachment when parents are unavailable and unresponsive to their physical and/or emotional needs. An avoidant pattern of attachment is a pattern typified by a child's lack of distress at the primary caregiver's absence or a lack of interest in a caregiver. Avoidant children lack an ability to discriminate relationships and maintain appropriate boundaries, and they react the same way to a stranger as they would to their primary caregivers. *Ambivalent* or *resistant* attachment patterns occur when children do not experience their primary caregivers as a secure base because of the caregivers' inconsistent and unpredictable parenting style. The caregivers of children who are ambivalent are sometimes nurturing and attuned to their child's needs, yet at other times they are insensitive, critical, or emotionally unavailable. These children tend to be highly stressed when removed from their caregiver's presence and frequently demonstrate affect inconsistency once the attention of the primary caregiver has been achieved. Finally, the *disorganized* style occurs when a child experiences inconsistent caregiving; the caregivers of children who are disorganized often have unresolved trauma struggles and engage their children in disorienting ways. For example, a disorganized parent may behave in overexaggerated, destructive, and/or fearful ways toward a child during times of increased stress and/or frustration.

Attachment theory suggests that as an infant ages and develops, certain attachment-related messages and experiences are placed into the unconscious, thus creating the formation of persistent, possibly pathological behaviors. For example, if a youth has experienced abuse and/or neglect in his or her child–caregiver relationship, he or she will unconsciously assume new relationships will also be abusive and may not trust others. From an attachment perspective, early abuse and neglect can greatly affect a child's self-concept (e.g., sense of self-worth, body image, guilt), attachment and relationships, ability to emotionally regulate (i.e., ability to tolerate and navigate painful internal states), behavioral control (e.g., impulse control), and even physical health (Briere & Lanktree, 2012). Consequently, counselors must continually work with children and parents to enhance parent–child attachment and attunement (e.g., psychoeducation, parent–child activities). Attachment theory suggests that a change in parenting behaviors and facilitating a child's attachment will inevitably promote positive youth development.

SEPARATION-INDIVIDUATION THEORY

Mahler's theory of separation-individuation is an example of an object relations theory that has a focus on intrapersonal processes (Mahler, Pine, & Bergman, 1973). Mahler focused on young children's abilities to establish a sense of separateness in relation to others, especially in relation to their primary **love object**, who most often is their mother (Mahler et al., 1973). Mahler's theory focuses on how children develop a sense of themselves as separate and unique from others. He believed that disruptions in the fundamental process of separation-individuation during the first 3 years of life could result in disturbances in the ability to maintain a reliable sense of individual identity later in life. Children whose needs are not met do not develop the healthy sense of security needed to appropriately separate, and individuate, from their caregivers. As such, they struggle to develop a healthy sense of themselves as unique, autonomous individuals.

The task of the child is to separate from their mothers and eventually become independent. Disturbances in this separation process can jeopardize the fundamental process of separation-individuation during the first few years of a child's life, resulting in disturbances in the child's ability to maintain a reliable sense of individual identity later in life. Youth whose needs are not fully met by their primary love object often do not develop the healthy sense of security needed to appropriately separate and individuate from these caregivers. As such, they may struggle to develop a healthy sense of themselves as unique, autonomous individuals. Mahler et al. (1973) contended this process reverberates throughout the life span of the individual and is constantly being reorganized.

SELF-PSYCHOLOGY

Another development in psychodynamic counseling and ego psychology has been self-psychology, which was pioneered by Heinz Kohut (1971, 1977). Kohut's self-psychology focused less on drives or ego and more on the development of a **healthy narcissism** or sense of self. Kohut (1977) understood narcissism as being innate in all individuals, and he believed people's infantile narcissism could mature into healthy adult narcissism over time. In addition, he contended that narcissism could be a motivating factor in the development of love because self-love precedes one's ability to love others.

According to Kohut (1977), children whose sense of self is bruised and/or neglected do not adequately develop the ability to tolerate and accept their own inadequacies, thereby, developing a **narcissistic injury**, which threatens the cohesiveness of the self. Repeated injuries or wounds can develop into pathological narcissism, resulting in repeated attempts to bolster one's sense of self through unending quests for love, approval, and success. These efforts to fill one's self in this way can be viewed as external attempts to shield one's self from vulnerability or as attempts to ensure narcissistic injuries or wounds are not exposed or exploited.

To put it simply, Kohut (1971) believed a child's sense of self develops early in life and is based on interactions with their early caregivers. If parents or caregivers do not respond with approval and empathy—which fosters a sense of self and competency—youth fail to develop a healthy self-esteem. Conversely, if parents respond to the youth with respect, empathy, and acceptance, then the youth will develop a healthy sense of self.

Kohut (1971, 1977) suggested that it is the construction of the self and how it plays out in human interactions that dictates what is normal and abnormal. In other words, psychopathology is viewed as a disturbance of the self, with severe psychopathology being rooted in very early disturbances of the caregiver–infant relationship.

Although differing definitions of the self exist, within this theory the self is the core of the person's subjective experience (Sharf, 2012). The self must be understood in relation to **self-objects**, which in the case of young children are persons who complete their self and are requisite to normal development and functioning. More simplistically, self-object is the shared experience with another that becomes an extension or continuation of the individual. The value of self-objects lies in the psychological functions they contribute to the child's developing self. Self-object responses such as praise or the induction of shame are absorbed by the child and experienced as pride or guilt. For children, self-objects can include attachments to objects (e.g., transitional items such as pacifiers, blankets) and can extend, as youth mature, to selection of romantic partners, career choices, or even cultural self-objects (e.g., strong allegiance to one's country or a football team because these contribute to the sense of self); basically, anything that can fill or serve a self-object function can become a self-object. Self-object responses are concrete, observable communications that comprise the caregiver–child interactions and form the building blocks of what ultimately comes to be known as the self.

There are two basic narcissistic needs that the child seeks to satisfy through early self-object relations. First is the need to demonstrate emerging capabilities and to be admired for them because this serves an important ego function (e.g., "If others see me as good, then I must be good."). This need involves the development of grandiose, exhibitionistic self-images and is filled by **mirroring** self-objects or those who reflect this sense of specialness and admiration.

The second healthy narcissistic need self-objects meet is that through the formation of an idealized image of one of the parents, usually the mother, a child experiences a sense of merger—or connection—thus feeling like he or she is the self-object and developing a sense of completeness and satisfaction with one's self (e.g., "This person who I idealize is good and we are one, so I must be good."). Self-images involving **fusion** evolve out of these interchanges with these **idealized self-objects** (e.g., "You are perfect, and I am part of you.")

Both needs are normal and healthy: the first (a need for admiration), a healthy sense of omnipotence, and the second (idealized images and fusion), a healthy desire for connectedness. The significance of these early self-object relationships is that they become incorporated into one's representational world. By means of **transmuting internalization**, the two types of external object relations are transformed into two inner relational configurations.

Psychopathology, according to this approach, can be described as a child having an incomplete self (secondary to disrupted mirroring from caregivers), and the use of nonrelational self-objects might be described as a self-prescribed remedy to this incompleteness. As a child develops, he or she has experiences that either sustain or diminish the self, and these self-objects—external figures—fulfill or frustrate the child's developmental needs (Kohut, 1971).

Kohut (1977) suggested that counselors should use empathy as a primary tool for creating a healthy youth–counselor relationship because this offers a coactive experience and sense of hope that heals problematic parental relationships. Transference is also an important counseling technique that plays a key role in Kohut's theory. **Twinship transference** or **alter ego transference** and **mirror transference** all relate to the child's need to believe the counselor possesses special characteristics similar to him- or herself or the child's need to have his or her specialness mirrored through the therapeutic relationship. Ideally, in the course of counseling, the child develops transferences with the counselor, and this serves a corrective function. With counselor mirroring, the child casts the counselor into the role of an admiring audience. When the child idealizes the counselor, or when he or she views the counselor as special or extraordinary, it helps to enhance the child's sense of self.

Counselors should, according to Kohut (1971, 1977), construct a therapeutic environment in which the youth has his or her narcissistic needs responded to as this allows the child to develop a more cohesive self-system. As an example, an adolescent may find his self-worth is based on his parents' love and praise; therefore, the youth has internalized an aspect of his parents as a self-object. With the increase of understanding and interpretations, insight can begin to lead this adolescent to becoming more self-reliant in defining his own self-worth, regardless of how his parents relate to him. Therefore, the youth–counselor therapeutic alliance becomes the transference vehicle for addressing, repairing, and building the youth's sense of self. Counselors' major role in counseling is to aid the youth in restoring **self-cohesion** or creating a unified personality out of the separate parts of self.

GOALS OF PSYCHODYNAMIC THEORY

Psychodynamic counseling is a multifaceted and versatile approach to working with youth. This theoretical approach can be used with youth who are dealing with internalizing disorders, externalizing disorders, maladaptive responses, and various life stressors (Kernberg, Ritvo, Keable, & American Academy of Child & Adolescent Psychiatry (AACAP) Committee on Quality Issues (CQI), 2012). Simplistically, the three essential mechanisms within all psychodynamic approaches include the creation of a strong therapeutic alliance, enhanced insight, and focus on the youth's affective awareness (Messer, 2013). More comprehensively, the goals of psychodynamic counseling with young people include:

- helping the client to focus on affect and the expression of emotions;
- increasing the client's ability to accept feelings and emotions (e.g., exploring attempts to avoid distressing thoughts and feelings);
- identifying recurrent themes and patterns (e.g., exploring past experiences);
- exploring wishes, desires, and fantasy life;
- focusing on and developing adaptive interpersonal relations (including the counselor–child relationship);
- enhancing self-understanding (i.e., new awareness to previously unconscious material); and
- replacing unconscious defense mechanisms with conscious coping strategies.

The phases of counseling within a psychodynamic counseling perspective consist of (a) an opening phase, (b) a middle phase, and (c) a termination phase. Table 6.4 provides a summary of the counseling goals associated with each phase of counseling from a psychodynamic perspective.

Table 6.4 Phases of Counseling with the Associated Psychodynamic Goals of Counseling

Phases of Counseling	Goals of Psychodynamic Counseling
Opening phase	• Establishing routines and arrangements for counseling (e.g., frequency, number of parent sessions versus number of child sessions) • Assessing initial observations and engaging youth and parents to garner their subjective experiences • Establishing a therapeutic alliance with youth and parents • Evaluating youth's strengths and struggles
Middle phase	• Maintaining a therapeutic alliance with youth and parents • Valuing the youth's expression (e.g., language, play, behaviors) • Understanding and identifying patterns in play and conversation • Using the transference relationship to reveal a youth's internal conflict, difficulties, or maladaptive relational patterns • Facilitating change in the youth's internal world (e.g., self-regulation, internal representation of self and others, defenses mechanism) through interpretations, play clarifications, and corrective emotional experiences • Maintaining flow of conversation with parents and helping parents adapt parenting style to the changing needs of the youth
Termination phase	• Consolidating and reviewing gains from counseling • Dealing with the reemergence of symptoms as counseling comes to an end • Constructing follow-up plans specific to the youth's situation • Considering any countertransference issues of the counselor • Addressing the issues of separation and loss that are consequences of termination • Addressing any issues of dependency that have arisen out of the counseling relationship

Regardless of the counseling phase, the three overarching goals to psychodynamic approaches include shaping the youth–counselor relationship, facilitating youth's awareness and self-understanding, and working with the parents to establish a collaborative alliance rooted in neutrality (i.e., not siding with the youth against the parents and, conversely, not siding with the parents against the child; Kernberg et al., 2012).

Psychodynamic counseling is generally open ended—meaning that the length of counseling depends on the youth meeting the established counseling treatment goals. Essentially, psychodynamic counselors contend that young people's behaviors are mostly governed by unconscious processes and that mental and emotional disturbances are directly connected to early childhood experiences (Kegerreis & Midgley, 2015). Therefore, psychodynamic counselors will use their therapeutic relationships to address young people's mental and emotional difficulties by increasing young people's awareness and insight into their inner world, which is fundamental to their emotional well-being (Kegerreis & Midgley, 2015).

Role of the Counselor in Psychodynamic Therapy

Psychodynamic counselors encourage youth to openly and freely share their thoughts, feelings, experiences, and history. The psychodynamic counselor purposefully maintains a neutral presence, with the goal of fostering transference from the youth to the counselor, while minimizing countertransference from the counselor onto the youth. **Transference**, simply put, is the client's projection of characteristics—positive, negative, or neutral—of another person onto the counselor. **Countertransference**, in contrast, is transference from the counselor onto the youth. If countertransference is not managed and used in a therapeutic way, counselors run the risk of losing their objectivity and potentially endangering or harming clients.

From a psychodynamic counseling perspective, the counselor and the youth–counselor relationship are the central interventions. To fully use the relationship as an intervention, counselors need to create a safe, caring, and accepting environment. A common misperception is that psychodynamic counselors are detached and aloof. The counselor should be calm and reflective and assume a curious style of exploration. Psychodynamic counselors remain neutral, yet they are emotionally available, sincere, and empathetic. As an example, they would share excitement with the youth when counseling gains are made or demonstrate compassion when a youth goes through a difficult time. In addition, contemporary psychodynamic counselors use observations, play, interactions, and interpretations *in vivo*, rather than from behind a "couch"—as much of traditional psychoanalysis was historically done.

Psychodynamic counselors establish appropriate limits within each session. Primarily, counselors establish safety limits to keep young people from hurting themselves or others. For example, if a young child is frustrated and angry with a counselor, she should not be permitted to be destructive or physically attack the counselor, but she can be offered the opportunity to substitute the counselor with a play doll. In this situation, the counselor can then direct the child to react to the doll "as if" he or she was the counselor, creating a sense of safety for all involved and increasing the youth's opportunity for self-expression.

The Psychodynamic Counseling Process

Psychodynamic counseling is a fluid process of discovery and recovery (Luborsky, O'Reilly-Landry, & Arlow, 2008). Therefore, psychodynamic counselors will not only attempt to bring about more insight and self-understanding in youth but will also help youth to acquire more productive and satisfying ways to manage their difficulties. Counselors must use assessment, establish a therapeutic alliance, deal with resistance, understand transference and countertransference, and be well versed in psychodynamic counseling interventions to aid youth in meeting their therapeutic goals.

ASSESSMENT

Although structured formal assessment is not normally used systemically within psychodynamic approaches, incorporation of play has always been one way these counselors assess for impediments in young people's normal development (Wagner, 2008). Especially in children who are less verbal, play becomes the central means for self-expression. Play can be unstructured or more structured cooperative play that involves the use of action figures, dolls, and/or puppets to elicit more information about the family and family members' presenting issues.

In some cases, psychodynamic counselors may use assessments to increase their understanding of young people's personality, ego, or sense of self. Because psychodynamic counselors are especially interested in the unconscious, projective testing can be incorporated into the assessment phase of treatment. Projective tests such as the Rorschach Inkblot Test (Rorschach, 1921/1942) and the Children's Apperception Test (CAT; Bellak & Bellak, 1949) are grounded in the assumption that children will project their negative feelings and emotions onto less threatening inkblots or pictures, thus revealing their unconscious anxiety, anger, and/or conflict (Wagner, 2008). One example of a projective assessment frequently used with youth early on in the counseling process is the House-Tree-Person Projective Drawing Technique (HTP; Buck, 1970). In the HTP assessment, youth are asked to draw one person, one house, and one tree with a crayon. After each drawing has been fully completed, a counselor can ask the youth a series of probing questions:

- *House:* Who lives here? Are the people who live here happy? What is it like in this house at night? What happens when the doors close?
- *Person:* Who is this person? What does he or she like to do? What does he or she not like to do? Has anyone ever tried to hurt him or her? Who takes care of him or her? Is this person loved?
- *Tree:* What kind of tree is this? How old is the tree? Has anyone ever tried to cut down this tree? Does this tree get enough water and sunshine?

Another example of a psychodynamic projective test often used with children and adolescents is sentence completion. The sentences completion test (SCT) is a semistructured projective test that involves youth being presented with the beginning idea of the sentence—or the stem—and then being asked to complete the sentence/thought (Frick, Barry, & Kamphaus, 2005). The central assumption underlying the use of SCT is that youth—through their responses and answers—will provide insight into their concealed mental state, attitudes, motivations, beliefs, and/or feelings. Here is a brief list of frequently used sentence completion *stems*:

- I wish my parents would _____.
- I am most worried about _____.
- I am most scared of _____.
- The person who helps me the most is _____.
- I am the happiest when _____.
- When I grow up, I want to _____.
- I get most frustrated when _____.
- The greatest thing that has ever happened to me was _____.
- The worst thing that has ever happened to me was _____.
- I remember _____.
- I regret _____.
- My biggest problem is _____.
- My teacher is _____.
- Students at my school _____.
- My three wishes are _____, _____, and _____.

The psychodynamic assessment process continues throughout counseling. As with other approaches covered in this text, parents and family members are asked to provide a complete history to shed light on the young person's physical and psychological development. Therefore, the ultimate aim of assessment is discovery (Luborsky et al., 2008), and discovery will only be possible if counselors establish an effective rapport with youth through the cultivation of a positive therapeutic alliance.

ESTABLISHMENT OF RAPPORT AND THERAPEUTIC ALLIANCE

As the counseling sessions begin, the therapeutic alliance becomes foundational, especially when working with young children and adolescents. The counselor may need to become the "good enough" parent for the youth during the course of counseling (Winnicott, 1953) and be the *secure base attachment* that the youth requires for growth and exploration (Bowlby, 1988).

Given this, it is important for counselors to recognize the need to form a therapeutic relationship and a strong working alliance with the youth. Therefore, counselors should consider establishing and continually strengthening the therapeutic alliance by (Messer, 2013):

- attending to the experiences of the youth and family members;
- using an active, caring, and affirming style;
- being reflective and supportive of the youth and family members;
- facilitating expression of affect and emotions;
- exploring interpersonal themes or conflicts;
- making accurate interpretations and thus increasing insight;
- collaborating with the youth and family to establish counseling goals; and
- highlighting the youth's past and current counseling successes.

In addition to these previously mentioned considerations, counselors must consider the youth's development level. When working with younger children, play is counselors' language of choice because it is a well-established form of communication that emerges even before social skills are developed. Parallel play in sessions can give the young person enough space to acclimate to the counseling sessions and evaluate the counselor. In addition, the counselor will have enough space to adequately evaluate and observe the child—eventually, over time, counselors move between the roles of participant and observer. In this way, the space created during parallel play aids the younger child in viewing the counselor as nonthreatening. The primary goal for the counselor is to be seen by the youth as someone who is nonthreatening and who can be trusted. Therefore, parallel play is used throughout counseling as the means and method of working to create a strong therapeutic alliance with younger children.

In adolescence, the symbolic aspects of play frequently give way to more verbal interactions, yet these interactions are often action oriented (e.g., doing and talking versus sitting and talking; Kenny, 2013). Parallel play transitions to more cooperative or competitive play with adolescents and may involve drawing or playing a game of cards, chess, or basketball. These action orientations may in turn present the counselor with a problem—that is, some adolescents will begin to push back against the counselor. These pushbacks are to be expected in an adolescent and should generally be confronted head-on. A counselor may say to an adolescent who has become nonparticipative with a counseling session "This is your time—what would you like to do this week while we talk?" This level of directness and confrontation may prove to be a way of facilitating transference.

CLIENT RESISTANCE

Counseling sessions not only provide the opportunity for young people to talk about their concerns and difficulties, but they can also be a time when difficulties, emotions, interactions, and behaviors manifest. **Resistance** is the blocking of counseling progress and involves the client ceasing to discuss, address, think about, or accept an interpretation from a counselor. From a psychodynamic perspective, resistance is an unconscious defense used in the context of counseling to thwart progress (Cramer, 2006).

As an example, avoiding discussion of painful events, wasting time within sessions, showing up late for sessions, or arriving unprepared for sessions can all be considered ways youth are being resistant to counseling. Some possible examples of how resistance may be displayed by youth in counseling sessions include:

- irrelevant or off-topic discussions;
- silence or minimal responsiveness;
- insulting and disrupting comments and/or disposition;
- perseverating on an object, toy, or game;
- preoccupation with someone else (e.g., parent, peer, counselor);
- ignoring or not attending to the counselor; and
- excessive wordiness or verbosity that is lacking in content.

Although these behaviors can be frustrating to counselors, using them as opportunities to learn about youth's internal dynamics and to bring unconscious obstacles closer to the conscious is the essence of a psychodynamic approach. In these situations, counselors need to reframe resistance to be not an obstacle to overcome but an authentic means of exploring and addressing how clients are attempting to defend their ego in real life. In addition, counselors need to consider that resistance has little to do with them and more to do with clients' frustrations, defenses, pain, and lived experiences. In dealing with a resistant youth, counselors should attempt to respect the youth; express honest, authentic curiosity about the youth's resistance; slow down the pace of the session and explore the details (e.g., meaning of behaviors, feelings, and pain); and honor the youth's resistance by making it the focus (e.g., use immediacy to talk about it in the present; Elliott, 2015; Wagner, 2008).

TRANSFERENCE

Once a counselor achieves a strong therapeutic relationship with a youth, transference can occur. Simplistically, when a young person feels safe and comfortable in his or her environment, he or she may begin to project attitudes, motives, and characteristics from other relationships onto the counselor. For example, the client may project feelings and emotions onto the counselor and respond as though the counselor is her mother. A youth's projection could be related to anyone he or she considers significant enough to warrant this position (e.g., teacher, coach, grandparent, older sibling).

Youth experience these transferences as being authentically real, and they are relatively unaware of the connection between these attitudes, motives, and characteristics with other relationships. When analyzing the transference relationship, the counselor's primary goal is to uncover the content of transference, including (a) who the youth is projecting onto the counselor and (b) a clear and relevant picture of the repressed, unconscious content, which may comprise actual events, situations, attitudes, and motives. For example, an adolescent may project parental qualities onto the counselor that involve issues of control, independence, and self-expression (e.g., "You always want me to look presentable for your sake. You don't understand that it's my body and I should be able to express myself."). In classic psychoanalytic theory, working through the transference is critical to the success of counseling; without it, there can be no counseling gains (Freud, 1912/2001).

New counselors should be mindful of their own personal reactions to youth who may direct or transfer their highly charged emotional experiences onto the counselor, and counselors should attempt to remain neutral in these situations. The use of immediacy (i.e., talking about the here and now) can be challenging, especially with youth who, because of their developmental readiness, may not be able to discuss their feelings in the here and now. In addition, when making interpretations concerning clients' transference reactions, counselors should monitor clients' reactions and seek their input. With younger children, and if the child is unable to gain insight from the interpretation, these interpretations may be best shared with the parent. With younger children, play and resolution through play can be a developmentally appropriate approach to dealing with transference. Regardless of whether the client is a child or an adolescent, the analysis of transference is an important aspect of providing interpretations and engaging in psychodynamic play, which is presented in more detail in the Counseling Intervention section.

COUNTERTRANSFERENCE

If the analysis of transference is critical in understanding the young person, the analysis of countertransference is helpful to counselors not only in understanding youth but also in examining their thoughts and feelings. Countertransference is the act of a counselor projecting attitudes, motives, and characteristics from other relationships onto the client. These can stem from current relationships, past relationships, or even the counselors' perceptions of themselves as a child. Usually, the first inclination that a counselor has that countertransference has occurred is when the counselor begins to have an emotional reaction (e.g., internal shift) to the young person that is often incongruent with presented content or material. For example, a counselor may feel the need to overly protect a young child by taking on additional responsibilities within and outside of counseling sessions.

Traditionally, countertransference was an indication that a counselor was treading into dangerous waters; yet, many now view countertransference as an opportunity to reveal valuable information and insight to the counselor about their clients and themselves. Countertransference with a young person can allow counselors to get in touch with their own self-as-child (Bonovitz, 2009). Therefore, when counselors are working with youth and these *remnants* of childhood emerge in their conscious minds, counselors should thoroughly explore them through self-reflection and ongoing supervision (e.g., Is this a normal reaction for me to have as a counselor? How does the counselor-as-person understand this reaction? How does the counselor-as-child understand this reaction?).

COUNSELING INTERVENTIONS

A central aim in psychodynamic counseling is to help youth make unconscious material that is impeding current development conscious. This process is vital to the effectiveness of psychodynamic counseling. Psychodynamic counseling interventions such as play, catharsis, dream analysis, free association, insight, and interpretations are presented.

PLAY

At the core of psychodynamic theory with youth is the use of play (Kernberg et al., 2012). Play therapy, which has fundamentally grown out of the psychodynamic approach, is conceptualized as a means for children to communicate their inner world, emotions, thoughts, and conflict with an attentive, yet neutral counselor (Bratton, Purswell, & Jayne, 2015; Wagner, 2008). Play therapy is a co-constructed process between the counselor and the young person during which the counselor assumes an observer and a participant role (Yanof, 2013). For example, while a counselor engages a youth in imaginary play as an active participant who constructs imaginary friends, the counselor can begin to observe the youth's socialization and interpersonal interactions with these imagined friends and with the counselor.

Play, especially pretend or imaginative play, allows youth to become freer in their expression of affect, conflict, fantasies, wishes, and forbidden aspects of their emotions and lived stories (Yanof, 2013). Pretend play allows youth to have freedom and control over the therapeutic situations in which normally—in real life—they may have limited or no control. In many ways, play itself is an object with which the child interacts and can experience his or her world; therefore, it can take many forms. From a psychodynamic approach, activities used in play therapy can involve imaginary play with the counselor as participant, the use of physical activities, creative projects, and solo imaginary play with established rules (Kernberg et al., 2012).

Essentially, play therapy is a vehicle used not only to facilitate the therapeutic alliance and set the stage for a transference relationship but also to increase the youth's socialization. Although many options within play exist, a counselor should be cautious to not have too much unstructured space within play (Coppolillo, 1987). Too much freedom within play can inadvertently create anxiety within the youth, thus derailing the therapeutic process. Play in conjunction with some intermittent, structured activities appears to be the most effective use of play therapy from a psychodynamic perspective (Yanof, 2013). In addition to structured activities, boundaries or parameters are important for counselors to establish, thus preventing harm to participants.

A young person's play communicates to the counselor information about (a) past experiences, (b) current experiences, (c) fears, conflicts, fantasies, and imagined solutions to conflict, (d) reenacted aspects of important relationships (i.e., transferences), and (e) the current youth–counselor relationship (Yanof, 2013). Counselors need to enter the younger person's world of play, being careful to continue to develop play rather than always attempting to find direct meaning in particular components of the play. Relaying direct, unconscious meaning during play can slow or even halt the play process (Yanof, 2013). Therefore, the aim of the counselor is to continually promote elaboration of the play, which can allow play to continue, develop, and become an optimally effective therapeutic tool.

Interpretations must be made, but timing is everything because often an interpretation can shut down the safe place play represents (Yanof, 2013). In addition, counselors track potential meanings involved in the symbolic content of the youth's play. When an interpretation is required (or seems beneficial for the youth), the most effective way for counselors to communicate these interpretations or comments in the play space is through one of the following potential avenues:

- Making interpretations and comments from outside the play as an outside observer
- Making interpretations and comments from inside the play as a character or participant
- Making interpretations and comments by creating a new character or using parallel play (i.e., adjacent play to another) and/or telling a story that will draw the youth into realizing and understanding the interpretation

The central aim of play is for youth to communicate their inner world, including their emotions, thoughts, and conflict with a neutral and attentive counselor (Bratton et al., 2015). Through play and the therapeutic relationship, these emotional expressions can emerge into clients' consciousness.

CATHARSIS

From a psychodynamic counseling perspective, **catharsis**—the self-expression of emotional issues underlying a concern or problem—can often reduce internal conflict symptomology. Psychodynamic counselors attempt to provide youth with a clinical environment to help the youth to fully express his or her emotions or feelings. These emotions or feelings may have been blocked due to anxiety, shame, or fear connected to an event or a relationship. Catharsis has the potential to provide a significant amount of emotional relief. Often, this emotional relief completes some unfinished business for the youth, thus decreasing symptomology and enhancing the youth's personal relationships (Messer, 2013).

Psychodynamic counseling approaches do not presuppose cognitive understanding and learning as a requirement for change; rather, expression of emotions is critical in evoking change (Messer, 2013). As such, this approach can be very effective with youth who may not be able to—because of their developmental levels—understand situations cognitively, but they can have emotions and reactions and express and heal from these on an emotional level. From a psychodynamic perspective, emotions are not just impulses or drives; rather, they suggest important information that counselors seek to address. These emotions are the motivators of behaviors, and if they are not brought forward from the unconscious to the conscious, they can evolve into more automatic, maladaptive behaviors. Therefore, counselors need to aid youth in making their emotions more conscious through a process called **corrective emotional experiences**. These corrective emotional experiences are the reexperiencing or transformation of an unsettled conflict (e.g., painful situation or relationship) through the use of the therapeutic relationship (Alexander & French, 1946). The psychodynamic counselor works from an accepting, encouraging, and compassionate stance, and the therapeutic relationship is an integral aspect. These corrective emotional experiences—occurring within the safety of the therapeutic relationship—consist of four essential components (Bridges, 2006), which include:

- *emotional arousal* (e.g., physiological reactions and aspects of emotions);
- *emotional experience* (e.g., subjective quality and intensity of emotions);
- *emotional expression* (e.g., expressed verbal and nonverbal expression of emotions); and
- *emotional processing* (e.g., the meaningful cognitive processing of emotions leading to insight, adaptability, and/or ability to solve problems more effectively).

The counselor verbally walks a youth though the components of emotional arousal, experience, expression of emotions, and emotional processing, thus facilitating increased insight and a corrective emotional experience. From a psychodynamic perspective, as youth's intense emotions become tolerable, the use of repressive or regressive defense mechanisms diminishes and becomes less necessary. Dream analysis and free association are two interventions that can promote the self-expression of emotional issues, which often underlie presenting problems in counseling.

DREAM ANALYSIS

According to Freud, there is no more direct path to the unconscious mind and its content than through the path of dreams (Freud, 1910). Therefore, dream analysis has historically been an essential part of Freud's drive theory. In **dream analysis**, clients recount the latent and manifest content of the dream. Manifest content is the actual content of the dream—such as a fox walking through the woods or a bearded lady playing a steel drum. Conversely, the latent content is the underlying pattern and meaning of the content interpreted from the manifest content. For example, consider that a female adolescent expresses that she dreamed she was in jail, her mother was the warden, and her cell smelled of jasmine. The manifest content is the jail and the smell of jasmine, yet the latent content behind those representations may be her desire to be free from her mother whom she feels is holding her captive with her rules and expectations. In addition to dreams, the daydreams of youth are ripe with manifest and latent content (Freud, 1946). Therefore, Anna Freud contended that counselors should conduct dream and daydream analysis when working with younger people. Although traditional psychoanalysis focused considerable time in session on the interpretative meaning (i.e., latent content) of dreams, contemporary psychodynamic counseling focuses on the actual content of the dream (i.e., manifest content) as being connected with the youth's self-concept, internal conflicts, ego defense mechanisms, and transference reactions (Lane, 1997).

FREE ASSOCIATION

Another mainstay for exploring the unconscious mind in psychoanalysis is free association. During free association, the youth is encouraged to speak on any topics that come to mind. In younger children, uninhibited play can be used similarly. It is important that children's play is not censored or restricted and that children can freely express themselves. Counselors must monitor any judgment or inhibiting comments, which have the potential to interrupt the flow from the unconscious. The main purpose of free association is to allow the manifest content of the unconscious mind to come forth via the content being shared. The counselor must dissect the contents divulged during the free association and connect themes from other sessions. Another use of free association is to facilitate the release of repressed emotions and promote catharsis. Anna Freud (1946) recommends against engagement of youth in verbal free association and recommends only the use of play to draw out these free associations from the observations of the child's play. Others argue that the verbal use of free association is a valuable tool for use in psychodynamic counseling, especially when working with older children and adolescents (Coppolillo, 1987). Based on the contention that youth naturally make mental connections, counselors should be attuned to any associations or connections they may make.

During free association, counselors look for continuity of emotions, thoughts, and behaviors, which can be displayed in the clients' interactions, play, and resistance to the counseling process, as well as in the youth–counselor relationship (i.e., transference). Counselors should attempt to look beyond the surface level of youth's behaviors and verbalizations to examine the underlying connectedness of their mental processes (e.g., emotions, thoughts). There are three pragmatic ways to further assess and explore these underlying processes, which include looking for discrepancies, omissions, and excesses (Shapiro, 2015):

- *Discrepancies* are the observed disagreement between things that are said and/or done. For example, a young child might state she does not care about a fight she had with her best friend in school, yet she appears to perseverate over it all night and even to become emotionally reactive when an adult brings the situation up in conversation.
- *Omissions* are things that were not said, done, or felt but likely should have been said, done, or felt given the situation. For example, a child experiences violence and trauma within his home, yet he says everything at home is "great." The child may refuse to talk about these situations and display avoidance behavior to keep from expressing his anxiety, sadness, or anger.
- *Excesses* are overreactions, overdramatic emotions, or extreme behaviors related to benign events that do not justify such behavior. Youth may find their overreactions to these events difficult and/or threatening to discuss. For example, a child has a tantrum and yells at the counselor "I hate you, I hate you!" after the counselor asks the child "to please return all of her play toys" to the assigned places at the end of a session.

From a drive theory perspective, counselors are continually exploring and assessing these emerging patterns within youth's emotions, thoughts, and/or behaviors (e.g., clinical symptomology and presentation) and attempting to understand and explain youth's difficulties or concerns as internal conflicts of personality structures (e.g., id, ego, superego), thus moving the unconscious into the conscious by increasing insight.

INTERPRETATIONS AND INSIGHT

Within the psychodynamic approach, another significant catalyst for change is insight that increases a youth's self-understanding. Simply explained, the aim of psychodynamic counseling is to make the unconscious conscious. Inherent in this approach to counseling, insight is a catalyst significant enough to increase self-understanding and therefore resolve symptomology (e.g., anxiety, disruptive behaviors). Counselors aim to increase a young person's self-understanding or insight through accurate interpretations. An interpretation is a comment or statement that brings an unconscious process to a person's attention. More than paraphrasing or reflecting a feeling, interpretation is helping a youth to understand something that he or she did not know or was not aware of previously.

Interpretations link the conscious behaviors, thoughts, and feelings with the youth's unconscious (a) defenses, (b) wishes, (b) past experiences, and/or (c) dreams (Kernberg et al., 2012). Interpretations can be shared in numerous ways:

- *Direct observation*—"You look irritated today."
- *Indirect presentation*—During imaginary play with the counselor, the counselor says "Sophia, the lion, seems to be really sad because no one asks her to play today. What should Sophia do next?"
- *Using the youth–counselor relationship*—"I wonder if you are thinking of me as a strict teacher or a parent who only asks you all the questions?"
- *Revealing the counselors' perspective*—In a game where the youth is cheating, the counselor can say "If I was a kid playing this game, I wouldn't want to play anymore because I'm feeling angry." Thus, the youth may realize that others might avoid playing with him because of these antagonistic behaviors (Kernberg et al., 2012).

When presenting interpretations or even confronting defense mechanisms, a counselor should consider working within the client's perception of reality, demonstrating the defense mechanism while interacting with the youth or posing a question rather than being direct.

Insight becomes the catalyst for change, especially when youths are armed with why they feel the way they do or why they do what they do. These insights often help youth to feel less confused, irritated, and out of control. From a psychodynamic perspective, once a youth is able to think about a previous unconscious process consciously, he or she is able to use a more mature ego to deal with the now-known internal conflict. Simplistically, insight is not compatible with defenses because defenses decrease as insight increases (Lacewing, 2014). Therefore, the counselor's interpretation can be the catalyst for the youth's increase of self-understanding and movement toward change. The youth can then apply his or her more developed, rational, and adaptive thinking to the long-buried conflict.

Family Interventions and Involvement

Each psychodynamic approach places a different emphasis on the role and importance of involving families in counseling (Wagner, 2008). Minimally, counselors should know the people who are part of the youth's environment and understand those family relationships (Freud, 1946). Historically, psychodynamic counselors have used encounters with parents to gain information about young people's behaviors outside counseling, and they have avoided disclosing information derived from the counselor–youth sessions (Klein, 1921/1959). Although family therapy and parent involvement vary depending on the age and needs of the youth, counselors should consider that parents are a primary source of information and potentially have the ability to underscore what occurs within counseling sessions.

Some counselors may decide to bring parents and family members into the counseling process through the use of **psychodynamic family therapy** (Ackerman, 1958; Gerson, 2010; Wagner, 2008). Psychodynamic family therapists consider how a young person's and his or her family members' internal conflicts are related to the way they interact with each other (Ackerman, 1966; Wagner, 2008). In addition, the parent–child relationship is viewed as the primary means of the child's identification with self, yet over time the desired separation of self from this relationship could be expanded into further identification with other family members. Thus, each family member—including the child—creates his or her identity based on the organization of the family, role adaptation and expectation, rules for governing family interactions, and individual personalities (Ackerman, 1966; Wagner, 2008).

Counselors attempt to understand youth within the context of their primary system (i.e., family) and how their interactions with their family members affect and/or maintain their internal conflict (Ackerman, 1958). In addition, because young people's self-identity is interrelated and influenced by their family identities, each identity directly affects the balance and stability of the family system. For example, if parents impose a rigid controlling approach during times of conflict, a younger person's interpersonal and personal growth will be stymied. Counselors aim to disentangle pathologies within and between family members, thus creating an increase in **role complementarity** or patterns of role relations that produce positive, healthy outcomes relative to family conflict (Ackerman, 1958).

Object relations family therapy is another psychodynamic family therapy approach. As previously stated, parent–child interactions are the essence of an object relations theory approach. Counselors using object relations family therapy explore not only parent–child interactions but also the youth's interactions with the family and the external world (Scharff & Scharff, 1987). For example, a parent who has unresolved child–parent conflict from her family of origin may project negative feeling onto her child because of her dysfunctional internal objects. Not only is this process intrapsychic and interpersonal; indeed, it is also intergenerational and potentially repeated in multiple future intimate relationships. These unresolved conflicts and relationship patterns are reenacted between family members and can become internalized patterns of self. For example, marital relationships can be extremely important in young people's development of internal objects (Scharff & Scharff, 1987). Therefore, if parents are engaged in a caring and loving relationship with each other, then the child often will develop a healthy sense of object relations. Conversely, if parents are engaged in marital discord and conflict, youth may develop apprehension toward their future romantic relationships. Counselors working within this approach conceptualize youth and their struggles within the context of their families.

Although not all psychodynamic-oriented counselors choose to incorporate aspects of family therapy into counseling, they will often attempt to engage the family in some capacity. Pragmatically speaking, one of the most standard means of increasing family involvement within a psychodynamic approach is to incorporate parents through parent education. Parent education can help parents to build healthier relationships and parenting patterns with their child, thus enriching the parent–child connectedness and relatedness (e.g., attachment, emotional intimacy, sharing of feelings and experiences; Paris, 2013). Although parent education may look similar to other approaches discussed in this text, counselors working from a psychodynamic orientation should especially emphasize (a) teaching the parent the process of attachment and bonding (e.g., providing the child with safety and thus increasing attachment and trust), (b) mirroring and communicating (e.g., providing the child with the experience of being heard, seen, understood, and valued), and (c) differentiating (e.g., distinguishing self from child; Paris, 2013).

Clinical Toolbox 6.2

In the Pearson eText, click here for a summary of recommendations on how counselors can work with parents from a psychodynamic perspective.

Counselors may need to serve as consultants to parents by being a supportive and educational resource. Counselors can assist parents by (a) maintaining neutrality (e.g., not siding with the parent against the youth and not siding with child against her or his parents), (b) addressing any parental negative feelings about counseling, (c) improving the parent–child relationship, (d) exchanging information (e.g., increasing parents' awareness of how their struggles and/or conflict can be played out with their youth), and (e) treating the parent as a collaborative partner in the counseling process (Kernberg et al., 2012; Yanof, 2013). In addition to establishing a healthy, therapeutic alliance with parents, counselors can aid parents in establishing realistic and collaborative goals for their youth (e.g., especially concerning social and academic goals (Kernberg et al., 2012). Some parents may require their own individual counseling services. Parent counseling referrals are appropriate if the parent's own psychological difficulties begin to surface and significantly interfere with the youth's counseling sessions and progress.

ADLERIAN THERAPY: INDIVIDUAL PSYCHOLOGY

Adler's (1958) theory, individual psychology, is based on a strength-based perspective, and it emphasizes the idea that each individual is naturally oriented toward growth and change. The source of mental health difficulties is not believed to come from a deficit in any part of development; instead, mental health problems are viewed as simply an extension or exaggeration of typical developmental processes. Individual psychology also holds that youth have a basic human need to be accepted by others and to contribute positively to society. Adler believed individuals are constantly doing their best to improve themselves and the world using the resources to which they have access, and counselors work to harness these resources for them. In Adlerian counseling, counselors also identify and enhance the positive traits, characteristics, and inherent drives of each youth so any undesirable drives or motivations are overcome.

Adler (1958) was a humanistic theorist who developed individual psychology as an alternative to psychoanalytic explanations of mental health. Although the term *individual psychology* might seem to suggest the isolation of the client from others, Adlerian concepts actually highlight the unique experience of the individual in relation to his or her social context (e.g., society, family, peers, society). In fact, Adlerian theory is one of the most comprehensive counseling theories because it highlights the way that biological, psychological, and genetic factors interact with environmental and social influences in explaining human behavior and helping people change. Adler promoted a holistic model for viewing the individual in context, noting that human development is the product of both nature and nurture—that is, every child is born with an inherent personality, and external factors determine how the personality is expressed over time.

Adler (1958) specifically addressed youth development and explored the various ways young people are influenced by their early life experiences. He theorized that one of the primary reasons people develop mental health difficulties is because of discouragement from others and a lack of meaningful connections. Individuals who experience difficulty coping with life's struggles and overcoming interpersonal barriers often feel discouraged (Adler, 1958). Discouraged youth develop unhelpful thoughts and behaviors to cope with feelings of inferiority. Conversely, youth who feel loved, valued, and encouraged are likely to behave in ways that benefit themselves and society.

Feelings of connectedness and contribution can allow youth to overcome feelings of inferiority across three domains: friendship/social, work/occupation, and love/intimacy (Kelly & Lee, 2007). A major focus of development for youth is forming social relationships that are consistent with the self-concept and produce feelings of acceptance and self-worth. Youth also need to feel as though they are contributing to society or making the world a better place, and they can achieve this goal by helping others, excelling in a sport, or achieving academic goals.

Finally, Adler (1958) believed youth have a need to feel loved by others. In childhood, youth experience intimacy with their family members and close friends. As young people transition through adolescence, intimacy is generally extended to romantic partners. Overall, the motivation for youth behaviors lies in a need to feel positive about one's self socially, occupationally, and intimately. In this chapter, the core concepts of individual psychology are reviewed. The role of the counselor in the therapeutic process, as well as specific Adlerian interventions and techniques, are provided.

Core Concepts and Goals of Counseling

Individual psychology is widely considered to be one of the most expansive theories, and it covers many broad concepts. Table 6.5 provides a summary of the multiple concepts associated with Adlerian theory.

Adlerian theory is strength based in that it promotes the inherent worth of every individual, but also highlighted in individual psychology is a key human struggle of feeling unvalued, incompetent, inadequate, or generally less acceptable than others. This feeling of inadequacy is referred to as a **felt minus** in Adlerian theory (Schultz & Schultz, 2013). Youth are particularly observant and notice the behaviors and conditions of other humans, but they do not always excel at accurate interpretations of the meaning behind others' behaviors due to their limited cognitive and emotional development (e.g., a youth might think it is his fault his parents are divorcing). Youth often interpret the fact that they are smaller and less capable than older individuals as an inherent inferiority, although this is simply a reflection of the human developmental process. Regardless, though, Adler (1958) believed all humans were born with a felt minus because they are fully dependent on caregivers until significant developmental milestones are reached. The felt minus functions as a motivator for youth to strive and achieve throughout life.

All youth crave attention, affection, and acceptance from others. Humans are inherently **social beings** who need connection with others and generally want to contribute in positive ways to society (Sweeney, 2009). Youth often gauge their worth by comparing themselves to others. Those who have especially discouraging social interactions or who experience difficulty finding their own unique strengths will experience a felt minus in their particular areas of struggle. As a culture, we tend to promote the idealized self

Table 6.5	Key Principles of Individual Psychology
Concept	Definition
Adult models	Youth look to the important people in their lives for guidance on how to be an ideal citizen, how to resolve difficulties in life, and how to interact with others.
Analytic	The motivation for most youth behaviors is unconscious, but youth are able to understand their underlying motivations if prompted through a process of self-exploration and self-analysis.
Birth order	Initial impressions of the world are made as youth interact with their siblings. Youth learn about their roles in the world as a reflection of their roles in the family, which include birth order (e.g., first child, second child, middle child, youngest child, or only child). The personality is highly influenced by birth order.
Felt minus	Babies are inherently weak and dependent on others when they are born, which creates an inherent, lingering sense of inequality known as a *felt minus*; this sense lingers into adulthood and directs much of young people's behaviors.
Fictive final goal	All youth behaviors are an attempt to become the prototype of who a youth believes he or she should be. However, the prototype is often unrealistic, creating a final goal that is fictional or unachievable.
Forward motion/creativity	People are future oriented, and all youth strive to build self-esteem and a unique sense of belonging.
Holism	All parts of an individual are connected, and all thoughts, feelings, and beliefs of an individual are associated with their consistent short- and long-term goals.
Inferiority complex	Youth who have a difficult time identifying behaviors that provide them with a perceived plus might develop a poor self-concept and low self-esteem, as well as difficulty contributing to society.
Lifestyle	The lifestyle is a pattern of behaviors that youth use to strive toward their unique fictive final goals.
Mistaken goals	When youth experience disheartening interactions with others (e.g., rejection, aggression), their goals shift away from social interest and can become unhealthy or unhelpful.
Perceived plus	Youth strive to gain a sense of mastery and competency in one or two particular areas (e.g., friendships, sports, academics) to overcome a felt minus or inferiority complex.
Private logic	Youth often create their own reasoning to support their lifestyle; private logic is often faulty and typically benefits the individual rather than society.
Safeguarding behaviors	When faced with a struggle, youth might make excuses, blame others for their problems, or regress to developmentally inappropriate behaviors to avoid the felt minus.
Social interest	Every young person craves intimacy and interpersonal connection. Interacting positively with others creates a sense of community and belonging. Individuals are motivated to help others because they want to contribute positively to the world.
Superiority complex	Youth who lack a felt minus in early development might not feel a need to perform behaviors that benefit others. Conversely, youth might overexert themselves to prove their superiority.
Teleo	Youth are constantly striving to become better versions of themselves, and they do the best they can with the resources to which they have access. All behavior is purposeful and forward moving.

Note: Schltz & Schultz (2013); Sweeney (2009).

through celebrities, who are often photoshopped or spend much of every workday making their bodies look ideal. This promotion of idealized standards further contributes to the felt minus in youth (Schultz & Schultz, 2013). Individuals might choose healthy ways to overcome a felt minus (e.g., reaching out to others who can help), or they might use unhealthy ways of overcoming a felt minus (e.g., being mean to a peer to feel superior to them).

Clinical Toolbox 6.3

In the Pearson eText, click here to review a music therapy activity that can be used to facilitate the therapeutic relationship.

Although the initial felt minus is a universal experience caused by helplessness at birth, the felt minus can fade away in early childhood or it can linger (and even grow) throughout early development. Adler (1958) posited that life experiences inform the way that the felt minus is uniquely experienced by each individual.

Related to the felt minus, an **inferiority complex**, or internalized negative belief about the self, can be caused by three basic felt minus themes. The basic sources of an inferiority complex include:

- organic inferiority (e.g., deficiencies in the body such as a chronic illness, physical or learning disabilities, various mental disorders such as ADHD);
- overattentive parents who teach the youth unrealistic social expectations; and
- underattentive parents, which suggests to the youth that he or she is unlovable (Schultz & Schultz, 2013).

Youth who have an inferiority complex will often behave in ways that counteract the specific theme of the complex. For example, youth who hold unrealistic social expectations might go to great lengths for people to notice them (e.g., class clown, bully) because they have learned to associate being noticed with being worthy. Alternatively, individuals can compensate for their inferiority complexes in helpful ways (e.g., serving as class president).

To overcome a felt minus or an inferiority complex, youth work to find certain behaviors at which they feel especially successful or talented. The areas in which a youth excels contribute to a **perceived plus** or the subjective perception that the youth has achieved an area of mastery above peers. Often, individuals pursue a perceived plus in an area that compensates for their sense of a felt minus. For example, a youth who was sick throughout childhood might feel physically inferior to others and focus on sports to gain a sense of perceived plus. Some youth develop unhealthy behaviors to compensate for a felt minus. For example, a neglected child might feel unlovable and engage in early sexual behaviors to experience a perceived plus.

Although some youth use unhelpful behaviors to achieve a perceived plus, Adler (1958) proposed that all humans are inherently on a path of **forward motion and creativity**. As a result of the felt minus, youth are constantly growing and reinventing themselves to create a life that is progressively more similar to their perceived plus. Youth are viewed as creative and responsible individuals who are in a trajectory of growth and development toward their healthiest and happiest capabilities (Watts, 2013). Essentially, all individuals are doing the best they can to achieve social significance and contribute positively to society.

Youth behaviors are often aligned with successive approximations toward an idealized version of the self. Youth often create a mental schema of the perfect self, known as the **fictive final goal**. The fictive final goal is developed early in life as the result of individual qualities, social interactions (especially with caregivers and peers), and environmental influences/popular culture. These life goals are unique for every individual and can be created to overcome perceived inferiorities or deficiencies in:

- intellectual ability;
- physical appearance;
- personal level of ambition;
- level of cooperation or opposition from others; and
- degree of independence/dependence with others. (Kelly & Lee, 2007)

All individuals develop a fictive final goal to find ways to feel good about themselves and experience the social validation they crave. A youth's **lifestyle**, or way of being, is fundamentally informed by his or her fictive final goals.

Adler (1958) posited that people adopt one of four typical lifestyle patterns. These patterns of interacting with the world are used to overcome difficulties and achieve a perceived plus. The four general lifestyles are as follows:

- *Dominant lifestyle*—youth work to assert control over others.
- *Getting lifestyle*—youth receive personal satisfaction from the way others treat them.
- *Avoiding lifestyle*—youth avoid acknowledging social difficulties and/or uncomfortable feelings.
- *Socially useful lifestyle*—youth perform behaviors that promote the well-being of the self and society. (Schultz & Schultz, 2013)

The *getting lifestyle* is most commonly used by youth, but the *socially useful lifestyle* is most beneficial to society (Schultz & Schultz, 2013). The socially useful lifestyle is also the most effective in facilitating and supporting youth mental health because youth are able to achieve a perceived plus in ways that benefit themselves and others simultaneously. Helping others further contributes to a sense of perceived plus, and helpful and productive behaviors are cyclically reinforced. As such, counselors should strive toward supporting the development of a socially useful lifestyle when counseling young people. To do so, counselors will benefit from having an understanding of lifestyle assessment components and how they relate to the therapeutic process.

Role of the Counselor in Adlerian Therapy

The therapeutic relationship is at the heart of individual psychology, and counselors must strive to create a collaborative relationship with youth and their families. Counselors and clients work together to assess thoughts, feelings, and beliefs; identify underlying goals; and determine more helpful methods of interacting with the world. The therapeutic relationship in Adlerian counseling is egalitarian, in which the client is as much an expert as the counselor. The counselor and client work together to map the client's lifestyle, create insight, and foster change.

The counselor's role in the counseling process is to encourage the client to thoughtfully explore his or her lifestyle (Watts, 2013). Youth should be encouraged to explore their lifestyles, gain insight into aspects of incongruence or inaccuracy, and take action to correct any existing difficulties. It is necessary, also, to enlist help and cooperation from the important people in a youth's social world. Adlerian therapy with youth is holistic and enlists the help of siblings, parents, teachers, peers, and community members to support the client toward feelings of connectedness and contribution.

The Adlerian Therapy Counseling Process

When youth do not feel competent and important in social, occupational, or intimate domains, they often develop mental health difficulties (Watts, 2013). Mental health difficulties are the result of unhelpful thoughts and feelings that develop from difficult social interactions, and these unhelpful thoughts are manifested as unhealthy behaviors. Unhealthy or unhelpful youth behaviors suggest underlying feelings of discouragement in some part of their lives, and encouragement is a key component to an effective Adlerian counseling process.

Overall, Adler (1958) viewed every individual as inherently positive, creative, and desiring to contribute to society. Youth are no exception to this rule, and counselors can support healthy development in youth by encouraging them to meet their needs in socially useful ways. Counselors should also recruit the important people in youth's lives to provide encouragement. When counselors identify the motivations for youth behaviors, specific interventions can be implemented to highlight positive ways that youth can achieve their goals in desirable, helpful ways. For example, a youth who seeks attention by hitting his siblings should be given positive attention before the need to hit a sibling appears.

Individual psychology can be used to conceptualize individual, group, family, and school-based counseling with youth. Counselors should choose the format for Adlerian counseling interventions based on the clients' needs and availability of services. Sometimes, counselors will not be able to incorporate key stakeholders into treatment, but it is important to still conceptualize clients in a holistic, developmental context. Counselors can choose between individual, school-based, family, and group Adlerian interventions to address each client's unique circumstances and needs.

Adler held that youth sometimes have mistaken goals that they use to achieve a perceived plus. In Table 6.6, common mistaken goals—according to Adler's theory—are identified. Youth often use unhelpful behaviors to achieve these goals, and achievement of the mistaken goals provides youth with a perceived plus.

Counselors should work to understand the mistaken goals that motivate a youth's unhelpful behaviors—for example, a youth wanting others to feel hurt when he or she feels betrayed or disappointed. This mistaken goal is ineffective because it harms society, which contributes further to a felt minus, and does not actually support the fictive final goal of becoming a better person. Counselors should work with the client to

Table 6.6 Common Mistaken Goals in Individual Psychology

Mistaken Goal	Faulty Logic Example	Relevant Behaviors	Therapeutic Goals
Seeking attention	I need others to pay attention to me to feel valued.	Youth might throw tantrums, disobey the rules, or make loud/inappropriate noises in an attempt to garner attention.	• Identify and reframe faulty logic. • Help youth gain attention through healthy behaviors (e.g., sports). • Implement coping skills that make alone time enjoyable and satisfying. • Praise youth when behaving desirably.
Seeking power	I am only important when I have control of a situation.	Youth might throw tantrums, steal toys from peers, or refuse to follow directions in an attempt to feel powerful.	• Identify and reframe irrational beliefs. • Provide youth with healthy opportunities to assert personal preferences and control (e.g., dressing oneself). • Play games and other activities that allow youth to practice relinquishing control with satisfying results.
Seeking revenge	I want you to feel bad when I feel bad.	Youth might hit a parent or peer. Youth might say mean things to others.	• Identify and reframe irrational beliefs. • Help youth identify and express their feelings. • Complete activities, games, play, and worksheets that help youth to develop increased empathy for others.
Feelings of inadequacy	I am going to fail, so you shouldn't ask me to try.	Youth might begin crying or otherwise avoid difficult tasks. Youth might purposely perform poorly so no one asks them to do a task again.	• Identify and reframe irrational beliefs. • Praise youth for trying new things (regardless of the level of success). • Complete difficult tasks with youth to encourage a sense of mastery.

Note: Schultz & Schultz (2013); Sweeney (2009).

create insight around this mistaken goal and develop healthier methods for achieving a perceived plus in a socially useful manner (e.g., by helping others who have been wronged).

In the first few sessions, counselors should work to understand a youth's social experiences, fictive final goal, sources of perceived pluses and any felt minuses, mistaken goals, or inferiority complex. Counselors can use a **lifestyle assessment** to gain an intimate understanding of the client and his or her counseling needs.

Counselors can use assessment information to understand the biopsychosocial factors that interact to foster feelings of discouragement and inferiority in youth. Adlerian counselors use the results of the lifestyle assessment to understand a youth's:

- social relationships;
- thoughts, feelings, and behaviors;
- overarching goals;
- internal/external factors;
- felt minus; and
- fictive final goal.

Counselors gather information to complete the lifestyle assessment by directly asking the youth, observing the youth's behavior, and interviewing significant people in the youth's life. Adlerian counselors place a holistic conceptualization of youth at the heart of counseling (Drout, Habeck, & Rule, 2015). The lifestyle assessment is administered to learn about the youth's family system, neighborhood, community, social circle, and school/day care settings, along with individual-level factors (e.g., life experiences, personal development, genetics, and biology).

Clinical Toolbox 6.4

In the Pearson eText, click here to review an activity that helps youth to explore their social worlds.

A lifestyle assessment is much like any written assessment used by a counselor to systematically gather information about a client. However, an Adlerian lifestyle assessment is unique because it can be used to draw conclusions about a youth's consistent pattern of interacting with the world and others. Table 6.7 presents the main components of an Adlerian lifestyle assessment.

The **family constellation** is the most complex and dynamic aspect of an Adlerian lifestyle assessment. The family constellation is a culmination of all family-of-origin factors, including a brief description of every family member (including sibling birth order), description of any additional parental figures, typical interaction patterns with siblings and parents, the youth's inherent temperament and personality, and an exploration of the youth's core views about life.

Birth order is another key concept in Adlerian lifestyle assessments. Adler (1958) found that youth tend to have specific characteristics based on their positions and roles in the family. Also, Adlerian counselors believe that a youth's sibling who is closest in age has the most significant effect on that youth's development (Sweeney, 2009). For example, a child who was born 3 years after the first and 1 year before the third will be greatly influenced by the younger sibling.

Adler (1958) posited that the order in which youth enter the world in relation to their siblings can significantly affect their personalities and lifestyles. **Oldest children** have no other siblings with whom to compete for attention. Firstborn youth are often highly engaged with their parents. When the next sibling is born, however, the firstborn is no longer the center of attention. These children are the only ones in the family who know how it feels to be an only child and a child with siblings.

Secondborn children never have the opportunity to be the only child. As a result, secondborn children are never fully the center of attention, but they also do not have the experience of losing such power (as with the first child). Secondborn children often receive less attention and fewer rules than the first child did

Table 6.7	Components of the Adlerian Lifestyle Assessment
Assessment Category	**Therapeutic Relevance**
Birth order	Youth can be born first, second, or last, or they might be an only child. The birth order of each youth contributes to the formation of the personality and the fictive goal.
Childhood attributes	All youth have biological and genetic factors that make them organically unique. These attributes, combined with their own unique, subjective life experiences, form a youth's personality.
Cultural values	The values held within the family, neighborhood, community, and society shape the way a youth interprets and interacts with the world.
Dream analysis	Dreams can be used to highlight key feelings about current and relevant problems the youth is facing. Events in the dream can be interpreted to identify potential solutions to problems.
Early recollections	Memories from the first years of life (typically beginning around age 4 or 5) inform a youth's personality and lifestyle and provide insights into a young person's life roles.
Family constellation	The family is a unique subset of individuals who have a strong influence on the youth's personality. Family communication patterns, dynamics, and expectations can reveal information about youth behaviors.
Gender guidelines	The messages youth receive about their gender are key contributors to personality development. When youth's thoughts, feelings, and behaviors align with gender guidelines from family, friends, or society, a perceived plus is experienced; thoughts, feelings, and behaviors that are significantly different from the family's and society's messages about gender can contribute to a felt minus.
Hero identification	Youth often idolize individuals who embody their fictive goal. The behaviors and qualities of childhood heroes will likely be replicated by youth to strive toward a perceived plus.
Personal strengths	Youth can use their inherent talents (e.g., sports, academics) to contribute meaningfully to society and experience a perceived plus.
Physical development	Physical characteristics can be observed by others. Developmental delays in this domain can lead to a felt minus and/or an inferiority complex. Appropriate or above-average physical development can contribute to a perceived plus or even a superiority complex.
Sexual development	Sexuality and sexual relationships are inherent human needs, and these relate to social acceptance and social connection. Healthy sexual development can contribute to a perceived plus, and difficulty with sexual development can lead to a felt minus.
Strange early memories	Youth might remember a key event from their early years in a highly distorted way, and these memories highlight youth's key fears and struggles. For example, a little boy might remember a large clown yelling and chasing him. In reality, the clown might not have been all that big and was not actually aggressive, but the clown represents fear and inferiority for the boy, which distorts the memory.
Three wishes	Asking youth to identify three wishes that they hope will come true in the future is one way to identify areas of felt minus or perceived plus.

Note: Schultz & Schultz (2013); Sweeney (2009).

at the same age. Secondborn children often strive to be very different, almost opposite, from their older sibling, and the older sibling often resents the secondborn child, which can lead to power struggles and fights, often referred to as sibling rivalry.

The second child might also be the **middle child**—the child who is often squeezed between the oldest (and often more dominating) and the youngest children. Middle children might seek attention from their parents and need reassurance of their value in the family. These children might be rebellious and independent, but they are often emotionally sensitive. Middle children often learn to navigate the politics of family dynamics well, and they are able to apply these skills to their social relationships. When there are more than three children in a family, counselors should consider which birth order fits the youth best (e.g., a third child in a family of eight children might be considered a middle child).

Youngest children, who are often babied by parents—might experience the fewest rules of all the siblings because parents' enthusiasm for child-rearing wanes with time and experience. As a result of this freedom, youngest children might be highly self-sufficient and successful. However, youngest children who are spoiled might become just the opposite: highly dependent with a lack of motivation.

Only children remain the center of their parents' attention for their entire lives. Only children never have to compete with or share their resources with siblings. Only children can have unrealistic expectations for attention from others, which could result in an inferiority complex (Schultz & Schultz, 2013). In addition, youth who are born 6 years before or after the sibling who is closest in age often display only child tendencies (Sweeney, 2009).

Many factors can influence a youth's development, and thus birth order does not affect every youth in a standardized way. For example, blended families, single parents, and extended family member caregiving can moderate the generalities placed on birth order. However, birth order may be a helpful way to conceptualize how youth experience the world. All youth perceive their roles in the family constellation as the most difficult to bear, and counselors should work to validate these experiences and understand how youth development is affected accordingly.

There are multiple pieces of the lifestyle assessment, and some of the most popular and relevant concepts were highlighted in this section. The lifestyle assessment, as conceptualized in Adlerian theory, helps counselors to understand a youth's thoughts, feelings, and behaviors and determines how the youth interacts with the world. All individuals inherently experience a sense of felt minus, and counselors work to understand the unique source of each client's felt minus and identify ways to support healthy attainment of a perceived plus. Counselors should work to understand and validate a youth's fictive final goal and foster helpful social behaviors through the counseling process.

Family Interventions and Involvement

Ideally, counselors will include family members and other significant stakeholders in youth counseling. This might not always be possible, especially for school counselors, but the social focus of individual psychology lends itself to a therapeutic approach that is conducted within a social context. As such, school counselors might consider the importance of a youth's teachers and peers when using an Adlerian approach. Most mental health issues are experienced as a result of interpersonal difficulties, and the best way to overcome these deficits is by enlisting the help of the most important people in the youth's life.

Counselors typically begin the Adlerian counseling process with youth by intentionally building therapeutic rapport with the client and the family. Family-based Adlerian counseling is especially effective and uses the basic Adlerian framework to conceptualize the lifestyle of the identified client, as well as that of the family members. Counselors can implement proven systems for family therapy that were derived from Adlerian theory. Specifically, the Active Parenting model (Popkin, 2014; see www.activeparenting.com for more on this model) is a family-based intervention for children that is included in SAMHSA's National Registry of Evidence-Based Programs and Practices. *Active Parenting of Teens* (Popkin, 2009) is an evidence-based program for implementing Adlerian-based principles in family therapy with adolescent clients who have mental health and behavioral difficulties.

Counselors working with families aim to gain insight into youth's social needs and strive to understand what motivates youth behaviors. When using family-based interventions, parents are invited to evaluate the ways in which they might be contributing to youth's feelings of inadequacy and ways in which their children can be encouraged to get their needs met in more helpful ways. Some helpful techniques for creating insight and supporting behavioral change include Socratic questioning, creative activities that highlight social connections, role-plays, and systematically reframing thoughts to produce healthier feelings and behaviors. Counselors pay special attention to harnessing resources that meet youth's needs in healthy ways, such as membership in an afterschool program or increased quality time with parents. When possible, counselors teach parents and stakeholders to encourage desirable traits in youth, and they also praise positive youth behaviors in session.

The **CARE acronym** has been proposed as one way counselors can help parents interact with youth from an Adlerian perspective (Sweeney, 2009). First, parents should *Catch* themselves and avoid acting impulsively and emotionally in difficult situations because doing so can lead to unhelpful interactions with children. Next, instead of reacting out of frustration or anger, parents should *Assess* the goals of a child's behaviors—that is, counselors should help parents understand the child's social needs, their experience of the felt minus, mistaken goals, and fictive final goals. Counselors can educate parents about the ways that these factors, compounded by various other lifestyle factors, lead youth toward unhelpful behaviors. Parents who are able to understand the underlying motivations of youth behaviors are able to avoid taking such behaviors personally and are better able to *Respond* in empathic, encouraging ways. Finally, parent responses must be *Executed* consistently.

Counselors can teach parents to respond to youth in ways that allow the youth to grow and develop. As previously mentioned, encouragement is a key method for helping youth find healthy ways to meet their needs. Whenever possible, parents should be encouraged to highlight the youth's positive intention behind an unhelpful behavior and provide a more helpful alternative. For example, consider a youth who steals a sibling's toy to get his attention. A parent could respond "Johnny, it is so good that you want to make a connection with your brother. Could you please ask him to play with you instead of stealing his toy?"

Sometimes, parents or caregivers are faced with the need to prevent youth behaviors that are unsafe (e.g., a youth hitting a peer). For behaviors that must be reprimanded, parents should be encouraged to implement **logical consequences** that allow youth to learn from their actions. For example, a child who hits a peer can be placed in a time-out. Parents should preemptively explain logical consequences to youth and implement them every time an undesirable behavior occurs so the youth knows that the behavior will never be tolerated.

Sometimes **natural consequences** occur as the natural result of unhelpful behaviors. For example, a youth who was told not to run at the pool falls and gets a serious cut. Parents do not always have to implement logical consequences for youth to learn from their unhelpful behaviors because sometimes natural consequences are just as effective, if not more so.

Counselors can teach parents about basic Adlerian concepts and encourage parents to be supportive and empathic with their children. Parents should be encouraged to reflect on their own roles in their children's difficulties, and open communication should be used within the household to help youth to identify the motivations for their behaviors and healthier ways that they can achieve their goals. Finally, parents should be continually reminded that encouragement of desirable behaviors can often be the best way to bring the most positivity out of youth who are inherently kind and socially invested.

Individual psychology has applications for school counseling as well. School-based interventions can be used to closely attend to a specific student's mistaken goals. Counselors can help teachers to understand a youth's mistaken goal (e.g., seeking attention) and find ways to preemptively meet the youth's needs in the classroom. For example, a teacher might report that a youth is often out of his seat and joking with peers. To address this behavior, counselors can find socially useful ways for the youth to get positive attention, such as being a hallway monitor or having a special job in the classroom. They can even implement behavioral interventions (e.g., token reward system) in conjunction with Adlerian theory to shape desirable behaviors that meet the youth's underlying social needs while being more helpful in the classroom.

Because communication and cooperation between parents and teachers can increase consistency within the youth's lifestyle, counselors should implement family- and school-based interventions whenever possible. For example, counselors can educate parents and teachers about the motivations for youth's unhelpful behaviors. Counselors can also provide individual Adlerian counseling to youth to help them to understand their lifestyles, private logic, mistaken goals, and healthier ways to work toward the fictive final goal.

PERSON-CENTERED THERAPY

Deviating from the psychoanalytic and behavioral approaches that dominated the early part of the 20th century, Carl Rogers (1942) developed **person-centered therapy**—an approach to helping others that, at the time, was very controversial due to its emphasis on the counseling relationship as the necessary and essential vehicle for client change. This approach differed dramatically from the psychoanalysts' focus on uncovering clients' unconscious motives and internal conflicts to facilitate insight and resolution of problems. The person-centered approach also differed from the behaviorists' focus on the principles of classical and operant conditioning as a means of extinguishing or reinforcing learned behaviors. Rogers (1961) believed all people, including youth, had the innate capacity to resolve their own problems and work toward achieving their full potential if the appropriate therapeutic conditions were provided by the counselor.

As a leader in the **humanistic psychology** movement, Rogers (1957, 1970) advocated for a non-directive counseling approach in which counselor-generated techniques and interventions were not important and only the therapeutic relationship mattered. Because of this assumption, person-centered counselors strive to avoid formally assessing youth's presenting problems, diagnosing young clients with mental disorders, gathering a past history, making interpretations, giving advice, and/or setting goals for youth. Person-centered therapy is the original strength-based counseling approach because it holds an optimistic view of human nature and honors the unique, individual perspectives of each young person; values an egalitarian counselor–client relationship; and aims to facilitate young clients' natural growth processes and help them to live optimally authentic and thus optimally functioning lives.

When working from a person-centered approach, counseling is not designed to eliminate specific behavioral problems, alleviate symptoms associated with a diagnosis, or apply evidence-based practices. Rather, person-centered counselors seek to establish a trusting therapeutic relationship and provide an accepting counseling environment, thus inviting a sense of worth in young people and allowing them to engage in an individually guided counseling experience. The nonjudgmental and nurturing orientation of person-centered therapy is highly applicable to the developmental needs of youth. As young people are developing and learning more about themselves and their identity, the nondirective nature of a person-centered approach allows them the space they need to discover who they are and who they want to become. The empowering nature of a person-centered approach also facilitates young people's autonomy and thus helps them develop the sense of personal efficacy they will need to cope not only with their current distress but also with any future challenges they may face. Because many adolescents experience feelings of self-doubt and uncertainty while navigating the challenges inherent to identity development, the accepting, warm, understanding, and supportive therapeutic climate that the person-centered approach offers can be particularly advantageous to counseling adolescents, especially those who may initially present as hesitant, skeptical, or even reluctant to engage.

The philosophical framework of person-centered counseling has served as a foundation for various therapeutic modalities commonly used with children. **Child-centered play therapy** (CCPT; Axline, 1947a) and **person-centered expressive arts therapy** (Rogers, 1993, 2011) are two approaches that have been particularly influential and widely used among counselors who work with youth. Both child-centered play therapy and person-centered expressive arts therapy are grounded in Rogerian principles and rely on alternative mediums to talk therapy to facilitate children's expressions of thoughts, feelings, and experiences. Moreover, both approaches also emphasize the counselor's way of being, the therapeutic relationship and core conditions of counseling, and children's self-directed growth processes toward enhanced self-understanding, autonomy, and creativity.

Virginia Axline (1947) developed child-centered play therapy as a developmentally appropriate method for working with children. She integrated Carl Rogers's ideas on how people change and held that basic person-centered principles were necessary to encourage children's constructive growth and development. Axline believed play is children's language, or their natural means of communication, so she adapted Rogers's (1951) nondirective counseling approach and applied the theory to the playroom, where children are provided with various toys and play materials that allow them to explore, express, and discover different aspects of themselves. Child-centered play therapists aim to establish a safe, nonthreatening, and warm environment for children that fosters the emergence of their innate capacity to self-actualize and thus become more fully functioning. Child-centered play therapy has been identified as an effective therapeutic modality for use with various problems across diverse populations, and it has been implemented with adolescents and adults (Baggerly, Ray, & Bratton, 2010; Bratton & Ray, 2000; Carmichael, 2006; Demanchick, Cochran, & Cochran, 2003; Ray & Bratton, 2010).

Natalie Rogers (1993, 2011), the daughter of Carl Rogers, creatively adapted person-centered counseling to include music, drawing, movement, painting, improvisation, writing, and sculpting in a therapeutic approach she called *expressive arts therapy*. Rogers believed in the inherent capacities and self-actualizing tendencies of children, and she held that expressive arts was an effective vehicle for facilitating one's ability to grow, evolve, and resolve problems in living. The use of play and expressive arts in counseling and their foundations as vehicles of change are discussed in more detail later in this text.

Counselors can maintain a genuine, affirming, and empathic stance while working with reluctant adolescents through the implementation of **motivational interviewing** (MI; Miller & Rollnick, 2012). MI is an expansion of person-centered therapy that aims to enhance clients' intrinsic motivation to change by eliciting and exploring discrepancies between behaviors and personal goals, processing their ambivalence about change, reinforcing change talk, and exploring and capitalizing on signs of readiness to change (Miller & Rollnick, 2012). MI has been widely applied to various presenting concerns (Miller & Rollnick, 2012) and can be used to facilitate clients' commitment, self-efficacy, and positive behavioral change.

Core Concepts and Goals of Counseling

VIEW OF HUMAN NATURE

According to Carl Rogers (1957, 1961), youth are inherently trustworthy, positive, and resourceful, and they hold the potential for constructive change, self-direction, and personal growth. Founded on Abraham Maslow's (1954) notion of **self-actualization**, youth are believed to be naturally predisposed to move away from maladjustment or psychological distress, and motivated to achieve autonomy, realization, socialization, and self-fulfillment. These concepts suggest that youth are capable of arriving at their own conclusions about their thoughts, emotions, and behaviors, and in solving their problems, young people essentially serve as their own agents of change. Person-centered theory refutes directive or instructional counseling methods. In other words, value is not placed on learning or applying new skills. However, thorough consideration of the developmental, intellectual, and contextual specificities of each client is integral to sound counseling practice because not all youth enter into counseling with the competencies and skills required to independently resolve presenting concerns or even fully conceptualize what it is they need. Consequently, counselors should tailor their approach to the individual needs of youth to maximize therapeutic potentiality, and this may involve encouraging clients toward self-actualization at times.

It is important to note person-centered theory's emphasis on the youth's **phenomenological** experiences—that is, each young client has his or her own unique, subjective understanding of the world; self-concept; and awareness of his or her experiences in the world. Therefore, regardless of what is occurring in the lives of youth and in the world around them, their subjective perceptions of their environment, self-concept, and interactions with others are what inform their reality. For example, there are many barriers in a young client's external world that may deter or inhibit self-actualizing processes. When these barriers create a state of **incongruence** between a young client's phenomenological experience—or real self—and the perceived actualized self, he or she will experience distress. Youth may begin to exhibit maladaptive behavioral and psychological responses when their thoughts, emotions, and experiences are in opposition to their self-actualizing tendencies. Exploring incongruence between the real self and the actualized self may serve as a starting point for counselors working with youth who require a higher degree of collaborative guidance. As youth continue to explore, they will likely—because of their self-actualizing tendencies—experience therapeutic movement toward the discovery of problem resolution and, ultimately, a more integrated, congruent self.

Clinical Toolbox 6.5

In the Pearson eText, click here to review an activity that can help youth to identify and explore different aspects of self with the aim of increased congruence.

From a person-centered perspective, an environment that offers acceptance, love, and warmth needs to be provided if youth are to grow optimally. As such, counselors who apply person-centered theory should maintain a nondirective stance as well as demonstrate congruence, unconditional positive regard, and accurate empathic understanding to foster a therapeutic relationship that allows young clients to engage in a self-directed search for potential solutions to their problems and continued self-development. When working from a person-centered perspective, counselors do not choose counseling goals for clients, diagnose them with a particular disorder, or apply specific interventions to change clients' behaviors. Rather, with an inclination toward self-actualization and an innate capacity to identify and resolve their problems, youth are given the freedom to select their own goals and determine the direction and focus of their counseling. Adolescents and high-functioning children may possess the cognitive flexibility to verbally communicate their distresses; however, because language development is less advanced early in life, younger children communicate more through play behaviors. For them, a cognitive understanding of person-centered concepts is not important. What is important is that counselors provide a counseling environment that supports young people's growth.

SELF-ACTUALIZING PROCESSES

The principal goals of person-centered therapy are to help young clients to recognize who they want to be, realize the people they wish to be, and become all that they can be. Carl Rogers (1961, 1977) described this **self-actualizing** process as being one in which a young person develops into a more fully functioning person, a person who is autonomous, is self-directed, and experiences congruence between his or her real self and ideal self. According to Rogers (1961), youth who engage in constructive personal growth processes typically share the following attributes:

- Openness to experience
- Trusting of one's self and judgment
- Trustworthy behavior
- An internal source of evaluation
- Creativity

Counselors who use a person-centered approach attempt to promote these qualities among youth and believe counseling will naturally advance the development of these self-actualizing characteristics. By allowing youth to direct counseling sessions in a safe therapeutic climate that supports the open disclosure of thoughts, feelings, behaviors, and lived experiences, youth can discover the inner resources they hold, their ability to autonomously manage life's present and future challenges, and their ability to learn to accept and value themselves, as well as ultimately to become fully functioning.

Moreover, in an effort to facilitate the development of self-actualizing characteristics and promote an enhanced sense of autonomy, counselors may want to integrate associated themes such as mastery and self-efficacy. For example, counselors can frequently attend to and reflect the strengths and capabilities of youth, and they can find ways to *create* opportunities for youth to accomplish tasks during counseling sessions through play or other means that suit the unique capacities of individual clients. Presenting success opportunities can be beneficial when working with youth who may not be offered many achievement opportunities in their natural environment.

Counselors may need to use alternative language to reframe notions of the self when working with youth because such ideas may be too abstract for some young people to understand. The integration of developmentally appropriate creative interventions is one strategy that counselors and other helping professionals can use to establish more concrete conceptualizations of the self, personal growth, and change. For example, counselors can use metaphors such as a shooting star to explore the person the client wants to be or a tree or flower for growth process. They can also use other creative interventions that are conducive to self-exploration and personal growth and that will help clients to feel understood as unique individuals of worth.

Role of the Counselor in Person-Centered Therapy

The primary objective of the person-centered counselor is to nurture a safe, warm, and trusting therapeutic relationship and environment. Counselors maintain a disposition that is consistent with the person-centered philosophy, sometimes referred to as a **way of being**. The attitude and spirit of the counselor, along with the counselor's ability to establish rapport with youth, are assumed to transcend the use of any intervention or empirically validated therapeutic tools. Thus, counselors use themselves as a therapeutic tool and offer a relationship, environment, and counseling experience that facilitates youth's movement from incongruence to congruence. Carl Rogers (1957, 1961) described six **therapeutic core conditions** that provide an optimal opportunity for youth to experience constructive personality change. Among these core conditions, three hold the greatest significance and are fundamental to the person-centered way of being:

- *Congruence*, or genuineness, authenticity, or transparency
- *Unconditional positive regard*, or acceptance, warmth, and/or care
- *Accurate empathic understanding*, or a deep and accurate sense of a young client's subjective world and experiences

Carl Rogers (1957) believed these core conditions were both necessary *and* sufficient enough to facilitate client change—that is, a therapeutic relationship marked by congruence, unconditional positive regard, and accurate empathic understanding will foster personal development among youth and enable them to solve their own problems without the need for additional interventions. Although controversial at the time, Rogers's core conditions, or the importance of the counseling relationship, currently serve as the foundation of most therapeutic modalities regardless of the theoretical orientation, and a large body of research demonstrates the important role these factors play in counseling.

The core condition of empathy has been the focus of decades of empirical research and is frequently noted as one of Carl Rogers's (1942, 1977) most significant contributions to the field of counseling. Indeed, a breadth of empirical literature has consistently validated the critical role of empathy in effective counseling practice because it was found to be the most powerful predictor of client progress and successful treatment outcomes (Cain, 2010; Clark, 2010).

It is important to note, however, that the therapeutic core conditions of congruence, unconditional positive regard, and accurate empathic understanding may *not* be necessary and sufficient to yield self-growth and constructive change among youth, as Carl Rogers (1957) originally hypothesized. Indeed, Rogers's core conditions most certainly provide a solid foundation for counseling processes, but youth can experience various forms of distress that may require behavioral change, skill development, or, in some cases, pharmacological intervention. However, even when working with youth with more severe struggles, person-centered counselors aim to build a connected and meaningful therapeutic relationship founded in the core conditions, to join youth in their immediate experience, and to remain fully present as youth navigate the shared counseling journey. When these counselors genuinely attend to youth and reflect on, clarify, and summarize their moment-to-moment experiences and emotions, youth can become more open, explore and discover self-growth barriers, accept and integrate new aspects of themselves, and take constructive action toward becoming their desired selves.

Person-Centered Therapy Counseling Process

As previously described, Carl Rogers (1957, 1961) did not promote the use of diagnostic or assessment measures to obtain an understanding of the client's distress, nor did he advocate for the application of specific interventions to bring about client change. Instead, he placed an emphasis on the counselor's attitude and way of being, the therapeutic core conditions, and the quality of the relationship between the counselor and client. Person-centered counselors do not focus on *what they can do* to help youth, but *how* they can establish a relationship that will provide youth with an opportunity to become more fully functioning, self-aware, trusting, and autonomous. What follows are some of the characteristics that Rogers believed counselors must demonstrate to facilitate effective counseling.

COUNSELOR WAYS OF BEING WITH CLIENTS

The counselor plays an important role in person-centered therapy. Although person-centered counselors are nondirective, they are responsible for building a strong therapeutic relationship in which clients have the space to explore, gain insight, and make shifts toward more congruent thoughts, feelings, and behaviors. Counselors should intentionally display the core conditions of congruence, empathy, and unconditional positive regard when working with clients (Rogers, 1957).

Congruence.   Congruent counselors are genuine, real, open, and honest when interacting with youth because bearing a façade or attempting to disguise one's true sentiments during counseling sessions will impede the development of a genuine, relational connection. The external presentation of person-centered counselors, or the manner in which they interact with youth, should be consistent with their internal thoughts, emotions, reactions, and experience. However, being congruent does not mean counselors should freely express any thought or emotional reaction with the youth. Person-centered counselors use **appropriate self-disclosure** and **immediacy** to reinforce a genuine and authentic way of being, but they do so with therapeutic intent and in a deliberate, measured fashion.

Unconditional Positive Regard.   As youth are presumed to enter into counseling in a state of incongruence, whereby their self-regard is influenced by the approval or disapproval of others, counselors' unconditional positive regard for youth is of critical importance. Unconditional positive regard is characterized by counselor acceptance, warmth, care, and prizing or valuing the client as a person. Counselors work to convey the deep sense of value and respect they hold for young clients and accept each client as a unique person, along with the client's thoughts, feelings, behaviors, and individual characteristics, without judgment or evaluation. Counselors may not always accept or approve of the behaviors of youth, but they do not place conditions of worth on youth or value them based on their actions—youth are accepted as they are. When youth begin to feel compassion and acceptance through counselors' unconditional positive regard, they can also begin accepting themselves and develop a strong sense of positive self-regard.

Empathic Understanding.   Counselors must display empathy to be effective in counseling with youth. *Empathy* is the counselor's ability to gain a deep sense of understanding of the client's subjective world and experience it *with* the client, while never losing touch with his or her self—that is, by joining youth in their here-and-now, moment-to-moment experiences, counselors sense the feelings of youth as if they were their own, without ever losing a separate awareness of their own selves. Counselors' expressions of empathy allow youth to feel genuinely understood and cared for, further affirming unconditional positive regard and promoting their degrees of self-awareness.

INTERVENTIONS

Person-centered counseling does not embrace a template set of techniques; rather, strategies that promote the therapeutic relationship, foster the core conditions, engender self-directed growth processes among youth, and facilitate a sense of congruence in youth are held as primary interventions. What follows is a brief discussion of some of the techniques that Rogers believed to be essential in helping youth.

Active Listening.   As previously noted, person-centered interventions may be conceptualized as strategies counselors use to support their way of being with youth or, in other words, strategies that promote the therapeutic core conditions. Active listening is one technique that is consistent with the person-centered philosophy, and it is particularly important to a counselor's ability to understand and accurately communicate empathy to youth. Not only is it necessary for counselors to attentively listen to youth, but it is equally as important for youth to feel heard. A counselor's **presence**, or absolute engagement and full attention to youth, is a necessary element to convey genuineness, warmth, acceptance, and empathy. Counselors reveal their presence and show youth they are listening through verbal and nonverbal behaviors. With active listening, counselors remain silent and attend to youth's self-directed exploration processes while displaying their presence through such nonverbal actions as making frequent eye contact, maintaining an open posture, leaning in at times, and facial expressions that are congruent with youth's present-moment experience. Such behaviors nurture the therapeutic relationship, convey warmth, and support counselors' empathic identification with youth. Counselors provide verbal messages that are accurate, thoughtful, and related to the client's story.

Reflection of Feelings.   Although a counselor's ability to monitor and show his or her presence through nonverbal behaviors are meaningful skills for expressing empathy, young clients are not always cognizant of counselors' nonverbal behaviors and may require more concrete messages to know they are being heard. As such, counselors also verbally communicate their presence, understanding, way of being, and empathy through the reflection of youth's feelings. Counselors use their own words to provide a reflection of youth's explicit disclosures, or implicit emotions or experiences. Accurately reflecting the feelings of youth evidences the counselor's grasp of clients' subjective perceptions of reality and enhances the self-awareness of youth, bringing them more in tune with their emotions and worldview. Youth can then use this heightened awareness to better understand their current self and state of incongruence, their emotional responses to others, and how they can begin to engage in constructive actions to facilitate becoming a more fully functioning individual.

Paraphrasing.   Person-centered counselors aim to feel and experience with young clients in the here and now. They convey their presence and understanding through active listening and reflections of youth's emotions; however, because counselors can never fully understand all the idiosyncratic complexities of a young client's phenomenological experience and subjective inner world, counselors' reflections are not always accurate. Thus, counselors use concise statements to test their understanding of youth's feelings and experiences and paraphrase the core essence of what youth are saying. Reflecting on their feelings and paraphrasing their primary messages create opportunities for youth to correct counselors and further expound on their prior statements.

Immediacy.   Counselors can use the here-and-now emphasis of person-centered counseling as a therapeutic intervention through immediacy or by addressing the immediate experience, feeling, or situation between the counselor and child. Counselors use immediacy to call attention to the here-and-now dynamics within the therapeutic relationship, either focusing on their own feelings or responses to youth or on those they sense youth are experiencing.

Open-Ended Questions or Leads.   Although open-ended questions and leads are not traditional strategies of the person-centered approach, such techniques can be advantageous to stimulate the deeper exploration and disclosure of youth's thoughts, feelings, behaviors, and experiences. Counselors may pose open-ended questions that begin with "what," "how," or "when," such as "How did you respond in that situation?" Open-ended leads are statements rather than questions that begin with "I'm curious," "Tell me," or "I wonder," for example.

Family Interventions and Involvement

Person-centered therapy is a widely applicable and highly suitable therapeutic modality for working with parents because the approach's fundamental values naturally foster the development of positive family relationships. One method counselors can use to involve family members in treatment processes is **child–parent relationship therapy (CPRT)**. CPRT is a filial therapy model (Landreth & Bratton, 2006), based on the principles of CCPT, that aims to enhance the parent–child relationship and focuses on the growth and development of both parents and children. Counselors can implement this evidence-based model to address many different presenting concerns among youth (Bratton, Landreth, Kellum, & Blackard, 2006) and with families seeking a structured counseling experience that requires a high degree of commitment and involvement.

Counselors use the 10-session CPRT model (Bratton et al., 2006) to provide parents with education on the core tenets and skills of CCPT, including the establishment of an accepting, warm, nonjudgmental, and safe environment; promoting children's self-esteem; empathically responding to children; and engaging in relationship-building play behaviors. In an effort to empower parents to become the therapeutic agents of change for their children and to assist them with understanding and responding more effectively to their children's emotional needs, counselors coach parents during structured weekly play sessions with their children. Such supervised parent–child play processes provide parents with therapeutic training opportunities that are both didactic and experiential in nature, allowing them to receive support and feedback from counselors. CPRT is a well-researched and empirically supported model that has been used for many different presenting concerns and in various settings (Bratton et al., 2015).

Person-centered counselors can also focus on strengthening parent–child relationships in their everyday practice without the inclusion of supplemental interventions or the employment of techniques specifically designed for working with families. By displaying congruence, unconditional positive regard, and empathic understanding, the counselor functions as a model to the parent in which they can observe and learn new ways of interacting, connecting, and responding to youth. Counselors can educate parents about the importance of maintaining a consistently warm and secure relationship with their children. Counselors can also process core themes of genuineness, honesty, acceptance, empathy, and self-directed growth in an effort to promote the competency and efficacy of parents and can facilitate relationship-enhancing experiences between parents and their children. Additional strategies such as practicing active listening, reflecting feelings, and being present with youth can also be modeled and processed with parents, providing them with valuable skills to engage their children in meaningful, supportive, and loving ways.

Summary

This chapter discusses theoretical approaches focused on the role of clients' past experiences and the counseling relationship. These approaches are applicable in many settings, particularly family settings, and address many youth concerns. Each theory also fosters in the client a sense of control or empowerment and helps the client to reach his or her full potential.

Table 6.8 provides an overview of the three theories discussed in this chapter. More specifically, for each theory, the following components are addressed: basic philosophy, key concepts, goals of counseling, the therapeutic relationship, counseling techniques, applications/ approaches, multicultural considerations, and youth-specific approaches.

Table 6.8	Summary of Counseling Theories
Psychoanalytic Theory	
Basic philosophy	The interplay between the unconscious and conscious aspects of personality and the successful resolution of these stages of development are required for a young person to develop a healthy personality; when this does not occur, psychological and behavioral issues arise. Early childhood relationships and their experiences within these are central to understanding youth.
Key concepts	A young person's personality development requires the successful navigation of early stages of development, and these stages vary depending on the specific psychoanalytic theory. The use of ego-defense mechanisms serve to protect the ego from anxiety-producing memories or events. Repression is one such defense mechanism. When a youth does not successfully resolve a developmental stage, that youth becomes stuck and will manifest problematic psychological and behavioral concerns.
Goals of counseling	Make the unconscious conscious, and work through repressed conflicts. Reconstruct personality by working through and resolving previously unachieved developmental states. Increase awareness. With youth, it is best to head off developmental issues before they arise by preemptively reinforcing the ego. If repression has occurred, the temporal proximity of the event aids in uncovering and resolving the conflict. Familial influence invariably factors into a young person's behavior, as such that influence should be addressed accordingly via appropriate supportive education.
Therapeutic relationship	In classical psychoanalysis, counselors are anonymous so clients can develop projections that can be used to help them overcome the developmental struggles they need to resolve. A client may project onto the counselor the role of a surrogate parent, and the role the counselor chooses largely depends on the age, needs, and developmental stage of the youth. In contemporary psychoanalysis, the relationship is important, and counselors take a here-and-now approach and use immediacy as an important therapeutic tool.
Counseling techniques	Free association—through play observation and interpretation of representational objects, dream and daydream analysis, interpretation of transference, analysis of resistance, and psychodynamic play therapy—is just one technique in a counselor's toolbox. The associations and interpretations a counselor needs arise during the act of play, which functions as a normative language of children.
Application/approaches	This theory is not widely applied today due to the lengthy time requirements for proper analysis. It is influential in establishing many play therapy approaches. Brief treatment approaches have been developed. Although generally a one-on-one treatment approach, the theory has had successful application in group, family, and parent–child counseling.
Multicultural counseling	The emphasis on family and family dynamics is relevant cross-culturally. Some clients may be more comfortable with a counselor who is more distant professionally.
Limitations for multicultural counseling	The emphasis on insight and self-exploration may be alien to some, especially those who are living in poverty or in a circumstance in which they are in transition or crisis. Many clients desire quick changes, so the length associated with these approaches may be prohibitive.
Youth-specific approaches	Psychodynamic approaches have greatly informed many play therapy approaches. This approach is focused on early child development, which fits for those who work with youth.

Table 6.8	(Continued)

Adlerian Theory

Basic philosophy	Humans are social beings who are motivated to become better versions of themselves. Humans have an inherent drive to contribute positively to society, and individuals use self-comparison with peers to assess their competence in life. Some personal difficulties, especially physical setbacks and overbearing/underattentive parents, can lead to an inferiority complex. Individuals adopt one of four lifestyles (i.e., dominant, getting, avoiding, and socially useful) to achieve their short- and long-term goals. Factors that contribute to a youth's individual lifestyle include biology, birth order, family structure, life experiences, and social relationships. The positive capacities of youth should be encouraged to help them reach their full potential for benefitting society.
Key concepts	All perspectives are subjective and unique to the individual, and multiple factors are involved in the creation of a youth's unique lifestyle. Consistently encouraging young people and helping them to change in a prosocial direction are key. Youth are inherently motivated to develop a sense of direction and achieve socially useful life goals. Youth have an innate need for social connection, which creates meaning and fulfillment within the young person. Peer relationships are especially important during adolescence, when youth are developing rapidly and comparing their own growth to their peers' growth.
Goals of counseling	Youth sometimes use unhelpful behaviors to have their interpersonal needs met, and the primary goal of counseling is to provide encouragement for youth to accomplish goals in healthy ways. Counselors help youth to uncover unconscious reasoning and reframe it in more socially useful ways. Positive social relationships and movement toward broader social involvement should be encouraged. Counselors help young people to build self-understanding and insight, achieve new levels of self-confidence and courage, and promote social interest and social connectedness.
Therapeutic relationship	The therapeutic alliance, from an Adlerian perspective, is one of equality. The counselor should provide encouragement to the youth while sensitively uncovering mistaken goals and assumptions within the youth's lifestyle. The counselor and the youth are equals on the path toward achieving socially useful short- and long-term goals. The counselor fosters mutual trust and respect.
Counseling techniques	This theory is not a technique-heavy approach. Instead, the main focus is on the youth's subjective experience. The counselor works to understand the youth's unique lifestyle and identify healthier behaviors that can help the young person achieve socially motivated, short- and long-term goals. The counselor may collect information regarding life history, family constellation, and social history. In supporting youth during counseling, encouragement is critical to growth and socially useful functioning.
Application/approaches	Because it encourages a young person's growth toward more prosocial behaviors and attitudes, Adlerian theory is extremely applicable to a diverse range of professional fields, including personal and school counseling, parent and teacher education, and social advocacy.
Multicultural counseling	Adlerian theory is broadly applicable to individuals from diverse cultures. Its focus on the individual experience and the promotion of prosocial interests and social ties meshes well with many culture-based values from collectivistic and individualistic cultures. The holistic approach, emphasis on cooperation versus competition, and the acknowledgment of the subjective experiences of a young person also lend themselves to working with youth from diverse cultures.
Limitations for multicultural counseling	The egalitarian nature of the therapeutic alliance may not align with cultures that defer to the expertise of elders and professionals. Western ideas of family structure and growth toward autonomy may conflict with cultures that do not emphasize the individual experience. Youth who desire a brief, solution-focused counseling experience might lose patience when building insight into early memories and social experiences. Youth with limited cognitive abilities might have difficulty gaining insight into their behavioral motivations.

(Continued)

Table 6.8	Summary of Counseling Theories (*Continued*)
Youth-specific approaches	Adlerian play therapy provides a place for young people to examine perceptions and practice new roles, emotions, and behaviors. Creative activities can be integrated into individual Adlerian counseling with youth to help them to identify their social needs and gain insight into their lifestyles. Older children and adolescents are encouraged to explore their early recollections to identify any inferiority complexes or mistaken goals and overcome them in socially useful ways.
Person-Centered Theory	
Basic philosophy	Youth have an innate capacity to resolve their problems, grow, and reach self-actualization within a safe, warm, empathetic environment. Unconditional positive regard provides a nonjudgmental place for youth to flourish and individuate.
Key concepts	Maladaptive behaviors and feelings are the result of the incongruence between who young people want to be and who they are. The person-centered approach seeks to empower youth by establishing a warm, empathetic, and nonjudgmental environment in which to recognize this incongruence and manifest self-actualization toward becoming their genuine selves.
Goals of counseling	Counseling serves to encourage and assist youth in self-exploration, uncover and overcome blocks to their growth, increase openness of self, and promote self-directed growth in a safe, empathetic environment.
Therapeutic relationship	The therapeutic relationship is the most important factor in this approach. This relationship is typified by warmth, genuineness, empathy, and unconditional positive regard, as well as the counselor remaining congruent throughout the relationship.
Counseling techniques	Techniques that focus on promoting the therapeutic relationship are the most essential. Key techniques from person-centered theory include active listening, accurate reflections, empathetic understanding, and open-ended questions.
Application/approaches	The application and approach of the theory are applicable to nearly all counseling situations involving youth, including family interventions, parent–child relationships, individual or group counseling, community initiatives, or culturally diverse populations.
Multicultural counseling	Widely applicable to diverse populations due to the core values of genuineness, respect, unconditional positive regard, and empathy, which are nearly universal across cultures. This approach respects and honors youth and their experiences and perspectives.
Limitations for multicultural counseling	The minimal structuring of this approach may not be appropriate for youth from cultures that prize direction- and action-oriented interventions from an expert. Collectivistic cultures do not share the common Western themes of autonomy, individual preference, and self-actualization emphasized in person-centered counseling; thus, this approach may not fit those from all cultural backgrounds.
Youth-specific approaches	Core person-centered principles are effective with all youth. Child-centered play therapy is widely recognized for its application with youth. It provides a safe environment for the child or young adolescent to explore and grow within the boundaries set by the counselor. Nondirective empathetic support is provided to maintain the warm, congruent therapeutic environment.

MyLab Counseling: Counseling Children and Adolescents

In the Topic 4 Assignments: *Theoretical Foundations for Counseling Youth*, try Application Exercise 4.2: *Person-Centered Therapy with Adolescents* and Licensure Quiz 4.2: *Psychodynamic Therapy*.

Then try Licensure Quiz 4.3: *Adlerian and Person-Centered Therapy* and Application Exercise 4.4: *We Are Family*.

CHAPTER 7

Counseling Theories That Focus on Family Change Processes

In Chapters 5 and 6, theories that conceptualized youth counseling from an individual level of analysis are discussed. Although these approaches take into consideration the role family and caregivers play in the change process, the primary vehicle of change *from those perspectives* is at the individual level—that is, change is not incumbent on others changing.

Family therapy approaches, however, focus on the patterns of interactions between all family members, rather than on the characteristics or behaviors of just one family member (Goldenberg & Goldenberg, 2013). Family therapists argue that young people's problems originate and are maintained within families and that families play a critical role in helping youth to grow and change (Minuchin & Fishman, 1981). Specifically, problems do not exist within individuals, but they exist and are maintained within the context of a family system. As such, youth cannot make enduring, sustainable changes unless shifts are made within the family system. In family therapy, all members of the youth's family are charged with the responsibility of critically reflecting on themselves and making behavioral changes that support the well-being of all other family members.

In this chapter, theories that conceptualize youth from a family systems perspective are addressed. Because there are numerous family therapy theories, specific theories are not discussed in depth. Instead, common family therapy foundations, concepts, approaches, and counseling considerations are provided. This chapter provides the reader with a general sense of family therapy and how the major aspects of family therapy can be pragmatically implemented when counseling youth.

FAMILY THERAPY

Family therapy focuses on altering the exchanges between family members with the aim of improving the functioning of the family and/or individual members of the family (Gladding, 2011). Although the theories discussed in Chapters 5 and 6 have applications to working with parents, most of them involve helping parents to understand and/or manage their children's behaviors. These theories may encompass providing education or psychoeducation to parents, teaching parents how to apply different skills with their children, facilitating and prompting positive family interactions, and encouraging family members to engage in a supportive manner. Family therapy differs in several important ways in that it:

- involves meeting with the youth and parents together;
- focuses not only on the child who is identified as having a problem (i.e., the "identified client") but also on all family members who relate to or influence the child's problem;
- concentrates on the needs of all family members, not just the child's needs; and
- centers on the ways in which the family's interactions affect all members of the family unit and how this influences the child's behavior.

The basic premise of family therapy is that young people's behaviors are rooted in interactions within the family. Family therapists contend that the ways youth interact with members of the family repeat, and if repeated regularly, these interactions and ways of being within the family become an interactional pattern.

Family members have hundreds of regular interactions that include how they respond to predictable day-to-day tasks (e.g., homework, cleaning) and how they manage conflict, privacy, and needs for support. These patterns or ways of interacting within family systems can quickly become habits that are difficult to change.

This concept of problems being rooted in family or systemic interactions is a stark contrast to the idea that children's problems in living are due to medical model explanations (e.g., mental disorders) or problems, struggles, deficiencies, or a paucity of supportive and growth-promoting conditions within the child (Eriksen & Kress, 2005—that is, family therapists do not focus on individual-level considerations unless they are affecting system dynamics. Family counselors believe that what may look like a child's disturbance is most likely a manifestation of unhealthy family interactional patterns. Thus, they aim to change the patterns and relationships causing or supporting the child's problems, and they ask themselves how cyclical patterns within the family are encouraging and supporting a child's struggles (Haley, 1963). It is here—in altering these patterns—that family therapists believe meaningful change occurs.

It could be said that family therapists hold to the Aristotle quote that the "whole is greater than the sum of its parts." There are qualitatively unique dynamics that others cannot understand unless they come to understand a system and its inner functioning. As an example, a teenager and her mother might have a strained, conflictual relationship and regularly fight. Yet, they may have a pattern of healthy, nonconflictual relationships with others in their lives. Thus, it is not enough to say these two individuals are angry, aggressive people. One must understand their relationship in the system in which they function to understand the nature of their conflicts, and more important, the patterns that need to be addressed to influence change processes.

Core Concepts

Family is defined as a group of people who intimately share their lives with one another, and family can include any combination of parents (biological, step, and/or adoptive), siblings (biological, step, and/or adoptive), extended family (aunts, uncles, cousins, grandparents), and even friends or neighbors (Bosch, Segrin, & Curran, 2012; Council on Foundations, 2015). Any member of a family is seen as just one part of the larger family system; anything that affects one family member has an impact on the entire family system. In addition, every member of a family will have different experiences and perceptions of the interactions and relationships among family members.

It is common in families that one person, often the child, will be referred to as the **identified client** or **identified patient** (Becvar & Becvar, 2012). The identified client is the person who has come to counseling or who has been brought to counseling to address a specific mental health concern. Regardless of the youth's presenting problem (e.g., behavior difficulties, ADHD, depression, grief), family therapists believe the root of the problem lies within the family system dynamics. This is a key difference between family therapy and many other theoretical approaches: The individual who manifests mental health problems is not viewed as more or less pathological or disturbed than the rest of the family members.

Family therapy involves all family members working together to create intentional, long-term changes in relational and interactional patterns. The presenting problems of a youth are viewed as a product of the ways in which family members interact and relate with one another (Van Ryzin & Fosco, 2016). As such, family therapists—rather than working to change any one person within the family system—view the system as the mechanism of change. Table 7.1 provides an overview and key elements of most family therapies.

Clinical Toolbox 7.1

In the Pearson eText, click here to review a chart that provides an overview of the prominent family therapy approaches.

Although each family therapy theory has its own unique emphasis and flavor, many have overlapping concepts such as those of reciprocal influence and family functionality. These two concepts are presented more fully in the following sections.

Table 7.1	Key Elements of Family Therapy
Basic philosophy	The family is viewed as an interactive, living system that maintains its own internal balance. Dysfunction within this system is balanced by other parts of the system. Family therapists believe a disruption to the homeostasis of one part of the system will institute a change in the whole system.
Key concepts	Counseling is done within the family context and/or with the entire family unit because the youth's struggles are believed to be a manifestation of larger familial dynamics. Generational transmission of issues is common and manifests itself in the actions and thoughts of the family. Most often, the focus is on present functioning and working on verbal and nonverbal communication patterns within the family unit.
Goals of counseling	The aim of this type of therapy is to identify the family's current dysfunctional patterns and aid family members in developing new patterns of interaction. It is important to disrupt any dysfunctional maladaptive homeostasis that may be hampering the family unit from optimal functioning.
Therapeutic relationship	In most family therapy approaches, counselors work with the family unit as a whole and may act as coaches, experts, or teachers. At times, the relationship is personal and in-depth, and at other times, it is more distant. Some approaches will seek to intensify the maladaptive behaviors in session to highlight any dysfunctions. Regardless of the specific family therapy approach, a family therapist considers the primary relationship to be with the entire family unit.
Counseling techniques	Short-term techniques are generally preferred over long-term therapy, but the family therapist may draw on various techniques, depending on the specific family approach he or she uses. The counselor may draw on family mapping or genograms, joining with the family as a pseudomember, or use direct psychoeducation.
Application/approaches	In the context of working with youth, family systems approaches are highly applicable to situations involving conflict within the family, divorce, or relationship dysfunctions. When working with youth with disruptive behaviors, these approaches are helpful. In-home family therapy is useful for youth who have multiple needs and require a greater level of care than outpatient counseling.
Multicultural counseling	Many cultures have a focus on and place value on the family, with extended family sometimes being seen as an important part of the family. Family therapy appeals to many from diverse cultural backgrounds because the family is often considered the primary unit and greater than the individual members, and solutions to problems are often believed to be within the family.
Limitations for multicultural counseling	Concepts related to family boundaries and structure are culturally dependent, and navigating these can be difficult for counselors who are from a different culture than their clients. Concepts such as independence and self-expression may not be consistent with some clients' cultural values. In some cultures, it may be shameful to admit problems at all, and/or it may not be acceptable to discuss family struggles with an outsider. First-generation youth may more rapidly adapt to the host culture, and this may foster interfamily conflict, which can be difficult to address in family therapy.
Youth-specific approaches	This approach provides a place where a child's wants and needs can be heard and addressed. Family sculpting and other activities and interventions provide the youth with an opportunity to visually and verbally share their viewpoints with the family.

RECIPROCAL INFLUENCE

Systems thinking contends that one part of the family affects all other parts of the family. However, the mechanism through which one person affects another within a family is complex and synergistic. In its simplest form, the action of one individual leads another individual to respond (see Figure 7.1). This is known as **linear causality** because the effect pattern is in a straight, one-way line (Shapiro, 2015). However, family therapists do not generally focus on linear causality. Linear causality is too simplistic, and this type of logic typically misses the bigger picture at hand. Youth's thoughts, feelings, and behaviors develop across time as an intricate, underlying pattern of interactions that have fostered and maintained the youth's problems in living.

In contrast to linear causality, **circular causality** is believed to better explain most family system dynamics (Bertalanffy, 1968; Witherington, 2011). Circular causality goes beyond linear causality to identify a long-standing, complex spiral of interactions that includes all family dynamics and can become problematic over time. Often, circular causality is a subtle, long-term process in which one person says or does (or fails to do) something, and another family member interprets this behavior (correctly or incorrectly) and acts on it. Then, additional family members interpret these behaviors and act on them. With circular causality, a counselor can understand that a youth's behaviors come as the result of multiple family interactions, which must be addressed slowly and systematically. More important, family systems theorists are able to understand how a youth's behaviors are sustained by the family system and how family members' behaviors are influenced and affected by the youth (see Figure 7.2).

When counselors are able to identify intricate patterns of circular causality within the family, it becomes easier to view the interactions of the family as a whole instead of focusing on the presenting problems of one person within it. Family therapy is helpful for clients of all ages, but a systems approach is especially effective when working with youth because they are not able to physically separate themselves from the family; youth depend on their families for basic needs throughout childhood and adolescence (Satir, 1983). Even beyond childhood, most individuals live in some family context, and they depend on their nuclear and extended families for connection, love, and guidance (Bertalanffy, 1968; Sweeney, 2009).

The **dynamics**, or interactional patterns of a family, include the ways in which members' rules, beliefs, values, and experiences are expressed within the household and within the larger society as a whole (Walsh, 2012). Each family member plays a distinct role in the family, and the thoughts, feelings, and behaviors of each are typically consistent across situations. The family system is relatively stable, and its patterns have been built over time (Bertalanffy, 1968; Witherington, 2011). Family members respond and behave in predictable ways that serve an identifiable purpose or function within the family system. For example, one child might serve as the jokester in a family to create distractions and relieve tension between his parents. A pattern such as this might show up across settings and transfer into school or social situations.

Counselors cannot effectively address the presenting concerns of a client without considering the entire family system. Even if the client is able to make progress in individual counseling, positive family connections are a key component to strong mental health (Sweeney, 2009). Poor family dynamics and dysfunctional interactional patterns can serve as risk factors for youth and should be addressed whenever possible (Van Ryzin & Fosco, 2016). Furthermore, Olson (2011) developed the Circumplex model for explaining healthy and unproductive patterns of family dynamics and family relationships; this model outlined that

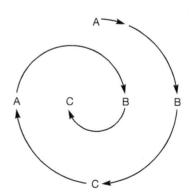

FIGURE 7.1 Linear Causality

FIGURE 7.2 Circular Causality

balanced levels of cohesiveness (e.g., closeness, loyalty, independence) and flexibility (e.g., leadership, disciple, roles, amount of change) in families is "most conducive to healthy family functioning" (p. 65). See Table 2.3 in Chapter 2 for a more complete overview of the Circumplex model.

FUNCTIONALITY IN THE FAMILY SYSTEM

To identify the mental health needs within a family system, counselors should work to understand the way a family typically functions or behaves. The **functionality** of a family system can be assessed by determining the flexibility of family members' subsystems and boundaries or the structure of the family. **Subsystems** within a family are smaller groupings of individuals who have unique ways of relating and interacting with one another (Bertalanffy, 1968; Bowen, 1978). Common subsystems include the dyad and the triad (Bowen, 1978). A **dyad** consists of two family members who interact in a unique way, and a **triad** is a close relationship between three family members. These basic components interact with one another in regular, predictable patterns to create subsystems within the larger family system.

Boundaries between two or more individuals in a family can be healthy, enmeshed, or disengaged (Minuchin, 1974; Olson, 2011). **Healthy boundaries** are achieved when individuals within the system are sufficiently attached to one another and can reach out to one another for support and guidance (Bowen, 1978). Similarly, though, individuals with healthy boundaries are able to separate themselves from their family members to gain a sense of independence and autonomy when appropriate. Individuals with **enmeshed boundaries** are overly invested in one another and have difficulty making decisions for themselves, taking responsibility for their own actions, and holding others accountable. Individuals with **disengaged boundaries** are not able to make meaningful connections with their family members and therefore lack the guidance and support that all people require.

Healthy and supportive families are able to adapt to change and celebrate the positive development of all family members (Minuchin, 1974). In fact, difficult events such as an illness or divorce can actually promote healthy relationships and development within the family if members are able to support one another and adapt to change as a system working together. It is especially important to foster healthy boundaries in youth who are experiencing pivotal developmental milestones.

Role of the Counselor in Family Therapy

Some counselors may find family therapy to be intimidating. It can be more difficult to build a therapeutic relationship with an entire family as opposed to one or two clients. Family therapists should take care to avoid aligning with any one family member because counselors are charged with serving all members of the family and the system as a whole. As such, counselors must carefully monitor their words and behaviors to ensure each family member is treated equitably and engaged in the therapeutic process.

Each person in the family system will have his or her own thoughts, opinions, needs, and presenting problems. Family therapists are responsible for working to learn and understand the unique perspectives of each family member, and they are charged with identifying the interactions and communication patterns within the system. Counselors should work to identify and address any biases they might hold and acknowledge that an accurate understanding of the complex family dynamics will evolve over time. Initially, as is true with individual counseling, counselors should take time to focus on building the therapeutic relationship.

When implementing family therapy, counselors may need to take a more directive role with clients (Haley, 1963). Family therapists are responsible for managing several people at once, and sometimes it might be necessary to interrupt clients, be assertive in directing clients to complete specific activities or behaviors, and encourage family members to participate.

Counselors can assume the role of teacher in family therapy and educate the members about interactional patterns, communication patterns, feedback loops, and circular causality. Counselors should implement various activities in the exploratory phase of counseling to encourage participation of family members and create memorable learning experiences for the family. For example, counselors might ask each family member to write his or her name at the top of a paper. The family members can take turns passing the papers to the right and writing one descriptive word for the person whose name is at the top. When the papers have reached their original owners, each family member can share their reactions to the ways family members perceive them. This activity helps the counselor to observe family dynamics while helping clients to learn about themselves and others.

Clinical Toolbox 7.2

In the Pearson eText, click here to review a creative activity that can be used to help family members to explore systemic norms and values related to emotional expression.

Throughout the exploration process, counselors might uncover emotional responses from clients, and counselors will often need to serve as mediators to promote healthy emotional expression and support for one another. Family members might get into arguments, and counselors should diffuse situations through validation and immediacy, as well as help clients to develop healthier ways of resolving their differences. Counselors can even model healthy emotional responses and behaviors in session (e.g., responding in an empathic way when a client displays genuine emotion) so the clients can learn through various mediums.

Counselors who work with families often have to act as advocates to assist family members in understanding the importance of each family member's values and needs. At times, counselors might especially need to advocate for youth, who have limited power within the family system due to their status as children and because of their inability to fully care for themselves (Whitaker & Keith, 1981). Counselors should educate parents and caregivers about children's developmental levels and the unique needs of each youth within that particular family system.

Overall, counselors should intentionally build therapeutic relationships with each family member and the family system as a whole. The counselor enters the family system as a participant and an observer, influencing the family's future history and contributing to future interactional patterns (Goldenberg & Goldenberg, 2013). Counselors should model appropriate behaviors and communication patterns with clients, and counselors should work to help clients gain insight into their own needs and the needs of others in their family systems.

Counseling Process

Initially, it is important that counselors **join** or build the therapeutic relationship with the family (Minuchin & Fishman, 1981). As part of the informed consent process, it should be clearly stated that counselors who operate from a family systems perspective view the entire family as the identified client, and the identified family members must participate in therapy to create a sustainable change in the identified client.

Some family members might be hesitant to participate in counseling. Perhaps they fear the discomfort that may come with counseling. Or perhaps these family members might not believe in the effectiveness of family therapy and believe their time, energy, and resources will be wasted. To overcome resistance to family therapy, counselors should take plenty of time to explain how family therapy works, and they should be open and transparent about the ultimate goal of shifting the communication and interactional patterns of the family system as a whole. Counselors can also work to overcome any resistance within the family by pulling on clients' strengths and highlighting their desires to help and support the identified client (Satir, 1983).

During the informed consent process, counselors should address if and how diagnoses will be issued. Counselors who operate strictly from a family systems perspective might not believe it is appropriate to ascribe a *DSM-5* diagnosis for an individual youth because the presenting problems are viewed as resulting from the overarching interactions and communication patterns of the family system as a whole. Even though family therapists will not make one person's diagnosis the focus of counseling, most third-party payers require a diagnosis to reimburse for services (Eriksen & Kress, 2005), and a diagnosis can often be assigned to the identified client.

Counselors should explain that family therapy requires hard work and dedication from all members of the family system, yet they should also communicate to family members a sense of hope and excitement.

Counselors should take time to explain the number, length, general content, and structure of counseling sessions. At first, counselors will work to help family members gain insight into their own behaviors, needs, desires, values, and communication styles. In addition, each member of the family system will be encouraged to explore the ways in which other members affect their own experiences and interactional patterns. Finally, clients will be encouraged to explore and understand ways in which their behaviors affect other members of the family system in an ongoing, cyclical pattern. After this insight has been fostered, clients can be encouraged to enact quantitative changes in their behaviors, which will effectively shift the dynamic of the system.

The assessment process in family therapy begins at the initial meeting and is ongoing throughout the counseling process. Assessment in family therapy is incredibly complex, and counselors should approach this portion of family therapy with an open mind and awareness that the patterns and mechanisms of the family system will become clearer with each session spent. Counselors will watch for interactional patterns, communication patterns, feedback loops, dyadic and triadic units, and circular causalities to understand the mechanisms that create and sustain youth behaviors. Figure 7.3 lists informal assessment questions counselors might use as part of the preliminary assessment process, when they are first getting to know clients.

All counseling assessment interventions serve the dual function of promoting exploration and insight within the family unit and providing information for ongoing conceptualization. New understandings and information will unfold over time, and counselors are likely to find that some of their preconceived notions are untrue or inaccurate. For example, a sibling who initially appears to be innocent and helpful might eventually be seen as unconsciously or subtly manipulating the family interactional patterns for his or her own benefit. Counselors should be patient and allow the process to unfold naturally.

Genograms are an especially relevant and effective assessment tool for use with youth and their families. A **genogram** is a visual representation of the family system and the many dynamics that exist within it. Genograms are essentially drawings that map out the family's dynamic relationships, and these drawings are often used to highlight patterns that relate to the client's presenting problems. For example, a counselor conducting family therapy with an identified client who is depressed would ask the family to create a genogram that shows the various family relationships and highlight anyone in the family who also experiences depression. Counselors can use process questions to highlight family dynamics and help clients to gain insight into patterns that have persisted in their family system. Clients can then explore and reframe any unhelpful or outdated interactional patterns in hopes of fostering new healthier ways of interacting and coping.

A genogram depicts all members in the immediate family and relevant members in the extended family. Counselors and clients might choose to include extended family members who are especially close with the identified client or extended family members who have relevant characteristics (e.g., those who experience addiction, those who share similar values). Clients use symbols to map out characteristics that occur across the family. Counselors can ask process-related questions to help clients to explore the therapeutic value of simply creating the genogram and identify any patterns or insights that were uncovered in the process.

- Who is the most warm-hearted person in the family?
- Who is the toughest person in the family?
- Who in the family is most emotional?
- Who usually gets angry first?
- How does each member of the family show anger?
- How does each member of the family show sadness?
- How does each member of the family show happiness?
- Describe a typical Tuesday night in your house.
- Describe a typical Sunday morning in your house.
- Who do each of you turn to for support?
- What is the best part of being a member of this family?
- What is the toughest part of being a member of this family?

FIGURE 7.3 Informal Family Assessment Questions

Step One: Determine the purpose of making the genogram. It might serve as a general exploration of the family system, or it could include just the immediate family or a larger extension of the family. Depending on its focus, the genogram could concentrate on family history of mental health disorders, communication patterns, or boundary issues. Its use depends on the purpose.

Step Two: Explain the purpose of the genogram to the family. Indicate that the counselor and family will initially map out all family members. Then, specific themes will be applied (if relevant).

Step Three: Determine the symbols that will be used to represent various factors and dynamics. Some common genogram symbols include:

☐ = Male

◯ = Female

------ = Relationship

——— = Marriage

—⫻— = Divorce

✕ = Death (inside the circle or square)

△ = Family secret

- Every genogram has its own key with unique symbols.
- The birth date/year is typically written above each individual's symbol.
- Names can be added to genograms when space is available.
- Additional symbols should be created to support the specific purpose of the genogram. For example, "Dx" might be written above any person who had or has a mental health disorder, or a wavy line might be used to indicate a stressed relationship.

Materials: Large writing surface (e.g., poster board, whiteboard), writing utensil.

Directions
The counselor begins by explaining the purpose and process of the activity to the family. Then, the family works together to draw the immediate family members. Next, extended family members are drawn in as necessary to accomplish the goal of the genogram. Finally, special symbols and details are added.

Process Questions
1. What is it like to see your family drawn like this?
2. What patterns do you notice in the genogram?
3. What can you learn from this exercise?
4. How was it to do this activity together?
5. What would you like to do with this genogram?

FIGURE 7.4   Implementing a Genogram in Family Therapy

Figure 7.4 shows the steps involved in creating and implementing a genogram, and Figure 7.5 depicts an example of a genogram.

Counselors should take plenty of time to help the family to explore and learn about each other and themselves. The process of exploration is therapeutic in itself as family members demonstrate vulnerability and spend quality time with one another when sharing and exploring. Family members' efforts in counseling demonstrate their dedication to becoming part of a healthier and happier interactional system. In addition, the time spent in counseling affirms that each member of the family system is valued.

Family-Based Interventions

Counselors do not need to create an *either–or* dichotomy between individual and family modalities of counseling but can blend these modalities as they deem necessary. Having the freedom to alter these different interventions and modalities within and even between sessions can be helpful. Some general family-based

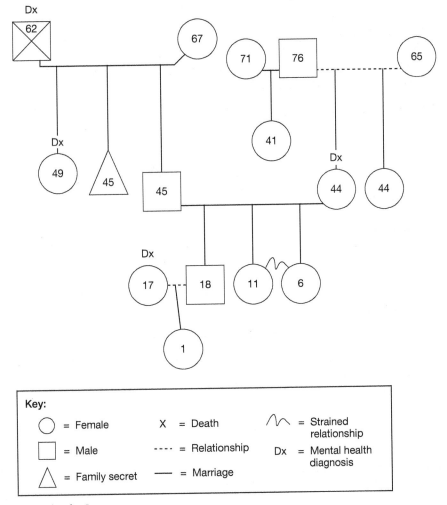

FIGURE 7.5   Example of a Genogram

interventions that can be especially useful with youth and their families are facilitating communication, promoting insight, reframing challenges and difficulties, addressing disengagement or enmeshment, altering feedback loops, and assigning directives and outside-of-session assignments. Each family-based intervention is discussed briefly in the following sections.

FACILITATING COMMUNICATION

Many families have difficulties managing boundaries (i.e., the separation of self and others) and maintaining clear parental roles. In addition, many parents engage in inconsistent parenting, which creates confusion and misunderstanding. In these times, family communication becomes essential in building family unity and consistency and in aiding families' ability to navigate the challenges of everyday life (McBride, 2008; Murdock, 2009). Therefore, awareness and communication skills building are vital and applicable to most family-related issues and struggles.

Simplistically, families need to listen to each other and address conflict in a clear and direct manner. They need to be open to sharing information and nurturing relationships within the family unit. Families can do this by (a) showing empathy and affection, (b) increasing discussions about everyday activities (e.g., name one positive and one negative thing that happened today), (c) attending to children's activities and extracurricular events, (d) establishing family rituals (e.g., eating one meal together, play board games every Tuesday night), and (e) being intentional about the verbal and nonverbal communication used toward each other (e.g., attempting to be kind, considerate, and caring; McBride, 2008; Murdock, 2009).

Furthermore, because one of the major assumptions of family therapy is that emotional and behavioral difficulties are primarily the result of disturbed family communication and interaction patterns, focusing on communication within the family tends to be the first course of action in most family-focused counseling approaches. **Family communication** is the verbal and nonverbal exchange of information (e.g., thoughts, feelings, values, beliefs) between family members, which involves not only talking but also listening to others. Communication is the means by which family members express their wants, desires, dreams, and concerns, attempting to express differences and admiration and even resolving unavoidable conflict.

Conversely, poor or dysfunctional communication can lead to an increase in conflict, a lack of bonding and intimacy, and the use of ineffective problem-solving skills (Murdock, 2009). In addition, dysfunctional communication often involves faulty communication patterns between family members that are unclear, incomplete, inaccurate, distorted, inappropriate, or indirect (Goldenberg & Goldenberg, 2013). For example, a parent may lecture a young child on the value of sharing but do so in a manner the child cannot comprehend. Similarly, in other situations, the use of yelling, blaming, name-calling, passive-aggressive statements (e.g., appearing angry, yet denying being angry), labeling a person as bad, using terms such as *always* or *never*, and engaging in the silent treatment can all lead to dysfunctional communication patterns. Conversely, when members within a family begin to understand each other more deeply, these same members begin to feel more validated and perceive that their feelings, thoughts, and beliefs are now being heard by other family members. Table 7.2 provides examples of family-based activities that can be used to increase family communication.

One of the most essential rules of communication is to be clear, direct, and explicit. Counselors will need to teach and model appropriate communication. Communicating properly will enable clients to better respond to counselors and each other. An emphasis can be placed on communicating thoughts, views, feelings, and needs.

Unfortunately, conflict exacerbates and even complicates existing difficulties in communicating. During these times of conflict, family members tend to react and respond to aspects they do not fully understand

Table 7.2 Family-Based Activities to Increase Communication

Activity	Description
Color Candy Crunch	Distribute a handful of small colored candies (e.g., M&Ms, Skittles) to each family member. Ask the family members to sort their candies by color. Each color corresponds to a question about the family. The question must be answered before the candy can be eaten. For example, yellow may be a word that describes the family, green might be ways the family has fun, red could be a concern or worry the person has about the family, and purple could be one thing that needs improvement in the family. Have one family member start by picking a color, answering the question, and eating one candy. Take turns until all candies are eaten. After all the candies are eaten, open up the discussion to the family to hear their reactions to some of the answers. Asking questions such as "What surprised you?" and "What did you learn?" and "What changes need to be made?" can facilitate discussion about family counseling goals.
52-Card Pick	For this activity, a standard 52-card deck and a bag of candy used to facilitate and increase family communication. In addition to the deck of cards, counselors should write family-focused questions on 10 to 15 index cards. Ask questions such as "What do you think needs change in the family?" "Who is helpful in times of need?" "How might family counseling help the family?" and "How will you feel if your family gets the help they need?" One at a time, each family member is asked to select a card from the top of the deck. If the card is an even number, then the family member answers the question. If the number is an odd number, then the family member asks someone else the question. When a family member picks a king, queen, or jack, he or she is to request a hug from another family member. Finally, when a family member picks an ace, he or she can pick a piece of candy from the bag.

or things they dislike about the individual family member, or they may even default to previous, unhelpful ways of interacting with each other (e.g., a child's defiant behavior leads to a parent's yelling). Often, instead of conveying and discussing the emotional impact and aspects of the interaction they are unsure of, the historical pattern of interacting emerges and can lead to the dehumanizing of family members. In such situations, empathy is replaced with anger, resentment, and frustration.

Even more than intense emotions, the inaccurate presentation of material can make communicating extremely difficult. For example, communication can be convoluted by disorganized thoughts, tangential comments, or even confusing or developmentally inappropriate content or logic. Although many family members may be unable to articulate their points succinctly and accurately, counselors can help clients to draw out the main feelings and meaning of what is being said within sessions. Doing this allows family members to feel better understood and helps them to articulate themselves more fully in present and future interactions. It also allows them to hear the more accurate intentions, meanings, and feelings of other family members. For example, an adolescent might assume that his mother does not want him to have any fun and her use of guilt as a form of discipline only pushes him to be later and later for his curfew. Conversely, a mother struggling to express her worry about her son's whereabouts (e.g., car accident), her inability to manage her own anxiety (e.g., pacing, perseverating), and even her pestering, all attempts to squash her fears, could be translated by a counselor to better communicate her true feelings and concerns.

Clinical Toolbox 7.3

In the Pearson eText, click here to review a summary of fair communication rules for families to use when dealing with conflict.

In many family situations, counselors will need to compensate for weak, underdeveloped, or nonexistent communication skills. For example, if Dad is the dominant figure in the household and he does most of the talking, a counselor may need to compensate by directly asking other family members about their perceptions of the issues and the concerns that brought them into counseling (e.g., "How do you feel about the issue?" "How does it affect you?" "What do you think is causing the problem?" "Are there times it bothers you more?" "Are there times it bothers you less?"). In families that have patterns of dysfunctional communication such as talking over others and not listening attentively, especially if they are unaware of these patterns, the counselor will need to make these implicit behaviors more explicit to all family members. For example, if family members do not listen to each other and frequently attempt to talk over each other, a counselor may stop the interaction, point out this behavior, and ask each member to discuss what he or she is feeling and thinking during the derailing of this conversation, as well as how he or she conceptualizes what is going on and being said at that moment.

Clinical Toolbox 7.4

In the Pearson eText, click here to review a psychoeducation and role-play activity that can be used to teach families how to make more positive requests of other family members and thus increase healthy communication.

Counselors who work with younger children might help them to improve their own communication skills, especially their listening skills. Ultimately, better listening skills will enhance the parent–child relationship. Listening skills are also vital to the child's ability to understand expectations and effectively communicate with adults. Younger children may benefit from learning how to pay attention to the person speaking and listen for "clues" that signal when it is time to listen, and they benefit from asking questions if something does not make sense. Having parents play games with their child such as *Simon Says*; *Red Light Green Light*; or *I Spy* can teach children to listen more intently and ask questions when they become confused about content. Counselors can help to accomplish this by instructing parents on how to *notice*, *catch*, *interpret*, and *alter* aspects of the parent–child interactions as a way of teaching younger children about the connection of the delivery of requests, the needs driving the request, and the most effective way to ask for what the child wants. To illuminate these concepts, they will be applied in an example of a child saying to a mother "Give me some cereal, I'm hungry." A parent might:

- *Notice:* I noticed that you didn't say "please" when you asked for your cereal this morning;
- *Catch:* I've heard you say "please" in the past, and I really feel good about helping you when you are polite and say "please";
- *Interpret:* I know you are really hungry and in a hurry to get the day started, but I don't want to help you when you are rude to me because it hurts my feelings; and
- *Alter:* What if you were to try this again? How might you ask me for help?

Counselors can help parents and youth to learn the skills they need to encourage healthy parent–child interactions and subsequently maximize family communication.

In other family situations, excessive venting can become an area of concern for counselors wanting to cultivate an increase in family communication. Excessive venting—by parents or youth—can distract and even derail family counseling goals. Blaming and excessive complaining can actually buffer and impede change attempts. Practically speaking, counselors may want to consider limiting parents who do this to only 5 minutes of venting per session before redirecting them to family therapy goals (Tuerk, McCart, & Henggeler, 2012).

Another issue that can thwart family communication is patterns of behavior that involve silencing or negating other family members. An example of this type of behavior is excessive interrupting of all or even certain family members. Often, this silencing can be directed by a parent toward a child. Counselors may need to establish rules such as allowing everyone to complete their thoughts before allowing another to talk, regardless of their position within the family (e.g., parent, grandparent, child, sibling). Counselors should be aware that some family members chronically interrupt as a way to protective themselves (e.g., "If I do not interrupt the speaker, he or she will continue to hurt me with his or her words"), whereas others may do it intentionally to derail further discussion of a topic (e.g., "If I monopolize these conversations, others may concede"). Furthermore, counselors can facilitate healthy communication processes by making these implicit patterns explicit and not allowing family members to continue to interrupt others or monopolize the conversation.

Ultimately, counselors need to inquire and facilitate discussions that pull out every family member's perspective on the presenting situations, family structure, and boundaries within the family. Although many family members will not know how other members think and/or feel about any one issue or topic, this new level of awareness can often promote an increase in curiosity, thus leading to an increased desire to communicate and engage other family members (Shapiro, 2015). Counselors can increase family communication by helping the family to increase the frequency with which they have positive interactions; use clear and direct communication; pay closer attention to verbal and nonverbal communication; enhance their ability to be active listeners; and develop positive attitudes toward all family members (Goldenberg & Goldenberg, 2013).

PROMOTING INSIGHT

Facilitating communication is often not enough to lead families to a higher level of functioning. As such, counselors are required to identify and help change the systemic processes occurring within the family system. Family therapists attempt to increase individuals' insight into their family system dynamics—in other words, family therapy helps family members to understand their family system and how each family member functions and operates within the family system (Williams, Edwards, Chamow, & Grauf-Grounds, 2009). The idea is that as insight increases, more effective behaviors and more adaptive patterns of interactions will emerge. Some family theorists believe insight is more critical than behavior change (e.g., Ackerman, 1958), whereas others argue that behavior change is more important than insight (e.g., White & Epston, 1990). Ultimately, most families respond best to a blended approach that involves facilitating family members' insights and behavior changes (Murdock, 2009).

Simplistically speaking, increasing systemic insight is making the implicit explicit, especially concerning family patterns and rules (Shapiro, 2015). Often, the logical content and the emotions involved in relationships get tangled, making communication and insight difficult (Shapiro, 2015). In addition, resentment may build, making it more difficult to follow the logical content of a contentious request or argument.

For example, a parent presents a reasonable expectation for her child but does so in an agitated and bitter way because of the child's previous noncompliant behaviors; thus, the child reacts emotionally to the logical but bitter-laden request. In this situation, the child is angry and responds with emotion, thus missing the logical aspect of the request because of the parent's delivery; in turn, the child's negative response escalates the mother.

To facilitate insight into the family system, counselors may need to point out that being right and rational is not processed well by someone who feels disrespected and belittled (Shapiro, 2015). Interaction patterns occur over time; yet, in many cases, they are picked up where the conflict last ended. Counselors should consider that if an individual's behaviors seem unreasonable and unexplainable within the current situation or in response to another family member's actions, the individual may be reacting to some past stimuli or encounter that may need to be explored before dealing with the current situation (Shapiro, 2015). Promoting exploration to facilitate insight into the family system is helpful in fully understanding current systemic interactions.

Exposing interaction and communication patterns within the family can also be accomplished through the use of circular questions (Patterson et al., 2009). **Circular questioning** is a family therapy technique used to gather more information and introduce new information and awareness into the family system. By asking all members about their perceptions of their relationships and differences among family members, circular questioning enhances the development of a more explicit family structure and thus an increased awareness of the nature of each relationship within the family can be revealed (Patterson et al., 2009). As an example, if an adolescent is chronically truant from school, circular questions a counselor might ask family members are as follows: "Who is usually the first to find out about Billy skipping school?" "What happens within the family after Billy is caught skipping school?" "How does Billy act when he does not skip school?" "What is happening in the family before Billy decides to skip school?" and "Can anyone predict when Billy might skip school?" These types of questions may lead to the realization that Billy skips school more frequently after his mother fights with his stepfather. Circular questions can increase family members' awareness not only about the process of the presenting issue but also how family interactions and behaviors can maintain, exacerbate, or even hinder the presenting issue.

More specifically, circular questions highlight perceptions and perspectives of individuals on their relationships (e.g., How do your parents interact and relate to you?), rank-order responses (e.g., Who is most upset about this divorce?), differences over time (e.g., How has the behavior changed during the separation and after the divorce?), and indirect information (e.g., Because your husband is not here, how would he talk about parenting challenges?; Patterson et al., 2009). Counselors must assume a position of curiosity, attempting to aid individuals in revealing and processing who and what needs to change while considering family members' interconnectedness with each other and with the issues being discussed.

REFRAMING CHALLENGES OR DIFFICULTIES

Family members can become entrenched in negatively viewing—and even demonizing—certain events or other family members' behaviors, actions, and/or intentions. Counselors will often need to assist family members in the process of **reframing** or aiding individuals in their reinterpretation of events and/or others' actions and/or intentions (Minuchin & Fishman, 1981). Counselors should consider using reframing when existing interpretations of family members' behaviors are inaccurate, incomplete, maladaptive, or unfairly blaming of another family member. The goal of reframing is to assist family members in changing their views of each other so their thinking is more positive and adaptive (Watzlawick, Weakland, & Fisch, 1974). For example, a father may erroneously conceptualize an action from his daughter as being deliberately cruel and selfish. A counselor might challenge the father to consider his daughter's behaviors in a new light, potentially as an inability to manage and/or select effective ways for dealing with her painful emotions. Ultimately, a counselor invites the father to assume another perspective characterized by more curiosity, empathy, and understanding. If not addressed, patterns of repeating disrespectful, cruel behaviors, and/or criticism are often continually followed by the person countering with similar behaviors that further entrench the unproductive dynamics.

Counselors can produce reframes by adhering to these three stages: (a) validate the perspective and view of the family member, (b) provide an alternative perspective that places behavior in a more adaptive or positive light, and (c) assess the level of agreement with the reframe (Tuerk et al., 2012). For example, consider an adolescent who believes her mother is overly controlling and does not provide adequate love and affection, and her mother has negative views about her daughter's lifestyle (e.g., clothing, tattoos and piercings, friend selection). A counselor's response for each reframing stage is provided:

- **Stage 1—Validate Their Perspectives**
  - *(To Daughter)* "I hear what you are saying. From what you have been saying, your mother ridicules your decisions and tries to control your future decisions. You feel like she doesn't really care about you and that she is more worried about how your decisions reflect on her parenting."
  - *(To Mother)* "I also see your point. You have tried to provide her with a good compass and the decisions she has made recently have been worrying you. You think some of her decisions are intentional and you feel hurt."

- **Stage 2—Provide an Alternative**
  - *(To Daughter)* "I wonder if your mother's behaviors are actually ways for you to see just how much she really loves you. I wonder if someone who really didn't care would make this type of effort. Maybe they would just say whatever you want and not provide you any oversight."
  - *(To Mother)* "I wonder if her piercings, tattoos, and friends have less to do with you and more to do with her trying to assert her independence and forge her own identity. I've also been wondering about what it would be like if we focused on some other considerations—like how she has not self-injured in months and how she is now attending school again."

- **Stage 3—Assess for Agreement**
  - *(To Both)* "What do you think about these ideas I presented, could this be another way to look at what is going on here? What would that be like for you to think of things in this new way?"

Reframing does not attempt to dispute or deny the facts of a situation or an encounter; rather, counselors can use this technique to assist family members in conceptualizing the undesirable behavior of another family member while maintaining a more positive or even neutral perception of that individual as a person. For example, a son's excessive crying may be reframed as his best attempt to get his father's undivided attention.

Central to most reframes is the assumption that individuals do not want to hurt others or be troublesome. Ultimately, reframes need to identify and conceptualize an aspect of a family member that has not been previously considered or has not been fully understood. In many situations, family members may have good intentions, but misjudgments, lack of psychosocial skills, or disruptive emotions may produce negative behaviors. Counselors will need to continually work with family members to build empathy and thus reduce anger and frustration.

ADDRESSING DISENGAGEMENT AND ENMESHMENT

In families, **boundaries**—or the unwritten ground rules of how family members distinguish self from others—are the established ways family members, subsystems (e.g., parental, siblings), and individuals interact and get their individual and collective needs met (Minuchin & Fishman, 1981). Boundaries, in a sense, can be considered on a continuum of closeness and autonomy with the ideal balance being in the middle of the continuum, attempting to have both the needs for closeness and autonomy met. Frequently, counselors will see the extreme ends of this continuum—enmeshed and disengaged families (see Figure 7.6).

A term that must be defined to fully understand family dynamics and boundaries is *differentiation of the self*. **Differentiation of the self** is conceptualized as one's ability to separate his or her own intellectual and emotional functioning from that of family members (Bowen, 1978). Bowen theorized that this development of the self was not confined to the individual but emerged more fully within the context of family. He further contended that therapy is less about uncovering family communication patterns and more about

[---Enmeshed ------------------------- Balanced ------------------------- Disengaged ---]

FIGURE 7.6 Family Boundaries Continuum

differentiation of the self from other family members (Bowen, 1978). For example, less differentiated individuals—or those who have a greater sense of **fusion** (i.e., too much togetherness) with other members—attempt to gain the approval of others within the family, thus maintaining a pseudo or pretend sense of self. Simplistically, these individuals struggle to differentiate between their own thoughts and feelings and the thoughts and feelings of other family members. Conversely, more differentiated individuals can concurrently hold defined beliefs, values, and convictions while also recognizing their own need and dependence on other members of the family (Bowen, 1978). Therefore, the goal of family therapy—from this family perspective—is to increase differentiation of all family members.

Disengagement and enmeshment can be understood on a similar continuum with enmeshed closeness on one side and total autonomy or disengagement on the other side. **Enmeshment** can be understood as inappropriate, boundary-violating closeness in which family members are emotionally overreactive to one another (Minuchin, 1974). Conversely, **disengagement** occurs when there is too much emotional distance between family members. In an enmeshed family, a parent may be upset and take it personally if a child does not finish her dinner; in a disengaged family, a parent may not even make a child dinner or be concerned if the child does not eat (Minuchin, 1974). Enmeshed families are often characterized by:

- guilt used to control or motivate behaviors;
- family members who do not share family matters with others outside the family;
- a lack of separation between members on thoughts, feeling, and ideas (children may remain enmeshed with their parents into adulthood);
- indoctrination of children to what they *should* think and feel;
- members speaking for each other; and
- a fear that if one becomes too different, they will run the risk of being cut off from the family.

Conversely, disengaged families are often characterized by:

- a lack of consistent engagement or experiences with some or all family members;
- a pervasive sense that unrequested permission to do as one pleases is always available;
- a tendency to seek guidance and support from those outside the family;
- family members who seek isolation and privacy more than being available for other members;
- a fear of intimacy rooted in rejection, discomfort with closeness, fear of losing oneself within relationships, and fear of ridicule; and
- rarely sharing opinions, feelings, and thoughts, especially by parents to their children.

When working with enmeshed families, counselors can be helpful by aiming to enhance insight and awareness around family members' discomfort with separation. When working with disengaged families, counselors can aid family members in exploring what it is that feels threatening about closeness and reliance on other members of the family. In both enmeshed and disengaged families, the goal is to create open discussion and conscious thought so each type of family will gravitate toward the middle of the continuum and achieve balance (Shapiro, 2015).

Counselors can highlight the way of being in the family that has been overemphasized, while deciphering and encouraging the ideal that has been underemphasized. Ultimately, counselors will need to strike a balance between family members' need for autonomy and their need to feel a sense of belonging and connectedness. Counselors will need to aid family members in realizing that moving back and forth between autonomy and connectedness can enhance both aspects of this continuum (e.g., independence and togetherness) for the individual and the family, ultimately allowing children the security and strength they need to venture into the external world.

ALTERING FEEDBACK LOOPS

As previously mentioned, families seek to maintain their customary organization and functioning over time and tend to resist change. Family therapists use the concept of **homeostasis** to explain that families have an inherent pull to maintain a sense of equilibrium or balance or to keep the status quo. If homeostasis is disrupted, then the rules, interactions, and dynamics of the family will need to be altered to maintain the family's sense of balance (Goldenberg & Goldenberg, 2013; Minuchin & Fishman, 1981).

Homeostasis can be healthy or unhealthy, and counselors will be able to observe a family system's natural way of being as the therapeutic relationship builds. For example, over time, a counselor might learn that the father in a family tends to be disengaged from the child subsystem. He asks his children to complete their homework or daily chores when they get home from school. The children might have learned through past experiences that there will be no set consequences if they ignore their father's demands, so they typically make excuses, act uncontrollably, and fight with each other instead of doing their chores. After a while, the father typically becomes so exhausted and frustrated that he screams at the children to do their chores. This is their cue to stop playing around and actually do their work because they have learned in the past that consequences occur when dad gets mad. This pattern might not be the best way to manage the demands of a household; however, over time, circular causation has created this pattern of homeostasis within the family system.

To understand the motivation for youth behaviors, family therapists believe the communication patterns and their consequences within a particular family system must be understood and changed. A **negative feedback loop** is a method of communicating and interacting that creates a pattern of moving away from homeostasis and then quickly returning back to homeostasis (Bertalanffy, 1968). Consider the following example of this concept: A thermostat controls the heating and cooling in a home. The thermostat is set at 72 degrees, which is the homeostasis for that home. When the temperature drops below 72 degrees, the thermostat commands the heat to come on to bring the temperature back to homeostasis. Also, when the temperature rises above homeostasis, the thermostat signals the air conditioning to come on and bring the home back to 72 degrees.

Consider the following family therapy example of a negative feedback loop: A family seems to function in a constant state of chaos (e.g., neighbors in and out of the house, dog chewing things up). If household dynamics begin to get repetitive or calm, a youth might misbehave to bring the dynamics back into a heightened state of activity and put the focus on her. Chaos feels comfortable and familiar to the youth, and it serves the function of keeping the typically disengaged parents—who rarely talk and who the child has heard discussing divorce—engage with each other as she becomes the focus. This is called a negative feedback loop because family members' behaviors function to bring families back into their same, familiar patterns. The term *negative* does not indicate that behaviors are healthy or unhealthy; rather, it indicates that a stressor or unnatural process is being removed from the system. The goal of counseling when a negative feedback loop is present is to promote a healthy state of homeostasis.

Families who start with a healthy homeostasis use negative feedback loops in supportive, growth-oriented ways. For example, a youth might typically be independent when getting home from school, completing his or her assigned homework and chores while Mom prepares dinner. The youth might begin to struggle in school, and Mom might have to start spending extra time doing homework with the youth after school (a slight shift away from homeostasis). Eventually, the youth will overcome the academic struggle, and the family dynamics will return to a state similar to the previous homeostasis. The overall system will be strengthened by the two individuals joining together to overcome the system disruption in a healthy way.

Families with an unhealthy homeostasis experience negative feedback loops that do not allow for positive growth of its members. For example, a youth might want to go to college (which would be a shift away from previously established homeostasis), but a parent might discourage the youth so he or she stays close to home. Thus, negative feedback loops can be helpful or unhelpful based on the original state of homeostasis, and the negative pattern refers to a disruption in homeostasis and family members' behaviors that facilitate a return to homeostasis.

A **positive feedback loop** facilitates a process of change and forward movement in a family. The term *positive* does not have an evaluative component; the communication pattern is observed regardless of whether family behaviors are helpful or unhelpful. Essentially, a positive feedback loop indicates that the communication pattern between two or more family members results in movement further and further away from homeostasis. Eventually, though, because this is a feedback loop, some external force often enters the picture and brings the family back to homeostasis. The external force might be counseling interventions or a distraction that is bigger than the feedback loop itself (e.g., a death in the family, a community tragedy).

Just as in a negative feedback loop, the positive feedback loop can be healthy or unhealthy. As an example of a healthy positive feedback loop, imagine a family system that is relatively docile and inactive. Let's say a mother and her daughter decide to train for a 5K together, and as a result both members of the subsystem motivate each other to become more physically active each day. With every word of encouragement and hour spent training, the family moves further away from the previous state of homeostasis. After the race, this positive feedback loop might naturally decline, with family dynamics returning to a state of homeostasis. Alternatively, the positive feedback loop might even out, and a more interactive dynamic might become the family's new homeostasis.

A positive feedback loop can also move families away from homeostasis in unhelpful ways. For example, a mother who typically has a good relationship with her daughter might yell at the daughter in a moment of frustration, and the daughter might yell back. As a result, the daughter might get grounded. These incidents are moving the family away from a previously healthy homeostasis. The next day, the youth harbors resentment toward her mother and does not come home from school. Mom retaliates by giving away the new clothes she recently bought for her daughter. This positive feedback loop can potentially become destructive, and the turbulent relationship between the mother and daughter will undoubtedly affect the functioning of the entire family system.

Counselors can make feedback loops explicit and explain how difficulties are being maintained, how new behaviors can alter these feedback loops, and how new self-reinforcing solutions can remedy the family's presenting problems. In some situations, counselors might empower family members to write up and sign feedback loop contracts. These contracts might outline each family member's contribution as he or she moves forward in altering the dysfunctional feedback loops.

Introduction of new elements into the family's patterns of behaviors and communication can often be enough to disrupt the normalcy and habitual sequence of family behavioral patterns of interacting. Family therapists often engage in the use of **indirect directives**—or directives made by counselors whereby they anticipate clients will not follow completely but will likely resist—thus creating more spontaneous responses or movements that are opposite the counselors' directives (Haley, 1987). For example, when positive change does occur, a counselor using an indirect directive might say "It seems like progress is occurring too quickly—maybe you all need to slow this process down a bit." Such a statement not only affirms that a family is in charge of the change process and capable of making changes but also that the family can ultimately dictate the rate and speed of these changes.

ASSIGNING DIRECTIVES AND OUTSIDE-OF-SESSION ASSIGNMENTS

A central aspect of family therapy is directing family members to engage in new patterns of behaviors. Family therapists often invite clients to take part in behavioral experiments as a means of helping them to understand their maladaptive ways of interacting and to bring about changes to maladaptive **intergenerational patterns** (i.e., patterns of interacting that are shared and transmitted throughout generations of a family; Haley, 1963; Minuchin & Fishman, 1981). These directives are intended to help family members go beyond their own limitations to experience new ways of engaging family members. The rationale behind this technique is that the new behaviors or experiences can often produce positive change by disrupting the older engrained ways of interacting. Ideally, these behaviors become part of the family's new way of being and interacting. Directives or assignments might involve inviting family members to engage others in unfamiliar ways. For example, someone who is known to be a know-it-all might ask other family members questions, or an authoritarian parent might be asked to discuss her softer side or vulnerabilities with her children. Someone known to be a talker in the family might be asked to practice carefully listening to other family members.

A commonly used directive within family therapy is a paradoxical injunction. **Paradoxical injunctions** (Haley, 1963, 1996) are directives from the counselor that initially appear to be opposed to the goals of counseling. A counselor may "prescribe the problem" for a certain day and time with the explanation that the client needs to practice the problem a bit more before reducing it. For example, assigning a specific time to be anxious (Monday from 8:00 to 9:00 a.m.) or scheduling arguments for a specific time and place (e.g., Wednesday at 7:00 p.m. in the bathroom). The intention is not to reenact the problem but rather to disrupt individuals' attempts to resolve it. In addition, if clients do not comply with these interventions, then the problem can often be resolved because the prescribed behavior did not occur. Paradoxical injunctions can often include asking family members to interact or argue in a new place (e.g., move arguments to the bathroom if fighting normally occurs in the kitchen), interacting in a different way (e.g., move from *you* statements to *I* statements), change something about the process (e.g., stop fighting and change into formal clothing to argue), or change the physical environment in some way (e.g., play jazz music in the background; Becvar & Becvar, 2012).

In addition, one specific paradoxical directive that is commonly used in family therapy is the use of a **pretend directive**. This directive involves the symptomology or the presenting problem being prescribed within the counseling session—or within some other structured context—to be acted out or role-played by the individual or family (Madanes, 1981). For example, a counselor working with an adolescent who is anxious could prescribe that he pretends to be anxious from 12:00 to 1:00 p.m. each day and then go on with his normal daily routine. This process of pretending to have or experience the symptom makes individuals more aware of the need their behavior serves (e.g., attention, distraction) and their ability to control the behavior (Becvar & Becvar, 2012).

As previously stated, these directives can be implemented within or outside sessions (Dattilio, 2002, 2010). In-session directives allow counselors to not only evaluate the individual's ability to perform the new behavior but also to monitor their responses and reactions, thus enabling counselors to provide individuals with immediate feedback. Conversely, out-of-session assignments occur in a natural setting and may be more organic. Examples of out-of-session assignments include asking family members to engage in a pleasant activity during the week to strengthen their family relationships, alter their usual interactions or routine patterns, discover new aspects of other family members, and find new ways of relating to each other that can produce sustaining changes in family interaction patterns (Murdock, 2009; Shapiro, 2015; Wagner, 2008).

In addition to enhancing family interactions, outside-of-session assignments can also include practicing learned techniques from in-session work, such as assertiveness, active listening skills, and I-statements; completing assigned readings; and performing activities to enhance documenting or processing between-session symptomology and/or family interactions (e.g., journaling, behavioral logs; Goldenberg & Goldenberg, 2013). It can be especially helpful for counselors to collaborate with school personnel to determine out-of-session assignments that support work the youth is doing in schools. In Table 7.3, examples of strength-based activities that can be used to develop family cohesion are provided.

Table 7.3	Strength-Based Outside-of-Session Family Assignments
Assignment	**Descriptions**
Create a family mission statement	Ask the family to select a time outside of session to construct a mission statement. The counselor can develop questions that will guide the family's process. Such questions might include the following: "What is the purpose of our family?" "When are we at our best?" "When are we at our worst?" "What do we love to do together?" "How can we better serve each other?" "What can we improve on?" "What kind of family do we want?" "What are the values that we believe are important?" Using the responses to these questions, ask the family to construct a three- to four-sentence mission statement that can be shared in the next family therapy session. This mission statement could be displayed in a central location in the home as a reminder of the family's focus.
Construct a coat of arms	Ask the family to construct a coat of arms (a family shield). This coat of arms should be divided into five sections: members of the family, favorite family activities and hobbies, strengths of the family, positive family accomplishments, and events that have positively defined or affected the family. These sections can be displayed through text, pictures, and/or drawings. Ask each family member to assist in the construction of this coat of arms.
Fill a bucket	Ask the family to engage in a bucket-filling activity. Using the metaphor of filling up each other's invisible buckets with good and positive actions, ask members to construct a list of actions that can be used to fill each other's buckets. For example, family members could list smiling at each other, providing hugs, giving compliments, sharing toys with siblings, helping with chores around the house, using manners at mealtimes, or making requests with kind words and in a calm voice. Put this list in a prominent place in the home and have members who experience or witness these acts make marks next to the family members' names—listed on the piece of paper— who fill other members' buckets.

Summary

Family therapy involves working collaboratively with youth, parents, siblings, and extended family members, as needed. The focus of family therapy is on the intricate pattern of interactions and relationships that occur on an ongoing basis between all members of the family system.

In this chapter, the core concepts of family therapy were explored. Specifically, the reciprocal influence family members have within the family system was discussed, along with concepts related to family boundaries. Healthy boundaries can be observed when each member of the family system can reach out to one another for support while maintaining a unique sense of identity and independence. Healthy families are flexible and support one another in achieving their goals. Unhealthy family boundaries present as enmeshment (i.e., certain members of the system are highly dependent on one another) or disengagement (i.e., family members do not turn toward each other in times of need).

Counselors can assist family members in creating healthy boundaries and better ways of communicating that may include more clear and explicit boundaries with each other. In family therapy, counselors tend to be more directive and work to form a therapeutic relationship with every member of the family. Counselors may temporarily join with the family as a member of the system, and the assessment process begins at the first meeting and spans the length of the family therapy relationship. The assessment process can include formal and informal assessments, creation of various genograms, and tracking and exploring family feedback loops.

The primary goals of family therapy include facilitating helpful and supportive verbal and nonverbal communication patterns between all members of the family, promoting systemwide insight, and addressing any unhealthy boundaries within the family system. Overall, family therapy is a complex, ongoing engagement in which all family members, including the counselor, work to openly and honestly address the needs of the family system.

MyLab Counseling: Counseling Children and Adolescents

Try the Topic 5 Assignments: *Theoretical Foundations for Counseling Youth and Their Families.*

CHAPTER **8**

The Use of Play and Creative Arts in Counseling

Imagination, resiliency, and a zest for life are key strengths that all youth naturally possess, and play and creative arts counseling approaches pull on these strengths. Imagination can facilitate the counseling process, and the integration of both play and creativity are essential when counseling youth. Both play and creative arts counseling are rooted in empirically supported mental health theories, and these interventions are effective with a broad range of clients (Gladding, 2011; Lin & Bratton, 2015; Ray, Armstrong, Balkin, & Jayne, 2015). The interventions discussed in this chapter are developmentally appropriate for counseling with youth; however, play and creative arts interventions should be adjusted according to clients' verbal, physical, emotional, and cognitive abilities, and interests.

Counselors are ethically obligated to communicate with clients in developmentally appropriate ways (American Counseling Association [ACA], 2014, Section A.2.c.), and because many play and creative arts techniques are nonverbal in nature, they can be effective even if clients have minimal verbal skills (Packman & Bratton, 2003). In Table 8.1 an overview of play/creative arts approaches and the associated therapeutic

Table 8.1 Goals of Play and Creative Counseling

Play/Creative Medium	Examples of Associated Goals
Pretend/Imaginative play	• Enables youth to express underlying thoughts • Helps youth to build self-concepts and express emotional issues • Helps youth to improve communication skills • Helps youth to develop new behaviors by acting out different roles • Helps youth to act out ideas, fears, and fantasies by taking on imaginary roles
Sand ray	• Helps youth to explore specific ideas and events in their lives • Helps youth to explore their fantasies and ideas • Gives youth a sense of power over their stories • Helps youth to articulate ideas and solutions • Helps youth to gain a cognitive understanding of elements in their lives
Games	• Helps youth to explore strengths and weaknesses • Helps youth to practice communication skills • Enhances collaboration and cooperation skills • Helps youth to practice problem-solving and decision-making skills • Helps youth to practice appropriate responses to discouragement and success
Drawing/Painting	• Allows for expression of emotion and thoughts • Enables youth to tell their stories on their terms • Helps youth to express emotions through symbolic representation • Gives youth a sense of power over their ideas and emotions • Helps youth to gain a sense of mastery over events in their lives

Table 8.1	(Continued)
Play/Creative Medium	**Examples of Associated Goals**
Clay	• Enables youth to tell their stories using clay to illustrate specific events • Helps youth to recognize thoughts and emotions by creating specific events • Gives youth an opportunity to act out their stories by creating representations of it • Helps youth to act out their emotions physically (e.g., pounding on the clay, smoothing out the clay) • Helps youth to gain insight on representation and symbolism

goals are provided. Table 8.2 includes an abbreviated list of materials counselors might have available when using creativity and play in session. Additional information on creative and play interventions, associated goals, and needed materials will be provided throughout this chapter.

Play therapy is effective in addressing a wide range of behavioral difficulties in youth (Henggeler & Schaeffer, 2010; Ray et al., 2015). Specific play approaches have been developed for use with youth who have certain disorders or presenting issues. For example, youth with autism spectrum disorder can benefit from general play therapy interventions, but a focused play-based approach called *Floortime* is an optimal approach with this population (Ware Balch & Ray, 2015).

Sometimes counselors will need to implement additional, specific treatment approaches along with play-based interventions to address a youth's holistic needs. For example, a young person who has attention-deficit/hyperactivity disorder might benefit from medication management and cognitive behavioral interventions in addition to child-centered play therapy (Döpfner, Metternich-Kaizman, Schürmann, Rademacher, & Breuer, 2015; Naderi, Heidarie, Bouron, & Asgari, 2010). Overall, play-based and creative interventions are appropriate for a wide range of clients, and counselors should use their knowledge of the client's context and needs to determine the best course of action for each unique individual.

Table 8.2	Toys and Materials That Can Be Used in Play and Creative Counseling
Play/Creative Medium	**Toys and Materials**
Pretend Play	Small dolls (e.g., Barbie dolls, Polly Pocket), dollhouses, stuffed animals, toy cars, race tracks, dress-up clothes, baby dolls, building blocks (e.g., Legos), hats and masks, toy telephones, paper money, cash registers, and puppets
Sand Tray	Small toys such as plastic trees, planes, boats, people and superhero figurines, small toy animals, toy blocks, small toy cars, rocks, stones, pebbles, marbles, and small mirrors
Drawing/Painting	White and colored paper, pencils, pens, markers, paint, crayons, brushes, aprons, tape, glue, scissors, yarn, string, fabric, glitter, feathers, sequins, popsicle sticks, and plastic containers
Games	Games that involve motor skills, emotional regulation, and cognitive development, such as board games (e.g., *Operation*, *Mouse Trap*, *Hungry Hippo*) and strategy games (e.g., *Connect Four*, chess, card)
Clay	Blocks of clay, a groundsheet to control any messes, aprons, wire to cut the clay, sculpting tools, water, and paper
Sports	Baseballs, basketballs, soccer balls, jump ropes, footballs, Frisbees, tennis balls, Nerf balls, and ping pong equipment
Music/Technology	Electronic music and video players

SPECIALIZED CERTIFICATION AND REGISTRATION

Play therapy is a process through which children's natural play behaviors are used to support changes in their thoughts, feelings, and/or behaviors. The Association for Play Therapy (APT; 1997) defined play therapy as "The systematic use of a theoretical model to establish an interpersonal process wherein trained play therapists use the therapeutic powers of play to help clients to prevent or resolve psychosocial difficulties and achieve optimal growth and development" (p. 7). Counselors do not need to be registered **play therapists** to use therapeutic play techniques with youth, but they should not refer to themselves as *play therapist*s or suggest they conduct *play therapy* unless they have proper play therapy certification. Such certification suggests advanced training and adds a layer of expertise to one's counseling practice. That said, to maintain simplicity in this chapter, the terms *play therapy* and *play therapist* are used generically to refer to the use of play in counseling.

In addition to play therapy interventions, counselors can use creative arts in counseling to foster young people's growth and change processes. Creative arts counseling approaches involve various therapeutic interventions that engage clients in artistic ways and promote unique forms of self-exploration and self-expression (Gladding, 2011; Rosen & Atkins, 2014). *Creative arts therapy, expressive therapy,* or *expressive arts therapy* are terms that can be used by licensed mental health professionals who are not certified or licensed as art therapists to refer to the creative counseling work they do (Gladding, 2011; Rosen & Atkins, 2014). Mental health professionals can use creative arts in counseling without being certified, but additional training can be helpful because it facilitates and communicates expertise.

As is true with regard to the term *play therapist*, counselors should be cautious to avoid referring to themselves as **art therapists** unless they have received such certification and/or licensure (if applicable in one's state). The American Art Therapy Association (2013b) explained that **art therapy** is a "mental health profession in which clients, facilitated by the art therapist, use art media, the creative process, and the resulting artwork to explore their feelings, reconcile emotional conflicts, foster self-awareness, manage behavior and addictions, develop social skills, improve reality orientation, reduce anxiety, and increase self-esteem" (para. 1). In this chapter, the terms *creativity in counseling* and *creative arts in counseling* are used as umbrella terms to describe the use of artistic, creativity-focused therapeutic interventions.

Mental health professionals can become credentialed as play therapists and/or art therapists through a combination of education and supervised training. A master's degree in art therapy is needed to become an entry-level **Registered Art Therapist** (ATR). Art therapists can pursue additional education and training to advance to a **Board Certified Art Therapist** (ATR-BC) or an **Art Therapy Certified Supervisor** (ATCS). Individuals interested in becoming art therapists should visit www.arttherapy.org and www.atcb.org for more information.

Mental health professionals who already have a state-recognized license to engage in counseling and/or psychotherapy (e.g., counselors, social workers, psychologists, family therapists, art therapists) can become certified as play therapists to communicate their specialized knowledge and additional training in play therapy. Mental health professionals who are interested in seeking play therapy credentials should visit www.a4pt.org to learn more about becoming a **Registered Play Therapist** (RPT), **Registered Play Therapist–Supervisor** (RPT-S), and/or a **School Based–Registered Play Therapist** (SB-RPT).

Because of the importance of play and creativity when counseling youth, we examine both approaches in more depth in this chapter. The history and foundations of play and expressive arts in counseling are discussed, and attention is paid to the theoretical frameworks used to support the effectiveness of play and creative activities. In addition, specific techniques associated with the two approaches are provided.

PLAY THERAPY AND THE USE OF PLAY IN COUNSELING

Play therapy is a counseling approach in which the naturally occurring playful behaviors of young people are used to facilitate the counseling process and support client goals (APT, 2015). Play interventions can be used with clients of any age, but play techniques are often a primary vehicle for engaging in therapy with young clients ages 3 to 13 (Ray et al., 2015; Rye, 2010). Although play therapy uses the same natural play behaviors in which children engage on a daily basis, it is qualitatively different from regular play in that the play behaviors take on a therapeutic purpose that is not otherwise present.

Play is not only fun and engaging for youth, but it is an effective way to support desired mental health outcomes. More than 25 empirical studies showed that play therapy significantly helped youth to change their externalized behavior problems (e.g., hitting, vandalism) and their internalized behavior problems (e.g., social withdraw, somatic symptoms; Lin & Bratton, 2015; Ray et al., 2015). Play therapy also helped youth to achieve greater levels of self-efficacy and academic achievement (Ray et al., 2015).

Play therapy or play methods can be used—in one way or another—to address the needs of many youth. Sometimes it can be difficult for clients, families, and third-party payers to understand how play can be a therapeutic intervention. Figure 8.1 outlines some of the ways play therapy can be therapeutic.

Youth play behaviors generally occur spontaneously and allow for self-expression demonstrated through movements, actions, patterns, verbalizations, and nonverbal messages. Play behaviors are a youth's language, and toys are the words. Play therapy can be used to address a wide variety of presenting problems in youth, including:

- abuse and neglect;
- adjustment difficulties;
- anxiety/depression;
- attachment struggles;
- attentional challenges;
- behavioral problems;
- bullying;
- chronic illness in youth or family members;
- family transitions or struggles;
- fears or phobias;
- grief;
- parental mental health difficulties;

- Invites access to the creative unconscious
- Increases youth autonomy
- Facilitates catharsis
- Channels painful thoughts and feelings
- Facilitates congruence of thoughts, feelings, and behaviors
- Facilitates development of skill competency and proficiency
- Facilitates development of coping skills
- Defines self-imposed boundaries and encourages self-control
- Enhances critical and divergent thinking skills
- Enhances problem-solving skills
- Enhances interpersonal skills
- Facilitates a sense of personal identity
- Builds parental connections
- Facilitates healthy attachments
- Deepens emotional expression
- Enhances emotion regulation
- Facilitates exploration and insight
- Aids in learning more about oneself, others, and the world
- Encourages remembering and integrating traumatic events from a safe place
- Facilitates self-expression
- Facilitates stress relief
- Encourages healing via the therapeutic relationship
- Invites vicarious learning through counselor modeling
- Achieves other goals associated with specific play therapy theories and approaches

FIGURE 8.1 How Is Play Therapeutic?
Note: Degges-White & Davis (2011).

- school attendance problems;
- social skill deficits; and
- traumatic experiences. (Drewes & Schaefer, 2010; Kottman, 2001; Rye, 2010)

In play therapy, play behaviors are intentionally used to facilitate client expression of thoughts and feelings, encourage insight, develop problem-solving skills, and foster new, more adaptive behaviors.

Play Therapy: The Setting

Although play therapy can be used in both clinical and school settings, it is especially well suited for school-based interventions (Drewes & Schaefer, 2010). Counselors who use play therapy in the school setting will likely focus on the young person's mental health difficulties that are interfering with academic success, whereas clinically based counselors are more likely to address the young person's holistic mental health concerns. To address specific school-based concerns, counselors might choose nondirective play, which allows the client to create his or her own insights, or they might use a more directive approach. Both non-directive and directive play interventions are discussed in greater depth later in this chapter.

Counselors using play therapy in the school should keep in mind that youth likely need to return to class after session, so they should be given plenty of time to transition from play to class. To link the work done in session to the classroom, counselors can ask the youth how he or she will apply any new insights to the classroom (e.g., "You showed me today that you can count blocks and not throw them. That is exciting! How will this help you with Miss Suzie?"). Counselors can also ask the student what he or she expects to do on returning to class and what skills he or she will use to be successful. These approaches can also be useful for clinical counselors as they help youth to transition to their homes or other community settings after a session.

Counselors who choose to integrate play therapy techniques into their practice should intentionally set up a designated space for play therapy and for play therapy materials. This space can be located within the counselor's main office or in a separate playroom. There should be plenty of space so play materials can be used freely and stored in a well-organized fashion (Landreth, 2012). Effective play therapy rooms can be created using a limited amount of space, but larger rooms might be needed depending on the types of toys or objects provided.

The objects included in a play therapy room should be carefully selected to facilitate therapeutic play behaviors (Landreth, 2012). Counselors should take care to respect clients' cultural backgrounds when determining the most theoretically sound play therapy interventions for youth. For example, parents who value strict gender roles might request that a youth only play with gender-conforming toys (e.g., dolls for a girl, trucks for a boy). Counselors should validate and uphold the parents' wishes while advocating for clients' needs throughout the therapeutic process.

Toys should also be adjusted to accommodate youth's presenting concerns. For example, if a client has a fear of clowns, clowns may be removed from the therapy room so they do not distract from the natural play therapy process. Clowns might be added back into the playroom when—or if—they become therapeutically relevant or helpful.

Youth use toys as their words, so counselors should have available a wide variety of toys that convey respect for all types of diversity (e.g., ethnicity, gender, age, disability, physical appearance, religion). The types, sizes, textures, and colors of toys should also be varied to facilitate maximum exploration and client expression. The types of toys chosen might include feminine toys, masculine toys, big toys, small toys, scary toys, pretty toys, realistic toys, fantasy-based toys, old toys, new toys, figurines, dolls, and plush toys. This list only begins to cover the many toys that can contribute to creating a productive play therapy space. See Figure 8.2 for a more comprehensive list of items that may be useful in a play therapy room. Each room will be created based on the counselor's approach, client needs, and availability of resources.

Foundations of Play Therapy

Mental health professionals have used play therapeutically since the early 1900s (Homeyer & Morrison, 2008). Not long after Freud (1905/2011) developed his theory of psychoanalysis, play was used with youth as a form of free association. In a traditional use of free association, adults were guided to clear their minds

• Baby blankets	• Dollhouse	• Mop
• Baby bottles	• Dolls	• Musical instruments
• Baby dolls	• Dress-up clothes	• Paper rolls
• Balls	• Dustpan	• Play-Doh
• Bandaids	• Egg cartons	• Pretend makeup
• Barbies	• Empty food containers	• Pretend stove
• Binoculars	• Fake money	• Pretend televisions
• Blocks	• Fake telephone	• Puppets
• Boxes	• Fake television	• Purse/wallet
• Broom	• Fake tools	• Racetrack
• Cars	• Hats	• Rope
• Cash register	• Games	• Rubber sword
• Chalk	• Hairbrush	• Shelves
• Chalkboard	• Handcuffs	• Stuffed animals
• Cleaning items	• Hard animals	• Tarps
• Clocks	• Jars	• Telephone
• Costumes	• Jewelry	• Towels
• Cotton balls	• Legos	• Toy soldiers
• Craft sticks	• Magic wand	• Trinkets
• Darts	• Masks	• Trucks
• Dishes/silverware	• Medical kit	• Wood blocks
• Doll furniture	• Money	• Work bench

FIGURE 8.2   List of Possible Play Therapy Objects

and say aloud any words or thoughts that emerged. These words and thoughts were used to make meaning of dreams and facilitate other insights for clients. When applied to children, youth were encouraged to make any play behaviors as a form of free association, and these behaviors (as opposed to words) were used for interpretation and insight.

As the 20th century progressed, play interventions were viewed as intrinsically therapeutic, and almost all major mental health theories were adapted for use with youth through play (e.g., person-centered, cognitive behavioral, Gestalt; Landreth, 2012). The APT was formed late in the 20th century, and new play techniques and interventions have continued to emerge (APT, 2015). Overall, play therapy is regarded as an effective way to facilitate therapeutic growth through play behaviors and through nonverbal and verbal messages.

Play is a youth's natural language; it is fun, free, exciting, satisfying, creative, and engaging. Play can improve young people's moods and help them to connect emotionally with others (Landreth, 2012). Play is used by young people to communicate, explore, gain autonomy, learn about the self, and build new relationships with others and the world. In the therapeutic setting, counselors might refer to play behaviors as a child's **work** because play is a youth's way of making important contributions.

The therapeutic relationship can be fostered and supported through play because youth are naturally interested in playing and find it to be fun (Schaefer & Drewes, 2013). Many youth are brought to counseling involuntarily, yet they are able to let go of any feelings of resistance due to the naturally engaging nature of play therapy. Counselors are able to further build the therapeutic relationship by meeting clients at developmentally appropriate levels and communicating with them in a play language with which youth are comfortable and skilled. Youth might not typically have the opportunity to engage with adults who are willing to speak to them through play, and therapists who use play can communicate mutual respect and increase feelings of safety in session.

When the therapeutic relationship is established and enhanced through the use of play, youth learn that they are worthy of being loved and gain an increased sense of trust in others and the world (Landreth, 2012; Schaefer & Drewes, 2013). Youth who enjoy counseling are able to build healthy attachments with their counselors, and these bonds can be transferred outside of session to parents and other important attachment figures. Overall, play fosters a genuine human connection—a connection needed and valued by individuals of all ages, especially youth.

Youth, when engaging in play in the context of counseling, generally experience positive emotions as they are doing something they enjoy in a safe environment with an encouraging, supportive person. When they are ready and feel safe, counseling provides them with an opportunity and space to come into contact with unpleasant emotions, such as anger or sadness (Landreth, 2012). It is important for youth to have the space they need to fully express their emotions because this provides an opportunity for **catharsis**, which is the therapeutic release of important emotions (Ray, 2014). Through play, youth are also able to process emotions and work toward replacing unhelpful emotions with healthier thoughts and feelings (Schaefer & Drewes, 2013).

In addition to promoting creativity, relationship building, and catharsis, play therapy provides a safe space for youth to learn new ways of interacting with the world—that is, play scenarios often act as metaphors that can be transferred to real-life events (Schaefer & Drewes, 2013). For example, a youth might play with a dragon that eats princesses. The dragon might represent a real-life person who has hurt the youth, and the youth can develop ways to protect the princess, which might translate to real-life strategies for protecting one's self.

Play behaviors serve an important role in youth development: When youth are given the opportunity to display their abilities through play, they gain an increased sense of purpose (Schaefer & Drewes, 2013). Play can be viewed as a youth's life work, and youth who are praised for working hard, effectively, and creatively in their play can gain an improved sense of self-confidence and purpose in the world.

Play modalities are also inherently culturally sensitive in that they allow counselors to account for many cultural factors, such as age, gender, race, ethnicity, religion, communication patterns, and family dynamics in their play interventions (Carmichael, 2006). It is important for counselors to take a balanced approach between understanding general trends within certain cultures and accounting for the unique variances within each family.

Counselors should be sensitive to cultural variations in nonverbal and verbal communication as well. For example, African American clients might tend to use more eye contact when speaking than when listening (Sue & Sue, 2013). Counselors should acknowledge that a lack of eye contact from clients does not indicate a lack of interest or respect, and counselors can choose whether to match or mismatch this aspect of nonverbal communication. Overall, counselors who use play modalities should use nonverbal communication to appear interested and relaxed (Ray, 2014). This can be done by maintaining an open posture, leaning forward, using a voice tone that is congruent with the youth's, providing supportive eye contact, and using minimal encouragers to convey interest in the client (Ray, 2014).

Cultural considerations are important factors in all counseling relationships and interventions (Sue & Sue, 2015). When working with youth, counselors should clearly explain the therapeutic play process and the roles of the client, family members, and counselor. Counselors should intentionally check with clients and their families to ensure the planned interventions are culturally appropriate and have a promise of being helpful and effective.

When implementing play interventions, the following strategies might be useful:

- Take a nonjudgmental approach.
- Establish a strong therapeutic relationship with the youth and relevant family members.
- Uphold relevant ethical principles and codes.
- Maintain confidentiality for the youth and the family.
- Engage in ongoing assessment and treatment planning.
- Collaborate with key stakeholders (e.g., parents, teachers).
- Provide informed services that are likely to help clients to achieve their goals.
- Keep a wide variety of toys and other creative mediums in the counseling setting.
- Use a client's play behaviors to inform case conceptualization and interventions.
- Provide directive and/or nondirective play interventions.
- Use various creative mediums, including storytelling, metaphors, acting, singing, art, sculpture, sand tray, games, and/or free play, in the counseling session.
- Involve parents and other stakeholders when relevant and possible (Gladding, 2011; Homeyer & Morrison, 2008).

The participation of parents or caregivers can be integral to the therapeutic play process (Plastow, 2011). Although it is not always possible to include parents in counseling due to scheduling difficulties or a lack of parental willingness to participate, counselors should try to include them in play interventions whenever possible. Parents can be involved in play therapy sessions with their children to:

- learn to enjoy playing with their children;
- learn to communicate and cooperate with their children;
- develop new ways of understanding their children;
- develop new skills for supporting their children;
- learn how to set helpful limits for their children;
- develop trust in their children; and
- develop trust in themselves.

The needs of the youth and the theoretical orientation of the counselor will determine how parents are integrated into play techniques.

Counselors using play interventions might ask parents to (a) actively participate in play therapy sessions, (b) quietly observe all play therapy sessions with a debriefing at the end, or (c) attend just the end of play therapy sessions for a debriefing (Schaefer & Kaduson, 2007). Parents might also be asked to attend group or individual counseling without their children to learn skills they can use in everyday interactions with their children. Filial therapy and theraplay are two of the most common play therapy modalities that highlight attachment relationships within the family, and these two types of interventions are explained in detail in the next section.

There are many play therapy approaches rooted in different counseling theories. Counselors who use play techniques will create an individualized plan or approach for each client. This plan will be informed by the client's presenting struggles and shift according to the counselor's and client's theoretical orientation. For example, a person-centered counselor might need to integrate some psychoanalytic techniques when working with clients who require interpretation (e.g., a youth who has difficulty with self-expression might be encouraged to use play as a form of free association). Counselors should be aware of the many theoretical frameworks that can inform play interventions and choose the theories that best suit both his or her style and the client's needs. Therapeutic play theories and techniques are outlined in greater detail in the next section.

Techniques and Interventions

Although there are many different techniques and interventions used in play therapy, some basic counseling skills cut across most theoretical play approaches. As is the case with all counseling approaches, play therapy sessions are tailored to each individual client. Play therapy sessions can last up to 50 minutes, and the session length should be adjusted according to clients' developmental levels (Menassa, 2009). Some youth might only be able to follow the rules or play for 10 to 15 minutes, whereas others might benefit from a full 50-minute session. Counselors should consider the theory that guides their practice, clients' presenting concerns, and clients' developmental considerations when making decisions regarding the length of sessions.

Counselors who use play take care to set safe boundaries before youth are allowed to play (Ray, 2014). These boundaries might include explaining (a) how long the youth can play, (b) where the youth may go while playing, (c) what will happen if the youth plays aggressively or dangerously, and (d) how and when the session will be ended (Rye, 2010). Landreth (2012) suggested the use of the acronym **ACT** (Acknowledge, Communicate, Target alternatives) as a model that can be used to set healthy and safe in-session boundaries with children. Figure 8.3 shows an example of a counselor using the ACT model to set boundaries during play therapy.

When youth are told how long play therapy sessions will last, they should also be informed about cleanup procedures. Counselors should intentionally determine whether it is important or therapeutic for clients to clean up their toys before the end of a session. Cleanup can be a way to teach and facilitate personal responsibility and self-control. Some other practitioners suggest supporting clients' freedom to leave the playroom in a state of creativity and self-expression, thus requiring the counselor to clean up after the client has left (Landreth, 2012; Schaefer & Kaduson, 2007). Counselors should give clients a warning when therapy is coming to a close so they can therapeutically disengage from play behaviors before the end of the session.

Scenario: A youth is slamming a toy against the wall. The youth could get injured if a piece of the toy breaks. Property could also be damaged as a result of the child hitting the wall.

Solution: Implement the ACT model for setting boundaries in play therapy.

Step 1: Acknowledge the feeling that is producing the unhelpful behavior.
   Example: "You feel angry."

Step 2: Communicate the limit.
   Example: "One of our counseling rules is that you cannot break toys."

Step 3: Target alternatives.
   Example: "Consider telling the toy why you are angry."

Additional Considerations
If the child does not easily redirect to target alternatives, counselors should state what will happen if the unhelpful behavior is continued.
   Example: "If you slam that toy again, I will take it away."

Nonjudgmentally and consistently implement reasonable consequences every time it is relevant in session and help caregivers to apply this method outside of session.

Counselors can end the play therapy session if the youth refuses to abide by the rules.

If the youth consistently experiences difficulty abiding by rules in play sessions, this might indicate that the youth is not currently a good candidate for play therapy (Landreth, 2012).

FIGURE 8.3 The ACT Model for Setting Boundaries in Play Therapy
Note: Adapted from Landreth (2012).

Counselors who use therapeutic play can be **directive** or **nondirective** in session. In nondirective play therapy, the child is not given any directions about how to play (Menassa, 2009). The counselor can set some general guidelines for safety and logistics, but youth are not given any further guidance or instructions regarding their play behaviors. Nondirective approaches to play therapy are discussed further in the next section. When using nondirective approaches, counselors serve as witnesses to youth play behaviors and choices in session.

Throughout play sessions, most counselors will use **verbal tracking** in which they say aloud, or narrate, the youth's play behaviors. Counselors should verbally reflect content and feelings that occur in session to encourage creativity, spontaneity, relationship building, and development of personal strengths and positive identity in youth (Ray, 2014). More directive counselors can also use verbal tracking to identify themes/patterns and facilitate decision-making and problem-solving skills (Ray, 2014). The nature and directiveness of verbal tracking will be determined by the theoretical underpinning of the therapeutic play process.

Ultimately, the theoretical orientation of the counselor will inform how play therapy interventions are conceptualized, introduced, implemented, and processed. Nondirective counseling is generally supported through a person-centered, humanistic framework (Menassa, 2009). Directive play interventions can be supported by various theoretical orientations, which include:

- Adlerian play therapy;
- cognitive behavioral play therapy;
- developmental play therapy;
- dynamic play therapy;
- ecosystem play therapy;
- Gestalt play therapy;
- group play therapy;
- Jungian play therapy;
- narrative play therapy;
- object relations play therapy;
- prescriptive play therapy;

- psychoanalytic play therapy;
- release play therapy;
- solution-oriented play therapy;
- theraplay; and
- time-limited play therapy. (Menassa, 2009; Schaefer & Kaduson, 2007)

In summary, play therapy can be directive or nondirective, and many different theories can be used to support the implementation of play techniques in therapy. An overview of popular play therapy approaches is provided in Table 8.3. Counselors should complete a biopsychosocial assessment with youth and/or significant others to choose a play therapy approach that aligns with the counselor's skill set and the client's needs. Some of the most popular directive and nondirective play modalities are discussed in more detail in the following sections.

NONDIRECTIVE PLAY MODALITIES

Nondirective play therapists believe young clients already possess the strength, knowledge, and resources needed to overcome struggles and achieve their goals (Menassa, 2009). The child knows exactly what to do

Table 8.3 Overview of Popular Play Therapy Approaches

Theory	Type	Overview
Child-centered play therapy	Nondirective	Counselors provide empathy, congruence, and unconditional positive regard to youth. Youth uncover their personal values and sources of resiliency. Mental health difficulties diminish as congruence between the youth's ideal and real self increases.
Experiential play therapy	Nondirective	Youth progress through five stages: exploratory, testing, dependency, therapeutic, and termination. Real-life experiences are reenacted organically through play, and internal conflicts are resolved as a natural part of youth resiliency.
Filial therapy	Nondirective	Youth are allowed to engage in organic play while parents, siblings, and other important family members are present. Family members are encouraged to provide the core conditions of child-centered play therapy (i.e., empathy, congruence, and unconditional positive regard), and youth are ideally able to achieve healthier/more helpful relationships with themselves and their family members.
Adlerian play therapy	Directive	A lifestyle assessment is performed to understand the youth's unique context and social relationships. Healthy ways to meet youth's basic needs are uncovered through play behaviors. The methods for meeting the youth's basic needs are reenacted in real life with key people in the youth's life.
Cognitive behavioral play therapy	Directive	Counselors work to help youth to explore and understand the link between thoughts, feelings, and behaviors. Thoughts are systematically reframed while play occurs to promote healthier feelings and behaviors.
Release play therapy	Directive	Counselors intentionally create play situations that act as metaphors for difficult youth experiences. Youth are given unlimited opportunities to overcome the various metaphors and apply their newly found skills to real life.
Theraplay	Directive	Parents are viewed as the primary vehicles of change in youth and are taught to improve attachment bonds with their youth throughout three stages: beginning, middle, and end. Parents provide praise and consistency in play and outside of session to create a sense of safety and well-being for youth.

and how to do it, and the counselor's job is to simply provide the resources, safety, and space required to facilitate this process. There is no need for the counselor to interpret the child's play or understand any underlying meaning; clients know exactly how to process and overcome adversity, and in fact they have a natural inclination to do so. The counselor's main job in nondirective therapy is to build a strong therapeutic relationship and hold an open, safe space for client self-expression and self-discovery. There are many theoretical frameworks for nondirective play therapy, and two common types of individual approaches are child-centered play therapy and experiential play therapy. A third approach, filial therapy, is a long-standing nondirective play therapy theory that integrates the client and family members/significant others. These three nondirective play therapy approaches are explained in this section.

Child-Centered Play.   Child-centered play therapy is firmly grounded in a humanistic approach and is highly supported as an effective mental health intervention (Axline, 1947a; Ray et al., 2015). In a child-centered play therapy approach, the necessary and sufficient components of play therapy include empathy, congruence, and unconditional positive regard. The counselor joins the client in the therapeutic process, which is highly collaborative with few rules, directions, or boundaries. The counselor holds the client in the highest regard and actively works to eliminate all judgment in the play therapy process—that is, no play behaviors can be right or wrong; nothing about the play process is correct or incorrect. As such, counselors simply join clients on a therapeutic play therapy journey when implementing child-centered play therapy.

During session, counselors should reinforce the message that the client is in control (Rye, 2010). For example, if a client asks permission to play with a certain toy, the counselor should not grant permission but rather should reflect the client's choice by saying "You are going to play with the big ball" or "You chose to pick up the truck." This transfer of power demonstrates that the counseling process is different from other settings or relationships the youth experiences outside of session.

Unconditional positive regard is used to describe a counselor's ability to understand a youth from his or her unique point of view and accept that the youth is functioning as well as possible with the resources he or she has. To uphold unconditional positive regard, child-centered therapists take care to avoid passing any judgment (positive or negative) on client behaviors (APT, 2015; Rye, 2010). It might seem natural to praise youth for cleaning up their toys, but a counselor can instill the concepts of autonomy and self-confidence by saying things such as "You cleaned up every last toy" or "You believe that it is important to clean up." These phrases are nonevaluative and help clients to uncover their true thoughts and feelings.

Although child-centered play therapists are nondirective in session, they are fully present and active throughout their time with clients. Child-centered therapists observe the youth's play behaviors and work to identify the associated thoughts and feelings. Counselors verbally track the youth's thoughts, feelings, and behaviors in an empathic, nonjudgmental manner (Rye, 2010).

Empathic responses are an important aspect of this approach, and they include thoughts and feelings that a client might experience (e.g., feeling scared, angry, or worthless). Counselors can provide empathic responses directly to the client (e.g., "You feel scared"). Alternatively, counselors can use metaphors by providing empathic responses to the toys with which the child is playing (Ray, 2014). For example, a client who experienced past trauma might pretend in session that an action figure is saving helpless animals. The counselor could highlight thoughts and feelings of the animals that might align with the client's own thoughts and feelings. In this case, the metaphorical empathic responses might include "The animals were scared, but now they are free" or "The animals are happy to get a helping hand." These statements normalize the youth's experiences while focusing on the play.

In child-centered play therapy, counselors provide a nonjudgmental space while empathically fostering **congruence** between clients' thoughts, feelings, and behaviors (Menassa, 2009; Rye, 2010—that is, youth are guided through a process of self-exploration in which they identify their values, needs, preferences, and personal goals. Youth are also encouraged to behave in ways that align with their individual values and preferences. For example, if youth like to build and create things, they should be able to spend time playing with blocks and other building materials.

Counselors approach the counseling relationship as a long-term process of client exploration, learning, and development. Specifically, counselors using this approach avoid guiding clients and instead set the tone that youth have full autonomy to make their own decisions in session. When youth ask permission to play in certain ways, counselors should respond with confirmation or reiterate their plans (rather than providing permission). Counselors give youth full autonomy of their decisions and thus allow youth to identify their true values and needs. Counselors should collaborate with parents, caregivers, teachers, and other stakeholders to harness emotional support for clients outside the counseling session, and they should encourage these key stakeholders to allow clients to have autonomy over their decisions as much as possible.

Experiential Play. Experiential play therapy was pioneered as a departure from child-centered play in the late 1900s (Norton & Norton, 1997). As is true with child-centered play therapy, experiential play therapists believe every child has an innate capacity to become more healthy and well. It is believed that youth will intuitively choose to reenact past events that are still unresolved in their play, and a nondirective stance is taken during play opportunities. Youth can use their own play behaviors to reach new levels of insight, control, and strength. Experiential play therapists interpret play behaviors as metaphors for fear, powerlessness, shame, sorrow, or anger.

Experiential play therapists are considered nondirective because they provide limited directions to youth, but they do reflect and track the underlying meaning of play behaviors. Whereas child-centered play therapists are more likely to track just the content of the play behaviors, experiential play therapists integrate some interpretations in their tracking. There are five stages in experiential play therapy: the exploratory stage, the testing stage, the dependency stage, the therapeutic stage, and the termination stage (Norton & Norton, 1997).

In the **exploratory stage**, the child builds a relationship with the counselor and gets comfortable with the play process. The child is then provided with basic instructions such as "You can play with any toys you'd like as long as you don't break them" or "We will play for twenty minutes, and I will tell you a few minutes before it is time to clean up." Otherwise, counselors make nonjudgmental verbal observations about the child's choices and behaviors. For example, "You played with the truck the whole time" or "You played with the truck for a while, and now you are playing with the dolls." Counselors should use a neutral, yet inviting tone of voice to verbally track the child's natural play behaviors.

In the **testing stage**, the child determines whether the counselor can be trusted. For example, the youth might hit a doll's head on the floor quite hard and then look to the counselor for a reaction. The counselor should work to validate and empower the youth in this stage using verbal tracking and reflection of content, feeling, and meaning. For example, "You decided that the doll deserved to be hurt" or "You are angry at the doll." Statements such as these are nonevaluative and show the client that counseling is a safe place for emotional expression.

If youth determine that the experiential play therapist is trustworthy, they will progress into the **dependency stage** in which they become willing to share difficult thoughts and feelings through their play behaviors. It is in this stage that youth gain the courage to reenact traumatic experiences in their play behaviors. For example, the youth might enact one doll lying on top of another (to symbolize molestation or physical abuse), and then the youth might slam the aggressive doll against the ground. Counselors can verbalize the significance of the youth's actions through statements such as "That doll was being mean, and you made it stop." A statement like this validates the youth's experience and empowers him or her.

In the dependency stage, youth behavior in the home or school might seem to become more problematic or unhealthy. An escalation of problematic behaviors, or regression, may be a natural result of youth uncovering traumatic and difficult experiences, and counselors should inform parents that youth behaviors will most likely improve when the therapeutic growth stage is reached (Norton & Norton, 1997).

The **therapeutic growth stage** involves youth regaining control and power over difficult situations by reenacting events metaphorically through play. Youth learn new problem-solving skills and gain greater self-confidence. For example, the youth who previously slammed an aggressive doll on the ground might eventually choose to have the doll arrested through play. Throughout the growth stage, counselors provide a safe space for clients to explore and learn more about themselves, gain insights into their worlds, and learn new ways of problem solving. Over time, youth will become increasingly able to transfer skills from session into real life to take initiative and gain control over their lives.

When youth have fully resolved their difficult experiences, they enter the **termination stage**. Youth should be given plenty of time to process the loss of the therapeutic relationship. The time needed for termination depends on client characteristics and developmental level. For example, clients with attachment difficulties should be given extra processing during the termination stage.

Experiential play modalities celebrate the inherent resilience of youth. Counselors who operate from this underpinning should create a safe space for youth to engage in any play behaviors they choose. Such play behaviors will provide the autonomy needed for youth to process and overcome difficulties in their lives. Through play experiences, youth learn to navigate the world in healthy, effective ways.

Filial Therapy.   Filial therapy (Gurney, Gurney, & Andronico, 1966) was developed in the mid-1900s. Filial therapy's foundations are closely related to child-centered play therapy foundations, but in filial play the primary attachment figures—generally, the parents—are viewed as the primary change agents. The key role that family members play in filial play modalities is a primary difference between child-centered play and filial play modalities. However, many of the other basic tenets between filial play and child-centered play remain the same.

Filial play interventions are rooted in child-centered play modalities, and they are effective in fostering healthy relationships within families (Gurney & Ryan, 2013; Munns, 2013). The theoretical underpinning of empathy, congruence, and unconditional positive regard are key considerations in filial therapy. In filial therapy, parents and other important attachment figures and/or siblings are taught healthy ways to interact with youth. Play behaviors are used in session to allow youth and their family members to practice healthy problem-solving and coping skills. Youth are provided with a safe space to express themselves and learn helpful ways of interacting with those they love the most. Filial play is a nondirective approach to helping youth build healthy relationships and a strong, positive self-concept.

When using filial therapy, parents are taught about helpful play techniques and the ways play benefits youth. As an example, to enhance the parent–child attachment, parents might be taught to respond to their child's demands in play scenarios consistently and happily. This supports the development of a safe base in session and translates outside the therapeutic setting.

Although filial play sessions are nondirective, parents are coached on the underlying mental health implications of certain parent–child interactions. For example, parents who allow their children to play autonomously are able to foster their child's sense of congruence, self-esteem, and identity (Gurney & Ryan, 2013).

In session, parents can allow the youth to take the lead and join with the youth in play behaviors. Parents can support autonomous play inside and outside of session by nonjudgmentally allowing youth to choose their toys and the play behaviors that are used throughout the session. Parents can also learn to extend this autonomy outside of session by allowing youth to pick their clothing or what they eat for dinner that night. Parents should strive for a comfortable balance between guiding their children and allowing them to make their own choices.

Overall, nondirective play therapies honor the inherent resiliency of youth. Nondirective play therapists allow youth to control the therapeutic process and bear witness to the youth's growth. Sometimes, though, counselors might need to—or elect to—take a more directive play therapy approach, and this is discussed in the following section.

DIRECTIVE PLAY MODALITIES

Directive play therapists take a more authoritative approach when implementing play therapy, and they intentionally instruct clients to participate in carefully chosen activities. Counselors may use a more directive play therapy approach when clients are stuck, have repressed emotions and unresolved difficulties, or are otherwise unable to resolve their mental health challenges independently (Menassa, 2009). Directive play therapy can be useful when time is limited and brief interventions are necessary. Older youth might require more structure in their sessions to meet their developmental levels. For example, a 12-year-old boy might quickly become bored or disconnected if encouraged to play freely with toys, and thus more engaging directives might be helpful. Younger clients might require more structure if they are unable to play on their own due to behavioral difficulties or developmental delays. Counselors should adjust their interventions and approach to play therapy according to relevant client characteristics.

Three directive play therapy theories that are quite popular include Adlerian play therapy, cognitive behavioral play therapy, and release play therapy (Drewes, 2009; Schaefer & Kaduson, 2007). Adlerian play therapists take a holistic approach, conceptualize youth in context, and pay special attention to the role of the family and how it affects a child's mental health. Cognitive behavioral play therapists place a high level of importance on cognitions because they believe negative or distorted thinking can lead to unhelpful feelings and behaviors. Release therapists place more of a focus on the role of emotions, which are viewed as the source of unhelpful thoughts and behaviors. Theraplay is also explored in this chapter as a directive approach to play therapy that integrates family members as an integral part of therapy. Although there are many directive play therapy theories, four theories are briefly discussed in this section.

Adlerian Play Therapy.   Adlerian play therapy is informed by a holistic conceptualization of the youth. Before any play takes place, counselors working from this theoretical perspective complete a **lifestyle assessment** to gather a unique understanding of the young client and the significant people in his or her life. A lifestyle assessment is a comprehensive questionnaire used to gather information about a person and his or her environment. It includes an assessment of:

- genetic/biological factors;
- family system considerations;
- family dynamics;
- neighborhood dynamics;
- community dynamics and politics;
- social relationships;
- hobbies;
- academic or career considerations; and/or
- other special considerations. (Adler, 1958; Drout, Habeck, & Rule, 2015)

Counselors can use the information gathered in the lifestyle assessment to inform the therapeutic play process.

When conceptualizing young people through an Adlerian lens, counselors spend a significant amount of time working to understand the client and to identify themes in play behaviors. The information from the lifestyle assessment is used to draw conclusions about a youth's thoughts, feelings, and behaviors. Counselors use therapeutic play interventions to understand a youth's behaviors and identify healthier thoughts and beliefs. These healthier thoughts are believed to create healthier behaviors and more positive emotions in youth. Healthier behaviors also improve one's social relationships.

Adler (1958) suggested that all individuals are inherently social beings, and all youth behaviors are goal directed—that is, youth are always working toward some end that is important to them (Drout et al., 2015). Counselors hypothesize the underlying meaning of youth play behaviors through one of the four motivations posed by Adler (1958): attention, power, revenge, and escape. Adlerian play therapists structure sessions to uncover the purpose of every client behavior and to identify more constructive ways for the client's needs to be met.

Regarding the need for **attention**, all individuals have a need to be noticed by others (Adler, 1958). A youth's need for attention can be satiated when parents and other key stakeholders praise a youth for doing something positive (e.g., cleaning the living room or being kind to a sibling). Youth who do not get the positive attention they require sometimes learn that unhelpful behaviors (e.g., hitting a sibling) result in the much-needed attention they are craving from parents or other key attachment figures. Counselors should work to help youth to identify healthy ways to get attention and educate parents on how to provide youth with the positive attention they need.

Although youth largely depend on their parents to help to get their basic needs met, all individuals—even youth—need to feel **powerful** and autonomous (Adler, 1958)—that is, youth need to feel as though they are capable of making decisions for themselves and following through with their choices. Counselors can provide youth with power in session by allowing them to choose their own toys and forms of play. Counselors can then work to link thoughts and feelings related to control to more helpful behaviors outside of session. For example, a youth can choose to put down a toy and begin playing with another. Counselors can help youth to identify the thoughts and feelings that contributed to this decision and to apply that same thought process to, say, walking away from a peer who is trying to start a fight. This behavior should then be reinforced through additional play scenarios and practiced outside of session as well.

Youth might display mental health or behavioral problems when feeling hurt by others. Feelings of rejection or betrayal from loved ones can result in anger toward the self and others (Adler, 1958). Acting on this anger, youth might try to get **revenge** on those who hurt them by saying or doing hurtful or disruptive things to others (e.g., hitting a parent or bullying a peer).

Sometimes, though, youth withdraw when they are faced with mental health difficulties, and they might try to escape uncomfortable situations by appearing incapable of complying with the demands of others. For example, youth might purposely do a poor job putting away their toys so they will no longer be asked to do it. Counselors should praise youth for working hard in counseling and find other ways to boost their confidence.

When implementing Adlerian play therapy, counselors first explain the counseling process to the youth and the family. Using an Adlerian approach, sometimes the counselor takes the lead, and sometimes the client takes the lead. Counselors might ask a youth to play with a certain set of toys if they want to learn more about a specific aspect of the youth's mental health. For example, counselors might ask youth to play with Jenga blocks to see if the youth gets angry when the tower falls down. The youth might also be asked to play with dolls to see how he or she approaches social relationships. Counselors might also simply allow youth to free play in session.

Clinical Toolbox 8.1

In the Pearson eText, click here to review an example of an Adlerian play therapy activity.

As counselors build rapport with youth through play behaviors, a safe space for therapeutic play is established. Counselors can work to facilitate youth development through verbal tracking and processing the meaning of the sessions with youth. As an example, counselors might initially begin with simple process-based verbal tracking (e.g., "You are playing with the truck"), and they progress to reflections that add interpretation and facilitate insight (e.g., "You are playing with the truck because you like strong things"). Clients' thoughts and feelings should be verbalized by the counselor, and the counselor should also help the client to link his or her thoughts and feelings with resulting behaviors. Ultimately, the goal of Adlerian play therapy is to help youth to overcome feelings of inferiority and reframe mistaken beliefs about the self and/or others.

Cognitive Behavioral Play Therapy.   Counselors might decide to use cognitive behavioral play interventions with clients who have difficulty with various presenting concerns, ranging from mood difficulties to phobias and specific behavior problems (Drewes, 2009). Cognitive behavioral play interventions can be used with youth as young as 4 years (Knell, 1995). It has been debated whether youth this young are able to understand their own thoughts, but it is generally agreed on that youth are able to learn simple, basic concepts about their thoughts, feelings, and behaviors (Knell, 1995).

Cognitive behavioral play therapists believe that young people's thoughts (conscious or unconscious) directly contribute to their feelings, and this determines their moods and behaviors. As such, cognitive behavioral play therapists structure sessions to foster and facilitate healthy thinking, which leads to desirable feelings and behaviors. To begin, counselors should educate parents and youth about the cognitive behavioral model in which a thought produces a feeling, which leads to a behavior (Drewes, 2009). This can be done through talking, drawing diagrams, or even playing games that demonstrate the link between thoughts, feelings, and behavior. Cognitive behavioral play therapists often spend several sessions building and establishing the therapeutic relationship and easing youth and their families into the thought-feeling-behavior framework or way of thinking.

Clinical Toolbox 8.2

In the Pearson eText, click here to review a cognitive behavioral therapy activity a counselor can use to teach young clients about the relationship between thoughts, feelings, and behaviors.

Counselors can use play interventions to tap into a youth's thought processes. For example, a counselor and client might play a game in session (e.g., checkers) and watch to see if the play behaviors evoke any strong emotions in the youth. A discussion might ensue about how the thoughts, feelings, and behaviors in this situation translate to other aspects of the child's life. Counselors might also encourage free play and ask the client what thoughts occurred and what feeling came as a result. Whether using free play or structured games, play can offer an opportunity for young people to begin to link their thoughts with their feelings and behaviors. In addition to games and free play, cognitive behavioral play therapists often use puppets, sand tray, dolls, or other vehicles for play to help youth to begin to understand the relationship between their thoughts, feelings, and behaviors. Cognitive behavioral interventions might not be appropriate or necessary for every client, but it is a popular mode of play intervention that can be practiced in session and applied in clients' daily lives.

Release Play.   **Release play** is based on the belief that play behaviors mimic a youth's real-life experiences and that youth are able to experience and thus release emotions in play therapy. Youth are able to develop healthy emotional responses and coping behaviors in play sessions that can then be transferred to daily activities outside of session.

Counselors who practice release therapy believe that youth independently overcome many difficult life experiences through their play behaviors—that is, youth are naturally resilient and are able to process the thoughts and feelings that accompany a wide range of common life stressors, including getting disciplined by a parent or getting into a fight with a friend. However, they also believe that some life stressors are too difficult and complex for youth to overcome on their own (e.g., parental divorce, trauma). Through the use of structured counseling interventions, youth can work through their struggles.

Using release therapy, counselors intentionally create metaphorical scenarios that represent a specific event or difficulty that happened to the client. Often, the specific event was scary or uncomfortable (e.g., physical abuse). Every time the event is reexperienced, counselors work with clients to process their thoughts and feelings. Counselors strive to facilitate catharsis in session to create emotional release for the client. Counselors also use clients' emotional reactions as indicators that unresolved thoughts still exist in regard to that specific topic. As such, release therapists work to re-create troubling scenarios in safe ways until the youth has developed healthy thoughts, feelings, and coping skills to navigate the world without significant distress.

Clinical Toolbox 8.3

In the Pearson eText, click here to review an example case note for a release therapy session.

It is important to note that counselors who use release therapy believe youth gain mental health benefits from their play behaviors, not from insight or interpretations provided by the counselors—that is, the counselor's job is to guide the youth toward specific play behaviors that are relevant to the problem at hand, but the counselor does not need to interpret youth play behaviors. In the moment, verbal tracking of thoughts and feelings is sufficient and effective (Levy, 1938/2015).

Theraplay.   **Theraplay** is a directive therapy that is used to foster healthy attachment bonds between youth and their caregivers. In theraplay, parents are viewed as the primary change agents for youth (Munns, 2013). The foundation of theraplay is built on attachment theory and the belief that youth need to form secure attachment bonds early in life to experience healthy development and fulfilling social relationships throughout their lives.

A secure attachment bond is developed when youth's physical and emotional needs are consistently met by their caregivers. As a result, youth with secure attachment models view the world as a safe place and are able to develop their own autonomy while knowing they will receive unconditional love and support from those who matter. Unhealthy, or insecure, attachment develops when youth's needs are not consistently met, and they learn the world is not a safe place.

In theraplay, the primary goal is to correct any unhealthy attachments in youth to foster their sense of safety and independence (Munns, 2013). In addition, counselors work to enhance parents' and young people's self-esteem/self-efficacy. Similarly, counselors who use theraplay aim to increase youth's abilities to regulate their thoughts, feelings, and behaviors when they are alone and when they are interacting with family members and significant others. To achieve these goals, counselors provide theraplay in three phases: beginning, middle, and end (Munns, 2013).

In the *beginning stage* of theraplay, the youth is invited to explore the concept of play therapy, and the counselor and client get to know each other by playing with each other. In this stage, counselors should pay special attention to learning about the youth's home structure, home-based challenges, and level of engagement with his or her parents (Munns, 2013). The beginning stage of theraplay also involves a *honeymoon period* in which youth are engaged in the theraplay process but directive interventions have not yet been employed. Instead, free play is a primary activity in the beginning stage.

In the *middle stage* of theraplay, a *negative period* replaces the honeymoon period in which youth begin to feel challenged by the counselor who gradually increases the directiveness and structure of sessions. This directiveness is also taught to parents and caregivers for replication at home and in other important settings (e.g., school, day care). Youth begin to learn that the theraplay process may change or shake up the current family structure and that the process will take them out of their comfort zones. In the negative stage of theraplay, parents might observe that youth's mental health problems get worse (before they begin to improve). This phenomenon should be normalized for parents by the counselor.

As the middle stage progresses, youth let go of the resistance they held in the negative period, and a period of *growth and trust* emerges. In this stage, the child learns to trust the genuineness and consistency of the counselor, and this model is transferred to the parents; youth learn to expect safe and consistent boundaries within and outside of play sessions. A healthy attachment bond is fostered between youth and their parents, and the youth's mental health goals are progressively achieved.

The final phase of theraplay includes *termination*. When the youth's presenting problems have been sufficiently addressed, counselors should broach the topic of termination and process the implications with youth and their families. Parents are encouraged to maintain the new behaviors that were learned in theraplay outside of sessions, and it is expected that youth will be able to engage in healthy cognitive and emotional development on termination of theraplay.

Overall, directive play modalities allow the counselor to actively guide youth and family members toward therapeutic growth. Counselors should account for relevant cultural and clinical considerations when working with youth in therapeutic play. Clients might require both directive and nondirective counseling modalities at different times in the counseling process, and clients might also require special play modalities, such as sandplay, throughout the therapeutic process.

Sandplay.   **Sandplay** is a unique subset of play therapy that can be used to supplement various directive or nondirective play modalities. In sandplay, youth are encouraged to create miniature representations of their worlds in a tray filled with sand or a similar material (e.g., rice, small pebbles). Mental health professionals can become registered or certified in sandplay after earning a graduate degree in a helping profession. Counselors can become **Registered Sandplay Therapists** (STRs) through the Association for Sandplay Therapy (www.sandplayassociation.com). Alternatively, individuals can become **Certified Sandplay Therapists** (CSTs) through the Sandplay Therapists of America (www.sandplay.org) and the International Society for Sandplay Therapy (http://www.isst-society.com). Additional sandplay credentials can be obtained through other associations and organizations as well.

Sandplay can be supported by various play and family theories. Counselors should implement sandplay according to each client's unique developmental needs and presenting concerns. Counselors should also integrate their preferred theoretical orientations as appropriate.

Sandplay, often referred to as sand tray, originated in the early 1900s (Rae, 2013). Sandplay occurs in vessels in various shapes, sizes, and heights. Some counselors might use a baby pool filled with sand, and other sand trays might be quite small and portable (e.g., a small plastic container). Some trays sit on the ground, and others are built into a table or bench. Some people may elect, too, to use other materials—for example, rice— instead of sand in the sand trays.

Using sandplay, youth are invited to place small toys in the sand. As clients submerge into sandplay, they are able to construct a representation of their worlds using various small toys. As in all play modalities, counselors should ensure youth are provided with a wide variety of toys, figurines, blocks, and other objects that can be used to construct a subjective model of the client's world (Rae, 2013). Often, metaphors are used for youth to create a safe world that includes symbols for real people, places, and things. In sandplay, the tray acts as a microcosm (or miniature version) of the real world.

When using sandplay, counselors first assess a client's readiness to engage in therapeutic play. Sandplay activates various senses (especially touch, sight, and sound). Clients who are asked to engage in sandplay should be comfortable using their sense of touch, and clients who are overly reactive to touch—for example, as the result of traumatic experiences or genetic factors—might not be good candidates for this type of play therapy (Rae, 2013).

When it has been determined that a client is a good fit for sandplay, a counselor should explain the process to the client and the family if relevant. Counselors should create a safe space by allowing one or more silent sessions in which the youth is allowed to play freely with the sand tray toys. Counselors might explain that the silent, nondirective play will eventually transition into a more directive pace, or it might be explained that all sand tray sessions will be nondirective in nature.

Counselors should assume the role of a witness in the sandplay process (Rae, 2013). For at least some sessions, and perhaps for all nondirective sessions, counselors should allow clients to have the autonomy they need to construct their worlds—within the sand tray—and gain control over their lives. Directive counselors can use various play techniques and theories to guide directive sandplay, and this might include reflections, verbal tracking, and/or use of specific directions. As an example, counselors who work from an Adlerian approach might, when working with a youth whose parents recently got divorced, direct the youth to create a sand tray representing the youth's home. The counselor could gather valuable information from this exercise by observing the setting that the youth chooses as "home" and the toys used to represent each member of the family. Counselors should also take note if key family members are missing and/or where they are placed in relation to the rest of the family.

In sandplay, counselors can enter into the worlds of their clients and support an interactive and effective process of exploration and insight. Counselors should summarize each sandplay session privately or in conjunction with the client/family. A plan to facilitate behavioral change based on the insight created in sandplay can be constructed with the client and family when appropriate. Again, counselors can be as directive or nondirective as client need dictates.

In this section regarding play therapy, directive and nondirective play interventions were outlined. Play therapy interventions are helpful when working with young clients, but they can also be quite effective when used with older adolescents and even adult family members. Counselors should involve parents in play sessions as much as possible, and counselors should consistently work to make play interventions applicable in the youth's daily life.

Counselors are not necessarily required to choose just one of the play theories explored in this section. Counselors can integrate several play theories to create a meaningful combination that best suits the client circumstances. In addition to play therapy, counselors might also choose to integrate creative arts interventions—which can be conceptualized as a type of play—into counseling sessions with clients.

CREATIVE ARTS IN COUNSELING

Creative arts engage the imagination and the senses in meaningful ways. When used in counseling, creative arts methods can be used to connect with young people in ways not always possible via talk therapy methods. Art is an imaginative and stimulating process that often results in some sort of final product (Degges-White & Davis, 2011). The final product of a creative arts intervention could be intangible, such as an imaginary box of coping skills, or it could be quite tangible, like a painting of one's feelings. Creative arts interventions are helpful for clients of all ages, but creative activities are especially effective with youth in counseling because these activities are process oriented, developmental, diverse, flexible, and engaging.

Counseling is an artistic, goal-oriented process in itself, and counselors can harness the power of creativity when working to support client goals. Conversation, the hallmark of talk therapy, is an art in which counselor and client join together to pursue an agreed-on goal, the creative product of counseling.

Creativity in counseling goes beyond talk therapy to engage one's senses and brain in unique ways. The use of creative arts in counseling creates a bridge between the logical and creative parts of the brain. Therapeutic interventions become even more effective when the entire brain is stimulated and connections are made in creative ways (Rae, 2013). The use of creative arts in counseling can serve as a vehicle that facilitates a meaningful, holistic connection.

The use of expressive techniques in session allows counselors to connect with clients in unique ways, and the intentional incorporation of creative activities and interventions can increase the effectiveness of counseling (Degges-White & Davis, 2011). Counselors have an ethical responsibility to provide interventions that can help clients to reach their goals (ACA, 2014, A.1.c.), and creativity can be used in session to support this ethical imperative.

Art therapists—and many other mental health professionals—believe that the construction of art is therapeutic in and of itself (Rosen & Atkins, 2014)—that is, expressive arts therapies are intrinsically valuable and do not require direction or guidance from a helper other than to introduce the activity. Many mental health professionals integrate creative or expressive arts interventions with various theoretical approaches. As an example, consider that a counselor invites a client to make a sculpture—in session—of his anger. For this client, the act of creating the sculpture is relaxing, engaging, and facilitates insight into his anger. In addition to the inherent therapeutic value of this experience, counselors can use various techniques and interventions associated with specific theories to supplement any creative arts intervention. Conversely, creative arts interventions can be used as vehicles that facilitate the application of specific theoretical approaches. To effectively implement creative arts in counseling, mental health professionals should know the foundations of the use of creative arts in counseling and apply them intentionally.

Foundations of Creative Arts in Counseling

Since ancient times, creativity has held a therapeutic value in society (Gladding, 2011). Creativity was a driving force that influenced culture and societal growth through the Middle Ages, the Renaissance period, and into modern times. Creativity is a foundation of the counseling process, and creative interventions in counseling are supported by most theoretical orientations (Gladding, 2011). All counselors can integrate creative arts and expressive techniques into their daily counseling as long as they are intentional about the activities chosen (Gladding, 2011).

When planning creative interventions for youth, the counselor should first gather information about the client and work to understand the youth's presenting problem, developmental level, and any relevant cultural considerations (Gladding, 2011). Counselors should complete thorough assessments and engage in ongoing treatment planning to determine the nature and types of creative interventions that are most appropriate for each individual client. For example, a counselor teaching cognitive behavioral concepts to a child who stifles his emotions as the result of posttraumatic stress disorder might use a flashcard game in which the client acts out specific feelings to earn points. This is just one creative way that counselors can highlight important treatment concepts and make the interventions more meaningful to clients.

Creative Techniques and Interventions

Creativity can be woven into the counseling process in ways that fit with the counselor's theoretical approach and the client's unique needs. There is an endless list of creative interventions that counselors might integrate into their sessions, and the use of art, music, and writing/storytelling is briefly discussed in more detail in the following sections.

ART

Art can include drawing, painting, sculpting, sketching, coloring, decorating, crafting, scrapbooking, creating collages, and any other activities that involve visual expression. Some common drawing and painting materials counselors might want to use include white and colored paper, pencils, pens, markers, paint, crayons, brushes, aprons, tape, glue, scissors, yarn, string, fabric, glitter, feathers, sequins, popsicle sticks, and plastic containers. If choosing to use sculpture as a medium, counselors will need blocks of clay, a groundsheet, aprons, wire to cut the clay, sculpting tools, water, and paper.

Art interventions can be especially relevant when counseling youth who struggle with verbal expression, but all youth benefit from various forms of visual self-exploration and expression. Art can be used in the school setting, in the home, or in a clinical setting, and art is an effective tool in group, family, and individual counseling.

The act of creating art can be therapeutic in itself, and counselors can further increase the effectiveness of art interventions by designing, implementing, and processing creative activities through a theoretical lens (Rosen & Atkins, 2014). Examples of theoretically supported art activities for counseling are provided in Table 8.4. It is the counselor's responsibility to determine which theory fits best with each client and to develop creative techniques that have a reasonable promise of success. When used intentionally, art activities allow clients to tap into their creative talents, express themselves in unique ways, explore thoughts and feelings, gain insight, and process emotions (Garrett, 2015). Art invites clients to engage in the counseling process, facilitates the therapeutic process, and promotes new behaviors and skills.

Table 8.4 Examples of Creative Arts Counseling Activities

Activity	Counseling Goal	Theoretical Orientation	Description
Look at My Worries	To reduce client anxiety	Cognitive behavioral theory	The client is given a blank piece of paper (larger than standard paper is preferred but not required). The client is also given various art supplies such as paint, crayons, glue, and glitter. The client is asked to draw a picture of his or her worries and fears on the paper. After the client completes the drawing, the counselor processes the activity with questions such as "Where does the fear/worry come from?" "Where does the fear/worry live?" "What makes the fear/worry loud or quiet?" "What does the fear and worry say to you?" "When the fear and worry bother you, what do you do differently?" Counselors can write down the thoughts the client identifies and the behaviors that accompany the thoughts. Counselors can then ask the client to draw a picture of the thoughts and behaviors he or she will use to fight the worry and fear.
Who Am I?	To enhance identity and self-esteem	Person-centered theory	The counselor provides the client with various artistic materials and asks him or her to draw a self-portrait. When the client is finished, the counselor works with him or her to explore how it felt to create something and how it felt to draw one's self. The counselor should also ask the client what the person in the portrait likes, dislikes, values, and worries about. These thoughts and feelings should be validated to promote congruence.
Where Am I Going?	To increase healthy and positive behaviors	Behavioral theory	The client is asked to draw a portrait of his or her current self. Then, on completion, the client is asked to draw a picture of him- or herself in 2 years (or a developmentally appropriate time gap). The counselor and client work to determine how the two portraits are different and to identify specific behaviors that can be used to strive toward the future self.
The Serenity Activity	To reduce anger outbursts	Adlerian theory	The client is directed to draw a large circle on a piece of paper, with the circle representing a hula hoop. Much like using a hula hoop, the client is able to control what happens inside the circle (e.g., moving hips to balance the hoop) but not what happens outside the circle (e.g., someone bumping into it). The counselor works with the client to identify social situations that are especially upsetting or distressing (e.g., parents fighting, dealing with a bully at school). The counselor and client then focus on one social situation that is frustrating for the client, and the client writes down the things he or she can control on the inside of the circle and the things that cannot be controlled on the outside of the circle.

MUSIC

Music is a collection of sounds that can be created through various mediums such as instruments, voices, or other common objects (e.g., trash cans, spoons). Music has been an important part of culture for centuries, and it is a powerful tool that can allow youth to express themselves verbally or audibly. Music is used as a way to connect with one another, tap into emotions, spark old memories, or generally heighten daily experiences (Land, 2015).

In session, counselors can allow youth to create their own music as a form of self-expression. Music might be created in session using drums, chimes, or other items that create nice sounds. Clients can be given direction for the type of music they should create (e.g., "Play a tune that sounds like your relationship with your mother"). Alternatively, youth can be given freedom to create any sounds or write any lyrics that come to mind. Counselors can then work with clients to interpret or make sense of the music. Alternatively, the music-making experience can serve as a source of self-expression and catharsis that does not require interpretation.

Counselors can also use preexisting music to create a sense of human connection and similarity. Songs are inherently a source of self-expression, and it is common for several people to experience a similar difficulty that is expressed through music. For example, a counselor working with a client who has depression might choose a song that explores the song artist's experience of depression and ends with a hopeful message. The counselor and client can explore how the client's experience of depression is similar or different from the artist's, and the client can identify hopes and coping skills for the future. Youth—especially adolescents—are tuned into popular culture, and it is helpful when counselors can use music that the client already connects with and enjoys.

Clients can also be asked to bring their own music into counseling. Counselors might ask youth to bring a copy of their favorite song, a song they particularly dislike, or a song that seems relevant to the presenting problem. The counselor and client can build the therapeutic relationship by joining together in listening to the client's music, and the client can share thoughts and feelings that might have previously been kept inside. Finally, the counselor and client can join together to plan for the future using new coping skills and insights that come from the lyrics of the song. Counselors can help clients to process the meaning of the song and potentially create a new viewpoint or a renewed sense of hope.

Clinical Toolbox 8.5

In the Pearson eText, click here to review a therapeutic music activity.

Music is a fun and effective tool that can be used in counseling. Music interventions can be used in a group or individual setting. In a group, members can listen to one song provided by the counselor or an assigned group member, and the common experience of the artist and group members can be explored. Similarly, groups can be asked to create music together using instruments or written lyrics. Creating music together creates a shared experience, bonds the group, and can lead to a renewed sense of hope or direction. Music activities can be adapted to fit whatever theoretical approach the counselor practices from. Examples of music activities that can be used in counseling are provided in Table 8.5.

WRITING AND STORYTELLING

Writing and storytelling methods are also potentially helpful creative techniques that can be used in counseling. Counselors can choose to use various creative communication tools to facilitate client self-expression and insight. Some creative forms of writing and storytelling include:

- journaling;
- completing worksheets;
- making lists;
- reading and writing poetry;
- telling written and oral stories;
- writing and performing drama;
- writing letters;

Table 8.5 Examples of Music-Based Activities That Can Be Used in Counseling

Activity	Counseling Goal	Theoretical Orientation	Description
Sharing My Story	To facilitate client self-expression	Cognitive behavioral theory	The counselor asks the client his or her current favorite song and what about the song the client particularly enjoys. The counselor can find the song online and play it on an office computer or the client's device if applicable (the censored versions of songs should be used based on client developmental level). The counselor and client can listen to the song together and verbally process lyrics that are especially poignant and relevant to the client's mental health needs. The counselor can work to identify and challenge any unhelpful cognitions that might be uncovered, and the client should be encouraged to use music as a coping skill when having a difficult time.
Sharing the Moment (group activity)	To validate a common experience between individuals	Cognitive behavioral theory	The group facilitator chooses a popular song that relates to a common theme within the group. For example, Justin Bieber's song "Sorry" could be used in a group on dating and relationships. The counselor explains the theme of the group and provides an overview of the activity: A song will be played, and after the song is over, group members can be invited to share how they relate to the song (e.g., a lesson learned, a feeling that was highlighted). The group leader can link group members' experiences and ask group members to list other songs that might be helpful in times of need.
The Song of Today (group activity)	To increase group cohesion	Person-centered theory	Each group member is given an everyday object that also makes noise (e.g., a pair of spoons, a plastic bowl). Each group member takes a turn showing the group the noise of his or her instrument, and then the group members begin to make a song. One member begins by making the same sound repeatedly, the next member joins with a different sound that matches the pace of the initial member, and eventually all members play their instruments simultaneously. The group members name their song and brainstorm lyrics that would fit with the music. Optionally, a group member can sing while the others play. The counselor takes time at the end to highlight how the group members worked together and created a common experience.
"Shake It Off"	To increase emotional regulation	Dialectical behavioral theory	The counselor and client pinpoint an experience that was especially difficult for the client. All possible responses to the situation are explored (e.g., an aggressive response, an assertive response, walking away). If walking away seems to be the most helpful response, the counselor should play the song "Shake It Off" by Taylor Swift while the counselor and client practice shaking it off (a bit of body movement/dance could even be incorporated). Clients are encouraged to "shake it off" when faced with challenging situations in real life.
Express Yourself	To facilitate client self-expression	Adlerian theory	Clients who prefer not to express themselves verbally can express themselves through dance. Counselors should bring up an incident that relates to the client's struggles, and the client can be asked to identify a song or beat that matches the associated feeling. Counselors can play the song and ask the client to do a dance that shows how he or she feels about that incident. The counselor verbally processes how the dance is perceived and the feelings that were represented in the dance. The counselor can also respond to the client's dance with a dance of his or her own. This process is repeated whenever appropriate or necessary.

- sharing myths and fables;
- researching and writing essays;
- creating therapeutic stories;
- use of puppets by the client and/or counselor;
- watching movies;
- listening to books on tape;
- reading psychoeducation books;
- writing short or long stories; and
- writing and delivering speeches. (Land, 2015)

Counselors should choose the types of writing and storytelling appropriate for each client and his or her unique needs.

Narrative therapy (White & Epston, 1990) can be used as a framework to support the use of writing as a therapeutic medium. Using narrative therapy, individuals are given the power to create and rewrite their own stories. For example, a youth might write a story about a fight with a friend. Then, the child might go back through the story and identify parts that are not necessarily true (e.g., "I hate her") and rewrite those portions in more realistic terms ("I don't hate her. I was angry at her"). The youth might even write a new ending in which he or she apologizes to the friend. The new story allows youth to act differently in the future and can lead to therapeutic movement.

When using writing activities, youth are often able to express things that they could not otherwise say aloud. Some youth might have developmental delays that inhibit their verbal skills. Other youth might have experiences that are too difficult to say aloud. Counselors can sometimes use written words as a safe and effective way to communicate with clients nonverbally.

There are numerous ways youth can be engaged in therapeutic writing. Youth might be asked to keep a daily journal to facilitate self-expression and provide a centering experience that can support self-regulation (Land, 2015). Daily journals might also be used to track thoughts, feelings, and behaviors, as well as to facilitate insight. Youth might be invited to write at times when they are experiencing emotional difficulties because writing can reduce anxiety and other unhelpful feelings (Park, Ramirez, & Beilock, 2014). Writing exercises can serve as powerful tools to help youth to calm down, focus on a specific activity, express themselves in a nonthreatening manner, claim power over their environments, and gain new and helpful insights.

Counselors can use therapeutic storytelling to inspire youth to continue changing and growing in resilient ways. Stories related to a youth's mental health needs can be carefully selected by counselors, or counselors and clients can write stories together to facilitate movement through the use of metaphors and fantasy (Kress, Adamson, & Yensel, 2010). The use of storytelling in counseling can be supported by various theoretical orientations (e.g., person-centered, cognitive behavioral, narrative) and serves to increase trust in the therapeutic relationship, foster client motivation and empowerment, and promote cognitive organization (Bergner, 2007; Carlson, 2001; Erickson & Rossi, 1989). Guidelines for the use of therapeutic storytelling include:

- choose a story that is appropriate;
- determine if a prewritten story or personalized story will work best;
- time the intervention carefully;
- incorporate the client's goals and resources;
- make sure the client can connect to the story;
- ensure the message of the story is positive and realistic;
- know the story well when presenting it;
- introduce the client to the storytelling process and ask permission to use the story; and
- process the story intentionally. (Kress et al., 2010)

When selecting a story for a client, counselors should consider the client's developmental level, presenting concerns, and current mental health needs (Kress et al., 2010). If the counselor is able to locate a prewritten story that is likely to resonate with the client, the story can be read aloud in session by the counselor or client or the client can take the story home to read (for older children and adolescents). Counselors can ask process questions afterward to help clients to apply the story to their own lives. Reading is a helpful tool that can be used in counseling to normalize client experiences and teach new skills. Counselors can read stories with their clients in session to address key issues such as the death of a loved one, interpersonal difficulties, personal development, and emotion regulation (Eppler, Olsen, & Hidano, 2009; Slyter, 2012). Stories can provide normalization for the client because the story is evidence that others have experienced similar struggles.

Counselors can also provide books to clients that they can read based on their specific needs. For example, a counselor might give a teenage girl a text about interpersonal relationships that she can read at home and then process any questions or insights in session. Through the text, the girl can learn helpful and unhelpful behaviors for interpersonal relationships, and she can also learn new ways of interacting with her peers. Youth can read poems, fables, fairytales, myths, essays, and religious passages to learn about themselves and the world around them.

Sometimes, counselors are not able to locate a book, story, poem, or passage that provides an alternative way of viewing a problem or that is likely to promote insight and growth in the client. In that case, counselors can write stories for their clients (Kress et al., 2010). For example, a young girl who was sexually abused might benefit from a story about a tomcat (her favorite animal) having a scary and painful experience that was out of his control (e.g., getting his tail caught under a pile of rocks). Counselors should incorporate similar resources to which the client has access to inspire the client (Kress et al., 2010). Counselors can even coauthor stories with clients to explore and process conflicts and achieve mental health goals.

Finally, drama can be used in counseling to allow clients to express themselves through writing and performing scripts. Psychodrama, originally developed by Moreno (1932), is a theoretical foundation that can be used to support interventions related to drama and performance. In psychodrama, individuals are encouraged to enact important life events that still linger or feel unfinished. Psychodrama can be used in a group or individual format; if the group members have all experienced a similar life difficulty (e.g., divorce of parents), the entire group might benefit from a particular act, but sometimes group members can serve as a support system for one individual enacting something that is particularly important to him or her.

Scripts and performances can be based on the real-life events or consist of metaphors that address the youth's presenting problems in nonthreatening ways. Drama allows youth to gain a sense of power and control in session, and youth are able to express themselves and learn how to create new life stories (Land, 2015; Slyter, 2012). Overall, writing and storytelling in counseling can take many creative, engaging, and effective forms. Examples of theoretically supported writing and storytelling activities for counseling are provided in Table 8.6.

The use of creative arts in counseling is an effective way for counselors to build genuine connections with their clients. People of all ages enjoy using their imaginations and creating. Counselors should trust in the power of the counseling process to design and implement creative counseling interventions that will help clients to reach their goals.

Table 8.6	Examples of Writing and Storytelling Activities That Can Be Used in Counseling		
Activity	Counseling Goal	Theoretical Orientation	Description
Tell Me a Story	To increase client understanding and coping skills	Bibliotherapy	The counselor chooses a storybook that is developmentally appropriate for the client and addresses a struggle that is relevant (e.g., potty training, social anxiety, divorce in the household). The counselor reminds the client of the specific issue the book addresses and then reads the book to the client. The counselor and client then process how the story relates to the client and how the client can learn from the story and apply it in the future.
ReStory-Telling	To encourage rational and helpful cognitions	Narrative theory and cognitive behavioral theory	The client is asked to write the details of an event that occurred and was especially troubling (e.g., a recent fight with a friend, an instance of abuse or neglect). The counselor and client can read the story together, identify any details that might be unhelpful or irrational, and then work to rewrite the story with a more desirable ending.

(Continued)

Table 8.6			Examples of Writing and Storytelling Activities That Can Be Used in Counseling (*Continued*)
Activity	Counseling Goal	Theoretical Orientation	Description
Freewriting	To increase self-expression and facilitate catharsis	Person-Centered theory	Clients spend 5–10 minutes per day writing in a journal or diary. Clients write about their daily experiences and their thoughts and feelings. This activity is inherently therapeutic because it allows clients to reflect on and organize their thoughts. Counselors can ask clients to share important passages as appropriate or helpful.
Act It Out (group activity)	To increase group rapport and create a shared group experience	Psychodrama therapy	Group members work together to create a play. They decide on a title and a main theme for the play. This theme should relate to the purpose of the group (e.g., grief, substance use). The play should have a meaningful ending that incorporates healthy coping skills, and the group members may act out the play for an audience (e.g., parents) if possible or therapeutic.
Share Yourself	To facilitate self-exploration, self-expression, and catharsis	Gestalt theory	Clients are encouraged to write poems about their presenting struggles. This poem can be written in session or assigned as homework. The client reads the poem aloud for the counselor, who validates and processes the meaning with the client.

Summary

In this chapter, the foundations, techniques, and interventions associated with play and creative arts were explored. Many terms are used to describe the use of creativity, art, expression, and play in therapy, and mental health professionals should take care to advertise and implement these interventions in accordance with their licensure and credentials. Counselors should create individualized treatment plans to meet their clients' needs and support all creative interventions with sound theoretical frameworks.

Play therapy is an expressive type of mental health intervention in which play behaviors are used to facilitate exploration, insight, and growth in clients. Play therapy can be used with all age ranges, but it is especially relevant for use with youth due to its developmental nature. Play therapy is effective with various mental health concerns, including trauma, mood difficulties, phobias, grief, and adjustment struggles and transitions.

The two primary approaches to using play therapy are nondirective play and directive play. As the names suggest, counselors are more directive and manipulate interventions in directive play therapy, and nondirective counselors believe clients have the ability to heal themselves given the proper tools and circumstances. Examples of nondirective play therapy are child-centered play therapy, experiential play therapy, and filial therapy. Directive play therapies include various theories, and those explored in this chapter include Adlerian play therapy, cognitive behavioral play therapy, release play therapy, and theraplay. Sandplay and the use of sand tray were also explained as approaches or techniques that can be used when counseling youth.

Creative arts activities engage the imagination and spark unique connections that may not be achieved via more traditional talk therapy. Creative arts have been used as a therapeutic tool since the beginning of formal mental health theorization and therapy. Some broad categories of creativity that can be used in counseling include art, music, and writing or storytelling. The foundations for each of these categories were explored, and examples of creative activities were provided. It is important to note that creative activities can be incorporated into interventions associated with all counseling theories.

Overall, counselors might consider integrating play and creativity into their practices whenever possible. Play and creative interventions can be therapeutic for a broad range of clients who have an array of presenting problems.

Try the Topic 10 Assignments: *The Use of Play and Creativity in Counseling Youth.*

CHAPTER 9

Conceptualizing Young Clients' Situations and Directing Counseling

---

THE CASE OF DAQUAN

Daquan is 8 years old and lives with his younger sister and his mom. He has not been his usual self since learning about his father's 3-year sentence for selling marijuana. Daquan has a loving relationship with his mother, sister, and grandparents. His mom told me that when she told Daquan and his sister about their father's incarceration, Daquan became extremely upset and locked himself in the bathroom for several hours, refusing to open the door until his grandfather persuaded him to join the family for dinner. Daquan has a strong attachment to his father because they spent a lot of time together throughout Daquan's childhood. Daquan is outgoing, funny, and popular among his peers, and he is a kid who has good manners—a really respectful student. Daquan typically earns good grades, demonstrates positive behavior at school, and has excellent attendance.

Over the past 3 weeks, I have noticed that Daquan's academic performance, classroom behavior, and peer interactions have drastically changed. Following his 3-day suspension due to fighting with a classmate, I noticed a slight change in Daquan's classroom participation; he no longer desires to answer questions during group discussions or serve as a classroom helper—a role that I use to reward model students and that Daquan had always enjoyed. Daquan appears irritable, angry, and sad at times; seems to become highly reactive when annoyed; and has been playing less with his peers.

There have been several incidences, including Daquan throwing his books on the floor during a temper outburst, storming out of the classroom after accidentally breaking a crayon, and breaking down in tears when he was not chosen to be the line leader for a restroom break. Since then, Daquan has become increasingly argumentative and has refused to complete many of his academic assignments. His grades have dropped.

Numerous students have stated that Daquan has been bullying them on the bus and during recess. His peers reported that Daquan has been calling them names, yelling curse words at them, and threatening to punch them for not playing games by his rules. When I met with Daquan, he did not provide any explanations for his uncharacteristic behaviors. This is a special kid, and something is very wrong here. Can you help him?

—Daquan's teacher

WHERE TO BEGIN: SUGGESTIONS FOR DIRECTING COUNSELING AND DEVELOPING A TREATMENT PLAN

Most young people in counseling have layered and complex life circumstances, and conceptualizing their situations and determining the best way to help them can be confusing; focusing and directing counseling is no easy task. In a short amount of time, counselors are required to develop a thoughtful understanding of a client's situation (i.e., case conceptualization) and determine a plan for helping him or her. School counselors may have as little as 15 minutes to assess a student's situation and figure out what the student needs, and counselors working in clinical settings generally have about 1 hour to do so. It is important that counselors have theories and models they can use to direct their thinking because failure to be thorough and thoughtful could result in harm to their clients (Kress & Paylo, 2015).

The material presented in this chapter is intended to aid counselors in their ability to conceptualize young people's situations and create comprehensive counseling and treatment plans. The first section of the chapter introduces practice principles that counselors can use to guide their thinking and planning when counseling youth. The second section presents a comprehensive, strength-based treatment planning model (i.e., the I CAN START model; Kress & Paylo, 2015).

The setting in which a counselor works will likely determine how detailed he or she will need to be in planning and structuring counseling. School counselors do not typically develop formal counseling and/or treatment plans. However, clinical mental health counselors, who work in community agencies, hospitals, residential treatment facilities, or any other clinical setting, are typically required to develop formal treatment plans. Although the information presented in this chapter is geared toward counselors who engage in formal treatment planning, the principles, concepts, and information can be equally useful to school counselors and counselors who are not required to develop formal treatment plans.

There is no shortage of available resources that counselors can use to identify objectives and goals that can be used when counseling clients who have various problems and mental disorders. As an example, the Jongsma (e.g., Jongsma, Peterson, & Bruce, 2014) treatment planning series includes numerous treatment planning books, which provide examples of short-term objectives, long-term goals, and therapeutic interventions that relate to youth and the problems they experience. There has also been a trend toward agencies' use of computer software systems that generate predetermined counseling goals, objectives, and interventions.

These resources can be helpful, but counselors must have a comprehensive model that can guide their conceptualization of their clients' situations and help them to create thorough, effective counseling plans (Kress & Paylo, 2015). In addition, counselors must understand the basic foundations of good counseling and treatment planning. Good counseling plans are unique to each youth's needs and strengths; counselors should not cut and paste predetermined treatment goals, objectives, and interventions developed by others into a client's treatment plan (Kress & Paylo, 2015). Counselors who rely on treatment goals, objectives, and interventions that are determined by others run the risk of creating treatment plans that are prescriptive, lack individualization, are too generic, and do not optimally meet clients' needs (Kress & Paylo, 2015).

Good youth counseling is evidence based, individualized, relational, strength based, and contextually sensitive (Kress & Paylo, 2015). The following guiding principles can be used in the process of developing and focusing counseling. These principles are also integrated into the I CAN START model, which is presented later in this chapter. The principles are intended to serve as a starting place for counselors as they develop treatment plans or otherwise focus the direction of counseling.

Take a Relational, Collaborative, and Strength-Based Approach with Clients

A strong counseling relationship is the most important predictor of successful counseling. A healthy **therapeutic alliance** has an effect on clients' satisfaction with counseling services, how much and what they feel safe disclosing, their optimism or faith in the counselor and counseling, and their sense of hope that their situation can change (Norcross, 2011). A counselor's ability to convey relationship-building characteristics such as empathy, congruence, positive regard, and affirmation in the counseling relationship is essential, and the importance of counselors communicating these factors cannot be overstated (Norcross, 2011). When a strong relationship is present, counselors and clients will communicate well, be in agreement on the goals and tasks of counseling, and be able to collaboratively develop counseling goals.

Counselors must be genuine and congruent; they must be perceived as truthful, honest, and who they suggest they are. Youth are particularly adept at sensing when those around them are not being congruent. Adolescents in particular tend to test to see if the counselor really is the person he or she is presenting (i.e., if the counselor is authentic) and may take longer to build a solid relationship foundation with the counselor (Whitmarsh & Mullette, 2009). Many adolescents distrust adults or authority figures; thus, early in counseling they are less likely to demonstrate an interest in collaborating with counselors (Whitmarsh & Mullette, 2009). Building rapport and trust early in a counseling relationship is not impossible, but counselors should be patient during the trust-building process.

When building a counseling relationship, the counselor must be able to connect with young clients' experiences. Although counselors were children at one time, they have often lost their connection with the perspective or experience of being a child or adolescent. Counselors who are able to put themselves in their clients' shoes and at their developmental level will be better at helping them to make changes. Related to this idea, counselors should be aware of the developmental distinctions between children and adolescents. As an example, adolescents generally tend to be better aware of the counseling process, skeptical of its ability to be helpful, and less trusting of authority figures; these factors will influence how a counselor responds to the client (Whitmarsh & Mullette, 2009). Even a year's difference in age (e.g., a 12-year-old and a 13-year-old), can make a world of difference in terms of how a client responds to a counselor and the counseling process. Being sensitive to developmental matters and recalling their own experiences during their youth can help counselors to build a therapeutic, trusting relationship.

Counseling goals and treatment plans should be individualized to the client's needs and preferences and should be developed in collaboration with feedback from the client and his or her family (Kress & Paylo, 2015). Young people should have a voice in counseling, and this collaborative approach complies with the various ethical codes that guide counselor practice (e.g., the American Counseling Association's [ACA] *Code of Ethics,* 2014; the American Mental Health Counselors Association's *Code of Ethics*, 2015). In addition, third-party payers require that clients' preferences direct the focus of counseling.

The idea that young people should be active participants in counseling is rooted in a strength-based philosophy and the assumption that clients and their families best know their problems and the solutions to their problems. A **strength-based approach** is grounded in the assumption that the development and amplification of strengths and assets within and around the individual provide clients with a greater sense of resiliency against problems in living and/or mental illness (Smith, 2006). Counselors who work from a strength-based perspective actively focus on enhancing, developing, and highlighting clients' resources, strengths, times of resiliency, and ability to cope and persevere.

Counseling is not something that is done to clients; rather clients and their families are active participants in the counseling process (Kress & Paylo, 2015). Engaging clients in counseling can foster a sense of resiliency and strength, which may foster young people's self-efficacy and thus can facilitate their motivation to make the life changes they need to be successful (Carney, 2007). A strength-based focus is empowering and thus enhances clients' sense of self-esteem by increasing their sense of self-determination, sense of mastery of life, and ability to endure and persevere.

Counselors should discuss with their clients and their families the advantages and disadvantages of different counseling approaches and counseling goals. They should determine clients' and families' strengths, capacities, and resources and discuss how these will be integrated into counseling and how they will focus counseling. If young clients collaboratively identify the goals and the direction of counseling, they will be more personally invested in change, and the counseling process will be demystified. Even very young clients can have a voice—as developmentally appropriate—in counseling goals and the counseling process.

Focus on Evidence-Based Counseling Approaches and Interventions

Evidence-based practices are research-based interventions and treatments that have demonstrated effectiveness in addressing the various struggles that clients present. Because they have demonstrated success, evidence-based practices should reduce clients' mental health symptoms, thus improving their level of functioning and/or their ability to thrive within their families and communities (Kress & Paylo, 2015). Evidence-based practices have been supported as effective by randomized controlled trials, the gold standard for clinical health care research (Kress & Paylo, 2015). **Randomized controlled trials** are research studies that are *controlled*, meaning they have a nontreatment group (i.e., a control group) that the treatment group is compared to, and *randomized*, meaning that a participant has an equal or random chance of being assigned to any of the treatment groups or the control group. Such studies are rigorous, and knowing that certain approaches or interventions have demonstrated success even under these well-controlled circumstances helps to give counselors confidence that the approaches they select for use with clients are supported as effective. In this book, we make every attempt to indicate evidence-based approaches and interventions that can be used to address many of the problems that young people present.

Consider Context and Culture

When conceptualizing clients' situations and developing counseling plans, counselors should also be sensitive to contextual and cultural considerations. A focus on, and a sensitivity to, culture and context are important because clients need to be understood in the context of their unique situations if counseling is to be effective (Kress & Paylo, 2015).

Context refers to the interrelated conditions in which clients' experiences and behaviors occur. In considering clients' situations from a contextual perspective, culture, gender, and various developmental factors are just a few of the important factors that should be considered.

Culture and gender are exceptionally important contextual considerations; culture defines, expresses, and interprets people's beliefs and worldviews, values, customs, and gender-role expectations. Multicultural considerations can have a significant impact on how counselors and clients think about their problems in living and on what they perceive they need to do to resolve these problems. In fact, the *ACA Code of Ethics* (2014) emphasizes that culture influences the way that clients' problems are understood, so counselors must consider culture throughout the counseling process. Counselors cannot understand clients' situations and how best to help them if they do not consider cultural factors. An understanding of clients' culture in relation to counseling and treatment planning includes a focus on cultural explanations of illness experiences and help-seeking behaviors, the cultural framework of clients' identity, cultural meanings of healthy functioning, and cultural aspects that relate to the counselor–client relationship.

Culture dictates what people see as normal and abnormal. For example, families often bring young clients into counseling for problems that they perceive as being some form of misbehavior. Youth's behaviors—good and bad—are interpreted through a lens that is clouded by cultural norms and expectations. Parenting and discipline are highly culturally dependent factors that relate to youth counseling. Culture influences what behaviors or symptoms are permitted as appropriate and how individuals are permitted or encouraged to manage their distress. Culture also determines how friends, family, and the community respond to distress or problematic behaviors, especially in terms of determining the type and severity of the problems that must be evident before family or community intervention is deemed necessary. Culture also determines acceptable help-seeking behaviors and interventions, as well as who is expected to intervene.

Counselors must consider not only the interaction of culture, race, ethnicity, and gender when considering the development, maintenance, and treatment of problems but also the influence of socioeconomic status. Individuals living in poverty are among the most marginalized and stigmatized people in the United States (Foss, Generali, & Kress, 2017). Counselors need to be sensitive to the myriad considerations that relate to poverty. Those who live in poverty experience both system barriers (e.g., stereotypes about those who live in poverty, social structures that are not supportive of this population) and internal barriers. Common barriers include financial instability (e.g., food insecurity), abuse experiences, chronic mental or physical illnesses, young pregnancies, and/or interpersonal partner violence or living in unsafe relationships (Foss et al., 2017).

Despite the need this population has for counseling services, the values, expectations, and requirements for obtaining and successfully participating in counseling may be at odds; traditional counseling models may be more consistent with middle-class values rather than the values of individuals from diverse backgrounds. Clients need to see counseling as relevant to their immediate needs (Foss et al., 2017). For example, people who live in poverty are typically focused on the present; many do not have the luxury of planning for the future. Counselors are generally interested in helping clients think about their future—in the context of their mental health—but clients may not be able do so if they are barely making it in the present moment. Supporting clients in getting their basic needs met is critical, and doing so can be a wonderful way to develop a warm, trusting counseling relationship (Foss et al., 2017).

As an example, if a young client's mother is struggling to feed her children and her electricity has been turned off, the focus of counseling may need to be on supporting the mother in attending to these basic needs. Discussions about future-oriented matters may be irrelevant and feel insensitive to the mother because her needs are so immediate. In addition, the trend in community mental health treatment is for counselors to provide case management to their clients; thus, the line between counseling and case management has become thin, and counselors need to adapt and help those who live in poverty to garner the resources they need to be successful. In some contexts and situations, it may be helpful for these objectives to be reflected in clients' counseling plans.

Overall, culture and gender influence clients in multiple ways, including their experiences of problems, their internal sense of distress in different situations, their interpretations of problems after experiencing their reactions or symptoms, and their presentation of complaints (Eriksen & Kress, 2008). Culture and gender also affect counselors' perceptions of clients' presenting problems, their understanding of mental disorders, their style of interviewing, and their choice of theoretical perspectives and counseling approaches (Eriksen & Kress, 2008).

Development is another important aspect of client context that needs to be considered when focusing counseling and developing a counseling plan. Counselors value a developmental perspective which holds that many young people's problems in living are rooted in disruptions to their normal developmental processes. As such, helping clients get back on their normal developmental track can foster health. Counselors also believe that many young clients' problems in living are not necessarily problems but rather normal developmental transitions that they are traversing. For example, consider a young boy who has just switched schools and is struggling with feelings of sadness and loss secondary to this transition. Considering this situation from a developmental perspective, loss and sadness would be considered a normal reaction, the resolution of which will provide an opportunity for the boy to become better connected with his sense of resiliency and to manage transitions in the future.

A developmental focus depicts youth as dynamic—rather than static—organisms, and it highlights their natural inclinations toward growth and health. Developmental perspectives offer hope because client problems or positions are not permanent; instead, they are constantly changing and growing. Inherent in a developmental perspective is the understanding that young people have the capacity to move forward, to change, to adapt, to heal, and to attain optimal mental health.

Fully considering and integrating relevant knowledge, skills, and awareness with regard to cultural, gender, and developmental issues can be challenging. People are complex, and it is difficult to fully understand all of the factors that influence youth. Contextually sensitive case conceptualization and counseling are easier to talk about than to actually do, but clients benefit if counselors push themselves to understand clients in their context. Counselors must consider how they can integrate various contextual factors into clients' counseling and treatment plans.

Follow the Golden Thread

When developing counseling and treatment plans, clinical and community counselors must consider numerous factors. Counseling agencies all have accrediting bodies that dictate different required aspects of a formal treatment plan (Kress & Paylo, 2015). Counselors also often have to work around session and service limits applied by third-party payer sources, and this can influence a treatment plan. Counselors must also consider a client's diagnosis and its potential for reimbursement because not all diagnoses are eligible for the same level of care or allotted session numbers. All of these considerations affect the types of approaches counselors use, the types of services that can be integrated into a treatment plan, the number of counseling sessions, and the types of treatment theories and models that can be applied and considered as part of the client's treatment plan (Kress & Paylo, 2015).

In clinical settings, the client's *Diagnostic and Statistical Manual of Mental Disorders* (*DSM*; American Psychiatric Association [APA], 2013a) diagnosis is typically the starting place for the development of the treatment plan and the goals, and interventions identified in the treatment plan are directly related to the indicated diagnosis. For example, a counselor cannot provide a diagnosis of attention-deficit/hyperactivity disorder (ADHD) and select goals and interventions aimed at treating conduct disorder. The **Golden Thread** refers to the idea that the treatment, and just as important the documentation, progresses in a logical fashion as follows: The diagnosis and the client's goal in seeking counseling lead to the development of aims and objectives of treatment, which lead to counselor-prescribed interventions. Related to this idea of the Golden Thread, the interventions that are identified in the treatment plan must be the same interventions presented and addressed in the progress notes. Counselors cannot begin to provide interventions that do not relate to the diagnosis, goals, and interventions addressed in the treatment plan without modifying the treatment plan. Finally, as clients conclude their counseling, their treatment summary documentation should also present a unified, cohesive treatment approach that follows the Golden Thread philosophy. A thoughtful, careful presentation in practice and in documentation communicates a deliberate, thoughtful approach to counseling, and it demonstrates that the counselor is working to a certain standard of care.

Be Flexible: Treatment Plans Are Not Static

In our experience, new counselors often identify too many counseling goals and objectives. Counseling and treatment plans are evolving documents, and over time the treatment plan will be revisited and edited and additions will be made. When developing a preliminary treatment plan, counselors pull on a limited amount of information—generally information they have been provided with at one or two points in time. As counselors get to know their clients and their families better, they are privy to additional information that may shift the focus of the initial plan. Counselors should also be aware that clients, as counseling progresses, will have experiences that change their situations; successes and new struggles will emerge, and clients and their families may want to change the focus of counseling. Counselors have an ethical responsibility to be flexible in how they conceptualize clients' treatment plans.

As clients' diagnoses, symptoms, or presenting problems evolve, the treatment plan must be updated to reflect these changes. As an example, a client may have initially presented with severe disruptive behaviors associated with conduct disorder, but after 3 months of intervention he or she may experience lessened disruptive behaviors but still need to address ongoing depressive symptoms. In this situation, the treatment plan objectives must be updated to reflect the client's current needs.

Related to the idea of being flexible, clients will also present with life crises that may require a counselor to take a detour in his or her approach, either in a select session or overall. All clients face changing life circumstances, and counselors need to be flexible and know when detours are appropriate. As an example, a school counselor might be meeting with a youth to address classroom behavior, but if the child's dog just died and he is upset about this, it may be more appropriate to address the child's loss.

Finally, counselors are often called on to work as part of a team, and this can require flexibility in their counseling approach. Counselors sometimes need to adapt their counseling plan to include team input or the team's consensus.

The principles discussed in this section can help counselors to approach and focus counseling and, where applicable, develop treatment plans. The following section presents a model that counselors can use to focus counseling and guide their treatment planning process.

A CONCEPTUAL FRAMEWORK FOR CASE CONCEPTUALIZATION AND TREATMENT PLANNING

The material presented elsewhere in this text and earlier in this chapter informs the treatment planning model presented in this section. The essential elements needed for a counselor to construct a comprehensive strength-based treatment plan are organized within the presented model. This systematic model is represented by the acronym **I CAN START** (see Figure 9.1; Kress & Paylo, 2015). This mnemonic code is intended to assist counselors in the relevant recall of the important aspects of the model.

I	Individual
C	Contextual assessment
A	Assessment and diagnosis
N	Necessary level of care
S	Strengths
T	Treatment approach
A	Aim and objectives of counseling
R	Research-based interventions
T	Therapeutic support services

FIGURE 9.1   A Conceptual Framework for Case Conceptualization and Treatment Planning

Components of the Conceptual Framework

INDIVIDUAL (I)

Just as every client is unique, so is every counselor. Counselors should consider who they are as individuals as they approach each client. Because counselors' personal and professional experiences are so important and frame their experience with clients, the model's first component is an *I*, which stands for *Individual*: Who is the counselor as an individual, and how do his or her personal and professional qualities and factors relate to his or her work with a given client?

This aspect of the model includes both professional and personal characteristics. An example of a professional characteristic is the counselor's personal scope of practice. Each counselor has unique training experiences and competencies with clients' presenting issues and populations. Ethically, counselors must know their professional competencies so they can ensure they are competent to work with certain populations. Counselor personal characteristics may influence their professional practice and their:

- theoretical approach;
- interventions selected;
- pacing and structuring of counseling;
- demeanor and style; and
- approach to engaging families and community partners.

Personal characteristics or qualities are more elusive and have to do with the essence, or the personhood, of the counselor. Personal characteristics also include any experiences counselors have over the course of their lives that influence their perceptions and values, and thus their counseling practice.

Counselors bring their personal qualities, lived experiences, and professional training into each counseling relationship. As such, they must be aware of how clients perceive them and how their characteristics may affect the counseling relationship. Research suggests that counselor qualities such as being over- or understructuring, defensive, critical, demanding, or unsupportive have poorer therapeutic alliances and counseling outcomes (Sharpless, Muran, & Barber, 2010). Some counselor traits have little to no influence on counseling outcomes (e.g., age, sex, ethnicity), but counselors who are perceived as empathic, authentic, warm, interested, open-minded, confident, flexible in practice, and accepting of clients have better counseling outcomes, form stronger working alliances, and have more successful counseling outcomes (Sharpless et al., 2010; Zuroff, Kelly, Leybman, Blatt, & Wampold, 2010). Counselor optimism, emotional health, and emotional stability can also affect counseling in positive ways, thus suggesting the importance of counselors monitoring their own mental health (Zuroff et al., 2010).

As counselors consider themselves in relation to their counseling practice, they should be aware of their personal strengths, capacities, and resources and leverage these in their work. Often, a counselor's strengths and weaknesses are different sides of the same coin. For instance, consider a counselor who is very focused, action oriented, and eager to set goals and move forward in supporting clients in the change process. This counselor's weakness may be moving forward too fast and not paying attention to subtle shifts in the client's situation that may affect the focus and direction of counseling. Counselors should develop an awareness of their personal strengths and take steps to optimize these, while also being aware of their weaknesses and ensuring these do not have an adverse impact on clients (Kress & Paylo, 2015).

Counselors are not static beings; like all people, they are constantly changing. As counselors evolve, they should pay attention to how their experiences and personal changes affect their work with clients. As counselors age and have different experiences with youth in their personal lives, they may find themselves professionally positioned in different roles relative to their young clients. Counselors' relationships and approaches toward young people may be affected by their age, developmental level, and/or changing life roles. As an example, a counselor in her 20s might have a certain approach she prefers, and then in her 30s have children and find that she begins to develop a different approach or different reactions toward her work with young clients and/or their families. This new approach may be helpful—or not—but what is important is that she is aware of these changes and makes an effort to ensure her counseling practices are productive and helpful.

With regard to the individual aspect of the I CAN START model, counselors might consider, among other factors, countertransference reactions specific to youth and families and their own cultural worldviews. Both of these factors are briefly addressed in the following sections.

Countertransference.   When working with young clients and families, counselors will experience countertransference reactions. **Countertransference** is defined as redirection of a counselor's feelings toward a client—or, more generally, as a counselor's emotional entanglement with a client. These reactions are not always harmful, and in fact they can be helpful. Countertransference can serve as an interpersonal barometer—an instrument—that provides valuable information about the client or family members. As an example, if a counselor feels frustrated with a young client's father's lack of follow-through, the child or other family members may respond to the father in this way too, thus providing the counselor with valuable insight.

Before becoming youth counselors, counselor trainees must spend time reflecting on their own childhood and adult experiences and how these experiences may influence them because these experiences will significantly affect their ideas about how to help children and families. It is obvious that traumatic or difficult childhood experiences have a significant impact on counselors, but normal childhood experiences can also affect counselors' perceptions of how to help children. These values, beliefs, and ideas are typically so ingrained that counselors do not realize their existence.

The impact of countertransference is constantly present when counseling children and adolescents, perhaps even more so than when counseling adults. Because youth counselors typically work with multiple adults around the child, both within and outside the child's family, these counselors may experience many countertransference reactions (e.g., with case workers or teachers; Rasic, 2010). Counselors must be aware of any positive or negative feelings that arise when working with youth because these emotions may create problems and affect counseling practice.

Because counseling with youth and their families can bring up so many personal reactions that are rooted in past experiences and cultural beliefs and values, counselors should be aware of and consider their reactions and how these reactions influence counseling. Reactions that suggest countertransference include:

- overidentification with the client or one of the family members;
- attempts to rescue or save the client from others or from his or her natural consequences;
- perceiving oneself as playing an overly important role in the client's life;
- projecting personal views on parenting and discipline onto parents;
- placing personal views of appropriate youth behavior on the youth and family members;
- attempting to solve or fix the client's problems;
- attempting to parent the client;
- thinking about the client or family outside of counseling sessions;
- disregarding the parents as ineffective or otherwise vilifying the parents; and
- wanting to see the client outside of sessions or for more sessions than warranted.

When acted on or not managed, these countertransference reactions may manifest in boundary violations. Boundary violations can be subtle (e.g., allowing sessions to go 5 minutes over) or more extreme (e.g., initiating relationships with youth outside of the counseling relationship). Counselors should monitor for these reactions and stop them before they become problematic.

The way clients respond to counselors can also trigger countertransference reactions. It is common for adolescents in particular to be disengaged, bored, or otherwise uninterested in participating in counseling, and this may trigger feelings of inadequacy in the counselor (Rasic, 2010). The change process may be slow with youth, and this too can trigger feelings of frustration in the counselor. It is important for counselors to recognize any feelings of frustration or thoughts of being ineffective that such client behavior might trigger and to discuss their reactions with a trusted colleague or supervisor.

To illuminate the idea that counselors' background experiences affect their work with youth, consider one of the more divisive issues that almost always emerges when counseling youth: corporal punishment. **Corporal punishment** is the use of physical punishment (e.g., spanking, slapping) that involves the infliction of pain as retribution for an offense or for the purpose of disciplining or reforming behavior. It is legal in the home in all U.S. states (attempts to ban it in several states have been unsuccessful), and it is, at this writing, banned in public schools in 31 states. Corporal punishment is connected to various negative physical, emotional, social, behavioral, and neurophysiological issues, including increased potential for aggressive behavior or even, in some contexts, the development of mental disorders (Taylor, Moeller, Hamvas, & Rice, 2012).

Because most American families use corporal punishment (Taylor et al., 2012), all counselors who work with youth will need to consider their own ideas on corporal punishment. Perspectives on corporal punishment are influenced by numerous cultural variables, including socioeconomic status, ethnic background, and social class, as well as personal experiences.

Although many counselors are not comfortable with the idea of corporal punishment as a form of discipline, they must be aware of it and should not make family members feel intimidated while they explore alternative ways to manage and influence their children's behavior. This corporal punishment example is just one of many situations counselors face that require an awareness and sensitivity to one's personal values and beliefs.

Another topic that relates to countertransference is how any personal abuse and/or trauma experiences affect counselors' reactions to young clients and their families. Research suggests that the majority of women who become counselors have experienced some form of trauma or abuse (Pope & Feldman-Summers, 1992). No recent research has been conducted on the prevalence of mental health professionals' abuse experiences, but one classic study's finding indicated that 70% of female psychologists had experienced some form of abuse (inclusive of adult and child victimization), with 39% of female psychologists and 26% of male psychologists having experienced some form of child abuse (Pope & Feldman-Summers, 1992). These findings suggest that the majority of people reading this text have some past victimization experience. Counselors must ask themselves how their past victimization experiences affect their work with clients. Counselors' decision making and ability to objectively counsel clients may be compromised if they are struggling with unaddressed abuse material. As an example, a counselor might find it difficult to hear details of a client's abuse experiences because it may trigger personal reactions. Yet, counselors need to help a client who has been abused or traumatized to integrate and process his or her activating memories (Cohen, Mannarino, & Deblinger, 2006).

Culture. Effective counselors are aware of their personal context and culture and how these factors may affect their work with clients. Counselor beliefs and attitudes are culturally rooted, and they may bump into or even clash with some of the clients' beliefs and attitudes (Sue & Sue, 2015). An important aspect of establishing one's identity is coming to terms with and developing a clear understanding of one's cultural, ethnic, gender, and racial identity. To provide culturally sensitive counseling, counselors should be sensitive to their own values, assumptions, and biases. Related to this idea, counselors must understand oppression, racism, and discrimination and be aware of how their own attitudes, values, and personal reactions might have an impact on clients or hinder the counseling relationship and process. This awareness should include an understanding of the counselor's immediate and extended family structure, as well as social and community groups and their influence on their development and worldviews.

Clinical Toolbox 9.1

In the Pearson etext, click here to read about important counselor considerations that relate to counseling diverse clients.

Gender is also an important aspect of culture. Sexuality and sexual identity are closely related to ideas about gender, and counselors should have a clear sense of their gender and sexual identity and their ideas and values toward those who have different ideas from theirs so they can effectively help clients.

Lesbian, gay, bisexual, transgender, and questioning (LGBTQ) youth face a unique set of diverse challenges when coming to terms with their sexuality and gender identity, and if counselors are struggling with their own issues, these issues will likely get in the way of the counselors' ability to help clients. Counselors must be prepared to guide clients through many phases of self-awareness, realization, and acceptance.

Personal counseling can help counselors to enhance their self-awareness of who they are and how their unique constellation of characteristics affects their counseling practices. Personal counseling can serve as a vehicle for enhancing self-awareness of one's strengths and weaknesses and can facilitate personal development.

Certain clients or client situations will trigger strong reactions, and counselors working with youth and families can experience reactions that are exponentially greater than reactions they experience when working with adult clients. All counselors have family experiences that they carry with them, and these experiences cloud how they think about the families with whom they work. Awareness and self-honesty about their reactions is important, and this awareness is the first step in ensuring these reactions do not affect their judgment and harm their clients.

To best understand their personal characteristics and how they are affecting counseling, or the *I* aspect of this model, counselors should engage in regular supervision and peer consultation, in addition to participating in their own personal counseling (Sue & Sue, 2015). A transparent, open conversation about counselors' experiences and reactions can help them to self-monitor and sharpen the most important tool they use in counseling: themselves. Good self-awareness and an ability to thoughtfully maximize one's strengths within a counseling relationship—while minimizing one's limitations or weaknesses—lays the foundation for working with clients and helping to direct counseling.

Clinical Toolbox 9.2

In the Pearson etext, click here to read more about questions counselors should ask themselves when developing a counseling/treatment plan.

CONTEXTUAL ASSESSMENT (C)

An assessment of a client's **context** involves three interrelated contexts: intrapersonal context, or variables within an individual; interpersonal context, or relationships with others; and macro-level context, or relationships with one's community and culture (Wenar & Kerig, 2005). Clients' situations should be considered in their lived context, not just at an individual level of analysis.

First, young clients' intrapersonal context should be considered. Counselors might consider the following characteristics when assessing a client's context and considering a treatment plan or a direction for counseling:

- **Developmental considerations**—Young clients are constantly developing and changing, yet they grow and change at different rates. Many factors, including nutrition, environmental stimulation, and trauma and abuse experiences, can have an impact on the rate at which a young person meets developmental milestones. Even as they meet these milestones, there is individual variability in their capabilities. Counselors must consider clients' developmental level and unique capacities when creating their treatment plans. Some of the developmental factors that influence a young person's treatment plan include:
  - Cognitive development (e.g., egocentrism, perspective taking, information processing)
  - Social and emotional development (e.g., social skills, self-awareness and ability to self-regulate behaviors and emotions)
  - Moral development (e.g., morality, personal connection with concepts such as justice and equality)
  - Physical development (e.g., physical health and growth)
  - Educational development (e.g., reading ability)
  - Sexual development (e.g., gender identity, sexual orientation)
- **Emotions or feeling**—Counselors should be aware of their young clients' ability to identify, understand, regulate, release, and manage feelings. Although these abilities develop over time, clients vary in their ability to engage in such activities. Counselors should consider their clients' abilities in this regard as they construct treatment plans.
- **Attachment**—Attachment has to do with the bonds that youth develop with their caregivers and their subsequent ability to trust and develop emotional connections with others. Disrupted attachments can have a serious impact on a youth's development, and if there are attachment-related struggles, these will need to be considered in developing a treatment plan and establishing the young person's needs.
- **Personality**—Personality has to do with the interrelatedness of cognitions, feelings, and behaviors and how these factors interact to form consistent ways of responding. Personality is often regarded as

innate rather than learned. The Big Five personality dimensions, which have the most evidence of remaining stable over time, are conscientiousness, openness to experience, agreeableness, neuroticism, and extraversion (Terracciano, McCrae, Brant, & Costa, 2005).

- **Behaviors or actions**—Although many factors influence youth behaviors, young people are shaped in large part by their environment and the various principles of learning discussed previously in this text. Young clients are often brought to counseling to address behaviors of concern to the adults around them, and the youths' unique behaviors—adaptive and not adaptive—should be considered when developing treatment plans.
- **Biology or organic context**—Each youth has a unique genetic and biological blueprint. Genetics, biochemical considerations, and various factors such as innate intelligence or physical abilities influence youth and must be considered when treatment planning.
- **Cognitions or thinking**—Young people have unique mental processes, which include learning, memory, language, problem solving, reasoning, attention, and decision making. Although this factor is linked to developmental level, young people vary in their ability to engage in these mental processes.

The next context to consider when conceptualizing clients is their unique interactions and relationships with others, or their interpersonal context. Interpersonal context involves the client's environmental circumstance and the impact it has on growth and development. Consider two children, Madison and Hailey.

- Madison, an 8-year-old girl, lives in a safe middle-class community and attends an excellent school. She is the same race and religion as most of her community. Her family is intact, and she lives with both of her biological parents, who have stable employment. Madison has been diagnosed with ADHD and has some reading struggles, but her school has been responsive, and she receives regular response-to-intervention remediation through the school to help facilitate her academic success. Her parents also pay for private tutoring to help her with her schoolwork. Her parents spend 2 to 3 hours each night helping Madison with her homework, and she earns As and Bs in school. Madison also goes to weekly counseling, where she works on developing coping skills she uses to manage her ADHD symptoms. Madison plays soccer and takes swim lessons, which help her to redirect her energy, and she is active in her Girl Scout troop. She hopes to be a veterinarian when she grows up.
- Hailey is also an 8-year-old girl, but she lives in an economically disadvantaged, racially diverse community with crowded schools that lack the resources they need to manage the multiple needs of their students. Her parents were teenagers when Hailey was born; they never married, and Hailey has never met her father. Hailey lives with her grandmother because her mother works second shift as a server at a local truck stop on weekdays. Her grandmother has multiple health issues and has a difficult time getting around. Hailey spends the weekends with her mother. Like Madison, Hailey has ADHD and reading struggles, but she has never been identified or diagnosed. Although her struggles are significant, they pale in comparison to the needs the other children in her school experience. Neither her family nor her school has flagged Hailey as requiring intervention, even though she is barely passing the third grade. Her grandmother and mother think she just needs to try harder. After school, Hailey plays video games for most of the evening, and she rarely leaves the home except to go to school. Her grandmother has tried to help her with her schoolwork, but she herself struggles to understand the new ways of calculating math problems, and she gets frustrated with Hailey's inability to read. Hailey thinks she is "stupid," and her self-esteem and self-efficacy are beginning to plummet. She does not consider future careers, and when pressed she suggests she will be a movie star when she grows up.

Hailey and Madison have similar struggles, yet their contexts and the communities in which they live play an important role in how their struggles are addressed. Madison enjoys access to family, school, and community supports that Hailey does not have, and this comparison highlights the important role that context can play in understanding youth and the resources that may best help them.

Bronfenbrenner's (1979) **ecological systems theory** suggested that five environmental factors affect an individual's development:

- **Microsystem**—the environment in which the person lives; the family siblings, peers, school, work, and neighborhood

- **Mesosytem**—the interaction between each microsytem; experiences at home related to experiences at school
- **Exosystem**—links between a social setting in which the client does not have an active role and the individual's immediate context; the economic system, political system, educational system, religious system, and government
- **Macrosystem**—the overarching beliefs and values of that culture and society; political or religious norms of the culture
- **Chronosystem**—sociohistorical circumstances or the cumulative experiences a person has over the course of his or her lifetime; birth of a sibling

Counselors should consider young clients within their immediate relational context (e.g., the environment where they live), the interactions between these relationships (e.g., family and school; parents and friends), the interactions with societal systems (e.g., educational system, economic), and the culture of the society. As an example, a newly emigrated 10-year-old Lebanese American girl who lives in an economically disadvantaged, crime-ridden community where she is a racial minority may have overprotective parents who have restricted her ability to create and form close peer and community relationships. Because of this lack of trust, she might not develop ties to her peer groups, the school, and/or the resources in her community. Because of the conflicted interaction between her parents and the community, and her feelings of alienation within her school and community, the girl may avoid going to school and be truant. This could lead to new, more problematic systems becoming involved in the family's life, such as children's services and the legal system. This example highlights the multiple factors that can have an impact on a young person's interpersonal context. Bronfenbrenner's model can be applied to young clients and help counselors to conceptualize their contextual circumstances.

In addition to Bronfenbrenner's systems, another context to consider when conceptualizing clients' context is their macro-level context, or their demographics. Closely related to this is the concept of culture, or shared worldviews, traditions, and cultural practices—all of which significantly affect an individual's personal identity (Sue & Sue, 2015). If a counselor desires to understand clients, their context, and their worldview, he or she must also understand their affiliations. The following are important in considering clients' context (Sue & Sue, 2015):

- **Age**—the accumulation of multidimensional [physical, psychological, developmental] change over years
- **Gender**—the range of characteristics [behavioral, mental, physical] on the continuum of femininity and masculinity; social gender roles and gender identity
- **Race**—national, cultural, ethnic, geographic, linguistic, and religious affiliations
- **Ethnicity**—national or cultural affiliations
- **Socioeconomic class**—a class system based on the affiliation of stratifications or hierarchical categories [lower, middle, upper class] based on economic recourses
- **Sexual orientation**—the inclination, attraction, or enduring quality that draws an individual to another person of the opposite gender or sex, the same gender or sex, or both genders or sexes
- **Disability/ability**—impairments, limitations, or extreme strengths in physical, mental, emotional, cognitive, sensory, or developmental abilities, or some combination of these abilities
- **Religious preferences/spirituality**—an affiliation with an organized set of beliefs, worldviews, and traditions related to spirituality and humanity
- **Geographic location**—where the client lives

Counselors must be aware of their own assumptions and personal reactions to diverse groups and affiliations, attempt to fully understand individuals within their unique context, and allow these understandings to adequately inform appropriate treatment planning (Sue & Sue, 2015). This meta-theoretical approach to counseling, or multicultural counseling, allows counselors to clarify clients' definition of the problem, perceptions of the cause, the problem's context, factors affecting their self-coping, and their ability to seek help in a culturally sensitive context (Sue & Sue, 2015). Attending to the clients' intrapersonal, interpersonal, and macro-level contexts, while allowing them to engage and share their stories and perceptions of their lived experiences, relationships, and the problem's formation, can help to facilitate counselors' optimal understanding of their clients.

Creative Toolbox Activity   Community Strengths and Resources Genogram

Activity Overview

In this activity, clients and their families can create a visual representation of the relationships in their lives. This activity helps clients to understand the context in which they live. This activity can help clients and their families to identify strengths and resources within their environment and community. Identifying healthy and supportive relationships can bring attention to the positive aspects of clients' lives.

Counseling Goal Addressed

The exercise can be used as an assessment tool to help clients, families, and counselors to identify strengths that can be useful in developing treatment plans. The primary goal of this activity is to encourage clients to examine the ways in which individuals function and develop within a community. Clients explore their support networks and identify strengths and resources with which they had not previously connected. This exercise can also help clients to identify strengths within their community.

Directions

1. Instruct clients and/or their family members to choose a piece of paper to represent their community.
2. Ask them to draw themselves within the community, represented by any symbol or depiction.
3. Invite them to draw their family, friends, and other people who are important in their lives (e.g., teachers, religious leaders, social or sports groups).
4. Instruct clients to draw lines between themselves and the other identified individuals. Encourage clients to use different types of lines to depict different types of relationships among the individuals. For example:

   positive and supportive relationships: ~~~~~~~~~~~~~~~~~~~~~~~~~~~~~
   distant relationships: \/
   problematic/conflictual relationships: ============================

Process Questions

1. What is it like for you to see the support and resources you have?
2. Who can you lean on for support?
3. What other identified individuals or groups might you add to your current support network?
4. Are there any changes you would like to make to your support network?
5. How can you enhance your network to gain more supportive people and resources?

One resource that counselors can use in conducting a contextual assessment is the Cultural Formulation Interview (CFI; this measure can be found in the *DSM-5*; APA, 2013). The CFI is a standardized 16-question interview tool. The CFI can be used to enhance counselors' understanding of information that relates to a client's culture. This systematic interview should be used in initial counseling sessions and involves four lines of inquiry (APA, 2013):

1. Cultural definition of the problem (e.g., the client's definition of the problem; defining the problem through the perspective of the client's family, friends, or relevant community members)
2. Cultural perceptions of cause, context, and support (e.g., personal perceptions of the causes of the problem; problem causes that family, friends, or relevant community members might prescribe; supports and stressors; components of the client's background/identity or cultural identity)
3. Cultural factors affecting self-coping and past help seeking (e.g., coping skills; past advisement, help, and treatment; barriers to past attempts at help seeking)
4. Cultural factors affecting current help seeking (e.g., preferences of counseling style and approach; concerns about the present counseling relationship)

Armed with a solid understanding of a young person's individual, family, community, and cultural context, the counselor is ready to explore the more formal components of the assessment process. Contextual information can affect counselors' ability to determine which formal assessment might be necessary and to select, if applicable, the most descriptive, appropriate *DSM* diagnosis. Figure 9.2 provides questions counselors can ask to assess culture and cultural understandings of problems.

The following are questions for young clients and/or their families to assess their culture and the cultural understanding of the problems they bring to counseling. Developmental considerations should be taken into account when asking any questions.

ASSESSING THE CLIENT'S/FAMILY'S CULTURAL BACKGROUND

How do you identify yourself (i.e., age, race, ethnicity, culture, socioeconomic status, sexual orientation, disability/ability)?

What is your country of origin?

Where were your parents born? Where were your children born?

Where do you call home?

Have you always lived in the United States? If not, when did you come to the United States?

What was life like before you came to the United States?

What was it like when you first came to the United States? How is it now?

Why did you leave your country of origin?

Which languages do you speak? Which languages do you prefer to speak? Which language is spoken at home/with your family members/in your community?

How would you describe your culture? Your ethnicity? What are your foundational values and beliefs?

How would you describe your family? Who are the members of your family?

Who raised you?

Do you want your extended family or other important people in your life included in counseling? Would you like me to talk with any of them?

In what ways does your family affect and support you?

How would you describe your community? Do you belong to any groups or organizations?

What do you view as important sources of support?

What activities are you associated with or do you participate in?

Are religion and/or spirituality important to you?

Are you comfortable talking about values, beliefs, and spirituality with me?

Is religion or spirituality an important aspect of treatment you wish to address?

Is there a religious, spiritual, or healing person who should be part of counseling?

Do you feel that others have discriminated against you because of your culture? Have you seen this at school (for older family members: at work), in the community, in relationships, or in other settings?

Have you ever felt people discriminated against you or judged you because of your religious, spiritual, political, or ethnic worldview?

Have you ever been discriminated against due to your race, socioeconomic class, sexual orientation, gender, or disability, or for any other reason that you would like to talk about and make me aware of?

What is your sexual orientation?

How would you describe your gender identity?

How would you define your socioeconomic status?

Do you have any customs or practices that you would like me to know about or pull into counseling?

UNDERSTANDING THE PROBLEM

How would you/the family describe what is going on with you? How would you/the family define the problem?

How might your other family members, friends, or others within your community define the problem?

FIGURE 9.2 Interview Questions to Assess Clients' and Families' Cultural Context

What is the most troubling part of the problem?

What would you like to be doing that you are not able to do?

Have you/the family sought help for this problem in the past? If so, from whom? What parts of reaching out to others were helpful? What parts were not?

Have you ever had times when you thought you would have the problem but did not?

How would you name or label what is happening (i.e., the presenting problem)?

Are there any beliefs or cultural considerations that you would like to discuss concerning the problem?

Is there anything you are afraid of or fear related to the problem?

Do your family members, friends, or others within your community support your decision to seek help?

What do you/the family think caused or is causing this problem?

What would your family members, friends, or others within your community say is causing your problem?

Is there any kind or type of support that makes the problem better?

Do you/the family feel supported by family members, friends, and others within the community?

What seems to make the problem worse? What stressors make the problem more difficult to deal with or tolerate?

How have you/the family dealt with the problem in the past?

How are you/the family currently coping with this problem?

BARRIERS TO COUNSELING/INTERVENTION

Has anything ever gotten in the way of you seeking help for this problem?

What barriers have prevented you from seeking help in the past?

Do you think the services here will help you and your family?

Do you see any potential challenges in your receiving counseling?

Considering what you know about counseling, is there anything you feel uncomfortable about?

POSSIBLE SOLUTIONS

How have you dealt with the problem in the past?

Has anything been helpful?

How are you currently coping with this problem?

COUNSELING AND COUNSELING RELATIONSHIP PREFERENCES

What kind or type of help is most useful to you/the family?

What kinds of help would your family members, friends, or others within your community deem as most useful?

What would you/the family like from me in this relationship?

What expectations do you have for me in this relationship?

What expectations do you have for yourself in this relationship?

What expectations do you have for your child/the family in this relationship?

How do you see counseling progressing?

What type of pace is ideal?

How often would you like to attend sessions?

What would indicate to you that counseling or this counseling relationship is not working?

Do you have any reservation that I will not understand your situation, your culture, or your lived experience? If so, what do you think I need to know?

Is there anything I have failed to ask you that would be helpful in facilitating counseling and making you feel safe here?

FIGURE 9.2   Interview Questions to Assess Clients' and Families' Cultural Context (*Continued*)

ASSESSMENT AND DIAGNOSIS (A)

Counselors assess clients to get information they need to determine the clients' needs to develop a solid treatment plan. Formal or informal **assessment** processes can be used to gain a thorough understanding of clients' presenting concerns, get an accurate conceptualization of clients' experiences, identify counseling needs, and monitor the impact of counseling (Whiston, 2012). Formal assessment (i.e., the use of formal assessment measures) can help counselors to determine if further, more advanced testing is warranted, and it is required to determine some aspects of young people's functioning (e.g., an IQ test is required as part of the process of diagnosing a youth with an intellectual disability).

As part of the informal assessment process, counselors should gather the following information during the preliminary assessment (Sadock & Sadock, 2007):

- Identifying information (i.e., name, age, sex, grade level, language, religion)
- Description of the presenting issues (i.e., In the client's and the parent's own words, why was the client brought into counseling?)
- History of the presenting issues (i.e., development of the problems or symptoms, behavior changes over time, time of onset, level of impairment)
- Medical history (i.e., medical conditions, neurological disorders)
- Past counseling experiences (i.e., Were they successful? What was helpful and not helpful?)
- Family history (i.e., ethnicity, composition of the home, important relationships, illness in the family, community and neighborhood)
- Personal history (i.e., developmental considerations [personality, temperament, social interactions, cognitive]; past history of abuse, neglect, or traumatic experiences; educational history)
- Mental status examination data (discussed later in this chapter)
- Referrals or further diagnostic considerations (i.e., physical examination, neurological examination, interviews with other family members)

Depending on the presenting issue and the setting in which they work, counselors may elect to review medical records or prior health or mental health treatment information as part of their assessment process. This information, along with information from collateral reports (i.e., family or the school), can help counselors to develop a comprehensive clinical picture. Collateral reports are especially necessary when counseling young people as they may be poor historians or lack insight into their situation or context (Kress & Paylo, 2015). Counselors may also want to use formal assessment measures such as structured interviews, personality inventories, specific symptoms assessments, and/or a mental status examination. A **mental status examination** provides counselors with a model they can use to assess a client's self-presentation, and this information can be helpful in diagnosing clients and in assessing their needs. A mental status examination includes an assessment of (Sommers-Flanagan & Sommers-Flanagan, 2009):

- appearance;
- behaviors/psychomotor activity;
- attitudes;
- affect and mood;
- memory and intelligence;
- reliability, judgment; and insight
- speech and thought;
- perceptual disturbances; and
- orientation and consciousness;

Clinical Toolbox 9.3

In the Pearson etext, click here to read more about mental status observations and assessment.

Formal and informal assessments help to facilitate accurate client diagnosis and a thoughtful case conceptualization, thus facilitating the development of a comprehensive treatment plan (Kress & Paylo, 2015; Whiston, 2012). The results of the formal assessment will provide counselors with information that can help them to best determine the most appropriate *DSM* diagnosis, if one is applicable, and/or the areas in which clients are struggling and need support. Diagnosing mental disorders requires a very complex skill set. A discussion of the *DSM* diagnosis process and all of its complexities is beyond the scope of this text, but readers are encouraged to receive training on the use of the *DSM* if they will be working in clinical settings. Assessment and development of an accurate diagnosis of the problem—whether it be a mental disorder or some other problem—and an associated prognosis aids counselors in determining how to move forward in determining the level of care the client requires.

NECESSARY LEVEL OF CARE (N)

All counselors, as part of the counseling process, are called on to determine the level of care their clients require. **Level of care** refers to the setting and intensity of services that a client (and members of the community) require to be safe and successful in meeting their counseling goals. Clients ideally will be placed in the least restrictive level of care that they require. In terms of level of care decisions, counselors must consider differing treatment settings (i.e., residential treatment hospitalization, outpatient treatment), types of treatment (i.e., individual, group, family), and the pacing of treatment (i.e., daily, weekly, monthly).

As an example, consider a 10-year-old who repeatedly sexually abused his sister and niece and was just released from a juvenile detention center. Family reunification was the goal of Child Protective Services, but the client has not had treatment and is not deemed safe to reenter the home or the community. As such, an appropriate level of care as a step down from the juvenile justice center may be a residential treatment facility where the client can receive sexual offender treatment services and the community can be protected from the risk of potential victimization.

A continuum of care refers to a treatment system in which clients enter treatment at a level appropriate to their needs and then, as needed, step up to more intense treatment levels or step down to less intense treatment levels. The trend in community mental health is toward close collaboration across providers and agencies, and the merging of agencies and services to be able to provide a greater number of services to clients in one place and with the greatest ease.

Some issues that counselors should consider when determining appropriate treatment settings, types of treatments, and pacing include:

- the severity of the mental health symptoms;
- any mental health diagnoses (i.e., mental disorders) and their associated prognoses;
- physical limitations or medical conditions;
- suicidal ideation (i.e., threat to self) and homicidal ideation (i.e., harm to others), or a client's ability to be safe in the community and/or not harm others;
- ability to care for oneself (i.e., activities of daily living [ADLs], such as showering, eating, using the toilet, dressing);
- past treatment settings and responsiveness to those settings;
- aims and goals of treatment;
- social and community support systems and resources; and
- the desired level of care from the client's/family's perspective.

Counselors take into consideration the client's diagnosis, specific needs, the severity of the symptoms, any situation-specific matters, and client characteristics when matching clients with the appropriate level of care. Residential treatment, inpatient hospitalization, day treatment/partial hospitalization, in-home family services, and outpatient treatment are the most common settings or youth levels of care (see Figure 9.3 for an overview of these levels of care).

STRENGTHS (S)

The importance of a strength-based lens has already been discussed and punctuated numerous times throughout this text. As such, we refer readers to prior discussions.

	Service restrictiveness				
	More			**Less**	
Aspects of service	Inpatient hospitalization	Residential treatment	Partial hospitalization/day treatment	In-home treatment programs	Community treatment
Level of restriction	• Most restrictive and highly structured environment • Involves staying at a facility under 24-hour supervision	• Highly structured 24-hour or intermittent supervision • Involves temporarily living in a facility	• Permitted to live in the community but in a highly structured environment • Involves attending an office-based program during the day	• In-home counseling • Manualized and highly structured treatment model	• Least restrictive and structured • Outpatient, home-based, and/or school-based counseling
Primary foci	• Safety of youth and others • Symptom stabilization (e.g., reduce suicidal behavior, psychosis) • Medication titration • Discharge to less restrictive level of care once stable	• Reduce symptom severity and improve functioning • Prepare youth and families for a less restrictive level of care and continued engagement in treatment	• Continue to reduce symptom severity, develop skills, and restore adaptive functioning • Prevent hospitalization and/or deterioration • Facilitate aftercare through case management	• Prevent inpatient and/or higher levels of care • Address other psychosocial/ environmental concerns (e.g., family, school, needs) • Link family to community resources and services	• Eliminate or reduce symptom severity to a level of minimal distress • Enhance wellness (e.g., leisure activities, friendships)
Intensity of services	• Intensive psychiatric evaluation (i.e., risk assessment, mental status exam, medication management) • Intensive brief counseling	• Ongoing evaluation and medication management • Individual, group, and/or family counseling • Educational services provided	• Between 2 and 5 days per week at a minimum of 3 hours per day • Individual, group, family, and/or rehabilitative therapies (e.g., daily living and social skills)	• In-home visits 1–3 times per week • Typically 4–6 direct hours per week • Indirect hours are commonly needed to collaborate with or obtain other services	• Dependent on clinical necessity • Weekly, every other week, or monthly sessions • Individual, group, and/or family counseling • Advocacy as needed
Duration of services	• Overnight stay to less than 1 month • Shorter periods than residential treatment	• Extended period of stay • Duration not typically prescribed in advance	• Timely discharge intended • Typically 2–6 weeks, with some programs lasting up to 6 months	• Extended period of services • Duration typically 60–120 days but can extend longer	• Time-limited service • Discharge after goals or effective functioning are achieved

FIGURE 9.3   Level of Care Continuum

Clinical Toolbox 9.4

In the Pearson etext, click here to read about a creative activity that can be used to help young clients and their families to identify family strengths collaboratively.

In the context of treatment planning, when using a strength-based perspective, clients' strengths and resources can be used to help them to overcome their struggles. Most clients and their families present for counseling because there is some identified problem they want help to resolve. At these points in time, they are generally far removed from a place of considering their strengths. Counselors play an important role in identifying and connecting clients and their families with their strengths, resources, and competencies. Table 2.5 (in Chapter 2) provides information that can be used to assess young people's strengths; specific character strengths and questions that can be used to tap into strengths are provided in this table. Table 9.1 provides strength-based exercises counselors may use when counseling youth. Additional examples of strength-based counseling activities are provided in the Creative Toolboxes later in this chapter.

TREATMENT APPROACH (T)

The treatment aspect of the model has to do with the theory, model, or approach that is selected for use with clients (e.g., cognitive behavioral play therapy). The selected theory will direct the research-based interventions, which are addressed at a later point in the model.

When selecting a theoretical/treatment approach, counselors should consider evidence-based practices. However, they must also consider the approaches they are trained to use, clients' preferences, the

Table 9.1	Strength-Based Exercises
Title	**Description**
My Strength Bracelet	Materials for this exercise include string or wire, beads, stones, paint, stickers, and/or markers. Counselors instruct youth to first think of their different strengths. For example, youth may say they are funny, kind, athletic, and creative. Youth then select a bead or stone that best represents that strength. For example, a yellow bead might represent having a lot of energy. Youth may decorate the bead or leave it as is. Symbols, such as color, shape, and design of the bead or stone, will represent the strength. Counselors instruct youth to place the bead or stone on the wire or string to create a strength bracelet.
Power Animals	Counselors instruct youth to identify their various strengths. Youth should be challenged to identify at least five. With the strengths and positive qualities in mind, youth are asked to assign each one of the strengths to a different animal of his or her choice. For example, if caring was chosen as a strength or quality, youth may assign that quality to an elephant. Once the animals are created and defined, youth can create a story using the animals. The story may be about how the animals interact in a fantasy environment using the powers and strengths they possess. The goal of this exercise is to make youth self-aware of their strengths and qualities and to show how each one contributes and defines them in a unique, positive way.
My Strength Book	In this exercise, counselors help youth to create a strength book. Materials used for this exercise may include markers, colorful paper, scissors, stickers, a hole puncher, and string. Counselors instruct youth to consider their strengths. Then, youth write each strength on a piece of paper in the book. Youth then create a page dedicated to each strength, including ways they use that strength, a picture of the strength, or an example of when that strength was used last. Pictures, words, and/or images can be used to communicate the strength. Youth can work on the book during each session or between sessions.
The Positive Puzzle	With this activity, counselors help clients to develop a puzzle that is a metaphor for the clients' individual strengths. Counselors can trace and cut out puzzle pieces with the client or in advance of the session. Materials for this exercise may include the created puzzle pieces, markers, paint, glue, paintbrushes, and pens. Clients create a puzzle with pieces on which they have identified their goals, strengths, and positive qualities. Counselors may create a puzzle that is a picture or a straight line. After youth create the pieces and put the puzzle together, counselors can discuss how the clients' various strengths make up a larger whole and how this combination of strengths can be used to help the client to achieve his or her goals.

confines of the setting in which they work, and a myriad of additional considerations. When considering the use of an evidence-based treatment, theory, or approach, counselors need to consider what is already known based on the research literature. Some helpful guidelines that may assist counselors in evaluating whether a theory, approach, or intervention should be deemed evidenced based and used in clinical practice follow (Substance Abuse and Mental Health Services Administration [SAMHSA], 2009):

- **Guideline 1:** Approaches and interventions need to be based on some documented, clear conceptual model of change.
- **Guideline 2:** Approaches and interventions need to be similar to, or found in, federal registries and/or the peer-reviewed literature.
- **Guideline 3:** Approaches and interventions should be supported by the documentation of multiple scientific enquiries that seem credible, are rigorous, and evidence consistent positive effects.
- **Guideline 4:** Approaches and interventions should be reviewed and deemed credible by informed experts in that treatment area.

In addition, when determining an appropriate treatment approach, counselors also need to consider the following (Sommers-Flanagan & Sommers-Flanagan, 2009):

- Does the counselor fully understand the client's/family's issue or concern for entering counseling?
- Does the counselor use empirically supported research on the clinical relationship to address the client, counselor, and treatment variables (e.g., therapeutic alliance, collaboration, client feedback)?
- Has the counselor considered how the client's/family's preferences may intersect (e.g., the counselor's theoretical orientation and the client's/family's desired form/modality of intervention)?
- Has the counselor previously implemented evidence-based treatment approaches for that issue or concern?
- Is the counselor working within or outside of his or her skill or competency level?

Adhering to these considerations can be helpful in selecting an evidence-based approach that also takes into account clients' preferences and uniqueness.

AIM AND OBJECTIVES OF COUNSELING (A)

Counseling aims and objectives are rooted in clients' goals for counseling, counselors' perceptions of what may help clients to reach their goals, the selected treatment or theoretical approach (i.e., the T aspect of the model), and the research-based interventions (i.e., the R aspect of the model, discussed in the following section). The aims and objectives of counseling may affect the treatment approach the counselor takes, and vice versa, the treatment approach will have an impact on the clients' counseling aims and objectives.

The aims and objectives of counseling should be well defined, with objectives stated in measurable, behavioral terms so they can be evaluated and used to assess clients' progress. Clinical counselors are required by third-party payers to develop treatment plans with well-defined objectives, and failure to do so can result in counselors and agencies not being reimbursed for counseling services. Agencies can even be cited or required to pay back money for counseling services deemed as unclear or inconsistent with the client's diagnosis or needs. Well-defined counseling aims and objectives communicate to clients, families, and external reviewers what counselors and clients are working toward in counseling. They also help to keep clients and counselors working toward established, collaboratively determined goals.

Counseling objectives should be specific, simple, realistic, and measurable (Kress & Paylo, 2015). Consider a child who has posttraumatic stress disorder secondary to years of repeated sexual and physical abuse; the client may only be able to achieve several counseling goals in a 3-month period. An example of a goal that is broad and difficult to measure might be "The client will experience decreased trauma symptoms." This objective lacks specificity as to what symptoms will be addressed, and it does not include a measure of evaluation. A better objective might be "The client will learn and use a relaxation exercise 75% of the time when experiencing flashbacks." This objective clearly states what the client will do, when the client will do it, and how the objective's achievement will be measured. This objective is also realistic because a client with severe trauma may only be able to use skills 75% of the time early in the counseling process.

The objectives that clients and their families present are generally broad (e.g., to get along with my mom, to not get in trouble at school, to make more friends), and clients' goals often involve other people changing (i.e., "I want my mom to stop nagging me"; "I want my teacher to treat me better"; "I want my child to listen more"). Counselors' challenge is to take clients' presented goals and help to reframe them in a way that is operationalized and defined so that success in meeting the goals can be determined, while still ensuring the goals are meaningful to clients. Solution-focused questioning (e.g., If a miracle occurred, and you were feeling more *happy*, what would be different?) can be helpful in narrowing the client's focus to specific areas of change (De Shazer, Dolan, Korman, Trepper, & McCollum, 2007).

Simple counseling goals are generally best. Counselors should develop counseling treatment goals and objectives that can realistically be achieved by the client within the specified time frame. For example, a client who is in a residential youth treatment facility for short-term psychiatric stabilization because of a suicide attempt needs objectives framed accordingly. Three realistic short-term goals might be "0 suicide attempts," "Learn one skill that can be used to prevent suicide attempts," and "Develop a safety plan that can be used in the future when suicidal thoughts emerge." These goals are appropriate to the level of care and setting the client is in, and they can realistically be attained in a short amount of time.

It is important for counselors to recognize that short-term and long-term goals can be developed and addressed simultaneously, and not all goals need to have the same aspirational achievement date. A client with generalized anxiety disorder who has just moved to a new school and is having adjustment difficulties may need to address the short-term goal of adjusting to the new school before he or she can work on the broader anxiety problems.

When developing counseling objectives, counselors should be realistic in their expectations of client change, and these expectations should be reflected in the actual objectives, as well as the anticipated dates the goals are expected to be achieved. Numerous client factors should be considered when developing counseling goals that are realistic for a given client, and these include, but are not limited to, the nature of the problem; clients' past functioning levels; clients' response to past interventions; various unique internal or external limitations; clients' unique strengths and resources; and family, community and school supports.

In recent years, an increased emphasis has been placed on assessing and measuring client change. Client self-report or family report of client symptom reduction is the usual mode of assessment of client change. One helpful and simple way to assess for change is to have clients—or their families if more age appropriate—rate young clients' symptom or behavior severity on a scale from 1 to 10 (with 1 reflecting the worst functioning and 10 reflecting the highest functioning). Informal client self-report or family report assessments can easily be integrated into the client's counseling plan. For example, a goal might be "The client will self-report an increased ability to manage his anger by moving from a 4 to a 6 on a 10-point scale."

The use of a structured model can be helpful when co-developing clients' counseling aims and objectives. The **S.M.A.R.T. model** (SAMHSA, 2006) can be helpful when developing counseling aims and objectives, with S.M.A.R.T. being an acronym for goals that characterized by the following traits:

- **Specific**—concrete, uses action verbs (e.g., *attend, identify, utilize, begin, obtain, transition, report, communicate, process*)
- **Measurable**—numeric or descriptive, quantity, quality (e.g., client will identify 3 strategies and attempt to implement 1 of them in the midst of personal crisis; client will engage in 20 minutes of an activity on Monday, Wednesday, and Friday after breakfast)
- **Attainable**—appropriately limited in scope, feasible (e.g., over the next 2 months, the client will use the strategy to increase her tolerance of being in school)
- **Results oriented**—measures output or results, includes accomplishments (e.g., client will examine thoughts/beliefs 75% of the time each day and will engage in the replacement behavior 75% of the time; client will have 0 acts of negative behavior and will use his anger management skills 90% of the time)
- **Timely**—identifies target dates, includes interim steps to monitor progress (e.g., within 2 months, the client will learn and identify strategies and will gradually tolerate the activity 70% of the time; through the use of the strategy the client will identify, tolerate, and act on an alternative behavior 90% of the time)

Clinical Toolbox 9.5

In the Pearson etext, click here to view a S.M.A.R.T. goal worksheet that can be used to develop counseling goals.

RESEARCH-BASED INTERVENTIONS (R)

Research-based interventions and treatments are evidence based, meaning they have been researched and found to be efficacious in treating a client's specific presenting problems or mental disorders. **Research-based interventions** are those that have been validated through scientific inquiry, peer review, and/or consensus. The interventions identified in this part of the model are used to tailor the specific treatment aims and objectives (i.e., alleviation of a certain symptom; reducing the need for more restrictive placements).

This stage of the I CAN START model does not necessarily follow the identification of the aims and objectives of counseling in a linear fashion. In fact, the two are integrally related, with research-based interventions typically informing the aims and objectives and with the counselor- and client-generated aims and objectives potentially influencing the selection of research-based interventions to be used in counseling. For example, if a young client who has depression is having difficulty sleeping at night—in part because she takes naps after school—and her objective is to fall and stay asleep through the night, the counselor can move to this stage of the model to select a research-based intervention that can help the client with her sleep issues (e.g., the use of sleep hygiene procedures). This girl's counseling aim and objective might be "The client will take zero naps after school and go to bed and get up at the same time each day to promote healthy sleep patterns."

In addition, when applying the I CAN START model, the interventions should be grounded in the selected treatment or theoretical approach (i.e., the *T* aspect of this model). Thus, the treatment/theoretical approach (the *T* aspect of the model) will inform the aims and objectives (the *A* aspect of this model) of counseling and the research-based interventions (the *R* aspect of this model) as well.

When considering the interventions they will use with a client, counselors should consider the client's unique situation, developmental and contextual factors, and the client's and family's counseling preferences. Research-based interventions only matter if they are individually tailored and clients are actively involved in the development of their counseling plans. Counselors should empower their clients so that they are actively involved in the selection of various interventions (Kress & Paylo, 2015).

THERAPEUTIC SUPPORT SERVICES (T)

Many clients need more than just counseling services to be successful. **Therapeutic support services** complement counseling interventions and provide services that counselors alone cannot provide. Supportive services may involve education around different topics. As an example, a girl who has an eating disorder may need support services related to healthy nutrition, diet, and exercise, information that is out of the scope of practice of counselors.

Targeted skills training is another area that can be addressed by therapeutic supports. For example, the family of a youth who has disruptive behaviors and a conduct disorder diagnosis might benefit from parent training, or a youth who has posttraumatic stress disorder might benefit from biofeedback training (provided by a different provider) as an adjunct to receiving trauma-focused cognitive behavioral counseling.

Support services that integrate socialization or social activities might also be a helpful aspect of a client's counseling plan. Young clients may benefit from various support groups (e.g., a support group for children whose parents are divorcing) and opportunities to socialize with peers or mentors (e.g., a Big Brother/Big Sister program, Al-Anon). Support services might also be related to ancillary matters involving the legal system, the school system, or any other system in which the client functions (e.g., a court-appointed guardian ad litem).

The types of therapeutic support services young people require will depend on the severity of their symptoms, the nature of the setting in which they reside (e.g., home [outpatient therapy], hospital, juvenile justice center, residential facility), their diagnosis, their strengths, and multiple other factors. Support services can complement counseling treatment goals and align with clients' goals and their situations.

As an example, a client with severe disruptive behavior problems who is living in residential treatment and aging out of the child welfare system may benefit from case management, consistent psychiatric evaluation for medication responsiveness, and transitional support services. In addition to support from the school counselor, an elementary school student who was recently diagnosed with a learning disorder related to reading may benefit from staff involvement and support around the development of an individualized education program (IEP), from a peer reading tutor, or from a grant-funded afterschool reading/tutoring program.

Creative Toolbox Activity   Personal Strengths and Resources Collage

Activity Overview

Clients (and families, if applicable) use collage techniques to identify strengths and resources that can be used in helping them overcome their identified struggles. This activity can help clients to identify strengths and resources within themselves and within their circle of influence.

Treatment Goal Addressed

This exercise can be used as an assessment tool to help clients and counselors to identify strengths that can be useful in developing clients' treatment plans. The goal of this activity is to encourage the client to identify his or her personal strengths and resources and to begin to punctuate and amplify them for use in overcoming struggles.

Directions

1. The counselor and client discuss how all people have strengths and resources.
2. The counselor presents the client with various magazines, catalogues, or any other source that contains different pictures.
3. The counselor invites the client to cut out pictures or words that represent his or her strengths, resources, and competencies across various domains (e.g., his or her personal capacities, resources, personal interests).
4. The client then assembles these words and pictures on a piece of paper in a collage format.

Process Questions

1. What was it like for you to see the strengths, resources, and capacities you possess?
2. What most surprised you about this activity?
3. How do you see yourself using these strengths, resources, and capacities to overcome the problems with which you have been struggling?
4. Which struggles have these strengths, resources, and capacities helped you to overcome in the past?
5. Which strengths, resources, and capacities mean the most to you?
6. How can you use your strengths, resources, and capacities to help others or contribute to your community?
7. How do your unique strengths, resources, and capacities make you special?
8. How are your strengths, resources, and capacities different from those of others?
9. How could you use these strengths, resources, and capacities to build a more positive future?
10. Are there any other strengths, resources, and capacities you want to develop? How can you achieve this?
11. What have you learned from this activity?

I CAN START COUNSELING PLAN FOR DAQUAN

As discussed at the beginning of this chapter, Daquan's demonstration of bullying and physical aggression toward peers, noncompliance in the classroom, labile mood (i.e., irritable, angry, and sad), and emotional outbursts represent a cluster of symptoms and behaviors that are characteristic of several mood and disruptive behavior disorders. When considering the recent incarceration of his father, however, Daquan's deterioration in academic, behavioral, and social–emotional functioning most appropriately indicates an adjustment disorder with a mixed disturbance of emotions and conduct. Although clinical and school settings each present unique factors that differentiate the implementation and provision of counseling practices, school counselors, too, must consider contextual factors, diagnosis, and the necessary levels of care before moving ahead with a comprehensive, strength-based counseling approach. The following I CAN START conceptual framework outlines counseling considerations that may be helpful to a school counselor or a clinical counselor who works with Daquan.

C = Contextual Assessment

Attachment (strong familial bonds, temporary absence of father); exosystem environmental impacts (father's incarceration); family support (extended family members are present and provide Daquan's mother with caregiving assistance); African American and Puerto Rican culture (connectedness with family); Roman Catholic religious affiliation (routinely attends Mass with grandparents); low socioeconomic status (basic needs are met, but father's absence may present new financial challenges); healthy childhood development as evidenced by previous academic, social/emotional, and personality functioning (e.g., typically earns good grades, has many friends, respects others).

A = Assessment and Diagnosis

Diagnosis = 309.4 (F43.25) Adjustment Disorder with mixed disturbance of emotions and conduct

Assessment of Suicidality (monitor potential suicidality, and continue assessment on a weekly basis if necessary as adjustment disorders are associated with an elevated risk of suicidal behaviors).

N = Necessary Level of Care

Weekly meetings with the school counselor; peers may be included as needed to provide support, to promote skills development, or for mediation purposes.

Outpatient, individual weekly clinical counseling sessions; family members may be included as desired by Daquan, per his mother's request, or if determined advantageous to the counseling processes. Because Daquan previously denied suicidal ideation, an acute level of care (i.e., inpatient hospitalization) would likely not be necessary over the course of treatment, unless suicidal behaviors escalated.

S = Strengths

Self: Daquan is intelligent, humorous, athletic, and generally loving. His friendly and outgoing personality has enabled him to establish and maintain many positive relationships with his peers.

Family: Daquan shares strong attachments and loving relationships with his nuclear and extended family members. Both his maternal and paternal grandparents have demonstrated a commitment to increase their presence and provide additional familial support while Daquan's father is absent. Daquan's time spent with his grandparents and other extended family members each Sunday not only provides him with a sense of warmth and connectedness but also serves to add structure, security, and consistency to his weekly routine.

School/community: Daquan has always enjoyed going to school and has excellent attendance. He is well liked by his teachers and has become recognized as a model student for his peers due to his respectful attitude, active engagement, and general leadership in the classroom. His history of positive school behavior provides evidence that he already possesses the competencies and abilities to perform at a high academic level, adhere to school rules and meet classroom expectations, interact with his peers in an age-appropriate manner, and resolve conflicts without engaging in verbally or physically aggressive behaviors. His school counselor and teacher want to support Daquan and assist him with achieving his goals throughout the counseling process. Daquan enjoys running around outdoors and playing sports with his friends at the neighborhood playground and community park; these experiences foster his development of positive peer relationships and engagement in pleasurable leisure activities that support his overall wellness.

T = Treatment Approach

Cognitive behavioral therapy; supportive counseling

A = Aim and Objectives of Counseling (1-month objectives)

School counseling objectives aim to restore Daquan's prior degree of functioning in the school environment, particularly related to bullying, peer interactions, and classroom behavior, so he and others can be successful academically.

Daquan will refrain from engaging in bullying behaviors. Daquan will have 0 incidences of physically aggressive behavior, threatening his peers, name calling, or using inappropriate language as determined by self, peer, and teacher reports.

Daquan will improve his interactions with peers. Daquan will explore and identify how bullying behaviors affect his peer relationships (i.e., peers' feelings and responses, relational consequences) and interact with his peers in a positive, age-appropriate manner (e.g., treating others with respect and kindness) in 5 out of 5 presented peer interactions.

Daquan will increase his classroom compliance. Daquan will follow his teachers' directions and complete academic assignments within 2 prompts in 4 out of 5 presented opportunities.

Daquan's teacher will reinforce his compliant behavior. Daquan's teacher will provide clear expectations and directives in a supportive manner and use Daquan's individualized token economy system to reinforce his compliance with academic tasks in 5 out of 5 presented opportunities (i.e., provide Daquan with a sticker to place on his behavior chart immediately following the completion of an assignment, verbally praise Daquan and the specific behavior being reinforced, and provide Daquan with a predetermined reward after earning 5 stickers).

Outpatient counseling treatment objectives primarily aim to improve Daquan's adjustment to his father's incarceration and associated mood and behavioral concerns.

Daquan will explore his feelings surrounding his father's incarceration. Daquan will identify and express a minimum of 1 feeling each session associated with his father's incarceration.

Daquan will explore the connection between his behaviors and feelings. Daquan will identify a minimum of 3 behaviors and 3 associated feelings each session.

Daquan will effectively regulate his emotions. Daquan will learn and use coping and/or problem-solving skills to manage distressing emotions at home and school without engaging in outburst or aggressive behaviors in 4 out of 5 presented opportunities.

R = Research-Based Interventions (Based on Cognitive Behavioral Therapy)

School counselor will help Daquan to eliminate bullying behaviors by developing empathy and perspective-taking ability and understanding of his peers' feelings, his own feelings, and the function of bullying.

School counselor will help Daquan to improve peer relationships by increasing his awareness of the consequences of positive interactions and bullying behaviors.

School counselor will help Daquan to increase his compliance through positive reinforcement, shaping, and token economy systems.

Clinical counselor will help Daquan to manage emotions by providing skills training (e.g., practicing coping strategies and problem-solving skills, modeling, role-playing).

Clinical counselor will help Daquan to increase awareness of feelings by making connections with behaviors and engaging in expressive activities and role-plays to allow for open expression and processing of feelings.

Clinical counselor will help Daquan to increase communication of his feelings by conducting family sessions and facilitating open communication of feelings, wants, and needs.

T = Therapeutic Support Services

School counselor will need to make a referral to a clinical mental health provider in an outpatient counseling setting and will need to consult and collaborate with the clinical counselor to promote congruent treatment processes and generalize skills across settings.

Referral to a counseling group that has a focus on grief, loss, or adjustment.

Referral to a community Big Brother program where Daquan can connect with an older male role model.

Summary

This chapter provided suggestions and principles that can guide counseling and treatment planning efforts. Good counseling and treatment plans include certain elements. First, treatment plans must be individualized to the client's and family's needs and preferences, and they must be developed collaboratively with the client and family. The severity of the client's impairments and how these might relate to the counseling plan and outcomes should also be considered. Next, the counselor should develop treatment objectives that follow the S.M.A.R.T. model (SAMHSA, 2006) or are specific, measurable, attainable, results oriented, and timely. The concept of the Golden Thread is a way to ensure counselors' counseling and treatment plans flow and progress in a logical fashion. This progression involves the identification of an overarching problem or disorder (if relevant), struggle, or counseling goal, which leads to the development of the aims and objectives of treatment, which in turn leads to specific forms of intervention.

Finally, it is important to view counseling and treatment planning as a fluid, evolving process that develops in response to clients' changing needs.

Next, the chapter presented the I CAN START counseling and treatment planning model and applied it to a case from both a school and clinical counseling perspective. This model is comprehensive in that it addresses multiple layers of factors (e.g., contextual and cultural issues) that affect clients' and families' functioning and counseling needs. The model is strength based in that it highlights the strengths, competencies, and resources that clients and families have and integrates these into counseling. In being strength based and contextually and culturally focused, the model is consistent with the theoretical and philosophical foundations of professional counseling. The model also emphasizes the use of evidence-based practices as essential in all counseling. In the following chapters, the I CAN START model is applied to different case examples.

MyLab Counseling: Counseling Children and Adolescents

Try the Topic 6 Assignments: *Case Conceptualization for Counseling Youth.*

CHAPTER 10

Youth Suicide, Self-Injury, and Homicide

Counselors of young clients should always make safety considerations a top priority; they have an ethical and legal obligation to do all they can to enhance client safety. Safety measures, when relevant, should be integrated into counseling. Emphasizing safety considerations helps to keep clients safe, reinforces the value of safety to young clients and their families, and helps to protect counselors from legal liability.

This chapter discusses select safety-related issues that are relevant to counseling youth. Practical steps counselors can take to promote and support their clients' safety are provided. The safety-related topics presented are those that counselors who work with youth encounter with the greatest frequency (i.e., suicide and self-injury) and/or those that have the most serious risk implications (e.g., homicide).

Topics associated with self-violence are explored first. Counselors identify client self-violence as one of the most distressing client behaviors they encounter (King, Ewell Foster, & Rogalski, 2013). As such, suicide is explored, and assessment and intervention techniques and resources useful to counselors who work with youth are provided. Client self-injury is also discussed, with an emphasis on clinical considerations and interventions that counselors can use to help manage and address clients' self-injury. Although it is a topic that can feel uncomfortable to consider, some young people are at risk for initiating homicide. Homicide risk is explored later in the chapter, with an eye to how counselors can assess and prevent homicide risk.

SUICIDE

Suicide is the third leading cause of death in adolescents, accounting for 20% of all adolescent deaths annually (Centers for Disease Control and Prevention [CDC], 2012a). Data on attempted suicide are not systematically collected; thus, it is difficult to assess the frequency of attempts that do not end in death. However, it is estimated that almost 16% of high school students have seriously considered attempting suicide, 12% have made a plan to attempt suicide, and 7% have attempted suicide, with 2% of students making an attempt that resulted in injury or hospitalization (CDC, 2012a).

Clinical Toolbox 10.1

In the Pearson etext, click here to read the definitions of commonly used terms related to suicide.

Clients who are seen in counseling settings are at a greater risk for suicide attempts and completed suicide, and counselors must be vigilant about assessing for suicide risk in young clients. Developmentally young people are impulsive, and they may have difficulty thinking through the consequences of their actions (Klonsky & May, 2013). They are especially vulnerable to suicide attempts. A common misconception is that only clients who have depressive or bipolar disorders will experience suicidal ideation. In fact, suicidal ideation, and even suicide attempts, can occur with young people who have no documented mental disorder as well as with those diagnosed with any variety of mental illnesses, including posttraumatic stress disorder, emerging personality pathology, eating disorders, and anxiety disorders (King et al., 2013). Counselors have a responsibility to regularly assess suicide with any client who demonstrates the potential for self-harm, regardless of his or her presenting issue. Throughout the counseling process with a suicidal adolescent, counselors must conduct regular assessments of suicidal ideation or risk (Buchman-Schmitt, Chiurliza, Chu, Michaels, & Joiner, 2014).

Young people who consider or attempt suicide are trying to avoid pain and suffering, gain a sense of control over a situation in which they feel helpless, or make an attempt to communicate in the only way they can identify to do so (Granello & Granello, 2006). As such, counselors' role is to help youth to manage their strong negative emotions via counseling and possibly medication if necessary, help them to regain some sense of control over their lives, and help them to communicate what they need to the appropriate people. Counseling should help young clients to identify the function the suicidal ideation serves so the clients' needs can be met in an adaptive way (Granello & Granello, 2006).

Counselor Considerations

A natural initial reaction of counselors working with young clients who have suicidal ideation is to feel anxious, but it is important that counselors obtain the knowledge and skills required to feel confident in effectively responding to a potential crisis situation. Core competencies for mental health professionals who work with clients at risk for suicide include (Berman et al., 2004): (a) managing one's own reactions to suicide, (b) maintaining a sense of collaboration in treatment, (c) understanding the construct of suicide, (d) possessing appropriate risk assessment and intervention skills, (e) developing an effective crisis plan, (f) keeping appropriate documentation related to suicidality, and (g) understanding potential legal and ethical issues in the treatment of those who are suicidal.

Counselors who work with young clients who are suicidal should be aware of the ethical and legal considerations associated with counseling this population. Related to ethics and legal considerations, counselors should take concrete measures to facilitate client safety. Safety measures should also be integrated into clients' counseling objectives, with an example of an appropriate objective for youth being "0 suicide attempts."

Counselors should document the steps they take to enhance and encourage client safety. If they do not, they may be accused of not taking the appropriate steps to support a young client's safety. It is especially important that counselors clearly communicate to young people—and their parents—that they have an obligation to encourage safety, which may result in breaching confidentiality.

Another important ethical/legal issue related to suicide is the use of safety plans. Safety plans are discussed in greater detail in the "Interventions" section. All counselors should have at least one suicide assessment, one suicide decision-making model, and one safety planning model for use with young clients.

Next, counselors need to be aware of more restrictive settings, or higher levels of care, where young clients at risk of suicide can be stabilized until they are safe to be in the community. Related to this, counselors should know their state's guidelines related to hospitalization of underage minors. In some states, counselors can have clients admitted to hospitals only with the consent of a parent or legal guardian; in other states, professionals such as physicians are able to hospitalize a minor patient in emergency situations (King et al., 2013). In any case, counselors must be familiar with the laws of the state in which they practice.

Client Characteristics

Suicidality is a complex concept, and there are many reasons why young clients experience suicidal thoughts or behaviors. Suicidal behavior ultimately results from the interaction of environmental circumstances and individual factors (King et al., 2013). Certain demographic risk factors predict suicide, and counselors should take these factors into consideration when working with youth. For example, gender may be a suicide predictor because adolescent boys (15–19 years old) are more likely to use violent means in attempting suicide (e.g., firearms) and are therefore more likely to die by suicide; however, adolescent girls are almost twice as likely to attempt suicide compared to their male counterparts (King et al., 2013). Another important demographic feature related to suicide is race. Among adolescents, the ethnic group considered most at risk for suicide or suicide attempts is American Indian and Alaskan Natives, who are more than twice as likely to attempt or complete suicide than their non-Hispanic Caucasian peers (King et al., 2013). Age is another important factor to consider when treating youth who are at risk for suicide. Although suicide is rather rare in children younger than 9, the risk increases for youth age 10–14, with a dramatic jump occurring in adolescents age 15–19 (King et al., 2013).

Demographic information cannot predict whether an individual will attempt suicide. However, the following factors have been identified as potential indicators of suicidality: (a) past suicide attempts; (b) substance abuse problems; (c) sexual orientation or gender identity struggles; (d) being the victim of bullying; (e) thoughts of suicide; (f) hopelessness; (g) exposure to suicide; and (h) the presence of a mental health disorder, especially bipolar disorder or depression (Goldblum, Espelage, Chu, & Bongar, 2015; King et al., 2013). Parent–child discord and parental psychiatric illness are among the chief common family contributors to suicide risk (Brent, Poling, & Goldstein, 2011). Various biological risk factors (e.g., biologically based mental or brain disorders, impulsivity, hyperactivity), cognitive factors (e.g., limited problem-solving skills, rigid thinking), emotional risk factors (e.g., various mental disorders, low self-esteem, identity struggles, anger and aggressive and defiant behaviors), and environmental risk factors (e.g., recent stressful life situations, peer relationship problems, early separation from and/or loss of caregivers, maltreatment, family violence) may also serve as suicide risk factors (Granello & Granello, 2006).

Of special importance with regard to suicidality and youth is the topic of sexual orientation and gender identity. Multiple studies have demonstrated that approximately 30% of lesbian, gay, bisexual, transgender, and questioning (LGBTQ) youth attempt suicide at least once (Goldblum et al., 2015). Family and peer support plays an especially important role for this population; developmentally, adolescents seek acceptance, and if they cannot find it, they are at risk. The stress they face as they question their sexual orientation or gender identity, the adversities they face in terms of homophobia, weak social support (especially in certain cultures and communities), and victimization experiences leave this population vulnerable and at risk for suicide (Goldblum et al., 2015; Liu & Mustanski, 2012).

In addition, counselors must be aware of any recent life stressors, such as parental divorce, a relationship breakup or loss of friendship, rejection from the client's peer group, or problems at school because these may also predict suicide attempts (Klott, 2012). Any abrupt changes in mood (e.g., moving from significant depression to uncharacteristic euphoria) should also be considered potential warning signs of suicide risk (McGlothlin, 2008), as should recent discharge from a psychiatric hospital (King et al., 2013). Table 10.1 provides an overview of the risk factors for adolescent suicide.

Assessment

Potential suicide risk should be assessed at each of the following points in time: (a) at intake or the initial counseling session, (b) at any time suicidal ideation arises or the counselor suspects possible suicidal ideation, (c) when a client experiences a sudden change in affect or behavior, and (d) at the time of discharge from counseling (Granello, 2010; King et al., 2013). When assessing clients who have suicidal ideation, counselors should consider the following: (a) the presence of psychiatric symptoms (e.g., aggression,

Table 10.1 Risk Factors for Adolescent Suicide

Clinical Risk Factors	Family and Interpersonal Risk Factors	Contextual Risk Factors
• Previous suicide attempt • Suicidal ideation and intent • Nonsuicidal self-injury • Psychiatric disorders • Emerging personality disorder traits • Hopelessness • Learning disorders and difficulties • Sleep disturbances • Recent discharge from psychiatric hospital	• Family psychiatric history • Sexual, physical, and/or emotional abuse or neglect • Family violence • Bullying/victimization experiences • Peer relationship problems • Sexual orientation and gender identity struggles	• Exposure to suicide • Access to suicide attempt methods (especially a lethal means)

Note: Adapted from *Teen Suicide Risk: A Practitioner Guide to Screening, Assessment, and Management* by C. A. King, C. Ewell Foster, & R. M. Rogalski, 2013, New York, NY: Guilford.

impulsiveness, hopelessness, agitation); (b) past suicidal behavior, including the presence of self-injury, number of past suicide attempts, and access to lethal means; (c) socioeconomic and family factors (e.g., young people who come from a disadvantaged background are more likely to experience suicidal ideation, as are those whose parents have a history of mental illness or substance abuse); (d) exposure and access to means; (e) recent negative life events (e.g., interpersonal relationship changes, alcohol or drug use, intense emotional changes; Buchman-Schmitt et al., 2014; Wolfe, Foxwell, & Kennard, 2014). Of course, counselors should remain sensitive to the fact that no two clients are alike, and the assessment process can be complicated and widely varied for each client (Granello, 2010). Counselors may also consider administering or consulting self-report screening tests or other evaluation tools available to them (King et al., 2013). In addition, assessment should be an ongoing process, and multiple others' perspectives on the young person's behavior should be gathered and considered (Granello & Granello, 2006).

When working with youth, counselors might consider using a mnemonic to facilitate their assessment process. SAD PERSONS is one example of such a mnemonic (Patterson, Dohn, Bird, & Patterson, 1983). Since its creation, an adaptation of the SAD PERSONS tool has been created for youth (i.e., the A-SPS; Juhnke, 1996). A description of the mnemonic device is provided in Figure 10.1. Once the counselor determines that the client possesses any of the suggested risk indicators, he or she should conduct a more detailed risk assessment. A detailed assessment of risk should generally involve the client, family/significant others, and any other potential informants (e.g., teacher, physician). An effective risk assessment will include questions related to the client's thoughts of death and dying (e.g., Have you ever thought about hurting yourself?). An effective assessment will also include questions about substance abuse because there appears to be a strong connection between youth suicide risk and the use of substances (King et al., 2013).

Clinical Toolbox 10.2

In the Pearson etext, click here to review two additional mnemonic devices that have been created to identify proximal (e.g., immediate or pressing issues) and distal (e.g., not imminent but can become imminent with passage of time) suicide risk factors.

Signs of acute (i.e., imminent) suicide risk include verbalized threats to harm or kill oneself (e.g., "I'm going to kill myself today"), actively seeking a means to harm or kill oneself (e.g., "I am going to get my dad's gun from the cabinet in the garage"), and talking or writing about suicide or death (e.g., "Things are going to be so much better once I'm dead"). In the event that these signs are observed, further assessment and possibly immediate intervention (e.g., psychiatric hospitalization) are necessary. When youth display signs of acute suicide risk, they should be viewed as being in a state of psychiatric crisis, and emergency personnel (e.g., police, paramedics) may need to be contacted to help to ensure their entry into a secured setting.

S—Sex (heightened risk if male)
A—Age (heightened risk for those between ages 15 and 25)
D—Depressive or bipolar disorder
P—Previous suicide attempts or psychiatric care
E—Excessive alcohol or substance use
R—Rational thinking loss (e.g., psychotic symptoms such as hallucinations or delusions)
S—Social support is lacking (e.g., Does the youth have friends? Does the youth perceive he or she fits in with a group of friends or his or her family system? Is the youth isolated and frequently alone?)
O—Organized suicide plan or serious suicide attempt
N—Negligent parenting
S—School problems

FIGURE 10.1   SAD PERSONS Suicide Assessment Mnemonic (Adapted for Youth)

Note: Adapted from "The Adapted-SAD PERSONS: A suicide assessment scale designed for use with children" by G. A. Juhnke, 1996, *Elementary School Guidance & Counseling, 30*(4), pp. 252–258.

1. Have you ever felt so low that you thought about death or wished you were dead?
2. You've been experiencing so much pain, I wonder if you've had thoughts of suicide? Can you tell me about your pain and feelings associated with your thoughts?
3. You have been so brave and strong during this difficult time, but sometimes people find it hard to hang in there. Is there any part of you that thinks about what it would be like to no longer exist?
4. Have you ever tried to hurt yourself in the past? Have you ever attempted suicide in the past? Can you tell me about that time/those times? What happened to cause you to take that step? Do you remember what you were thinking about at the time? What was helpful in your recovery then?
5. Who else knows about your thoughts of killing yourself? Is there anyone you really trust whom you could talk to now, someone outside of this room?
6. When you think about suicide, do you have a specific plan, or is it just thoughts? Tell me more about the thoughts you do have. Share some of that plan with me (if there is a plan). What would it be like for you to follow up on your plan? How easy do you think it would be for you to follow up on your plan? What types of resources (i.e., means) are available to you to help you to carry out your plan?
7. What stops you from hurting yourself? What are some reasons you can think of to keep living for the next week? Next month? Next year?
8. How do you feel people would react if you hurt or killed yourself?
9. Would you be willing to construct a safety plan with me?

FIGURE 10.2 Suicide Assessment Questions

Counselors should be persistent when questioning adolescents about suicide. An initial inquiry into thoughts of suicide may scare or startle young clients, causing them to become defensive or hide their true feelings (King et al., 2013). Therefore, counselors may want to be creative in how they phrase questions to open the door for young clients to share difficult information (e.g., "Listening to you talk, I can hear that you are bearing a lot of pain right now. Some people find they start to go to lonely places when facing so much pain. Have you ever gone to any lonely or dark places?"). Counselors may also specifically frame questions in relation to current problems (e.g., "I can hear that failing that class has really shaken you. Between that and your family's reaction to failing the class, I'm wondering if you've ever thought about hurting yourself?"). Figure 10.2 provides questions that counselors might ask to assess a client's suicide risk. Finally, counselors should not wait until the end of a session to address possible suicidal thoughts, ideations, or risk factors; ample time needs to be allotted to process suicidal ideation (King et al., 2013).

Intervention

SAFETY PLANS AND INTERVENTION
Counselors who work with suicidal youth must first establish a therapeutic alliance and quickly move to supporting and enhancing clients' reasons for living (King et al., 2013). When attempting to establish a therapeutic alliance with a potentially suicidal youth, counselors may need to first inquire about how the client is hurting and how the counselor can be helpful (e.g., "How do you hurt?" "How can I help you?") while also instilling hope that the client can feel better.

Clinical Toolbox 10.3

In the Pearson etext, click here to read about an activity that can be used to help young clients with suicidal ideation to connect with their reasons for living.

Counselors should involve the parents of young clients who have attempted suicide or are experiencing suicidal ideation. Parents ideally will take a collaborative, supportive role in their child's counseling. Counselors should be open to parents' questions and suggestions. Counselors should also offer concrete ways parents can assist their child. Collaboration with family allows young clients and their families to feel in control of their experience. It creates a space where their ideas about what they need can be expressed, and it helps children and their families to take ownership of their safety (Brent et al., 2011).

One counselor response to suicidal ideation may be an attempt to contract for safety, or use a *no-suicide contract*; the client agrees, typically on paper, not to kill him- or herself within a specific time frame (e.g., hours, days). Although there may be some benefits to using a no-suicide contract (e.g., the contract emphasizes the common goal of treatment, which is client safety and the reduction of imminent suicide risk; Brent et al., 2011), there are also numerous potential limitations. The use of no-suicide contracts may lead the client and/or parents to mistakenly believe that the counselor is only concerned with protecting him- or herself against legal action. Another possible disadvantage is that the no-suicide contract may serve to inadvertently silence clients; they may feel discouraged, embarrassed, or ashamed if they do experience suicidal ideation (Lee & Bartlett, 2005). The word *contract* may also be problematic because it implies a legally binding agreement. Last, no-suicide contracts may inadvertently lead counselors to believe that they are legally protected against malpractice in the event a client does complete suicide; however, in reality, no such protection exists.

An alternative to the no-suicide contract is the *Commitment to Counseling Statement,* which emphasizes other dimensions of the therapeutic relationship and avoids focusing solely on what the client should not do (Rudd, Mandrusiak, & Joiner, 2006). Commitment to Counseling Statements emphasize positive client coping behaviors (e.g., forms of positive self-soothing behaviors, such as talking or listening to music), focus on what the client is doing well (e.g., commitment to change), and delineate the therapeutic responsibilities of both the client and the counselor. An example of a Commitment to Counseling Statement is provided in Figure 10.3.

This is my commitment to counseling plan. By signing this plan, I agree to engage and participate in the counseling process with my counselor during our sessions. I also agree to carry out the information I learn and the insight I gain during sessions in my everyday life and to the best of my ability.

I understand that part of the counseling process involves setting goals. I will be responsible for setting goals with my counselor. I understand that part of achieving these goals may involve applying the things I have learned in counseling in between our sessions, and I agree to apply the strategies and skills learned in counseling to the best of my ability.

I know that counseling may not always be easy, and we may discuss some things that make me feel uncomfortable. Sometimes it will be difficult for me to discuss certain topics. I agree to openly and honestly communicate any discomfort or fear with my counselor when we approach these subjects. Even if my feelings are negative, I know I can respectfully share them with my counselor without hurting anyone's feelings.

I will continue taking any medication I am currently prescribed. If there is any change in my medication, I will communicate this with my counselor.

I will also willingly implement my safety plan when necessary.

I understand that if there are any thoughts of suicide or suicide-related attempts, I will follow the suicidal ideation steps included in my safety plan.

If at any time I become uncomfortable with the direction my counseling is going, I will openly communicate my concern with my counselor.

Client	Date
Parent	Date
Counselor	Date

FIGURE 10.3 Example of a Youth Commitment to Counseling Statement

Determining the appropriate level of care for the client (i.e., inpatient, partial hospitalization, outpatient) may be the most important element of effective suicide intervention. Containment in an inpatient psychiatric facility is generally necessary when clients present an imminent risk of violence to themselves. Clients with suicidal thoughts who are not at immediate risk of acting on these thoughts can generally be managed in a less restrictive (i.e., partial hospitalization, outpatient) level of care. Counselors may use decision trees to determine an appropriate level of care for a suicidal client. Ultimately, a detailed risk assessment, or safety plan (see Figure 10.4 for an example of a safety plan), and appropriate consultation and supervision will help counselors to determine the best course of action with a young client who is suicidal.

Step 1: Identify triggers leading to suicidal thoughts and behaviors:
1. *Feeling empty and lonely*
2. *Pressure to do things that I feel I can't do (e.g., meet new people, do hard assignments)*
3. *Being left out of weekend plans made by my friends and/or family members*

Step 2: Identify warning signs that a crisis may be developing:
1. *Thinking "everyone is too busy or important to talk to me" or "no one likes me"*
2. *Isolating myself (going to my room and spending most of the evening there, sitting in the first row of the bus)*
3. *Arguing with my parents (more angry than normal)*

Step 3: Identify internal strategies (things I can do without contacting someone):
1. *Play my drums*
2. *Go for a walk with my dog*
3. *Listen to music*
4. *Take a hot shower*
5. *Journal about how I am thinking and feeling*
6. *Do deep breathing exercises*
7. *Tell myself, "People do like me" and "They would be sad if I was gone"*

Step 4: Identify external strategies (things I can do with others or people I can ask for help):
1. *Play basketball with my older brother*
2. *Go to the mall with my friend Bobby*
3. *Call my Uncle Carl and talk about how I'm feeling*
4. *Talk/meet with my school counselor*
5. *Talk with my parents (especially my mother)*
6. *Talk with my counselor*
7. *Call the suicide hotline*
8. *Call 911*

Step 5: Internal resources:
1. The most important thing to me that is worth living for is *my future—I have dreams for my future (e.g., be in a band, go to college, own a car, maybe be a school counselor).*
2. Things I like about myself (that I sometimes forget)
   a. *I am really nice person who cares about others.*
   b. *People say I'm a good listener.*
   c. *I think I can help other people in the future.*

Step 6: External resources: Contact information (friends, family, mental health agencies)
1. *Add names, numbers, and addresses of individuals and agencies that will help you to remain safe.*
2. *Suicide Prevention Hotline: 1-800-273-TALK (a national free suicide hotline)*
3. *Suicide Prevention Website (Chat): http://www.suicidepreventionlifeline.org/ (Contains a free suicide chat room for those at risk)*

Step 7: Identify safety strategies (steps I can take when I have suicidal thoughts):
1. If I believe I am in immediate danger of harming myself, I will:
   a. *Not harm myself*
   b. *Tell my parents*

FIGURE 10.4 Safety Plan for Use with Youth Who Are Suicidal

c. *Call 911*
d. *Call the suicide hotline*
e. *Go directly to an adult who can help me*

Commitment Statement:
If I plan to hurt myself, I am committed to following through on my safety plan and remaining safe.

Signed:

_____   _____
Client   Date

_____   _____
Counselor   Date

_____   _____
Parent   Date

FIGURE 10.4   Safety Plan for Use with Youth Who Are Suicidal (*Continued*)

Clinical Toolbox 10.5

In the Pearson etext, click here to review a decision-making tree resource that can be used to help counselors to assess young clients' suicide risk.

Similar to commitment to counseling statements, safety plans are intended to enhance clients' adaptive, life-sustaining behaviors. Counselors implement safety plans with youth as a means to aid them in controlling and managing suicidal ideations, thus reducing the impact of these thoughts and behaviors. Parents and youth should also be informed and aware of the necessary steps to take in case youth suicidal ideation or suicidal behaviors emerge or escalate. Safety plans for suicidal youth should include: (a) the associated triggers and warning signs that trigger suicidal thoughts and behaviors; (b) ways for clients to manage these triggers and warning signs; (c) a designated social support network (e.g., friends, family members, parents, professionals); (d) steps to take should youth's thoughts escalate to suicidal intent or behavior; and (e) unique internal and external protective resources (King et al., 2013).

Safety plans with suicidal youth need to have an immediate effect so they can be implemented the moment they are created for use in multiple settings (e.g., home, school, community). Counselors can approach the construction of a safety plan as a problem-solving intervention for youth and integrate parents throughout the creation and implementation of the plan. In addition, safety plans should be written or typed out and provided to youth and their families to allow them to have constant access to the plan. Figure 10.4 provides an example of a youth safety plan.

SUICIDE INTERVENTION/PREVENTION AND THE SCHOOLS

School staff can play an important role in suicide assessment, prevention, and intervention. First, school staff can support youth who are identified as at risk. Community-based counselors can reach out to school staff as needed, and these staff can play a role in the development and implementation of safety plans (e.g., allowing the client to listen to music in the nurse's office, asking teachers for extensions on assignments, extending a *flash pass* to leave class during an emergency situation; King et al., 2013). Creating a collaborative treatment plan that allows a cohesive, communicative relationship between counselors, treating physicians, school officials, and select family members can be a key step in maximizing client success (King et al., 2013).

School counselors also play an important role in the assessment, prevention, and intervention of youth at risk for suicide. However, much of the current literature about school counselors' role in counseling suicidal youth involves the postvention treatment of students who have lost a peer to suicide (Fineran, 2012). Although it is important to be prepared to help students grieving such a loss, especially because it creates risk for more suicidal behavior (Finernan, 2012; Ward & Odegard, 2011), it is imperative that schools implement suicide intervention programs as well. One group of researchers analyzed multiple school-based suicide intervention programs and found that the best interventions are long-term (e.g., last throughout the school year); engage not only students but also their parents, teachers, school staff, and community members; provide students with access to mental health services on campus and in the community; and address all potential risk factors associated with suicide (Balaguru, Sharma, & Waheed, 2013). Suicide interventions that prove to be successful are those that address the use of drugs and alcohol, improve problem-solving skills, and are tailored to the cultural group being addressed (Balaguru et al., 2013).

School counselors can also play an active role in the lives of students returning to school following a suicide attempt. Because adolescents spend the majority of their time in school, it is important that school interventions be set in place (Balaguru et al., 2013). Unfortunately, many adolescents express reservations about going back to school after a suicide attempt, and some may even completely refuse to do so because of fear or embarrassment (King et al., 2013). School counselors can most positively intervene by working with clients and their parents to accommodate requests (e.g., extra time between classes, permission to leave class and stay in the nurse's or school counselor's office if necessary; King et al., 2013). By keeping school counselors and officials in the loop, clients are more likely to receive a successful continuum of care.

NONSUICIDAL SELF-INJURY

Nonsuicidal self-injury (hereafter referred to as *self-injury*) is "the intentional destruction of one's body tissue without suicidal intent and for purposes not socially sanctioned" (Klonsky, Muehlenkamp, Lewis, & Walsh, 2011, p. 6). Self-injury can include, but is not limited to self-hitting, pin-pricking, skin-picking, embedding, burning, swallowing foreign objects, head-banging, and, most commonly seen, self-cutting. Prevalence research suggests that self-injury rates in youth vary depending on the population assessed, with rates within various populations being estimated as follows: 1%–37%, among general adolescent populations; 5%–47% in outpatient clinical samples of adolescents; and 39%–61% of adolescents in acute care settings (Dyl, 2008). Preadolescent populations may also self-injure, with one study indicating that almost 8% of this population reported having self-injured (Turner, Austin, & Chapman, 2014). Most research, though, suggests that the typical age range for the onset of self-injury is between 12 and 14 (Courtney-Seidler, Burns, Ziber, & Miller, 2014; Jarvi, Jackson, Swenson, & Crawford, 2013). Because of its increasing relevance, nonsuicidal self-injury was added to the *Diagnostic and Statistical Manual of Mental Disorders, Fifth Edition (DSM-5)* as a "condition for future study" (American Psychiatric Association [APA], 2013a).

Counselor Considerations

Some counselors feel intimidated by the prospect of working with clients who self-injure because of the possible health risks (e.g., cutting too deeply, medical complications such as infections) that can occur secondary to self-injury. In addition to client suicidal behaviors, client self-injury is often identified by counselors as one of the most distressing client behaviors encountered in clinical practice (King et al., 2013). Writers on self-injury frequently address the importance of counselors managing their personal reactions to young clients who self-injure (Kress, Drouhard, & Costin, 2010). Counselors may feel frustrated with clients' self-injury, and they may try to control clients by forcing them to cease the behavior. It is important that counselors constantly monitor their own reactions to the behavior and be self-aware, intentional, and reflective about their counseling methods when working with those who self-injure (Kress et al., 2010). Self-awareness, along with ongoing consultation and/or supervision, can help to ensure counselors maintain an objective perspective when working with this population.

Although self-injury does not always indicate a client is experiencing suicidal ideation, research does indicate that individuals who self-injure have an increased risk of suicide attempts, especially those who are also being treated for depression (Brausch & Girresch, 2012; Ougrin, Tranah, Leigh, Taylor, & Rosenbaum Asarnow, 2012; Turner et al., 2014). Although some have suggested that self-injury is a stronger predictor of suicide attempts than a history of suicide attempts or other established risk factors such as depression, anxiety, impulsivity, or bipolar disorder, there is no finite evidence linking self-injury with a higher risk of completed suicide (Klonsky, Victor, & Saffer, 2014; Ougrin et al., 2012).

Clients who self-injure may also benefit from a counseling approach that is relational, active, dynamic, and focused on facilitating the client's desire to change, while also providing the client with the tools he or she requires to make changes. Counseling interventions that target self-injury are most effective when they are used in the context of a nurturing, nonjudgmental, and collaborative counseling relationship (Walsh, 2012).

Client Characteristics

There is no profile of a young person who self-injures (Walsh, 2012). Male and female clients tend to engage in self-injury at the same rate; however, male clients tend to cut, hit, or burn as their methods of self-injury, whereas female clients tend to cut (Klonsky et al., 2014). Several studies have demonstrated that rates of self-injury are highest among individuals who experience emotional distress and dysregulation; have depressive, anxiety, or eating disorders; or have experienced trauma or child abuse (Gonzales & Bergstrom, 2013; Jarvi et al., 2013; Klonsky et al., 2014).

The reasons people self-injure vary, but the behavior can serve various evolving functions that are informed by lived experiences and the environment (Walsh, 2012). Self-injury can function (a) as a form of affect regulation; (b) as a method to influence others with the intention of communicating anger, hurt, or rebellion in a manner that does not involve verbally speaking of these emotions; (c) as a means of decreasing feelings of isolation and loneliness; or (d) as a means of self-stimulation with the intention of increasing emotional arousal (e.g., euphoric sensation; Klonsky et al., 2014; Walsh, 2012). There is also evidence that self-injury may be triggered by interpersonal forces such as internal conflicts or anticipated losses (Jacobson & Mufson, 2012), and there is mounting evidence that self-injury can be "contagious" (e.g., young people who are exposed to self-injury through their peers or media exposure are likely to replicate the behavior; Jarvi et al., 2013).

Although there is variability in the underlying functions self-injury serves, the typical progression of a self-injury event involves a precipitating stressful event such as rejection, which escalates the youth's dysphoria and agitation; an attempt to forestall the self-injury; a self-injury event; and then a subsequent tension release (Walsh, 2012). The dysphoria associated with the self-injury is often described by clients as feelings of shame and helplessness (Jacobson & Mufson, 2012), fear, anger, loneliness, and/or panic. Some clients may also describe dissociative experiences such as feeling numb, empty, and dead immediately prior to the self-injury (Walsh, 2012).

Assessment

People who self-injure have various personal contexts and presentations that contribute in unique ways to the development and maintenance of the behavior. The complex nature of self-injury can make it difficult for counselors to conceptualize and determine young clients' counseling needs. When working with youth who self-injure, counselors may find it helpful to first engage in a comprehensive assessment of the frequency, duration, severity, and onset of the self-injury as well as the behavior's supporting consequences, antecedents, functions, and dynamics (Hoffman & Kress, 2010). Counselors might inquire about the age of onset, the course of the behavior, the longest period free of the behavior, the lifetime and current frequency of self-injury, changes in the behavior over time, emotional states when injuring, triggers leading to the self-injury, the immediate and more long-term aftermath of injuring, use of substances before and after injuring, past attempts to stop injuring, medical complications (e.g., infections, stitches), resistance (e.g., effort to stop oneself), control (e.g., success in stopping oneself), the impulsivity of self-injury, and dystonicity (e.g., a wish to stop oneself from injuring).

Clinical Toolbox 10.6

In the Pearson etext, click here to review assessment questions that counselors might use for a client's self-injury.

In addition, ongoing medical assessment and evaluation will be necessary for young clients who engage in frequent, severe self-injury. Because medical assessment is outside of the scope of a counselor's practice, counselors should obtain consent to speak to and consult with the client's medical treatment providers (e.g., pediatrician, school nurse). Counselors should also speak with the youth's parents about the importance of communicating with their child's medical providers about any medical complications associated with the self-injury. Related to this, counselors should also encourage the family to work with the medical team around proper wound care.

Another important early assessment consideration is determining whether the client shares cutting implements, which is a practice more common in environments where clients have limited access to cutting implements (e.g., secure treatment facilities). Clients with a history of sharing cutting implements should be encouraged to consult with their medical team about concomitant health-related issues (e.g., HIV, hepatitis C, infection).

Counselors working with clients who self-injure should implement a standard suicide assessment to facilitate client safety. However, self-injury should only be thought of as suicidal if the client indicates intent to die; overreacting to a client's self-injury may rupture the therapeutic relationship. The issue of suicidal ideation is complicated because clients can have suicidal ideation while engaging in an act of self-injury. As previously mentioned, self-injury can also be a clinical marker for subsequent suicide attempts (Ougrin et al., 2012; Turner et al., 2014; Wilkinson, Kelvin, Dubicka, & Goodyer, 2011); therefore, counselors should regularly assess both self-injury and suicide risk.

Counselors can invite their young clients—and their parents—to monitor and document self-injury between sessions and map the frequency, triggers, cues, and self-injury reducers that relate to the self-injury. Many young clients do not voluntarily report self-injury, so counselors should ask all young clients about such activity. A generic question such as "Have you ever deliberately, physically hurt yourself in any way?" can be asked to inquire not only about past suicidal behaviors, but also about self-injury.

Intervention

Because the profiles and needs of people who self-injure are so unique, self-injury per se is not often a targeted and researched behavior in treatment studies. There is limited research that identifies effective treatments for self-injury, with only a few studies applying randomized controlled treatments to assess the effectiveness of approaches to address self-injury (Brausch & Girresch, 2012; Klonsky et al., 2011). The research findings to date suggest that behavior therapy and cognitive behavioral therapy (CBT) approaches and interventions that emphasize problem solving, cognitive restructuring, emotion regulation, and functional assessment and analysis of the behavior (i.e., developing an understanding of which thoughts, feelings, and behaviors led to the self-injury, and which behaviors could be altered to preclude further injury; see Kinch & Kress, 2012) in the context of a strong therapeutic relationship may be most effective in treating and reducing the occurrence of self-injury (Klonsky et al., 2011; Washburn et al., 2012). Maladaptive beliefs and distorted cognitions (e.g., self-criticism) and self-deprecation commonly demonstrated in those who self-injure may sustain self-injury; cognitive therapy may be useful in addressing these destructive thought patterns (Klonsky et al., 2011).

Dialectical behavior therapy (DBT; Linehan, 2014) is one treatment approach that shows promise in addressing self-injury, especially among adolescent clients who have emerging borderline personality disorder features (Muehlenkamp, 2006). DBT helps clients to develop alternative coping skills, identify obstacles to the use of alternative skills, and enhance skill generalization to real-world environments via the use of various modalities, including group skills training, individual therapy, and treatment team consultation, in which a group of professionals consult on interventions and modifications that need to be made to best support the youth.

Problem-solving therapy (PST) is a type of CBT that may be helpful when counseling youth who self-injure (Muehlenkamp, 2006). PST helps clients to cope with stressful life experiences by adapting. It was one of the first treatments for self-injury to use randomized control trials in evaluation (Washburn et al., 2012). As applied to self-injury, this approach is based on the idea that self-injury can be understood as an ineffective, maladaptive coping skill. The approach aims to help clients to develop their coping skills, better understand the role that emotion plays in understanding and coping with problems, reduce problem-solving avoidance, and develop action plans geared toward reducing psychological distress and enhancing well-being (Washburn et al., 2012). Interventions used in PST include: psychoeducation, interactive problem-solving exercises, and motivational homework assignments.

Clinical Toolbox 10.7

In the Pearson etext, click here to read about a counseling activity that may help clients to develop an increased awareness of the function of their self-injury, its impact on others, and the value of using alternative coping skills.

Because environmental and intrapersonal triggers (e.g., conflicts and frustrations in relationships) often trigger and support self-injury, behavior management strategies, or interventions that target changing behaviors or learning new behaviors, may be helpful (Klonsky et al., 2011). For example, guided imagery is a behavior therapy technique that involves the use of descriptive language to invoke strong mental imagery that can be used to invite relaxation as a form of distraction from uncomfortable feelings or as a means of directing clients toward more positive and optimistic outlooks.

Clinical Toolbox 10.8

In the Pearson etext, click here to read an example of a creative application of a behavioral guided imagery technique that can be used to help young clients to cope with overwhelming feelings and thus prevent self-injury.

Functional assessment is a behavior therapy technique that involves identifying factors that motivate and reinforce self-injury. By identifying and addressing the experiences that reinforce and maintain self-injury, clients can change these patterns and ultimately stop self-injuring. Related to functional assessment, counselors can invite clients to restrict the means of self-injury or to delay self-injury to either prevent or postpone self-injury (Klonsky et al., 2011). Examples include the use of behavioral alternatives (see Wester & Trepal, 2005), healthy alternatives (e.g., exercise, meditation), and distraction techniques (e.g., being with friends, listening to music). Means restriction and delay techniques may not facilitate long-term change and should be used as one part of a more detailed treatment plan (Klonsky et al., 2011).

Clinical Toolbox 10.9

In the Pearson etext, click here to read about how to use behavioral chain analyses when counseling youth who self-injure.

Negative replacement activities (e.g., holding a cold ice cube, snapping one's wrist with a rubber band) are controversial as a means of preventing self-injury. Some argue that the use of negative replacement activities as a means of coping reinforces the self-injury dynamic, or a focus on pain—or self-aggression—as a means of coping, which is not effective or socially appropriate in natural settings (e.g., Conterio, Lader, & Bloom, 1999). For example, if an adolescent has an upsetting interaction before a class, it is not feasible or socially acceptable for him to hold an ice cube in his hand during class, but the adolescent could employ a guided imagery exercise, challenge his thinking, or engage in a deep breathing exercise to help regulate strong emotions. Others (e.g., Walsh, 2012) argue that negative replacement activities may serve a transitional function and be useful in the early stages of counseling youth who self-injure.

Many youth who self-injure do not view the behavior as problematic and may not wish to cease the behavior. Even those who view the self-injury as problematic may not feel ready to stop self-injuring. Counselors are charged with determining how to facilitate a client's desire to change while avoiding power struggles and attempts to control the client (i.e., forcing or demanding clients to stop injuring). Attempts to control clients often increase their resistance to change and are typically considered contraindicated and unethical (Kress et al., 2010).

Motivational interviewing (MI) techniques can enhance clients' motivation to change (Kress & Hoffman, 2008). When working with a client who self-injures, counselors should assess whether the client is ready to change, is contemplating change, or is in a precontemplation stage of change (see Chapter 6 for a more detailed discussion of MI; Miller & Rollnick, 2012). To deepen a client's motivation to change, counselors should explore and process the client's ambivalence around change. In other words, counselors should explore the reasons the client does and does not want to change. MI highlights the importance of not attempting to define clients' problems and not persuading them that they should stop self-injuring. Counselors use a nonjudgmental, empathetic stance to develop and deepen clients' motivation to change. MI allows counselors to address the issues that brought the client into counseling via a humanizing, collaborative, respectful, and empowering means that increases the client's level of engagement in the counseling process and decreases resistance (Kress & Hoffman, 2008).

Clinical Toolbox 10.10

In the Pearson etext, click here to review a guided imagery activity that clients can use to resist impulses to self-injure.

Table 10.2 provides activities counselors might use with youth who self-injure.

Table 10.2 Nonsuicidal Self-injury Counseling Activities

Title	Description
My Creations	This activity can be used to help youth to (a) increase their awareness of self-injury, and (b) distract themselves to prevent self-injury. Youth draw a picture when they have an urge to injure. They express their emotions via drawing and bring awareness to the situation. Some questions clients can respond to include: • What are the feelings you have when you want to self-injure? • What could protect you from the self-injury influence? • Does this protector have a shape or color? Youth may use paints, markers, collage items, or any other items to express the image, drawing, words, or symbols. Youth can use their internal representation of this image—or the image they construct—when they have urges to self-injure.
Self-Injury Prevention Plan	This activity involves counselors helping youth develop a self-injury prevention plan that they can use to help prevent instances of self-injury. Youth write down situations that trigger their urge to self-injure. Then, they identify distracting activities they can use when they have an urge to self-injure. For example, painting, calling a friend, or going for a run are all distracting, healthy alternatives to self-injury. Next, youth may write down three positive self-affirmations that they can use to encourage themselves to use their coping skills. Finally, youth identify people who are supportive and can help them to achieve their goals. Youth sign and date the plan and use it during times when they want to self-injure.
Safety Animal	This activity focuses on helping youth to recognize a support system they can pull on during times when they want to self-injure, and it provides them with imagery of a safe person they can use to control self-injury impulses. Counselors help youth to identify a support system, or the people they can lean on when they have urges to self-injure. After youth identify and discuss their support system, they identify one person and select a safety animal that they believe best describes the person. The safety animal represents a loved one who is a protector and who wants to take care of them and not hurt them. For example, if a client identifies a best friend as a support figure, a bunny may be the safety animal. When youth want to self-injure and the support person is not available, they can draw the animal and use this as a means of avoiding self-injury impulses.

(Continued)

Table 10.2	Nonsuicidal Self-injury Counseling Activities (*Continued*)
Title	Description
Impulse Control Log	This activity involves clients creating a log that they can write in to avoid impulses to self-injure. Youth write down the date and location where they had the urge to self-injure as well as their thoughts and emotions at that time. For example, youth may write down, "I think I am bad, and I feel guilty." Youth then identify what function they think the self-injury would serve and how they can meet that need in other ways. For example, youth may say, "Self-injury would distract the hurt I am feeling, but I can write a letter to my pain instead and express my anger in that way." This log may be used each time youth have an urge to self-injure, and this activity can provide youth with a sense of control over their self-injurious impulses.
My Progress in Color	This activity involves clients documenting the times they resisted self-injury on pieces of paper that are linked together like a chain. These links represent the clients' progress and can serve as a source of encouragement and empowerment. Clients cut out a symbolic chain link that represents a day without self-injury and/or a time when they resisted an urge to self-injure. Youth may elect to use different colored pieces of paper to represent different experiences (e.g., yellow paper represents an exceptionally positive day). Youth write a positive message on the link that suggests their strength. For example, "I was strong today even though I was provoked by my sister." Youth might write on the opposite side of the piece of paper what they did as an alternative to fight the urge (e.g., taking a walk, reading a book). If youth relapse, a black chain might be added for that day instead of a colored one. Over time and with counseling, the chain will generally become longer, with more colored chains in a row and fewer black chains. This activity can serve as a motivator and may prevent self-injury.

HOMICIDE

In one survey, 16% of high school students (grades 9–12) reported carrying a weapon on more than 1 day in the 30 days preceding the survey, and 5% reported carrying a gun (CDC, 2012b). Violence perpetrated by youth is a serious issue, especially for young men. Much of the violence perpetrated by young people is aimed at their peers, which in turn contributes to high homicide rates among youth (Loeber & Farrington, 2011). During the 2012–2013 school year, 31 homicides of school-age youth ranging in age from 5 to 18 years occurred on school property (CDC, 2016). In fact, homicide is the second leading cause of death among youth age 15–24, and older adolescents have the highest homicide victimization and offending rates of any age group (CDC, 2012b).

Counselor Considerations

Reflecting on homicidal risk—especially in youth—can be uncomfortable for counselors; the grave consequences and legal and ethical responsibilities involved can be intimidating. Because client disclosure of homicidal ideation can prevent the loss of life, it is crucial that counselors remain open to encouraging client disclosure and monitor for homicide risk. Those at risk for homicide are often guarded; thus, nonjudgmental responding and neutral body language can be helpful in getting clients to share critical information about their ideation and information that is needed for assessment (i.e., their plan, availability of weapons). Counselors should continually monitor their verbal and nonverbal responses for signs of discomfort. Clients at risk for homicidal behavior typically experience feelings of fear, confusion, and ambivalence, and counselors should maintain a calm demeanor in approaching them.

Counselors should be aware of and explore their feelings about working with those at risk for homicide. Counselors should not underestimate a young client's potential for violent behavior because of preconceived stereotypes (e.g., youth or younger children are not vulnerable to homicide). Regular consultation and supervision are recommended when working with this population.

Although less than 2.6% of homicides carried out by school-age youth occur at school (CDC, 2016), all counselors who work in school settings should be aware of how to handle and facilitate safety. School violence occurs on school property, and youth, including younger children, can be victims, witnesses, and perpetrators of such violence. To prevent school violence, counselors, teachers, and administrators can use several prevention strategies, including school-based and outreach programs as well as parent- and family-based programs (CDC, 2016; Jaycox, Stein, & Wong, 2014). Counselors must understand youth violence prevention strategies as well as appropriate safety measures.

Primary, secondary, and tertiary prevention strategies can be used to prevent and address school crises. Primary prevention strategies often include creating a safe, nurturing environment and school community; identifying students at risk for self or other violence; teaching social skills; adopting a zero tolerance policy; and providing counseling services for students who have emotional difficulties. Secondary prevention strategies refer to the actions that take place immediately following a crisis; these efforts are intended to minimize traumatization. Examples of secondary prevention strategies include evacuating students to a safe place, leading classroom discussions about the crisis, and answering any questions students or staff may have following the crisis. Tertiary intervention involves debriefing strategies with students and caring for and intervening with victims following a crisis (Schargel, 2014; Studer & Salter, 2010). Figure 10.5 provides ideas for how counselors can establish a homicide crisis plan.

As mentioned previously, counselors of suicidal clients should facilitate safety and should document the steps they have taken to enhance safety. Likewise, counselors working with homicidal youth should understand homicide risk factors and have a safety planning model or approach that they can use. Safety measures should also be explicitly integrated into clients' counseling plans, with an appropriate objective being "0 episodes of aggression toward others."

Again, as with counselors of suicidal clients, counselors of homicidal clients need to be aware of community resources and more restrictive settings where clients at risk of homicide can stay and be treated until they are safe. In addition to knowing the state guidelines related to hospitalization, counselors should also know their state's guidelines related to their duty to warn others of possible harm because these laws vary by state. Counselors must respond to risk, especially when children are involved. They must be aware of their obligation to report concerns about safety to child welfare agencies or legal authorities.

Client Characteristics

Because perpetrators of homicide have diverse motivations for their actions, a single personality profile for a client with homicidal potential is not feasible; however, clusters of personality traits of violent offenders have been identified. Clients who pose a risk to others may display a lack of empathy and understanding of others' emotions; the welfare and needs of others are considered secondary to their own personal needs and goals (Loeber & Farrington, 2011). They may have a history of harming people or animals, and engaging in destructive behaviors such as fire setting and vandalizing property are also common (Loeber & Farrington, 2011). This at-risk population may display a marked disregard for social norms and the rights

- Coordinate with community support people (i.e., fire department, police, and other medical emergency staff) to have resources on site, should they be needed.
- Facilitate good communication with parents to ensure intervention plans are in place and parents know how communication will be set up during a crisis.
- Identify crisis team leader roles to plan training sessions and provide overall coordination during crisis response.
- Have in place defusing and debriefing activities that can provide ways to identify students and staff in need of aftermath care. Also, have in place evaluation procedures so interventions can be evaluated.
- Practice intervention plans with students, teachers, and administration so everyone is familiar with how to respond during a crisis (i.e., where to go, who to call).
- Set up a resource/supply kit (i.e., map of school, extra keys, teacher/employee roster) that can be used in a time of crisis.

FIGURE 10.5 Establishing Homicide Crisis Plan Activities in Schools

Note: Adapted from *The Role of the School Counselor in Crisis Planning and Intervention*, by J. R. Studer, & S. E. Salter, 2010, Retrieved from http://counselingoutfitters.com/vistas/vistas10/Article_92.pdf

of others, and they may have a history of criminal activity. Perpetrators may also have negative family influences such as history of abuse, harsh punishment, violent cultural influences, and weakened family support structures (Loeber & Farrington, 2011). Potentially homicidal individuals may have previously threatened or perpetrated violence against themselves and others. Peer influence is also a factor, and having delinquent friendships may influence negative behaviors (i.e., drugs and alcohol) and violence (Loeber & Farrington, 2011). Clients at risk for homicide may also have a pattern of impulsive behavior with little consideration for consequences, and they may lack remorse for their behavior (Hammond, 2007; Loeber & Farrington, 2011).

Conduct disorders, emerging personality disorders, schizophrenia and other psychotic disorders, and substance use disorders are often comorbid in those at risk for homicide (Hammond, 2007). Young clients who are experiencing a psychotic or manic episode may also be impulsive and act out violently. Although particular diagnoses may be associated with homicidal ideation, most clients diagnosed with mental disorders are not at an increased risk of committing a violent crime (Purcell et al., 2012). Youth who come from large families with a young mother and absent or problematic father or who have parents with substance abuse problems are also more likely to commit homicidal offenses (Loeber & Farrington, 2011).

Although there is no finite set of traits that describes potentially homicidal clients, there are some commonalities among young homicidal offenders (Loeber & Farrington, 2011). Figure 10.6 lists risk factors associated with homicide risk in youth.

Assessment

Counselors must use clinical judgment when determining whether an assessment for homicidal ideation is needed. They should ask clients about homicidal ideation in a clear, direct manner. As with suicide assessment, the counselor should inquire directly if the client has intentions of harming another person, if a plan exists, the method of carrying out the plan, and whether the client has access to the means to fulfill the plan (e.g., access to a firearm). Counselors must be mindful of their ethical duty to notify intended targets and the authorities. In addition, counselors should be alert for reasons that clients may over- or underexaggerate their potential for violence. Within the confines of appropriate ethical boundaries, counselors should consult family members and other possible informants to gain richer assessment information.

Counselors can begin to assess the level of risk by determining the client's current level of distress, recent behaviors that may suggest risk, and communication of ideation. If the client poses a safety risk to the counselor, the session should take place in a safe environment; the counseling setting should be free of dangerous objects, have alarms or a means of communicating a need for assistance, and have quick access to an exit that is not blocked by the client. Assessments should include questions about ideation and attitudes, current life stressors, past reactions to stressors, a psychosocial history, mental health status, and protective

- School truancy
- Peer delinquency (e.g., aggressive or disruptive behavior with peer group)
- Single-parent household or limited adult supervision and support
- Criminal behavior (e.g., convicted of a violent crime or robbery)
- School suspensions
- Old for their grade (e.g., held back in previous grade[s] or enrolled in school at late age)
- Cruel to others
- Disruptive behavior disorder (e.g., conduct disorder, oppositional defiant disorder)
- Low academic achievement
- Violent and/or high-crime neighborhood
- Devaluation of school/academic success
- Nonphysical aggression (e.g., verbal bullying)
- Poor communication skills
- Poor relationships with peers

FIGURE 10.6 Key Risk Factors of Homicide Offenders in Youth

Note: Adapted from *Young Homicide Offenders and Victims: Risk Factors, Prediction, and Preventions from Childhood*, by R. Loeber & D. P. Farrington, 2011, New York, NY: Springer.

S—Suicidal/homicidal ideation. Are you thinking of killing yourself or somebody else?

I—Ideation. How likely are you to kill somebody else?

M—Method. How would you kill somebody else? Are the means available to you to do so? How easy would it be for you to do this?

P—Pain. How much emotional pain are you feeling? What makes this pain worse?

L—Loss. Have you recently experienced significant losses? Have you experienced a loss in your past that you have not been able to move on from?

E—Earlier attempts. Have you ever tried to kill somebody else before? When? How? What interfered?

S—Substance use. Do you use drugs or alcohol?

T—Troubleshooting. How much of your ideation has to do with school, family, or other stressors, and can these stressors be managed? If things were better, what would they look like?

E—Emotions/diagnosis. Have you ever been diagnosed with a mental, emotional, or medical disorder? How are you being treated? Are you complying with treatment?

P—Parental/family history. Has anybody in your family thought about or completed suicide or an act of homicide?

S—Stressors and life events. Which events and feelings have made you think that killing somebody else will be a solution?

FIGURE 10.7 SIMPLE STEPS Homicide Assessment Mnemonic

Note: Adapted from *Developing Clinical Skills in Suicide Assessment, Prevention, and Treatment,* by J. M. McGlothlin, 2008, Alexandria, VA: American Counseling Association.

factors that could prevent homicidal behavior (see Appendix 10.1 for a list of questions that can be used to assess for risk in each of these areas).

All threats of homicidal behavior should be taken seriously. The SIMPLE STEPS mnemonic can be used to assess risk of homicidal behavior (McGlothlin, 2008; see Figure 10.7 for an overview of this assessment tool). After completing an assessment, counselors should determine the level of risk that the client poses—low, medium, or high—and implement appropriate interventions.

Intervention

Research on ways to intervene with homicidal youth is sparse, and counselors must consider each youth's unique situation. Counselors should work with parents and take steps to limit the client's access to weapons. Working within the confines of ethics and laws, counselors should notify intended victims or structures to which the client poses a risk (e.g., a school) as well as law enforcement.

After careful assessment, if the counselor determines that the client poses a significant risk to others, the client should be placed in a more restrictive level of care. If the client and his or her family do not voluntarily agree to a higher level of care, dependent on the state's laws the counselor may need to have the client admitted to a secure setting or contact law enforcement to implement forced hospitalization. Medical staff may apply pharmacological interventions to immediately reduce the client's level of distress, including antianxiety, fast-acting antipsychotic, and sedative medications. A deeper exploration into the young client's presenting issues will be more useful once the client has stabilized and is not at immediate risk. Counseling sessions with a high-risk client will focus on ascertaining the nature of the client's violent ideation, potential targets, motivations, and ongoing assessment of risk. Consistent follow-up contact is highly recommended in the days following release from hospitalization to continually assess client risk.

Counseling interventions that involve the development of coping skills and the exploration of alternatives to violence are appropriate with clients who have stabilized and are not an imminent threat to others. The counselor can address the emotions that the client is experiencing and help the client to identify more adaptive coping methods. Pointing out emotional triggers and encouraging self-awareness can be helpful in promoting the development of new coping skills. Working to establish and strengthen social support networks should also be a part of the intervention process with homicidal youth because social supports are a protective factor against violent behavior (David-Ferdon & Simon, 2014).

In addition, crisis cards with information about warning signs, a reminder of useful coping skills, and a plan of action to prevent homicidal behavior can be given to clients and their families (James & Gilliland, 2013). A safety plan should be implemented with any youth at risk for homicide. The safety plan template discussed in the "Suicide" section can be applied when counseling homicidal youth. A client's level of risk

People usually have mixed feelings about harming someone else. What are some reasons that may prevent you from trying to harm somebody?
If you did decide to try to harm somebody, how would you do it? How easy would it be for you to do this? Do you have access to the method (e.g., weapon, substance)?
What are some of the things that could happen in your life that would make you more or less likely to actually try to harm somebody?
What is something you can do if you start feeling as if you want to hurt somebody (e.g., practice coping skills, contact crisis line, talk to your school counselor)?
If you start feeling as if you want to hurt somebody, who can you call for help? (Include contact information.)
What things have helped you to not hurt others in the past (e.g., coping skills, protective factors)?
What can your counselor do to help you make safe decisions (e.g., take crisis phone calls)?
Which family members and friends can provide you with information about warning signs and emergency contact numbers so they can help you to monitor your behavior (e.g., my mother, Joe)?

FIGURE 10.8 Homicide Safety Plan Prompts

may ebb and flow, and interventions must be adapted accordingly. If a counselor assesses homicidal ideation in a youth directed at a specific individual and the client seems intent and able to implement the plan, then a counselor has an ethical duty to warn the victim. Figure 10.8 provides questions that can be asked to help clients to establish a homicide safety plan.

Summary

This chapter reviewed suicide, self-injury, and homicide in youth, three client behaviors that counselors find challenging to navigate. Above all else, counselors must remember that they have an obligation to facilitate client safety. Safety plans, commitment to counseling plans, risk mnemonics, and other practical resources and tools were provided with the hope that this information will empower counselors in their practice.

Moving forward in the text, we will begin to address various problems that youth present in counseling. Many of the topics discussed will require a consideration of suicide, self-injury, or homicide. The resources provided in this chapter can serve as a guide to inform counselor practice with additional, not explicitly addressed issues that involve risk. For example, the concept of safety planning can be applied to work with youth who are in violent relationships or who are living in violent homes, or the risk factors and mnemonics discussed can be applied to assess a parent for risk.

MyLab Counseling: Counseling Children and Adolescents

Try the Topic 7 Assignments: *Strategies for Addressing Suicidal, Homicidal, and Self-Injurious Behavior in Youth.*

Questions for Assessing Facets of Homicide Risk

IDEATION AND ATTITUDES

1. Do you have thoughts of hurting yourself or others?
2. Would you like to hurt a certain person or group of people?
3. Do you feel that you are a threat to somebody else's safety?
4. Do you think that anybody else views you as a threat to his or her safety?
5. How often do you have thoughts of hurting others?
6. How long have you been having these thoughts?
7. Are there any times when these thoughts are more intense? Are there any triggers?
8. Have you told others about your thoughts of harming yourself/others?
9. If you wanted to hurt somebody else, how would you do it?
10. Do you have a plan for how you might hurt someone else?
11. Have you ever played out your plan in your head?
12. Do you have access to how you might carry out the plan (i.e., the means)?
13. Do you have weapons in your home? What are they, and where are they located?
14. Do you have access to weapons? What are they, and where are they located? Do they belong to you or somebody else?
15. When do you feel it is appropriate to use a weapon?
16. Do you think weapons should be used to solve conflicts?
17. Describe the most violent thing you have witnessed in person. How about in a TV show, movie, or video game? What is it like for you to think about this?

CURRENT STRESSORS

1. How are things going with your friends, family, and school?
2. Are you experiencing any conflicts?
3. What would you like to do about this situation?
4. Is there a reason that you want to hurt somebody or yourself?
5. Are you going through any changes right now?
6. Has anything been bothering you recently?
7. Have you experienced any losses lately? Have you experienced any losses that you don't feel you have been able to get over (e.g., loss of relationship, death)?
8. Have you felt victimized, treated unfairly, or humiliated?
9. Have you felt bullied recently? How did you react? What were your thoughts and feelings? Did you want to seek revenge?
10. Describe significant relationships in your life.
11. Do you feel jealous of your boyfriend/girlfriend (if applicable)? Do you think he or she will be unfaithful or leave you? How do you react?
12. What events in your life have affected you the most? How do they still affect you?

PAST REACTIONS TO STRESSORS

1. When somebody or something upsets you, what is that like? What do you think? How do you react? If I were a fly on the wall, what would I see?
2. If you could react the way you would like to when somebody hurts or bothers you, what would you do?
3. Do you ever have thoughts of hurting others? Can you describe those thoughts?
4. How have you reacted in the past when someone or something made you upset?
5. Do you ever feel as if you are being treated unfairly? How do you react? What thoughts do you have?
6. When you become upset, what happens to you physically? Do you ever feel out of control?

HISTORY

1. Have you been seen by a mental health professional before? If so, for what?
2. Have you ever been diagnosed with a psychiatric disorder?
3. Were you ever treated with medication? Do you currently take medication?
4. Have you or do you currently use drugs or alcohol?
5. What is your history with weapons? Have you ever used one? Would you like to?
6. Have you ever been in a physical fight?
7. Have you ever used violence or threats of violence to solve a conflict?
8. Have you thought of hurting yourself or others in the past?
9. Have you ever tried to hurt yourself or somebody else in the past? What interfered?
10. Have you ever felt as if you were not in control of your actions?

ADDITIONAL MENTAL HEALTH QUESTIONS

1. Do you take prescription drugs that are not yours, or in incorrect dosages?
2. Have you ever seen things or heard things that others do not?
3. How do you picture your future?
4. Do you think that your life is getting better or worse?
5. What activities do you enjoy? How often do you engage in them? Have you been enjoying them less recently?
6. Do you have trouble sleeping? Do you sleep too little or too much?
7. Have you done things lately without thinking of the consequences?
8. Have you made any impulsive decisions recently?
9. What is your current level of anxiety? Do you feel this way most of the time?
10. Have you been more easily irritated by things that didn't bother you before?

PROTECTIVE FACTORS

1. What are your religious or spiritual beliefs? How might these help you to deal with the problems you are experiencing? Do your religious/spiritual beliefs support your thoughts of hurting others or yourself?
2. What are your core values?
3. What skills have you used to cope with your troubles in the past? Did they work?
4. Do you have supportive family members or friends that you can talk to?
5. Who is the person you are closest to?
6. Do you have a person whom you can count on to discuss problems in your life?
7. What or who has helped you to deal with your problems in the past?
8. What has prevented you from hurting yourself or others in the past?
9. Are there safe places you can go or people you can contact if you are having thoughts of hurting yourself or others?
10. How can I (counselor) help you?
11. How can your significant other, family members, or friends help you?

Family-Related Transitions and Struggles

THE CASE OF MALIK

Malik has not been the same since his father passed away from a heart attack while in prison last year. Malik's father had five more years to serve for an aggravated assault charge. Now, Malik no longer talks about his father. Malik seems distracted and avoids spending time with our family. I know he's only ten, but sometimes he gets really moody and just plain nasty, acting like he's in charge. I try to ask him about his dad and his feelings and stuff, but he just denies his father is even dead or says stuff like, "I don't believe you" or "You're lying." I just don't know what to say to him anymore. Also, I hear him up late at night. I'm not sure he is even sleeping; it sounds like he is just rolling around in his bed. Lately, I've been getting calls from the school nurse that he either has a stomachache or headache. This is happening a lot, and I am getting worried. Then he wants me to leave work and take him home, but my boss sure doesn't have time for that. What can I do? Shouldn't he be talking about this with someone?

—Malik's mother

The family is the most basic, indispensable unit in society. The structure of families has evolved and changed (e.g., single parent, stepfamilies, same-sex partner families), yet the significance of the family unit continues to remain crucial to a child's development and wellness (Broderick & Blewitt, 2014). Regardless of the family's composition, each family is a unique and sustaining social system, and each family has its own (a) set of rules, (b) power structure (e.g., parent, caregiver, grandparent, aunt), (c) assigned roles (e.g., provider, caregiver, disciplinarian), (d) forms of communication (e.g., implicit and explicit), and (e) means of problem solving (Goldenberg & Goldenberg, 2013).

Families are essentially microsystems that create their own "microculture" rooted in shared history and sense of purpose and consisting of their own assumptions and beliefs about the world (Goldenberg & Goldenberg, 2013). Within families, children are *socialized* and taught how to navigate their worlds. Relationships between family members (e.g., parent–child, extended family member–child, caregiver–child) ideally provide youth with a healthy sense of stability in emotional, intellectual, and social domains. Youth who experience family stress and dissonance, violence, inconsistent parenting, illness (e.g., mental or physical), parental substance abuse, and/or poverty are less likely to enjoy such emotional, cognitive, and social stability (Zolkoski & Bullock, 2012). Some youth experience stressful, chaotic living situations and continue to thrive despite these difficulties and challenges, whereas others are less successful. Those children who are successful appear to be resilient despite these difficulties and benefit from **protective factors** within the family and the community.

This chapter discusses family-related transitions and struggles that may have a negative impact on young people's development and wellness. We discuss how counselors can address and counsel youth who are navigating family-related transitions and struggles. These transitions and struggles are complex, and not all youth respond and react to them in the same way. The mere presence of any of the transitions or struggles addressed in this chapter does not mean a young person will require counseling. Each child and family should be assessed individually to determine counseling-related needs. This chapter also explores protective factors that families and counselors may cultivate and strengthen to increase children's resilience.

THE NATURE OF FAMILY-RELATED TRANSITIONS AND STRUGGLES IN YOUTH

The "traditional" family consisting of two married individuals who have biological children is less prevalent now than ever before in U.S. history (Broderick & Blewitt, 2014; U.S. Census Bureau, 2014). Although families continue to make up the nucleus of society in the United States, they come in all shapes and sizes. For example, families that have single parents, same-sex partners, cohabitating partners, members who are immigrants or refugees, blended or stepfamily members, and extended family members (e.g., grandparents, aunts, uncles, cousins) have become more prevalent (Centers for Disease Control and Prevention [CDC], 2010; U.S. Census Bureau, 2014). Children being raised with two biological parents in the same home appear to have an advantage (e.g., fewer emotional or behavioral disorders) over children living in other family structures (CDC, 2010). Yet, regardless of family structure, parents who are directly involved and exhibit positive attitudes toward their children have children who achieve more academically, are more socially competent, and can tolerate new, stressful situations and settings (Stallman & Sanders, 2014). There is no doubt that parents play an important role in cultivating and enhancing children's resiliency.

Clinical Toolbox 11.1

In the Pearson e-text, click here to review recommendations on how counselors can work effectively and empathetically with immigrant families and youth.

Children can become at risk for negative life outcomes due to numerous family-level factors, such as poverty, parents' educational level, family conflict, negative life experiences, (e.g., maltreatment, neglect, abuse, intimate partner violence), and racial discrimination (Masten, 2011). Examples of negative life outcomes include substance-related problems, violent behaviors, poor academic achievement, dropping out of school, teenage pregnancy, criminal behaviors, mental health disorders, and greater emotional distress (Zolkoski & Bullock, 2012). These negative life outcomes are often exacerbated by problems in the family, such as parenting weaknesses and external challenges (e.g., poverty, discrimination, grief and loss).

Clinical Toolbox 11.2

In the Pearson e-text, click here for counselor recommendations on how to work with low socioeconomic status families and youth.

This chapter explores family-related transitions and struggles that counselors frequently help young people to navigate. These family-related transitions and/or struggles include family-structure transitions (i.e., divorce, stepfamilies, adoption), parental substance abuse (one or both parents), and grief, loss, and bereavement.

TYPES OF FAMILY-RELATED TRANSITIONS AND STRUGGLES

Transitions that alter the family structure, including divorce, blending families, parental remarriage, and adoption, all have the potential to affect youth's ability to function. These transitions may bring challenges, yet they can also provide opportunities for children and families.

Family-Structure Transitions

DIVORCE/PARENTAL SEPARATION

In U.S. society, about half of all marriages end in divorce (National Center for Health Statistics, 2015). The divorce rate has remained stable since the 1990s, with slightly higher divorce rates in the African American population and slightly lower rates in Hispanic American and Asian American populations (Emery, 2013; National Center for Health Statistics, 2015). Parents who are unmarried but live together present youth with a similar situation as divorce if they choose to separate (Lucas, Nicholson, & Erbas, 2013; Pedro-Carroll, 2010); therefore, the terms *parental separation* and *divorce* are used interchangeably in this chapter.

Divorce affects youth in unique ways. Some experience the impact of divorce initially, whereas others have delayed reactions or experience the impact over time (Weaver & Schofield, 2015). Some youth do not experience any obvious adverse effects related to a divorce or parental separation. Youth who experience a divorce may feel confused, fearful, trapped, angry, unloved, guilty, and afraid. Counselors need to consider that, for these children, their family composition, rules, power structure, forms of communication, and assigned roles in the family drastically change secondary to divorce and may be in flux both during and after the divorce. Children often feel unsure about a host of pragmatic questions, such as the following (Pedro-Carroll, 2010): When will I see my parents? Will we have enough money? Where will I live? Will I still go to the same school? Was it something I said or did that caused the divorce?

Divorce generally alters young people's family structure. Although divorce can be a positive development in some family situations (e.g., the elimination of parental and family conflict, removal of an abusive parent from the home), this transition is still disorienting for most youth because family composition and dynamics (e.g., patterns of relating and interacting) are altered. Many young people struggle with the circumstances that occur around or following the divorce. These circumstances are unique to each young person's lived experience, yet they frequently include (a) parental conflict (e.g., resulting in emotionally strained relationships), (b) parents' attempts to save or salvage the relationship (e.g., resulting in diminished attention to the child), (c) parents' decision to separate or divorce (e.g., feelings of anger, pain, longing, and guilt), (d) parents and family members grieving the divorce (e.g., feelings of loss and grief—the essential emotion involved in divorce), and (e) the renegotiating of former relationships (e.g., redefining the parent–child relationship; Emery, 2012). Divorce is a complex process that plays out on multiple fronts (i.e., emotional, legal, economic, parental; Emery, 2013), and it has the potential to affect parents and their parenting. In addition, adults involved in divorce often report feeling less happiness, increased social isolation, and depression, and they experience more negative life events—all of which may affect their children (Amato, 2014).

For some youth, divorce creates a loss of certain dreams, hopes, and family expectations. A youth's problematic reactions to divorce commonly fall into one of three categories: (a) normal reactions to crisis, which include fear, anger, grief, and a desire to reconnect the original family, (b) age-specific exaggerations (e.g., aggression and defiance in younger children, emotional distancing and a more conflicted parent–child relationship in older children), and/or (c) emerging psychopathology, such as depression, night terrors, enuresis, and other mental illness symptomology (e.g., anxiety, failure to cope; Oppawsky, 2014). Regardless of age, youth may experience psychosomatic symptoms (e.g., headaches, stomachaches, nausea, insomnia), which are often responses to feelings of abandonment, anger, grief, and loss (Oppawsky, 2014). Table 11.1 presents a

Table 11.1	Young People's Common Reactions to Divorce and How to Ease this Transition	
Age	Overall Understandings and Reactions	Ways to Ease the Transition
Early Childhood (3–5)	• Young children have limited understanding of divorce. • They typically want their parents to stay together regardless of any family difficulties or discord. • They tend to internalize self as the cause of the divorce. • Young children may imitate behaviors displayed in divorce (e.g., yelling, fighting, screaming) in play. • They may have uneasiness about the future and struggle with separation anxiety with parental figures. • They keep emotions and feelings bottled up or internalized. • They may experience unpleasant thoughts, ideas, or nightmares concerning the divorce.	• Handle the divorce in an open, positive manner. • Keep the message clear and simple (e.g., "Mom and Dad will be happier, and this will make things easier on you. You will have two homes where you will be loved. We will both still be a big part of your life"). • Reiterate that the child is loved by both parents. • Reiterate that the divorce is not the child's fault. • Use age-appropriate books or resources on divorce to engage the child. • Discuss and implement a regular visitation schedule.

(Continued)

Table 11.1	Young People's Common Reactions to Divorce and How to Ease this Transition (*Continued*)	
Age	Overall Understandings and Reactions	Ways to Ease the Transition
Middle Childhood (6–12)	• Youth may feel as if parents are leaving or divorcing them. • They may fear loss, abandonment, and rejection. • They may fantasize about getting parents back together or may feel the need to rescue the marriage. • Youth may blame one parent more than the other and may align with this "good" parent. • They may express their anger toward parents or others through the use of fights, disrespect, or defiance. In some children, this anger is internalized and is displayed through agitation, anxiety, and withdrawal. • They may display academic struggles (e.g., concentrating, nervousness at school, low academic success). • Some youth experience night terrors, enuresis, and other regressive behaviors (e.g., tantrums, nail biting, thumb sucking).	• Present a consistent and clear plan to maintain the child's normal routine as much as possible. • Attempt to rebuild or maintain the child's sense of security and esteem by spending quality time with the child. • Request that the child talk about and process his or her feelings with both parents. • Reiterate that divorce is not the child's fault. • Encourage the child to participate in extracurricular activities so he or she has structure and social support. • Implement a regular visitation schedule.
Adolescence (12–18)	• Divorce can intensify relationships or exacerbate preexisting grievances between the youth and parent(s). • Youth may feel betrayed by broken promises and commitments to family. • Youth may become angry and communicate less frequently with one or both parents. • Some youth seek more independence from the family by spending more time with friends; others may feel the need for more dependency on the family.	• Be flexible with visitation due to the adolescent's changing social needs. (One idea is to allow a teenager to bring a peer along, which may be an effective compromise.) • Create a working alliance for the child's greater good, which can help to restore the adolescent's trust in the divorcing parents. • Show the adolescent—through one's behavior—that even though the marriage commitment is over, the parental commitment to the child is unchanged.

Note: Adapted from Broderick & Blewitt (2014).

summary of young people's understandings and reactions to divorce and how adults can ease this transition (Broderick & Blewitt, 2014).

Although children react differently to divorce, younger children may experience more consequences of divorce based on their gender (i.e., male), socioeconomic status (i.e., low), and postdivorce parental conflict (Amato, 2014; Lambie, 2008). These consequences often consist of a negative impact on academic functioning, an increase in acting-out behaviors (e.g., conduct and behavior problems), an increased risk of internalizing problems (e.g., depression, anxiety), and a decrease in social support (Amato, 2014; Broderick & Blewitt, 2014; Lambie, 2008). Adolescents may (a) struggle with forming and maintaining intimate relationships, (b) engage in early sexual activity, (c) drop out of school sooner, (d) use drugs and alcohol more frequently, and (e) display increased delinquent behaviors (Amato, 2014; Broderick & Blewitt, 2014). Drug and alcohol use and abuse may be of concern for adolescents making the transition through divorce. More specifically, there appears to be an increased risk of adolescent alcohol abuse prior to the divorce (often 2–4 years before the divorce) and increased use and abuse of alcohol, marijuana, and other drugs after the divorce (Arkes, 2013). Negative divorce outcomes appear to be exacerbated by exposure to parental conflict and discord (Baker & Ben-Ami, 2011).

Marital conflict and discord before, during, and after a divorce can be a significant stressor for youth. In particular, parental conflict may contribute to youth sadness, anger, fear, and insecurity (Baker & Brassard, 2013). Because parents are often in a state of crisis as their marriage unfolds, they may demonstrate poor communication with family members, struggle with appropriate parent–child relationship boundaries, and engage in inconsistent parenting, all of which can have a negative impact on youth (Stallman & Sanders, 2014). Exposure to marital conflict is the single biggest predictor of negative outcomes for children and adolescents making the transition through divorce (Baker & Ben-Ami, 2011). Negative long-term outcomes of divorce (e.g., conflicted parent–child relationships, decreased life satisfaction) have been more frequently associated with parental conflict than divorce per se (Baker & Brassard, 2013). In addition, parental conflict has been linked with quality of parenting (e.g., lack of responsiveness to the child, inconsistent discipline measures, inappropriate parent–child boundaries), which affects parent–child interactions and relationships.

After a divorce or separation, youth may live in a single-parent home. In these situations, a parent may need to work longer hours to provide financially, may seek out support from adult relationships (e.g., friends, new romantic partners), and may struggle to perform household duties that were previously shared with the partner (e.g., laundry, buying groceries). Youth may feel an increased sense of alienation postdivorce (Webb, 2011b). In some situations, an older child may assume a caregiving role (e.g., for other siblings), thus forgoing his or her normal developmental activities (e.g., social interactions, extracurricular activities) and potentially blurring the parental boundaries in the family system.

Generally speaking, higher family income after the divorce, increased parental sensitivity (e.g., responsiveness to the child, appropriate boundaries, consistent parenting), and higher youth IQ serve as protective factors, helping to diminish the internalizing consequences (e.g., sadness, anger, depression) children of divorce may experience (Weaver & Schofield, 2015). One of the most effective protective factors that can enhance a youth's ability to cope with the negative effects of divorce is the quantity and quality of positive parent–child interactions (Velez, Wolchik, Tein, & Sandler, 2011). When parents increase positive interactions (e.g., engaging the child, setting clear limits, using praise), youth are more resilient to the long-term effects of divorce. Youth are more likely to have behavior problems (e.g., substance use, aggression) if their postdivorce homes are less stimulating (e.g., limited supervision and resources), less supportive, and less responsive to developing and cultivating the parent–child relationship (Weaver & Schofield, 2015). Table 11.2 presents family risk and protective factors that affect children experiencing a divorce.

Counselors helping youth who are navigating a divorce can review six psychological tasks that show how youth progress through a divorce experience (Wallerstein & Blakeslee, 1989). These psychological tasks, which have been embedded into numerous child-focused approaches, are as follows:

- Recognizing and acknowledging what is going on in their lived situation (i.e., divorce is imminent)
- Identifying and reducing parental conflict and maintaining previous living friendships and activities
- Resolving the loss (e.g., family structure, dynamics)
- Resolving intense emotions (e.g., anger, self-blame)

Table 11.2 Family Risk and Protective Factors That Affect Children Experiencing a Divorce

Family Risk Factors	Family Protective Factors
• Poor parenting (e.g., inconsistency, lack of supervision)	• Positive parenting (e.g., co-parenting by both parents)
• Marital conflict (especially when abusive and/or child focused)	• Protection of child from parental conflict
• Multiple family transitions (e.g., moving, remarriage)	• Stable home environment
• Unstable or chaotic home environment	• Predictable and consistent family structure
• Parental mental health and/or substance-related challenges	• Healthy psychological well-being
• Impaired parent–child relationship (e.g., limited interactions)	• Healthy relationship between child and parent
• Economic hardship (e.g., decline in family resources)	• Supportive sibling and extended family relationships
	• Financial stability

- Accepting their lived situation (i.e., inevitability of divorce)
- Achieving hope for their future relationships (e.g., friendships, intimate relationships; Pedro-Carroll, 2008; Webb, 2011b).

Counselors who work with children and families who are managing a divorce should be aware of their own personal views on divorce. Counselors need to be mindful of their own family-of-origin difficulties and any potential personal biases related to divorce when working with youth in divorce situations. Some counselors have an increased risk of countertransference when working with youth in these situations, and this can lead a counselor to move beyond his or her clinical role (e.g., to become personally involved, to label or even demonize a parent, to overidentify with the child; Zimmerman et al., 2009). When working with issues of divorce in youth, some of the most effective ways for counselors to counteract countertransference include being aware of potential blind spots (e.g., unresolved family-of-origin challenges), using personal counseling to resolve such personal difficulties, and seeking supervision to enhance their ability to understand and conceptualize the youth's situation (Zimmerman et al., 2009).

Counselors should be aware that although divorce can have significant and adverse impacts on some youth, not every child experiencing divorce warrants counseling services, and not all youth experience adverse effects secondary to a divorce. In fact, some younger youth may become more resilient, adaptable, self-sufficient, and empathic after a divorce secondary to more strongly established relationships with both parents (Golombok & Tasker, 2015). Nonetheless, some youth may experience adverse effects due to divorce; therefore, counselors may rely on parenting education programming and preventive interventions, which often include cognitive behavioral therapy (CBT) and/or expressive therapy such as play-based approaches. Each of these counseling interventions is discussed briefly.

Because quality parenting is a protective factor for children of divorce, counseling interventions aimed at increasing **positive parenting** may be helpful in reducing the behavioral and emotional consequences associated with divorce (Amato, 2014; Stallman & Sanders, 2014). In general, positive parenting programs aim to increase parental warmth, reassure the child he or she is loved, and create consistent expectations in the home through appropriate limit setting and discipline. In addition, the parent–child relationship is an essential protective factor. Thus, counselors should aid parents in strengthening and cultivating their parent–child relationship (Amato, 2014). There are various ways this relationship can be developed and promoted. Parents might regularly or even systematically express their appreciation and gratitude, parents might highlight their child's strengths or positive behaviors, and parents might write kind words or positive affirmations for their child (e.g., "You are such a kind, thoughtful person, and I love you so much") on a napkin and place it with the child's lunch. Encouraging and expressing appreciation in the parent–child relationship will promote communication and strengthen the bond between the parent and child.

Prevention programs for youth of divorce attempt to provide children with support proactively, reduce the potentially adverse impacts of divorce, and increase children's well-being. These prevention programs specifically aim to reduce the distress associated with divorce and increase young people's ability to cope via the acquisition of skills (e.g., emotion identification and expression, problem solving). Often occurring in a group format, these prevention programs follow a similar process, which includes (a) helping the youth to acknowledge, express, and share his or her feelings and experiences related to the divorce, such as anger, isolation, self-blame, and/or feelings of loss; (b) increasing the youth's skills to deal with interpersonal difficulties and the expression of emotions to others appropriately; and (c) increasing the youth's self-esteem and adjustment to new circumstances (Amato, 2014; Botha & Wild, 2013).

One example of an evidence-based prevention program for youth experiencing divorce is the Children of Divorce Intervention Program (CODIP; Pedro-Carroll, 2008). The CODIP is a 15-week manual-based prevention program that addresses the risks of divorce through the implementation of protective factors; it uses a group format (e.g., outpatient, school based). The overarching goal of CODIP is to reduce youth's stress, to provide a supportive environment, and to teach specific coping skills that can be used to mitigate the possible adverse consequences of divorce (Pedro-Carroll, 2008). Counselors using CODIP attempt to:

- provide youth with peer-based social support (e.g., help youth to realize they are not alone; attempt to normalize the youth's experience);

- aid youth in the education, identification, and expression of emotions and divorce-related thoughts and feelings;
- educate youth on divorce-related misconceptions and thus promote greater understanding (e.g., divorce is not your fault; you did not cause this to happen);
- teach youth problem-solving skills (e.g., generate alternative solutions and prepare for any anticipated reactions/consequences) and emotion regulation (e.g., stress, anxiety, depression); and
- enhance young people's positive regard for self and their families (e.g., highlight their unique and special qualities; highlight the positive changes since the separation occurred in the family; Pedro-Carroll, 2008).

CODIP ultimately aids youth in their ability to adjust positively to divorce by assisting youth in externalizing their thoughts and connecting emotions and feelings with events (Pedro-Carroll, 2008). Figure 11.1 provides an activity to help youth to identify, verbalize, and process significant life events through the use of a self-created personal time line.

In summary, counseling interventions can benefit children making the transition through divorce (Carr, 2009). Interventions that can be effective with this population include developing coping skills and increasing positive parenting, reducing youth's negative moods, adapting divorce-related beliefs, encouraging healthy relationships (e.g., parent, family members, peers), and supporting positive behaviors at home and school (Carr, 2009).

Activity Overview
The personal history activity helps clients to identify, verbalize, and process significant life events through the use of a self-created personal time line.

Activity Objectives
The primary goals of this activity are to help clients to (a) become better aware of their feelings, life events, and personal experiences; (b) increase their ability to verbalize these feelings, events, and personal experiences; and (c) discuss these past events as well as future hopes and dreams in the context of a counseling relationship.

Directions
1. Ascertain client preparedness to engage in this creative intervention. This intervention may be inappropriate for clients who lack awareness of their lived experiences and struggle with reading and writing. Counselors could modify this activity with younger children by having them draw pictures of events instead of writing about them.
2. This time-line activity can work with any child but may be especially helpful for a youth dealing with divorce. The only materials needed to complete the activity are a pencil and paper.
3. The counselor asks the child to draw a horizontal line lengthwise across the sheet of paper. On the left-hand side of the line, the counselor instructs the child to place a star to signify his or her beginning or birth.
4. Next, the child places a line in the middle of the paper to distinguish the present time.
5. Then, the child labels the significant events that have occurred from his or her birth to present time. The time-line events may include birth of siblings, starting school, moving, divorce, remarriage, playing a sport, riding a bike, death of a loved one, learning to read, and so on.
6. Finally, the counselor instructs the child to mark all the events from the present moment to the future that he or she hopes to experience.
7. The counselor can use this activity to process past events as well, as future hopes and dreams.

Process Questions
1. What was this activity like for you?
2. What feelings or emotions did you have as you created your personal history time line?
3. Were any of your past event(s) hard to write down (or to draw)? Why?
4. Tell me about one of your past events, one that means a lot to you.
5. Tell me about one of your future hopes or dreams.

FIGURE 11.1 Personal History Time Line

STEP AND BLENDED FAMILIES

High divorce rates and nonmarital childbirths have dramatically reshaped the traditional structure of families in the United States (Copen, Daniels, Vespa, & Mosher, 2012; Sweeney, 2010). In addition, rates of cohabitation continue to rise regardless of ethnicity (Copen et al., 2012). High divorce rates, cohabitation, and nonmarital childbirths have led to an increase in the family structure known as step or blended families. In blended families, one or both adult partners have children from previous relationships whom they bring into the new family unit.

Approximately one third of children in the United States younger than 18 will live in a stepfamily over the course of their childhood (Copen et al., 2012). Generally speaking, youth living with a stepparent do not fare as well cognitively, emotionally, educationally, and behaviorally as those who live with two married biological parents (Sweeney, 2010). Many young people appear to do better (i.e., cognitively, emotionally, educationally, and behaviorally) with a married stepparent than with a cohabitating stepparent (Sweeney, 2010).

Stepfamilies are different from first-time families because (a) they are formed secondary to a loss (e.g., death of partner, divorce, change in partner), (b) the parent–child relationship has existed longer than the relationship with the new partnership, (c) in the case of divorce, the biological parent (e.g., ex-spouse) is typically in another physical location, (d) the child typically becomes a member of two households, (e) the stepparent may be required to assume a parental role before strong emotional ties with the child have been established, and (f) there is often no legal relationship between the child and the stepparent (National Stepfamily Resource Center, 2015). In stepfamilies, the addition of new members means that once agreed-on rules, the power structure, forms of communication, and problem solving to accomplish tasks must be renegotiated (Goldenberg & Goldenberg, 2013). This process of renegotiating family dynamics can be confusing, frustrating, and inconsistent for children and parents.

During this renegotiation process, youth often feel left out as the family structure and composition change. In some situations, youth may feel they need to divide their loyalty between their "new" family and the parent who is no longer part of their in-home family structure (Gonzales, 2009). In addition, the young person must learn to navigate a new parent, who will typically have a different parenting style and approach, while building relationships with other stepfamily members (e.g., stepsiblings). Finally, the young person's schedule and daily routine change with the introduction of new family members, which can be a complicated transition (Gonzales, 2009).

Clinical Toolbox 11.3

In the Pearson e-text, click here to review an activity that can be used with children with stepfamilies. This activity helps youth to identify family membership and highlight each family member's role.

Youth who have not adequately processed their loss of a parent (through death or reduced contact with the parent), loss of stability, and loss of original family structure may experience unexpected feelings of jealousy, anger, and betrayal (National Stepfamily Resource Center, 2015). If youth are unable to resolve these feelings, they may become hostile toward the stepparent and have difficulty accepting him or her. Many parents and stepparents believe these feelings and behaviors will resolve over time, so they fail to invest the time needed to foster new family relationships and communication.

Adults entering into a stepfamily must take proactive measures to ensure a successful transition. They should (a) nurture and enrich their relationship with the new partner (e.g., show affection, spend "alone" time together), (b) communicate about the transition regularly, (c) reveal feelings of loss and attempt to understand all family members' emotions (e.g., dealing with loss and pain of previous relationships; expressing thoughts and emotions positively), (d) have realistic expectations for assimilation (e.g., family members need to get to know each other before a remarriage takes place), and (e) develop new roles in the stepfamily (National Stepfamily Resource Center, 2015). Parents need to temper their own expectations and allow ample time for each child to adjust to the new living arrangement.

- Involve the youth in counseling and family decision making.
- Acknowledge that forming a new family is time consuming, involves work, and can be an emotionally intensive process.
- Teach the new family to establish and maintain clear but flexible boundaries.
- Aid the family in establishing consistent rules in the home; instruct parents to allow for a transition period for their youth, especially if they go to another parent's home during the week/weekends.
- Advise parents and stepparents to keep messages about their former partners positive.
- Teach stepparents to acclimate to the new family structure and not rush into being a new parent or the disciplinarian for the youth.
- Encourage all family members (e.g., parents, stepparents, youth) to increase trust, communication, and sharing of ideas, activities, and interests in the family.
- Increase parental awareness of their behaviors, speech, and attitudes toward the family and youth.

FIGURE 11.2   Strategies for Counseling Youth and Stepfamilies

The most common challenges that bring stepfamilies into counseling are parenting and communication difficulties (Pace, Schafer, Jensen, & Larson, 2015). In addition, unclear expectations, boundaries, and relationships can disrupt the family system and homeostasis (Pace et al., 2015). Counselors working with stepfamilies often work directly with parents in the context of parent education (e.g., parenting, family dynamics) and with the entire family to increase overall communication.

Some stepfamilies have difficulty managing boundaries and maintaining clear parental roles. Therefore, communication skills are vital and applicable to most family-related transition struggles. Families need to listen to each other and address conflict in a direct manner. They need to be open to sharing information together and need to nurture multiple relationships in the family unit. Families can do this by (a) showing affection, (b) engaging in discussion about everyday activities (e.g., "How was school?" "What was one positive thing that happened today?"), (c) attending children's activities and extracurricular events, (d) establishing family activities and/or rituals (e.g., family game night, eating one meal together), and (e) being intentional about the words used toward each other (e.g., respectful, kind; McBride, 2008). Figure 11.2 presents strategies for counseling stepfamilies.

As families go through transition (e.g., adding and subtracting members), parents and stepparents should use clear communication with children, especially concerning the stepparents' parental role in the family. This may alleviate some of the negative difficulties and challenges associated with stepparenting and increase relationship stability and overall family satisfaction (Pace et al., 2015). Stepparents should remain neutral regarding past family struggles, be supportive of the current parental plan (e.g., rewards, bedtimes, allowances, rules, punishments), and build positive relationships with youth before exercising parental discipline. In addition, stepparents should work on their relationship with the children by participating in shared interests with them and getting to know them on their terms.

When working with younger children, counselors can facilitate interactions between parents and children that enhance their relationship and increase communication. Counselors can coach parents and stepparents with younger children how to use play to enhance parent–child interactions (McNeil & Hembree-Kigin, 2010). In addition, counselors can train parents to use skills that enhance and encourage positive interactions. The PRIDE acronym is one example of skills that might be used:

- *Praise* (e.g., "You did a really good job saying 'please' and 'thank you'")
- *Reflection* (e.g., verbally restating what the child stated to show the parent is listening)
- *Imitation* (e.g., doing what the child is doing to show approval and aid the child in playing with others)
- *Describing behaviors or actions* (e.g., describing what the child is doing, such as "It looks like you are working hard to build that castle with all of those blocks"); and
- *Enjoyment* (e.g., using verbal and nonverbal behaviors to show excitement about something the child is doing; McNeil & Hembree-Kigin, 2010)

The PRIDE acronym highlights how parents can use simple and practical means to enhance the parent–child relationship. Communication with older children is a process of giving and receiving information. Counselors can help parents and children by teaching them basic attending skills (Meichenbaum, Fabiano, &

Fincham, 2002). Some skills that can be helpful in reducing parent–child conflict and increasing parent–child communication are:

- *encouraging* (e.g., asking for more information to better understand the other's positions, requests, or statements);
- *restating* (e.g., putting the other person's words into your own words);
- *reflecting* (e.g., attempting to restate what you feel the other is going through, experiencing);
- *clarifying* (e.g., asking additional questions to see if you are understanding the other person);
- *summarizing* (e.g., pulling together the ideas, themes, and/or emotions of the conversation into one statement); and
- *validating* (e.g., acknowledging and showing appreciation for what someone has to say even if you do not agree with it).

Counselors should use in-session time to work on these communication skills and help family members to create expectations of how members will interact with each other. In addition, the new family should attempt to communicate—when necessary—with the nonresidential biological parents, thus strengthening family boundaries and continuity of communication (DiVerniero, 2013). For example, members of the nonresidential biological parent's family (e.g., grandparents, cousins, aunts, uncles) may continue to be part of the child's daily life and routines (e.g., extracurricular activities, sporting events, family celebrations, holidays). In addition, because the child is not living with the parent, communication and interactions may naturally decrease with the nonresidential parent's side of the family. If appropriate, youth should be encouraged to spend time with both of their biological parents and their families (DiVerniero, 2013).

The development of parenting skills is another critical task for stepfamilies. The central aim of skill-based parent training in stepfamilies is to (a) aid parents in creating safe, nurturing family environments, (b) develop caring family relationships, and (c) develop effective strategies to deal with and manage common behavioral and developmental struggles with children in times of stress. One such evidence-based parenting training program that has empirical support is the Positive Parenting Program, or the Triple P program (Stallman & Sanders, 2014). This program can be applied individually or in group formats. The Positive Parenting Program can be helpful with all types of families (e.g., single parent, stepfamilies), and it is directed to parents and children of all age ranges, from infancy to adolescence (Stallman & Sanders, 2014). Parents using the positive parenting techniques have reported feeling less distressed, less angry, and better able to communicate with their children (Stallman & Sanders, 2014). Table 11.3 provides positive parenting tips and examples.

Table 11.3 Positive Parenting Tips and Examples

Positive Parenting Tips	Examples
1. Engage your child in dialogue.	Be intentional when asking your child how his or her day was and what the child learned at school, as well as about things that interest him or her.
2. Pay attention to your child's actions.	If your child is talking to you, stop what you are doing and engage your child verbally. Making even brief time for your child can increase communication and enhance the parent–child relationship.
3. Give your child physical attention.	Be sure to occasionally give your child a hug, hold hands, or give a kiss before he or she leaves for school.
4. Provide your child with verbal praise.	Point out to your child when you notice something you appreciated, such as "I really liked how you said thank you. I really want to help you when you are so polite."
5. Encourage your child to engage in activities (indoor and outdoor).	Sometimes children get in trouble when they are bored. Consider suggesting things you know your child likes to do (e.g., build with cardboard boxes, play sports, read, play with toys or sibling).
6. Stay calm, and provide clear instruction during stressful times.	If your child is misbehaving, remain calm and tell your child exactly what you would like him or her to do. For example, "Please do not swing that stick around. Take it over to the woodpile and set it down."

(Continued)

Positive Parenting Tips	Examples

Table 11.3 (Continued)

Positive Parenting Tips	Examples
7. Have realistic expectations for your parenting and your child's behaviors.	Remember that your child is a child. He or she is not perfect, and you are not a perfect parent.
8. Set clear limits and expectations for behaviors in and outside the home.	As a family, outline your rules and expectations for the house. You may want to write the rules and expectations on a poster board and place it in the kitchen—for example, "Respect others and treat them like you would like to be treated."
9. Model coping skills before teaching your children the same skills.	Teaching a child a coping skill by displaying it is one of the best ways. If your child yells at you, take a deep breath and speak directly to him or her: "I do not appreciate it when you raise your voice at me. I do not feel appreciated, and I do not want to help you in your time of need. If you speak more politely to me I'd be more than happy to help you out. Do you see how I responded to someone as they were yelling at me? I spoke calmly and presented my thoughts and feelings calmly and directly. How did that feel?"
10. Make sure you are taking care of your own health and wellness.	Find time every day/week to unwind and recharge. Take a few minutes and do something that can help you remain calm (e.g., read, look on the Internet, go for a short walk).

KINSHIP CAREGIVERS

In some communities and populations, it is common for individuals who are not biological parents but are members of the family (e.g., grandparents) to serve as primary caregivers for youth (Daly & Glenwick, 2000; Lee, Choi, & Clarkson-Henderix, 2016). Nonparental family members who serve as the primary guardians for youth are known as kinship caregivers, and youth might be placed with a kinship caregiver for various reasons, ranging from parental mental illness or incarceration to child abuse or neglect (Daly & Glenwick, 2000). The prevalence of kinship caregivers is sometimes higher in families with fewer resources and higher levels of poverty and/or oppression (Daly & Glenwick, 2000; Lee et al., 2016; Sue & Sue, 2013). Often, individuals who serve as kinship caregivers have their own mental health needs and difficulties with their families of origin (Lee et al., 2016). As such, youth and families involved with kinship care might be in an especially vulnerable position.

Youth under kinship care might be placed with an aunt, uncle, older sibling, cousin, grandparent, or other relative by blood, marriage, or adoption. It is increasingly common for youth to be placed with grandparents specifically, and grandparents often assume care for youth under difficult circumstances (Daly & Glenwick, 2000; Goodman & Silverstein, 2002). For example, a youth's father might be incarcerated and the youth's mother might be incapable of caring for her child on her own; thus, the child may live with a grandmother. Sometimes, a youth's parent might maintain a relationship with the youth while grandparents assume responsibility for providing for the child's basic needs. Parents might ask for assistance from grandparents, or they might live in the same household with the youth and grandparents. Counselors should work to understand the unique dynamics that exist in each youth's household to develop interventions that are individually tailored for effectiveness. Important adults (and children) in the child's life should be integrated into the counseling process as appropriate.

When working with matters of child custody, counselors should consider various legal factors. The laws in each state vary, and counselors should obtain supervision and consultation as necessary. To begin, counselors might ask kinship caregivers a series of questions, including the following:

- Even though you have physical custody of the youth, who has formal legal custody of the youth?
- May I have a copy of any signed paperwork that documents your custody arrangement with the youth?
- Do you anticipate that you will be going to court in the future?
- Do you anticipate that this counseling process will become part of future court proceedings?

- Will anyone from other agencies want or need to collaborate with me as this youth's mental health professional?
- Will you give me permission to collaborate with any necessary outside agencies or health professionals with your prior consent and approval?

Counselors should use the answers to questions such as these to plan their work with youth and their families.

Kinship caregivers typically are involved with multiple legal and community agencies as they work with social services to keep youth safe, attend court proceedings as necessary, obtain financial assistance to help with raising the youth, and connect with various community organizations that can offer additional support for the youth, the youth's siblings, the youth's biological parents, or the kinship caregivers (Sampson & Hertlein, 2015). Involvement in multiple agencies can be time-consuming and stressful for kinship caregivers. These processes can provide the resources kinship caregivers need to succeed but can also take time and energy away from raising and attending to the youth. In addition, kinship caregivers might be responsible for more than one youth, most often the client's siblings, which can create added sources of stress and responsibility for the caregiver; this situation must be intentionally addressed by the counselor as well.

The presence or absence of siblings in the home can be a source of stress for youth and their kinship caregivers. Youth who have been separated from their siblings might experience feelings of loss and grief and need therapy that focuses on validation of emotions and reframing irrational thoughts. Youth whose siblings are under the care of the same kinship caregiver might contribute to unhelpful dynamics in the family, creating the need for family therapy and mental health referrals for the siblings.

Youth who are being cared for by their grandparents have likely experienced disruption and trauma in their lives (Sampson & Hertlein, 2015), which—along with a lack of resources—might contribute to emotional or behavioral difficulties. Many grandparents in kinship caregiver roles experience lower levels of satisfaction and higher levels of stress and mood disruptions (e.g., anxiety, depression) when the children in their care display emotional or behavioral difficulties (Doley, Bell, Watt, & Simpson, 2015), and grandparents' reactions to youth's challenges can potentially exacerbate the youth's behavioral and emotional symptoms. This cycle can be harmful if youth and their caregivers are not offered the mental health services they need individually and as a family.

Although serving as a kinship caregiver can be quite challenging, grandparents can provide their grandchildren with many benefits. For various reasons, many grandparents are able to give their grandchildren more time and attention than they were able to give their biological children. Grandparents may have fewer competing demands, increased schedule flexibility, and wisdom related to parenting that they did not have in their younger years, all of which may benefit a child (Sampson & Hertlein, 2015). Grandparents who have informal supports (e.g., community agencies, church communities, close family members, supportive friends) experience less depression than grandparents who feel isolated or have to face their challenges alone (Doley et al., 2015), so the mental health needs of grandparents and other kinship caregivers are important to address as a holistic method of supporting young clients. Some things that counselors, schools, and agencies can do to help to support grandparents who care for their grandchildren include:

- providing psychoeducation and relevant resources to kinship caregivers;
- applying for grants that can be used to offer therapeutic services to kinship caregivers;
- advocating for kinship caregivers to local, state, and federal legislators;
- providing reasonable and accessible mental health referrals to kinship caregivers and any other relevant family members;
- creating and running support groups or peer mentorship programs for kinship caregivers;
- helping grandparents create and run their own support groups or peer mentorship programs;
- creating and distributing lists of helpful community resources;
- creating and distributing lists of helpful informal resources;
- organizing a toy or food drive for local families involved with kinship care;
- organizing days or weeks dedicated to thanking kinship caregivers in the schools and communities;
- helping youth identify ways to show their appreciation for their caregivers; and
- providing kinship caregivers with frequent updates regarding the progress and needs of the youth in their care.

When providing counseling interventions to youth, counselors should address the mental health needs associated with the events that led them to be placed in kinship care (e.g., abuse, neglect, trauma; Sampson & Hertlein, 2015). Counselors should also work to address the mental health needs that are associated with being adopted or placed in foster care (see the next section). Finally, counselors should provide family therapy and mental health referrals for family members when necessary and appropriate. Counselors should work to understand the unique circumstances experienced by each youth and his or her caregivers and family members through a process of ongoing assessment, and case conceptualization and intervention should be approached with a nonjudgmental, supportive attitude.

ADOPTION

On average, 120,000 younger people are adopted each year in the United States (American Academy of Child & Adolescent Psychiatry [AACAP], 2011b). Unlike the adults in the process (e.g., birth parents, adoptive parents), youth who have been adopted often possess little power and voice in the adoption process; therefore, counselors need to empower these children during the counseling process (Baden, Gibbons, Wilson, & McGinnis, 2013). Empowerment efforts could be as simple as letting young people discuss their adoption stories in their own way—especially if they are uncomfortable with certain aspects or parts of their story—to empower them to decide who they want to share with and how much of their story they feel comfortable sharing with others.

Generally speaking, adoptions can be either open or closed. Youth involved in a closed adoption have no ongoing contact with their biological parents, and they have limited identifying information about their biological families. In contrast, in an open adoption there is some expectation that the youth will have intermediary or open contact with parents (e.g., visits, letters, phone calls, emails). Many adoptions with older children or adolescents are open due to the youth's existing knowledge and lived experience with the biological family.

In addition, adoptions can be domestic (e.g., within the United States) or international. Domestic adoptions often occur in one of the following ways: (a) youth are adopted out of the foster care system, (b) youth come to a potential adoptive parent in a foster parent role, and the foster parents have the expectation of adoption eventually occurring (i.e., a foster-to-adopt situation), (c) youth, usually infants or young children, come to an adoptive parent through a private adoption, and (d) youth come to an adoptive parent independent of an agency, most often through a legal proceeding (e.g., an aunt takes custody of and adopts her niece). In international adoptions, youth frequently spend some time in orphanages or government institutions, where they often experience inconsistent caregiving, limited child interactions, and limited appropriate emotional involvement because of high child-to-caregiver ratios (Baden et al., 2013). Despite these limitations, many of the potential risk factors caused by these caregiving challenges can be ameliorated with subsequent, responsive caregiving from the adoptive parents.

Although the parent–child attachment requires considerable work on the part of all members involved, most youth and their families do not require the direct assistance of a counselor or mental health professional to manage this process. Counselors can be a helpful resource in promoting healthy parent–child attachment, parent education, and strategies to implement in the home postadoption. Therefore, counselors should be consulted for assessment and counseling when warranted. Families and children may warrant consideration for counseling if the youth:

- shows signs of distress (e.g., wetting the bed, using baby talk, hoarding, experiencing separation anxiety, being aggressive toward others or animals);
- displays rage or fear out of proportion to a given situation;
- is unable to talk about the adoption process;
- displays attention or learning-related struggles;
- does not seem to be establishing an attachment with the parent and/or does not seem motivated to form one;
- has a history of physical or sexual abuse, including neglect and/or extreme deprivation;
- is demonstrating signs of having a mental illness; and/or
- has witnessed violence in the previous home or community (Gray, 2012).

In addition, adolescents who are adopted may struggle with identity issues, understanding their role in the family, social and peer interactions, and navigating the demands of the outside world (AACAP, 2011b).

As adolescents, many young people who have been adopted have an increased interest in contacting and connecting with their biological parents. This desire to reconnect appears to be part of a normal process, and adoptive parents should not view this desire as a rejection (Baden et al., 2013).

One of the essential tasks when working with adoptive children and families is to facilitate **attachment** and **attunement**. Adoptive parents with younger children especially need to facilitate attachment by being responsive to their child's needs. Building a secure attachment takes time, but counselors can support adoptive parents by providing them with skills that can enhance attunement. Table 11.4 presents a summary of the ways parents can enhance attunement with younger children.

Table 11.4   Ways to Increase Parental Attunement in Adoptive Families

Parenting Skill	Overview	Example
Collaboration	The parent mirrors a reaction to the child's nonverbal behaviors, such as eye contact, voice tone, vocal noise, and/or facial expressions.	A young child is coloring and frowns sadly at her mother. The mother can mirror this facial expression (slanting her head to the left side) as their eyes meet. This allows the two to connect with a similar nonverbal behavior and connect on an emotional level.
Reflective dialogue	The parent verbally communicates a reaction to the child's nonverbal behaviors with a narrative. The narrative should capture the connection of observed behaviors with an interpretation of cognitions and/or feelings. These can involve emotions, intentions, thoughts, beliefs, and attitudes.	A parent might say "I noticed you didn't make eye contact with me when you told me about the broken picture frame. You look really upset, and I'm wondering if you thought I'd be mad at you because you broke it?"
Repair	When there are disconnections or communication is disrupted, parents need to repair or reestablish a connection with their child. This action teaches the child that although misunderstandings and misconnection are part of life, parents will respond to the child in a predictable, intentional way.	The child is having difficulties (e.g., crying, having a tantrum). Due to the parent being on the phone and attending to household responsibilities, the parent has missed the child's cues that she is ready for her nap. Instead of using a time-out or some form of discipline, the parent may need to repair the connection with the child: "It seems like you're getting really tired. How about if I cover you up with a blanket and snuggle with you for your nap. And, if you want, I can read you your favorite story."
Coherent narratives	When a parent reconstructs a story about the child's past, present, or future, the child can integrate these experiences into a more coherent narrative. Taking time to reminisce and retell old narratives (e.g., a memorable story involving the parent and child) increases emotional connection and enables more communication to follow.	A parent might say "Remember when we went to the river outside of the city and fished all day? Even though we didn't catch anything, I think I had more fun just putting bait on the line and casting it out. We probably didn't catch anything because we were laughing so much, telling stories about places and people we'd like to meet."
Emotional communication	The parent shares in and amplifies emotions (whether positive or negative) with the child. The child can learn that his or her parent will not abandon him or her, especially during negative emotional states. The child will also learn how to reduce his or her emotional state and ways to soothe distress.	A parent might say "I know you are feeling really upset right now, and it is totally okay to feel this way. I'm just going to sit here with you while you feel this way. I know when I'm upset I take some deep breaths. I wonder if you take a few deep breaths if that might help you."

Note: Adapted from Lacher, Nichols, Nichols, & May (2012).

The major task of adolescence is **identity formation** (e.g., Who am I? What do I believe? What do I want to do in life?) and separation (e.g., individuating oneself from caregivers), but adopted adolescents—both those who were adopted in adolescence and those who were adopted in childhood—have an extra layer of identity formation and separation, which includes understanding and integrating their experiences as an adoptee (Webb, 2011b). Counselors should aid adopted adolescents in formulating their own identity by addressing the following questions in the context of counseling sessions:

- Who am I? What do I believe in?
- Who are my role models? Do I want role models who share my birth parents' ethnicity, nationality, and/or culture?
- How am I like my adoptive parents? In what ways do I want to be like them? Do they respect my culture, my ethnicity, and me?
- How am I like my birth parents? Do I know enough about my birth parents? How much of what I know about my ethnicity, birth country, and culture will I incorporate into my identity?
- Do I want to be more like my birth parents? Do I want to have others (e.g., friends, role models) in my life who share my birth parents' culture, ethnicity, and/or nationality?

Counselors can assist adolescents in separating, or individuating, themselves by addressing the following questions:

- Once my adoptive parents are done caring for me, what will be my role or connection with them?
- Can they still be my parents if they are not my birth parents?
- If I am different from them, will they still love me?
- Even if I am different from them, will I still be part of their family?

Through this counseling process, counselors can help adolescents to address identity and separation issues, address any existing adoption issues from the youth's past, realize their unique role in their family, and increase their ability to navigate the demands of the outside world (AACAP, 2011b).

Parental Substance Abuse

An estimated 8 million youth younger than 18 live with an adult who has a substance use disorder (Lander, Howsare, & Bryne, 2013). Youth who live in families in which one or both parents abuse substances may not have their basic physical and/or emotional needs met. Although each circumstance is unique, these families may be at risk for experiencing economic difficulties, emotional distress, legal issues, and, in some cases, violence in the home (Lander et al., 2013). In addition, youth in these families often experience a lack of appropriate parental supervision and inconsistent parenting, and in some cases, youth may even compensate by catapulting themselves into a caregiver or parental role (Child Welfare Gateway, 2009).

Maternal substance abuse can also have an effect in utero. The use and abuse of alcohol and drugs during pregnancy can have irreversible effects on an unborn fetus (Broderick & Blewitt, 2014). Although not all children exposed to alcohol and drugs prenatally will develop adverse effects, in the most severe cases a child will have defects in his or her major organs and/or central nervous system. For example, **alcohol-related neurodevelopmental disorder** (ARND; formerly known as fetal alcohol syndrome) is a commonly known birth defect resulting from prenatal drug or alcohol exposure. ARND can manifest in a child in the following ways: reduced head and brain size; overall growth deficits; intelligence quotient (IQ) in the mild to severe range; joint, limb, and ear malformations; problems with the central nervous system, and poor optic nerve development (Broderick & Blewitt, 2014). Different consequences ensue with the use of other substances during pregnancy. Youth whose mothers abuse substances while pregnant are at risk for low birth weight, physical malformations, premature birth, attention-related struggles, behavior problems, and decreased brain functioning as compared to youth who were not prenatally exposed to drugs or alcohol.

Youth being raised in families with a parent who has substance-related problems are at a greater risk for emotional and behavioral difficulties (AACAP, 2011a). More specifically, these children are at an increased risk for mental illness, substance-related problems, physical health difficulties, behavior problems, learning issues, neglect, and abuse (AACAP, 2011a; Child Welfare Gateway, 2009; Lander et al., 2013; Osborne & Berger, 2009).

In addition, because of various factors, including unpredictable interactions with the substance-abusing parent, they often struggle to form secure attachment with parents. As a consequence, these children may have difficulties forming and maintaining relationships with others, regulating their emotions, and relating to others. They may struggle with their self-esteem, self-image, and confidence; and they may experience a general mistrust of others' motives and intentions, which can affect their social relationships (Child Welfare Gateway, 2009).

These young people may struggle with school attendance and academic performance, social relationships, physical complaints (e.g., stomachaches, headaches), and delinquent behaviors (e.g., substance use, stealing, violence; AACAP, 2011a). The young person's safety is a paramount concern; therefore, counselors should continually assess the young person's safety in the home (Webb, 2011b). In situations of neglect and maltreatment, counselors must report concerns to child protective services.

Some youth may assume a parental role in the family—to care for themselves, as well as for younger children. Although these young people often present as being in control and may appear to be overachievers (e.g., academically successful, motivated, hypervigilant), these childhood experiences may lead youth to be socially isolated and experience painful emotions (e.g., fear, sadness, guilt) that can lead to emotional difficulties later in life (e.g., depression, anxiety; AACAP, 2011a).

A broad counseling approach that includes educational, psychological, and behavioral interventions is useful when working with these families and youth (Webb, 2011b). Counseling treatment historically has only involved the parent who has the substance abuse problem, but some argue this is a missed opportunity to intervene at the systemic, family level (Lander et al., 2013). Counselors ultimately must treat parents who abuse substances or refer them to an appropriate treatment facility that best can meet their needed level of care (e.g., detox treatment facility, day treatment, outpatient facility). Counseling treatment cannot be effective if it does not address the parent's substance abuse directly. A counselor working with a youth in family situations can assume a child-focused approach, a family-focused approach, or some type of blended child-and-family approach to counseling. If the sessions tend to be more family focused, counselors should:

- provide a thorough assessment of substance-related difficulties in the family and with all family members;
- require the treatment goal of abstinence/sobriety for the parent who abuses substances;
- provide education for all family members on the substance use and abuse;
- create a climate for the family members to openly discuss the problem and the associated consequences; and
- highlight and address the specific needs of the youth living in the family. (Webb, 2011b)

If a counselor decides to assume a more child-focused approach, treatment focuses on the needs of the child. In child-focused counseling with school-age children, counselors may need to focus on providing the youth with emotional support, educating the child about the nature of substance use disorders (e.g., dispelling the notion that the child is the cause of the substance abuse), helping the youth develop the coping skills needed to deal with the family environment, reducing isolating behaviors, and strengthening self-image. Adolescents in these family situations are at a greater risk of developing substance use disorders. Therefore, education and prevention are essential components of counseling treatment, regardless of whether counseling is child, parent, or family focused.

Younger people who have substance-abusing family members often feel intense shame and guilt and may be reluctant to discuss feelings, thoughts, and experiences (Straussner & Fewell, 2015). Play-based and expressive arts activities are a means for younger children to convey their lived experience through self-expression (Seymour, 2014; Webb, 2011a). When working with older children and adolescents, counselors can use a cognitive approach that addresses the following three Cs of treatment: (a) they did not *cause* this substance use disorder, (b) they cannot *control* their parent's substance use disorder, and (c) they cannot *cure* the parent's substance use disorder (Child Welfare Gateway, 2009).

Adolescents who have substance-abusing family members may benefit from insight-oriented and cognitive behavioral approaches with a primary focus on increasing the youth's ability to care for their physical, emotional, social, and educational needs. Counselors should facilitate the discussion of their thoughts and emotions, which often include guilt, anxiety, embarrassment, confusion, anger, and sadness (AACAP, 2011a). For example, the young person may feel that he or she is the cause of the parental substance use, worry excessively about his or her parent (e.g., safety, well-being), be ashamed of how his or her parent behaves in public, and become distrustful of others; these feelings have an indirect impact on his or her ability to form close relationships. Counselors can help youth to identify, verbalize, and discuss these thoughts and emotions (e.g., the influence on their behaviors), which ultimately can enhance adolescents' ability to problem solve, communicate, handle conflict, and manage or shift any non-adaptive cognitive processes (e.g., "If I was a better kid, my mom wouldn't drink so much"; Straussner & Fewell, 2015).

In addition to counseling services, counselors may also recommend youth participate in support groups. These support groups provide an opportunity for youth to discuss their thoughts, feelings, and experiences while feeling supported by others who live in similar situations. The curriculum for these types of groups varies, but the content often includes education on the disease model of chemical dependency, identification and discussion of the youth's feelings and emotions, problem-solving and decision-making skills, and activities aimed at increasing youth self-esteem (Webb, 2011b).

Clinical Toolbox 11.4

In the Pearson e-text, click here for an activity that can be used with youth who have a parent who has substance abuse problems. This activity aids youth in identifying and verbalizing their feelings and lived experiences.

In many support groups for youth, the use of workbooks, videos, and storybooks allows group members to see how other youth have dealt with and overcome these difficult living situations.

Grief, Loss, and Bereavement

During their formative childhood years, many youth experience the death and loss of a grandparent, parent, sibling, or pet. Although most children are able to navigate this grieving process, some children struggle (Cohen & Mannarino, 2011). Grief symptoms in youth may involve emotional shock (e.g., a lack of feelings), regression to immature behaviors (e.g., wanting to sleep in the parent's bed, needing to be held), and explosive behaviors (e.g., outbursts, demanding and aggressive behaviors), and younger children might repeat questions over and over (e.g., "Where is grandpa?").

Clinical Toolbox 11.5

In the Pearson e-text, click here for 10 facts counselors can share with parents and youth regarding youth grief in the context of death and loss.

Kubler-Ross (2014) was the West's pioneer of conceptualizing grief and loss, and she created a stage model (i.e., denial, anger, bargaining, depression, and acceptance) for individuals coming to terms with their own impending death. Similar to the adult grief process, childhood grief is thought to include (a) denial (e.g., unwillingness to discuss loss), (b) anger (e.g., blaming others for the loss), (c) bargaining (e.g., a means of regaining some sense of control by making promises or changes in one's situation or life), (d) sorrow (e.g., loss of energy, appetite, and motivation), and (e) acceptance (e.g., acceptance that loss is real, final, and painful; National Association of School Psychologists [NASP], 2010).

Current understanding of grief and loss is built on Kubler-Ross's model, yet newer models focus on grief as occurring in a nonprescriptive and often circular fashion. Table 11.5 provides the behaviors youth typically express at different points in their grief process.

Table 11.5	Youth Grief and Loss Behaviors
Grief Process	**Possible Behaviors**
Denial	• Youth refuse to accept, acknowledge, or talk about the deceased person. • They share stories about having "felt" or "seen" the deceased person. • They experience regression of behaviors (e.g., urine or bowel accidents such as bedwetting). • They experience increased somatic complaints (e.g., nausea, headaches). • Younger children often do not understand the concept of death, and they may believe that death is temporary or reversible.
Anger	• Youth engage in more conflict with parents, siblings, or peers. • They display an increase in verbal or physical aggression. • They display an increase in temper tantrums. • They display more risk-taking behaviors (e.g., substance use). • They exhibit destructive behaviors (e.g., ripping up pictures or letters). • They show an increase in oppositional or argumentative behaviors. • They have an increase in delinquency (i.e., disregard for norms or rules).
Bargaining	• Youth express remorse or guilt for past actions. • They reach out more to others (e.g., struggle to find meaning in what happened).
Sorrow/anxiety	• Youth experience changes in eating, sleeping, and activity levels. • They have more nightmares. • They display more avoidant behaviors. • They have more somatic complaints (e.g., nausea, headaches). • They have mood changes (e.g., flat affect). • They are tearful (e.g., excessively cry). • They isolate themselves from others or excessively cling to others (e.g., separation anxiety). • They have diminished ability to concentrate. • They experience a decline in academic performance.
Acceptance	• Youth slowly return to normal functioning and routine.

Youth ideally will move to a place of integrated acceptance relative to the loss. Once youth have adapted and dealt with their grief, they are able to:

• understand and experience the pain of a loss in a developmentally appropriate way;
• tolerate talking and thinking about the deceased individual (e.g., often finding some comfort in the process);
• adjust to the change and slowly engage the deceased individual in a new way (i.e., as a memory); and
• move forward on a healthy developmental trajectory unencumbered by the energy it takes to manage unresolved grief (Cohen & Mannarino, 2011).

Preschool children often view death as temporary, not final, and in some cases even reversible. Although children in middle childhood are able to view death as final, they often do not believe death will or could happen to anyone they know. Anger and sadness are the typical and normal responses to grief, but some younger children may regress (e.g., become more infantile) and demand more attention, thumb suck, engage in regressed talk, experience bedwetting, and/or demand to be fed (AACAP, 2013). In contrast to adolescents, younger children who are experiencing grief and loss often feel isolated, feel powerless, and have more difficulty regulating their emotions (Biank & Werner-Lin, 2011). Table 11.6 provides a brief summary of young people's age-related understanding of death.

In some situations, youth's symptoms may escalate to the point that they meet the criteria for a *Diagnostic and Statistical Manual of Mental Disorders,* Fifth Edition (*DSM-5;* American Psychiatric Association [APA], 2013a), mental disorder diagnosis (e.g., major depressive disorder). In most situations,

Table 11.6	Age-Related Understanding of Death

Age Level	Conception of Death
Early childhood (3–5)	• Children believe that death is reversible. For example, someone is only temporarily dead and can come back to life. • Death is associated with sleep. Children lack conceptualization of the finality of death. • Children lack understanding that everyone will die. • Children believe that they can cause death with their thoughts. Often, youth will assume responsibility due to bad thoughts or behavior and subsequently experience intense feelings of guilt and shame.
Middle childhood (6–12)	• Youth begin to understand the finality of death. • Youth believe that death is often associated with bad behaviors, evil, or evil forces. • Youth become more interested and even fascinated with the specific details of death. • An intense fear of the mutilation of death arises. • Youth continue to believe that their actions may have caused the death.
Adolescence (12–18)	• Youth have a mature understanding of death and dying. • Youth begin to speculate on the ramifications of death. • Youth may still feel shame and guilt but realize they did not cause the death with their thoughts and/or behaviors.

children will display symptoms of grief for weeks, but that can extend to months or even years. Some signs of extreme childhood grief include (a) extended periods of depressed and/or irritable mood, (b) loss of interest in normal activities, (c) inability to sleep, (d) loss of appetite, (e) fear of being alone, (f) behavioral regression (e.g., acting younger than chronological age), (g) excessive statements of wanting to join the deceased person, (h) withdrawal from friends and activities, and (i) decline in academic performance (AACAP, 2013). Children who are unable to progress through the normal grieving process may begin to develop trauma like symptoms (e.g., reexperiencing, avoidance, hyperarousal, maladaptive cognitions). This concept is referred to as childhood traumatic grief (CTG) and often occurs when the loss is traumatic (e.g., murder) or witnessed directly by the youth (Cohen & Mannarino, 2011). Table 11.7 presents trauma symptoms associated with CTG.

Similar to other types of trauma, certain reminders can and may trigger unpleasant thoughts, feelings, and reactions associated with the young person's loss (Cohen & Mannarino, 2011). These reminders may be as straightforward as certain people, places, situations, or things that remind the youth of the deceased person. For example, sitting around the Sunday dinner table may trigger a youth to remember her grandmother because she often sat in a certain seat at the kitchen table. In addition, youth may have negative reactions (e.g., thoughts, emotions, memories) associated with changes that occurred during their time of loss. For example, a youth visiting a relative's home where he stayed during the final stages and eventual death of his father may experience this home as an emotional trigger (e.g., reexperience feelings of grief and loss). Counselors can support parents to identify these triggers, which will help the younger person to connect his or her reexperiencing, arousal, avoidance, and emotional reactions to a specific trigger (Cohen & Mannarino, 2011).

Counselors need to be mindful of cultural and religious factors that may have an impact on the process and presentation of grief. For example, some cultures may be more private and manage their losses on their own or in their families, whereas others may be more communal and open about loss. In addition, all religions adhere to unique grief observances, and these religious convictions often form the context in which the family will interpret, make meaning (e.g., resurrection, afterlife), and react to death. Counselors should not assume that they fully understand how anyone will progress through grief, loss, and bereavement, even if they are familiar with the family's culture, ethnicity, or religion. Counselors should allow family members to

| Table 11.7 | Trauma Symptoms Associated with Childhood Traumatic Grief (CTG) |

Symptoms	Examples
Reexperiencing	• Intrusive thoughts, memories, and/or dreams of the deceased person • Fixation on how the deceased person died • Nightmares and scary dreams that may appear to be unrelated (specifically in younger children)
Avoidance	• Avoidance of thoughts, including happy memories • Not celebrating activities or holidays that remind the child of the deceased person • Not wanting the family to talk about or discuss the deceased person • Becoming angry or agitated • Withdrawing from activities (e.g., celebrations, birthdays, discussion of certain topics)
Hyperarousal	• Difficulty sleeping • Increased anger, agitation, and/or irritability • Psychosomatic complaints (e.g., headaches, stomachaches, nausea) • Increased jumpiness or being keyed up • Difficulty concentrating or paying attention
Emotional, behavioral deregulation, or maladaptive cognitions	• Increased moodiness (or anger and/or irritability) • Increased anxiety and/or fears • Increased emotional sensitivity (e.g., crying or outbursts with minimal stimuli) • Increased sense of self-blame (e.g., "I should have known this would have happened and stopped her from leaving")

Note: Adapted from Cohen and Mannarino (2011).

guide and educate the counselor on their cultural and religious grief considerations (Webb, 2011b). For example, a young person may come from a deeply spiritual family that believes in an afterlife, as well as the idea that the deceased soul watches over the youth and may be present in times of need. Therefore, counselors should be aware of these cultural and spiritual identities so they can allow these identities to inform and guide the grieving and counseling process.

CBT is an effective approach to address grief and loss in youth (Cohen & Mannarino, 2011; Cohen, Mannarino, & Deblinger, 2012). Grief psychoeducation using CBT is important because younger youth often have misconceptions about death (e.g., thinking a deceased person will return) and need assistance (e.g., reminders) in identifying grief, loss, and triggers (Cohen & Mannarino, 2011). Adults in the youth's life should normalize the sadness and feelings of loss associated with grief. This can be accomplished by educating children and families about the normal stages of grief and loss. With younger children, counselors and family members may need to help them to define death (e.g., address the difference between being alive and being dead, such as the beating of the heart and breath moving through lungs), answer questions about the finality of death (e.g., "When will she come back?" "Why can't she move?" "Can she hear me?" "Is she sleeping?" "Why can't they fix her?"), and use simple details and language to clarify death (e.g., "Dad's heart stopped working, and he died"; "Grandma was very old, and her body stopped working"). Through this process, counselors and family members should address the child's feelings of sadness, clarify causation (e.g., assuring the child that the death was not his or her fault), and allow the child to ask questions and receive truthful answers. Counselors should be mindful that children process this type of information in small increments and may ask the same question over and over again.

In addition to grief education, counselors need to allow youth to tell their story in their own words (i.e., creating a grief and loss narrative). Processing this loss in counseling allows the child to experience gradual exposure as they slowly incorporate the loss into either a verbal or written narrative (Cohen & Mannarino, 2011). Exposure to the loss is essential and helps the youth to tolerate and integrate the experiences, which is a requirement of the grieving process. Grief counseling helps youth to increase communication and reduces common tendencies to avoid discussing or processing the loss.

As part of grief counseling, youth will need to grieve their loss. This process allows youth to discuss and present what they miss about the deceased person. An example of an activity that can be used to help youth to process their loss is a name anagram activity. In this activity, youth assign a memory, activity, or positive thought to each letter of the deceased person's name. For example, a young girl who is grieving the loss of her mother, Katie, may construct an anagram as follows:

- **K**—Kind and caring
- **A**—Always in my heart
- **T**—Took walks with me
- **I**—I could always talk to her
- **E**—Was always excited to see me!

Some youth may have ambivalence about the loss, so addressing ambivalence is another important part of the grief process. Ambivalence involves those aspects of the lost person that will not be missed (Cohen & Mannarino, 2011). Contexts that might lead a young person to have ambivalence about a loss include abuse by the deceased, unresolved anger toward the deceased, shame around the type of death (e.g., suicide, drug overdose), and anger over the death not being necessary (e.g., loved one elected not to get medical care). Counselor can ask older children to write a letter to the lost person in which the youth wrestles with his or her unresolved struggles. If the youth is too young to write, the counselor could write down the young person's words. These letters can be therapeutic, and themes such as "You didn't care about me" or "Why didn't you think about how I'd feel" may begin to emerge. Counselors may also want to help the youth to process any regrets related to the relationship. Having an older child or adolescent process questions related to regret may be therapeutic. Incomplete sentences may be helpful to this end: "If only I had . . ."; "I am sorry that . . ."; I blame myself for . . ."; "It was my fault that . . ."; "I wish I had. . . ." Answering these questions can help young people to navigate their ambivalence toward the deceased person.

In counseling, it may also be therapeutic to help a younger person to identify and preserve the positive memories of the deceased person. These positive memories help the youth to progress through the bereavement process (e.g., tolerating sadness, processing how his or her world will be without the deceased) and commemorate the deceased person (e.g., celebrating his or her life). As the youth and family build their level of tolerance for discussion about the deceased person, counselors can increase in-session reminiscing of positive memories about the deceased person. Counselors may even assign a specific reminiscing activity for homework that requires the youth and family to set aside time during the week to recall or present one positive memory of the deceased. Another example of preserving memories of the deceased person could be to have the younger person create a memory book or box. The youth could cut and glue photos, drawings, letters, and mementos of the loved one into a binder or photo album. In addition, the counselor can have the youth create an enduring positive memory item such as a poem, video recording, or collage full of pictures and memories. Table 11.8 provides a summary of group activities for grief and loss counseling with youth.

In addition, counselors can aid young clients in integrating their memories and experiences with the deceased and helping them to be able to move forward with their new reality. The mantra of this stage is that a person "may be gone, but their memory lives on in us." The counselor and family members can begin to use the past tense when referring to the deceased. An important task in grief counseling is distinguishing what of the person still remains—in spirit—and what has been lost through his or her death. The balloon exercise is an activity that can help a younger person to identify the parts of the relationship the youth still has with the deceased person and the parts of the relationship he or she will need to relinquish (e.g., letting go; Cohen et al., 2012). The counselor can invite the client to draw a picture of a balloon and to list or draw inside the balloon things he or she wants to hold onto in the context of the deceased (e.g., memories, love they shared). Next, the youth draws another balloon that is floating away. Inside, the youth can draw or write the things that represent what he or she needs to let go of (e.g., being able to see that person, trips to the park with the person). The counselor can also use a real balloon and let it go with the client as a way of symbolically letting go.

Another important aspect of the grief process has to do with addressing a youth's loss in the context of his or her expectations for the future. An exploration of these issues will depend on the age and developmental

Table 11.8	Group Activities for Grief and Loss Counseling with Youth
Title	**Descriptions**
Finish the sentence	Provide each youth with a piece of paper and a writing utensil. Ask group members to finish the following sentences: "The thing that makes me the saddest is . . ."; "If I could talk to that person again, I would ask him or her . . ."; "My worst memory is . . ."; "If I could change anything, I would . . ."; "When I am alone . . ."; "One thing I would like to do with that person is . . ."; "Who will I share these answers with?" Next, ask each group member to share only what he or she feels comfortable sharing. Attempt to process each young person's answers and his or her underlying emotions connected with his or her responses.
All about my loved one	Provide each youth with a prepared worksheet and coloring supplies. Ask each group member to draw pictures responding to the following prompts on the provided worksheet: (a) things he or she enjoyed about that person, (b) things he or she did with the loved one, (c) what he or she will miss most about that person, and (d) one happy event or memory that he or she will always remember about the loved one. Allow each group member to present his or her worksheet to the group.
Family picture	Provide each group member with a piece of paper. Ask the youth to fold the paper in half. On the left half, ask the youth to draw a picture of the family doing an activity before the loved one's death. On the right half, ask the youth to draw a picture of the family engaging in an activity after the loved one's death. Facilitate a discussion with the youth around the process of the drawing, the idea of living without the loved one, and the underlying emotions and feelings.
When you get sad	Discuss with each group member the variety of ways that people express and deal with sadness. After some positive ways have been identified, hand out a prepared list of age-appropriate ways to cope with sadness. For example, this sheet could include telling someone about feelings, taking deep breaths, writing a letter, playing a sport, running around outside, getting a hug, watching a funny television show or movie, walking the dog, drawing a picture, journaling, calling a friend or other family member, playing a game, listening to music, or reading a book or magazine. Allow each group member to discuss these additional ideas, and then ask him or her to create a reminder sheet of what he or she can do when getting sad in the future. After the sheet has been completed, each group member can discuss how he or she plans to use these ideas/skills in the future. In addition, group members can discuss where they will place this sheet as a way to remind them of the skills for dealing with sadness.

level of the youth, and this exploration will be more appropriate with adolescents. Youth have expectations of things they would have been doing or experiencing with the deceased, and it can be helpful to process these expectations. Counselors might consider talking with the youth about the future events they will experience and what these will be like without the deceased (e.g., holidays, future celebrations such as the youth's prom, graduation, or wedding).

Counselors might also explore with clients how their roles with others may evolve or change secondary to the loss. Youth may need to look to others around them for various supports, and counselors can help clients to navigate these changes. Exploring options for the client to have his or her needs met in the context of current relationships may also be helpful.

As a part of counseling, the counselor might also help the client and his or her family to plan for future triggers and reminders. These reminders often include significant dates (e.g., date deceased passed, birthday of deceased, family holidays and celebrations), events (e.g., weddings, marriages, Father's or Mother's Day), and changes (e.g., in family living situation, of schools). Planning for these events in advance and finding ways to commemorate the deceased around these events can facilitate youth's grieving.

Counselors can also help young people and families to make meaning of the grief they experienced. When youth are able to express their feelings of loss and feel understood by others, they can begin to create meaning from their experiences. The following statement made by an adolescent demonstrates how he is making sense of his grief and transforming his loss in a productive way.

CLIENT: My mother used to always say I was "special" to her. I miss her so much, and that she thought I was special makes me feel special, even though she is gone. She is in my heart and will always be with me. I hope that one day I will love someone so much that they might feel special, too.

At some point in counseling it may be helpful to facilitate a memorial service activity for the deceased person. This activity can be as simple as having each family member prepare and share a few remarks and memories that they will miss most about the person. In addition to sharing those memories, the counselor may want to aid the youth in preparing to share the parts of that relationship he or she will keep (e.g., love, life lessons, memories) and how that relationship has prepared him or her to go forward in the future.

Younger children may have difficulties verbally expressing their thoughts and feelings, especially related to grief, loss, and death. Younger children can become silent and nonverbal when asked about these emotionally charged thoughts and feelings, which frequently involve intense and emotional situations. Play can be an effective means of communicating with the child about his or her experiences with the loss. The counselor can engage the child in play verbally or symbolically, allowing the child to "play out" his or her frustrations, anxiety, and confusion (Webb, 2011a). In the context of grief counseling, the goal of play therapy is for children to work out their feelings and to ultimately express their concerns through play, thus progressing toward a higher level of functioning and preventing or decreasing behavioral and emotional difficulties associated with the loss (Webb, 2011a).

Although play therapy approaches can be directive and nondirective, the success of play therapy rests on a counselor's ability to establish and maintain a helping relationship (Webb, 2011a). This helping relationship is initiated and maintained through the use of child-friendly activities that use various play materials (e.g., art supplies, toys, dolls, sand trays, costumes, building blocks, musical instruments). In a more directive approach, a counselor could use play therapy with a child who is experiencing grief by asking the youth to play with a specific material (e.g., dolls, action figures, puppets) and recreate some of the memorable or last interactions with the deceased person. A less directive counselor may allow a youth to choose between a group of play materials (e.g., toys, dress-up costumes, puppets, art supplies) and self-select an activity or play medium.

I CAN START COUNSELING PLAN FOR MALIK

This chapter opened with quotes from Malik's mother. Malik is a 10-year-old, biracial boy whose father recently passed away in prison. The following I CAN START conceptual framework outlines counseling considerations that may be helpful to a school counselor or a clinical counselor who works with Malik.

C = Contextual Assessment

Malik is a 10-year-old biracial boy. His father recently died from a heart attack in a maximum-security prison, where he was serving an 8- to 10-year sentence for aggravated assault. Malik lives with his mother, grandmother, and three half-siblings (i.e., Tyrone, 1; Deshawna, 4; and Nevaeh, 6). His family lives in a two-bedroom government-subsidized apartment. Malik's mother works as a full-time janitor at a local university. Malik's grandmother is retired and is the primary caregiver in the home.

It has been 4 months since his father's death, and Malik's mother is concerned with her son's behavior. Malik was close with his father, and he avoids talking about him (e.g., memories, activities associated with his father). He does not want to be around the rest of the family either. Sometimes, he even denies that his father has passed away. Malik's mother states that he is increasingly moody, irritable, and "just nasty to his half-brother and sisters." She also reports changes in his ability to concentrate and sleep and an increase in physical complaints (i.e., headaches, stomachaches, nausea).

Malik's mother is invested in supporting Malik, and she has sought help. She expresses the need to learn parenting strategies to deal with his behaviors, and she is eager to learn how to support her son.

In addition, Malik's mother has a history of depressive struggles, and she has been diagnosed with major depressive disorder. Although Malik's basic needs are being met, he lives in a very small government-subsidized apartment with his grandmother, mother, and three half-siblings.

A = Assessment and Diagnosis

Diagnosis = V62.82 (Z63.4) Uncomplicated Bereavement

N = Necessary Level of Care

> Family counseling (once per week)
> Individual counseling (once per week)

S = Strengths

> **Self:** Malik is of above-average intelligence, and his test scores indicate his potential to excel as a student. Malik believes he is a talented soccer and football player. He enjoys playing sports with the kids in the neighborhood. Malik appears willing to participate in counseling services.
>
> **Family:** Malik's mother is loving and supportive. Malik's grandmother is a consistent caregiver in the home. Malik has a bond with his three half-siblings.
>
> **School/community:** Although Malik's community is in a lower socioeconomic area, his family is close to transportation (i.e., bus line), parks, and the YMCA.

T = Treatment Approach

- CBT primarily focused on Childhood Grief and Loss

A = Aim and Objective of Counseling (90-day objectives)

Malik will learn to recognize and identify his grief experiences. Malik will identify and report to his counselor physical, cognitive, and behavioral symptoms of grief.

Malik will increase his ability to tolerate memories of his father. Malik will develop a constructed list of positive memories of his father. He will share at least one of these positive memories daily with his grandmother or mother.

Malik will integrate and organize his memories of his father. Malik will create a grief and loss narrative (i.e., tell his story in his own words), paying attention to the things he will miss about his father and the special challenges surrounding his father dying in prison, and will complete a collage or memory book (e.g., with pictures that remind, represent, and/or capture components of his relationship with his father) as a reminder of his father. He will share this narrative and collage or book with his mother during a conjoint counseling session.

Malik's mother will reinforce Malik's participation in desired family activities. Malik will participate in one family activity each week. In return, he will get one additional privilege per week in the family setting (e.g., a later bedtime, longer television time).

R = Research-Based Interventions (Based on CBT)

Counselor will help Malik to learn, develop, and/or apply the following skills:

- Grief psychoeducation (discussion about death, misconceptions about death, and cultural consideration related to death)
- Complete a grief and loss narrative and share it with his mother in session
- Conjoint sessions to increase communication in the family
- Participation in family-based activities (in and out of session)

T = Therapeutic Support Services

> Medication evaluation with a psychiatrist (if symptoms remain or intensify)
> Youth grief and loss support groups
> YMCA programming (e.g., flag football)
> Referral for Malik's mother (i.e., individual counseling to address her depression symptoms; possible medication evaluation with a psychiatrist)

Summary

Family is one of the most essential units in society, and it is vital to a young person's development and wellness (Broderick & Blewitt, 2014). Families are unique. They are governed by their own set of rules, structure, communication patterns, and problem-solving abilities (Goldenberg & Goldenberg, 2013). Transitions and struggles in families are normal and frequently complex. Youth often respond to these transitions and struggles in unique ways. In many of these cases, counseling may not be warranted. However, each child and family should be assessed individually to determine if counseling-related needs exist.

Some examples of family-related transitions and/or struggles include family-structure transitions, such as divorce, stepfamilies, kinship caregivers, and adoption. Counseling may be necessary for youth whose parents (one or both) abuse substances and youth who are experiencing grief, loss, and bereavement. Counselors working with young people and families in these unique situations should be mindful of their own personal views and family-related experiences. More specifically, counselors need to mindful of their own family-of-origin experiences and any potential personal biases that may impede working with these young people and their families.

Although youth who experience family stress, violence, inconsistent parenting, parental substance abuse, parental illness (e.g., mental or physical), and/or poverty exhibit less emotional and cognitive stability, all young people appear to benefit from cultivating protective factors in the family and the community (Zolkoski & Bullock, 2012). Counselors should foster and increase family involvement, positive parenting skills, and open communication, which can cultivate and enhance children's resiliency. These family-based interventions, along with CBT, can be effective approaches, especially when counselors are addressing grief, loss, and bereavement in youth (Cohen et al., 2012).

MyLab Counseling: Counseling Children and Adolescents

In the Topic 8 Assignments: *Family-Based Challenges for Youth*, try Application Exercise 8.1: A *Real Father* and Licensure Quiz 8.1: *Family-Related Transitions and Struggles*.

Then try Application Exercise 8.3: *Grief and Loss* and Application Exercise 8.4: *Kinship Caregivers and Adoptive Parents*.

CHAPTER **12**

Academic and Social–Emotional Transitions and Struggles

THE CASE OF GUDETA

Yeah, I like it here. I want to go back and play with my friends though. Mom told me it isn't safe in Kenya anymore; that's why we came here. I went to school there, but this school is way different. It is bigger, and there are more people! I do really good in school. Mom and Dad are proud. They tell me that all the time. Mom asks if I have any friends, but I just don't know. I don't play with them. I only talk to Ms. Cindy.

—Gudeta, age 6

outh experience an array of transitions and potential struggles during their school-age years. All youth are vulnerable when going through major life changes or experiencing increased stress. Often, young people's difficulties can be overcome with brief counseling interventions, especially if the issues are addressed early. Other times, academic, career, or social–emotional struggles can require more intentional and long-term counseling interventions and supports.

School counselors are specifically charged with fostering academic, career, and social–emotional growth, but all counselors address these important domains as part of a comprehensive and holistic counseling approach (American Counseling Association [ACA], 2014; American School Counselor Association [ASCA], 2012). If left unaddressed, the transitions and struggles discussed in this chapter could progress and eventually contribute to the young person developing a mental health disorder. Academic and social–emotional considerations are intimately intertwined, and counselors should maintain a broad awareness of the difficulties youth face as part of their developmental processes.

ACADEMIC STRUGGLES

All young people—and their families—define academic success differently. For some, it might mean all *A*s on a report card; for others, academic success might be indicated by an ability to maintain a *C* grade or better in all classes. Intelligence plays a role in academic success, but genetics, biology, family values, social–emotional well-being, and personal motivation all contribute to a youth's performance in the school setting.

Regardless of how academic success is defined, academic achievements lead to an increased sense of identity and purpose in youth (ASCA, 2012; Organization for Economic Cooperation and Development [OECD], 2013). Youth who do well in school have increased confidence and experience greater long-term success with interpersonal relationships and career achievements (OECD, 2013; Zhu, Tse, Cheung, & Oyserman, 2014). As such, it is important for counselors—especially school counselors who are charged with promoting academic success—to understand the factors that can interfere with a youth's academic and career success, and to implement interventions that support healthy development across the life span.

Time Management Difficulties

Young people today receive more homework than ever, and even elementary school students are charged with completing in-class assignments and homework in a timely fashion. Students must exercise willpower and self-regulation to do most academic tasks, such as completing homework, writing papers, and studying for exams (Job, Walton, Bernecker, & Dweck, 2015). Successful time management also requires executive functioning abilities in which dynamic cognitive processes allow youth to identify the steps required to complete a project and employ emotion regulation and self-control while completing the task at hand.

Some young people experience time management difficulties because of a lack of organizational or planning skills. Procrastination, or avoiding unpleasant tasks, is another time management–related academic struggle in youth. Youth who procrastinate on academic tasks have poorer mental health and lower grades than their peers (Glick & Orsillo, 2015). Youth who procrastinate often believe that willpower is a limited resource (rather than readily accessible for any task) and often avoid unpleasant tasks in the moment while not considering the long-term consequences. As a result, youth who procrastinate often delay beginning tasks and are not able to complete their academic tasks in a satisfactory way or on time.

Some youth experience developmentally inappropriate difficulties regulating emotions and behaviors, and this can interfere with their abilities to manage time appropriately. Young people learn self-regulation and executive functioning skills from their environments and through trial and error. Time management difficulties can result in poor self-esteem and inhibited motivation to continue pursuing academic success (Glick & Orsillo, 2015; Job et al., 2015).

Counselors should look for signs of time management difficulties in youth who have high aptitude yet are not performing well in the classroom. These signs include a tendency to procrastinate, difficulty with emotion regulation or self-control, and limited executive processing abilities. While viewing a youth in a developmental context, counselors should identify the sources of academic struggle and offer appropriate interventions. The ultimate goal of counseling youth who have time management difficulties is to increase willpower, self-control, emotion regulation, and organizational skills.

Counselors working with youth who display deficits in time management skills should first assess for differential diagnoses, such as attention-deficit/hyperactivity disorder (ADHD) or depression. The symptoms of ADHD in children often include a lack of self-control and an inability to focus (American Psychiatric Association [APA], 2013a). Depression often manifests in youth as aggression or inability to focus, which could easily be mistaken for general time management difficulties (APA, 2013a). Counselors should gain a full understanding of risk factors in a youth's life, as well as any comorbid diagnoses. Counselors should also assess youth's developmental levels and adjust all interventions accordingly.

Cognitive interventions can be useful for youth who experience time management difficulties (Glick & Orsillo, 2015; Job et al., 2015). When assessing young people's cognitions and patterns related to time management, counselors might ask the following questions:

- "What is your favorite type of homework assignment?"
- "What is your least favorite type of homework assignment?"
- "When do you typically complete your homework?"
- "Where do you typically complete your homework?"
- "Who typically helps you to complete your homework?"
- "What is the hardest part of doing your homework?"
- "What gets in the way of you completing your schoolwork?"
- "What do you do that helps you to complete your schoolwork?"
- "Why do teachers make students do assignments?"
- "Is homework important to you?"
- "Is homework important to your family members?"
- "Is homework important to your friends?"

These types of questions can help counselors to gauge youth's beliefs regarding academics and identify the types of time management skills they might be lacking. For example, youth might have trouble with organization or planning if they are unable to tell where and when they typically complete their homework.

Or, youth might have difficulty completing difficult tasks if they report a belief that teachers give assignments to make students' lives difficult.

Cognitive interventions that might be helpful with youth include Socratic questioning and reframing. Socratic questioning is used by counselors to help youth to see errors in their thinking. For example, if a counselor asks a youth "Why do teachers give students homework assignments?" a student might reply "To make my life horrible." The counselor can then ask for a concrete example: "What is the toughest assignment your teacher has given you?" and the counselor should validate the youth's answer by saying "That really made your life tough!" This validation should be followed with a Socratic question, which the counselor likely already knows the response to but pretends not to: "What was the teacher thinking? Was there any point to the assignment at all?" The youth might then respond "She says she wants us to know this so we can learn. . . ." The counselor could respond "Oh, wow. That is tough. So, it feels like she is just trying to make your life horrible, but homework also helps you learn." From this process, the youth's cognition has been reframed from "She wants to make my life horrible" to "Homework is horrible, but my teacher wants me to learn."

When working with youth who have time management difficulties, concrete behavioral and solution-focused interventions that focus on learning and using skills are essential. Self-control and emotion regulation can be practiced through the use of games and role-plays. For example, counselors can present a client with an age-appropriate board game. As the game is played, the counselor can highlight times when the client has to wait for a turn or is disappointed with the outcome. If the youth handles these situations well, the counselor can praise the youth and encourage the same behavior in relation to academics (e.g., "Tell me about how you waited so patiently"; "Tell me about times when you wait patiently in the classroom"). If the youth does not handle the stressors well (e.g., temper tantrum, avoidance), the counselor can point out specific behaviors and help the student to practice more helpful behaviors. Counselors can also have clients engage in their actual schoolwork and practice the previously learned self-control and emotion regulation skills throughout the process of completing the assignments.

Youth benefit from a set routine that offers a sense of predictability and safety in daily life. Routines also help to reduce procrastination because schoolwork or chores are completed at a specific, predictable time and place. Especially for younger youth, high levels of parental involvement are required so youth learn how to manage their time effectively. As youth grow older, especially if they have learned basic skills earlier in life, they can begin to implement their own routines and uphold their schedules independently.

When working with children who have time management difficulties, counselors should assess the youth's current daily routine by talking to the child and the parents. Counselors should ask about a typical school day from start to finish and write down the flow of events on a piece of paper. Counselors should identify any areas in which a routine does not seem apparent. For example, parents might report that they sometimes give a youth a bath before bed and sometimes the youth bathes in the morning. If this variation cannot be avoided due to the parent's work schedule (or some other reason), youth should still wake up at the same time each day, and all other elements of the routine should remain stable. Parents ideally should find a way to make routines as consistent as possible, even if it is sometimes inconvenient for themselves.

Time management and self-discipline are critical skills, and youth benefit from developing these skills early in life. These skills can be fostered through a daily routine, which will vary based on developmental level. Youth younger than age 5 or 6 might not have as many chores or school tasks to complete, but they also might require more sleep. Counselors should know generally how much sleep youth require to help parents to develop an appropriate daily routine for their children. See Table 12.1 for an overview of sleep requirements by age.

Although sleep is important for a youth's overall functioning, it is common for children and adolescents to avoid sleeping in lieu of more entertaining activities (e.g., television, video games). Youth need parental guidance and encouragement at all ages, and parents should guide youth through difficult tasks. This might entail sitting with a youth while he or she completes homework and guiding the youth when he or she gets stuck on difficult concepts. Or, it might require completing chores with the youth until he or she fully learns the steps. It is also important for parents to praise youth as much as possible while offering constructive feedback when necessary.

As youth get older, parents might not need to monitor tasks such as homework and chore time as carefully, but routines should remain in place and shift according to developmental needs. Consistent consequences should be enforced at all times if a youth does not complete his or her required tasks.

Table 12.1	Hours of Sleep Needed According to Age
Age	Hours of Sleep Needed per Day
0–3 months	10–18 hours (irregular schedule)
4–11 months	9–12 hours with naps through the day
1–2 years	11–14 hours with one nap per day
3–5 years	11–13 hours
6–13 years	9–11 hours
14 years and up	8–10 hours

Note: Adapted from National Sleep Foundation (2016).

For example, youth should not be allowed to play until all homework is complete. Parenting is hard work, and it requires diligence, patience, and much energy to help youth to develop the skills needed to succeed in the world.

In summary, time management skills are imperative to a youth's academic success, and time management deficits can affect all other difficulties addressed in this section. Counselors should use cognitive and behavioral interventions to help youth to develop positive and effective beliefs about the importance of academics and their ability to succeed. Counselors can help youth to practice self-control and emotion regulation skills in order to increase students' willpower and organization. Counselors should always remember to complete holistic assessments and incorporate significant others into the treatment process whenever possible.

Study Skills Deficits

Many youth experience difficulties when preparing for graded academic assessments. This can be due to time management difficulties or deficits in information processing, information recall, critical thinking, and/or vocabulary. Although a teacher's approach to classroom learning has a significant effect on a student's learning (Meng, 2015), effective study skills are also a key component to academic success, and these skills can be learned.

Study skills help youth to transfer short-term information into long-term knowledge. In addition, more advanced study skills allow youth to employ critical thinking and apply new knowledge to abstract concepts. The young person's developmental level and factors unique to the young person's classroom should be considered when determining the types of study skills youth should be using to prepare for in-class assignments and exams.

For multiple-choice tests, youth need to be able to identify the information that is likely to be on an exam and develop methods for remembering key information. Some study skills for memorization include reading comprehension, note-taking, repetition, creating outlines, developing pneumonic phrases, and reviewing flash cards. For short-answer and essay tests, youth need to understand concepts rather than to memorize facts. Youth will need to recall key concepts and overlap this skill with strong organizational and vocabulary skills.

Clinical Toolbox 12.1

In the Pearson etext, click here to review an activity that can help youth to learn how to develop and use flash cards as a study tool.

It might seem as though study skills should be addressed by teachers or parents rather than counselors. However, teachers often do not have the time to teach their students these skills, and many parents lack awareness of these skills or how to teach them to their children. Study skills also relate to mental health in that youth who experience academic difficulties can develop poor self-efficacy and depressive symptoms

(Perera & Chang, 2015). Youth who experience academic success experience an increased sense of identity, confidence, and purpose (Zhu et al., 2014). Therefore, it is appropriate for counselors in various settings to address study skills with youth and to support young people in developing the skills they need to be successful. If it is not appropriate to the counselor's setting or function to facilitate the development of these skills, the counselor can connect the young client to resources and other services that provide this type of support.

In terms of intervention and study skills development, counselors should first work to understand a youth's time management skill deficits and other differential diagnoses (e.g., ADHD, depression) and address these considerations as necessary. Counselors should then explore the youth's ability to read and comprehend written material in meaningful ways. Even if youth have developmentally appropriate reading and retention abilities, they might struggle with note-taking skills, retention of key pieces of information, or use of an outline, all of which help youth to organize and can be applied to other tasks (e.g., time management). In addition, youth might not know the proper structure of a sentence or paragraph, or they might have limited vocabularies.

When counseling youth who have deficits in reading or note-taking skills, counselors might spend time teaching key concepts (e.g., note-taking, outlining) and have the youth practice these skills. Counselors can reinforce these skills by having clients practice between sessions or in future sessions. If clients need more support than their counselors can provide, the counselors can make referrals to resources or services at the school or with community-based tutors and services (e.g., various learning centers, local nonprofit organizations that provide academic support through grant programs).

Group interventions in school can be particularly helpful for youth who are experiencing study skills deficits. Such groups might emphasize a youth's ability to study smarter rather than harder. In these groups, counselors can provide strategies for note-taking, outlining, writing, and remembering key concepts. Counselors can also ask group members to share their tips and tricks in specific areas, which helps peers while increasing self-confidence. Group members can support each other and normalize study skills deficits.

All youth have academic strengths and weaknesses. Counselors can help clients to use these strengths to address their academic struggles. For example, if youth have writing difficulties but are well organized, they can practice creating outlines to guide and support growth in writing. Time management is essential to academic success; youth must have the motivation and behavioral restraint to systematically create a routine and spend time working toward academic success. See Table 12.2 for goals that

Table 12.2	Common Counseling Goals for Youth Who Have Time Management Difficulties
Child focused	• Develop a consistent daily schedule.
	• Increase self-efficacy related to time management.
	• Increase self-efficacy in relation to academic abilities.
	• Complete schoolwork and chores before engaging in leisure activities.
	• Identify triggers for emotional distress.
	• Use healthy coping skills when faced with difficulties.
Parent education/ training	• Establish routine and structure in the home.
	• Establish rewards and consequences for completing required tasks.
	• Use brief and specific commands to guide youth toward desired behaviors.
	• Establish communication between school and home to ensure all required tasks are addressed.
School based	• Provide concrete steps toward each behavioral goal.
	• Carefully monitor and redirect student progress.
	• Consistently reward desired behavior in the youth.
	• Establish a behavior chart with rewards and consequences for the whole class.
	• Use a time-out program when youth are not engaging in helpful behavior. (Ignore minor infractions.)
	• Communicate with parents regularly.

Table 12.3	Common Counseling Goals for Youth Who Have Study Skills Deficits
Child focused	• Identify specific study skills deficits (e.g., memorization, reading comprehension). • Identify empirical strategies that address the specific study skills deficit (e.g., using a blank note card to guide reading across the line). • Reduce study-related anxiety. • Increase self-efficacy regarding studying and testing. • Improve organizational skills (e.g., creating and referencing a daily schedule).
Parent education/ training	• Practice various study skills in the home to determine which are most effective for the youth. • Establish rewards and consequences for implementing study skills when needed. • Maintain communication with the school for any helpful feedback from teachers. • Contact referral sources as needed.
School based	• Provide youth with various study skills to choose from. • Practice implementing various study skills, and determine which are most helpful for each student. • Provide specific information regarding the format and types of questions on upcoming exams.

counselors might create with youth who have time management difficulties and Table 12.3 for goals that counselors might use to address study skills deficits.

Some youth do not have difficulty with time management or study skills but still perform poorly on in-class exams. This is especially apparent if the student earns satisfactory grades on in-class assignments and homework but has comparatively low test scores. In this case, counselors should consider the possibility of test anxiety.

Test Anxiety

Many young people struggle with text anxiety. Various anxiety disorders are discussed in Chapter 17. In this section, we discuss anxiety that is specific to the school setting. Many youth are anxious about the high-stakes standardized testing that schools have moved toward, and sometimes this anxiety can become debilitating (Thames et al., 2015). **Test anxiety** is situational and occurs specifically in relation to tests. It can occur just for specific types of tests (e.g., multiple choice, standardized), especially when commonly held stereotypes are a factor (e.g., a female student might be especially anxious about her math tests; Thames et al., 2015).

Test anxiety can manifest in various ways. Some youth might report that they cannot eat or sleep the night before a test. Others might explain that they overeat or oversleep before an exam. Feelings of hopelessness, dread, or difficulty concentrating might occur during test preparation, and students might have feelings of dread, confusion, or panic during an exam. The sense of panic might lead to dizziness, shortness of breath, sweating, headaches, stomachaches, or mental block/blankness. After exams, youth might feel guilty and blame themselves for not working hard enough or preparing adequately (even though there is evidence to contradict this).

Counselors should use cognitive behavioral approaches when counseling youth who have test anxiety (Dundas, Wormnes, & Hauge, 2009; Garber et al., 2016). The cognitive and behavioral components of test anxiety go hand in hand; test anxiety manifests as physical symptoms intertwined with unhelpful or ineffective thoughts. Counselors can help youth to untangle their thoughts, feelings, and behaviors and organize them so their reactions to tests are adaptive and students feel empowered to tackle the test without the anxiety dominating their experience.

First, counselors should educate youth about test anxiety and the physical, emotional, and cognitive cues that can be associated with tests. After psychoeducation is provided, counselors can help the client to explore symptoms—or cues—that indicate the onset of anxiety. Youth almost always experience physical symptoms of anxiety, such as stomachaches and a subsequent fear of vomiting. Counselors should also help clients to identify their thoughts because they contribute to the anxiety and are under youth's control to change. Negative self-talk (e.g., "I am going to fail this exam") is typical in test anxiety situations, and clients need to develop an awareness of their self-talk as the first step to helping them to change their thinking.

Next, counselors should work with youth to develop adaptive coping skills that help them to manage the anxiety. Cognitive coping skills include, but are not limited to, time-outs, meditation, creative visualization, setting goals, thought-stopping, and developing positive self-talk. When youth notice cognitive symptoms of anxiety, they can practice taking time-outs in which they allow themselves to zone out and think about something pleasant (e.g., clothing, afterschool activities, weekend plans). Youth might also meditate during a time-out by repeating a positive mantra (e.g., "I am good enough") or focusing on deep, soothing breaths. Youth can visualize themselves receiving a positive test score the next day and might return from a time-out with a specific goal (e.g., complete 10 questions before taking another time-out). Their anxiety cues and their coping skills might even be written on a note card and stored in their desks.

Behavioral coping skills might include preemptive physical exertion. For example, before an exam, youth might take time to do pushups against a wall, complete a set of jumping jacks, or take a lap outside. If feasible, this can be an effective technique to improve youth's motivation and academic success. Teachers might even be willing to schedule a short period of physical activity for the whole class before important exams. Counselors should advocate for students to teachers or administrators if special accommodations are needed in school.

Youth can also be taught to, while taking a test, complete a body scan to assess for any physical signs of anxiety. Counselors can guide youth through this process in counseling, beginning with the top of the scalp, moving down to the ears, progressing down the throat, past the chest, and across the belly, eventually reaching the tips of the big toes. In this process, youth can identify the specific body parts that feel tense or uneasy. As a method for relaxing these tense body parts, youth should intentionally squeeze and contract the body parts for 3 to 5 seconds and end with a full release of the tension. In addition, youth can take deep breaths (perhaps 5 seconds on the inhale), hold for a few seconds, and then slowly release to ease tension throughout the body.

Youth who experience test anxiety might develop feelings of frustration and self-doubt that reciprocally make the test anxiety worse. Youth should be encouraged to externalize test anxiety and focus on the desired outcome they wish to have in a specific situation. This solution-focused approach helps to break the self-perpetuating cycle: youth have anxiety from the possibility of poor performance, which ultimately leads to poor performance. Counselors can help youth to move away from focusing on the anxiety and focus on performing well on academic tests.

Youth who learn about the realities of test anxiety, have their experiences normalized, and learn specific skills they can use to manage their anxiety can experience an increased sense of efficacy in taking exams and in their ability to self-soothe. Counselors should continually assess for external stressors that might sustain test anxiety (e.g., lack of teacher support, bullying) while implementing cognitive behavioral approaches that meet each student's unique needs.

School Attendance Problems

School attendance is compulsory for American youth. Although most students miss some school, excessive absenteeism can suggest emotional or behavior difficulties and can have long-term consequences on a youth's well-being. Two types of school attendance problems exist: school refusal and truancy. School refusal typically occurs as the result of emotional difficulties such as separation anxiety, fear of being bullied, fear of academic struggles, fear of being mistreated by school personnel, social phobia, anxiety, or depression (APA, 2013; Darwich, Hymel, & Waterhouse, 2012). Youth who refuse school often prefer to stay home with their families, whereas youth who display chronic truancy often avoid both the school and home settings.

Truancy is defined as a youth missing school due to behavior problems (e.g., conduct disorder, difficulty following school rules) (APA, 2013), and youth often hide their lack of school attendance from their parents. Unlike school refusal, truancy is not accompanied by feelings of fear, anxiety, or worry. Rather, youth might skip school to engage in delinquent behaviors, such as drinking alcohol or socializing with peers while parents are at work. Some parents might learn about their children's chronic truancy from school personnel, but some truancy might be related to a lack of parental involvement. Counselors should ask youth and their parents about school attendance behaviors, and counselors should request a release to talk with school personnel when necessary.

Intervention strategies for school refusal and chronic truancy are similar because counselors will address the underlying mental health concerns of a youth; however, the resources and approaches counselors use will likely be different. In general, individual counseling that incorporates the support of parents and other important stakeholders can help youth who display school refusal, but youth who display chronic truancy will likely need multisystemic interventions in which all areas of the youth's life are addressed.

Counselors who work with youth who refuse school or are chronically truant should complete a holistic assessment to determine the root causes of the behaviors. The first step of intervention is to determine if the youth's absenteeism is considered school refusal (i.e., the result of emotional difficulties) or truancy (i.e., the result of behavior difficulties). Referrals might be necessary for youth to attend regular counseling in which interventions that have a reasonable promise of supporting school attendance can be provided.

If emotional difficulties (e.g., a specific phobia, separation anxiety, depression) are suspected as the source of school refusal, counselors should conduct a thorough assessment to determine the specific difficulty with which the youth is struggling. Counselors should work with parents and school personnel to address the underlying contributors to the emotional difficulties. Specific assessment and treatment protocols for youth experiencing various forms of anxiety and depression are outlined in the designated chapters of this text.

If counselors determine that a youth's school absenteeism can be classified as truancy, they should address the behavior problems multisystemically. Behavior problems develop as the result of multiple biopsychosocial factors, and interventions should be intentional and multifaceted. Chronic school refusal and truancy are symptoms of underlying mental health concerns, and counselors should work with school, community, neighborhood, and family resources to help youth to get the support they need. School refusal or truancy might develop over time, or attendance behaviors might occur as the result of a specific event, such as making the transition to a new school.

Changing Schools

All youth are required to attend school, although the ages at which students begin school and the grade levels included at each school vary by state and district. All students will experience several school transitions throughout their academic careers. During these times of transition, youth are vulnerable and may struggle. There are two types of school transitions: normative and nonnormative. Normative school transitions are routine shifts from one school to another that all students in a particular grade or school navigate (Temkin, Gest, Osgood, Feinberg, & Moody, 2015). Examples of normative transitions include students from three local elementary schools making the transition to the local middle school, or students from the elementary school moving to high school.

Nonnormative school transitions include times youth change schools outside the typical transition periods for the school district. Nonnormative transitions can occur for a multitude of reasons, such as a family move, youth going to live with another parent in a new school district, or parents choosing to place students in a new school for better opportunities. Nonnormative school relocations can occur during the academic year or over summer break. Normative and nonnormative school transitions are often unavoidable, but the vast array of changes associated with school transition can be quite stressful for youth (Shell, Gazelle, & Faldowski, 2014).

NORMATIVE SCHOOL TRANSITIONS

The normative transitions from elementary school to middle school and from middle school to high school are typically experienced by all youth (Temkin et al., 2015). Many students also experience transitions from home to kindergarten, preschool to kindergarten, and/or from kindergarten to elementary school as stressful. Sources of stress during normative transitions include uncertainty of the new school's culture, rules, teachers, building layout, and class structure. Schoolwork progressively becomes more difficult, and gradually increasing levels of freedom require increased self-discipline and time management skills (Jackson & Schulenberg, 2013). Also, youth often have to renegotiate their social relationships after normative transitions, and social relationships play a major role in identity development throughout childhood and adolescence (Shell et al., 2014).

Not all young people attend preschool, but preschool is the first experience youth have in an academic environment. Some youth attend day care as early as 6 weeks of age, but youth typically attend preschool between the ages of 2 and 5 years. Preschool is a structured environment in which youth are under the care of a teacher (rather than their parents) and interact with peers of a similar age. After preschool, youth make the transition to kindergarten, which is required in most states by age 5 to 8 years. Youth who have not attended preschool will need to adjust to being away from their parents or caregivers for the first time. Youth who attended preschool will have to adjust to a new teacher, a demanding and structured curriculum, and new friends.

From kindergarten, youth make the transition into elementary school, which can be in a new building. In first grade, youth need to adjust to full days away from their parents, an increasingly difficult curriculum, new teachers, new classroom rules, and new friends. Stressors for youth during the transition from kindergarten to first grade include an increased focus on academics (as opposed to play), stricter rules, and increased teacher expectations (Loizou, 2011). However, many aspects of the transition to elementary school can be exciting and empowering if youth receive adequate preparation and support.

The transition from elementary to middle school can be especially challenging. First, youth spend several years in elementary school and make important social relationships. Sometimes multiple elementary schools feed into a single middle school, and social relationships are often renegotiated, which can be especially difficult for youth who are anxious or shy, or those who have limited social skills or have social skill impairments (Shell et al., 2014; Temkin et al., 2015). Social relationships tend to remain more steady when a single elementary school feeds into a single middle school, but the classroom structure might still create a need to renegotiate social relationships; elementary students often stay with the same teacher and classmates for most subjects, but middle school students sometimes change classrooms and teachers for many or all subjects. The frequent classroom changes also create more freedom and responsibility for middle school students, who must make responsible choices throughout the day.

Another stressful normative transition includes the shift from middle school to high school, which can present many of the same challenges found in the middle school transition, such as new social relationships, the increasingly challenging curriculum, and greater freedom and responsibility (Jackson & Schulenberg, 2013). Substance use, risky sexual behavior, and delinquency often increase during puberty, which coincides with the transition from middle school to high school, and youth are especially vulnerable at this age. The stress of the transition itself, combined with the importance of social relationships, can put youth at particular risk during the middle school to high school transition (Jackson & Schulenberg, 2013).

The final normative transition for youth occurs as youth prepare to leave secondary school and shift into postsecondary endeavors. After high school graduation, youth can enter postsecondary education or the workforce. **College readiness** is a broad term that encompasses a youth's ability to succeed in a 4-year college or university, a 2-year college, or a technical/vocational school (Curry & Milsom, 2014). Youth who pursue postsecondary education must have sufficient academic abilities, as well as noncognitive factors, that support success (e.g., self-discipline, an understanding of the postsecondary culture). Youth who enter the workforce after high school must possess career readiness skills, which include concrete application of academic concepts, employability skills (e.g., self-discipline, responsibility), and technical skills that are needed for a specific career (Curry & Milsom, 2014).

Youth ideally engage in an ongoing cycle of career exploration, commitment, and reconsideration across childhood and adolescence (Porfeli & Lee, 2012). Career development continues throughout the life span but is especially important in late adolescence, when youth determine their plans after high school (ASCA, 2012). Counselors should intentionally work to support youth from kindergarten (and sometimes preschool) through 12th grade so every student gains the academic and social–emotional skills needed for postsecondary success.

During times of normative school transitions, youth can experience complex feelings of happiness and excitement mixed with depression and anxiety (Symonds & Hargreaves, 2016). When supporting youth through transitions, counselors should work to validate the unpleasant feelings youth experience while highlighting the hopeful and exciting possibilities that accompany transitions. In addition, counselors should work with students and families to help youth to preemptively plan and prepare for transitions as much as possible.

Counselors and parents can work to prepare children entering preschool or kindergarten by implementing rules and routines in the home that are likely to be replicated in the school setting, such as a set time for snacks and toy cleanup. It is especially beneficial if the counselor or parents contact the preschool to determine the typical daily happenings. Then, counselors and parents can tell the youth what to expect when entering preschool, as well as remind the youth of the multiple benefits of attending school (e.g., learning, making friends). Parents should also monitor their own reactions when taking their children to school; they should remain relaxed and say goodbye casually to indicate that preschool is a normal and desirable activity.

Preparation is an essential component for transition at any age. When youth are preparing to move from kindergarten to first grade, counselors can work with parents to help youth to understand the new requirements they will face, as well as the new opportunities they will have (Loizou, 2011; Symonds & Hargreaves, 2016). Counselors should intentionally prepare youth for transitions to middle and high school in much the same manner. Counselors can work individually with youth and their families, and school counselors can deliver classroom guidance lessons to prepare an entire class for their next phases of education.

In classroom guidance presentations, counselors can present the details of what to expect at the next school, highlighting the new rules, social opportunities, and academic requirements. Counselors can use process questions to ask youth what they think they will like and dislike about their new schools; it is important to validate the students' conflicting feelings and allow them to grieve their anticipated losses. Counselors should also review strategies for making friends, positive coping skills, and time management concepts.

Clinical Toolbox 12.2

In the Pearson etext, click here for a guidance lesson that can be used to support youth in their transition from elementary school to middle school.

In addition to preparation, counselors can support youth after transitions, as they adjust and immerse themselves into their new school environments. This can be done through classroom guidance units that explore and validate students' experiences and feelings. Counselors can also organize support groups for youth who might have a particularly hard time adjusting, such as youth who do not have many friends or who are also experiencing challenging transitions at home (e.g., divorce, death of a loved one). In addition, counselors can work with youth individually to highlight students' positive qualities, teach social skills, and validate feelings of anxiety or depression.

Preparation and support for the postsecondary transition is slightly more complex than for the normative transitions youth experience from preschool through high school. Career exploration ideally will have begun as early as preschool with play-based activities that allow children to explore the careers that might suit them well. As youth prepare to make the transition to postsecondary endeavors, they need concrete information about the many choices available after high school graduation. Some youth might desire to enter the workforce after graduation and will need information about resumes, job applications, and adjusting to the workforce. Other youth might wish to pursue postsecondary education and need information about standardized testing, school applications, and transcripts.

When working with youth through the various normative school transitions they will face, counselors should offer preparation before the transition and support after the transition, when possible. Parents and other loved ones should be involved with school transitions as appropriate, and counselors should work to deliver interventions in an effective and time-efficient format. Some youth will experience nonnormative school transitions in addition to normative school transitions, which require an additional layer of preparation and support.

NONNORMATIVE SCHOOL TRANSITIONS

Some youth change schools between times of normative school transitions for various reasons. Sometimes youth have to change schools or school districts due to family relocation for employment. This is especially common in military families. Others experience nonnormative school transitions when parents get divorced or when parents choose to send their child to a new school that has open enrollment (Metzger, Fowler, Anderson, & Lindsay, 2015). Youth who experience one nonnormative school transition in their academic careers have a lower likelihood of earning a high school diploma (Metzger et al., 2015).

This phenomenon exists regardless of the type of move (e.g., to a school with more or less resources) or the reason for the move (e.g., parental divorce, relocation for work).

Nonnormative school transitions can be especially challenging for youth because they commonly occur in isolation, unlike normative transitions that are experienced by a group of classmates. In addition, nonnormative transitions often entail a youth moving to an entirely new school or school district with completely new peers, teachers, and school personnel. Also, the new school will have new classroom norms and schoolwide expectations, which require additional adjustments.

Sometimes nonnormative school transitions can have positive consequences. Youth who move from a poorer school district to a less poor school district can sometimes receive a higher quality of education and greater support in the neighborhood and community (Long, 2014; Metzger et al., 2015). Some youth might move to a school with less rigorous standards and gain an increased sense of self-efficacy. Finally, youth entering a new school by themselves are easily recognized by others in the school, and they can experience increased popularity due to being new and different.

Nonnormative school transitions are quite common, and the educational and long-term effects vary for each student. However, these transitions tend to be overlooked by many parents, teachers, school personnel, and counselors. Counselors should be aware that changing schools is very stressful for youth and can result in educational underachievement, which has long-term career implications for healthy youth development. As with normative school transitions, the focus of counseling should be on preemptive preparation for leaving the student's current school and responsive support while the youth adjusts to the new school.

In preparation for a nonnormative school transition, counselors can do their best to learn about the student's new school, including the classes he or she will be taking, the layout of the building, the schedule of events for a typical day, schoolwide rules, and teacher expectations. Counselors can work with students to visualize positive opportunities at their new schools and identify things that make the students feel confident and happy. Students should also develop a list of coping skills that can be used when things seem overwhelming or tough, which might include meditation, listening to music, going for a walk, calling a friend from the previous school, watching a favorite movie, or talking to a parent. Students might also create a list of mantras to build confidence before the first day at a new school, such as "I am smart and kind" or "I am a great friend; I have a lot to offer." Students can review these statements during school and may keep these mantras and coping skills on a note card.

Counselors might also work with youth to practice social skills for making new friends; throughout childhood and adolescence, friendships are an imperative source of identity and self-exploration for youth. Students can plan the outfits they will wear on the first day because this may make them feel confident and happy. Counselors can work with local organizations to obtain clothing for youth who have limited financial resources. Counselors should also help youth to practice conversation starters, such as "Hi, my name is ___. I'm new to the school. What are some of your favorite afterschool clubs?" Counselors might also take the opportunity to help youth to identify the qualities they look for in a friend, as well as the friend qualities they want to avoid (e.g., students who drink alcohol or skip school).

Finally, as students prepare to change schools, counselors can provide space for students to grieve the loss of their current schools. In its simplest form, counselors should use feeling reflections to allow students to fully experience feelings of sadness, anger, and fear. Students might be invited to write goodbye letters to the teachers they like the most or to the friends they will miss. Counselors should validate such feelings and help students to reframe their losses as new opportunities. Counselors can also explain to parents that youth are likely to experience negative feelings in regard to the transition, and these feelings should be nonjudgmentally validated. Parents might even share their own fears and sadness with their children, and they should ask youth how they can help to support them. Even if youth cannot identify any ways they need help in the current moment, they will likely feel more comfortable seeking support from their parents when needed. Overall, counselors should support youth through a nonnormative school transition by validating how scary and difficult such a move can be and assessing for academic and social–emotional wellness every couple of weeks for the first few months the student is at the new school.

Youth academic success is important for many reasons, including a strong sense of self-efficacy, a positive sense of identity, and long-term career success (Zhu et al., 2014). Youth might experience academic difficulties for a variety of important but relatively elusive reasons, and counselors should work to identify and address these needs. It is first necessary to rule out any diagnosable disorders that might inhibit academic success, such as ADHD or intellectual disabilities. These disorders require unique treatment protocols that are addressed elsewhere in this text. Next, counselors should complete a holistic assessment to identify sources of academic stress and difficulty, and they should not forget to assess for strengths.

Youth might have academic struggles due to time management difficulties, which require a broad range of skills, including willpower, self-regulation, strength to complete unpleasant tasks, organizational and problem-solving skills, and the ability to regulate and control emotions. Youth might also have study skills deficits, in which information is not effectively processed and recalled. Test anxiety is another major factor that can inhibit academic achievement in otherwise high-functioning youth. Finally, school transitions can be a major source of stress and struggle for youth in the academic realm.

Counselors should preemptively work to identify and address academic and career-related issues before they lead to long-term consequences. School counselors are in a unique position to offer support and interventions on a large-scale and short-term basis, and community referrals should be made for youth who need more intense or long-term interventions. Overall, counselors should know that academic and career success is imperative for holistic wellness in youth. They should work with families, school personnel, and other available resources to support youth in academic and career domains, which are closely intertwined with social–emotional considerations.

SOCIAL–EMOTIONAL TRANSITIONS AND STRUGGLES

Social–emotional wellness is a broad concept that includes a youth's ability to form a strong, positive sense of identity as well as healthy, supportive peer relationships. Although the school setting is traditionally associated with academic growth, it also serves as a key platform for social–emotional development (Shin & Ryan, 2014). Emotional wellness is a key requirement for a healthy lifestyle in childhood, adolescence, and adulthood, and social relationships contribute to, and are affected by, emotional development.

Difficulty Making and Maintaining Friendships

Friendship is a reciprocal relationship between two or more people who share developmental similarities (Bagwell & Schmidt, 2011). Reciprocity is at the heart of friendship, in which individuals exchange thoughts, feelings, or behaviors nonjudgmentally with one another. Children engage in reciprocal play behaviors, and more intimate exchanges of thoughts and feelings become important as youth grow older (Bagwell & Schmidt, 2011). Girls are more likely to experience high levels of intimacy and emotional involvement with their friends than boys, which increases social and emotional self-efficacy and increases academic satisfaction (Asahi & Aoki, 2010).

Social competence is a key component to a youth's ability to make and maintain friendships. Social competence encompasses a youth's ability to read others' social cues and respond in a way that is helpful and desirable. Youth with poor social competence are commonly seen as outcasts or otherwise rejected by their peers, which can leave youth feeling lonely and lacking in confidence (Olsen, Parra, Cohen, Schoffstall, & Egli, 2012). Poor social competence could be the result of a diagnosable disorder (e.g., autism spectrum disorder, ADHD), or it could be due to a lack of exposure to reciprocal relationships. Counselors should assess a youth's social competence if he or she is having trouble making and maintaining friendships.

Friendships typically develop between youth who share similarities. In social settings, youth tend to form subgroups of friends, known as cliques (Knecht, Burk, Weesie, & Steglich, 2011). Within each clique, dyadic pairs of friends develop. Youth tend to select cliques and best friends who are similar in ethnicity and of the same sex (Foelsch et al., 2014). Youth who are members of the minority race or sex (in the community or at school) might inherently find it difficult to make connections with peers, which can also inhibit their sense of self-worth (Titzmann, 2014).

In addition to physical characteristics, children tend to associate with youth who experience similar struggles and hobbies (Mercer & DeRosier, 2010). Although it can be helpful for youth with similar needs and interests to validate and support one another, it can become problematic if a youth's friends use unhealthy coping skills (e.g., drugs, alcohol, risky sexual behaviors). In addition, youth who experience loneliness, depression, and anxiety are likely to become friends with one another, and youth become even more similar to their friends across time (Mercer & DeRosier, 2010). As such, youth can become increasingly anxious and depressed as a result of their friendships. Counselors should pay close attention to a youth's friendships as a gauge of overall well-being and as a potential source of difficulty in healthy development.

Counselors can provide education to teachers, school personnel, parents, and youth about the importance of social development during childhood and adolescence. Counselors should remember the intertwined nature of academic, career, and social–emotional growth in youth, and holistic assessment should be completed to rule out any diagnosable disorders that might be interfering with healthy friendship development (e.g., anxiety, depression, ADHD). Next, counselors should identify the specific factors that are contributing to friendship difficulties, including poor social competence, negative identity development, or exposure to peers who are hostile or otherwise unwelcoming.

For youth who lack social competence, counselors can employ multiple methods to teach social skills and provide opportunities for practice. School counselors might offer classroom guidance lessons in which youth can learn about social cues at a developmentally appropriate level. Youth in elementary school might be shown various faces and asked to identify the associated feeling. Youth in middle school might be given scenarios and asked to identify a friendly way to respond. Counselors can implement similar activities in a group setting, and youth can share their own experiences of friendship difficulties while validating one another. Group counseling might be especially helpful for boys, who are not always socialized to be empathic and supportive (Asahi & Aoki, 2010).

In individual counseling, counselors might teach youth about social cues and reciprocity and then offer role-plays as a way to practice the skills in a safe setting. Counselors should also encourage parents to teach social skills at home, and positive social skills should be modeled in the classroom.

Clinical Toolbox 12.3

In the Pearson etext, click here for a list of role-play scenarios counselors can use to help elementary students to increase social competence.

A positive self-concept is also a key component for healthy friendships. Counselors can encourage healthy self-concepts in children by helping them to identify the things they are good at and the things that are harder for them. Counselors can help youth to embrace and accept themselves just as they are. Counselors can also use age-appropriate cognitive behavioral interventions to help youth to identify irrational or unhelpful automatic thoughts and work to reframe these into more healthy and positive self-statements.

Counselors can choose to work individually with students to explore friendship difficulties and validate feelings of loneliness or sadness while also supporting a positive self-concept. Counselors could choose to organize group interventions that focus on general mental health topics (e.g., self-esteem, study skills) to foster friendships. Counselors can also provide referrals to afterschool programs or other resources that might be helpful for students with friendship difficulties.

Bullying

Bullying is a relatively new mental health concept that has been heavily researched since the late 1970s. Bullying includes all interpersonal acts in which one person intentionally causes physical or emotional harm to another (Bradshaw, Waasdorp, & Johnson, 2015). Bullying can occur in real life or on the online platform. Examples of bullying include:

- fighting;
- hacking into social media accounts or making inappropriate posts;
- hitting;
- ignoring;
- kicking;
- name-calling;

- "outing" people on social media;
- pranking;
- punching;
- relational aggression;
- sending malicious messages via technology;
- sending malicious written notes in person;
- spreading rumors or damaging one's reputation;
- staring down;
- starting fights between friends;
- stealing belongings;
- teasing; and
- threatening.

Bullying behaviors develop as the result of intertwined biopsychosocial factors. Often, youth use bullying behaviors to express and displace their own uncomfortable emotions onto others. These emotions might include fear, sorrow, anger, sadness, lack of self-confidence, or anxiety, which develop as the result of multiple biopsychosocial factors. Bullying can also occur when youth experience a lack of order, adult supervision, and predictable rules in the home, neighborhood, or school (Bradshaw et al., 2015). Youth who have chaotic home or classroom experiences might use bullying as a predictable way to get attention from others or as a way to alleviate boredom or frustration.

Bullies often choose victims who are smaller and more timid than themselves. Youth with noticeable physical and cognitive difficulties are more at risk for being bullied. Sometimes victims learn bullying behaviors to protect themselves, and in these cases they are labeled as bully-victims (McGuckin & Minton, 2014). Youth who have mental health difficulties (e.g., emotion dysregulation, disruptive behaviors) are at a higher risk for becoming bully-victims. Although it is helpful to conceptualize bullying dynamics using labels, it is important to view all youth involved with bullying as individuals with unique feelings and needs.

Children and adolescents who are friends with bullies might not approve of the behaviors but might not want to jeopardize their friendships. These youth might occasionally join in the bullying behaviors to maintain social status. Some youth might actively avoid either the bully or the victim, and sometimes these youth want to stand up for the victim but do not know how to do so. Finally, some youth might actually insert themselves into the bullying event to stand up and protect the victim, which can sometimes result in harm to the protector.

Adults who witness bullying should intervene immediately with a nonjudgmental stance. After privately collecting details about the incident, adults should arrange for bullies and victims to receive the support they need from parents, caregivers, teachers, and peers. Bullying behaviors should never be ignored because bullying is associated with a slew of harmful side effects in all youth involved, including:

- low self-esteem;
- low self-efficacy;
- decreased academic performance;
- depression;
- suicide;
- homicide;
- behavior problems;
- emotional difficulties;
- academic difficulties; and
- other violent behaviors (Bradshaw et al., 2015; Connolly et al., 2015; McGuckin & Minton, 2014).

Counselors should take bullying very seriously and should respond in a multifaceted way that involves bullies, victims, and adults. Proactive approaches are especially helpful and are most appropriate for the school environment. Responsive counseling can also be used to address the mental health needs of bullies, victims, and bystanders. It is not often recommended that a bully and victim engage in counseling together because the vulnerability required to participate in counseling can be used to fuel future bullying behaviors.

However, counselors can work with youth individually to identify motivations for bullying (e.g., a lack of support at home, low self-esteem) or to address any effects of bullying (e.g., feelings of guilt, perceived helplessness).

Many specific anti-bullying programs exist to help to prevent and end bullying. Often, these programs are implemented in the school setting, where counselors can reach individuals who are bullied, bystanders, and those who engage in bullying behaviors. Common components of bullying prevention programs include:

- building awareness (for youth and adults);
- building social–emotional skills;
- educating parents, school personnel, youth, and community members;
- increasing a sense of personal responsibility in bullies and bystanders;
- increasing self-reflection;
- modeling prosocial and intervention behaviors in the media;
- modifying behaviors of bullies, victims, and bystanders;
- role-playing; and
- social–cognitive training. (Polanin, Espelage, & Pigott, 2012)

Counselors should take a holistic approach to bullying prevention and intervention whenever possible. Often, bullying prevention programs have the ultimate goal of engaging the help of bystanders, and other programs try to teach victims to defend themselves or otherwise flee the bullying situation (Polanin et al., 2012). In a meta-analysis of 12 programs, Polanin and colleagues (2012) found that school-based bullying prevention programs increase bystander intervention behaviors.

Counselors should choose a school-based bullying prevention program that meets their students' needs and fits well with the school dynamics (e.g., age level, budgetary restrictions, time constraints, degree of need). **KiVa** (Kärnä et al., 2011) is an evidence-based program that can help to prevent bullying and provide specific interventions for addressing existing cases of bullying (http://www.kivaprogram.net). KiVa was found to increase bystander intervention and increase empathy for others (Polanin et al., 2012). **Expect Respect** (Positive Behavioral Interventions & Supports, 2017) is another program found to be effective for elementary/high school students (https://www.pbis.org/resource/900) and elementary school students (https://www.pbis.org/resource/785) in a meta-analysis (Polanin et al., 2012). The Olweus Bullying Prevention Program (Olweus, 2013) is another highly regarded bullying prevention program used to address bullying in community, school, and classroom settings, as well as the individual level (http://www.violencepreventionworks.org).

Character development can also be used as a way to teach youth prosocial behaviors as a preemptive approach to bullying prevention and cessation. If youth develop empathy and healthy ways to express emotions and needs, they might not feel the need to bully. Many character development programs are available for use by counselors, but Core Essentials is a popular program that highlights helpful characteristics that youth should exhibit in the school, community, neighborhood, and home settings. As part of the Core Essentials program, behaviors that are incompatible with bullying are promoted for youth enactment, including:

- wisdom;
- initiative;
- individuality;
- service;
- compassion;
- self-control;
- cooperation;
- hope;
- friendship; and
- contentment. (Core Essential Values, 2016)

The Core Essentials program provides a monthly toolkit of posters, flyers, classroom guidance activities, and plans for small group or individual interventions. Counselors can also find other character development programs online or develop their own methods to teach prosocial character traits to youth.

Counselors must also be able to respond to instances of bullying that occur despite preventative measures. The main goals when working with youth who have been bullied include:

- increasing problem-based and emotion-based coping skills;
- increasing self-defense strategies;
- increasing connections with allies;
- promoting less predictable behaviors to reduce the bully's confidence;
- teaching physical, verbal, and social assertiveness skills; and
- teaching how, where, and when to seek support. (Carney & Hazler, 2015)

The main goals for working with bullies include:

- holding youth accountable;
- developing relationships with bullies;
- providing experiences to promote acceptance of others; and
- teaching empathy skills. (Carney & Hazler, 2015)

Finally, the main goals for counseling bystanders include:

- teaching methods for recognizing and acting on feelings of discomfort;
- staying calm and demonstrating casual (rather than assertive or aggressive) disapproval;
- telling the person to stop;
- gathering more people to the scene;
- stopping actions that do not work and trying something different;
- getting help;
- teaching methods for supporting youth who are bullied; and
- teaching methods for supporting youth who enact bullying behaviors. (Carney & Hazler, 2015)

Counselors can respond to reports of bullying by providing individual, dyadic, group, or family counseling to address issues of self-esteem, family rules and values, classroom rules and norms, and appropriate ways to express emotions and needs. Bullying should be addressed on an individual basis to identify the specific stressors, contributors, and consequences, but counselors can also preemptively educate youth about bullying on a larger scale.

Sexual Orientation Struggles

Late childhood and early adolescence is a time of sexual exploration. The concepts of sex and gender are especially important during this time. Sex refers to a youth's biological reproductive functioning, and gender refers to emotional manifestations of biological sex. Youth become aware of the physical differences between boys and girls at various ages (perhaps as young as age 2 or 3), and they begin to understand the differences between male and female gender characteristics as young as age 6 (American Academy of Pediatrics, 2016).

Some youth's thoughts, feelings, and behaviors do not align with their biological sex; **gender-nonconforming** youth accept their biological sex but do not behave in gender-conforming ways (e.g., a biological man wears female clothing). **Transgender** youth do not accept their biological sex and experience the world through the viewpoint of the opposite sex and gender (Diamond, 2013). Some youth are able to express their gender identities early in life (e.g., age 6), but others might not be able to clearly understand and articulate their gendered experiences until adolescence or even later (American Academy of Pediatrics, 2016). Many factors will contribute to a youth's understanding of gender identity, including individual developmental characteristics, cultural factors, and life experiences. Keeping in mind that many youth are not yet able to understand and articulate their gender identities, counselors should complete ongoing assessment with youth as the therapeutic relationship builds and grows. Most youth feel comfortable acting in ways that align with their sex and gender, but youth whose gender and sex do not align often know they are different by the age of 5 or 6 (American Academy of Pediatrics, 2016), and they might verbalize these feelings if they are given an open and supporting forum to do so.

Once a counselor understands a young person's gender self-perceptions, the relationship between gender and sexuality can be explored. Sexuality begins to develop around puberty, which is roughly at age 12 (American Academy of Pediatrics, 2016). Most youth are attracted to members of the opposite sex (although gender expression can widely vary, as previously explained), but some youth are attracted to members of the same sex (Diamond, 2013). The acronym LGBTQQIA refers to lesbian, gay, bisexual, transgender, queer, questioning, intersex, and ally individuals (Association for Lesbian Gay, Bisexual, Transgender Issues in Counseling [ALGBTIC] LGBTQQIA Competencies Taskforce, 2013). However, the acronyms LGBT or LGBTQ are commonly used to refer to this population as well. See Table 12.4 for definitions of commonly used LGBTQQIA terms.

Overall, sexuality is unique to every individual. In the past, individuals who did not conform to typical gender or sexual norms were considered to have a mental illness, and therapy was aimed at correcting or fixing deviant sexuality (Diamond, 2013). However, counselors currently believe that healthy and developmentally appropriate sexuality exists along a continuum, and sexual expression is only a problem if it causes significant distress for an individual or those around them (APA, 2013). Sometimes sexual minority or gender nonconforming youth can experience judgment from others, and their distresses are actually a result of the judgment rather than their inherent sexualities or genders.

LGBTQ individuals can be discriminated against in the home, neighborhood, community, school, or work and often face a wide variety of social and emotional challenges, including:

- social marginalization;
- peer victimization;
- lack of self-esteem;
- diminished self-concept;
- lack of school belonging;
- poor school performance;
- traumatic experiences;

Table 12.4	Key Terms Related to Sexual Orientation and Sexual Identity
Affectional orientation	*Affectional orientation* is used to describe the type of people (e.g., sex, gender identity) with whom an individual prefers to bond in an emotional, physical, spiritual, or cognitive sense. The term *affectional orientation* is used instead of *sexual orientation* to capture the complexity of sexual identity and intimate relationships.
Ally	*Ally* is used to describe an individual who provides support to any individual who identifies as LGBTQ.
Bisexual	*Bisexual* is used to describe a man or woman who has an affectional orientation toward men and women.
Gay	*Gay* is used to describe a man who has an affectional orientation toward men. This term can be used sometimes to refer to anyone who identifies as LGBTQ.
Intersex	*Intersex* is used to describe an individual who was born with both male and female sex organs, hormones, chromosomes, and/or secondary sex characteristics. The term has generally replaced the word *hermaphrodite*.
Lesbian	*Lesbian* is used to describe a woman who has an affectional orientation toward women.
Queer	*Queer* is used to describe individuals who identify outside of the male or female gender categories. This term can be used sometimes to refer to anyone who identifies as LGBTQ.
Questioning	*Questioning* is used to describe individuals who are unsure of their affectional orientations.
Transgender	Transgender (or trans) is used to describe people who do not adhere to gender norms.

Note: Adapted from Association for Lesbian Gay, Bisexual, Transgender Issues in Counseling (ALGBTIC) LGBTQQIA Competencies Taskforce (2013).

- increased stress;
- alcohol and substance use;
- family judgment and rejection;
- anger;
- depression; and
- suicidality. (Beauregard & Moore, 2011; Collier, van Beusekom, Bos, & Sandfort, 2013)

Counselors can play key roles in supporting the mental health of LGBTQ individuals. Overall, it is important to promote acceptance of others and to help youth to find healthy and appropriate ways to explore and express their sexualities. Counselors should work to ensure sexuality is just one part of a youth's holistic identity. Counselors should also work to harness a youth's resources while addressing any harmful environmental factors to promote wellness and a positive sense of self.

Although American culture seems to be gradually becoming more accepting of LGBTQ individuals, this population still faces many barriers in their homes, communities, and schools. Counselors who work with LGBTQ individuals should regularly seek supervision (and possibly their own counseling) to experience continued personal and professional development in the areas of gender and sexuality. Counselors should monitor any potential biases or issues of countertransference to provide a safe, supportive counseling space for LGBTQ youth (Beauregard & Moore, 2011). Competency standards for working with LGBTQ youth can be located through the ALGBTIC LGBTQQIA Competencies Taskforce (2013) and the ALGBTIC Transgender Committee (2010). Mental health theory and research have historically pathologized LGBTQ individuals. As a result, counselors should validate LGBTQ youth's inherent mistrust of the mental health system while also working to validate and explore every youth's sexuality and gender identity as a unique expression of self.

Clinical Toolbox 12.4

In the Pearson etext, click here to review a summary of competencies for working with LGBQQIA youth.

When working with LGBTQ youth, counselors should aim to assess the areas in which they are thriving, identify opportunities for LGBTQ youth, and use available resources to overcome areas in which LGBTQ youth typically struggle. Struggles typically associated with LGBTQ status include:

- identity confusion;
- anxiety and depression;
- suicidal ideation and behavior;
- academic failure;
- substance abuse, physical, sexual, and verbal abuse;
- homelessness;
- prostitution; and
- sexually transmitted diseases/HIV infection. (ALGBTIC LGBTQQIA Competencies Taskforce, 2013)

It is especially important to note that individuals who identify as LGBTQ might face discrimination from religious institutions. Youth whose families ascribe to a religion that does not support LGBTQ identities might face heightened difficulties with their loved ones. In addition, LGBTQ individuals might face discrimination in the school and/or workplace, although it is illegal. Accompanied by the other academic struggles that are often faced by LGBTQ youth, career endeavors can be quite limited and difficult.

The primary focus of counseling LGBTQ individuals is on reducing or eliminating environmental factors that threaten a youth's healthy development and increasing factors that support positive identity formation (Diamond, 2013). These broad goals can be met through a combination of psychoeducation and individual, group, and family counseling. School counselors can advocate for LGBTQ youth in many ways by doing things such as educating the community or developing classroom guidance curricula. School counselors can also develop or attend a SafeZone training that creates safe spaces for LBGTQ individuals (Gay Alliance, 2016).

In individual counseling, youth can be taught about healthy coping skills, healthy sexual practices, and ways to build self-esteem and a positive sense of identity. Counselors should work to harness family and community resources, such as parents or grandparents who are allies, allied school personnel, and support groups (Craig & Smith, 2014; Ehrensaft, 2013). Counselors can use creative activities that are theoretically supported by cognitive behavioral therapy (CBT) or narrative therapy to identify unhelpful or irrational automatic thoughts and restructure personal narratives in healthier, more productive ways.

Overall, counselors should work to validate any difficulties experienced by LGBTQ youth and the uncomfortable emotions that come as a result. Counselors should help youth to understand the social and political history of persecution toward LGBTQ individuals and explain that sexuality is unique and complex. Counselors should help youth to identify healthy methods of self-expression and work to harness resources that can help LGBTQ youth to develop and grow.

Intimacy and Dating

Youth typically begin to explore romantic intimacy in adolescence. Romantic intimacy occurs when two people who are sexually attracted to one another share a reciprocal relationship that involves the exchange of thoughts, feelings, and behaviors. Romantic behaviors might be sexual in nature, but they also include nonsexual activities such as spending time together and participating in enjoyable events.

Childhood interpersonal experiences contribute to a youth's experiences in the dating arena (Rauer, Pettit, Lansford, Bates, & Dodge, 2013). Youth often observe the interactions between their parents, extended family members, older siblings, and media characters to develop ideas of how intimate partners interact. Often, the healthy or unhealthy models of attachment developed between youth and caregivers persist into romantic relationships later in life.

Although youth relationships with family and friends create scaffolding for romantic relationships, the addition of sexuality can create an added layer of complexity and confusion (Rauer et al., 2013). Puberty is a confusing time in which youth's bodies and feelings are rapidly changing, and youth often experience wavering senses of identity. In addition, physical desires for sexual connection are not often aligned with emotional readiness. For example, girls who experience puberty earlier than their peers often have sexual intercourse earlier as well (Moore, Harden, & Mendle, 2014). Although their bodies indicate sexual maturity and desire, their emotion regulation and interpersonal insight skills are still lacking, which leads to more unstable and unhealthy relationships for these youth.

Perceptions of unreciprocated love in which youth desire to become romantic with someone who does not desire the same thing can also be a source of difficulty. Unreciprocated love is especially challenging if two youth have experimented sexually but one partner does not wish to make a commitment to date or be in a relationship with the other (Howard et al., 2015). Even when love is reciprocated, breakups at this age can occur for various reasons (e.g., competing interests, lack of communication or compromise). Breakups can be especially devastating for youth because abstract reasoning is not fully developed and heartbreak can seem unending.

Previous experiences of abuse can also affect the ways in which youth conceptualize and enact their sexuality and needs for intimacy. Emotional, physical, and sexual abuse can result in lowered self-esteem, difficulty sustaining healthy attachments, anger, depression, anxiety, and hypersexualization (Centers for Disease Control [CDC], 2015c; U.S. Department of Health and Human Services, 2013). Youth who have experienced abuse might have unique difficulties with intimate relationships above and beyond those that are developmentally indicated.

When youth experience romantic difficulties, they are at higher risk for developing problems at school and work. Youth experiencing romantic difficulties often have trouble regulating emotions (even if they have previously been able to do so) and might engage in self-destructive behaviors (e.g., promiscuity, drugs, alcohol, avoiding the school setting; Foelsch et al., 2014). Youth who experience difficulties with romantic relationships often carry their frustrations into their friendships and family relationships, which can cause further isolation and use of unhealthy coping skills (Foelsch et al., 2014). Intimacy and dating are part of typical youth development that requires close attention from adults, especially counselors.

Sexual education is an effective way to help youth to understand their sexuality and reduce sexually transmitted infections and crisis pregnancy (Bourke, Boduszek, Kelleher, McBride, & Morgan, 2014).

Sexual education can be provided at a schoolwide level through guidance programs, in small group settings, or individually. Youth as young as 7 years can experience puberty, and even tweens may have sexual experiences (Moore et al., 2014). Sexual education, especially with younger youth, can be a controversial subject for some people, and counselors should try to get parental consent to provide sexual health education while maintaining the confidentiality of the counseling relationship.

Counselors can help youth to identify a healthy sense of self so they are able to navigate romantic relationships in healthy, objective ways. Counselors can use various creative activities to help youth to identify who they are, what they like, and their values, beliefs, and personal goals. This might be done through classroom guidance units in which youth are asked to draw a picture of themselves and write 10 things they like about themselves. Or counselors might ask youth to create collages that represent their future hopes and goals. Counselors might invite youth to list the ways their romantic relationships support their personal growth and development, and youth can imagine how their lives will unfold if they remain in their current relationships.

Counselors should also work to help youth to identify the relationship models they have experienced in their homes, neighborhoods, and communities. Counselors can help youth to identify healthy boundaries in relationships and ways to maintain a healthy balance of work, family, friends, personal time, and time for romantic endeavors. Counselors can help youth to identify their beliefs and perceptions about the ways romantic relationships should be, as well as ways in which this might differ from the thoughts of their peers or their romantic partners. Each of these activities helps foster abstract thinking and insight into the many gray areas that arise in the navigation of romantic relationships.

Counselors should take special care to address any previous trauma or abuse that might inhibit a youth's development of healthy intimate relationships. Assessment and intervention strategies for youth who have experienced abuse or trauma are explored elsewhere in this text. In general, counselors should watch for any red flags that indicate difficulties that go beyond typical developmental concerns. Counselors should make referrals as necessary to support youth during this crucial time of social–emotional development.

In addition, counselors should focus on helping youth develop skills in emotion regulation, communication, and coping strategies for the times when romantic relationships become difficult. Counselors can help youth to identify past or possible scenarios in which the youth felt sad, helpless, angry, or scared. Counselors should validate these feelings and allow youth to fully experience them through creative activities, such as writing a song or drawing the emotions on paper. Next, counselors should explore positive coping skills youth can use in the moment to overcome difficult feelings, such as taking a walk, talking to a friend, or writing a letter. Counselors might praise youth's abilities to control their emotions and explore assertive communication techniques for negotiating needs in a relationship, highlighting the positive results that often come as a result.

Youth can utilize many of the skills they have used in previous friendships and academic endeavors to navigate intimate relationships in helpful, healthy ways. However, some new difficulties arise when sexuality is intertwined, and counselors should work to build a deep understanding of each youth's individual experiences, beliefs, and values regarding sexuality. Sometimes counselors find that youth are involved in relationships that are not necessarily healthy, and additional interventions might be needed.

Intimate Partner Violence

Another consideration for youth in romantic relationships is the possibility of intimate partner violence (IPV). IPV can manifest through physical violence, in which one or both partners use hitting, kicking, or other methods of force to coerce the other. Sexual violence, stalking, and psychological aggression are also considered IPV when these behaviors occur within the context of a romantic relationship (CDC, 2014c). Several types of IPV may occur in a single relationship, and IPV can range from a single incident to an ongoing struggle between two individuals.

IPV can be devastating to youth in many ways. The effects of IPV include, but are not limited to:

- anger;
- chronic pain;
- death;

- depression;
- difficulty leaving unhealthy relationships;
- difficulty maintaining relationships;
- difficulty sleeping;
- difficulty trusting others;
- eating disorders;
- flashbacks;
- limited social activity;
- low self-esteem;
- minor injuries (e.g., cuts, scratches, bruises, welts);
- panic attacks;
- physical, emotional, or intellectual disabilities;
- serious injuries (e.g., burns, broken bones, head trauma, organ damage);
- stress;
- suicidality; and
- unhealthy coping skills (e.g., drugs, alcohol, promiscuity). (CDC, 2014c)

Many youth do not report IPV to anyone, and they may remain in unhealthy relationships for extended periods of time. Longer and more frequent IPV leads to more harmful effects (CDC, 2014c).

Various risk factors that might lead to youth hurting their partners have been identified. Male youth who observe IPV in the home are more likely to reproduce this behavior in their own relationships (Chen & Foshee, 2015; Foshee et al., 2015). Youth who experience more stressful events in the home, with their peers, in the school setting, and with health-related issues are more likely to engage in IPV (Chen & Foshee, 2015). In addition to stress, having high levels of anger is also a risk factor for male and female youth (Foshee et al., 2015). For girls, higher levels of anxiety have been associated with higher levels of IPV, and neighborhood violence can also be a contributor. For boys, heavy alcohol use is also associated with IPV (Foshee et al., 2015).

Prosocial beliefs in youth and parental monitoring can serve as protective factors against IPV. It is also helpful to identify and address IPV in youth before the behaviors persist into adulthood (CDC, 2014c). Parents, school personnel, and mental health professionals can learn about the risk factors of IPV and work to prevent such relationship difficulties before they manifest.

Promoting client safety is the foundation of any interventions addressing IPV. After assessing immediate safety, counselors should work with clients to collaboratively develop safety plans. Youth often need their parents' support in designing and implementing safety plans, so counselors should assess legal and ethical considerations regarding parental involvement. If youth are open to parental involvement, counselors in the school and clinical settings should involve parents in safety planning. Some youth might not want their parents to know about their IPV experiences, which can be challenging for counselors. School counselors should assess any system policies regarding confidentiality and inform parents about the student's IPV experiences if the policy determines it is necessary or if the youth is deemed to be in danger. Clinical counselors should encourage youth to involve their parents in safety planning and should divulge information as necessary to protect the safety of the youth.

Safety plans address various ways that clients can promote their emotional and physical safety. First, strategies for preventing high-risk situations are determined. Next, healthy ways clients can respond in violent situations are explored.

Clinical Toolbox 12.5

In the Pearson etext, click here for a list of questions that counselors can use to develop safety plans with adolescents.

Because IPV is a serious safety issue, counselors should consider making referrals to medical professionals for the assessment and treatment of physical wounds incurred during or associated with

IPV experiences. Although providing medical treatment is outside of counselors' scope of practice, discussion of basic wound care and circumstances in which youth should seek immediate medical attention can be discussed in treatment. Counselors should work with youth to involve their parents whenever possible. Counselors should tell youth frequently that for safety reasons their parents need to be informed about the IPV.

Fears of reporting abuse may prevent youth from using medical services, and the various medical complications associated with IPV can go unaddressed. With female clients, referrals may be made to address gynecological concerns associated with IPV (e.g., sexually transmitted diseases, physical trauma, complications of terminated pregnancy). In youth presenting with co-occurring substance abuse issues, a medical referral can be used to assess for and treat associated health concerns (e.g., hepatitis C, HIV). Counselors may also need to provide referrals for legal resources, transportation, and a safe living environment in the event that the client's safety is compromised at home.

Interventions must be tailored to each youth's presenting symptoms and circumstances. Promoting safety, self-esteem, and self-efficacy and managing mental health symptoms are the primary goals of all interventions addressing IPV. Helping youth to build healthy support networks and reengage in activities that they enjoy can build resiliency and promote the healing process. Trauma-Focused CBT (TF-CBT; Cohen, Mannarino, & Deblinger, 2006) and Child and Family Traumatic Stress Interventions (CFTSI; Berkowitz, Stover, & Marans, 2011) are evidence-based practices used with children and adolescents presenting with issues related to traumatic experiences (e.g., depression, anxiety, posttraumatic stress disorder) and parental reactions to these events, and they are used with those ages 3 to 18 and 7 to 18, respectively. The Seeking Safety treatment model is frequently used to treat co-occurring trauma and substance abuse disorders in adults and can also be used with adolescents (i.e., 13–17; Najavits, Gallop, & Weiss, 2006).

Several prevention programs have been developed to address IPV, including Safe Dates (Foshee et al., 1998) for ages 13 to 17, Relationship Smart Plus (RS+; Adler-Baeder, Kerpelman, Schramm, Higginbotham, & Paulk, 2007) for ages 13 to 17, and Dating Matters: Strategies to Promote Healthy Teen Relationships (Tharpe et al., 2011) for ages 11 to 14. Joven Noble (Tello, Cervantes, Cordova, & Santos, 2010) is an evidence-based prevention program designed to promote positive character development in Latino men and boys ages 10 to 24 to decrease engagement in IPV, substance abuse, and unplanned pregnancies. Prevention programs often focus on building communication, conflict management, and decision-making skills related to intimate relationships and developing an understanding of healthy and unhealthy relationships to decrease the likelihood of verbal or physically aggressive behaviors.

Social and emotional development in youth is intimately intertwined with biological, psychological, genetic, and family factors. A youth's social–emotional well-being often supports or inhibits his or her academic performance, which contributes to long-term career success and overall mental health and wellness. Some youth have diagnosable mental health disorders that inhibit their social–emotional well-being, but other youth will experience developmentally appropriate social–emotional difficulties that require a counselor's attention.

When working with youth, counselors should focus on youth's ability to make and maintain friendships, which can be used as an indicator of social competence. Youth must be able to reciprocate thoughts, feelings, and behaviors with their peers, and difficulties with these tasks can indicate a lack of positive identity, self-esteem, self-regulation skills, or social competence. Counselors should also remember that some youth with emotional or behavior difficulties use bullying in their social interactions, which can have negative consequences for the bully, the victim, and bystanders. Counselors should use various intentional counseling interventions that are appropriate for youth's unique needs in the counseling setting and context.

Counselors might also need to address issues related to sexuality, intimacy, dating, and IPV. Each of these complex issues requires counselors to form a holistic understanding of a youth while also assessing environmental risk and protective factors. Counselors must have working knowledge in each one of these social–emotional issues to accurately identify the course of a youth's struggles and employ effective counseling interventions. Overall, academic, career, and social–emotional wellness are intimately intertwined, and counselors should work to address deficits in any area, which likely affect a youth's overall mental health.

I CAN START COUNSELING PLAN FOR GUDETA

This chapter opened with a short description of Gudeta, a 6-year-old boy who is struggling to make friends after arriving in the United States from Kenya. The following I CAN START conceptual framework outlines counseling considerations that may be helpful to a school counselor or a clinical counselor who works with Gudeta.

C = Contextual Assessment

Gudeta is a 6-year-old boy of Ethiopian descent. He was born in a Kenyan refugee camp, where he lived for 6 years, and his family moved to the United States less than 6 months ago. Gudeta went to an English-speaking school in Kenya. He has attended a diverse elementary school in the southern United States for the past 3 months, and he excels academically. However, Gudeta avoids raising his hand in class, and he tends to play and eat lunch by himself. Gudeta's teacher describes him as a "sweet, shy boy who needs some support making friends." Gudeta's parents speak little English, but they explained that they want "everything that is good for him." Gudeta plays by himself at recess and sits quietly at the end of a table during lunch.

A = Assessment and Diagnosis

Gudeta has experienced a nonnormative school transition in which he left the only environment he ever knew to move to a new country. He is still with his parents, but he has lost all his previous friends and familiar surroundings. Although no formal diagnosis will be given at this time, counseling interventions will be used to address his social skills deficits.

N = Necessary Level of Care

- School-based individual counseling (once per week)
- School-based group counseling (once per week)

S = Strengths

Self: Gudeta is highly motivated in his schoolwork. He diligently and capably works on all class assignments. Gudeta is a handsome young man; he is well groomed and well dressed. Gudeta has a warm, inviting smile, and he is easygoing. Gudeta likes to build model cars, and he is able to entertain himself with various games, such as building blocks or playing with cards.

Family: Gudeta's parents are highly invested in his well-being, as evidenced by frequent attendance at school events and quick response to any communication from the school. Gudeta's parents are resilient, as evidenced by their move from their homeland to a refugee camp and their ability to secure residence in the United States.

School/community: Gudeta's family lives in a moderate-size city in which various resources are available, including social services, free libraries, free afterschool programs for economically disadvantaged families, and various social groups and summer camps for youth.

T = Treatment Approach

- Social skills training
- Group therapy

A = Aim and Objectives of Counseling (90-day objectives)

Gudeta will identify three ways he can initiate conversations with peers. Gudeta will use one conversation strategy at least once per school day.

Gudeta will identify three social skills that work for him. Gudeta will use one social skill per day.

Gudeta will identify three peers with whom he can be friendly. Gudeta will play at recess or eat lunch with one of these peers at least once per school day.

R = Research-Based Interventions

Counselor will help Gudeta to

- create a list of mantras to build confidence in social situations;
- practice social skills for making new friends;
- practice conversation starters; and
- identify desired qualities in a friend.

T = Therapeutic Support Services

In-school peer support group

Free afterschool program at the school

YMCA programming (e.g., swim lessons, Boy Scouts)

Summary

Academic and social–emotional development are intimately intertwined throughout the formative years. School counselors are specifically charged with addressing these developmental domains (ASCA, 2012), but all counselors who work with youth should understand the importance of youth's success in these areas. Overall, healthy social and emotional development allows youth to focus on their academic endeavors, which ultimately supports a fulfilling career in adulthood. Counselors should be aware of the developmental struggles associated with academic, career, and social–emotional issues in youth. Counselors should also harness strengths and resiliencies of youth to support healthy growth in these key domains.

Youth who experience academic struggles might have inherent disabilities that create extra challenges in this area. Academic struggles can lead to low self-esteem, depression, and anxiety, and counselors should assess and address academic needs in youth. Even if youth do not have documented disorders that affect academic achievement, they might struggle with time management, study skills, or test anxiety. Counselors should implement appropriate counseling interventions to support youth through these difficulties while providing appropriate advocacy and referral sources.

Youth might also experience academic struggles as the result of changing schools. Normative transitions can be expected for every youth in America, but they can still be overwhelming and anxiety provoking. Not all youth experience nonnormative transitions, but those who do often experience harmful academic consequences. Counselors should offer support and appropriate interventions for youth during times of school transition.

As highlighted in this chapter, solid social–emotional development is necessary for a youth's academic and career success. Some youth do not attend school due to emotional or behavior difficulties, which is known as school refusal or chronic truancy (depending on the root cause). Counselors should work to resolve underlying social–emotional issues that lead to youth missing school, which often results in poor academic and career achievement.

Additional social–emotional difficulties that youth typically encounter during the formative years include struggles with making and maintaining friendships, bullying, sexual orientation, intimacy and dating, and IPV. Counselors should implement individual and group interventions to address the issues that can inhibit healthy growth and development in youth.

Overall, childhood and adolescence are filled with developmental changes and related struggles. All youth will experience some adversity in their lives, some more than others. Counselors should be aware of the multiple challenges youth might face and should address these issues to support youth toward healthy development into adulthood.

MyLab Counseling: Counseling Children and Adolescents

In the Topic 9 Assignments: *Academic and Social–Emotional Challenges for Youth*, try Application Exercise 9.1: *Flashcards are Fun* and Licensure Quiz 9.1: *Academic Struggles and Career Success.*

Then try Application Exercise 9.3: *Understanding and Addressing Bullying* and Licensure Quiz 9.3: *Social–Emotional Transitions and Struggles.*

CHAPTER 13

Neurodevelopmental and Intellectual Impairments

THE CASE OF SOFÍA

Sofía is full of energy, life, and excitement. We could not love her more. Last week, her first-grade teacher asked that we come in for an impromptu parent–teacher meeting. She told us how much she enjoys Sofía and how she believes that academically Sofía is a smart kid. Her teacher then told us that she does have some concerns regarding several things she is seeing in the classroom. She said that Sofía often seems out of control, blurts out answers, and is unable to wait her turn. She also said that she has observed Sofía interrupting other students, and she believes Sofía is having some difficulties getting along with her classmates. Her teacher said that she seems to talk excessively and is not able to engage in quiet or independent activities.

My husband and I have seen some of these behaviors at home—like interrupting others, not waiting her turn, and being physically out of control. Since she is the youngest of five children—you know we are a big Catholic family—she seems to fit right in with the chaos of our busy world. Sofía is spirited, and she's often on the go all day, and most nights she has trouble getting into bed and sleeping; we have grown to just accept that is who she is. But the teacher is concerned, and I'm wondering if something is maybe wrong. What do you think? Do you have any ideas on how we can help Sofía?

—Sofía's mother

As young people grow, they achieve various developmental milestones, including the development of gross and fine motor movements, language, and cognitive and social skills. The development of these skills helps young people to meet the demands of their evolving worlds (Broderick & Blewitt, 2014). Some children experience intellectual and neurodevelopmental problems that are characterized by developmental deficits (e.g., limitations in learning, impairments in social skills, struggles with executive functioning), which can impair their personal, social, and academic functioning. Developmental deficits or impairments affect youth's **adaptive functioning**, or the basic skills needed to handle and meet the demands of everyday life. Examples of skills that young people need to possess to navigate their worlds include communication, socialization skills (e.g., social rules, obeying laws, detecting motivation of others), and personal self-care skills (e.g., feeding, bathing, dressing, occupational skills; American Psychiatric Association [APA], 2013a; Ashwood et al., 2015). Without some mastery of these general adaptive functioning skills, young people struggle at school, at home, and in their community. Parents of youth who have developmental deficits often present with fears (e.g., "Why is this happening to me?" "Did I do something to cause this in my child?") and concerns for their child's well-being and future. Counselors can be instrumental in supporting parents through the process of identification, diagnosis, and treatment, as well as the associated feelings often connected with this process (e.g., anxiety, guilt, denial, disbelief).

This chapter discusses the diagnosis, assessment, and counseling approaches that are useful when working with youth who have neurodevelopmental and intellectual impairments. These impairments typically manifest early in childhood, often before the child enters school. Although these impairments involve numerous disorders and disabilities, this chapter highlights the most frequently diagnosed childhood disorders: attention-deficit/hyperactivity disorder (ADHD), autistic spectrum disorder, intellectual disabilities, and specific learning disorders.

All intellectual and/or neurodevelopmental problems involve a disruption of brain-related developmental processes, which result in some type of impairment in cognitive functioning that ranges from mild to severe. Intellectual and neurodevelopmental impairments can present as a wide array of symptoms and experiences, but they are often congenital disorders. Although most intellectual and neurodevelopmental disorders are present at birth, impairments are often not fully manifested or observed until the child faces the academic and social demands associated with the school environment. During the transition to school, the difficulties that the child experiences often become more obvious, which leads to referrals for testing and assessment and needed educational services.

Intellectual and neurodevelopmental problems present a host of potential challenges for youth and their families. Early diagnosis, counseling intervention, and parental participation in counseling have all been associated with more positive outcomes (Kendall & Comer, 2010).

ATTENTION-DEFICIT/HYPERACTIVITY DISORDER (ADHD)

ADHD is a neurodevelopmental disorder characterized by difficulties with attention. Youth who have ADHD experience difficulties with attention/inattention, impulsivity, and/or hyperactivity across multiple settings (e.g., home, school, interpersonal contexts). ADHD is one of the most commonly diagnosed disorders, and while a popular misconception is that youth grow out of ADHD, the vast majority experience ADHD symptoms throughout their lives (Centers for Disease Control and Prevention [CDC], 2015a). ADHD can affect young people's well-being, social interactions, and academic achievement (American Academy of Pediatrics, 2011a). Approximately 5% of school-age children are diagnosed with ADHD. Although boys are diagnosed with it twice as frequently as girls, many believe the disorder is underdiagnosed in girls because they tend to display fewer signs of hyperactivity (which often leads to disruptiveness and attracts the attention of teachers) and greater inattentiveness (APA, 2013). Diagnostically, there are three types of attention-deficit/hyperactive disorders:

- *Attention-deficit/hyperactive disorder, predominantly inattentive type:* These young people may fail to give sustained or close attention to details/directions, make careless mistakes, have difficulties with organization, be easily distracted, be forgetful or lose things, appear not to listen, and/or struggle to follow instructions.
- *Attention-deficit/hyperactive disorder, predominantly hyperactive/impulsive type:* These young people may fidget with their hands and/or feet, have difficulties waiting or taking turns, blurt out answers, have difficulties remaining seated, run or climb indiscriminately, have difficulties working independently, talk excessively, appear to be driven by a motor, and/or interrupt others.
- *Attention-deficit/hyperactive disorder, combined type:* These young people have both inattentive and hyperactive/impulsive symptoms.

ADHD is a neurological processing disorder that traditionally has a symptom onset before 7 years of age (APA, 2013). The inattention aspect of ADHD is often misunderstood and may be better characterized as attention irregularities (Rausch, Williams, & Kress, 2015). Although some children with ADHD may struggle to maintain focused attention for an extended duration, many children with ADHD oscillate between difficulties attending and overfocusing, with the latter often referred to as an ability to **hyperfocus** and be extremely attentive for extended time periods, especially when the task is of interest. Generally speaking, inattentiveness is demonstrated by difficulties with listening/attending, short-term memory or remembering things they were told, following directions or completing assigned tasks, rapidly shifting attention from one activity to another without fully engaging or completing the initial task, and shifting their attention to new demands when engaged in an enjoyable task (Kendall & Comer, 2010). These inattention struggles can manifest as a child's inability to sustain attention for a developmentally appropriate length of time. For example, a younger child may move from playing with one toy to another without a focused, directed sense of play, seemingly jumping from one item to another. Or the child may often daydream and seem distracted when engaged in play.

Although impulsivity and hyperactivity are both based on the same criteria (e.g., ADHD impulsive/hyperactive type) and may appear to overlap, these constructs are unique and are covered independently in this chapter. **Impulsivity**, or the inclination to act without fully considering the impact and/or consequences of an action, is one symptom of ADHD. Although impulsivity is developmentally appropriate throughout childhood, children with ADHD differ in that they often display impulsivity in their schoolwork and social interactions, and these differences generally become most apparent in the school setting (Kendall & Comer, 2010). Furthermore, these young people often have impairments in their "planning, inhibition, and executive control," which is why they are more likely to adopt a rushed pathway in their decision-making process (Hickson & Khemka, 2013, p. 214). For example, young people who have ADHD and struggle with impulsivity may, in the school setting, fail to wait their turn, get out of their seat, move on to another activity before completion, blurt out answers without raising their hand, and interrupt others; thus, these difficulties can often inhibit adequate responses to others. This impulsivity has the potential to interfere with schoolwork and to strain a child's social interactions, thus making the development of appropriate peer relationships and friendships more difficult. Table 13.1 provides two activities that address impulsivity and restlessness.

Hyperactivity involves excessive physical activity and movement that are not appropriate and/or desirable. It is behaviorally manifested as excessive fidgeting, restlessness, wandering around (e.g., inability to sit still), excessive talking, and difficulties with quiet, self-directed activities (e.g., reading, homework). Parents and teachers often report that children with hyperactivity are "on the go" or act as if they are "driven by a motor," and they often struggle to make the transition from a nonstructured activity to a more structured activity. For example, a child may seem to do well at recess, where he or she experiences limited directedness, yet struggle to settle and make the transition back to the classroom after recess.

Counselor Considerations

Struggles with inattention, impulsivity, and hyperactivity affect young people's peer relationships and academic performance (Kendall & Comer, 2010). Many children with ADHD find it difficult to initiate, engage in, and maintain appropriate peer relationships. In some cases, these young people may be perceived as intrusive. They often violate the rules of social engagement (e.g., neglect to ask others questions, struggle

Table 13.1 Activities to Address Impulsivity and Restlessness in Youth

Title	Description
Daily Impulsiveness Cards	Work collaboratively with the client, parents, and/or educators to identify the main areas where impulsive behaviors occur. Next, list those behaviors and areas on an index card, explaining to the client that he or she will be observed in these areas. Ask educators, parents, and/or the client to rate the youth's ability to manage his or her impulsive behaviors in a given area (e.g., assigned English worksheets at a desk in school). At the end of the day or a specified time period, review the young person's daily evaluation, and discuss how the client felt he or she did, what successes occurred, and what changes may need to be considered for the following school day.
Fidget Toy/ Stress Ball	Explain to the client that he or she will receive a stress ball or fidget toy to use when he or she feels restless (e.g., unfocused, nervous, anxious, fidgety). Tell the client this item may be used to help him or her to focus and/or to manage feelings of anxiety or nervousness. Instruct the client in the appropriate and inappropriate uses of the stress ball or fidget toy, allowing the client to either keep the item with him or her or to select an accessible place where the item can be retrieved when needed.

Activity Overview

Clients with intellectual and neurodevelopmental issues often have difficulties engaging and interacting with others socially. This creative intervention is an awareness-based activity that aims to increase clients' understanding of their (or others') behaviors that may be complicating or exacerbating social interactions. As the title of the activity implies, clients are given an opportunity to consider things that may irritate or "bug" others versus things that others do that may irritate or "bug" them.

Activity Objectives

The primary goals of this activity are to help youth to (a) become aware of behaviors that might have a negative impact on their social interactions with others and (b) identify and discard certain behaviors that may be getting in the way of forming and maintaining social relationships.

Directions

1. Ascertain client preparedness to engage in this creative intervention. This intervention may be inappropriate for clients who lack some awareness into their behaviors involved in social interactions.
2. Print a picture of a bug or have the client draw a picture of a bug at the start of the activity. This bug should cover an entire sheet of paper and be broken into numerous parts (e.g., head, thorax, abdomen, legs, antennae).
3. Ask the client to think about some of his or her interactions with children at school. Help guide this discussion to address some things that really irritate or "bug" this child about other children at school. If the child struggles to identify these things, suggest a list of behaviors (e.g., tattling, name calling, yelling, breaking promises, taking things, being bossy) that may help the child to remember. These behaviors should be specific to the client's concerns and issues in treatment. Have the child write or draw each one of these behaviors on the bug.
4. Next, ask the client if he or she has ever engaged in any of these behaviors with others at school. Ask the client if he or she thinks that others liked or disliked the behaviors. Finally, ask the client to consider behaviors that might be better received by his or her peers in the future.

Process Questions

1. What was this exercise like for you?
2. What behaviors that "bug" others might you need to stop doing to have more positive interactions with others?
3. What behaviors "bug" you, and how can you manage and respond to these behaviors?

FIGURE 13.1   Social Bug Activity

with conversation reciprocity, jump from one conversation to another) and may be perceived as rude, short, or even verbally aggressive (Kendall & Comer, 2010). Figure 13.1 provides an activity to assist youth in understanding behaviors associated with engaging and interacting with others.

As academic demands increase in middle childhood, schoolwork often becomes more difficult for children who have ADHD. Difficulties with sustained attention and focus in the classroom can contribute to negative teacher evaluations and poor grades. In addition, these young people may face consequences secondary to their behaviors (often related to their inattentiveness or impulsivity), which can include referrals for mental health intervention and disciplinary action in educational settings (e.g., detention, suspension; Rausch et al., 2015). Youth who have ADHD often fail to complete assignments, struggle with organizational skills, and find it difficult to maintain the focus needed to complete multiple-step assignments throughout the school day.

In conjunction with social and academic struggles, youth with ADHD often have trouble listening, have difficulty sitting still, are easily distracted, struggle with time management, and become bored easily, which can make the provision of counseling services challenging. Therefore, counselors must select counseling approaches that are creative, multidisciplined, and multifaceted and must take into consideration multiple settings and supportive others. The counseling treatment team frequently will include parents, youth, counselors, physicians, school psychologists, and an educational specialist.

Because counseling services often include a parental component known as parent education or parent training, counselors must understand the family context and dynamics. The rationale for this assertion is twofold. First, counselors must understand that parent–child and sibling–child interactions may be strained and conflicted in families that have a youth with ADHD (Barkley, 2013b). Although these environmental interaction patterns are not the cause of ADHD, negative interactions may contribute to oppositional behavior and conduct-related problems (APA, 2013). Second, because ADHD has a strong genetic component,

Be compassionate (e.g., praise their ability to focus and sustain effort).

Be flexible and willing to focus on what motivates them.

Do work in bursts (e.g., 8–10 minutes), and reward them with short counseling breaks.

Create a visual outline for the session and have it displayed for the youth to see.

Engage the youth in physical activity in the session as needed.

Focus on the youth's strengths (e.g., resourcefulness, individuality, creativity, self-determination).

Provide a box of fidget toys (e.g., squeeze balls, bags, putty, bands, rubber bangle bracelets) to use during sessions.

Provide the youth with opportunities to be creative (e.g., drawing, clay, puppets, blocks, toys).

Use therapeutic books, workbooks, or a smartphone/tablet (e.g., creative apps).

Create a sign or a code (e.g., touching ear, putting hands together) so you can remind the youth to stay on task, slow down, focus on the task/activity at hand, and so forth.

Be willing to change or alter the youth's environment during counseling sessions.

Provide the youth with choices (e.g., bring music, game, or project into the counseling session).

FIGURE 13.2   Counselor Strategies for Engaging Youth Who Have ADHD

the disorder may be present in other family members (e.g., parents, siblings), and this can play a role in family dynamics. In some cases, parents may even begin to recognize symptoms in themselves as their youth are diagnosed and progress through counseling. One detail must be clarified: Parents are not the cause of these disruptive or conduct-related behaviors, but negative interactions can exacerbate the severity of the youth's symptomology and conduct-related problems, and parents' own ADHD dynamics can affect how they perceive and respond to their child's behavior (Barkley, 2013b).

Ultimately, counselors must consider ways to engage and support parents and youth in and during the counseling process. Because attention, impulsivity, and/or hyperactivity are some of the primary symptoms of ADHD, counselors must consider ways they can enhance counseling engagement with both parents and youth. Figure 13.2 provides a summary of counseling engagement strategies that can be used with youth who have ADHD.

Assessment of ADHD

When assessing for ADHD, counselors need to obtain information from parents, teachers, previous schools, and mental health professionals. Counselors should consider conducting separate interviews with the child, parents, and teachers; investigating the child's behavior from multiple perspectives and evaluating the child's behaviors in multiple settings can be helpful. Clinical interviews can reveal situations or conditions that may be exacerbating problematic behaviors, and they can be invaluable not only in the diagnosis of ADHD but also for treatment planning considerations.

Attitudes toward and interpretations of youth's ADHD symptomology can affect the identification of ADHD. There is a relationship between behaviors that are identified as problematic—or attributed to ADHD—and the diagnosis of ADHD (Gómez-Benito, Van de Vijver, Balluerka, & Caterino, 2015). For example, prevalence rates of ADHD have steadily increased in African American and Latino/a American youth, but parents do not always perceive the related behaviors as problematic or do not initiate or seek counseling or psychological intervention (APA, 2013). Parents' lower recognition of ADHD symptoms as problematic may be attributed to (a) their viewing the behaviors associated with ADHD as culturally appropriate, (b) their not seeking intervention because they have concerns about the impact of an ADHD diagnosis (e.g., lack of knowledge of symptoms or treatment options, fear of overdiagnosing and/or misdiagnosing ADHD as oppositional defiant disorder), and/or (c) their perceiving that the various systems around them may not be trustworthy or support their needs (Bailey et al., 2010). As is true with all counseling, counselors should assume a culturally sensitive stance by attempting to understand the youth and family's cultural identity, their conceptualization of the distress, their psychosocial stressors, and cultural differences between the counselor and the client.

Clinical Toolbox 13.2

In the Pearson e-text, click here for counselor recommendations for reducing racial and ethnic disparities when diagnosing ADHD.

Numerous assessment measures (e.g., the Child Behavioral Checklist [Achenbach & Rescorla, 2001]; Conners 3rd Edition [Conners, 2008]; ADHD Rating Scales–5 [DuPaul, Power, Anatopoulos, & Reid, 2016]; the NICHQ Vanderbilt Assessment Scales—2nd Edition [American Academy of Pediatrics, 2011b]) can aid counselors in assessing youth for ADHD. Although checklists and rating scales are helpful, direct observation and task performance are among the most reliable means of assessing ADHD in younger children (Kendall & Comer, 2010). In addition to these mentioned assessments, an emerging computer-based assessment of attention is the Test of Variables of Attention (T.O.V.A.; Leark, Greenberg, Kindschi, Dupuy, & Hughes, 2007). Table 13.2 provides a summary of several commonly used ADHD assessment measures.

Table 13.2 Common ADHD Assessment Measures

Assessment Measure or Scale	Age Range	Overview of Assessment Measure
The Child Behavior Checklist (CBCL)	6–18 years	The CBCL is a 124-item parent-rated measure that assesses a child's prosocial and maladaptive behaviors. This measure contains possible areas of competence (e.g., extracurricular activities, relationships, academic performance) and problematic areas (e.g., affective disorders, anxiety disorders, attention-deficit/hyperactivity disorder, oppositional defiant disorder). This measure can also be used as an outcome measure to assess progress. The CBCL has a Teacher's Report Form (TRF), Youth Self-Report (YSR), and Child Behavior Checklist for Ages 1½–5 (CBCL/1½–5).
Conners, 3rd Edition (Conners 3)	6–18 years (teacher and parent forms) 8–18 years (self-report form)	The Conners 3 is a behavioral rating scale that uses parent, teacher, and self-report to identify and diagnose ADHD in children and adolescents. The Conners 3 comes in a full form (which takes 20 minutes to administer) and a short form (which takes 10 minutes to administer). This measure can be completed with a pencil and paper or on a computer. In addition to assessing ADHD, the Conners 3 also assesses comorbid disorders (i.e., oppositional defiant disorder and conduct disorder) and related difficulties (i.e., learning problems, defiance, aggression, peer relations, and family relations) often associated with ADHD.
ADHD Rating Scales–5	5–17 years	The ADHD Rating Scales–5 is an 18-item parent- and teacher-rated measure used to assess youth for ADHD. Organized to align with the two diagnostic categorizes for ADHD in the *Diagnostic and Statistical Manual of Mental Disorders* (i.e., inattention and hyperactivity-impulsivity; APA, 2013), this measure provides counselors with the frequency of each symptom depending on the context (i.e., home or school). In addition, two age-specific versions (i.e., children and adolescents) have been created to identify ADHD across development. Although the ADHD Rating Scales–5 is helpful in the identification of ADHD, it also can be used to measure improvements over the course of counseling treatment.

(Continued)

Table 13.2	Common ADHD Assessment Measures (*Continued*)	

Assessment Measure or Scale	Age Range	Overview of Assessment Measure
NICHQ Vanderbilt Assessment Scales, Second Edition	6–12 years (may be used with preschool children)	The NICHQ Vanderbilt Assessment Scales, Second Edition, is a 64-item parent- and teacher-rated measure used to assess children for ADHD. The NICHQ measures the manifestation of symptoms (e.g., attention issues, makes careless detail mistakes, easily distracted), performance (e.g., reading, writing, math, relationships), other conditions (e.g., tics), and previous diagnosis and treatment (e.g., anxiety or depression diagnosis, previous medication). The assessment of symptoms can be organized into the following categories: predominantly inattentive; predominantly hyperactive; ADHD combined inattentive/hyperactive; and oppositional-defiant/conduct disorder. The NICHQ also has a corresponding follow-up measure for parents and teachers to evaluate symptomology and treatment effects.
The Test of Variables of Attention (T.O.V.A.)	4 years and older	The T.O.V.A. is a computerized performance measure that assesses attention and impulsivity in youth and adults. There are two T.O.V.A. examinations: one that measures visual processing, one that measures auditory processing. Both measure response times, consistency of the response times, how quickly youth's performance worsens, errors (or responding to a nontarget), anticipatory responses (or guessing responses), and the number of times a switch is pressed compared to the number of targets. This assessment measure can be used in conjunction with clinical interviews, behavioral measures, and symptom checklists to accurately diagnose ADHD.

ADHD has a high degree of comorbidity with oppositional defiant disorder and learning disorders. ADHD can also co-occur with anxiety, depression (e.g., disruptive mood dysregulation disorder), substance use, and conduct and intermittent explosive disorders (American Academy of Pediatrics, 2011a; APA, 2013; Nigg & Barkley, 2014). Counselors may want to consider medical evaluation to assess clients for physical conditions that are sometimes related to ADHD, such as tics, motor coordination issues, or sleep apnea, all of which may exacerbate ADHD symptoms (American Academy of Pediatrics, 2011a; Nigg & Barkley, 2014).

Counseling Interventions

Counseling interventions with children who are diagnosed with ADHD should target all relevant settings (e.g., home, school, community) and pull together multiple people and systems in the young person's life (e.g., family members, school professionals, and health professionals; Erk, 2008). Cognitive behavioral therapy (CBT), in conjunction with medication management, has the most significant impact on reducing ADHD symptomology (Döpfner et al., 2015). Counselors working with younger children who may not have the cognitive skills required to benefit from CBT should emphasize concrete behavior changes and the development of specific skills they can use to manage their ADHD symptoms (Fabiano et al., 2009). This approach generally involves training parents in behavioral interventions (e.g., reinforcements, token economies, time-outs), as well as consultation with school personnel (Antshel et al., 2011).

One additional note on the current literature on effective ADHD treatment: A body of literature suggests **neurofeedback** may be an effective treatment for adolescents who have ADHD (Lofthouse, Arnold, Hersch, Hurt, & DeBeus, 2011). Neurofeedback (e.g., electroencephalography, or EEG) is a learning process that involves youth retraining their brainwaves to self-regulate impulsivity and distractibility (Duric, Assmus, Gundersen, & Elgen, 2012). Using a cap lined with electrodes, the counselor aids youth to produce brainwave patterns that are associated with a more focused state. For example, a youth wears the electrode-filled cap to monitor his or her brainwaves while playing a video game that is programmed to shut off when the youth exhibits a diminished level of focused attention, as measured by his or her brainwaves. This form of operant conditioning allows youth to monitor and regulate their attention and distractibility. Counselors must acquire additional training before engaging in neurofeedback.

Young people learn skills in CBT counseling that they can use to manage their ADHD symptoms (e.g., hyperactivity, impulsivity, attention issues). Child-focused interventions are directed at increasing youth's cognitive and behavioral skill acquisition (e.g., attentiveness, self-regulation, self-mediation). The primary focus of CBT with children who have ADHD is enhancing impulse control, problem solving, attention span, social skills, organizational skills, and emotion regulation skills (e.g., the ability to self-soothe, the ability to manage anger and emotional reactivity). Parent training is often integrated into CBT approaches. Counselors can also coordinate treatment goals with school personnel to implement school-based interventions. Table 13.3 provides a summary of common counseling goals for children who have ADHD.

The counseling goals discussed in Table 13.3 can also be applied to work with adolescents. Figure 13.3 provides a summary of common counseling goals for adolescents who have ADHD.

Adolescents can also benefit from learning practical behavioral strategies to manage difficulties with planning, organization, and time management (Rausch et al., 2015). For example, an adolescent who struggles with organizational skills may benefit from a visual planner (e.g., calendar on a wall) or an electronic alarm system on a smartphone to prevent distractions, to remain on task, and to aid in self-regulated time management. Children can also benefit from developing their organizational skills, including the use of:

- different colored notebooks with matching folders that align with certain subjects (e.g., blue is for English, red is for math);

Table 13.3 Common Counseling Goals for Children Who Have ADHD

Parent education/ training	• Establish house rules and structure.
	• Learn to praise positive behaviors and ignore minor inappropriate behaviors.
	• Use appropriate commands. (Be brief and specific on exactly what is expected of the youth.)
	• Plan ahead to deal with disruptive behaviors in new and public settings.
	• Use time-outs consistently and appropriately.
	• Create a token economy and a daily behavior chart (e.g., with rewards and consequences).
	• Establish a school-to-home communication note system (e.g., rewarding behaviors from school at home, tracking homework completion).
School based	• Praise appropriate behaviors, and ignore minor inappropriate ones.
	• Use appropriate commands (specific, manageable).
	• Increase academic performance (e.g., deconstruct tasks, offer task choice, provide peer tutoring, use computer-assisted instruction).
	• Accommodate the youth (e.g., change placement of the desk, pair the youth with another student, allow for breaks, provide immediate/frequent feedback, require the youth to make corrections before moving on to new material).
	• Establish a behavior chart with rewards and consequences (e.g., for the individual and the whole class).
	• Use a time-out program (e.g., often only for a few minutes—less time for younger children).
	• Write a daily school-to-home note.
Child focused	• Teach social skills (e.g., communication, cooperation, being positive, participation, sharing, coping with distractions).
	• Increase the youth's ability to identify and regulate emotions.
	• Help the youth to develop peer friendships.
	• Increase organizational skills at school and at home.
	• Increase social problem solving (i.e., identifying the problem, brainstorming, choosing a solution, implementing the solution, and evaluating outcomes).
	• Decrease undesirable and antisocial behaviors (e.g., intrusiveness, aggression).

Increase Organizational and Planning Skills
- Use a documentation system (e.g., calendar, smartphone app, planner) to improve organizational skills, homework completion, and planning for academic expectations.
- Deconstruct larger assignments and projects into smaller, more manageable steps.
- Create an action plan, including a time line for any anxiety-producing, overwhelming tasks.

Reduce Distractibility
- Increase awareness of the amount of sustained attention (e.g., in minutes) the youth is able to employ before needing a break.
- Learn to divide larger tasks into chunks (e.g., smaller segments) that do not exceed the amount of sustained attention time.
- Use timers and alarms to aid in staying on task.
- Write down distractions as they occur instead of acting on them (e.g., delay distractibility).

Increase Problem-Solving Skills
- Learn and practice problem-solving techniques (e.g., identify the problem, brainstorm possible solutions, break down solutions into manageable steps, try the best solution, and assess the outcome).

Learn and Apply Cognitive Restructuring Techniques
- Identify and challenge self-critical thoughts and beliefs (e.g., consider alternative thoughts and strategies for addressing problematic, irrational thoughts).

Reduce Procrastination
- Use learned problem-solving techniques to address areas of procrastination.

Improve Communication Skills
- Learn, practice, and implement active listening skills (e.g., eye contact, rephrasing, empathic statements); allow others to finish statements before adding to the conversation.
- Learn to intercept the social cues and intentions of others.
- Learn social problem-solving techniques (e.g., generating ideas/solutions to social situations/problems).

Learn and Apply Anger and Frustration Management Techniques
- Learn and implement stress reduction techniques (e.g., progressive muscle relaxation).
- Engage others assertively, not aggressively.

FIGURE 13.3 Common Treatment Goals for Adolescents Who Have ADHD

- a homework assignment notebook (e.g., class, assignment, book and materials needed);
- a monthly assignment calendar (e.g., placed in the locker, bedroom, or kitchen);
- periodic clean-out days (e.g., desk, backpack, any place that may store assignments); and
- a specific distraction-free work location in the home where they can complete schoolwork.

Organizational tools can help young people to learn the self-regulation and self-mediation skills they need to regulate impulsivity, attention, and organization. Parents of both younger and older youth can implement academic-based interventions at home to enhance academic success (Bertin, 2011).

Clinical Toolbox 13.3

In the Pearson e-text, click here for a summary of academic-based interventions parents can incorporate in the home.

Counselors can also use CBT interventions to aid youth—especially older youth who have developed **metacognitive skills**—in developing helpful and productive thought patterns. Secondary to the symptoms associated with ADHD (e.g., forgetfulness, losing items, impulsive behaviors), young people with ADHD often develop a negative view of themselves and their capabilities. Counselors can help young people to learn to challenge these negative views and unproductive thoughts. For example, youth who have ADHD are often hesitant to engage in activities with which they have struggled in the past. Counselors can help youth to challenge and alter their thoughts by entering a new situation with a new way of thinking. In the following CBT intervention, a counselor helps a 13-year-old youth to challenge one of her negative, unproductive thoughts that is keeping her from approaching a new activity.

COUNSELOR:	So, tell me more about when your teacher asked you if you could be the leader of your team project. What kinds of things did you say to yourself about how well you thought you could do that?
CLIENT:	Well, I didn't think I could do it very well. The last time I did that I forgot the project on the bus and my whole team lost points. I can't do anything right, and I mess everything up.
COUNSELOR:	Let's look at that thought, the "I mess everything up" thought. Talk to me about times when you do things right.
CLIENT:	Well, yeah. I guess I sometimes do things right. But most of the time I forget stuff or lose things, I can't stay on track, and then I mess things up.
COUNSELOR:	Talk to me about times when you do turn your homework in, times when you participate in classroom discussions, times when you complete activities.
CLIENT:	Um, yeah. I guess I see what you're saying. A lot of what I do is right. I mean, most of the time I do things right, but it's hard to forget the times when I goof up.
COUNSELOR:	It's almost like the negative thinking is trying to bully you and get you to not even try.
CLIENT:	Yeah, it is. It is telling me I'll just make a mistake again, so why even bother.
COUNSELOR:	What advice would you give a friend whose thinking was bullying her to give up before she even tried? What would you say to her?
CLIENT:	Well, I don't know. I mean, maybe I would just say "Of course you'll fail if you don't even try."
COUNSELOR:	What else would you say to your friend whose thinking was bullying her?
CLIENT:	I guess I'd tell her to tell the thinking that just because she made a mistake before that doesn't mean she'll make a mistake again.
COUNSELOR:	Talk to me about what it would be like for you if you took that advice and changed your way of thinking.

CBT interventions are highly structured, are direct, and involve concrete interventions that can be used with young people to help them to change their thoughts and behaviors. Instead of belaboring the emotions behind a situation, a counselor working from a CBT perspective focuses on young people's thinking and how their beliefs about self and their world may be affecting their feelings and ultimately their behaviors. CBT interventions can be developmentally appropriate for young people who have ADHD and are aware of their thought patterns. When using CBT approaches, counselors take a firm, yet supportive role and redirect clients in an attempt to help them to focus on desired tasks and on working toward counseling goals. For example, an adolescent may know what needs to be done in social situations (e.g., engaging in positive social interactions) but not know how to bring it to fruition. The counselor can help the youth to identify any irrational thoughts, beliefs, or expectations that have gotten in the way, as well as assist the youth in breaking this complex behavior into smaller, more manageable tasks (e.g., communication, self-management, social problem solving). CBT therapy can enhance young people's attention span, impulse control, and problem-solving skills.

Although ADHD invites many struggles, those who have ADHD also possess unique capacitates and strengths that can be highlighted as a part of the counseling process (Young & Bramham, 2012). Figure 13.4 provides a list of potential strengths of youth who have ADHD.

A strength-based focus can, from a CBT perspective, punctuate a client's strengths and reframe struggles as positives. Many young people who have ADHD struggle with their self-esteem and feel "different" from

Are adventurous and courageous

Can be hyperfocused on certain tasks

Are creative and artistic (e.g., design, music, art)

Are optimistic and hold a strong belief in self

Are charismatic, are humorous, and have a bright personality

Have ingenuity (e.g., inventive, unique, original thinking)

Have ebullience and infectious enthusiasm (e.g., witty, entertaining, fun to be around)

Are resilient and possess learned persistence

Have a strong sense of fairness, generosity, and compassion

Are willing to take risks (e.g., are initiators, are not afraid to act)

Have spontaneity

Have high energy, passion, and the ability to motivate others

FIGURE 13.4   Potential Strengths of Youth Who Have ADHD

other kids. This emphasis on their special abilities can help them to shift how they think—and thus feel—about themselves. Using in-session opportunities to offer praise for completion of tasks, counselors can help the client to work toward counseling goals while promoting the young person's self-esteem and sense of mastery.

Parent education/training is another important component of a comprehensive treatment plan for youth who have ADHD (see Table 13.3). Parent education/training begins with a detailed account of the youth's behavioral struggles (e.g., what, when, under what conditions) and how adults respond and react to those behaviors (Antshel et al., 2011). Counselors can assist parents in exploring what conditions might be triggering, exacerbating, or even maintaining their child's behavioral struggles. In addition, counselors can use parent education/training to help parents to incorporate behavioral interventions (e.g., reinforcements such as praise, implementation of token economies, use of time-outs) that can increase their child's adaptive behaviors (Erk, 2008).

Parents should attempt to use clear and concise verbal feedback composed of both praise and corrective feedback. Corrective statements can be simple redirections concerning the youth's disruptive behaviors. These redirections should be consistently implemented, be timely or immediately administered, be clear and specifically articulated (i.e., state the behavior, consequences, and reinforcements), and address, correct, and empower the youth (Tresco, Lefler, & Power, 2010). For example, instead of a parent telling an interrupting youth, "Don't you interrupt your sister," the parent can remind the youth of the rule in the home and offer an alternative such as, "Please allow your sister to finish talking. While you wait to talk, you can listen to your sister or think about what you want to say next."

Some youth with ADHD may also have oppositional defiant disorder, and parents may struggle to manage oppositional behaviors. Counselors can teach parents to pause before making a request of the youth—to see if a choice or redirection may be offered instead—and to monitor their own reactions to the youth's behaviors by not allowing anger or irritation to color the feedback they provide (Bertin, 2011). Role-plays can be used to teach parents these skills.

Parent training should also include education about (a) ADHD symptoms and how they can be regulated, (b) reinforcing and attending to positive behaviors, (c) adopting a positive parenting style, (d) using token economies to influence behaviors, (e) using time-outs appropriately, and (f) planning for future behaviors. Counselors can explain to parents that although consistent parenting can modulate ADHD symptoms, biology is ultimately driving the behaviors, so these young people need unique parental supports (Bertin, 2011). Figure 13.5 provides a list of tips for parents of youth with ADHD.

Establish specific, measurable, and daily goals for your child.

Set clear boundaries and consequences that are practical and fit the child's situation (level of ability and understanding) and the setting (home, school, community).

Maintain a structured, predictable daily routine (e.g., transitions, free time, mealtimes, bedtimes). Consider using clocks and timers to allow your child the time needed to make the transition from one activity to an other, to complete homework, to take free-time breaks, and to get ready for bed.

Establish a private, quiet place for your child. Make sure it is not the same place the child goes for time-outs. This space is a place where the child can be away from other family members and gather his or her thoughts.

Consider what is happening in the family system (e.g., parents, siblings, changes, stressors) that may be adding to and exacerbating your child's ADHD symptoms. Take measures to limit their impact on the child.

Provide your child with clear and appropriate commands, and use additional prompts (e.g., gestures, verbal) as needed.

Highlight your child's accomplishments, strengths, and progress through the use of verbal praise (i.e., positive reinforcement).

Provide rewards (e.g., token economy, behavior chart) in the home to encourage desired behaviors.

Help your child with social interactions by speaking gently to him or her, engaging him or her in role-plays of potential social situations (e.g., meeting new people), selecting and establishing play dates (e.g., no more than one or two friends at a time), and making time to play and talk with your child (e.g., modeling appropriate social behaviors and interactions).

Use daily correspondence (e.g., daily report card, narrative report) with your child's school and teachers to increase communication between home and school.

Ignore negative behaviors that can be ignored. In situations where discipline is warranted, consider using appropriate, non-physical punishment (e.g., time-outs, removal of privileges) to discourage behaviors and provide your child with additional time to consider alternative behaviors.

Help your child to prepare for bedtime and sleep by decreasing stimuli (e.g., video games, television time), eliminating caffeine, decreasing physical activity (e.g., allowing him or her to engage in drawing, reading, or coloring), and spending time cuddling or talking with your child before bedtime. Try to create a consistent bedtime routine.

If a medical provider determines medication is warranted, work to find the right medication and the right physician for your child, and adhere to the outlined medication regime.

FIGURE 13.5 Tips for the Parents of Youth Who Have ADHD

With regard to psychopharmacotherapy, stimulant medications (e.g., Adderall, Ritalin, Concerta, Focalin) can be effective in reducing symptomology in youth who have ADHD (American Academy of Pediatrics, 2011a). Some of the common side effects of stimulants in children include headaches, abdominal pains, loss of appetite, and sleep disturbances (American Academy of Pediatrics, 2011a). Extended-release stimulants may be considered to increase medication compliance (e.g., less treatment doses needed to reach desired medication levels) and because extended-release medications last throughout the school day. Stimulant medications are addictive, and parents should review the risks and benefits of such medications with the prescribing physician. Some youth may not respond to stimulant medications or may not be able to tolerate the side effects.

Nonstimulant medications (e.g., Strattera, Intuniv, Kapvay) can also be effective in treating ADHD symptomology (American Academy of Pediatrics, 2011a). These medications have not been approved for use with preschool-age children, but they can be helpful in improving attention span, working memory, and impulse control. Table 13.4 provides a summary of the medications commonly used to treat youth who have ADHD.

Table 13.4	Common Medications Used to Treat Youth with ADHD		
Category	Types	How the Medicine Works	Advantages
Stimulants	Adderall Ritalin Concerta Focalin	Stimulant medications stimulate central nervous system activity; they stimulate cells in the brain to produce more of the deficient neurotransmitters. Stimulant medications work to decrease hyperactivity, increase attention, and increase impulse control.	• Stimulant medications are very effective (i.e., 70%–80% of youth respond to this type of treatment). • Stimulant medications tend to work quickly.
Nonstimulants	Strattera Intuniv Kapvay	Nonstimulant medications either increase the amount of norepinephrine (e.g., Strattera) or affect the receptors in the brain (e.g., Intuniv and Kapvay). They improve attention span, working memory, and impulse control.	• Nonstimulant medications tend to cause less insomnia, agitation, and appetite suppression than stimulants. • Nonstimulant medications tend to have a diminished risk of abuse and/or addiction. • Nonstimulant medications do not wear off as abruptly as stimulants.

AUTISM SPECTRUM DISORDER

Autism spectrum disorder (also referred to as autism) is a neurological disorder with both genetic and environmental risk factors (Klinger, Dawson, Barnes, & Crisler, 2014). Genetics may play a significant role in the development of autism (Klinger et al., 2014). In addition, environmental factors such as **prenatal** and **perinatal risk factors** (e.g., maternal infections, birth complications, advanced maternal/paternal age) and environmental toxins (e.g., pollutants, pesticides) may affect and influence the development of autism (Klinger et al., 2014). Although the specific cause of autism is not fully understood, the suspected link between childhood vaccinations has been largely discredited in numerous research studies (DeStefano, Price, & Weintraub, 2013).

Youth who have autism experience significant deficits in their ability to socialize and communicate with others (APA, 2013). These youth display atypical communication styles (e.g., poor eye contact, repetition of words or phrases, lack of facial affect), lack a desire for social interactions (e.g., often are more focused on an object than a person), and react atypically to stimuli in their environment (e.g., do not respond to someone calling their name or prompting; Gray & Zide, 2013). Approximately 1% of the U.S. population (APA, 2013), or 1 in 88 children in the United States, have autism spectrum disorder (Centers for Disease Control and Prevention [CDC], 2012). An autism diagnosis is 4 times more common in boys than girls. Autism is often first diagnosed in children under the age of 3 (APA, 2013), although some children may be diagnosed later in life (depending on the severity and how soon the family seeks intervention). Autism is well documented in youth throughout the world and across all social–economic classes (Kendall & Comer, 2010).

In addition to social-communication deficits, children with autism have behaviors, interests, or activities that are restrictive and repetitive in nature. For example, youth who have autism may engage in **repetitive behaviors** (e.g., insist on lining up toys) or **repetitive speech** (e.g., quoting material from television or books), have **echolalia** (e.g., repeating what is heard), be inflexible to changes in their routines, fixate on a specific interest or object (e.g., talk only about U.S. presidents or trains), or engage in stereotypical behaviors such as **self-stimulatory behaviors** (e.g., rocking back and forth, hand-flapping; APA, 2013). Along with the aforementioned symptoms, children with autism may experience limitations in cognitive and adaptive functioning. Autism can be placed on a continuum of severity related to a child's social communication and restricted, repetitive behaviors (i.e., Level 1: Requiring Support; Level 2: Requiring Substantial Support; and Level 3: Requiring Very Substantial Support; APA, 2013, p. 52). Table 13.5 presents a summary of the severity levels of autism.

Because of the wide range of symptoms, behaviors, and functioning levels associated with autism, the disorder can manifest differently, thus complicating early and accurate diagnosis. One child with autism

Table 13.5	Levels of Severity in Autism Spectrum Disorder (ASD)		
	Severity Level for ASD		
	Level 1: **Requiring Support**	**Level 2:** **Requiring Substantial** **Support**	**Level 3:** **Requiring Very** **Substantial Support**
Social communication	• Without support, noticeable social impairments and social skills deficits are apparent. • Youth has some difficulties initiating and maintaining social interactions. • Youth appears to have a diminished interest in social interactions or relationships.	• Youth has marked deficits in verbal and nonverbal communication. • Youth has limited interest in and initiation of social interactions. • Youth has reduced or abnormal responses to social cues/overtures from others.	• Youth has severe deficits in verbal and nonverbal communication. • Youth has very limited social interactions. • Youth has minimal responses to social cues/overtures.
Restricted/ repetitive behaviors	• Rituals and repetitive behaviors cause interference with functioning in at least one setting. • Youth resists attempts by others to interrupt or redirect restricted/repetitive behaviors. • Youth has difficulty making the transition from one activity to another.	• Restricted/repetitive behaviors occur frequently enough to be observed and interfere with functioning in multiple settings. • Distress is apparent when restricted/repetitive behaviors are interfered with or interrupted. • Youth has difficulty with any change in schedule, environment, and/or routine.	• Youth displays fixation, preoccupation, and restricted/repetitive behaviors that markedly interfere in all areas of functioning and settings. • Marked distress is apparent when restricted/repetitive behaviors are interfered with or interrupted; redirection is difficult. • Youth experiences extreme distress with changes in the schedule, environment, and/or routine.

Note: Adapted from APA (2013).

might present with a high intelligence quotient (IQ) score yet struggle with interpersonal interactions and communication (i.e., engaging and playing with other children). Another child with autism may have a low IQ score, have more severe symptomology related to social interactions and communication, and manifest more severe behavior problems (e.g., self-injury, aggressive outbursts).

Counselor Considerations

Early identification and intervention for autism are critical and can optimize long-term functioning. Some of the signs that suggest a young person may have autism include not meeting normal developmental milestones in a timely fashion, having limited eye contact, having restricted social interactions, and experiencing limited language development. The diagnosis of autism is based on observable behaviors. Counselors must consider that these behaviors are not just isolated actions but a form of communication (Sicile-Kira, 2014). Behaviors—even confounding behaviors—are a means of communicating, especially for youth who are nonverbal. For example, consider a young child who is nonverbal and continually disrobes. This disrobing behavior may be the child's attempt to convey or communicate with the adults around him. Thus, if counselors can identify a pattern (e.g., disrobing only happens when certain clothes are worn), then they can determine that the youth is having a tactile response or sensitivity to a certain cloth or brand of fabric softener. Therefore, counselors should assume all behaviors communicate a message, even when words are not used.

Children with autism often struggle with sensory processing problems—that is, processing information acquired through their senses. Some children may be **overly sensitive** (e.g., unable to tolerate loud noises, bright lights, or touch), whereas others may be **undersensitive** (e.g., extremely tolerant of pain, unaware of their own physical strength, less sensitive to personal boundaries by touching others excessively). In connection with sensory processing issues, youth with autism often experience physical and emotional dysregulation. In many cases, young people's inability to regulate their emotions results in tantrums and/or acting-out behaviors (e.g., verbal outbursts, physical aggression), thus exacerbating already strained interpersonal interactions and relationships. Counselors will need to help parents and youth to strike the balance between trying to change the environment versus changing the youth's behavior (Sicile-Kira, 2014). For example, if a child with sensory processing difficulty reacts with increased agitation (e.g., tantrums) around fluorescent lighting, it may be helpful to develop alternative behaviors (e.g., time-outs, going for a walk) rather than attempt to eliminate fluorescent lighting in every setting.

Counselors should be sensitive to the fact that raising youth with autism can be difficult for parents. These youth may require a great deal of care and attention. They do not typically reciprocate love and affection the same ways other children do, and they can react strongly when family routines and activities are disrupted and altered. In addition, siblings of youth with autism may struggle if they have awkward social interactions with their sibling, experience the stress of their parents, or receive less attention from their parents because they are asked to be caregivers for their sibling (Sicile-Kira, 2014). Because autism affects the whole family, family involvement and investment are critical to counseling's success. Counselors should integrate family members and the young person's support system into treatment and strive to validate their experiences.

Youth who have autism have deficits in communication, so counseling is not always done through traditional talk-therapy formats. Alternative communication vehicles may be used, and youth with more severe limitations in communication may use **augmentative and alternative communication** (AAC) devices to initiate conversations and support their daily activities (e.g., communicating basic needs such as hunger, needing to use the bathroom). Parent training and education can focus on verbal communication, but behavioral interventions (e.g., applied behavioral analysis) generally are the treatment of choice. The treatment goals for youth with autism typically include addressing sensory processing challenges (e.g., over- or underreacting to sensory stimuli), increasing communication (e.g., nonverbal, speech and language), altering socially inappropriate behaviors (e.g., head banging, aggression), increasing social skills and relationships, and increasing adaptive functioning (e.g., self-care, occupational therapy, academic skills).

Assessment of Autism Spectrum Disorder

When assessing for autism, counselors should conduct thorough clinical interviews that take into account the young person's developmental milestones, any history of abnormal behavior, a three-generation family history, the youth's medical history, and any mental health treatments and their effectiveness (Butler, Youngs, Roberts, & Hellings, 2012). Standard interviewing assessments such as the Autism Diagnostic Interview–Revised (ADI-R; Le Couteur, Lord, & Rutter, 2003) are an effective means of assessing autism in children as young as 36 months. Autism assessments historically have relied on parent interviews, as well as retrospective and collateral reports of the child's behavior; however, gathering collateral reports and historical data can take time and delay diagnosis. Advances in the development of structured behavioral observation measures (e.g., Childhood Autism Rating Scale, Second Edition [CARS-2; Schopler, Van Bourgondien, Wellman, & Love, 2010]; The Autism Diagnostic Observation Schedule, Second Edition [ADOS-2; Lord, Luyster, Gotham, & Guthrie, 2012]) have facilitated quicker and more reliable diagnosis by the second year of life through evaluation of communication, social interactions, and play (Kendall & Comer, 2010). Table 13.6 provides a summary of several autism assessment measures.

Children with autism frequently have co-occurring mental disorders (APA, 2013), and many children with autism (i.e., more than 31%) have intellectual disabilities (Butler et al., 2012; Klinger et al., 2014). Because of their communication struggles, this population's ability to self-report additional symptoms may be limited, and caregivers are important sources of information. Young people who have autism may also have ADHD and/or developmental coordination disorder, as well as various medical problems (e.g., epilepsy, sleep issues, constipation; APA, 2013). Counselors should be aware of these co-occurring mental and physical disorders and ensure the client has a comprehensive treatment plan that addresses all of his or her needs.

Table 13.6	Summary of Commonly Used Autism Assessment Measures	
Assessment Measure	Age Range	Overview of Assessment Measure
Autism Diagnostic Interview–Revised (ADI-R)	18–36 months and up	The ADI-R is a 93-item semi-structured clinical interview that caregivers of children complete to assess for autism spectrum disorder. The ADI-R focuses on three main areas: quality of social interactions, use of language and communication, and restrictive and repetitive (e.g., stereotyped) behaviors and interests. In addition, the measure aids in treatment planning by assessing areas such as self-injury, memory, motor skills, and overactivity. The interview often requires 90 minutes to administer.
Childhood Autism Rating Scales, Second Edition (CARS-2)	24 months and up	The CARS-2 is a 15-item observational measure that comes in two forms: a standard and a high-functioning version (e.g., verbally fluent, above 80 IQ score). In addition, both forms assess ability to relate to people, use of body and/or objects in the correct way, ability to adapt to change, visual response, listening response, nonverbal communication, activity level, intellectual response, and ability to imitate. This measure can be used for assessment and for evaluating counseling progress.
Autism Diagnostic Observation Schedule, Second Edition (ADOS-2)	12 months and up	The ADOS-2 is a semi-structured observational measure that aids in the assessment of autism spectrum disorder across age, development, and language skill. The ADOS-2 assesses communication, social interaction, and repetitive and restrictive behaviors by eliciting behaviors through various controlled activities (e.g., play, cartoons, demonstration tasks) via the use of interactive stimuli (e.g., toys, dolls, blocks). Differing modules are provided depending on the child's verbal fluency and age.

Counseling Interventions

Counseling approaches for youth with autism should be focused on addressing specific symptoms and increasing adaptive functioning. A comprehensive treatment approach that combines applied behavior analysis (ABA) interventions and social skills training with supplemental therapies (e.g., educational, speech, and occupational therapies) and parent training is most effective in treating youth who have autism (Butler et al., 2012). ABA is widely accepted as the gold standard of treatment when working with children who have autism (e.g., Boutot & Hume, 2012; Matson et al., 2012). ABA is rooted in Skinner's behavioral principle of operant conditioning, which is rooted in the concept that any behavior can be changed through differential reinforcement. ABA treatment principles can be applied to either increase or decrease the occurrence of any behavior. For example, ABA can be used to reduce the occurrence of a child's tantrums or outbursts and increase the occurrence of adaptive behaviors and learned social-communication skills.

ABA helps a child to break down a task into smaller steps and, through the reinforcement of adaptive behaviors, teaches the child the sequence of actions needed to complete the behavior. For example, teaching a youth with autism to brush her teeth may reinforce the following steps: finding her toothbrush, finding the toothpaste, opening up the toothpaste, putting the right amount of toothpaste onto the toothbrush, brushing her top teeth, brushing her bottom teeth, brushing her tongue, spitting out toothpaste, rinsing her mouth with water, and putting all items away.

The wide scope of ABA allows counselors to engage children and families in addressing the problem behaviors often connected with autism (e.g., communication; social skills; adaptive living, including eating, dressing, toileting, and personal self-care), as well as specific problems that may be unique to the youth. The versatility of ABA allows counselors to deliver treatment in a group or family setting or one-on-one. ABA can also be used in a host of settings (e.g., school, home, clinic). For example, a counselor can deliver ABA in a group setting and include children who do not have autism to model adaptive social interactions. **Peer training** is often integrated into ABA treatment. Table 13.7 provides a summary of several ABA techniques and examples of their application.

There are numerous comprehensive behavioral treatment models derived from ABA, including Pivotal Response Treatment (PRT; Koegel, Koegel, Vernon, & Brookman-Frazee, 2010), the Early Start Denver Model (ESDM; Rogers & Dawson, 2009), and the Early Intensive Behavioral Intervention (EIBI; Smith, 2010). Table 13.8 provides a summary of interventions that have been derived from ABA approaches, along with a general overview of each.

Table 13.7 Add Continued line.

ABA Technique	Brief Summary	Example
Discrete trial training (DTT)	DTT attempts to decrease problem behaviors and increase adaptive behaviors. DTT involves (a) identifying and presenting a behavior, (b) providing a prompt, (c) allowing the child to respond to the prompt, (d) providing a consequence, and (e) after a pause, beginning another trial.	The counselor presents a behavior (e.g., to pick up the hair brush), provides a prompt (e.g., "Please pick up the hairbrush"), allows the child to respond (e.g., either by picking up the brush or not), provides a consequence (i.e., either reinforcement or a correction), and after a short pause (i.e., inter-trial interval), begins another trial. Once this behavior is mastered (e.g., picking up the hairbrush), the counselor can introduce another associated behavior (e.g., using the brush to brush hair) following the same process.
Joint attention intervention	This technique increases the child's ability to respond to the social requests of others. Two individuals focus on an activity, object, or each other at the same time. Sharing an activity is an essential component of communication and can be learned.	The counselor brings attention to an object, such as a set of toy blocks (e.g., the counselor verbally prompts or places his or her hand close to the youth's line of sight and points to the object). The counselor should select something that the youth may want to play with because he or she will engage better with such items. The counselor then applies a specific skill (e.g., sharing) he or she would like to address with this intervention.
Modeling	One person demonstrates the behavior that the counselor wants the child to engage in. Anyone can model these adaptive behaviors (e.g., the counselor, peers, parents, siblings).	The counselor demonstrates a behavior (e.g., asking for a toy and waiting patiently) to teach the child a predetermined skill. The youth must be engaged in the observation. The counselor may videotape a play interaction between two toy figures that involves an adaptive skill such as sharing. The counselor can then have the child watch this taped play interaction. Finally, the child can recreate this play interaction—including verbal dialogue and actions—with the provided toys.
Naturalistic teaching strategies	This technique engages the child in his or her natural environment to teach functional skills. The counselor can use the child's natural environment or objects in it to engage the child and increase his or her adaptive functioning.	The counselor selects a ball in the youth's natural play area. The counselor uses language to describe it ("This is a ball; it is round") and shows the action of it (rolls the ball back and forth). After a brief pause, the counselor asks the child to repeat these actions. The counselor can provide running comments on what is happening ("You ask for the ball so nicely"; "You are doing a great job rolling the ball back and forth"; "I love to see you play like this").

(Continued)

Table 13.7	(*Continued*)	
ABA Technique	**Brief Summary**	**Example**
Peer training	Because youth with autism often spend less time interacting with others, this technique allows them to spend time with accessible and competent peers, who model social interactions in intentional ways. This can affect the youth's ability to initiate and interact socially.	The counselor can use a group setting, peer networks, and peer-mediated social interactions to increase awareness and use of social skills. The counselor needs to plan these interactions thoughtfully by training peers how to get the attention of the youth, facilitate sharing, model appropriate play, and help to organize activities. The counselor may decide to integrate a few children without social skills deficits into a group setting to aid those with deficits by demonstrating the target behaviors in the context of the group.
Schedules	This technique involves following a task list (pictures or words) through a series of steps to complete an activity.	The counselor shows the youth a group of sequential pictures depicting the steps for preparing for bedtime (e.g., changing clothes, brushing teeth, washing face).
Self-management	The child regulates his or her reactions or behaviors by recording each occurrence of the target behavior.	The counselor aids the child in recording the occurrence of a desired behavior in some concrete, meaningful way (e.g., a behavior chart placed in a prominent place). The youth can place a star on the behavior chart for each day he completes his chores, which may include cleaning his room and helping with dinner cleanup.
Story-based interventions	The counselor shares stories that present situations with the specific target behaviors.	The counselor shows a visual narrative depiction of the target behavior (e.g., introducing oneself to a new person, keeping hands to oneself). These stories deconstruct the complicated behaviors into small tasks, thus teaching the child through a narrative/story context the who, when, why, and how of social interactions and how they can be strengthened.

Note: Adapted from National Autism Center (2009).

Table 13.8	Examples of Treatment Models Derived from ABA
ABA Approach	**Description**
Pivotal Response Treatment (PRT)	PRT is a child-centered, play-based ABA approach that focuses on naturally occurring reinforcements in critical (i.e., pivotal) areas such as motivation, self-management, reacting to cues, and initiation of social interactions. These areas are pivotal because they become the focus for improvements in communication, interpersonal interactions, behavior, and social skills.
Early Start Denver Model (ESDM)	ESDM is a play-based form of ABA for younger children (e.g., 1–4 years old) who have more severe learning challenges. ESDM involves teaching developmental skills through a set of teaching procedures. It is an intensive program, sometimes requiring 20 hours of participation per week. It focuses on teaching developmental skills and uses play as the medium of engagement. ESDM focuses on creating good therapeutic relationships with the youth, highlighted by positive interactions, language development, and an increase in communication in the context of play.
Early Intensive Behavioral Intervention (EIBI)	EIBI involves one-on-one focused coaching/interacting with a child and typically requires 20–40 hours per week of intensive intervention. EIBI aims to increase a child's communication skills, social skills, and adaptive functioning through constant and consistent corrective responses and reinforcements (e.g., DTT) in the child's natural environment. Parents or caregivers are also incorporated into treatment because they are critical to the long-term success of this intervention.

Another autism treatment approach—often used in conjunction with ABA—is **Floortime** (Greenspan & Wieder, 2009). Floortime is a developmental, relationship-oriented, and play-based approach for treating children who have autism. This approach helps children to increase their communication and interpersonal skills. As the name (Floortime) suggests, an adult (e.g., counselor, parent) will join the child in developmentally appropriate play. More opportunities are gradually added to increase communication and interpersonal skills. As the adult follows the child in his or her play, the adult can slowly direct and redirect the child to increasingly more complex interactions using new play, media, and materials, thus increasing the child's circle of communication (e.g., a look, words, sounds, gestures; Greenspan & Wieder, 2009). For example, if the child begins to pound his hand on a toy truck, the adult could tap the top of a toy car. Once the child visually responds to the adult, the adult may place the car next to the child's truck and say, "Let's drive these trucks over there to the work site and get to work." Floortime is intended to increase a child's interest in the world, communication, social engagement, and emotion identification. In particular, this play-based approach seems to be effective with younger children who have autism (Casenhiser, Shanker, & Stieben, 2013; Pajareya & Nopmaneejumruslers, 2011).

Although parental education (e.g., about the disorder, techniques) is very important, counselors must also consider providing parents with emotional and social support. Parents often go through the diagnosis and treatment process with a sense of denial, followed by a sense of grief; they need to let go of some of the expectations they had of their child and make the transition to a new way of thinking about their child and his or her future. Many parents feel frustrated because of their child's frequent difficult behaviors (e.g., tantrums, aggressive behaviors, repetitive behaviors). They often feel alienated and perceive others as judging them. Parents may also experience a lack of support and struggle to find much-needed respite. The impacts of raising a child with autism (e.g., on intimate relationships, other siblings, and extended family) can also be significant and stressful (Ludlow, Skelly, & Rohleder, 2012). Counselors should consider connecting parents with other parents in similar situations for additional social support, for social comparison (e.g., evaluation of self and others), to express negative emotions and share common experiences, and to learn about others' successes (Hodges & Dibb, 2010; Ludlow et al., 2012). However, many parents struggle to identify and use social support systems because of time constraints and lack of resources (e.g., transportation, childcare). Counselors can aid parents in finding supports, respite, and community resources that may support them and their children.

With regard to psychopharmacotherapy, there are no medications identified to treat autism per se, but various medications can address symptoms associated with autism (e.g., self-injury, anxiety, depression, hyperactivity). For example, in situations where youth display severe agitation, aggressive behaviors, or impulse control problems, physicians may prescribe antipsychotic medications (e.g., risperidone, aripiprazole; CDC, 2013).

INTELLECTUAL DISABILITIES

Youth who have **intellectual disabilities** have below-average general intelligence (e.g., below or around an IQ score of 70), limited adaptive functioning, and a greater need for assistance in meeting the demands of everyday life (APA, 2013). These limitations or difficulties primarily present when a child is engaging in academic or intellectual pursuits, "such as reasoning, problem solving, planning, abstract thinking, judgment, academic learning, and learning from experience" (APA, 2013, p. 31).

The prevalence rate for intellectual disabilities in the general population is 1% (APA, 2013). Intellectual disabilities are categorized on a continuum of severity (i.e., mild, moderate, severe, and profound). Of those children diagnosed with intellectual disabilities, the majority fall in the mild category (89%), some in the moderate category (7%), few in the severe category (3%), and only a very few in the profound category (1%; Kendall & Comer, 2010). Although intellectual disabilities affect youth from all cultures and ethnicities, more boys (2 to 1), more African Americans, and more youth from lower socioeconomic backgrounds are diagnosed with intellectual disabilities (Kendall & Comer, 2010).

Genetic and environmental circumstances can increase the risk of developing an intellectual disability. For example, genetic conditions (e.g., Down syndrome, fragile X syndrome) and prenatal/perinatal environments (e.g., alcohol consumption, drug use, poor nutrition, smoking, radiation, infections) have been associated with an increased risk of being diagnosed with an intellectual disability (APA, 2013; Kendall & Comer, 2010).

Counselor Considerations

To meet the criteria for the diagnosis of intellectual disability, youth must have an IQ score that is two standard deviations below the mean average on an intelligence examination and an impairment in **adaptive functioning** (e.g., communication, socialization, independent living) that occurs across multiple life domains (e.g., home, school, community). Although standardized intelligence tests are highly debated, their use is required to determine and apply an intellectual disability diagnosis. When diagnosing an intellectual disability, counselors should always conduct a thorough clinical assessment of adaptive functioning and consider this information in conjunction with standardized intelligence test scores. Assessment across the following three adaptive functioning domains can help in determining if a young person has an intellectual disability:

- *Conceptual skills* (e.g., reading, writing, communication, language, money, time, numbers)
- *Social skills* (e.g., interpersonal skills, following social norms or rules, understanding motives of others, social problem solving, social responsibility, gullibility)
- *Practical life skills* (e.g., safety, use of schedules, daily living skills such as bathing, dressing, and feeding; APA, 2013)

As previously stated, intellectual disabilities range on a continuum of severity, with varying levels of intelligence and adaptive functioning. They are categorized into four levels of severity: mild, moderate, severe, and profound. Table 13.9 provides a summary of characteristics that relate to each level of severity.

Table 13.9   Intellectual Disabilities: Characteristics of the Levels of Severity

Level of Severity	Characteristics
Mild	These children will experience some difficulties with academic skills (e.g., reading, writing, mathematics) and may require one-on-one assistance to meet classroom and grade-level expectations. Although these young people typically require special education services, they may still have some functional academic skills. Adolescents may experience increased difficulties with executive functioning (e.g., cognitive flexibility, planning, problem solving) and struggle with abstract thinking. Social interactions may appear more immature (e.g., language, conversation) than age appropriate, and these children often struggle to regulate their emotions. This immaturity in judgment may also contribute to these children being more readily manipulated by other students. In most cases, these children are able to perform age-appropriate personal care (e.g., showering, brushing teeth).
Moderate	These children may experience some progress in academic skills (e.g., reading, writing, mathematics), but it will be slow, and they will not be able to master most traditional academic concepts (Witwer et al., 2014). Middle and high school academic course work becomes increasingly difficult and more frustrating. Social communication exists, but social skills are less complex than those of same-age peers. The ability to read social cues and make decisions is often limited, so these children require significant social support. Although these children are able to perform daily living activities, significant time and instruction are required for them to be independent and successful.
Severe	These children are unable to read, write, problem solve, and/or understand concepts that involve numbers (e.g., math, time, money; Witwer et al., 2014). Although some basic social and communication skills may be present, limited vocabulary and spoken language restrict the youth's social relationships and communication. Because of the supervision level these children require, family members and caregivers are the primary source of social interactions. These youth require a great deal of support with daily living activities (e.g., eating, dressing, bathing), and they are unable to make responsible decisions or independently care for themselves.

(Continued)

Table 13.9	Intellectual Disabilities: Characteristics of the Levels of Severity (*Continued*)
Level of Severity	Characteristics
Profound	Significant motor and sensory impairments often limit these children's ability to use objects functionally (e.g., use a brush to brush hair). These children typically have extremely limited use and understanding of language and symbolic communication (i.e., nonverbal). Communication is primarily nonverbal. These children may respond predictably to gestures and cues. Co-occurring sensory and physical impairments may prevent these children from engaging in social activities. They typically require constant and daily aid from family members and caregivers to meet basic physical needs and ensure safety. These children may be able to participate in some concrete work tasks if no co-occurring sensory or physical impairments exist.

Note: Adapted from APA (2013) and Witwer, Lawton, & Aman (2014).

Assessment of Intellectual Disabilities

To confirm the diagnosis of intellectual disability, counselors need to assess adaptive functioning—that is, the ability to engage in everyday life skills independently—along with IQ score. A youth may have a below-average IQ score yet be able to accomplish most everyday life activities and thus not meet the criteria for an intellectual disability diagnosis. In addition, research suggests that intelligence is more fluid than previously hypothesized and that schooling and education-related programming may affect intelligence (Nisbett et al., 2012). Although differences do appear to exist based on race, ethnicity, and gender, some of that variability may be attributed to environment (e.g., school, educational resources, home situation) and learning opportunities. Thus, youth may, through educational or environmental interventions (e.g., reasoning skills, cognitive exercises), be empowered and make progress (Nisbett et al., 2012). Counselors, especially in the school environment, can be critical in advocating for sufficient and comprehensive educational interventions for at-risk youth.

Although a standardized intellectual test (e.g., Wechsler Intelligence Scale for Children, Fifth Edition [WISC-V; Wechsler, 2014]; Stanford-Binet Intelligence Scales, Fifth Edition [SB5; Roid, 2003]; Kaufman Brief Intelligence Test, Second Edition [KBIT-2; Kaufman & Kaufman, 2004]) is required to diagnose an intellectual disability, some children may warrant an assessment that uses a nonverbal measure of intelligence (e.g., Leiter-3 International Performance Scale, Third Edition [Roid, Miller, Pomplun, & Kock, 2013]).

Clinical Toolbox 13.4

In the Pearson e-text, click here to review a summary of several of the most commonly used measures of intelligence.

Children diagnosed with intellectual disabilities are at a higher risk of co-occurring mental health diagnoses, such as disruptive behavior disorders (i.e., conduct and/or impulse control disorders), anxiety disorders, ADHD, and depressive disorders (Witwer et al., 2014). In addition, these children may engage in self-injurious behaviors (e.g., head banging; Kendall & Comer, 2010). Having a child with an intellectual disability can be very stressful for families because of the multiple needs of this population. Counselors should take the family's needs into account when working with these youth (Tsai & Wang, 2009).

Although intellectual impairments and disabilities bear some resemblance to and may even be comorbid with autism spectrum disorder, youth display differences in repetitive behaviors, social interactions, and/or the ability to communicate. In young children, these differences may be difficult to differentiate, especially in situations where children have not yet developed language (APA, 2013). Counselors must learn to differentiate between intellectual disabilities and autism spectrum disorder, taking special heed to recognize and thoroughly examine any discrepancies "between the level of social-communicative skills and other intellectual skills" (APA, 2013, p. 58).

Counseling Interventions

Similar to autism, early identification and intervention (e.g., in the first 5 years of life) for intellectual disabilities is important and can optimize long-term functioning (Witwer et al., 2014). Youth with intellectual disabilities often become involved in counseling secondary to the following concerns: emotional and/or behavior disturbances, development of adaptive skills in home and school settings, and/or difficulties with daily living skills (e.g., personal care). Counseling approaches and interventions vary and depend heavily on the youth's level of intellectual disability severity and his or her adaptive functioning. Young people with moderate to severe intellectual disabilities often benefit from behavioral approaches (e.g., ABA), whereas youth with mild intellectual disabilities may benefit from an integrated approach including cognitive and behavioral interventions (Kendall & Comer, 2010).

Case management—collaborative, comprehensive care coordination that meets the health care needs of an individual or family—is one of the most essential counseling components when working with youth with intellectual disabilities. Counselors can link clients and their families to various community resources to meet their needs. Comprehensive services for children with intellectual disabilities generally include placement opportunities (e.g., living arrangements that place an emphasis on the least restrictive environment needed to meet the child's needs), counseling interventions (e.g., ABA, behavioral treatments), and school-based educational interventions (e.g., special education [either inclusion or segregated classrooms]; Kendall & Comer, 2010).

Family involvement is crucial in counseling children with intellectual disabilities. Collaborations with parents will aid them in encouraging their youth's abilities. Family involvement often increases the probability that a young person will learn, implement, and integrate skills into real-life situations. In addition, counselors can assist parents with any educational and vocational concerns they have for their child.

Behavior therapy and CBT with modifications are effective counseling approaches with this population (Campbell, Robertson, & Jahoda, 2014; Kendall & Comer, 2010). Counseling interventions for higher functioning youth often include social skills training, problem solving, feelings identification and expression, and managing interpersonal relationships. Counselors may also use ABA (Campbell et al., 2014).

Counselors should consider that insight-oriented and purely humanistic approaches are less effective with those who have intellectual disabilities (Kendall & Comer, 2010). Active and concrete counseling approaches can help children with intellectual disabilities to capture concepts and ideas. For example, counselors can implement visual schedules, token economies (i.e., reward systems that use symbols or tokens), and other forms of positive reinforcement (e.g., verbal praise, rewards) to increase the use of adaptive behaviors. Another example of how counselors can be concrete in sessions is to visually write or draw the outline for each counseling session on a piece of paper and review with the client the important concepts that will be addressed in a given session. Providing frequent summaries during a session and asking clients to explain, in their own words, what they are learning may also be helpful. In addition, clients should practice any identified skills during the session.

Counselors might also model how the skill will look and then ask the client to try it. Through the use of role-play, the counselor can slowly walk through a social situation identifying an emotion (e.g., anger), expressing that emotion appropriately (e.g., looking directly at another and saying "I was angry when you did not listen to me"), and managing intense feelings in relation to behaviors (e.g., not stomping or hitting anything, waiting for the other person to verbally respond before saying anything else). Figure 13.6 provides a summary of counseling considerations for youth with intellectual disabilities.

Most children who have an intellectual disability benefit from medication that addresses specific behavior problems and/or emotional conditions associated with the intellectual disability (e.g., impulsive behaviors, self-injury, anxiety, agitation; Kendall & Comer, 2010). Youth with intellectual disabilities who display impulsivity, attention difficulties, and/or hyperactivity are often prescribed methylphenidate (Ritalin; Ageranioti-Bélanger et al., 2012). The antipsychotic medication risperidone (Risperdal) or olanzapine (Zyprexa) is often used to decrease aggression and/or self-injurious behaviors (Ageranioti-Bélanger et al., 2012). In most situations, behavioral approaches are used in conjunction with psychopharmacotherapy.

Consider bringing in someone the youth knows well—at least for the first few sessions, to build rapport and ascertain an accurate picture of what is occurring at home and school.

Consider meeting more frequently than once per week and meeting for shorter periods of time.

Consider spending more time than usual building trust and rapport with the youth. Often, these young people have been bullied, made fun of, and disrespected by others, and they may be apprehensive about meeting someone new.

Use concrete language (e.g., reduce use of abstractions and metaphors), and limit the use of skills that involve multistep directions. If talk therapy is used, conversations and interchanges need to be slowed down to allow youth time to process what was discussed, think about it, and express themselves.

Plan to be directive, and incorporate teaching and modeling into counseling sessions, including repetition and reminders of learned and practiced skills.

Consider that expressive language in youth with intellectual disabilities is an area of growth; receptive language may be more developed. Therefore, counselors should not underestimate what a youth understands and should make a regular effort to assess what the youth comprehends.

Youth with intellectual disabilities often have learned to please others. Therefore, counselors will need to make sure that they are being understood, even if the youth is providing nonverbal communication (e.g., nodding).

Consider using action-oriented counseling techniques, such as role-plays, expressive arts, and objects (e.g., toys, puppets, dolls) to depict what has occurred in a given situation.

Consider that youth will often act out their feelings and emotions (e.g., pound chair or stomp feet when angry, cry or be despondent when sad, hug or be excessively talkative when happy).

Consider homework that is specific, concrete, and can be done between sessions. In some cases, it is helpful to ask for assistance from a family member to support the homework assignment.

FIGURE 13.6   Youth with Intellectual Disabilities: Counseling Considerations

SPECIFIC LEARNING DISORDERS

The essence of a specific learning disorder is a discrepancy between a child's performance on an intelligence test and his or her performance in a specific area of academic achievement (Kendall & Comer, 2010). According to the *Diagnostic and Statistical Manual of Mental Disorders,* Fifth Edition *(DSM-5)* criteria for a specific learning disorder, the discrepancy is significantly below the expected grade level or age of the child (APA, 2013). Although all youth benefit from early diagnosis and treatment, many youth are not identified, and they manage these learning impairments by avoiding activities that demand some proficiency in the academic area with which they struggle (e.g., reading, arithmetic; Gross, 2011).

Specific learning disorders are fairly common, with an estimated 5% to 15% of school-age children experiencing a learning disorder related to reading, writing, and/or mathematics (APA, 2013). Learning disorders are more frequently diagnosed in boys (i.e., 2 to 1), and the most common type of learning disorder is a reading disorder (Kendall & Comer, 2010). Genetic and environmental factors appear to have combined influences on the prevalence of specific learning disorders, especially in families with histories of first-degree relatives with specific learning disorders, reading difficulties (e.g., dyslexia), and deficits in parental literacy skills (APA, 2013).

As a point of clarification, **learning disability** is a legal term used to refer to someone who experiences significant impairments in academic functioning (Rausch et al., 2015). Although the terms *learning disorder* and *learning disability* are often used interchangeably, *specific learning disorder* is the term that refers to the actual mental disorder, according to the *DSM-5* (APA, 2013).

Counselor Considerations

Children with learning disorders have difficulties with learning the fundamental academic skills needed to be successful in educational settings. These academic skills involve children's ability to listen, speak, read, write, and do mathematics (e.g., arithmetic, binary operations). Learning disorders capture difficulties for children that occur in the following areas/domains (APA, 2013):

- *Reading and fluency* (e.g., reading words incorrectly, reading slowly with tremendous hesitation, trying to guess the correct word when reading)
- *Reading comprehension* (e.g., not understanding the sequence, the plot, the meaning, and/or the inferences being made in the narrative)
- *Spelling* (e.g., frequently adding, omitting, or substituting consonants or vowels into the spelling of a word)
- *Written expression* (e.g., lacking clarity of ideas in writings, making multiple grammatical errors, having poor sentence or paragraph organization)
- *Arithmetic calculations* (e.g., lacking an understanding of numbers, numerical relationships, and how to do simple calculations)
- *Mathematic reasoning* (e.g., having difficulty solving mathematical problems and understanding mathematical concepts and application)

Although there is variability in terms of how a child's relationship with a learning disorder develops, most children with learning disorders follow a similar developmental process. Children with learning disorders often have (a) an initial failure in a specific academic skill, (b) an increased sense of doubt in their abilities, leading to lowered self-worth, and (c) decreased effort in future endeavors related to the academic skill (Kendall & Comer, 2010). Parents may be slow to accept or even react to these learning difficulties, believing their child will naturally overcome these impairments in due time (Gross, 2011). Counselors can be helpful in educating and supporting parents and children as they seek the educational and support services they require.

Assessment of Learning Disorders

The assessment and diagnosis of a learning disorder are often conducted and specified by school psychologists working in an educational setting. These professionals compile teachers' and school counselors' observations, the youth's responses to academic interventions, standardized test scores, and a complete history (e.g., family, educational, medical, developmental) before diagnosing a learning disorder.

When assessing a child for a learning disorder, counselors should consider that a child cannot be diagnosed with a learning disorder if that child meets the criteria for an intellectual disability, external factors are affecting the learning disorder (e.g., lack of education, absenteeism, consistently poor instruction, learning in a second language), or if a neurological disorder (e.g., pediatric stroke, traumatic brain injury) is the cause of the learning disorder (APA, 2013). In terms of assessment, the use of standardized assessments is critical. Standardized measures allow the counselor to gain a more complete and objective picture of the client's academic functioning, thus allowing the counselor to plan appropriate educational and counseling options.

Standardized measures that are useful in ascertaining an accurate diagnosis in children with learning disorders include the Scholastic Reading Inventory (SRI; Salvia & Ysseldyke, 1998); the Woodcock Reading Mastery Tests, Third Edition (WRMT-III; Woodcock, 2011); the Gray Oral Reading Test, Fifth Edition (GORT-5; Wiederholt & Bryant, 2012); and the Wide Range Achievement Test 4 (WRAT 4: Wilkinson & Robertson, 2006). Although standardized measures must be used to diagnose learning disorders, counselors must also be mindful that these measures have frequently been criticized because certain populations (e.g., youth from low-income areas, African and Hispanic Americans) often score lower regardless of their ability levels (Martin, 2012).

Clinical Toolbox 13.5

In the Pearson e-text, click here to review a summary of several commonly used learning disorder assessments.

Complicating the clinical presentation of learning disorders is the fact that they are often comorbid (e.g., co-occurring) with other neurological disorders that involve emotional and behavior problems. In particular, children with learning disabilities often have co-occurring neurodevelopmental disorders (e.g., ADHD, autism;

Kendall & Comer, 2010). In addition, learning disorders are sometimes associated with certain childhood medical conditions (e.g., epilepsy, central nervous system infections, neurological problems; Kendall & Comer, 2010). Counselors must also differentiate learning disorders from other neurodevelopmental disorders such as intellectual disabilities. In cases where symptoms of ADHD are present, counselors need to assess if the young person's learning issues are due to deficits in ability to learn (i.e., specific learning disorder) or pertain better to deficits in performing (e.g., inattention, impulsivity, hyperactivity; APA, 2013).

Counseling Interventions

Learning disorders are addressed in the general education setting through special education accommodations. If a child does meet the criteria for a learning disorder, he or she may qualify for an **individualized education program** (IEP) or a **504 plan**, in which special accommodations and modifications are outlined and provided by the educational institution (Swanson, Harris, & Graham, 2013). School professionals (e.g., school psychologist, school counselors) attempt to increase youth's academic success, often providing interventions that aim to increase academic competency, achievement, and educational functioning. School counselors may (a) provide short-term, goal-directed individual or group counseling, (b) advocate for these students in the school and community, (c) consult and collaborate with school professionals and families about adaptations and modification needed in the classroom for personal and academics success, and (d) develop and implement academic and transition plans for students with specific learning disorders (American School Counselor Association [ASCA], 2013). Mental health counselors frequently complement these services by addressing the students' co-occurring disorders (e.g., oppositional defiant disorder, ADHD, depression, anxiety) and the other struggles that stem from the learning disorder, such as self-esteem and self-worth issues. Counselors frequently use group counseling as a modality because being around other children who have similar struggles can normalize the youth's experience and enhance self-worth in children with learning disorders (Mishna, Muskat, & Wiener, 2010).

Children with learning disorders tend to be a heterogeneous group, and their learning difficulties change over time. Children who have learning disorders are often misunderstood by school staff and parents, who may characterize them as indifferent or unmotivated. Counselors can work from a strength-based perspective, assume a nonjudgmental stance, and focus interventions on the emotional difficulties related to having a learning disorder (e.g., low self-esteem, anxiety, depression). Counselors should focus on these emotional, social, and/or family issues that exacerbate children's academic difficulties if doing so may help young people to better focus on the skills they need to navigate their learning disorder.

Counseling goals for youth with learning disorders often involve, psychoeducation about the disorder, overcoming a sense of failure, facilitating a positive attitude toward school/academics, increasing the use of adaptive coping skills, using and enhancing social skills, and learning academic strategies (e.g., modeling, practice, feedback; Kendall & Comer, 2010).

To reach these counseling goals, counselors may incorporate expressive art activities (e.g., collage, drawing, sculpting), role-plays, and therapeutic games to maximize children's ability to express themselves and the emotions surrounding the learning disorder (Mishna et al., 2010). For example, a counselor can help a youth in a group setting to create a mantra or an affirming sentence that can be shared with the group and ultimately written on his bathroom mirror (or on anything that the child sees often). Possible mantras are "Be brave, and work hard today!" and "You are amazing—so go do your best!" The child could be instructed to look at this positive affirmation every morning while brushing his teeth. This positive affirmation can change over time and be a reminder for the child of his strengths, inherent worth, and competency.

I CAN START COUNSELING PLAN FOR SOFÍA

This chapter opened with a statement from Sofía's mother. Sofía is a 7-year-old Latina girl who is having difficulties in school and in the home. The following I CAN START conceptual framework outlines counseling considerations that may be helpful to a school counselor or a clinical counselor who works with Sofía.

C = Contextual Assessment

Sofía is a 7-year-old Latina girl whose parents are first-generation American citizens from Colombia. Sofía lives with her father, mother, grandmother, and four older siblings. Her family lives in a three-bedroom home; Sofía and her sisters share one bedroom. Sofía's father owns his own landscaping business, and her mother does not work out of the home. Sofía's grandmother also lives in the home, occupying a room in the basement.

Sofía is having some difficulties settling into the first grade. Her classroom teacher reports that although Sofía does fine academically, she struggles with her behavior in the classroom (e.g., blurting out answers, unable to wait her turn). In addition, her teacher reports that Sofía is having social difficulties and interrupts other students, and she is struggling to connect with her peers.

Sofía's parents are invested in supporting Sofía and getting her the help she needs. Sofía's mother expresses that she needs to learn strategies she can use to manage her daughter's behaviors. Sofía's mother's attention is being pulled by her four other children and her aging mother, who lives in the home. Sofía's father owns his own business, so he often works long hours and is absent from family activities.

A = Assessment and Diagnosis

Diagnosis = 314.01 (F90.1) Attention-Deficit/Hyperactivity Disorder predominantly hyperactive/impulsive presentation (moderate)

Conners 3—Parent Assessment Scores

- Elevated hyperactivity/impulsivity 64; elevated learning problems 61; and elevated peer relations 60

Conners 3—Teacher Assessment Scores

- Very elevated hyperactivity/impulsivity 72; elevated learning problems 62; and elevated peer relations 64

N = Necessary Level of Care

Outpatient parent training and education (every other week)

Outpatient individual counseling (once per week)

S = Strengths

Self: Sofía is of above-average intelligence, and her teacher's report shows potential to excel as a student. Sofía is creative, outgoing, energetic, and enthusiastic, and she has many interests (e.g., animals, nature). She loves being outside and playing with her siblings. In addition, Sofía is interested and willing to participate in counseling services.

Family: Sofía's parents are loving and supportive but unsure of the best way to support and parent their daughter. Her mother is eager to receive support and has taken the initiative to seek out counseling services. Sofía's grandmother is another supportive caregiver in the home, and she helps Sofía's mother with chores and parenting. Sofía has a close bond with her four siblings, although these children are engaged in numerous athletics or extracurricular activities outside the home.

School/community: Sofía's family lives in a middle-class area in the suburbs of a local city, and they enjoy reasonable community resources, such as parks, libraries, and transportation options. Sofía's teacher seems to really like her and seems to have an interest in her being socially and academically successful.

T = Treatment Approach

- CBT (focus on behavioral interventions)

A = Aim and Objectives of Counseling (30-day objectives)

(Parent training) *Sofía's parents will implement a token economy in the home.* They will select three behaviors to target (e.g., not interrupting others, waiting her turn, interacting with others positively) and will create a visual reward system that consist of a means to earn extra privileges and rewards. This will be displayed in a central area and be updated every day.

(Parent training) *Sofía's parents will establish a school-to-home communication system.* They will correspond with Sofía's teacher every school day by providing a blank report card of behaviors in the classroom, including

(a) not interrupting others, (b) waiting her turn, (c) interacting with peers, and (d) being physically under control. Sofía's parents will reward her behaviors from school in the home by using their established token economy system in the home every day after school. This system can also be used to track homework and homework completion.

Sofía will increase her ability to control her interrupting others and not waiting her turn at home and at school. Sofía will slow down, stop and think, and generate at least two alternative solutions to interrupting others and not waiting her turn. She will implement at least one of these solutions and avoid impulsive behaviors at least 80% of the time.

R = Research-Based Interventions

The counselor will help Sofía's parents to develop and apply the following skills: increasing communication with Sofía's teacher, becoming more aware of parent–child interactions, increasing use of positive reinforcements, using time-outs when needed, using a token economy, knowing when to attend to behaviors and when to ignore behaviors, and implementing learned skills through role-play in sessions.

In addition, the counselor will help Sofía to develop more effective social problem-solving and decision-making skills to deal with impulsivity through the use of role-playing activities, coaching techniques to model problem-solving skills, positive reinforcement, and corrective feedback on ways to handle future situations.

T = Therapeutic Support Services

Medication evaluation with a psychiatrist

Weekly individual counseling and family sessions

Consulting with Sofía's teacher about behaviors and school-based interventions

Check-ins as needed with Sofía's elementary school counselor

Summary

Although most children achieve developmental milestones, some young people experience intellectual and neurodevelopmental problems that are characterized by developmental delays or even impairments (e.g., limitations in learning, struggles with executive functioning, impairments in social skills; Broderick & Blewitt, 2014). In addition, these developmental impairments often affect young people's adaptive functioning, particularly their communication, socialization skills, and personal self-care skills (Ashwood et al., 2015). If adaptive functioning skills are lacking, young people will often struggle in the home, in school, and in the community.

These delays and impairments may consist of numerous disorders and disabilities. The most frequently diagnosed intellectual and neurodevelopmental disorders in childhood include ADHD, autistic spectrum disorder, intellectual disabilities, and specific learning disorders. Early diagnosis, specific evidence-based counseling interventions,

and parental participation have all been associated with more positive outcomes (Kendall & Comer, 2010). Early identification and specific interventions are important to optimizing the young person's long-term functioning.

Counselors need to understand the signs and symptoms of these neurodevelopmental and intellectual impairments; incorporate testing, assessment measures, and other educational support services to confirm these diagnoses; and measure the impact on youth's functioning. During the assessment process, counselors can be especially instrumental in helping to support parents through identification, diagnosis, and treatment. Counselors can also discuss any emotions parents are experiencing during the process. Counselors should always consider ways to engage and support parents and youth during the counseling process. In addition, counselors should assume a comprehensive and collaborative care approach, attempting to meet the specific health care needs of each young person and her or his family.

MyLab Counseling: Counseling Children and Adolescents

In the Topic 9 Assignments: *Academic and Social–Emotional Challenges for Youth,* try Application Exercise 9.2: *A Sibling with Autism* and Licensure Quiz 9.2: *Neurodevelopmental and Intellectual Impairments.*

Then try Application Exercise 9.4: *Understanding and Addressing ADHD.*

CHAPTER 14

Disruptive Behavior Problems

THE CASE OF JACE

The only time I lose it is when other people get on me about what I should or shouldn't do. That teacher deserved to hear it from me, and I'm glad I threw my book at him. He gave me an *F* last semester, and he's always been after me. He told me that I needed to go to class even though I told him I was getting something from my locker. He is the one who pushed it with me. The teachers at school are on me about everything, just like my stupid mom. My little brother hates it when I go off on Mom and we fight, but she's always all over me. I don't need to be in counseling—everyone just needs to leave me alone.

—Jace, age 14

Behavior problems include a wide range of child and adolescent actions that are harmful or unhelpful to the self, others, or property. Examples of behavior problems include, but are not limited to, screaming, crying; hitting; kicking; biting; throwing objects; having temper outbursts; lying; disrespecting authority figures; arguing; destroying property; setting fires; stealing; defecating inappropriately; and showing aggression toward people, animals, or objects (American Psychiatric Association [APA], 2013a; Liu, Lewis, & Evans, 2012). Despite the disruptiveness associated with youth behavior problems, the prognosis for these youth can be positive, especially for those who enter counseling early and have stable and solid social supports (APA, 2013a; Sadock, Sadock, & Ruiz, 2014).

Some behavior problems in youth are developmentally appropriate. For example, babies and toddlers commonly express their feelings and desires by crying, screaming, or hitting; the *terrible twos* is a common term used to describe difficult behaviors that toddlers use to communicate thoughts, feelings, and needs (Liu et al., 2012). Although youth typically grow out of the terrible twos by childhood, most children occasionally engage in problem behaviors when they are feeling especially tired, emotional, or frustrated. In later years, adolescents may become more aggressive, defiant, and irritable as the result of developmentally appropriate physical changes and puberty (Liu et al., 2012). Although many behavior problems in youth are developmentally appropriate, counseling interventions might still be needed to support parents, family members, and youth.

Youth behavior problems that do not meet the criteria for a diagnosable behavior disorder are referred to as **subthreshold behavior problems**. Prevalence rates for subthreshold behavior problems fluctuate depending on the nature and severity of the behaviors, but many youth experience some behavior difficulties at different points in childhood (APA, 2013a; Sadock et al., 2014). When behavior problems become increasingly severe or cause significant impairment for youth or their loved ones, the youth might meet the criteria for a formal *Diagnostic and Statistical Manual of Mental Disorders,* Fifth Edition (*DSM-5*; APA, 2013a) diagnosis, and he or she may require treatment services to address the behaviors.

The diagnoses that directly pertain to disruptive behavior problems are found under the *DSM-5* classification *Disruptive, Impulse-Control, and Conduct Disorders,* and these diagnoses include oppositional defiant disorder, conduct disorder, intermittent explosive disorder, pyromania, and kleptomania (APA, 2013a). Because counselors are more likely to work with youth who have oppositional defiant disorder and conduct disorder, this chapter focuses on these two disorders. However, most of the considerations and interventions discussed can be adapted to address other behavior difficulties that might be found in youth (e.g., subthreshold behavioral problems, intermittent explosive disorder).

This chapter provides a discussion of the characteristics, symptoms, and types of youth disruptive behavior problems. It also presents assessment measures that can be used to assess behavior problems and counseling interventions that have been found to be effective with youth who display disruptive behaviors. Later in the chapter, a counseling plan is applied to the case of Jace.

THE NATURE OF DISRUPTIVE BEHAVIOR PROBLEMS IN YOUTH

Many factors contribute to the course and development of behavior problems and behavior disorders in youth (APA, 2013a; Burke, Hipwell, & Loeber, 2011). Disruptive behaviors develop over time, and they are intimately intertwined with genetics, biological factors, family dynamics, cultural factors, environment, and learned behaviors.

Genetics and biology can increase the likelihood of behavior problems in youth. Youth with low intelligence quotient (IQ) scores or brain abnormalities might have difficulties regulating emotions, expressing themselves verbally, or forming satisfying peer relationships (APA, 2013a).

Temperament influences the way youth process and react to external stimuli. Youth who have behavior problems often experience high levels of emotional intensity (especially anger and fear), oversensitive personalities, lower frustration tolerance, and fewer emotion regulation skills (MacDonald, 2012). These factors contribute to a more volatile temperament that is often observed early in life and persists across the life span (APA, 2013a; MacDonald, 2012).

Some argue that the internal circuitry in youth with behavior disorders is wired for greater sensation seeking, higher levels of aggression, and more social dominance than in their peers (MacDonald, 2012). In addition, youth whose parents have conduct disorder, alcohol use disorder, depression, bipolar disorder, schizophrenia, and attention-deficit/hyperactivity disorder (ADHD) are more likely to display behavior problems (APA, 2013a).

A youth's environment and social context can also contribute to behavior problems. Youth who live in violent and high-crime neighborhoods often learn unhealthy coping skills and form unhealthy peer relationships (APA, 2013a; Search Institute, 2015). Socioeconomic status dictates a youth's access to resources, ultimately influencing youth's behaviors in the home, school, and community (Holcomb-McCoy, 2007).

Parental rejection, neglect, and abuse are also often linked to youth behavior problems (APA, 2013a). Poor parental goodness of fit is another risk factor for youth behavior problems. Various factors can contribute to a poor fit between a parent and child (e.g., incompatible personality traits, difficult youth temperament, financial hardship). Harsh or inconsistent parenting also contributes to disruptive behaviors in youth because these parenting approaches can leave youth feeling agitated, helpless, and frustrated (MacDonald, 2012). Youth who do not experience warm and nurturing parent bonding early in life tend to be more callous, and this may contribute to difficulties empathizing with others and may even, in extreme cases, lead to victimizing others (MacDonald, 2012).

In addition, culture can play an important role in the way disruptive behaviors are understood and displayed. **Culture** is defined as an agreed-on set of norms, values, characteristics, and beliefs shared by a group of people and used to inform their thoughts, feelings, attitudes, behaviors, and customs (France, Rodriguez, & Hett, 2013). Culture affects the ways youth learn to understand behavioral norms and rules and the ways in which behaviors are used to communicate. Table 14.1 provides a snapshot of behavioral norms—in the context of disruptive behaviors—that are characteristic of certain ethnicities and potential biases that can be held by some cultural outsiders about these behaviors. It is important to note that these general characteristics should be used to inform the exploration of each youth; there are always risks and limitations when making cultural generalizations about any group.

When working with youth who display behavior problems, counselors should integrate cultural considerations into their assessment processes. Many criteria that distinguish appropriate youth behaviors from inappropriate behaviors are arbitrary and determined by cultural norms, and some disruptive, impulse-control,

Table 14.1 Behavioral Characteristics and Cultural Biases by Ethnicity

Cultural Group	Possible Behavioral Norms	Potential Biases
African American	• Individuals use various nonverbal behaviors (e.g., hand gestures, voice tone). • Individuals look for signs of genuineness in others. • Individuals use eye contact when speaking but not when listening.	• Youth's nonverbal expressions might be interpreted as aggressive. • Youth might experience poor fit with people whom they perceive as being insincere or untrustworthy. • Youth's lack of eye contact can be interpreted by others as being rude or a sign that the youth is disinterested.
Asian	• Individuals prefer personal space. • Individuals use few nonverbal behaviors. • Individuals avoid confrontation. • Individuals smile when uncomfortable. • Individuals defer eye contact when listening and talking to respected people.	• Youth might have difficulty relating to others who use verbal and nonverbal expressions heavily. • Youth might have trouble standing up for themselves in bullying situations. • Youth's lack of eye contact could be interpreted by others as the youth being disengaged, shy, or disrespectful.
Caucasian	• Individuals use expressive nonverbal gestures. • Individuals are verbally expressive. • Individuals are inclined to use touch to greet others (e.g., handshake). • Individuals use regular, direct eye contact.	• Youth's behaviors might be considered loud, rude, or aggressive. • Youth might unknowingly violate others' personal space boundaries. • Youth's use of eye contact could be interpreted by others as aggressive.
Hispanic/Latino/Latina	• Individuals use expressive nonverbal gestures and voice tones. • Individuals readily use touch when interacting. • Individuals use regular, direct eye contact.	• Youth's verbal and nonverbal behaviors might be interpreted as overwhelming or aggressive. • Youth might unknowingly violate others' personal space boundaries. • Youth's use of eye contact could be interpreted by others as aggressive.
Native American	• Individuals have modest and restrained nonverbal behaviors. • Individuals look for signs of genuineness in others. • Individuals defer direct eye contact when possible.	• Youth might have difficulty relating to others who use animated verbal and nonverbal expressions. • Youth might have difficulty asserting themselves in social situations. • Youth's lack of eye contact could be interpreted by others as the youth being disengaged or shy.

Note: Adapted from "What is your body saying? The use of nonverbal immediacy behaviors to support multicultural therapeutic relationships," by N. A. Stargell & K. Duong, in press, *North Carolina Counseling Journal*; *Counseling the Culturally Diverse: Theory and Practice*, by D. W. Sue & D. Sue, 2016, Hoboken, NJ: John Wiley & Sons.

and conduct disorders are diagnosed more frequently in certain cultures than others (APA, 2013a; Norbury & Sparks, 2013). Youth behaviors ultimately are the result of complex interactions, and counselors should work to understand the etiology of a youth's behaviors before making a formal diagnosis.

Youth behaviors must be understood in the context of genetics, biology, temperament, environment, family dynamics, and culture. Youth do not typically understand or have insight into the complex underlying motivations for their behaviors. Instead, they learn to perform behaviors that feel comfortable and rewarding, even if the behaviors have negative or harmful long-term consequences

(Westbrook, Kennerly, & Kirk, 2014)—that is, problem behaviors are often developed by youth because such behaviors have worked in the past to achieve their needs. For example, a youth might observe that a younger sibling gets attention when crying and screaming. The youth might replicate this behavior, which results in attention from others. This attention might be negative (e.g., being reprimanded or punished), but some youth will take whatever attention they can get. Overall, almost all youth behaviors, whether helpful or problematic, serve a purpose. A deeper understanding of the various disruptive behavior problems can help counselors and stakeholders to understand the underlying motivations and identify healthier ways of meeting a youth's needs.

Description of Disruptive Behavior Problems

Youth behavior problems tend to cluster around three problem areas: conflicts with authority, destruction of property and theft, and aggression toward self, others, or animals (Loeber & Burke, 2011; MacDonald, 2012). Table 14.2 presents the common symptoms associated with each of these categories of behavior problems. Disruptive behavior problems often become progressively more problematic across time if unaddressed (APA, 2013a; Loeber & Burke, 2011).

Table 14.2	Evolution of Disruptive Behaviors in Youth		
Theme	**Less Severe** ——————————————————→		**More Severe**
Conflicts with authority	Stubborn behavior • Temper outbursts • Interrupting adults • Responding to authority figures with a negative attitude • Arguing • Negative affect	Defiance/disobedience • Ignoring rules at home and school • Noncompliance for authority figures • Retreating and withdrawing • Defecating in inappropriate places (not related to potty training)	Authority problems • School truancy • Running away • Breaking curfew • Attainment, distribution, and/or use of illegal or controlled substances
Destruction of property and theft	Minor covert acts • Shoplifting • Lying	Property damage • Vandalism • Fire setting • Breaking objects	Moderate to serious delinquency • Fraud • Pickpocketing • Auto theft • Burglary • Stealing while confronting the victim
Aggression toward self, others, or animals	Minor aggression • Bullying • Annoying others • Touchiness • Anger management problems • Playing rough • Aggressive language • Pinching, hitting, kicking, biting, slapping, hair pulling, or spitting	Physical aggression • One-on-one fights • Gang fights • Nonsuicidal self-injurious behavior • Cruelty to animals • Spiteful and vindictive behaviors	Severe violence • Sexual assault and rape • Physical assault • Attack with a deadly weapon • Murder

Note: Adapted from "Developmental pathways in juvenile externalizing and internalizing problems," R. Loeber & J. D. Burke, 2011, *Journal of Research on Adolescence, 21,* pp. 34–46, doi:10.1111/j.1532-7795.2010.00713.x

Counselors should remember that some problem behaviors can be considered developmentally—or culturally—appropriate (APA, 2013a). When diagnosing conduct disorder, counselors should be sensitive to clients' contexts. For example, if a young boy lives in a high-crime, violent neighborhood and uses violence to protect his safety or property, these protective actions might not be considered disruptive or meet diagnostic criteria. However, violent behavior is still a cause for concern—regardless of cultural origins—and counseling interventions can be used to help youth to identify and implement healthier coping skills.

DSM-5 Disorders Associated with Disruptive Behavior Problems

Two common disruptive behavior disorders diagnosed in youth are oppositional defiant disorder and conduct disorder. The relationship between these two disorders can be viewed on a continuum in which oppositional defiant disorder progresses into conduct disorder if left unaddressed (APA, 2013a). In general, conduct disorder is characterized by more severe forms of oppositional defiant disorder behaviors. However, either diagnosis can be assigned to a youth at any age, and a diagnosis of oppositional defiant disorder does not necessarily have to precede a conduct disorder diagnosis (APA, 2013a).

In the *DSM-5*, intermittent explosive disorder, pyromania, and kleptomania are also listed under Disruptive, Impulse-Control, and Conduct Disorder, along with oppositional defiant disorder and conduct disorder. Table 14.3 provides a brief overview of the symptoms associated with each of the *DSM-5* (APA, 2013a) disruptive, impulse-control, and conduct disorders.

The focus of this chapter is on oppositional defiant disorder, conduct disorder, and subthreshold disruptive behavior problems because they are the most commonly presented counseling concerns. The overall

Table 14.3 Summary of the *DSM-5* Disruptive, Impulse-Control, and Conduct Disorders

Diagnosis	Criteria	Example
Oppositional defiant disorder	• Youth has angry/irritable mood (loses temper; is touchy, easily annoyed, angry, or resentful). • Youth is argumentative or defiant (argues with adults and authority figures, defies rules, annoys others, blames others). • Youth is vindictive or spiteful. • These behaviors cause distress or impairment to the youth or others. • Persistence and frequency must be greater than what is developmentally appropriate.	A 9-year-old girl frequently gets in trouble at school for not following rules; she often bickers and argues with her peers, and she is verbally disrespectful to her teachers at least once per week. At home, she frequently throws temper tantrums and yells at her parents and siblings.
Conduct disorder	• Youth shows a consistent pattern of violating social norms and the rights of others (bullying, threatening, fighting, using a weapon, cruelty to people or animals, stealing, forcing sexual activity). • Youth destroys property. • Youth is deceitful or steals. • Youth has serious rule violations (staying out all night, running away from home, skipping school). • Youth has significant impairment in social, academic, or occupational functioning. • Conduct disorder can be diagnosed at any age.	A 12-year-old-boy has become increasingly aggressive toward his parents and siblings; he recently hit his brother in the head with a toy bat and then threatened his mother with a kitchen knife when she attempted to correct him. His father found a dead squirrel he had killed in a shoebox in the garage; the tail had been cut off the body.

(Continued)

| | Table 14.3 | Summary of the *DSM-5* Disruptive, Impulse-Control, and Conduct Disorders (*Continued*) |

Diagnosis	Criteria	Example
Intermittent explosive disorder	• Youth has verbal/physical outbursts toward property, animals, or others (occurs twice per week for 3 months; at least three outbursts have caused destruction or physical harm in the past year). • Aggression is out of proportion to the stressor. • Aggression not premeditated or used to gain a tangible object. • These behaviors cause impairment or distress in the youth. • Youth must be at least 6 years old to receive this diagnosis.	A 10-year-old boy becomes noticeably irritated when navigating a peer altercation or struggling with a concept in class. The youth will typically find ways to self-soothe, but once or twice per week the youth "blows up" and throws objects, kicks things, and pulls his hair. On occasion, he has hit another person during one of these outbursts.
Pyromania	• Youth participates in deliberate and purposeful fire setting. • Youth experiences tension or arousal before the act. • Youth has a fascination with fire. • Youth experiences pleasure and relief when setting fires or participating in the aftermath. • Fire setting is not used for monetary gain or self-expression or when judgment is impaired (e.g., during a psychotic episode, while under the influence of a substance).	A 14-year-old boy is not particularly aggressive or rebellious but has been caught on three occasions setting fires. He recently set his parents' garage on fire. When asked why he did it, he responded, "I don't know. I like fire."
Kleptomania	• Youth steals objects that are not needed for monetary value. • Youth experiences tension before committing theft. • Youth experiences pleasure and relief after the act.	A 16-year-old girl has a large closet full of clothes and makeup, but she has been caught stealing underwear, nail polish, and lipstick on two separate occasions. She already owned many of the same items she was attempting to steal, but she reported an intense need and desire to commit the acts despite attempts to stop herself.

Note: Adapted from *Diagnostic and Statistical Manual of Mental Disorders* (5th ed.), by American Psychiatric Association (APA), 2013, Washington, DC: Author.

prevalence rate for diagnosable behavior disorders in children and adolescents is 19%, with these disorders being diagnosed more frequently in boys than girls (APA, 2013a; Merikangas et al., 2010).

Oppositional defiant disorder is characterized by a pattern of noncompliance in which youth are angry, irritable, and vindictive (APA, 2013a). Oppositional defiant disorder is found in up to 3% of youth, and the symptoms usually begin in early childhood; it is rare for symptoms to first appear after early adolescence (APA, 2013a).

Youth who have oppositional defiant disorder are highly emotional and experience high levels of interpersonal conflict at least once per week (APA, 2013a). In addition to outward defiance of authority figures and rules, youth with oppositional defiant disorder often intentionally annoy others, shirk responsibility for their behaviors, and blame others for their troubles (APA, 2013a). Many oppositional defiant symptoms can be developmentally appropriate in moderation, so the behaviors must create a significant amount of social, educational, or occupational impairment to warrant a formal diagnosis. To be diagnosed with oppositional defiant disorder, youth under the age of 5 must experience the symptoms on most days for at least 6 months, as opposed to once per week for youth ages 6 and older (APA, 2013a).

The symptoms of conduct disorder are similar to oppositional defiant disorder but are more severe and harmful than the symptoms found in oppositional defiant disorder. Conduct disorder is diagnosed in up to 4% of youth, and symptoms of the disorder typically emerge in middle childhood or adolescence. It is rare for symptoms of conduct disorder to begin after age 16 (APA, 2013a). If their symptoms are left unaddressed, youth who have oppositional defiant disorder and conduct disorder are at greater risk for developing depression, anxiety, and escalated antisocial behaviors later in life (Burke et al., 2011).

A primary way to distinguish between oppositional defiant disorder and conduct disorder is that youth with conduct disorder repeatedly violate the basic rights of others and disregard major social norms (APA, 2013a). In addition to the anger, irritability, and interpersonal conflict seen in youth with oppositional defiant disorder, youth with conduct disorder act on these difficulties with aggression and cruelty toward people, animals, or property. These aggressive behaviors can include bullying, threatening, physical fighting, using a weapon, hurting animals, stealing while confronting the victim, sexually assaulting others, setting fires, destroying objects, lying and conning, and swindling others.

Youth with conduct disorder violate social norms that carry serious consequences, such as breaking into a car, house, or building and stealing valuable items. The defiant behaviors found in conduct disorder might include staying out all night, running away from home, and/or skipping school. Overall, the same emotional difficulties and behavior patterns are found in oppositional defiant disorder and conduct disorder, but individuals with conduct disorder blatantly disregard the rights of others and societal norms (APA, 2013a).

Differential Diagnoses

Some counselors have the privilege and responsibility to diagnose clients, and others do not because they work with youth in the schools or other exempt settings. However, all counselors should know the indicators of diagnosable behavior problems to make accurate referrals. In addition, they should be able to distinguish disruptive behavior problems from other mental health concerns that have emotional or behavioral components that might manifest as disruptive behaviors (APA, 2013a). Counselors should consider the possibility of differential or comorbid diagnoses that might exacerbate or account for a youth's behavior problems. **Differential diagnosis**, or exploring alternative diagnoses that might fit better, is an important component of selecting appropriate and effective counseling interventions.

NEURODEVELOPMENTAL DISORDERS

Intellectual disability, autism spectrum disorder, and ADHD are present in 1% to 5% of youth, and the behavioral manifestations of these disorders can be mistaken for disorders rooted in behavior problems (Ageranioti-Bélanger et al., 2012; APA, 2013a). Basic behavioral manifestations of these disorders are as follows:

- Youth with intellectual disabilities can experience sleep difficulties, chronic pain, or medication side effects that result in irritability or loss of inhibition.
- Youth with autism spectrum disorder have difficulties with information processing, communication, and changes in daily routines, which might lead to hypersensitivity and behavioral expressions of needs (National Autistic Society, 2015).
- Youth who have ADHD are often impulsive, experience fidgeting, have difficulty sitting still, run or climb when inappropriate, have difficulty engaging in quiet leisure activities, talk excessively, blurt out answers, interrupt others, and avoid tasks that require sustained attention (APA, 2013a).

Many behaviors associated with common neurodevelopmental disorders in youth could be mistaken for a diagnosable disruptive, impulse-control, or conduct disorder. In addition, the symptoms of a neurodevelopmental disorder could contribute to, or worsen, the symptoms of a diagnosable or subthreshold behavior problem.

ANXIETY OR DEPRESSION

Disruptive mood dysregulation disorder, major depression, and persistent depressive disorder are found in 0.5% to 2% of youth and can manifest behaviorally as angry outbursts and irritability (APA, 2013a). Separation anxiety disorder and generalized anxiety disorder occur in 1.6% to 4% of youth, and youth often have temper outbursts or behavioral protests as a way to avoid anxiety-provoking stimuli (APA, 2013a). Sleep disturbances are common in youth with anxiety, and depression is commonly associated with youth who also have neurodevelopmental disorders (APA, 2013a). Any of these behavioral symptoms associated with anxiety or depression should be considered when assessing for disruptive, impulse-control, or conduct disorders in youth.

STRESS AND TRAUMA

Among youth, 3% to 8% have posttraumatic stress disorder, and many youth experience traumatic events (e.g., physical, emotional, or sexual abuse). Trauma experiences can contribute to irritability, angry outbursts, and behavioral protests (Centers for Disease Control and Prevention [CDC], 2014a). Youth who experience trauma can experience externalized responses (e.g., aggression, disregarding authority figures) in addition to internalized responses (e.g., anxiety, depression; Milne & Collin-Vézina, 2015). Youth who have experienced trauma might display irritability, aggression, sleep disturbances, avoidant behaviors, hypersexualization, self-injurious behaviors, and substance use (Milne & Collin-Vezina, 2015).

PHYSICAL DISCOMFORT

Behavior problems can occur as the result of physical discomfort. Counselors should ensure youth with behavior problems have their basic needs met and are not reacting to physical irritants such as hunger, stomachaches, earaches, toothaches, and medication side effects. In addition, youth have trouble concentrating if they are tired; they should get between 8 and 11 hours of sleep each night, yet many young people lack adequate sleep (Hirshkowitz et al., 2015). In addition, youth can become irritable if they are hungry, are cold, cannot see or hear well, or are otherwise uncomfortable. Counselors working with youth who display behavior problems should assess and consider their physical comfort.

ASSESSMENT OF DISRUPTIVE BEHAVIOR PROBLEMS

Depending on the setting in which counselors work, they may use specific assessment tools to measure disruptive behavior problems in youth. When assessing behavior problems, counselors should assess for comorbid disorders and differential diagnoses to ensure diagnostic accuracy. Counselors should refer youth for a basic medical examination to rule out any physical causes of the disruptive behaviors. At the beginning of the counseling relationship, they should conduct an assessment of the youth's developmental history, risk factors, and demographics.

Parents, siblings, peers, teachers, and other important people (e.g., coach, babysitter) can serve as important sources of information about a youth's behaviors. If possible, parents should be interviewed privately to provide any information they are not comfortable sharing in front of the youth (e.g., pending divorce). Counselors should interview both parents if possible because each person will have a unique perspective on the youth's behaviors. The youth should also be interviewed individually in case he or she has information that was not shared in the family interview (e.g., possible abuse).

Diagnostic Interview

If a counselor suspects that a young client may have a disruptive behavior disorder, he or she should determine the pervasiveness of the client's behavior problems by asking about the settings in which the behaviors occur. Diagnosable behavior disorders persist across various settings and create significant impairment in the school, neighborhood, and home (APA, 2013a). Counselors can use the questions in Figure 14.1 to complete a diagnostic interview for oppositional defiant disorder or conduct disorder.

Standardized Assessments

In addition to informal diagnostic interviews, counselors can use standardized assessments to support accurate diagnosis of behavior problems. Table 14.4 provides an overview of formal assessments that can be used to assess for disruptive behavior problems in youth.

Oppositional Defiant Disorder
- Does the child lose his or her temper?
- Is the child touchy or easily annoyed?
- Is the child angry or resentful?
- Does the child argue with authority figures or adults?
- Does the child actively defy rules?
- Does the child refuse to comply with requests from authority figures?
- Does the child deliberately annoy others?
- Does the child blame others for his or her misbehavior?
- Has the child been spiteful or vindictive?

Conduct Disorder
- Does the child bully, threaten, or intimidate others?
- Does the child initiate physical fights?
- Has the child used a weapon that can cause serious physical harm to others?
- Has the child been physically cruel to people or animals?
- Has the child stolen while confronting the victim?
- Has the child forced someone into sexual activity?
- Has the child deliberately engaged in fire setting to cause damage?
- Has the child damaged others' property?
- Has the child broken into someone else's house, car, or building?
- Does the child lie to obtain goods or favors or to avoid obligations?
- Has the child stolen items of nontrivial value?
- Is the child truant from school?

FIGURE 14.1 Questions Counselors Should Consider When Assessing for Disruptive Behavior Disorders
Note: Adapted from *Diagnostic and Statistical Manual of Mental Disorders* (5th ed.), by American Psychiatric Association (APA), 2013, Washington, DC: Author.

Table 14.4 Summary of Youth Disruptive Behavior Assessment Measures

Assessment Measure	Age Range	Overview
Beck Youth Inventories (2nd ed.)	7–18 years old	This youth-completed assessment consists of five, 20-question measures (Beck, Beck, Jolly, & Steer, 2005). The purpose of this assessment is to measure young people's emotional and social impairment, including depression, anxiety, anger, disruptive behavior, and self-concept.
DSM-5 Parent/ Guardian-Rated Level 1 Cross-Cutting Symptom Measure	6–17 years old	This assessment consists of 25 questions (19 five-point scale questions and 6 yes/no questions) and is completed by a caregiver (APA, 2013b). The purpose of this assessment is to differentiate categories of youth problems, including somatic, sleep, inattention, depression, anger, irritability, mania, anxiety, psychosis, repetitive thought/behavior, substance use, and suicidality. It is available as a free download.
Inventory of Callous-Unemotional Traits	12–20 years old	This assessment consists of 24 questions and can be completed by the youth, a parent, and/or a teacher (University of New Orleans, 2014). The purpose of this assessment is to identify traits linked to aggressive and antisocial behaviors, including callousness, lack of caring, and lack of emotion.

(Continued)

| Table 14.4 | Summary of Youth Disruptive Behavior Assessment Measures (*Continued*) |

Assessment Measure	Age Range	Overview
Achenbach System of Empirically Based Assessment (ASEBA)	1.5–18 years old	This assessment system consists of multiple measures of various lengths (Achenbach & Rescorla, 2001). Counselors can strategically choose which ones to use based on the client's initial presentation. The purpose of this assessment is to identify subthreshold behavior problems, as well as behaviors that meet diagnostic criteria.
Behavior Assessment System for Children (2nd ed.; BASC-2)	2–21 years old	This assessment system consists of multiple measures of various lengths (Reynolds & Kamphaus, 2004). Counselors can strategically choose which ones to use. The purpose of this assessment is to understand youth behaviors through teacher ratings, parent ratings, and youth self-report. Counselors can also use the observation system and structured developmental history process to form a comprehensive understanding of child and adolescent behaviors.

INTEGRATED TREATMENT COMPONENTS FOR YOUTH WHO HAVE DISRUPTIVE BEHAVIOR PROBLEMS

Counselors might encounter disruptive behavior problems in various settings. School counselors might use the treatment components outlined in this chapter in brief counseling interventions with youth and in long-term behavior plans with teachers and caregivers. Counselors who work in the community and clinical settings might use many of the treatment components provided in this section; they should determine the nature and duration of interventions based on the client's unique needs and resources.

The development of a strong therapeutic relationship is essential when working with youth who have disruptive behavior problems and their families. Relationship development factors are discussed elsewhere in this book, but suffice it to say that because of the nature of this population's struggles, special attention must be paid to the counseling relationship.

Counselors should carefully identify counseling interventions that have a reasonable promise of meeting their clients' treatment goals (American Counseling Association [ACA], 2014). Because of various risk factors (e.g., violence), the stakes can be high when working with this population, and counselors must employ best practices. The interventions discussed in this section are empirically supported for use with youth who have disruptive behavior problems.

Individual counseling with a youth is convenient because family participation is not required. However, counseling is most helpful when the young person's family is engaged in counseling and can create a more supportive environment for the youth (Barkley, 2013; Henggeler & Schaeffer, 2010). The following section discusses basic behavioral and emotion regulation interventions, followed by cognitive restructuring techniques. Next, problem-solving skills training (PSST) is explored as a tool that can be used with multi-dimensional counseling approaches. Dialectical behavior therapy (DBT), multisystemic therapy (MST), and family interventions are discussed as part of a multidimensional approach. Counselors should intentionally choose their interventions based on their clients' needs and the availability of resources.

Behavioral Interventions

Problem behaviors are the area of concern for youth who have disruptive behavior disorders, so it makes sense that counselors commonly use interventions that target behavior change. Basic behavioral concepts such as classical and operant conditioning can be used as a foundation for understanding, targeting, and changing youth behavior. In **classical conditioning**, a stimulus that is not otherwise significant to an individual becomes associated with a stimulus that is inherently important; thus, the insignificant stimulus also becomes important. This concept was originally researched in dogs; the neutral stimulus was a bell, and the unconditioned stimulus was food. Researchers rang a bell, but the dogs did not react. Next, they rang a bell while giving food to the dogs, and the dogs salivated. Soon, the dogs salivated when the bell rang, even if the food was not present. The concept of classical conditioning can be applied to youth to hypothesize the reinforcements and motivations for certain behaviors.

Operant conditioning is a process that uses rewards and punishments to reinforce or distinguish certain behaviors. Rewards are desirable consequences (e.g., candy, extra movie time), and punishments are undesirable consequences (e.g., losing a privilege, extra chores). Operant conditioning is especially relevant for youth because parents have control over various rewards and consequences. Counselors can use operant conditioning to identify the consequences that reinforce problem behaviors, and they can help parents, caregivers, teachers, and other important people to adjust the environment so unwanted behaviors are no longer reinforced and desirable behaviors are reinforced.

Incompatible behaviors are two behaviors that cannot occur simultaneously. For example, youth cannot throw a temper tantrum while quietly watching their favorite show. Important people in a youth's life can reinforce desirable behaviors, especially those that are incompatible with unwanted behaviors. As a result, unwanted behaviors are not reinforced and will eventually become extinct.

Punishment is not always needed to shape behavior. In fact, punishment can actually be harmful if it causes youth to feel unloved or unsupported. Punishment may be necessary when youth pose a threat to their safety or the safety of others around them. Otherwise, reinforcement is a much more effective way to shape behavior.

There are two types of reinforcement: positive and negative. **Positive reinforcement** occurs when youth are given something desirable (e.g., praise, a hug, a cookie), and **negative reinforcement** occurs when an unwanted consequence is removed (e.g., excusing a youth from chores for the day). Positive and negative punishments work in much the same way. Table 14.5 provides an overview of the types of consequences. Counselors should note that verbal praise and affection are highly effective and free reinforcement for youth.

The first step in behavioral intervention is to understand the motivation for the youth's behavior. Counselors should list the youth's problem behaviors. Next, they should work with the youth, his or her parents, and other important people to identify the circumstances that typically occur before (i.e., antecedent) and after (i.e., consequence) the behaviors.

Once counselors understand the reason that youth act out, efforts can be made to remove the consequences that are reinforcing such behaviors. For example, youth who typically get attention when misbehaving in class should be ignored when possible (Barkley, 2013). Desirable behaviors should be reinforced with praise and tangible reinforcements. General behavioral concepts can be used to identify factors in the environment that are reinforcing behavior problems and restructuring the ways that youth achieve their desired goals.

Behavioral interventions can be practiced in counseling sessions through role-plays and consistent enforcement of rules and consequences. Counselors can also help teachers to implement behavioral concepts in the classroom through the use of behavior charts and token economies. In addition, parents can implement behavior changes in the home to reduce unwanted behaviors and increase healthier expressions of needs.

Although behavioral interventions can be used to understand the basic motivations for unhealthy behaviors in youth, thoughts and feelings also play a role in producing and reinforcing behavior problems. This is especially relevant for older youth who experience behavior problems across settings and have made unhealthy cognitive, behavioral, and emotional associations—that have been reinforced—over many years. Counselors will often have to integrate affective and cognitive interventions to supplement basic behavioral interventions.

Table 14.5 Types of Consequences: Reinforcements and Punishments

	Add Stimulus	Remove Stimulus
Increase Behavior	Positive reinforcement (Give youth praise)	Negative reinforcement (Take away youth's chores)
Decrease Behavior	Positive punishment (Give youth extra chores)	Negative punishment (Take away youth's iPad)

Mindfulness-Based Skills

Affective awareness, or the ability to recognize and control emotions, is central to effective counseling with this population. Many disruptive behaviors (e.g., angry outbursts, fights) by definition are rooted in difficulties with emotion regulation. Youth ideally will express uncomfortable emotions verbally or through creative activities (e.g., writing, drawing). Some youth, however, lack awareness of their emotions and/or do not know how to use adaptive means to express their emotions. Youth who lack such skills may, when feeling particularly overwhelmed, express their emotions in disruptive ways. There are many reasons youth might develop unhealthy emotion regulation skills, including observing unhealthy models (e.g., physical aggression in the home) and having biological sensitivities that make it inherently difficult for them to understand and control their emotions.

Counselors should help youth to understand the connection between their feelings and behaviors. Youth must first be able to identify their feelings, which are typically unconscious or otherwise unacknowledged by the youth. Counselors might use mindfulness techniques to bring active awareness to youth's emotions.

Mindfulness is a process of becoming consciously aware of one's inner workings, and mindfulness techniques have been used to successfully support healthy behaviors in youth (Swart & Apsche, 2014). Through the use of mindfulness techniques, youth can become actively aware of their thoughts and the associated feelings experienced in their bodies. As a result of becoming consciously aware of these thoughts and feelings, youth can learn the basic drives that motivate behavior and work to redirect their behaviors toward more helpful and healthy ways of interacting. Youth are especially good candidates for mindfulness work because they tend to be open to new opportunities and experiences.

Mindfulness techniques call attention to youth's thoughts and feelings in the present moment. When being mindful, youth do not focus on the past or the future. Rather, they focus on the current moment and nonjudgmentally observe their inner thoughts and feelings without placing any evaluation of good or bad, right or wrong. Youth accept their thoughts and feelings in the present moment as valid and view their current experience as a passing moment in time. Using mindfulness, youth acknowledge that life is exactly as it should be, and they are perfectly fine in that moment in time. What has happened in the past is over, and what might happen in the future is not known. All that is known is that the youth are alive and well in the current moment.

Mindfulness techniques bring youth into a centered, calm state of consciousness in which there is no room to put unnecessary energy into judgment, sorrow, regret, remorse, anxiety, or worry. Instead, youth practicing mindfulness realize that thoughts and feelings can be observed, identified, explored, and redirected to motivate desirable and healthy behaviors. Through mindfulness techniques, youth can become aware of their inherent power to fully experience their thoughts and feelings in the moment and then move toward a happier, healthier way of interacting with the world around them.

Counselors might begin and end sessions with mindfulness activities and encourage youth to practice mindfulness on their own when feeling irritable or uncomfortable. A first step in the mindfulness process is inviting youth to become aware of their internal processes and their surroundings (Swart & Apsche, 2014). Counselors should then guide clients to close their eyes and notice the feelings they are experiencing, such as sadness or worry. Clients should take time to acknowledge and fully experience their feelings without judgment—that is, youth should be observers looking in on their experiences. In doing this, they should be totally present and aware without worrying and thinking about the past or the future. The specific feeling being experienced in the moment is perfectly valid and important; the feeling does not indicate that anything is wrong or is going to go wrong in the future. Rather, it just indicates how clients are currently feeling, in the present.

To bring youth to a present-moment focus, counselors should ask them to open their eyes and describe what they see in the room (e.g., the television, the counselor in a chair, the computer in the background). Youth should then share how they feel in the current setting (e.g., anxious, sad, hopeful), and counselors should validate and process these feelings nonjudgmentally.

Breathing exercises are a key mindfulness component, and they involve youth intentionally focusing on their lungs and chest as breath enters and leaves the body. Counselors can guide clients to make a long, slow inhalation; hold the breath for a moment or two; and enjoy a calm, controlled exhalation. Clients can repeat the deep breaths five times. In this exercise, youth become relaxed and connected to their bodies. Clients accept themselves as individuals with basic human needs and recognize the power of mindfulness in controlling feelings of anger and putting life into perspective.

Youth should notice the calm, soothing feeling that comes with mindfulness practices. Counselors should encourage youth to practice mindfulness when they experience uncomfortable emotions so they can express and process the feelings in healthy ways. If youth notice that interpersonal relationships are a key source of emotional reactivity and distress, counselors can build on key mindfulness techniques to integrate additional healthy behaviors.

Clinical Toolbox 14.1

In the Pearson e-text, click here to review a mindfulness activity for youth who experience anxiety.

Cognitive Restructuring Abilities

Youth's thoughts are directly tied to their feelings and behaviors. An important counseling goal with this population is identifying and changing maladaptive thoughts as needed to prevent disruptive behaviors from occurring. Cognitive restructuring can help youth to gain insight into how their thoughts affect their behaviors and how they can make better behavioral choices. Table 14.6 provides common treatment goals for addressing the cognitive aspects of disruptive behavior problems.

Cognitive behavioral therapy (CBT) is an integrative theory that merges theories of thought (i.e., cognitive theory), feeling (i.e., affective regulation), and behavior (i.e., behavioral theory; Benjamin, Puleo, & Kendall, 2011; Westbrook et al., 2014). CBT is a holistic approach that helps youth to identify the

Table 14.6 Cognitive Treatment Goals for Youth with Behavior Problems

Behavior Disorder	Beliefs	Assumptions	Behaviors	Possible Treatment Goals
Oppositional defiant disorder	I do not have control over my own life and personal needs.	Others place unreasonable demands on me. I can control my environment through my behaviors. Others are trying to manipulate or take advantage of me. I do not have to do things others tell me to do. Nothing is my fault.	Youth experience temper tantrums and an angry or resentful attitude. Youth disrespect others.	Treatment aims to increase personal reflection and social sensitivity, build empathy and self-confidence, improve interpersonal skills, and increase anger management.
Conduct disorder	Others do not have the same rights as I do.	I have the right to hurt others. Other people deserve to be hurt the way I have been hurt. I can control others through violence. Destroying property is a good way to express my feelings. I do not have to follow rules. I do not have to respect others.	Youth are involved in bullying, fighting, physical cruelty to people or animals, and property damage. Youth lie, steal, and ignore rules.	Treatment targets empathy building, emotion regulation, anger management, and personal reflection.
Intermittent explosive disorder	I cannot control my impulses.	My behaviors are reasonable/appropriate for the situation. My anger is out of control. Other people make me uncontrollably angry.	Youth display verbal aggression, temper tantrums, and physical aggression.	Treatment aims to decrease impulsivity, improve emotion regulation skills, teach social skills training, and increase anger management.

(Continued)

Table 14.6	Cognitive Treatment Goals for Youth with Behavior Problems (*Continued*)			
Behavior Disorder	Beliefs	Assumptions	Behaviors	Possible Treatment Goals
Pyromania	I must set fires to feel better.	The only way to calm my nerves is to set a fire. Setting fires is a good way to deal with my emotions. Fire setting is the only way I can experience pleasure or relief.	Youth set fires repeatedly.	Treatment aims to increase self-discipline, self-control, self-reflection, and coping skills.
Kleptomania	I must steal to feel better.	Stealing will make me feel better. Stealing is a good way to reduce the tension I feel. Stealing is the only way I can feel good.	Youth steal items not needed for survival.	Treatment aims to increase self-discipline, self-control, self-reflection, self-awareness, and coping skills.

cognitive and emotional triggers that influence behaviors. CBT has been shown to be effective with youth ages 7 and up who have the developmental ability to connect thoughts with feelings and behaviors (Benjamin et al., 2011; Sigelman & Rider, 2012; Westbrook et al., 2014).

To help youth to see the connection between thoughts and feelings, counselors might use **Socratic questioning** (i.e., pretending not to know the answer) to lead clients to insight rather than telling them. Counselors should avoid interrogating clients and should use encouragement, validation, and reflection as part of this process. For example, a counselor working with a young person who has angry outbursts when asked to do chores might use questions such as the following: "What happened right before you got angry at your mom?" "How were you feeling right before you got angry?" "What happened after you became angry?" "What were you thinking about?" "How did you feel after you got angry?" The counselor can then highlight that the youth was angry when forced to do chores but felt better when the chores were avoided. The counselor can also highlight that the youth was able to escape chores but was grounded for 3 days, which actually caused more serious consequences than completing the chores.

After exploring the thoughts, feelings, and behaviors associated with several behavior incidents, counselors can help youth to track their cycle of thoughts, feelings, and behaviors to facilitate youth insight. Figure 14.2 depicts *Beck's Cognitive Triad,* often called a CBT triangle (Beck, Rush, Shaw, & Emery, 1979). This triangle is simple to understand and developmentally appropriate for younger children. The idea of the triangle is that thoughts are connected to feelings, and feelings motivate behaviors; thus, identifying and reframing irrational or unhelpful thoughts can help youth to feel better, which produces more desirable behaviors.

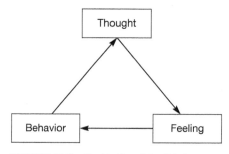

FIGURE 14.2   Beck's Cognitive Triad

Clinical Toolbox 14.2

In the Pearson e-text, click here to review a mindfulness activity that can be used with youth who experience anxiety.

Counselors can also assign a thought journal to older children and adolescents. Clients can review the journal contents with counselors to practice linking thoughts, feelings, and behaviors. Youth will eventually be able to track the cycle independently and thus implement prevention strategies to live a healthier, happier life.

Clinical Toolbox 14.3

In the Pearson e-text, click here for a blank copy of a log that can be used to track thoughts, feelings, and behaviors.

Tracking the cycle of thoughts, feelings, and behaviors is therapeutic in itself because youth gain insight into their inner experiences and their reactions to these experiences. Counselors can help youth to identify the thoughts and feelings that often lead to disruptive behaviors. Counselors should ask youth for specific examples of when they used unhelpful behaviors. For example, a counselor might ask "When was the last time you got in trouble in class?" The counselor can help the client to determine what was happening before he got upset. For example, the counselor might say "So, you were in class doing your math exercises. You were sitting at your desk minding your own business."

Next, the counselor should identify the thoughts and feelings that led to unhelpful behaviors. For example, the counselor can ask "What happened then to make you upset?" The youth might answer that his peer threw a pencil at him. The counselor should then clarify exactly what happened by asking about details, such as if the youth saw the peer throw the pencil or if it startled him because he was looking down. (This could indicate if the throw was intentional or if the youth instigated the incident.) Counselors should summarize the precipitating events and the trigger. For example, the counselor can say "So you were looking down while you kicked a piece of gum. It hit your peer, and he then threw a pencil at you."

In the next step of CBT, the counselor should ask why the student kicked the gum, discuss reasons why the behavior was unhelpful (e.g., it didn't solve any problems, it upset his peer), and discuss alternative behaviors (e.g., deep breathing, taking a break). The counselor can also show the chain of events. —that is, the youth kicking the gum actually led to the pencil being thrown, which led to the disruptive classroom behavior.

Next, the counselor should discuss the main trigger (i.e., the youth being hit by a pencil) and the associated thoughts and feelings. This process will likely take some time because internal thoughts and feelings are not easily accessible. The counselor can ask "How did you feel when the pencil hit you?" It would be helpful to have a feelings chart available for the student to pick from. The counselor should then ask "What thoughts did you have at that moment?" If the youth is unable to generate thoughts, the counselor might guess "You thought to yourself, 'I'm not going to let him get away with that.' Is that correct?" The counselor might need to make several guesses and allow the youth to clarify until the accurate thoughts are identified.

The counselor can take time to identify the youth's thoughts and potentially replace them with more helpful thoughts. For example, the counselor can explain that "I'm not going to let him get away with that" could be shifted to "He did something I didn't like. I'll tell the teacher." In addition, the counselor can help the youth to link his thoughts, feelings, and behaviors. The youth can learn to notice the physical cues in his body that indicate strong feelings (e.g., racing heart, flushed face) and learn other coping skills to deal with these feelings, such as coloring, journaling, exercising, or calling a friend.

After practicing the CBT process with the youth several times, the counselor can teach the young client how to track his thoughts and combat triggering thoughts with more productive thoughts. As part of the process of challenging thoughts, the youth can engage in healthier and more effective behaviors. CBT is traditionally a talk therapy method, but creative interventions should be implemented whenever possible because creative applications and modifications are developmentally appropriate for young people.

Clinical Toolbox 14.4

In the Pearson e-text, click here to review a creative CBT activity that can be used with youth.

Problem-Solving Skills

Problem-solving skills training (PSST) is a CBT approach that focuses on restructuring the cognitive processes of youth, which are thought to be at the heart of disruptive behaviors. PSST can help youth to engage in effective problem solving and avoid disruptive or otherwise unproductive behaviors. PSST can help youth to:

- identify the consequences of their actions;
- hold others accountable for their actions;
- better perceive how others feel;
- generate alternative solutions to interpersonal problems; and
- identify ways that they can get their needs/desires met in a way that is respectful to themselves and others.

PSST is a highly structured intervention, and it can be conducted in individual or group sessions (Weisz & Kazdin, 2010).

When applying PSST, counselors should first introduce the verbal problem-solving steps. (There are many different problem-solving models that can be used, but all have similar steps.) The steps are as follows:

- What am I supposed to do?
- What else can I do?
- What will happen if I do this?
- What choice should I make?
- How did I do?

When introducing the steps, counselors should take time to explain and process each step with the youth. The first step focuses on ensuring the youth is able to identify and understand what is being asked of him or her by an adult or other authority figure. For example, a young person must ensure her bedroom is clean and must clean her room when asked by her parents. The youth should consciously evaluate her options. She can choose to clean her room, or she can choose to engage in alternative tasks, such as watching TV or playing a video game. The youth can also refuse to clean her room by screaming, throwing things, or storming out of the room. The youth should take time to consider all her options and what will happen if she makes any of those choices. She will likely determine that she will be permitted to play or will be praised for cleaning her room, whereas she will be punished for any of the other actions. Next, counselors can help the youth to determine what choice she should make based on the options and the likely consequences. Finally, the youth makes a choice and evaluates that decision.

After learning the steps, youth can practice applying the steps to various problems in session through talk therapy and role-playing. Counselors can use games and real-life scenarios to teach youth how to use the problem-solving skills. PSST is especially relevant in residential treatment facilities that facilitate real-life problem solving in a controlled environment. Counselors can teach PSST to the youth in the facility, as can the staff who supervise the youth throughout the day (direct care workers). When youth are faced with a difficult situation or a situation that has historically led to unhelpful behaviors, staff can guide the youth through the PSST process to foster healthier adaptive behaviors.

Counselors might also incorporate the use of operant conditioning into a young person's counseling plan to motivate the youth to apply PSST. Parents or caregivers can learn to implement the operant conditioning system. In PSST, a token economy system is encouraged; tokens serve as positive reinforcement for working hard. At first, tokens should be given to the youth each time he or she performs a desirable behavior. Over time, tokens should be given randomly, every few times the youth behaves well or participates. Tokens can also be taken away as a form of negative punishment for undesirable behaviors in counseling. The youth can exchange the tokens for a small treat at the end of sessions or in the home or treatment environment.

As an example of PSST in action, consider an incident at school in which a client was bullying another child. The counselor might ask the client "When it comes to bullying, what are you supposed to do?" If the child answers that he is supposed to talk with someone about how to handle the bully, the counselor can give a token. If the youth answers with sarcasm or silliness (e.g., "I'm supposed to hit them"), the counselor can take away a token. The counselor can then inquire about other ways to handle the situation. After identifying the undesired consequences that come as the result of bullying, the youth can identify the more helpful and appropriate choices. The counselor and client can then role-play alternative, more adaptive behaviors to rehearse the more desirable behavior. By the end of counseling, the youth should ideally use the steps automatically and not need to verbally process the problem-solving steps.

PSST is a targeted intervention that can be used to help youth to understand the consequences of their behaviors. It is an effective intervention for helping youth to change their perceptions, beliefs, and experiences. The PSST model is one tool that can be integrated into a holistic counseling approach.

Dialectical Behavior Therapy

Dialectical behavior therapy (DBT) is a multipronged approach that can be used preventively with youth who display subthreshold behavior problems or as an intervention for youth with diagnosable disruptive behavior problems (Rathus & Miller, 2015). Central to DBT is a focus on helping clients to develop their ability to effectively regulate their emotions. Counselors who use DBT help youth to address personal and environmental factors that might trigger unhelpful behaviors. Next, counselors guide youth to develop healthy emotion regulation skills and address any barriers to implementing such skills. Table 14.7 provides an overview of the skills and interventions that would be used for specific types of behavior problems.

Table 14.7 DBT Interventions to Address Disruptive Behaviors

DBT Skill Module	Disruptive Behaviors Addressed	Example Interventions
Emotion regulation	• Emotional outbursts • Mood swings • Depression • Shame/guilt • Anxiety	• Understanding and changing emotions • Reframing subjective experiences • Reducing emotional vulnerability • Applying the PLEASE (treat **p**hysical illness, balance **ea**ting, avoid mood-altering drugs, get **s**leep and **e**xercise) acronym
Distress tolerance	• Impulsivity • Risky sexual behavior • Truancy • Substance use • Aggression • Suicidality • Nonsuicidal self-injury	• Self-soothing with six senses: IMPROVE (**i**magery, **m**eaning, **p**rayer, **r**elaxing, **o**ne thing in the moment, **v**acation, **e**ncouragement) • Exploring pros and cons

Walking the middle path	• Black-or-white thinking
	• Limited empathy
	• Limited conflict resolution skills
	• Difficulty making desired changes
		• Identifying dialectical dilemmas:
		  ◦ Emotional vulnerability versus self-invalidation
		  ◦ Crisis versus inhibited experiencing
		  ◦ Autonomy versus dependence
		• Validating self and others
		• Changing behaviors (reinforcement and shaping, punishment and extinction)

Core mindfulness	• Limited insight into personal thoughts, feelings, and behaviors
	• Inattentiveness
	• Difficulty accepting uncomfortable feelings
	• Difficulty producing desired feelings
	• Lack of personal identity
	• Sense of emptiness/dissociation
		• Using core mindfulness skills
		  ◦ Positive, nonjudgmental state of mind
		  ◦ Observe surroundings
		  ◦ Stay focused
		  ◦ Do what works

Note: Adapted from *DBT Skills Manual for Adolescents*, by J. H. Rathus & A. L. Miller, 2015, New York, NY: Guilford.

Counselors can use various DBT concepts to promote emotion regulation skills, distress-tolerance skills, and mindfulness skills (Rathus & Miller, 2015). Affective education can help youth to understand their behaviors and find emotional relief in healthier ways. DBT interventions also can help youth to understand how their thoughts, feelings, and behaviors affect, and are affected by, others. Counselors might also choose to integrate key stakeholders into the therapeutic process (e.g., family, friends, teachers) to provide holistic interventions for behavior problems.

Integrating Family

When working to integrate family members into the therapeutic process, counselors should educate those closest to the youth about the potential sources of behavior problems. As previously discussed, there are many types of behavior problems (i.e., subthreshold and diagnosable disorders), and there are many ways that behavior problems develop (e.g., as a coping skill, in reaction to a traumatic event). In addition, there are many factors that support the use of inappropriate or unhelpful behaviors in youth (e.g., unintentional reinforcement from others, feelings of power or control). Counselors can inform family members about the youth's developmental trajectory and the mechanisms through which his or her behaviors seem to be supported in the environment and through interpersonal relationships.

Counselors should inform family members up front about the level of care and the type of support needed by the youth from his or her family and social support people. Younger children will inherently require more investment from their families, but youth of all ages need support from their families to succeed in counseling. Some youth might simply require encouragement and occasional support from their parents. For example, a youth who is struggling with slight behavior difficulties in class might be able to attend counseling in school with minimal involvement from his or her parents. However, other youth might need to engage in more intensive family therapy to overcome difficulties that originate in the family system and are manifested behaviorally (e.g., paternal substance use, familial abuse, unhelpful family dynamics).

Parents are often the point of contact between a youth and his or her counselor. Parents can serve as vital sources of information; they have unique perspectives and often share details that the youth otherwise would not divulge. Parents can also serve as collaborators to monitor youth behaviors, implement protocols in the home setting, enforce rules consistently, and/or practice new skills learned in counseling.

Engaging family members in the therapeutic process can sometimes be challenging. It is often difficult to schedule times when all family members are available for counseling sessions. Some members of the family might not be invested in the therapeutic process, and others might not be ready to change. In addition, many parents have multiple responsibilities, and it might be difficult for them to find the time and energy to invest in counseling-related endeavors. Counselors should do their best to secure the help of family members whenever possible while remaining realistic about the limitations associated with integrating family members into counseling. Family involvement is a key component to addressing behavior problems in youth. The following sections discuss parent management training (PMT) and MST, two of the more commonly used approaches that integrate family.

PARENT MANAGEMENT TRAINING

Youth are intimately connected to their families, and the home environment is a key consideration in effective counseling interventions for youth who have disruptive behavior problems (APA, 2013a; Weisz & Kazdin, 2010). Family counseling interventions should be implemented whenever possible, and counselors should work to engage family members—as appropriate—so the family is involved in the development and implementation of the treatment plan.

Many family therapy models can be applied when working with youth who have disruptive behavior disorders, but several models have evidence to support their use; they are described later in this section. Because of the nature of disruptive behavior disorders, counselors should clearly delineate therapy rules and expectations when engaging in family therapy.

Behaviorally based family interventions have the most evidence of success for youth who have disruptive behavior disorders (Barkley, 2013; Weisz & Kazdin, 2010). **Parent management training (PMT)** is one program that provides a clear, effective, targeted strategy for family behavior change. PMT is a highly structured, manualized approach to counseling this population, and it includes various assessments and worksheets that accompany each step of the program (Barkley, 2013).

In PMT, parents are viewed as key predictors of youth behaviors. The goals of PMT include:

- increasing parents' ability to communicate rules and expectations in the home;
- increasing children's understanding of consequences when family rules are breeched;
- increasing parents' focus on positive reinforcement; and
- building on children's successes. (Barkley, 2013; Weisz & Kazdin, 2010)

The first step in PMT is to educate parents about the basic motivations for youth misbehavior. In this step, parents learn about individual characteristics of the child that might lead to disruptive behavior (e.g., a difficult temperament, high levels of anxiety) and parental characteristics that might exacerbate such factors (e.g., inconsistent rule enforcement, limited ability to express feelings). Family stress events (e.g., a divorce) and environmental factors (e.g., limited access to resources) are also explained in the early stages of counseling.

Next, parents are asked to pay attention to their child's behaviors and identify the triggers that most often lead to misbehavior (e.g., going to the grocery store, chore time). Parents are encouraged to ignore undesirable behavior and reinforce desired behaviors through praise and quality time. Some parents might think that rewarding is synonymous with bribing; counselors should explain that bribes are given before a desired behavior is carried out (e.g., "Here's a candy bar; go clean the kitchen"). Rewards are given after a behavior has been completed, which ideally reinforces the youth's desire to use desirable behaviors without being prompted or redirected.

If reinforcement is not enough to eliminate disruptive behaviors, parents can implement a token economy system. They can give the youth an item (e.g., poker chip, sticker, point on a chart) for desirable behaviors and take away the item for undesirable behaviors. Time-outs can be used to supplement the token economy as needed (Barkley, 2013).

It is important for parents to anticipate problematic situations for youth and to provide clear rules preemptively. For example, if a child tends to misbehave at the grocery store, parents should clearly identify the consequence for misbehavior and ask the youth to list behaviors that are inappropriate or unhelpful while at the store. Parents should praise the youth when desired behaviors occur in the store; they might even consider a token award at the end of a store trip that goes well. If youth misbehave in the store, parents should leave immediately and implement the predetermined, reasonable behavior (e.g., no television for the rest of the day). Parents should be as consistent as possible with rule enforcement and punishments.

Clinical Toolbox 14.5

In the Pearson e-text, click here to read more information about PMT skills.

Counselors should remind parents that youth and parent behavior change requires a significant amount of time and energy, and PMT is a long-term lifestyle change, rather than a quick fix. Counselors should take time to validate parents' struggles and make referrals for individual or couples counseling as necessary.

Counselors who work with youth individually and in the context of the home will be able to address the majority of contributors to disruptive behavior. However, counselors working with youth who have especially severe behavior problems should consider integrating the school and community, in addition to individual and family counseling, to implement a holistic intervention plan.

MULTISYSTEMIC THERAPY

Multisystemic therapy (MST) is a comprehensive approach for addressing serious behavior problems in children and adolescents (Henggeler & Schaeffer, 2010). This comprehensive treatment approach blends CBT, family therapy, and community psychology foundations (MST Services, 2015). Although all systems play a role in youth development, the primary caregivers for youth with behavior problems are viewed as the most influential elements of change (Henggeler & Schaeffer, 2010). MST focuses on harnessing resources in multiple settings to work toward nine key principles:

1. Identifying the function that each behavior problem serves in the youth's life
2. Focusing on strengths and protective factors in the youth and in his or her surroundings
3. Encouraging and developing responsible youth and family behaviors
4. Creating goals and objectives that provide concrete definitions of the problem and measurable solutions

5. Identifying and altering the home, school, and community interactions that support youth behavior problems
6. Implementing developmentally appropriate interventions that support the youth's academic, career, and personal–social growth
7. Implementing interventions that require weekly or daily family participation
8. Regularly assessing readiness to change and progress
9. Providing the primary caregivers with the tools needed to generalize the therapeutic interventions so long-term behavior change can be maintained (MST Services, 2015)

The MST assessment process begins in vivo after the initial referral. Counselors visit the home, the school, and places where the youth spends a considerable amount of time (e.g., the park, an afterschool club). Next, the family and other important people (e.g., the youth's teacher, a protective services agent) identify desired outcomes. The MST provider develops overarching goals and works to understand the purpose that the youth's maladaptive behavior serves in the family system (e.g., to meet a need for attention, as an unhealthy coping skill, to avoid unwanted stressors). With this information, the counselor prioritizes the overarching goals into smaller goals.

Next, counselors employ empirically supported interventions (e.g., CBT, PSST, PMT) to reduce risk factors and harness strengths in the youth's environment (Henggeler & Schaeffer, 2010). Counselors measure progress toward change and reevaluate the treatment goals accordingly. Many MST programs are implemented through the juvenile justice system, and such programs are intensive, with counselors spending time in the home and in the community with the youth and his or her family.

Psychopharmacotherapy

Medication is not commonly supported for use with disruptive behavior problems. Often, though, comorbid disorders such as ADHD or depression can be addressed with medication. Medication should always be used in conjunction with mental health interventions to address the core difficulties and promote sustainable wellness.

Although medication is not highly indicated for use with disruptive behavior problems, psychopharmacotherapy interventions have been studied for use with this population. Some medications may target specific symptoms that cause problems (e.g., impulsiveness, irritability). Medications that have been used to address behavioral symptoms in youth include mood stabilizers, antidepressants, stimulants, selective norepinephrine reuptake inhibitors, and antipsychotics (Smith & Coghill, 2010). Of these interventions, risperidone—an atypical antipsychotic medication—holds promise in targeting aggression, severe irritability, and mood dysregulation behaviors in youth who do not have comorbid disorders (Pringsheim, Hirsch, Gardner, & Gorman, 2015).

Psychopharmacotherapy interventions can be helpful in various ways. Medications may provide quick relief from problematic symptoms. Also, medications can bring youth to a baseline so they can attend, comprehend, and fully participate in mental health interventions. Medications can be systematically tapered as youth's bodies become acclimated to chemical levels, and as youth are better able to implement newly learned skills and manage their behavior.

I CAN START COUNSELING PLAN FOR JACE

This chapter opened with a quote from Jace, a 14-year-old Hispanic boy who is displaying disruptive behavior problems. The following I CAN START conceptual framework outlines counseling considerations that may be helpful to a school counselor or a clinical counselor who works with Jace.

C = Contextual Assessment

Jace is a 14-year-old Hispanic boy who has one younger brother and a mother who works two jobs. Jace's mother reported that her pregnancy with Jace was difficult because his father was in jail, and Jace was born with colic. Jace was bullied in elementary school because he is overweight and has some learning difficulties. Jace is currently friends with two boys with similar home lives, cultural backgrounds, and behavior problems.

Jace's father used to verbally and physically abuse Jace and his mother when he used alcohol. He no longer lives in the home and is facing criminal charges for a fourth offense of driving while intoxicated. Although Jace is no longer exposed to harsh parenting, he does experience a lack of supervision; when his mom is not at work, she often complains that her "nerves are shot" and she needs to "sleep it off." Jace's neighborhood has limited resources, and many members of his immediate community use violence to obtain what they want.

A = Assessment and Diagnosis

Diagnosis = 313.81 (F91.3) Oppositional Defiant Disorder, Moderate

N = Necessary Level of Care

> In-home family counseling (once per week)
>
> Individual counseling (once per week)

S = Strengths

> **Self:** Jace has strong family values as evidenced by the way he protects his brother from bullies, spends quality time with him, and makes sure his needs are met. Jace is independent and assertive, and he is able to make and maintain friendships.
>
> **Family:** Jace has a strong bond with his younger brother and has a dedicated and caring mother. He knows his father and can contact him when desired. Jace has several supportive aunts, uncles, and cousins in the same or nearby neighborhoods.
>
> **School/Community:** Jace and his family have local public transportation that offers access to all necessary shopping and social outlets. Several churches in the community offer afterschool programs, and the community has a YMCA, Boys & Girls Club, and Big Brothers/Big Sisters. There are also many sliding-scale mental health facilities in the community, and the school employs a full-time school counselor.

T = Treatment Approach

- CBT focusing primarily on affective education, relaxation, and exposure-based approaches
- PMT to increase his mother's involvement and consistency in the home

A = Aim and Objective of Counseling (90-day objectives)

Jace will learn to identify the connection between his thoughts, feelings, and behaviors. Jace will identify 5 triggers and 5 anger cues that occur before disruptive behaviors and will record these in a journal. Jace will create a list of 10 anger reducers that he can use when he notices anger cues.

Jace will learn and use mindfulness techniques. Jace will notice the physical and cognitive symptoms that typically precede disruptive behaviors and will use mindfulness practices to avoid disruptive behaviors 4 out of 5 times.

Jace will increase his ability to tolerate uncomfortable emotions. Jace will express emotions verbally and through expressive arts at least 3 times per week. Jace will use 1 mindfulness activity per day.

Jace's mother will support healthier behaviors in Jace. Jace's mother will spend quality time with her sons twice per week, will reinforce desirable behaviors in Jace every time she notices them, and will provide consistent and reasonable consequences for undesirable behaviors.

R = Research-Based Interventions

Counselor will help Jace to learn, develop, and/or apply the following skills:

- Affective education—understanding what he is experiencing in his body and mind and the impact it has on his behaviors
- Cognitive restructuring
- Problem-solving skills
- Mindfulness
- PMT

T = Therapeutic Support Services

> Physical evaluation/medication assessment with a primary care doctor
>
> Big Brothers/Big Sisters referral
>
> Mental health referral for Jace's mother

Summary

Many youth experience some disruptive behavior problems that are harmful or unhelpful to themselves, others, or property. The two main behavior diagnoses in youth include oppositional defiant disorder and conduct disorder. Subthreshold behavior problems do not meet the criteria for formal diagnosis, but counselors can address these struggles, as well as a wide array of behavior problems.

Disruptive behaviors develop across time as the result of genetics, biological factors, family dynamics, environments, and learned behaviors (APA, 2013a; Liu et al., 2012). When working to understand disruptive behavior problems in youth, counselors should use informal and formal assessment tools. Counselors should also assess for comorbid and differential diagnoses (APA 2013a; Barry, Golmaryami, Rivera-Hudson, & Frick, 2013).

The common treatment components for addressing behavior problems focus on learning skills that can be used to prevent disruptive behaviors. Behavioral interventions, cognitive restructuring, and affective education can be implemented with the youth individually, but integrating the family, school, and community is ideal because doing so typically results in better outcomes. MST is the most comprehensive intervention to address a youth's holistic context, but it requires an abundance of resources, access to such programs, and a significant time investment from clients, counselors, and family members. Counselors can strive for a holistic intervention process that pulls on a CBT framework and integrates specific techniques, such as PSST. To best support this population, counselors should also engage parents and use PMT principles whenever possible.

MyLab Counseling: Counseling Children and Adolescents

Try the Topic 11 Assignments: *Strategies for Addressing Disruptive Behavior Problems in Youth.*

CHAPTER 15

Abuse and Trauma

THE CASE OF JIA

Jia is my everything. You need to know that from the start—I'd do anything for her. She's been through so much—more than any kid should for her age. Her father died a few years ago, and now all of this has happened.

Okay, so my brother used to pick up Jia from her preschool, and then he would drop her off at my house down the street. Since my mother is elderly and lives with me, she would watch her until I got home from work. He did this for most of the school year. I remember him telling me he was happy to help out since I had a lot on my plate—you know, with mom and work.

I am completely heartbroken and betrayed by what happened to her. You know it's all my fault. I should have seen this coming. My brother and I were beaten and sexually abused by our father when we were little, and we swore we'd never be that way. We were going to be good parents, the ones that went to church and loved our kids. I thought he was better. I thought God made us both better. Or so I thought until a month or so ago, when it all came crashing down on me.

It came out that not only was my bother sexually abusing his kids but my little Jia, too. I guess his wife came home early from work and found him taking pictures of the kids naked. He said it was not how it looked, but she called the cops and then called me. I'm so angry and hurt. How could he do that, and how could I be so stupid?

I mean, I saw the signs. Like for the last few months, Jia, who used to love school, now never wants to go. She has trouble sleeping and wakes up a lot just screaming at the top of her lungs. She needs to be comforted to go back to sleep. She used to be so sweet, and lately she has been really nasty. If I say anything to her, she just snaps at me. Last week, I came into her room, and she almost jumped through the roof. I could not have scared her. She's been so withdrawn lately and doesn't want to play with her friends in the courtyard and just stays in her room a lot.

And this was really disturbing: I found her touching herself down there in the bathroom. I mean, I saw her, and then when I asked her what was she doing, she denied it all. But I know what I saw. What am I going to do? I can't even find the words to talk to her. Can you help us?

—Jia's mother

Over half of all youth in America will experience at least one or more traumatic events in their lifetime (Nader & Fletcher, 2014). Because of the high prevalence with which trauma affects youth, counselors must be aware of and understand trauma-informed practices, and they must know how to counsel youth who have experienced traumatic events. Counselors can treat the adverse consequences brought on by traumatic events, and it is important that they know the physical and psychological impacts and the associated risks and preventive factors of trauma.

This chapter addresses the **trauma-** and **stressor-related disorders** presented in the *Diagnostic and Statistical Manual of Mental Disorders,* Fifth Edition (*DSM-5*; American Psychiatric Association [APA], 2013a). Not all youth who experience trauma or are abused will have long-term trauma symptoms, but all youth who are abused benefit from counseling that helps them to process and integrate their experiences (Kress, Moorhead, & Zoldan, 2015). Because youth who are abused and/or traumatized share similar risk and protective factors and benefit from similar counseling interventions, these two topics are combined in many places in this chapter.

This chapter discusses the diagnostic criteria, assessment, and counseling approaches that are useful and effective when working with youth who have experienced abuse and traumatic events. Although many youth manifest natural reactions to traumatic events (e.g., sadness, irritability, concentration issues) and only require short-term counseling services, other youth are affected more severely (e.g., experience overwhelming fear, lose interest in activities, have depressive symptoms, are hypervigilant, experience decline in academic performance, have difficulties sleeping and eating) and thus require longer-term counseling (American Academy of Child and Adolescent Psychiatry [AACAP], 2010a; American Psychological Association, 2008). Adverse effects and difficulties may, in some cases, develop into mental health disorders.

This chapter highlights the most frequent causes of trauma-related difficulties in American youth—youth maltreatment, disaster, and violence—and the common associated reactions, which include **reactive attachment disorder**, **posttraumatic stress disorder (PTSD)**, and **complex trauma** reactions.

THE NATURE OF ABUSE AND TRAUMA-RELATED DIFFICULTIES IN YOUTH

Trauma, in the technical sense, is not a reaction but an event. More specifically, trauma or a traumatic event is the "exposure to actual or threatened death, serious injury, or sexual violence" either by direct personal experience, witnessing an event happening to another person, learning about an event that happened to someone close to the youth (e.g., parent, sibling), or the repeated exposure to the details of traumatic events (APA, 2013a, p. 271).

Traumatic events include diverse experiences, such as exposure to natural disasters, mass interpersonal violence, transportation accidents, fires, motor vehicle accidents, assault, rape, partner violence, torture, war, animal attacks, and child abuse (Briere & Scott, 2015). Researchers have attempted to differentiate and categorize traumatic events, and they identify a traumatic event that happens only once (Type 1) versus traumatic events that have an ongoing, chronic quality and include ongoing abuse (Type 2; Nader & Fletcher, 2014). Table 15.1 provides a summary of Type 1 and Type 2 traumatic events. Type 2 traumatic events are associated with a poorer prognosis due to the more adverse and complicated reactions they invoke; yet, some individuals who experience Type 1 traumatic events may have similar reactions (Nader & Fletcher, 2014)

Because trauma reactions and experiences are diverse, there is variability in how youth respond to such events, and not all youth require intensive counseling treatment (American Psychological Association, 2008). For many youth, the emotional response to traumatic events includes anxiety, terror, guilt, shock, irritability, hostility, and depression (American Psychological Association, 2008). Youth may have difficulty concentrating, experience confusion, self-blame, have intrusive thoughts (or flashbacks), have lower self-efficacy, fear they will lose control, and fear reoccurrence of the traumatic event. Because abuse and trauma occur at different ages and developmental points in a youth's life, the impact of trauma is case by case and

Table 15.1 Type 1 and Type 2 Traumatic Events	
Type 1: Single-Incident Traumas	**Type 2: Complex or Repetitive Traumas**
• Natural disasters, such as earthquakes, avalanches, hurricanes, floods, wildfires, typhoons, mudslides, drought, tornados, and volcanic eruptions	• Witnessing or being a victim of domestic, interpersonal, and/or community violence
• Accidental traumatic events, such as motor vehicle accidents (e.g., automobiles, trains, airplanes) and explosions	• Continued and ongoing traumatic events caused by parent and/or caregiver, such as youth maltreatment, domestic violence, and child sexual abuse
• Nonaccidental, one-time traumatic events, such as animal attacks, robbery, assault, and invasive medical procedures	• Deliberate traumatic events caused by another, such as rape, assault, war, torture, and forced displacement (e.g., political persecution)
	• Chronic injury or illness of self or others
	• Being a victim of bullying or school violence
	• System-induced trauma, such as removal from the home, multiple community placements, traumatic foster placements, and separation from siblings

situation dependent. For example, a young person with good prior functioning, a supportive family and peer network, adaptive skills and attitudes, and positive prior experiences may interpret a traumatic event differently than might a youth who has historically received little support, has complicating family adversities and challenges, and has experienced many vulnerabilities prior to the traumatic event's occurrence.

Trauma exposure can affect a young person's developing brain, ability to emotionally regulate (i.e., tolerate and regulate painful internal states), self-concept (e.g., poor self-worth and body image, guilt), attachment and ability to feel safe and connected in relationships, behavior control (e.g., poor impulse control), dissociation (e.g., impaired memory), and physical health (e.g., difficulty sleeping and eating, somatic complaints; Briere & Lanktree, 2012). In addition, abuse and trauma can influence brain activity, brain receptors, and connectivity, which affect youth's cognitive functioning and may make it difficult for them to manage their emotional responses, regulate their mood and affect, and form and maintain relationships (Nader & Fletcher, 2014).

Normal brain development progresses in a predictable fashion. For example, over time young people master **self-regulatory processes**, which include learning from their mistakes, problem solving, having emotional awareness, and developing distress tolerance skills (Underwood & Dailey, 2017). Traumatic events can shift young people's development in such a way that their brains function in "survival mode" (Underwood & Dailey, 2017). Depending on the stage of development and the youth, the shift may result in stunted emotional growth and development, and youth may attempt to reduce trauma-related stress by engaging in maladaptive, harmful activities (e.g., substance abuse, aggression, reckless sexual behaviors, self-injury) to numb their emotions, thoughts, and pain (Briere & Scott, 2015).

In many cases, youth who are exposed to traumatic events display a sense of resiliency and adaptability and return to their prior level of functioning (AACAP, 2010a; American Psychological Association, 2008). Only a minority of youth exposed to traumatic events are diagnosed with PTSD, suggesting that vulnerability or certain risk factors likely increase the probability of youth developing PTSD (Nader & Fletcher, 2014). Various resiliency factors seem to be insulative and help to prevent trauma reactions (American Psychological Association, 2008). Table 15.2 provides a summary of risk and resiliency factors associated with youth

Table 15.2	Risk and Resiliency Factors Associated with Youth Developing a Mental Illness Due to a Traumatic Event
Category	**Overview**
Characteristics of the event	This category describes the severity, frequency, duration, cause, and nature of the event. The more severe, frequent, and violent the event, the greater the associated risk. In situations involving maltreatment, the closeness of the perpetrator, type of violence used, and lack of social and emotional support can exacerbate the associated risks.
Characteristics of the young person	This category describes the young person's emotional, cognitive, psychobiological, and behavioral responses to the event. The category includes young people's developmental stage, age, gender, and ability to employ coping skills. Factors affecting young people's resiliency include cognitive processing skills (e.g., problem-solving abilities, coping skills, flexibility and adaptability, accurately perceiving their ability to control the situation), help-seeking behaviors or seeking out assistance from social support systems, ability to self-regulate intense emotions (e.g., sadness, anger), ability to attribute the experience to external factors (understanding the event was not their fault or something that could be controlled), and engagement with others (e.g., peers) and their community (e.g., school, athletics, employment, culture, religion). In addition, the younger the child and the more intense his or her perception of fear and hopelessness, the greater the associated risk.
Characteristics of the young person's environment	The young person's family, including the level of support, safety, resources, family cohesiveness, and dynamics, can all affect how the youth experiences a traumatic event. Community support and resources available to the youth and the family also support youth resiliency. Less parent, family, and community support increases risk. Resiliency is fostered by family, peer, and community support.

Note: Adapted from "Childhood posttraumatic stress disorder," by K. Nader & K. E. Fletcher, 2014. In E. J. Mash & R. A. Barkley (Eds.), *Child Psychopathology* (3rd ed.), pp. 476–528, New York, NY: Guilford.

developing a mental illness due to a traumatic event. With all youth who have experienced abuse and trauma, counselors should identify, cultivate, and enhance these protective factors to increase and maximize their resiliency.

In addition, studies have shown that early, prolonged, and/or multiple traumatic events are associated with poorer outcomes, including more severe, long-standing trauma-related symptomology and reactions (Nader & Fletcher, 2014). Table 15.3 provides a summary of the reactions and responses to traumatic events in youth of different ages.

If violence is a component of the traumatic event, youth have an increased risk of developing a conduct and/or substance-related difficulty (Cerdá, Tracy, Sánchez, & Galea, 2011). They are at an increased risk for repeated victimizations, and they are prone to victimization later in their lives (Widom, Czaja, & Dutton, 2008). Revictimization—or victimization over multiple periods of time and incidents—is thought to be related to the individual's inability to detect danger, recognize risky situations, and say 'no' to others and to the likelihood of freezing in stressful situations (Nader & Fletcher, 2014). A small minority of those who experience repeated victimization may initiate or perpetrate victimization on others (Nader & Fletcher, 2014).

Table 15.3 Reactions and Responses to Traumatic Events in Youth of Different Ages

Ages	Reactions
Infant (0–2 years)	• Difficulties forming attachments with parents and caregivers • Difficulties or inconsistencies with feeding, eating, and sleep • Exaggerated startle reactions • Repetitive play (i.e., play that does not change, may mimic autism spectrum disorder) • Blank facial expressions • Fear of others as demonstrated by overreaction to strangers
Young children (2–5 years)	• Delays in reaching language milestones • Irritability, agitation, or fussiness • Increased number of tantrums • Clinginess to parent • Over- or underactivity • Traumatic or adult content in play and conversations (e.g., acting out traumatic events in play)
School-age children (6–12 years)	• Impairments in concentration and attention • Frequent reports of somatic complaints (e.g., headache, stomachache, nausea) • Exaggerated emotions (e.g., excessive tears or crying, sadness) • Difficulties making the transition to new activities and environments • Excessive discussion of fears and scary thoughts/ideas • Regressed behaviors, such as bedwetting, thumb-sucking, and infantile fears • Increased aggressive behaviors with peers and siblings
Adolescents (12–18 years)	• Excessive conversations about trauma, death, and scary thoughts and feelings • Defiant behaviors (e.g., refusal to comply with rules, disrespectful speech, running away from home) • Increased aggressive behaviors (e.g., fighting, property destruction) • Increased need for sleep • Decreased desire to engage in previously pleasurable activities (e.g., sports, clubs, dancing, hanging out with friends) • Increased use of alcohol and/or drugs

Note: Adapted from *Parenting a Child Who Has Experienced Trauma,* by Child Welfare Information Gateway (CWIG), 2014, Washington, DC: U.S. Department of Health and Human Services, Children's Bureau.

TYPES OF ABUSE AND TRAUMA-RELATED DIFFICULTIES

This chapter highlights the most frequent causes of traumatic events that youth experience and explores the ways such events can affect youth.

Youth Maltreatment

Counselors who work with youth frequently find themselves counseling those who have been, or currently are, **maltreated** or are experiencing abuse and/or neglect. Unfortunately, child maltreatment is somewhat prevalent. According to the U.S. Department of Health and Human Services (USDHHS; 2016), more than 3 million reports of maltreatment were made in 2014, with over 700,000 cases being founded and over 1,500 resulting in death. Professionals made more than 60% of these reports, so counselors must know the signs and symptoms of youth maltreatment and be prepared to report such instances (USDHHS, 2016).

According to the USDHHS (2016), youth maltreatment, at a minimum, is:

> Any recent act or failure to act on the part of a parent or caretaker which results in death, serious physical or emotional harm, sexual abuse or exploitation; or an act or failure to act, which presents an imminent risk of serious harm.(p. 17)

Although most states determine their own response and procedure for dealing with and investigating accusations or allegations of maltreatment, these inquires will ultimately result in either a substantiated determination (i.e., a support or founded allegation) or an unsubstantiated determination (i.e., insufficient evidence to move forward with a case). Counselors need to be mindful of their state laws, policies, and procedures concerning child maltreatment.

Counseling youth who have experienced maltreatment is not easy, and it frequently stirs up complex feelings and emotions for counselors. Feelings of anger, frustration, and agitation may arise toward the parent and/or perpetrator of the maltreatment. In some cases, counselors may get overinvolved in the young person's situation; they may feel anxious and compelled to protect and rescue the maltreated youth. In extreme cases, counselors may even consider violating professional boundaries to advocate for the youth. Counselors must intentionally monitor their thoughts and feelings when working with this population. They should seek regular supervision and peer consultation that aims to highlight youth's resiliency and hope for the future because these perceptions of youth protect counselors from boundary violations, emotional fatigue, compassion fatigue, and vicarious trauma (Silveira & Boyer, 2015).

Youth maltreatment is the overarching term that includes child abuse and neglect. Child abuse consists of physical, sexual, and emotional abuse, whereas neglect is the failure of parents to attend to the basic needs of the youth (e.g., adequately meeting a youth's emotional and physical needs). Although the differing forms of child abuse often receive more societal and media attention, child neglect is actually more prevalent. Child neglect is the most pervasive type of maltreatment (75%), followed by physical abuse (17%) and sexual abuse (8%; USDHHS, 2016). The following sections briefly present the signs and symptoms associated with each form of youth maltreatment.

CHILD ABUSE

Child abuse is the action or inaction that results in the emotional, physical, or sexual harm of a youth. It is sadly a prevalent phenomenon in the United States and around the world (AACAP, 2014; USDHHS, 2016).

A small percentage of youth who have experienced abuse ultimately die. Those who survive abuse are left with emotional bruises that often warrant counseling consideration and treatment (AACAP, 2014). Many researchers agree that early detection and treatment comprise the most effective approach to thwarting the long-term consequences of these types of abuse, and this requires that counselors take the signs, symptoms, and reports of abuse seriously (Nader & Fletcher, 2014). Youth who have been abused often display a compilation of the following symptomology: attachment and relationship difficulties; poor self-image; aggressive, disruptive, and sometimes illegal behaviors; self-destructive behaviors (e.g., self-mutilation, suicide); excessive fear and anxiety; feelings of helplessness and hopelessness; sleep issues and nightmares; substance use; and sexual acting-out behaviors (AACAP, 2014). Many of these symptoms will not surface until adolescence or later (AACAP, 2014; London, Bruck, Ceci, & Shuman, 2005).

Although parents and adults are the predominant abusers of youth, peers are also common perpetrators of abuse (Turner, Finkelhor, Hamby, Shattuck, & Ormrod, 2011). **Peer victimization** involves a youth becoming the target of another young person's physical, emotional, social, or emotional harm. Peer victimization can take many forms (e.g., bullying, assault, sexual assault, intimidation), and prevalence rates increase with age (Turner et al., 2011). Historically, researchers assumed that most peer victimization occurs in the school setting, but a considerable portion of peer victimization occurs outside traditional school settings (e.g., in the community, in online formats). Peer victimization can be devastating and carry long-term consequences for youth. It can contribute to poor adjustments in the academic, physical, social, personal, and mental health domains, and many youth carry these adverse consequences into adulthood (McDougall & Vaillancourt, 2015).

The following sections briefly present the signs and symptoms of physical, sexual, and emotional abuse of youth. The assessment, counseling approaches, and interventions associated with abuse and/or trauma reactions are covered later in this chapter.

Physical Abuse.   **Physical abuse** is the nonaccidental injury of a youth that may include hitting, punching, spanking, kicking, throwing, choking, shoving, pulling hair, burning, or any other action that physically hurts, impairs, or injures youth (Child Welfare Information Gateway [CWIG], 2013). Although physical abuse is often more prevalent in middle childhood and adolescence, boys tend to have a higher prevalence rate regardless of their age (Finkelhor, Turner, Shattuck, & Hamby, 2013). Often, the observable effects of these types of physical abuse are visible to the counselor. For example, physical abuse may manifest as scrapes, cuts, bruises, and sprains. In more severe situations, physical abuse can result in broken bones, internal injuries, and even brain damage.

Parents and caregivers may struggle to explain these physical injuries to others, and they may have difficulty providing a story that justifies the injury. They may also require the youth to wear inappropriate clothing to cover the injuries (e.g., long sleeves and long pants on warm days), and they may delay medical care for the youth out of fear of consequences. Parents or caregivers who physically abuse their children may have a history of outbursts, aggression, and violence, and they may even display aggression toward the child in social contexts. Abusers may also attempt to rationalize their behaviors by conceptualizing the youth as out of control or a troublemaker, or they may demonize the youth as "bad" (CWIG, 2013).

In most cases, the effects of physical abuse are visible, but sometimes a young person's behaviors lead a counselor to suspect abuse. Youth who are being abused may be overly harsh and aggressive, fearful and afraid of their parents, or withdrawn and depressed. They may report nightmares and insomnia, present with regressed behaviors, report injuries, and report that parents or caregivers severely discipline them (CWIG, 2013). Some signs and symptoms that physical abuse may be occurring in youth include (CWIG, 2013):

- unexplained injuries, including bruises, bites, burns, broken bones, or black eyes;
- noticeable bruises or scars after an absence from school;
- fear or nervousness during interactions with adults;
- reports of injuries, severe discipline, or nightmares;
- fear around parents or when it is time to return to parents (e.g., end of day at school);
- regressed behaviors (e.g., bedwetting, thumb-sucking);
- abuse or aggression toward peers, animals, or household pets; and
- violent themes or situations in play and in conversations.

Parents may display the following signs and symptoms in physical abuse situations:

- Unconvincing or conflicting information regarding the youth's injury (e.g., the child has lacerations on his arms, yet the parent states the child rolled down the steps)
- Harsh, demeaning disciplining of the youth
- Aggression toward the youth in social situations
- Avoiding medical attention (or using multiple doctors and hospitals if medical attention is sought)
- History of abuse and/or history of abusing animals
- Demonizing the child and his or her behaviors (e.g., she is evil)

Sexual Abuse.   **Sexual abuse** occurs when a person forces or exposes a youth to sexual activities for the person's own sexual purposes. Sexual abuse can include contact abuse, such as fondling, penetration, making the youth perform sexual acts (e.g., oral sex), and child pornography and prostitution. Some sexual abuse does not involve contact, such as making the youth view the perpetrator's sex organs, having the youth view others engaging in sexual acts, or engaging the youth in inappropriate perverse sexual talk.

Sexual abuse is prevalent in the United States and around the world. In the United States, 1 in 4 girls and 1 in 5 boys will be sexually abused over the course of their childhood (Finkelhor, Shattuck, Turner, & Hamby, 2014). Girls have a higher prevalence rate of sexual abuse and sexual assault perpetrated by adults and peers, especially in adolescence, as compared to their male counterparts (i.e., 27% vs. 5%; Finkelhor et al., 2014). Although childhood abuse and sexual assault are predictive of mental health disorders such as PTSD, sexual abuse and/or assault that occurs in conjunction with intimidation and physical abuse significantly increases a young person's risk of developing severe mental health disorders in the future (James, 2008).

The physical symptoms of sexual abuse are often focused on problems with the young person's genital area and may include pain, bleeding, bruising, and swelling. Youth may also present with medical diagnoses related to sexually transmitted diseases, urinary tract infections, and bowel problems (CWIG, 2013). Although the physical symptoms of sexual abuse may not be readily visible to counselors, behavioral observations may be clinically helpful in suggesting sexual abuse. Counselors need to be aware that youth who have been sexually abused often (a) possess extensive sexual knowledge or behaviors and may discuss sexual matters beyond their development level, (b) have difficulties with sleep, including nightmares, bedwetting, sleep disturbance, and fear of bedtime, (c) engage in excessive masturbation, (d) engage in acting-out behaviors, such as running away, aggression, and substance abuse to regulate strong emotions, and (e) become withdrawn, depressed, or anxious (CWIG, 2013). In addition, counselors need to consider that the majority of children do not reveal their sexual abuse or will retract claims of sexual abuse due to feelings of helplessness or entrapment, the pressure of secrecy by abusers, and poor responses or outcomes after past disclosures of abuse (London et al., 2005). Being mindful of these considerations, counselors should thoroughly explore all claims of sexual abuse and report all allegations. In youth, some signs and symptoms that sexual abuse may be occurring include (CWIG, 2013):

- bleeding, pain, and bruises in genital area;
- sexual behaviors or sophisticated sexual knowledge at a young age;
- quickly attaching to new or unknown adults;
- repetitive self-soothing behaviors (e.g., rocking, pacing);
- sleep disturbances, nightmares, and/or bedwetting;
- changes in appetite;
- decline in academic performance or attendance;
- refusal to change clothes in gym class and/or participate in physical activities;
- reporting sexual abuse of a parent or another person;
- running away from home; and
- substance use and/or reckless risk-taking behaviors.

Parents who sexually abuse youth may display the following sign and symptoms:

- They present as being overly protective of the youth (e.g., excessively limit the youth's ability to have contact with other children) or fail to provide any supervision of the child.
- They have high levels of secrecy and/or isolate the child from interactions with other adults (e.g., other family members).
- They experience jealousy related to other relationships the child has or seeks.
- They have a high reliance on the youth to provide emotional support.

Emotional Abuse.   **Emotional abuse** is psychological abuse that affects a youth's self-worth and emotional development (CWIG, 2013). This form of abuse is more difficult to detect and address because of differing perceptions of what defines emotional abuse. A diverse set of behaviors can constitute emotional abuse, but all of these behaviors leave internal bruises on the youth's self-worth, self-esteem, and internal world.

Emotional abuse often involves a pattern of behaviors that continually and repeatedly affect the youth. Emotional abuse may include, but is not limited to, the following:

- *Rejecting:* The adult will convince the youth that he or she is not wanted, is worthless, and is unlovable.
- *Ignoring:* The adult will make little to no attempt to initiate or return affection, show interest in, or even validate and encourage the youth.
- *Humiliating:* The adult will belittle, mock, criticize, shame, and demean the youth to make the youth feel worthless.
- *Intimidating:* The adult will threaten, manipulate, punish, and take advantage of the fact that the child needs to be cared for by an adult. In severe cases of emotional abuse, the adult will attempt to force the child's complete submission.
- *Isolating:* The adult will seclude, confine, and forbid the youth from engaging with other peers or being part of prosocial activities. In severe cases, the adult will confine the youth in a small space for extended periods of time (e.g., locking the child in the closest for hours).
- *Corrupting:* The adult will encourage the youth to engage in illegal acts or to misbehave (e.g., telling the youth that the strong always take what they want and the weak give it to them).

Although emotional abuse is frequently difficult to prove in child protective situations, this type of abuse appears to have the most significant impact on the development of trauma-related symptomology in youth (Turner et al., 2011). In addition, counselors should consider that emotional abuse is almost always present in other forms of abuse (CWIG, 2013). Some signs and symptoms that emotional abuse may be occurring in youth include (CWIG, 2013):

- extreme behaviors (e.g., being demanding, overly compliant, passive, and/or aggressive);
- indifference and/or lack of attachment with parents;
- delayed physical and/or emotional development;
- socially inappropriate behavior with other youth (e.g., demeaning and/or parenting other youth);
- displaying regressed behaviors such as head banging and excessive whining or crying;
- anxiety and possibly having an anxiety disorder;
- destructive behaviors, such as vandalism, stealing, lying, cruelty, and violence; and
- previous suicide attempts.

Parents who are emotionally abusive may display the following characteristics:

- Rejecting the youth (e.g., routinely criticizes, yells at, or blames the youth)
- Indifference to the well-being of the youth (e.g., refuses any offers of help, refuses to comply with school expectations for parents)
- Poor anger management or emotion regulation
- Difficulties with other adults, especially those in authority positions
- Frequently blaming or belittling the youth, especially in front of others
- Untreated mental illness and/or substance-related issue

CHILD NEGLECT

According to the USDHHS (2016), **neglect** is the most prevalent form of youth maltreatment. Neglect is characterized by lack of the supervision, provision, affection, and support needed for a youth to meet his or her needs for safety and well-being (CWIG, 2013). Neglect can affect multiple areas and domains in young people's lives, including their physical, emotional, medical, and educational worlds:

- *Physical neglect* could include excessively leaving the child with others, not adequately supervising the child, and not providing adequate basic needs for the youth, such as food, clothing, and shelter.
- *Emotional neglect* is similar to emotional abuse in that the parent ignores the youth's basic emotional needs for respect, love, acceptance, and affection. Parents in these situations often expose youth to violence, inconsistency, and substance use/abuse and may even isolate the youth from others.
- *Medical neglect* is not addressing the youth's emergent health needs (e.g., not taking the child to the hospital after a serious injury) or preventive care (e.g., not providing the child with vaccinations,

yearly doctor visits, or regular dentist appointments). For example, the parent does not take the youth to the dentist for most of his childhood, which results in the need to extract numerous permanent teeth.
- *Educational neglect* can include allowing the youth to excessively miss school, refusing the youth educational services in the school (e.g., not allowing the youth to be in special education services), and not enrolling the youth in any schooling.

Neglect is prevalent and poses severe consequences for youth. It is often the most significant predictor of violent crimes, property offending, nonviolent crimes, and status offending (e.g., consuming alcohol, running away, truancy; Evans & Burton, 2013). Some signs and symptoms that neglect may be occurring in youth include (CWIG, 2013):

- lack of medical and/or dental care (e.g., youth requires eyeglasses but does not have them);
- reports that no one is at home providing care;
- lack of adequate clothing or food;
- hygiene issues, such as body odor and bad breath;
- low body weight and smaller height and stature than other children his or her age;
- reckless behaviors (e.g., abuses alcohol or drugs); and
- frequent truancy from school or changing schools frequently.

Parents who neglect youth may display the following characteristics:

- Indifference to the well-being of the youth
- Irrational or bizarre behavior (e.g., leaving for a few days without telling anyone where he or she is going)
- Apathy toward the child
- Blaming the youth for his or her problems
- Abusing alcohol and/or other drugs or suffering from severe mental health issues that affect his or her ability to tend to the child

Adult Partner Violence in the Home (or Intimate Partner Violence)

Whether in the home or the community, many youth witness violence, with prevalence estimates being upwards of 35% to 85%—and exposure to violence increases a young person's chances of future victimization (American Psychological Association, 2008). Violence in the home, or **intimate partner violence (IPV)**, is a growing public concern, with approximately 5 million incidents of IPV reported annually (Rizo, Macy, Ermentrout, & Johns, 2011). IPV involves any physical, sexual, or emotional abuse by a past or current partner meant to intimidate, control, or manipulate. This type of violence does not require sexual intimacy and can occur in a hetero- or homosexual relationship. IPV exposure affects children and can cause devastating consequences. An estimated 8% of children between the ages of 2 and 17 have witnessed IPV incidents in the previous year (Finkelhor et al., 2013).

Exposure to IPV is associated with higher rates of child neglect and abuse (Herrenkohl, Sousa, Tajima, Herrenkohl, & Moylan, 2008) and increases the likelihood of cognitive, emotional, academic, and behavior problems in youth. IPV and family violence often co-occur with parental substance abuse, unemployment, and financial stress (Herrenkohl et al., 2008). In some cases, children appear resilient to the effects of IPV and family violence, and factors such as a high intelligence, positive coping skills, and access to community and social support resources seem to be the most protective factors in supporting this population's resilience (Herrenkohl et al., 2008).

Young clients who have witnessed IPV are likely to display various symptoms, including increased anxiety, fear, and/or guilt for being unable to protect the abused parent; excessive worry about the parent's well-being; gastrointestinal symptoms, such as ulcers or ongoing stomachaches; speech troubles; and age-inappropriate behaviors, such as bedwetting, thumb-sucking, or clinginess to the abused parent (Herrenkohl et al., 2008). Common behavior problems for this population include hyperactivity, difficulty controlling anger, aggressiveness, truancy, running away, or other attention-seeking behaviors (Herrenkohl et al., 2008). They may have trouble making friends or forming functional relationships with others. Children and teens who witness IPV are often distrustful of others, are distractible, and have difficulty concentrating. They may also experience suicidal ideation, depression, or PTSD, and they may practice self-injury (Finkelhor et al., 2013; Herrenkohl et al., 2008).

An additional concern for many young clients living in IPV situations is that there is often instability of caregivers. Parents and caregivers may divorce or separate, the child may be removed from the home, the abuser may be arrested or sentenced to a prison term, and the abused parent and/or children may need to stay at a shelter (Huth-Bocks, Schettini, & Shebroe, 2001). Young clients may also be manipulated by the perpetrator of the abuse. For example, they may be asked to spy on the victim of abuse, or they may be used as a tool to get the abused parent to return home (Edleson et al., 2007).

Witnessing IPV is a highly emotional and personal topic, and young clients may be hesitant to discuss their experiences out of fear, embarrassment, shame, or guilt. Also, abusers may have instructed them to never tell anyone about the violence they witness at home. Establishing rapport and creating a safe, comfortable environment is crucial in encouraging disclosure of abuse. Counselors should also explore their feelings toward IPV to ensure their attitudes and feelings will not hinder the counseling experience or make young clients feel uncomfortable or judged while disclosing their experiences.

Another concern for counselors working with young clients who witness IPV is the risk that they themselves may become victims of IPV. Physical harm may come to them unintentionally; they may try to intercede on the abused parent's behalf or try to protect a sibling who is being abused and may be physically harmed in the process. They may also be threatened or emotionally abused by the aggressor. Youth living with violent family members are at risk for neglect, abuse, or even homicide. Counselors must carefully address young clients' safety at home. In addition, counselors working with young clients who witness IPV should be aware of community resources that can assist witnesses, as well as victims of IPV. Counselors should also be familiar with state laws that explain or mandate their obligation to report IPV.

Mass Violence, Terror, or Disaster

Every year, millions of youth are directly or indirectly affected by natural or human-made disasters (Masten & Narayan, 2012). Although these disasters frequently only last seconds or days, the effects of these events can be devastating, taking communities and individuals months—if not years—to recover, reach equilibrium, and restore what was damaged. Incidents can range from human-caused disasters, such as mass shootings or acts of terror, to natural disasters, such as typhoons, hurricanes, or floods, to name just a few. Regardless of the type of event, these kinds of experiences disrupt young people's perception of the world, their sense of safety, and their general sense of social order. In addition, even youth who are not directly affected by these disasters can have immediate access to them through mass media, which can potentially confuse them, cause them uncertainty, or even make them perceive a threat to their own well-being (APA, 2013a; Masten & Narayan, 2012).

For youth, exposure to mass violence, terror, or disasters can contribute to significant emotional distress, an increased susceptibility to mental illness, and developmental delays (Felix, You, & Canino, 2013; Kletter et al., 2013). Furthermore, youth who are traumatized early in life can adopt unhealthy or irrational beliefs about their world, their community, and themselves, thus limiting their ability to form a strong personal identity and engage in meaningful interpersonal relationships (Briere & Lanktree, 2012). To complicate these adverse effects, in some situations young people may lose loved ones in these traumatic events. Young people's reactions to these events are diverse; Table 15.4 provides a summary of the most common youth reactions to mass violence, terror, or disaster.

These reactions to unplanned natural or human-made events are normal, and they may last days to weeks. Unfortunately, for some youth, these reactions persist, increase in severity, and affect their overall functioning. These developing reactions may evolve into a mental health disorder such as PTSD, which is characterized by continued hyperarousal, emotional numbing, intrusive re-experiencing, and excessive attempts to avoid disturbing memories (APA, 2013a; National Center for PTSD, 2010).

Although there is a general relationship between exposure to disaster or violence and PTSD symptomology, this exposure appears to be moderated significantly by social support (Salami, 2010). Youth who have adequate social support are more likely to have increased adaptive coping skills, reduced risk-taking

Table 15.4 Common Youth Reactions to Mass Violence, Terror, or Disaster

Reactions	Specific Symptoms
Emotional reactions	Shock Anger and/or irritability Sadness and grief Excessive nervousness and worry (e.g., rumination) Guilt Loss of pleasure in once pleasurable activities Difficulty being and remaining happy Difficulty expressing positive and/or loving emotions
Cognitive reactions	Disbelief Inability to concentrate Impaired decision making Memory impairments Nightmares and intrusive thoughts or memories Self-blame (e.g., younger children may even think they caused the event) Confusion and uncertainty Dissociation (e.g., feeling like they are in a fog, feeling as if the world is not real)
Physical reactions	Insomnia or sleep disturbances Increased bedwetting Decreased appetite Hyperarousal Increased startle response Somatic complaints (e.g., headaches, pain, fatigue)
Interpersonal reactions	Isolation and/or becoming socially withdrawn Impaired performance on schoolwork Increased relational tension and conflict Distrust of others (e.g., feeling abandoned)

Note: Adapted from *Mental Health Reactions After Disaster*, by National Center for PTSD, 2010, Washington, DC: U.S. Department of Veterans Affairs.

behaviors, increased feelings of self-worth, and reduced risk of loneliness, as well as the ability to understand their experience in the context of the totality of their lives (Salami, 2010). Social support is not the only moderator of reactions to disasters. Premorbid functioning and factors, such as the ability to self-regulate, cognitive skills (e.g., intelligence, cognitive flexibility), religious beliefs, community supports, hope, and self-efficacy (i.e., sense of competency), have all been associated with a young person's ability to adapt to severe threats of violence, terror, and disaster (Masten & Narayan, 2012). Counselors need to use counseling approaches that do not disrupt the naturally occurring process of resilience and recovery but, rather, aid in the cultivation of safety, hope, connectedness, equilibrium, and the efficacy of individuals, families, and the community (Masten & Narayan, 2012).

Counselors who continually work with these young people must monitor themselves for burnout, compassion fatigue, and vicarious trauma (Smith et al., 2014). **Vicarious trauma** is when helpers who were not directly exposed to the natural or human-made disaster begin to experience trauma-related symptoms similar to those who were associated with the event (Smith et al., 2014). This secondary type of trauma may be correlated with counselors' direct exposure to the clients' trauma stories, and counselors' reactions may be similar to the clients' reactions. In these situations, counselors must seek supervision, peer consultation, continuing education, and, if warranted, their own personal counseling.

Trauma-Related Disorders

As previously stated, not all youth who experience child maltreatment will develop long-term psychological problems; however, many do struggle with the aftereffects of these experiences. In some situations, youth exposure to a traumatic or stressful event may result in significant impairment that warrants clinical attention. Counselors may need to address the treatment of trauma- and stressor-related disorders, which may include reactive attachment disorder, disinhibited social engagement disorder, PTSD, acute stress disorder, and complex trauma. The following sections discuss these disorders associated with early traumatic experiences and child maltreatment.

REACTIVE ATTACHMENT DISORDER AND DISINHIBITED SOCIAL ENGAGEMENT DISORDER

Youth who have experienced seriously negligent care by their parents or caregivers often struggle with disorders rooted in attachment problems. These disorders include reactive attachment disorder and disinhibited social engagement disorder (APA, 2013a). **Reactive attachment disorder** is characterized by inhibited and emotionally withdrawn behaviors regardless of situations or stress, whereas **disinhibited social engagement disorder** is characterized by a disinhibited and emotional intrusiveness related to engaging and interacting with unfamiliar adults. Table 15.5 provides a summary of the differences between reactive attachment disorder and disinhibited social engagement disorder.

According to **attachment theory** (Bowlby, 1969), young children must have their basic needs met constantly and consistently by their parents throughout their early developmental years if they are to form

Table 15.5	Differences Between Reactive Attachment Disorder and Disinhibited Social Engagement Disorder	
	Reactive Attachment Disorder	Disinhibited Social Engagement Disorder
Emotional responsiveness	Youth are emotionally withdrawn, lack remorse and empathy, and lack social and emotional responsiveness. For example, a child who has a favorite toy taken will not respond but will stare blankly toward the individual who took it. Unexplained episodes of irritability and sadness may occur, but limited expressions of positive affect are displayed.	Youth are overly emotional and lack regard for the social norm of only sharing personal and private information with known individuals. For example, a youth tells an unfamiliar adult about a traumatic event on the first encounter.
Desire to form attachments	Youth lack the desire or are unwilling to form attachments with others, especially parents and central caregivers.	Youth are overzealous to form attachments. They may even wander off with unfamiliar adults and not check back with parents. Youth engage in lavish hugging and displays of affection with unknown adults.
Desire to be comforted	Youth have limited expressions or response when comforted by adults or parents.	Youth are overly needy and clingy with adults, regardless of the situation. They can be verbally and socially intrusive and even engage in attention-seeking behaviors to attain attention and comfort.
Internalized versus externalized symptomology	Youth have internalized symptomology.	Youth have externalized symptomology.

healthy attachment to others. If these needs are unmet, youth are at risk for developing unhealthy behaviors that they use in an attempt to have their basic social and belonging needs met. Young people's present and future abilities to form attachments, trust others, and build healthy relationships are compromised when their attachment needs are not met (Bowlby, 1969).

Youth who are abused and/or neglected are at serious risk for developing attachment problems because of the nature of these experiences. In addition to overt abuse and neglect, severely inconsistent parenting may also result in a young person developing attachment problems. For example, youth who are shuffled between caregivers and live in and out of foster care placements may not establish healthy attachments and are at risk for developing attachment disorders (Lehmann, Havik, Havik, & Heiervang, 2013).

Abuse and neglect do not always explain or result in an attachment-related disorder. Some youth remain resilient despite significant child maltreatment (Kress et al., 2015). The variability in youth responses to difficult situations may be attributed to the youth's temperament and internal resources, as well as the role of protective factors that insulate youth.

Complications associated with attachment disorders include academic and learning disorders, depressive and bipolar disorders, anxiety disorders, feeding disorders, and developmental delays (e.g., emotional, physical, and cognitive; Kress et al., 2015). Often, disinhibited social engagement disorder is comorbid with attention-deficit/hyperactivity disorder (ADHD), and depressive disorders are often comorbid with reactive attachment disorder (APA, 2013a). In addition, youth with attachment disorders sometimes struggle with antisocial behaviors (e.g., aggression, lack of remorse and empathy) and substance-related difficulties as they make the transition into adulthood (Kress et al., 2015). Treatment considerations and counseling intervention options are presented later in this chapter.

POSTTRAUMATIC STRESS DISORDER AND ACUTE STRESS DISORDER

Acute stress disorder and PTSD are the primary *DSM-5* trauma-related disorders associated with youth maltreatment and child traumatic experiences (APA, 2013a). Although differences exist in the duration of symptoms of acute stress disorder and PTSD, with acute stress disorder involving trauma symptoms of a briefer duration, we refer to these two disorders collectively as PTSD because of their significant overlap in symptomology, clinical presentation, and counseling treatment approaches.

Generally speaking, PTSD is characterized by the following symptoms: reexperiencing the traumatic event (e.g., recurrent flashbacks or nightmares), avoidance symptoms (e.g., avoiding situations, aspects, and/or places that remind the youth of the experiences; emotional numbing to avoid or block the pain), and a general sense of increased emotional arousal and reactivity (APA, 2013a). Youth who have PTSD frequently (a) experience somatic complaints, such as stomachaches and headaches, (b) demonstrate a diminished interest in activities, (c) are worried about death and dying, (d) are alert and hypervigilant, (e) demonstrate increased levels of irritability and aggression, (f) appear moody and seem to overreact emotionally, (g) struggle to fall and stay asleep, (h) have concentration difficulties, (i) display regressed behaviors (e.g., bedwetting, clinginess, thumb-sucking), and/or (j) act out or repeat behaviors associated with the trauma in their lives or in play (APA, 2013a; Kress et al., 2015).

In children age 6 and younger, PTSD symptoms may present in unique ways and may appear as fear when meeting strangers, irritableness and aggressiveness, difficulties with sleep (e.g., nightmares), behavioral regression, and demonstration of traumatic themes in their play (i.e., posttraumatic play). Table 15.6 provides a summary of the differences in clinical presentation between children and adolescents.

Traumatized youth live in a state of hypervigilance, anxiety, and fear of reexperiencing the traumatic event (Nader, 2008). If anger and PTSD symptoms are left untreated, youth may remain irritable and aggressive, even after the abuse has ceased (Runyon, Deblinger, & Schroeder, 2009). In addition, youth may experience dissociative symptoms (APA, 2013a), such as **depersonalization**, or feeling detached from their minds and/or bodies. For example, youth may feel that in certain situations—when aspects of the traumatic event are present—they are in a dreamlike state watching themselves go through the motions of life. Some youth may also experience the dissociative symptom called **derealization**, or the feeling that the world around them is unreal or dreamlike.

Cultural risk factors may increase a young person's likelihood of experiencing trauma and thus being diagnosed with trauma-related disorders, including a history of exposure to traumatic events, low socioeconomic

Table 15.6	How PTSD/Acute Stress Disorder May Present at Various Developmental Levels
Age	Clinical Presentation
School-age youth (5–12 years)	• Youth *may not* experience visual flashbacks. • Youth *may not* experience amnesia for aspects of the traumatic event. • Youth may have difficulty sequencing the trauma-related events (i.e., time skew). This may lead youth to believe that if they are alert (hypervigilant) they can predict future traumatic events and therefore avoid these events (i.e., omen formation). • Youth may exhibit posttraumatic play, which is a literal representation of the event and does not relieve the associated anxiety.
Adolescents (12–18 years)	• Presentation closely resembles the presentation of PTSD in adults (reexperiencing, increased avoidance, negative cognition/mood, and high arousal/reactivity). • Although younger children may exhibit posttraumatic play, older children may engage in trauma reenactment in their everyday lives (e.g., attempting to protect self by overreacting to a situation with too much aggression, displaying extreme recklessness, exhibiting avoidant behaviors that may interfere with their ability to create social connections). • Youth may exhibit impulsive and aggressive behaviors.

status, and minority racial or ethnic status (APA, 2013a). For example, youth living in poverty are at an increased risk for experiencing traumatic events that are related to a lack of community support and resources (e.g., community violence, fewer childcare options, poor schools, more prevalent mental illness and substance abuse).

COMPLEX TRAUMA

Complex trauma is a type of trauma that occurs continually and pervasively, potentially occurring over a given period of time within a specific context (Courtois, 2004). Complex trauma is often associated with chronic, severe child abuse and may be seen in youth who have experienced multiple traumatic events starting early in childhood. In the literature, the complex trauma concept has also been referred to as developmental trauma disorder (van der Kolk, 2005).

Complex trauma is uniquely different from PTSD. Although PTSD is often associated with experiencing one traumatic event, complex trauma is associated with chronic, ongoing traumatic events that can continue for days, months, or even years. Six areas of potential impairment in youth who have experienced complex trauma are (a) the ability to regulate affect, which can manifest as difficulties with anger and/or self-destructive behaviors, (b) the ability to process information and focus, which can manifest as issues with attention, concentration, and learning-related difficulties, (c) self-concept difficulties, including feelings of shame and guilt, (d) difficulties with impulse or self-control, which can manifest as aggression and substance abuse, (e) difficulties with forming and maintaining interpersonal relationships, which can manifest as trust and intimacy problems in relationships, and (f) problems with biological processes, including the delayed development of sensorimotor skills (Margolin & Vickerman, 2007; van der Kolk, 2005).

The following behaviors might alert counselors to the possibility of complex trauma: cognitive distortions, such as worthlessness, helplessness, and hopelessness; identity disturbances, including boundary issues and/or a lack of self-awareness; interpersonal difficulties, such as forming attachments and relationship with others; affect regulation difficulties; dissociation difficulties; substance use; somatization; nonsuicidal self-injury; and suicidality (Briere & Lanktree, 2012). Youth may appear to present with characterological disorders when in fact their behaviors are traits associated with the adverse effects of complex trauma.

ASSESSMENT OF ABUSE AND TRAUMA-RELATED DIFFICULTIES

Clinical interviews with youth who have experienced abuse and trauma-related difficulties is one of the most effective means for assessing immediate safety, traumatic history exposure, and the effects of the trauma on the youth's level of functioning (Briere & Lanktree, 2012). The first area counselors must assess is the young person's immediate safety. More specifically, counselors must assess whether the youth is in immediate danger. The following are preliminary assessment questions counselors may ask themselves to assess a young person's risk of immediate danger (Briere & Scott, 2015):

- Is the youth hurt, or does the youth have sustained injuries that need to be addressed?
- Does the youth have an immediate need for medical attention and medication consultation?
- Is the youth currently incapacitated?
- Is the youth suicidal?
- Is the youth a danger to someone else?
- Is the youth living in an unsafe, violent environment?

If any of these immediate dangers are present, counselors must initiate and coordinate additional services to ensure the physical health and safety of the youth and others. In these types of situations, counselors need to collaborate with other professionals, such as law enforcement, emergency services, psychiatric services, and child protective services.

If the youth does not appear to be in immediate danger, counselors can begin to assess the client's trauma exposure history. Counselors could consider asking the youth and/or parent about the types of traumatic events and the onset, frequency, duration, and severity of these events. Youth do not often recognize their traumatic experiences as something meaningful to counselors, and they do not often share such information until they feel a sense of safety and rapport in the counseling relationship (Briere & Lanktree, 2012). Parents and family members can be invaluable assets in the assessment phase, providing the counselor with additional psychological and social functioning information, family and mental health history, developmental considerations, and trauma-related information. Although counselors should consider integrating parents into the assessment process, they must also consider that parents may have certain biases due to the nature of the trauma, their own psychological difficulties or limitations, their level of investment in the youth's progress, and their own emotional responses to the youth and the youth's trauma experiences (Briere & Lanktree, 2012). Young clients may feel more comfortable disclosing abuse, trauma, and violence they witness in the home when parents or other family members are not present. If counselors suspect abuse and/or violence may be occurring in the client's home, they should schedule one-on-one time with the client to allow him or her to address concerns or feelings.

Clinical Toolbox 15.1

In the Pearson etext, click here for a summary of ways counselors can support youth who disclose abuse and/or witnessing violence.

Although clinical interviews with youth and their associated family members can be vital to the assessment process, counselors should also use trauma-related assessments and trauma checklists to increase reliability of assessment and diagnosis and to aid in treatment planning considerations. For example, the Clinician-Administered PTSD Scale for *DSM-5*—Child/Adolescent Version (CAPS-CA-5; Pynoos et al., 2015), which is the youth-modified version of the Clinician-Administered PTSD Scale (CAPS; Blake et al., 1995), is the gold standard in assessing PTSD (Briere & Scott, 2015). In addition, counselors may want to consider using the following assessment measures: the Children's PTSD Inventory (CPTSDI; Saigh et al., 2000); the Child PTSD Symptom Scale (Foa, Johnson, Feeny, & Treadwell, 2001); and the Trauma Symptom Checklist for Children (TSCC; Briere, 1996). Table 15.7 provides summaries of these youth trauma-related assessments.

When assessing trauma symptomology, counselors need to consider youth's symptoms and reactions in relation to their developmental level. Developmental considerations are important, and early childhood trauma and maltreatment can be significant and produce greater impairment and dysfunction than if a similar situation occurred in adolescence or early adulthood (Nader, 2014). As developmental skills acquisition

Table 15.7 Summary of Youth Trauma-Related Assessment Measures

Assessment Measure	Age Range	Overview of Assessment Measure
Clinician-Administered PTSD Scale for *DSM-5*—Child/Adolescent Version (CAPS-CA-5)	7–18 years	The CAPS-CA-5 (a modified version of the CAPS-5) is a 30-item assessment that is based on the *DSM-5* criteria for PTSD in children and adolescents. This counselor-administered assessment assesses each of the 20 PTSD symptoms by providing counselors with structured questions and probes for each symptom. In addition, questions targeting onset, severity, duration, distress, impact on functioning, overall validity, dissociative type (e.g., depersonalization, derealization), and overall improvement since last administration are included. The CAPS-CA-5 can be used to assess and evaluate counseling progress.
Children's PTSD Inventory (CPTSDI)	6–18 years	The CPTSDI is a counselor-administered assessment that measures the presence and severity of PTSD symptomology in youth related to specific traumatic events. Using this measure, counselors provide youth with multiple examples of traumatic events and ask youth if they have ever experienced a similar event. If they have, counselors ask if the situation was scary or upsetting and if they felt powerless. If an event meets screen criteria, the counselor will follow up with 34 items to assess reexperiencing, avoidance, and arousal in reference to that event. The CPTSDI yields clinical scores for impairment, reactivity, arousal, avoidance, reexperiencing and severity. These scores can be used in the initial diagnosis and assessment and for continued evaluation of counseling progress.
Child PTSD Symptom Scale (CPSS)	8–18 years	The CPSS is a 26-item assessment measure used to assess PTSSD criteria and symptomology in children. This self-report measure evaluates traumatic events, symptoms, and the youth's functional impairment. The CPSS provides two cumulative scores (i.e., symptom severity and impairment score), which can be clinically useful. The CPSS is the child version of the Posttraumatic Diagnosis Scales (PDS; Foa, 1996) and can be used to assess and evaluate progress.
Trauma Symptom Checklist for Children (TSCC)	8–16 years	The TSCC is a 54-item assessment designed to evaluate the traumatic exposure history of a youth. This self-report assessment presents youth with thoughts, feelings, and behaviors and asks them to rate how often they experience them (i.e., 4-point scale with 0 = *never* to 3 = *almost all the time*). The TSCC consists of two validity scales (e.g., overreporting and underreporting) and six clinical scales that highlight levels of anxiety, depression, posttraumatic stress, sexual issues, dissociation, and anger. Written at an 8-year-old reading level, the TSCC can be used to assess and evaluate progress in counseling.

varies, counselors need to consider preexisting functioning and be alert to trauma reactions because the presentation and the trajectory of PTSD symptomology can shift over time. For example, PTSD is often missed in preschool children, but observable acting-out or externalizing symptoms—symptoms that alert counselors to problems—often become more obvious as youth age and become adolescents (Cohen & Scheeringa, 2009).

In addition, the clinical presentation of trauma-related difficulties may involve multiple comorbid clinical diagnoses that are often rooted in or caused by traumatic experiences (Briere & Scott, 2015). Trauma-related difficulties, especially PTSD, have been commonly comorbid with depressive disorders, anxiety disorders, phobias, ADHD, oppositional defiant disorder, conduct disorders, and/or substance abuse disorders (APA, 2013a; Nader & Fletcher, 2014). Youth who experience trauma-related difficulties also frequently present with somatic complaints, health issues, and emotion regulation difficulties. Youth who experience multiple mental health diagnoses are at risk for a poorer counseling prognosis, more severe symptomology, and greater impairment in their social functioning (Nader & Fetcher, 2014).

COUNSELING INTERVENTIONS

Trauma-informed counseling should focus on establishing safety, should be appropriately focused on processing the traumatic experiences, and should focus on social reconnection and orientation to a more positive future (Herman, 1997). Counselors working with traumatized youth should consider trauma-focused counseling that (a) promotes youth safety, (b) incorporates psychoeducation, (c) enhances distress reduction and affect regulation skills, (d) facilitates emotional processing, (e) implements cognitive interventions, (f) enhances young people's identity, and (g) increases family involvement and relational functioning (Briere & Scott, 2015). **Trauma-informed counseling** should incorporate parents into the counseling process, as appropriate, and focus not only on symptom relief and reduction but also on resiliency, encouraging a typical developmental trajectory, and enhancing youth functioning (AACAP, 2010a). What follows is a brief explanation of each of the integral components of trauma-focused counseling.

Promoting Safety

Many people assume that children who have been involved with, or assessed by, a child protective agency are monitored and are in safe environments (Kress, Adamson, Paylo, DeMarco, & Bradley, 2012). The reality is that many abused children continue to live in, or are returned to, living environments that have the potential for serious violence (Castelino, 2009), and some research suggests that only 10% of children who are exposed to and experience some form of maltreatment are placed in out-of-home care settings (Black, Trocmé, Fallon, & MacLaurin, 2008).

The foundational component of counseling abused, neglected, or traumatized youth is promoting their safety (Kress et al., 2012; Underwood & Dailey, 2017). Counselors need to aid youth in promoting:

- safety related to reexperiencing trauma symptoms (e.g., intrusive thoughts, nightmares, being overwhelmed and not in control of emotions);
- safety in their day-to-day physical environment; and
- safety from recurring traumatic events.

Some strategies that can promote safety include (Substance Abuse and Mental Health Services Administration [SAMHSA], 2014):

- teaching youth how to use grounding exercises during times when they may feel overwhelmed and unsafe;
- establishing a consistent structure for individual, group, and/or family counseling sessions;
- discussing safe and unsafe behaviors that can promote safety or exacerbate unsafe feelings; and
- developing a safety plan to help the youth to feel safe in his or her environment and more in control.

In situations where a youth does not feel safe, such as when violence is prevalent in the home or maltreatment has occurred, or when clients are in abusive dating relationships, counselors should introduce the concept of safety planning. **Safety planning** empowers youth to take an active approach and may enhance their sense of safety. Safety planning increases a young person's awareness of warning signs and triggers, things that have not worked in the past related to safety, and self-initiated interventions that have the potential to be effective. Early in counseling, counselors often need to aid youth in avoiding unsafe coping skills, such as substance use, self-injury, and verbal and/or physical aggression. Figure 15.1 provides a summary of guidelines for creating a safety plan for youth in unsafe environments.

- Counselors should help youth to identify warning signs and triggers of unsafe situations and provide them with guidelines on when to implement the safety plan.
- Counselors should teach youth coping skills (e.g., removing themselves from the situation).
- Counselors should identify safe allies or individuals who will aid the youth should the need arise.
- Counselors should provide contact information for individuals and secondary support services, such as:
  ○ emergency service providers (fire, police, EMS);
  ○ crisis centers; and
  ○ help hotlines.
- Counselors should identify safe alternative locations, both inside and outside the home, for the youth to retreat to should the need arise.
- Counselors should aid the youth in creating a covert safety kit, which may include items such as:
  ○ emergency contact information;
  ○ supplies and personal items;
  ○ counselor contact information; and
  ○ a list of locations to go to for help.
- If possible, the youth should develop a code phrase for use when violence is likely. This code phrase is something that the child and a safety ally (e.g., a parent, sibling) could share ahead of time.
- For very young children, it may be best to set automatic dialing features on a cellular device.
- Counselors should rehearse and role-play implementation of the safety plan with the youth and help the youth to understand how to use the plan and associated resources.

FIGURE 15.1   Guidelines for Constructing a Safety Plan for Youth Living in Unsafe Environments
Note: Adapted from "The use of safety plans with children and adolescents living in violent families," by V. E. Kress, N. Adamson, M. J. Paylo, C. DeMarco, & N. Bradley, 2012, *The Family Journal, 20,* pp. 249–255. doi:10.1177/1066480712448833

Incorporating Psychoeducation

Psychoeducation can aid youth in better understanding their trauma-related symptoms and experiences. It can provide accurate information on the nature and effects of abuse and trauma and is an important component of any comprehensive abuse- and trauma-related counseling approach. Psychoeducation is often introduced early in the counseling process, and it is typically warranted throughout counseling, as the youth requires more information and gains understanding. Youth may benefit from psychoeducation because it validates and normalizes their experiences and creates new perspectives for them.

Counselors who integrate psychoeducation into counseling with youth who have experienced abuse and/or trauma might consider including the following material (Briere & Scott, 2015):

- Prevalence of abuse and/or trauma
- Commonly held misconceptions about abuse and trauma
- Possible reasons a perpetrator may engage in interpersonal violence
- Immediate reactions and responses to abuse and trauma
- Lasting posttraumatic responses to the abuse and trauma
- Reframing symptoms experienced as trauma processing or coping skills
- Safety plan discussions and implementation

Psychoeducation ideally should increase a youth's awareness of accurate information concerning the nature of abuse, the impact of abuse, and how the youth can integrate new information into his or her perspective and experiences of the trauma events. To be effective and helpful for youth, psychoeducation needs to individualized and integrated as appropriate throughout the counseling process (Briere & Scott, 2015).

Enhancing Distress Reduction and Affect Regulation Skills

Affect regulation or **mood management** relates to young people's attempts to manage their emotional states (Dvir, Ford, Hill, & Frazier, 2015). In early development, affect regulation is dependent on a parent soothing and nurturing the child when he or she is feeling distress. Youth ideally begin to model, imprint, and learn these behaviors so they can self-soothe; thus, the child learns to self-regulate. Youth who have these skills may fair better when exposed to trauma than youth who do not possess these skills (Briere & Scott, 2015).

As previously stated, youth who experience abuse and/or trauma often experience posttraumatic arousal and may have a difficult time regulating strong negative emotions. After the trauma, youth often experience negative emotional responses, sadness, and arousal associated with triggered memories, and this can lead to emotional avoidance, including dissociation, substance abuse, and external tension reduction activities (Briere & Scott, 2015). Emotional avoidance can inhibit recovery, and in some situations, excessive avoidance can lead to increased hyperarousal and emotional dysregulation, or poorly modulated emotional responses to stressors (Briere & Lanktree, 2012).

Distress reduction and affect regulation training focuses on helping youth to manage their arousal and combat sustained anxiety and hyperarousal. The major components of arousal reduction include relaxation training, identifying and countering nonproductive emotions and thoughts, and becoming aware of and intervening with trauma triggers (Briere & Scott, 2015). Counselors attempting to enhance young people's affect regulation or arousal reduction focus on teaching youth to do the following:

- Identify thoughts, feelings, and emotions
- Counter thoughts, feelings, and emotions
- Increase awareness of triggers and manage reactions to these triggers
- Hold off as long as possible on reacting to impulses or strong emotions (tension reduction behaviors)
- Manage affect during and after exposure-based interventions (e.g., trauma narrative)

As counselors encourage young people to identify their thoughts, feelings, and emotions, they will frequently need to assist youth in countering and/or managing strong emotions that emerge. In these situations, counselors should consider using the following emotion regulation questions: (a) *personal change questions* (e.g., What can I do differently? What can I personally control about this situation? What resources/strengths do I have?), (b) *accepting questions* (e.g., Is this a normal part of life? This may be how I feel now, but will it pass?), and/or (c) *letting go questions* (e.g., Can I let this go? What can I learn from this?; Harvey & Rathbone, 2013). These types of questions encourage youth to become more self-aware and proactive in regulating their feelings and emotions.

Another part of affect regulation involves helping youth to identify and manage trauma triggers. Clients may have triggering memories, have reactions to stimuli (e.g., noises, smells, situations), experience intrusive negative thoughts or flashbacks, or even have sudden panic attacks that leave them debilitated and unable to engage in counseling sessions (Briere & Scott, 2015). Counselors can teach youth how to use **grounding techniques**, which are strategies that help youth to stabilize, to be present, and to feel safe when triggering situations arise. Grounding techniques should be used in situations where the youth has clearly diminished his or her contact with the counselor and the counseling session. When used with clients in sessions, grounding techniques include the following steps (Briere & Scott, 2015):

1. Attempt to refocus the youth back on the counselor and the counseling session.
2. Ask the youth to talk about what he or she is thinking, feeling, and experiencing.
3. Orient the youth to the physical environment of the counseling room.
4. Apply relaxation and breathing techniques so the youth feels safe and comfortable.
5. Repeat any of the previous steps as needed.

Clinical Toolbox 15.2

In the Pearson e-text, click here to view a script for introducing a grounding activity to youth in trauma-focused counseling. This script provides counselors with the language to introduce and practice grounding.

As an example of a grounding technique, a counselor might ask a young client to assume a standing position and feel her feet become like roots of a tree grounding her to the floor. The counselor can guide the girl in allowing the roots to grow up from her feet as she takes deep, slow breaths. The girl can be directed to feel the energy of the tree grow toward the trunk, eventually moving toward her limbs, or the branches of the tree. Counselors will frequently use variations of certain relaxation and breath awareness techniques as grounding techniques. For example, a counselor might ask a client take 10 breaths, focusing his attention on each breath on the way in and on the way out; the client should say the number of each breath in his head as he exhales.

Clinical Toolbox 15.3

In the Pearson etext, click here to view a mindful breathing activity that can be used with youth. This activity cultivates mindfulness and promotes the use of deep breathing practices during times when a young person needs to orient to the present moment.

Clients can also use grounding techniques in their lives when they are not in session. Counselors can give clients a small item that they can carry in their pocket, and they can touch the item when they need a reminder to orient to the present and use their grounding tools.

Facilitating Emotional Processing

Emotional processing involves intentionally and therapeutically exposing youth to environmental triggers associated with their traumatic memories and helping them to manage their negative emotions and rescript the negative cognitions associated with these traumatic memories (Briere & Scott, 2015). The central contention of emotional processing is that as youth increase their exposure to trauma-related stimuli, they become more desensitized to their physical and psychological hyperarousal responses, and they can begin to separate their present thoughts and feelings from the painful thoughts and emotions associated with the traumatic experiences. Youth are then better organized and able to manage the associated feelings and memories of their traumatic experiences by integrating new thoughts and feelings into their experience, thus allowing for a more adaptive relationship with their past trauma experiences. Table 15.8 provides activities that may be helpful in processing youth trauma.

One of the essential techniques used in emotional processing is the creation of a **trauma narrative**. A trauma narrative is simply the youth's written description of the abuse and trauma experience. Trauma narratives are an exposure-based counseling technique frequently used in trauma counseling and associated with numerous theoretical approaches, including Trauma-Focused Cognitive Behavioral Therapy (TF-CBT; Cohen & Mannarino, 2008), trauma-focused integrated play therapy (TFIPT; Gil, 2012), and traumatic incident reduction (TIR; Descilo, Greenwald, Schmitt, & Reslan, 2010)—just to name a few.

Much of the effective trauma processing or the sharing of trauma narratives occurs spontaneously in the therapeutic conversation. However, there is value in being strategic about processing one's traumatic experiences. As a part of developing a trauma narrative, youth learn healthier ways to control their strong emotions, such as fear, anger, distress, and grief. In addition, the construction of a trauma narrative desensitizes the child to the thoughts, feelings, and triggers—or the reminders—of the traumatic experience (Cohen & Mannarino, 2008). The trauma narrative process enables youth to increase discussions about their thoughts and feelings more openly so they can begin to confront any reminders or triggers that incite fear and distress.

In addition, sharing narratives with themselves and family members has been associated with positive counseling outcomes, such as a reduction in trauma symptoms, an increase in feelings of safety, and increased coping skills (Cohen & Mannarino, 2008; Murray, Cohen, & Mannarino, 2013). Youth who tell their own story and hear that story retold by others (e.g., parents, family member) are better able to integrate their experiences; they are able to pick up the pieces of their experience they have avoided, examine them from a safe vantage point, integrate them into their past, and understand what it means for them in their future. In essence, they are able to co-create an identity as a survivor, or someone who has experienced traumatic events yet is moving forward (Lacher, Nichols, Nichols, & May, 2012). The integration of traumatic experiences helps youth to decrease self-blame, shame, and guilt and place the blame where it belongs: on their perpetrators (Lacher et al., 2012). The power of a trauma narrative lies in its ability to allow youth to

Title	Description
Story-Telling Basket	Before the session, prepare a basket that contains an array of toys and action figures. Consider including animals, dolls (e.g., varying ages, occupations, outfits), and an array of other objects. Ask the client to select any objects that remind him or her of traumatic experiences. After the client has selected the objects, permit the client to either describe why he or she selected each of the objects or act out how the client associates these objects with his or her experience. Process the objects and the underlying emotions associated with the client's experience.
My Mask	Ask the client to think about the feelings and emotions associated with his or her traumatic experience. Then ask the client to think about how he or she presents those emotions to the outside world. Allow the client to construct a mask for his or her emotions that are shared with the outside world (on one side of a paper plate or an actual mask) and then the emotions or feelings that are internal and not shared with the outside world (on the other side of the plate or mask). Next, ask the client to process his or her emotions on the outside and the inside of the mask. In addition, the counselor can ask the client what would happen if others saw what was inside and how they might react or respond to those thoughts and emotions.
Valley and Mountain	Ask the client to draw a valley and then a mountain on a large piece of paper. After the drawing is complete, ask the client to use colors and symbols to represent a valley or low point in his or her past. Ask the client to write words, emotions, and feelings that are associated with that valley in the past. Now ask the client to select colors and symbols to represent a more positive, healthy future. Ask the client to write the words, emotions, or feelings or images associated with the mountain in the future. Discuss with the client the tools that are necessary to climb up the mountain in the future, setting the stage for trauma-focused counseling.

Table 15.8 Trauma Processing Activities

re-author their stories by incorporating often forgotten and overlooked details of their experiences. This close examination takes away the power the trauma holds over their lives and psyches.

The process of constructing a trauma narrative involves youth sharing what information they think is important about their traumatic experiences. Their story may include information about other people (e.g., parents, caregivers, a deceased person, their abuser), events surrounding the trauma (e.g., least traumatic event first, then gradually building), and details involving the trauma (e.g., when it happened, what happened prior and after, leading to the worst time or their worst memory associated with their experience). The narrative is simply about the child telling—in his or her words—what has happened. The counselor should facilitate a thorough exploration of the thoughts, feelings, and actions that were involved in the traumatic experiences. Counselors working with younger children should write down the dictated story, allowing the youth to integrate drawings into the narrative when appropriate.

The process of helping clients to develop a trauma narrative is complex, and counselors must be sensitive to the pacing of the process and carefully read clients' reactions. First, counselors should be aware that clients will often back away from sharing their painful memories; in fact, it is a natural reaction to lean away from painful memories. Yet, an integration of these memories is essential if youth are to construct an appropriate trauma narrative. That said, counselors must also understand the importance of being sensitive to what material and experiences young clients are ready—and not ready—to examine. Counselors must make efforts to ensure youth are not retraumatized during the counseling process.

Counselors must ultimately use their clinical judgment and decipher how much and at what pace clients are ready to dig into their traumatic material. Therefore, counselors should be mindful to moderate and regulate the intensity of trauma processing by occasionally decreasing the overall intensity of the discussion by (a) asking content questions not specific to the trauma, (b) anchoring youth in the present (i.e., grounding techniques), (c) using a calm, hypnotic voice, and (d) stopping the intervention and asking clients to engage in a coping skill (e.g., relaxation activities) as needed.

When working with younger children and helping them to develop their narrative, counselors can use expressive techniques, including reading books (e.g., bibliotherapy), drawing pictures, writing songs or poems, or using a collage to create a visual depiction of their story. These expressive techniques are essential with younger youth but work equally well with older youth.

When working with youth to develop a trauma narrative, counselors can have clients rate their level of distress before, during, and after construction of the trauma narrative (e.g., "On a scale of 1 to 10, how uncomfortable or upsetting is this discussion making you. If 10 is the worst you have ever felt and 1 is not bad at all, what number are you feeling right now?"). Having youth rate their level of distress allows them to become more aware of their thoughts, feelings, and reactions concerning their story and trigger reminders, and it helps counselors to monitor clients' progress and know when clients may need to pull back or lean into their memories.

Clients differ in the amount of time required to construct a trauma narrative, with some clients requiring a handful of sessions and others requiring many sessions over an extended period of time. Clients who have experienced multiple traumas will generally require more time to fully process all of their traumatic experiences. Figure 15.2 provides a summary of the steps associated with assisting youth in constructing and processing a trauma narrative.

1. Before starting the trauma narrative process, counselors must ensure the youth has learned and can implement coping and relaxation skills during gradual exposure. In addition, counselors need to understand the theoretical foundation for their approach, communicate what the client can understand to him or her, and communicate that gradual exposure might increase discomfort and avoidance tendencies.
2. All youth are different, but many will do better discussing events verbally before writing them down or drawing pictures. Some children, though, may need to engage in creative expression before sharing verbally. Counselors need to assess the younger person's developmental readiness to engage in discussing his or her trauma narrative.
3. The counselor should consider aspects of trauma narratives that are important for the youth to cover. Either with the youth's assistance or independent of the youth, the counselor should construct a list of important aspects of the trauma narrative and a time line for addressing each aspect. Often, counselors introduce choices to allow the youth to talk about one or two important aspects of the trauma narrative. Talking about the facts of the experience and writing those down is a good place to begin. This can be followed up with the young person's thoughts and feelings associated with the experiences. This hierarchy can focus on the least to most painful aspects of the trauma. Some aspects that may be beneficial for the youth to add to the trauma narrative include the first time, the worst time, the last time, others' reactions, bravest moments, advice to other youth, and what he or she learned.
4. Youth do not need to write or detail every traumatic experience. Often, having the youth write about the worst and first traumatic experience can provide the most triggering information, and this may be sufficient material to help with the processing. If the youth has experienced multiple trauma events, counselors can have the youth address these trauma events over multiple sessions.
5. Counselors should attempt to keep the youth in the moment as he or she is processing. Once the trauma narrative has been completed and written down, the counselor can go back and begin processing the youth's inaccurate thoughts, often associated with self-blame. Productive, adaptive cognitions can be explored and integrated into the final trauma narrative.
6. Counselors should interrupt the youth to assist him or her in using coping or relaxation skills, as needed. In addition, it may be beneficial to have a feelings chart and/or thermometer of intensity to check in with the youth during his or her gradual exposure experiences. Counselors should be mindful that if the youth is experiencing a bit of anxiety and distress, it is advisable to continue. Counselors should not stop and impede the process because of their own discomfort. If a client is triggered and a coping or relaxation skill is used, counselors should then allow the youth to go back to sharing/writing the narrative.
7. Counselors can have the youth read and reread what has been written to not only desensitize the youth to the details but to refocus the youth back into the flow of the narrative. Any missed details or aspects of the narrative can be added as needed. As this process continues, the youth should progressively experience less and less emotional and psychological reactivity when exposed to his or her story.
8. As each session comes to a close, counselors should praise the youth for progress and allow 5 to 10 minutes to use psycho-education, to teach new coping and relaxation skills, or to engage in an activity the child selects. This will also allow

FIGURE 15.2 Suggestions for Assisting Youth in Constructing a Trauma Narrative

the client ample time to make the transition out of the session. It is also helpful to integrate a strength-based conversation into session endings so the client leaves with a sense of what is going well.

9. As sessions progress, counselors can summarize what the youth has learned, encourage the youth to consider advice he or she might have for other youth experiencing the same situation, and explain the benefit of sharing the narrative with another person (e.g., parent). At this point in the counseling process, the youth may have additional questions for a parent or care-giver, and this may be a good time to explore those questions. The youth may have questions about confusing aspects of the narrative or sequential details.

10. Finally, counselors should provide the rationale for this gradual exposure process to the young person's parents. In addition, the counselor should explain that all youth react differently, but this process may be difficult for the youth. The youth may experience increased behavior problems (e.g., acting out, sleep issues) and a decreased desire to stay engaged.

FIGURE 15.2 Suggestions for Assisting Youth in Constructing a Trauma Narrative (*Continued*)

As the story is shared, counselors should help the child to become more descriptive, thus desensitizing the child even more to the events (Cohen & Mannarino, 2008). During this time, counselors may want to discuss the idea of trauma reminders. Trauma reminders are the people, places, words, thoughts, sounds, smells, and sensations that might remind the youth of traumatic experiences. Counselors can assist youth in creating a plan to address each of these trauma reminders.

Parents play an important role in the trauma narrative process. In fact, the final aspect of a trauma narrative is sharing the story with parents, caregivers, and family members. Sharing the story with parents can be anxiety provoking for children and family members. Counselors, through the use of parallel parent sessions, should make efforts to ensure parents will be supportive, helpful, and ready for the possibility of an escalation in the child's distress once the narrative is shared. The counselor should facilitate the encounter with the parents, yet allow the child to present the narrative as it is developed (e.g., written, pictures, collage, song) and in the way he or she selects.

Clinical Toolbox 15.4

In the Pearson e-text, click here to view a script for introducing trauma narratives to youth. This script can provide counselors with language they can use to introduce the trauma narrative, to encourage understanding of trauma-focused counseling, and to increase motivation to engage in this aspect of trauma-focused counseling.

Implementing Cognitive Interventions

Youth who have experienced abuse and trauma often experience important shifts in their thinking about themselves, the world, and their place in the world. This population is susceptible to self-blame, guilt, overestimation of danger, negative beliefs about themselves and others, and lower self-esteem, all as a result of their thinking secondary to trauma experiences. Some youth will even believe that the traumatic event or abuse was their fault, that they "deserved it," or that they were the cause of it. Youth who have experienced abuse and trauma tend to develop thoughts of worthlessness, helplessness, and hopelessness. Therefore, counselors must aid youth in identifying, challenging, and replacing those negative and unhelpful thoughts. A youth's cognitive distortions frequently emerge in the discussion of the traumatic event or the trauma narrative (Briere & Scott, 2015).

In the following example, a 9-year-old boy, while discussing his trauma narrative, discloses his belief that he deserved to be physically tied to a chair and beaten when his father was upset.

CLIENT: I made him mad . . . that's why my dad would punish me.

COUNSELOR: Before, you told me that he would tie you up and beat you with a belt. Is this what you mean by he "would punish" you?

CLIENT: Yeah.

COUNSELOR: How did you make him mad?

CLIENT:	I would do something that would make him get up out of his chair in the living room, and he would drag me to the kitchen and punish me.
COUNSELOR:	So, what would you do that you think would make him get up out of the chair and punish you?
CLIENT:	I would knock something over or my mother would yell at me for not taking my shoes off in the house.
COUNSELOR:	So, the way you would think about it is this way: You would be punished for an accident or forgetting a house rule, and you deserved this . . .
CLIENT:	Yeah, I guess that's right.
COUNSELOR:	Tell me about a time when someone you know had an accident.
CLIENT:	Well, I guess (*pause*) . . . yesterday at lunch, my friend was talking and knocked his drink all over the lunch table. He got it all over his white shirt.
COUNSELOR:	OK, so what happened next?
CLIENT:	Ms. White, the lunch aid, brought over a towel and then took him to the bathroom to get cleaned up.
COUNSELOR:	So, when this accident happened did Ms. White "punish" him?
CLIENT:	No, because it was an accident.
COUNSELOR:	OK, so talk to me about accidents and what you think a fair response is to your accidents.

The counselor is attempting to identify and clarify the belief that abuse was deserved. As this cognitive pattern becomes clearer to the youth, the counselor can then aid the youth in disputing this maladaptive cognition and provide him with an in-session example of how to challenge such thoughts. The strategies most frequently associated with building cognitive skills in youth are cognitive restructuring, rehearsal, social reinforcement, and role-plays. (These cognitive skills are covered in more detail in Chapters 17 and 18.)

In addition to confronting these cognitive distortions and becoming more self-affirming, the youth can begin to develop a more detailed and coherent awareness and knowledge of the associated traumatic events (Briere & Scott, 2015). As youth develop and repeat their trauma narrative, their cognitions associated with their experiences become more clear, detailed, and organized, and they are better able to shift their thinking about themselves and their worlds. Figure 15.3 provides a therapeutic story for use with youth in trauma-focused counseling.

Enhancing Identity

Abuse and trauma experiences can create substantial and chronic problems that adversely affect a young person's identity and self-perceptions (Briere & Scott, 2015). The young person may struggle to assess his or her needs, to maintain a positive sense of self during times when he or she is experiencing strong emotions, and to predict how he or she will react or act in specific situations. For example, if an adult infrequently responds to a child's feelings or experiences, the youth may never have a sense of his or her legitimacy and thus may not develop a positive sense of self. Instead of developing a strong sense of self, the young person enters a state of self-preservation, needing to be **hyperalert** to the external environment, which includes being hyperaware of the actions of those around him or her and the ever-changing conditions in the home or environment (Herman, 1997). Introspection and self-exploration are not a priority because of the potential danger that could reappear at any moment.

Introspection—or the ability to observe one's own emotional and mental processes—is required to develop an internal sense of self. Yet, youth often feel uncomfortable when they attempt to introspect because it not only diverts their attention from their environment, which can make them feel unprepared to handle potential danger, but it can also make them feel uncomfortable because they have to face their emotional pain in isolation (Briere & Scott, 2015). Because insight and introspection help youth to develop their

Directions: Counselors can read a script that introduces a therapeutic story to use with youth who are engaged in trauma-focused counseling. This therapeutic story can help young people to change their cognitions and shift how they think about their trauma experiences, thus helping to increase their self-confidence and empowerment and to focus on their strength and resiliency.

In a far-off place, deep in a forest, there once was a little caterpillar named Claire. Claire thought, "Why am I not as beautiful and colorful as the birds in the trees? Why do I not flutter or fly like butterflies in the fields? Why do I not make beautiful music like crickets in the marsh? I'm so ordinary."

As the caterpillar grew, she noticed that children were often afraid of her. Occasionally, some children would say "ewwww" or "ick" when they came across her. Even when the children didn't say anything, Claire still believed the children did not like her. She wondered why she couldn't be like the others—the birds, butterflies, the crickets, or even the cuddly squirrels. She thought those other creatures must be so much happier than her. All she knew was she felt different.

Mostly though, Claire just didn't think anyone noticed her or cared about her at all. With all these sad thoughts, it's no wonder Claire felt so badly and sad. She would cry and think to herself, "Why did this happen to me? Why can't I be a beautiful bird? No one else knows how it feels to be me! Why, why, why? My destiny is to be ugly and repulsive."

Claire was afraid to tell others how hurt and alone she felt. Once she tried to tell someone how she felt, and she felt ignored. Being ignored made her hurt even more. She thought, "That's it. I can't trust anyone, and I can't even trust what I think and feel. I'm just a lonely and ugly caterpillar." So, Claire continued feeling horrible.

One day, she met several other caterpillars, and they all quickly became friends. Claire somehow mustered up the courage to tell these other caterpillars how she felt. They chuckled to themselves and told her that she was really beautiful inside and that someday she would realize this beauty. They told her, "Deep inside you are a beautiful butterfly!" She thought, "What? Yeah right! I'm beautiful? Come on. They're just saying that to make me feel better. I'm not beautiful on the inside or on the outside!"

These same caterpillars told her that to become a butterfly, Claire needed to look inside herself for her inner beauty. They told Claire she already possessed this strength and that she needed to believe in herself and have faith. It was only then that she could do what was necessary to change into a beautiful butterfly.

Claire thought this was hopeless; it was a very silly thing to dream so big. She even thought, "Maybe this is fine for my friends, but this dream is not for me. I'm too different. I'm way too ugly, and I can't be beautiful."

So, as time went on, she decided to do nothing. She just sat . . . and sat . . . and sat . . . and watched while all her friends turned into butterflies. One day, she became sick and tired of sitting. "That's it!" she said. "I'm going to really try to believe in myself. I am beautiful on the inside. I'm going to think positive thoughts, and I'm going to feel better even if a little part of me is afraid to do that. I'm going to really look inside of myself for my beauty. I'm not going to fight myself anymore."

And then she put all her energy into trying to find her inner beauty, thinking positive, and trying to be happy. It was hard work, but she was up for the fight!

As she tried and tried, Claire noticed she began to develop a warm, safe cocoon around her little caterpillar body. It happened gradually, but it happened. It felt a little scary and weird but also a little nice! She slowly began to feel safe. She didn't fight it; she embraced it.

And then, one day, she emerged from her cocoon a beautiful butterfly!

"Do you see it now? You were beautiful all along," exclaimed one of the butterflies. "You had to believe in yourself, and look what you've become!"

As a new butterfly, Claire thought about what had happened to her. She realized that her beauty had always been deep within her. It was always waiting to be found! Others could see it even before she could. Now, she can see the beauty that's always been inside of her!

FIGURE 15.3 The Caterpillar: A Therapeutic Story for Use with Youth in Trauma-Focused Counseling

identity, counselors must create a sense of safety within counseling sessions by honoring clients' boundaries, validating their needs and perceptions, and encouraging them to pursue self-explorations.

Self-exploration is an overarching theme in all trauma-focused approaches. Counselors can enhance clients' self-exploration by frequently encouraging them to focus on their own internal experiences.

In addition, counselors need to allow youth enough space to discover how they think about their current situation and their trauma experiences and to encourage exploration of their likes and dislikes and their view of self, others, and even the therapeutic relationship (Briere & Scott, 2015).

Counselors can describe to youth that they need to become detectives so they can discover what they think, feel, and believe distinct from what others think, feel, and believe. Promoting self-exploration can be one of the most useful components of trauma treatment. It requires the counselor to foster ongoing introspection and exploration and to assume a facilitator role with the youth (Briere & Scott, 2015).

One practical way to aid youth in the self-exploration process is to invite them—when it is appropriate to do so—to write a letter to their perpetrators. This letter can include young clients' thoughts and feelings about the abuse and the perpetrators, and how they have come to view the abuse and the abuser through their personal growth. Clients may also add elements of their choosing to the letter, such as what they might say or do the next time they see the abuser. The therapeutic letter may be sent to the perpetrator in some circumstances. The construction of the letter enables youth to continue to solidify their sense of identity and resiliency through this supportive and explorative process.

In addition to a diminished sense of self, youth who have experienced abuse and trauma may have strained and conflicted interpersonal relationship with parents, family members, and peers. These relationship difficulties may be rooted in clients' skewed perceptions of themselves and others, often stemming from negative perceptions of self and a distrust of others (Briere & Scott, 2015). As victims, these young people are sometimes involved in unhealthy and even violent relationships (Gopalan et al., 2010). Although continued safety, validation, and self-exploration can increase a youth's sense of self, counselors can aid them in developing healthy relationships and an adequate social support network. Counselors must intentionally develop and facilitate relational functioning in youth who have experienced abuse and trauma, and the counseling relationship can serve as an initial vehicle for such change.

Increasing Family Involvement

Family members can play a critical role in supporting youth who have been abused or traumatized. Counselors can monitor out-of-session symptomology, introduce learned coping skills, and integrate weekly check-ins with parents and family members to keep them engaged and updated on the counseling process. Because these young people often isolate themselves and avoid social support for fear of further exposure to the traumatic event, counselors should attempt to integrate parents, extended family, and siblings when appropriate (Gopalan et al., 2010). Youth who have adequate social support, especially parental support, are more likely to display adaptive coping skills, have a strong sense of self-worth, and feel less lonely (Salami, 2010).

One of the major considerations for increasing family involvement in counseling is dealing with parents' feelings, experiences, and reactions to their child's experiences. Counselors can aid parents in identifying, expressing, and regulating these reactions in parent, family, or conjoint sessions (Cobham et al., 2012). Some parents may feel guilty that they were unable to protect their youth from these traumas, and they may even avoid engaging in counseling; however, counselors should attempt to use psychoeducation with parents to explain the importance of treatment, normal reactions to traumatic events, and the process of trauma-related counseling (Gopalan et al., 2010). Counselors will primarily focus conjoint sessions on the impact of the trauma on the child–parent relationship and teaching parents the skills they need to create an emotionally safe home environment (Runyon et al., 2009).

Parents may have overwhelming reactions to their child's traumatic experiences, which can be exacerbated by any unresolved traumatic experiences they have had. Educating parents on the importance of identifying and addressing these experiences can be helpful. In some situations, counselors may need to make individual counseling referrals to parents if their trauma experiences are negatively affecting their child's trauma-related treatment (Cohen, Mannarino, & Deblinger, 2010). Counselors can reframe parents' well-being in the context of the whole family, thus allowing parents to realize that their own mental health affects their actions, their youth, and the family system.

Sometimes parents are the cause of young people's abuse experiences. Although initially the child may have been removed from the home, government agencies typically prioritize family reunification, even in these circumstances (CWIG, 2016). In cases where the parent is the perpetrator of the maltreatment, reunification is generally the overarching counseling goal. Although re-abuse and neglect rates for youth returning to abusive parents are high (i.e., 30%; Biehal, Sinclair, & Wade, 2015), positive outcomes in reunification are attributed to enhanced parenting skills and an increased ability to manage the child's behaviors in nonviolent ways (Biehal et al., 2015). Therefore, counselors should be mindful of ways that they can increase parental engagement and engage parents in counseling. Focusing on family communication, creating a safe home environment, and encouraging the development of parenting skills are several goals counselors might work toward (Cohen et al., 2010; Runyon et al., 2009). Counselors will need to be flexible and tailor parent and child sessions to reflect the various circumstances (e.g., maltreatment, domestic violence, substance abuse) that may have initially brought the family into counseling.

Youth who experience abuse and trauma yet have some supportive relationships with their family members and peers tend to have fewer trauma-related difficulties and symptomology moving forward (Nader & Fletcher, 2014). Comprehensive and effective trauma-related treatment addresses the development of social supports and encourages parent involvement and positive parenting, factors that have been associated with decreased impairment and symptomology (Nader & Fletcher, 2014).

Clinical Toolbox 15.5

In the Pearson e-text, click here to read about dyadic developmental psychotherapy, a family-based treatment for addressing chronic youth maltreatment initiated by parents. Dyadic developmental psychotherapy is a family-based approach used with youth who exhibit attachment-related difficulties, such as reactive attachment disorder.

SPECIFIC TRAUMA-FOCUSED AND DISASTER INTERVENTION APPROACHES

Considerable research exists on targeted approaches to address abuse- and trauma-related difficulties in youth. Numerous cognitive behavioral–based and developmental approaches that allow youth to explore and share their personal narrative, whether through words (Cohen & Mannarino, 2008; Lacher et al., 2012; May, 2005) or play-based approaches (Gil, 2012), are effective in treating abuse- and trauma-related difficulties. The following sections briefly present several approaches that can be used when counseling youth who have experienced abuse, disasters, and/or trauma.

Trauma-Focused Cognitive Behavioral Therapy (TF-CBT)

An example of an evidence-based approach that can be used with abused or traumatized children is Trauma-Focused Cognitive Behavioral Therapy (TF-CBT; Cohen et al., 2010; Murray et al., 2013). TF-CBT is a conjoint child and caregiver psychotherapy approach used with children and adolescents who are experiencing significant emotional and behavioral difficulties secondary to traumatic life events. This model integrates trauma-sensitive interventions with cognitive behavioral techniques, humanistic principles, and family involvement. Through TF-CBT, children and caregivers learn new skills to help them to process thoughts and feelings related to traumatic life events; manage and resolve distressing feelings, thoughts, and behaviors that are related to the traumatic life events; and develop an enhanced sense of safety, increased personal growth, better parenting skills, and improved family communication (Cohen et al., 2010).

A free 10-hour certificate training program on TF-CBT can be completed through TF-CBTWeb (https://tfcbt.musc.edu). This training program can be completed by students in field placement or practicing counselors, and it is an excellent means of deepening one's understanding of cognitive behavioral treatment principles in general and trauma treatment in particular.

TF-CBT involves young people discussing their trauma narratives while using anxiety reduction techniques to regulate their physical, emotional, cognitive, and biological responses to the memory of the trauma (Underwood & Dailey, 2017). Table 15.9 provides a summary of the components and tasks associated with TF-CBT.

Table 15.9	Components of Trauma Focused-Cognitive Behavioral Therapy and Associated Counseling Tasks

Essential Component	Associated Tasks
P Psychoeducation and parenting skills	• Increase knowledge of common reactions to trauma (e.g., physical, emotional, cognitive). • Identify trauma triggers and reminders. • Connect behaviors and reactions with trauma experiences. • Instill hope for recovery. • Increase parenting skills (e.g., praise, attention, use of reinforcements).
R Relaxation skills	• Learn and implement focused breathing. • Learn and implement progressive muscle relaxation. • Increase ability to relax or use relaxation skills (e.g., blowing bubbles). • Increase mindfulness (when appropriate for development and spirituality).
A Affective modulation skills	• Increase affective identification and expression. • Increase problem-solving skills. • Learn and implement anger management skills.
C Cognitive coping skills	• Increase awareness of the connection between thoughts, feelings, and behaviors. • Learn and implement cognitive restructuring (e.g., replacing unhelpful, inaccurate thoughts with more helpful, accurate ones).
T Trauma narrative and processing	• Develop a detailed trauma narrative. • Process the narrative and events involved in the youth's narrative. • Use cognitive processing and coping skills (e.g., relaxation and affective modulation).
I In vivo mastery	• Develop a fear/anxiety hierarchy.
C Conjoint sessions	• Implement family safety plans. • Share the child's trauma narrative. • Enhance family communication. • Increase healthy family interactions and relationships (e.g., reactions to family stress, family activities).
E Enhancing safety	• Develop and implement safety plans. • Learn and implement social skills. • Develop a discharge plan.

Note: Adapted from "Trauma-focused cognitive behavioral therapy for children and parents," by J. A. Cohen & A. P. Mannarino, 2008, *Child and Adolescent Mental Health, 13*(4), pp. 158–162. doi:10.1111/j.1475-3588.2008.00502.x

From a TF-CBT perspective, counselors will need to provide psychoeducation on trauma and teach clients basic skills before helping them to construct a trauma narrative. Counselor should ideally teach children specific relaxation skills (e.g., focused breathing, progressive muscle relaxation, engaging in relaxing activities such as blowing bubbles) and affective modulation skills (e.g., affect identification and expression, problem-solving skills, anger management) before constructing and sharing the child's narrative (Murray et al., 2013). These relaxation and affective modulation skills enable youth to more fully develop their narratives, to tolerate processing the events and triggers, and to use cognitive skills to increase their awareness of the connection between thoughts, feelings, and behaviors (Murray et al., 2013). In addition, counselors can teach children how and when to implement cognitive restructuring skills or, in other words, help them to challenge and replace unhelpful or inaccurate thoughts with more helpful and accurate ones. One nuance of trauma treatment versus grief and loss treatment is that counselors help children and families to address safety issues in the home and confront fear triggers (e.g., reminders) through in vivo exposure. (See Chapter 17 for a step-by-step approach to implementing in vivo techniques in counseling sessions.)

Cognitive Behavioral Intervention for Trauma in Schools (CBITS)

Cognitive Behavioral Intervention for Trauma in Schools (CBITS) is a school-based intervention aimed at decreasing PTSD symptomology for youth who are exposed to traumatic community events, such as school shootings or natural disasters (Langley, Nadeem, Kataoka, Stein, & Jaycox, 2010). CBITS is a 10-session group-based approach aimed at reducing PTSD symptomology in youth. CBITS includes cognitive behavioral skills–based components, such as relaxation, cognitive restructuring, creating a trauma narrative and processing memories, gradual exposure (e.g., in vivo), and social problem solving (Langley et al., 2010). CBITS is often used with students in middle and high school so counselors can incorporate teacher and parent education sessions to maximize client gains.

CBITS has been associated with enhanced academic functioning and a reduction in depressive symptoms (Morsette et al., 2009). CBITS has also been implemented with numerous populations (e.g., youth with lower socioeconomic status, immigrant youth, African American youth, American Indian youth, Latino youth), and it appears to be culturally adaptable to diverse populations (Morsette et al., 2009).

Combined Parent-Child Cognitive Behavioral Therapy (CPC-CBT)

Combined Parent-Child Cognitive Behavioral Therapy (CPC-CBT) is a structured family counseling approach that integrates components of other cognitive behavioral approaches, including positive reinforcement, time-outs, and trauma narrative and processing, as well as motivational interviewing and family systems theory (Runyon, Deblinger, Ryan, & Thakkar-Kolar, 2004). CPC-CBT is an appropriate approach when there is significant youth maltreatment and abuse, there are multiple referrals to child protective services, or the parents feel they may lose control and harm their children (Runyon et al., 2004).

CPC-CBT can be done in individual or group formats. In 16 to 20 sessions, counselors target youth and parents, who engage in coercive parenting strategies. Sessions are typically structured so the counselor meets with the youth and parent independently and then finishes with a joint session. As counseling progresses, the joint sessions become longer, focusing more on the parent's ability to manage the child's behaviors and on conflict resolution between the parent and the child. The structure of CPC-CBT involves:

- *engagement* (e.g., the use of motivational enhancement skills, rapport building, goal setting, psychoeducation, and education for parents);
- *skill building* (e.g., coping skills, such as assertiveness, anger management skills, relaxation skills, and problem-solving skills for both parents and youth; positive parenting skills);
- *safety* (e.g., developing a family safety plan); and
- *clarification* (e.g., youth write or share their abuse experiences with a focus on feelings and thoughts associated with their abuse; parents write a letter to their child aimed at increasing their own empathy and understanding of their child's perspective).

A unique aspect of this model over others is the clarification process by which parents and children gradually discuss the abuse experiences within parameters to reduce the PTSD symptomology of the youth (Runyon et al., 2009).

Throughout the course of counseling, counselors engage parents in positive parenting training. They aid parents in practicing these positive parenting skills, communicating more effectively, and using effective behavior management skills in their interactions with their youth. In addition, counselors must take an active approach in providing corrective feedback, offering encouragement, and reinforcing positive parenting skills to increase use of the skills (Runyon et al., 2009).

Eye Movement Desensitization and Reprocessing (EMDR)

Although evidence exists that eye movement desensitization and reprocessing (EMDR) reduces the PTSD and trauma-related symptoms of traumatized youth (Diehle, Opmeer, Boer, Mannarino, & Lindauer, 2015; Fleming, 2012), there is disagreement in the field about EMDR's effectiveness with this population. Some researchers have contended that EMDR is better suited for Type I trauma (one-time traumatic events) as compared to Type II trauma (chronic, ongoing traumatic events). Other researchers argue that EMDR does not have enough rigorous scientific research to be considered an evidence-based approach with youth (Greyber, Dulmus, & Cristalli, 2012). However, because some research studies have shown efficacy and usefulness with traumatized youth, counselors may benefit from specialized training in EMDR.

EMDR involves evoking a young person's traumatic memory (i.e., exposure), recognizing a negative thought associated with the memory (i.e., cognition), using breathing exercises (e.g., relaxation skills), and using guided eye movements to access, process, and resolve traumatic memories (Shapiro, 2001). EMDR addresses these items in an eight-phase sequential treatment approach (Shapiro, 2001):

Phase 1: The counselor takes the youth's history, which may include assessing the young person's mental health, family, and medical history; evaluating the youth's readiness to engage in EMDR (e.g., ability to identify distressing memories and current situations that are causing distress); and determining the skills and behaviors the youth needs to be more successful in the future.

Phase 2: The counselor strengthens the therapeutic relationship and provides the youth with additional ways to handle emotional distress, such as imagery and stress reduction techniques (e.g., relaxation skills, breathing).

Phases 3–6: A target is identified and processed using EMDR. The target is a visual image of the related memory, any negative thoughts or beliefs about oneself, and any related emotions and body sensations. The counselor aids the youth in identifying positive and negative beliefs associated with the traumatic event. The youth rates not only the beliefs but also the intensity of the belief and its accompanying emotions (e.g., 10 = *strong* vs. 1 = *almost nonexistent*). Next, the counselor asks the youth to focus on the memory (i.e., image), any negative thoughts, and the accompanying body sensations while engaging in bilateral stimulation (e.g., following the counselor's finger moving back and forth in front of the youth). The counselor asks the youth to let his or her mind go blank and then become aware of the emotions, thoughts, memories, and/or sensations that come to mind. If the youth has no distress, the counselor instructs the youth to reprocess and reintegrate the positive beliefs previously identified. If another negative focus emerges, the counselor can begin this process again.

Phase 7: The counselor brings the youth to closure on the traumatic experience. The counselor may ask the youth to keep a log during the week to document if any related material arises.

Phase 8: The counselor and youth examine progress and any new areas of focus, such as other past traumatic events, current incidents of distress, or events that require a different response from the youth.

Counselors using EMDR focus attention on the young person's past, present, and future. The focus on past traumatic events is linked with more adaptive thoughts, current situations that have caused distress, and imagined future events. The practice of EMDR requires counselors to seek specialized training and appropriate clinical supervision.

Trauma-Focused Integrated Play Therapy (TFIPT)

Trauma-Focused Integrated Play Therapy (TFIPT) currently has limited research support, yet this emerging play therapy approach incorporates numerous other evidence-based components (Gil, 2012). TFIPT is a 12-week manual-based program that uses a blend of nondirective and directive counseling approaches to foster a young person's discovery and use of posttraumatic play. It was created for use with youth who have experienced abuse, neglect, and violence in the home (Gil, 2012).

TFIPT allows a youth to naturally and gradually introduce the narrative formation and trauma processing. Techniques associated with expressive arts, such as art, play, music, and sand, are used as complements to counseling. The goals of TFIPT are (a) to identify trauma symptoms, (b) to allow the young person the space to explore thoughts and feelings associated with the abuse, (c) to increase the young person's coping strategies and self-esteem, and (d) to increase the young person's access to internal and external resources (Gil, 2012).

TFIPT is based on Herman's (1997) three phases of trauma treatment, which include (a) establishing safety for the youth, (b) focusing on the traumatic material and processing that material, and (c) making social connections to the future. The beginning and end of counseling sessions are often structured with affect identification and mindful breathing exercises (see Clinical Toolbox 15.3), but periods of nondirective play in a play therapy room are also used (Gil, 2012). As treatment progresses, counselors will become more directive in increasing the young person's awareness of traumatic play themes. Treatment from a TFIPT approach culminates with the creation and processing of a trauma narrative, which can be completed verbally or nonverbally (e.g., painting, drawing journal; Gil, 2012). Counselors of older children can aid youth in correcting negative thoughts, in addition to affect identification. Although TFIPT mainly focuses on counseling youth, counselors work with parents in a supportive way, providing education, coaching, and needed referrals and resources.

Psychological First Aid: One Crisis Intervention Model

Many approaches can be used to address youth who have recently experienced a crisis or disaster. **Psychological first aid** is one of the more commonly used approaches to support youth who have experienced a disaster, and it is the model endorsed by the American Red Cross (Underwood & Dailey, 2017). Psychological first aid is a crisis intervention model that can provide immediate relief and support to youth and families in the aftermath of traumatic events, such as acts of terrorism and natural disasters (Underwood & Dailey, 2017).

The intention of psychological first aid is to facilitate immediate physical and psychological safety, reduce stress-related symptoms, encourage recuperation, and connect youth with appropriate services and support (James & Gilliland, 2013). Psychological first aid should not be confused with trauma-focused counseling (e.g., TF-CBT, CPC-CBT, EMDR). Although trauma-focused counseling is intended to address, process, and resolve crisis-related trauma associated with traumatic events, psychological first aid is a first-response approach to helping an individual in immediate crisis. When applying psychological first aid, counselors are nonintrusive; they provide support, empathy, information, and assistance (James & Gilliland, 2013). Although there are many forms of psychological first aid, the following essential components are often involved (James, 2008):

- *Defining the problem:* Counselors explore the situation from the client's point of view using core listening skills, such as open questions, empathy, positive regard, and genuineness.
- *Ensuring client safety:* Counselors attempt to minimize physical and psychological danger.
- *Providing support:* Counselors communicate to the client that he or she is accepted, listened to, and valued.
- *Examining alternatives:* Counselors assist the client in exploring his or her available choices, including the people, actions steps, resources, and positive thinking patterns that are realistic and potentially helpful.
- *Making plans:* Counselors use systematic problem solving that identifies additional supports and definitive action steps that are realistic, reasonable, and useful to the client.
- *Obtaining commitment:* Counselors gain the client's commitment to take agreed-on action steps that move the client toward more equilibrium and stability.

Counselors applying psychological first aid should consider the ABCs of crisis assessment: (a) *affective state of the youth*, or assessing for abnormal or impaired affect, (b) *behavioral functioning of the youth*, or the ability to focus attention on acting, doing, and behaving, and (c) *cognitive state of the youth*, or assessing for signs of rationalizing, exaggerating, or exacerbating the crisis (James, 2008). Appropriately assessing the youth and the crisis situation enables counselors to be supportive, to more fully understand the severity of the crisis, and to gain enough clarity to make appropriate short- and long-term counseling referrals.

Psychopharmacotherapy

Selective serotonin reuptake inhibitors (SSRIs) are approved for use with adults who have been diagnosed with PTSD. However, there is only preliminary evidence that SSRIs may be beneficial in reducing PTSD symptomology in youth (AACAP, 2010a). Some researchers contend that evidence-based talk therapy approaches, such as TF-CBT, should be used as front-line interventions. Some suggest that SSRIs should only be used if the young person's symptoms are severe or intensify during the course of sessions, or if the youth has comorbid anxiety or depressive/bipolar disorder (AACAP, 2010a; Cohen, Mannarino, Perel, & Staron, 2007). In some young people, SSRIs may lead to increased irritability, inattention, or poor sleep, which may exacerbate the symptomology of PTSD (AACAP, 2010a).

I CAN START COUNSELING PLAN FOR JIA

This chapter opened with quotes from Jia's mother. Jia is a 5-year-old African American girl who has been sexually abused by her uncle. The following I CAN START conceptual framework outlines counseling considerations that may be helpful to a school counselor or a clinical counselor who works with Jia.

C = Contextual Assessment

Jia is a 5-year-old African American girl. Her father died a few years ago, and she is being raised by her mother and live-in grandmother. Jia's mother is not currently dating anyone and has a stable place of employment. Jia's family lives in a two-bedroom apartment, where they have converted their dining room into a bedroom for her grandmother.

Jia's mother reported that her brother has been sexually abusing her daughter for the past 4 to 6 months. She has witnessed numerous changes in Jia's disposition and behaviors over this time, including a sudden lack of interest in school, increased irritability, changes in sleep and nightmares (two to three per week), exaggerated startle responses and "jumpiness," masturbation, and avoidance of aspects connected with her alleged sexual abuse.

A = Assessment and Diagnosis

Diagnosis = 309.81 Posttraumatic Stress Disorder

N = Necessary Level of Care

Outpatient, individual counseling and parent education (once per week)

S = Strengths

Self: Jia is intelligent, and her preschool teacher has relayed to her mother that she is doing well at school. Jia is curious, is creative, and has many interests (e.g., fashion/clothing, drawing). In addition, Jia seems interested and willing to participate in counseling services.

Family: Jia's mother loves Jia and her family. Her mother is eager to receive support and has taken the initiative to seek out counseling services. Jia's grandmother is another supportive caregiver in the home and appears helpful to Jia's mother with childcare and parenting responsibilities.

School/community: Jia's family lives in a lower middle-class area in the downtown area of a big city with reliable transportation and community resources (e.g., libraries, parks, museums, YMCA). Jia's preschool teacher seems to like her and has an interest in her social and academic success.

T = Treatment Approach

Trauma-Focused Cognitive Behavioral Therapy (TF-CBT)

A = Aim and Objective of Counseling (90-day objectives)

Jia will learn and implement relaxation techniques as needed. Jia will learn focused breathing, progressive muscle relaxations, expressed movement, and mindfulness activities. She will practice and learn to implement at least one of these techniques outside of counseling sessions during times of frustration, anxiety, and irritability at least 80% of the time.

Jia will decrease hyperarousal symptoms. Jia will construct a trauma narrative (in a book form appropriate to her developmental level) highlighting her thoughts, feelings, and reactions associated with the events of the trauma. Jia will share her trauma narrative in session each week to elaborate the narrative, desensitize her physical and psychological responses (hyperarousal), and unpair thoughts, reminders, and discussion of events from the negative emotions (e.g., shame, guilt, terror). In addition, Jia will share her trauma narrative with her mother once by the end of the 90-day treatment plan.

Jia will learn to identify and challenge cognitive distortions related to her traumatic experience. Jia will learn about and challenge cognitive distortions to examine her thoughts/beliefs (e.g., It was my fault; I am a bad girl) and incorporate alternative and more accurate thoughts/beliefs 80% of the time.

Jia's mother will develop skills to assist Jia in reducing her level of psychological arousal during stressful or trauma-reminder situations. Jia's mother will assist Jia by introducing and participating in at least one predetermined coping skill (e.g., controlled breathing, progressive muscle relaxation, thought stopping) during the midst of stressful situations in the home at least 90% of the time.

R = Research-Based Interventions

The counselor will help Jia to develop and apply the following skills: increased knowledge of the reactions to trauma, identification of triggers and reminders of the traumatic event, relaxation skills, affective identification and expression, problem-solving skills, and increased connections between thoughts, feelings, and behaviors.

The counselor will help Jia's mother to develop and apply the following skills: implementing a family safety plan, enhancing parent–child communication, and increasing positive family interactions and healthy relationships (by increasing the number of family activities and improving responses to family stress).

In addition, the counselor will help Jia to develop more effective social problem-solving and decision-making skills to deal with the intrusive, arousing, and reexperiencing nature of her symptomology.

T = Therapeutic Support Services

Medical and physical evaluation with Jia's pediatrician
Weekly individual counseling and family sessions
Support group for Jia and her mother
Referral of Jia's mother for mental health counseling services

Summary

Many youth in America will experience at least one traumatic event during their lifetime. Youth frequently manifest normal reactions to these traumatic events and can often benefit from short-term counseling services. Others may experience more pervasive impairments, such as declining academic performance, loss of interest in activities, overwhelming fear, hypervigilance, depressive symptoms, and difficulties related to sleeping and eating, that require longer-term counseling options (AACAP, 2010a). In some cases, these adverse effects and reactions may develop into mental health disorders. Therefore, counselors need to recognize the physical and psychological impacts of traumatic events, know the associated risk factors and preventative factors, and understand how to implement trauma-informed practices.

Not every youth who experiences traumatic events will exhibit long-term trauma symptoms. However, youth who do experience trauma can benefit from counseling. Counselors can help these young people to process and integrate their experiences (Kress et al., 2015). More specifically, counselors working with traumatized youth should consider incorporating aspects of trauma-focused counseling, such as promoting safety, incorporating psychoeducation, enhancing distress reduction and affect regulation skills, facilitating emotional processing, applying cognitive interventions, enhancing identity, and increasing family involvement (Briere & Scott, 2015). Some examples of specific trauma-focused and disaster interventions counselors can consider—depending on the young person, family, specific situation, and setting—include TF-CBT, CBITS, CPC-CBT, EMDR, TFIPT, and psychological first aid.

CHAPTER **16**

Substance Abuse

with Amy Williams, Ph.D., Youngstown State University

THE CASE OF TYLER

When I was about 12, I started sneaking alcohol from my parents' liquor bottles when they weren't home. To be honest, I didn't even like the taste at first, but I liked how it made me feel, so I kept doing it. When I went into high school, I realized there were other kids who drank, and it became less of a secret I kept to myself and more of a thing to do with my friends. Sometimes we'd get together after school and drink or smoke weed. It really didn't seem like a big deal at the time since everyone I knew did the same thing.

After a while, it got so I was drinking or smoking almost every day, sometimes even before school. My parents had no idea what I was doing until I got caught with alcohol in my water bottle at school. They were really angry when they found out. They keep telling me I just needed to stop, but they just don't understand how hard it is. My brain just goes there—to thinking about drinking—and I don't want to do anything else. No matter how hard I try not to think about it, it just keeps coming back into my mind. I'm still drinking and smoking weed a couple of times a week, but my parents have no idea. If they found out, I don't know what they would do. I wish it were as easy as just deciding to stop, but it's just not.

—Tyler, age 16

Substance use among young people is a serious community problem; it creates difficulties for parents, schools, medical and mental health professionals, and the young people themselves. The National Survey on Drug Use and Health (NSDUH) is conducted annually to determine prevalence rates of substance use and mental health disorders among Americans. According to the 2014 results, 12% of young people ages 12 to 17 reported current alcohol use. In addition, 6% of these youth met the criteria for binge drinking, and 1% met the criteria for heavy alcohol use (Substance Abuse and Mental Health Services Administration [SAMHSA], 2015).

In the same survey, 9% of youth ages 12 to 17 reported current illicit drug use. Marijuana was the most common illicit drug, with 7% of youth reporting use, followed by 3% reporting nonmedical use of psychotherapeutic drugs, including pain relievers, stimulants, tranquilizers, or sedatives (SAMHSA, 2015). Other illicit drug use reported by young people ages 12 to 17 included 0.2% cocaine use, 0.1% heroin use, 0.5% hallucinogen use (including drugs such as LSD and ecstasy), and 0.6% inhalant use. In addition, 7% of young people in the study reported tobacco use (SAMHSA, 2015).

Overall in 2014 approximately 5% of youth met the criteria for one or more substance use disorders, with alcohol being the most commonly abused drug (SAMHSA, 2015). According to the National Institute on Drug Abuse (NIDA; 2014b), substance misuse is most likely to begin in adolescence and young adulthood. In fact, by the time students graduate from high school, almost 70% have used alcohol, and 50% have used an illicit substance. In addition, more than 20% of young people have used a pharmaceutical medication for a nonmedical reason by the time they reach adulthood (NIDA, 2014b).

Counselors play an important role in prevention and early identification and intervention for substance abuse. This chapter takes a closer look at the biological, psychological, and social aspects leading to and resulting from substance use among young people. It also considers treatment modalities and tools to support young people who are engaging in high-risk substance use and explores ways to support them throughout the counseling process.

THE NATURE OF SUBSTANCE USE DISORDERS IN YOUTH

Substance abuse involves numerous behavioral, cognitive, and physiological symptoms. Youth who have **substance use disorders** continue to use a substance despite significant substance-related problems and consequences (American Psychiatric Association [APA], 2013). In other words, substance use disorders involve a complicated and damaging relationship with a substance. Recreational use of alcohol or other drugs may develop into a substance use disorder over time, particularly when the person using the substance is doing so to cope with emotions, when the amount of a substance used increases or becomes more frequent, or when the individual is at risk of a substance use disorder due to biological or psychological factors. This section provides information on these risk factors, how substance misuse progresses to substance use disorders, and the negative consequences associated with substance misuse.

Risk Factors

Numerous factors increase the possibility that young people will develop a problematic relationship with substances. First, the presence of substance use disorders in biological family members is a risk factor for young people because genetic links and biological markers affect how some people's brains respond to alcohol and other drugs (Genetic Science Learning Center, 2013). If family members carry the genetic material that increases the reward response to these substances, young people, too, may carry these genes. Because the brain will respond differently to alcohol or drugs in these individuals, a family history of alcohol or other drug abuse is a vulnerability among youth who experiment with substances that may predispose them to problems with alcohol or drugs.

In addition to the biological risks, some young people also have psychological risks that predispose them to misusing alcohol or other drugs. Children and adolescents who are not able to cope with their emotions—for whatever reason—may find that alcohol or drug use helps them to numb or otherwise manage these feelings (NIDA, 2014b). Over time, the use of substances to manage emotions may evolve into a substance use disorder. Likewise, youth who have experienced traumatic events, such as abuse or neglect, may use substances to help them to cope with the aftereffects of the traumatic experience, particularly if they have never been supported in directly addressing the trauma (NIDA, 2014b). In addition, some mental health disorders may increase the risk of substance use disorders, either through an increase in risk-taking behaviors or as a result of difficulty coping with symptoms of the disorder (NIDA, 2014b). It can be particularly challenging to identify the presence of a mental health disorder when a young person is actively using alcohol or other drugs regularly because symptoms of intoxication and withdrawal may mimic or worsen some mental health disorders.

In addition to biological and psychological factors, there are also social factors that create a risk for substance misuse. Identity development in adolescence occurs in the context of social affiliation and connection to peers, and peer influences can have a tremendous impact on the choices a young person makes (Broderick & Blewett, 2014). Some young people begin to use alcohol or other drugs because it is considered acceptable or even desirable by their peers (NIDA, 2014b). Over time, this use may become habitual and begin to cause problems, and the youth may make the transition from using recreationally to having a substance use disorder.

The initiation of substance use while among peers may be a particular vulnerability for youth who lack social skills or a strong social support network. Young people who have difficulty fitting in with their peers may gravitate toward peers who offer them acceptance; sometimes these individuals are accepted by others who have also been rejected and who themselves may be coping with this rejection through the use of alcohol or other drugs. As a result, social rejection may increase the possibility that a child or teen may experiment with, and potentially end up experiencing problems due to, alcohol or other drugs (National Institute on Drug Abuse [NIDA], 2003).

Etiology

Although the risk factors described previously may predispose young people to substance use disorders, not all young people who find themselves in these circumstances develop problematic relationships with substances. At the same time, some young people who do exhibit symptoms of substance use disorders do not have any of the previously described risk factors. It is impossible to know exactly why an individual chooses to experiment with alcohol or other drugs for the first time. Once they begin to use, some individuals are able to control or stop using completely, whereas others find managing use difficult, if not impossible. The biological, psychological, and social effects of using alcohol or drugs make it difficult for some young people to moderate or stop their use once they have started. These effects explain why substance use evolves into substance use disorders.

BIOLOGICAL

Biological explanations have been proposed to describe how people develop a problematic relationship with substances. The biological actions of alcohol and other drugs directly and indirectly affect the brain's reward system (NIDA, 2014b). This system makes use of the neurochemical dopamine to reinforce behaviors that are good for survival and discourage behaviors that are not good for survival. Dopamine is released whenever people engage in activities that are pleasurable; eating, shopping, and time spent with friends may all trigger the release of dopamine to reinforce these behaviors and increase the likelihood that they will recur (McCauley & Reich, 2007).

A second neurochemical, glutamate, acts as a neurochemical messenger to recognize events and experiences that are likely to trigger higher-than-usual dopamine release (McCauley & Reich, 2007). When glutamate is released, the brain prepares for elevated levels of dopamine triggered by a familiar stimulus. In this way, glutamate is able to capture memories of previously rewarding experiences and alert the brain to the opportunity of another dopamine-rich experience (McCauley & Reich, 2007). In this way, behaviors that have a survival advantage are rewarded and reinforced through memory and pleasure via dopamine release, thus increasing the likelihood they will be repeated and promote survival.

The problem with alcohol and drugs is that they produce intense spikes in dopamine beyond what the body is able to produce naturally. Over time, these spikes in dopamine are locked into the brain via glutamate and are perceived as a highly superior reward compared to naturally occurring behaviors that trigger a dopamine release (McCauley & Reich, 2007). This process makes using alcohol or drugs neurochemically rewarding and thus reinforced; as a result, substance use can quickly become a habit that is difficult to break. If an individual continues using alcohol or drugs for an extended period of time, his or her ability to experience pleasure from things that used to be pleasurable diminishes because the brain adjusts to the immense release of dopamine produced by alcohol or drug use (McCauley & Reich, 2007). This can further reinforce substance use because the individual's ability to experience any pleasure is limited to alcohol or drug use. If use continues, the brain and body will become dependent on the drug as a perceived necessity for survival and will react negatively when the substance is not used (McCauley & Reich, 2007). This physiological response is called **withdrawal**, and it is described in more detail later in this chapter.

PSYCHOLOGICAL

Psychological explanations have also been developed for substance abuse. Substance use may begin as a response to stress, anxiety, or depression. During the transition from childhood to adolescence, youth are particularly vulnerable to negative affective states because the emotional center of the brain—the limbic system—becomes hyperactive and highly networked (Siegel, 2014). Emotional responses may be intense and changeable, and for some adolescents, this emotional lability and reactivity may be difficult to manage. Increased emotional sensitivity and reactivity are coupled with demands in all spheres of life, including increased family responsibility, increased academic rigor, increased engagement in social activities, increased self-reflection, and development of personal identity (Siegel, 2014).

Some young people begin using substances recreationally and find that, in the short term, their use helps them to cope with stress, anxiety, or depression, either by reducing the symptoms or by initiating an emotional disconnect from these feelings. This short-term affective response may increase the possibility of future substance use as a coping mechanism for uncomfortable emotions. Over time, the interaction of biological and psychological elements associated with both intoxication and withdrawal may increase the frequency and quantity of substance use, as well as the risk of experiencing negative consequences resulting from ongoing substance use.

SOCIAL

Peer networks are an important influence on young people, and these social ties may increase exposure to opportunities for experimenting with substances and eventual substance abuse. As youth age, they experience increased autonomy and more peer relationships; thus, they have ample opportunities to assert their growing independence and autonomy. The decrease in parental supervision that often accompanies the transition from childhood to adolescence, coupled with the increased risk-taking behaviors often seen in adolescence, may make experimentation with substances a desired social activity for some young people. Rejection by peers may push some youth toward social circles where substance misuse is the norm (NIDA, 2003). In either case, the result is that experimentation with substances becomes part of the youth's social experience. Although some young people refrain from regular substance use and others abstain completely, the risk of progressing from experimentation to problematic use exists for some young people, even if use began as experimentation with friends. Given the potential biological and psychological antecedents and consequences described previously, social circles may provide initial access to substances that may ultimately develop into a substance use disorder.

Developmental Considerations

Young people are not miniature adults; they have unique experiences, and counselors must consider these experiences when addressing their needs. Substance abuse in young people differs from adults in terms of biological, psychological, and social spheres. As previously discussed, problematic substance use patterns in young people have causes and effects that may be similar in some ways to those causes and effects experienced by adults. At the same time, some factors remain unique to young people who are using or abusing substances. Counselors should be aware of these factors and how substance abuse can affect youth, not just in the present but also across the life span.

BIOLOGICAL

Substance use affects the entire biological system of the user for both youth and adults. Depending on the substance being used, physiological processes such as breathing, blood pressure, and heart rate may increase or decrease (Hart & Ksir, 2015). The neurochemical reward pathways described previously respond to substance use in similar ways among adults and young people. In addition, cognitive processes, including reaction time, assessment of risk, and decision-making processes may be negatively affected by substance use (Hart & Ksir, 2015).

Although these biological impacts are consistent across age groups, they are particularly salient for young people. First and foremost, the brains of young people are still developing, particularly with regard to the neural pathways and connections between the limbic system and prefrontal cortex of the brain (Siegel, 2014). The prefrontal cortex is responsible for decision making, cost–benefit analysis, and delaying immediate gratification, whereas the limbic system is responsible for emotional responses and pursuit of pleasure. The still-developing brain of young people is less likely to engage in thinking about long-term risks related to substance use and is more likely to respond based on emotional stimuli and short-term rewards (Siegel, 2014). This makes impulsive and high-risk decisions an important risk factor among young people.

In addition to these brain-based differences, physiological differences between youth and adults may also be observed related to substance misuse. Most young people are inexperienced substance users, with a low physiological tolerance for substances. Certain routes of administration, such as smoking and intravenous injection, have the ability to speed the substance to the young person's central nervous system rapidly and produce intense immediate effects. Because of the combination of low tolerance and lack of knowledge related to routes of administration and dosage amounts, inexperienced substance users may be at an increased risk to experience negative physiological effects and overdosing due to taking too much of a substance (Hart & Ksir, 2015). As a result, young people, whose bodies are still growing and developing, may experience increased side effects or negative physiological reactions from substance use, particularly if they consume doses similar to those of adults despite their smaller physical stature. A young person may, therefore, be at a higher risk of overdose due to the physiological limitations of his or her body to adequately process the substance ingested.

Consistent substance use may also hinder the ongoing physical development of a young person. Stimulant use may decrease weight gain and growth (Swanson et al., 2007), whereas alcohol use may affect growth, liver functioning, bone development, endocrine functioning, and reproductive development and functioning (National Institute on Alcohol Abuse and Alcoholism [NIAAA], n.d.). Regular use of some substances at any age may also increase the risk of chronic diseases (NIDA, 2014a), and young people who use these substances regularly are at increased risk of exposure to the chemical agents associated with these diseases over time if they continue their use into adulthood. The potential long-term impact of consistent substance use by young people may negatively affect physical functioning in adulthood, particularly as individuals age.

PSYCHOLOGICAL

In both young people and adults, substance use has short-term and potential long-term impacts on psychological functioning and mental health. Substances have the potential to affect psychological functioning both during and as a result of use. For example, hallucinogens may trigger hallucinations and increase emotional reactions during use, whereas withdrawal from opioids such as heroin or pharmaceutical medications may cause anxiety, panic, and/or insomnia (Hart & Ksir, 2015).

Although the psychological risks associated with substance use hold for both young people and adults, the vulnerability of young people to these consequences is greater. As described previously, the young person's brain is still developing; this development continues through ages 25 to 30 (Siegel, 2014). The psychological impact of substance use, coupled with the increased reactivity of the limbic system (the emotional center of the brain) and the decreased engagement of the prefrontal cortex (the reasoning and logic center of the brain), may increase the propensity of young people to react to psychological symptoms such as suicidal ideation or impulsivity.

An added challenge to substance use and psychological functioning in young people is the fact that the emergence of mental health disorders such as anxiety, depression, bipolar disorder, and schizophrenia typically occurs in late adolescence or early adulthood (APA, 2013). In some individuals, the mental health disorder may precede the initiation of substance use, and substance use may become a coping mechanism for managing the psychological symptoms of an emerging mental health disorder. In other cases, substance use may predate the emergence of a mental health disorder and may exacerbate the onset of symptoms experienced on emergence of mental health symptoms (NIDA, 2014b). In either situation, the assessment and diagnosis of a possible mental health disorder are complicated and confounded by regular substance use because both intoxication and withdrawal can trigger psychological symptoms that may be similar to symptoms experienced by individuals with a chronic or severe mental health concern (APA, 2013).

SOCIAL

The impact of substance use on relationships exists as a consequence for young people and adults alike. Family, peer, and romantic relationships may all deteriorate due to problematic substance use, and family concern is often an important factor in motivating adults and young people to seek treatment (NIDA, 2014b). In both young people and adults, peer associations may change to support ongoing substance use, and changing social circles to maintain use may also increase the risk of engagement in behaviors that could trigger involvement with the criminal justice system (NIDA, 2003, 2014b).

Social consequences for young people and adults differ in important ways. A major difference lies in the legal responsibility of parents or guardians for their children until age 18. Although an adult who is engaged in problematic substance use may be removed from the household or left by a partner, young people cannot generally be put out on the street, regardless of how frustrated or overwhelmed their parents or guardians may be. In addition, the legal responsibility for substance-related consequences is often absorbed by family members. Although a young person may be involved in the juvenile justice system, parents are often the ones responsible for paying fines and court costs, as well as transporting the individual to court-related appointments.

The effort and energy that may be expended toward and on behalf of a young person who is engaged in problematic substance use typically causes family tension among parents, siblings, and extended family. Substance use is often a polarizing topic, particularly in families with a history of substance use disorders. The young person's substance use may cause ripples in relationships between parents, children, and extended family members that increase stress and decrease support for the family as a whole and for the family's individual members. The added impact of social stigma associated with having a child who is abusing substances may compound these stressors.

Although the family system typically bears the brunt of the impact of a young person's substance use, other social support systems may also be affected. A young person may change peer groups to facilitate ongoing substance use, and this may cause strain on former friends who are concerned about the young person's escalating use. The impact of social status and social reputation is particularly salient for young people, and changing social acceptance may affect the young person's self-concept and his or her feeling of belonging among peers. Social supports are particularly important for young people who are trying to change high-risk substance use patterns, and the impact of losing social status and social supports may be detrimental to the young person's efforts to change. Although adults may be able to overcome these challenges, young people—whose social landscape is often consistent throughout middle and high school—may have greater difficulty changing their reputation and reconnecting with peers who have withdrawn from them secondary to their substance use.

In adults, high-risk substance use often affects employment, including obtaining and maintaining employment, job performance, and the adequacy of employment to meet financial needs in light of increased money spent on substances. Although young people may not be employed, they are typically enrolled in school, and academic functioning in young people is often negatively affected by substance misuse. Because substance use affects memory, cognition, and other biological functions, young people who regularly use substances may find themselves unable to engage in the academic environment. Both acute intoxication and recovering from substance use (e.g., hangovers) may affect academic performance. Over time, decreased academic performance may have an impact on the student's access to afterschool activities, sports, rigorous coursework, or additional academic support. The possibility of increased absences due to intoxication or withdrawal may also negatively affect a young person's academic record. The long-term impact of these consequences may hinder future opportunities, such as college acceptance or employment, which can negatively affect the individual's quality of life well into adulthood.

Development of Substance Use Disorders

BIOLOGICAL AND PSYCHOLOGICAL PREDISPOSITIONS

General factors related to how substances interact with the brain in all individuals and specific factors related to personal and family history of substance use disorders, mental health symptoms, and emotion regulation and response to stress may predispose an individual to developing high-risk substance use patterns. These risks are compounded in young people, who typically are experimenting with substances for the first time and may not be aware of the potential risks of frequent or high-dose use. Over time, a young person may find him- or herself using more often to achieve a similar effect. As the aftereffects of use set in, the individual may also use the substance to avoid the negative effects of withdrawal or to attempt to sustain the euphoric feeling produced by using the substance. Tolerance and physiological dependence may develop, which necessitates use to avoid feeling physically uncomfortable or ill.

SOCIAL FACTORS

Peer groups play an important role in the psychosocial development of young people, particularly as adolescence progresses. Both social acceptance and social rejection may make a young person susceptible to experimenting with substances, depending on the norms of the peer group and the accessibility of the substances. An added social factor that may increase risk of developing high-risk substance use is the social contagion that surrounds some substances (Ali, Amialchuk, & Dwyer, 2011). Like other fads or trends, substance use may reflect a type of social currency; it may be difficult for individuals to refrain from substance use when it is ubiquitous or expected among a social group or in a specific setting, such as a high school. The perception of use as low risk and socially acceptable may conceal the serious dangers associated with even infrequent use. In past years, the use of and dire consequences associated with inhalants (i.e., paint fumes, aerosol spray), nonmedical use of prescription medication (i.e., opioids and stimulants), and synthetic marijuana (i.e., Spice) have garnered media attention due to increases in use among young people that appear to be due, at least in part, to social contagion.

DEVELOPMENTAL FACTORS

The developmental processes associated with making the transition from childhood to adolescence increase risk-taking behavior and emotional lability (triggered by increased limbic activity) without associated increases in assessment of risk and delaying of gratification typically associated with the prefrontal cortex of the brain. These changes in the brain, which are necessary for survival of the species and for launching the young person out of the family home and into independence, also increase the risk of experimentation with substance use and the risks associated with being under the influence (Siegel, 2014). The reduced ability to perceive risk in a situation, coupled with the increased need for immediate gratification, may lead a young person to perceive recreational substance use as harmless and as a mechanism for asserting independence or experiencing emotional release. While the youth is under the influence, his or her inhibitions and decision making may be further diminished, which may lead to poor decision making and high-risk behaviors. Serious negative consequences may be avoided when first initiating use due to the infrequent and covert nature typical of adolescent substance experimentation. Young people may come to the erroneous belief that risk of harm or consequences is minimal or nonexistent due to lack of immediate consequences and the adolescent's developmentally congruent perception of personal invincibility. These beliefs, coupled with the biological effects of substances, may contribute to a transition from experimentation to development of a substance use disorder in vulnerable youth.

Long-Term Effects of Substance Misuse

BIOLOGICAL AND PSYCHOLOGICAL

Youth who use substances are at risk for biological and psychological consequences that may affect them well into adulthood. Because the young person's brain is constantly developing, the use of substances that interfere with this development can have an impact on the brain and on the processes it regulates. In young people, this can cause increased emotional lability and reactivity, decreased self-regulation and ability to delay gratification and consider consequences, and difficulties with short-term memory (NIDA, 2003, 2014b). These consequences can also increase the possibility of ongoing substance use, given the reduced ability to assess risks and consequences and the brain's increased responsivity to the substances being used. Over time, the young person may become physiologically dependent on the substance. This dependence has a lasting impact on his or her ability to moderate the use of substances in the future and may put the individual at lifelong risk for misusing substances.

Depending on the substance being used and the route of administration, physical growth, hormone production and regulation, and major organ functioning may decline, either through the action of the substance or through diseases acquired through use, such as hepatitis or HIV. Over time, the physical impacts of substance abuse can cause lasting effects on a young person's ability to reach full growth potential, maintain physical health, and reproduce in the future. The impact on organ systems may also increase the individual's risk of chronic diseases, such as heart disease, cancer, or diabetes.

Some substances used by young people also carry the risk of death. For example, young people are more likely than adults to use inhalants due to their accessible nature (Hart & Ksir, 2015), and inhalation of substances that produce intoxicating fumes cuts off circulation of oxygen to the brain, which can lead to coma or death (NIDA, 2014b). Inhalants may be fatal regardless of the number of times a person has used them or the dose being used due to the constant risk of suffocation. Other substances may be fatal at higher doses. Opioids (e.g., heroin) and depressants (e.g., alcohol) carry a risk of death that increases as the user ingests more of the substance than the body is able to process at one time; other substances, including depressants (e.g., alcohol, benzodiazepines), carry a risk of death due to withdrawal from chronic use of high doses of the substance (Hart & Ksir, 2015). In all cases of substance use, counselors should assess and discuss physical safety and risk of death so young people and their families are aware of the short- and long-term risks of misusing these substances.

SOCIAL

Many young people see recreational substance use as a rite of passage associated with adolescence and young adulthood, so they do not reflect on the long-term social impact of their substance use. Because substance use can affect short-term memory, executive functioning, and the ability to weigh risk and reward, it can hinder academic performance, and high-risk or impulsive behaviors may cause further disruptions in the young person's academic pursuits and lead to disciplinary action that tarnishes the youth's legal or academic record. This impact on academic achievement may negatively affect the young person's ability to pursue higher education or employment. These difficulties can be exacerbated if the young person has also been involved in the criminal justice system because of his or her substance use. The lost wages, benefits, and opportunities of young people whose substance use has interfered with their ability to learn and succeed in school are tremendous and often unconsidered by young people, who are biologically wired to focus on the present rather than the far-off future.

CLASSIFICATION OF SUBSTANCE USE DISORDERS

The *DSM-5* classifies and diagnoses substance use disorders based on the specific substance being used, along with the severity of symptoms associated with the use of the substance (APA, 2013). Table 16.1 provides an overview of the classes, drug types and street names, and acute effects of substances often used by young people. It can be used as a reference for assessment, diagnosis, and treatment.

Symptoms can range in severity from mild (two to three symptoms), to moderate (four to five symptoms), to severe (six or more symptoms). These symptoms broadly describe four domains associated with problematic substance use: impaired control, social impairment, risky use, and pharmacological indicators (e.g., tolerance, withdrawal). Substance-related disorders, including intoxication, withdrawal, and substance-induced disorders, are also included in this diagnostic category.

In the case of substance use disorders, symptoms remain consistent across substances and include the presence of at least two of the following symptoms occurring during a 12-month time span:

- Use of the substance over longer periods of time or in larger amounts than intended
- Desire or unsuccessful efforts to cut down on use
- A great deal of time spent obtaining, using, and/or recovering from the effects of the substance
- Craving the substance
- Continuing use that causes failure to fulfill major work, school, or home obligations
- Continued substance use despite negative social or interpersonal problems caused or exacerbated by use
- Important social, occupational, or recreational activities are given up or decrease as a result of use
- Ongoing substance use in physically hazardous situations
- Continued use despite knowledge of persistent or recurrent physical or psychological consequences stemming from use
- **Tolerance** leading to increased amounts of the substance to obtain the desired effect or a diminished effect with continued use of the same amount of the substance

Table 16.1	Substance Classes, Names, and Effects	
Class	**Name (Trade or Street Names)**	**Effects**
Stimulants	Cocaine (coke, crack, base) Amphetamines (meth, ice, crystal) Pharmaceutical stimulants (Adderall, Ritalin, Provigil, Nuvigil, Cyclert)	• Alertness, euphoria, excitement • Elevated pulse rate and blood pressure • Insomnia, decreased appetite • *Overdose effects:* agitation, hyperthermia, seizures, hallucinations, risk of death
Depressants	Alcohol (many trade names) Benzodiazepines (Xanax, Atavan, Valium, Halcion, Librium) Barbiturates (Seconal, Amytal, Nembutal) Soporifics (Ambien, Lunesta)	• Disorientation, decreased reaction time and coordination, slurred speech • Loss of short-term memory encoding at high doses (e.g., blackouts) • *Overdose effects:* shallow breathing, cold and clammy skin, weak and high pulse rate, coma, risk of death
Opioids	Opium (Paregoric, Pantofen) Morphine Codeine (syrup, purple drank, lean) Heroin (dope, tar, H) Methadone (Dolophine) Other pharmaceutical opioids (Demerol, Fentanyl, OxyContin, Dilaudid)	• Drowsiness and euphoria • Slowed breathing and nausea • *Overdose effects:* shallow breathing, clammy skin, pupil constriction, coma, risk of death
Hallucinogens	LSD (acid) Psilocybin (mushrooms, shrooms) Mescaline/peyote (mesc, cactus, buttons) Phencyclidine (PCP, angel dust) MDMA/Molly/Ecstasy and related compounds	• Hallucinations, altered perceptual experiences, increased emotions • *Overdose effects:* long-lasting episodes of intoxication that may be similar to psychosis
Cannabis	Marijuana (pot, weed, grass) Tetrahydrocannabinol (THC, Marinol) Hashish (hash)	• Decreased inhibitions and euphoria • Increased appetite, decreased attention and memory • *Overdose effects:* paranoia, fatigue, a state similar to psychosis (at high doses)

Note: Adapted from *Drugs, Society, & Human Behavior* (16th ed.), by C. L. Hart & C. Ksir, 2015, New York, NY: McGraw-Hill.

In addition, substance use disorder diagnostic criteria for alcohol, cannabis, opioids, sedatives/hypnotics/anxiolytics, stimulants, and tobacco also include withdrawal symptoms as a diagnostic symptom. Several specifiers may be used to describe the context of the substance use disorder. Early remission includes absence of symptoms that meet the *DSM-5* criteria for the disorder for at least 3 but fewer than 12 months, and sustained remission includes the absence of these symptoms for 12 months or more. For individuals who are in treatment or incarcerated in the juvenile justice system, the specifier *in a controlled environment* may be used. For individuals who are using medication-assisted treatment (e.g., methadone, Suboxone), the specifier *on maintenance therapy* may be used. Additional information on the specific substance use and related disorder *DSM-5* diagnoses and examples are presented in Table 16.2.

Table 16.2   Summary of the Common *DSM-5* Substance Use and Related Disorders

DSM-5 Disorder Category	Specific *DSM-5* Diagnoses Included	Brief Example
Alcohol-related disorders	Alcohol Use Disorder, Alcohol Intoxication, Alcohol Withdrawal, Other Alcohol-Induced Disorders, Unspecified Alcohol-Related Disorder	A 17-year-old girl experiences negative consequences from alcohol use, including absenteeism from school and decreasing grades, social withdrawal from peers, and a need to drink more than she used to in order to feel the effects of drinking.
Caffeine-related disorders	Caffeine Intoxication, Caffeine Withdrawal, Other Caffeine-Induced Disorders, Unspecified Caffeine-Related Disorder	A 15-year-old boy who drinks caffeinated soda throughout the day wakes up with symptoms of headache, dry mouth, and fatigue; drinking a soda helps to ease these symptoms.
Cannabis-related disorders	Cannabis Use Disorder, Cannabis Intoxication, Cannabis Withdrawal, Other Cannabis-Induced Disorders, Unspecified Cannabis-Related Disorder	A 14-year-old girl who has been using marijuana consistently for over a year begins experiencing increased anxiety when not smoking marijuana; she also finds that her anxiety when she has smoked is greater than it was before she began using marijuana.
Hallucinogen-related disorders	Phencyclidine and Other Hallucinogen Use Disorders, Phencyclidine and Other Hallucinogen Intoxication, Phencyclidine and Other Hallucinogen Withdrawal, Other Phencyclidine- and Hallucinogen-Induced Disorders, Unspecified Phencyclidine- and Hallucinogen-Related Disorder	A 13-year-old boy describes strange perceptual experiences, including being able to hear colors and taste music, following ingestion of LSD. His description of his thoughts and feelings is incoherent and disorganized. In addition, the young man's heart rate and blood pressure are elevated, and his pupils are dilated.
Inhalant-related disorders	Inhalant Use Disorder, Inhalant Intoxication, Other Inhalant-Induced Disorders, Unspecified Inhalant-Related Disorder	A 12-year-old girl inhales fumes from rubber cement on infrequent occasions. She has reported that she experiences severe headaches that she did not experience at all before she began using inhalants, but she denies any other symptoms associated with her infrequent use.
Opioid-related disorders	Opioid Use Disorder, Opioid Intoxication, Opioid Withdrawal, Other Opioid-Induced Disorders, Unspecified Opioid-Related Disorder	A 16-year-old boy was prescribed pharmaceutical opioids following a serious football injury. At first, he took the medication as prescribed, but after about 2 weeks it was not working as well as it had been. As a result, he began taking more than he was prescribed and eventually began using similar medication from his parents' medicine cabinet to continue his regular schedule of use. He notices that when he does not take the medication, he becomes irritable, shaky, and nauseous and he begins craving its use. His friends regularly abuse prescription opioid-based pills, and he starts to take pills with his friends, which later evolves into him buying the pills off the street and taking them on a regular basis.

(Continued)

Table 16.2	Summary of the Common (*DSM-5*) Substance Use and Related Disorders (*Continued*)	
DSM-5 Disorder Category	Specific *DSM-5* Diagnoses Included	Brief Example
Sedative, hypnotic, or anxiolytic-related disorders	Sedative, Hypnotic, or Anxiolytic Use Disorder; Sedative, Hypnotic, or Anxiolytic Intoxication; Sedative, Hypnotic, or Anxiolytic Withdrawal; Other Sedative, Hypnotic, or Anxiolytic-Induced Disorders; Unspecified Sedative, Hypnotic, or Anxiolytic-Related Disorder	A 15-year-old girl appears to be under the influence of alcohol. Her speech is slurred and incoherent, she nods off intermittently, and her coordination is poor. She denies consuming any alcohol but does state that she took two doses of Xanax, which a friend gave to her.
Stimulant-related disorders	Stimulant Use Disorder, Stimulant Intoxication, Stimulant Withdrawal, Other Stimulant-Induced Disorders, Unspecified Stimulant-Related Disorder	A 16-year-old boy describes intrusive and paranoid thoughts surrounding the cameras in the school being placed there to watch his every move and report his actions to the government. This young man has been regularly using methamphetamine for the past 6 months; his paranoid thoughts emerged during this time and persist whether or not he is using methamphetamine.
Tobacco-related disorders	Tobacco Use Disorder, Tobacco Intoxication, Tobacco Withdrawal, Other Tobacco-Induced Disorders, Unspecified Tobacco-Related Disorder	A 17-year-old girl who smokes cigarettes daily craves a cigarette first thing in the morning after waking up. Until she has this cigarette, she is irritable, is fatigued, and experiences a mild headache.
Other (or unknown) substance-related disorders	Other (or Unknown) Use Disorder, Other (or Unknown) Intoxication, Other (or Unknown) Withdrawal, Other (or Unknown)-Induced Disorders, Unspecified Other (or Unknown)-Related Disorder	A 14-year-old boy has withdrawn from his social and athletic activities over the past month. In addition, his grades have dropped. He spends most of his free time in his room with the door locked. His parents report that sometimes his room smells like potpourri when they enter it, but they do not have any evidence to suggest that their son is using marijuana, alcohol, or pharmaceutical medications recreationally. They are not sure what he is using, but they believe that he is misusing some substance due to these symptoms.

Note: Adapted from *Diagnostic and Statistical Manual of Mental Disorders* (5th ed.), by American Psychiatric Association (APA), 2013a, Washington, DC: Author.

ASSESSMENT OF SUBSTANCE USE DISORDERS

Assessment of substance use disorders or substance abuse or misuse may involve collecting data related to the types of substances used, the frequency and quantity of use, consequences experienced secondary to use, and high-risk behaviors associated with substance use.

Clinical Toolbox 16.1

In the Pearson etext, click here to read about biological testing mechanisms used to measure the amount of a mood-altering substance in a client's system, as well as the benefits and limitations of these tests.

Assessment Measures

Assessment typically begins with a screening tool to determine whether additional assessments are needed. If more in-depth assessments are indicated, the assessment process may include a combination of paper-and-pencil instruments, interviews, and collection of collateral data from parents/guardians, teachers, and other professionals. The overall goal of assessment related to substance use disorders is to determine the degree of risk and the most appropriate level of care and types of interventions that will support the young person and his or her family in changing high-risk substance use patterns. Specific substance use assessment tools for youth are described in Table 16.3.

The questions presented in Figure 16.1 may be useful in screening for the presence of substance use disorders in young people. In addition, the American Society of Addiction Medicine (ASAM; 2013) provided specific guidelines for data collection across six domains of functioning. These guidelines, discussed later in this chapter, can be used to further assess the client's needed level of care.

Assessing Comorbidity

Throughout the assessment process, it is important to screen for the presence of other mental health disorders that may co-occur with the substance use disorder. If the individual regularly uses substances, it may be difficult to determine whether other mental health symptoms stem from substance use or whether they exist as separate primary disorders. For this reason, careful monitoring of symptoms commonly associated with other mental health disorders, such as anxiety, depression, bipolar disorder, and schizophrenia, should be undertaken throughout the process of substance use disorder assessment and treatment (APA, 2013). This is particularly important when working with young people because the age of onset of many of these disorders coincides with adolescence or young adulthood. Youth who have experienced child abuse, sexual assault, or any other traumatic events are also at risk for developing substance use disorders (APA, 2013).

Table 16.3 Summary of Substance Use Assessment Measures

Assessment Measure	Age Range	Overview of Assessment Measure
CRAFFT	Under 21 years	The CRAFFT is a six-item screening tool that assesses alcohol and other drug use (Knight, Sherritt, Shrier, Harris, & Chang, 2002). This assessment can be used in primary care and mental health service settings to provide a snapshot of an adolescent's engagement in risky substance use. The CRAAFT is used for screening purposes and is not appropriate for use as a diagnostic tool.
Personal Experience Screening Questionnaire (PESQ)	12–18 years	The PESQ is a 40-item screening that measures problem severity, psychosocial factors, and history of drug use (Winters, 1992). This screening tool is useful for determining whether a young person should be referred for further assessment and treatment.
Rutgers Alcohol Problem Index (RAPI)	12–21 years	The RAPI is a 23-item screening tool for assessing consequences experienced due to alcohol use (White & Labouvie, 1989). The RAPI's focus on consequences excludes information related to frequency, quantity, and substances used and instead focuses on possible hazards experienced by young people who use alcohol. The RAPI is a screening tool and is not appropriate for use as a diagnostic instrument.
Substance Abuse Subtle Screening Inventory–Adolescent Version (SASSI-A2)	12–18 years	The SASSI-A2 is an assessment used to determine the likelihood that a young person is experiencing a substance use disorder (Miller & Lazowski, 2005). The SASSI-A2 includes both face-value questions about alcohol and other drug use and subtle questions focused on risk factors, family dynamics, and deceptive response patterns that assist with determining risk of a substance use disorder.

- Does the child sometimes appear to be intoxicated, as evidenced by changes in affect, physiological response patterns, state of consciousness, or other observable symptoms of intoxication?
- Does the child use a substance more often or for a longer time period than intended?
- Does the child try to cut back or stop using with unsuccessful results?
- Does the child spend a great deal of time obtaining, using, and/or recovering from using the substance?
- Does the child experience cravings for the substance?
- Does the child fail to fulfill obligations at work, school, or home because of his or her substance use?
- Does the child continue to use the substance despite negative social or interpersonal problems that stem from use of the substance?
- Has the child given up important social, occupational, or recreational activities due to substance use?
- Does the child use the substance when it is physically hazardous to do so (e.g., driving while under the influence, use in spite of a medical condition)?
- Does the child continue to use the substance despite experiencing negative physical and/or psychological consequences?
- Does the child need more of the substance to obtain the same effect or experience a diminished effect from the same amount of the substance over time?
- Does the child experience symptoms of withdrawal when he or she stops using the substance?
- Does the child experience symptoms of another mental health disorder (e.g., anxiety, depression, schizophrenia) that coincide with onset of the use of the substance?

FIGURE 16.1 Questions Counselors Should Ask to Assess for Substance Use and Related Disorders
Note: Adapted from *Diagnostic and Statistical Manual of Mental Disorders* (5th ed.), American Psychiatric Association (APA), 2013, Washington, DC: Author.

Other disorders that may present alongside substance use disorders—or precipitate them—include post-traumatic stress disorder, conduct disorder, and oppositional defiant disorder (APA, 2013).

Assessing Needed Levels of Care

The ASAM (2013) describes a multidimensional model that can be used when assessing a client to determine the most appropriate and least restrictive **level of care** the youth requires. These dimensions include a consideration of various biological, psychological, and social domains, as well as the young person's strengths and limitations in functioning across each of the dimensions. The ASAM suggests taking into consideration (a) acute intoxication and/or withdrawal; (b) biomedical conditions and complications; (c) emotional, behavioral, or cognitive conditions or complications; (d) readiness to change; (e) relapse, continued use, or continued problem potential; and (f) recovery and living environment (ASAM, 2013).

Risk factors that necessitate medical monitoring include overdose, acute withdrawal, or concurrent medical or psychological conditions, all of which may warrant placement of the youth in a treatment facility where these issues can be monitored and addressed quickly. In other cases, where the risk of harm is less serious, a young person may be placed in outpatient services and interventions. When interviewing young people and their family members about substance use, practitioners should pay attention to each of these domains to determine the most appropriate placement for treatment and also gain a better understanding of the strengths and challenges the young person may face when trying to make changes to high-risk substance use patterns.

Levels of care for treating adolescents with substance use disorders include outpatient, intensive outpatient, partial hospitalization, residential, and inpatient treatment (NIDA, 2014b). Placement in each level of care requires consideration of the strengths, needs, and supports available for the young person, and an individual will often participate in more than one level of care over time. For youth who need medical monitoring, inpatient or residential treatment is often the first level of care recommended because these facilities operate with medical staff to monitor detoxification. Residential or inpatient treatment settings typically offer an array of services, including individual and group therapy, 12-step program attendance, family-based programming, and academic support. Young people may stay for several weeks or months in residential or inpatient treatment to ensure they have a foundation of sobriety prior to making the transition to the next level of care.

Partial hospitalization programs share many features with residential and inpatient treatment settings, such as providing a full day and week of treatment programming that balances individual, group, family, and peer-support programming. Partial hospitalization programs, however, allow the young person to return to his or her home in the evenings, and this helps the young person to begin experiencing substance-free independent living with adequate support and accountability to promote success.

Intensive outpatient treatment (IOP) represents a step down from partial hospitalization programs. A young person may attend group counseling and peer-support groups for 3 to 4 hours per day on 2 to 3 days per week. This step down from partial hospitalization programs allows the young person to increase his or her autonomy, yet still have the safety net associated with an IOP setting. The step down from IOP may include weekly individual, family, or group counseling sessions to support ongoing abstinence from substances. For young people who are experimenting with substances but have not yet manifested a substance use disorder, the outpatient level of care may provide the individual and family with the support, structure, and accountability needed to prevent the young person's substance use from escalating. In fact, most adolescent substance use disorder treatment occurs in the context of outpatient, community-based treatment (NIDA, 2014b).

COUNSELING INTERVENTIONS

When treating young people who have a substance use disorder, counselors must take into account the risk of continued substance use, the environment in which the individual functions, the individual's and family's motivation to make changes, and the possibility of other mental health or physiological disorders that may require concurrent treatment. In addition to these factors, counselors must consider the confidentiality of substance-related treatment records.

Legal and Ethical Considerations

Health privacy laws, professional ethical codes, and federal laws intersect in complex ways for practitioners who work with minors seeking treatment for substance use disorders. Ethical codes and legal statutes concur regarding immediate action that may necessitate breach of confidentiality in cases where there is eminent risk of harm to self or others. In other situations, practitioners who receive direct or indirect federal funding or hold tax-exempt status are required to adhere to the guidelines of **42 CFR**, a federal law that requires clearly documented written consent from the client before releasing any information related to his or her substance use disorder treatment (including disclosing that the individual is participating in treatment) to a third party, including parents or guardians (see Chapter 4). Although the **Health Insurance Portability and Accountability Act (HIPAA)** generally affords parents and guardians access to a minor's treatment records, 42 CFR conflicts with this law and typically takes precedence in protecting the confidentiality of minors who seek substance use treatment services. As a result, practitioners who provide substance use disorder treatment services to a minor client in a federally funded setting must obtain written consent that adheres to the guidelines set forth by 42 CFR to disclose information to or involve family members in the young person's treatment because involving the family requires disclosing the young person's engagement in treatment. As a result, negotiating the informed consent and release of information processes with minor clients and their families may present complexities for counselors when the young person is unwilling to provide consent to disclose any information to family members (Williams, 2015). Consultation on how to handle such matters is important.

Developmental Considerations

An important factor to consider when selecting level of care and specific treatment interventions for a young person with a substance use disorder is the youth's development across physical, affective, and social domains. Generally speaking, increased structure and support coupled with consistency, tangible reward systems for progress, and small, achievable, manageable goals and target behaviors work well for young people who are engaged in treatment for a substance use disorder. In addition, helping the family to increase structure, support, and consistency in the home may help the individual and the family system to change behaviors that enable, support, or encourage the young person's substance use (NIDA, 2014b). In all cases, decisions about level of care, treatment modalities, and family involvement should be based on the individual's and family's strengths, needs, and goals.

Family Involvement and Support

As previously described, a young person's substance use affects multiple domains of functioning and causes strain in interpersonal relationships. Families face many challenges, including experiencing fear, anger, and frustration; managing financial and legal consequences stemming from the young person's substance use; and coping with guilt, shame, and grief surrounding the many difficult experiences family members have to endure.

As a result of these challenges, the entire family system warrants attention and support throughout the treatment process. Family engagement in treatment is important for various reasons, ranging from establishing consistency, rules, and expectations for the young person, to allowing the family members to address their own feelings surrounding their experiences with the young person's substance use. Family treatment models and supports are described in more detail later in this chapter. Some of these supports may be helpful for family members regardless of whether the young person chooses to engage in treatment. Counseling allows family members to address the systemic and interpersonal processes associated with the young person's substance use, even if the young person chooses to engage in treatment independently.

Prognosis

The outlook for young people who engage in high-risk substance use or who meet the criteria for a substance use disorder is largely dependent on the interventions provided and the degree to which high-risk substance use is stopped. Not all young people who choose to use substances will develop a substance use disorder; in many cases, early intervention can help the young person to avoid the symptoms associated with these disorders altogether. Despite the challenges that treating young people with substance use disorders may present, treatment can be effective, especially when it is initiated early and involves the support of families, schools, peers, and communities (NIDA, 2003; 2014b).

INTEGRATED TREATMENT COMPONENTS

Table 16.4 describes the phases, goals, and treatment components associated with counseling youth who have substance use disorders. Specific elements and recommendations for treatment are made based on the individual's readiness for change, cultural background, strengths, needs, and severity of consequences and symptoms of substance use. In addition, treatment components may be influenced by mandates or requirements of agencies that are involved with the client as a result of his or her substance use. These agencies may include the criminal justice system, the school district, or the social services department. Although the primary consideration when selecting treatment goals and interventions must always be the well-being of the client, these additional stakeholders in the client's treatment may necessitate consultation, coordination of care, and integration of treatment elements that support the young person to function optimally in the biological, psychological, and social domains.

Clinical Toolbox 16.2

In the Pearson etext, click here to view an example of a relapse prevention plan.

Detoxification

Counselors should take several things into consideration when determining whether a young person requires medically monitored detoxification to withdraw safely from a substance. First and foremost, counselors must ensure the safety of the client. If a young person has been consistently using a depressant, such as alcohol or benzodiazepines, for a long period of time, it is particularly important to refer the individual to a medical professional to monitor and assist with the withdrawal process because risk of death is possible when withdrawing from these substances (Hart & Ksir, 2015).

Table 16.4	Phases, Goals, and Treatment Components Associated with Substance Use Disorders	
Phase of the Disorder	**Goals**	**Treatment Components**
Acute intoxication and withdrawal (detoxification)	Medical stabilization and monitoring of withdrawal, assessment, relationship building with the client and family	Medical monitoring (may include medications to manage withdrawal symptoms) Client safety Family engagement
Stabilization and treatment	Resolving intoxication and withdrawal symptoms, initiating abstinence from substances, motivating the client and family to engage in treatment, group counseling and/or participation in support groups for the client and family, psychoeducation on substance use disorders for the client and family	Psychoeducation Affective education Motivational interviewing Group counseling Support groups/12-step participation for client and family Family counseling Possible individual counseling, particularly if comorbid disorders or history of trauma are present Possible use of medication-assisted treatment Possible use of urine drug screens to monitor abstinence from substance use
Maintenance	Resolving intrapersonal and interpersonal difficulties, relapse prevention planning	Support group/12-step participation for client and family Family counseling Possible ongoing group counseling Possible ongoing individual counseling, particularly if comorbid disorders or history of trauma are present Possible use of medication-assisted treatment Possible use of urine drug screens to monitor abstinence from substance use

Although withdrawal from opiates, stimulants, and marijuana does not possess the same level of lethality as depressant withdrawal, the symptoms of withdrawal from these substances will still be uncomfortable for the client (Hart & Ksir, 2015). This discomfort, coupled with the possibility of experiencing cravings for the substance, make referral to a medical professional for withdrawal support advisable to support the client in detoxing as comfortably as possible from the substance.

Medically monitored detoxification is most likely to be needed when an individual is actively using substances on a consistent basis and has developed tolerance and physiological symptoms of withdrawal when stopping use. Even if detoxification is not warranted due to irregular patterns of use that have not resulted in acute withdrawal symptoms upon stopping, an important role of the counselor in supporting the client's transition from use to nonuse is providing therapeutic support for the possibility of psychological symptoms of stopping use of the substance.

Individual and Group Counseling

COGNITIVE BEHAVIORAL THERAPY (CBT)

Cognitive behavioral therapy (CBT) for young people who have a substance use disorder typically targets the faulty thoughts and beliefs that underlie the young person's use of substances. Because of young people's incomplete brain development, focusing on risks, rewards, and consequences and the underlying thoughts and beliefs surrounding the positive attributions made toward substances may be particularly helpful in raising awareness surrounding the risks associated with ongoing substance use. CBT is also useful in helping young people to learn how to develop self-control and coping skills, areas that may be negatively affected by ongoing substance use. Overall, CBT's focus on developing practical problem-solving and risk assessment skills is well coordinated with the unique challenges inherent in substance use among young people (NIDA, 2014b).

BEHAVIOR THERAPY AND CONTINGENCY MANAGEMENT

Numerous behavior therapy interventions are employed to encourage youth in residential, partial hospitalization, and IOP programs to participate in their treatment program and to help them to manage their behavior. Contingency management is one example of a behavior therapy intervention that is useful, especially with youth who are in residential treatment programs. Contingency management programs help the young person to develop habits and behaviors that do not involve using substances; these programs support the development of social and behavioral skills that make ongoing abstinence from substance use more likely. Contingency management is often used in conjunction with other treatment modalities, such as individual, group, or family therapy, to support the overall goals of treatment (NIDA, 2014b).

Contingency management involves the use of a coordinated system of rewards that are tied to expected behaviors to reinforce positive behaviors and reduce the occurrence of negative behaviors. Contingency management programs typically involve the use of tickets or vouchers that can be exchanged for prizes or money as a reward for clients. The schedule of reinforcements should be consistent and clear, and it may include positive reinforcement (e.g., ticket, voucher, token) for activities such as participating actively in group; demonstrating abstinence via a substance-free urine drug screen; participating appropriately in educational activities; following rules, directions, and procedures; and demonstrating prosocial behaviors during recreational activities.

In the context of outpatient family-based treatment, contingency management principles may be employed by the family in the home to reinforce and encourage similar behaviors. Consistency and predictability of expectations and rewards, coupled with follow-through of the reward system by parents, make contingency management a useful home-based intervention. The behavioral goals of contingency management are tied to abstinence-related behaviors, so the use of urine drug screens or other monitoring tools to ensure adherence to treatment is common.

MOTIVATIONAL ENHANCEMENT THERAPY

Motivational enhancement therapy is used to increase a young person's motivation to engage in treatment and to make changes to high-risk substance use patterns. This approach uses **motivational interviewing**—a collaborative approach for helping the client to resolve ambivalence and to elicit reasons for change—as an intervention tool to help the young person to identify benefits and challenges of change and to lay a foundation on which additional interventions can be built. Motivational enhancement therapy is often used at the onset of treatment and typically involves a brief intervention that leads to targeted interventions related to the client's goals, needs, and strengths (NIDA, 2014b).

Motivational interviewing is a client-centered intervention that is directive in its use of ongoing counselor attention to the client's thoughts, feelings, and behaviors related to the possibility of change (Miller & Rollnick, 2012). Throughout motivational interviewing–based interventions, the counselor takes a collaborative stance with the client, helping the client to identify reasons for and against change, to discern and begin resolving ambivalence about change, and to articulate a plan and act toward changes that the client believes are important to reduce the risks associated with problematic substance use.

Motivational interviewing involves helping the client to identify his or her most salient concerns, explore reasons for change, and identify and implement a change plan based on his or her goals and needs (Miller & Rollnick, 2012). The four key intervention activities of motivational interviewing are (a) expressing empathy toward the client throughout the intervention process, (b) developing discrepancies between client goals and values and his or her choices and actions to increase motivation to change and resolve ambivalence, (c) supporting client self-efficacy related to making changes, and (d) dealing with resistance that may occur between the client and counselor as a result of the client's ambivalence or fears surrounding the change process (Miller & Rollnick, 2012).

Motivational interviewing uses techniques that allow the counselor to intentionally engage the client in discussing his or her concerns, with a focus on identifying and capitalizing on motivation for change in the client's talk. The techniques, which include open-ended questions; affirmations of client strengths and values; reflections on content, feelings, and meaning; and summaries of the client's verbalizations surrounding change, are used to reflect to the client his or her own thoughts and feelings surrounding the change process (Miller & Rollnick, 2012).

By integrating these components and maintaining a client-centered and supportive attitude that reflects the counselor's genuine belief that the client is capable of change, the counselor is able to demonstrate the most important element of motivational interviewing: the spirit of motivational interviewing. The spirit of motivational interviewing is difficult to define operationally, but it is a collaborative, genuine, and sincere approach to working with the client; without this spirit, motivational interviewing may be perceived as coercive or mean-spirited by the client and may fail to help the client to harness his or her own motivation to change (Miller & Rollnick, 2012). Table 16.5 provides information about the goals and techniques associated with motivational interviewing.

Table 16.5 Motivational Interviewing Processes and Techniques

Process	Key Goals	Associated Techniques	Examples
Engage	Develop rapport. Explore the client's perspective on the value of counseling.	Open-ended questions Affirmations Reflection on content, feelings, and meaning Summaries	"Your parents are important to you, so even though you don't think you have a problem, you made the choice to come to this appointment because you care about them."
Focus	Explore concrete reasons for counseling. Assess the client's motivation to change. Identify the client's strengths and values as well as discrepancies between these and substance use.	Open-ended questions Affirmations Reflections on content, feelings, and meaning Summaries Double-sided reflections	"On the one hand, you don't think your alcohol use is a problem, and on the other hand, people you care about are really worried about you."
Evoke	Explore concrete reasons for and against change. Continue identifying discrepancies. Determine what the client is willing to do to make the problem as he or she sees it better.	Open-ended questions Affirmations Reflections on content, feelings, and meaning Summaries Double-sided reflections Importance and confidence-scaling questions	"You said that you see the biggest problem as your parents not trusting you. You also said you'd be willing to let them check your phone randomly so they'd start to trust you again. On a scale of 1 to 10, with 1 being *not important* and 10 being *super important*, how important is it to you that they start to trust you? On that same scale, how confident are you that you will be able to build trust by letting them check your phone randomly?"
Plan	Develop a client-centered, concrete plan for change. Troubleshoot and explore options. Provide the client with a menu of options if he or she is unable to articulate a plan but is ready to begin making one. Affirm the client's desire to change.	Open-ended questions Affirmations Reflections on content, feelings, and meaning Summaries Double-sided reflections Importance and confidence-scaling questions Providing feedback only after getting the client's permission	"I heard you mention that you had no idea where to start with making new friends. What would you think about me sharing some ideas other clients have found helpful?" The client agrees. "Some clients said they started by joining a school club. I have one client who really liked art and enrolled in a community art class and met people there. What thoughts do you have about this? What ideas do you have for your situation?"

Motivational interviewing uses the stages of change (Prochaska, 1995) as a framework for conceptualizing client readiness to change and matches interventions to these stages. The stages of change include the following: *precontemplation*, or lack of recognition that a problem exists; *contemplation*, or acknowledgement that a problem may exist but not yet experiencing motivation to change; *preparation*, or beginning to consider changes that might be made to address the problem; *action*, or taking consistent steps to address the problem; *maintenance*, or developing a way of living that supports ongoing management of the problem; and *relapse*, or return to behaviors that are indicative of the problem (Prochaska, 1995). Table 3.1 in Chapter 3 lists these stages and associated counseling goals and tasks in more depth. During a relapse, an individual typically does not return to precontemplation; instead, he or she may make the transition to contemplation, preparation, or action depending on his or her awareness of the significance of the relapse and his or her sense of urgency to avoid consequences associated with the relapse.

Clinical Toolbox 16.3

In the Pearson etext, click here to review an activity that helps clients to review the pros and cons of making a change.

PSYCHOEDUCATION

Psychoeducation is an important aspect of substance abuse treatment and is generally provided in individual, family, and group counseling contexts. Psychoeducation in the treatment of substance use disorders provides young people with information and skills that can help them to better understand the biology, psychology, and sociology of substance use disorders; risks associated with ongoing use; and tools for abstinence and recovery (Haddock & Sheperis, 2016). Topics of focus for psychoeducation groups may include the biology of substance use disorders, consequences and risks associated with use, the stages of change, tools for relapse prevention, social and coping skills, and exploration of activities that promote overall wellness. In selecting topics for psychoeducation, counselors should consider the biological, psychological, social, and developmental needs of the group members to ensure a fit between the topics and group members' needs.

GROUP THERAPY

The individual treatment modalities previously described may also be integrated into group therapy treatments for young people who have substance use disorders (NIDA, 2014b). CBT and contingency management may be used together or separately in a group setting to provide opportunities for skill development, relapse prevention, affective regulation, and positive reinforcement and monitoring. The added support of peers who are coping with similar challenges and who can provide added support and perspectives to one another may be particularly helpful for young people who are in need of positive social supports and accountability. Group therapy is the most common—and most effective—treatment modality for addressing substance use disorders (Haddock & Sheperis, 2016). As a result, residential, partial hospitalization, and IOP programs typically use group therapy as the primary form of treatment for substance use disorders. Figure 16.2 provides a group activity that can be used to help youth to develop coping skills.

TWELVE-STEP PROGRAMS

Twelve-step programs allow individuals to connect with others who have a desire to abstain from substance use. Through such programs, youth are able to receive and provide each other with support, encouragement, and hope. The most widely available peer support groups are 12-step groups, which include Alcoholics Anonymous (AA), Narcotics Anonymous (NA), and Cannabis Anonymous (CA), to name a few. These groups are facilitated by group members, promote engagement with the 12 steps, are free and widely available, and provide a community of support for individuals who want to maintain sobriety from mood-altering substances (NIDA, 2014b).

It is important to note that 12-step participation is not considered a form of treatment; however, counselors often integrate discussions regarding participation in 12-step programs into counseling when they work with young people who have substance use disorders. This infusion of 12-step preparation activities by

Activity Overview

This puzzle activity helps group members to come up with personal coping techniques that they can use in times of difficulty. Group members provide help and feedback to each other. This activity shows joint effort and group cohesion. It helps group members to recognize new coping strategies and develop a sense of empowerment over their situation (i.e., an addiction or stressor). Clients who suffer from addiction, grief, or various stressors can also use this activity individually as a mechanism of strength and support.

Activity Objectives

This activity teaches self-understanding by developing group members' coping strategies.

Directions

1. Introduce the exercise, and instruct group members to take a few moments to establish a connection with themselves. Ask them to connect with their hobbies and interests, likes, and other aspects of themselves.

2. Instruct group members to draw a large shape (e.g., square, heart, star) that has personal significance and then draw puzzle pieces inside the shape. Ask group members to cut out the pieces.

3. Instruct group members to write or draw pictures of coping skills on each of the pieces. These coping skills can represent any category that pertains to physical, spiritual, emotional, psychological, and personal self.

Examples include:
*   taking a walk with my dogs;
*   taking bubble baths;
*   taking a yoga class;
*   getting coffee with a friend;
*   learning a new language; and
*   reading a book.

Group members can provide suggestions and feedback to each other as needed.

1. Ask group members to connect the pieces of their puzzles. Discuss how each piece connects to another and how the pieces work together to create balance.

Process Questions

1. What was this activity like for you?
2. Talk about how you use the coping skills you selected.
3. What made you pick the puzzle shape you chose?
4. Talk about how your puzzle pieces go together.
5. Where do you run into problems with fitting your pieces together?
6. How can you use this activity to remind yourself of the skills you need to use to maintain your sobriety?

FIGURE 16.2   Filling in the Pieces to My Puzzle

the counselor into the treatment of substance use disorders is called **12-step facilitation**. This process typically provides clients with information on the benefits of attending a 12-step program, how to locate and participate in meetings, information on key 12-step components such as sponsorship and step work, ongoing support for participation and engagement in 12-step programs, and outside accountability and support for ongoing 12-step group participation. Counselors also check in with clients to see which steps they are working on and how the counselor can support them in progressing through the program.

Integrating Family into Treatment

PSYCHOEDUCATION

As with individual-level psychoeducation, family-based psychoeducation often focuses on topics related to bio-psycho-social elements of substance use. In addition, family-based psychoeducation may provide information on coping with the impact of the young person's use on the family system. Information related to common effects of a substance use disorder on family members' roles, ways of coping, communication, and emotion regulation may be included to validate the experiences of the family, to provide more information on ways to cope with the substance use disorder, and to support effective communication and behavior management strategies in the family system. Psychoeducation for family members may also include information on parental self-care and affect regulation skills, 12-step programs for family members (e.g., Al-Anon, Alateen), and special education laws, regulations, and procedures when the young person's education is negatively affected by his or her substance use disorder or a co-occurring condition that meets criteria for special education services.

FAMILY THERAPY

A key component of treatment for young people who have a substance use disorder is family involvement in treatment. Typical goals for engaging the family in the treatment process include promoting physical and psychological safety against triggers for substance use and allowing each family member to voice his or her lived experiences stemming from coping with the substance use disorder. Because the young person typically resides in the family home and the parents or guardians are legally responsible for the young person's safety and well-being, family involvement is crucial for the young person's success and for the well-being of the entire family system (NIDA, 2014b). Often, there are others in the family who abuse substances, and this adds an additional layer of importance for family involvement.

Family therapy treatments typically are offered on an outpatient basis and involve participation of all family members who are available to engage in services. In addition, families are encouraged to be involved throughout the young person's treatment in residential, partial hospitalization, or IOP programming. Therapeutic activities in these settings may include psychoeducation for family members; family counseling in the residential, partial hospitalization, or IOP setting; and meetings with the young person and family members to discuss treatment progress and discharge planning. The young person may receive passes permitting home visits while he or she is still in treatment to provide the young person and his or her family with opportunities to practice new behaviors and skills with the support of treatment to process these experiences.

Many family therapy approaches can be useful when working with youth who have an addiction. **Brief strategic family therapy** (**BSFT**; Szapocznik, Hervis, & Schwartz, 2003) addresses the interactions in the family system that may be perpetuating ineffective communication and poor coping skills among its members. The goal of BSFT is to help the family to change ineffective patterns of interaction to promote more effective ones (NIDA, 2014b).

Family behavior therapy (**FBT**; Donohue et al., 2009) is an approach that empowers the family system to provide consistent reinforcement for desired behaviors. This approach typically uses behavioral contracts, contingency management techniques, and consistent rewards and consequences to help the family to develop behavior and interactional patterns to function optimally (NIDA, 2014b). **Multidimensional family therapy** (**MDFT**; Liddle, 2010) and **multisystemic family therapy** (**MST**; Henggeler & Schaeffer, 2010) both view the family system in the context of a multisystems perspective; academic, social, legal, and community systems may all play a role in the treatment process in both of these family therapy models. MDFT typically empowers the family system to collaborate directly with these systems to increase the young person's awareness of potential consequences of ongoing substance use. MDFT may also support families in using community-based resources and provide a network of support for the family and the young person (NIDA, 2014b). In contrast, MST typically does not involve these other systems directly in treatment. Instead, it uses the relationship the young person and the family have with these systems to identify areas of strength and weakness and to support the young person and the family in making changes to promote more cohesive family functioning (NIDA, 2014a).

Clinical Toolbox 16.4

In the Pearson etext, click here to read about a creative activity that can be used with an individual and his or her family. The activity involves the use of a time line to explore significant events, emotions, and substance use and to make connections between these elements.

Community-Based Interventions

In addition to treatment modalities that focus on individual and family-level interventions, community-based interventions that rely on multisystemic supports across academic, social, and community systems have emerged that specifically target the unique needs of young people. These community-based interventions require collaboration within and across systems of support; when these collaborations are achieved, the impacts for young people who are making changes to high-risk substance use may be significant.

ADOLESCENT COMMUNITY REINFORCEMENT APPROACH (A-CRA)

Adolescent Community Reinforcement Approach (A-CRA; Godley, Smith, Meyers, & Godley, 2009) is a community-based intervention program that pulls on coordinated systems of care, reinforcement schedules, and multifaceted levels of support to help young people to make and maintain changes to high-risk substance use patterns. The goal of this program is to replace people, places, and things that the young person associated with his or her substance use with more positive people, places, and things that reinforce abstinence from use. In addition to providing support and positive reinforcement for abstaining from use, A-CRA also provides counseling for young people that focuses on coping skills, communication skills, and behavior management techniques to support ongoing abstinence from substance use (NIDA, 2014b). A-CRA uses behavioral and contingency management techniques and is typically facilitated on an outpatient basis. Counselors assess the client for areas of need related to substance use, social skills, and coping behaviors and use these areas as the focus of interventions that tie rewards to abstinence from substance use, prosocial behaviors, and engagement in positive coping mechanisms. In addition to meeting with the client, counselors hold family sessions without the client present to elicit support from the family, teach and model behavioral interventions and positive communication techniques, and assess the young person's progress. In addition, the counselor may collaborate with other community-based organizations, such as schools, recreational facilities, or the juvenile justice system, to promote consistency in expectations, supports, and reinforcements across settings. The overall goal of A-CRA is to make not using substances more rewarding than using them; this treatment modality aims to increase the rewards for not using substances, to decrease the young person's use, and to promote appropriate peer interactions and community engagement (Substance Abuse and Mental Health Services Administration [SAMHSA], 2007).

RECOVERY HIGH PROGRAMS

High schools that promote recovery for their students are a new tool for helping young people who have made changes to high-risk substance use. These Recovery High programs are typically affiliated with alternative school programs and use physical space and scheduling to create a separate educational environment for young people in recovery to promote positive social supports and a culture of abstinence from substances. Students enrolled in Recovery High programs often engage in outside treatment and supportive services in addition to their attendance at the school (NIDA, 2014b). The Association of Recovery Schools (ARS), the accrediting body for Recovery High programs, identifies five accredited schools nationally (ARS, 2016). In 2015, a total of 35 school-based recovery programs in public, private, alternative, and charter school settings were available to students in recovery nationally, although not all programs are accredited by the ARS (Coyle, 2015). Admission and enrollment to these schools is typically granted to any student who is in recovery who meets the eligibility criteria, such as living within the school system's boundaries (Coyle, 2015).

Clinical Toolbox 16.5

In the Pearson etext, click here to read about a creative activity that can be used to help youth to develop a positive view of themselves.

Psychopharmacotherapy

There is a lack of clinical data on the efficacy or appropriateness of the use of medications in treating young people who have substance use disorders (NIDA, 2014b). Medications generally are used to treat comorbid disorders, such as depression or anxiety. What is known about addictions and psychopharmacotherapy is grounded in research conducted with adults who have substance use disorders. Decisions surrounding the use of medication to assist young people being treated for a substance use disorder must be undertaken by trained medical professionals who have a firm understanding of the risks and benefits associated with the severity of the substance use disorder and with medication-assisted treatment for substance use disorders. The following information is provided as a reference for counselors working with young people who receive medication from a qualified medical professional as a component of their substance use disorder treatment.

Acamprosate (Campral) is a medication that may be used to promote a safe withdrawal from depressants, such as alcohol and benzodiazepines (NIDA, 2014b). In addition, the cross-tolerance that develops between alcohol and other depressants warrants the use of benzodiazepine medications, tapered over a brief period of time, to promote safe withdrawal from alcohol (Hart & Ksir, 2015).

Several medications exist to ease the symptoms of withdrawal from opioids. Buprenorphine (Subutex) and methadone are two medications that act on the brain's opiate receptors to reduce cravings and the physiological symptoms of withdrawal. These medications, when used as directed, do not produce the high associated with opioid use; they do, however, possess the potential for misuse. As a result, physicians who prescribe these medications hold special certifications and adhere to strict prescribing practices for these medications (NIDA, 2014b).

Although not formally approved by the U.S. Food and Drug Administration (FDA) for older adolescents and not recommended at all for use in pediatric clients, both buprenorphine and methadone may be used in special circumstances as ongoing medication-assisted treatment with older adolescents who have failed to maintain abstinence from opioid use after multiple treatment attempts (NIDA, 2014b). In addition, naltrexone, a medication that blocks the action of opioids, reduces cravings, and triggers acute withdrawal if opioids are used concurrently, may be used as a medication-assisted treatment to support young people who have completed the withdrawal process. Naltrexone is available as an oral medication and as a once-monthly injection (NIDA, 2014b), which may make treatment adherence more likely for some individuals. A combination medication that pairs naltrexone and buprenorphine, called Suboxone, may also be used as a medication-assisted treatment for older adolescents under special circumstances, although, again, this treatment is not approved by the FDA (NIDA, 2014b).

Clinical Toolbox 16.6

In the Pearson etext, click here to read about a creative activity that can be used to help youth to identify and process unresolved issues that may affect their ability to remain abstinent from substances.

I CAN START COUNSELING PLAN FOR TYLER

This chapter began with a direct quote from Tyler, a 16-year-old boy who described experiencing cravings and difficulty stopping his alcohol and marijuana use. Multiple factors should be considered in developing a treatment plan for a young person with a substance use disorder. The following I CAN START conceptual framework outlines counseling considerations that may be helpful to a school counselor or a clinical counselor who works with Tyler.

C = Contextual Assessment

Tyler is a 16-year old Caucasian boy in the 11th grade. His grades have slipped since he began high school, going from As and Bs to Ds. Tyler lives with his biological mother and father and a younger brother, age 12. Tyler's transition from middle to high school was difficult because he struggled to make friends and adapt to the frequent transitions associated with high school. Tyler has not been diagnosed with any other mental or medical disorder.

A = Assessment and Diagnosis

Assessment = SASSI-A2

Diagnosis = 303.90 Alcohol Use Disorder, Moderate; 304.30 Cannabis Use Disorder, Moderate

N = Necessary Level of Care

Outpatient, group, individual, and family counseling

S = Strengths

Self: Tyler enjoys sports and previously played soccer and basketball in middle school. Although he does not play for the high school, he does participate in an intramural soccer league each year in the fall. Tyler is articulate and emotionally aware; he is able to describe his thoughts and feelings surrounding his substance use congruently and reflectively. Tyler has begun making changes to his substance use by cutting down from daily use to twice-weekly use; this indicates he has a desire and is ready to make changes in this area.

Family: Tyler's parents have made a strong effort to respond consistently and as a unified front to his substance use. Tyler and his younger brother get along well, and Tyler is aware of and sensitive to the fact that his younger brother looks up to him.

School/community: Tyler lives in a safe middle-class neighborhood with his family. He has few close friends, but the friendships he has maintained are with individuals who are accepting of his desire to cut back on his alcohol and marijuana use.

T = Treatment Approach

Psychoeducation (for Tyler and family), CBT (Tyler), BSFT (for entire family)

A = Aim and Objective of Counseling (90-day objectives)

Tyler will abstain from the use of substances. Tyler will self-report abstinence from substances weekly during counseling sessions; monthly urine drug screens will be negative for substances.

Tyler will verbalize risks and consequences associated with his substance use. Tyler will report at least 5 negative consequences he has experienced due to substance use and identify at least 3 future risks he is likely to face if he continues to use.

Tyler will identify triggers for his use of substances. Tyler will identify thoughts, beliefs, and emotions that trigger his substance use by keeping a daily log of triggers and responses and sharing these triggers and his responses to these triggers weekly in individual counseling.

Tyler will learn coping skills he can use to manage cravings for substances. Tyler will identify cognitive, behavioral, and/or emotional cues (e.g., feelings of loneliness or boredom) and implement at least one coping strategy (e.g., urge surfing, distraction, support seeking) 100% of the time at the onset of cravings to use a substance.

Tyler will identify high-risk situations associated with triggering his urge to use substances. Tyler will identify situations in which he is likely to use substances, formulate a plan for avoiding or seeking support in these situations, and successfully negotiate these situations without using a substance 100% of the time.

Tyler and his family (i.e., mother, father and younger brother) will increase their use of effective communication skills. Tyler and his family will learn and practice effective communication strategies (e.g., reflective listening, use of "I" statements, scheduling serious conversations) weekly in family counseling; they will practice these communication techniques daily for a minimum of 15 minutes after dinner.

R = Research-Based Interventions

Counselor will help Tyler to develop and apply the following CBT and BSFT skills:

Learn and use healthy coping skills

Identify and change responses to cognitive, behavioral, and/or affective triggers associated with substance use

Identify and change responses to environmental cues associated with substance use

Develop problem-solving and risk-assessment techniques

Learn and implement effective communication skills

T = Therapeutic Support Services

Academic tutoring through Tyler's high school

Activities (i.e., soccer, basketball) with non-using peers

Twelve-step support group for Tyler and his family

Summary

This chapter provided an in-depth look at substance use disorders in youth. Risk factors in the biological, psychological, and social realms include family history of substance use, the role of coping mechanisms on substance use, and challenges associated with identity development and peer relationships. The chapter examined the etiology of substance use disorders in young people, the impact of mood-altering substances on the brain's pleasure centers and memory salience, and the physiological symptoms of withdrawal. Psychological factors include substance use as a coping mechanism. Social factors, including the strong need for peer affiliation and the use of substances within a social context, are also related to the development of high-risk substance use in young people. In addition, young people have unique developmental needs. Substance use can interact with developmental factors, including physiological and neurological development, reasoning and rational judgment, emotional expression and regulation, and relationship development and peer affiliation.

This chapter provided information on assessment, diagnosis, and treatment of substance use disorders in young people. The *DSM-5* diagnostic criteria were presented and applied to substance use among young people. Information was also provided on the eight classes of mood-altering substances, their effects, and their risks. The chapter also provided an assessment questionnaire that parallels the *DSM-5* criteria for substance use disorders and explained how the ASAM's multidimensional model and treatment placement criteria can be used to contextualize the process of assessment, diagnosis, and treatment. Specific treatment modalities include detoxification, individual and group counseling, family-based treatment, community-based interventions, psychopharmacology, and 12-step groups.

Counselors need to consider the ethical and legal guidelines for working with youth with a substance use disorder, particularly the federal regulations governing substance use treatment records (42 CFR). This chapter described recommendations for treatment planning and integrating multiple treatment modalities and provided a case study to explore the multidimensional contexts of substance use disorders in young people and to demonstrate the treatment planning process for young people with a substance use disorder.

MyLab Counseling: Counseling Children and Adolescents

In the Topic 13 Assignments: *Strategies for Addressing Physical Health Concerns in Youth*, try Licensure Quiz 13.1: *Substance Use and Abuse* and Application Exercise 13.3: *Understanding and Addressing Substance Use in Youth.*

CHAPTER 17

Anxiety, Obsessive-Compulsive, and Related Disorders

THE CASE OF CASSANDRA

When I was 10 years old, I started to notice that for no reason my heart would beat so fast. My chest would feel tight, and I'd have trouble breathing. I felt like I might even throw up. I was so embarrassed that I never talked about it with anyone. I felt like everyone would laugh at me, make fun of me.... I felt like I was crazy. I stopped going places, and I remember yelling, screaming, and throwing fits when my parents wanted me to go to school or leave our house. I felt really alone, like no one understood what I was going through. I was lonely and scared.

—**Cassandra, age 12**

nxiety is one of the most frequently diagnosed psychiatric disorders in youth (Beesdo, Knapp, & Pine, 2009; Waite & Creswell, 2014), with lifetime prevalence rates for anxiety in youth ranging from 15% to 20% (Beesdo et al., 2009). The most common anxiety disorders include separation anxiety disorder, generalized anxiety disorder, phobias, and panic disorders (Wilson, Smith, Monnin, & Wildman, 2016). Girls are more frequently diagnosed with an anxiety disorder than boys—a 2:1 to 3:1 ratio—with female anxiety rates increasing in adolescence (Beesdo et al., 2009).

Lifetime prevalence rates of obsessive-compulsive disorder in children and adolescents range from 1% to 3% (Franklin, Freeman, & March, 2010; Kendall & Comer, 2010). Boys are more frequently diagnosed with obsessive-compulsive disorder, with 25% experiencing an onset before 10 years old (American Psychiatric Association [APA], 2013). The most common obsessive-compulsive and related disorders diagnosed in youth are obsessive-compulsive disorder, body dysmorphic disorder, trichotillomania, and excoriation disorder. In this chapter, *obsessive-compulsive disorders* is used to describe all obsessive-compulsive and related disorders.

The *Diagnostic and Statistical Manual of Mental Disorders, Fifth Edition DSM-5* categorizes anxiety disorders and obsessive-compulsive disorders into two separate diagnostic categories, but in this chapter we present obsessive-compulsive disorders with anxiety disorders because of their historically close relationship and because of the overlap of these disorders and their treatment (APA, 2013).

THE NATURE OF ANXIETY AND OBSESSIVE-COMPULSIVE DISORDERS IN YOUTH

Anxiety is a normal, functional response to concerning events or unknown outcomes; it is a feeling that all people experience, often at multiple points in any given day. Most of the time, anxiety is adaptive in nature; it helps people to connect with the added oomph they need to adequately prepare for upcoming activities and accomplish tasks. For example, the anxiety adolescents feel as they prepare for examinations can drive them to read the textbook and study the course material to adequately meet the expectations of the exam.

Fear is commonly discussed in the context of anxiety. Fear and anxiety are similar, yet different. Quite simply, fear is an emotional reaction to a real perceived threat, whereas anxiety is the emotional reaction to an anticipated threat (APA, 2013).

Very young children begin their lives with fears and worries that are universal (e.g., fear of the dark) and/or imaginary in nature (e.g., monsters living under their bed). Over the course of time, as children move through childhood, they formulate more specific fears that are often grounded in events that could actually happen (e.g., a tornado could hit their home). A young girl, for example, may be afraid of shadows in the dark, fearing these shadows to be the Boogie Man, whereas an adolescent girl may perceive shadows to be an intruder who has broken into her home. Young people's fears have historically been classified into five domains: (a) fear of failure and criticism, (b) fear of the unknown, (c) fear of animals and injury, (d) fear of death and danger, and (e) medical fears (Muris, Ollendick, Roelofs, & Austin, 2014).

A degree of youth fear and anxiety is normal; however, fear and anxiety can become a problem, thus hindering youth's ability to function and perform academically or socially. Some youth become stuck in a perpetual state of excessive and unwarranted apprehension, worry, fear, and anxiety. This emotional state invariably frustrates their attempts to participate in social, family, community, and school/academic endeavors. When anxiety becomes debilitating and problematic, the young person needs additional assistance, and counseling may be helpful (Kendall, 2012).

Symptoms of Anxiety-Related Problems

Counselors should understand how to recognize anxiety-related problems in young clients. Although some presentations of anxiety in youth are obvious, others may be masked by co-occurring problems, behavior problems, environmental or developmental stressors, or dysfunctional family dynamics (Kendall, Crawford, Kagen, Furr, & Podell, 2017).

Anxiety typically presents in youth in three distinct, yet interrelated domains: (a) somatic, (b) cognitive, and (c) behavioral. Youth—especially younger children—almost always report somatic experiences of anxiety, and they often report nausea, stomachaches, tics (i.e., sudden, nonrhythmic movements or vocalizations), perspiration, palpations (i.e., perceived abnormal heart beats), or dizziness. Figure 17.1 presents a list of possible physical symptoms associated with youth anxiety.

Physical symptoms of anxiety affect the cognitive domain; these physical symptoms are either triggered by certain thoughts (e.g., "Everyone is looking at me and judging me") or trigger thoughts (e.g., "I can't breathe, so something is seriously wrong"). Thoughts of losing control, humiliation, and embarrassment are common in anxious youth. As a result of this fear of losing control, these youth often focus on their internal world—thoughts and emotions—and are less focused on things happening in their external world (e.g., social relationships, school, community activities). As a consequence, youth who have anxiety often

- Fast/pounding heartbeats (palpitations)
- Trembling or shaking
- Sweating or perspiration
- Shortness of breath
- Difficulty swallowing
- Stomach/abdominal pains
- Chest discomfort (sharp pains)
- Dizziness (lightheadedness)
- Tics (sudden, repetitive movement or vocalizations)
- Nausea or vomiting
- Frequent urination
- Hot or cold flashes
- Fatigue
- Sleep difficulties/insomnia

FIGURE 17.1 Possible Physical Symptoms of Youth Anxiety

learn to interact with their environments in unproductive, avoidant ways (e.g., withdrawing, a lack of interest in new activities or those that are out of their comfort zone; Kendall et al., 2017). Avoidance behaviors need to be unlearned to eliminate and alleviate physical and cognitive reactions to anxiety.

Anxious youth are not typically aware of the connection between somatic/physical, cognitive/mind, and behavioral/action processes and typically focus on the somatic aspects of their anxiety. For example, youth who have anxiety commonly express complaints of stomachaches, which then transfer into a fear of vomiting and being embarrassed, but they do not express thoughts or feelings associated with anxiety. Teaching youth to understand the connection between what is happening within their body and the accompanying thoughts and behaviors is the foundation for counseling anxious youth. Anxious youth often have high levels of perceived stress and predict negative outcomes, and they will frequently attempt to protect themselves by trying to control situations or outright avoid situations because of their apprehension, fear, and tension (Kress & Paylo, 2015). For example, an adolescent who has a fear of failure may avoid participating in school activities because her fear of rejection outweighs her perceived benefits of participating in the activity. Anxiety symptoms in youth also include a shaky voice, rigid posture, crying, nail-biting, thumb-sucking (in younger children), excessive questioning regarding sources of worry or fear, and physical or verbal outbursts.

The natural tendency for youth who are experiencing intense levels of apprehension, worry, fear, and anxiety is to turn inward and internalize these feelings; they avoid verbalizing or processing their fears and worries with others. Young people's avoidance behaviors are their best attempt to manage the intense, uncomfortable feelings, thoughts, and emotions associated with their fears, worries, and apprehensions (Kendall, 2012). Counselors need to aid clients in connecting their behaviors with their emotions and thoughts so counselors can empower them to make changes.

A counselor's means of intervention will vary depending on the characteristics and nature of the child's anxiety. For example, a young client who has significant difficulty creating connections with peers and making friends may experience intense anxiety in school and attempt to avoid school in general. Another young client may feel overwhelmed and fearful of the demands of school and avoid these expectations for fear of public embarrassment and humiliation. These two scenarios have the same behavioral reaction or end result—avoiding school—yet, one youth may benefit more from social skills training (SST), whereas the other may benefit from cognitive restructuring and controlled exposure. Youth who have anxiety-related struggles may also experience cognitive struggles, including perseveration, excessive fixation and worry, exacerbated fears or concerns in different situations, fear of performance evaluation and humiliation, and an excessive sense of embarrassment; these fears must be addressed in unique ways. Helping youth to understand the relationships between their cognitions and their behavior is an important counseling goal. The specific approaches to addressing anxiety are addressed later in this chapter.

Anxiety symptoms vary in intensity, duration, and frequency, and they are manifested differently in varied situations and settings. Although one young person may experience anxiety in an academic setting, another may be affected more in a family setting. Most youth who have anxiety though, experience a significant impact in their social interactions with others, regardless of the setting (Kendall, 2012). In addition, youth who have anxiety may have distorted thoughts, perceptions, and interpretations of social situations and events that unfold around them. They may selectively pay attention to certain aspects of their environment or interactions and choose to focus on those that reinforce their apprehension, worry, and fears. Early identification of anxiety is helpful in intervening and providing support to youth.

Types of Anxiety Disorders

Youth who have anxiety disorders experience different symptoms, yet in most cases they have an excessive, irrational fear and dread (APA, 2013). Symptoms include anxiety, worry, or fear in response to a specific object (e.g., a dog, blood), situation (e.g., being evaluated on performance, being in an elevator), or perceived threat (e.g., crowded grocery store, contamination) or general free-floating feelings of anxiety. Table 17.1 provides a summary of the *DSM-5* (APA, 2013) anxiety disorders. The anxiety disorders that youth may experience include separation anxiety disorder, selective mutism, specific phobias, social anxiety disorder, panic disorder, agoraphobia, and generalized anxiety disorder.

Table 17.1 Summary of the Common *DSM-5* Anxiety Disorders

DSM-5 Anxiety Disorder	Overview	Brief Example
Separation Anxiety Disorder	Excessive anxiety regarding separation from home and/or attachment figures (e.g., parents)	A 5-year-old boy refuses to leave his mother's side because he fears if he does something negative will happen to his mother (i.e., she will get in a car accident, be taken by a criminal, or will die).
Selective Mutism Disorder	Inability to speak and communicate effectively in certain settings (yet able to communicate sufficiently in other settings)	A 9-year-old girl does not speak at school (even when spoken to directly by her teacher) yet converses adequately at her home with parents and siblings.
Specific Phobia	Anxiety symptoms that are brought on by an identified object or situation (present or imagined)	A 6-year-old boy has tantrums and cries excessively every time he sees a bird. He avoids going outside to play with friends in the neighborhood for fear of having an encounter with a bird or group of birds.
Social Anxiety Disorder	Excessive fears of—and self-consciousness in—social situations, and a fear of being judged, evaluated, and embarrassed in such social situations	A 15-year-old girl fears eating around others at lunch and will frequently ask the lunch aides if she can sit in the hall and eat her lunch. She also has a severe fear of being called on in class and having to talk in front of the class (e.g., presentations, assignments).
Panic Disorder	Recurrent, intense episodes of excessive anxiety/panic that involves acute, intense, time-limited physical and psychological symptoms	A 13-year-old boy experiences unexpected panic attacks (i.e., abrupt, intense fear and discomfort that peak within 10 minutes) and often excessively worries about "losing control" in those moments and during future panic episodes.
Agoraphobia	Excessive anxiety and fear of being in open, crowed places where an escape or exit may be difficult	A 17-year-old girl experiences intense fears when in public spaces (i.e., parking lots, mall, grocery stores) and avoids going to these places, often refusing to leave her home because of the fear she will not be able to escape a crowd or potentially dangerous situation.
Generalized Anxiety Disorder	Excessive, uncontrollable, and often irrational worry and apprehension about numerous events or activities and accompanying physical symptoms of anxiety	An 11-year-old boy worries consistently and excessively about his grades, making friends, getting sick, and losing things. He is often irritable and has difficulty concentrating because he is constantly distracted by his worry.

Note: Adapted from *Diagnostic and Statistical Manual of Mental Disorders* (5th ed.), by American Psychiatric Association (APA), 2013, Washington, DC: Author.

Exaggeration and distortion of anxiety symptoms are common and can be evidenced by clients' reactions to their physical symptoms (e.g., "I can't breathe; I'm going to die"), cognitions (e.g., "Everyone will notice that I'm different, and they'll all make fun of me"), and coping strategies used to deal with their anxiety (e.g., "If I avoid all anxiety-producing situations, then I'll never have anxiety again"). Table 17.2 presents a summary of cognitions often associated with each of the anxiety disorders.

Table 17.2	Anxiety Disorders: Potential Associated Cognitions
DSM-5 Disorder	**Potential Associated Cognitions**
Separation Anxiety Disorder	Youth believe that if they are not always present with a major attachment figure something bad will happen (e.g., the caregiver will get hurt, sick, or separated). They often think the outside world is a dangerous place.
Selective Mutism Disorder	Youth believe others will think they are stupid, will not like what they say, or will laugh at them because of the way they talk. They often feel they will embarrass themselves if they speak.
Specific Phobia	Youth believe that phobic objects are dangerous and need to be avoided. They often believe they will get seriously injured/hurt or experience a bad outcome if they are exposed to the feared object/situation.
Social Anxiety Disorder	Youth believe others are judging and evaluating the way they act, dress, look, and interact with others. They often believe they will embarrass themselves.
Panic Disorder	Youth believe they are having a heart attack (or even dying) and something serious must be wrong. They often think they are losing control.
Agoraphobia	Youth believe that many public situations will end in embarrassment, humiliation, or pain. They often think the outside world is a dangerous place.
Generalized Anxiety Disorder	Youth believe they have done something wrong and will have a negative consequence (e.g., punishment, negative interaction). They may have concerns about their own safety and future. They often fear they are losing control over important aspects of their lives.

Note: Adapted from "Cognitive-behavioral treatments for anxiety disorders in children and adolescents," by R. R. Silva, R. Gallagher, & H. Minami, 2006, *Primary Psychiatry, 13*(5), pp. 68–76.

Assessment of Anxiety Disorders

A thorough anxiety assessment might include a compilation of clinical interviews, self-reports, behavioral observations, parent–teacher rating scales, and family assessments (Kendall, 2012). The assessments should include various methods, such as self-report, observation, anxiety scales, clinical interviews, and review of the youth's functioning in multiple settings (e.g., home, school, community) and from multiple perspectives (e.g., child/adolescent, parent, family members, teacher) including the youth's cognitive, behavioral, and psychological domains (Kendall et al., 2017).

A thorough assessment allows the counselor to garner a complete picture of the client's anxiety experiences and plan for appropriate counseling options and approaches. Although a diagnostic interview is the most effective means to assess anxiety disorders in youth, inventories such as the Beck Youth Inventories–Second Edition (BYI-II Anxiety Inventory; Beck, Beck, Jolly, & Steer, 2005), State-Trait Anxiety Inventory for Children (STAIC; Spielberger, 1983), Spence Children's Anxiety Scale (Spence, 1998), and the Revised Children's Manifest Anxiety Scales–Second Edition (RCMAS-2: Reynolds & Richmond, 2008) can provide more clinical clarity of anxiety symptomology (Wilson et al., 2016). Table 17.3 presents a summary of several anxiety assessment measures.

During the clinical interview and assessment process, counselors need to be mindful of the age of onset of anxiety symptoms, development (e.g., cognitive, emotional, social), and co-occurring disorders. Those who have anxiety-related problems typically begin to experience them, on some level, before the age of 12 (Beesdo et al., 2009). In terms of the frequency of specific anxiety disorders across developmental levels, younger children are more likely to be diagnosed with separation anxiety disorder than adolescents. Adolescents are more frequently diagnosed with social anxiety disorders and co-occurring depressive disorders, substance-use disorders, and irregular school attendance than are younger children (Beesdo et al., 2009; Waite & Creswell, 2014).

Table 17.3	Summary of Anxiety Assessment Measures for Youth	
Assessment Measure	Age Range	Overview of Assessment Measure
Beck Youth Inventory–Second Edition (BYI-II) Anxiety Inventory	7–18 years	The BAI is a 20-item self-report measure that assesses levels of anxiety in young people. The measure reflects a young person's specific worries about the future, school, performance, fears, and loss of control, as well as physiological symptoms associated with anxiety. This measure can be used for the assessment and evaluation of counseling progress and can be used in conjunction with the other four Beck Youth Inventories: depression, anger, disruptive behaviors, and self-concept.
State-Trait Anxiety Inventory for Children (STAIC)	9–12 years	The STAIC is a 40-item counselor-rated measure that assesses how a youth feels in a particular moment (i.e., state anxiety) and how he or she feels more generally (i.e., trait anxiety). The measure requires a seventh-grade reading level; therefore, it needs to be administered orally with children in elementary school. This measure can be used for assessment and evaluation of counseling progress.
Spence Children's Anxiety Scale	8–12 years	The Spence Children's Anxiety Scale is a 44-item measure that assesses six domains (i.e., generalized anxiety, panic/agoraphobia, separation anxiety, obsessive-compulsive disorder, and physical injury fears). This measure can be used for assessment and evaluation of counseling progress.
Revised Children's Manifest Anxiety Scales–Second Edition (RCMAS-2)	6–19 years	The RCMAS is a 49-item (i.e., yes or no) youth-rated measure that assesses youth global anxiety, worry, social anxiety, and defensiveness. The measure has a third-grade reading level and will require oral administration for younger children. This measure can be used for assessment and evaluation of counseling progress.

Clinical Toolbox 17.1

In the Pearson etext, click here for a list of questions counselors can ask parents to facilitate the assessment of anxiety in youth.

In children, anxiety often co-occurs with other anxiety disorders, oppositional defiant disorder, attention-deficit/hyperactivity disorder (ADHD), and depressive disorders (Liber et al., 2010). In adolescents, anxiety-related symptoms can also contribute to the development or maintenance of depressive disorders, suicidal ideation, substance use and abuse (due to the desire to self-medicate), and academic difficulties (Woo & Keatinge, 2016). Counselors should assess for possible co-occurring disorders or maladaptive coping skills. The sections that follow describe the symptoms, types, and diagnostic and assessment considerations associated with obsessive-compulsive and related disorders in youth.

Symptoms of Obsessive-Compulsive and Related Disorders

Obsessive-compulsive disorders are characterized by **obsessions** (i.e., recurrent and intrusive urges, thoughts, or images that are unwanted), **compulsions** (i.e., physical or mental acts that are repetitive), and/or persistent **body-focused repetitive behaviors** (e.g., hair pulling, skin picking). For example, a child may report that he or she feels "stuck" with a thought (e.g., "I'm worried about catching germs and getting sick") or a behavior (e.g., "I need to turn the lights on and off six times or something bad will happen"). Youth have usually tried—but have been unsuccessful—at stopping these urges, thoughts, and/or behaviors. These symptoms may be poorly articulated, and compulsions may exist without clearly defined obsessions (American Academy of

Child and Adolescent Psychiatry [AACAP], 2010). For example, a child may engage in repetitive blinking and breathing rituals (e.g., every time he enters a room he needs to blink five times and breathe deeply twice), yet he may be unable to articulate why he is engaging in these behaviors, only that he feels better after doing so. These recurrent obsessions, compulsions, and body-focused repetitive behaviors are time consuming, impair the child's level of functioning, and cause significant distress in all areas of the child's life (Kendall & Comer, 2010). Table 17.4 presents a list of types and examples of obsessive-compulsive symptoms.

Table 17.4 Summary of Obsessive-Compulsive Symptoms, Types, and Examples

Symptom	Types	Examples
Obsessions	Contamination	• Fear of touching door handles • Fear of germs and dirt • Fear of handling money
	Self-doubt	• Fear of misplacing possessions • Fear of forgetting assignments or homework
	Harm to self or others	• Fear of causing an accident • Fear of pushing someone down the stairs
	Religious	• Fear of being cursed
	Sexual themes	• Repeated pornographic images of a teacher • Intrusive sexual thoughts or images
Compulsions	Cleaning	• Handwashing • Brushing teeth until gums bleed
	Counting	• Performing a task in a certain number of steps (e.g., six) • Counting steps or cars that pass
	Checking	• Returning to check if the door is locked or the faucet is off • Repeatedly checking to see if a bike is put away
	Balancing	• Need for evenness (e.g., items on a desk are even in number, order, and symmetry)
	Demanding reassurance	• Excessively asking about the possibility of a tornado • Asking others excessively for feedback
	Repeating or redoing behaviors	• Tapping an object • Repeating holy verses or prayers • Repeating a word(s) over and over (e.g., "It's ok, it's ok, it's ok")
	Hoarding	• Hiding food under the bed • Refusing to throw away trash
Body-focused repetitive behaviors	Self-grooming	• Nail-biting • Picking cuticles • Nose picking • Hair pulling • Skin picking
	Other	• Biting the inside of cheeks • Biting skin (e.g., knuckles) • Thumb- or finger-sucking • Lip pinching

Obsessive-compulsive symptomology is similar in youth and adults (Hinkle, 2008). As is true with adults, youth commonly have obsessions related to dirt and germs and engage in repetitive washing, grooming, and checking behaviors. It is rare for a youth to experience only obsessions and not compulsions (Kendall & Comer, 2010). Some youth experience recurrent, persistent, body-focused repetitive behaviors (e.g., hair pulling, skin picking) as a result of anxiety, fear, excitement, or even boredom, and these behaviors frequently co-occur with ADHD (Panza, Pittenger, & Bloch, 2013). Adolescents are typically aware of these repetitive behaviors, and they may have insight into their occurrence and dynamics, whereas younger children often engage in these behaviors automatically (i.e., without their full awareness; Tompkins, 2014). Therefore, younger children will often need more assistance than adolescents to develop awareness of their obsessions, compulsions, and body-focused repetitive behaviors.

Types of Obsessive-Compulsive Disorders

This section discusses the types of obsessive-compulsive disorders common in young people. Table 17.5 presents a summary of the *DSM-5* obsessive-compulsive disorders (APA, 2013). The obsessive-compulsive and related disorders that most commonly affect youth are obsessive-compulsive disorder, body dysmorphic disorder, trichotillomania, and excoriation disorder. Although these disorders tend to overlap and are

Table 17.5 Summary of the Common *DSM-5* Obsessive-Compulsive and Related Disorders

DSM-5 Disorder	Overview	Brief Example
Obsessive-Compulsive Disorder	Intrusive thoughts that produce worry (i.e., obsessions), often accompanied by repetitive behaviors aimed at reducing this anxiety (i.e., compulsions)	An 8-year-old boy is fixated on germs and becoming sick. He performs excessive handwashing, checking, and ordering activities in an attempt to combat his intense, intrusive thoughts.
Body Dysmorphic Disorder	Preoccupation with a perceived flaw in physical appearance, often accompanied by repetitive behaviors (e.g., grooming, mirror checking) or mental acts (e.g., comparing appearance with others)	A 15-year-old girl is preoccupied with her nose. She obsesses about how her nose is "not right for her face." She believes her nose is too big and that she is ugly and disfigured. She spends considerable time examining and checking her nose in the mirror, often applying makeup and asking others if they think her nose is ugly.
Trichotillomania	Preoccupation with hair picking, resulting in hair loss; hair-pulling behaviors intensify in response to strong emotions; unsuccessful attempts have been made to decrease or stop the pulling behaviors	A 12-year old girl recurrently pulls her hair, and bald patches appear on her scalp. On some occasions, she pulls her eyebrows out with tweezers. She feels shame and embarrassment, often pulling her hair in isolation and hiding her behaviors from others. Stress and anxiety exacerbate her hair-pulling behaviors.
Excoriation Disorder	Preoccupation with skin picking, resulting in skin tissue damage and skin lesions; picking behaviors intensify in response to strong emotions; unsuccessful attempts have been made to decrease or stop picking behaviors	A 14-year old girl persistently picks the acne on her face (i.e., acne excoriée), her shoulder blades, and the back of her arms. She spends considerable time touching, scratching, and digging, and this results in skin lesions. She feels ashamed and embarrassed by her behaviors and engages in picking behaviors in secret.

Note: Adapted from *Diagnostic and Statistical Manual of Mental Disorders* (5th ed.), by American Psychiatric Association (APA), 2013, Washington, DC: Author.

Table 17.6	Obsessive-Compulsive and Related Disorders: Potential Associated Cognitions
DSM-5 Disorder	Potential Associated Cognitions
Obsessive-Compulsive Disorder	Youth believe that if they touch germs something bad will happen. They often think that if they do not count, check, or do something in the ritualistic pattern, a negative event will occur to them or to someone they love. The obsessive thoughts often revolve around a catastrophic family event (e.g., death of parent or guardian).
Body Dysmorphic Disorder	Youth experience intrusive, distressing thoughts about a perceived flaw in their physical appearance. This flaw or imperfection often is unnoticeable to others; it is small at most, yet they think their flaw (e.g., nose too big, legs too short, lips too thin, hips too big) is seen and experienced by others with the same intensity. They believe others will not like, love, or accept them because of their flaw.
Trichotillomania	Youth often think excessively about pulling their hair and worry about what others would think or say. They are often self-conscious about how their pulling behaviors affect their appearance and become frustrated and embarrassed. They often blame themselves for being unable to stop.
Excoriation Disorder	Youth often think excessively about picking their skin and worry about what others will think or say. They are often self-conscious about how their picking behaviors affect their appearance. They become frustrated and embarrassed, often feeling less confident socially and blaming themselves for being unable to stop.

Note: Adapted from "Cognitive-behavioral treatments for anxiety disorders in children and adolescents," by R. R. Silva, R. Gallagher, & H. Minami, 2006, *Primary Psychiatry, 13*(5), pp. 68–76.

frequently comorbid with anxiety disorders (APA, 2013), counselors should be cautious when differentiating the nuances of the associated behaviors and cognitions associated with each of the obsessive-compulsive and related disorders. Table 17.6 presents the cognitions associated with each of the obsessive-compulsive and related disorders.

Assessment of Obsessive-Compulsive and Related Disorders

A thorough assessment allows the counselor to acquire a complete picture of the youth's experience with obsessive-compulsive disorder and plan for appropriate counseling options and approaches. When assessing for these disorders, counselors need to evaluate the youth's (a) current and past obsessive-compulsive symptoms, (b) current level of severity and impairment of functioning, and (c) comorbid psychopathology (Franklin et al., 2010).

Although the diagnostic interview is the most effective means to assess obsessive-compulsive disorders in youth, the Children's Yale-Brown Obsessive Scale (CY-BOCS; Scahill et al., 1997) and/or the Child Obsessive-Compulsive Impact Scales–Revised (COIS-R; Piacentini, Peris, Bergman, Chang, & Jaffer, 2007) can provide more clinical clarity of obsessive-compulsive related symptomology (AACAP, 2010; Wilson et al., 2016). Table 17.7 provides a summary of two assessment measures that may be helpful in assessing obsessive-compulsive disorder in youth. There are no well-established assessment measures for assessing body-focused repetitive behaviors in youth; therefore, the diagnostic interview is the most effective means for assessing these disorders (McGuire et al., 2012).

A thorough youth assessment takes into account **differential diagnoses** (i.e., distinguishing one disorder from another) and comorbid disorders (i.e., co-occurring disorders). In assessing youth for obsessive-compulsive and related disorders, counselors will need to differentiate these disorders from other mental health disorders that can have a similar presentation of symptoms, including generalized anxiety disorder, autistic spectrum disorder, anorexia nervosa, and schizophrenia spectrum disorder

Table 17.7	Summary of Obsessive-Compulsive Assessment Measures	
Assessment Measure	**Age Range**	**Overview of Assessment Measure**
Children's Yale-Brown Obsessive Scales (CY-BOCS)	8–18 years	The CY-BOCS is a 10-item counselor-rated interview that assesses the severity of obsessive-compulsive disorder. The measure can provide a severity score for obsessions or compulsions and a total score. The measure involves two informants (i.e., the youth and at least one parent or guardian) and can be completed separately or in a conjoined session. The CY-BOCS can also be used for the assessment and evaluation of counseling progress.
Child Obsessive-Compulsive Impact Scales–Revised (COIS-R)	7–18 years	The COIS-RC is a 33-item youth-rated measure that assesses the impact of obsessive-compulsive symptoms on functioning (e.g., academic, social) over the past month. Guardians also complete a 58-item parent-rated form as part of the assessment process. The COIS-R can also be used for the assessment and evaluation of counseling progress.

(Lewin & Piacentini, 2010). Counselors also need to consider that obsessive-compulsive disorders are often comorbid or co-occurring with another mental health diagnosis. In children, obsessive-compulsive disorders often co-occur with anxiety disorders (e.g., generalized anxiety disorder, separation anxiety, phobias), ADHD, and tics disorder (Wilson et al., 2016). In adolescents, depressive and psychotic symptomology have been linked with more severe and treatment-resistant forms of obsessive-compulsive disorder (AACAP, 2010; Peris et al., 2010). Discussion of the specific approaches for addressing these obsessions, compulsions, and body-focused repetitive behaviors and the implementation of these approaches is provided in the following section.

COUNSELING INTERVENTIONS

Considerable research exists on the efficacy of counseling with anxious youth, but less research exists on effective counseling with youth who have obsessive-compulsive and related disorders (Wilson et al., 2016). The available research suggests that cognitive behavioral therapy (CBT) is the most evidence-based approach for use with children and adolescents who have anxiety and/or obsessive-compulsive disorders (Freeman et al., 2014; Hofmann, Asnaani, Vonk, Sawyer, & Fang, 2012), with many young clients even experiencing a complete cessation of anxiety symptoms (Seligman & Ollendick, 2011). In addition, there have been encouraging advances in the use of CBT in treating youth who have body-focused repetitive behaviors, with research suggesting that flexible application of multiple treatment strategies is most useful (e.g., CBT, exposure-based approaches, habit reversal training [HRT]; Flessner, 2011; Tompkins, 2014).

CBT approaches involve a mixture of cognitive restructuring, repeated exposure with reduction of avoidance behaviors (i.e., the distance youth will put between themselves and a feared object or situation), and skills training (Seligman & Ollendick, 2011). One issue with this line of research is that little theory or practical research has focused on treating adolescents (12–18 years old) who have anxiety disorders (Waite & Creswell, 2014). The adaption of treatments aimed at treating youth in middle childhood may or may not be sufficient to meet the needs of adolescents (Waite & Creswell, 2014). Therefore, counselors must tailor the recommended treatments to adolescents as needed.

Combined treatments that involve medication (i.e., selective serotonin reuptake inhibitor [SSRIs]) and CBT have the highest remission of anxiety symptoms with this population (Ginsburg et al., 2011). Factors that appear to influence the effectiveness of counseling include age (i.e., youth who are younger may have a better prognosis), lower baseline severity of anxiety symptoms, absence of multiple internalizing disorders (i.e., additional anxiety disorders, depression), and absence of social anxiety disorder

(Ginsburg et al., 2011). Because anxiety and obsessive-compulsive disorders involve physiological, cognitive, and behavioral components, counselors should consider a multifaceted approach (Freeman et al., 2014; Kendall et al., 2017).

Additional treatment approaches that have promising results when counseling youth with anxiety include acceptance and commitment therapy (ACT; Greco & Hayes, 2008) and dialectical behavioral therapy (DBT; Harvey & Rathbone, 2013). ACT is a type of CBT that integrates acceptance, mindfulness, and behavior-change principles. ACT involves clients intentionally living more in the moment (e.g., "here and now") and experiencing themselves without judgment, thus enhancing their cognitive flexibility and behavioral change process. DBT is another CBT approach that holds promise in counseling this population. It is often associated with treating individuals who have personality disorders (e.g., borderline personality disorder), yet more recently this approach has been used with numerous populations, including youth (Kress & Paylo, 2015). DBT stresses the importance of youth tolerating and coping with their strong negative emotions in intentional and prosocial ways.

INTEGRATED TREATMENT COMPONENTS: ANXIETY AND OBSESSIVE-COMPULSIVE DISORDERS

Counseling for youth who have anxiety generally focuses on (a) skills training and development and (b) skills practice (Kendall, 2012). A gradual progression equips children with skills, followed by real-world practice and application of these skills in either gradual or progressive exposure to anxiety-provoking activities. Most counseling approaches with youth who have anxiety involve (a) education, (b) learning cognitive coping skills, (c) learning somatic coping skills, and (d) behavioral exposure. Treatment protocols for obsessive-compulsive and related disorders often involve (a) education, (b) learning cognitive coping skills, (c) exposure and ritual prevention, and (d) relapse prevention (Franklin et al., 2010). These comprehensive components can be implemented in individual, family, or group counseling formats (Pahl & Barrett, 2010).

The following sections outline the essential counseling components for working with anxious youth. These components may be cobbled together or completely integrated, depending on the specific nature of the youth's presenting issue and his or her related symptomology (e.g., somatic, cognitive, and behavioral symptoms). The components of an integrated, comprehensive approach in counseling youth with anxiety include relaxation training, affective education, SST, cognitive skills training, problem solving, establishing a contingent reinforcement plan, HRT, exposure-based activities, integrating the family into the counseling process, and the use of medications. A brief explanation of each of these components follows.

Relaxation Training

Helping youth to tolerate anxiety-related situations is an important initial task in counseling. Teaching, practicing, and implementing relaxation training can help young clients to learn how to manage anxiety (Kendall, 2012). Relaxation training involves breathing, visualization, and in some cases muscle relaxation. The central task of relaxation training is to increase clients' awareness of apprehension, worry, and anxiety, thereby increasing their ability to counteract these feelings with their own physiological and muscular reactions to anxiety (Kendall, 2012; Kendall et al., 2017). These relaxation and imagery activities should be done in a quiet environment, free from the distractions of electronic and handheld devices. In addition, playing soft, relaxing music can assist young people in shutting out outside noises, thus increasing their engagement and compliance with this type of intervention. As clients practice these activities and skills in sessions, they will ideally begin to apply them in real-world settings. Table 17.8 provides examples of relaxation training and imagery activities.

Clinical Toolbox 17.2

In the Pearson etext, click here to read about an experiential deep breathing activity that can be used with youth to facilitate relaxation.

Table 17.8   Examples of Relaxation Training and Imagery Activities

Type	Title	Description
Deep breathing	Three-Counts-In and Three-Counts-Out	Have the client breathe in for "three-counts-in" and then breathe out for "three-counts-out." Invite the client to pay attention to the air as it travels through the nose to the stomach, and then back out of the nose. Have the client continue breathing in for three-counts-in and then out for three-counts-out for at least 10 full cycles.
Deep breathing with imagery	Just a Day at the Beach	Continue with the three-counts-in and three-counts-out breathing, but ask the client to close his or her eyes. Next, ask the client to envision standing on the edge of a beach. Walk the client through a visualization, such as the following: Envision the tide rolling in and out. The water covers your feet, and the sun begins to shine on your face. As your body becomes warmer, a soft breeze comes in, brushes your body, and envelops you. Finally, you begin to smell the sweet and salty sea air so vividly you begin to taste the salt on the tip of your tongue.
Progressive relaxation	Progressing to a State of Relaxation	Continue with the three-counts-in and three-counts-out breathing, and have the client continue to do deep breathing throughout this progressive relaxation activity. The client can place one hand on his or her stomach and allow it to move up and down with each cycle of breathing. Next, walk the client through a progressive muscle relaxation sequence, such as the following: "Pay attention to your feet. Allow them to sink deep into the ground as if you were standing at the edge of the ocean. Allow the sand to slowly sink beneath your feet. As your feet grab hold of the ground with each toe, allow your legs to straighten as stiff as possible and hold that . . . and then relax. Now, pretend you are flying out of the sand and into the sky. Stretch your leg muscles and stomach out so you are as tall as you can be, and hold that . . . and now relax." Continue this process, moving to the client's arms, hands, neck, and face.

Counselors can also integrate meditation, exercise, stretching, painting, reading, listening to music, dancing, or any other expressive activities to assist youth in their relaxation training. For example, clients can paint or draw a picture of a relaxing scene, and the counselor can use that scene as the foundation for the relaxing imagery activity. Figure 17.2 provides a relaxation script that can be used to help younger children to engage in muscle relaxation.

Affective Education

Affective education is an intervention aimed at increasing young clients' awareness of their feelings, beliefs, and attitudes and how these components affect their behaviors. Affective education is a foundational component to working with youth who have anxiety and obsessive-compulsive and related disorders (Franklin et al., 2010; Kendall, 2012; Tompkins, 2014). The aim of **affective education** is to make youth aware of what is happening within them (e.g., emotions, thoughts) and how they can learn to affect and influence what is

---

The following is a relaxation script that can be used to teach younger children (e.g., 5–8 years old) how to engage in progressive muscle relaxation.

"Today we are going to do an exercise to help you see how good it feels to be relaxed and to teach you how you can help your body become more relaxed. We are going to focus on different parts of the body, and when I tell you, you are going to tense that body part as much as you can. If you feel like you're ready and comfortable, please close your eyes and listen to the sound of my voice. We will start at the top, so let's start with your face. Pretend you just ate something really sour, like a piece of lemon. Scrunch your eyes and lips as much as you can because that lemon was SOUR! Now, relax your lips and eyes. Relax your lips so much that your mouth may even open a bit.

"Now, scrunch your nose and your forehead. See how tense you can make them. Picture your eyebrows getting so high that they almost touch your hair. Now, relax the muscles in your forehead, letting your muscles slide back into place. Doesn't it feel good to relax your face?

"Next, we will move to relaxing the lower part of your face. Pretend you have a big jawbreaker candy in your mouth and the jawbreaker has a piece of bubble gum in its center. You really want to get to that bubble gum, but you are going to have to bite down hard to break it open. Now, gently bite down and try to crack open the jawbreaker. It is really tough! Take a break and let your muscles relax. Give me one more good bite and the jawbreaker will break. Ready? Go! Fantastic! You did it! Now, relax your neck and jaw muscles—letting your chin roll down to your chest. Maybe even let your mouth hang open a little bit. It sure feels good to relax after biting down so hard, doesn't it?

"Next, bring your attention to your neck and shoulders. You already used your neck muscles a little bit to break the jaw-breaker, and we are going to use them again. Tense your back and shoulders up so much that your shoulders are close to your ears. Maybe try to make your shoulders like earrings. Squeeze your muscles and make them as tight as you can. See if you can get your shoulders just a little bit higher. Tuck your chin to your chest, and keep pushing your shoulders higher. Now, let go. Pay attention to how good it feels to let your muscles relax and go back to their natural places. Doesn't it feel much better to relax?

"Let's move to your belly. Pretend you are trying to suck your bellybutton in so hard that it is going to touch your back. Good. Now hold it in even tighter, like you are going to squeeze sideways through a tiny door. Make yourself as tiny as you can be. Now, let your muscles relax, and take a deep breath to fill up your tummy. That feels good, doesn't it?

"Bring your attention to your legs and feet. Stand up, and pretend you are on a sandy beach and you are pushing your feet into wet sand. Spread your toes down into the sand as the waves from the ocean are rolling by up to your waist. The waves are big, and you need to really make your legs strong and spread your toes into the sand so you don't get swept onto shore. You have to stand really strong. Flex your leg muscles as strong as you can; a really big wave is coming! You don't want to get washed onshore! Good job. Now, relax your muscles again.

"Think of how good it feels to relax your muscles after they have been tightened up. It feels much better to relax than to be tense, doesn't it? You can practice this exercise anytime to help you relax. Maybe you would like to practice this at bedtime to help you to relax before sleep. You can do these exercises anywhere, anytime you feel stressed or your muscles feel tense. You did a great job today! Keep practicing, and you will be an expert relaxer!"

FIGURE 17.2 Relaxation Script for Younger Children

happening to them (e.g., behaviors). Affective education explores the interrelated nature of the somatic, cognitive, and behavioral components of anxiety (Kendall, 2012). Young clients ultimately need to understand the dynamics of their anxiety and learn self-awareness and self-regulation skills if they are to make enduring changes (Kendall, 2012).

AWARENESS OF PHYSICAL SYMPTOMS

Affective education begins with counselors helping youth to recognize and identify emotions through others' words, facial expressions, and overall demeanor (Kingery et al., 2006). After clients are able to demonstrate some mastery of emotion identification, counselors can begin to facilitate their awareness of their physical symptoms of anxiety (e.g., shortness of breath, stomachaches, perspiration). Counselors encourage youth to become better aware of what is happening in their bodies when they feel anxious (i.e., before, during, and after).

Counselors can ask clients to list their anxiety-related physical symptoms. Clients can also think through their life experiences in a "movie" format. For example, the client can slowly walk through each experience or event and consider how he or she physically felt at the beginning, during, and after the anxiety-provoking situation. Counselors' aim in dissecting clients' anxiety experiences is to help clients to better understand their experience of anxiety, with the goal of helping them to identify their anxiety triggers and the early signs that these symptoms are occurring.

The use of a mirror to examine clients' posture and facial expressions is another way counselors can heighten young clients' awareness of the physical components of anxiety. The use of a mirror may allow the client to gain a different perspective—the perspective of others—re-creating how she or he "wears" anxiety. Young clients may lack awareness of how those who are anxious present compared to those who appear relaxed. Therefore, counselors may want to introduce differing postures or facial expressions through the use of visual aids such as magazines, pictures, or videos. After asking young clients to explain what emotion the images represent, they can also ask the youth to discuss a situation in which they had a similar feeling and expression.

AWARENESS OF COGNITIVE SYMPTOMS

Because their cognitive development is still maturing, young people may have a more limited awareness of their cognitive processes than most adults. The process of thinking about one's thoughts requires metacognition and can either exacerbate or mitigate anxiety symptoms, depending on how a youth interprets and relates to these cognitions (Kertz & Woodruff-Borden, 2013). Youth are typically unaware of their thoughts and how their self-talk affects their emotions, behaviors, and self-concept. Generally speaking, self-talk involves statements clients vocalize internally when they are anxious, worried, or apprehensive. These statements involve their expectations, self-evaluation, standards of performance (e.g., perfectionistic thoughts), and concerns for what others might be thinking about them or expecting from them. For example, a youth may think about an upcoming science exam on which he believes he will be unsuccessful. He allows biased, dysfunctional thinking (i.e., catastrophizing) to control his thoughts and thus experiences worry and fear.

> YOUTH: I won't pass this exam. I'll get an *F* in the class and then I'll probably get kicked out of school. My parents will be so angry with me that they'll either ground me forever or throw me out of the house. Everyone at school will laugh at me for being so stupid, and then I'll probably end up homeless.

Underlying these dysfunctional cognitions are the bigger issues and questions about the client's own sense of competence—the consequences of failure and his fear of humiliation, which maintain his low self-concept (i.e., perception of self). Assisting youth in becoming better aware of their tendencies to engage in negative self-talk can lead to identifying and challenging maladaptive cognitions. In addition, helping this population to identify, counter, and ultimately reduce negative thinking is often more powerful than just promoting positive thinking (Kendall, 2012).

AWARENESS OF BEHAVIORAL SYMPTOMS

As young clients begin to understand what is happening in their bodies and in their minds, they connect the ways that their thoughts trigger anxiety and cause cognitive and physical cues that have an impact on their behavior. These behavioral reactions—or responses to their physical experiences and thoughts—can include avoidance of anxiety-provoking stimuli, an excessive need for reassurance, withdrawing from friends or family, nervous tics, outbursts or tantrums, irritability, fatigue or difficulties with sleep, restlessness, difficulty concentrating, and compulsions (i.e., compensating behaviors in an attempt to rid oneself of anxiety-provoking, intrusive thoughts).

Youth are typically unaware of the ways that physical and cognitive symptoms affect their behavior. They typically require assistance in understanding the interrelatedness of these experiences. For example, consider a 12-year-old girl who is fearful of having panic attacks. When she is in crowded stores, she feels as if she is unable to escape. She subsequently selects avoidance as her means of coping, and she avoids any potentially crowded areas. Her parents find it is easier on the family to allow the girl to stay at home; thus, they inadvertently reinforce her avoidance dynamic. The girl notices that she has less anxiety and panic

| Table 17.9 | Affective Education Application: Feelings, Thoughts, and Behaviors |

Anxiety-related situation	What did you feel in your skin/body?	What thoughts did you have about the situation? About yourself?	How did you respond?	How did you feel after you responded?	How else could you have responded?
An Example with a 13-Year-Old					
I was told I had to do an impromptu presentation about an unassigned topic in class.	*I started sweating. My heart started to pound. I felt nauseous and hot.*	*I have to get out of here. I am going to make a fool of myself. I don't want anyone to laugh at me. I am going to be humiliated.*	*I told my teacher that my stomach was hurting and that I needed to see the nurse. Then, I left the classroom.*	*I felt relief, but later I felt embarrassed. How could I be such a "baby." I bet everyone knew I was faking it. I bet they even talked about me after I left.*	*I could have waited a little longer to see how others managed the task. I could have also tried to wait it out because there were only 10 minutes left in class. I could have discussed how I felt uncomfortable with the assignment.*

because she avoids crowded places, yet because she avoids most social encounters, she feels lonely and lacks friendships, which creates additional problems.

Because young clients are more cognitively concrete than adults, activities that help them to visually see the connection between their anxiety symptoms, thoughts, and behaviors are helpful. The use of worksheets, picture diagrams, or behavioral sequencing, for example, can facilitate therapeutic discussions and enhance clients' ability to comprehend concepts. Table 17.9 presents a clinical application of affective education training.

If a client is too young to write and/or complete a worksheet, the counselor or a parent can verbally walk the child through this process or use alternative media to display the concepts, such as drawing, playing games, finger-painting, making a collage, using a sand tray, using puppets, or using imaginary play (Geldard, Geldard, & Yin Foo, 2013). A counselor working on affective education with a younger child could have the child draw pictures in response to the following statements: (a) "When I am happy, I show it by . . ."; (b) "When I am sad, I show it by . . ."; (c) "When I am mad, I show it by . . ."; and (d) "When I am worried, I show it by. . . ." Following up on those statements, a counselor can select one of the child's emotions and ask him or her to draw a picture describing (a) how and where he or she felt that emotion (e.g., "Select a color associated with your feeling, and draw where you felt it in your body") and (b) what he or she was thinking concerning that emotion (e.g., "In this cartoon bubble floating above your head, draw what you were saying to yourself when you felt worried"). The use of these drawing activities can aid counselors in teaching young clients how their emotions are connected with their thoughts and behaviors.

Social Skills Training (SST)

The purpose of **social skills training (SST)** is to help youth to develop the skills they need to interact with others. Although SST can be integrated into the treatment of all anxiety disorders, it is especially useful for youth who have social anxiety disorder (Scharfstein & Beidel, 2011; Seligman & Ollendick, 2011). Youth who have social anxiety disorder commonly struggle with school-based situations, such as answering a question from a teacher, participating in classroom discussions, or initiating conversations with peers. Often, these young people withdraw and avoid these uncomfortable and potentially embarrassing situations, thus increasing their lack of adequate social problem-solving skills. Therefore, SST can offer practical and pragmatic skills to increase their ability to manage and maneuver social situations (Seligman & Ollendick, 2011).

SST often includes educating clients about the verbal and nonverbal components of social interactions. Most young people have never been explicitly instructed on how to identify their feelings, identify other people's feelings, or express their own feelings in the context of a social interaction. The components of most SST programs include (a) identification and expression of emotions, (b) communication of these emotions with others, and (c) an increased ability to self-manage (i.e., being aware of one's behavior in relation to others; Geldard et al., 2013).

The central assumption of SST is that as youth develop their social skills and their ability to interact with others (e.g., peers, adults, teachers), they will have more positive interactions with others, and their ability to handle everyday social interactions will improve, thus resulting in enhanced self-esteem and confidence (Geldard et al., 2013). Because youth anxiety is often related to social interactions, SST may be an important aspect of counseling with youth who have anxiety (Geldard et al., 2013).

SST involves deconstructing complex social interactions to better understand how they can be managed. For example, if a child is having difficulties making friends, the counselor can suggest analyzing a typical social interaction. Typical social interactions have beginning, middle, and end stages. The beginning stage involves the child starting a conversation using conversation starters (e.g., "Hi! My name is Aidan. What is your name?"). In the next phase of the social interaction, the child might use preconstructed questions (e.g., "What video games do you like?") to maintain and continue the conversation. During this phase, the client will need to develop a pattern of taking turns, listening, and commenting. These interaction skills can be practiced through role-play in counseling sessions. In the final phase of a social interaction, the child disengages and appropriately ends the conversation (e.g., "I'll see you soon. It was nice talking to you").

Self-management skills are embedded in SST; they involve behaving deliberately and thoughtfully. Clients can learn stop-and-think techniques to help them with reactivity, or behaving in an impulsive, reactive manner. For example, STOP (identify feelings and problems), THINK (think about solutions and consequences, and choose the best solution), and DO (try your plan, and evaluate how it went) is one commonly used self-management skill. Young clients might also learn to self-manage by considering consequences of behaviors (e.g., "If I do this, then that might happen"), or they may be taught how to use assertiveness as opposed to aggression (e.g., instead of attacking someone the child states "I feel this way when you do that to me, and I would like it if you would do this instead"). Some of the specific techniques used in SST involve practicing skills via role-plays, receiving feedback from others (e.g., counselor, parents, siblings), receiving reinforcement for positive behaviors, and modeling.

Modeling, a technique often used in SST, is based on social learning theory, which suggests that learning can occur through observing, imitating, and modeling another individual (Kendall, 2012). Counselors use modeling techniques as a way to teach youth more adaptive social skills (Kendall, 2012). When clients observe others responding in adaptive, positive ways to anxiety-provoking situations, they can then imitate and model better ways to handle these situations, thus reducing their anxiety. Modeling can be used in counseling sessions (e.g., watching a video interaction, role-playing with a counselor), in group settings (e.g., a role-play activity), or as homework assignments (e.g., watching others kids interact during recess).

Consider, for example, a young client who is overtly anxious (e.g., hiding behind his parents instead of talking and engaging with other children) and struggles with social skills. The counselor and client might watch a video of a productive social interaction (e.g., an educational video, an Internet video clip of a show the child likes, a cartoon) and process this social interaction (e.g., What did the child do? What did he or she say? How and where did the child stand? What things did the child talk about?). The counselor may have the client role-play and experiment by using certain facial expressions, introduction statements, and conversation starters. These learned skills should ultimately be attempted and implemented by the client in real-world social interactions.

Cognitive Skills Training

As discussed in Chapter 1, young people move through a predictable sequence of cognitive development. As they move through and interact with their worlds, children gradually become better problem solvers. However, children—like adults—can at times become stuck in distorted, unproductive thought patterns; thus, they may benefit from cognitive skills training. Cognitive skills training is an essential component to working with youth who have anxiety and obsessive-compulsive disorders (Franklin et al., 2010; Seligman & Ollendick, 2011; Tompkins, 2014).

Cognitive problems in anxious youth generally arise from cognitive deficiencies or cognitive distortions (Kendall, 2012). Cognitive deficiencies can be understood as problematic processing (e.g., an adolescent makes an impulsive decision without all the needed information). With this type of thinking, problem-solving strategies can be used to support processing and encourage healthier thought patterns. **Cognitive distortions** are biased, dysfunctional, unproductive thinking patterns that distort youth's beliefs about themselves, others, or the world around them. Table 17.10 provides common types of youth cognitive distortions.

Table 17.10 Types of Cognitive Distortions (or Dirty Tricks)

Types	Overview	Example Quote
One-Eyed Ogre (*Overgeneralizing*)	You come to a rigid, firm conclusion based on only one piece of evidence or one incident.	"I have no friends, and I will never have friends."
Too Fast Forward (*Jumping to conclusions*)	Without evidence or knowledge, you either (a) assume you know what someone else is feeling or thinking or why he or she acted in that way or (b) predict the future in a negative light.	"My teacher hates me because she didn't call on me when I had my hand raised. She probably thought I didn't really know the answer anyway."
Disaster Forecaster (*Catastrophizing*)	You expect and assume the worst will happen to you.	"I knew when I missed the bus that my whole day would be a disaster. I'll bet all my homework is wrong. I bet no one will sit with me at lunch. I bet I'll miss the bus going home, too."
No Middle Riddle (*Polarized thinking*)	You have all-or-nothing thinking that involves no middle ground or any realization of the complexity of a given interaction or situation.	"I can't believe I only got the second-highest grade on the math test. If I was really smart, I'd have got all of them right. I am so dumb. Everyone must be smarter than me."
Circus Mirror Thinking (*Filtering*)	You only integrate the negative components (details) and amplify them, while filtering out the positive aspects of interactions and situations.	"Sally didn't want to be my partner for that classroom assignment. She must really dislike being around me. I wonder how many other people hate being around me."
Tragic Magic Thinking (*Personalizing*)	You assume everything that others do or say is directed toward you.	"I saw those eighth graders looking over at me and laughing. They must have been talking about my big nose. I hate my nose. Why does it have to be so big!"
Maxi-Me Thinking (*Blaming*)	You hold yourself completely responsible for all your suffering/pain or you hold others responsible for your suffering/pain.	"Those other boys never want me to win or to be good at anything. They must have moved that mat in the gym knowing that I would slip and fall on it and then have to go to the nurse's office."
Prisoner of Feeling (*Emotional reasoning*)	You believe that what you feel must be truth. Your reasoning stems from your emotions.	"I feel worthless, so I must be worthless. I feel stupid, so I must be stupid."
Lame Blaming (*Labeling*)	You generalize a negative label for yourself or someone else instead of exploring the complexity of a specific situation or event.	"Bobby just walked by me without saying 'hi.' He is such a jerk!"
Mules Rules (*Excessive use of "should"*)	You criticize yourself and others with a created list of *musts, oughts,* and *shoulds,* outlining how others should interact, relate, and behave.	"I should be more popular. I should have more friends. I should be more likable. I should be more relaxed and chill."

Note: Adapted from *Cognitive Therapy Techniques for Children and Adolescents,* by R. D. Friedberg, J. M. McClure, & J. H. Garcia, 2009, New York, NY: Guilford.

Although adolescents may be able to identify their own cognitive distortions with education and support, younger children have limited metacognitive abilities, and this makes it difficult for them to be aware of their own thought processes. One helpful approach in aiding children to understand and identify cognitive distortions is to relabel them as the *dirty tricks your mind plays on you* (Friedberg, McClure, & Garcia, 2009). By allowing clients to be detectives who try to *spot these tricks* in action, children may improve their ability to recognize distortions.

Cognitions are linked with emotions and behaviors. Therefore, if clients have dysfunctional behaviors or emotions, then a reasonable means to address those domains is by addressing their cognitions. This is done by identifying maladaptive cognitions and challenging them. By highlighting maladaptive thinking and then aiding clients to see the connection with their behaviors, counselors can help clients to adjust their distorted cognitive process and move toward a more constructive way of thinking.

Clinical Toolbox 17.3

In the Pearson etext, click here to read about an insight-based activity that can be used to increase young people's understanding of anxiety and stress and help them to cope.

The aims of cognitive skills training are to (a) identify and reduce negative self-talk, (b) generate positive self-statements, (c) challenge unrealistic or dysfunctional self-statements, and (d) create a plan to cope with feared situations or objects in the future (Kress & Paylo, 2015). The strategies most frequently associated with building cognitive skills are cognitive restructuring, rehearsal, social reinforcement, and role-plays.

In the following example, a 9-year-old boy discusses an upcoming assignment, and negative self-talk emerges as he talks about how he will be unable to meet the demands of the assignment.

COUNSELOR:	Tell me about a recent time when you were really nervous.
CLIENT	Last week at school, my teacher was talking about this Wax Museum project where we have to dress up like someone famous and give a three- to five-minute speech to the whole class.
COUNSELOR:	What kinds of things were you thinking?
CLIENT:	I was thinking about how crazy this assignment was. How am I going to do this in front of everyone?
COUNSELOR:	You worried about your ability to be up in front of everyone. What thoughts were going through your head?
CLIENT:	I guess I thought I'd look stupid and the other kids would make fun of me.
COUNSELOR:	Talk more about "looking stupid" and the "other kids making fun of you."
CLIENT:	I don't know. I just always get so nervous. I'll probably forget my lines and stumble over my words. I am not as smart as those kids and they know it. They would talk about me.
COUNSELOR:	This sounds a lot like something you talked about a few weeks ago, concerning that interaction with Stacey. What did you do in that interaction that was helpful?
CLIENT:	Yes, I remember. I started jumping to conclusions. But this is different. I can't talk in front of others.
COUNSELOR:	How do you think the two events are similar?
CLIENT:	I don't know.
COUNSELOR:	You predicted something negative was going to happen before you looked at any of the facts of the situation. Let's look at the facts for and against what you said—"I can't talk in front of others."

This client is beginning to learn his cognitive pattern (i.e., Too Fast Forward [jumping to negative conclusions]), and the counselor is attempting to help him to not only identify negative self-talk but also to evaluate the evidence of the claim he is making and hopefully generate new positive statements about himself. The process of identifying cognitive patterns will aid the client in disputing maladaptive cognitions in the future and provide him with an example of how to challenge such unfounded claims.

One means to aid youth in building cognitive awareness and skills is to have them fill out a **thought record** when a situation becomes anxiety producing. Tables 17.11 and 17.12 provide thought records to be used in cognitive skills training with adolescents and children, respectively. Thought records can be an effective tool for teaching clients to notice their thought processes.

Clinical Toolbox 17.4

In the Pearson etext, click here to read about an insight-based activity that can be used to increase a client's understanding of the relationship between anxiety and cognitions.

Problem Solving

Problem-solving approaches have long been associated with the enhancement of social competence and a decrease in psychological distress (Bell & D'Zurilla, 2009; Malouff, Thorsteinsson, & Schutte, 2007). Problem-solving approaches train children to independently meet life's daily challenges. Effective problem-solving

Table 17.11 Using a Thought Record in Cognitive Skills Training (Adolescent)

Situation	Emotions or Feelings (1–10) What Is Happening in Your Body?	Unhelpful Thoughts	Facts for the Unhelpful Thought	Facts Against the Unhelpful Thought	Alternative Thought	New Emotion or Feeling (1–10)
What? When? Where? How? Alone or with others?	How did it make you feel? How intense? What did you notice happening in your body? Where did you feel it?	What thoughts were going through your mind at that time?	What facts show the thoughts are true?	What facts show the thoughts are NOT true?	What might someone else say about this situation? Is there another way to look at this?	What are you feeling now? Rate it from 1 to 10.

An Example with a 13-Year-Old

Yesterday, I made a mistake at school—I went to the wrong classroom for third period. Then, I hurried to the right classroom.	I felt so anxious (9). My face felt warm, my heart raced, and I felt sick in my stomach.	I thought—I am so stupid; If people really knew me they'd see I'm a mess (i.e., Lame Blaming [labeling]).	I went to the wrong classroom, and I should know my schedule. I made a dumb mistake.	I did go to the wrong classroom, but I was only two minutes late; my teacher and other students didn't say anything to me; I've seen this happen to other students.	My reaction may be over-the-top; I made a dumb mistake but that does not make me dumb/stupid or a failure—I was just distracted.	I feel less anxious and realize no one was even watching me, and I am not my thoughts (3).

Table 17.12	Using a Thought Record in Cognitive Skills Training (Children)		
What Happened?	Your Feeling(s)	Your Thought(s)	Your Action(s)
Tell me about the event. Draw it below.	How did it make you feel? How strong did you feel it? Rate it, and pick a color to describe your feeling.	What were you thinking during and after the event? Draw your thoughts during and after below.	What did you do? Draw it below.
An Example with a 7-Year-Old			
My mother left me with a baby sitter.	*I was mad and then sad.* *Rate it or pick a color.*	*DURING:* *She's not coming home.*	*Cried, yelled, and screamed*
(Drawing)	*1-2-3-4-5-6-7-8-9-10* *Red*	*AFTER:* *What if she died?*	*(Drawing)*

skills are essential for youth struggling with anxiety and obsessive-compulsive disorders, especially generalized anxiety disorder, social phobia, and separation anxiety disorder (Kendall, 2012; Kendall et al., 2017). There are numerous problem-solving models that can be taught to young clients—for example, (a) define the problem, (b) generate ways to address the problem, (c) make an educated decision, choice, or course of action based on the information you have, and (d) implement a solution and evaluation (Bell & D'Zurilla, 2009).

Counselors must help young clients to distinguish between solvable and unsolvable problems or worries. Solvable problems or worries are the ones that can be altered by actions (i.e., "If I am lonely, I can talk to someone"), whereas unsolvable worries (i.e., "What if I get cancer one day?" "What if my mother never comes home?") cannot be altered by actions. If a youth continues to perseverate on unsolvable problems or worries, the counselor can aid the client in managing uncertainty and ambiguity.

Problems require a degree of self-awareness, and youth need to realize and assess the origins of their problems. After identifying the problem, counselors can challenge youth to not only avoid these distressing situations but also to generate alternative actions. Once youth recognize how their emotions affect their behaviors and thinking, they often realize they can take actions to alter undesirable problems or situations (Stark, Streusand, Krumholz, & Patel, 2010). The next step in problem solving is generating alternatives. Youth need to generate options to address the problem or situation. After they generate solutions, they should determine what end each decision will produce and evaluate the merit of each idea until they identify a solution. Finally, clients need to implement their selected solution, which should be realistic and produce their intended result. Role-playing this process in sessions can be a helpful way to reinforce the problem-solving process and ensure some transferability happens. After implementation, the counselor and the client should reevaluate the outcome, allowing the client to assimilate the experience to lead to more effective decision making in the future. Table 17.13 presents an example of a basic problem-solving formula for use with youth.

With younger clients, counselors can get creative and use characters to communicate problem-solving concepts. For example, clients can think of a cartoon character (e.g., Jake and the Never Land Pirates) with whom they identify and who they think could handle their situation. Counselors can ask clients to talk about how that character would deal with the situation and ask them to pretend they are the character (e.g., act as if they are the person) in session role-plays and in upcoming real-life situations (Kendall, 2012).

Contingent Reinforcement

Contingent reinforcement is the intentional reinforcement of behaviors to encourage a desirable outcome. Based on operant conditioning principles (i.e., learning certain behaviors as a result of rewards or punishments), contingency management assumes that behaviors are controlled by consequences and can be increased by reinforcing them or reduced by not reinforcing them. Contingency management techniques

Table 17.13	Example of a Basic Problem-Solving Formula
Problem-Solving Question	**Example**
What is the problem?	"I worry about a lot of things. Recently, I started to worry about going to the end-of-the-year school dance. I want to go, but what if I do something stupid or what if I just sit all alone. What if no one talks to me?"
What can I do about it?	"I guess I could: 1. not go to the dance; 2. go to the dance from start to finish; or 3. go for part of the dance and call my mother to pick me up if I feel uncomfortable."
What will probably happen if I do each of those things?	"I would: 1. just sit at home by myself watching TV; 2. feel uncomfortable, but I guess I could leave." 3. feel lonely and embarrassed until my mother came to pick me up; or
What solution might work the best?	"I think option 3 is my best option."
After I have tried it, how did I do? How did it go?	"It went okay, I guess. I stayed at the dance longer than I thought I would—for like an hour and a half. I eventually called my mom, but after I had talked with two girls for a little bit."

Adapted from "Anxiety disorders in youth," by P. C. Kendall, 2012. In P. C. Kendall (Ed.), *Child and Adolescent Therapy: Cognitive-Behavioral Procedures* (4th ed., pp. 143–189), New York, NY: Guilford.

affect youth anxiety by altering their behaviors related to anxiety-provoking situations. These approaches are useful for reducing anxiety-related behaviors (e.g., avoidance), selective mutism (Vecchio & Kearney, 2009), and phobias (i.e., social, specific, agoraphobia; Kendall, 2012). The most common contingency management techniques are shaping and positive reinforcement.

SHAPING

Shaping is the gradual training or altering of behaviors by either (a) dividing the desired behavior into multiple parts and reinforcing those parts or (b) reinforcing any movement toward the desired behaviors. For example, if the counseling goal is for a youth to share two sentences in a fearful social situation, this goal can be broken down so the youth uses one word (not a gesture), then a few words (not one word), and then eventually says two sentences in the social situation. Counselors can use the following systematic approach to apply shaping principles with youth:

1. Label the desired behavior (e.g., tantrum behaviors, avoidance behaviors).
2. Determine the end goal of shaping (e.g., extinguishing the disruptive behavior).
3. Rate present performance in displaying the desired behavior (on a scale of 0–10, 0 = *none* to 10 = *all the time*).
4. Detail steps to move the client from the present level of performance to the desired behavior (i.e., end goal). The steps should be progressively more demanding. If they are too minimal, youth will become bored; if they are too demanding, youth will get frustrated. Either way the process will be ineffective unless it is graduated.
   a. When step 1 of the set of steps is accomplished, the youth should receive a predetermined reward.
   b. Once the youth has mastered that step (or a specified behavior), then he or she must move to the next stage to receive a reward.
   c. Repeat this process until all steps are complete.

POSITIVE REINFORCEMENT

The next contingency management concept, positive reinforcement, is simplistic in presentation yet often misunderstood. A positive reinforcement is something that is added to (a) increase the likelihood a behavior will reoccur or (b) maintain an existing behavior. For example, providing youth with positive reinforcement (e.g., later bedtime, extra television time, additional snacks, verbal praise) will increase the likelihood they will complete their homework. In contrast, extinction occurs when a certain behavior is no longer reinforced; therefore, in the absence of reinforcement, the behavior eventually stops. In the context of anxiety-related problems, positive reinforcements can be used to increase the likelihood of youth approaching situations they fear. The more clients experience these events and receive positive reinforcements for doing so, the more likely they are to engage in the feared behaviors. In addition, the use of positive reinforcement in a scheduled fashion can be helpful in addressing anxiety. For example, counselors can use a token economy system in which the young person receives positive reinforcement for engaging in identified behaviors. The youth can turn in the earned tokens to gain additional privileges or receive positive items. Steps for implementing a token economy include the following:

1. Select and define a target behavior to reinforce or strengthen (e.g., tantrum behaviors, avoidance behaviors).
2. Create a token system and a visual way to review and evaluate progress (e.g., stickers on a chart, tokens or chips).
3. Establish the reinforcement payout system with exchange criteria (e.g., for this behavior the youth receives this privilege or positive item).
4. Put the reinforcement schedule into place (e.g., provide tokens when behavior occurs in a designated time period).
5. Consider adding a response cost (e.g., a cost or fine for inappropriate behaviors).

Token economies are an effective means to teach youth new skills and to motivate new behaviors; however, continued implementation and consistency are difficult to maintain (Bailey, Gross, & Cotton, 2011). Counselors need to ensure parents are involved in the development of token economies, feel supported throughout implementation, and receive aid if difficulties arise.

Habit Reversal Training

HRT is a behavioral treatment approach that is effective in treating various body-focused repetitive behaviors (e.g., hair pulling, skin picking, nail-biting; Tompkins, 2014). HRT focuses on enhancing a youth's awareness of repetitive behaviors, developing a competing response to the repetitive behavior (e.g., bend arms 90 degrees, clench fists, and hold arms firmly at side for 90 seconds), and creating adequate social support through parent training (Tompkins, 2014).

In the initial stages of HRT, counselors enhance young clients' awareness of the existence of the problem behaviors and their antecedents. In adolescents, this awareness process can be straightforward; they typically have some awareness of the problem. Younger children who lack insight into these repetitive behaviors may be less aware, and sessions will typically need to be completed with young clients and their parents (Tompkins, 2014). Although adolescents can often identify warning signs for their repetitive behaviors, younger children frequently engage in automatic behaviors (i.e., out of their awareness) and will need parents' assistance to become more aware of behaviors and triggers. For example, a younger child may automatically pull her hair while watching television in the living room. The child may be rewarded for noticing and verbalizing: "I pull my hair in the living room."

Once young clients are aware of their repetitive behaviors and precursors, they can engage in competing responses (i.e., replacement behaviors). A competing response consists of three components: (a) the youth is not able to do both the competing response and repetitive behavior, (b) the youth can do the competing response easily in most situations, and (c) the competing response will not bring excessive attention to the youth (Tompkins, 2014). One common competing response children and adolescents use is placing hands to their sides and clenching their fists for at least a minute. In some situations, they can use doodling on a piece of paper, tying knots with a small piece of yarn, doing origami, or clenching silly putty in their hands.

Finally, the social support component is when the parents remind, reinforce, and instruct the youth on the skills learned in session within the home. For example, younger children often need to be reminded of the competing responses they decided to implement instead of the repetitive behaviors. Parents can reinforce these skills through verbal praise (e.g., "Great job!") and/or contingency management plans (e.g., positive reinforcements) to increase desired behaviors (e.g., competing responses).

Exposure-Based Procedures

Exposure-based procedures aim to decrease the avoidance behaviors associated with anxiety (i.e., not participating or not fully entering a situation or activity) by encouraging youth to approach and engage in anxiety-provoking situations. Exposure-based procedures, often incorporated into CBT, are effective in working with separation anxiety disorder, specific phobias, social phobia, selective mutism, and obsessive-compulsive disorder (Barlow, 2008; Franklin et al., 2010; Seligman & Ollendick, 2011; Vecchio & Kearney, 2009).

Exposure-based procedures are based on classical conditioning and the assumption that as clients are better able to tolerate a fearful situation over an extended time period, they will naturally progress through the process of extinction (i.e., behaviors are extinguished because of a lack of reinforcement) and habituation (i.e., decreased response to stimuli because of increased exposure). Exposure-based procedures can be gradually introduced (i.e., progressive exposure to the anxiety hierarchy) or exposure can be immediate (i.e., flooding).

When using gradual exposure procedures, counselors first aid young clients in developing an anxiety hierarchy (e.g., fear or anxiety ladder). Counselors help clients to identify and detail the least anxiety-provoking situation and move up to the most feared stimuli. The actual exposure to the feared stimuli can consist of imaginal (i.e., use of imagery to envision feared situation), in vivo in session (i.e., confronting a feared situation in session), and/or in vivo outside of session (i.e., confronting a feared situation outside of session). The aim of all types of exposure-based interventions is to help the client to acclimate to the distressing stimuli and to practice coping skills in a simulated, and eventually a real-life, situation, ceasing or decreasing the level of emotional activation caused by the anxiety-provoking situation, object, or obsession (i.e., process of habituation).

Flooding is the repeated and prolonged exposure of the feared situation or object (e.g., imaginal, in vivo) until the client's self-reported anxiety level dissipates. The assumption behind this approach is that anxiety can only reach a quantifiable level and will eventually dissipate, thus leaving the young client with a sense of enduring and of mastering the fearful situation. Flooding can create distress—more so than other exposure-based interventions—so youth should have some cognitive understanding of the rationale behind the intervention, and it may not be appropriate for younger children (Kendall, 2012).

Counselors using exposure-based procedures (e.g., gradual, flooding) must incorporate response prevention—prevention of the client's normal response (e.g., avoidance behaviors, compulsions) to the anxiety-provoking situation, object, or obsession—into the exposure-based protocol. Response or ritual prevention is critical to the use of exposure methods, especially with obsessive-compulsive disorders in youth (Franklin et al., 2010).

One CBT model that incorporates exposure-based procedures is Coping Cat (Kendall, Chourdhury, Hudson, & Webb, 2002). In the exposure portion of treatment, children and adolescents confront their own anxiety-provoking situation through a gradual hierarchy. Youth practice and implement four skills represented in the acronym FEAR:

- **F** *(feeling frightened):* Acknowledge your physiological responses to anxiety.
- **E** *(expecting bad things to happen):* Identify unhelpful anxious thoughts.
- **A** *(actions and attitudes that can help):* Focus on your learned skills to use during times of anxiety (e.g., relaxation, deep breathing, visualization, problem solving, positive thoughts).
- **R** *(results and reward):* Evaluate your performance when facing an anxiety-provoking situation.

Coping Cat is one example of how exposure-based approaches can be integrated into counseling children and adolescents with anxiety and obsessive-compulsive–related disorders.

Integrating Family

Parental involvement is essential in helping youth to address and overcome anxiety (Seligman & Ollendick, 2011). When working with parents, counselors should aim to (a) increase their awareness and education about anxiety and (b) solicit their support in implementing consistent reinforcements and in reinforcing skills and the young clients' counseling objectives. The extent to which family members and parents are engaged will vary and will depend on the nature of the client's anxiety, the client's age, the client's level of awareness, the clinical setting (e.g., outpatient, residential treatment facility, hospital, school, day treatment), and the family situation (e.g., members, motivation, resources). When working with younger children, the family will need to play a greater role in supporting the child in his or her application of skills. In addition, family dynamics and considerations may exacerbate anxiety in youth, and these considerations may need to be addressed in counseling.

Clinical Toolbox 17.5

In the Pearson etext, click here for a list of common stressors that counselors can relay to parents that may cause or worsen youth anxiety.

Parents typically participate in one or more of the following roles with regard to their child's counseling: (a) a consultant (e.g., fact-checking client-presented information, serving as an informant), (b) a collaborator (e.g., reinforcing skills learned in sessions, helping the child to role-play and/or practice new skills), or (c) a co-client (e.g., learning how to manage their own anxiety, learning how to parent youth in a new way; Kendall et al., 2017). The use of parents as consultants and collaborators can be done in individual sessions (i.e., meeting alone with the parents), in conjoined family sessions (i.e., sessions with youth and parents), or in private meetings with parents for a portion of the youth's session. Parental engagement can increase participation, increase collaboration on counseling objectives and goals, maintain treatment motivation, and foster more positive counseling outcomes secondary to parents' behavioral changes (e.g., being less intrusive, being more encouraging of autonomy, being less encouraging of avoidant behaviors). Table 17.14 provides common goals, topics, and skills that can be addressed in family sessions with youth who have anxiety.

Collaborative contact with parents and family members enhances family members' understanding and ability to implement their respective roles, thus increasing the probability that young clients with anxiety will complete homework assignments (Franklin et al., 2010; Seligman & Ollendick, 2011).

Psychopharmacotherapy

Psychopharmacotherapy is another intervention that may be used to address youth anxiety (Ipser, Stein, Hawkridge, & Hoppe, 2009; Strawn, Sakolsky, & Rynn, 2012). Parents, relevant family members, and youth must consider the pros and cons of using psychopharmacotherapy in addressing anxiety. When considering a referral for a psychiatric evaluation, counselors should evaluate the youth's current level of distress and functioning, severity of symptoms, and mental health history (e.g., the length of time the youth has felt anxious; Franklin et al., 2010). Medication side effects, the preference of the youth and family members to try medication as an option, and the family's ability to adhere to medication compliance and attend all follow-up medication management appointments may all influence a physician's decision to integrate medication into a young person's treatment plan (Hinkle, 2008). A general knowledge of commonly used anxiety medications and their side effects may aid counselors in their understanding of a client's treatment options. Table 17.15 presents the SSRIs used in anxiety and obsessive-compulsive disorder treatment and the associated side effects.

Table 17.14	Goals, Topics, and Skills for Family and/or Parent Sessions with Youth with Anxiety
General goals	Improving the parent–child relationship
	Strengthening family communication skills
	Strengthening family problem-solving skills
	Encouraging a parental style focused on the autonomy and healthy coping of the child (e.g., helping the parent to realize only the child can face his or her fears)
General topics discussed	Family communication patterns and styles
	Parenting style (e.g., parental overinvolvement, criticism, and control)
	Impact of the child's anxiety on parents' behaviors
	Impact of the child's anxiety on siblings
	Problem-solving patterns and styles
Specific skills	Helping parents to feel knowledgeable about the impacts of anxiety
	Connecting the youth's symptoms with behaviors, thoughts, and emotions
	Using positive reinforcements to increase desired behaviors
	Ignoring unwanted behaviors
	Modeling calm problem-solving approaches
	Reminding the child of learned skills from sessions (e.g., relaxation, coping skills, positive self-talk)
	Parents as collaborators or "coaches"
	• Implementing exposure-based homework assignments; challenging avoidance responses
	• Viewing the child as resilient, not vulnerable (e.g., in need of protection)
	Focusing on small, positive successes to build courage and competence

Current research supports the use of medications with youth with anxiety disorders (Ipser et al., 2009; Strawn et al., 2012). More specifically, SSRIs have consistently been the most effective medication for treating youth with anxiety disorders (Strawn et al., 2012) and obsessive-compulsive disorders (Ipser et al., 2009). In addition to SSRIs, buspirone (BuSpar) has demonstrated some effectiveness in treating anxiety disorders; yet, with limited research support it should be used with caution (Kodish, Rockhill, & Varley, 2011). Benzodiazepines (Ativan, Valium, Klonopin) have not been found to be effective in treating youth with anxiety disorders, and their use warrants more research and exploration (Ipser et al., 2009; Strawn et al., 2012).

Table 17.15	SSRIs Commonly Used to Treat Youth Anxiety and Associated Side Effects
SSRIs used in the treatment of anxiety and obsessive-compulsive disorder	• Fluoxetine (Prozac)
	• Sertraline (Zoloft)
	• Paroxetine (Paxil)
	• Citalopram (Celexa)
	• Escitalopram (Lexapro)
General side effects of these SSRIs	• Headache, which often dissipates within a few days
	• Nausea (i.e., feeling sick to your stomach), which often dissipates within a few days
	• Agitation (i.e., jittery).
	• Sleeplessness or drowsiness, which often dissipates within a few weeks

I CAN START COUNSELING PLAN FOR CASSANDRA

This chapter opened with quotes from Cassandra, a 12-year-old girl who experiences severe anxiety. The following I CAN START conceptual framework outlines counseling considerations that may be helpful to a school counselor or a clinical counselor who works with Cassandra.

C = Contextual Assessment

Cassandra is a 12-year-old Caucasian girl whose father left when she was young. She becomes anxious when engaging in any new activities or when she is required to leave her home. She reports experiencing panic attacks and avoiding unfamiliar situations (e.g., other people's homes, school trips, grocery stores). Cassandra's mother is invested in supporting Cassandra, but she needs assistance with parenting strategies to quell Cassandra's anxiety. Mom often allows Cassandra to avoid anxiety-producing situations, and this reaffirms Cassandra's belief that the world is a scary place. In addition, Cassandra's mother has her own anxiety struggles and has been diagnosed with generalized anxiety disorder. Cassandra's basic needs are met, but her family lives in an urban lower socioeconomic area that is engulfed in poverty, and her family has limited access to resources.

A = Assessment and Diagnosis

Diagnosis = 300.01 (F41.0) Panic Disorder

N = Necessary Level of Care

Outpatient family counseling (once per week)

Outpatient individual counseling (once per week)

S = Strengths

Self: Cassandra has above-average intelligence, and her teachers indicate her potential to excel as a student. Cassandra believes she is a talented dancer and enjoys playing with her dog. She appears willing to participate in counseling services.

Family: Cassandra's mother is loving and supportive but unsure of how to parent her daughter. Although Cassandra is an only child, she enjoys playing with several cousins on the weekends.

School/community: Cassandra's family lives in an urban area with access to transportation, therapeutic resources (e.g., YMCA), and nearby parks.

T = Treatment Approach

- CBT focusing primarily on affective education, relaxation, and exposure-based approaches
- Family therapy

A = Aim and Objective of Counseling (90-day objectives)

Cassandra will learn to recognize and identify anxiety symptoms. Cassandra will identify physical, cognitive, and behavioral symptoms that precede, occur concurrent to, and occur after each panic or anxiety-related incident, and she will chart these symptoms.

Cassandra will increase her ability to tolerate panic, anxiety, and discomfort. Cassandra will use at least one relaxation technique (e.g., deep breathing, progressive muscle relaxation) at the onset of intense anxiety. She will use at least one of these learned relaxation skills 100% of the time.

Cassandra will increase her ability to tolerate and approach panic and anxiety-invoking situations. Cassandra will create a hierarchy of anxiety-inducing stimuli (e.g., walking in a neighborhood [further from home], going to a crowded place, being in a grocery line with Mom). She will gradually be exposed to these situations and resist avoiding them at least 75% of the time.

Cassandra's mother will reinforce Cassandra's participation in desired activities, even if doing so is anxiety producing. Cassandra's mother, Cassandra, and the counselor will co-create a token economy, providing

Cassandra with positive reinforcement (e.g., later bedtime, extra TV/computer time, verbal praise) each time Cassandra participates in an anxiety-producing activity (e.g., walking in the neighborhood, going to the store with mom).

R = Research-Based Interventions (based on CBT)

Counselor will help Cassandra to learn, develop, and/or apply the following skills:

- Affective education—understanding what she is experiencing in her body and mind, and the impact that has on her behaviors
- Relaxation skills
- Anxiety management skills
- Participation in exposure-based activities (in and out of session)
- Identifying and challenging cognitive distortions associated with her panic anxiety and discomfort

T = Therapeutic Support Services

Medication evaluation with a psychiatrist

Youth and/or parent anxiety support groups

YMCA programming (e.g., dance)

Referral for Cassandra's mother (i.e., individual counseling to address her anxiety symptoms)

Summary

Anxiety disorders are extremely common in children and adolescents, and they are one of the most prevalent types of disorders in childhood (Waite & Creswell, 2014). Obsessive-compulsive disorders are less common in children and adolescents. Although anxiety disorders are characterized by excessive fear and worry of an anticipated threat, obsessive-compulsive disorders are characterized by obsessions, compulsions, and/or persistent body-focused repetitive behaviors.

Due to the vast variety of anxiety and obsessive-compulsive disorders, counselors must garner a complete picture of the client's experiences to confirm an accurate diagnosis and to plan for the appropriate counseling options and approaches. Therefore, counselors must complete an assessment that includes clinical interviews, self-reports, behavioral observations, parent–teacher rating scales, and a thorough family history review (Kendall, 2012). Furthermore, counselors should employ assessment methods from multiple perspectives to consider the young person's distinct settings (Kendall, 2012; Kendall et al., 2017). Because these disorders will often co-occur with other mental health disorders, counselors should always consider if any comorbid diagnoses exist. In addition, counselors should assess for suicidal ideation, substance use and abuse, and academic difficulties.

Significant research exists on the efficacy of counseling youth with anxiety disorders. However, less research exists on the effectiveness of counseling youth who have obsessive-compulsive disorders (Wilson et al., 2016). CBT is among the most effective approaches for children and adolescents (Freeman et al., 2014). Counselors should consider taking an integrative–comprehensive approach to working with these youth, which could include relaxation training, affective education, SST, cognitive skills training, problem solving, establishing a contingent reinforcement plan, HRT, exposure-based activities, integrating the family, and use of medications.

MyLab Counseling: Counseling Children and Adolescents

In the Topic 12 Assignments: *Strategies for Addressing Mood Disorders in Youth*, try Application Exercise 12.1: *Assessing and Addressing Anxiety in Childhood.*

Then try Licensure Quiz 12.2: *Understanding Anxiety, Obsessive-Compulsive, and Related Disorders* and Application Exercise 12.3: *Assessing and Addressing Obsessive-Compulsive Disorder in Youth.*

CHAPTER 18

Depressive and Bipolar Disorders

THE CASE OF KEANDRA

I always knew I was different. While others seemed to float along, I trudged. A dark cloud followed my every move. I wish it would just disappear, but it never does. I feel hopeless and alone. I hurt. It's a deep, down-to-my-core kind of hurt. Sometimes I just feel numb. I know people think I should just "get over it." Don't they get that I try? I'm scared. What if this feeling never leaves? I can't tell anyone how bad I feel. So, I just keep it all to myself. I don't know why I feel so bad. Sometimes I tell myself "I'm ok," but I'm not; I'm in pain. I say to myself "It's nothing," but it's everything. I keep telling myself "I'm fine," but I'm not. I'm anything but fine. Sometimes I wish it would all end. It isn't that I want to kill myself or anything like that; I just want to stop living . . . so I can stop hurting.

—Keandra, age 17

Depression (i.e., major depressive disorder, persistent depressive disorder) is the third most prevalent mental illness in youth behind phobias (i.e., social and specific) and oppositional defiant disorder (Merikangas et al., 2010). Prevalence rates for depression are around 11% in adolescents, with more severe cases around 9% (Merikangas et al., 2010). Although prevalence rates of depression steadily increase from middle childhood through adolescence, depression appears less frequently in younger children (i.e., ages 1–3 years old; Kendall & Comer, 2010; Merikangas et al., 2010). Adolescent girls appear to be twice as likely to be diagnosed with depression as adolescent boys (Merikangas et al., 2010). However, no apparent gender differences exist in the childhood. The most predictive risk factor associated with the development of a depressive disorder in youth is family history of depressive disorders (i.e., number of first-degree relatives with depressive disorders), with clear evidence of family transmission of depression (e.g., 24%–58%; American Academy of Child and Adolescent Psychiatry [AACAP], 2007; Rao & Chen, 2009).

General prevalence rates for bipolar disorders are around 3% for the youth population, with prevalence rates increasing steadily throughout adolescence and into adulthood (Merikangas et al., 2010). No apparent gender differences exist in prevalence rates (Merikangas et al., 2010). Similar to depressive disorders, bipolar disorders appear to have a significant genetic component, with the risk of bipolar disorders increasing significantly (i.e., up to 5 times) when a youth has a family history of bipolar disorders (i.e., if one or both of the parents are diagnosed with bipolar disorder; Youngstrom, Freeman, & McKeown-Jenkins, 2009).

We have intentionally chosen to present bipolar disorders with depressive disorders because of the close relationship and overlap of counseling considerations and approaches associated with these conditions (American Psychiatric Association [APA], 2013). What follows is a description of the general characteristics of these disorders, along with the specific symptoms, types, and assessment considerations of depressive and bipolar disorders.

THE NATURE OF DEPRESSIVE AND BIPOLAR DISORDERS IN YOUTH

Depression is a term that is often casually used to refer to a person feeling sunken, dejected, or sad. Most people acknowledge feeling sad from time to time due to the death of a loved one, a missed opportunity, a broken relationship, or a failed dream. Over time, those feelings typically subside, and the cloud lifts. For youth who experience a depressive disorder, the cloud does not lift, and they experience a sense of sadness

---

Manic episode: A distinct period of time when a person has a persistent, elevated, expansive mood that may be irritable in nature, which generally consists of an inflated sense of self; a decreased need for sleep; talkativeness; flight of ideas and racing thoughts; distractibility; and an increase in goal-directed activities, risk-taking activities.

Hypomanic episode: A distinct period of time when a person has a persistently elevated or irritable mood. No psychotic symptoms exist, and the child or adolescent is generally able to function better than those who are in a manic episode. Many of the same qualities of a manic episode are present but at a lower level, and they may include an inflated sense of self, a decreased need for sleep, talkativeness, flight of ideas and racing thoughts, distractibility, and an increase in goal-directed, risk-taking activities.

Depressive episode: A distinct period of time when a person has a persistent, prolonged (i.e., at least 2 weeks) period of unhappiness and irritability; decreased interest in pleasurable activities; a bleak outlook on life and oneself; an inability to enjoy things, people, or activities; and changes in sleep and appetite.

FIGURE 18.1 Summary of the Episodes Associated with Depressive and Bipolar Disorders

and melancholy that affects their energy levels (e.g., fatigue, lethargy) and their thoughts about themselves (e.g., "I am hopeless"; "I am worthless"). Those around the youth often inadvertently communicate the message that the youth should just snap out of it or cheer up, but those who have depressive and bipolar disorders require mental health intervention and support.

Compared to youth with depression (e.g., depressive episodes only), youth who have bipolar disorders experience episodes of **mania** or **hypomania**, which involve an elevated emotional state characterized by a frenzy of activity (e.g., goal-directed, risk-taking behavior), energy (e.g., lack of need for sleep), grandiosity (i.e., inflated sense of self and abilities), and elation of mood. Figure 18.1 presents a summary of the episodes associated with depressive and bipolar disorders. Bipolar disorder is characterized by unusual mood changes, which may present as an expansive mood; agitated, high "up" period; and/or escalated, goal-directed activities (e.g., "I have to complete this Lego house and this puzzle, play that video game, and make a fort outside").

When this frenzy of mood, energy, and activity subsides, youth with bipolar disorders typically experience a swing back to the other extreme of depression and experience sadness or a lower-than-low "down" period that includes the previously mentioned depressive symptoms. For example, a child with bipolar disorder may explain that he feels as if he is on "an emotional roller coaster" that he cannot "get off," which may leave him frustrated, agitated, and irritable. Youth with bipolar disorder typically alternate between manic/hypomanic and depressive states. The diagnostic specifier **with mixed features** can be applied to youth who simultaneously display episodes and symptomology consistent with mania/hypomania and depressive features (APA, 2013). Children and adolescents frequently present diagnostically with mixed features, which is not usually the case in adults (Singh, 2008).

Depression and bipolar disorder were once believed to only affect adults, which is why they were not historically diagnosed in childhood (Kendall & Comer, 2010; Parens & Johnston, 2010). The explanations for why depression and bipolar disorders may be overlooked in counseling include (a) bipolar youth enter counseling because the adults in their lives perceive they have behavior problems (e.g., conduct, aggression, disruptive behaviors), so behavior becomes the focus of counseling, (b) youth who display depressive symptoms are overlooked and not referred to counseling because their symptoms are not disruptive, and (c) depression in youth can look different from depression in adulthood, so it can be easily missed (Kendall & Comer, 2010). The following sections outline the symptoms, types, and assessment considerations for depressive disorders.

Symptoms of Depression

The same criteria used to define adult depression have historically been used to diagnose youth depression. Although there are many similarities between youth and adult depression, depressive symptoms in youth are unique and are influenced by factors such as age and developmental considerations. For example, in younger children, depression is frequently expressed as physical symptoms (e.g., aches, pains, stomachaches), temper tantrums, and irritability (as opposed to sadness in adults; Field, Seligman, & Albrecht, 2008). Older children may convey more subjective depressive symptoms, such as helplessness, hopelessness, sadness, and pessimism, than younger children (Kendall & Comer, 2010). One of the most consistent qualities present in depressed adolescents is a hypersensitivity to criticism (Kendall & Comer, 2010). Adolescents also frequently disengage from their peers, parents, teachers, and family members as a means of protection. Unlike adults with depression, who withdraw or isolate entirely, adolescents with depression frequently maintain some social connection, even though they find maintaining these relationships to be difficult (Field et al., 2008). Adolescents with depression typically socialize less frequently and reduce communication with their parents and may attempt to find alternative friends or social groups. Table 18.1 presents descriptions of developmental differences in the presentation of depression in youth.

Depressed youth tend to interpret and think about experiences in a negative way—the proverbial glass is half empty, not half full. Depressed youth in late childhood and adolescence often fixate on their deficiencies and their thoughts of worthlessness, helplessness, and hopelessness, and they often perceive any unpleasant

Table 18.1 Developmental Differences in the Presentation of Depression in Youth

Developmental Stage	Presentation of Symptoms
Early childhood	Is socially withdrawn • Has decreased interest in people, things, and activities (e.g., "bored") • Shows decreased activity (e.g., decreased play) • Avoids interactions and contact with others (e.g., not interested in siblings or playing with others) Has depressed/irritable mood • Lacks enthusiasm • Is angry and verbally aggressive • Has physical complaints (e.g., headaches, stomach problems) • Is unhappy or cranky • Is tearful and cries excessively • Is tired and needs a lot of sleep
Middle and late childhood	• Has physical/somatic complaints • Displays regression (e.g., clinging behaviors) • Displays aggressive behaviors (i.e., both physical and verbal) • Experiences marked loss of pleasure and interest in activities • Has increase or decrease in appetite • Has sleep disturbances • Has increased or decreased activity level • Has fatigue or loss of energy
Adolescents	• Has negative self-image: self-blame and self-loathing • Displays anger, irritability, and/or agitation • Has physical complaints • Has morbid thinking • Has suicidal thoughts and/or actions • Displays acting-out behaviors (e.g., defiance, running away, aggression, nonresponsive) • Is restless • Has excessive worry or inappropriate guilt (e.g., low self-esteem) • Has sleep disturbances • Is uncommunicative • Is hypersensitive to criticism • Isolates self from others

experience, interaction, or event as being due to their lack of competence, ability, or control over their lives (Kendall & Comer, 2010). Youth who are depressed often have a negative perception of (a) self (e.g., "I'm no good"), (b) the world around them (e.g., "The world is a bad place"), and (c) their future (e.g., "I will never be good at anything"; Beck & Alford, 2009). Young people with depression perceive that they are less competent, less resourceful, and less worthy than others, and they consider their situation as uniquely hopeless. This population also experiences a significant reduction in positive affect (e.g., confidence, enthusiasm, attentiveness, excitement) and positive events secondary to their sustained, persistent negative affect and outlook.

Some depressed youth present as removed and passive, whereas others present as angry irritable, argumentative, aggressive, and even violent (Jacobson & Mufson, 2010). Regardless of presentation, youth with depression generally become socially withdrawn and struggle socially and often academically (Kendall & Comer, 2010). Social and academic performances are often exacerbated by their difficulties not only with affect but also with concentration, motivation, and interest levels. Some adolescents with depression experience weight loss/gain, engage in substance use (i.e., self-medication), have hypersomnia (i.e., excessive sleeping), and display self-harm behaviors (Kendall & Comer, 2010). All of these behaviors contribute to a sustained negative perception of self, the world, and the future. Table 18.2 presents the emotions, cognitions, and behaviors commonly associated with depression in youth.

As previously stated, youth with depression often have a difficult time restraining and managing negative perceptions of themselves, their world, and their future. Negative thinking contributes to impairments in their ability to regulate negative emotions (Joormann & Gotlib, 2010). Depressed youth often feel an array of emotions, including sadness, emotional lability, frustration, irritability, and guilt, and they often do not enjoy experiences that are typically pleasurable (i.e., anhedonia; Field et al., 2008; Kendall & Comer, 2010). Because of these emotional difficulties, emotion management and regulation constitute a central goal when counseling youth with depression (Stark, Streusand, Prerna, & Patel, 2012).

Furthermore, the concept of **emotion regulation** involves (a) restraining impulsive or inappropriate reactions to strong emotions (e.g., negative or positive), (b) being goal directed and not emotion or mood dependent, (c) having the ability to self-soothe strong emotions (i.e., calm or relieve emotional tension or distress),

Table 18.2 Emotions, Cognitions, and Behaviors Associated with Youth Depression		
Emotions Associated with Depression	Cognitions Associated with Depression	Behaviors Associated with Depression
• Depressed and/or irritable mood • Sadness • Anhedonia (i.e., inability to experience/feel pleasure) • Feelings of guilt • Feelings of being overwhelmed • Feelings of hopelessness • Feelings of frustration, agitation, anger, or excessive irritability	• Thoughts of being a failure (low self-worth) • Loss of interest in normal pleasurable activities • Thoughts of being inherently flawed • Thoughts of self-loathing • Wishing "I were a better person" • Wondering "Why can't I be better at things?" • Wondering "Why doesn't anyone like me?" • Thoughts of not measuring up to a standard (e.g., their own or someone else's expectation) • Thoughts of self-harm, death, and/or suicide • Thoughts that are negative or distorted (e.g., "I am worthless")	• Changes in sleep or appetite • Difficulty concentrating (e.g., forgetfulness) • Indecisiveness • Overreacting to criticism • Frequent crying or tantrums • Withdrawing from friends or family • Suicidal behaviors (i.e., suicide, attempted suicide, nonsuicidal self-injury) • Changes in academic performance (e.g., grades, getting into trouble at school)

and (d) having the ability to maintain attention in the "here and now" in the midst of strong emotions (Linehan, 2014; Trosper, Buzzella, Bennett, & Ehrenreich, 2009). Youth with depression may not know how to regulate their emotions to facilitate a more positive emotional experience. Depressed youth tend to use strategies and techniques that exacerbate interpersonal conflict and increase distress (e.g., verbal aggression, being argumentative; Stark et al., 2012).

In girls, depressive symptoms can also be manifested and associated with menstruation (APA, 2013); these adolescents experience a cyclical pattern of symptoms occurring most months in the last week of their menstrual cycle, all of which resolve in early to mid menses. These symptoms characterize premenstrual dysphoric disorder, which is a newly added depressive disorder in the *Diagnostic and Statistical Manual of Mental Disorders* (*DSM-5*; APA, 2013). Those with premenstrual dysphoric disorder often present with a range of symptoms, including sadness, feeling overwhelmed, emotional lability, persistent irritability, decreased interest in usual activities, difficulty concentrating, lack of energy, marked changes in appetite, changes in sleep, and physical discomfort (e.g., breast tenderness, headaches, bloating), all of which are associated with menstruation.

Finally, suicide is an important consideration when working with youth who have depression because some youth who have depression may have suicidal ideation (e.g., thoughts or preoccupation with suicide; Cash & Bridge, 2009). Counselors must constantly assess suicidal ideation in youth who are depressed and must consider hospitalization in some situations. (See Chapter 10 for assessment information on suicide in youth.) The following sections briefly discuss the types of depressive disorders and assessment considerations.

Types of Depressive Disorders

According to the *DSM-5* (APA, 2013), youth with depressive disorders can experience different symptoms. Yet, in most cases they have a depressed mood and/or loss of interest in normally pleasurable activities (e.g., sports, dance, school). They often experience intense and persistent sadness, loss of interest, changes in sleep and appetite, somatic complaints (e.g., aches, pains), school absenteeism, poor academic performance, and thoughts of death and/or suicide (APA, 2013). Table 18.3 presents a summary of the depressive disorders. Disruptive mood dysregulation disorder (DMDD), major depressive disorder, persistent depressive disorder, and premenstrual dysphoric disorder are depressive disorders that may affect youth.

Table 18.3 Summary of the *DSM-5* Depressive Disorders

DSM-5 Depressive Disorders	Overview	Brief Example
Disruptive Mood Dysregulation Disorder	Intense temper outbursts (which are out of proportion with a situation), with irritable, angry mood present between incidents most of the time	An 8-year-old boy frequently (i.e., at least three times a week) has verbal outbursts and tantrums that are excessive. Between these incidents, he seems tense and agitated, and his mother thinks he is always "keyed up."
Major Depressive Disorder	Intense, discrete periods of mood disturbances, often consisting of depressed mood, loss of interest, sleep issues, weight loss, fatigue, restlessness, and feelings of worthlessness, guilt, and/or death/suicide (*Meeting criteria currently or in past for a major depressive episode is required; see Figure 18.1 for mood episode criteria.*)	A 12-year-old girl, who used to be outgoing at school, has recently become withdrawn, sleeping excessively, crying, and complaining of not wanting to go to gymnastics or school or even hang out with friends. Her parents report that she often makes self-loathing remarks, such as "I'm so ugly" or "I'm a worthless loser." She was recently caught stealing liquor from her father's study.

(Continued)

Table 18.3	(Continued)	
DSM-5 Depressive Disorders	Overview	Brief Example
Persistent Depressive Disorder	Chronic or ongoing depression, which is a lower grade version of major depressive disorder and may be observed as depression or irritability, most of the time, on most days	A 16-year-old boy lacks diverse interests and motivation and frequently displays a flat affect. His parents report that he is consistently irritable and agitated in most of the interactions they observe. He spends a considerable amount of time on the Internet engaged in violent gaming.
Premenstrual Dysphoric Disorder	Depressive symptoms, irritability, and tension before menstruation, often diminishing after menses begins	A 12-year-old girl becomes considerably more "down in the dumps" every week before menstruation. During these times, she often cries excessively, feels out of control, binge eats, and verbally attacks others in her family and at school. These symptoms usually begin to subside a day after her period starts.

Note: Adapted from *Diagnostic and Statistical Manual of Mental Disorders* (5th ed.), by American Psychiatric Association (APA), 2013, Washington, DC: Author.

Assessment of Depressive Disorders

Procedures for assessing those who have depressive disorders vary and depend on age. Because younger children have more difficulty articulating emotions, thoughts, and past history, counselors will need to rely on parents to capture a complete diagnostic picture. Because of the subjective nature of depression, normal assessment procedures such as clinical interviews, behavioral observations, parent–teacher rating scales, and family assessments can sometimes present conflicting results (Kendall & Comer, 2010). Disagreement or conflicting results can often reflect differences in behavioral expectations relative to the setting or observers; some behaviors may occur in one setting or not another, or in front of one person and not another. Observers' perceptions will also influence the assessment of a youth's behavior, and each observer will have his or her personal biases, standards for evaluating the behavior, and understanding of age-appropriate behaviors (Lempp, de Lange, Radeloff, & Bachmann, 2012). Although more weight should be given to reliable, credible sources, multiple perspectives increase a counselor's understanding of the situation in context, thus leading to more accurate assessments of depressive disorders.

Although the clinical diagnostic interview is the most effective means to assess depressive disorders in youth, the use of inventories such as the Children's Depression Inventory (CDI; Kovacs, 1992) or the Beck Depression Inventory for Youth (BDI-Y; Beck, Beck, & Jolly, 2001) can provide more clinical clarity of depressive-related symptomology (Wilson, Smith, Monnin, & Wildman, 2016). In addition, the Hopelessness Scale for Children (HSC; Kazdin, Rodgers, & Colbus, 1986) is a measure that may be useful with youth who are depressed and present with suicidal ideation. Table 18.4 presents a summary of depressive assessment measures used for assessing depression in youth. Although parent–teacher rating forms capture the evaluator's perceptions of the child's behavior, they do not adequately measure the youth's unique experience of depression. Counselors will generally need to use self-report measures or clinical interviews because these are the most effective means for assessing youth's emotional distress levels (Kendall & Comer, 2010).

Counselors should never diagnose a young client with a depressive disorder without first conducting a thorough mania/hypomania assessment to rule out bipolar disorder. Many of the medications used to treat depressive disorders can cause manic/hypomanic symptoms to flare or worsen, and it is important that an accurate diagnosis be communicated so physicians can make appropriate medication-related decisions (Evan-Lacko, dosReis, Kastelic, Paula, & Steinwachs, 2010).

Table 18.4	Summary of Youth Depression Assessment Measures	
Assessment Measure	**Age Range**	**Overview of Assessment Measure**
Children's Depression Inventory (CDI)	7–17 years	The CDI is a 27-item youth-rated measure that assesses depression in children and adolescents for the previous 2-week period. This measure evaluates five factors (i.e., negative mood, interpersonal problems, ineffectiveness, anhedonia, and negative self-esteem) and has one item assessing suicidal ideation. For younger children or those with difficulties reading, the CDI can be administered orally. In addition, the CDI has parent (17 items) and teacher (12 item) versions. The CDI can be used for assessment and evaluation of progress in counseling.
Beck Depression Inventory for Youth (BDI-Y)	7–14 years	The BDI-Y is a 20-item youth-rated measure that identifies symptoms of depression in children and adolescents. This measure assesses feelings of sadness, guilt, negative thoughts (i.e., self, life, future), and disturbances (e.g., sleep, appetite). Written at a second-grade reading level, the BDI-Y can be used for assessment and evaluation of progress in counseling.
Hopelessness Scale for Children (HSC)	6–13 years	The HSC is a 17-item youth-rated measure that assesses the construct of hopelessness, which has been linked to depression and suicide. Generally speaking, higher levels of hopelessness tend to be an accurate predictor of suicide. Therefore, this measure has a great deal of clinical utility in exploring the extent of a young person's negative expectations for the future. The HSC is written at a first-grade reading level and can be used for assessment and evaluation of progress in counseling.

Because irritability is a central symptom of depression in youth, counselors should thoroughly assess irritability in situations where acting-out behaviors are present. For example, acting-out behaviors, especially in young boys, are often associated with behavior disorders (e.g., oppositional defiant disorder, attention-deficit/hyperactivity disorder [ADHD]); therefore, depression may be missed. This concept of **masked depression** is characterized by the presentation of acting-out behaviors, aggressive behaviors, school refusal, and/or somatic complaints, which are thought to conceal underlying feelings of depression; in addition, masked depression or acting-out behaviors have been associated with more overt presentations of depression in later years (Schneider, 2014). In some situations, trauma and trauma-related experiences (e.g., abuse, neglect) may also be associated with an inability to display behavioral control, regulate emotions, and maintain a positive self-concept (Briere & Lanktree, 2012). Therefore, counselors need to fully assess early acting-out behaviors because in certain situations these behaviors may be concealing depressive feelings, trauma-related experiences, or even depressive or trauma-related disorders.

Youth who are diagnosed with depressive disorders are significantly more prone to be diagnosed with another mental disorder (Field et al., 2008; Kendall & Comer, 2010), and counselors should take this into consideration. In particular, depressive and anxiety disorders are frequently comorbid because of the overlap of features—especially negative cognitions—between the two disorders (Kendall & Comer, 2010). The disorders most commonly comorbid in youth are disruptive behavior disorders (i.e., oppositional defiant disorder), anxiety disorders (i.e., social phobia, specific phobias, generalized), and ADHD (Small et al., 2008). In some situations, children and adolescents will attempt to self-medicate with substances (e.g., alcohol, marijuana), which can become a lethal combination (Field et al., 2008). These risk-taking behaviors warrant a counselor to assess suicidal ideation. Considering gender, boys tend to be at a greater risk for being diagnosed with a comorbid diagnosis (especially oppositional defiant disorder, substance related, and ADHD) than girls (Kendall & Comer, 2010). The following sections outline the symptoms, types, and assessment considerations of bipolar disorders.

Symptoms of Bipolar Disorders

Once considered to be rare or even nonexistent in children, the diagnosis of bipolar disorder has dramatically increased in recent years in both child and adolescent populations, even in the early childhood population (Luby & Belden, 2006; Parens & Johnston, 2010). The hallmark symptoms of bipolar disorder include **manic** or **hypomanic** symptoms, which involve extreme, dramatic changes in mood, energy, thinking, perceptions of reality, and behavior (e.g., poor judgment; excessive involvement in risky, pleasurable activities; APA, 2013). Younger children who have bipolar disorder typically present with fewer acute symptoms and better **interepisodic** (e.g., between manic and depressed periods) functioning than adolescents (Field et al., 2008). Adolescents experiencing their first manic phase may have especially dramatic symptoms, and they may require hospitalization to facilitate psychiatric stabilization (Kress & Paylo, 2015). Table 18.5 provides a summary of nine common manic/hypomanic features in youth.

Table 18.5	Nine Common Manic and Hypomanic Features of Childhood Bipolar Disorder with Examples
Manic/Hypomanic Feature	**Examples of Features Displayed in Young People**
1. Elevated or expansive mood	• Inflated self-esteem/grandiosity (overconfidence in self) • Excessive worrying about rejection and/or failure • Irritability • Oversensitivity to emotional and environmental triggers • Rage and/or explosive temper tantrums
2. Decreased need for sleep	• Feeling restless (fidgety) • Requiring minimal sleep
3. Talkative	• Pressured speech • Silliness or giddiness • Bossiness and/or overbearing
4. Flight of ideas or racing thoughts	• Racing or pressured thoughts • Lots of new ideas and plans • Paranoia and/or delusional thinking • Anxiety (e.g., social and/or separation anxiety)
5. Distractible	• Distractibility • Hyperactivity • Impulsivity (or making rash decisions without thinking of the consequences)
6. Increased goal-directed activities	• Hyperfocused, thus having difficulty making transitions to other activities • Lying and/or other manipulative behaviors relative to goal-directed activities • Obsessive thoughts and behaviors relative to goal-directed activities
7. High involvement in risky activities	• Risk-taking and/or dare-devil behaviors (decreased inhibition) • Aggressive and oppositional behaviors • Inappropriate or precocious sexual behavior • Destruction of property
8. Duration of features	*Mania:* Lasts at least 1 week and may require immediate hospitalization *Hypomania:* Lasting at least 4 days

(Continued)

Table 18.5	Nine Common Manic and Hypomanic Features of Childhood Bipolar Disorder with Examples (*Continued*)
Manic/Hypomanic Feature	**Examples of Features Displayed in Young People**
9. Intensity of features	*Mania:* Significant dysfunctionality or requiring hospitalization due to inability to keep self or others safe and/or the presence of psychotic symptoms
	Hypomania: Marked dysfunctionality or an elevated and persistent mood, not requiring hospitalization to keep self and others safe

Note: Adapted from *Diagnostic and Statistical Manual of Mental Disorders* (5th ed.), by American Psychiatric Association (APA), 2013, Washington, DC: Author; *The bipolar child: The definitive and reassuring guide to childhood's most misunderstood disorder* (3rd ed.), by D. S. Papolos & J. Papolos, 2006, New York, NY: Broadway Books.

During a manic/hypomanic phase, youth with bipolar disorder have unrealistic beliefs and thoughts about their own abilities, which in some cases may border on psychotic (APA, 2013). These exaggerated, grandiose beliefs are frequently centered on ideas of inflated self-worth, power, knowledge, identity, or a relationship to someone famous, and the youth believes these ideas regardless of reason, logic, or proof (Sadock, Sadock, & Ruiz, 2014). Grandiose, manic thought processes are illustrated in the following case:

> A 13-year-old girl who happens to be a good writer begins her seventh-grade English class with a declaration: "You all may not know this, but I'm sure you do, especially you, Mr. Johnson. Anyway, I'm a talented poet and writer. I do it all. I'm currently writing a masterpiece that Taylor Swift will eventually sing. I know she'll love it. I'm in the market for a publisher to publish my first of many science fiction and romantic novels. These are based on my life story."

Grandiose beliefs and thoughts can strain, if not fracture, relationships with classmates. Classmates may perceive youth who are manic as rude, conceited, and condescending. Manic thinking also impairs youth's ability to be productive and engage in good decision-making skills. In addition to grandiose thinking, youth with bipolar disorders are easily distracted and find it difficult to concentrate; racing thoughts, having multiple thoughts simultaneously, and jumping from thought to thought with little to no connections (i.e., flight of ideas) all contribute to concentration difficulties. In more severe cases, youth with bipolar disorder may manifest psychotic symptoms (i.e., hallucinations and delusions) and show difficulties with their reality-testing abilities (i.e., inability to distinguish between internal thoughts, feelings, and the external world). Bipolar with psychotic features is associated with poor overall levels of functioning (e.g., academic, social) and higher rates of comorbid psychopathology (Hua et al., 2011).

Youth with bipolar disorder have elevated moods, increased energy, and increased, yet unfocused, activity levels. Often, this population displays risky behaviors, inappropriate sexual remarks and behaviors, and in general, poor decision-making skills. Hypersexuality can also be a behavioral component of mania (Field et al., 2008). A 12-year-old boy, for example, may make overtly sexual comments to school personnel and students. He may attempt to rub up against others without their consent and even inappropriately touch himself in front of others. When hypersexuality is present, counselors need to carefully assess youth for history of physical and sexual abuse versus manic-induced hypersexuality (Field et al., 2008).

Elevated emotions, excessive energy, and increased activity all contribute to bipolar youth experiencing severe emotion regulation difficulties. Emotional dysregulation is an inability—even under normal circumstances that are not stressful—to regulate one's response to emotionally triggering stimuli, resulting in impulsive behavioral responses (Trosper et al., 2009). An inability to regulate emotional responses can manifest as excessive anger, verbal outbursts, destruction of property, and aggression toward self or others. The development of emotion regulation skills is a central goal when counseling youth who have bipolar disorder (Trosper et al., 2009).

In addition to struggles with emotion regulation, this population may present with an inappropriate affect, which often includes excessive giddiness and silliness. Inappropriate behaviors persist regardless of the seriousness of a situation, setting, or consequences. During manic episodes, youth often exhibit pressured speech (speaking faster than normal), a loud voice, and difficulty focusing (Kendall & Comer, 2010). To the listener, this type of speech seems accelerated, frenetic, and cluttered, and the youth jumps from topic to topic. It is difficult to follow the thoughts of youth who are manic; thus, it is difficult to engage with them. Counselors may need to be more direct than normal and use agreed-on hand signals to slow down young clients (e.g., putting up a hand to signal talking time) or use a talking stick. If the client is in the midst of a manic episode, techniques used to focus clients will likely not be helpful.

Types of Bipolar Disorders

Three mental disorders are recognized in the bipolar and related disorders section of the *DSM-5* (APA, 2013). Table 18.6 provides a summary of the disorders affecting children and adolescents in the category of bipolar disorders: bipolar I disorder, bipolar II disorder, and cyclothymic disorder.

Table 18.6 Summary of the *DSM-5* Bipolar and Related Disorders

DSM-5 Bipolar and Related Disorder	Overview	Brief Example
Bipolar I Disorder	Intense, severe shifts in affect, energy, activity, and ability to complete day-to-day tasks, often connected with major depressive episodes *(Must have at least once met the criteria for a manic episode; see Figure 18.1 for episode criteria.)*	A 15-year-old boy presents with elevated mood and excessive talking. He appears to be unable to sit down in the office and is easily distracted. He was referred because of inappropriate sexual remarks and behaviors he made in the hallway at school. He becomes more agitated and increasingly more hostile as the conversation continues. His thoughts and speech jump around, and he seems to have delusions of grandeur (e.g., "Stephen Hawking has nothing on me, and you want me to do this simple-ass math assignment? I'm going be rich, you ignoramus, and making the laws. What's wrong with you? I should be teaching this class—not you. You don't even know how to do your own taxes. Let me show you how to do that problem! How are you going to teach me anything?").
Bipolar II Disorder	Less-intense shifts in affect, energy, activity, and ability to complete day-to-day tasks compared to bipolar I disorder *(Must have at least once met the criteria for a major depressive and a hypomanic episode; see Figure 18.1 for episode criteria.)*	A 14-year-old girl presents as extremely despondent with a flat affect, expressing a loss in appetite and sleep and thoughts of suicide. Her mother reports that she seems to fluctuate in mood and energy. Sometimes she seems elated, driven, and active (i.e., taking on new hobbies and interests). Her mother appears confused by the presentation of these symptoms, saying the down periods are often 2–3 weeks and the up periods are never more than 5 days.
Cyclothymic Disorder	Less extreme chronic fluctuations of disturbances in affect, energy, activity, and ability to perform day-to-day tasks; disturbances do not reach the level or qualify as hypomania or major depressive episodes but involve hypomanic and depressive symptoms	An 8-year-old boy presents as irritable, jumpy, and energetic. His mother reports that he has "episodes" like this, during which he doesn't need much sleep. The up episodes only last a day or two. She said he was a much different child a few days ago, when he seemed dejected and sad and refused to go out and play with his friends. She also adds that it seems as if her son is often on an emotional roller coaster.

Note: Adapted from *Diagnostic and Statistical Manual of Mental Disorders* (5th ed.), by American Psychiatric Association (APA), 2013, Washington, DC: Author.

Assessment of Bipolar Disorders

Bipolar disorder is one of the more complex disorders to accurately identify and diagnose; it often goes unrecognized when present, yet it can also be overdiagnosed in some contexts (Youngstrom et al., 2009). Therefore, counselors need to complete a thorough assessment to ensure the criteria for manic/hypomanic episodes are met before diagnosing bipolar disorder (e.g., see Table 18.5). As previously stated, youth—especially younger children—have difficulty articulating emotions and thoughts and recalling past history, and counselors will generally need to rely on parents to capture a complete diagnostic picture.

Bipolar disorder in youth is frequently misdiagnosed, ascribed inaccurately, and missed altogether (Youngstrom et al., 2009). Often youth with bipolar disorder are misdiagnosed with ADHD, depression, borderline personality disorder, or posttraumatic stress disorder (Kendall & Comer, 2010; Singh, 2008). Care should be taken when diagnosing bipolar disorder, and counselors should garner multiple reports from different adults in the child's life before ascribing the diagnosis (Youngstrom et al., 2009). There are also assessment measures that can be used to aid counselors in accurately assessing bipolar disorders in youth. These assessment measures include the Youth Mania Rating Scale (YMRS; Young, Biggs, Ziegler, & Meyer, 1978), the Child Mania Rating Scale–Parent Version (CMRS-P; West, Celio, Henry, & Pavuluri, 2011), and the Child Bipolar Questionnaire (CBQ; Papolos, Hennen, Cockerham, Thode, & Younstrom, 2006). Table 18.7 presents a summary of bipolar assessment measures.

Because parents and family members influence children and adolescents, it is important to interview youth and parents separately when assessing for depressive and bipolar disorders. Parents may be able to accurately provide behavioral observation and past history, whereas the youth can share his or her internal, private experience (Kendall & Comer, 2010).

Clinical Toolbox 18.1

In the Pearson etext, click here to view a list of questions counselors should ask themselves and/or parents to assess for depressive/bipolar disorders.

A thorough youth assessment involves consideration of differential diagnoses (i.e., distinguishing one disorder from another). In assessing youth for bipolar disorders, counselors will need to differentiate bipolar disorder from DMDD. DMDD is a new diagnosis in the *DSM-5* (APA, 2013) that was developed and included to address the misdiagnosis or overdiagnosis of bipolar disorder in children (Leibenluft, 2011; Margulies,

Table 18.7   Summary of Bipolar Assessment Measures

Assessment Measure	Age Range	Overview of Assessment Measure
Youth Mania Rating Scale (YMRS)	5–17 years	The YMRS is an 11-item client-rated measure that assesses the severity of manic symptoms over the last 48 hours. The measure assesses elevated mood, increased activity, sexual interest, sleep, irritability, speech, language, aggressive behaviors, appearance, and insight. A parent version (P-YMRS) has also been created for use with younger children (5–12 years old).
Child Mania Rating Scale–Parent Version (CMRS-P)	8–18 years	The CMRS-P is a 21-item parent-rated measure assessing mania symptoms over the past month. This measure also assesses psychotic symptoms (e.g., hearing voices that nobody else can hear, seeing things that nobody else can see).
Child Bipolar Questionnaire (CBQ)	5–17 years	The CBQ is a 65-item counselor- or parent-rated measure that assesses for bipolar disorders, as well as other comorbid disorders (i.e., ADHD, generalized anxiety disorder, major depressive disorder). In addition, this measure reports the frequency and severity of symptomology rather than only the presence or absence of symptoms.

Weintraub, Basile, Grover, & Carlson, 2012). DMDD applies to children who have chronically unstable moods, heightened irritability, and intense and disruptive behaviors (e.g., temper tantrums, verbal outbursts, or physical aggression three or more times in a given week over a 12-month period) that are out of proportion to their situational stressors (APA, 2013). When children with DMDD are not acting out verbally or aggressively, they are often perceived as being irritable, angry, or sad (APA, 2013). Therefore, when distinguishing DMDD from bipolar disorders in youth, counselors need to evaluate if a manic/hypomanic episode is or has ever been present and if these symptoms happen in discrete periods of time (i.e., episodic in nature; Leibenluft, 2011).

In addition, there is a high occurrence of comorbid (i.e., co-occurring) disorders in youth diagnosed with bipolar disorders, and this co-occurrence should be assessed for (Field et al., 2008; Singh, 2008). Some children who are diagnosed with bipolar disorders are also diagnosed with ADHD, substance use, anxiety, and/or depressive disorders (APA, 2013; Singh, 2008). Figure 18.2 provides a decision-making flow chart for diagnosing bipolar-related disorders in youth.

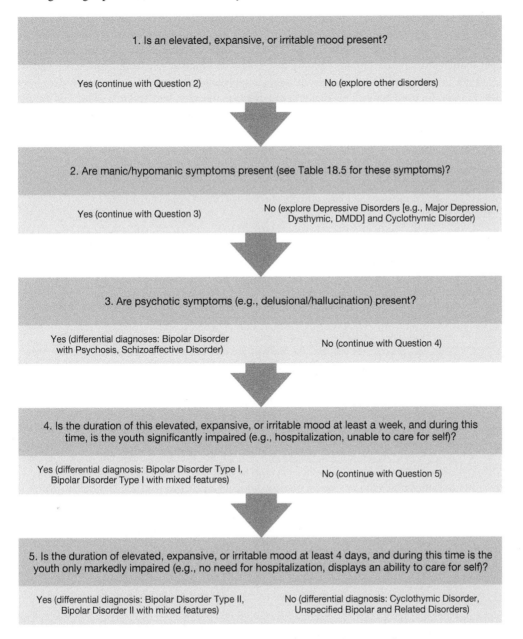

FIGURE 18.2 Decision-Making Flow Chart for Bipolar-Related Disorders in Youth

COUNSELING INTERVENTIONS

Considerable research exists on the efficacy of counseling with youth who have depressive disorders. In particular, cognitive behavioral therapy (CBT) used in the context of a strong counseling relationship appears to be the most effective counseling approach for use with this population (Hofmann, Asnaani, Vonk, Sawyer, & Fang, 2012; Klein, Jacobs, & Reinecke, 2007). In clinical trials, CBT was as effective as treatments in which only medication was used (DeRubeis et al., 2005; Hofmann et al., 2012). Numerous experts suggest that medication should only be used in conjunction with counseling when treating youth who have depression (Sommers-Flanagan & Campbell, 2009). In addition to individual CBT formats, group CBT formats are effective, especially with adolescents who have depression (Clarke & DeBar, 2010).

Although CBT can be a stand-alone approach with youth who have mild to moderate depression, it is not sufficient for treating bipolar disorder, and medications are generally required (Hofmann et al., 2012). Once manic symptoms are stabilized through the use of medication, CBT can address symptoms, thus delaying—and in some cases preventing—symptom relapses (Lam, Burbeck, Wright, & Pilling, 2009).

Although CBT is the most researched counseling approach used with this population, other effective counseling options exist. Behavioral activation therapy (BAT), interpersonal therapy, and pharmacotherapy are all prominent therapeutic approaches for treating depression in youth (Chartier & Provencher, 2013; Kress & Paylo, 2015). In addition to CBT, numerous adjunct approaches exist for treating youth who have bipolar disorder. Family-focused treatment, dialectical behavior therapy, and Interpersonal and Social Rhythm Therapy (IPSRT) all demonstrate positive counseling outcomes when used in conjunction with pharmacotherapy (West & Pavuluri, 2009). Table 18.8 presents a summary of the commonly used treatment approaches for depressed and bipolar youth.

Table 18.8	Effective Counseling Approaches for Use with Youth Who Have Depressive and Bipolar Disorders
Approach	**Overview**
Cognitive behavioral therapy (CBT; Friedberg, McClure, & Garcia, 2009; Stark et al., 2012)	Depressed youth often ruminate and fixate on negative thoughts of self, their world, and their future. CBT focuses on altering clients' thoughts, which in turn has an impact on their depressive symptoms, affect, and behavior. CBT holds that if youth change their maladaptive thinking, their affect and behaviors will change. CBT aims to help youth to identify, challenge, and modify their thoughts, beliefs, and assumptions, thus facilitating more adaptive thought processes. This approach teaches youth to recognize and manage their reactions to depressive symptoms via the use of cognitive and behavioral strategies.
Behavioral activation therapy (BAT; Chartier & Provencher, 2013)	Youth with depressive symptoms cease to engage in activities because of a lack of positive reinforcement and a belief that the activities will not be enjoyable. They often isolate from others and fail to engage in activities that could bring them pleasure. BAT is a type of behavior therapy that involves altering clients' behavior, which in turn has an impact on their depressive symptoms, affect, and thoughts. By engaging in pleasurable activities and connecting that these activities make one feel better, clients are behaviorally activated and come to engage in more pleasurable activities that have an impact on their affect in a positive way. Thus, this change in affect decreases their depression.
Interpersonal therapy (IPT; Jacobson & Mufson, 2010)	IPT is a brief psychodynamic approach that conceptualizes depression as being rooted in—and linked with—interpersonal patterns and concerns. This approach attempts to enhance clients' social supports, decrease their interpersonal stress, facilitate the processing of emotions, and improve their interpersonal skills. Symptom relief often can be accomplished by focusing on relationship development and shifts, depressive symptoms, and the connection between affect and interpersonal factors.

(Continued)

Table 18.8	(Continued)
Approach	**Overview**
Interpersonal and Social Rhythm Therapy (IPSRT; Hlastala, Kotler, McClellan, & McCauley, 2010).	IPSRT is a behavioral therapy approach that aids clients with bipolar disorders in recognizing how their everyday actions (e.g., sleeping, eating, socializing, exercise patterns) can be altered to avoid an escalation of symptoms. This approach focuses on how daily activities can hinder or enhance stabilization and relapse prevention. Breaking down and charting a young client's normal 24-hour day, and identifying areas where positive changes can be implemented, can help youth—and their families—to better structure their days to regulate affect and avoid symptom relapse.
Family-focused treatment (Miklowitz et al., 2008)	Family-focused treatment is a 9-month, 21-session counseling approach that involves psychoeducation on bipolar disorder for the family, encouraging adherence to pharmacotherapy, and teaching, identifying, and using relapse-prevention skills (Miklowitz et al., 2008). This approach teaches communication skills (e.g., active listening, providing positive feedback and constructive criticism) and problem-solving skills (e.g., identifying, generating, and implementing solutions), and it involves the whole family.
Dialectical behavior therapy (Harvey & Rathbone, 2013)	DBT is a CBT approach that stresses the importance of youth taking a proactive approach to their depression and learning the skills they need to tolerate, cope with, and regulate their intense negative emotions. DBT involves the development of mindfulness, distress tolerance, interpersonal effectiveness, and emotion regulation skills.

INTEGRATED TREATMENT COMPONENTS WITH YOUTH WHO HAVE DEPRESSIVE AND BIPOLAR DISORDERS

When counseling youth who have depressive and/or bipolar disorders and are in the stabilization and maintenance phases of counseling (i.e., they are psychiatrically stabilized), treatment generally addresses four areas: (a) affective education, (b) coping and problem-solving skills, (c) cognitive restructuring, and (d) developing positive beliefs and feelings about oneself (Stark, Streusand, Krumholz, & Patel, 2010). After building a strong counseling working alliance, counselors help youth to identify how their emotions, thoughts, and behaviors relate, and then move to learning and applying coping and problem-solving skills within and then outside sessions. In addition, parent training is often an essential component of counseling, and this involves the development of effective communication and conflict resolution skills, positive behavior management of the child's behaviors, effective family problem-solving abilities, and altering behaviors that may maintain the youth's depressive core beliefs or symptoms (Stark et al., 2010).

Bipolar treatment is tailored to the stage of the disorder, with the stages being (a) acute (i.e., initial period of manic or depressive symptoms), (b) stabilization (i.e., 2–6 months after acute symptoms have resolved), and (c) maintenance (i.e., prevention period with an awareness to possible relapse; Miklowitz, 2008; Miklowitz et al., 2008). Table 18.9 provides the treatment goals and the treatment components that relate to each of the phases of depressive and bipolar disorders.

The following sections outline the essential counseling components associated with the treatment of depressive and bipolar disorders in youth. Individual components may be integrated into clients' counseling, and the components used will depend on the nature of the setting where the youth is seen, the counselor's theoretical orientation, and the needs of the client and family. The components of an integrated, comprehensive approach to counseling these populations include psychoeducation (affective education), cognitive restructuring, problem-solving approaches, activity scheduling, family involvement, and psychopharmacotherapy. Because of the high comorbidity between anxiety and depression, counselors might also consider integrating some of the previously discussed components (i.e., relaxation training, social skills training, cognitive skills training, establishing a contingent reinforcement plan, and exposure-based activities) from

Table 18.9	Phases, Goals, and Treatment Components Associated with Depressive and Bipolar Disorders	
Phase of the Disorder	**Goals**	**Treatment Components**
Acute	Medication referral; hospitalization (when a danger to self or others); assessment; relationship building; and work toward affect stability	Pharmacotherapy Client safety Family engagement
Stabilization	Awareness and education of depressive and/or bipolar disorder; symptoms, patterns, and signs of mood cycles/relapse; self-care interventions; stress-management training; and challenging maladaptive cognitions	Pharmacotherapy Psychoeducation (affective education) Relaxation training (if needed, to help with self-soothing) Structured scheduling (Interpersonal and Social Rhythm Therapy) Problem solving Activity scheduling Cognitive restructuring (if needed) Family involvement
Maintenance	Resolving intrapersonal and interpersonal difficulties and relapse prevention planning	Pharmacotherapy Family involvement

Chapter 17 when counseling this population. What follows is a brief explanation of each of the components that are important when counseling this population.

Psychoeducation (Affective Education)

Psychoeducation—or, when used in reference to depressive and bipolar disorders, affective education—involves educating and empowering youth and their families on the impacts and patterns of depressive and bipolar issues and is associated with more positive outcomes (Smith, Jones, & Simpson, 2010). Affective education is a foundational component for working with the depressive and bipolar-related disorders in youth (Smith et al., 2010; Stark et al., 2010). This intervention increases young clients' awareness of their emotions and cognitions (i.e., thoughts, beliefs, and attitudes) and how these influences have an impact on their behaviors (Stark et al., 2010). Through psychoeducation, young clients can increase their understanding and awareness of their disorder and eventually develop their ability to function more optimally by self-regulating their emotions. An awareness of their affective processes and how they can identify, manage, and influence these processes is an important part of counseling.

Therefore, the focus of affective education is for youth to recognize their emotions and better understand how those emotions affect their thoughts and eventually their behaviors. Young clients ideally will realize that it is because of their negative emotions that they distance themselves from others, and not the other way around.

When counseling younger children, counselors need to use creative approaches and introduce different mediums (e.g., writing, drawing, play) to help youth to develop an awareness of their emotional experiences and affective education concepts. One creative way to help younger children to identify and become more aware of these emotion–mind connections is to empower them to become *emotional detectives* (Stark et al., 2010). This concept requires youth to explore what is happening in their body (i.e., "How is my body reacting?"), their brain (i.e., "What am I thinking?"), and their behaviors (i.e., "What am I doing?"; Stark et al., 2010). By helping youth to connect the internal and external cues (e.g., thoughts, behaviors) of emotions, counselors can help them to *catch* the link between emotions, thoughts, and behaviors, and this lays the foundation for youth to engage in self-monitoring, self-initiating, and self-regulating skills (e.g., coping, problem solving, cognitive skills) in future situations. Figure 18.3 provides

Activity Overview

The counselor reads a scenario in which a magic key opens a door to "happiness." The client is instructed to draw what he or she imagines would be found behind his or her door of happiness. The drawing can represent numerous feelings, wishes, dreams, and hopes the child may be harboring, and it will identify the issues to address throughout the counseling process.

Activity Objectives

The goal of this activity is to increase awareness of the key issues to address with the client and to facilitate a meaningful dialogue concerning these issues.

Directions

1. Read the following to the client:

   "Imagine you are at the front door of a giant beautiful castle. You turn the handle to enter, and it is unlocked. When you step inside, you find a key on the floor that has your name engraved on it. You decide that this key must be special and magical, and you begin to wander through the castle to find what door this key belongs to. You walk the halls and the floors of the castle, and it seems that the key does not work for any door, until you reach the fourth and final floor. You turn your magic key into the lock, and it opens. Because this is a magic key, it only opens this door when you turn the key. Behind this door, you will see the one thing money cannot buy that leads you to happiness. What do you see in this room? What is one thing that has been missing to make you happy? Take your time to think of a clear picture of what this one thing is, and please draw it as best you can.

2. Allow the client ample time to draw.
3. When the client is finished, ask the client to explain what he or she drew.

Process Questions

1. Can you talk about why you drew this as the one thing you need to be happy?
2. What are some other things you thought about drawing?
3. What are some things you have right now that make you happy?

Process Questions for Parent/Caregiver

1. What was this activity like for you?
2. What was the easiest part of this activity? What was the hardest part of this activity?
3. Have you ever talked about this "one thing" in session?

FIGURE 18.3   The Magic Door to Happiness Activity

an activity that can be used to increase young people's awareness of their own happiness and potential areas of exploration in counseling.

Psychoeducation is flexible, and it can be used individually, in a group setting, and/or in family formats. Counselors need to use a wide range of media (e.g., written, audio, video, interactive) to present information in a thoughtful, concise, developmentally appropriate, and engaging manner. Psychoeducation with youth who have bipolar disorders may cover topics such as medication management, bipolar patterns and cycles, signs of relapse, self-care (i.e., diet, exercise, sleep, minimal use of caffeine and alcohol), stress management, identification of stressors, and the value of self-monitoring (e.g., mood and sleep, activity, substance use, suicide ideation).

Cognitive Restructuring

Youth who have depressive and bipolar disorders often interpret and think about themselves and the events around them in a negative way. Fixating on their deficiencies, this population tends to have thoughts of worthlessness, helplessness, and hopelessness. Unpleasant experiences, interactions, and events are often attributed to their being less competent, less resourceful, and less worthy of being happy, accepted, or valued than others. Therefore, identifying, challenging, and replacing these thoughts is essential when counseling those who have depressive and bipolar disorders (Field et al., 2008). In Chapter 17, CBT was discussed related to anxiety, as well as the common cognitive distortions and the ways self-talk and thought records can be used in counseling. When counseling youth with depressive or bipolar disorders, counselors can pull on the general CBT techniques discussed in Chapter 17 in relation to anxiety. This section focuses on the process of cognitive restructuring (or cognitive reframing), a specific CBT technique in cognitive skills training.

Cognitive restructuring is the systematic identification and replacement of distorted cognitions with more positive, adaptive beliefs. The first step in cognitive restructuring is identifying cognitive distortions (e.g., see Chapter 17: Table 17.10). The following application highlights a 13-year-old girl's cognitive distortions:

COUNSELOR: So, you said earlier that, although you like school, recently it's been more difficult. What's happening at school that's making it difficult?

YOUTH: Other kids just don't like me. I'm different from everyone else. It's like there's something wrong with me. I mean, who wants to be friends with a loser like me?

The girl's cognitive distortions are beginning to present (i.e., Lame Blaming [labeling] and Too Fast Forward [jumping to negative conclusions]). Using cognitive restructuring, the counselor would attempt to help the client to identify her cognitive distortions and to evaluate the evidence of her claim. She will generate new, positive statements about herself.

COUNSELOR: "Kids don't like me" and "I'm a loser"—these are strong statements. Do they say this to you?

YOUTH: No, but I really am a loser. I know they all think it, too.

COUNSELOR: Sometimes what we think about ourselves or to ourselves is different from what others think. Talk to me more about what you said: "I really am a loser." Let's take a look at if that is what they think or if that is what you think they think.

Counselors need to help youth to identify cognitive distortions and to flesh out their interpretations and assumptions. Moving forward, the counselor will need to have the client evaluate the proof of her claim (i.e., "I really am a loser"). In addressing the proof of the client's claim, the counselor should progress through the following steps: (a) ask "What is the evidence that supports that statement?"; (b) ask "Could there be another way to look at it?"; (c) ask "What if this happened to someone else? What would you think of him or her?"; and (d) engage in a behavioral experiment (i.e., testing the validity of one's beliefs through an experiment). Writing out a list of evidence that supports and refutes the distortions may help older children and adolescents to visualize and challenge their maladaptive cognitions. In situations with younger children, counselors may need to be more creative and use alternative mediums (e.g., drawing, painting, puppets, clay) to identify and challenge a child's dysfunctional or distorted thoughts.

For example, a counselor could have a child participate in a drawing activity called Change the Channel. This activity involves using two paper images of blank television screens. In the first screen, the client draws how this channel (e.g., his or her feelings, thoughts, situation) feels in his or her head. Next, the counselor asks the child to consider *changing the channel* (e.g., "What might this new channel look like?"). In the second television screen, the counselor asks the child to change the channel to a calmer, more positive channel. The child draws what this new channel looks like in his or her head. As a follow-up to this activity, the counselor can discuss how the child possesses the ability to affect his or her thoughts by changing the channel in his or her head.

Allowing youth to conduct a behavioral experiment is an effective way of altering their thinking. A behavioral experiment is an experiential activity used to test the validity of the client's beliefs or a new belief, or to gather more information about an existing maladaptive cognition. In order for a behavioral experiment to be successful, the counselor must make the youth aware of the maladaptive cognition, establish enough evidence to consider refuting or supporting the thought or cognition, and devise a BAT to test the validity of the cognition or thought (Stark et al., 2012).

COUNSELOR: So, you said that the kids at school don't like you and they think you're a loser. You said you're 100 percent sure on this—right? (*She nods her head*). Let's test out that thought with an experiment. What would be the evidence that those kids actually like you?

YOUTH: Well, I guess at least a few of them would sit with me at lunch.

COUNSELOR: Okay. But how about some other things that these kids might do to tell you they like you. What if they said hi to you, smiled at you, stood by you, opened a door for you, and talked with you—even about school stuff. Let's list all these things and anything else we can come up with on this piece of paper. I'd then like you to mark a line next to each time one of these things actually occurs during the school day. *(She nods her head.)* Let's have you rewrite this list and check the list each day at school. Then, we'll review the results next week.

The ultimate intention of cognitive restructuring is to alter the youth's negative self-evaluation. As youth are challenged to evaluate their thoughts, their thinking will shift, and they will become more aware of their positive attributes and skills, reduce negative self-talk, generate more accurate and positive statements, and challenge unrealistic and/or dysfunctional self-statements (Kress & Paylo, 2015). Table 18.10 provides a summary of cognitive restructuring activities aimed at increasing clients' ability to evaluate and substitute these negative thoughts with more positive ones.

Problem-Solving Approaches

Problem solving is a foundational component to working with youth who are depressed (Stark et al., 2010). Depressed youth's negative thinking often distracts them and impairs their problem-solving endeavors. In many cases, depressed youth are so overwhelmed by their emotions, thoughts, and past experiences that they feel immobilized and hopeless. Problem-solving approaches can train youth to meet everyday challenges on their own, thus empowering them and improving their affect. Problem-solving approaches can enhance social competence and decrease the psychological distress of youth who have depressive and bipolar disorders (Bell & D'Zurilla, 2009; Malouff, Thorsteinsson, & Schutte, 2007).

Table 18.10	Cognitive Restructuring Activities
Title	**Description**
Positive Thinking Cards	Create or purchase index cards. Ask the client to write all his or her negative thoughts on them, placing each one on a separate index card. Next, ask the client to flip over each card and replace that thought with a more accurate, positive thought. Have the client review and use the cards inside sessions initially, and then move to using them outside sessions.
An Advice Letter	Ask the client to think about what words or advice he or she might have for another youth experiencing depression. Next, ask the client to construct a letter to this individual with advice on what he or she has learned and how that individual can combat negative thoughts. Assist the client in sharing with the fictitious youth the successes and struggles associated with changing negative thinking.
Positive Self-Talk Shield	Ask the client to draw and then cut out a shield from a piece of construction paper. Next, ask the client to write and/or draw positive self-talk messages in the middle of the shield (i.e., messages that can be used to combat negative thinking). Examples might include "I can do this"; "I believe in myself"; "I am strong"; and "I know I am important and valuable." Finally, ask the client to write positive messages he or she hears from others that might support his or her positive thinking (e.g., "I love you"; "I am proud of you"; "You are so important to me"). Discuss how the client can use this shield to combat negative thinking.
My Comic Strip	Ask the client to draw a recent time when he or she felt depressed, agitated, or angry. Ask the client to consider his or her behaviors and thoughts and the people who were around at the time. After the client completes and discusses this comic strip, ask the client to consider a new way of responding to his or her emotions, thoughts, or feelings. Instruct the client to construct a comic strip depicting his or her ability to alter his or her situation and therefore alter his or her thoughts, feelings, and emotions.

Clinical Toolbox 18.2

In the Pearson etext, click here to view an activity that can be used to help youth to develop self-understanding and awareness of emotions and behaviors.

The problem-solving model discussed in Chapter 17 (i.e., define the problem; generate ways to address the problem; make an educated decision, choice, or course of action based on the information you have; and implement a solution and evaluation; Bell & D'Zurilla, 2009) can be useful with this population, but the inclusion of another step—addressing youth apprehension and pessimism—is helpful when working with youth with depression (Stark et al., 2012). Counselors can integrate a focus on pessimism and apprehension into the *generate ways to address the problem* stage (i.e., the second stage) of the model. Counselors generally need to be active and directive in helping young clients with depression to identify alternative solutions during this second stage. Encouraging clients to brainstorm and refrain from judging the feasibility of various solutions may be a helpful approach when generating alternatives (Stark et al., 2012). Consider the following example of a 12-year-old boy who is having a difficult time generating alternative solutions for a peer problem.

COUNSELOR: What are some things you can do when Tommy starts trying to talk with you during class?

YOUTH: I don't know. (*Pause*) No, I really don't know.

COUNSELOR: Remember, at this point there are no bad ideas. We're just brainstorming your options. Sit with it for a minute.

YOUTH: Well, I guess I could ignore him, but he is pretty annoying and usually keeps it up. So, I guess I could just crack him in his face. I bet he'd stop then.

COUNSELOR: So ignoring or hitting. What other options do you have?

YOUTH: I just don't know.

COUNSELOR: What do other kids do when Tommy annoys them?

YOUTH: They tell the teacher, but I'm not doing that. My dad always says "Snitches get stitches!"

COUNSELOR: Okay. So, you are not going to tell the teacher. Let's keep looking for other options. I'm wondering about last week and how you dealt with your cousin. He was saying all kinds of things to you, and it was making you angry. Right? (*He nods his head.*) You felt pretty bad about yourself? (*He nods again.*) What did you do in that situation?

YOUTH: You mean when I told him how it was? That he was bothering me, and I wasn't going to hang out with him if he was going to be like that?

COUNSELOR: Exactly! That is what I'm talking about. So another option is to just lay out the consequences with Tommy: "Tommy if you keep doing this, I'm not going to hang out with you."

This client is slow in providing potential solutions, and in some cases he quickly discards any possible solutions; this scenario is fairly typical when counseling youth. The counselor can help the client to compile all potential solutions without evaluating them, pulling out alternative solutions that the client is unaware of or unable to connect with. After ample solutions are generated, the counselor can help the client to progress through the additional steps in the problem-solving model.

With younger children, the problem-solving process should be more simplistic. It may be helpful to have a child progress through the If-Then-But activity (Geldard, Geldard, & Yin Foo, 2013). The If-Then-But activity aids the child in quickly exploring problems or situations and the consequences or end result of his or her behaviors. Consider the following example of 6-year-old boy who is having a difficult time dealing with a peer problem:

COUNSELOR: Remember, we can talk about this situation using the If-Then-But activity. Let's think about Andy, that kid who says mean things to you at school. So, if he says something mean to you, what will you do?

YOUTH: Maybe I'll just be mean right back to him.

COUNSELOR: Okay, then what might happen?

YOUTH: Then I'd feel better.

COUNSELOR: But?

YOUTH: But then he'd probably feel mad and do it even more.

COUNSELOR: Okay, let's go through this again with a different solution, and we'll see how it turns out.

Young clients can repeat this process, evaluating the potential solutions and discarding solutions that do not help them to reach their desired end. This problem-solving process can aid youth in developing and increasing their ability to better meet everyday challenges, thus empowering them and improving their affect.

Activity Scheduling

Central features of depression are withdrawal and inactivity. Behavioral Activation Therapy, or BAT, is an approach or tool that can help youth to fight passivity, withdrawal, and stagnation and re-engage in pleasurable and desirable activities (Chu, Colognori, Weissman, & Bannon, 2009; Stark et al., 2012). **Activity scheduling** is based on the assumption that if life stressors can have a negative impact on affect, then normal, predictable, or planned experiences can have a positive impact on affect. Youth may have resistance to this intervention because it counters this population's tendency to withdraw from everyday living (e.g., socializing, participating in activities). The central premise of activity scheduling is that by increasing the client's engagement in desirable or pleasurable activities, the youth will experience a more positive affect. Changes in affect ideally will affect their thinking and perceptions (e.g., the world is an enjoyable place) and result in diminished depressive symptoms.

The first step in BAT is identifying the client's perceptions of the activities that are still—or have historically been—pleasurable. Youth with depression will often indicate they find little enjoyment in any activities. It can be helpful to invite clients to consider past activities they have found enjoyable and to offer potential activity suggestions that are age appropriate and align with the youth's interests. By working together with the youth—and maybe his or her family—the counselor can construct a comprehensive list of potentially enjoyable activities. These activities can then be listed and scheduled on an activity sheet. Between sessions, clients can self-manage and self-monitor their engagement in the identified activities; they can indicate if they participated and, if so, what their mood was post participation. They can bring these documents to their counseling sessions for review with the counselor. Documenting these activities and the accompanying reactions generally highlights for clients that participation in pleasurable activities improves their energy level, positive affective states, and overall well-being.

Clinical Toolbox 18.3

In the Pearson etext, click here to view an example of a completed and blank activity scheduling sheet.

The following questions might be asked to process the between-session application of activity scheduling:

- What was it like doing the different activities this week?
- What activity did you most enjoy?
- What activity did you least enjoy?
- What activities should we add to the list?
- When you think about the connection between the activities and how you felt, what stands out for you?

Another technique for self-monitoring is to have a young client use a 24-hour social rhythm worksheet. The use of such worksheets can reveal sleeping, eating, interacting, and mood patterns that occur throughout a given day. Counselors can use these worksheets to help youth and families to create a balanced, structured schedule, which helps to regulate youth's sleeping, eating, and activity levels. By creating and attempting to maintain a balanced, structured daily schedule consisting of wake time, active time, mealtime, and bedtime, youth can create regular routines and have more stable moods, thoughts, and behaviors.

Clinical Toolbox 18.4

In the Pearson etext, click here to view an example of a 24-hour self-monitoring worksheet.

Family Involvement

Parent and family involvement in the counseling process creates a vital link between the awareness, knowledge, and skills acquired in counseling sessions and the youth's natural environments (Stark et al., 2012). Parent and family involvement helps to (a) increase support for the individual counseling with the youth, (b) facilitate the development of improved self-evaluation and cognitive skills, (c) encourage the use of all skills outside counseling sessions, and (d) alter environmental and family structures and events that may be contributing to the cognitive, interpersonal, and family disturbances that underlie depressive and bipolar symptoms (Stark et al., 2012). For example, families often need assistance in developing communication skills. Counselors can teach families how to communicate more effectively. Effective communication includes expressing positive feelings, using active listening, making positive requests to alter or change behaviors, and appropriately expressing negative feelings about specific behaviors or situations.

Parent training often becomes a central component of a comprehensive approach when working with youth with depressive and bipolar disorders. Parent training ideally consists of a compilation of education, communication, and conflict resolution skills, behavior management skills, problem-solving skills, and identification of any behaviors that may maintain depressive and bipolar core beliefs or symptoms (Stark et al., 2010). In some situations, in particular with bipolar youth, education is essential in addressing the high comorbidity of bipolar disorder with other mental health diagnoses such as anxiety disorders, ADHD, and substance use disorders. For example, counselors can discuss the destabilizing effect substance use and abuse can have on depressive and bipolar symptoms. In other cases, parent and family training may center more on the family environment, including the family's ability to integrate positive behavior management, reduce conflict, increase the family decision-making process, and improve the youth's self-esteem. In some cases, it may focus on parent skills and the parent's reactions to the youth's symptoms in the home.

Clinical Toolbox 18.5

In the Pearson etext, click here to view a list of tips that can be shared about parenting youth who have bipolar disorder.

Families and parents of youth who have depressive and bipolar disorder may fail to engage in fun recreational activities (Stark et al., 2012). Assigning families to engage in activities and events that are fun can be a good way for them to work together on problem-solving skills and have positive interactions that insulate their child against mood symptoms. Family members might brainstorm and select a weekly activity that they all agree will be enjoyable. In addition, counselors should invite parents to monitor the impact of activities on their family and child—as done with activity scheduling—and use this information to inform their decisions regarding scheduling future activities.

Psychopharmacotherapy

Research supports the use of medications with youth who have depressive and bipolar disorders, specifically selective serotonin reuptake inhibitors (SSRIs) for depression, and mood stabilizers (e.g., lithium), atypical antipsychotics (e.g., risperidone, aripiprazole), and anticonvulsants (i.e., lamotrigine, valproic acid, divalproex sodium) for youth with bipolar disorder (Field et al., 2008; Kendall & Comer, 2010; McKeage, 2014; Pavuluri, West, Hill, Jindal, & Sweeney, 2009). However, it should be noted that the U.S. Food and Drug Administration (FDA) has only approved lithium, risperidone, and aripiprazole to treat bipolar disorder in youth, yet anticonvulsants (e.g., lamotrigine) do appear to be clinically useful with certain bipolar youth (Pavuluri et al., 2009). Although antidepressants are often used in conjunction with other bipolar medications (e.g., mood stabilizers, atypical antipsychotics, anticonvulsants), use of antidepressants exclusively with bipolar youth is not recommended because they can induce manic symptoms (Evan-Lacko et al., 2010).

Medication is essential and typically required to address the acute symptoms of severe depression and bipolar disorders (AACAP, 2007; Evan-Lacko et al., 2010). Medication should always be used in conjunction with counseling-based interventions when counseling youth with depressive and bipolar disorders (Hofmann et al., 2012).

Although the use of antidepressants has been associated with the reduction of depressive symptoms, this group of medications has also been associated with an increased risk of suicidality (i.e., suicidal thoughts and behaviors) in adolescents (AACAP, 2007; Barbui, Esposito, & Cipriani, 2009). In fact, the FDA requires a "black box" warning label be added to all antidepressants, thus highlighting this increased risk. Therefore, counselors and mental health professionals must consistently evaluate suicidal ideation, especially with youth who are depressed and taking antidepressant medication because increased suicidality is a possibility.

Medication compliance is an important treatment goal with all youth who take psychotropic medication, but especially with youth with bipolar and depressive disorders. Counselors can play an important role in working with the psychiatrist/physician and the young client and his or her family to construct a plan that helps the young client to successfully take his or her medication as prescribed. Table 18.11 presents the types and side effects of medications commonly used to treat depressive and bipolar youth.

Although counselors' scope of practice does not include prescribing these medications, they often are in a unique position to recognize negative side effects that may warrant collaboration or consultation with other medical professionals. For example, if a client has an increase in suicidal ideation while taking a newly prescribed SSRI, then counselors need to seek supervision and consultation with other medical professionals (e.g., psychiatrist, family physician).

Table 18.11 Types and Side Effects of Medications Commonly Used to Treat Youth Who Have Depressive and Bipolar Disorders

Medication Class	Selective Serotonin Reuptake Inhibitors (SSRIs)	Mood Stabilizers	Atypical Antipsychotics	Anticonvulsants
Medications	• Fluoxetine (Prozac) • Sertraline (Zoloft) • Paroxetine (Paxil) • Citalopram (Celexa) • Escitalopram (Lexapro)	• Lithium (Eskalith)	• Risperidone (Risperdal) • Aripiprazole (Abilify)	• Lamotrigine (Lamictal) • Valproic acid or divalproex sodium (Depakote)
Side effects of medication	• Headache • Nausea • Agitation • Sleeplessness or drowsiness • Sexual functioning problems • Increased risk of suicidality	• Restlessness • Dry mouth • Bloating and indigestion • Joint or muscle pain • Frequent urination • Acne • Brittle hair and nails • Lithium poisoning (including diarrhea, drowsiness, muscle weakness, vomiting, lack of coordination)	• Weight gain • Drowsiness • Dizziness • Menstrual issues in girls • Skin rashes • Rapid heartbeat • Blurred vision • Sensitivity to the sun	• Headache • Diarrhea • Heartburn • Stuffy or runny nose (coldlike symptoms) • Constipation • Drowsiness • Dizziness • Life-threatening rash (i.e., Stevens-Johnson syndrome)

In treatment-resistant depression (e.g., depression that does not respond to or improve with the use of one medication), the addition of another medication may be added to the existing antidepressant treatment (Trivedi & Chang, 2012); this is referred to as **augmenting medication**. Augmenting medication is often done when a youth has some symptom reduction with a certain medication; therefore, adding an augmented medication is more ideal than switching and trying another antidepressant (Trivedi & Chang, 2012). Although the research is relatively scarce on augmenting medication in youth populations, some youth benefit from augmenting with lithium, atypical antipsychotics, other antidepressants, and buspirone (Trivedi & Chang, 2012). Although benefits may exist, augmenting medications can also increase the risk of adverse effects (e.g., side effects).

I CAN START COUNSELING PLAN FOR KEANDRA

This chapter began with a direct quote from Keandra, a 17-year-old girl who experiences intense periods of depressed affect. Myriad factors should be considered in developing a treatment plan. The following I CAN START conceptual framework outlines counseling considerations that may be helpful to a school counselor or a clinical counselor who works with Keandra.

C = Contextual Assessment

Keandra is 17-year-old African American girl with a strong cultural identity. She is from an influential and affluent family. Although she identifies as Christian, she expresses that religion and spirituality are not important to her. Keandra experiences normal adolescent developmental struggles (e.g., identity, relationships), yet these struggles have been exacerbated because of her isolative behaviors.

A = Assessment and Diagnosis

Diagnosis = 296.22 (F32.1) Major Depressive Disorder, Moderate Single Episode

N = Necessary Level of Care

Outpatient individual counseling (once per week)

S = Strengths

Self: Keandra is intelligent and has potential to be a strong student, as indicated by previous high school grades. She reports a love of exercise but has stopped engaging in healthy eating and physical fitness practices.

Family: Keandra lives with her family (i.e., her mother, father, and four younger siblings). She describes her parents as loving and supportive and appears to have strong relationships with her siblings and extended family.

School/community: Keandra lives in a safe, stable community with her family. She has numerous friends but does not feel close with any of them. She recently removed herself from regular interactions with friends and relatives.

T = Treatment Approach

CBT

A = Aim and Objective of Counseling (90-day objectives)

Keandra will report an improved affect. Keandra will report an increase in positive affect—from a 4 to a 6 on a 10-point scale.

Keandra will engage in activity scheduling/BAT. Keandra will schedule and engage in one exercise activity (e.g., walking around neighborhood, yoga class, running on treadmill) at least 3 days per week.

Keandra will learn coping skills she can use to manage depression. Keandra will identify emotional cues (e.g., feelings of helplessness and hopelessness) and implement at least one coping strategy (e.g., problem solving, activity scheduling, cognitive restructuring) 90% of the time at the onset of sadness (e.g., helplessness, hopelessness).

Keandra will learn to identify and challenge cognitive distortions. Keandra will use cognitive restructuring to examine her unhelpful thoughts/beliefs (e.g., "I'm hopeless"), evidence-review for the accuracy of those thoughts/beliefs, and engage in behavioral experimentation of alternative thoughts/beliefs 80% of the time.

Keandra will increase positive interactions with all family members (i.e., mother, father, and four younger siblings). Keandra and her family will plan and engage in a family recreational activity (e.g., dinner at the park, family game night, movie night) 2 times a month.

R = Research-Based Interventions (based on CBT)

Counselor will help Keandra to develop and apply the following CBT skills:

Learn and use healthy coping skills

Identify and challenge cognitive distortions

Learn and use relaxation skills

Use activity scheduling/BAT

Learn and implement cognitive restructuring techniques (e.g., evidence for that belief, assuming other perspectives, engaging in behavioral experiments)

T = Therapeutic Support Services

Medication evaluation with a psychiatrist

Academic tutoring through Keandra's high school

Support group for adolescents with depression

Summary

Youth were historically not diagnosed with depressive and bipolar-related disorders, possibly because depression presents differently in children than adults (Parens & Johnston, 2010). Many youth experience depressive disorders, which affects their thoughts about themselves, about the world around them, and their energy levels (Beck & Alford, 2009). Many young people have bipolar disorders, which are characterized by an elevated emotional state. They may experience fevered activity, increased levels of energy, grandiosity of thought, and an elation of mood (APA, 2013).

Young people often have difficulty articulating emotions and thoughts and recalling past history. Counselors can use clinical interviews, inventories, and assessments and garner multiple perspectives from adults who are familiar with the young person to capture the youth's complete diagnostic picture. In addition, bipolar disorders are one of the more difficult disorders to accurately diagnosis in youth. Therefore, counselors should never diagnose a young person with a depressive disorder without first conducting a thorough mania/hypomania assessment to rule out bipolar-related disorders. Assessing for mania/hypomania is also critical in distinguishing bipolar-related disorders from DMDD.

Significant research exists about treating depressive and bipolar-related disorders (Kress & Paylo, 2015). Although CBT is the most researched counseling approach for youth who are depressed, BAT, interpersonal therapy, and pharmacotherapy are also effective approaches for treating depression in youth (Chartier & Provencher, 2013; Kress & Paylo, 2015). The most effective counseling treatments for youth with bipolar-related disorders include CBT, dialectical behavior therapy, family-focused treatment, Interpersonal and Social Rhythm Therapy, and pharmacotherapy (Kress & Paylo, 2015; West & Pavuluri, 2009).

As previously stated, youth who are in an acute state require stabilization first and foremost. Young people who are more psychologically stable will often benefit from affective education, coping and problem-solving skills, cognitive restructuring, and the development of more positive beliefs and feelings about oneself (Stark et al., 2010). In youth with depressive or bipolar-related disorders, pharmacotherapy is important. Counselors should aid youth and families in ascertaining evaluations for pharmacotherapy—especially in conjunction with their more psychosocial counseling approaches (Hofmann et al., 2012).

MyLab Counseling: Counseling Children and Adolescents

In the Topic 12 Assignments: *Strategies for Addressing Mood Disorders in Youth,* try Application Exercise 12.2: *Assessing and Addressing Depression in Adolescence* and Application Exercise 12.4: *Assessing and Addressing Bipolar Disorder in Youth.*

Then try Licensure Quiz 12.1: *Understanding Depression and Bipolar Disorders* and Licensure Quiz 12.3: *Strategies for Addressing Mood Disorders in Youth.*

Physical Health-Related Counseling Issues: Eating Disorders, Elimination Disorders, and Chronic Illness/Disability Counseling

Denise D. Ben-Porath, Ph.D., John Carroll University
Kelly Bhatnagar, Ph.D., The Emily Program
Stephanie Sedall, MA, Youngstown State University

THE CASE OF ELLA

When I was 15, the director at my ballet company told me that I could be competitive for lead roles if I lost 5 to 10 pounds. For me, that was it; it was on. At first, I stopped eating junk food. Then I stopped eating breakfast. Once I cut out all carbs, my appetite went away, and it got easier to not eat. My mom started to notice that I wasn't eating the dinners she packed for me to eat at the studio, so now I throw the food away before she picks me up. At home, I just avoid eating, and if my parents force me to eat, I vomit. I've been eating about 400 calories a day, and I've really been feeling good—like I am finally getting closer to the weight I want to be. Mostly I eat lettuce and celery, but I'll eat a bit of chicken here and there, too. Last week, I passed out at practice . . . and that is how I landed here.

—Ella, age 16

This chapter discusses physical health–related mental health problems that some youth face. More specifically, two categories of *Diagnostic and Statistical Manual of Mental Disorders, Fifth Edition* (*DSM-5*; American Psychiatric Association [APA], 2013a), mental disorders—eating disorders and elimination disorders—are explored, as well as counseling considerations relative to youth who have a chronic physical illness or health-related disability.

All of the topics discussed in this chapter involve physical health matters. Medical professionals play a critical role in working with and supporting these youth and their families, and counselors need to be one part of an interdisciplinary team of professionals who help youth who struggle with these issues.

EATING DISORDERS OVERVIEW

Eating disorders, such as anorexia nervosa and bulimia nervosa, are serious conditions characterized by a persistent disturbance of eating behaviors, resulting in the altered consumption or absorption of food (APA, 2013a). Eating disorder behaviors may include extreme attempts to limit food intake and/or other weight management behaviors, such as self-induced vomiting, excessive/compulsive exercise, and laxative or diuretic abuse. Overvaluation of shape and weight is often (but not always) present in eating disorders, which may manifest in frequent weighing, repetitive checking of body parts, avoidance of information related to one's shape (e.g., refusal to look in mirrors), and extreme body dissatisfaction (Fairburn et al., 2009).

In anorexia, youth may also present with a persistent lack of recognition of the seriousness of low body weight (APA, 2013a).

The dangerous behaviors that accompany eating disorders can be life-threatening and have dire medical consequences. For example, excessive dietary restriction causes decreased bone density, dry and thin skin, abdominal bloating, delayed gastric emptying, cardiac abnormalities, renal complications, and endocrine and metabolic irregularities (Pomeroy, Mitchell, Roerig, & Crow, 2002). In addition, excessive malnutrition that begins in early adolescence can stunt physical development and interfere with adolescents reaching their maximum growth potential if it is left untreated. Recurrent compensatory behaviors, such as self-induced vomiting and laxative abuse, cause cardiac hypotension, permanent erosion of dental enamel, esophageal tears, and a depletion of the body's sodium and potassium (Pomeroy et al., 2002). The combined medical and psychological consequences of eating disorders lead to substantially high mortality rates when compared to other mental health disorders (Klump, Bulik, Kaye, Treasure, & Tyson, 2009).

Because of these life-threatening medical consequences, immediate treatment is warranted on identification of eating disorder symptomatology. In other words, time is of the essence when treating those who have eating disorders, and counselors, mental health professionals, and medical professionals must be aggressive in their efforts to support these youth and their families. Eating disorders negatively influence brain functioning (Muhlau et al., 2007), metabolism (Katzman, 2005), and neurochemistry (Kaye, Strober, & Jimerson, 2009), thus impairing cognitive functioning (Southgate, Tchanturia, & Treasure, 2008), decision making (Cavedini et al., 2004), and emotional stability, and severely limiting the life activities of these youth (de la Rie, Noordenbos, Donker, & Van Furth, 2007). Counselors should have specialized training if they counsel youth who have eatings disorders. All counselors working with clients who have disordered eating should regularly consult other professionals, get specialized supervision, and engage in ongoing education.

The level of impairment associated with eating disorders requires that counselors' attention be immediately drawn to variables thought to be maintaining the illness rather than variables thought to have caused the illness. Sessions initially focusing too heavily on the "root" of the illness may be doing so at the expense of resolving disordered eating behaviors that have the potential to lead to death. In addition, youth and their parents may find insight-oriented counseling difficult, frustrating, and unproductive while the client is in a malnourished state, and these discussions may be better suited for a time when physical and psychological functioning have been fully restored.

The typical age of onset for both anorexia and bulimia is age 12 (Swanson, Crow, LeGrange, Swendsen, & Merigankis, 2011). Because these disorders often begin in adolescence, counselors who work with young people are in a unique position to be able to diagnose and intervene early, before symptoms become entrenched.

Eating disorders are serious disorders with life-threatening implications, but there is an emerging treatment literature suggesting that with the application of evidence-based treatments and a comprehensive, team-based approach, eating disorders can be turned around. In general, research suggests that approximately 50% of those who have anorexia have good outcomes, 25% have moderate outcomes, and about 25% do poorly after treatment (Lock et al., 2010). What makes anorexia so dangerous, however, is that it has the highest mortality rate of any psychiatric illness listed in the *DSM*, including depression and substance use disorders. The crude mortality rate is approximately 5% per decade for this population (APA, 2013a). It is critical that intervention occur as early as possible to prevent chronicity. There is strong evidence to suggest that adolescents who are not ill for a long duration (less than 3 years) can make a full psychological and weight recovery if treatment is immediate and intensive (Lock et al., 2010).

Recovery rates for bulimia vary considerably depending on the study cited, with rates of remission ranging from 31% to 74% (Bogh, Rokkedal, & Valbak, 2005; Fairburn, Agras, Walsh, Wilson, & Stice, 2004). A rapid reduction in symptoms during the first 4 weeks of treatment has been linked to a positive course for those diagnosed with bulimia (Bogh et al., 2005; Fairburn et al., 2004). In one review of the literature that involved studies conducted since the 1990s, poorer long-term outcomes were found with earlier age of onset, severity of symptoms, comorbid diagnoses (e.g., substance use disorders), and certain personality characteristics (e.g., introversion, perfectionism, emotional lability, neuroticism; Steinhausen & Weber, 2009).

Many parents and adults around youth who have eating disorders struggle to understand how to respond to this population. Table 19.1 provides some of the dos and don'ts of responding to this population. These suggestions may be useful for counselors, family, and friends of youth who have an eating disorder.

Table 19.1 Dos and Don'ts for Interacting with Youth with Eating Disorders	
Do	**Don't**
Involve a medical provider who can monitor the client's physical health: It is not within the counselors' scope of practice to monitor the physical health symptoms associated with an eating disorder, but counselors should pay attention to signs of escalating symptoms (e.g., blood in vomit, dizziness). A medical provider should always be engaged when a client has an eating disorder. A team approach should be taken to work with this population, with various medical providers involved (e.g., dietitian, physician, psychiatrist).	*Hesitate to refer for a higher level of care if there is no progress or symptoms worsen after six sessions:* An alternative treatment or a higher level of care should be tried if no progress is seen after six sessions (Agras et al., 2000). Eating disorders have the highest mortality rate of any mental health disorders, and counselors should not be conservative in their responses and should not delay medical and more intensive treatment referrals.
Involve family and other culturally appropriate members of the youth's community in counseling: The client needs support and accountability, and others serve this function. Others can also help with objective evaluation and reporting of the youth's behaviors.	*Expect the client to make changes in isolation of others:* Overcoming an eating disorder is extraordinarily difficult, and supports are required, especially with youth.
Understand an eating disorder is a biologically based illness: Eating disorders are rooted in and maintained by complex genetic and biological factors. As an eating disorder takes a greater hold, it becomes increasingly hard for a young person to fight its influence. Physical monitoring and refeeding are required.	*Blame the parents or the client for the eating disorder:* Parents and clients are not responsible for the development and maintenance of an eating disorder. They already feel a great deal of shame, and their fears that the disorder is their fault should be assuaged.
Externalize the client's eating disorder: The client is not the problem; the eating disorder is the problem. The client and the family must come to recognize that the client is not the eating disorder. The client has various personal strengths, capacities, and characteristics—and struggles— that make him or her unique.	*Reinforce an eating disorder–saturated identity:* Clients with eating disorders often come to see themselves as the eating disorder. Letting go of the eating disorder can feel as if they are letting go of themselves. Avoid reinforcing the idea that the client is the eating disorder.
Encourage friendships and social connections: Support friendships with peers who are positive and confident. Collaborative activities can help the youth to connect with others.	*Allow isolation:* Many youth who have an eating disorder isolate from their peer group. Isolation can perpetuate feelings of low self-worth and shame and should be avoided.
Tell the person you care about him or her: Tell the youth you want him or her to be healthy and at peace. Tell the youth you will continue to be there for him or her, with compassion and support. Let the youth know he or she always has someone to lean on.	*Tell the person he or she looks too thin or comment on appearance:* Do not comment on the youth's weight— "You look too thin"; "You look like you've gained some weight"; or "You look healthier." It is best to not comment on the youth's appearance at all.
Eat as a family: Provide balanced, nutritious meals with all food groups represented. Try to make mealtimes enjoyable by including the entire family in food preparation, dedicating time to talk, and creating a relaxing ambiance.	*Allow the youth to skip meals:* Family meals are an important aspect of many approaches to treating eating disorders. Time spent together eating is believed to be central to helping youth to recover from an eating disorder.
Validate and support: Validate the youth and his or her struggles. Take time to listen closely to young people's experiences without trying to convince them their feelings, thoughts, or behaviors are wrong.	*Blame, shame, or guilt:* Don't blame the youth for having an eating disorder or judge the associated behaviors. The youth is not trying to be difficult; he or she is in pain and struggling, and the behaviors are not about you.

(Continued)

Table 19.1	Dos and Don'ts for Interacting with Youth with Eating Disorders (*Continued*)
Do	**Don't**
Get educated: To understand the youth better, learn about the disorder, and educate others on the consequences and risks an eating disorder entails. Parents can join a support group, receive counseling, and seek supports.	*Let your fears override your emotions:* Fear can cause people to control those who have an eating disorder, and this can cause damage. Remind yourself that the eating disorder is not your fault or the child's because this thinking will lead to unproductive attempts to control and will harm.
Encourage healthy habits: Help the youth to find activities and hobbies to deal with stress and loneliness. Encourage the youth's interests, and help the youth to find ways to become more involved with these. For example, if the youth likes to paint and draw, encourage him or her to take an art class or even offer to go with him or her.	*Self-limit and lose hope:* Youth may not feel motivated to pursue interests or hobbies. They may lose interest or feel they are not capable enough to pursue a hobby, such as drawing.
Use "I" statements when communicating: Communication with youth is very important, especially when they are going through hardships and struggles. Using "I" statements such as "I think you should take an art class" or "I am worried about how often you stay in your room" may help without sounding accusatory. Using "I" statements shows the youth you care and you feel this way versus sounding as if the youth is doing something wrong. Using these statements will encourage conversation rather than make the youth get defensive and refuse to talk.	*Use "you" statements when communicating:* Changing communication style with the youth to sound more sincere and gentle will help with feelings of self-blame and guilt. Using statements such as "You stay in your room too much" or "You need to spend more time drawing" sounds as if you are blaming the youth for such actions. Changing the tone and wording will help the youth to understand these are your feelings and thoughts and you are not placing them on the youth as if they are his or her fault.

Note: Adapted from Stephanie Konesky, LPCC, Site Director at the Emily Program–Cleveland, personal communication, January 30, 2017.

Anorexia: Symptoms and Counselor Considerations

Anorexia nervosa is a serious and potentially life-threatening mental health disorder characterized by dietary restriction that leads to a significantly low body weight (APA, 2013a). Significantly low body weight is defined as a weight that is less than minimally normal relative to one's age, sex, developmental trajectory, and/or physical health. For children and adolescents, this includes maintaining a weight that is less than that minimally expected based on historic growth patterns. In healthy children, weight and height increase along a fairly constant growth curve. When an adolescent falls off the growth curve, or is not making the expected gains in height and weight, an investigation into the cause is warranted. Although other medical issues, such as inflammatory bowel disease or food allergies, may be responsible, inquiry into eating habits and weight management should be explored. Most children who are followed by a pediatrician will have a growth chart in their medical record that examines their weight and height trends from birth until early adulthood. These records are important assessment tools that counselors can use to establish that an adolescent is indeed experiencing weight loss that is atypical for his or her developmental trajectory.

There are two subtypes of anorexia: *restricting type* and *binge-eating/purging type. Restricting type* anorexia describes presentations in which weight loss is attained primarily through dieting and sometimes exercise. Individuals with restricting type do not regularly engage in binge-eating or purging/compensatory behaviors such as self-induced vomiting; excessive exercise; or misuse of laxatives, diuretics, or enemas. Those with *binge-eating/purging type* anorexia regularly engage in binge-eating and/or compensatory purging behaviors, which may further complicate the diagnostic picture. Other characteristics of anorexia include maladaptive beliefs surrounding weight, shape, and appearance and often a persistent disregard for the seriousness of low body weight. Individuals with anorexia can demonstrate an intense fear of gaining weight or becoming fat, even though they are at a significantly low body weight or engage in persistent behavior that interferes with weight gain (APA, 2013a).

Approximately 0.5%–1% of the adolescent population has anorexia, and it is estimated to be 10 times more common in girls than in boys (APA, 2013a). It is important to note, however, that estimates of anorexia in boys are likely misrepresented due to the cultural stigma of anorexia being a "female disease."

Treatment of anorexia is complex and requires attention to the broad medical, nutritional, and psychological aspects of the disease. Counselors working with clients with anorexia must be closely connected with a multidisciplinary treatment team that ideally includes a physician, dietitian, and psychiatrist, all of whom hold expertise in the treatment of eating disorders.

A thorough medical evaluation by a medical professional is a key step in the initial assessment and in the ongoing treatment of anorexia. The medical evaluation includes a complete physical and laboratory tests (e.g., blood tests, electrocardiogram, blood urea nitrogen, creatinine, thyroid study, urine specific gravity) to test for the physical effects of anorexia on the body. Chronic malnutrition can lead to major medical complications, including dehydration, orthostasis (drastic changes in heart rate and blood pressure when moving from lying down to standing up, which manifests as dizziness), bradycardia (low heart rate) and heart arrhythmias (irregular heartbeats), hypothermia (low body temperature), cold intolerance, skin changes, and lanugo (sudden growth of fine hair on one's body). Clients who have anorexia and engage in self-induced vomiting may also experience hypokalemia (low potassium levels), esophageal tears, and tooth erosion (Academy of Eating Disorders, 2011).

Clinical Toolbox 19.1

In the Pearson etext, click here to read about a therapeutic meal support intervention.

Partnership with a psychiatry professional specializing in eating disorders can help counselors to manage comorbid disorders that often complicate treatment. Counselors working with this population should be aware of common regularly co-occurring psychiatric disorders. Depressive and bipolar disorders, anxiety, and especially obsessive-compulsive disorder are found in relatively high rates among adults and adolescents who have anorexia (Keel, Klump, Miller, McGue, & Iacono, 2005). Risk factors for developing anorexia include the co-occurrence of anxiety and depressive/bipolar disorders, family history of eating disorders, teasing by peers, low self-esteem, poor body image, and belonging to a family that is heavily preoccupied with dieting (Jacobi, Hayward, de Zwaan, Kraemer, & Agras, 2004).

Adolescence is also a time period when adolescents are exploring extracurricular activities, including high school sports and teams. Extracurricular activities, particularly those for which success in a particular sport is linked with a certain body type, may also place an adolescent at risk for developing an eating disorder. Dancers, gymnasts, wrestlers, and distance runners tend to be at greater risk, whereas swimmers and football players tend to be at less risk.

Treating clients who have eating disorders, particularly those who have anorexia, requires an awareness of important ethical considerations. Because treatment with these individuals is often rife with life-threatening medical complications, counselors must be certain that they are adequately trained to treat this population and to assess when a higher level of care is warranted. Not making referrals as required can potentially involve death when working with this high-risk population. Because clients who are malnourished are unable to think logically, it is important that the family is active and engaged in counseling so clients' needs can be aggressively supported.

Counselors can play an important role in educating youth and others on the prevention and early intervention of eating disorders and body and weight concerns. Figure 19.1 provides guidance on how parents and those around youth can prevent eating disorders from developing.

Table 19.2 provides body-image exercises counselors can use to promote self-esteem and a healthy body image.

Bulimia: Symptoms and Counselor Considerations

Bulimia is characterized by recurrent episodes of binge eating coupled with compensatory behaviors that are used to prevent weight gain. A **binge** is defined as the rapid consumption of an objectively large amount of food in a short time period (within 2 hours) accompanied by a feeling of loss of control (APA, 2013a).

- *Avoid a Culture of Dieting:* The implicit message behind dieting is "my body is not okay as it is." Many consider dieting the gateway to an eating disorder. Educate parents about the importance of modeling a healthy relationship with food for their child by eating well-balanced meals.
- *Encourage physical activities for enjoyment rather than weight loss:* Encourage parents to find physical activities for their child that the child enjoys. Remind parents to focus on the positive aspects of the activity, such as teamwork, strength, endurance, and commitment, rather than weight loss.
- *Be aware that certain sports place children at risk for an eating disorder and/or body dissatisfaction:* Sports in which bodily aesthetics are judged can place youth at risk for poor body image and thus an eating disorder. These sports/activities include competitive gymnastics, dance, and body building. In addition, sports where "making weight" or being underweight provides a competitive edge (e.g., wrestling, martial arts, distance running) can also place individuals at risk for an eating disorder. Educate parents about these higher risk activities. Educate coaches/instructors to ensure they are not inadvertently encouraging and/or reinforcing eating disordered behaviors.
- *Be aware of media messages:* Society places a strong emphasis on media/social media, and youth are bombarded daily with harmful messages on how their bodies "should" look. Educate youth on the value of different body shapes, and help them to understand there are limits to what they can and cannot control about their appearance. Encourage youth to focus on embracing a positive body image (e.g., remind them of their strengths and the functions their bodies serve), and discourage a focus on unrealistic social ideals.
- *Do not judge food:* Prevent labeling foods as good or bad. Separating foods into these categories can encourage youth to only eat certain foods while depriving themselves of others. Labeling foods as good or bad can also invite guilt or shame, which can threaten self-esteem and thus encourage eating disorders. Encourage food choices based on nutritional value and nourishment versus good or bad categories.
- *Positive support and relationships:* Encourage positive, strong relationships with others because these people can serve as role models for youth and insulate them from harmful societal ideas about appearance. Remind parents to show youth how much they love them for who they are—not how they look—and always encourage good communication. Communicating about struggles and coping skills will help youth to feel comfortable in times of distress and need.

FIGURE 19.1 Preventing Eating Disorders in Youth

Table 19.2	Body Image–Related Exercises	
Title	**Description**
Body Wellness Checklist	Provide youth with materials, such as paper, pens, pencils, markers, and stickers. Youth can create a checklist they can use to assess their body self-care and wellness. The goal of this exercise is to help youth to become better aware of their body at a functional level—not based on appearance—and to become empowered to take an active approach to their wellness. Instruct youth to use whatever media they want to complete the checklist. Provide a list of about 10 *yes* or *no* questions, such as the following: Did my body get enough sleep last night? Does my body have enough energy right now? Right now, have I provided my body with enough nutrients? Am I nurturing my body? If youth answer *no* to a question, they can consider ways a *no* can be changed to a *yes*. After discussion, youth use the checklists to enhance their self-awareness and mindfulness related to their body and health.
My Body Agreement	This exercise involves clients creating an agreement in which they express their commitment to accepting their body as it is and treating it—and themselves—with kindness and respect. The format of the agreement might include "I" statements such as "I will," "I choose to," or "I have the power to." The agreement may state "I understand that from this day on, I will move forward in a positive way and treat my body with care and respect because it is a part of who I am." Underneath the opening statement, clients can use "I will" statements, such as "I will accept my body the way it is," "I will give my body positive talk and love," and "I will not deny my body of physical activity and proper nutrients." Agreements might also include a signature line.

(Continued)

Table 19.2	Body Image–Related Exercises (*Continued*)
Title	**Description**
A Message to My Body	Instruct youth to write a letter or construct a collage in which they send a message to their body and apologize for abusing and/or neglecting it. Youth can use pictures or words from magazines if it is difficult to identify words. The message might start out with "Dear Body," and the client can use prompts such as "I am so sorry for. . . ." For example, youth may write "I am so sorry, Body, for not respecting you, for ignoring your needs, and for depriving you of the proper health and care."
Love Your Image	In this exercise, youth draw an image of their body on a regular-size piece of paper and identify positive words and images they can associate with their body and their health. Provide youth with materials such as stickers, pictures, paint, markers, pens, crayons, yarn, scissors, buttons, and whatever other media they want to use. After they create a picture of their body, they fill the actual body with positive messages, colors, textures, and symbols that are personal and unique and are geared toward health. For example, the words "I am strong" may be written on the legs, or a heart may be placed on the chest to suggest kindness. Youth can be as creative as they want. Encourage positive imagery and associations.
What My Body Gives Me	This writing exercise can be used to help youth to reframe their body as something that is functional and critical to their well-being. Counselors ask clients to respond to the following prompts either in or out of session: How is my body important? What would it be like if I had a physical disability? In what ways is my body strong? What can I do to help my body to stay strong and healthy? What do I love about my body? How can I treat my body with respect and nurture it? Encourage clients to write as much as they can relative to each prompt. Youth can draw a picture, identify a word, or identify a small object they can use to connect with their strength.

Those diagnosed with bulimia also engage in inappropriate compensatory behaviors to prevent weight gain. These behaviors may include self-induced vomiting, misuse of laxatives, diuretics, enemas, excessive exercise, and/or fasting. Youth who have diabetes may also abuse their insulin levels in an attempt to control their weight. A common misperception is that people must engage in purging behaviors to receive a bulimia diagnosis. However, nonpurging methods (e.g., fasting, exercise) can also be used to compensate for the binge episodes. Individuals may receive the diagnosis of bulimia if they have been engaging in binge behaviors and some form of inappropriate compensatory behaviors (purging or nonpurging) approximately once a week for the prior 3 months (APA, 2013a). To receive the diagnosis, the *DSM-5* also requires that the person's self-evaluation be significantly influenced by his or her body shape and weight.

The prevalence rate of bulimia in adolescents is generally found to be 1% (Swanson et al., 2011). Girls are more often diagnosed with this disorder, with an estimated gender ratio of 10:1. Therefore, the diagnosis of bulimia may be missed in boys because it is less common and because societal perceptions lean toward viewing bulimia as a female problem. Despite this, an estimated 10% to 15% of those with bulimia are male. Higher rates of bulimia are sometimes found in male athletes, suggesting that sports, particularly those where weight control and muscle mass are linked to athletic success (e.g., wrestling, long-distance running, gymnastics), may place some boys at an increased risk for bulimia. In addition, sexual orientation may play a role in the development of bulimia. Some research suggests a higher percentage of gay (15%) versus heterosexual males (5%) have an eating disorder. However, when these percentages are applied to population figures, the majority of boys with an eating disorder are heterosexual (Feldman & Meyer, 2007). Thus, boys should be carefully assessed for bulimia, particularly those who participate in at-risk sports or are gay.

Counselors who work with those who have bulimia must understand the medical consequences and complications that can result from the disease. Because excessive purging behaviors (e.g., diuretics, laxatives, vomiting, ipecac use) can result in an electrolyte imbalance that places the individual at risk for death (secondary to heart failure), counselors must coordinate client care with a medical professional. A routine physical, including a blood panel that assesses the levels of potassium (K+), magnesium (Mg+), and calcium (Ca+) in the blood, should be performed to rule out electrolyte disturbances. Esophageal tears are a rare, but serious, medical complication associated with self-induced vomiting. Esophageal tears most commonly occur when the individual is using objects or instruments to produce a gag reflex. Although not generally life-threatening, self-induced vomiting can also result in erosion of the tooth enamel, leaving the person vulnerable to dental disease. Swelling of the salivary (parotid) glands can also occur secondary to self-induced vomiting (Academy of Eating Disorders, 2011).

A second important consideration in treating individuals with bulimia is determining the proper level of care. Several studies indicate that the first four sessions are a good indicator of longer term treatment success (Bogh et al., 2005; Fairburn et al., 2004). Thus, if clients with bulimia cannot greatly reduce their incidents of purging in an unstructured setting, or if medical complications are not resolving, the counselor should consider a more structured setting, such as day treatment or residential hospitalization (Friedman et al., 2016).

Several studies indicate that those with bulimia, particularly those who exhibit the purging subtype, are more prone to impulsive behaviors, affective instability, and disinhibition (Godt, 2008; Keel, Wolfe, Liddle, De Young, & Jimerson, 2007). Psychological impulsivity combined with adolescence—a time when, developmentally, young people are generally prone to impulsive behavior anyway—could lead to risky and dangerous behavior. Thus, counselors should assess for possible comorbid impulsive behaviors in youth who have bulimia, including substance abuse, unprotected sexual encounters, multiple sexual partners, and any other impulsive, risky behaviors.

With respect to cultural issues, there appears to be less variability of bulimia in culture-specific prevalence rates than with anorexia. In the United States, those who present for treatment with bulimia are primarily Caucasian, but the disorder occurs in other ethnic groups, with prevalence rates comparable to those of Caucasian samples (APA, 2013a).

COUNSELING INTERVENTIONS AND TREATMENT FOR YOUTH WHO HAVE EATING DISORDERS

Although there is a great deal of overlap in the treatment for anorexia and bulimia, these two populations have unique treatment needs. In 2004, the National Institute for Health and Care Excellence (NICE) published guidelines for core interventions in the treatment and management of eating disorders. The guidelines are considered to be the gold standard by those who specialize in working with those who have eating disorders. They list family-based treatment (FBT; also known as the Maudsley Method; Lock & Le Grange, 2012) as the treatment of choice for adolescent anorexia nervosa, and FBT and cognitive behavioral therapy (CBT) with family involvement as the treatment of choice for adolescent bulimia nervosa.

Anorexia Nervosa: Treatment Models and Interventions

A significant body of research has emerged suggesting evidence-based approaches to treat anorexia. In recent years, FBT (i.e., Maudsley Method) has been demonstrated to have a high success rate in treating adolescents who have anorexia. CBT approaches also have some demonstrated success. As previously mentioned, early intervention and a comprehensive team approach to treating anorexia are critical.

FAMILY-BASED TREATMENT (THE MAUDSLEY METHOD)
In adolescents, anorexia severely affects physical, emotional, and social development, and it is important that treatment addresses each of these components. **Family-based treatment (FBT)**, or the **Maudsley Method** (Lock et al., 2010; Lock & Le Grange, 2012), is an outpatient treatment model developed at the

Maudsley Hospital in London. FBT is intended to take approximately 1 year to complete, and it was origi-nally designed to treat adolescents age 18 or younger who live at home with their families.

The overall philosophy of FBT is that the adolescent is embedded in the family and that family involvement, particularly from the parents, is critical for treatment success. The adolescent is viewed as too ill to make sound decisions about eating and related behaviors. As such, it is the parents' responsibil-ity to take control of their child's eating and activity behaviors until the child is less physically and psy-chologically involved with the eating disorder. FBT is also highly focused on adolescent development and aims to guide parents in assisting their adolescent with navigating normal developmental tasks (Lock et al., 2012).

FBT typically proceeds through three clearly defined phases. *Phase I: Weight Restoration* usually lasts 3 to 5 months, with counseling sessions scheduled at weekly intervals. Counseling in Phase I is almost entirely focused on the eating and weight management behaviors. Parents are encouraged to work out for themselves how best to help their child to gain weight and return to normalized eating while the counselor provides ongoing support of these efforts. Problem solving is a key therapeutic tool used to assist parents in making appropriate decisions for their child's food intake. The family meal, which occurs during Session 2, is an opportunity to assess and provide feedback surrounding mealtime family dynamics and to empower parents to take charge of the illness by successfully coaching the child to take "just one more bite" than he or she was originally prepared to eat. In Phase I, parents may have to sit at the table with their children, sometimes for hours, to wait for them to finish a meal. Parents may also be required to supervise their child for 30 minutes or longer after the meal to block any compensatory methods, such as vomiting. Given that adolescence is a time of struggle regarding autonomy and independence, counselors need to alert family members that Phase I treatment will be difficult and challenging. Although CBT-focused interventions may employ a nutritionist or dietitian at this stage of treatment, in FBT parents are empowered to be leaders of the weight restoration process. Reliance on a nutritionist/dietitian is discouraged, except when there is a risk for refeeding syndrome.

When steady weight gain is evident and parents believe they have a manageable grasp on the ill-ness, *Phase II: Transitioning Control of Eating Back to the Adolescent* begins. During Phase II, sessions are held every 2 to 3 weeks over the course of approximately 3 months. Eating disorder symptoms remain central in discussions, and the counselor works with the family to slowly move developmentally appropriate control over eating and activity back to the adolescent (under close parental supervision). As Phase II progresses, other familial issues that had to be postponed to focus on weight restoration may now be introduced. The issues are only processed, however, in relation to the effect that they have on the family's ability to continue refeeding and/or to support maintenance of a healthy weight for the adolescent.

Phase III: Adolescent Issues and Termination is initiated when the client achieves a stable weight (e.g., minimum of approximately 95% of his or her expected body weight) and eating disordered behaviors are no longer occurring. Sessions are held monthly or every other month over the course of approximately 3 months. The primary goal of Phase III is to help the adolescent to establish a healthy relationship with parents so the distorted eating does not make up the basis of the familial interactions. This entails working toward achieving personal autonomy, establishing appropriate familial boundaries, practicing effective problem solving, and preparing for upcoming transitions in the stages of life.

FBT is currently considered the first-line treatment for adolescents who have anorexia (NICE, 2004). There is substantial evidence supporting FBT as an effective immediate and long-term treatment option for adolescent anorexia (Downs & Blow, 2013; Lock et al., 2012). Overall, the data indicate that FBT, used with young clients (i.e., ages 19 or below) with anorexia who have a relatively short duration of illness (i.e., less than 3 years), is promising and that the beneficial effects of the treatment appear to be sustained in 2- to 5-year follow-up studies (Eisler, Simic, Russell, & Dare, 2007; Lock et al., 2012).

COGNITIVE BEHAVIOR THERAPY (CBT)

CBT focuses on the cognitive, affective, and behavioral dimensions of the disorder that initiate and maintain the eating disorder. Fairburn's (1981) approach is a classic CBT treatment for use with this population. It is divided into three stages, with each stage progressively treating the eating disorder.

Stage 1 is primarily behavioral in nature. In this stage, clients keep a diary of eating disordered behaviors (e.g., bingeing, inappropriate compensatory behaviors) and engage in self-monitoring of food intake. In addition, clients are encouraged to establish a regular pattern of eating, which includes eating foods from many different food groups. In session, clients review their self-monitoring forms with their counselor, and the counselor and clients work together to identify triggers for eating disordered behaviors and to problem-solve how to change or avoid them. Stage 1 treatment also consists of psychoeducation about nutrition. Because many clients with an eating disorder have misinformation or distorted information about nutrition, psychoeducation designed to teach clients about balanced nutrition is important. Collaboration with a specialized dietitian can help counselors working with this population to better understand clients' nutritional needs. Meal plans are frequently used for clients with anorexia and can assist in monitoring caloric intake to make sure clients are eating adequately to reverse malnutrition. Counselors using a CBT approach often work with a dietitian to ensure sound nutritional recommendations are made to parents, especially as they work to refeed their malnourished child and avoid nutrition-related complications such as refeeding syndrome (i.e., a metabolic disorder that occurs as a result of reinstitution of food to those who have been severely malnourished).

Stage 2 of therapy is designed to teach clients how to problem-solve life's difficulties without resorting to eating disordered behaviors. The problem-solving strategies include (a) identifying the problem, (b) describing the problem as accurately and objectively as possible, (c) brainstorming solutions to the problem, (d) generating consequences to each solution, (e) choosing the best response, and (f) following through with the action.

The last stage, Stage 3, assists clients in identifying cognitions and behaviors that may lead to relapse. For example, dichotomous or black-and-white thinking (e.g., "No one will think I am special unless I am thin") may set up clients for relapse. In this instance, the counselor may ask clients to develop alternative cognitions that refute their current beliefs. For example, the counselor may ask clients to observe individuals they know whom others value and respect who are not thin. Recognizing these cognitive distortions and challenging them is an important goal in preventing relapse in CBT treatment.

Several studies have demonstrated the effectiveness of CBT in treating those who have anorexia. For example, CBT has been demonstrated to be superior to nutritional counseling with respect to relapse prevention in those with anorexia (Pike, Walsh, Vitousek, Wilson, & Bauer, 2003). Furthermore, in a nonrandomized clinical trial, individuals diagnosed with anorexia who were treated with CBT had significantly longer periods without relapse as compared to those individuals who were provided a standard treatment (Carter et al., 2009).

ENHANCED COGNITIVE BEHAVIOR THERAPY FOR EATING DISORDERS (CBT-E)

CBT-E is an adaptation of CBT that was specifically designed for use in treating all eating disorders (Fairburn, 2008; Fairburn et al., 2009; Fairburn Cooper, & Shafran, 2003). CBT-E was originally designed for use with adults; however, adaptations have been made so it can be used with adolescents.

CBT-E constructs a clinical formulation of the processes hypothesized to be maintaining the eating disorder. This clinical formulation is used to identify and prioritize features of the illness that need to be targeted in counseling. Thus, an individualized formulation (or treatment plan) is developed in the very beginning and revised throughout counseling.

The standard course of treatment for CBT-E is 20 treatment sessions over 20 weeks. It focuses on using specific strategies and procedures to address the targeted symptoms. CBT-E is conducted in four stages. Stage 1 (weeks 1–4) goals include orienting and engaging the client to treatment, developing the personalized formulation, providing psychoeducation on eating disorders and weight change, and establishing a pattern of "regular eating" and "in-session weighing." Stage 2 (weeks 5–6) is considered a transitional stage in which the client and counselor review treatment progress, identify emerging barriers to change, and modify the personalized formulation. Stage 3 (weeks 7–14) is considered the crux of treatment, and the goal is to address the main mechanisms (mostly cognitive) thought to be maintaining the eating disorder. Stage 4 (weeks 15–20) is the final stage of treatment and focuses on relapse prevention planning for the long term. A review session held 20 weeks posttreatment is also offered to ensure changes are maintained over time.

Clinical Toolbox 19.2

In the Pearson etext, click here for an activity that can be used to help youth who have eating disorders to challenge distorted cognitions that support the eating disorder.

PSYCHOPHARMACOTHERAPY

Unlike the research on adults with eating disorders, the efficacy of psychotropic medications in treating adolescents who have anorexia is limited. The one retrospective study that was conducted compared adolescents diagnosed with anorexia who were prescribed selective serotonin reuptake inhibitors (SSRIs) to adolescents diagnosed with anorexia who were not prescribed medication. No differences were found between the two groups on body mass index (BMI), eating disorder symptoms, depression, or obsessive-compulsive symptoms at discharge or at 1-year follow-up (Holtkamp et al., 2005). Furthermore, the U.S. Food and Drug Administration (FDA) concluded that prescribing antidepressant medication to adolescents may pose serious life-threatening side effects (U.S. Department of Health and Human Services, 2004). After reviewing numerous clinical reports and studying 3,300 adolescents who were prescribed antidepressant medication, the FDA concluded that antidepressants increase the risk of suicide in a real but small number of adolescents. As such, the FDA has issued a "black box warning" on SSRIs that indicates that these drugs may increase suicidal thinking and behavior in youth (U.S. Department of Health and Human Services, 2004).

Because body image disturbance in those with anorexia can be severe and profound, many researchers have conceptualized this distortion as bordering on delusional thinking. Many have subsequently explored the use of antipsychotic medications in treating those diagnosed with anorexia. Furthermore, antipsychotic medications are known to stimulate hunger and promote weight gain, an additional benefit for those needing weight restoration. The most promising antipsychotic agent used to date with adults with eating disorders is olanzapine (e.g., Zyprexa), which is an atypical antipsychotic agent (Attia et al., 2011); however, the research in the adolescent population is severely lagging, and no clear conclusions can be drawn about the effectiveness of the atypical antipsychotics. The few case studies that have been reported suggest that atypical antipsychotics may increase weight gain and decrease agitation and anxiety in adolescents who have anorexia. However, given the side-effect profile of atypical antipsychotics and the limited data to support their efficacy, treatment guidelines suggest that medication should not be the first line of defense, but rather family-based therapy is most important when treating adolescents with eating disorders (NICE, 2004).

Bulimia Nervosa: Treatment Models and Interventions

The treatment literature suggests several effective treatments to address bulimia. CBT, dialectical behavior therapy (DBT), FBT, and interpersonal psychotherapy (IPT) appear to be effective in treating bulimia in the short and long term.

COGNITIVE BEHAVIOR THERAPY (CBT)

CBT (e.g., Fairburn, 1981) and CBT-E (Fairburn, 2008) have been applied to the treatment of bulimia nervosa with success. For a more detailed description of these treatment approaches, please see the "Anorexia Nervosa: Treatment Models and Interventions" section. To date, CBT has the strongest empirical support for the treatment of bulimia, with studies suggesting that approximately 50% of clients diagnosed with bulimia recover with CBT treatment (Hay, 2013). A prospective treatment study found that those who have bulimia who were treated with CBT did markedly better on treatment outcomes—and had a better prognosis—than those treated with just behavior therapy (Haslam, Meyer, & Waller, 2011; Poulsen et al., 2014).

DIALECTICAL BEHAVIOR THERAPY (DBT)

The previously mentioned approaches do not fully address issues associated with affect regulation, which often contributes to the development and maintenance of bulimia. Although DBT was originally developed to treat emotion dysregulation in those with borderline personality disorder (Linehan, 1993), it has subsequently been applied in counseling those who have bulimia and other eating disorders (Johnston, O'Gara, Koman, Baker, & Anderson, 2015).

Although still considered experimental in nature, DBT is emerging as a potential adjunctive or alternative treatment model, particularly for youth who struggle with comorbid affect regulation difficulties that interfere with the success of the first-line treatment models such as FBT or CBT. Thus, DBT may be particularly effective for those adolescents with eating disorders who have difficulties with mood regulation, engage in self-injury, and/or exhibit risky, impulsive social behaviors. Early results from a handful of studies that have examined adapted DBT models for adolescents with eating disorders suggest DBT aids in the reduction of eating disorder symptoms, depression symptoms, and general psychopathology (Johnston et al., 2015; Safer, Couturier, & Lock, 2007; Salbach-Andrae, Bohnekamp, Pfeiffer, Lehmkuhl, & Miller, 2008). Some research suggests that DBT treatment may increase the BMI of adolescents who have anorexia (Johnston et al., 2015).

When using DBT with youth who have bulimia or anorexia, counselors work with adolescents to replace maladaptive behaviors with more skillful and adaptive behaviors. Toward this end, behavior chain analyses and diary cards are used to address and track dysfunctional behaviors, including bingeing and purging and suicidal/nonsuicidal self-injurious behaviors. Figure 19.2 illustrates a *self-soothing kit* that can be used to help youth to regulate their emotions, thus avoiding eating-disordered behaviors.

Activity Overview

Clients with eating disorders often have difficulty regulating their emotions. Linehan (1993) described self-soothing as a helpful intervention to reduce distress and assist clients in re-regulating strong emotions. An important therapeutic goal is to teach clients how to self-soothe and regulate intense painful emotions.

Activity Objectives

This intervention provides clients with a tool they can use to self-soothe and regulate their emotions, thus avoiding eating-disordered behaviors.

Directions

1. One week before the activity (which can be used in individual or groups sessions), orient the group to the exercise. State "Next week we will be making a self-soothing kit. This will be a kit that you can use when you are feeling intense emotions and need to re-regulate those emotions." Next, state "Your only homework for the following week is to choose and bring in a recording of your favorite soothing song. This is a song that relaxes and calms you. It may be that the lyrics are meaningful to you, or it may just be that the tune is comforting. The most important part of your assignment is that the song you choose is comforting. Bring this with you to our next group session."
2. Next session, have your clients sit at a long table. Give each client a shoebox and construction paper. Have them cover the shoebox lid and the box in construction paper.
3. Next, provide them with several magazines. Have them look for inspirational quotes or messages in ads or titles. Examples may include "You are amazing!" "Take time to smell the roses"; or "Respect yourself." Have them clip out these inspirational sayings and paste them to the outside of their boxes. While they are working on this activity, you can explain that the outside of the box with its inspirational quotes will be a way for them to visually self-soothe.
4. When they are finished, hand them each a stress ball. Explain that squeezing the stress ball is a tactile way they can self-soothe.
5. Next, give each client a small candle. Explain that various scents are known to relax and calm people. Have them smell the candle and then place it in their boxes. Explain that the candle will be a way for them to self-soothe using their sense of smell.
6. Now, ask them to play the soothing song selected during the week. Explain that music can be a way for them to self-soothe using their auditory senses. Ask them to commit to using their self-soothing kit before the next session.

Process Questions

1. Did you use your self-soothing kit this week?
2. What sense did you find worked best for you when you needed to self-soothe?
3. Did you notice yourself feeling more calm and relaxed after using your self-soothing kit? If so, how long did it take before it started working?
4. What other items might be helpful to include in your self-soothing kit?
5. What else can you add to your kit to help you to self-soothe?

FIGURE 19.2 Self-Soothing Kit

A treatment hierarchy that prioritizes life-threatening behaviors is constructed. The first behaviors to be addressed, the Level 1 target behaviors, are imminently life-threatening behaviors, including suicidal behaviors and eating disorder–related medical complications that can result in imminent death (e.g., electrolyte disturbances). With respect to the target hierarchy, therapy-interfering behaviors should be addressed once life-threatening behaviors are stabilized, and these may include noncollaborative behaviors, such as engaging in deceptive weight gain measures such as "water loading" prior to weigh in, not adhering to the prescribed meal plan, or simply refusing to collaborate with the counselor on a treatment plan. Last, behaviors that interfere with quality of life are addressed. These may include relationship difficulties, school issues, or eating-disorder symptoms that are not life-threatening.

FAMILY-BASED TREATMENT MODEL (FBT)

FBT, the current gold standard approach for treating adolescent anorexia, has also been adapted to treat youth with bulimia (FBT-BN; Le Grange & Lock, 2007). Manualized FBT-BN includes 20 sessions that occur over the course of 6 months. Three individual sessions between the adolescent and the counselor are also recommended during the course of FBT-BN.

Similar to FBT-AN (i.e., for use in treating anorexia nervosa), FBT-BN has three well-defined phases. In *Phase I,* parents assist their adolescent in reestablishing healthy patterns of eating. In *Phase II,* parents oversee the adolescent's return to independence regarding eating behaviors. FBT-BN concludes with *Phase III,* in which the primary task is to discuss issues related to adolescent development in the context of the eating disorder.

When compared to FBT-AN, FBT-BN is considered more collaborative in Phase I, and the adolescent is more directly involved in plans for a return to normalized eating. FBT-BN emphasizes regulating food intake, breaking the binge–purge cycle, and addressing the secretive nature of these behaviors as key to successful treatment. Also, counselors using FBT-BN can exercise greater flexibility and creativity in their approach and style because of the heterogeneous presentation of adolescents with bulimia (as compared to those with anorexia nervosa; Le Grange & Lock, 2007). There is strong research support for the use of this approach in treating bulimia (Le Grange, Lock, & Dymek, 2003; Le Grange & Schmidt, 2005).

PSYCHOPHARMACOTHERAPY

Limited research is available on the effectiveness of psychotropic medications with youth who have eating disorders. However, SSRIs have been supported and shown to be effective in addressing depression, anxiety, and suicidal ideation, symptoms sometimes associated with anorexia and bulimia, although they have not been proven to facilitate weight restoration or prevent relapse (Harrington, Jimerson, Haxton, & Jimerson, 2015; Lock & La Via, 2015). A clinical trial in which fluoxetine was used to treat adolescents found a decrease in weekly binge and purge episodes, and the FDA suggested that this medication is effective in decreasing the frequency of binge eating and purging (Kotler, Devlin, Davies, & Walsh, 2003; Lock & La Via, 2015; FDA, 2017). Fluoxetine is the only FDA-approved medication for use in treating bulimia in youth (Lock & La Via, 2015; FDA, 2017). Because so little data on the use of medications with youth who have bulimia are available, the National Institute for Clinical Excellence (2004) suggested that CBT adapted for the treatment of bulimia should be offered as a first-line treatment, with fluoxetine added as an adjunctive treatment for adolescents with bulimia who are not responding to CBT.

ELIMINATION DISORDERS

Enuresis and encopresis are both elimination disorders that involve difficulties with the elimination of bodily waste. **Enuresis** is characterized by inappropriate elimination of urine into bedding or clothing, and encopresis is defined as the involuntary or intentional passage of fecal matter into inappropriate places (e.g., clothing, bedding; APA, 2013a). According to the *DSM-5,* encopresis cannot be diagnosed in an individual before the age of 4, and enuresis cannot be diagnosed before the age of 5 (APA, 2013a). Before these ages, it is not uncommon for children to have accidents; thus, it would not be appropriate to label elimination difficulties as being a mental health disorder.

Most children master toilet training by the time they are 4 or 5 years old. During childhood, there is potential for toilet training to be inconsistent, especially since early toileting behavior can be dependent on adult involvement. As an example, a caregiver might be inconsistent and encourage the child to use the toilet one day but allow the child to wear a diaper the next day. However, according to the APA (2013a), after the ages of 4 or 5, caregiver inconsistency is not generally considered to be a warranted reason for enuresis or encopresis.

The only time a child older than 4 or 5 might display the symptoms of an elimination disorder but not warrant a diagnosis is in the case of a developmental delay. If the chronological age of the child is 4 or 5 years or older but he or she has a developmental delay (e.g., physical, cognitive, neurological) that prevents achievement of age-appropriate milestones, the child's difficulties with elimination would be considered a result of the primary disorder. That said, all elimination difficulties that cause significant distress should be addressed, and youth who have intellectual or other developmental delays may be diagnosed with elimination disorders at some point if it is determined that they are developmentally able to control their elimination but are not doing so.

Counselors should consider whether elimination difficulties are related to physical illnesses. They should thoroughly explore physical explanations for the child's elimination problems before ascribing a mental health diagnosis. For example, children who have seizure disorders might lose control of their bladders during the course of a seizure, and this would not require psychosocial intervention.

Because youth who have these disorders might eliminate waste on their clothing or in other visible places, others are often aware of their difficulties. The presence of enuresis or encopresis can be embarrassing for youth, and it can create a great deal of shame. The extent to which children with elimination disorders are stigmatized by peers can exacerbate the mental health difficulties already associated with these disorders.

There are many causes of elimination disorders, including psychological factors, genetics, and biology. Many children who have been the victims of emotional or physical abuse experience enuresis (APA, 2013a), but certainly not all children with an elimination disorder have an abuse history. However, as is true when counseling all youth, counselors should rule out the possibility of abuse when working with a young population.

Coping with elimination disorders can be especially challenging for parents and caregivers (e.g., preschool teachers, day care workers). Adult caregivers are often charged with the responsibility of cleaning the child's waste from clothes, bed linens, or other household surfaces. This requires time and energy, and it can fatigue caregivers. Some children with elimination disorders might need to wear diapers to bed, or even throughout the day. This can be financially and emotionally taxing for caregivers, and they may be subtle— or even overt—in communicating their frustrations. If the child experiences this frustration, it may further exacerbate his or her symptoms and elimination difficulties. It is important for counselors to explore ways to address not only the specific symptoms of the elimination disorder but also the anxiety and shame that might develop as a result.

Enuresis: Symptoms and Counselor Considerations

According to the *DSM-5*, symptoms of enuresis include urination in the bed or clothing at least twice per week for 3 consecutive months, or to the extent that it causes significant client distress (APA, 2013a). As previously mentioned, clients diagnosed with enuresis must be at least 5 years of age, and the problem must not be due to a general medical condition.

In the *DSM-5*, there are three specifiers for enuresis used to indicate that the symptoms only occur at certain times of the day (APA, 2013a). *Nocturnal only* means that the client only experiences difficulty urinating in a proper facility during the nighttime. *Diurnal only* indicates that the client experiences the symptoms of enuresis only during the daytime. *Nocturnal and diurnal* involves a combination of the two subtypes. In addition, *primary enuresis* is used to indicate that the client has never experienced a period of urinary continence, and *secondary enuresis* indicates a setback from a previous period of urinary continence.

Enuresis is one of the most common disorders diagnosed in young people (Shapira & Dahlen, 2010). It can affect up to 19% of children ages 5 to 12 years (Hodgkinson, Josephs, & Hegney, 2010). However, it only affects approximately 1% of people age 15 years or older (APA, 2013a). Nocturnal enuresis is more common in boys, and diurnal incontinence is more common in girls (APA, 2013a).

Environmental considerations are a potential risk factor for children who develop enuresis because this disorder is more common in children who live in childcare systems, institutions, and organizations such as orphanages (APA, 2013a). Stressful life events or stressful family dynamics can lead to increased levels of anxiety in youth, which is also associated with the symptoms of enuresis (Shapira & Dahlen, 2010). For example, youth who experience harsh potty-training practices might have difficulty relaxing and fully draining the bladder when urinating. This can lead to bladder infections or overactive bladder muscles that contract frequently. When contractions of the bladder occur unexpectedly, accidental urination can occur.

Youth might also avoid urinating because they are uncomfortable going to the restroom (e.g., in a public place or school) or because they do not want to take time away from a fun activity. Delayed voiding of urine can cause urine to leak onto clothing. Delayed voiding can also cause the bladder to become stressed, weakened, or overactive. Many youth experience difficulties achieving a regular bathroom schedule, and small difficulties can cycle into a larger problem if ignored. In fact, the stress of enuresis symptoms can actually further contribute to the development of more severe symptoms of urinary incontinence.

In addition to environmental factors and stress, genetic and biological factors are primary contributors to enuresis (Shapira & Dahlen, 2010). About two thirds of children who have enuresis have a biological relative who experienced similar symptoms (APA, 2013a). Potential biological contributors to the disorder are a lack of sleep arousal, low levels of antidiuretic hormones (leading to increased urine production), reduced bladder capacity, weak bladder muscles, or delayed ability to recognize when the bladder is full and needs to be emptied (Shapira & Dahlen, 2010).

Also, a neurological pathway between the bladder and the brain must be formed so the youth's internal alarm can signal the need to wake up and go to the bathroom. The connection between children's brains and physical mechanisms for holding and voiding urine typically forms by the age of 5, but some youth develop more slowly, even if they have otherwise average cognitive abilities. In addition, youth sleep schedules fluctuate during childhood, and youth who need to sleep for extended periods of time might experience an increased or new difficulty waking up to urinate.

Youth who are constipated might also experience some urinary incontinence due to the pressure on the bladder. Caffeine can also increase urine production in youth and should be avoided if potentially related to urinary difficulties. In addition to any other general medical conditions that might cause enuresis symptoms (e.g., sleep apnea, urinary tract infection, urinary reflux), physical and biological contributors to enuresis should be screened by a medical professional and addressed by counselors via psychoeducation only.

There are many factors that contribute to the symptoms of enuresis, and the prognosis is good because most children grow out of enuresis on their own and counseling can effectively support the process. Most children who have enuresis are otherwise happy and well adjusted. As such, counselors should have a working understanding of the biological and genetic contributors to the disorder, the ways in which these can be assessed by a medical professional, and the ways that counselors can develop and implement proven interventions to reduce or eliminate the symptoms.

Encopresis: Symptoms and Counselor Considerations

Encopresis is characterized by repeated voiding of feces in inappropriate places (i.e., places other than the toilet) at least once every 3 months. Approximately 1% of 5-year-olds have encopresis, and it is more common in boys (APA, 2013a). To receive a formal diagnosis of encopresis, the behavior must occur at least once per month for at least 3 months, and the client must be age 4 or older. In addition, the behavior must not be due to a general medical condition. One exception to this is constipation, which can be considered a medical condition but does not negate diagnosis of the disorder.

There are two subtypes of encopresis. The most common subtype that is generally considered to be involuntary is referred to as *with constipation and overflow incontinence*. *Without constipation and overflow incontinence* indicates that constipation is not a consideration with regard to the encopresis, and this subtype is often believed to be voluntary and could possibly be related to the presence of oppositional defiant disorder, conduct disorder, or some other type of behavior problem (APA, 2013a).

There are several ways that encopresis can develop as the result of constipation. To begin, youth might experience *constipation,* or a large mass of hardened feces stuck in the colon, due to various causes: holding feces in the colon for too long, eating foods that cause constipation (e.g., bananas, caffeine, sugar), or drinking too little water. When youth become constipated, it might hurt to pass the hardened feces, and youth might further avoid going to the bathroom. As the feces build in the colon, more water is removed, and the mass becomes larger and harder. At a certain point, watery feces begin to leak around the hard mass, and the rectum is not able to hold in the leakage. The rectum might be so stretched that the youth cannot even feel the leakage.

Some youth might avoid voiding their feces due to psychological reasons. Youth might avoid going to the bathroom because they are scared or embarrassed or because they do not want to miss a fun activity in which they are participating when they receive the signal to go to the bathroom. Youth might not consciously choose to avoid going to the bathroom, and constipation might also come as the result of being required to sit for extended periods of time (e.g., at school, at home) and not having the opportunity to use the restroom.

Harsh potty-training methods (e.g., yelling, hitting) might make it difficult for youth to relax when passing feces because they fear consequences related to going to the bathroom. Stressful life events or changes may also cause youth to refrain from defecating and become constipated. Encopresis can be *primary,* which indicates that the client has never reached a point of consistently defecating in a proper facility, or *secondary,* which indicates that the client has intermittently displayed desirable defecating behaviors. Secondary encopresis might indicate that youth have experienced some other difficulty that has contributed to the development of encopresis.

Although various factors can lead to initial symptoms of encopresis with constipation and overflow incontinence, the maintenance of this disorder is often psychologically based. Youth become quite frustrated with their difficulty controlling their bowels, which leads to further stress and anxiety that further contributes to constipation and difficulty. Voluntary encopresis (without constipation) has a strong psychological component, and it is not uncommon to find that those who have this disorder have been abused or neglected.

Individuals who have encopresis without constipation and overflow incontinence often deposit well-formed stool (as opposed to fecal leakage) into inappropriate places. This form of encopresis is more rare than the type caused by constipation, and defecation behaviors are often associated with behavior problems in youth. Often, youth with this subtype of encopresis use defecation as a way to assert power or express disapproval. In this case, counselors should address the related mental health difficulties in addition to the encopresis.

Sometimes youth who have overcome encopresis with constipation might still experience difficulty defecating in appropriate places due to a damaged colon that might be weakened or desensitized. Counselors should encourage youth to continue the techniques that have resolved the constipation, refer clients to medical professionals who can provide options to strengthen the colon, and support youth with the emotional consequences of this frustrating and uncomfortable disorder.

Finally, some youth might become constipated or experience decreased colon sensitivity/functioning as the result of sexual abuse. Although the majority of encopresis is caused by other sources of constipation and stress, it is always important to remember the link between elimination disorders and sexual abuse in youth. Counselors should complete a holistic, ongoing assessment of youth before determining the best course of action.

Counseling Interventions and Treatment for Youth Who Have Elimination Disorders

Counselors should remember that psychological factors can, but do not always, contribute to the development of elimination disorders. Counselors should thoroughly assess the client's psychosocial experiences and familial relationships. Any potential stressors should be addressed in addition to addressing the elimination disorder per se. Any biological and genetic contributors should be assessed by a medical professional, and counselors should focus on the use of psychosocial interventions.

The most highly supported interventions for clients who have enuresis involve the application of behavior therapy principles that help clients to retrain their bodies to respond to physical cues to urinate. In addition to counseling interventions that directly focus on the wetting behaviors, clients can also benefit from counseling interventions that focus on any emotional needs that have emerged as a result of the enuresis.

For both encopresis and enuresis, behavior therapy techniques and interventions are highly supported once any medical explanations have been ruled out. With regard to enuresis, only 1% of cases are not resolved once medical and/or psychosocial treatments have been applied, and in fact, many cases of enuresis spontaneously resolve without intentional interventions (APA, 2013a).

For both disorders, it is important to involve the families of the client and to begin counseling as early as possible. Enuresis and encopresis have a strong behavioral component, which suggests that clients who have these diagnoses are able to control the symptoms in some way (von Gontard, 2013). Early intervention allows clients to maintain a sense of control over their bodies, and the longer the symptoms persist, the longer the clients will believe that they are powerless over their difficulties. Also, behavior patterns can form quickly; habits that exist for shorter periods of time become less engrained in the child's behavior routine. Thus, early intervention is important. Family can serve as a strong source of motivation and encouragement for clients as they work together to find more helpful ways to deal with waste elimination.

With intervention, enuresis has an excellent prognosis. The prognosis for encopresis is not as straightforward as it is for enuresis. Treatment can require up to a year of dedicated, consistent interventions from parents, medical professionals, and mental health professionals. Encopresis in certain populations (e.g., those who have intellectual disabilities) could require extensive, ongoing intervention and may involve a reoccurrence of symptoms. Interventions must be holistic and address cognitive, behavioral, and dietary changes.

Enuresis Interventions and Treatment

ENURESIS ALARMS

The primary psychosocial treatment for nocturnal enuresis is the use of an enuresis alarm (Hodgkinson et al., 2010; Shapira & Dahlen, 2010). Via the alarm, clients can learn to better control their urination. The alarm goes off when it detects increased moisture levels. Because nocturnal bedwetting occurs while the child is sleeping, it is always an unintentional behavior. The use of an enuresis alarm at night can translate to helping the child to learn to control any daytime wetting symptoms.

Some children wet during the day. With these children who wet during the day, an enuresis alarm may be used during the day as well. Enuresis alarms are helpful pieces of technology that can be worn underneath clothing to help youth to learn how to intentionally regulate their biological processes. For youth who experience enuresis during the day, an alarm can help them to learn the cues and signals they need to understand when they need to urinate.

Bioregulatory wearable technology protocols involve the use of various alarms that can be independently purchased at online retailers. The search term for online purchases is *enuresis alarm,* and they range in cost from $50 to $100. Depending on the specific brand, the components and features of the alarm will vary. However, two main features are a sensor that indicates the moisture level of the child's undergarments and an alarm that sounds (and/or vibrates) when moisture levels increase. The sensor can be wireless and typically clips onto the outside of the client's undergarments, which can be covered with clothing or pajamas.

This alarm system pulls on two behavioral principles to decrease (and eventually eliminate) enuresis. First, with regard to nocturnal enuresis, classical conditioning links the body's sensation of having to urinate with the act of waking up. At first, the association is mediated by the noise of the alarm. Thus, the association links sensation of urination to a loud noise (or vibration) and then to waking up. The client's body eventually begins to link the urination sensation with the act of waking up. Next, the alarm promotes behavior rehearsal of getting up and going to the bathroom in the midst of sleeping. Coupled with the client's ability to wake when feeling the need to urinate, the client begins to independently use the restroom during the night instead of urinating in the bedding. It is especially effective to link the use of an enuresis alarm with other operant behavioral interventions (as discussed in the next section).

Clinical Toolbox 19.3

In the Pearson etext, click here for an example of how to implement an enuresis alarm as an effective behavioral intervention for enuresis.

OPERANT CONDITIONING INTERVENTIONS

When treating nocturnal enuresis, operant conditioning interventions pair nicely with the classical conditioning provided by an enuresis alarm. These techniques are also useful in treating children who experience diurnal enuresis (or symptoms throughout the waking hours). Operant conditioning interventions reward clients for desired behaviors, and they have been found to have a small but significant effect on treating enuresis (Hodgkinson et al., 2010).

Operant conditioning interventions come in two forms: reinforcement and punishment. Reinforcement increases the likelihood of desired behaviors, and punishment decreases the likelihood of unhelpful behaviors. However, reinforcement is generally more effective than punishment in motivating children— that is, children are more easily motivated to alter behaviors to obtain something desirable than to alter behaviors to avoid punishment. Counselors should reward behaviors that are inconsistent with the unwanted behaviors (e.g., going to the bathroom every 2 hours). Counselors should also help caregivers to find ways to reward the client's behaviors when the youth gets out of bed to go the bathroom or goes an extended period of time without urinating inappropriately.

Reinforcement schedules are an important component in using operant conditioning. At first, a 1:1 ratio should be used—that is, every time clients complete a desired behavior, they receive a reward. At first, successive approximations might need to be reinforced to shape the desired behaviors—that is, behaviors that are closer to the target behavior (e.g., running to the toilet as the client is urinating in clothing) should be reinforced. The target behavior eventually will be reached as their efforts and practices continue to increase. Once clients achieve the desired behavior on a consistent basis, verbal praise should remain high, but tangible reinforcers can be systematically reduced from a 1:1 ratio to 2:1, 3:1, and eventually a random reinforcement schedule.

PSYCHOPHARMACOTHERAPY

Medications may be used to treat youth who have enuresis in conjunction with behavioral interventions to support their improvement. One possible reason for difficulty in controlling urination is that hormones are not at the levels required to control elimination. Medications such as desmopressin (e.g., DDAVP), a synthetic hormone, are sometimes used to simulate the hormone in the body that encourages water retention. This medication increases the client's ability to physically contain urine for longer periods of time.

It has been hypothesized that clients with enuresis have trouble identifying when they need to use the restroom. Tricyclic antidepressants (e.g., Tofranil) have been used to stimulate the body's responsiveness to recognizing and controlling the urge to eliminate waste (Shapira & Dahlen, 2010). These antidepressants may increase clients' awareness and ability to use the restroom properly.

Although medication may help to address enuresis, there is a significant risk of relapse after clients cease taking the medication (Hodgkinson et al., 2010). If mental health and behavioral interventions are not used in conjunction with the medications, clients do not learn how to maintain their progress without the medications. The aforementioned counseling interventions should be used in lieu of or in conjunction with medicinal interventions, if at all possible.

Encopresis Interventions and Treatment

TOILET EDUCATION AND TRAINING

At some point, children learn to use the toilet to expel waste, and it is important to ensure young people who have encopresis be taught these skills. Proper toilet training is an important aspect of treatment for clients who are experiencing encopresis as the result of physiological difficulties, cognitive difficulties, or anxiety surrounding the process of defecating. It is important to ensure clients can verbalize the steps of defecating in a toilet (e.g., notice the urge to defecate, go to the bathroom, sit on the toilet, defecate, wipe, flush, and wash hands) and their readiness to do so. It is also important to determine that clients are physically able to complete the steps associated with using a toilet to defecate, such as pulling pants up and down, wiping properly, and flushing the toilet on completion.

Caregivers should model toilet-training behaviors to children and clearly teach children how to implement the behaviors independently (Coehlo, 2011). In addition, counselors can teach caregivers that punishment related to undesirable toilet-training behaviors is unproductive. Punishment further contributes to clients' anxiety around defecating. Parents should focus on praising positive behaviors associated with appropriate defecation.

Counselors can also help parents to develop a schedule for the client to take quiet time and sit on the toilet for a few minutes. This is especially effective after meals. Clients can learn to associate time on the toilet as enjoyable if they get rewarded at the end, and clients can learn how to have a consistent, successful bathroom schedule.

Counselors and caregivers should work together to ensure the client has a developmentally appropriate understanding of toilet training. This can be done through talk therapy, bibliotherapy (i.e., reading and processing stories), or other creative media interventions (e.g., viewing shows that address the topic of toilet use). When choosing a story about proper toilet behaviors, it can be helpful to select media that has a main character who is similar to the client in age and gender. It can be helpful to process ways in which the client's toileting behaviors are similar to the character and ways in which they differ.

BEHAVIOR MANAGEMENT

Behavior therapy principles play an important role in helping youth to engage in appropriate elimination. As mentioned, many caregivers use punishment as a way to control their child's elimination behaviors, but punishment is an ineffective way to handle encopresis (Coehlo, 2011). Children can, however, be involved in cleaning up any improper defecation because this may help them to become more personally invested in managing their behaviors. However, cleanup should never be introduced in a punitive manner. Parents should simply explain that every person is responsible for cleaning up after him- or herself.

To change these elimination behaviors, families must be engaged and supportive of the youth. Caregivers can help the child to develop a routine around his or her use of the bathroom, and any dietary and medication recommendations should be made by a medical professional.

Caregivers should implement a reinforcement schedule to solidify the child's healthy routine. As was mentioned with regard to enuresis, there are two types of reinforcers: positive and negative. Positive reinforcers give children something they want, such as extra time with friends, toys, prizes, or parental praise. The most effective (and free) reinforcer is verbal praise (e.g., "Nice work!"). Negative reinforcers remove something the child does not want, such as a chore or extra household responsibilities. As an example, if the child uses the facilities successfully, she may be let out of doing a chore that day.

Both positive or negative reinforcement occurs after the child has successfully completed a desired behavior. This distinguishes operant conditioning from bribery in the sense that bribery uses a reward first to make an individual complete a desired behavior. Bribery is ineffective because the client does not learn to engage in the desired behavior spontaneously on his or her own. Thus, all reinforcers should be given after the client independently completes a desired behavior (e.g., using the restroom instead of soiling his or her clothing).

Reinforcement schedules are an important component to using operant conditioning. At first, a 1:1 ratio should be used—that is, every time clients complete a desired behavior, they receive a reward. At first, successive approximations might need to be reinforced to shape the desired behaviors; behaviors that are closer to the target behavior (e.g., running to the toilet as a client is defecating in clothing) should be reinforced. The reinforcement schedule can eventually be reduced to 2:1, 3:1, and then an unpredictable schedule. Continued use of these principles will shape the child's behavior, hopefully with positive end results.

NUTRITIONAL CHANGES/MEDICATIONS

It is not generally appropriate for counselors to make dietary recommendations (unless they have specialized medical training and this is within the scope of practice of the license under which they practice). However, counselors should encourage clients to work with a medical professional to discuss nutritional changes or the use of laxatives or stool softeners, all of which may support the circumstances required to have appropriate toilet behaviors.

When treating encopresis, increased fiber in a youth's diet may facilitate success (Coehlo, 2011). Counselors can be helpful in working with clients and families to develop behavior schedules that facilitate fiber consumption recommendations provided by a medical professional. The fiber should improve the texture of the client's stool (e.g., higher water content, improved texture), which should make it easier to pass fecal matter.

A physician may also recommend a reduction in the youth's fat and sugar intake and any foods that increase constipation (e.g., bananas; Coehlo, 2011). Again, counselors should refer clients to medical professionals for specific directions regarding a change in diet, but counselors can focus on lifting the barriers that might prevent clients from making such changes.

If clients have constipation, which leads to loss of bowel control, a laxative might help them to increase their ability to properly control and expel waste. Over time, a medical professional may taper the laxative as clients gain greater efficacy around defecation.

Another over-the-counter medication that is often suggested by medical professionals to treat encopresis is stool softeners. Stool softeners allow the client to have more predictable, less painful bowel movements. Stool softeners are helpful for clients who have painful or hard bowel movements, which often result from their diet (e.g., not enough water, too much cheese), food allergies, or may even be a side effect of different medications. Some youth who have painful or otherwise difficult bowel movements may appear to have encopresis, when in actuality they have a more straightforward physiological difficulty. Over-the-counter stool softeners such as MiraLax, Senokot, or mineral oil might be prescribed to youth (by medical professionals) to rule out physiological causes of the encopretic symptoms.

CHRONIC ILLNESS/DISABILITY COUNSELING

Over the life span, all people experience some health-related problems, but physical illness and disability are commonly thought of as something that adults experience. However, some youth—at birth and throughout their childhood—are diagnosed with and experience chronic health disorders and illness that may affect not just their physical development, but also their psychological development. Youth who have chronic health conditions are faced with difficulties that affect their daily life and living and can create problems across multiple life domains. In addition, when a child has a chronic illness or health condition, it can place stress on the family unit and affect both parents and siblings.

The impact of a childhood illness is constant, and the challenges are difficult, thus leaving these children and their families emotionally, physically, and mentally stressed and/or exhausted. Studies suggest that as many as 1 out of 4 children in the United States, or 15 to 18 million children age 17 years and younger, have at least one chronic health problem (Compass, Jaser, Dunn, & Rodriguez, 2011). The most commonly diagnosed disease in children is asthma (about 9% of children; Compass et al., 2011). In the United States alone, over 13,000 children are diagnosed with cancer each year; 13,000 children are diagnosed with type 1 diabetes annually; 200,000 children live with either type 1 or type 2 diabetes; and 9 million children have asthma (Compass et al., 2011).

The degree of attention chronic illnesses require varies, with some youth requiring little regular medical attention and others requiring frequent attention that may involve both outpatient and inpatient health care treatment. For both families and youth, the process of accepting and managing a child's chronic health challenges can be difficult. Psychosocial adaptations and the development of necessary skills and coping mechanisms are important for the child, family, and caregivers. Counselors can play an important role in supporting youth and their families so they can navigate the challenges associated with a chronic health illness and/or disability. In this section, we discuss the challenges faced by young people and parents when a child has a chronic health problem and how counselors can support youth and their families. Because chronic illnesses do not affect just the child, family adaptation and stress management are also discussed.

Physical and Health-Related Conditions

Although different definitions exist, a **chronic health condition** is often defined as a health concern that lasts 3 months or longer, affects the child's day-to-day activities, and requires specific medical attention

(Compass et al., 2011). Some examples of chronic illnesses include asthma, diabetes, cerebral palsy, sickle cell anemia, cystic fibrosis, cancer, HIV/AIDS, epilepsy, spina bifida, severe food allergies/food intolerances, and congenital heart defects, just to name a few (Compass et al., 2011). Chronic illness can be a result of genetics, environmental factors, or a combination of both (Compass et al., 2011).

Many children who have a chronic illness experience symptoms of discomfort and pain that may affect their functioning. As an example, children who have **cystic fibrosis**—a chronic illness that targets the gastrointestinal and respiratory system—may have malnutrition, an inability to maintain weight, frequent coughing spells, and respiratory infections (Storlie & Baltrinic, 2015). Children with cystic fibrosis may spend many hours per day on breathing treatments and take an abundance of medications to improve their digestion (Storlie & Baltrinic, 2015).

A chronic illness can consume a great deal of a young person's time and energy. As an example, children who have **type 1 diabetes**, also known as insulin dependence or juvenile diabetes, require consistent care that includes blood monitoring and insulin injections (Anderson & Wolpert, 2004). Long-term complications of diabetes develop gradually over the lifetime and can affect almost every organ in the body if care is not taken to follow an insulin-adherence regime (Whiteman, 2015). As another example, food allergies can cause youth and their families stress. According to the National Institutes of Health (NIH), 5% of children have a food allergy, and the numbers are only rising; between 1997 and 2007, there was an 18% increase of food allergies diagnosed in children 18 and under (National Institute of Allergy and Infectious Disease [NIAID], 2016). Unfortunately, children who have severe food allergies live with at least some negative effects, making the allergies a subject of concern and a possible focus in counseling. Accidental food exposure can be risky, and reactions can cause gastrointestinal symptoms, rashes, and even death (NIAID, 2016). Living with a food allergy is difficult, and navigating potential exposures may affect the quality of life of the child and family.

Adjustment to Chronic Illness/Disability

Youth and parents have unique reactions to a chronic illness diagnosis, and how they respond may have to do with personal characteristics; levels of familial, community, and social support; the rarity of the illness (which may relate to medical and community support); the nature of the treatment; the course of the illness; and the severity and nature of the illness (Edwards & Davis, 1997). Youth at different stages of development respond differently to medical diagnoses, and how they cope and understand the situation will depend in large part on their developmental stage. The major stages of development and how youth may respond based on their developmental level follow (Denby, 2016):

- *Infants and toddlers:* In this stage of development, there is little to no understanding of the illness or its implications. These youth require a sense of parental trust and security, and parents should make their children feel safe during hospitalizations, doctors' appointments, and medical procedures.
- *Preschool-age youth:* In this stage of development, the child knows what it feels like and means to be sick, but there is still little to no understanding of what causes the illness or the implications of the illness. The child depends on the parents to take care of him or her in times of pain, confusion, and stress.
- *Early school-age youth:* In this stage of development, the child can understand the reasons for his or her illness, although the reasons may not be logical. The youth has **magical thinking**, or the belief that what he or she wishes or thinks can influence the external world (Ryan, 2015). For example, the child may believe the illness was caused by bad behavior. Parents still play a primarily role in helping to manage the illness and the associated stress.
- *Older school-age youth:* In this stage of development, the child is more capable of understanding the illness and the effects it is having on him or her, family members, and friends. Peers are important in this stage, as is participation in school-related activities. Often, a feeling of being left out can emerge if the child is unable to participate in certain activities because of the illness or its associated obligations, such as appointments, procedures, and/or hospitalizations.
- *Adolescents:* In this stage of development, independence and self-image are very important. Teenagers often form independence away from family, which can cause a rift between parents and the

teenager, and this can create problems in illness management if the youth begins to neglect his or her treatment plan. Hormone and body changes occur, which can cause different symptoms depending on the illness.

Research suggests that age is an important factor in terms of how a child adjusts to a diagnosis, so the stage of development is important to consider when counseling children who have a chronic illness (Cheeson, Chisholm, & Zaw, 2004). Children will gradually acquire more knowledge of their condition as their developmental level progresses. As children go through each stage, their understanding of their illness will vary, making development an important factor for counselors to consider.

Counselors should also be aware of the family's adjustment process. Family members often experience the classic stages of grief, progressing from anger and denial to bargaining and depression, all before acceptance (Guthrie, Bartsocus, Jarosz-Chabot, & Konstantinova, 2003). Youth and family members may also go through differing adjustment processes. For example, some research suggests that adjustment to a diagnosis of diabetes can take up to 9 months for children and up to 12 months for parents (Guthrie et al., 2003). The nature of the disease, severity, complexity of treatment, and financial cost often cause a burden on the family, and minimization of the illness's impacts—or even denial—is a common familial reaction.

Families facing chronic illness, such as diabetes, must deal with daily assessment and management considerations, and counselors must be sensitive to the ongoing stress this places on parents and caregivers, who are often already pushed to the limits by the demands of their day-to-day lives. The entire family has to adapt to the disease as each member accommodates to the needs of the child. For the parents, responsibilities may include catering to dietary needs, managing medication, providing home-based treatments, and facilitating medical appointments and procedures (Edwards & Davis, 1997). Therefore, it is normal for the parents to feel a sense of disappointment or grief for the child because adaptation is a complex process that continuously influences the daily life and emotions of both the child and parents.

Apart from the parents, siblings are also affected. They are often required to help and take on more responsibility around the house than they might have otherwise. Siblings might experience the following shifts as a result of an ill sibling: performing more household chores, supervising other children in the family, coping with alternative care arrangements during medical visits, and receiving less parental attention (Edwards & Davis, 1997; Midence, 1994). Parents may restrict siblings' participation in social events and limit peer contact because of their child's medical needs. Siblings may begin to feel less important than the child who is ill, and parents must be mindful of this dynamic because it can breed resentment toward the child who has the illness. In addition, extended family may also be affected by the child's illness if they are called on often for childcare and practical arrangements (Edwards & Davis, 1997).

Parents may experience internal, external, and physiological stress when their child has a physical illness. **Internal parental stressors** are those that originate within parents, and these include unrealistic expectations of themselves, self-blame, confusion, worry about the future, and unrealistic perceptions about what others think (Cheeson et al., 2004). Parents' expectations of themselves may be one of the biggest stressors brought on by their child's illness. The reason for this is because of the responsibility and pressure they take on for the child to the exclusion of their own needs (Edwards & Davis, 1997; Midence, 1994).

External parental stressors include those stressors that are beyond or outside of parents' control that relate to the illness. This includes child/sibling discord that results from the illness, financial burdens, difficult child/sibling behaviors, conflicts that may emerge with the significant other, difficulties managing the child's school or educational needs, the stress the illness places on extended family or caregivers, and difficulties finding medical care for the child (Midence, 1994).

Physiological stressors have to do with physiological ways the stress affects parents. Sleeping and eating patterns may be disturbed, as well as daily exercise and self-care activities (Cheeson et al., 2004). Counselors might highlight that the youth benefits when parents engage in self-care.

Management of Stress

The recognition and management of stress are essential for parents and youth who are navigating a child's chronic illness. Although all people experience stress in unique ways, some physical signs of stress include headaches, sleep difficulties, an upset stomach, and muscle aches and pains (Cheeson et al., 2004). Mental and

---

Education: Education can facilitate parent empowerment. Parents should learn all they can about their child's illness (e.g., treatment, symptoms, causes). Participation in support groups or talking with other parents who have had similar experiences may also be educational.

Social support: Encourage parents to seek out opportunities for social support. Social support can involve close or extended family, friends, or support groups. Supports help to take some of the burden off parents. Parents can also receive outside support from the community (e.g., churches, online blogs). Supportive others or support groups provide an outlet for parents to receive emotional support.

Plan: Staying organized and planning for the future can give parents a sense of control and help them to prepare for the future. The use of agendas to organize appointments, plan for medical procedures, and monitor medications/side effects is helpful. Parents can document questions they plan to ask the physician, financial budgets, medications, and resources such as cards and medical information needed for appointments.

Financial budget and support: Chronic illness can be draining on a family's budget, and budgeting and seeking financial assistance can be helpful. Medical services and medication bills can be intimidating to parents; monitoring expenses and the use of a budget may be helpful in alleviating parental stress. Planning for future expenses is necessary as well. Parents can also explore various financial resources, such as government and private programs, charities, and volunteer programs that are available and offer financial support.

Self-care: It is helpful for parents to develop a self-care routine so they can be their best. Explaining to parents that self-care is crucial to both their physical and mental health can be helpful. It may also be helpful to explain to parents that self-care makes them better parents, and it provides a good example for their child with a chronic illness.

FIGURE 19.3   Suggestions for Empowering Parents of Youth with Chronic Illnesses

mood changes, including anxiety, anger, sadness, depression, lack of motivation, lack of attention, and lowered self-esteem, may also occur (Midence, 1994). Figure 19.3 provides suggestions counselors might share with parents who are navigating a child's illness.

Counseling Interventions

Counselors can play an important role in helping young people who have an illness by supporting them during their initial adjustment period and during the course of the illness. When counseling a young person who has a chronic illness, counselors should develop an understanding of what the chronic illness means to the child. Young people struggle to understand their condition, and they will attempt to make sense of the illness in their own ways. Often, this means that what information they have is distorted, and they may misunderstand much of the information. Counselors can play a role in helping youth to get access to the information and resources they need to adequately make sense of their condition.

Counselors treating this population should take time to develop a therapeutic relationship. They should consider the circumstances of the illness, how it is affecting the child's emotions, and how that may influence the youth's comfort level and expression of his or her experiences. In conjunction with understanding the illness and the client's reactions to the illness, counselors should consider the child's unique concerns that relate to his or her condition (e.g., peer worries, worries about not being able to play, worries about future plans such as marriage, having a family, and college; Edwards & Davis, 1997). Frequent medical appointments may affect a client's flexibility, and counselors should also be aware of these time demands. It is also important for the counselor to consider the other treatment professionals the family will be involved with (i.e., primary care physicians, physical therapists, dietitians, school counselors and nurses) and obtain releases to communicate with these people as necessary. Counselors may also, at times, need to initiate family sessions and/or meetings with other health care professionals about the child. The counselor should make sure youth understand the decisions and roles of the parents, counselor, and other medical professionals in their treatment (Storlie & Baltrinic, 2015). For example, the counselor can explain the role of counselors and explain what counseling methods include and do not include (e.g., no needles are involved in counseling).

As counselors get acquainted with a child who has an illness, they should learn about the characteristics of the illness and the ways in which the condition challenges developmental and daily living tasks (Edwards & Davis, 1997). Such information can point counselors in the direction they need to head to help the child.

Children will experience the burdens and hindrances of their illness in unique ways. For example, many illnesses require isolation from others, and youth may experience this isolation in different ways depending on their developmental level. A child who has a comprised immune system following chemotherapy is required to stay away from others because of the risk of infection. Young people at different ages often have a different understanding of why they are being isolated and may place a different value on being isolated from their friends and peer groups. Counselors can provide education and information about why youth are being isolated, and they can help youth to develop ways to cope with and manage this isolation.

Counselors can also help young people to process the uncertainty of their illness and its prognosis. Some medical conditions (e.g., cancer) may have an unpredictable prognosis, whereas others (e.g., diabetes) are lifelong conditions that will need to be managed by the young clients more independently as they age.

Counselors can also help young clients to develop the skills they need to manage their illness. Some medical conditions, such as severe food allergies, celiac disease, or diabetes, require that the youth take some amount of responsibility in managing their illness, but this can be difficult for many young people. Parents typically encourage their child with food-related problems to become aware of and avoid triggering foods, yet many young people may not have the skills required to do so. Counselors can help young people to develop the skills they need to avoid such triggering foods. For example, when working with a child who has nut allergies, a counselor might role-play with the child how she can ask if a food has nuts in it and how to explain to others that she has a life-threatening nut allergy.

For many youth, diet is an important aspect of their wellness. Counselors can help young people to develop the skills they need to manage a food diary, which can help them to self-mediate their food intake. For example, a counselor might help a child who has diabetes and food allergies and his parents to keep a diary of the foods the child is allergic to and other alternative foods the child can have. This can also serve as an outlet for the child to express concerns and identify safety strategies. The counselor might help the youth to implement the meal plans developed by a nutritionist and develop the motivation and skills he requires to select healthy food alternatives versus foods that are unhealthy for him. The diary can also include strategies and safety preventions when glucose levels rise and drop. The counselor can use role-play to educate the youth on how to ask for help when he is not feeling well due to the rise or drop of glucose levels. Figure 19.4 provides practice suggestions for counselors who work with youth who have a chronic illness.

Several counseling theories can be applied to work with this population. What follows are several approaches and interventions that can be helpful when counseling youth and their families when children have a chronic illness.

CBT has demonstrated success in helping youth who are managing a chronic illness, with some research suggesting that it can improve young people's functioning in the context of their illness (Ehde, Dillworth, & Turner, 2014). The goal of CBT when working with this population is to help children to recognize and manage any distorted or unproductive thinking related to the illness and to teach them the

---

Understand the child's physical pain or symptoms and how they are affecting him or her; counselors need to understand the child's physical experience—what it is like and how it affects his or her daily life.

Understand the child's developmental level and how it affects his or her experience with and understanding of the illness, and how the illness may affect his or her psychological development.

Address illness-related considerations and concerns that may influence the counseling process, such as scheduling, physical comfort level in counseling, and communications with medical providers.

Empower the child and family to get information and resources they need to feel in control of the illness.

Help the child and family to recognize the emotional impact that the illness has on the child and family and help them to develop the skills they need to cope with these illness-related life changes.

Be available as stable support for the child and his or her family; predictability and consistency are helpful to youth and their families who are managing an unpredictable chronic illness.

FIGURE 19.4   Practice Suggestions for Counselors Who Work with Children Who Have a Chronic Illness

skills they require to manage different aspects of their functioning. When using CBT, the areas that counselors may take into consideration are managing (a) the distress related to the diagnosis or the progression of the illness, (b) the pain associated with the illness or treatment (if applicable), (c) any related psychosocial distress, (d) the treatment/medication routine, and (e) the development of any needed social or disease management skills (Pao & Bosk, 2011). CBT techniques have been shown to be effective on children with cancer, specifically children with leukemia receiving bone marrow aspirates (BMA; Pao & Bosk, 2011).

Behavior therapy techniques such as relaxation training and biofeedback are also frequently used with this population (Ehde et al., 2014). Techniques such as filmed modeling of breathing exercises, imagery/distractions, the use of positive incentives, and behavioral rehearsal can be used to manage the distress associated with medical procedures (Pao & Bosk, 2011). Biofeedback interventions—in conjunction with relaxation techniques—can be used to reduce anxiety and pain symptoms (Pao & Bosk, 2011). CBT techniques have also been used with success to help youth to manage depressive symptoms secondary to a chronic illness diagnosis (Pao & Bosk, 2011).

Solution-focused brief therapy (SFBT) has also been used with some success in counseling youth who have a chronic illness (Frels, Soto-Leggett, & Larocca, 2009). The SFBT model focuses on creative solution building as a means of helping the child and family to make sense of the illness. Three main concepts are used when counseling youth using the SFBT model: (a) counseling is centered on the clients' concerns because they are the experts on their experiences and their solutions, (b) counseling focuses on helping clients to create new, more adaptive meanings and realities around their illness, and (c) counseling draws on clients' strengths and past successes to resolve struggles related to the illness (Frels et al., 2009). When applied to younger children, creative expression and play therapy are used to facilitate the goals of an SFBT approach. SFBT aims to empower clients and their families, help them to set clear goals, and help them to reframe struggles caused by the chronic illness (Frels et al., 2009). In addition, SFBT-focused counseling helps youth to discover new ways of handling the stress of the illness.

As previously mentioned, adjustment to chronic illness is difficult on the child and the family. Therefore, family involvement is critical to the youth's success, and family members should be part of counseling when working with young people around illness adjustment and management. Counselors working with the family must provide a predictable, comfortable setting to help the parents and the child during the process. Counselors may also recommend parents obtain other emotional supports, such as their own personal counseling (Storlie & Baltrinic, 2015). Figure 19.5 provides provides suggestions for how parents may be advised to respond to their children who have a chronic illness.

Understand your child's physical/psychological needs related to the illness.

Listen to your child's issues, fears, and confusions about the illness.

Value support from others, such as close and extended family and friends.

Consider the family dynamic and how it is affecting your child.

Maintain self-care for yourself.

Plan for time, money, and anything extra the illness brings.

Validate the difficulties and challenges of the illness.

Nurture your child's emotions, thoughts, and self-awareness.

Stay educated and involved about the illness.

Recognize the emotions the illness brings.

Know the risks and challenges ahead.

Remain calm.

Be hopeful.

FIGURE 19.5 Suggestions for Parents of Youth Who Have a Chronic Illness/Disability

Different programs have been suggested for helping families to adjust to and manage a chronic illness/disability. Mastering Each New Direction (MEND; Distelberg, Williams-Reade, Tapanes, Montgomery, & Pandit, 2014) is one example of a program that focuses on helping the child and family to increase medical treatment adherence and improve disease-specific outcomes (Distelberg et al., 2014). MEND integrates and focuses on individual, family, social, and health care systems and pulls on techniques associated with cognitive, behavioral, emotional, and social processes. This intervention is a 21-day, 7-days-a-week, comprehensive, intensive, outpatient, family-based model. Each session lasts about 3 hours. During those 3 hours, children participate in group therapy with 8 to 10 other children. The groups use creative interventions, play therapy, talk therapy, and stress management techniques. Parents engage in education and process groups (without the child) during the first 2 hours. During the last hour, the parents and child come together for multifamily groups. Family dynamics are assessed—specifically stress response patterns and emotional patterns—to help the family to respond in a positive and understanding manner to the child. Outside the regular 3-hour sessions, additional individual and family therapy is available (Distelberg et al., 2014). This is just one example of a model that can be applied when counseling youth who are navigating a chronic illness/disability.

I CAN START COUNSELING PLAN FOR ELLA

This chapter began with a discussion of a 15-year-old girl who restricts food intake and engages in purging behaviors. Ella meets the diagnostic criteria for anorexia nervosa, purging subtype. A counselor must consider various factors before moving ahead with a strength-based treatment approach. The following I CAN START conceptual framework outlines counseling considerations that may be helpful to a school counselor or a clinical counselor who works with Ella.

C = Contextual Assessment

Ella is a 16-year-old Caucasian girl from a middle-class urban family. Her family is intact, and she has two younger siblings. Ella has a supportive family, and they are actively involved in her life. Ella experiences normal adolescent developmental struggles (e.g., identity, relationships), yet these struggles have been complicated by the anorexia nervosa. Her struggle to achieve identity development is twisted with the eating disorder; being a dancer and being thin is central to her identity, and this poses struggles. Her eating disorder has become an accomplice in helping her to maintain and promote this identity. The stress of perfectionism and her lack of identity outside of being a dancer could be exacerbating the eating disorder symptoms, and these issues should be integrated into her treatment plan as her behavior stabilizes.

A = Assessment and Diagnosis

Diagnosis = 307.51 (F50.2) Anorexia Nervosa

The Children's Eating Disorder Examination (ChEDE; conducted at initial assessment)

Eating Disorder Examination–Questionnaire (EDE-Q; Fairburn & Beglin, 1994) at initial session and then administered every 4 weeks to assess symptom severity

Physical examination by a physician to determine if there are any long-standing medical complications secondary to restriction and purging behaviors that need to be immediately addressed

Formal assessment by a psychiatrist to determine if psychiatric medication may be helpful

N = Necessary Level of Care

Outpatient treatment plus family therapy (once per week)

A higher level of care should be considered if symptoms do not improve and/or there is no evidence of weight gain within 4–6 sessions.

S = Strengths

Self: Ella is an intelligent, determined, and tenacious young woman. She is passionate and is goal focused. She is taking advanced classes in high school and plans to be a physician's assistant. She is sociable, gregarious, and friendly.

Family: Ella's family is supportive. They are committed to treatment and willing to do whatever is necessary to help their daughter. They also possess the financial means to assist in covering treatment expenses that insurance may not cover. Her family is well educated, and her father has already begun to do his own research on eating disorders to better help his daughter.

School/community: Ella lives in a safe, stable community and has access to excellent mental health care resources. Her community has a residential eating disorder unit and an outpatient center that specializes in eating disorders. Her community also has a wellness center that offers yoga and mindfulness retreats for members.

T = Treatment Approach

FBT (Maudsley Method)

A = Aim and Objective of Counseling (three-phase objectives)

Phase I (Sessions 1–10)

Ella's parents will be empowered to take over management of Ella's meals and physical activity to promote weight restoration. Parents will be responsible for selecting her food, preparing her food, portioning her food, serving her food, and monitoring her meals so they can ensure everything has been consumed. Ella's parents will collaborate on a parent-driven plan for monitoring food consumption and time after meals. Ella will achieve at least 95% Expected Body Weight by the end of Phase I, with a minimum of 4 lb gained in the first 4 weeks (Doyle, le Grange, Loeb, Doyle, & Crosby, 2010).

Phase II (Sessions 11–17)

Ella and her parents will collaborate on a family-driven plan designed to slowly return developmentally appropriate control to Ella in a manner that supports weight maintenance. Ella and her parents will assign Ella responsibilities for food and weight management (e.g., eating lunch in the cafeteria with friends as opposed to eating in the nurse's office with her parents) until Ella is managing her food and activity to what one would expect from a typical 15-year-old.

Phase III (Sessions 18–20)

Ella and her family will generalize problem-solving skills learned in earlier treatment phases to issues related to typical adolescent development. Ella's family will identify risks factors for relapse and an eating disorder action plan for managing these risks, should they arise. Ella's family will select one issue not related to an eating disorder to discuss and problem solve using the support of the counselor.

R = Research-Based Interventions (based on FBT)

Counselor will help Ella and her parents to develop and apply the following FBT interventions:

- Parent Empowerment
- Blame Reduction Strategies
- Externalization Strategies
- Laser Focus on Symptom Management Strategies

T = Therapeutic Support Services

Ongoing medication management by a psychiatrist (if medication is needed)

Ongoing medical evaluation by a medical provider who has an expertise in eating disorders

Access to a higher level of care if needed

Coordination of care with school personnel

Summary

This chapter discussed physical health-related problems that youth navigate. Youth who have eating disorders, elimination disorders, and chronic illnesses and disabilities face a unique set of challenges. Counselors working with youth who have physical and health-related concerns should take a proactive, holistic approach to counseling and advocating for clients' needs.

Eating disorders are serious, potentially life-threatening disorders that counselors need to be aware of and swiftly respond to. The longer a young person has an eating disorder, the more deeply entrenched he or she can become in the disorder, thus making it harder to move away from it. Early intervention is essential. In this chapter, we focused on eating disorders, but we did not discuss counselors' role in the prevention of eating disorders and the promotion of a healthy body image. Counselors, especially school counselors, can provide prevention programming in their work settings. Awareness and prevention programming not only prevent eating disorders but also help young people to develop a healthy body image. In addition, youth can struggle with a poor body image, and this may affect their mental health and self-esteem. Counselors should—in the context of a warm, safe, supportive relationship—work to empower youth who struggle with poor body image and help them to understand the roots of their dissatisfaction and techniques they can use to enhance their self-image.

Next, the chapter discussed two elimination disorders: enuresis and encopresis. Enuresis is the repeated voiding of urine in inappropriate places, and youth with this disorder are typically well-adjusted individuals who have met other developmental milestones at expected times. Most youth outgrow the symptoms of enuresis by adolescence, but counselors can implement behavioral interventions to train the body. Medication can, in some situations, be helpful if the enuresis is related to biological factors.

Encopresis is the repeated voiding of feces into inappropriate places, and this behavior is most often the result of constipation. Youth can become constipated when they avoid regularly going to the bathroom because they are stressed, scared, embarrassed, or distracted. As a result, a large, uncomfortable mass of feces gathers in the colon, and looser stool leaks out around it. Youth rarely expel fully formed stool that is not related to constipation in any way, and this is typically associated with behavior disorders. Counselors can address encopresis with cognitive and behavioral interventions, and medical providers can use medication to help youth to manage constipation.

Overall, the mind–body connection is strong, and counselors provide holistic services with a close eye to the mental health implications that are associated with physical health-related issues. Counselors are able to provide youth and their families with psychoeducation regarding a wide variety of physical health-related problems, and counselors can also provide referrals and work in conjunction with medical professionals. Counselors should work within their area of competence to provide comprehensive support for youth who experience a wide variety of physical health-related stressors and difficulties.

MyLab Counseling: Counseling Children and Adolescents

In the Topic 13 Assignments: *Strategies for Addressing Physical Health Concerns in Youth*, try Application Exercise 13.1: *Strategies for Preventing Eating Disorders,* Application Exercise 13.2: *Strategies for Addressing Enuresis,* and Licensure Quiz 13.2: *Eating Disorders.*

Then try Licensure Quiz 13.3: *Elimination Disorders* and Application Exercise 13.4: *Understanding and Addressing the Effects of Chronic Illness/Disability in Youth.*

REFERENCES

Academy of Eating Disorders. (2011). *Eating disorders: Critical points for early recognition and medical risk management in the care of individuals with eating disorders* (2nd ed.). Retrieved from http://www.aedweb.org

Achenbach, T. M., & Rescorla, L. A. (2001). *Manual for the ASEBA School-Age Forms & Profiles*. Burlington: University of Vermont, Research Center for Children, Youth, & Families.

Ackerman, N. W. (1958). *The psychodynamics of family life*. New York, NY: Basic Books.

Ackerman, N. W. (1966). *Treating the troubled family*. New York, NY: Basic Books.

Adamson, N., & Kress, V. E. (2011). "Green" counseling: Integrating reused household materials into creative counseling interventions. *Journal of Creativity in Mental Health, 6*(3), 193–201. doi:10.1080/15401383.2011.605103

Adler, A. (1958). *The practice and theory of individual psychology*. Paterson, NJ: Littlefield, Adams.

Adler-Baeder, F., Kerpelman, J. L., Schramm, D. G., Higginbotham, B., & Paulk, A. (2007). The impact of relationship education on adolescents of diverse backgrounds. *Family Relations: Interdisciplinary Journal of Applied Family Studies, 56*, 291–303. doi:10.1111/j.1741-3729.2007.00460.x

Ageranioti-Bélanger, S., Brunet, S., D'Anjou, G., Tellier, G., Boivin, J., & Gauthier, M. (2012). Behaviour disorders in children with an intellectual disability. *Paediatrics & Child Health, 17*, 84–88. Retrieved from http://www.pulsus.com/journals/journalHome.jsp?sCurrPg=journal&jnlKy=5&/home.htm

Agras, S., Crow, S. J., Halmi, K. A., Mitchell, J. E., Wilson, G. T., & Kraemer, H. C. (2000). Outcome predictors for the cognitive behavioral treatment of bulimia nervosa: Data from a multisite study. *American Journal of Psychiatry, 157*, 1302–1308.

Ainsworth, B., Eddershaw, R., Meron, D., Baldwin, D. S., & Garner, M. (2013). The effect of focused attention and open monitoring meditation on attention network function in healthy volunteers. *Psychiatry Research, 210*, 1226–1231. doi:10.1016/j.psychres.2013.09.002

Ainsworth, M. D. S., & Bell, S. M. (1970). Attachment, exploration, and separation: Illustrated by the behavior of one-year-olds in a strange situation. *Child Development, 41*, 49–67.

Ainsworth, M. D. S., Blehar, M. C., Waters, E., & Wall, S. (2014). *Patterns of attachment: A psychological study of the strange situation*. New York, NY: Psychology.

Aizer, A. (2008, February). *Neighborhood violence and urban youth* (National Bureau of Economic Research [NBER] Working Paper No. 13773). Retrieved from http://www.nber.org/papers/w13773.pdf

Alexander, F. G., & French, T. M. (1946). *Psychoanalytic therapy: Principles and applications*. New York, NY: Ronald.

Ali, M. M., Amialchuk, A., & Dwyer, D. S. (2011). The social contagion effect of marijuana use among adolescents. *PLoS One, 6*, e16183. doi:10.1371/journal.pone.0016183

Amato, P. R. (2014). The consequences of divorce for adults and children: An update. *Journal for General Social Issues, 1*, 5–25. doi:10.5559/di.23.1.01

American Academy of Child and Adolescent Psychiatry (AACAP). (2007). Practice parameter for the assessment and treatment of children and adolescents with depressive disorders. *Journal of the American Academy of Child and Adolescent Psychiatry, 46*(11), 1503–1526. doi:10.1097/chi.0b013e318 14ae1c

American Academy of Child and Adolescent Psychiatry (AACAP). (2010a). Practice parameter for the assessment and treatment of children and adolescents with posttraumatic stress disorder. *Journal of the American Academy of Child and Adolescent Psychiatry, 49*(4), 414–430.

American Academy of Child and Adolescent Psychiatry (AACAP). (2010b). Practice parameter for the assessment and treatment of children and adolescents with obsessive-compulsive disorder. *Journal of the American Academy of Child and Adolescent Psychiatry, 51*(1), 98–113. doi:10.1016/j.jaac.2011.09.019

American Academy of Child & Adolescent Psychiatry (AACAP). (2011a). *Facts for families: Children of alcoholics*. Retrieved from https://www.aacap.org/App_Themes/AACAP/docs/facts_for_families/17_children_of_alcoholics.pdf

American Academy of Child & Adolescent Psychiatry (AACAP). (2011b). *Facts for families: The adopted child*. Retrieved from https://www.aacap.org/App_Themes/AACAP/docs/facts_for_families/15_the_adopted_child.pdf

American Academy of Child & Adolescent Psychiatry (AACAP). (2013). *Facts for families: Children and grief*. Retrieved from http://www.aacap.org/App_Themes/AACAP/docs/facts_for_families/08_children_and_grief.pdf

American Academy of Child and Adolescent Psychiatry (AACAP). (2014). *Child abuse: The hidden bruises*. Washington, DC: Author.

American Academy of Pediatrics. (2011a). ADHD: Clinical practice guideline for the diagnosis, evaluation, and treatment of attention-deficit/hyperactivity disorder in children and adolescents. *Pediatrics, 128*(5), 1007–1022. doi:10.1542/peds.2011-2654

American Academy of Pediatrics. (2011b). *Caring for children with ADHD: A resource toolkit for clinicians*. Elk Grove Village, IL: Author.

American Academy of Pediatrics. (2016). *Supporting and caring for transgender children*. Retrieved from http://www.aap.org

American Art Therapy Association. (2013a). *Ethical principles for art therapists*. Alexandria, VA: Author.

American Art Therapy Association. (2013b). *What is art therapy?* Retrieved from http://www.arttherapy.org/upload/whatisarttherapy.pdf

American Association for Marriage and Family Therapy. (2012). *Code of ethics*. Alexandria, VA: Author.

American Association of Pastoral Counselors. (2012). *Code of ethics*. Fairfax, VA: Author.

American Counseling Association (ACA). (2014). *ACA Code of Ethics*. Alexandria, VA: Author.

American Counseling Association (ACA). (2015). *About us. What is counseling?* Retrieved from http://www.counseling.org/about-us/about-aca

American Mental Health Counselors Association. (2015). *Code of ethics*. Alexandria, VA: Author.

American Psychiatric Association (APA). (2006). Treatment recommendations for patients with eating disorders. *American Journal of Psychiatry, 163*(7 Suppl. 7), 1–54. Retrieved from http://www.edtreatmenthelp.org/references/8_published_practice_guidelines.html

American Psychiatric Association (APA). (2013a). *Diagnostic and statistical manual of mental disorders* (5th ed.). Washington, DC: Author.

American Psychiatric Association (APA). (2013b). *DSM-5 Parent/Guardian-Rated Level 1 Cross-Cutting Symptom Measure— Child age 6–17*. Retrieved from http://www.psychiatry.org

American Psychological Association (2008). *Children and trauma: Update for mental health professionals.* Washington, DC: Author.

American Psychological Association (2010). *Publication Manual of the American Psychological Association.* Washington, DC: Author.

American School Counselor Association (ASCA). (2010). *Ethical standards for school counselors.* Alexandria, VA: Author.

American School Counselor Association (ASCA). (2012). *The ASCA National Model: A framework for school counseling programs* (3rd ed.). Alexandria, VA: Author.

American School Counselor Association (ASCA). (2013). *The school counselor and students with disabilities.* Washington, DC: Author.

American School Counselor Association (ASCA). (2016). *Ethical standards for school counselors.* Alexandria VA: Author.

American Society of Addiction Medicine (ASAM). (2013). *The ASAM Criteria.* Retrieved from https://www.asam.org/resources/the-asam-criteria/about

Anderson, B. J., & Wolpert, H. A. (2004). A developmental perspective on the challenges of diabetes education and care during the young adult period. *Patient Education and Counseling, 53,* 347–352.

Antony, M. M., & Roemer, L. (2011). *Behavior therapy.* Washington, DC: American Psychological Association.

Antshel, K. M., Faraone, S. V., & Gordan, M. (2012). Cognitive behavioral treatment outcomes in adolescent ADHD. *Journal of Attention Disorders, 18*(6), 483–495. doi:10.1177/1087054712443155

Antshel, K. M., Hargrave, T. M., Simonescu, M., Prashant, K., Hendrricks, K., & Faraone, S. V. (2011). Advances in understanding and treating ADHD. *BMC Medicine, 9,* 72. doi:10.1186/1741-7015-9-72

Anyon, Y., Ong, S. L., & Whitaker, K. (2014). School-based mental health prevention for Asian American adolescents: Risk behaviors, protective factors, and service use. *Asian American Journal of Psychology, 5*(2), 134–144. doi:10.1037/a0035300

Arkes, J. (2013). The temporal effects of parental divorce on youth substance use. *Substance Use & Misuse, 48*(3), 290–297. doi:10.3109/10826084.2012.755703

Aronson-Fontes, L. (2005). *Child abuse and culture: Working with diverse families.* New York, NY: Guilford.

Asahi, K., & Aoki, K. (2010). Developmental changes in preadolescent friendships: From the perspective of close friendship and mental health. *Japanese Journal of Counseling Science, 43*(3), 182–191.

Retrieved from https://www.jstage.jst.go.jp/article/cou/43/3/43_182/_pdf

Ashwood, K. L., Tye, C., Azadi, B., Cartwright, S., Asherson, P., & Bolton, P. (2015). Brief report: Adaptive functioning in children with ASD, ADHD and ASD + ADHD. *Journal of Autism and Developmental Disorders, 45*(7), 2235–2242. doi:10.1007/s10803-014-2352-y

Association for Lesbian Gay, Bisexual, Transgender Issues in Counseling (ALGBTIC) LGBTQQIA Competencies Taskforce. (2013). Association for Lesbian, Gay, Bisexual, and Transgender Issues in Counseling competencies for counseling with lesbian, gay, bisexual, queer, questioning, intersex, and ally individuals. *Journal of LGBTQ Issues in Counseling, 7,* 2–43. doi:10.1080/15538605.2013.755444

Association for Lesbian Gay, Bisexual, Transgender Issues in Counseling (ALGBTIC) Transgender Committee. (2010). American Counseling Association competencies for counseling with transgender clients. *Journal of LGBT Issues in Counseling, 4,* 135–159. doi:10.1080/15538605.210.524839

Association for Play Therapy (APT). (1997). A definition of play therapy. *The Association for Play Therapy Newsletter, 16*(1), 7. Retrieved from http://www.a4pt.org

Association for Play Therapy (APT). (2015). *Evidence-based practice statement: Play therapy.* Retrieved from http://www.a4pt.org

Association of Recovery Schools. (2016). *Accreditation.* Retrieved from https://recoveryschools.org/accreditation

Attia, E., Kaplan, A. S., Walsh, B. T., Gershkovich, M., Yilmaz, Z., Musante, D., . . . Wang, Y. (2011). Olanzapine versus placebo for out-patients with anorexia nervosa. *Psychological Medicine, 41,* 2177–2182.

Axline, V. (1947). *Play therapy: The inner dynamics of childhood.* Cambridge, MA: Houghton Mifflin.

Baden, A. L., Gibbons, J. L., Wilson, S. L., & McGinnis, H. (2013). International adoption: Counseling and the adoption triad. *Adoption Quarterly, 16,* 213–237. doi:10.1080/10926755.2013.794440

Baer, R. A., Hopkins, J., Krietemeyer, J., Smith, G. T., & Toney, L. (2006). Using self-report assessment methods to explore facets of mindfulness. *Assessment, 13,* 27–45. doi:10.1177/1073191105283504

Baggerly, J., Ray, D., & Bratton, S. (2010). *Child-centered play therapy research: The evidence base for effective practice.* Hoboken, NJ: Wiley.

Bagwell, C. L., & Schmidt, M. E. (2011). *Friendships in childhood and adolescence.* New York, NY: Guilford.

Bailey, J. R., Gross, A. M., & Cotton, C. R. (2011). Challenges associated with establishing a token economy in a residential care facility. *Clinical Case Studies, 10,* 278–290. doi:10.1177/1534650111410969

Bailey, R. K., Ali, S., Jabeen, S., Akpudo, H., Avenido, J. U., Bailey, T., . . . Whitehead, A. A. (2010). Attention-deficit/hyperactivity disorder in African American youth. *Current Psychiatry Report, 12*(5), 396–402. doi:10.1006/s11920-010-0144-4

Baker, A. J. L., & Ben-Ami, N. (2011). To turn a child against a parent is to turn a child against himself: The direct and indirect effects of exposure to parental alienation strategies on self-esteem and well-being. *Journal of Divorce & Remarriage, 52,* 472–489. doi:10.1080/10502556.2011.609424

Baker, A. J. L., & Brassard, M. R. (2013). Adolescents caught in parental loyalty conflicts. *Journal of Divorce & Remarriage, 54*(5), 393–413. doi:10.1080/10502556.2013.800398

Balaguru, V., Sharma, J., & Waheed, W. (2012). Understanding the effectiveness of school-based interventions to prevent suicide: A realist review. *Child and Adolescent Mental Health, 18*(3), 131–139.

Bandura, A. (1977). Self-efficacy: Toward a unifying theory of behavioral change. *Psychological Review, 84*(2), 191–215.

Bandura, A. (1986). *Social foundations of thought and action: A social cognitive theory.* Englewood Cliffs, NJ: Prentice Hall.

Barbui, C., Esposito, E., & Cipriani, A. (2009). Selective serotonin reuptake inhibitors and risk of suicide: A systematic review of observational studies. *Canadian Medical Association Journal, 180*(3), 291–297. doi:10.1503/cmaj.081514

Barkley, R. A. (2013a). *Defiant children: A clinician's manual for assessment and parent training* (3rd ed.). New York, NY: Guilford.

Barkley, R. A. (2013b). *Taking charge of ADHD: The complete, authoritative guide for parents* (3rd ed.). New York, NY: Guilford.

Barlow, D. H. (Ed.). (2008). *Clinical handbook of psychological disorders: A step-by-step treatment manual* (4th ed.). New York, NY: Guilford.

Barry, C. T., Golmaryami, F. N., Rivera-Hudson, N., & Frick, P. J. (2013). Evidence-based assessment of conduct disorder: Current considerations and preparation for *DSM-5. Professional Psychology: Research and Practice, 44,* 56–63. doi:10.1037/a0029202

Bartholow, R. G., Willhite, R. G., Brokaw, S. P., & Wolf, J. (2011, September). *Adler Graduate School Life Style Assessment.* Retrieved from http://alfredadler.edu/sites/default/files/515_LifeStyle_Assessment_2011%20Final.pdf

Baruch, G., Vrouva, I., & Fearon, P. (2009). A follow-up study of characteristics of young people that dropout [sic] and continue psychotherapy: Service implications for a clinic in the community. *Child and Adolescent Mental Health, 14*(2), 69–75. doi:10.1111/j.14753588.2008.00492.x

Beauregard, M., & Moore, D. (2011). Creative approaches to working with gender variant and sexual minority boys. In C. Haen & C. Haen (Eds.), *Engaging boys in treatment: Creative approaches to the therapy process* (pp. 293–316). New York, NY: Routledge.

Beck, A. T. (1963). Thinking and depression: Idiosyncratic content and cognitive distortions. *Archives of General Psychiatry, 9*(4), 324–333. doi:10.1001/archpsyc.1963.01720160014002

Beck, A. T. (1964). Thinking and depression: Theory and therapy. *Archives of General Psychiatry, 10*, 561–571. Retrieved from http://jamanetwork.com/journals/jamapsychiatry

Beck, A. T. (1967). *Depression.* New York, NY: Harper & Row.

Beck, A. T. (2005). The current state of cognitive therapy: A 40-year retrospective. *Archives of General Psychiatry, 62*(9), 953–959. doi:10.1001/archpsyc.62.9.953

Beck, A. T., & Alford, B. A. (2009). *Depression: Causes and treatment* (2nd ed.). Philadelphia: University of Pennsylvania Press.

Beck, A. T., Freeman, A., & Davis, D. (2004). *Cognitive therapy of personality disorders* (2nd ed.). New York, NY: Guilford.

Beck, A. T., Rush, A. J., Shaw, B. F., & Emery, G. (1979). *Cognitive therapy of depression.* New York, NY: Guilford.

Beck, J. S. (2005). *Cognitive therapy for challenging problems: What to do when the basics don't work.* New York, NY: Guilford.

Beck, J. S., Beck, A. T., & Jolly, J. B. (2001). *Beck Youth Inventories.* San Antonio, TX: The Psychological Corporation.

Beck, J. S., Beck, A. T., Jolly, J. B., & Steer, R. A. (2005). *Beck Youth Inventories for Children and Adolescents: Manual* (2nd ed.). San Antonio, TX: Harcourt.

Becker, D. (2013). The impact of teachers' expectations on students' educational opportunities in the life course: An empirical test of a subjective expected utility explanation. *Rationality and Society, 25*(4), 422–469. doi:10.1177/1043463113504448

Becker-Weidman, A. (2008). Treatment for children with reactive attachment disorder: Dyadic development psychotherapy. *Child and Adolescent Mental Health, 13*, 52. doi:10.1111/j.1475-3588.2006.004

Becker-Weidman, A., & Hughes, D. (2008). Dyadic developmental psychotherapy: An evidence-based treatment for children with complex trauma and disorders of attachment. *Child and Family Social Work, 13*, 329–337. doi:10.1111/j.1365-2206.2008.00557.x

Becvar, D. S., & Becvar, R. J. (2012). *Family therapy: A systemic integration* (8th ed.). Upper Saddle River, NJ: Pearson.

Beesdo, K. B., Knapp, S., & Pine, D. S. (2009). Anxiety and anxiety disorder in children and adolescents: Developmental issues and implications for *DSM-V. Psychiatric Clinics of North America, 32*, 483–534. doi:10.1016/j.psc.2009.06.002

Bell, A. C., & D'Zurilla, T. J. (2009). Problem-solving therapy for depression: A meta-analysis. *Clinical Psychology Review, 29*, 348–353. doi:1016/j.cpr.2009.02.003

Bellak, L., & Bellak, S. S. (1949). *The Children's Apperception Test.* New York, NY: CPS.

Benard, B. (2004). *Resiliency: What do we know?* San Francisco, CA: WestEd.

Benjamin, C. L., Puleo, C. M., & Kendall, P. C. (2011). History of cognitive–behavioral therapy (CBT) in youth. *Child and Adolescent Psychiatric Clinics of North America, 20*, 197–189. doi:10.1016/j.chc.2011.01.011

Ben-Porath, D. D. (2010). Dialectical behavior therapy applied to parent skills training: Adjunctive treatment for parents with difficulties in affect regulation. *Cognitive and Behavioral Practice, 17*(4), 458–465. doi:10.1016/j.cbpra.2009.07.005

Bergin, C. C., & Bergin, D. A. (2015). *Child and adolescent development in your classroom* (2nd ed.). Stamford, CT: Cengage.

Bergner, R. M. (2007). Therapeutic storytelling revisited. *American Journal of Psychotherapy, 61*, 149–162. Retrieved from www.ajp.org

Berk, L. E. (2003). *Child development* (6th ed). Boston, MA: Pearson.

Berkowitz, S. J., Stover, C. S., & Marans, S. R. (2011). The Child and Family Traumatic Stress Intervention: Secondary prevention for youth at risk of developing PTSD. *Journal of Child Psychology and Psychiatry, 52*(6), 676–685. doi:111/j.1469-7610.2010.02321.x

Berman, A., Ellis, T. E., Jobes, D., Kaslow, N., King, C., & Linehan, M. (2004). *Core competencies for the assessment and management of individuals at risk for suicide.* Retrieved from http://www.suicidology.org/Portals/14/docs/Training/RRSR_Core_Competencies.pdf

Bertalanffy, L. V. (1968). *General systems theory: Foundation, development, applications.* New York, NY: Braziller.

Bertin, M. (2011). *The family ADHD solution: A scientific approach to maximizing your child's attention and minimizing parental stress.* New York, NY: St. Martin's Press.

Biank, N. M., & Werner-Lin, A. (2011). Growing up with grief: Revisiting the death of a parent over the life course. *Journal of Death & Dying, 63*(3), 271–290. doi:10.2190/OM.63.3.e

Biehal, N., Sinclair, I., & Wade, J. (2015). Reunifying abused or neglected children: Decision-making and outcomes. *Child Abuse & Neglect, 49*, 107–118. doi:10.1016/j.chiabu.2015.04.0414.

Bitsika, V., Sharpley, C. F., & Mailli, R. (2015). The influence of gender, age, psychological resilience and family interaction factors upon anxiety and depression in non-autism spectrum disorder siblings of children with an autism spectrum disorder. *British Journal of Guidance & Counselling, 43*(2), 216–228. doi:10.1080/03069885.2014.950944

Black, T., Trocmé, N., Fallon, B., & MacLaurin, B. (2008). The Canadian child welfare system response to exposure to domestic violence investigations. *Child Abuse & Neglect, 32*(3), 393–404. doi:10.1016/j.chiabu.2007.10.002

Blake, D. D., Weathers, F. W., Nagy, L. M., Kaloupek, D. G., Gusman, F. D., Charney, D. S., . . . Keane, T. M. (1995). The development of a clinician-administered PTSD scale. *Journal of Traumatic Stress, 8*, 75–90.

Bogh, E. H., Rokkedal, K., & Valbak, K. (2005). A 4-year follow-up on bulimia nervosa. *European Eating Disorders Review, 13*, 48–53.

Bohart, A. C., & Wade, A. G. (2013). The client in psychotherapy. In M. J. Lambert (Ed.), *Bergin and Garfield''s handbook of psychotherapy and behavior change* (6th ed., pp. 219–257). New York, NY: Wiley.

Bonovitz, C. (2009). Countertransference in child psychoanalytic psychotherapy. *Psychoanalytic Psychology, 26*(3), 235–245. doi:10.1037/a0016445.

Bordin, E. S. (1979). The generalizability of the psychoanalytic concept of the working alliance. *Psychotherapy: Theory, Research & Practice, 16*(3), 252–260. doi:10.1037/h0085885

Bosch, L. A., Segrin, C., & Curran, M. A. (2012). Identity style during the transition to adulthood: The role of family communication patterns, perceived support, and affect. *Identity: An International Journal of Theory and Research, 12*(4), 275–295. doi:10.1080/15283488.2012.716379

Botha, C. J., & Wild, L. G. (2013). Evaluation of a school-based intervention programme for South African children of divorce. *Journal of Child and Adolescent Mental*

Health, 25(1), 81–91. doi:10.2989/17280583. 2013.768528

Bourke, A., Boduszek, D., Kelleher, C., McBride, O., & Morgan, K. (2014). Sex education, first sex and sexual health outcomes in adulthood: Findings from a nationally representative sexual health survey. *Sex Education, 14*(3), 299–309. doi: 10.1080/14681811.2014.887008

Boutot, E., & Hume, K. (2012). Beyond time out and table time: Today's applied behavior analysis for students with autism. *Education and Training in Autism and Developmental Disabilities, 47*(1), 23–38.

Bowen, M. (1978). *Family therapy in clinical practice.* New York, NY: Jason Aronson.

Bowlby, J. (1969). *Attachment and loss* (Vol. 1). New York, NY: Basic Books.

Bowlby, J. (1988). *A secure base: Parent–child attachment and healthy human development.* New York, NY: Basic Books.

Bradshaw, C. P., Waasdorp, T. E., & Johnson, S. L. (2015). Overlapping verbal, relational, physical, and electronic forms of bullying in adolescence: Influence of school context. *Journal of Clinical Child & Adolescent Psychology, 44*(3), 494–508. doi:10.1080/15374416.2014.893516

Bratton, S., Landreth, G., Kellam, T., & Blackard, S. R. (2006). *Child parent relationship therapy (CPRT) treatment manual: A 10-session filial therapy model for training parents.* New York, NY: Routledge.

Bratton, S., Purswell, K., & Jayne, K. (2015). Play therapy: A child-centered approach. In H. Thompson Prout & A. L. Fedewa (Eds.), *Counseling and psychotherapy with children and adolescents* (5th ed., pp. 91–113). Hoboken, NJ: Wiley.

Bratton, S., & Ray, D. (2000). What the research shows about play therapy. *International Journal of Play Therapy, 9*(1), 47–88.

Brausch, A. M., & Girresch, S. K. (2012). A review of empirical treatment studies for adolescent nonsuicidal self-injury. *Journal of Cognitive Psychotherapy: An International Quarterly, 26*(1), 3–18. doi:10. 1891/0889-8391.26.1.3

Breda, C. S., & Riemer, M. (2012). Motivation for Youth's Treatment Scale (MYTS): A new tool for measuring motivation among youths and their caregivers. *Administration and Policy Mental Health and Mental Health Services Research, 39*(1–2), 118–132. doi:10.1007/s10488-012-0408-x

Breiding, M. J., Basile, K. C., Smith, S. G., Black, M. C., & Mahendra, R. R. (2015). *Intimate partner violence surveillance: Uniform definitions and recommended data elements, version 2.0.* Atlanta, GA: National Center for Injury Prevention and Control, Centers for Disease Control and Prevention.

Brent, D. A., Poling, K. D., & Goldstein, T. R. (2011). *Treating depressed and suicidal adolescents.* New York, NY: Guilford.

Bridges, M. R. (2006). Activating the corrective emotional experience. *Journal of Clinical Psychology: In Sessions, 62*(5), 551–568. doi:10.1002/jclp.20248

Brier, J. N., & Scott, C. (2014). *Principles of trauma therapy: A guide to symptoms, evaluation, and treatment (2nd ed.), DSM-5 update.* Thousand Oaks, CA: SAGE.

Briere, J. (1996). *Trauma Symptom Checklist for Children: Professional manual.* Odessa, FL: Psychological Assessment Resources.

Briere, J., & Lanktree, C. B. (2012). *Treating complex trauma in adolescents and young adults.* Thousand Oaks, CA: Sage.

Briere, J., & Scott, C. (2015). *Principles of trauma therapy: A guide to symptoms, evaluation, and treatment* (2nd ed.). Thousand Oaks, CA: Sage.

Broderick, P. C., & Blewitt, P. (2015). *The life span: Human development for helping professionals* (4th ed.). Upper Saddle River, NJ: Pearson.

Bronfenbrenner, U. (1979). *The ecology of human development: Experiments by nature and design.* Cambridge, MA: Harvard University Press.

Brown, A. P., Marquis, A., & Guiffrida, D. A. (2013). Mindfulness-based interventions in counseling. *Journal of Counseling & Development, 91*(1), 96–104. doi:10.1002/ j.1556-6676.2013.00077.x

Brummelman, E., Thomaes, S., Overbeek, G., Orobio de Castro, B., van den Hout, M. A., & Bushman, B. J. (2014). On feeding those hungry for praise: Person praise backfires in children with low self-esteem. *Journal of Experimental Psychology: General, 143*(1), 9–14. doi:10.1037/ a0031917

Buchman-Schmitt, J. M., Chiurliza, B., Chu, C., Michaels, M. S., & Joiner, T. E. (2014). Suicidality in adolescent populations: A review of the extant literature through the lens of the interpersonal theory of suicide. *International Journal of Behavioral Consultation and Therapy, 9*(3), 26–31.

Buck, J. N. (1970). *House-Tree-Person Technique: Manual.* Los Angeles, CA: Western Psychological Services.

Burke, J. D., Hipwell, A. E., & Loeber, R. (2011). Dimensions of oppositional defiant disorder as predictors of depression and conduct disorder in preadolescent girls. *Journal of the American Academy of Child and Adolescent Psychiatry, 49,* 484–492. Retrieved from http://www.jaacap.com

Butler, A. C., Chapman, J. E., Forman, E. M., & Beck, A. T. (2006). The empirical status of cognitive-behavioral therapy: A review of meta-analyses. *Clinical Psychology Review, 26*(1), 17–31. doi:10.1016/j.cpr.2005.07.003

Butler, J. B., & Ciarrochi, J. (2007). Psychological acceptance and quality of life in the elderly. *Quality Life Research, 16,* 607–615. Retrieved from http://www.isoqol.org/research-publications/quality-of-life-research

Butler, M. G., Youngs, E. L., Roberts, J. L., & Hellings, J. A. (2012). Assessment and treatment in autism spectrum disorders: A focus on genetics and psychiatry. *Autism Research and Treatment,* 242537. doi:10.1155/ 2012/242537

Cain, D. J. (2010). *Person-centered psychotherapies.* Washington, DC: American Psychological Association.

Campbell, M., Robertson, A., & Jahoda, A. (2014). Psychological therapies for people with intellectual disabilities: Comments on a matrix of evidence for interventions in challenging behaviour. *Journal of Intellectual Disability Research, 58*(2), 172–188. doi:10.111/j.1365-2788.2012. 01646.x

Capuzzi, D., & Stauffer, M. D. (2016). *Human growth and development across the lifespan: Applications for counselors.* Hoboken, NJ: Wiley.

Carlson, R. (2001). Therapeutic use of story in therapy with children. *Guidance and Counseling, 16,* 92–99. Retrieved from http://www.utpguidancecentre.com

Carmichael, K. D. (2006). *Play therapy: An introduction.* Upper Saddle River, NJ: Pearson.

Carney, J. V. (2007). Humanistic wellness services for community mental health providers. *Journal of Humanistic Counseling, 46,* 154–171.

Carney, J. V., & Hazler, R. J. (2015). Bullying intervention practice brief. *American Counseling Association: Practice Briefs.* Retrieved from http://www.counseling.org/ knowledge-center/center-for-counseling-practice-policy-and-research/practice-briefs

Carr, A. (2009). *What works with children, adolescents, and adults? A review of research on the effectiveness of psychotherapy.* New York, NY: Routledge.

Carter, J. C., McFarlane, T. L., Bewell, C., Olmsted, M. P., Woodside, D. B., Kaplan, A. S., . . . Crosby, R. D. (2009).

Maintenance treatment for anorexia nervosa: A comparison of cognitive behavior therapy and treatment as usual. *International Journal of Eating Disorders, 42,* 202–207.

Casenhiser, D. M., Shanker, S. G., & Stieben, J. (2013). Learning through interaction in children with autism: Preliminary data from a social-communication-based intervention. *Autism, 17*(2), 220–241.

Cash, S. J., & Bridge, J. A. (2009). Epidemiology of youth suicide and suicidal behavior. *Current Opinions in Pediatrics, 5*(3), 613–619. doi:10.1097/MOP.0b013e 32833063e1

Castelino, T. (2009). Making children's safety and well-being matter. *Australian Social Work, 62*(1), 61–73. doi:10.1080/03124 070802430726

Castro-Blanco, D., & Karver, M. S. (2010). *Elusive alliance: Treatment engagement strategies with high-risk adolescents.* Washington, DC: American Psychological Association.

Cavedini, P., Bassi, T., Ubbiali, A., Casolari, A., Giordani, S., & Zorzi, C. (2004). Neuropsychological investigation of decision-making in anorexia nervosa. *Psychiatry Residency, 127,* 259–266.

Center for Children and Families in the Justice System (CCFJS). (2002). *Children exposed to domestic violence.* Retrieved from http://www.lfcc.on.ca/teacher-us.pdf

Center for Community Health and Development (CCHD), University of Kansas. (2017). Section 4: Asset development. In *Learn a skill* (Chapter 2). Retrieved from http://ctb.ku.edu/en/table-of-contents/overview/models-for-community-health-and-development/asset-development/main

Centers for Disease Control and Prevention (CDC). (2010). Family structure and children's health in the United States: Findings from the National Health Interview Survey, 2001–2007. *Vital and Health Statistics, 10,* 246. Retrieved from http://www.cdc.gov/nchs/data/series/sr_10/sr10_246.pdf

Centers for Disease Control and Prevention (CDC). (2012). *Prevalence of autism spectrum disorders—Autism and Developmental Disabilities Monitoring Network, 14 sites, United States, 2008. MMWR 2012, 61*(SS03), 1–19. Retrieved from http://www.cdc.gov/mmwr/preview/mmwrhtml/ss6103a1.htm?s_cid=ss6103a

Centers for Disease Control and Prevention (CDC). (2013). *Autism spectrum disorder (ASD).* Retrieved from http://www.cdc.gov/ncbddd/autism/treatment.html

Centers for Disease Control and Prevention (CDC). (2014a). *Child maltreatment.* Retrieved from http://www.cdc.gov/violenceprevention/pdf/childmaltreatment-facts-at-a-glance.pdf

Centers for Disease Control and Prevention (CDC). (2014b). *Facts about Down syndrome.* Retrieved from http://www.cdc.gov/ncbddd/birthdefects/downsyndrome.html

Centers for Disease Control and Prevention (CDC). (2014c). *Understanding intimate partner violence* (Division of Violence Prevention). Retrieved from http://www.cdc.gov/violenceprevention/pdf/ipv-factsheet.pdf

Centers for Disease Control and Prevention (CDC). (2015a). *Attention-deficit/hyperactivity disorder (ADHD).* Retrieved from http://www.cdc.gov/ncbddd/adhd/facts.html

Centers for Disease Control and Prevention (CDC). (2015b). *Child abuse and neglect prevention.* Retrieved from http://www.cdc.gov/violenceprevention/childmaltreatment

Centers for Disease Control and Prevention (CDC). (2015c). *Child maltreatment prevention* (National Center for Injury Prevention and Control). Retrieved from http://www.cdc.gov/violenceprevention/childmaltreatment

Centers for Disease Control and Prevention (CDC). (2016). *Positive parenting tips for healthy child development: Middle childhood (9-11 years old).* Retrieved from http://growachild.org/documents/DevelopmentalMilestonesTipSheets/Milestones%20for%209-11%20Year%20Olds.pdf

Centers for Disease Control and Prevention (CDC). (2017a). *Child abuse and neglect prevention.* Retrieved from: https://www.cdc.gov/violenceprevention/childmaltreatment/index.html

Centers for Disease Control and Prevention (CDC). (2017b). *Child abuse and neglect: Definitions.* Retrieved from: https://www.cdc.gov/violenceprevention/childmaltreatment/definitions.html

Centers for Disease Control and Prevention (CDC), National Center for Injury Prevention and Control. (2012a). *Suicide: Facts at a glance* [online]. Retrieved from http://www.cdc.gov/violenceprevention/pdf/suicide-datasheet-a.pdf

Centers for Disease Control and Prevention (CDC), National Center for Injury Prevention and Control. (2012b). *Youth violence: Facts at a glance.* Retrieved from http://www.cdc.gov/violenceprevention/pdf/yv-datasheet-a.pdf

Centers for Disease Control and Prevention (CDC), National Center for Injury Prevention and Control. (2016). *Understanding school violence: Fact sheet.* Retrieved from http://www.cdc.gov/violenceprevention/pdf/school_violence_fact_sheet-a.pdf

Centers for Disease Control and Prevention (CDC), National Center for Chronic Disease Prevention and Health Promotion, Office on Smoking and Health. (2014). *Youth and tobacco use.* Retrieved from http://www.cdc.gov/tobacco/data_statistics/fact_sheets/youth_data/tobacco_use/index.htm

Centers for Disease Control and Prevention (CDC), National Center for Injury Prevention and Control, Division of Violence Prevention. (2014). *Promoting positive community norms.* Retrieved from http://www.cdc.gov/violenceprevention/pdf/efc-promoting-positive-community-norms.pdf.pdf

Centers for Disease Control and Prevention (CDC), National Center for Injury Prevention and Control, Division of Violence Prevention. (2015a). *About school violence.* Retrieved from http://www.cdc.gov/violenceprevention/youthviolence/schoolviolence

Centers for Disease Control and Prevention (CDC), National Center for Injury Prevention and Control, Division of Violence Prevention. (2015b). *Child abuse and neglect prevention.* Retrieved from http://www.cdc.gov/violenceprevention/childmaltreatment

Centers for Disease Control and Prevention (CDC), National Center for Injury Prevention and Control, Division of Violence Prevention. (2015c). *Youth violence: Risk and protective factors.* Retrieved from http://www.cdc.gov/violenceprevention/youthviolence/riskprotectivefactors.html

Cerdá, M., Tracy, M., Sánchez, B., & Galea, S. (2011). Comorbidity among depression, conduct disorder, and drug use from adolescence to young adulthood: Examining the role of violence exposure. *Journal of Traumatic Stress, 24*(6), 641–659. doi:10.1002/jts.20696

Chartier, I. S., & Provencher, M. D. (2013). Behavioural activation for depression: Efficacy, effectiveness and dissemination. *Journal of Affective Disorders, 145*(3), 292–299.

Cheeson, R. A., Chisholm, D., & Zaw, W. (2004). Counseling children with chronic physical illness. *Patient and Counseling Education, 55,* 331–338

Chen, M., & Foshee, V. (2015). Stressful life events and the perpetration of adolescent dating abuse. *Journal of Youth & Adolescence, 44*(3), 696–707. doi:10.1007/s10964-014-0181-0

Chen, S. H., Hua, M., Zhou, Q., Tao, A., Lee, E. H., Ly, J., . . . Main, A. (2014). Parent–child cultural orientations and child adjustment in Chinese American immigrant families. *Developmental Psychology, 50*(1), 189–201. doi:10.1037/a0032473

Child Welfare Information Gateway (CWIG). (2009) *Protecting children in families affected by substance use disorders.* Washington, DC: U.S. Department of Health and Human Services, Children's Bureau.

Child Welfare Information Gateway (CWIG). (2013). *What is child abuse and neglect? Recognizing the signs and symptoms.* Washington, DC: U.S. Department of Health and Human Services, Children's Bureau.

Child Welfare Information Gateway (CWIG). (2014). *Parenting a child who has experienced trauma.* Washington, DC: U.S. Department of Health and Human Services, Children's Bureau.

Child Welfare Information Gateway (CWIG). (2016). *Reunification: Bringing your children home from foster care.* Washington, DC: U.S. Department of Health and Human Services, Children's Bureau.

Choudhury, S., Blakemore, S. J., & Charman, T. (2006). Social cognitive development during adolescence. *Social Cognitive and Affective Neuroscience, 1*(3), 165–174.

Chronis-Tuscano, A., Rubin, K. H., O'Brien, K. A., Coplan, R. J., Thomas, S. R., Dougherty, L. R., . . . Wimsatt, M. (2015). Preliminary evaluation of a multimodal early intervention program for behaviorally inhibited preschoolers. *Journal of Consulting and Clinical Psychology, 83*(3), 534–540. doi:10.1037/a0039043

Chu, B. C., Colognori, D., Weissman, A. S., & Bannon, K. (2009). An initial description and pilot of group behavioral activation therapy for anxious and depressed youth. *Cognitive and Behavioral Practice, 16*, 408–419.

Clark, A. J. (2010). Empathy: An internal model in the counseling process. *Journal of Counseling & Development, 88*(3), 348–356.

Clarke, G. N., & DeBar, L. L. (2010). Group cognitive-behavioral treatment for adolescent depression. In J. R. Weisz & A. E. Kazdin (Eds.), *Evidence-based psychotherapies for children and adolescents* (2nd ed., pp. 110–125). New York, NY: Guilford.

Cobham, V. E., March, S., De Young, A., Leeson, F., Nixon, R., McDermott, B., . . . Kenardy, J. (2012). Involving parents in indicated early intervention for childhood PTSD following accidental injury. *Clinical Child and Family Psychology Review, 15,* 345–363. doi:10.1007/s10567-012-0124-9

Coehlo, D. P. (2011). Encopresis: A medical and family approach. *Pediatric Nursing, 37,* 107–112.

Cohen, J. A., Berliner, L., & Mannarino, A. (2010). Trauma focused CBT for children with co-occurring trauma and behaviour problems. *Child Abuse & Neglect, 34,* 215–224. doi:10.1016/j.chiabu.2009.12.003

Cohen, J. A., & Mannarino, A. P. (2008). Trauma-focused cognitive behavioral therapy for children and parents. *Child and Adolescent Mental Health, 13*(4), 158–162. doi:10.1111/j.1475-3588.2008.00502.x

Cohen, J. A., & Mannarino, A. P. (2011). Supporting children with traumatic grief: What educators need to know. *School Psychology International, 32*(2), 117–131. doi:10.1177/0143034311400827

Cohen, J. A., Mannarino, A. P., & Deblinger, E. (2006). *Treating trauma and traumatic grief in children and adolescents.* New York, NY: Guilford.

Cohen, J. A., Mannarino, A. P., & Deblinger, E. (2010). Trauma-focused cognitive-behavioral therapy for traumatized children. In J. R. Weisz & A. E. Kazdin (Eds.), *Evidence-based psychotherapies for children and adolescents* (2nd ed., pp. 295–311). New York, NY: Guilford.

Cohen, J. A., Mannarino, A. P., & Deblinger, E. (2012). *Trauma-focused CBT for children and adolescents: Treatment applications.* New York, NY: Guilford.

Cohen, J. A., Mannarino, A. P., Kliethermes, M., & Murray, L. A. (2012). Trauma-focused CBT for youth with complex trauma. *Child Abuse and Neglect, 36*(6), 528–541. doi:10.1016/j.chiabu.2012.03.007

Cohen, J. A., Mannarino, A. P., Perel, J. M., & Staron, V. A. (2007). A pilot randomized trial of combined trauma-focused CBT and sertraline for childhood PTSD symptoms. *Journal of the American Academy of Child & Adolescent Psychiatry, 46*(7), 811–819.

Cohen, J. A., & Scheeringa, M. S. (2009). Posttraumatic stress disorders diagnosis in children: Challenges and promise. *Dialogues in Clinical Neurosciences, 11*(1), 91–99.

Collier, K. L., van Beusekom, G., Bos, H. W., & Sandfort, T. M. (2013). Sexual orientation and gender identity/expression related peer victimization in adolescence: A systematic review of associated psychosocial and health outcomes. *Journal of Sex Research, 50*(3–4), 299–317. doi:10.1080/00224499.2012.750639

Compass, B. E., Jaser, S. S., Dunn, M. J., & Rodriguez, E. M. (2011). Coping with chronic illness in childhood and adolescence. *Annual Review of Clinical Psychology, 8,* 455–480.

Conners, C. K. (2008). *Conners manual (3rd ed.).* North Tonawanda, NY: Multi-Health Systems.

Connolly, J., Josephson, W., Schnoll, J., Simkins-Strong, E., Pepler, D., MacPherson, A., . . . Jiang, D. (2015). Evaluation of a youth-led program for preventing bullying, sexual harassment, and dating aggression in middle schools. *Journal of Early Adolescence, 35*(3), 403–434. doi:10.1177/0272431614535090

Constantino, M. J., Arnkoff, D. B., Glass, C. R., Ametrano, R. M., & Smith, J. Z. (2011). Expectations. *Journal of Clinical Psychology, 67*(2), 184–192. doi:10.1002/jclp.20754

Conterio, K., Lader, W., & Bloom, J. K. (1999). *Bodily harm: The breakthrough healing program for self-injurers.* New York, NY: Hachette.

Cook-Cottone, C. P., Kane, L. S., & Anderson, L. M. (2015). *The elements of counseling children and adolescents.* New York, NY: Springer.

Copen, C. E., Daniels, K., Vespa, J., & Mosher, W. D. (2012). *First marriage in the United States: Data from 2006–2010 National Survey of Family Growth.* Atlanta, GA: U.S. Department of Health and Human Services.

Coppolillo, H. P. (1987). *Psychodynamic psychotherapy of children: An introduction to the art and the techniques.* Madison, CT: International Universities.

Core Essential Values. (2016). *Core essential values 2015–2016.* Retrieved from http://www.coreessentials.org/us-1/schools/2014-2015.html

Corey, G., Corey, M., Corey, C., & Callanan, P. (2015). *Issues and ethics in the helping professions* (9th ed.). Belmont, CA: Brooks/Cole.

Council on Foundations. (n.d.). *The effects of family culture on family foundations.* Retrieved from http://www.cof.org/content/effects-family-culture-family-foundations

Council on Foundations. (2015). *The effects of family culture on family foundations.* Retrieved from http://www.cof.org/content/effects-family-culture-family-foundations

Courtney-Seidler, E. A., Burns, K., Ziber, I., & Miller, A. L. (2014). Adolescent suicide and self-injury: Deepening the understanding of the biosocial theory and applying dialectical behavior therapy. *International Journal of Behavioral Consultation and Therapy, 9*(3), 35–40.

Courtois, C. A. (2004). Complex trauma, complex reactions: Assessment and treatment. *Psychotherapy: Theory, Research, Practice, Training, 41*(4), 412–425.

Coyle, S. (2015). Recovery high schools: Getting an education and learning to stay clean and sober. *Social Work Today, 15*(3), 18. Retrieved from http://www.socialworktoday.com/archive/051815p18.shtml

Craig, S. L., & Smith, M. S. (2014). The impact of perceived discrimination and social support on the school performance of multiethnic sexual minority youth. *Youth & Society, 46*(1), 30–50. doi:10.1177/0044118X11424915

Cramer, P. (2006). *Protecting self: Defense mechanism in action.* New York, NY: Guilford.

Crean, H. F. (2012). Youth activity involvement, neighborhood adult support, individual decision making skills, and early adolescent delinquent behaviors: Testing a conceptual model. *Journal of Applied Developmental Psychology, 33*(4), 175–188. doi:10.1016/j.appdev.2012.04.003

Culbert, T., & Banez, G. A. (2016). Pediatric applications. In M. S. Schwartz & F. Andrasik (Eds.), *Biofeedback: A practitioner's guide* (4th ed., pp. 629–650). New York, NY: Guilford.

Curry, J., & Milsom, A. (2014). *Career counseling in P–12 schools.* New York, NY: Springer.

Daly, S. L., & Glenwick, D. S. (2000). Personal adjustment and perceptions of grandchild behavior in custodial grandmothers. *Journal of Clinical Child Psychology, 29,* 108–118. doi:10.1207/S15374424jccp2901_11

Darwich, L., Hymel, S., & Waterhouse, T. (2012). School avoidance and substance use among lesbian, gay, bisexual, and questioning youths: The impact of peer victimization and adult support. *Journal of Educational Psychology, 104*(2), 381–392. doi:10.1037/a0026684

Dattilio, F. M. (2002). Homework assignments in couple and family therapy. *Journal of Clinical Psychology: In Session, 58*(5), 535–547. doi:10.1002/jclp.10031

Dattilio, F. M. (2010). *Cognitive-behavioral therapy with couples and families: A comprehensive guide for clinicians.* New York, NY: Guilford.

David-Ferdon, C., & Simon, T. R. (2014). *Preventing youth violence: Opportunities for action.* Atlanta, GA: Centers for Disease Control and Prevention, National Center for Injury Prevention and Control. Retrieved from http://www.cdc.gov/violenceprevention/youthviolence/pdf/opportunities-for-action.pdf

Davies, D. (2011). *Child development: A practitioner's guide* (3rd ed.). New York, NY: Guilford.

de Haan, A. M., Boon, A. E., de Jong, J. T., Geluk, C. A., & Vermeiren, R. R. (2014). Therapeutic relationship and dropout in youth mental health care with ethnic minority children and adolescents. *Clinical Psychologist, 18,* 1–9. doi:10.1111/cp.12030

de la Rie, S., Noordenbos, G., Donker, M., & Van Furth, E. F. (2007). The patient's view on quality of life and eating disorders. *International Journal of Eating Disorders, 40,* 13–20.

de Santana, C. P., de Souza, W. C., & Feitosa, M. G. (2014). Recognition of facial emotional expressions and its correlation with cognitive abilities in children with Down syndrome. *Psychology & Neuroscience, 7*(2), 73–81. doi:10.3922/j.psns.2014.017

de Shazer, S., & Dolan, Y. (2007). *More than miracles: The state of the art of solution-focused brief therapy.* New York, NY: Routledge.

de Shazer, S., Dolan, Y. M., Korman, H., Trepper, T., & McCollum, E. E. (2007). *More than miracles: The state of the art of solution-focused brief therapy.* New York, NY: Haworth.

Deakin, E., Gastaud, M., & Nunes, M. L. T. (2012). Child psychotherapy dropout: An empirical research review. *Journal of Child Psychotherapy, 38*(2), 199–209. doi:10.1080/0075417X.2012.684489

Deblinger, E., Runyon, M. K., & Steer, R. A. (2014). Profiles of personal resiliency in youth who have experienced physical or sexual abuse. *Journal of Psychoeducational Assessment, 32*(6), 558–566. doi:10.1177/0734282914527407

Decker, S. L., Englund, J. A., Carboni, J. A., & Brooks, J. H. (2011). Cognitive and developmental influences in visual-motor integration skills in young children. *Psychological Assessment, 23*(4), 1010–1016. doi:10.1037/a0024079

Degges-White, S., & Davis, N. L. (2011). *Integrating the expressive arts into counseling practice: Theory-based interventions.* New York, NY: Springer.

Delgado, S. V. (2008). Psychodynamic psychotherapy for children and adolescents: An old friend revisited. *Psychiatry (Edgmont), 5*(5), 67–72.

Della Selva, P. C. (2004). *Intensive short-term dynamic psychotherapy: Theory and technique synopsis.* New York, NY: Karnac.

Demanchick, S. P., Cochran, N. H., & Cochran, J. L. (2003). Person-centered play therapy for adults with developmental disabilities. *International Journal of Play Therapy, 12*(1), 47–65. doi:10.1037/h0088871

DeNavas-Walt, C., Proctor, B. D., & Smith, J. C. (2011). *U.S. Census Bureau, population reports: Income, poverty, and health insurance coverage in the United States.* Washington, DC: U.S. Department of Commerce.

Denby, R. W. (2016). *Kinship care: Increasing child well-being through practice, policy, and research.* New York, NY: Springer.

DeRubeis, R. J., Hollon, S. D., Amsterdam, J. D., Shelton, R. C., Young, P. R., Salomon, R. M., . . . Gallop, R. (2005). Cognitive therapy vs medications in treatment of moderate to severe depression. *Archives of General Psychiatry, 62,* 409–416.

Descilo, T., Greenwald, R., Schmitt, T. A., & Reslan, S. (2010). Traumatic incident reduction for urban at-risk youth and unaccompanied minor refugees: Two open trails. *Journal of Child & Adolescent Trauma, 3,* 181–191. doi:10.1080/19361521.2010.495936

DeStefano, F., Price, C. S., & Weintraub, E. S. (2013). Increasing exposure to antibody-stimulating proteins and polysaccharides in vaccines is not associated with risk of autism. *Journal of Pediatrics, 163*(2), 561–567.

DeVore, E. R., & Ginsburg, K. R. (2005). The protective effects of good parenting on adolescents. *Current Opinion in Pediatrics, 17*(4), 460–465.

Diamond, L. M. (2013). Sexual-minority, gender-nonconforming, and transgender youths. In D. S. Bromberg, W. T. O'Donohue, D. S. Bromberg, & W. T. O'Donohue (Eds.), *Handbook of child and adolescent sexuality: Developmental and forensic psychology* (pp. 275–300). San Diego, CA: Elsevier. doi:10.1016/B978-0-12-387759-8.00011-8

Dickerson Mayes, S., Baweja, R., Calhoun, S., Syed, E., Mahr, F., & Siddiqui, F. (2014). Suicide ideation and attempts and bullying in children and adolescents: Psychiatric and general population samples. *Crisis: The Journal of Crisis Intervention and Suicide Prevention, 35*(5), 301–309. doi:10.1027/0227-5910/a000264

Diehle, J., Opmeer, B. C., Boer, F., Mannarino, A. P., & Lindauer, R. J. L. (2015). Trauma-focused cognitive behavioral therapy or eye movement desensitization and reprocessing: What works in children with posttraumatic stress symptoms? A randomized controlled trial. *European Child & Adolescent Psychiatry, 24,* 227–236. doi:10.1007/s00787-014-0572.5

Diemer, M. A., Kauffman, A., Koenig, N., Trahan, E., & Hsieh, C. (2006). Challenging racism, sexism, and social injustice: Support for urban adolescents' critical consciousness development. *Cultural Diversity and Ethnic Minority Psychology, 12*(3), 444–460. doi:10.1037/1099-9809.12.3.444

Distelberg, B., Williams-Reade, J., Tapanes, D., Montgomery, S., & Pandit, M. (2014).

Evaluation of a family systems intervention for managing pediatric chronic illness: Mastering each new direction (MEND). *Family Process, 53,* 194–213.

DiVerniero, R. (2013). Children of divorce and their nonresidential parent's family: Examining perceptions of communication accommodation. *Journal of Family Communication, 13,* 301–320. doi:10.1080/15267431.2013.823429

Dixon, A. L., Rice, R. E., & Rumsey, A. (2017). Counseling with young adolescents (12–14). In S. Smith-Adcock & C. Tucker (Eds.), *Counseling children and adolescents* (pp. 320–342). Thousand Oaks, CA: Sage.

Dodge, K. A., Lansford, J. E., Burks, V. S., Bates, J. E., Pettit, G. S., Fontaine, R., . . . Price, J. M. (2003). Peer rejection and social information-processing factors in the development of aggressive behavior problems in children. *Child Development, 74*(2), 374–393. doi:10.1111/1467-8624.7402004

Doley, R., Bell, R., Watt, B., & Simpson, H. (2015). Grandparents raising grandchildren: Investigating factors associated with distress among custodial grandparent. *Journal of Family Studies, 21,* 101–119. doi:10.1080/13229400.2015.1015215

Donohue, B., Azrin, N., Allen, D. N., Romero, V., Hill, H. H., Tracy, K., . . . Van Hasselt, V. B. (2009). Family behavior therapy for substance abuse: A review of its intervention components and applicability. *Behavior Modification, 33,* 495–519.

Döpfner, M., Ise, E., Metternich-Kaizman, T. W., Schürmann, S., Rademacher, C., & Breuer, D. (2015). Adaptive multimodal treatment for children with attention-deficit/hyperactivity disorder: An 18-month follow-up. *Child Psychiatry & Human Development, 46*(1), 44–56. doi:10.1007/s10578-014-0452-8

Dowell, N. M., & Berman, J. S. (2013). Therapist nonverbal behavior and perceptions of empathy, alliance, and treatment credibility. *Journal of Psychotherapy Integration, 23*(2), 158–165. doi:10.1037/a0031421

Downing, J., & Bellis, M. (2009). Early pubertal onset and its relationship with sexual risk-taking, substance use and anti-social behaviors: A preliminary cross-sectional study. *BioMed Central Public Health, 9,* 436. doi:10.1186/1471-2458-9-446

Downs, K. J., & Blow, A. J. (2013). A substantive and methodological review of family-based treatment for eating disorders: The last 25 years of research. *Journal of Family Therapy, 35,* 3–28.

Doyle, P. M., le Grange, D., Loeb, K., Doyle, A. C., & Crosby, R. D. (2010). Early response to family-based treatment for adolescent anorexia nervosa. *International Journal of Eating Disorders, 43*(7), 659–662.

Drewes, A. A. (2009). *Blending play therapy with cognitive behavioral therapy: Evidence-based and other effective treatments and techniques.* Hoboken, NJ: Wiley.

Drewes, A. A., & Schaefer, C. E. (2010). *School-based play therapy* (2nd ed.). Hoboken, NJ: Wiley.

Drout, M. O., Habeck, R. V., & Rule, W. R. (2015). Adlerian therapy. In F. Chan, N. L. Berven, & K. R. Thomas (Eds.), *Counseling theories and techniques for rehabilitation and mental health professionals* (2nd ed., pp. 205–226). New York, NY: Springer.

Dundas, I., Wormnes, B., & Hauge, H. (2009). Making exams a manageable task. *Nordic Psychology, 61*(1), 26–41. doi:10.1027/1901-2276.61.1.26

Dunn, M. S., Kitts, C., Lewis, S., Goodrow, B., & Scherzer, G. D. (2011). Effects of youth assets on adolescent alcohol, tobacco, marijuana use, and sexual behavior. *Journal of Alcohol and Drug Education, 55*(3), 23–40. Retrieved from http://jadejournal.com/Data/Sites/1/assets/2011_Vol_55_December.pdf

DuPaul, G. J., Power, T. J., Anatopoulos, A. D., & Reid, R. (2016). *ADHD Rating Scales–5 for children and adolescents: Checklist, norms, and clinical interpretations.* New York, NY: Guilford.

Duric, N., Assmus, J., Gundersen, D., & Elgen, I. B. (2012). Neurofeedback for the treatment of children and adolescents with ADHD: A randomized and controlled clinical trial using parental reposts. *BioMed Central Psychiatry, 12,* 107. doi:10.1186/1471-244X-12-107

Dvir, Y., Ford, J. D., Hill, M., & Frazier, J. A. (2015). Childhood maltreatment, emotional dysregulation, and psychiatric comorbidities. *Harvard Review of Psychiatry, 22*(3), 149–161. doi:10.1097/HRP.0000000000000014

Dyl, J. (2008). Understanding cutting in adolescents: Prevalence, prevention, and intervention. *Brown University Child and Adolescent Behavior Letter, 24*(3), 1–8.

Dyson, M. W., Olino, T. M., Durbin, C. E., Goldsmith, H. H., Bufferd, S. J., Miller, A. R., & Klein, D. N. (2015). The structural and rank-order stability of temperament in young children based on a laboratory-observational measure. *Psychological Assessment, 27*(4), 1388–1401. doi:10.1037/pas0000104

Eaton, D. K., Kann, L., Kinchen, S., Shanklin, S., Flint, K. H., Hawkins, J., . . . Wechsler, H. (2012). Youth risk behavior surveillance—United States, 2011. *Morbidity and Mortality Weekly Report: Surveillance Summaries, 61*(SS04), 1–162. Retrieved from http://www.cdc.gov/mmwr/preview/mmwrhtml/ss6104a1.htm

Edleson, J. L., Ellerton, A. L., Seagren, E. A., Kirchberg, S. L., Schmidt, S. O., & Ambrose, A. T. (2007). Assessing child exposure to adult domestic violence. *Child and Youth Services Review, 29,* 961–971. doi:10.1016/j.childyouth.2006.12.009

Edlund, J. N., & Carlberg, G. (2016). Psychodynamic psychotherapy with adolescents and young adults: Outcomes in routine practice. *Clinical Child Psychology and Psychiatry, 21*(1), 66–80. doi:10.1177/1359104554311

Edwards, K. M., Probst, D. R., Rodenhizer-Stämpfli, K. A., Gidycz, C. A., & Tansill, E. C. (2014). Multiplicity of child maltreatment and biopsychosocial outcomes in young adulthood: The moderating role of resiliency characteristics among female survivors. *Child Maltreatment, 19*(3/4), 188–198. doi:10.1177/1077559514543354

Edwards, M., & Davis, H. (1997). *Counseling children with chronic medical conditions.* Baltimore, MD: Wiley-Blackwell.

Ehde, D. M., Dillworth, T. M., & Turner, J. A. (2014). Cognitive-behavioral therapy for individuals with chronic pain. *American Psychologist, 69,* 153–166.

Ehrensaft, D. (2013). "Look, Mom, I'm a boy—Don't tell anyone I was a girl." *Journal of LGBT Youth, 10*(1–2), 9–28. doi10.1080/19361653.2012.717474

Eisler, I., Simic, M., Russell, G., & Dare, C. (2007). A randomised controlled treatment trial of two forms of family therapy in adolescent anorexia nervosa: A five-year follow-up. *Journal of Child Psychology and Psychiatry, 48,* 552–560.

Elliot, D. S., Menard, S., Rankin, B., Elliot, A., Wilson, W. J., & Huizinga, D. (2006). *Good kids from bad neighborhoods: Successful development in social context.* New York, NY: Cambridge.

Elliott, A. (2015). *Psychoanalytic theory: An introduction* (3rd ed.). New York, NY: Palgrave Macmillan.

Ellis, A. (1962). *Reason and emotion in psychotherapy.* New York, NY: Stuart.

Ellis, A. (2001). *Overcoming destructive beliefs, feelings, and behaviors.* New York, NY: Prometheus Books.

Ellis, A. (2004). Why rational emotive behavior therapy is the most comprehensive and effective form of behavior therapy. *Journal of Rational-Emotive & Cognitive Behavior Therapy, 22*(2), 85–92. doi:10.1023/B:JORE.0000025439.78389.52

Emery, R. E. (2012). *Renegotiating family relationships: Divorce, child custody, and mediation* (2nd ed.). New York, NY: Guilford.

Emery, R. E. (2013). *Cultural sociology of divorce: An encyclopedia.* Thousand Oaks, CA: Sage.

Eppler, C., Olsen, J. A., & Hidano, L. (2009). Using stories in elementary school counseling: Brief, narrative techniques. *Professional School Counseling, 12,* 387–391. Retrieved from http://www.schoolcounselor.org

Erford, B. T., Paul, L. E., Oncken, C., Kress, V. E., & Erford, M. R. (2014). Counseling outcomes for youth with oppositional defiant disorder. *Journal of Counseling & Development, 92*(1), 13–24. doi:10.1002/j.1556-6676.2014.00125.x

Erickson, M. H., & Rossi, E. L. (1989). *February man: Evolving consciousness and identity in hypnotherapy.* New York, NY: Taylor & Francis.

Eriksen, K., & Kress, V. E. (2005). *Beyond the DSM story: Ethical quandaries, challenges, and best practices.* Thousand Oaks, CA: Sage.

Eriksen, K., & Kress, V. E. (2008). Gender and diagnosis: Struggles and suggestions for counselors. *Journal of Counseling & Development, 86,* 152–162. doi:10.1002/j.1556-6678.2008.tb00492.x

Erikson, E. H. (1950). *Childhood and society.* New York, NY: Norton.

Erikson, E. H. (1963). *Childhood and society.* New York, NY: Norton.

Erikson, E. H. (1968). *Identity, youth, and crisis.* New York, NY: W.W. Norton.

Erk, R. R. (2008). Attention-deficit/hyperactivity disorder in children and adolescents. In R. R. Erk (Ed.), *Counseling treatment for children and adolescents with DSM-IV-TR disorders* (2nd ed., pp. 114–162). Upper Saddle River, NJ: Pearson.

Evan-Lacko, S. E., dosReis, S., Kastelic, E. A., Paula, C. S., & Steinwachs, D. M. (2010). Evaluation of guideline-concordant care for bipolar disorder among privately insured youth. *Primary Care Companion to the Journal of Clinical Psychiatry, 12,* 3. doi:10.4088/PCC.09m00837gry

Evans, C. B. R., & Burton, D. L. (2013). Five types of child maltreatment and subsequent delinquency: Physical neglect as the most significant predictor. *Journal of Child & Adolescent Trauma, 6,* 231–245. doi:10.1080/19361521.2013.837567

Fabiano, G. A., Pelham, W. E., Coles, E. K., Gnagy, E. M., Chronis-Tuscano, A., & O'Connor, B. C. (2009). A meta-analysis of behavioral treatments for attention-deficit/hyperactivity disorder. *Clinical Psychology Review, 29*(20), 129–140. doi:10.1016/j.cpr.2008.11.001

Fairburn, C. G. (1981). A cognitive behavioural approach to the management of bulimia. *Psychological Medicine, 11,* 707–711.

Fairburn, C. G. (2008). *Cognitive behavior therapy and eating disorders.* New York, NY: Guilford.

Fairburn, C. G., Agras, W. S., Walsh, B. T., Wilson, G. T., & Stice, E. (2004). Prediction of outcome in bulimia nervosa by early change in treatment. *American Journal of Psychiatry, 161,* 2322–2324.

Fairburn, C. G., & Beglin, S. J. (1994). Assessment of eating disorders: Interview or self-report questionnaire. *International Journal of Eating Disorders, 16,* 363–370.

Fairburn, C. G., Cooper, Z., Doll, H. A., O'Connor, M. E., Bohn, K., Hawker, D. M., . . . Palmer, R. L. (2009). Transdiagnostic cognitive–behavioral therapy for patients with eating disorders: A two-site trial with 60-week follow-up. *American Journal of Psychiatry, 166,* 311–319.

Fairburn C. G., Cooper, Z., & Shafran, R. (2003). Cognitive behaviour therapy for eating disorders: A "transdiagnostic" theory and treatment. *Behaviour Research and Therapy, 41,* 509–528.

Falco, L. D., & Bauman, S. (2014). Group work in schools. In J. L. DeLucia-Waak, C. R. Kalodner, & M. T. Riva (Eds.), *Handbook of group counseling and psychotherapy* (2nd ed., pp. 318–328). Thousand Oaks, CA: Sage.

Fall, K. A., Holden, J. A., & Marquis, A. (2010). *Theoretical models of counseling and psychotherapy* (2nd ed.). New York, NY: Routledge.

Family Educational Rights and Privacy Act of 1974 (FERPA), 20 U.S.C. § 1232g; 34 CFR Part 99 (1974).

Feldman, M., & Meyer, I. (2007). Eating disorders in diverse lesbian, gay, and bisexual populations. *International Journal of Eating Disorders, 40,* 218–226.

Felix, E., You, S., & Canino, G. (2013). School and community influences on the long term post disaster recovery of children and youth following Hurricane Georges. *Journal of Community Psychology, 41*(8), 1021–1038. doi:10.1002/jcop.21590

Field, A., & Cottrell, D. (2011). Eye movement desensitization and reprocessing as a therapeutic intervention for traumatized children and adolescents: A systematic review of the evidence for family therapists. *Journal of Family Therapy, 33*(4), 374–388. doi:10.1111/j.1467-6427.2011.00548.x

Field, L. F., Seligman, L., & Albrecht, A. C. (2008). Mood disorders in children and adolescents. In R. R. Erk (Ed.), *Counseling*

treatment for children and adolescents with *DSM-IV-TR disorders* (2nd ed., pp. 253–293). Upper Saddle River, NJ: Pearson.

Fineran, K. R. (2012). Suicide postvention in schools: The role of the school counselor. *Professional Counseling, 39*(2), 14–28.

Finkelhor, D., Shattuck, A., Turner, H. A., & Hamby, S. L. (2014). The lifetime prevalence of child sexual abuse and sexual assault assessed in late adolescence. *Journal of Adolescent Health, 55,* 329–333. doi:10.1016/j.jadohealth.2013.12.026

Finkelhor, D., Turner, H., Shattuck, A., & Hamby, S. L. (2013). Violence, crime, and abuse exposure in a national sample of children and youth: An update. *JAMA Pediatrics, 167,* 614–621. doi:10.10001/jamapediatrics.2013.42

Finnan, C. (2008). *Upper elementary years: Ensuring success in grades 3–6.* Thousand Oaks, CA: Corwin.

Fleck, J. R., & Fleck, D. T. (2013). The immigrant family: Parent–child dilemmas and therapy considerations. *American International Journal of Contemporary Research, 3*(8), 13–17.

Fleming, J. (2012). The effectiveness of eye movement desensitization and reprocessing in the treatment of traumatized children and youth. *Journal of EMDR Practice and Research, 6*(1), 16–26. doi:10.1891/1933-3196.6.1.16

Flessner, C. A. (2011). Cognitive-behavioral therapy for childhood repetitive behavior disorders: Tic disorders and trichotillomania. *Child and Adolescent Psychiatric Clinics of North America, 20*(2), 319–328. doi:10.1016/j.chc.2011.01.007

Flynn, S. D., & Lo, Y. (2016). Teacher implementation of trail-based functional analysis and differential reinforcement of alternative behavior for students with challenging behavior. *Journal of Behavior Education, 25*(1), 1–31. doi:10.1007/s10864-015-9231-2

Foa, E. B. (1996). *Posttraumatic Diagnostic Scale manual.* Minneapolis, MN: National Computer Systems.

Foa, E. B., Johnson, K. M., Feeny, N. C., & Treadwell, K. R. H. (2001). The Child PTSD Symptom Scale: A preliminary examination of its psychometric properties. *Journal of Clinical Child Psychology, 30,* 376–384.

Foelsch, P. A., Schlüter-Müller, S., Odom, A. E., Arena, H. T., Borzutzky H. A., & Schmeck, K. (2014). *Adolescent identity treatment: An integrative approach for personality pathology.* Cham, Switzerland: Springer.

Food and Drug Administration (FDA). (2017). *Label for fluoxetine tablets.* (Reference ID:

4036396). Retrieved from http://www. accessdata.fda.gov/drugsatfda_docs/ label/2017/202133s004s005lbl.pdf

Foshee, V. A., Bauman, K. E., Arriaga, X. B., Helms, R. W., Koch, G. G., & Linder, G. F. (1998). An evaluation of Safe Dates, an adolescent dating violence prevention program. *American Journal of Public Health, 88*(1), 45–50. Retrieved from http://ajph.aphapublications.org

Foshee, V. A., McNaughton Reyes, L., Tharp, A. T., Chang, L., Ennett, S. T., Simon, T. R., . . . Suchindran, C. (2015). Shared longitudinal predictors of physical peer and dating violence. *Journal of Adolescent Health, 56*(1), 106–112. doi:10.1016/j. jadohealth.2014.08.003

Foss, L., Generali, M., & Kress, V. E. (2017). Counseling strategies for empowering people living in poverty: The I-CARE Model. *Journal of Multicultural Counseling and Development, 45,* 201–213.

France, M. H., Rodriguez, M. D., & Hett, G. G. (2013). *Diversity, culture, and counselling* (2nd ed.). Alberta, Canada: Brush Education.

Frank, J. D., & Frank, J. B. (1993). *Persuasion and healing: A comparative study of psychotherapy*. Baltimore, MD: Johns Hopkins University Press.

Franklin, M. E., Freeman, J., & March, J. S. (2010). Treating pediatric obsessive-compulsive disorder using exposure-based cognitive-behavioral therapy. In J. R. Weisz & A. E. Kazdin (Eds.), *Evidence-based psychotherapies for children and adolescents* (2nd ed., pp. 80–92). New York, NY: Guilford.

Franzese, R. J., Covey, H. C., Tucker, A. S., McCoy, L., & Menard, S. (2014). Adolescent exposure to violence and adult physical and mental health problems. *Child Abuse & Neglect, 38*(12), 1955–1965. doi:10.1016/j.chiabu.2014.10.017

Freeman, J., Garcia, A., Frank, H., Benito, K., Conelea, C., Walther, M., . . . Edmunds, J. (2014). Evidence base update for psychosocial treatments for pediatric obsessive-compulsive disorder. *Journal of Clinical Child & Adolescent Psychology, 43*(3), 7–26. doi:10.1080/15374416.2013.804386

Frels, R. K., Soto-Leggett, E., & Larocca, P. S. (2009). Creativity and solution-focused counseling for a child with chronic illness. *Journal of Creativity in Mental Health, 4,* 308–319.

Freud, A. (1946). *The psycho-analytical treatment of children*. New York, NY: International Universities.

Freud, A. (1954). *The ego and the mechanisms of defence*. New York, NY: International University.

Freud, S. (1905/2011). *Three essays on the theory of sexuality*. Eastford, CT: Martino Fine Books.

Freud, S. (1910). The origin and development of psycho-analysis: First and second lectures. *American Journal of Psychology, 21*(2), 181–218.

Freud, S. (1912/2001). The dynamics of transference. In *The standard edition of the complete psychological works of Sigmund Freud, Volume XII (1911–1913): The case of Schreber, papers on technique and other works* (pp. 97–108). London, UK: Hogarth.

Freud, S. (1922/1953). Two encyclopedia articles. In E. Jones (Eds.), *Sigmund Freud: Collected papers* (Vol. 5, pp. 107–135). London, UK: Hogart.

Freud, S. (1943). *A general introduction to psychoanalysis*. New York, NY: Garden City.

Frick, P. J., Barry, C. T., & Kamphaus, R. W. (2005). *Clinical assessment of child and adolescent personality and behavior* (3rd ed.). New York, NY: Springer.

Friedberg, R. D., McClure, J. M., & Garcia, J. H. (2009). *Cognitive therapy techniques for children and adolescents*. New York, NY: Guilford.

Friedman, K., Ramirez, A. L., Murray, S. B., Anderson, L. K., Cusack, A., Boutelle, K. N., & Kaye, W. H. (2016). A narrative review of outcome studies for residential and partial hospital-based treatment of eating disorders. *European Eating Disorders Review, 24*(4), 263–276. doi:10.1002/erv.2449

Froiland, J. M., & Davison, M. L. (2014). Parental expectations and school relationships as contributors to adolescents' positive outcomes. *Social Psychology of Education, 17*(1), 1–17. doi:10.1007/s11218-013-9237-3

Froiland, J. M., Peterson, A., & Davison, M. L. (2013). The long-term effects of early parent involvement and parent expectation in the USA. *School Psychology International, 34*(1), 33–50. doi:10.1177/0143034312454361

Fulton, C., & Cashwell, C. S. (2015). Mindfulness-based awareness and compassion: Predictors of counselor empathy and anxiety. *Counselor Education and Supervision, 54,* 122–133. doi:10.1002/ceas.12009

Garber, J., Brunwasser, S. M., Zerr, A. A., Schwartz, K. T., Sova, K., & Weersing, V. R. (2016). Treatment and prevention of depression and anxiety in youth: Test of cross-over effects. *Depression & Anxiety, 33*(10), 939–959. doi:10.1002/da.22519

Garrett, M. (2015). Using artist trading cards as an expressive arts intervention in counseling. *Journal of Creativity in Mental Health, 10,* 77–88. doi:10.1080/15401383.2014.914455

Gassman-Pines, A. (2015). Effects of Mexican immigrant parents' daily workplace discrimination on child behavior and family functioning. *Child Development, 86*(4), 1175–1190. doi:10.1111/cdev.12378

Gay Alliance. (2016). *SafeZone programs*. The Gay Alliance of the Genesee Valley. Retrieved from http://www.gayalliance.org/programs/education-safezone/safezone-programs

Geldard, K., & Geldard, D. (2010). *Counselling adolescents: The proactive approach for young people* (3rd ed.). Thousand Oaks, CA: Sage.

Geldard, K., Geldard, D., & Yin Foo, R. (2013). *Counselling children: A practical introduction* (4th ed.). Thousand Oaks, CA: Sage.

Genetic Science Learning Center. (2013, August 30). *Genes and addiction*. Retrieved from http://learn.genetics.utah.edu/content/addiction/genes

Gerson, M. J. (2010). *The embedded self: An integrative psychodynamic and systemic perspective on couples and family therapy* (2nd ed.). New York, NY: Routledge.

Gil, E. (2012). Trauma-Focused Integrated Play Therapy. In P. G. Brown (Ed.), *Handbook of child sexual abuse: Identification, assessment, and treatment* (pp. 251–278). New York, NY: Wiley & Sons.

Ginsburg, G. S., Kendall, P. C., Sakolsky, D., Compton, S. N., Piacentini, J., Albano, A. M., . . . March, J. (2011). Remission after acute treatment in children and adolescents with anxiety disorders: Findings from CAMS. *Journal of Consulting and Clinical Psychology, 79*(6), 806–813. doi:10.1037/a0025933

Girio-Herrera, E., Dvorsky, M. R., & Owens, J. S. (2015). Mental health screening in kindergarten youth: A multistudy examination of the concurrent and diagnostic validity of the Impairment Rating Scale. *Psychological Assessment, 27*(1), 215–227. doi:10.1037/a0037787

Gladding, S. T. (2011). *The creative arts in counseling* (4th ed.). Alexandria, VA: American Counseling Association.

Gladding, S. T. (2012). *Groups: A counseling specialty* (6th ed.). Upper Saddle River, NJ: Pearson.

Glasser, W. (1961). *Mental health or mental illness?* New York, NY: Harper & Row.

Glasser, W. (1965). *Reality therapy*. New York, NY: Harper & Row.

Glasser, W. (1969). *Schools without failure*. New York, NY: Harper & Row.

Glasser, W. (1972). *The identity society*. New York, NY: Harper & Row.

Glasser, W. (1976). *Positive addiction.* New York, NY: Harper & Row.

Glasser, W. (1984). *Take effective control of your life.* New York, NY: Harper & Row.

Glasser, W. (1985). *Control theory: A new explanation of how we control our lives.* New York, NY: Harper & Row.

Glasser, W. (1992). *The quality school: Managing students without coercion.* New York, NY: Harper Perennial.

Glasser, W. (1998). *Choice theory: A new psychology for personal freedom.* New York, NY: HarperCollins.

Glasser, W. (2000). *Counseling with choice theory.* New York, NY: HarperCollins.

Glasser, W. (2001). *Counseling with choice theory: The new reality therapy.* New York, NY: Harper Collins.

Glasser, W. (2003). *Warning: Psychiatry can be hazardous to your mental health.* New York, NY: Harper Collins.

Glasser, W. (2005). *Defining mental health as a public health issue: A new leadership role for the helping and teaching professions.* Chatsworth, CA: Author.

Glasser, W. (2011). *Taking charge of your life: How to get what you need with choice theory psychology.* Bloomington, IN: Universe.

Glasser, W., & Glasser, C. (2000). *Getting together and staying together.* New York, NY: HarperCollins.

Glasser, W., & Glasser, C. (2007). *Eight lessons for a happier marriage.* New York, NY: HarperCollins.

Glick, D. M., & Orsillo, S. M. (2015). An investigation of the efficacy of acceptance-based behavioral therapy for academic procrastination. *Journal of Experimental Psychology: General, 144*(2), 400–409. doi:10.1037/xge0000050

Godley, S. H., Smith, J. E., Meyers, R. J., & Godley, M. D. (2009). Adolescent community reinforcement approach. In D. W. Springer & A. Rubin (Eds.), *Substance abuse treatment for youth and adults: Clinician's guide to evidence-based practice* (pp. 109–201). Hoboken, NJ: John Wiley & Sons.

Godt, K. (2008). Personality disorders in 545 patients with eating disorders. *European Eating Disorders Review, 16,* 94–99.

Goel, K., Amatya, K., Jones, R., & Ollendick, T. (2014). Child and adolescent resiliency following a residential fire: The role of social support and ethnicity. *Journal of Child & Family Studies, 23*(3), 537–547. doi:10.1007/s10826-013-9715-4

Goldblum, P., Espelage, D. L., Chu, J., & Bongar, B. (2015). *Youth suicide and bullying: Challenges and strategies for prevention and intervention.* New York, NY: Oxford.

Goldenberg, H., & Goldenberg, I. (2013). *Family therapy: An overview* (8th ed.). Belmont, CA: Brooks/Cole/Cengage.

Goleman, D. (2013). *Focus: The hidden driver of excellence.* New York, NY: HarperCollins.

Golombok, S., & Tasker, F. (2015). Socioemotional development in changing families. In M. E. Lamb (Ed.), *Handbook of child psychology and developmental science* (pp. 419–463). Hoboken, NJ: Wiley.

Gómez-Benito, J., Van de Vijver, F. J. R., Balluerka, N., & Caterino, L. (2015). Cross-cultural and gender differences in ADHD among young adults. *Journal of Attention Disorders* (Advance online publication). doi:10.1177/1087054715611748

Gonzales, A. H., & Bergstrom, L. (2013). Adolescent non-suicidal self-injury (NSSI) interventions. *Journal of Child and Adolescent Psychiatric Nursing, 26,* 124–130. doi:10.1111/jcap.12035

Gonzales, J. (2009). Prefamily counseling: Working with blended families. *Journal of Divorce & Remarriage, 50*(2), 148–157. doi:10.1080/10502550802365862

Goodman, C., & Silverstein, M. (2002). Grandmothers raising grandchildren: Family structure and well-being in culturally diverse families. *Gerontologist, 42*(2), 676–689.

Gopalan, G., Goldstein, L., Klingenstein, K., Sicher, C., Blake, C., & McKay, M. M. (2010). Engaging families into child mental health treatment: Updates and special considerations. *Journal of Canadian Academy of Child & Adolescent Psychiatry, 19*(3), 182–196

Gottfried, M. A. (2014). Can neighbor attributes predict school absences? *Urban Education, 49*(2), 216–250. doi:10.1177/0042085913475634

Graham, M. A., Sauerheber, J. D., & Britzman, M. J. (2012). Choice theory and family counseling: A pragmatic, culturally sensitive approach. *Family Journal: Counseling and Therapy for Couples and Families, 21*(2), 230–234.

Granello, D. H. (2010). The process of suicide risk assessment: Twelve core principles. *Journal of Counseling & Development, 88,* 363–370.

Granello, D. H., & Granello, P. F. (2006). *Suicide: An essential guide for helping professionals and educators.* Boston, MA: Pearson.

Gray, D. D. (2012). *Attaching in adoption: Practical tools for today's parents.* London, UK Kingsley Publishers. (Original work published 2002)

Gray, S. W., & Zide, M. R. (2013). *Psychopathology: A competency-based assessment model for social workers.* Belmont, CA: Brooks/Cole.

Greco, L. A., & Hayes, S. C. (2008). *Acceptance & mindfulness treatments for children & adolescents: A practitioner's guide.* Oakland, CA: New Harbinger.

Greenspan, L., & Deardorff, J. (2014). *The new puberty: How to navigate early development in today's girls.* New York, NY: Rodale.

Greenspan, S. I., & Wieder, S. (2009). *Engaging autism: Using the Floortime approach to help children relate, communicate, and think.* Philadelphia, PA: Da Capo Press.

Greyber, L. R., Dulmus, C. N., & Cristalli, M. E. (2012). Eye movement desensitization reprocessing, posttraumatic stress disorder, and trauma: A review of randomized controlled trials with children and adolescents. *Child and Adolescent Social Work Journal, 29*(5), 409–425. doi:10.1007/s10560-012-0266-0

Groark, C. J., McCall, R. B., McCarthy, S. K., Eichner, J. C., & Gee, A. D. (2013). Structure, caregiver–child interactions, and children's general physical and behavioral development in three Central American institutions. *International Perspectives in Psychology: Research, Practice, Consultation, 2*(3), 207–224. doi:10.1037/ipp0000007

Gross, C. M. (2011). Parenting a child with learning disabilities: A viewpoint from a teacher and parent. *Issues in Teacher Education, 1,* 85–93.

Gulley, L. D., Oppenheimer, C. W., & Hankin, B. L. (2014). Associations among negative parenting, attention bias to anger, and social anxiety among youth. *Developmental Psychology, 50*(2), 577–585. doi:10.1037/a0033624

Gurney, B. G., Jr., Gurney, L., & Andronico, M. (1966). Filial therapy. *Yale Scientific Magazine, 40,* 6–14. Retrieved from http://www.yalescientific.org

Gurney, L., & Ryan, V. (2013). *Group filial therapy: Training parents to conduct special play sessions with their own children.* London, UK: Jessica Kingsley.

Guthrie, D. W., Bartsocus, C., Jarosz-Chabot, P., & Konstantinova, M. (2003). Psychosocial issues for children and adolescents with diabetes: Overview and recommendations. *Diabetes Spectrum, 16,* 7–12.

Haddock, L. R., & Sheperis, D. S. (2016). Group therapy for treatment of addictions. In D. Capuzzi & M. D. Stauffer (Eds.), *Foundations of addiction counseling* (3rd ed., pp. 217–239). Boston, MA: Pearson.

Haley, J. (1963). *Strategies of psychotherapy.* New York, NY: Grune & Stratton.

Haley, J. (1987). *Problem-solving therapy* (2nd ed.). San Francisco, CA: Jossey-Bass.

Haley, J. (1996). *Learning and teaching therapy.* New York, NY: Guilford.

Halim, M. L., Yoshikawa, H., & Amodio, D. M. (2013). Cross-generational effects of discrimination among immigrant mothers: Perceived discrimination predicts child's healthcare visits for illness. *Health Psychology, 32*(2), 203–211. doi:10.1037/a0027279

Hamm, J. V., Farmer, T. W., Lambert, K., & Gravelle, M. (2014). Enhancing peer cultures of academic effort and achievement in early adolescence: Promotive effects of the SEALS intervention. *Developmental Psychology, 50*(1), 216–228. doi:10.1037/a0032979

Hammond, S. (2007). *Mental health needs of juvenile offenders.* Denver, CO: National Conference of State Legislatures. Retrieved from http://www.ncsl.org/print/cj/mentaljjneeds.pdf

Harrington, B. C., Jimerson, M., Haxton, C., & Jimerson, D. C. (2015). Initial evaluation, diagnosis, and treatment of anorexia nervosa and bulimia nervosa. *American Family Physician, 91*(1), 46–52.

Harrison, A. M. (2009). Setting up the doll house: A developmental perspective on termination. *Psychoanalytic Inquiry, 29*(2), 174–187. doi:10.1080/07351690802274918

Hart, C. L., & Ksir, C. (2015). *Drugs, society, & human behavior* (16th ed.). New York, NY: McGraw-Hill.

Harter, S. (2006). The self. In W. Damon & R. M. Lerner (Eds.), *Handbook of child psychology* (pp. 505–570). Hoboken, NJ: John Wiley & Sons.

Harvey, M. T., Luiselli, J. K., & Wong, S. E. (2009). Application of applied behavior analysis to mental health issues. *Psychological Services, 6*(3), 212–222. doi:10.1037/a0016495

Harvey, P., & Penzo, J. A. (2009). *Parenting a child who has intense emotions: Dialectical behavior therapy skills to help your child regulate emotional outbursts and aggressive behaviors.* Oakland, CA: New Harbinger.

Harvey, P., & Rathbone, B. H. (2013). *Dialectical behavior therapy for at-risk adolescents: A practitioner's guide to treating challenging behavior problems.* Oakland, CA: New Harbinger.

Harvey, P., & Rathbone, B. H. (2015). *Parenting a teen with intense emotions: Skills to help your teen navigate emotional & behavioral challenges.* Oakland, CA: New Harbinger.

Haslam, M., Meyer, C., & Waller, G. (2011). Do eating attitudes predict early change in eating behaviors among women with bulimic disorders who are treated with cognitive behavioral therapy? *International Journal of Eating Disorders, 44*(8), 741–744.

Hawley, K. M., & Garland, A. F. (2008). Working alliance in adolescent outpatient therapy: Youth, parent and therapist reports and associations with therapy outcomes. *Child and Youth Care Forum: Journal of Research and Practice in Children's Services, 37*(2), 59–74. doi:10.1007/s10566-008-9050-x

Hay, P. (2013). A systematic review of evidence for psychological treatments in eating disorders: 2005–2012. *International Journal of Eating Disorders, 46,* 462–469.

Hayes, S. C. (2004). Acceptance and commitment therapy, relational frame theory, and the third wave of behavioral and cognitive therapies. *Behavior Therapy, 35*(4), 639–665. doi:10.1016/S0005-7894(04)80013-3

Hayes, S. C., Strosahl, K. D., & Wilson, K. G. (1999). *Acceptance and commitment therapy: An experiential approach to behavior change.* New York, NY: Guilford.

Hayes, S. C., Strosahl, K. D., & Wilson, K. G. (2011). *Acceptance and commitment therapy: The process and practice of mindful change* (2nd ed.). New York, NY: Guilford.

He, A. S., Fulginiti, A., & Finno-Velasquez, M. (2015). Connectedness and suicidal ideation among adolescents involved with child welfare: A national survey. *Child Abuse & Neglect, 42,* 54–62. doi:10.1016/j.chiabu.2015.02.016

Headley, J. A., Kautzman-East, M., Pusateri, C. G., & Kress, V. E. (2015). Making the intangible tangible: Using expressive art during termination to co-construct meaning. *Journal of Creativity in Mental Health, 10*(1), 89–99. doi:10.1080/15401383.2014.938185

Health Insurance Portability and Accountability Act of 1996 (HIPAA), Pub. L. 104-191, 110 Stat. 1936 (1996).

Henggeler, S. W., & Schaeffer, C. (2010). Treating serious antisocial behavior with multisystemic therapy. In J. R. Weisz & A. E. Kazdin (Eds.), *Evidence-based psychotherapies for children and adolescents* (2nd ed., pp. 259–276). New York, NY: Guilford.

Henggeler, S. W., & Schaeffer, C. M. (2010). Treating serious emotional and behavioural problems using multisystemic therapy. *Australian and New Zealand Journal of Family Therapy, 31*(2), 149–164.

Herbert, J. D., & Forman, E. M. (Eds.). (2011). *Acceptance and mindfulness in cognitive behavior therapy: Understanding and applying the new therapies.* Hoboken, NJ: Wiley.

Herlihy, B., & Corey, G. (2015). *ACA ethical standards casebook* (7th ed.). Alexandria, VA: American Counseling Association.

Herman, J. (1997). *Trauma and recovery.* New York, NY: Basic Books.

Hermann, M. A., Remley, T. P. Jr., & Huey, W. C. (Eds.). (2010). *Ethical and legal issues in school counseling* (3rd ed.). Alexandria, VA: American School Counselor Association.

Herrenkohl, T. I., Sousa, C., Tajima, E. A., Herrenkohl, R. C., & Moylan, C. A. (2008). Intersection of child abuse and children's exposure to domestic violence. *Trauma, Violence, & Abuse, 9*(2), 84–99. doi:10.1177/1524838008314797

Hervey-Jumper, H., Douyon, K., Falcone, T., & Franco, K. N. (2008). Identifying, evaluating, diagnosing, and treating ADHD in minority youth. *Journal of Attention Disorders, 11*(5), 522–528. doi:10.1177/1087054707311054

Hickson, L., & Khemka, I. (2013). Problem solving and decision making. In M. L. Wehmeyer (Ed.), *The Oxford handbook of positive psychology and disability* (pp. 198–225). New York, NY: Oxford University Press.

Hill, J. P., & den Dulk, K. R. (2013). Religion, volunteering, and educational setting: The effect of youth schooling type on civic engagement. *Journal for the Scientific Study of Religion, 52,* 179–197. doi:10.1111/jssr.12011

Hinkle, J. S. (2008). Anxiety disorders in children and adolescents. In R. R. Erk (Ed.), *Counseling treatment for children and adolescents with DSM-IV-TR disorders* (2nd ed., pp. 216–252). Upper Saddle River, NJ: Pearson.

Hirshkowitz, M., Whiton, K., Albert, S. M., Alessi, C., Bruni, O., DonCarlos, L., . . . Hillard, P. J. A. (2015). The National Sleep Foundation's sleep time duration recommendation and results summary. *Sleep Health, 1,* 40–43. doi:10.1016/j.sleh.2014.12.010

Hlastala, S., Kotler, S., McClellan, M., & McCauley, E. (2010). Interpersonal and Social Rhythm Therapy for adolescents with bipolar disorder: Treatment development and results from an open trial. *Depression and Anxiety, 27*(5), 457–464. doi:10.1002/da.20668

Hodges, L., & Dibb, B. (2010). Social comparison within self-help groups. *Journal of Health Psychology, 15*(4), 483–492. doi:10.1177/139105309355491

Hodgkinson, B., Josephs, K., & Hegney, D. (2010). Best practice in the management of primary nocturnal enuresis in children: A systematic review. *JBI Library of Systematic Reviews, 8*(5), 173–254.

Hoffman, R., & Kress, V. E. (2010). Adolescent non-suicidal self-injury: Minimizing client and counselor risk and enhancing client care. *Journal of Mental Health Counseling, 32*(4), 342–353.

Hofmann, S. G., Asnaani, A., Vonk, I. J., Sawyer, A. T., & Fang, A. (2012). The efficacy of cognitive behavioral therapy: A review of meta-analyses. *Cognitive Therapy and Research, 36*(5), 427–440. doi:10.1007/s10608-012-9476-1

Hohl, B. C. (2013). *Working with the community to develop a new measure of neighborhood youth support* (Unpublished doctoral dissertation). Temple University, Philadelphia, PA.

Holcomb-McCoy, C. H. (2007). *School counseling to close the achievement gap: A social justice framework for success.* Thousand Oaks, CA: Corwin.

Holdsworth, C., & Brewis, G. (2014). Volunteering, choice and control: A case study of higher education student volunteering. *Journal of Youth Studies, 17*(2), 204–219. doi:10.1080/13676261.2013.815702

Holtkamp, K., Konrad, K., Kaiser, N., Ploenes, Y., Heussen, N., Grzella, I., . . . Herpertz-Dahlmann, B. (2005). A retrospective study of SSRI treatment in adolescent anorexia nervosa: Insufficient evidence for efficacy. *Journal of Psychiatric Research, 39,* 303–310.

Homeyer, L. W., & Morrison, M. O. (2008). Play therapy: Practice, issues, and trends. *American Journal of Play, 1,* 210–228. Retrieved from http://www.journalofplay.org

Hopson, L. M., & Lee, E. (2011). Mitigating the effect of family poverty on academic and behavioral outcomes: The role of school climate in middle and high school. *Children and Youth Services Review, 33*(11), 2221–2229. doi:10.1016/j.childyouth.2011.07.006

Hopson, L. M., & Weldon, P. (2013). Parental expectations and academic success in the context of school climate effects. *Families in Society, 94*(1), 45–52. doi:10.1606/1044-3894.4258

Howard, D. E., Debnam, K. J., Cham, H. J., Czinn, A., Aiken, N., Jordan, J., . . . Goldman, R. (2015). The (mal) adaptive value of mid-adolescent dating relationship labels. *The Journal of Primary Prevention, 36*(3), 187–203. doi:10.1007/s10935-015-0387-2

Hua, L. L., Wilens, T. E., Martelon, M., Wong, P., Wozniak, J., & Biederman, J. (2011). Psychosocial functioning, familiarity, and psychiatric comorbidity in bipolar youth with and without psychotic features. *Journal of Clinical Psychiatry, 72*(3), 397–405. doi:10.4088/jcp.10m06025yel

Hussey, D. (2008). Understanding minor clients. In K. Strom Gottfried, *The ethics of practice with minors* (pp. 47–63). Chicago, IL: Lyceum Press.

Huston, A. C., Bobbitt, K. C., & Bentley, A. (2015). Time spent in child care: How and why does it affect social development? *Developmental Psychology, 51*(5), 621–634. doi:10.1037/a0038951

Huth-Bocks, A., Schettini, A., & Shebroe, V. (2001). Group play therapy for preschoolers exposed to domestic violence. *Journal of Child and Adolescent Group Therapy, 11*(1), 19–34.

Individuals with Disabilities Education Act (IDEA) of 2004, 20 U.S.C. § 1400. (2004).

Ipser, J. C., Stein, D. J., Hawkridge, S., & Hoppe, L. (2009). Pharmacotherapy for anxiety disorders in children and adolescents. *Cochrane Database of Systematic Review, 3.* Retrieved from http://onlinelibrary.wiley.com/doi/10.1002/14651858.CD005170.pub2/abstract;jsessionid=E99A0302697F008F56AB9F5C5F6B75BB.f03t03

Isaacs, M. L., & Stone, C. (1999). School counselors and confidentiality: Factors affecting professional choices. *Professional School Counseling, 2*(4), 258–266.

Ivers, N. N., Johnson, D. A., Clarke, P. B., Newsome, D. W., & Berry, R. A. (2016). The relationship between mindfulness and multicultural counseling competence. *Journal of Counseling and Development, 94,* 72–82. doi:10.1002/jcad.12063

Jackson, K. M., & Schulenberg, J. E. (2013). Alcohol use during the transition from middle school to high school: National panel data on prevalence and moderators. *Developmental Psychology, 49*(11), 2147–2158. doi:10.1037/a0031843

Jacobi, C., Hayward, C., de Zwaan, M., Kraemer, H. C., & Agras, W. S. (2004). Coming to terms with risk factors for eating disorders: Application of risk terminology and suggestions for a general taxonomy. *Psychological Bulletin, 130*(1), 19–65.

Jacobs, E. E., Schimmel, C. J., Masson, R. L., & Harvill, R. L. (2015). *Group counseling; Strategies and skills* (8th ed.). Boston, MA: Cengage.

Jacobson, C. M., & Mufson, L. (2010). Treating adolescent depression using interpersonal psychotherapy. In J. R. Weisz & A. E. Kazdin (Eds.), *Evidence-based psychotherapies for children and adolescents* (2nd ed., pp. 140–155). New York, NY: Guilford.

Jacobson, C. M., & Mufson, L. M. (2012). Interpersonal psychotherapy for depressed adolescents adapted for self-injury (IPT-ASI): Rationale, overview, and case summary. *American Journal of Psychotherapy, 66*(4), 349–374.

Jacobson, E. (1938). *Progressive muscle relaxation.* Chicago: University of Chicago Press.

James, R. K. (2008). *Crisis intervention strategies* (6th ed.). Belmont, CA: Brooks/Cole.

James, R. K., & Gilliland, B. E. (2013). Crisis of lethality. In *Crisis intervention strategies* (7th ed., pp. 209–247). Pacific Grove, CA: Brooks/Cole.

Jarvi, S., Jackson, B., Swenson, L., & Crawford, H. (2013). The impact of social contagion on non-suicidal self-injury: A review of the literature. *Archives of Suicide Research, 17*(1), 1–19. doi:10.1080/13811118.2013.748404

Jaycox, L. H., Stein, B. D., & Wong, M. (2014). School intervention related to school and community violence. *Child and Adolescent Psychiatric Clinics of North America, 23*(2), 281–293.

Jenson, J. M., & Bender, K. A. (2014). *Preventing child and adolescent problem behavior: Evidence-based strategies in schools, families, and communities.* New York, NY: Oxford.

Jenson, J. M., & Fraser, M. W. (2015). A risk and resilience framework for child, youth and family policy. In M. J. Jenson & M. W. Fraser (Eds.), *Social policy for children and families: A risk and resilience perspective* (3rd ed., pp. 5–22). Thousand Oaks, CA: Sage.

Jimerson, S. R., Swearer, S. M., & Espelage, D. L. (Eds.). (2010). *Handbook of bullying in schools: An international perspective.* London, UK: Routledge.

Job, V., Walton, G. M., Bernecker, K., & Dweck, C. S. (2015). Implicit theories about willpower predict self-regulation and grades in everyday life. *Journal of Personality and Social Psychology, 108*(4), 637–647. doi:10.1037/pspp0000014

Johnson, S., Blum, R., & Giedd, J. (2009). Adolescent maturity and the brain: The promise and pitfalls of neuroscience research in adolescent health policy. *Journal of Adolescent Health, 45*(3), 216–221.

Johnston, J. A. Y., O'Gara, J. S. X., Koman, S. L., Baker, C. W., & Anderson, D. A. (2015). A pilot study of Maudsley Family Therapy with group dialectical behavior therapy skills training in an intensive outpatient program for adolescent eating disorders. *Journal of Clinical Psychology, 71,* 527–543.

Jongsma, A. E., Jr., Peterson, M. L., & Bruce, T. J. (2014). *The complete adult psychopathy treatment planner* (5th ed.). Hoboken, NJ: Wiley.

Joormann, J., & Gotlib, I. H. (2010). Emotional regulation in depression: Relation to cognitive inhibition. *Cognition & Emotion, 24*(2), 281–298. doi:10.1080/02699930903407948

Joyce, A. S., Piper, W. E., Ogrodniczuk, J. S., & Klein, R. H. (2007). *Termination in psychotherapy.* Washington, DC: American Psychological Association.

Juhnke, G. A. (1996). The Adapted-SAD PERSONS: A suicide assessment scale designed for use with children. *Elementary*

School Guidance & Counseling, 30(4), 252–258.

Jungbluth, N., & Shirk, S. (2009). Therapist strategies for building involvement in cognitive-behavioral therapy for adolescent depression. *Journal of Consulting and Clinical Psychology, 77*(6), 1179–1184. doi:10.1037/a0017325

Kabat-Zinn, J. (1990). *Full catastrophe living: Using the wisdom of your body and mind to face stress, pain, and illness.* New York, NY: Dell.

Kabat-Zinn, J. (1994). *Wherever you go, there you are: Mindfulness meditation in everyday life.* New York, NY: Hyperion Books.

Kalra, G., & Bhugra, D. (2010). Cross cultural psychiatry: Context and issues [Guest editorial]. *Journal of Pakistan Psychiatric Society, 7*(2), 51–54. Retrieved from http://jpps.com.pk/article/crosscultur-alpsychiatrycontextandissues_2403.html

Kaplan, D. M., Tarvydas, V. M., & Gladding, S. T. (2014). 20/20: A vision for the future of counseling: The new consensus definition of counseling. *Journal of Counseling & Development, 92*, 366–372. doi:10.1002/j.1556-6676.2014.00164.x

Kärnä, A., Voeten, M., Little, T., Poskiparta, E., Kaljonen, A., & Salmivalli, C. (2011). A large-scale evaluation of the KiVa anti-bullying program. *Child Development, 82*, 311–330. doi:10.1111/j.1467-8624.2010.01557.x

Katsiaficas, D., Suárez-Orozco, C., Sirin, S. R., & Gupta, T. (2013). Mediators of the relationship between acculturative stress and internalization symptoms for immigrant origin youth. *Cultural Diversity and Ethnic Minority Psychology, 19*(1), 27–37. doi:10.1037/a0031094

Katzman, D. K. (2005). Medical complications in adolescents with anorexia nervosa: A review of the literature. *International Journal of Eating Disorders, 37* (Suppl.), 552–559.

Kaufman, A. S., & Kaufman, N. L. (2004). *Kaufman Brief Intelligence Test, Second Edition.* Bloomington, MN: Pearson, Inc.

Kaye, W. H., Strober, M., & Jimerson, D. C. (2009). *The neurobiology of eating disorders.* New York, NY: Oxford.

Kazdin, A. E. (1978). *History of behavior modification: Experimental foundations of contemporary research.* Baltimore, MD: University Park Press.

Kazdin, A. E. (2005). *Parent management training: Treatment for oppositional, aggressive, and antisocial behavior in children and adolescents.* New York, NY: Oxford.

Kazdin, A. E., Rodgers A., & Colbus, D. (1986). The Hopelessness Scale for Children:

Psychometric characteristics and concurrent validity. *Journal of Consulting and Clinical Psychology, 54*(2), 241–245.

Keel, P. K., Klump, K. L., Miller, K. B., McGue, M., & Iacono, W. G. (2005). Shared transmission of eating disorders and anxiety disorders. *International Journal of Eating Disorders, 38,* 99–105.

Keel, P. K., Wolfe, B. E., Liddle, R. A., De Young, K. P., & Jimerson, D. C. (2007). Clinical features and physiological response to a test meal in purging disorder and bulimia nervosa. *Archives of General Psychiatry, 64,* 1058–1066.

Kegerreis, S., & Midgley, N. (2015). Psychodynamic approaches. In S. Pattison, M. Robson, & A. Beynon (Eds.), *The handbook of counselling children and young people* (pp. 35–48). Washington, DC: Sage.

Kelly, D. F., & Lee, D. (2007). Adlerian approaches to counseling with children and adolescents. In H. T. Prout & D. T. Brown (Eds.), *Counseling and psychotherapy with children and adolescents: Theory and practice for school and clinical settings* (4th ed., pp. 131–179). Hoboken, NJ: Wiley.

Kelly, D. R., Matthews, M. D., & Bartone, P. T. (2014). Grit and hardiness as predictors of performance among West Point cadets. *Military Psychology, 26*(4), 327–342. doi:10.1037/mil0000050

Kemp, M., Drummond, P., & McDermott, B. (2009). A wait-list controlled pilot study of eye movement desensitization and reprocessing (EMDR) for children with post-traumatic stress disorder (PTSD) symptoms from motor vehicle accidents. *Clinical Child Psychology and Psychiatry, 15*(1), 5–25. doi:10.1177/1359104509339086

Kendall, P. C. (2012). Anxiety disorders in youth. In P. C. Kendall (Ed.), *Child and adolescent therapy: Cognitive-behavioral procedures* (4th ed., pp. 143–189). New York, NY: Guilford.

Kendall, P. C., Choudhury, M., Hudson, J., & Webb, A. (2002). *"The C.A.T. Project" manual for the cognitive behavioral treatment of anxious adolescents workbook.* Ardmore, PA: Workbook.

Kendall, P. C., & Comer, J. S. (2010). *Childhood disorders* (2nd ed.). New York, NY: Psychology Press.

Kendall, P. C., Crawford, E. A., Kagen, E. R., Furr, J. M., & Podell, J. L. (2017). Child-focused treatment of anxiety. In J. R. Weisz & A. E. Kazdin (Eds.), *Evidence-based psychotherapies for children and adolescents* (3rd ed., pp. 17–34). New York, NY: Guilford.

Kendall, P. C., & Hedtke, K. (2006a). *Cognitive-behavioral therapy for anxious*

children: Therapist manual (3rd ed.). Admore, PA: Workbook.

Kendall, P. C., & Hedtke, K. (2006b). *Coping Cat workbook* (2nd ed.). Admore, PA: Workbook.

Kenny, E. (2013). "Action" in psychoanalysis: A comparison between adult and adolescent analysis. *Journal of the American Psychoanalytic Association, 61*(4), 787–803. doi:10.1177/0003065113496272

Kernberg, P. F., Ritvo, R., Keable, H., & American Academy of Child & Adolescent Psychiatry (AACAP) Committee on Quality Issues (CQI). (2012). Practice parameters for psychodynamic psychotherapy with children. *Journal of the American Academy of Child & Adolescent Psychiatry, 51*(5), 541–557. doi:10.1016/j.jaac.2012.02.015

Kertz, S., & Woodruff-Borden, J. (2013). The role of metacognition, intolerance of uncertainty, and negative problem orientation in children's worry. *Behavioural and Cognitive Psychotherapy, 41*(2), 243–248. doi:10.1017/s1352465812000641

Kinch, S., & Kress, V. E. (2012). The creative use of chain analysis techniques in counseling clients who engage in non-suicidal self-injury. *Journal of Creativity in Mental Health, 7,* 343–354.

King, C. A., Ewell Foster, C., & Rogalski, R. M. (2013). *Teen suicide risk: A practitioner guide to screening, assessment, and management.* New York, NY: Guilford.

Kingery, J. N., Roblek, T. L., Suveg, C., Grover, R. L., Sherrill, J. T., & Bergman, R. L. (2006). They're not just "little adults": Developmental considerations for implementing cognitive-behavioral therapy with anxious kids. *Journal of Cognitive Psychotherapy: An International Quarterly, 20*(3), 263–273.

Kirkcaldy, B. D., Siefen, G. R., & Merrick, J. (2007). A review of risk factors for adolescent suicidal behavior. In J. Merrick & H. A. Omar (Eds.), *Adolescent behavior research: International perspectives* (pp. 29–38). New York, NY: Nova Science.

Klaus, N. M., Algorta, G. P., Young, A. S., & Fristad, M. A. (2015). Validity of the Expressed Emotion Adjective Checklist (EEAC) in caregivers of children with mood disorders. *Couple and Family Psychology: Research and Practice, 4,* 27–38. doi:10.1037/cfp0000036

Klein, J. B., Jacobs, R. H., & Reinecke, M. A. (2007). Cognitive-behavioral therapy for adolescent depression: A meta-analytic investigation of changes in effect-size estimates. *Journal of the American Academy of Child and Adolescent Psychiatry, 46*(11), 1403–1413. doi:10.1097/chi.0b013e3180592aaa

Klein, M. (1921/1959). *The psycho-analysis of children*. London, UK: Hogarth.

Kletter, H., Rialon, R., Laor, N., Brom, D., Pat-Horenczyk, R., Shaheen, M., . . . Carrion, V. G. (2013). Helping children exposed to war and violence: Perspectives from an international work group on interventions for youth and families. *Child & Youth Care Forum, 42*(4), 371–388.

Klinger, L. G., Dawson, G., Barnes, K., & Crisler, M. (2014). Autism spectrum disorder. In R. A. Barkley & E. J. Mash (Eds.), *Child psychopathology* (3rd ed., pp. 531–572). New York, NY: Guilford.

Klonsky, E. D., & May, A. M. (2013). Differentiating suicide attempters from suicide ideators: A critical frontier for suicidology research. *Suicide and Life-Threatening Behavior, 44*(1), 1–5. doi:10.1111/sltb.12068

Klonsky, E. D., Muehlenkamp, J. J., Lewis, S. P., & Walsh, B. (2011). *Nonsuicidal self-injury*. Cambridge, MA: Hogrefe.

Klonsky, E. D., Victor, S. E., & Saffer, B. Y. (2014). Nonsuicidal self-injury: What we know, what we need to know. *The Canadian Journal of Psychiatry, 59*(11), 565–568.

Klott, J. (2012). *Suicide & psychological pain: Prevention that works*. Eau Claire, WI: Premier Publishing and Media.

Klump, K. L., Bulik, C. M., Kaye, W. H., Treasure, J., & Tyson, E. (2009). Academy for eating disorders position paper: Eating disorders are serious mental illnesses. *International Journal of Eating Disorders, 42*, 97–103.

Knecht, A. B., Burk, W. J., Weesie, J., & Steglich, C. (2011). Friendship and alcohol use in early adolescence: A multilevel social network approach. *Journal of Research on Adolescence, 21*(2), 475–487. doi:10.1111/j.1532-7795.2010.00685.x

Knell, S. M. (1995). *Cognitive-behavioral play therapy*. Landham, MD: Rowman & Littlefield.

Knight, J. R., Sherritt, L., Shrier, L. A., Harris, S. K., & Chang, G. (2002). Validity of the CRAFFT substance abuse screening test among adolescent clinic patients. *Archives of Pediatric Adolescent Medicine, 156*(6), 607–614.

Knox, M., Lentini, J., Cummings, T. S., McGrady, A., Whearty, K., & Sancrant, L. (2011). Game-based biofeedback for pediatric anxiety and depression. *Mental Health in Family Medicine, 8*(3), 195–203.

Kodish, I., Rockhill, C., & Varley, C. (2011). Pharmacotherapy for anxiety disorders in children and adolescents. *Dialogues in Clinical Neuroscience, 13*(4), 439–452.

Koegel, R. L., Koegel, L. K., Vernon, T. W., & Brookman-Frazee, L. I. (2010). Empirically supported Pivotal Response Treatment for children with autism spectrum disorders. In J. R. Weisz & A. E. Kazdin (Eds.), *Evidence-based psychotherapies for children and adolescents* (2nd ed., pp. 327–344). New York, NY: Guilford.

Kohut, H. H. (1971). *The analysis of self*. New York, NY: International University.

Kohut, H. H. (1977). *Restoration of the self*. New York, NY: International University.

Kolko, D., Simonich, H., & Loiterstein, A. (2014). Alternatives for families: A cognitive-behavioral therapy: An overview and case example. In A. Urquiza & S. Timmer (Eds.), *Evidence-based approaches for the treatment of child maltreatment* (pp. 187–212). New York, NY: Springer.

Koocher, G. P. (2008). Ethical challenges in mental health services to children and families. *Journal of Clinical Psychology, 64*, 601–612.

Kotler, L. A., Devlin, M. J., Davies, M., & Walsh, B. T. (2003). An open trial of fluoxetine for adolescents with bulimia nervosa. *Journal of Child and Adolescent Psychopharmacology, 13*, 329–335.

Kottman, T. (2001). *Play therapy: Basics and beyond*. Alexandria, VA: American Counseling Association.

Kovacs, M. (1992). *The Children's Depression Inventory manual*. North Tonawanda, NY: Multi-Health Systems.

Kress, V. E., Adamson, N., Paylo, M. J., DeMarco, C., & Bradley, N. (2012). The use of safety plans with children and adolescents living in violent families. *The Family Journal, 20*, 249–255. doi:10.1177/1066480712448833

Kress, V. E., Adamson, N. A., & Yensel, J. (2010). The use of therapeutic stories in counseling child and adolescent sexual abuse survivors. *Journal of Creativity in Mental Health, 5*, 243–259. doi:10.1080/15401383.2010.507657

Kress, V. E., Dixon, A., & Shannonhouse, L. (2018). Multicultural diagnosis and conceptualization. In D. G. Hays & B. T. Erford (Eds.), *Developing multicultural counseling competence: A systems approach* (3rd ed., pp. 558–590). Columbus, OH: Pearson.

Kress, V. E., Drouhard, N., & Costin, A. (2010). Students who self-injure: School counselor ethical and legal considerations. In M. A. Hermann, T. P. Remley, Jr., & W. C. Huey (Eds.), *Ethical and legal issues in school counseling* (3rd ed., pp. 158–170). Alexandria, VA: American School Counselor Association.

Kress, V. E., & Hoffman, R. (2008). Non-suicidal self-injury and motivational interviewing: Enhancing readiness for change. *Journal of Mental Health Counseling, 30*(4), 311–329.

Kress, V. E., Moorhead, H. H., & Zoldan, C. A. (2015). Trauma- and stress-related disorders. In V. E. Kress & M. J. Paylo (Eds.), *Treating those with mental disorders: A comprehensive approach to case conceptualization and treatment* (pp. 194–224). Upper Saddle River, NJ: Pearson.

Kress, V. E., & Paylo, M. J. (2015). *Treating those with mental disorders: A comprehensive approach to case conceptualization and treatment*. Upper Saddle River, NJ: Pearson.

Kubler-Ross, M. (2014). *On death and dying: What the dying have to teach doctors, nurses, clergy and their own families*. New York, NY: Scribner. (Original work published in 1969)

Kuther, T. L. (2017). *Lifespan development: Lives in context*. Thousand Oaks, CA: Sage.

Lacewing, M. (2014). Psychodynamic psychotherapy, insight, and therapeutic action. *Clinical Psychology: Science and Practice, 21*(2), 154–171.

Lacher, D. B., Nichols, T., Nichols, M., & May, J. C. (2012). *Connecting with kids through stories: Using narrative to facilitate attachment in adopted children*. Philadelphia, PA: Jessica Kingsley Publishers.

Lam, D. H., Burbeck, R., Wright, K., & Pilling, S. (2009). Psychological therapies in bipolar disorder: The effects of illness history on relapse prevention—A systematic review. *Bipolar Disorder, 11*(5), 474–482. doi:10.1111/j.1399-5618.2009.00724.x

Lambert, M. J. (2013). *Bergin and Garfield's handbook of psychotherapy and behavior change* (6th ed.). New York, NY: Wiley.

Lambie, R. (2008). *Family systems within educational and community context: Understanding children who are at risk or have special needs*. Denver, CO: Love.

Land, H. (2015). *Spirituality, religion, and faith in psychotherapy: Evidence-based expressive methods for mind, brain, and body*. Chicago, IL: Lyceum.

Lander, L., Howsare, J., & Bryne, M. (2013). The impact of substance use disorders on families and children: From theory to practice. *Social Work in Public Health, 28*, 194–205. doi:10.1080/19371918.2013.759005

Landreth, G., & Bratton, S. (2006). *Child Parent Relationship Therapy (CPRT):*

A 10-session filial therapy model. New York, NY: Routledge.

Landreth, G. L. (2012). *Play therapy: The art of the relationship* (3rd ed.). New York, NY: Routledge.

Lane, R. C. (1997). Dream controversies. *Psychotherapy in Private Practice, 16*(1), 39–68. doi:10.1300/J294v16n01_04

Langley, A. K., Nadeem, E., Kataoka, S. H., Stein, B. D., & Jaycox, L. H. (2010). Evidence-based mental health programs in schools: Barriers and facilitators of successful implementation. *School Mental Health, 2,* 105–113. doi:10.1007/s12310-010-9038-1

Lansford, J. E. (2010). The special problem of cultural differences in effects of corporal punishment. *Law and Contemporary Problems, 73,* 89–106.

Laughlin, L. (2014, December). *A child's day: Living arrangements, nativity, and family transitions: 2011 (selected indicators of child well-being)* (Current Population Reports, P70-139, U.S. Census Bureau). Retrieved from http://www.census.gov/library/publications/2014/demo/p70-139.html

Le Couteur, A., Lord, C., & Rutter, M. (2003). *Autism Diagnosis Interview–Revised (ADI-R)*. Los Angeles, CA: Western Psychological Services.

Le Grange, D., & Lock, J. (2007). *Treating bulimia in adolescents: A family-based approach*. New York, NY: Guilford.

Le Grange, D., Lock, J., & Dymek, M. (2003). Family-based therapy for adolescents with bulimia nervosa. *American Journal of Psychotherapy, 57,* 237–251.

Le Grange, D., & Schmidt, U. (2005). The treatment of adolescents with bulimia nervosa. *Journal of Mental Health, 14,* 587–597.

Leaf, J. B., Leaf, R., McEachin, J., Taubman, M., Ala'i-Rosales, S., Ross, R. K., . . . Weiss, M. J. (2016). Applied behavior analysis is a science and, therefore, progressive. *Journal of Autism and Developmental Disorders, 46*(2), 720–731. doi:10.1007/s10803-015-2591-6

Leark, R. A., Greenberg, L. K., Kindschi, C. L., Dupuy, T. R., & Hughes, S. J. (2007). *Test of Variables of Attention: Clinical manual*. Los Alamitos, CA: The TOVA Company.

Lee, E., Choi, M. J., & Clarkson-Henderix, M. (2016). Examining needs of informal kinship families: Validating the Family Needs Scale. *Child and Youth Services Review, 62,* 97–104. doi:10.1016/j.childyouth.2016.01.021

Lee, J. B., & Bartlett, L. (2005). Suicide prevention: Critical elements for managing suicidal clients and counselor liability without the use of a no-suicide contract. *Death Studies, 29,* 847–865.

Lehmann, S., Havik, O. E., Havik, T., & Heiervang, E. R. (2013). Mental disorders in foster children: A study of prevalence, comorbidity, and risk factors. *Child and Adolescent Psychiatry and Mental Health, 7,* 39. doi:10.1186/1753-2000-7-39

Leibenluft, E. (2011). Severe mood dysregulation, irritability, and the diagnostic boundaries of bipolar disorder in youths. *American Journal of Psychiatry, 168*(2), 129–142. doi:10.1176/appi.ajp.2010.10050766

Leibowitz, G. S., Burton, D. L., & Howard, A. (2012). Part II: Differences between sexually victimized and nonsexually victimized male adolescent sexual abusers and delinquent youth: Further group comparisons of developmental antecedents and behavioral challenges. *Journal of Child Sexual Abuse, 21*(3), 315–326. doi:10.1080/10538712.2012.675421

Lempp, T., de Lange, D., Radeloff, D., & Bachmann, C. (2012). The clinical examination of children, adolescents and their families. In J. M. Rey (Ed.), *IACAPAP e-textbook of child and adolescent mental health* (pp. 1–25). Geneva, Switzerland: International Association for Child and Adolescent Psychiatry and Allied Professionals.

Lereya, S. T., Copeland, W. E., Costello, E. J., & Wolke, D. (2015). Adult mental health consequences of peer bullying and maltreatment in childhood: Two cohorts in two countries. *The Lancet Psychiatry, 2*(6), 524–531. doi:10.1016/S2215-0366(15)00165-0

Leventhal, T., Fauth, R. C., & Brooks-Gunn, J. (2005). Neighborhood poverty and public policy: A 5-year follow-up of children's educational outcomes in the New York City moving to opportunity demonstration. *Developmental Psychology, 41*(6), 933–952. doi:10.1037/0012-1649.41.6.933

Levy, D. M. (1938/2015). "Release therapy" in young children. *Psychiatry, 1,* 387–390. doi:10.1521/00332747.1938.11022205

Lewin, A. B., & Piacentini, J. (2010). Evidence-based assessment of child obsessive-compulsive disorder: Recommendation for clinical practice and treatment research. *Child & Youth Care Forum, 39*(2), 73–89. doi:10.1007/s10566-009-9092-8

Liber, J. M., van Widenfelt, B. M., van der Leeden, A. J. M., Goedhart, A. W., Utens, E. M. W., & Treffers, P. D. A. (2010). The relation of severity and comorbidity to treatment outcomes with cognitive behavioral therapy for childhood anxiety disorders. *Journal of Abnormal Child Psychology, 38,* 683–694. doi:10.1007/s10802-010-9394-1

Liddle, H. A. (2010). Treating adolescent substance abuse using multidimensional family therapy. In J. Weisz & A. Kazdin (Eds.), *Evidence-based psychotherapies for children and adolescents* (pp. 416–432). New York, NY: Guilford.

Lin, D., & Bratton, S. (2015). A meta-analytic review of child-centered play therapy approaches. *Journal of Counseling & Development, 93,* 45–58. doi:10.1002/j.1556-6676.2015.00180.x

Lindahl, K. M., Bregman, H. R., & Malik, N. M. (2012). Family boundary structures and child adjustment: The indirect role of emotional reactivity. *Journal of Family Psychology, 26*(6), 839–847. doi:10.1037/a0030444

Linehan, M. M. (1993). *Cognitive-behavioral treatment of borderline personality disorder*. New York, NY: Guilford.

Linehan, M. M. (2014). *DBT skills training manual* (2nd ed.). New York, NY: Guilford.

Liu, J., Lewis, G., & Evans, L. (2012). Understanding aggressive behavior across the life span. *Journal of Psychiatric Mental Health Nursing, 20,* 156–168. doi:10.1111/j.1365-2850.2012.01902.x

Liu, R. T., & Mustanski, B. (2012). Suicidal ideation and self-harm in lesbian, gay, bisexual, and transgender youth. *American Journal of Preventive Medicine, 42*(3), 221–228.

Lock, J., Brandt, H., Woodside, B., Agras, S., Halmi, W., Johnson, C., . . . Wilfley, D. (2012). Challenges in conducting a multi-site randomized clinical trial comparing treatments for adolescent anorexia nervosa. *International Journal of Eating Disorders, 45,* 202–213.

Lock, J., & La Via, M. C. (2015). Practice parameter for the assessment and treatment of children and adolescents with eating disorders. *Journal of the American Academy of Child & Adolescent Psychiatry, 54*(5), 412–425.

Lock, J., & Le Grange, D. (2012). *Treatment manual for anorexia nervosa: A family-based approach* (2nd ed.). New York, NY: Guilford.

Lock, J., Le Grange, D., Agras, W., Moye, A., Bryson, S., & Jo, B. (2010). Randomized clinical trial comparing family-based treatment with adolescent-focused individual therapy for adolescents with anorexia nervosa. *Archives of General Psychiatry, 67,* 1025–1032.

Loeber, R., & Burke, J. D. (2011). Developmental pathways in juvenile externalizing and internalizing problems. *Journal of Research on Adolescence, 21,* 34–46. doi:10.1111/j.1532-7795.2010.00713.x

Loeber, R., & Farrington, D. P. (2011). *Young homicide offenders and victims: Risk factors, prediction, and preventions from childhood.* New York, NY: Springer.

Lofthouse, N. L., Arnold, L. E., Hersch, S., Hurt, E., & DeBeus, R. (2011). A review of neurofeedback treatment for pediatric ADHD. *Journal of Attention Disorders, 16,* 351–372.

Loizou, E. (2011). Empowering aspects of transition from kindergarten to first grade through children's voices. *Early Years: Journal of International Research & Development, 31*(1), 43–55. doi:10.1080/09575146.2010.515943

London, K., Bruck, M., Ceci, S. J., & Shuman, D. W. (2005). Disclosures of child sexual abuse: What does the research tell us about the ways that children tell? *Psychology, Public Policy, and Law, 11*(1), 194–226.

London, M. J., Lilly, M. M., & Pittman, L. (2015). Attachment as a mediator between community violence and posttraumatic stress symptoms among adolescents with a history of maltreatment. *Child Abuse & Neglect, 42,* 1–9. doi:10.1016/j.chiabu.2014.11.002

Long, C. (2014). Education, mobility and the zone defense in suburban American narratives. *European Journal of American Culture, 33*(2), 97–115. doi:10.1386/ejac.33.2.97_1

Lopata, C. (2003). Progressive muscle relaxation and aggression among elementary students with emotional or behavioral disorders. *Behavioral Disorders, 28*(2), 162–172.

Lord, C., Luyster, R. J., Gotham, K., & Guthrie, W. (2012). *Autism Diagnostic Observation Schedule, Second Edition (ADOS-2).* Los Angeles, CA: Western Psychological Services.

Luborsky, E. B., O'Reilly-Landry, M., & Arlow, J. A. (2008). Psychoanalysis. In R. J. Corsini & D. Wedding (Eds.), *Current psychotherapies* (8th ed., pp. 15–62). Belmont, CA: Thomson.

Luby, J. L., & Belden, A. C. (2006). Mood disorders: Phenomenology and a developmental emotion reactivity model. In J. L. Luby (Ed.), *Handbook of preschool mental health: Development, disorders, and treatment* (pp. 209–230). New York, NY: Guilford Press.

Lucas, N., Nicholson, J. M., & Erbas, B. (2013). Child mental health after parental separation: The impact of resident/non-resident parenting, parent mental health, conflict and socioeconomics. *Journal of Family Studies, 19*(1), 53–69. doi:10.5172/jfs.2013.19.1.53

Ludlow, A., Skelly, C., & Rohleder, P. (2012). Challenges faced by parents of children diagnosed with autism spectrum disorder. *Journal of Health Psychology, 17*(5), 702–711. doi:10.1177/1359105311422955

Lundberg, S. (2014). The results from a two-year case study of an information and communication technology support system for family caregivers. *Disability and Rehabilitation: Assistive Technology, 9*(4), 353–358. doi:10.3109/17483107.2013.814170

Ma, N., Roberts, R., Winefield, H., & Furber, G. (2015). The prevalence of psychopathology in siblings of children with mental health problems: A 20-year systematic review. *Child Psychiatry & Human Development, 46*(1), 130–149. doi:10.1007/s10578-014-0459-1

MacDonald, K. (2012). Cutting nature at its joints: Toward an evolutionarily informed theory of natural types of conduct disorder. *Journal of Social, Evolutionary, and Cultural Psychology, 6*(3), 260–291. doi:10.1037/h0099251

Mackrell, S. M., Sheikh, H. I., Kotelnikova, Y., Kryski, K. R., Jordan, P. L., Singh, S. M., . . . Hayden, E. P. (2014). Child temperament and parental depression predict cortisol reactivity to stress in middle childhood. *Journal of Abnormal Psychology, 123*(1), 106–116. doi:10.1037/a0035612

Madanes, C. (1981). *Strategic family therapy.* San Francisco, CA: Jossey-Bass.

Mahler, S., Pine, F., & Bergman, A. (1973). *The psychological birth of the human infant.* New York, NY: Basic Books.

Malchiodi, C. A. (2013). *Expressive therapies.* New York, NY: Guilford.

Malouff, J. M., Thorsteinsson, E. B., & Schutte, N. S. (2007). The efficacy of problem solving therapy in reducing mental and physical health problems: A meta-analysis. *Clinical Psychology Review, 27,* 46–57. doi:10.1016/j.cpr.2005.12.005

Many, M. M. (2009). Termination as a therapeutic intervention when treating children who have experienced multiple losses. *Infant Mental Health Journal, 30*(1), 23–39. doi:10.1002/imhj.20201

Marcia, J. E. (1967). Ego identity status: Relationship to change in self-esteem, "general maladjustment," and authoritarianism. *Journal of Personality, 35,* 118–133. doi:10.1111/j.1467-6494.1967.tb01419.x

Margolin, G., & Vickerman, K. A. (2007). Post-traumatic stress in children and adolescents exposed to family violence: Overview and issues. *Professional Psychology: Research and Practice, 38*(6), 613–619. doi:10.1037/0735-7028.38.6.613

Margulies, D. M., Weintraub, S., Basile, J., Grover, P. J., & Carlson, G. A. (2012). Will disruptive mood dysregulation disorder reduce false diagnosis of bipolar disorders in children? *Bipolar Disorders, 14*(5), 488–496. doi:10.1111/j.1399-5618.2012.01029.x

Martin, A., Gardner, M., & Brooks-Gunn, J. (2012). The mediated and moderated effects of family support on child maltreatment. *Journal of Family Issues, 33*(7), 920–941. doi:10.1177/0192513X11431683

Martin, P. C. (2012). Misuse of high-stakes test scores for evaluative purposes: Neglecting the reality of schools and students. *Current Issues in Education, 15,* 1–11.

Masarik, A. S., & Conger, R. D. (2017). Stress and child development: A review of the family stress model. *Current Opinion in Psychology, 13,* 85–90.

Maslow, A. (1954). *Motivation and personality.* New York, NY: Harper & Brothers.

Masten, A. S. (2011). Resilience in children threatened by extreme adversity: Frameworks for research, practice, and translational synergy. *Development and Psychopathology, 23,* 493–506.

Masten, A. S., & Narayan, A. J. (2012). Child development in context of disaster, war, and terrorism: Pathways of risk and resilience. *Annual Review of Psychology, 63,* 227–257. doi:10.1146/annurev-psch-120710-100356

Matson, J. L., Turygin, N. C., Beighley, J., Rieske, R., Tureck, K., & Matson, M. L. (2012). Applied behavior analysis in autism spectrum disorders: Recent developments, strengths, and pitfalls. *Research in Autism Spectrum Disorders, 6,* 144–150.

May, J. C. (2005). Family attachment narrative therapy: Healing the experience of early childhood maltreatment. *Journal of Marital and Family Therapy, 31,* 221–237.

McBride, J. (2008). *Quick steps: Information to help your stepfamily thrive.* Hyattsville, MD: U.S. Department of Health & Human Services.

McCauley, K., & Reich, C. A. (2007). *Addiction: New understanding, fresh hope, real healing.* Salt Lake City, UT: The Institute for Addiction Study.

McDougall, P., & Vaillancourt, T. (2015). Long-term adult outcomes of peer victimization in childhood and adolescence: Pathways to adjustment and maladjustment. *American Psychologist, 70,* 300–309. doi:10.1037/a0039174

McGlothlin, J. M. (2008). *Developing clinical skills in suicide assessment, prevention, and treatment.* Alexandria, VA: American Counseling Association.

McGuckin, C., & Minton, S. J. (2014). From theory to practice: Two ecosystemic approaches and their applications to understanding school bullying. *Australian Journal of Guidance & Counseling, 24,* 36–48. doi:10.1017/jgc.2013.10

McGuiness, T. (1977). *Idea book for the parent involvement program.* Los Angeles, CA: Educator Training Center.

McGuire, J. F., Kugler, B. B., Park, J. M., Horng, B., Lewin, A. B., Murphy, T. K., . . . Storch, E. A. (2012). Evidence-based assessment of compulsive skin picking, chronic tic disorder and trichotillomania in children. *Child Psychiatry & Human Development, 43*(4), 855–883. doi:10.1007/s10578-0120300-7

McKeage, K. (2014). Aripiprazole: A review of its use in the treatment of manic episodes in adolescents with bipolar I disorder. *CNS Drugs, 28*(2), 171–183. doi:0.1007/s40263-013-0134-2

McNeil, C. B., & Hembree-Kigin, T. L. (2010). *Parent–child interaction therapy* (2nd ed.). New York, NY: Springer.

Medical University of South Carolina. (2005). *TF-CBT-Web: A web-based learning course for trauma-focused cognitive-behavioral therapy.* Retrieved from https://tfcbt.musc.edu

Meichenbaum, D. L., Fabiano, G.A., & Fincham, F. (2002). Communication in relationships with adolescents. In F. W. Kaslow & T. Patterson (Eds.), *Comprehensive handbook of psychotherapy: Vol. 2* (pp. 141– 166). New York, NY: Wiley.

Menard, S., Covey, H. C., & Franzese, R. J. (2015). Adolescent exposure to violence and adult illicit drug use. *Child Abuse & Neglect, 42,* 30–39. doi:10.1016/j.chiabu.2015.01.006

Menassa, B. M. (2009). Theoretical orientation and play therapy: Examining therapist role, session structure, and therapeutic objectives. *Journal of Professional Counseling: Practice, Theory, and Research, 37,* 13–26. Retrieved from http://www.txca.org/tca/TCA_Publications.asp

Mendle, J., Harden, K. P., Brooks-Gunn, J., & Graber, J. A. (2012). Peer relationships and depressive symptomatology in boys at puberty. *Developmental Psychology, 48*(2), 429–435. doi:10.1037/a0026425

Meng, C. (2015). Classroom quality and academic skills: Approaches to learning as a moderator. *School Psychology Quarterly, 30*(4), 553–563. doi:10.1037/spq0000108

Mercer, S. H., & DeRosier, M. E. (2010). Selection and socialization of internalizing problems in middle childhood. *Journal of Social and Clinical Psychology, 29*(9), 1031–1056. doi:10.1521/jscp.2010.29.9.1031

Merikangas, K. R., He, J., Burstein, M., Swanson, S. A., Avenevoli, S., Cui, L., . . . Swendsen, J. (2010). Lifetime prevalence of mental disorders in U.S. adolescents: Results from the National Comorbidity Survey Replication–Adolescent Supplement (NCS-A). *Journal of American Academy of Child & Adolescent Psychiatry, 49*(10), 980–989. doi:10.1016/j.jaac.2010.05.017

Messer, S. B. (2013). Three mechanisms of change in psychodynamic therapy: Insight, affect, and alliance. *Psychotherapy, 50*(3), 408–412. doi:10.1037/a0032414

Metzger, M. W., Fowler, P. J., Anderson, C. L., & Lindsay, C. A. (2015). Residential mobility during adolescence: Do even "upward" moves predict dropout risk? *Social Science Research, 53,* 218–230. doi:10.1016/j.ssresearch.2015.05.004

Micali, N., Ploubidis, G., De Stavola, B., Simonoff, S., & Treasure, J. (2014). Frequency and patterns of eating disorder symptoms in early adolescence. *Journal of Adolescent Health, 54*(4), 574–581. doi:10.1016/j.jadohealth.2013.10.200

Midence, K. (1994). The effects of chronic illness on children and their families: An overview. *Genetic, Social & General Psychology Monograph, 120,* 311–327.

Miklowitz, D. J. (2008). *Bipolar disorder: A family-focused treatment approach* (2nd ed.). New York, NY: Guilford.

Miklowitz, D. J., Axelson, D. A., Birmaher, B., George, E. L., Taylor, D. O., Schneck, C. D., . . . Brent, D. A. (2008). Family-focused treatment for adolescents with bipolar disorder: Results of a 2-year randomized trial. *Archives of General Psychiatry, 65*(9), 1053–1061. doi:10.1001/archpsyc.65.9.1053

Miller, A. L., Rathus, J. H., & Linehan, M. M. (2007). *Dialectical behavior with suicidal adolescents.* New York, NY: Guilford.

Miller, F. G., & Lazowski, L. E. (2005). Substance Abuse Subtle Screening Inventory for Adolescents–Second Version. In T. Grisso, G. Vincent, & D. Seagrave (Eds.), *Mental health screening and assessment in juvenile justice* (pp. 139–151). New York, NY: Guilford.

Miller, W. R., & Rollnick, S. (2012). *Motivational interviewing: Helping people change* (3rd ed.). New York, NY: Guilford.

Milne, L., & Collin-Vézina, D. (2015). Assessment of children and youth in child protective services out-of-home care: An overview of trauma measures. *Psychology of Violence, 5*(2), 122–132. doi:10.1037/a0037865

Miltenberger, R. G. (2012). *Behavior modification: Principles and procedures* (5th ed.). Belmont, CA: Brooks/Cole.

Minuchin, S. (1974). *Families and family therapy.* Cambridge, MA: Harvard University Press.

Minuchin, S., & Fishman, H. C. (1981). *Family therapy techniques.* Cambridge, MA: Harvard University Press.

Mishna, F., Muskat, B., & Wiener, J. (2010). "I'm not lazy; it's just that I learn differently": Development and implementation of a manualized school-based group for students with learning disabilities. *Social Works with Groups, 33,* 139–159.

Mitchell, P., & Ziegler, F. (2012). *Fundamentals of developmental psychology.* New York, NY: Psychology Press.

Moore, S. R., Harden, K. P., & Mendle, J. (2014). Pubertal timing and adolescent sexual behavior in girls. *Developmental Psychology, 50*(6), 1734–1745. doi:10.1037/a0036027

Moreno, J. L. (1932). *First Book on Group Therapy.* Beacon, NY: Beacon House.

Morgan, P. L., Staff, J., Hillemeier, M. M., Farkas, G., & Maczuga, S. (2013). Racial and ethnic disparities in ADHD diagnosis from kindergarten to fifth grade. *Pediatrics, 132*(1), 85–93. doi:10.1542/peds.2012-2390

Morsette, A., Swaney, G., Stolle, D., Schuldberg, D., van den Pol, R., & Young, M. (2009). *Journal of Behavior Therapy and Experimental Psychiatry, 40,* 169–178. doi:10.1016/j.jbtep.2008.07.0067

Morsy, L., & Rothstein, R. (2015, June 10). *Five social disadvantages that depress student performance: Why schools alone can't close achievement gaps* (A report for the Economic Policy Institute). Retrieved from http://www.epi.org/publication/five-social-disadvantages-that-depress-student-performance-why-schools-alone-cant-close-achievement-gaps

MST Services. (2015). *Breaking the cycle of criminal behaviors by keeping teens at home, in school and out of trouble.* Retrieved from http://mstservices.com/index.php

Muehlenkamp, J. J. (2006). Empirically supported treatments and general therapy guidelines for non-suicidal self-injury. *Journal of Mental Health Counseling, 28*(2), 166–185.

Muhlau, M., Gaser, C., Ilg, R., Conrad, B., Leibl, C., & Cebulla, M. H. (2007). Gray matter decreases of the anterior cingulate cortex in anorexia nervosa. *American Journal of Psychiatry, 164,* 1850–1857.

Munns, E. (2013). Filial therapy and theraplay. In N. R. Bowers (Ed.), *Play therapy with families: A collaborative approach to healing* (pp. 147–160). New York, NY: Jason Aronson.

Murdock, N. L. (2009). *Theories of counseling and psychotherapy: A case approach* (2nd ed.). Upper Saddle River, NJ: Pearson.

Muris, P., Ollendick, T. H., Roelofs, J., & Austin, K. (2014). The Short Form of the Fear Survey Schedule for Children–Revised (FSSC-R-SF): An efficient, reliable, and valid scale for measuring fear in children and adolescents. *Journal of Anxiety Disorders, 28*(8), 957–965. doi:10.1016/j.janxdis.2014.09.020

Murray, L. K., Cohen, J. A., & Mannarino, A. P. (2013). Trauma-focused cognitive behavioral therapy for youth who experience continuous traumatic exposure. *Peace and Conflict: Journal of Peace Psychology, 19*, 180–195. doi:10.1037/a0032533

Myers, J. E., & Young, J. S. (2012). Brain wave biofeedback: Benefits of integrating neurofeedback in counseling. *Journal of Counseling & Development, 90*(1), 20–28. doi:10.1111/j.1556-6676.2012.00003.x

Nader, K. (2008). *Understanding and assessing trauma in children and adolescents: Measures, methods, and youth in context.* New York, NY: Routledge.

Nader, K. (2014). *Assessment of trauma in youth: Understanding issues of age, complexity, and associated variables.* New York, NY: Routledge.

Nader, K., & Fletcher, K. E. (2014). Childhood posttraumatic stress disorder. In E. J. Mash & R. A. Barkley (Eds.), *Child psychopathology* (3rd ed., pp. 476–528). New York, NY: Guilford.

Naderi, F., Heidarie, L., Bouron, L., & Asgari, P. (2010). The efficacy of play therapy on ADHD, anxiety and social maturity in 8 to 12 years aged clientele children of Ahwaz Metropolitan Counseling Clinics. *Journal of Applied Sciences, 10*, 189–195. doi:10.3923/jas.2010.189.195

Najavits, L. M., Gallop, R. J., & Weiss, R. D. (2006). Seeking Safety therapy for adolescent girls with PTSD and substance use disorder: A randomized controlled trial. *Journal of Behavioral Health Services and Research, 33*, 453–463. doi:10.1007/s11414-006-9034-2

Nasvytienė, D., Lazdauskas, T., & Leonavičienė, T. (2012). Child's resilience in face of maltreatment: A meta-analysis of empirical studies. *Psichologija, 46*, 7–26. Retrieved from http://www.psichologijatau.lt/

National Alliance of Children's Trust and Prevention Funds. (2014). *Bringing the protective factors framework to life in your work—A resource for action* [Online Training Course]. Retrieved from http://www.ctfalliance.org/onlinetraining.htm

National Association of School Psychologists (NASP). (2010). *Death and grief: Supporting children and youth.* Bethesda, MD: NASP.

National Association of Social Workers. (2008). *Code of ethics.* Washington, DC: Author.

National Autism Center. (2009). *National standards report* (Phase 1). Retrieved from http://www.nationalautismcenter.org/reports

National Autistic Society. (2015). *Challenging behavior in children with an ASD.* Retrieved from http://www.autism.org.uk/about/behaviour/challenging-behaviour.aspx

National Board for Certified Counselors. (2012). *Code of ethics.* Greensboro, NC: Author.

National Center for Health Statistics. (2015). *National marriage and divorce rate trends.* Hyattsville, MD: U.S. Department of Health & Human Services.

National Center for PTSD. (2010). *Mental health reactions after disaster.* Washington, DC: U.S. Department of Veterans Affairs.

National Center for Victims of Crime. (n.d.). *Reporting on child sexual abuse.* Retrieved from https://victimsofcrime.org/media/reporting-on-child-sexual-abuse

National Center for Youth Law. (2010). *California minor consent law—Mental health services: Minor consent services and parents access rules.* Retrieved from www.teenhealthlaw.org

National Child Traumatic Stress Network Child Sexual Abuse Committee. (2009). *Caring for kids: What parents need to know about sexual abuse.* Los Angeles, CA, & Durham, NC: National Center for Child Traumatic Stress. Retrieved from http://www.nctsn.org/sites/default/files/assets/pdfs/caring_for_kids.pdf

National Coalition for Child Protection Reform. (2009). *The evidence is in: Foster care vs. keeping families together: The definitive studies.* Retrieved from http://nfpcar.org/Archive/evidence_NCCPR.pdf

National Eating Disorders Association (NEDA). (n.d.). *For family and friends.* Retrieved from http://www.nationaleatingdisorders.org/family-and-friends

National Gang Center. (n.d.). *National youth gang survey analysis.* Retrieved from http://www.nationalgangcenter.gov/Survey-Analysis

National Institute for Health and Care Excellence (NICE). (2004). *Core interventions in the treatment and management of anorexia nervosa, bulimia nervosa, and binge eating disorder* (National Clinical Practice Guideline CG9). Retrieved from https://www.nice.org.uk/guidance/cg9

National Institute of Allergy and Infectious Disease (NIAID). (2016). *Food allergy.* Retrieved from https://www.niaid.nih.gov/topics/foodallergy/Pages/default.aspx

National Institute on Alcohol Abuse and Alcoholism (NIAAA). (n.d.). *The effects of alcohol on physiological processes and biological development.* Retrieved from http://pubs.niaaa.nih.gov/publications/arh283/125-132.htm

National Institute on Drug Abuse (NIDA). (2003). *Preventing drug use among children and adolescents: A research-based guide for parents, educators, and community leaders* (2nd ed.). Bethesda, MD: Author. Retrieved from https://www.drugabuse.gov/sites/default/files/preventingdruguse_2.pdf

National Institute on Drug Abuse (NIDA). (2014a). *Addiction and health.* Retrieved from https://www.drugabuse.gov/publications/drugs-brains-behavior-science-addiction/addiction-health

National Institute on Drug Abuse (NIDA). (2014b). *Principles of adolescent substance use disorder treatment: A research-based guide.* Bethesda, MD: NIDA. Retrieved from https://www.drugabuse.gov/sites/default/files/podata_1_17_14.pdf

National Sleep Foundation. (2016). *Children and sleep.* Retrieved from https://sleepfoundation.org/sleep-topics/children-and-sleep

National Stepfamily Resource Center. (2015). *Stepfamily FAQs.* Hyattsville, MD: U.S. Department of Health & Human Services.

Nezu, C. M., & Nezu, A. M. (Eds.). (2016). *The Oxford handbook of cognitive and behavioral therapies.* New York, NY: Oxford.

Ng, M. Y., & Weisz, J. R. (2016). Annual research review: Building a science of personalized intervention for youth mental health. *Journal of Child Psychology and Psychiatry, 57*(3), 216–236. doi:10.1111/jcpp.12470

Niepel, C., Brunner, M., & Preckel, F. (2014). The longitudinal interplay of students' academic self-concepts and achievements within and across domains: Replicating and extending the reciprocal internal/external frame of reference model. *Journal of Educational Psychology, 106*(4), 1170–1191. doi:10.1037/a0036307

Nigg, J. T., & Barkley, R. A. (2014). Attention-deficit/hyperactivity disorder. In R. A. Barkley & E. J. Mash (Eds.), *Child psychopathology* (3rd ed., pp. 75–144). New York, NY: Guilford.

Nisbett, R. E., Aronson, J., Blair, C., Dickens, W., Flynn, J., Halpern, D. F., & Turkheimer, E. (2012). Intelligence: New findings and theoretical developments. *American Psychologist, 67*(2), 130–159. doi:10.1037/a0026699

Norbury, C. F., & Sparks, A. (2013). Difference or disorder? Cultural issues in understanding neurodevelopmental disorders. *Developmental Psychology, 49*(1), 45–58. doi:10.1037/a0027446

Norcross, J. C. (Ed.). (2011). *Psychotherapy relationships that work: Evidence-based responsiveness* (2nd ed.). New York, NY: Oxford University Press.

Norcross, J. C., Krebs, P. M., & Prochaska, J. O. (2011). Stages of change. *Journal of Clinical Psychology, 67*(2), 143–154. doi:10.1002/jclp.20758

Norcross, J. C., & Wampold, B. E. (2011a). Evidence-based therapy relationships: Research conclusions and clinical practices. In J. C. Norcross (Ed.), *Psychotherapy relationships that work: Evidence-based responsiveness* (2nd ed., 423–430). New York, NY: Oxford.

Norcross, J. C., & Wampold, B. E. (2011b). Research conclusions and clinical practices. In J. C. Norcross (Ed.), *Psychotherapy relationships that work: Evidence-based responsiveness* (2nd ed., pp. 423–430). New York, NY: Oxford.

Norton, C. C., & Norton, B. E. (1997). *Reaching children through play therapy: An experiential approach.* Fulton, CA: Publishing Cooperative.

Ohio Counselor, Social Worker, & Marriage and Family Therapy Board, Laws and Rules, Revised. (2017). Retrieved from http://cswmft.ohio.gov/Portals/0/pdf/CSWMFT%20Board%20Laws%20and%20Rules%204757.pdf

O'Malley, M., Voight, A., Renshaw, T. L., & Eklund, K. (2015). School climate, family structure, and academic achievement: A study of moderation effects. *School Psychology Quarterly, 30*(1), 142–157. doi:10.1037/spq0000076

Oliver, A. C., Pratt, L. A., & Normand, M. P. (2015). A survey of functional behavior assessment methods used by behavior analysts in practice. *Journal of Applied Behavior Analysis, 48*(4), 817–829. doi:10.1002/jaba.256

Olsen, J. P., Parra, G. R., Cohen, R., Schoffstall, C. L., & Egli, C. J. (2012). Beyond relationship reciprocity: A consideration of varied forms of children's relationships. *Personal Relationships, 19*(1), 72–88. doi:10.1111/j.1475-6811.2010.01339.x

Olson, D. (2011). FACES IV and the Circumplex model: Validation study. *Journal of Marital and Family Therapy, 37*(1), 64–80. doi:10.1111/j.1752-0606.2009.00175.x

Olweus, D. (2013). School bullying: Development and some important challenges. *Annual Review of Clinical Psychology, 9*, 751–80. doi:10.1146/annurev-clinpsy-050212-185516

Oppawsky, J. (2014). The nurse sees it first: The effects of parental divorce on children and adolescents. *Annals of Psychotherapy & Integrative Heath*, 1–8.

Ordway, A. M., & Moore, R. O. (2015, October). Stuck in the middle. *Counseling Today.* Retrieved from http://ct.counseling.org/2015/10/stuck-in-the-middle

Organization for Economic Cooperation and Development (OECD). (2013). *Education indicators in focus.* Retrieved from http://www.oecd.org/education/skills-beyond-school/EDIF%202013--N%C2%B010%20%28eng%29--v9%20FINAL%20bis.pdf

Orton, G. L. (1997). *Strategies for counseling with children and their parents.* Boston, MA: Brooks/Cole.

Osborne, C., & Berger, L. M. (2009). Parental substance abuse and child well-being: A consideration of parents' gender and coresidence. *Journal of Family Issues, 30*, 341–370. doi:10.1177/0192513X08326225

Osofsky, J. D., & Lieberman, A. F. (2011). A call for integrating a mental health perspective into systems of care for abused and neglected infants and young children. *American Psychologist, 66*(2), 120–128. doi:10.1037/a0021630

Osypuk, T. L., Tchetgen, E. J., Acevedo-Garcia, D., Earls, F. J., Lincoln, A., Schmidt, N. M., . . . Glymour, M. M. (2012). Differential mental health effects of neighborhood relocation among youth in vulnerable families: Results from a randomized trial. *Archives of General Psychiatry, 69*, 1284–1294. doi:10.1001/archgenpsychiatry.2012.449

Ougrin, D., Tranah, T., Leigh, E., Taylor, L., & Rosenbaum Asarnow, J. (2012). Practitioner review: Self-harm in adolescents. *The Journal of Child Psychology and Psychiatry, 53*(4), 337–350. doi:10.1111/j.1469-7610.2012.02525.x

Pace, G. T., Schafer, K., Jensen, T. M., & Larson, J. H. (2015). Stepparenting issues and relationship quality: The role of clear communication. *Journal of Social Work, 15*(1), 24–44. doi:10.1177/1468017313504508

Packman, J., & Bratton, S. (2003). A school based play/activity therapy intervention with learning disabled preadolescents exhibiting behavior problems. *International Journal of Play Therapy, 12*(2), 7–29. doi:10.1037/h0088876

Pahl, K. M., & Barrett, P. M. (2010). Interventions for anxiety disorders in children using group cognitive-behavioral therapy with family involvement. In J. R. Weisz & A. E. Kazdin (Eds.), *Evidence-based psychotherapies for children and adolescents* (2nd ed., pp. 45–60). New York, NY: Guilford.

Pajareya, K., & Nopmaneejumruslers, K. (2011). A pilot randomized controlled trial of DIR/Floortime parent training intervention for pre-school children with autistic spectrum disorders. *Autism, 15*, 1–15.

Paladino, D., & DeLorenzi, L. (2017). Counseling with older adolescents (15–19). In S. Smith-Adcock & C. Tucker (Eds.), *Counseling children and adolescents* (pp. 343–372). Thousand Oaks, CA: Sage.

Panasenko, N. (2013). Czech and Slovak family patterns and family values in historical, social and cultural context. *Journal of Comparative Family Studies, 44*, 79–98. Retrieved from https://soci.ucalgary.ca/jcfs

Panza, K. E., Pittenger, C., & Bloch, M. H. (2013). Age and gender correlates of pulling in pediatric trichotillomania. *Journal of the American Academy of Child and Adolescent Psychiatry, 52*(3), 241–249. doi:10.1016/j.jaac.2012.12.019

Pao, M., & Bosk, A. (2011). Anxiety in medically ill children/adolescents. *Depression and Anxiety, 28*, 40–49.

Papolos, D., Hennen, J., Cockerham, M. S., Thode, H. C., & Younstrom, E. A. (2006). The child bipolar questionnaire: A dimensional approach to screening for pediatric bipolar disorder. *Journal of Affective Disorders, 95*, 149–158. doi:10.1016/j.jad.2006.03.026

Papolos, D. S., & Papolos, J. (2006). *The bipolar child: The definitive and reassuring guide to childhood's most misunderstood disorder* (3rd ed.). New York, NY: Broadway Books.

Parens, E., & Johnston, J. (2010). Controversies concerning the diagnosis and treatment of bipolar disorder in children. *Child and Adolescent Psychiatry and Mental Health, 4*, 9. Retrieved at http://www.capmh.com/content/4/1

Paris, E. (2013). Interrupting trauma and advancing development: Considering parent education in contemporary psychoanalytic treatment. *Clinical Social Work Journal 41*, 84–92. doi:10.1007/s10645-012-0412-3

Park, D., Ramirez, G., & Beilock, S. L. (2014). The role of expressive writing in math anxiety. *Journal of Experimental*

Psychology: Applied, 20(2), 103–111. doi:10.1037/xap0000013

Patterson, J., Williams, L., Edwards, T. M., Chamow, L., & Grauf-Grounds, C. (2009). *Essential skills in family therapy* (2nd ed.). New York, NY: Guilford.

Patterson, W. M., Dohn, H. H., Bird, J., & Patterson, G. A. (1983). Evaluation of suicidal patients: The SAD PERSONS scale. *Psychosomatics: Journal of Consultation and Liaison Psychiatry, 24*(4), 343–349.

Pavuluri, M. N., West, A., Hill, S. K., Jindal, K., & Sweeney, J. A. (2009). Neurocognitive function in pediatric bipolar disorder: 3-year follow-up shows cognitive development lagging behind healthy youths. *Journal of the American Academy of Child & Adolescent Psychiatry, 48*(3), 299–307. doi:10.1097/CHI.0b013e318196b907

Paylo, M. J., Darby, A., Kinch, S., & Kress, V. E. (2014). Creative rituals for use with traumatized adolescents. *Journal of Creativity in Mental Health, 9,* 111–121. doi:10.1080/15401383.2013.859992

Pedro-Carroll, J. (2008). The children of divorce intervention program: Fostering children resilience through group support and skill building. In C. W. LeCroy (Ed.), *Handbook of evidence-based treatment manuals for children and adolescents* (pp. 314–359). New York, NY: Oxford.

Pedro-Carroll, J. (2010). *Putting children first: Proven parenting strategies for helping children thrive through divorce.* New York, NY: Avery.

Perera, M. J., & Chang, E. C. (2015). Depressive symptoms in South Asian, East Asian, and European Americans: Evidence for ethnic differences in coping with academic versus interpersonal stress? *Asian American Journal of Psychology, 6*(4), 350–358. doi:10.1037/aap0000030

Peris, T. S., Bergman, R. L., Asarnow, J. R., Langley, A., McCraken, J. T., & Piacentini, J. (2010). Clinical and cognitive correlates of depressive symptoms among youth with obsessive-compulsive disorder. *Journal of Clinical Child & Adolescent Psychology, 39*(5), 616–626. doi:10.1080/15374416.210.501285

Piacentini, J., Peris, T. S., Bergman, R. L., Chang, S., & Jaffer, M. (2007). Functional impairment in childhood OCD: Development and psychometrics properties of the Child Obsessive-Compulsive Impact Scale–Revised (COIS-R). *Journal of Clinical Child & Adolescent Psychology, 36*(4), 645–653. doi:10.1080/15374410701662790

Piaget, J. (1928/2002). *Judgment and reasoning in the child.* New York, NY: Routledge.

Piaget, J. (1952). *The origins of intelligence in children.* New York, NY: International Universities.

Piaget, J. (1954). *The construction of reality in the child.* New York, NY: Basic Books.

Piaget, J. (1970). *Science of education and the psychology of the child.* New York, NY: Orion Press.

Pike, K. M., Walsh, B. T., Vitousek, K., Wilson, G. T., & Bauer, J. (2003). Cognitive behavior therapy in the posthospitalization treatment of anorexia nervosa. *American Journal of Psychiatry, 160,* 2046–2049.

Plastow, M. (2011). Hermine Hug-Hellmuth, the first child psychoanalyst: Legacy and dilemmas. *Australasian Psychiatry, 19,* 206–210. doi:10.3109/10398562.2010.526213

Podell, J. L., Mychailyszyn, M., Edmunds, J., Puleo, C. M., & Kendall, P. C. (2010). Coping Cat program for anxious youth: The FEAR plan comes to life. *Cognitive and Behavioral Practice, 17*(2), 132–141. doi:10.1016/j.cbpra.2009.11.001

Polanin, J. R., Espelage, D. L., & Pigott, T. D. (2012). A meta-analysis of school-based bullying prevention programs' effects on bystander intervention behavior. *School Psychology Review, 41,* 47–65. Retrieved from http://naspjournals.org

Pomeroy, C., Mitchell, J. E., Roerig, J., & Crow, S. (2002). *Medical complications of psychiatric illness.* Washington, DC: American Psychiatric Press.

Pope, K. S., & Feldman-Summers, S. (1992). National survey of psychologists' sexual and physical abuse history and their evaluation of training and competence in these areas. *Professional Psychology: Research and Practice, 23,* 353–361.

Popkin, M. H. (2009). *Active parenting of teens: Parent's guide* (3rd ed.). Marietta, GA: Active Parenting.

Popkin, M. H. (2014). *Active parenting: A parent's guide to raising happy and successful children* (4th ed.). Marietta, GA: Active Parenting.

Porfeli, E. J., & Lee, B. (2012). Career development during childhood and adolescence. *New Directions for Youth Development,* (134), 11–22. doi:10.1002/yd.20011

Positive Behavioral Interventions & Supports. (2017). *OSEP technical assistance center.* Retrieved from http://www.pbis.org

Poulsen, S., Lunn, S., Daniel, S., Folke, S., Mathiesen, B. B., Katznelson, H., . . . Fairburn, C. G. (2014). A randomized controlled trial of psychoanalytic psychotherapy or cognitive behavioral therapy for bulimia nervosa. *American Journal of Psychiatry, 171,* 109–116.

Pringsheim, T., Hirsch, L., Gardner, D., & Gorman, D. A. (2015). The pharmacological management of oppositional behaviour, conduct problems, and aggression in children and adolescents with attention-deficit hyperactivity disorder, oppositional defiant disorder, and conduct disorder: A systematic review and meta-analysis. Part 2: Antipsychotics and traditional mood stabilizers. *The Canadian Journal of Psychiatry/La Revue Canadienne De Psychiatrie, 60*(2), 52–61. Retrieved from http://www.cpa-apc.org/clinical-resources/the-canadian-journal-of-psychiatry/

Prochaska, J. O. (1995). An eclectic and integrative approach: Transtheoretical theory. In A. S. Gurman & S. B. Messer (Eds.), *Essential psychotherapies: Theory and practice* (pp. 403–440). New York, NY: Guilford.

Prochaska, J. O., DiClemente, C. C., & Norcross, J. C. (1992). In search of how people change: Applications to addictive behaviors. *The American Psychologist, 47*(9), 1102–1114. doi:10.1037/003-066X.47.9.1102

Prout, H. T., & Fedewa, A. L. (2015). *Counseling and psychotherapy with children and adolescents: Theory and practice for school and clinical settings* (5th ed.). Hoboken, NJ: Wiley.

Pugh, R. (2007). Dual relationships: Personal and professional in rural social work. *The British Journal of Social Work, 37*(8), 1405–1423. doi:10.1093/bjsw/bcl088

Purcell, R., Fraser, R., Greenwood-Smith, C., Baksheev, G. N., McCarthy, J., Reid, D., . . . Sullivan, D. H. (2012). Managing risks of violence in a youth mental health service: A service model description. *Early Intervention in Psychiatry, 6,* 469–475. doi:10.1111/j.1751-7893.2012.00372.x

Pynoos, R. S., Weathers, F. W., Steinberg, A. M., Marx, B. P., Layne, C. M., Kaloupek, D. G., . . . Kriegler, J. A. (2015). *Clinician-Administered PTSD Scale for DSM-5—Child/Adolescent Version.* White River Junction, VT: National Center for PTSD.

Rabiner, D. (2012). New study shows teens with ADHD helped by cognitive behavioral therapy. *Sharp Brains.* Retrieved from http://sharpbrains.com/blog/2012/08/29/new-study-shows-teens-with-adhd-helped-by-cognitive-behavioral-therapy

Rae, R. (2013). *Sandtray: Playing to heal, recover, and grow.* New York, NY: Jason Aronson.

Rao, U., & Chen, L. (2009). Characteristics, correlates, and outcomes of childhood and adolescent depressive disorders. *Dialogues in Clinical Neuroscience, 11*(1), 45–62.

Rappleyea, D. L., Harris, S. M., White, M., & Simon, K. (2009). Termination: Legal and ethical considerations for marriage and family therapists. *The American Journal of Family Therapy, 37*(1), 12–27. doi:10.1080/01926180801960617

Rasic, D. (2010). Countertransference in child and adolescent psychiatry—A forgotten concept? *Journal of Canadian Academy of Child and Adolescent Psychiatry, 19,* 249–254.

Rathus, J. H., & Miller, A. L. (2015). *DBT skills manual for adolescents.* New York, NY: Guilford.

Rauer, A. J., Pettit, G. S., Lansford, J. E., Bates, J. E., & Dodge, K. A. (2013). Romantic relationship patterns in young adulthood and their developmental antecedents. *Developmental Psychology, 49*(11), 2159–2171. doi:10.1037/a0031845

Rausch, M. A., Williams, N. F., & Kress, V. E. (2015). Neurodevelopmental and neurocognitive disorders. In V. E. Kress & M. J. Paylo (Eds.), *Treating those with mental disorders: A comprehensive approach to case conceptualization and treatment* (pp. 421–463). Upper Saddle River, NJ: Pearson.

Ray, D. (2014). Supervision of basic and advanced skills in play therapy. *Journal of Professional Counseling: Practice, Theory, & Research, 32,* 28–41. Retrieved from https://txca.submittable.com/submit/30127

Ray, D., Armstrong, S., Balkin, R., & Jayne, K. (2015). Child centered play therapy in the schools: Review and meta-analysis. *Psychology in the Schools, 52,* 107–123. doi:10.1002/pits.21798

Ray, D., & Bratton, S. (2010). What the research shows about play therapy: 21st century update. In J. Baggerly, D. Ray, & S. Bratton (Eds.), *Child-centered play therapy research: The evidence base for effective practice* (pp. 3–36). New York, NY: Wiley.

Ray, D. C., Lee, K. R., Meany-Walen, K. K., Carlson, S. E., Carnes-Holt, K. L., & Ware, J. N. (2013). Use of toys in child-centered play therapy. *International Journal of Play Therapy, 22*(1), 43–57. doi:10.1037/a0031430

Raz, S., Newman, J. B., DeBastos, A. K., Peters, B. N., & Batton, D. G. (2014). Postnatal growth and neuropsychological performance in preterm-birth preschoolers. *Neuropsychology, 28*(2), 188–201. doi:10.1037/neu0000038

Remley, T. P., & Herlihy, B. (2016). *Ethical, legal, and professional issues in counseling* (5th ed.). Upper Saddle River, NJ: Pearson.

Reynolds, C. R., & Kamphaus, R. W. (2004). *BASC-2: Behavior Assessment System for Children* (2nd ed.). Upper Saddle River, NJ: Pearson.

Reynolds, C. R., & Richmond, B. O. (2008). *Revised Children's Manifest Anxiety Scales* (2nd ed.). Torrance, CA: Western Psychological Services.

Rivera, J., Docter, P., & del Carmen, R. (2015). *Inside out* (DVD). Emeryville, CA Disney Pixar.

Rizo, C. F., Macy, R. J., Ermentrout, D. M., & Johns, N. B. (2011). A review of family interventions for intimate partner violence with a child focus or component. *Aggression and Violent Behaviors, 16,* 14–166. doi:10.1016/j.avb.2011.02.004

Rodenburg, R., Benjamin, A., de Roos, C., Meijer, A. M., & Stams, G. J. (2009). Efficacy of EMDR in children: A meta-analysis. *Clinical Psychology Review, 29*(7), 599–606. doi:10.1016/j.cpr.2009.06.008

Rogers, C. R. (1942). *Counseling and psychotherapy.* Boston, MA: Houghton Mifflin.

Rogers, C. R. (1951). *Client-centered therapy: Its current practice, implications and theory.* Boston, MA: Houghton Mifflin.

Rogers, C. R. (1957). The necessary and sufficient conditions of therapeutic personality change. *Journal of Counseling Psychology, 21,* 95–103.

Rogers, C. R. (1961). *On becoming a person.* Boston, MA: Houghton Mifflin.

Rogers, C. R. (1970). *Carl Rogers on encounter groups.* New York, NY: Harper & Row.

Rogers, C. R. (1977). *Carl Rogers on personal power.* New York, NY: Delacorte.

Rogers, N. (1993). *The creative connection: Expressive arts as healing.* Palo Alto, CA: Science and Behavior Books.

Rogers, N. (2011). *The creative connection for groups: Person-centered expressive arts for healing and social change.* Palo Alto, CA: Science and Behavior Books.

Rogers, S. J., & Dawson, G. (2009). *Play and engagement in early autism: The Early Start Denver Model. Volume 1: The treatment.* New York, NY: Guilford.

Roid, G. H. (2003). *Stanford–Binet Intelligence Scales, Fifth Edition: Technical manual.* Itasca, IL: Riverside.

Roid, G. H., Miller, L. J., Pomplun, M., & Kock, C. (2013). *Leiter-3 International Performance Scale, Third Edition.* Wood Dale, IL: Stoelting.

Romer, D. (2010). Adolescent risk taking, impulsivity, and brain development: Implication for prevention. *Developmental Psychobiology, 52*(3), 263–276. doi:10.1002/dev.20442

Rorschach, H. (1921/1942). *Psychodiagnostik.* Bern, Switzerland: Bircher (Hans Huber Verlag, trans.).

Rosario, M., Reisner, S. L., Corliss, H. L., Wypij, D., Frazier, A. L., & Austin, S. B. (2014). Disparities in depressive distress by sexual orientation in emerging adults: The roles of attachment and stress paradigms. *Archives of Sexual Behavior, 43,* 901–916. doi:10.1007/s10508-013-0129-6

Rosen, C. M., & Atkins, S. S. (2014). Am I doing expressive arts therapy or creativity in counseling? *Journal of Creativity in Mental Health, 9*(2), 292–303. Retrieved from http://www.creativecounselor.org/Journal.html

Rossano, M. J. (2012). The essential role of ritual in the transmission and reinforcement of social norms. *Psychological Bulletin, 138*(3), 529–549. doi:10.1037/a0027038

Roy, A. L., McCoy, D. C., & Raver, C. C. (2014). Instability versus quality: Residential mobility, neighborhood poverty, and children's self-regulation. *Developmental Psychology, 50*(7), 1891–1896. doi:10.1037/a0036984

Rudd, M. D., Mandrusiak, M., & Joiner, T. (2006). The case against no-suicide contracts: The commitment to treatment statement as a practice alternative. *Journal of Clinical Psychology, 62,* 243–251.

Runyon, M. K., Deblinger, E., Ryan, E. E., & Thakkar-Kolar, R. (2004). An overview of child physical abuse: Developing an integrated parent–child cognitive-behavioral treatment approach. *Trauma, Violence, & Abuse, 5*(1), 65–85.

Runyon, M. K., Deblinger, E., & Schroeder, C. M. (2009). Pilot evaluation of combined parent–child cognitive-behavioral group therapy for families at risk for child physical abuse. *Cognitive and Behavioral Practice, 16,* 101–118.

Ryan, M. (2015, December 17). *Signs of magical thinking in small children.* Retrieved from https://www.verywell.com/the-signs-of-magical-thinking-in-children-290168

Rye, N. (2010). Child-centered play therapy. In Center for International Rehabilitation Research Information and Exchange (CIRRIE) (Ed.), *International encyclopedia of rehabilitation.* Buffalo, NY: University at Buffalo. Retrieved from http://cirrie.buffalo.edu/encyclopedia/en/article/275

Sadock, B. J., & Sadock, V. A. (2007). *Kaplan and Sadock's synopsis of psychiatry: Behavioral sciences/clinical psychiatry* (10th ed.). Philadelphia, PA: Lippincott Williams & Wilkins.

Sadock, B. J., Sadock, V. A., & Ruiz, P. (2014). *Kaplan and Sadock's synopsis of psychiatry: Behavioral sciences/clinical psychiatry* (11th ed.). Philadelphia, PA: Lippincott Williams & Wilkins.

Safer, D. L., Courturier, J. L., & Lock, J. (2007). Dialectical behavior therapy modified for adolescent binge eating disorder: A case report. *Cognitive and Behavioral Practice, 14,* 157–167.

Saigh, P., Yaski, A. E., Oberfield, R. A., Green, B. L., Halamandaris, P. V., Rubenstein, H., . . . McHugh, M. (2000). The Children's PTSD Inventory: Development and reliability. *Journal of Traumatic Stress, 30,* 369–380.

Salami, S. O. (2010). Moderating effects of resilience, self-esteem, and social support on adolescents' reactions to violence. *Asian Social Sciences, 6,* 101–110.

Salbach-Andrae, H., Bohnekamp, I., Pfeiffer, E., Lehmkuhl, U., & Miller, A. L. (2008). Dialectical behavior therapy of anorexia and bulimia nervosa among adolescents: A case series. *Cognitive and Behavioral Practice, 15,* 415–425

Salo, M. (2015). Counseling minor clients. In B. Herlihy & G. Corey (Eds.), *ACA ethical standards casebook* (7th ed., pp. 205–214). Alexandria, VA: American Counseling Association.

Saltzman, A., & Goldin, P. (2008). Mindfulness-based stress reduction for school-age children. In L. A. Greco & S. C. Hayes (Eds.), *Acceptance and mindfulness treatments for children and adolescents: A practitioner's guide* (pp. 139–162). Oakland, CA: Raincoast.

Salvia, J., & Ysseldyke, J. E. (1998). *Assessment* (7th ed.). Boston, MA: Houghton Mifflin.

Sampson, D., & Hertlein, K. (2015). The experience of grandparents raising grandchildren. *The Contemporary Journal of Research, Practice and Policy, 2,* 75–96. Retrieved from http://scholarworks.wmich.edu/grandfamilies/vol2/iss1/4

Sanders, J., Munford, R., Thimasarn-Anwar, T., Liebenberg, L., & Ungar, M. (2015). The role of positive youth development practices in building resilience and enhancing wellbeing for at-risk youth. *Child Abuse & Neglect, 42,* 40–53. doi:10.1016/j.chiabu.2015.02.006

Sanderson, J. A. (2011). *Neighborhood, family, peer, and youth center experiences as predictors of urban youth development* (Doctoral dissertation). Retrieved from DigitalCommons@UConn (AAI3468068)

Santiago, C. D., Kaltman, S., & Miranda, J. (2013). Poverty and mental health: How do low-income adults and children fare in psychotherapy? *Journal of Clinical Psychology, 69,* 115–126. doi:10.1002/jclp.21951

Santiago, C. D., Kataoka, S., Cordova, M., Alvarado-Goldberg, K., Maher, L. M., & Escudero, P. (2015). Preliminary evaluation of family treatment component to augment a school-based intervention serving low-income families. *Journal of Emotional and Behavioral Disorders, 23*(1), 28–39. doi:10.1037/t19482-000

Santrock, J. W. (2011). *Child development* (13th ed.) New York, NY: McGraw-Hill.

Satir, V. (1983). *Conjoint family therapy.* Palo Alto, CA: Science and Behavior Books.

Scahill, L., Riddle, M. A., McSwiggin-Hardin, M., Ort, S., King, R. A., Goodman, W. K., . . . Leckman, J. F. (1997). Children's Yale-Brown Obsessive-Compulsive Scale: Reliability and validity. *Journal of the American Academy of Child and Adolescent Psychiatry, 36*(6), 844–852.

Schaefer, C. E., & Drewes, A. A. (2013). *The therapeutic powers of play: 20 core agents of change* (2nd ed.). Hoboken, NJ: Wiley.

Schaefer, C. E., & Kaduson, H. G. (Eds.). (2007). *Contemporary play therapy: Theory, research, and practice.* New York, NY: Guilford.

Schaeffer, J. A., & Kaiser, E. M. (2013). A structured approach to processing clients' unilateral termination decisions. *American Journal of Psychotherapy, 67*(2), 165–183.

Scharff, D. E., & Scharff, J. S. (1987). *Object relations family therapy.* Northvale, NJ: Jason Aronson.

Scharfstein, L., & Beidel, D. C. (2011). Behavioral and cognitive-behavioral treatments for youth with social phobia. *Journal of Experimental Psychopathology, 2,* 615–628. doi:10.5127/jep.014011

Schargel, F. P. (2014). *Creating safe schools: A guide for school leaders, teachers, counselors, and parents.* New York, NY: Routledge.

Schneider, B. H. (2014). *Child psychopathology: From infancy to adolescence.* New York, NY: Cambridge University Press.

Schomaker, S. A., & Ricard, R. J. (2015). Effect of a mindfulness-based intervention on counselor–client attunement. *Journal of Counseling and Development, 93,* 491–498. doi:10.1002/jcad.12047

Schopler, E., Van Bourgondien, M. E., Wellman, G. J., & Love, S. R. (2010). *Childhood Autism Rating Scale, Second Edition* (CARS). Los Angeles, CA: Western Psychological Services.

Schore, A. (2012). *The science of the art of psychotherapy.* New York, NY: Norton.

Schultz, D. P., & Schultz, E. S. (2013). *Theories of personality* (11th ed.). Boston, MA: Cengage.

Schultz, D. P., & Schultz, S. E. (2017). *Theories of personality* (11th ed.). Boston, MA: Cengage.

Search Institute. (2007). *Forty developmental assets for adolescents.* Retrieved from www.search-institute.org/content/40-developmental-assets-adolescents-ages-12-18

Search Institute. (2015). *Discovering what kids need to succeed.* Retrieved from www.search-institute.org

Section 504 of the Rehabilitation Act of 1973, 29 U.S.C. § 701.

Segal, Z. V., Williams, J. M. G., & Teasdale, J. D. (2002). *Mindfulness-based cognitive therapy for depression: A new approach to preventing relapse.* New York, NY: Guilford.

Selfhout, M. W., Branje, S. T., Delsing, M., ter Bogt, T. M., & Meeu, W. J. (2009). Different types of internet use, depression, and social anxiety: The role of perceived friendship quality. *Journal of Adolescence, 32*(2), 819–833. doi:10.1016/j.adolescence.2008.10.011

Seligman, L. D., & Ollendick, T. H. (2011). Cognitive behavioral therapy for anxiety disorders in youth. *Adolescent Psychiatric Clinics of North America, 20*(2), 217–238. doi:10.1016/j.chc.2011.01.003

Seligman, L. W., & Reichenberg, L. W. (2014). *Theories of counseling and psychotherapy: Systems, strategies, and skills* (4th ed.). Upper Saddle River, NJ: Pearson.

Seligman, M. E. P. (2012). *Flourish: A visionary new understanding of happiness and well-being.* New York, NY: Simon & Schuster.

Semple, R. J., Reid, E. F. G., & Miller, L. (2005). Treating anxiety with mindfulness: An open trial of mindfulness training for anxious children. *Journal of Cognitive Psychotherapy, 19,* 379–392. doi:10.1891/jcop.2005.19.4.379

Senn, D. S. (2004). *Small group counseling for children.* Chapin, SC: Youthlight.

Seymour, J. W. (2014). Integrating play therapy with childhood traumatic grief. In C. A. Malchiodi & D. A. Crenshaw (Eds.), *Creative arts and play therapy for attachment problems* (pp. 259–274). New York, NY: Guilford.

Shapira, B. E., & Dahlen, P. (2010). Therapeutic treatment protocol for enuresis using an enuresis alarm. *Journal of Counseling & Development, 88,* 246–252.

Shapiro, D. N. (2012). *Parent and child mental health in nontraditional families: The intersecting roles of gender, dyadic support, and communication* (Unpublished doctoral dissertation). The University of Michigan, Ann Arbor.

Shapiro, F. (2001). *Eye movement desensitization and reprocessing: Basic principles, protocols, and procedures* (2nd ed.). New York, NY: Guilford.

Shapiro, J. P. (2015). *Child and adolescent therapy: Science and art* (2nd ed.). Hoboken, NJ: John Wiley & Sons.

Sharf, R. S. (2012). *Theories of psychotherapy and counseling* (5th ed.). Belmont, CA: Brooks/Cole.

Sharkey, J. D., Ruderman, M. A., Mayworm, A. M., Green, J. G., Furlong, M. J., Rivera, N., . . . Purisch, L. (2015). Psychosocial functioning of bullied youth who adopt versus deny the bully-victim label. *School Psychology Quarterly, 30*(1), 91–104. doi:10.1037/spq0000077

Sharpless, B. A., Muran, C. J., & Barber, J. P. (2010). Coda: Recommendations for practice and training. In J. C. Muran & J. P. Barber (Eds.), *The therapeutic alliance: An evidence-based guide to practice* (pp. 341–354). New York, NY: Guilford.

Shaw, T. V., Bright, C. L., & Sharpe, T. L. (2015). Child welfare outcomes for youth in care as a result of parental death or parental incarceration. *Child Abuse & Neglect, 42,* 112–120. doi:10.1016/j.chiabu.2015.01.002

Shell, M. D., Gazelle, H., & Faldowski, R. A. (2014). Anxious solitude and the middle school transition: A diathesis × stress model of peer exclusion and victimization trajectories. *Developmental Psychology, 50*(5), 1569–1583. doi:10.1037/a0035528

Sheridan, D., Coffee, P., & Lavallee, D. (2014). A systematic review of social support in youth sport. *International Review of Sport and Exercise Psychology, 7*(1), 198–228. doi:10.1080/1750984X.2014.931999

Shields, M. K., & Behrman, R. E. (2004). Children of immigrant families: Analysis and recommendations. *Future of Children, 14*(2), 4–15.

Shin, H., & Ryan, A. M. (2014). Friendship networks and achievement goals: An examination of selection and influence processes and variations by gender. *Journal of Youth and Adolescence, 43*(9), 1453–1464. doi:10.1007/s10964-014-0132-9

Shlafer, R. J., McMorris, B. J., Sieving, R. E., & Gower, A. L. (2013). The impact of family and peer protective factors on girls' violence perpetration and victimization. *Journal of Adolescent Health, 53,* 365–371. doi:10.1016/j.jadohealth.2012.07.015

Shriver, M. D., Anderson, C. M., & Proctor, B. (2001). Evaluating the validity of functional behavior assessment. *School Psychology Review, 30*(2), 180–192.

Shulman, C. (2016). *Research and practice in infant and early childhood mental health.* New York, NY: Springer.

Sicile-Kira, C. (2014). *Autism spectrum disorder: The complete guide to understanding autism* (Rev. ed.). New York, NY: Penguin Group.

Siegel, D. J. (2014). *Brainstorm: The power and purpose of the teenage brain.* New York, NY: Penguin Group.

Sigal, A. B., Wolchik, S. A., Tein, J., & Sandler, I. N. (2012). Enhancing youth outcomes following parental divorce: A longitudinal study of the effects of the new beginnings program on educational and occupational goals. *Journal of Clinical Child and Adolescent Psychology, 41*(2), 150–165. doi:10.1080/15374416.2012.651992

Sigelman, C. K., & Rider, E. A. (2012). *Life-span human development* (7th ed.). Belmont, CA: Wadsworth.

Silva, R. R., Gallagher, R., & Minami, H. (2006). Cognitive-behavioral treatments for anxiety disorders in children and adolescents. *Primary Psychiatry, 13*(5), 68–76.

Silveira, F. A., & Boyer, W. (2015). Vicarious resilience in counselors of child and youth victims of interpersonal trauma. *Qualitative Health Research, 25*(4), 513–526. doi:10.1177/1049732314552284

Simpson, A., Flood, C., Rowe, J., Quigley, J., Henry, S., Hall, C., . . . Bowers, L. (2014). Results of a pilot randomised controlled trial to measure the clinical and cost effectiveness of peer support in increasing hope and quality of life in mental health patients discharged from hospital in the UK. *BioMed Central Psychiatry, 14*(1), 30. doi:10.1186/1471-244X-14-30

Simpson, J. A., Collins, W. A., & Salvatore, J. E. (2011). The impact of early interpersonal experience on adult romantic relationship functioning: Recent findings from the Minnesota Longitudinal Study of Risk and Adaptation. *Current Directions in Psychological Science, 20,* 355–359. doi:10.1177/0963721411418468

Singh, T. (2008). Pediatric bipolar disorder: Diagnostic challenges in identifying symptoms and course of illness. *Psychiatry (Edgmont), 5*(6), 34–42.

Skapinakis, P., Bellos, S., Gkatsa, T., Magklara, K., Lewis, G., Araya, R., . . . Mavreas, V. (2011). The association between bullying and early stages of suicidal ideation in late adolescents in Greece. *BioMed Central Psychiatry, 11,* 22. doi:10.1186/1471-244X-11-22

Skinner, B. F. (1971). *Beyond freedom and dignity.* New York, NY: Knopf.

Skinner, E. A., & Zimmer-Gembeck, M. J. (2016). *Development of coping: Stress, neurophysiology, social relationships, and resilience during childhood and adolescence.* New York, NY: Springer.

Slyter, M. (2012). Creative counseling interventions for grieving adolescents. *Journal of Creativity in Mental Health, 7*(1), 17–34. doi:10.1080/15401383.2012.657593

Small, D. M., Simons, A. D., Yovanoff, P., Silva, S. G., Lewis, C. C., Murakami, J. L., & March, J. (2008). Depressed adolescents and comorbid psychiatric disorders: Are there differences in the presentation of depression. *Journal of Abnormal Child Psychology, 36,* 1015–1028. doi:10.1007/s10802-008-9237-5

Smith, D., Jones, I., & Simpson, S. (2010). Psychoeducation for bipolar disorder. *Advances in Psychiatric Treatment, 16*(2), 147–154. doi:10.1192/apt.bp.108.006403

Smith, E. J. (2006). The strength-based counseling model. *The Counseling Psychologist, 34*(1), 13–79. doi:10.1177/0011000005277018

Smith, H. L., & Coghill, D. R. (2010). Pharmacotherapy for children and adolescents with conduct problems. In R. C. Murrihy, A. D. Kidman, T. H. Ollendick, R. C. Murrihy, A. D. Kidman, & T. H. Ollendick (Eds.), *Clinical handbook of assessing and treating conduct problems in youth* (pp. 383–404). New York, NY: Springer.

Smith, L. E., Bernal, D. R., Schwartz, B. S., Whitt, C. L., Christman, S. T., Donnelly, S., . . . Kobetz, E. (2014). Coping with vicarious trauma in the aftermath of a natural disaster. *Journal of Multicultural Counseling and Development, 42,* 2–12. doi:10.1002/j.2161-1912.2014.00040.x

Smith, T. (2010). Early and intensive behavioral interventions for autism. In J. R. Weisz & A. E. Kazdin (Eds.), *Evidence-based psychotherapies for children and adolescents* (2nd ed., pp. 312–326). New York, NY: Guilford.

Smith, T. B., & Silva, L. (2011). Ethnic identity and personal well-being of people of color: A meta-analysis. *Journal of Counseling Psychology, 58,* 42–60. doi:10.1037/a0021528

Smith-Adcock, S., & Tucker, C. (2016). *Counseling children and adolescents: Connecting theory, development, and diversity (counseling and professional identity).* Thousand Oaks, CA: Sage.

Sommers-Flanagan, J., & Campbell, D. G. (2009). Psychotherapy and (or) medication for depressed youth? An evidence-based review with recommendations for treatment. *Journal of Contemporary Psychotherapy, 39,* 111–120. doi:10.1007/s10879-008-9106-0

Sommers-Flanagan, J., & Sommers-Flanagan, R. (2009). *Clinical interviewing* (4th ed.). Hoboken, NJ: Wiley.

Sorhagen, N. S. (2013). Early teacher expectations disproportionately affect poor children's high school performance. *Journal of Educational Psychology, 105*(2), 465–477. doi:10.1037/a0031754

Southgate, L., Tchanturia, K., & Treasure, J. (2008). Information processing bias in anorexia nervosa. *Psychiatry Residency, 160,* 221–227.

Spence, S. H. (1998). A measure of anxiety symptoms among children. *Behaviour Research and Therapy, 36,* 545–566.

Spiegler, M. D., & Guevremont, D. C. (2016). *Contemporary behavior therapy* (6th ed.). Boston, MA: Cengage.

Spielberger, C. D. (1983). *Manual for the State-Trait Anxiety Inventory for Children.* Palo Alto, CA: Consulting Psychologists Press.

Stallman, H. M., & Sanders, M. R. (2014). A randomized controlled trial of family transitions triple P: A group-administered parenting program to minimize the adverse effects of parent divorce on children. *Journal of Divorce & Remarriage, 55,* 33–48. doi:10.1080/10502556.2013.862091

Stalvey, S., & Brasell, H. (2006). Using stress balls to focus the attention of sixth-grade learners. *Journal of At-Risk Issues, 12*(2), 7–16.

Stargell, N. A., & Duong, K. (in press). What is your body saying? The use of nonverbal immediacy behaviors to support multicultural therapeutic relationships. *North Carolina Counseling Journal.*

Stark, K. D., Streusand, W., Krumholz, L. S., & Patel, P. (2010). Cognitive-behavioral therapy for depression: The ACTION treatment program for girls. In J. R. Weisz & A. E. Kazdin (Eds.), *Evidence-based psychotherapies for children and adolescents* (2nd ed., pp. 93–109). New York, NY: Guilford.

Stark, K. D., Streusand, W., Prerna, A., & Patel, P. (2012). Childhood depression: The ACTION treatment program. In P. C. Kendall (Ed.), *Child and adolescent therapy: Cognitive-behavioral procedures* (4th ed., pp. 190–223). New York, NY: Guilford.

Steeger, C. M., Gondoli, D. M., & Gibson, B. S. (2015). Combined cognitive and parent training interventions for adolescents with ADHD and their mothers: A randomized controlled trial. *Child Neuropsychology, 3,* 1–26. doi:10.1080/09297049.2014.994485

Steinhausen, H. C., & Weber, S. (2009). The outcome of bulimia nervosa: Findings from one-quarter century of research. *American Journal of Psychiatry, 166,* 1331–1341.

Stein-Steele, E. C. (2013). *Perspectives of foster parents on interactions and involvement with K–12 public schools in a county in southern California* (Unpublished doctoral dissertation). Azusa Pacific University, Azusa, California.

Stone, C. (2003, November 1). Case notes, educational records and subpoenas. *ASCA School Counselor.* Retrieved from https://www.schoolcounselor.org/magazine/blogs/november-december-2003/case-notes,-educational-records-and-subpoenas

Stone, C. (2014, September 1). Informed consent: Is it attainable with students in schools? *ASCA School Counselor.* Retrieved from http://www.schoolcounselor.org/magazine/blogs/september-october-2014/informed-consent-is-it-attainable-with-students-i

Storlie, C. A., & Baltrinic, E. R. (2015). Counseling children with cystic fibrosis: Recommendations for practice and counselor self-care. *The Professional Counselor, 5,* 293–303. Retrieved from http://tpcjournal.nbcc.org/counseling-children-with-cystic-fibrosis-recommendations-for-practice-and-counselor-self-care

Straussner, S. L. A., & Fewell, C. H. (2015). Children of parents who abuse alcohol and other drugs. In A. Reupert, D. Maybery, J. Nicolson, M. Göpfert, & M. V. Seeman (Eds.), *Parental psychiatric disorders: Distressed parents and their families* (3rd ed., pp. 138–144). Cambridge, UK: Cambridge University Press.

Strawn, J. R., Sakolsky, D. J., & Rynn, M. A. (2012). Psychopharmacologic treatment of children and adolescents with anxiety disorders. *Child and Adolescent Psychiatric Clinics of North America, 21*(3), 527–539. doi:10.1016/j.chc.2012.05.003

Studer, J. R., & Salter, S. E. (2010). *The role of the school counselor in crisis planning and intervention.* Retrieved from https://www.counseling.org/Resources/Library/VISTAS/2010-V-Online/Article_92.pdf

Substance Abuse and Mental Health Services Administration (SAMHSA). (2006). *S.M.A.R.T. treatment planning.* Retrieved from http://www.samhsa.gov/samhsa_news/volumexiv_5/article2.htm

Substance Abuse and Mental Health Services Administration (SAMHSA). (2007). *Cannabis youth treatment series: Vol. 4. The adolescent community reinforcement approach for adolescent cannabis users.* Rockville, MD: Author. Retrieved from https://store.samhsa.gov/shin/content/SMA08-3864/SMA08-3864.pdf

Substance Abuse and Mental Health Services Administration (SAMHSA). (2009). *Identifying and selecting evidence-based interventions.* Retrieved from http://store.samhsa.gov/product/Identifying-and-Selecting-Evidence-Based-Interventions-for-Substance-Abuse-Prevention/SMA09-4205

Substance Abuse and Mental Health Services Administration (SAMHSA). (2014). *Trauma-informed care in behavioral health services: Treatment improvement protocol (TIP) series 57.* Retrieved from http://store.samhsa.gov/shin/content//SMA14-4816/SMA14-4816.pdf

Substance Abuse and Mental Health Services Administration (SAMHSA). (2015). *Behavioral health trends in the United States: Results from the 2014 National Survey on Drug Use and Health.* Rockville, MD: Author. Retrieved from http://www.samhsa.gov/data/sites/default/files/NSDUH-FRR1-2014/NSDUH-FRR1-2014.pdf

Sue, D. W., & Sue, D. (2013). *Counseling the culturally diverse: Theory and practice* (6th ed.). Hoboken, NJ: John Wiley & Sons.

Sue, D. W., & Sue, D. (2015). *Counseling the culturally diverse: Theory and practice* (7th ed.). Hoboken, NJ: Wiley.

Suldo, M. S., Hearon, B. V., Dickinson, S., Esposito, E., Wesley, K. L., Lynn, C., . . . Lam, G. Y. H. (2015a). Adapting positive psychology interventions for use with elementary school children. *NASP Communique, 43*(8), 4–8. Retrieved from http://www.nasponline.org

Suldo, S. M., Hearon, B. V., Bander, B., McCullough, M., Garofano, J., & Roth, R. A., & Tan, S. Y. (2015b). Increasing elementary school student's subjective well-being through a classwide positive psychology intervention: Results of a pilot study. *Contemporary School Psychology, 19*(4), 300-311.

Swanson, H. L., Harris, K. R., & Graham, S. (2013). *Handbook of learning disabilities* (2nd ed.). New York, NY: Guilford.

Swanson, J. M., Elliot, G. R., Greenhill, L. L., Wigal, T., Arnold, L. E., Vitiello, B., . . . Volkow, N. D. (2007). Effects of stimulant medication on growth rates across 3 years in the MTA follow-up. *Child and Adolescent Psychiatry, 46*(8), 1015–1027. doi:http://dx.doi.org/10.1097/chi.0b013e3180686d7e

Swanson, S. A., Crow, S. J., LeGrange, D., Swendsen, J., & Merigankis, K. R. (2011). Prevalence and correlates of eating disorders. *Archives of General Psychiatry, 68*(7), 714–723.

Swart, J., & Apsche, J. (2014). Family mode deactivation therapy (FMDT) as a contextual treatment. *International Journal of Behavioral Consultation and Therapy, 9*(1), 30–37. doi:10.1037/h0101012

Sweeney, M. M. (2010). Remarriage and stepfamilies: Strategies sites for family scholarship in the 21st century. *Journal of Marriage and Family, 72*(3), 667–684. doi:10.1111/j.1741-3737.2010.00724.x

Sweeney, T. J. (2009). *Adlerian counseling and psychotherapy: A practitioner's approach* (5th ed.). New York, NY: Routledge.

Swendsen, J., Burstein, M., Case, B., Conway, K., Dierker, L., He, J., . . . Merikangas, K. R. (2012). Use and abuse of alcohol and illicit drugs in US adolescents: Results of the national comorbidity survey—Adolescent supplement. *Archives of*

General Psychiatry, 69(4), 390–398. doi:10.1001/archgenpsychiatry.2011.1503

Swift, J. K., & Greenberg, R. P. (2015). Premature termination in psychotherapy. Washington, DC: American Psychological Association.

Symonds, J., & Hargreaves, L. (2016). Emotional and motivational engagement at school transition: A qualitative stage-environment fit study. Journal of Early Adolescence, 36(1), 54–85. doi:0.1177/0272431614556348

Szapocznik, J., Hervis, O. E., & Schwartz, S. (2003). Brief strategic family therapy for adolescent drug abuse (NIH Publication No. 03–4751). Rockville, MD: U.S. Department of Health and Human Services, National Institutes of Health, National Institute on Drug Abuse.

Tailor, K., Stewart-Tufescu, A., & Piotrowski, C. (2015). Children exposed to intimate partner violence: Influences of parenting, family distress, and siblings. Journal of Family Psychology, 29(1), 29–38. doi:10.1037/a0038584

Tandoc, E. C., Ferrucci, P., & Duffy, M. (2015). Facebook use, envy, and depression among college students: Is Facebooking depressing? Computers in Human Behavior, 43, 139–146. doi:10.1016/j.chb.2014.10.053

Taylor, C. A., Moeller, W., Hamvas, L., & Rice, J. C. (2012). Parents' professional sources of advice regarding child discipline and their use of corporal punishment. Journal of Clinical Pediatrics, 52, 147–155.

Taylor, D. M., & de la Sablonnière, R. (2013). Why interventions in dysfunctional communities fail: The need for a truly collective approach. Canadian Psychology, 54, 22–29. doi:10.1037/a0031124

Tello, J., Cervantes, R. C., Cordova, D., & Santos, S. M. (2010). Joven Noble: Evaluation of a culturally focused youth development program. Journal of Community Psychology, 38(6), 799–811. doi:10.1002/jcop.20396

Temkin, D. A., Gest, S. D., Osgood, D. W., Feinberg, M., & Moody, J. (2015). Social network implications of normative school transitions in non-urban school district. Youth & Society (Advance online publication). doi:10.1177/0044118X15607164

Terracciano, A., McCrae, R. R., Brant, L. J., & Costa, P. T., Jr. (2005). Hierarchical linear modeling analyses of the NEO-PI-R scales in the Baltimore Longitudinal Study of Aging. Psychology and Aging, 20, 493–506.

Thames, A. D., Panos, S. E., Arentoft, A., Byrd, D. A., Hinkin, C. H., & Arbid, N. (2015). Mild test anxiety influences neurocognitive performance among African Americans and European Americans: Identifying interfering and facilitating sources. Cultural Diversity and Ethnic Minority Psychology, 21, 105–113. doi:10.1037/a0037530

Tharpe, A. T., Burton, T., Freire, K., Hall, D. M., Harrier, S., Latzman, N. E., . . . Vagi, K. J. (2011). Dating matters: Strategies to promote healthy teen relationships. Journal of Women's Health, 20(12), 1761–1765. doi:10.1089/jwh.2011.3177

Thompson, L., Thompson, M., & Reid, A. (2010). Neurofeedback outcomes in clients with Asperger's syndrome. Applied Psychophysiology and Biofeedback, 35(1), 63–81. doi:10.1007/s10484-009-9120-3

Titzmann, P. F. (2014). Immigrant adolescents' adaptation to a new context: Ethnic friendship homophily and its predictors. Child Development Perspectives, 8(2), 107–112. doi:10.1111/cdep.12072

Tompkins, M. A. (2014). Cognitive-behavior therapy for pediatric trichotillomania. Journal of Rational-Emotive & Cognitive-Behavior Therapy, 32, 98–109. doi:101007/s10942-014-0186-3

Tresco, K. E., Lefler, E. K., & Power, T. J. (2010). Psychosocial interventions to improve the school performance of students with attention-deficit/hyperactivity disorder. Mind Brain, 1(2), 69–74.

Trivedi, H. K., & Chang, K. (2012). Psychopharmacology: An issue of Child and Adolescent Psychiatric Clinics of North America. Philadelphia, PA: Saunders.

Trosper, S. E., Buzzella, B. A., Bennett, S. M., & Ehrenreich, J. T. (2009). Emotion regulation in youth with emotional disorders: Implication for a unified treatment approach. Clinical Child and Family Psychology Review, 12, 234–254. doi:10.1007/s10567-009-0043-6

Tsai, S. M., & Wang, H. H., (2009). The relationship between caregiver's strain and social support among mothers with intellectually disabled children. Journal of Clinical Nursing, 18, 539–548.

Tucker, C., & Dixon, A. (2009). Low-income African male youth with ADHD symptoms in the United States: Recommendations for clinical mental health counselors. Journal of Mental Health Counseling, 31(4), 309–322.

Tuerk, E. H., McCart, M. R., & Henggeler, S. W. (2012). Collaboration in family therapy. Journal of Clinical Psychology: In Session, 68(2), 168–178. doi:10.1002/jclp.21833

Turner, B. J., Austin, S. B., & Chapman, A. L. (2014). Treating nonsuicidal self-injury: A systematic review of psychological and pharmacological interventions. The Canadian Journal of Psychiatry, 59(11), 576–585.

Turner, H. A., Finkelhor, D., Hamby, S. L., Shattuck, A., & Ormrod, R. K. (2011). Specifying type and location of peer victimization in a national sample of children and youth. Journal of Youth and Adolescence, 40, 1052–1067. doi:10.1007/s10964-011-9639-5

Twenge, J. M. (2014). Time period and birth cohort differences in depressive symptoms in the U.S., 1982–2013. Social Indicators Research, 121, 437–454. doi:10.1007/s11205-014-0647-1

U.S. Census Bureau. (2014). Family and living arrangements: Households by types. Retrieved from http://www.census.gov/hhes/families/data/households.html

U.S. Census Bureau. (2015). Projections of the size and composition of the U.S. population: 2014 to 2060. Retrieved from https://www.census.gov/library/publications/2015/demo/p25-1143.html

U.S. Department of Health and Human Services (USDHHS). (n.d). Health information privacy. Retrieved from http://www.hhs.gov/hipaa/index.html

U.S. Department of Health and Human Services (USDHHS). (2004). Black box warning for antidepressants. Retrieved from http://www.fda.gov/downloads/safety/fdapatientsafetynews/ucm417804.pdf

U.S. Department of Health and Human Services (USDHHS). (2013). Child maltreatment. Administration for Children and Families, Administration on Children, Youth and Families Children's Bureau. Retrieved from http://www.acf.hhs.gov/sites/default/files/cb/cm2013.pdf

U.S. Department of Health and Human Services (USDHHS). (2016). Child Maltreatment 2014. Retrieved from http://www.acf.hhs.gov/sites/default/files/cb/cm2014.pdf

U.S. Department of Health and Human Services (USDHHS), Administration for Children and Families, Administration on Children, Youth and Families, Children's Bureau. (2015). Child maltreatment 2013. Retrieved from http://www.acf.hhs.gov/sites/default/files/cb/cm2013.pdf

U.S. Department of Health & Human Services (USDHHS), Administration for Children and Families, Administration on Children, Youth and Families, Children's Bureau. (2016). Child maltreatment 2014. Retrieved from http://www.acf.hhs.gov/programs/cb/research-data-technology/statistics-research/child-maltreatment

Ugoani, J. N., & Ewuzie, M. A. (2013). Imperatives of emotional intelligence on psychological wellbeing among adolescents. American Journal of Applied Psychology, 1(3), 44–48. doi:10.1269/ajap-1-3-3

Underwood, L. A., & Dailey, F. L. (2017). Counseling adolescents competently. Thousand Oaks, CA: Sage.

United Nations. (1989, November 20). Convention on the Rights of the Child. Treaty Series, 1577, 3.

University of New Orleans. (2014). *Developmental psychopathology lab: Inventory of Callous–Unemotional Traits.* Retrieved from http://labs.uno.edu/developmental-psychopathology/ICU.html

van der Kolk, B. A. (2005). Developmental trauma disorder. *Psychiatric Annals, 35,* 401–408.

Van Ryzin, M. J., & Fosco, G. M. (2016). Family-based approached to prevention. In M. J. Van Ryzin, K. L. Kumpfer, G. M. Fosco, & M. T. Greenberg (Eds.), *Family-based prevention programs for children and adolescents: Theory, research, and large-scale dissemination* (pp. 1–20). New York, NY: Taylor & Francis.

Vandell, D. L., Belskey, J., Burchinal, M., Vangergrift, N., & Steinburg, L. (2010). Do effects of early child care extend to age 15 years? Results from the NICHD study of early child care and youth development. *Child Development, 81*(3), 737–756. doi:10.1111/j.1467-8624.2010.01431.x

Vecchio, J., & Kearney, C. A. (2009). Treating youths with selective mutism with an alternating design of exposure-based practice and contingency management. *Behavior Therapy, 40,* 380–392. doi:10.1016/j.beth.2008.10.005

Velez, C. E., Wolchik, S. A., Tein, J. Y., & Sandler, I. (2011). Protecting children from the consequences of divorce: A longitudinal study of the effects of parenting on children's coping processes. *Child Development, 82*(1), 244–257.

Vereen, L. G., Hill, N. R., Sosa, G. A., & Kress, V. (2014). The synonymic nature of professional counseling and humanism: Presuppositions that guide our identities. *Journal of Humanistic Counseling, 53*(3), 191–201. doi:10.1002/j.2161-1939.2014.00056.x

Vernon, A. (2009). *Counseling children and adolescents* (4th ed.). Denver, CO: Love.

Vigo, D. E., Simonelli, G., Cardinali, D. P., Tuñón, I., Pérez Chada, D., & Golombek, D. (2014). School characteristics, child work, and other daily activities as sleep deficit predictors in adolescents from households with unsatisfied basic needs. *Mind, Brain & Education, 8*(4), 175–181. doi:10.1111/mbe.12058

Voisin, D., & Hong, J. (2012). A meditational model linking witnessing intimate partner violence and bullying behaviors and victimization among youth. *Educational Psychology Review, 24*(4), 479–498. doi:10.1007/s10648-012-9197-8

von Gontard, A. (2013). The impact of *DSM-5* and guidelines for assessment and treatment of elimination disorders. *European Child & Adolescent Psychiatry, 22,* 61–67.

Wagner, M. F., Milner, J. S., McCarthy, R. J., Crouch, J. L., McCanne, T. R., & Skowronski, J. J. (2015). Facial emotion recognition accuracy and child physical abuse: An experiment and a meta-analysis. *Psychology of Violence, 5*(2), 154–162. doi:10.1037/a0036014

Wagner, W. G. (2008). *Counseling, psychology, and children* (2nd ed.). Upper Saddle River, NJ: Pearson.

Waite, P., & Creswell, C. (2014). Children and adolescents referred for treatment of anxiety disorders: Differences in clinical characteristics. *Journal of Affective Disorders, 167,* 326–332. doi:10.1016/j.jad.2014.06.028

Wallerstein, J. S., & Blakeslee, S. (1989). *Second chances: Men, women, and children a decade after divorce.* New York, NY: Ticknor & Fields.

Walsh, B. M. (2012). *Treating self-injury: A practical guide* (2nd ed.). New York, NY: Guilford.

Wampold, B. E. (2010). *The basics of psychotherapy: An introduction to theory and practice.* Washington, DC: American Psychological Association.

Ward, J. E., & Odegard, M. A. (2011). A proposal for increasing student safety through suicide prevention in schools. *The Clearing House: A Journal of Educational Strategies and Ideas, 84*(4), 144–149.

Ware Balch, J., & Ray, D. (2015). Emotional assets of children with autism spectrum disorder: A single case outcome therapeutic experiment. *Journal of Counseling and Development, 93,* 429–439. doi:10.1002/jcad.12041

Washburn, J. J., Richardt, S. L., Styer, D. M., Gebhart, M., Juzwin, K. R., Yourek, A., . . . Aldridge, D. (2012). Psychotherapeutic approaches to non-suicidal self-injury in adolescents. *Child & Adolescent Psychiatry & Mental Health, 6*(14), 1–8. Retrieved from https://www.ncbi.nlm.nih.gov/pmc/articles/PMC3782878/pdf/1753-2000-6-14.pdf

Watts, R. E. (2013). Adlerian counseling. In B. J. Irby, G. Brown, R. Lara-Alecio, S. Jackson, B. J. Irby, G. Brown, . . . S. Jackson (Eds.), *The handbook of educational theories* (pp. 459–472). Charlotte, NC: IAP.

Watzlawick, P., Weakland, J., & Fisch, R. (1974). *Change: Principles of problem formation and problem resolution.* New York, NY: Norton.

Weaver, J. M., & Schofield, T. J. (2015). Mediation and moderation of divorce effects on children's behavior problems. *Journal of Family Psychology, 29*(1), 39–48.

Webb, N. B. (2011a). Play therapy for bereaved children: Adapting strategies to communities, school, and home settings. *School Psychology International, 32*(2), 132–143. doi:10.1177/0143034311400832

Webb, N. B. (2011b). *Social work practice with children* (3rd ed.). New York, NY: Guilford.

Wechsler, D. (2014). *The Wechsler Intelligence Scale for Children, Fifth Edition: Technical and interpretive manual and supplement.* Bloomington, MN: PsychCorp.

Weisz, J. R., & Kazdin, A. E. (2010). *Evidence-based psychotherapies for children and adolescents* (2nd ed.). New York, NY: Guilford.

Welfel, E. R. (2010). *Ethics in counseling and psychotherapy: Standards, research, and emerging issues* (4th ed.). Belmont, CA: Thompson.

Welfel, E. R. (2013). *Ethics in counseling and psychotherapy: Standards, research, and emerging issues* (5th ed.). Belmont, CA: Brooks/Cole.

Wenar, C., & Kerig, P. (2005). *Developmental psychopathology: From infancy through adolescence* (5th ed.). New York, NY: McGraw-Hill.

West, A. E., Celio, C. I., Henry, D., & Pavuluri, M. N. (2011). Child Mania Rating Scale–Parent Version: A valid measure of symptom change due to pharmacotherapy. *Journal of Affective Disorders, 128,* 112–119. doi:10.1016/j.jad.2010.06.013

West, A. E., & Pavuluri, M. N. (2009). Psychosocial treatments for childhood and adolescent bipolar. *Child and Adolescent Psychiatric Clinics of North America, 18,* 471–482.

Westbrook, D., Kennerly, H., & Kirk, J. (2014). *An introduction to cognitive behavior therapy* (2nd ed.). Thousand Oaks, CA: Sage.

Wester, K. J., & Trepal, H. C. (2005). Working with clients who self-injure: Providing alternatives. *Journal of College Counseling, 8*(2), 180–189.

Whiston, S. C. (2012). *Principles and applications of assessment in counseling* (6th ed.). Belmont, CA: Brooks/Cole.

Whitaker, C. A., & Keith, D. V. (1981). Symbolic-experiential family therapy. In A. S. Gurman & D. P. Kniskern (Eds.), *Handbook of family therapy* (pp. 187–225). New York, NY: Brunner/Mazel.

White, H. R., & Labouvie, E. W. (1989). Towards the assessment of adolescent problem drinking. *Journal of Studies on Alcohol and Drugs, 50,* 30–37.

White, M., & Epston, D. (1990). *Narrative means to therapeutic ends.* New York, NY: Norton & Company.

White, T. G., Kim, J. S., Kingston, H. C., & Foster, L. (2014). Replicating the effects of a teacher-scaffolded voluntary summer reading program: The role of poverty. *Reading Research Quarterly, 49,* 5–30. doi:10.1002/rrq.62

Whiteman, H. (2015, June 5). *Child diabetes: Signs and symptoms.* Retrieved from http://www.medicalnewstoday.com/articles/284974.php

Whitmarsh, L., & Mullette, J. (2009). An integrated model for counseling adolescents. *Journal of Humanistic Counseling, 48,* 144–159.

Widom, C. S., Czaja, S. J., & Dutton, M. A. (2008). Childhood victimization and lifetime revictimization. *Child Abuse & Neglect, 32,* 785–796. doi:10.1016/j.chiabu.2007.12.006

Wiederholt, J. L., & Bryant, B. R. (2012). *Gray Oral Reading Test, Fifth Edition* (GORT-5). Austin, TX: PRO-ED.

Wigderson, S., & Lynch, M. (2013). Cyber- and traditional peer victimization: Unique relationships with adolescent well-being. *Psychology of Violence, 3*(4), 297–309. doi:10.1037/a0033657

Wilkinson, G. S., & Robertson, G. J. (2006). *Wide Range Achievement Test, Fourth Edition.* Lutz, FL: Psychological Assessment Resources.

Wilkinson, P., Kelvin, R., Roberts, C., Dubicka, B., & Goodyer, I. (2011). Clinical and psychosocial predictors of suicide attempts and nonsuicidal self-injury in the Adolescent Depression Antidepressants and Psychotherapy Trial (ADAPT). *American Journal of Psychiatry, 168*(5), 495–501. doi:10.1176/appi.ajp.2010.10050718

Williams, A. E. (2015). Ethical issues in providing substance abuse treatment within a family counseling setting. *Virginia Counselors Journal, 34,* 14–19.

Williams, J. M. (2010). Does neurofeedback help reduce attention-deficit hyperactivity disorder? *Journal of Neurotherapy, 14(4),* 261–279. *doi:*10.1080/10874208.2010.523331

Wilson, S. M., Smith, A. W., Monnin, K., & Wildman, B. G. (2016). Treating common childhood mental and behavioral health concerns. In C. L. Juntunen & J. P. Schwartz (Eds.), *Counseling across the lifespan* (2nd ed., pp. 91–108). Thousand Oaks, CA: Sage.

Winnicott, D. W. (1953). Transitional objects and transitional phenomena—A study of the first not-me possession. *International Journal of Psycho-Analysis, 34*(2), 89–97.

Winters, K. C. (1992). Development of an adolescent alcohol and other drug abuse screening scale: Personal Experiences Screening Questionnaire. *Addictive Behaviors, 17,* 479–490.

Witherington, D. C. (2011). Taking emergence seriously: The centrality of circular causality for dynamic systems approaches to development. *Human Development, 54*(2), 66–92. doi:10.1159/000326814

Witwer, A. N., Lawton, K., & Aman, M. G. (2014). Intellectual disabilities. In R. A. Barkley & E. J. Mash (Eds.), *Child psychopathology* (3rd ed., pp. 593–624). New York, NY: Guilford.

Wolfe, K. L., Foxwell, A., & Kennard, B. (2014). Identifying and treating risk factors for suicidal behaviors in youth.

International Journal of Behavioral Consultation and Therapy, 9(3), 11–14.

Wolpe, J. (1958). *Psychotherapy by reciprocal inhibition.* Stanford, CA: Stanford University.

Wolpe, J. (1969). *The practice of behavior therapy.* New York, NY: Pergamon.

Wolpe, J. (1990). *The practice of behavior therapy* (4th ed.). Elmsford, NY: Pergamon.

Wong, D. W., Hall, K. R., Justice, C. A., & Hernandez, L. W. (2015). *Counseling individuals through the lifespan.* Thousand Oaks, CA: Sage.

Woo, S. M., & Keatinge, C. (2016). *Diagnosis and treatment of mental disorders across the lifespan* (2nd ed.). Hoboken, NJ: John Wiley & Sons.

Wood, J. J., McLeod, B. D., Piacentini, J. C., & Sigman, M. (2009). One-year follow-up of family versus child CBT for anxiety disorders: Exploring the roles of child age and parental intrusiveness. *Child Psychiatry and Human Development, 40*, 301–316.

Woodcock, R. W. (2011). *Woodcock Reading Mastery Tests, Third Edition* (WRMT-III). Upper Saddle River, NJ: Pearson.

Wright, J. H., Brown, G. K., Thase, M. E., & Basco, M. R. (2017). *Learning cognitive-behavior therapy: An illustrated guide* (2nd ed.). Arlington, VA: American Psychiatric Association.

Wubbolding, R. E. (1988). *Using reality therapy.* New York, NY: Harper & Row.

Wubbolding, R. E. (1989). Radio station WDEP and other metaphors used in teaching reality therapy. *Journal of Reality Therapy, 8*(2), 74–79.

Wubbolding, R. E. (1991). *Understanding reality therapy.* New York, NY: HarperCollins.

Wubbolding, R. E. (2000). *Reality therapy for the 21st century.* Philadelphia, PA: Brunner-Routledge.

Wubbolding, R. E. (2007). Reality therapy theory. In D. Capuzzi & D. R. Gross (Eds.), *Counseling and psychotherapy: Theories and interventions* (4th ed., pp. 289–312). Upper Saddle River, NJ: Pearson.

Wubbolding, R. E. (2011). *Reality therapy: Theories of psychotherapy series.* Washington, DC: American Psychological Association.

Wubbolding, R. E., Robey, P., & Brickell, J. (2010). A partial and tentative look at the future of choice theory, reality therapy, and lead management. *International Journal of Choice Theory and Reality Therapy, 24,* 25–35. Retrieved from www.ctrtjournal.com

Yanof, J. A. (2013). Play technique in psychodynamic psychotherapy. *Child and Adolescent Psychiatric Clinics of North America, 22*(2), 261–282. doi:10.1016/j.chc.2012.12.002.

Young, R. C., Biggs, J. T., Ziegler, V. E., & Meyer, D. A. (1978). A rating scale for

mania: Reliability, validity and sensitivity. *British Journal of Psychiatry, 133,* 429–435.

Young, S., & Bramham, J. (2012). *Cognitive-behavioural therapy for ADHD in adolescents and adults: A psychological guide to practice* (2nd ed.). West Sussex, UK: Wiley-Blackwell.

Youngstrom, E. A., Freeman, A. J., & McKeown-Jenkins, M. (2009). The assessment of children and adolescents with bipolar disorder. *Child & Adolescent Psychiatric Clinics North America, 18,* 353–390. doi:10.1016/j.chc.2008.12.002

Zárate, M. A., Quezada, S. A., Shenberger, J. M., & Lupo, A. K. (2014). Reducing racism and prejudice. In F. L. Leong, L. Comas-Díaz, G. C. Nagayama Hall, V. C. McLoyd, J. E. Trimble, F. L. Leong, . . . J. E. Trimble (Eds.), *APA handbook of multicultural psychology, Vol. 2: Applications and training* (pp. 593–606). Washington, DC: American Psychological Association. doi:10.1037/14187-033

Zeanah, C. H. (2009). *The handbook of infant mental health* (3rd ed.). New York, NY: Guilford.

Zembar, M. J., & Blume, L. B. (2009). *Middle childhood development: A contextual approach.* Upper Saddle River, NJ: Pearson.

Zhu, S., Tse, S., Cheung, S., & Oyserman, D. (2014). Will I get there? Effects of parental support on children's possible selves. *British Journal of Educational Psychology, 84*(3), 435–453. doi:10.1111/bjep.12044

Zilberstein, K. (2014). The use and limitations of attachment theory in child psychotherapy. *Psychotherapy, 51*(1), 93–103. doi:10.1037/a0030930

Zimmerman, J., Hess, A. K., McGarrah, N. A., Benjamin, G. A. H., Ally, G. A., Gollan, J. K., & Kaser-Boyd, N. (2009). Ethical and professional consideration in divorce and child custody cases. *Professional Psychology: Research and Practice, 40*(6), 539–549. doi:10.1037/a0017853

Zolkoski, S. M., & Bullock, L. M. (2012). Resilience in children and youth: A review. *Children and Youth Services Review 34,* 2295–2303.

Zullig, K. J., Collins, R., Ghani, N., Hunter, A. A., Patton, J. M., Huebner, E. S., . . . Zhang, J. (2015). Preliminary development of a revised version of the school climate measure. *Psychological Assessment,* 1–10. doi:10.1037/pas0000070

Zuroff, D. C., Kelly, A. C., Leybman, M. J., Blatt, S. J., & Wampold, B. E. (2010). Between-therapist and within-therapist differences in the quality of the therapeutic relationship: Effects on maladjustment and self-critical perfectionism. *Journal of Clinical Psychology, 66*(7), 681–697. doi:10.1002/jclp.20683

NAME INDEX

A

Academy of Eating Disorders, 510, 513
Achenbach, T. M., 353
Ackerman, N. W., 189, 220
Adamson, N., 61, 250, 413
Adler, A., 171, 190–199, 240–242
Adler-Baeder, F., 345
Ageranioti-Bélanger, S., 369
Agras, W. S., 507, 510
Ainsworth, B., 143
Ainsworth, M. D. S., 178
Aizer, A., 53
Albrecht, A. C., 483, 485
Alexander, F. G., 187
Alford, B. A., 485
Algorta, G. P., 12
Ali, M. M., 436
Amato, P. R., 301–302, 304
Amatya, K., 43
American Academy of Child & Adolescent
    Psychiatry (AACAP), 181, 311–316, 398, 401,
    413, 427, 460–464, 482, 503
American Academy of Pediatrics, 339, 353–354,
    359
American Counseling Association (ACA), 76, 82, 95,
    113, 324, 384
American Psychiatric Association (APA), 12, 38,
    42–43, 45, 53, 325, 330, 348–349, 351, 354,
    360, 366, 368, 370, 375, 379–382, 398, 406,
    408–410, 431, 457, 482, 490, 493, 506–507,
    509–511, 519–520
American Psychological Association, 398, 405
American School Counselor Association (ASCA),
    47–49, 52, 102–103, 113, 324, 332, 372
Ametrano, R. M., 64–65, 72
Amialchuk, A., 436
Anatopoulos, A. D., 353
Anderson, B. J., 526
Anderson, C. L., 333–334
Anderson, C. M., 128, 137
Anderson, D. A., 516–517
Anderson, L. M., 28, 32
Andronico, M., 240
Antony, M. M., 123
Antshel, K. M., 358
Anyon, Y., 49, 51
Aoki, K., 335–336
Apsche, J., 386
Arkes, J., 42, 302
Armstrong, S., 228, 230–231
Arnkoff, D. B., 64–65, 72
Arnold, L. E., 354
Aronson-Fontes, L., 103–104
Asahi, K., 335–336
Asgari, P., 229
Ashwood, K. L., 348
Asnaani, A., 464, 494
Assmus, J., 354
Association for Lesbian Gay, Bisexual, Transgender
    Issues in Counseling [ALGBTIC], 340–342
Association for Play Therapy (APT), 230, 233, 238
Atkins, S. S., 230, 246–247
Attia, E., 516
Austin, K., 456

Austin, S. B., 287, 289
Axline, Virginia, 200, 238

B

Bachmann, C., 487
Baden, A. L., 311
Baer, R. A., 143
Baggerly, J., 201
Bagwell, C. L., 335
Bailey, J. R., 476
Bailey, R. K., 352
Baker, A. J. L., 302–303
Baker, C. W., 516–517
Balaguru, V., 287
Baldwin, D. S., 143
Balkin, R., 228, 230–231
Balluerka, N., 352
Baltrinic, E. R., 526, 530
Bandura, A., 125
Banez, G. A., 136
Bannon, K., 501
Barber, J. P., 70, 259
Barbui, C., 503
Barkley, R. A., 12, 41–42, 48, 51, 61–62, 64,
    351–352, 354, 384–385, 392
Barlow, D. H., 477
Barnes, K., 360, 362
Barrett, P. M., 465
Barry, C. T., 183
Bartholow, R. G., 196
Bartone, P. T., 2
Bartsocus, C., 527
Baruch, F., 62, 90
Basco, M. R., 148–149
Basile, J., 493
Basile, K. C., 45–46
Bates, J. E., 342
Batlett, L., 284
Batton, D. G., 5
Bauer, J., 514
Bauman, S., 28, 32
Beauregard, M., 341
Beck, A. T., 122, 138, 139, 141–142, 148, 388–389,
    459, 485, 487
Beck, J. S., 148, 459, 487
Becker, D., 48–49
Becvar, D. S., 210, 225–226
Becvar, R. J., 210, 225–226
Beesdo, K. B., 455, 459
Beidel, D. C., 469
Beilock, S. L., 250
Belden, A. C., 489
Bell, A. C., 474–475, 499–500
Bell, R., 43, 310
Bell, S. M., 178
Bellak, L., 183
Bellak, S. S., 183
Bellis, M., 23
Belsky, J., 27
Ben-Ami, N., 302–303
Benard, B., 37
Bender, K. A., 23, 25–28, 30–31, 57
Benjamin, A., 134
Benjamin, C. L., 387–388

Bennett, S. M., 486, 490
Ben-Porath, D. D., 159
Bentley, A., 11, 13
Berger, L. M., 313–314
Bergin, C. C., 24, 26–27, 30–31
Bergin, D. A., 24, 26–27, 30–31
Bergman, A., 179
Bergman, R. L., 463
Bergner, R. M., 250
Berk, L. E., 15, 19
Berkowitz, S. J., 345
Berliner, L., 76, 261, 318, 345
Berman, A., 280
Berman, J. S., 61, 71
Bernecker, K., 325
Berry, R. A., 147
Bertalanffy, L. V., 212–213, 224
Bertin, M., 356, 358
Bhugra, D., 35
Biank, N. M., 316
Biehal, N., 423
Biggs, J. T., 492
Bird, J., 282
Bitsika, V., 43
Black, M. C., 45–46
Black, T., 413
Blackard, S. R., 205
Blake, D. D., 411
Blakemore, S. J., 6
Blakeslee, S., 303
Blatt, S. J., 69, 259
Blehar, M. C., 178
Blewitt, P., 1, 6–8, 10–12, 15, 17–18, 23–24, 26–29,
    31, 57, 61, 71–72, 299–300, 302, 313, 323,
    348, 374, 431
Bloch, M. H., 462
Bloom, J. K., 290
Blow, A. J., 514
Blum, R., 24
Blume, L. B., 16
Bobbitt, K. C., 11, 13
Boduszek, D., 342
Boer, F., 425
Bogh, E. H., 507, 513
Bohart, A. C., 57, 69
Bohnekamp, I., 517
Bongar, B., 281
Bonovitz, C., 185
Boon, A. E., 65, 91
Bordin, E. S., 68
Bos, H. W., 341
Bosch, L. A., 40–42, 210
Bosk, A., 530
Botha, C. J., 304
Bourke, A., 342
Bouron, L., 229
Boutot, E., 363
Bowen, M., 213, 222–223
Bowlby, J., 178, 183, 408–409
Boyer, W., 401
Bradley, N., 413
Bradshaw, C. P., 336–337
Bramham, J., 357
Branje, S. T., 31

Brant, L. J., 263
Brassard, M. R., 303
Brassell, H., 61
Bratton, S., 186–187, 201, 205, 228, 231
Brausch, A. M., 287, 289
Breda, C. S., 76
Bregman, H. R., 40–42
Breiding, M. J., 45–46
Brent, D. A., 281, 283–284
Brewis, G., 53–54
Brickell, J., 163
Bridges, M. R., 187
Briere, J. N., 69, 179, 398–399, 406, 410–416, 419–420, 422, 488
Bright, C. L., 40
Britzman, M. J., 167
Broderick, P. C., 1, 6–8, 10–12, 15, 17–18, 23–24, 26–29, 31, 57, 61, 71–72, 299–300, 302, 313, 323, 348, 374, 431
Brokaw, S. P., 196
Bronfenbrenner, U., 263–264
Brookman-Frazee, L. I., 364
Brooks, J. H., 5
Brooks-Gunn, J., 40, 43, 45, 48, 53
Brown, A. P., 143, 147
Brown, G. K., 148–149
Bruce, T. J., 254
Bruck, M., 401, 403
Brummelman, E., 7–8, 10–11
Bryant, B. R., 371
Buchman-Schmitt, J. M., 280, 282
Buck, J. N., 183
Bulik, C. M., 507
Bullock, L. M., 299–300, 323
Bunner, M., 5, 7, 10–11
Burbeck, R., 494
Burchinal, M., 27
Burk, W. J., 335
Burke, J. D., 376, 378–379, 381
Burns, K., 287
Burton, D. L., 54, 405
Butler, A. C., 122, 139
Butler, J. B., 144, 362
Butler, M. G., 362
Buzella, B. A., 486, 490
Byrne, M., 313–314

C

Cain, D. J., 203
Callanan, P., 95, 98, 102–104, 113–116, 119
Campbell, D. G., 494
Campbell, M., 369
Canino, G., 406
Capuzzi, D., 6
Carboni, J. A., 5
Carlson, G. A., 493
Carlson, R., 250
Carmichael, K. D., 201, 234
Carney, J. V., 255, 339
Carr, A., 305
Carter, J. C., 514
Casenhiser, D. M., 365
Cashwell, C. S., 147
Castelino, T., 413
Castro-Blanco, D., 69
Caterino, L., 352
Ceci, S. J., 401, 403
Celio, C. I., 492

Center for Community Health and Development (CCHD), 39, 42, 49
Centers for Disease Control and Prevention (CDC), 12, 21, 43–44, 48, 50–53, 103, 279, 292–293, 300, 342–344, 360
Cerdá, M., 400
Cervantes, R. C., 345
Chang, E. C., 328
Chang, K., 504
Chang, S., 463
Chapman, A. L., 287, 289
Chapman, J. E., 122, 139
Charman, T., 6
Chartier, I. S., 494
Cheeson, R. A., 527
Chen, L., 482
Chen, M., 344–345
Cheung, S., 43, 324, 328, 334
Child Welfare Information Gateway (CWIG), 313–314, 402–405, 422
Chisholm, D., 527
Choi, M. J., 309
Choudhury, M., 159, 477
Choudhury, S., 6
Chronis-Tuscano, A., 6, 10, 12–13, 57
Chu, B. C., 501
Chu, C., 280, 282
Chu, J., 281
Churliza, B., 280, 282
Ciarrochi, J., 144, 362
Cipriani, A., 503
Clark, A. J., 203
Clarke, G. N., 494
Clarke, P. B., 147
Clarkson-Hendrix, M., 309
Cobham, V. E., 422
Cochran, J. L., 201
Cochran, N. H., 201
Coelho, D. P., 523–525
Coffee, P., 52
Coghill, D. R., 394
Cohen, J. A., 76, 159, 261, 315–319, 345, 416, 419, 422–424, 427
Cohen, R., 335
Colbus, D., 487
Collier, K. L., 341
Collins, W. A., 1–2
Colognori, D., 501
Comer, J. S., 349–351, 360, 362, 366, 368–372, 455–456, 461–462, 482–485, 487–488, 491–492, 503
Compass, B. E., 525–526
Conger, R. D., 20
Conners, C. K., 353
Connolly, J., 337
Constantino, M. J., 64–65, 72
Conterio, K., 290
Cook-Cottone, C., 28, 32
Cooper, Z., 515
Copeland, W. E., 7, 49–50
Copen, C. E., 306
Coppolillo, H. P., 186, 188
Cordova, D., 345
Corey, C., 95, 98, 102–104, 113–116, 119
Corey, G., 95, 96, 98, 102–104, 113–116, 115, 119
Corey, M., 95, 98, 102–104, 113–116, 119
Costa, P. T., 263

Costello, E. J., 7, 49–50
Costin, A., 287
Cotton, C. R., 476
Cottrell, D., 134
Council on Foundations, 40, 210
Courtney-Seidler, E. A., 287
Courtois, C. A., 410
Courturier, J. L., 517
Covey, H. C., 45–46
Coyle, S., 451
Craig, S. L., 342
Cramer, P., 184
Crawford, E. A., 456–459, 465
Crawford, H., 287–288
Crean, H. F., 43
Cresswell, C., 455, 459, 464
Crisler, M., 360, 362
Cristalli, M., 134, 426
Crow, S., 507
Crow, S. J., 507, 512
Culbert, T., 136
Curran, M. A., 40–42, 210
Curry, J., 332
Czaja, S. J., 400

D

Dahlen, P., 519–520, 522–523
Dailey, F. L., 399, 413, 427
Daly, S. L., 309
Daniels, K., 306
Darby, A., 87
Dare, C., 514
Darwich, L., 330
Dattilio, F. M., 226
David-Ferdon, C., 295
Davies, M., 518
Davis, D., 141
Davis, H., 526–528
Davis, N. L., 245–246
Davison, M. L., 41, 48
Dawson, G., 360, 362, 364
Deakin, E., 65, 90–91
Deardorff, J., 23
DeBar, L. L., 494
DeBastos, A. K., 5
DeBeus, R., 354
Deblinger, E., 44–45, 261, 318, 345, 409, 422–423, 425
Decker, S. L., 5
Degges-White, S., 245–246
de Haan, A. M., 65, 91
de Jong, J. T., 65, 91
de Lange, D., 487
de la Rie, S., 507
de la Sablonnière, R., 40, 43, 48, 52–53
Delgado, S. V., 173, 175
Della Selva, P. C., 175
DeLorenzi, L., 24, 31–32
Delsing, M., 31
Demanchick, S. P., 201
DeMarco, C., 413
Denby, R. W., 526
den Dulk, K. R., 52
de Roos, C., 134
DeRosier, M. E., 335–336
DeRubeis, R. J., 494
de Santana, C. P., 9, 12, 65
Descilo, T., 416

de Shazer, S., 273
de Shazer, 64
de Souza, W. C., 9, 12, 65
De Stavola, B., 27
DeStefano, F., 360
Devlin, M. J., 518
DeVore, E. R., 18
De Young, K. P., 513
de Zqaan, M., 510
Diamond, L. M., 339–341
Dibb, B., 365
Dickerson Mayes, S., 50
DiClemente, C. C., 77–78
Diehle, J., 425
Diemer, M. A., 52–53
Dillworth, T. M., 529–530
Distelberg, B., 531
DiVerniero, R., 308
Dixon, A., 36
Dixon, A. L., 24, 26, 28–29
Dmith, L. E., 407
Dodge, K. A., 50, 342
Dohn, H. H., 282
Dolan, Y., 273
Doley, R., 43, 310
Donker, M., 507
Donohue, B., 450
Döpfner, M., 229, 354
dosReis, S., 487
Dowell, N. M., 61, 71
Downing, J., 23
Downs, K. J., 514
Drewes, A. A., 232–234, 240, 242
Drouhard, N., 287
Drout, M. O., 196, 241
Drummond, P., 134
Dtone, C., 102, 109
Dubicka, B., 289
Due, D., 52
Duffy, M., 54
Dulmus, C. N., 134, 426
Dundas, I., 329
Dunn, M. J., 525–526
Dunn, M. S., 31
DuPaul, G. J., 353
Duric, N., 354
Dutton, M. A., 400
Dvir, Y., 414
Dvorsky, M. R., 8
Dweck, C. S., 325
Dwyer, D. S., 436
Dyl, J., 287
Dymek, M., 518
Dyson, M. W., 10, 65
D'Zurilla, T. J., 474–475, 499–500

E

Eddershaw, R., 143
Edleson, J. L., 406
Edmunds, J., 159
Edwards, K. M., 44–45
Edwards, M., 526–528
Edwards, T. M., 220–221
Egli, C. J., 335
Ehde, D. M., 529–530
Ehrenreich, J. T., 486, 490
Ehrensaft, D., 342
Eichner, J. C., 5, 9

Eisler, I., 514
Elgen, I. B., 354
Elliot, D. S., 51, 53
Elliott, A., 184
Ellis, A., 138, 140–141, 147, 149
Emery, G., 388–389
Emery, R. E., 300–301
Englund, J. A., 5
Eppler, C., 251
Epston, D., 220, 250
Erbas, B., 300
Erford, B. T., 137
Erford, M. R., 137
Erickson, M. R., 250
Eriksen, K., 35–36, 210, 213, 257
Erikson, Erik, 7–8, 11, 18–19, 24–25, 26, 27, 30, 172, 175, 177
Erk, R. R., 354, 358
Espelage, D. L., 20, 281, 338
Esposito, E., 503
Evan-Lacko, S. E., 487
Evans, C. B. R., 405
Evans, L., 375
Ewell Foster, C., 279–283, 286–287
Ewuzie, M. A., 27

F

Fabiano, G., 354
Fabiano, G. A., 307–308
Fairburn, C. G., 506–507, 514–516
Falco, L. D., 28, 32
Faldowski, R. A., 331–332
Fall, K. A., 121–123
Fallon, B., 413
Fang, A., 464, 494
Farmer, T. W., 48–49, 51
Farrington, D. P., 293–294
Fauth, R. C., 40, 43, 48
Fearon, P., 62, 90
Fedewa, A., 6, 9–11, 22
Feeny, N. C., 411
Feinberg, M., 331–332
Feitosa, M. G., 9, 12, 65
Feldman, M., 512
Feldman-Summers, S., 261
Felix, E., 406
Ferrucci, P., 54
Fewell, C. H., 314–315
Field, A., 134, 488, 490, 493, 497, 503
Field, L. F., 483, 485
Fincham, F., 307–308
Fineran, K. R., 286
Finkelhor, D., 402–403, 404, 405–406
Finnan, C., 19
Finno-Velasquez, M., 45
Fisch, R., 221
Fishman, H. C., 209, 213, 221–223, 225
Fleming, J., 425
Flessner, C. A., 464
Fletcher, K. E., 397–401, 413, 423
Flynn, S. D., 128
Foa, E. B., 411
Foelsch, P. A., 335, 342
Ford, J. D., 414
Forman, E. M., 122, 139, 143–144
Fosco, G. M., 210
Foshee, V., 344–345
Foss, L., 256

Foster, L., 9–11
Fowler, P. J., 333–334
Foxwell, A., 282
France, M. H., 376
Frank, J. B., 61, 65, 71
Frank, J. D., 61, 65, 71
Franklin, M. E., 455, 465–466, 470, 477–478
Franzese, R. J., 45–46
Fraser, M. W., 23
Frazier, J. A., 414
Freeman, A., 141
Freeman, A. J., 482, 492
Freeman, J., 455, 464–465
Frels, R. K., 530
French, T. M., 187
Freud, A., 172, 175–177, 188, 189
Freud, S., 172–175, 177, 185, 187–188, 232
Frick, P. J., 183
Friedberg, R. D., 472
Fristad, M. A., 12
Froiland, J. M., 41–42, 48
Fulginiti, A., 45
Fulton, C., 147
Furber, G., 43
Furr, J. M., 456–459, 465

G

Galea, S., 400
Gallop, R. J., 345
Garber, J., 329
Garcia, J. H., 472
Gardner, D., 394
Gardner, M., 45, 53
Garland, A. F., 69
Garner, M., 143
Garrett, M., 247
Gastaud, M., 65, 90–91
Gazelle, H., 331–332
Gee, A. D., 5, 9
Geldard, D., 27–28, 30–31, 470, 500–501
Geldard, K., 27–28, 30–31, 470, 500–501
Geluk, C. A., 65, 91
Generali, M., 256
Genetic Science Learning Center, 431
Gerson, M. J., 189
Gest, S. D., 331–332
Gibbons, J. L., 311
Gibson, B., 5, 9
Gidycz, C. A., 44–45
Giedd, J., 24
Gil, E., 416, 426–427
Gilliland, B. E., 295, 427
Ginsburg, G. S., 464–465
Ginsburg, K. R., 18
Girio-Herrera, E., 8
Girresch, S. K., 287, 289
Giufridda, D. A., 143
Gladding, S., 1, 35
Gladding, S. T., 49, 71, 228, 230, 234, 246
Glass, C. R., 64–65, 72
Glasser, W., 160–164, 167–168
Glenwick, D. S., 309
Glick, D. M., 325
Godley, M. D., 451
Godley, S. H., 451
Godt, K., 513
Goel, K., 43
Goldblum, P., 281

Goldenberg, H., 209, 214, 218, 226, 299, 306, 323
Goldenberg, I., 209, 214, 218, 226, 299, 302, 323
Goldin, P., 155, 159–160
Goldstein, T. R., 281, 283–284
Goleman, D., 155
Golombok, S., 304
Gómez-Benito, J., 352
Gondoli, D. M., 5, 9
Gonzales, A. H., 306
Goodman, C., 309
Goodrow, B., 31
Goodyer, I., 289
Gopalan, G., 422
Gorman, D. A., 394
Gotham, K., 362
Gotlib, I. H., 485
Gottfried, M. A., 54
Gower, A. L., 49
Graham, M. A., 167
Graham, S., 372, 434
Granello, D. H., 280–282
Granello, P. F., 280–282
Gravelle, M., 48–49, 51
Gray, D. D., 311
Gray, S. W., 360
Greco, L. A., 143, 465
Greenberg, R. P., 90, 92
Greenspan, L., 23
Greenspan, S. I., 365
Greenwald, R., 416
Greyber, L. R., 134, 426
Groark, C. J., 5, 9
Gross, A. M., 476
Gross, C. M., 370–371
Grover, P. J., 493
Guevremont, D. C., 122–124, 126
Gulley, L. D., 8
Gundersen, D., 354
Gupta, T., 52
Gurney, B. G., 240
Gurney, L., 240
Guthrie, D. W., 527
Guthrie, W., 362

H

Habeck, R. V., 196, 241
Haddock, L. R., 448
Haley, J., 213, 225
Hall, K. R., 22–23, 26–28, 30
Hamby, S. L., 402–403, 404, 405–406
Hamm, J. V., 48–49, 51
Hammond, S., 294
Hamvas, L., 261
Hankin, B. L., 8
Harden, K. P., 5, 342
Hargreaves, L., 332
Harrington, B. C., 518
Harris, K. R., 372, 434
Harris, S. M., 83, 86, 92
Harrison, A. M., 83–84, 92
Hart, C. L., 433–434, 437, 444–445, 452
Harter, S., 17
Hartman, H., 175–177
Harvey, M. T., 126
Harvey, P., 144, 159, 415, 465
Haslam, M., 516
Hauge, H., 329

Havik, O., 409
Havik, T., 409
Hawkridge, S., 478–479
Hawley, K. M., 69
Haxton, C., 518
Hay, P., 516
Hayes, S. C., 138, 143, 145, 465
Hayward, C., 510
Hazler, R. J., 339
He, A. S., 45
Headley, J. A., 72, 86–87, 92
Hedtke, K., 159
Hegarty, W., 94, 111–112
Hegney, D., 519, 522–523
Heidarie, L., 229
Heiervang, E. R., 409
Hellings, J. A., 362
Hembree-Kigin, T. L., 307
Henggeler, S. W., 220, 222, 229, 384, 393–394, 450
Henry, D., 492
Herbert, J. D., 143–144
Herlihy, B., 95–101, 96, 104–109, 111–113, 115–117
Herman, J., 413, 420, 426
Hernandez, L. W., 22–23, 26–28, 30
Herrenkohl, R. C., 405–406
Herrenkohl, T. I., 405–406
Hersch, S., 354
Hertlein, K., 310–311
Hervis, O. E., 450
Hett, G. G., 376
Hickson, L., 350
Hidano, L., 251
Higginbotham, B., 345
Hill, J. P., 52
Hill, M., 414
Hill, N. R., 1, 36
Hill, S. K., 503
Hinkle, J. S., 462, 478
Hipwell, A. E., 376, 381
Hirsch, L., 394
Hirshkowitz, M., 382
Hodges, L., 365
Hodgkinson, B., 519, 522–523
Hoffman, R., 288, 291
Hofmann, S. G., 464, 494
Hohl, B. C., 51, 53–54
Holcomb-McCoy, C. H., 376
Holden, J. A., 121–123
Holdsworth, C., 53–54
Holtkamp, K., 516
Homeyer, L. W., 232, 234
Hong, J., 46, 50
Hopkins, J., 143
Hoppe, L., 478–479
Hopson, L. M., 6, 10, 42, 45, 48, 51
Howard, A., 54
Howard, D. E., 342
Howsare, J., 313–314
Hsieh, C., 52–53
Hua, L. L., 490
Hudson, J., 159, 477
Hume, K., 363
Hurt, E., 354
Hussey, D., 97–98
Huston, A. C., 11, 13
Huth-Bocks, A., 406
Hymel, S., 330

I

Iacono, W. G., 510
Ipser, J. C., 478–479
Ivers, N. N., 147

J

Jackson, B., 287–288
Jackson, K. M., 331–332
Jacobi, C., 510
Jacobs, R. H., 494
Jacobson, C. M., 288, 485
Jacobson, E., 132
Jaffer, M., 463
Jahoda, A., 369
James, R. K., 295, 403, 427
Jarosz-Chabot, P., 527
Jarvi, S., 287–288
Jaser, S. S., 525–526
Jaycox, L. H., 293, 425
Jayne, K., 186–187, 228, 230–231
Jensen, T. M., 307
Jenson, J. M., 23–31, 57
Jimerson, D. C., 507, 513, 518
Jimerson, M., 518
Jimerson, S. R., 20
Jindal, K., 503
Job, V., 325
Johnson, D. A., 147
Johnson, K. M., 411
Johnson, S., 24
Johnson, S. L., 336–337
Johnston, J., 483, 489
Johnston, J. A. Y., 516–517
Joiner, T. E., 280, 282, 284
Jolly, J. B., 148, 459, 487
Jones, I., 496
Jones, R., 43
Jongsma, A. E., 254
Joorman, J., 485
Josephs, K., 519, 522–523
Joyce, A. S., 82, 84–86
Jungbluth, N., 70
Justice, C. A., 22–23, 26–28, 30

K

Kabat-Zinn, J., 138, 143, 145–146
Kaduson, H. G., 235, 237, 240
Kagen, E. R., 456–459, 465
Kaiser, E. M., 85, 90
Kalra, G., 35
Kamphaus, R. W., 183
Kane, L. S., 28, 32
Kaplan, D. M., 1, 35
Karver, M. S., 69
Kastelic, E. A., 487
Kataoka, S. H., 425
Katsiaficas, D., 52
Kauffman, A., 52–53
Kaufman, A. S., 368
Kaufman, N. L., 368
Kautzman-East, M., 72, 86–87, 92
Kaye, W. H., 507
Kazdin, A. E., 13, 58, 122, 123, 137, 139, 390, 392–393, 487

Keable, H., 181–182, 186, 189–190
Kearney, C. A., 475, 477
Keatinge, C., 460
Keel, P. K., 510, 513
Kegerreis, S., 172–173, 182
Keith, D. V., 214
Kellam, T., 205
Kelleher, C., 342
Kelly, A. C., 69
Kelly, D. F., 191, 193
Kelly, D. R., 2
Kelvin, R., 289
Kemp, M., 134
Kendall, P. C., 159, 349–351, 360, 362, 366,
    368–372, 387–388, 455–459, 461–462,
    465–471, 477–478, 482–485, 487–488,
    491–492, 503
Kennard, B., 282
Kennerly, H., 378, 387–388
Kenny, E., 184
Kerig, P., 262
Kernberg, P. F., 181–182, 186, 189–190
Kerpelman, F., 345
Kertz, S., 468
Khemka, I., 350
Kim, J. S., 9–11
Kinch, S., 87, 289
King, C. A., 279–283, 286–287
Kingston, H. C., 9–11
Kirk, J., 378, 387–388
Kirkcaldy, B. D., 26
Kitts, C., 31
Klaus, N. M., 12
Klein, J. B., 494
Klein, M., 172, 178, 189
Klein, R. H., 84–86
Kletter, H., 406
Kliethermes, M., 159
Klinger, L. G., 360, 362
Klonsky, E. D., 279, 287–290
Klott, J., 281
Klump, K. L., 507, 510
Knapp, S., 455, 459
Knecht, A. B., 335
Knell, S. M., 242
Knox, M., 136
Kock, C., 368
Kodish, I., 479
Koegel, L. K., 364
Koegel, R. L., 364
Koenig, N., 52–53
Kohut, H., 179–180
Kolko, D., 159–160
Koman, S. L., 516–517
Konstantinova, M., 527
Koocher, G. P., 112
Korman, H., 273
Kotler, L. A., 518
Kovacs, M., 487
Kraemer, H. C., 510
Krebs, P. M., 77–80
Kress, V. E., 1, 35–36, 52, 61, 64, 69, 72, 86–87, 92,
    107, 137, 210, 213, 250–251, 253–258, 257,
    268–269, 272, 287–289, 290, 291, 355, 397,
    409, 413, 457, 465, 472, 489, 494, 499
Kreumholz, L. S., 474, 485–486, 495–496, 500–502
Krietemeyer, J., 143
Kris, E., 175–177
Ksir, C., 433–434, 437, 444–445, 452

Kubler-Ross, E., 315–316
Kuther, T. L., 28, 32

L

Lacewing, M., 189
Lacher, D. B., 416
Lader, W., 290
Lam, D. H., 494
Lambert, K., 48–49, 51
Lambert, M. J., 65, 69, 76
Lambie, R., 302
Land, H., 248, 250–251
Lander, L., 313–314
Landreth, G., 205, 232–235
Lane, R. C., 188
Langley, A. K., 425
Lanktree, C. B., 179, 406, 410–411, 415, 488
Lansford, J. E., 103, 342
Larocca, P. S., 530
Larson, J. H., 307
Laughlin, L., 39
Lavallee, D., 52
La Via, M. C., 518
Lazdauskas, T., 44–45
Leaf, J. B., 128
Le Couteur, A., 362
Lee, B., 332
Lee, D., 191, 193
Lee, E., 42, 45, 51, 309
Lee, J. B., 284
Lefler, E. K., 358
LeGrange, D., 507, 512, 513–514, 518
Lehmann, S., 409
Lehmkuhl, U., 517
Leibenluft, E., 492–493
Leibowitz, G. S., 54
Leigh, E., 287, 289
Lempp, T., 487
Leonavičienė, T., 44–45
Lereya, S. T., 7, 49–50
Leventhal, T., 40, 43, 48
Levy, D. M., 243
Lewin, A. B., 464
Lewis, G., 375
Lewis, S., 31, 287–290
Leybman, Blatt, & Wampold, 69, 259
LGBTQQIA Competencies Taskforce, 340–342
Liber, J. M., 460
Liddle, R. A., 513
Liebenberg, L., 37–38, 44–45
Lieberman, A. F., 5–6
Lilly, M. M., 45, 53
Lin, D., 228, 231
Lindahl, K. M., 40–42
Lindauer, R. J. L., 425
Lindsay, C. A., 333–334
Linehan, M. M., 138, 143–144, 151–155, 159, 289,
    486, 516
Liu, J., 375
Liu, R. T., 281
Lo, Y., 128
Lock, J., 507, 513–514, 517, 518
Loeber, R., 293–294, 376, 378–379, 381
Lofthouse, N. L., 354
Loiterstein, A., 159–160
Loizou, E., 332–333
London, K., 45, 53, 401, 403
Long, C., 334
Lopata, C., 132

Lord, C., 362
Love, S. R., 362
Luborsky, E. B., 183
Luby, J. L., 489
Lucas, N., 300
Ludlow, A., 365
Luiselli, J. K., 126
Lundberg, S., 43
Lupo, A. K., 53
Luyster, R. J., 362
Lynch, M., 49–50

M

Ma, N., 43
MacDonald, K., 376, 378–379
Mackrell, S. M., 9, 11–12
MacLaurin, B., 413
Madanes, C., 226
Mahendra, R. R., 45–46
Mahler, S., 179
Mailli, R., 43
Malchiodi, C., 22
Malik, N., 40–42
Malouff, J. M., 474, 499
Mandrusiak, M., 284
Mannarino, A. P., 76, 159, 261, 315–319, 318, 345,
    416, 419, 422–424, 425, 427
Many, M., 83–85
Marans, S. R., 345
March, J. S., 455
Marcia, J. E., 24, 30
Margolin, G., 410
Margulies, D. M., 492–493
Marquis, A., 121–123, 143
Martin, A., 45, 53
Martin, P. C., 371
Masarik, A. S., 20
Maslow, A., 11, 201
Masten, A. S., 300, 406–407
Matson, J. L., 363
Matthews, M. D., 2
May, A. M., 279
May, J. C., 416
McBride, J., 217, 307
McBride, O., 342
McCall, R. B., 5, 9
McCart, M. R., 220, 222
McCarthy, S. K., 5, 9
McCauley, K., 432
McClure, J. M., 472
McCollum, E. E., 273
McCoy, D. C., 40, 43, 48
McCoy, L., 45–46
McCrae, R. R., 263
McDermott, B., 134
McDougall, P., 400
McGinnis, H., 311
McGlothlin, J. M., 281, 295
McGuckin, C., 337
McGue, M., 510
McGuinness, T., 167
McGuire, J. F., 463
McKeage, K., 503
McKeown-Jenkins, M., 482, 492
McLeod, B. D., 159
McMorris, B. J., 49
McNeil, C., 307
Medical University of South Carolina, 159
Meeu, W. J., 31

Meichenbaum, D. L., 307–308
Meijr, A. M., 134
Menard, S., 45–46
Menassa, B. M., 6, 235–238, 240–245
Mendle, J., 5–6, 8, 342
Meng, C., 327
Mercer, S. H., 335–336
Merikangas, K. R., 1, 27, 31, 380, 482, 507, 512
Meron, D., 143
Merrick, J., 26
Messer, S. B., 181, 184, 187
Metzger, M. F., 333–334
Meyer, C., 516
Meyer, D. A., 492
Meyer, I., 512
Meyers, R. J., 451
Micali, N., 27
Michaels, M. S., 280, 282
Mideley, N., 172–173, 182
Midence, K., 527
Miklowitz, D. J., 495
Miller, A. L., 144, 159, 287, 391–392, 517
Miller, K. B., 510
Miller, L. J., 368
Miller, W. R., 76–78, 172, 201, 291, 446–448
Milsom, A., 332
Miltenberger, R. G., 125–126, 136
Minton, S. J., 337
Minuchin, S., 209, 213, 221–223, 225
Mishna, F., 372
Mitchell, J. E., 507
Mitchell, P., 21
Moeller, W., 261
Monnin, K., 455, 459, 463–465, 487
Montgomery, S., 531
Moody, J., 331–332
Moore, D., 341
Moore, R. O., 112
Moore, S. R., 5, 7, 342–343
Moorhead, H. H., 397
Moreno, J. L., 251
Morgan, K., 342
Morrison, M. O., 232, 234
Morsette, A., 425
Morsy, L., 9
Mosher, W. D., 306
Moylan, C. A., 405–406
Muehlenkamp, J. J., 287–290
Mufson, L. M., 288, 485
Muhlau, M., 507
Mullette, J., 254–255
Munford, R., 37–38, 44–45
Munns, E., 240
Mura, C. J., 70, 259
Murdock, N. L., 217–218, 220, 226
Muris, P., 456
Murray, L. A., 159
Murray, L. K., 416, 424–425
Muskat, B., 372
Mustanski, B., 281
Mychailyszyn, M., 159
Myers, J. E., 136

N

Nadeem, E., 425
Nader, K., 397–401, 409, 411, 413, 423
Naderi, F., 229
Najavits, L. M., 345
Narayan, A. J., 406–407

Nasvytiené, D., 44–45
National Alliance of Children's Trust and Prevention Funds, 45
National Association of School Psychologists (NASP), 315
National Center for Health Statistics, 300
National Center for PTSD, 406
National Center for Youth Law, 98
National Child Trauma Stress Network, 103
National Coalition for Child Protection Reform, 44–45
National Eating Disorders Association, 49
National Gang Center, 53
National Institute for Health and Care Excellence (NICE), 513–514, 516, 518
National Institute of Allergy and Infectious Disease, 526
National Institute on Alcohol Abuse and Alcoholism (NIAAA), 434
National Institute on Drug Abuse (NIDA), 430–437, 442–443, 445–452
National Step-Family Resource Center, 306
Newman, J. B., 5
Newsome, D. W., 147
Nezu, A. M., 122, 139
Nezu, C. M., 122, 139
Ng, M. Y., 122, 139
Nichols, M., 416
Nichols, T., 416
Nicholson, J. M., 300
Niepel, C., 5, 7, 10–11
Nigg, J. T., 354
Nisbett, R. E., 368
Noordenbos, G., 507
Nopmaneejumruslers, K., 365
Norbury, C. F., 377
Norcross, J. C., 35, 57–58, 66–71, 77–80, 254–255
Normand, M. P., 128
Norton, B. E., 239
Norton, C. C., 239
Nunes, M. L. T., 65, 90–91

O

Odegard, M. A., 286
O'Gara, J. S. X., 516–517
Ogrodniczuk, J. S., 84–86
Oliver, A. C., 128
Ollendick, T. H., 43, 456, 464, 469–470, 477–478
Olsen, J. P., 251, 335
Olson, D., 41–42, 212–213
Olweus, D., 338
O'Malley, Voight, Renshaw, & Eklund, 48–49
Oncken, C., 137
Ong, S. L., 49, 51
Opmeer, B., 425
Oppawsky, J., 301
Oppenheimer, C. W., 8
Ordway, A. M., 112
Organization for Economic Cooperation and Development (OECD), 324–325
Ormrod, R. K., 402, 404
Orsillo, S. M., 325
Orton, G. L., 67
Osborne, C., 313–314
Osgood, D. W., 331–332
Osofsky, T. L., 5–6
Osypuk, T. L., 43
Ougrin, D., 287, 289
Owens, J. S., 8
Oyserman, D., 43, 324, 328, 334

P

Pace, G. T., 307
Packman, J., 228
Pahl, K. M., 465
Pajareya, K., 365
Paladino, D., 24, 31–32
Panasenko, N., 48
Pandit, M., 531
Panza, K. E., 462
Pao, M., 530
Papolos, D., 492
Parens, E., 483, 489
Park, D., 250
Parra, G. R., 335
Patel, P., 474, 485–486, 495–496, 500–502
Patterson, G. A., 282
Patterson, J., 220–221
Patterson, W. M., 282
Paul, L. E., 137
Paula, C. S., 487
Paulk, A., 345
Pavlov, I., 123
Pavuluri, M. N., 492, 503
Paylo, M. J., 64, 69, 87, 253–258, 268–269, 272, 413, 457, 465, 472, 489, 494, 499
Pedro-Carroll, J., 16, 300, 304–305
Penzo, J. A., 144
Perel, J. M., 427
Perera, M. J., 328
Peris, T. S., 463–464
Peters, B. N., 5
Peterson, A., 42
Peterson, M. L., 254
Pettit, G. S., 342
Pfeiffer, E., 517
Piacentini, J., 159, 463–464
Piaget, J., 5–6, 10, 16–17, 24, 29–30, 140
Piggott, T. D., 338
Pike, K. M., 514
Pilling, S., 494
Pine, D. S., 455, 459
Pine, F., 179
Piotrowski, C., 45
Piper, W. E., 82, 84–86
Pittenberger, C., 462
Pittman, L., 45, 53
Plastow, M., 235
Ploubidis, G., 27
Podell, J. L., 159, 456–459, 465
Polanin, J. R., 338
Poling, K. D., 281, 283–284
Pomeroy, C., 507
Pomplun, M., 368
Pope, K. S., 261
Popkin, M. H., 198
Porfeli, E. J., 332
Poulsen, S., 516
Power, T. J., 353, 358
Pratt, L. A., 128
Preckel, F., 5, 7, 10–11
Price, C. S., 360
Pringsheim, T., 394
Probst, D. R., 44–45
Prochaska, J. O., 77–80, 448
Proctor, B., 128, 137
Prout, H. T., 6, 9–11, 22
Provencher, M. D., 494
Pugh, R., 114
Puleo, C. M., 159, 387–388

Purcell, R., 294
Purswell, K., 186–187
Pusateri, C. G., 72, 86–87, 92
Pynoos, R. S., 411

Q

Quezada, S. A., 53

R

Radeloff, D., 487
Rae, R., 244–246
Ramirez, G., 250
Rao, U., 482
Rapaport, D., 175–177
Rappleyea, D. L., 83, 86, 92
Rasic, D., 260
Rathaus, J. H., 144, 287
Rathbone, B. H., 159, 415, 465
Rathus, J. J., 391–392
Rauer, A. J., 342
Rausch, M. A., 349, 355
Raver, C. C., 40, 43, 48
Ray, D., 61, 72, 201, 228–231, 229, 234–235, 238
Raz, S., 5
Reich, C. A., 432
Reichenberg, L. W., 122
Reid, A., 136
Reid, R., 353
Reinecke, M. A., 494
Remley, T. P., 95–101, 104–109, 111–113, 115–117
Rescorla, L. A., 353
Reslan, S., 416
Reynolds, C. R., 459
Ricard, R. J., 147
Rice, J. C., 261
Rice, R. E., 24, 26
Richmond, B. O., 459
Rider, E. A., 5–6, 10–11, 19–20, 388
Riemer, M., 76
Ritvo, R., 181–182, 186, 189–190
Roberts, C., 289
Roberts, J. L., 362
Roberts, R., 43
Robertson, A., 369
Robertson, G. J., 371
Robey, P., 163
Rockhill, C., 479
Rodenburg, R., 134
Rodenhizer-Stämpfli, K. A., 44–45
Rodgers, A., 487
Rodriguez, E. M., 525–526
Rodriguez, M. D., 376
Roelofs, J., 456
Roemer, L., 123
Roerig, J., 507
Rogalski, R., 279–283, 286–287
Rogers, C., 200–205
Rogers, N., 172, 200–201
Rogers, S. J., 364
Rohleder, P., 365
Roid, G. H., 368
Rokkedal, K., 507, 513
Rollnick, S., 76–78, 172, 201, 291, 446–448
Romer, D., 29
Rorschach, H., 183
Rosen, C. M., 230, 246–247
Rosenbaum Asarnow, J., 287, 289

Rossano, M., 52
Rossi, E. L., 250
Rothstein, R., 9
Roy, A. L., 40, 43, 48
Rudd, M. D., 284
Ruiz, P., 490
Rule, W. R., 196, 241
Rumsey, A., 24, 26, 28–29
Rush, A. J., 388–389
Russell, G., 514
Rutter, M., 362
Ryan, A. M., 335
Ryan, E. E., 409, 425
Ryan, M., 526
Ryan, M. A., 478–479
Ryan, V., 240
Rye, N., 230, 235, 238

S

Sadock, B. J., 268, 375, 490
Sadock, V. A., 268, 375, 490
Safer, D. L., 517
Saffer, B. Y., 288
Saigh, P., 411
Sakolsky, D. J., 478–479
Salami, S. O., 406–407, 422
Salbach-Andrae, H., 517
Salo, M., 94
Salter, S. E., 293
Saltzman, A., 155, 159–160
Salvatore, J., 1–2
Salvia, J., 371
Sampson, D., 310–311
Sánchez, B., 400
Sanders, J., 37–38, 44–45
Sanders, M. R., 304, 308
Sanderson, J. A., 49, 53
Sandfort, T. M., 341
Sandler, I. N., 42, 303
Santos, S. M., 345
Santrock, J. W., 18
Satir, V., 213
Sauerheber, J. D., 167
Sawyer, A. T., 464, 494
Scahill, L., 463
Schaefer, C. E., 232–235, 237, 240
Schaefer, K., 307
Schaeffer, C., 229, 384, 393–394, 450
Schaeffer, J. A., 85, 90
Scharff, D. E., 190
Scharff, J. S., 190
Scharfstein, L., 469
Schargel, F. P., 293
Scharmm, D. G., 345
Schettini, A., 406
Schimmel, Masson & Harvill, 22
Schmidt, M. E., 335
Schmidt, U., 518
Schmitt, T. A., 416
Schneider, B. H., 488
Schoffstall, C. L., 335
Schofield, T. J., 301, 303
Schomaker, S. A., 147
Schopler, E., 362
Schore, A., 10
Schroeder, C., 409, 422–423
Schulenberg, J. E., 331–332
Schultz, D. P., 43, 191, 193, 198

Schultz, E. S., 43, 191, 193, 198
Schutte, N. S., 474, 499
Schwartz, S., 450
Scott, C., 69, 398–399, 411–416, 419–420, 422
Se, D., 234, 261–262, 264, 309
Search Institute, 10–11, 37, 39, 41–43, 45, 48–54, 376
Seer, R. A., 44–45, 148, 459, 487
Segal, Z. V., 138, 143
Segrin, C., 40–42, 210
Selfhout, M. W., 31
Seligman, L., 483, 485
Seligman, L. D., 464, 469–470, 477–478
Seligman, L. W., 122
Seligman, M. E. P., 37
Semple, R. J., 155, 159–160
Senn, D. S., 22
Seymour, J. W., 314
Shafran, R., 515
Shanker, S. G., 365
Shannonhouse, L., 36
Shapira, B. F., 519–520, 522–523
Shapiro, F., 40, 42, 134, 178, 188, 212, 220–221, 223, 226, 426
Sharf, R. S., 177, 180
Sharkey, J. D., 49–50
Sharma, J., 287
Sharpe, T. L., 40
Sharpless, B. A., 70, 259
Sharpley, C. F., 43
Shattuck, A., 402–403, 404, 405–406
Shaw, B. F., 388–389
Shaw, T. F., 40, 44–45
Shebroe, V., 406
Shell, M. D., 331–332
Shenberger, J., 53
Sheperis, D. S., 448
Sheridan, D., 52
Shin, H., 335
Shirk, S., 70
Shlafer, R. J., 49
Shriver, M. D., 128, 137
Shulman, C., 9
Shuman, D. W., 401, 403
Sicile-Kira, C., 361–362
Siefen, G. R., 26
Siegel, D. J., 432–434, 436
Sieving, R. E., 49
Sigal, A. B., 42
Sigelman, C. K., 5–6, 10–11, 19–20, 388
Sigman, M., 159
Silva, L., 30
Silveira, F. A., 401
Silverstein, M., 309
Simic, M., 514
Simon, K., 83, 86, 92
Simon, T. R., 295
Simonich, H., 159–160
Simonoff, S., 27
Simpson, A., 43, 49
Simpson, H., 43, 310
Simpson, J. A., 1–2
Simpson, S., 496
Sinclair, I., 423
Singh, T., 382, 492–493
Sirin, S. R., 52
Skapinakis, P., 32

Skelly, C., 365
Skinner, B. F., 123–124, 363
Skinner, E. A., 2, 6, 9–10, 22
Slyter, M., 251
Smith, A. W., 455, 459, 463–465, 487
Smith, D., 496
Smith, E. J., 37, 255
Smith, G. T., 143
Smith, H. L., 364, 394
Smith, J. E., 451
Smith, J. Z., 64–65, 72
Smith, L. E., 407
Smith, M. S., 342
Smith, S. G., 45–46
Smith, T. B., 30
Smith-Adcock, S., 115
Sommers-Flanagan, J., 268, 272, 494
Sommers-Flanagan, R., 268, 272
Sorhagen, N. S., 48–49
Soto-Leggett, E., 530
Sousa, C., 405–406
Sousa, G. A., 1, 36
Southgate, L., 507
Sparks, A., 377
Spence, S. H., 459
Spiegler, M. D., 122–124, 126
Spielberger, C. D., 459
Stallman, H. M., 304, 308
Stalvey, S., 61
Stams, G. J., 134
Stark, K. D., 474, 485–486, 495–496, 500–502
Staron, V. A., 427
Stauffer, M. D., 6
Steeger, C. M., 5, 9
Steglich, C., 335
Stein, B. D., 293, 425
Stein, D. J., 478–479
Steinburg, L., 27
Steinhausen, H. C., 507
Stein-Steele, E. C, 44–45
Steinwachs, D. M., 487
Stewart-Tufescu, A., 45
Stice, E., 507
Stieben, J., 365
Stone, C., 102
Storlie, C. A., 526, 530
Stover, C. S., 345
Straussner, S. L. A., 314–315
Strawn, J. R., 478–479
Streusand, W., 474, 485–486, 495–496, 500–502
Strober, M., 507
Strosahl, K. D., 138, 143, 145
Studer, J. R., 293
Suárez-Orozco, C., 52
Sue, D., 36
Sue, D. W., 36, 52, 234, 261–262, 264, 309
Suldo, M. S., 7–8, 57
Swanson, H. L., 372, 434
Swanson, S. A., 507, 512
Swart, J., 386
Swearer, S. M., 20
Sweeney, J. A., 503
Sweeney, M. M., 15, 191, 198–199, 212, 306
Swendsen, J., 27, 31, 507, 512
Swenson, L., 287–288
Swift, J. K., 90, 92
Symonds, J., 332
Szapocznik, J., 450

T

Tailor, K., 45
Tajima, E. A., 405–406
Tandoc, E. C., 54
Tansill, E. C., 44–45
Tapanes, D., 531
Tarvydas, V. M., 1, 35
Tasker, F., 304
Taylor, C. A., 261
Taylor, D. M., 40, 43, 48, 52–53
Taylor, L., 287, 289
Tchanturia, K., 507
Teasdale, J. D., 138, 143
Tein, J., 42, 303
Tello, J., 345
Temkin, D. A., 331–332
ter Bogt, T. M., 31
Terracciano, A., 263
Thakkar-Kolar, R., 409, 425
Thames, A. D., 329
Tharpe, A. T., 345
Thase, M. E., 148–149
Thimasarn-Anwar, T., 37–38, 44–45
Thompson, L., 136
Thompson, M., 136
Thornsteinsson, E. B., 474, 499
Titzmann, P. F., 335
Tompkins, M. A., 462, 464, 466, 470, 476
Toney, L., 143
Tracy, M., 400
Trahan, E., 52–53
Tranah, T., 287, 289
Treadwell, K. R. H., 411
Treasure, J., 27, 507
Trepal, H. C., 290
Trepper, T., 273
Tresco, K. E., 358
Trivedi, H. K., 504
Trocmé, N., 413
Trosper, S. E., 486, 490
Tsai, S. M., 368
Tse, S., 324, 334
Tucker, A. S., 45–46
Tucker, C., 115
Tuerk, E. H., 220, 222
Turner, B. J., 287, 289
Turner, H. A., 402–403, 405–406
Turner, J. A., 529–530
Twenge, J. M., 54
Tyson, E., 507

U

Ugoani, J. N., 27
Underwood, L. A., 399, 413, 427
Ungar, M., 37–38, 44–45
U.S. Census Bureau, 36, 300
U.S. Department of Health and Human Services, 44, 103, 342, 401

V

Vaillancourt, T., 400
Valbak, K., 507, 513
van Beusekom, G., 341
Vandell, D. L., 27
van der Kolk, B. A., 410
Van de Vijver, F. J. R., 352

Van Furth, E. F., 507
Vangergrift, N., 27
Van Ryzin, M. J., 210
Varley, C., 479
Vecchio, J., 475, 477
Velez, C. E., 303
Vereen, L. G., 1, 36
Vermeiren, R. A., 65, 91
Vernon, A., 60–61, 63, 67, 72
Vernon, T. W., 364
Vespa, J., 306
Vickerman, K. A., 410
Victor, S. E., 288
Vigo, D. E., 48
Vitousek, K., 514
Voisin, D., 46, 50
Von Bourgondien, M. E., 362
Vonk, I. J., 464, 494
Vrouva, I., 62, 90

W

Waasdorp, T. E., 336–337
Wade, A. G., 57, 69
Wade, J., 423
Wagner, M. F., 12, 124, 173, 182–183, 185–186, 189, 226
Waheed, W., 287
Waite, P., 455, 459, 464
Wall, S., 178
Waller, G., 516
Wallerstein, J. S., 303
Walsh, B. M., 212, 288, 290
Walsh, B. T., 287–290, 507, 514, 518
Walton, G. M., 325
Wampold, B. E., 35, 57–58, 66–71, 69, 72, 259
Wang, H. H., 368
Ward, J. E., 286
Ware Balch, J., 229
Washburn, J. J., 289–290
Waterhouse, T., 330
Waters, E., 178
Watson, J., 123
Watt, B., 43, 310
Watts, R. E., 193–194
Watzlawick, P., 221
Weakland, J., 221
Weaver, J. M., 301, 303
Webb, A., 159, 477
Webb, N. B., 303–304, 313–315, 321
Weber, S., 507
Wechsler, D., 368
Weesie, J., 335
Weider, S., 365
Weintraub, E. S., 360
Weintraub, S., 493
Weiss, R. D., 345
Weissman, A. S., 501
Weisz, J. R., 13, 58, 122, 139, 390, 392–393
Weldon, P., 6, 10, 48
Welfel, E. R., 99, 115
Wellman, G. J., 362
Wenar, C., 262
Werner-Lin, A., 316
West, A., 503
West, A. E., 492
Westbrook, D., 378, 387–388

Wester, K. J., 290
Whiston, S. C., 268–269
Whitaker, C. A., 214
Whitaker, K., 49, 51
White, M., 83, 86, 92, 220, 250
White, T. G., 9–11
Whiteman, H., 526
Whitmarsh, L., 254–255
Widom, C. S., 400
Wiederholt, J. L., 371
Wiener, J., 372
Wigderson, S., 49–50
Wild, L. G., 304
Wildman, B. G., 455, 459, 463–465, 487
Wilkinson, G. S., 371
Wilkinson, P., 289
Willhite, R. G., 196
Williams, A. E., 136, 443
Williams, J. M. G., 138, 143
Williams, L., 220–221
Williams, N. F., 349, 355
Williams-Reade, J., 531
Wilson, G. T., 507, 514
Wilson, K. G., 138, 143, 145
Wilson, S. L., 311
Wilson, S. M., 455, 459, 463–465, 487
Winefield, H., 43

Winnicott, D. W., 183
Witherington, D. C., 212
Witwer, A. N., 368–369
Wolchik, S. A., 42, 303
Wolf, J., 196
Wolfe, B. E., 513
Wolfe, K. L., 282
Wolke, D., 7, 49–50
Wolpe, J., 124, 132
Wolpert, H. A., 526
Wong, D. W., 22–23, 26–28, 30
Wong, M., 293
Wong, S. E., 126
Woo, S. M., 460
Wood, J. J., 159
Woodcock, R. W., 371
Woodruff-Borden, J., 468
Wormnes, B., 329
Wright, J. H., 148–149
Wright, K., 494
Wubbolding, R. E., 160–167

Y

Yanof, J. A., 186, 190
Yensel, J., 250
Yin Foo, R., 500–501
You, S., 406

Young, A. S., 12
Young, J. S., 136
Young, R. C., 492
Young, S., 357
Youngs, E. L., 362
Youngstrom, E. A., 482, 492
Ysseldyke, J. E., 371

Z

Zárate, M. A., 53
Zaw, W., 527
Zeanah, C. H., 9, 11, 35
Zembar, M. J., 16
Zhu, S., 43, 324, 328, 334
Ziber, I., 287
Zide, M. R., 360
Ziegler, F., 21
Ziegler, V. E., 492
Zilberstein, K., 1, 5, 7–8, 11
Zimmer-Gembeck, M. J., 2, 6, 9–10, 22
Zimmerman, J., 304
Zoldan, C. A., 397
Zolkoski, S. M., 299–300, 323
Zullig, K. J., 48–49
Zuroff, D. C., 69

SUBJECT INDEX

A

ABCDEFG approach, reality therapy, 164
ABCDEF Model, 149–151
ABC model
  behavior assessment, 128
  cognitive behavior therapy, 141, 149–151
abuse. *See also* child abuse; emotional abuse;
    physical abuse; sexual abuse
  assessment of, 410–413
  countertransference, 261
  youth development and, 398–400
  youth maltreatment, 401
ACA Code of Ethics
  children's rights and, 95
  context and culture in, 35–36
  cultural context in counseling, 256
  developmental counseling and, 1–2
  informed consent in, 98–99
  prohibitions of discrimination, 96
academic achievement
  ADHD and, 351–352
  family influence on, 47–48
  problems in, 324–331
  school transitions and, 331–335
  study skills deficits, 327–329
  test anxiety, 329–330
  time management problems, 325–328
acamprosate, 452
acceptance and commitment therapy (ACT), 138,
    143–145, 465
ACCEPTS script, wise mind and, 154
acculturation, norms, 52
Achenbach System of Empirically Based Assessment
    (ASEBA), 283
acting with awareness, 143
action plans, termination process, 86
action stage of change, 77–80
active listening, 204
Active Parenting Model, 198–199
Active Parenting of Teens, 198–199
activity scheduling, 501–502
ACT model, play therapy, 235–236
acute stress disorder, 409–410
adaptive functioning, 348, 367
  chronic illness/disability, 526–527
  trauma and, 399
ADHD Rating Scales-5, 353
Adlerian play therapy, 240–242
Adolescent Community Reinforcement Approach
    (A-CRA), 451
adolescents. *See also* early adolescence; late
    adolescence
  communicating with, 74
  divorce/parental separation impact on,
    301–305
  parental substance abuse and, 314–315
  psychodynamic therapy with, 183–184
  substance use and, 431–433
  suicide in, 279–287
  working alliance challenges with, 69–70
adoption, families and family systems, 311–313
Advice Letters, 499
advocacy, in reality therapy, 164
affect, early childhood, 10

affective education, 466–469
  depressive and bipolar disorders, 496–497
affect regulation, 414–415
age factors, suicide and, 280–281
age of consent, ethics in counseling and, 98
aggression/death, drive theory and, 173–175
aims and objectives of counseling, 272–273
alcohol-related neurodevelopmental disorder
    (ARND), 313–315
all about my loved one, 319
Aloha Lei, 88
alter ego transference, 180
Alternatives for Families-A Cognitive Behavioral
    Therapy (AF-CBT), 159–160
ambivalent/resistance attachment, 178–179
American Art Therapy Association, 230
American Society of Addiction Medicine (ASAM),
    441–443
anal explosive personality, 174–175
anal retentive personality, 174–175
anal stage of development, 174–175
animal parade exercise, 156
anorexia nervosa
  binge-eating/purging anorexia, 509–510
  counselor's role concerning, 509–510
  incidence and prevalence, 506–509
  treatment models and interventions, 513–516
antecedent events, behavior assessment, 128–129
anxiety disorders
  assessment, 459–460
  characteristics, 455–456
  disruptive behavior problems, 381–382
  incidence and prevalence, 455
  symptoms, 456–457
  types of, 457–459
anxiety hierarchy, 132
applied behavior analysis (ABA), 126, 128
  autism spectrum disorder, 363–365
appropriate self-disclosure, 204
arbitrary inference, 142
art therapy, 230, 246–252
  interventions, 246–247
Art Therapy Certified Supervisor, 230
assent
  ethics in counseling and, 98–99
  school setting, 102–103
assessment process, 62–64
  abuse and trauma-related disorders, 410–413
  ADHD, 352–354
  anxiety disorders, 459–460
  autism spectrum disorder, 362–363
  behavior therapy, 128–129
  bipolar disorders, 492–493
  child maltreatment/abuse, 106
  cognitive behavioral therapy, 148
  conceptual framework, 268–269
  contextual assessment, 262–267
  disruptive behavior problems, 382–384
  family therapy, 215–216
  homicide risk, 294–298
  intellectual disabilities, 368
  learning disorders, 371–372
  lifestyle assessment, 196–197
  nonsuicidal self-injury, 288–289

obsessive-compulsive disorders, 463–464
  psychodynamic therapy, 182–183
  substance abuse, 440–442
  suicide risk, 281–283
Association of Recovery Schools (ARS), 451
attachment bonds, 7
  adoption, 311–313
  context in counseling and, 262
  early childhood, 11
attachment theory, 178–179, 408–409
attention
  Adlerian play therapy, 241
  behavior assessment, 129
attention-deficit/hyperactivity disorder (ADHD),
    349–360
  assessment, 352–354
  counseling issues, 350–352
  interventions, 354–360
  time management and, 325
attorneys, consultation with, 117
attunement, 312–313
augmentative and alternative communication (AAC),
    362
augmenting medication, 504
authoritarian parenting, 18
authoritative parenting, 18
Autism Diagnostic Interview-Revised (ADI-R),
    362–363
Autism Diagnostic Observation Schedule, Second
    Edition (ADOS-2), 362–363
autism spectrum disorder, 360–365
  assessment, 362–363
  counseling role, 361–362
  interventions, 363–365
  levels of severity, 361
automatic thoughts, 141
autonomy
  change and, 78–80
  in early adolescence, 25–26
  vs. shame & doubt, early childhood, 11
avoidant attachment, 178–179
avoiding lifestyle, 192, 194

B

bare attention, 143
Beck Depression Inventory of Youth (BDI-Y),
    487–488
Beck's cognitive triad, 142, 148, 388–389
Beck Youth Inventories-Second Edition, 148, 383,
    459–460
behavior. *See also* disruptive behavior problems
  contextual framework, 263
  culture and context for, 35–36
  neighborhood norms of, 52–53
behavioral activation therapy, 494, 501–502
behavioral experiments, 150–151
behavioral symptoms, of OCD, 468–469
Behavior Assessment System for Children, 384
behavior contracts, 130–131
behavior rehearsal, 136
behavior therapy
  assessment, 128–129
  basic principles, 121–122
  biofeedback, 136

behavior therapy *(continued)*
chronic illness and training, 530
classical conditioning, 124
core concepts and counseling goals, 124–125
counseling processes and procedures, 128–136
counselor's role in, 126–127
elimination disorders, 524
family interventions and involvement, 136–138
historical evolution of, 123–124
intellectual disabilities clients, 369–370
nonsuicidal self-injury, 289
operant conditioning, 124–125, 129–130
parent management training, 137–138
psychoeducation, 137
social learning, 125
social skills training, 135–136
substance abuse, 446
belly-breathing friend exercise, 155–156
bereavement. *See* grief, loss and bereavement
Big Five personality dimensions, 263
binge eating, 510–513
biofeedback, 136
chronic illness and training, 530
biological factors
behavior therapy, 123
contextual framework, 263
disruptive behavior, 376–378
substance abuse, 432–433, 435–437
suicide and, 281
biosocial theory, 144
bipolar disorders
assessment, 492–493
decision-making flow chart, 493
integrated treatment, 495–504
interventions, 494–495
symptoms, 489–491
types of, 491
birth order, individual psychology, 196–198
blended families. *See* step- and blended families
Board-Certified Art Therapist (ATR-BC), 230
body dysmorphic disorder, 462–463
body-focused repetitive behaviors, 460–462
body image-related exercises, 511–512
Body Wellness Checklist, 511
brain development
early adolescence, 24
middle childhood, 16–17
trauma and, 399
breathing exercises, 386
brief strategic family therapy (BSFT), 450
Building Blocks, 88
bulimia nervosa
incidence and prevalence, 506–509
symptoms and counseling guidelines, 510–513
treatment and interventions, 516–518
bullying/cyberbulling
late adolescence, 32
school counseling and, 336–339
school system and, 50–51
suicide and, 281
buprenorphine, 452

C

CARE acronym, individual psychology, 199
case conceptualization, 253–278
framework for, 258–275

relational, collaborative, and strength-based approach, 254–255
Case for Counseling Box, 89
catastrophizing, 142
catharsis
play therapy, 234
psychodynamic therapy, 187
causality, family therapy, 212
cause-effect correlations, 128
CBT. *See* cognitive behavioral therapy
Certified Sandplay Therapists (CSTs), 244
change, motivation for, 76–80
Change the Channel activity, 498–499
character development, bullying prevention and, 338
Child and Family Traumatic Stress Interventions (CFTSI), 345
Child Behavioral Checklist, 353
Child Bipolar Questionnaire (CBQ), 492
child-centered play therapy (CCPT), 200–201, 205, 237–240
child custody proceedings, 111–113
Childhood Autism Rating Scale, Second Edition (CARS-2), 362–363
childhood traumatic grief (CTG), 317–321
child maltreatment (child abuse), 397–429. *See also* abuse
assessment, 106
defined, 103
families and, 43–44
incidence and prevalence, 401–402
reporting, 103–108
working alliance development in cases of, 69
Child Mania Rating Scale-Parent Version (CMRS-P), 492
child neglect, 44
incidence of, 103, 404–405
reporting, 103–108
Child Obsessive-Compulsive Impact Scales-Revised (COIS-R), 463–464
Child–Parent Relationship Therapy (CPRT), 205
Child PTSD Symptom Scale, 411–412
Children of Divorce Intervention Program (CODIP), 304–305
Children's Apperception Test (CAT), 183
Children's Depression Inventory (CDI), 487–488
Children's PTSD Inventory (CPTSDI), 411–412
children's rights, ethics in counseling and, 94–120
Children's Yale-Brown Obsessive Scale (CY-BOS), 463–464
child-to-child abuse, 103
choice theory
axioms of, 163
changes to environments and relationships, 165
counseling concepts and goals, 161–163
development of, 160
family involvement and intervention, 167–168
process and procedures, 164–165
self-evaluation, 166–167
chronic illness counseling, 525–531
chronic health conditions, 525–526
chronosystem, 264
circular causality, 212
circular questioning, 221
classical conditioning
behavior therapy, 124
disruptive behavior, 384–385
interventions, 131–135

classroom management, 48–49
classroom resources, 49
client-centered therapy, 171–172
client expectations
in counseling, 64–66
counseling approaches and, 254–255
premature termination and, 90–93
client resistance, psychodynamic therapy, 184–185
climate, school climate, 48–49
Clinician-Administered PTSD Scales, 411–412
cliques, 335
closed adoption, 311–313
cognition
behavior therapy, 123
contextual framework, 263
suicide and, 281
Cognitive Behavioral Intervention for Trauma in Schools (CBITS), 425
cognitive behavioral play therapy, 240, 242–243
divorce and, 304
cognitive behavior therapy (CBT)
ADHD, 354–360
anorexia nervosa, 514–516
assessment, 148
basic principles, 122
bulimia nervosa, 516
chronic illness and disability, 529–531
core concepts and counseling goals, 140–146
counselor's role in, 146–147
depressive disorders, 494–495
disruptive behavior problems, 386–389
family interventions and involvement, 157–160
historical evolution, 138–140
intellectual disabilities clients, 369–370
nonsuicidal self-injury, 289
OCD, 464–465, 477–478
parental substance abuse, 314–315
process and procedures, 147–160
resistance to, 76
substance abuse, 445–446
test anxiety, 329–330
traditional interventions, 148–151
trauma, 416–420
cognitive development
early adolescence, 24
in early childhood, 9–10
late adolescence, 29–30
middle childhood, 16–17
stage theory, 5–6
cognitive disorders, middle childhood, 16
cognitive distortions, 142
OCD and awareness of, 468, 470–473
cognitive model of depression, 142
cognitive restructuring, 141
depressive and bipolar disorders, 497–499
disruptive behavior problems, 386–389
cognitive skills training, 470–473
cognitive therapy, 138, 141–142
time management and academic achievement, 325–326
collaboration
approaches using, 254–255
on change, 78–80
collaborative empiricism, 147
college readiness, 332
Color Candy Crunch, 218
Combined Parent-Child Cognitive Behavioral Therapy (CPC-CBT), 425

commitment
    in early adolescence, 24–25
    promotion in reality therapy of, 164
Commitment to Counseling Statement, 284–286
committed actions, acceptance and commitment
        therapy, 145
communication skills
    autism spectrum disorders, 360
    in counseling process, 59, 116–117
    emotion expression exercises, 74–75
    family, 42, 218–220
    family therapy, 217–218
    middle childhood, 19
    step- and blended families, 307–309
    working stage of counseling, 71–75
community
    defined, 51
    genogram of resources and strengths, 265
    neighborhood norms, 52–53
    risk and protective factors, 38–39, 51–55
    substance abuse interventions, 450–451
    technology and, 54
    violence and crime in, 53–54
competence in counseling
    requirements for, 97
    suicide counseling, 280
complex emotions, middle childhood, 19–20
complex trauma, 410
Comprehensive Alcohol Abuse and Alcoholism
        Prevention, Treatment, and Rehabilitation Act,
        109–110
conceptual framework
    assessment process, 268–269
    components, 259–275
concrete operational cognitive development, 5–6
    middle childhood, 16
conduct disorder, assessment, 383
confidentiality, 99–101
    in counseling, 63
    of documents, 108–110
    federal laws, 108–110
    school setting, 102–103
congruence, 201–204, 238
Connecting the Smell, 157
conscious, in psychodynamic theory, 175
consciousness, 175
consent for treatment
    child custody cases, 111–113
    ethics and, 97–98
consequences
    behavior assessment, 129
    logical and natural, 199
constipation, 520–525
contemplation stage, of change, 77–80
context
    evidence-based counseling, 255–257
    systemically informed youth counseling, 35–36
    understanding of, 116
contextual assessment, 262–267
contingency management, 129–130
    substance abuse, 446
contingent reinforcement, OCD and, 474–476
continuum of care, 269–271
Coping Cat exercise, 159, 477
core beliefs, 142
core conditions, 203
Core Essentials program, 338–339
corporal punishment, 260–261

corrective emotional experiences, 187
counseling
    aims and objectives, 272–274
    defined, 1, 57
    early adolescence, 27–29
    early childhood, 12–15
    family therapy, 209–227
    foundational skills, 58–60
    late adolescence, 31–32
    middle childhood, 20–22
    motivation and, 75–80
    physical setting, 60–61
    play and creative arts in, 228–252
    predictable structure in, 62
    preliminary considerations, 60–71
    structuring of, 66–69
    summary of behavioral experiential theories,
        206–208
    summary of behavioral theories, 168–170
    technology and, 80–81
    termination, 81–93
    working stage of, 71–81
counselors
    evaluation of, 64–66
    reaction to child abuse reporting, 104–105
counterconditioning, 132
countertransference, 182
    defined, 260
    psychodynamic therapy, 185–186
court testimony, child custody proceedings, 112–113
creative arts
    in counseling, 228–229, 245–252
    specialization and certification for counseling, 230
creativity
    in art counseling, 246–252
    in termination of counseling, 87–89
crime, in community, 53–54
crises, in early adolescence, 24–25
crisis cards, 295–296
crisis intervention models, 427–429
Cultural Formulation Interview (CFI), 265–267
culture
    child abuse and, 103–104
    conceptual framework and, 261
    demographics and, 264–267
    disruptive behavior and, 376–384
    evidence-based counseling, 255–257
    family communication and, 42
    grief, loss, and bereavement and, 315–321
    play therapy and, 234–235
    premature termination and, 91
    PTSD and, 409–410
    systemically informed youth counseling, 34–35
    understanding of, 116
cycle of counseling, 164–165
cystic fibrosis, 526

D

Dating Matters: Strategies to Promote Healthy Teen
        Relationships, 345
DBT Skills Training Manual, 151
DEAR MAN GIVE FAST script, 155
death, youth perceptions of, 316–321
decentering, 144
decision making
    bipolar disorder flowchart, 493
    client/guardian involvement in, 117
    ethical guidelines, 115–120

defense mechanisms, 175–177
demographics
    contextual framework and, 264–267
    suicide prediction, 280–281
dependency stage, experiential play therapy, 239
depersonalization, 409
depressive disorders
    assessment, 487–488
    cognitive model of, 142
    disruptive behavior problems, 381–382
    incidence and prevalence, 482
    integrated treatment, 495–504
    interventions, 494–495
    mixed features, 483
    symptoms, 483–486
    time management and, 325
    types, 486–487
derealization, 409
desensitization, 132
determinism, drive theory and, 173–175
detoxification programs, 444–445
development
    context in counseling and, 257, 262
    defined, 1
    early adolescence, 23–29
    early childhood, 9–15
    late adolescence, 29–33
    middle childhood, 15–23
    milestones, 1–2
    psychosexual stages of, 174–175
    psychosocial, 7–8, 177
    risk factors, 2–3
    self-development, 7
    substance abuse and, 433–436, 443–444
    youth development, 4–8
developmentally informed youth counseling,
        1–34
diabetes, 526–531
*Diagnostic and Statistical Manual of Mental
        Disorders, Fifth Edition* (APA), 64,
        257, 287
    anxiety and obsessive-compulsive disorders, 455,
        457–459, 462–463
    bipolar disorders, 491
    depressive disorders, 486–487
    disruptive behaviors, 375, 379–380
    eating disorders, 506
    elimination disorders, 518–519
    grief, loss, and bereavement, 316–317
    substance abuse disorders, 437–440
    trauma and stressor-related disorders, 397
diagnostic interview, disruptive behavior assessment,
        382
dialectical behavior therapy (DBT), 138,
        143–144
    bulimia nervosa, 516–518
    depressive disorders, 495
    disruptive behaviors, 384, 391–392
    family involvement, 159
    interventions, 151–155
    nonsuicidal self-injury, 289
    OCD, 465
    stages and goals, 152
dialectical biosocial theory, 144
dichotomous think, 142
diffusion, 144
direction, in reality therapy, 166
DIRECTION decision-making model, 119–120

directive play therapy, 236, 240–245
directives, in family therapy, 225–226
disability counseling, 525–531
discharge plans, termination process, 86
discrepancies, free association, 188
discrete trial training, 364
disengagement, 213, 222–223
disinhibited social engagement disorder, 408–409
disorganized attachment, 178–179
disruptive behavior problems, 375–396
    anxiety or depression, 381–382
    assessment, 382–384
    cognitive restructuring abilities, 386–389
    dialectical behavior therapy, 384, 391–392
    differential diagnoses, 381–382
    evolution, 378–379
    integrated treatment, 384
    interventions, 384–386
    mindfulness skills, 386–387
    neurodevelopmental disorders, 381
    problem-solving skills training (PSST), 384, 390–391
    in youth, 376–384
distress reduction, 414–415
distress tolerance, 153–154
divorce/parental separation, 300–305
    child custody proceedings, 111–113
documentation guidelines, 115
    suicide counseling, 280
doing, in reality therapy, 166
domestic adoption, 311–313
dominant lifestyle, 192, 194
Down syndrome, 9
dream analysis, 175, 187–188
drive theory, 173–175
    free association, 188
DSM-5 Parent/Guardian-Rated Level 1 Cross-Cutting Symptom Measure, 383
dyad, 213
dynamics, family therapy, 212
dysphoric disorder, 486

E

early adolescence, 23–29
    cognitive development, 24
    counseling in, 27–29
    emotional development, 26–27
    physical development, 23–24
    psychosocial development, 26
    self-development, 24–25
early childhood
    cognitive development in, 9–10
    communication skills for, 73
    counseling in, 12–15
    defined, 9
    development in, 9–15
    divorce/parental separation impact on, 301–305
    emotional development, 12
    group counseling, 13–15
    physical development, 9
    problems in, 12–13
    psychosocial development, 11
    self-development, 10–11
Early Intensive Behavioral Intervention (EIBI), 364–365
Early Start Denver Model (ESDM), 364–365
eating disorders
    interventions, 513–518
    overview, 506–509

echolalia, 360
ecological systems theory, 263–264
ego
    functioning, 175
    psychology, 175–177
    structural model of personality, 174–175
egocentrism, in early adolescence, 26
elimination disorders, 518–525
emotional abuse, 403–404
emotional detectives exercise, 496
emotional development, 8–9
    early adolescence, 26–27
    early childhood, 12
    late adolescence, 31
    middle childhood, 19–20
emotional mind, 153
emotional processing, trauma interventions, 416
emotional reasoning, 142
emotional regulation, early childhood, 12
emotional schema therapy, 143
emotional wellness, 335–336
emotion expression exercises, 74–75
emotion identification, early childhood, 12
emotion regulation, 151–152, 485
emotions
    behavior therapy, 123
    context in counseling and, 262
empathic understanding, 204
encopresis, 518–525
    interventions and treatment, 523–525
Enhanced Cognitive Behavior Therapy for Eating Disorders (CBT-E), 515–516
enmeshment, 213, 222–223
enuresis, 518–525
    intervention and treatment, 522
environmental factors
    autism spectrum disorder, 360
    intellectual disabilities, 366
environments, reality therapy and changes to, 165
equanimity, 143
escape, behavior assessment, 129
ethical decision-making model, 118–119
Ethical Standards for School Counselors, 102–103
ethics in counseling
    case study, 96–97
    child maltreatment reporting, 103–108
    codes of ethics, 95–96
    competence, 97
    consent issues, 97–98
    decision-making guidelines, 115–120
    definitions, 95–96
    legal foundations, 94–120
    minors' rights, 97–98
    professional standards, 117
    suicide, 280
ethnicity
    behavioral characteristics, 376–384
    culture and context and, 35–36
    family structure and boundaries and, 40–42
    neighborhood norms and, 52
    suicide and, 280–281
everyday mindfulness activities, 157
evidence-based counseling, 255–257
evocation, change and, 78–80
excesses, free association, 188
excoriation disorder, 463
exosystems, 264

Expect Respect program, 338
experiential avoidance, 145
experiential play therapy, 238–240
exploratory stage, experiential play therapy, 239
exposure-based intervention, 132–134
    OCD and, 477
expressive arts therapy, 200–201, 228–252, 230
    divorce and, 304
extinction techniques, 125
eye movement desensitization and reprocessing (EMDR), 132, 134, 425–426

F

families and family systems
    academic development, 47–48
    adoption, 311–313
    adult partner violence, 405–406
    anorexia nervosa intervention, 513–516
    behavior therapy interventions and involvement, 136–138
    child abuse and, 43–44
    chronic illness and disability and, 527–531
    cognitive behavioral therapy interventions and involvement, 157–160
    communication, 42
    communication, in, 42, 218–220
    defined, 40, 210
    depression and bipolar therapy and, 502
    disruptive behavior and, 376, 392–394
    divorce/parental separation, 300–305
    early adolescence, 26
    goals and interventions in counseling, 47
    grief, loss and bereavement, 315–321
    individual psychology interventions and involvement, 198–199
    intellectual disabilities clients, 369–370
    involvement and support, 42–43
    involvement in counseling, 116
    kinship caregivers, 309–311
    late adolescence, 30–31
    parental substance abuse, 313–315
    person-centered therapy, 205
    premature termination and expectations of, 90–93
    protective factors, 38–47
    psychodynamic therapy interventions and involvement, 189–190
    reality therapy involvement and intervention, 167–168
    school attendance and, 330–331
    step- and blended families, 306–309
    structural transitions in, 300–313
    structure and boundaries, 42–43, 213, 222–223, 300–301
    substance abuse interventions, 443, 449–450
    transitions and struggles of, 299–323
    trauma intervention and, 422–423
family-based treatment (FBT), 513–516, 518
family behavior therapy (FBT), 450
family constellation, 196
Family Educational Rights and Privacy Act, 108–109
Family picture exercise, 319
family therapy, 209–227
    basic principles, 209–210
    boundaries in, 42–43, 213, 222–223
    communication facilitation, 217–218
    core concepts, 210–213
    counselor's role, 213–214

depressive disorders, 495
directives and out-of-session assignments, 225–226
family CBT, 159
feedback loops, 223–224
functionality in family system, 213
interventions, 216–226
processes in, 214–216
promoting insight, 220–221
reciprocal influence, 212
reframing in, 221–222
substance abuse, 450
FEAR Plan, 159, 477–478
federal law, confidentiality, 108–110
feedback loops, family therapy, 223–225
feelings
  awareness of, 116
  context in counseling and, 262
  reflection of, 204–205
felt minus, 191–193
fetal alcohol syndrome. *See* alcohol-related neurodevelopmental disorder
fictive final goal, 192–193
52-Card Pick, 218
filial play therapy, 238, 240
Finish the Sentence, 319
504 Plan, 372
flexibility, in counseling process, 59
flooding, 133–134, 477
floortime, 365
focused attention, 143
food allergies, 526
formal operational cognitive development, 5–6
  in early adolescence, 24
  in late adolescence, 29–30
fortune telling, 142
42 CFR guidelines, 443
forward motion and creativity, 192–193
free association, 175, 188
  play therapy and, 232–233
friendships
  difficulties with, 335–336
  early adolescence, 27
  middle childhood, 19–20
functional analysis, 126
  nonsuicidal self-injury, 290
functional behavior assessment (FBA), 126, 128–129
functionality, family system, 213
fusion, 180, 223

G

gender
  anorexia and, 510
  bulimia and, 512
  community norms and, 52–53
  conceptual framework and, 261–262
  depressive disorders and, 482, 486
  divorce/parental separation impact and, 302–305
  evidence-based counseling approach, 256–257
  nonsuicidal self-injury, 288–289
  puberty onset and, 23
  suicide and, 280–281
gender-nonconforming clients, 339
generalization, operant conditioning, 125
genital stage of development, 174–175
genogram
  community strengths and resources, 265
  example, 215–217

getting lifestyle, 192, 194
Golden Thread, 257
Goodbye Letter, 88
grandparents, as kinship caregivers, 310–311
Gray Oral Reading Test, 371
grief, loss, and bereavement, 315–321
grounding techniques, trauma therapy, 415–416
group counseling
  early childhood, 13–15
  grief, loss, and bereavement, 319–321
  late adolescence, 32–33
  mindfulness-based group programs, 145–146
  social skills training, 135–136
  substance abuse, 445–449
group norms, early adolescence, 26
guardian *ad litem,* 113
guardians, 95
  confidentiality laws and, 108–110
  kinship caregivers, 309–311
  legal rights of, 97–98
guided discovery, 147, 150

H

habit reversal training (HRT), 476–477
Health Insurance Portability and Accountability Act (HIPAA), 108, 443
healthy boundaries, in families, 213
healthy narcissism, 179–180
hierarchical structural organization model, 141–142
homeostasis, family therapy, 223–225
homework assignments
  social skills training, 136
  time management problems, 325–327
homicide, 292–296
  client characteristics, 293–294
  counselor considerations, 292–293
  incidence and prevalence, 292
  interventions, 295–296
  risk assessment, 294–298
Hopelessness Scale for Children (HSC), 487–488
House-Tree-Person Projective Drawing Technique (HTP), 183
humanistic psychology, 200
hyperactivity, in ADHD, 349–350
hyperalertness, trauma intervention, 420
hyperfocus ability, 349
hypersexuality, bipolar disorder and, 490
hypomania, 483, 489–490

I

I CAN START model, 254, 258–275
  anxiety and OCD disorders, 480
  case study, 275–276
  depressive and bipolar disorders, 504–505
  disruptive behaviors, 394–395
  eating disorders, 531–532
  grief, loss, and bereavement, 321–322
  learning disabilities, 372–373
  social–emotional transitions, 346–347
  substance abuse, 452–453
  trauma-related disorders, 428–429
id, structural model of personality, 174–175
idealized self-objects, 180
identified client/patient, family therapy, 210
identity
  early adolescence, 24–25
  late adolescence, 30–31

middle childhood, 17–18
  trauma intervention and enhancement of, 420–422
identity formation, adoption, 313
identity vs. identity role confusion, 24–25
If-Then-But activity, 500–501
imagery activities, 465–466
imaginary audience, in early adolescence, 26
immediacy, 204–205
implosion, 133–134
IMPROVE process, dialectical behavior therapy, 153–155
impulse-control disorders, 379–380
Impulse Control Log, 292
impulsivity, in ADHD, 350
incentives, in counseling sessions, 61–62
incompatible behaviors, 385
incomplete sentence activities, 42
incongruence, 201–202
indirect directives, 225
individual counseling
  counseling process, 194–198
  counselor's role in, 194
  foundations of, 57–93
  substance abuse, 445–449
Individualized Education Plan (IEP), 110–111, 372
individual psychology, 171, 190–199
  core concepts and counseling, 191–194
  family interventions and involvement, 198–199
  lifestyle assessment, 196–197
  mistaken goals in, 195
Individuals with Disabilities Education Act (IDEA), 109–110
industry vs. inferiority, 18–19
inferiority complex, 193
informed consent, 62, 98–100
  child custody proceedings, 112–113
  family therapy, 214–216
  guidelines for obtaining, 117
  school setting, 102–103
initiative vs. guilt, 11
inner experience observations, 143, 172
insight, in psychodynamic therapy, 188–189
insight-oriented counseling, parental substance abuse, 314–315
instrumental conditioning, 124–125
intake process, 62
integrated treatment
  depressive and bipolar disorders, 495–504
  disruptive behavior problems, 384, 392–394
  obsessive-compulsive disorders, 465–479
  substance abuse, 444–452
intellectual disabilities, 366–370
  assessment, 368
  autism and, 362
  case management, intellectual disabilities, 369–370
  counseling role in, 367
  interventions, 369–370
  levels of severity, 367–368
intellectual impairment, 348–374
intelligence quotient (IQ)
  autism spectrum disorder, 361
  intellectual disabilities, 366–370
intensive outpatient treatment (IOP), substance abuse, 442–443
intergenerational patterns, 225–226
intermediate beliefs, 141
international adoption, 311–313
interpersonal and social rhythm therapy (ISRT), 495
interpersonal effectiveness, 153–155

interpersonal relationships, culture and context and, 36
interpersonal skills, in counseling, 58
interpersonal therapy, 494
interpretations, in psychodynamic therapy, 188–189
interventions
    ADHD, 354–360
    autism spectrum disorder, 363–365
    chronic illness and disability, 528–531
    classical conditioning, 131–135
    cognitive behavioral therapy, 148–151
    community-based, 450–451
    creative counseling, 246–252
    dialectical behavior therapy, 151–155
    disruptive behavior, 384–386
    eating disorders, 513–518
    elimination disorders, 521–522
    evidence-based approaches, 255–257
    family therapy, 216–226
    grief, loss, and bereavement, 319–321
    homicide, 295–296
    impulsivity and restlessness, 350–351
    intellectual disabilities, 369–370
    learning disabilities, 372
    mindfulness-based therapies, 155–157
    nonsuicidal self-injury, 289–292
    operant conditioning, 129–131
    person-centered therapy, 204–205
    play therapy, 235–245
    psychodynamic therapy, 186, 189–190
    reality therapy, 167–168
    research-based interventions, 274
    substance abuse, 443–444, 450–451
    suicide prevention, 283–287
    trauma counseling, 413–423
intimacy and dating, 342–343
intimate partner violence, 45–47, 343–345
    incidence and prevalence, 405–406
introspection, trauma therapy and, 420–422
in vivo exposure, 133–134

J

joint attention intervention, 364
Joven Noble program, 345

K

KATIE model, grief, loss, and bereavement, 319
Kaufman Brief Intelligence Test, 368
kinship caregivers, 309–311
KiVa bullying prevention program, 338

L

labeling/mislabeling, 142
late adolescence
    cognitive development, 29–30
    counseling in, 31–32
    development, 29–33
    emotional development, 31
    physical development, 29
    psychosocial development, 30–31
    self-development, 30
latency stage of development, 174–175
law, ethics and, 96
learning, behavior therapy and, 123
learning disability, 370–372

learning disorders, 370–372
legitimate education interest, confidentiality and, 109
Leiter-3 International Performance Scale, 368
lesbian, gay, bisexual, transgender, and questioning (LGBTQ) youth, 339–342
    counseling framework and, 261–262
    suicide and, 281
letting go exercise, 143, 156–157
level of care, 269–271
    substance abuse, 442–443
LGBTQQIA. See lesbian, gay, bisexual, transgender, and questioning (LGBTQ) youth
licensure boards, 96
lifestyle patterns, 192, 194
    assessment process, 196, 241–242
limitations of counseling, 116
linear causality, 212
Listening Dance, 157
logical consequences, 199
loss behaviors. See grief, loss, and bereavement
love object, 179
Love Your Image, 512

M

macrosystem, 264
magical thinking, 526
Magic Door to Happiness Activity, 497
magnification, 142
maintenance plans, termination process, 86
maintenance stage of change, 77–80
mania, 483, 489–490
masked depression, 488
Maslow's hierarchy of needs, early childhood and, 11
mass violence, terror, or disaster, 406–407
Mastering Each New Direction (MEND) program, 531
Maudsley Method, 513–516
MBSR for School-Age Children, 159–160
media, in counseling sessions, 61
Memory Book, 89
mental disability
    IDEA and, 110
    Section 504, 110–111
mental disorders
    co-occurrence with autism, 362
    depression and, 488
    intellectual disabilities and, 368
    nonsuicidal self-injury, 288–289
    substance abuse and, 441–442
    suicide and, 281
mental filtering, 142
mental status examination, 268–269
mesosystems, 264
Message to My Body activity, 512
metacognition, 143–144
    ADHD therapies, 356–360
methadone, 452
microaggressions, 36
microsystems, 263
    families as, 299–300
middle child, individual psychology, 198
middle childhood
    cognitive development, 16–17
    communication skills for, 73
    counseling in, 20–22
    development, 15–23
    divorce/parental separation impact on, 301–305
    emotional development, 19–20

physical development, 15–16
    psychosocial development, 18–19
    puberty in, 15–16
    self-development, 17–18
mindfulness
    dialectical behavior therapy, 152–155
    disruptive behavior problems, 386–387
mindfulness-based cognitive therapy (MBCT), 138, 143, 146
mindfulness-based cognitive therapy for children (MBCT-C), 146, 155–157, 159–160
mindfulness-based stress reduction (MBSR), 138, 143, 145–146, 155–157, 159–160
mindfulness-based therapies, 138, 142–144
    family involvement, 160
    group programs, 145–146
    interventions, 155–157
mind reading, 142
minimization, 142
minors
    defined, 95
    rights of, 97–98
mirroring, 180
mirror transference, 180
modeling
    autism spectrum disorder, 364
    social learning and, 125
    social skills training, 136
monitoring, in counseling process, 59
mood management, 414–415
motivation, in counseling, 75–80
motivational interviewing (MI), 77–78, 201
    nonsuicidal self-injury, 291
    substance abuse, 446–448
multidimensional family therapy (MDFT), 450
multiple relationships, in counseling, 113–114
multisystemic therapy, 384, 393–394
    family therapy, 450
music therapy, 248–249
My Body Agreement, 511
My Colorful Emotions, 157
My Comic Strip, 499
My Creations, 291
My Mask, 417
My Pretend Image, 157
My Progress in Color, 292
My Self-Care Assessment, 118
Mystery Bag activity, 156
My Strength Book, 271
My Strength Bracelet, 271

N

narcissistic injury, 179–180
narrative therapy, 250
    trauma, 416–419
National Survey on Drug Use and Health (NSDUH), 430
natural consequences, 199
natural termination, 82–89
necessary level of care, 269–271
needs
    reality therapy and, 161–163
    WDEP system, 166
negative feedback loop, 224
negative reinforcement, 125
    disruptive behaviors, 385
negative replacement exercises, 290
neglect, 44, 103–108, 404–405
neighborhood norms, 52–53

neurodevelopmental disorders, 348–374
　　ADHD, 349–360
　　autism spectrum disorder, 360–365
　　disruptive behaviors, 381
neurofeedback, 354
NICHQ Vanderbilt Assessment Scales, 353
nondirective play therapy, 236–240
nonjudgment of inner experience, 143
nonnormative school transitions, 331, 333–335
nonreactivity, 143
nonstimulation medications, ADHD, 359–360
nonstriving, 143
nonsuicidal self-injury, 287–292
　　assessment, 288–289
　　client characteristics, 288–289
　　counseling considerations, 287–288
　　intervention, 289–292
nonverbal communication
　　early childhood, 12
　　in working stage of counseling, 71–75
normative school transitions, 331–333
norms, neighborhood, 52–53
no-suicide contract, 284
nutrition, elimination disorders, 524–525

O

object relations theory
　　family therapy, 190
　　psychodynamic therapy, 177–178
obsessive-compulsive disorders (OCDs)
　　assessment, 463–464
　　counseling interventions, 464–465
　　differential diagnosis, 463–464
　　incidence and prevalence, 455
　　integrated treatment, 465–479
　　physical symptoms, awareness of, 467–468
　　symptoms, 460–462
　　types of, 462–463
oldest children, individual psychology, 196–198
Olewus Bullying Prevention Program, 338
Olson Circumplex Model, 41–42, 212–213
omissions, free association, 188
only children, 198
open adoption, 311–313
open-ended questions, 205
operant conditioning
　　behavior therapy, 124–125
　　disruptive behavior, 385
　　elimination disorders, 523
　　interventions, 129–131
opioids, 452
oppositional defiant disorder, assessment, 383
oral stage of development, 174–175
outcomes assessment, 115
outside-of-session assignments, 225–226
overgeneralization, 142
oversensitivity, 361–362

P

paining behaviors, 162
paradoxical injunctions, 225
parallel play, 184
paraphrasing, person-centered therapy, 205
parental rights
　　confidentiality and, 99–101
　　ethics in counseling and, 95–120
parental separation. *See* divorce/parental
　　separation

parenting
　　academic development and influence of, 48
　　for ADHD children, 354–360
　　adoption, 311–313
　　anorexia interventions, 513–516
　　for autistic clients, 362–365
　　behavior therapy interventions and involvement,
　　　136–138
　　child-parent relationship therapy (CPRT), 205
　　chronic illness and disability and, 527
　　cognitive behavioral therapy interventions and
　　　involvement, 157–160
　　communication skills in, 217–220
　　disruptive behavior and, 376
　　in divorce, 304–305
　　divorce and separation and, 301–305
　　eating disorders and, 506–507
　　individual psychology interventions and
　　　involvement, 198–199
　　intellectual disabilities clients, 369–370
　　in middle childhood, 18
　　object relations family therapy, 190
　　OCD therapy, 477–479
　　parental substance abuse, 313–315
　　play therapy and, 234–235
　　reality therapy interventions and, 167–168
　　school attendance and, 330–331
　　step- and blended families, 307–309
　　trauma therapy and, 422–423
Parent Involvement Program (PIP), 167–168
parent management training (PMT), 137–138,
　　392–393
peer relationships
　　early adolescence, 26
　　late adolescence, 30–32
　　in school, 49–50
　　self-development and, 7
　　victimization, 402
peer training, 364–365
perceived plus, 191–193
perceptions, WDEP system, 166
performance therapy, 251
perinatal risk factors, autism spectrum disorder, 360
permissive parenting, 18
personal attitudes, values and beliefs, awareness of, 116
personal identity, late adolescence, 30–31
personality
　　context in counseling and, 262–263
　　structural model of, 174–175
personalization, 142
personally held principles, ethics and, 96
personal strengths and resources collage, 275
person-centered therapy, 171–172, 200–205
　　core concepts and counseling goals, 201–202
　　counselor's role in, 202–203
　　expressive arts therapy, 200
　　family interventions and involvement, 205
　　process, 203–204
phallic stage of development, 174–175
phenomenological experience, 201
physical abuse, 402
physical development
　　early adolescence, 23–24
　　early childhood, 9
　　late adolescence, 29
　　middle childhood, 15–16
physical disability
　　counseling for, 525–526
　　IDEA and, 110

Section 504, 110–111
physical discomfort
　　disruptive behavior and, 382
　　OCD and awareness of, 467–468
physical effects, behavior assessment, 129
physical setting, counseling and, 60–61
picture album, 161
Pivotal Response Treatment (PRT), 364–365
planning, in reality therapy, 167
play, 175
　　assessment in, 182–183
　　in counseling, 228, 230–252
　　parallel play, 184
play therapy
　　child-centered, 200–201
　　cleanup procedures, 235
　　directive, 236, 240–245
　　foundations, 232–233
　　goals of, 228–245
　　grief, loss, and bereavement, 321
　　nondirective, 236–240
　　overview of approaches, 237
　　psychodynamic theory and, 186–187
　　setting, 232
　　specialization and certification, 230
　　techniques and interventions, 235–245
　　toys and materials, 229
　　trauma, 416–417
positive feedback loop, 224–225
positive parenting, 304
Positive Parenting Program, 308–309
Positive Puzzle, 271
positive reinforcement, 125
　　disruptive behaviors, 385
　　obsessive-compulsive disorder, 476
Positive Self-Talk Shield, 499
Positive Thinking Cards, 499
posttraumatic stress disorder (PTSD), 398
　　characteristics, 409–410
　　child abuse and neglect, 44
　　mass violence, terror and disaster, 406–407
　　risk factors, 399
power, Adlerian play therapy, 241
Power Animals, 271
practices and methods, articulation of, 116–117
preconscious, in psychodynamic theory, 175
precontemplation stage, changes and, 77–80
predictability, in counseling process, 62
premature termination, 82, 90–93
　　avoidance of, 91–92
　　culture and, 91
prenatal risk factors, autism spectrum
　　disorder, 360
preoperative cognitive development stage, 5–6
　　early childhood, 10
preparation stage, for change, 77–80
presence, person-centered interventions, 204
pretend directive, 226
prevention plans, termination process, 86
PRIDE model, step- and blended families,
　　307–308
privacy, 99–100
privileged communication, 100
problem definition in counseling, 115–116
problem-solving skills training (PSST), 384,
　　390–391
problem-solving therapy, 289–290
　　depressive and bipolar disorders, 499–500
　　OCD and, 473–475

processing disorders, ADHD, 349
procrastination, time management and, 325–327
professional counseling associations, 117
professional development, ethics in counseling and, 117
professional liability insurance, 117
progressive muscle relaxation (PMR), 132–133
protective factors
    bullying and school violence, 50–51
    community, 38–39, 51–55
    divorce, 303
    family system, 38–47, 299
    intimate partner violence, 46–47
    school system, 47–51
psychodrama, 251
psychodynamic theory and therapy
    asssessment, 182–183
    attachment theory, 178–179
    basic principles, 171–173
    catharsis, 187
    client resistance, 184–185
    core concepts and counseling goals, 173–182
    counseling process, 182–189
    counselor's goal, 182
    countertransference, 185–186
    dream analysis, 187–188
    drive theory, 173–175
    ego psychology, 175–177
    family interventions and involvement, 189–190
    free association, 175, 188
    goals, 181–182
    interpretations and insight, 188–189
    interventions, 186
    object relations theory, 177–178
    phases of counseling, 181
    play, 186–187
    rapport in, 183–184
    self-psychology, 179–180
    separation-individuation theory, 179
psychoeducation, 137
    depressive and bipolar disorders, 496–497
    grief, loss, and bereavement, 318–321
    substance abuse, 448–450
    test anxiety, 329–330
    trauma intervention, 414
psychological factors, substance abuse, 432–437
psychological first aid, 427
psychopathology, self-psychology and, 180
psychopharmacotherapy
    ADHD, 359
    anxiety and OCD disorders, 464–465, 478–479
    bulimia nervosa, 518
    depressive and bipolar disorders, 502–504
    disruptive behaviors, 394
    eating disorders, 516
    enuresis, 523
    for intellectual disabilities clients, 369–370
    substance abuse, 451–452
    trauma-related disorders, 427
psychosexual stages of development, 174–175
psychosocial crises, 7–8
psychosocial development, 7–8, 177
    early adolescence, 26
    early childhood, 11
    late adolescence, 30–31
    middle childhood, 18–19
puberty
    early adolescence, 23–24

    intimacy and dating and, 342–343
    middle childhood, 15–16
punishment, 125
    disruptive behavior, 385

Q

quality world, 161

R

race
    child abuse and, 103–104
    community norms and, 52–53
    culture and context and, 35–36
    family structure and boundaries and, 40–42
    intellectual disabilities, 366
    suicide and, 280–281
randomized controlled trials, 255
rapport
    in psychodynamic therapy, 183–184
    in reality therapy, 163–164
rational emotive behavior therapy (REBT), 138, 140–141, 147, 149–150
rational mind, 153
reactive attachment disorder, 398, 408–409
reading disabilities, 371–372
reading therapy, 250–251
reality therapy
    basic principles, 122
    changes to environments and relationships, 165
    counseling concepts and goals, 161–163
    counselor's role in, 163–164
    development of, 160
    family involvement and intervention, 167–168
    planning in, 167
    process and procedures, 164–167
    rapport establishment in, 163–164
    responsibility and commitment in, 164
    self-evaluation in, 166–167
    teaching and advocacy in, 164
reciprocal influence, 212
reciprocal inhibition, 132
reciprocity, friendship and, 335–336
Recovery High programs, 451
referral, termination and, 92–93
reflection of feelings, 204–205
reframing
    in family therapy, 221–222
    time management and academic achievement, 326–327
Registered Art Therapist (ATR), 230
Registered Play Therapist (RPT), 230
Registered Play Therapist-Supervisor (RPT-S), 230
Registered Sandplay Therapists (STRs), 244
regressive defenses, 175–177
Rehabilitation Act of 1973, Section 504. See Section 504
reinforcement, operant conditioning, 124–125
relational counseling approach, 254–255
relational factors, behavior therapy, 126
relational frame theory, 145
relationships
    reality therapy and changes to, 165
    strategies for building, 70–71
Relationship Smart Plus, 345
relaxation training, 465–466
    chronic illness and training, 530
release play therapy, 240, 243

religion, grief, loss, and bereavement and, 317–321
Reminder Jar, 118
repetitive behavior/speech, autism spectrum disorder, 360
child maltreatment/abuse reporting guidelines
    aftermath of filing, 107–108
    assessment, 106
    child abuse and neglect, 103–108
    components of report, 106–107
    counselors' personal reactions, 104–105
    statutory requirements, 105
repressive defenses, 175–177
research-based interventions, 274
resiliency factors
    child abuse and neglect and, 44–45
    school violence, 51
    strength-based perspective and, 37–38
    trauma and, 399
    youth development, 2, 4
resistance, in counseling, 76
respondent conditioning, 124
response cost, 131
responsibility, promotion in reality therapy of, 164
restricting type anorexia, 509–510
revenge, Adlerian play therapy, 242
revictimization, trauma and, 400
Revised Children's Manifest Anxiety Scales-Second Edition (RCMAS-2), 459–460
risk factors
    autism spectrum disorder, 360
    bullying and school violence, 50–51
    community, 38–39, 51–55
    divorce, 303
    family system, 38–47
    homicide, 293–294
    intellectual disabilities, 366
    intimate partner violence, 46–47, 344–345
    nonsuicidal self-injury, 288–289
    posttraumatic stress disorder, 399
    psychosocial development, 11
    school system, 47–51
    substance abuse, 431–432
    suicide, 281–283
    youth development, 2–3
risk-taking, late adolescence, 31–32
rituals, in counseling termination, 87–89
role complementarity, 189
role models, violence reduction and, 54
role-playing, social skills training, 136
Rorschach Inkblot Test, 183

S

SAD PERSONS assessment tool, 282–283
Safe Dates, 345
Safety Animal exercise, 291
safety plans
    child maltreatment/abuse, 107
    homicide intervention, 295
    intimate partner violence, 344–345
    suicide counseling, 280
    trauma counseling, 413–414
SAMHSA National Registry of Evidence-Based Programs and Practices, 198–199, 272, 413, 430, 451
sandplay, 244–245
scheduling technique, autism spectrum disorder, 365
schemas, 142
Scholastic Reading Inventory (SRI), 371

School Based-Registered Play Therapist (SB-RPT), 230
school counseling
    academic problems, 324–331
    attendance problems, 330–331
    social–emotional transitions and, 335–345
    substance abuse interventions, 451
school refusal, 330–331
school setting
    bullying and violence in, 50–51
    climate in, 48–49
    disability laws and, 110–111
    informed consent/assent and confidentiality in, 102–103
    peer relationships in, 49–50
    risk and protective factors, 38–39, 47–51
    school transitions, 331–335
    suicide prevention and intervention, 286–287
school transitions, 331–335
scope of practice, 116
scripting therapy, 251
secondborn children, 196–198
Section 504, 110–111
secure attachment, 178–179, 183–184
selective abstractions, 142
selective serotonin reuptake inhibitors (SSRIs), 427, 478–479, 516
    bulimia nervosa, 518
self-actualization, 201–202
self-awareness, in counseling process, 59
self-care, for counselors, 117–118
Self-Care Action Plan, 118
Self-Care Calendar, 118
self-cohesion, 180
self-compassion, 143
self-concepts, 7
    early childhood, 10–11
    friendship and, 336
    intimacy and dating and, 343
    in school, 49
self-development
    early adolescence, 24–25
    early childhood, 10–11
    late adolescence, 30
    middle childhood, 17–18
    youth, 7
self-differentiation, 222–223
self-discipline, time management and academic achievement, 326–327
self-disclosure, 204
self-esteem, 7
    early childhood, 10–11
    in school, 49
self-evaluation, in reality therapy, 166–167
self-injury, nonsuicidal, 287–292
Self-Injury Prevention Plan, 291
self-management
    autism spectrum disorder, 365
    OCD and, 470
self-objects, 180
self-psychology, 179–180
self-soothing kit, 517
self-stimulatory behaviors, autism spectrum disorders, 360
self-support, for counselors, 117
self-talk, 141
sensorimotor cognitive development stage, 5–6
    early childhood, 10

sensory stimulation
    autism spectrum disorders, 361–362
    behavior assessment, 129
sentences completion test (SCT), 183
separation-individuation theory, 179
sex/life, drive theory and, 173–175
sexual abuse, 403
sexual drive
    early adolescence, 23
    late adolescence, 29
sexual education, 342–343
sexual identity
    early adolescence, 23
    late adolescence, 29
    social–emotional transitions about, 339–342
sexuality, gender and, 340–342
sexual orientation
    early adolescence, 23
    late adolescence, 29
    school counseling and, 339–342
    suicide and, 281
shaping therapy, OCD and, 475
siblings
    of autistic clients, 362
    chronic illness and disability and, 527
    kinship caregivers, 310–311
    step- and blended families, 307–309
SIMPLE STEPS procedure, homicide risk, 295
single parents
    divorce and separation and, 303–305
    involvement and support, 43
sleep problems, time management and academic achievement, 326–327
S.M.A.R.T. model, 273
snacks, in counseling sessions, 61–62
social beings concept, 191–193
Social Bug activity, 351
social cognitive theory, 125
social competence, 335–336
    autism spectrum disorders, 360–365
social–emotional transitions, 335–345
    bullying, 336–339
    friendships, 335–336
    intimacy and dating, 342–343
    intimate partner violence, 343–345
    sexual orientation, 339–342
    substance abuse and, 433–437
social learning, behavioral therapy and, 125
socially useful lifestyle, 192, 194
social media, community and, 54
social rhythm worksheet, 502
social skills training (SST), 135–136, 457, 469–470
socioeconomic status
    academic development and, 48
    contextual framework and, 264–267
    counseling process and, 59
    culture and context and, 36
    disruptive behavior, 376–377
    divorce/parental separation impact and, 302–305
    intellectual disabilities, 366
    premature termination and, 91
    substance abuse and, 433
Socratic questioning/dialogue, 150
    disruptive behavior, 388
    time management and academic achievement, 326–327
solution-focused brief therapy (SFBT), 530
Spence Children's Anxiety Scale, 459–460
Stages of Change model, 77–80

stage theory, 5–6
Stanford-Binet Intelligence Scales, 368
state laws, ethics in counseling and, 105, 117
State-Trait Anxiety Inventory for Children (STAIC), 459–460
statutory requirements, child abuse reporting, 105
step- and blended families, 306–309
stimulant medications, ADHD, 359–360
STOP/THINK/DO exercise, OCD and, 470
story-based interventions, 365
Story-Telling Basket, 417
storytelling therapy, 248, 250–252
strength-based perspective, 36–38
    case conceptualization, 254–255
    counseling theories, 171–208
    exercises, 271
stress, 382
    chronic illness and disability and, 527–531
stressor-related disorders, 397–429
structural model of personality, 174–175
study skills deficits, 327–329
subjective units of distress (SUDs), 132, 134
Suboxone, 452
substance abuse, 430–454
    assessment, 440–442
    biological factors, 432
    classification, 437–440
    comorbidity with, 441–442
    counseling interventions, 443–444
    development of, 435–436
    etiology, 432
    incidence and prevalence, 430–431
    individual and group counseling, 445–449
    integrated treatment, 444–452
    levels of care for, 442–443
    long-term effects, 436–437
    parental, 313–315
    risk factors, 431–432
    suicide and, 281
subsystems of families, 213
subthreshold behavior problems, 375
suicide
    client characteristics, 280–281
    counselor considerations, 280
    depressive disorders and, 486
    incidence and prevalence, 279–280
    interventions and prevention, 283–287
    risk assessment, 281–283
    school-based prevention programs, 286–287
    self-injury and risk of, 287–289
superego, structural model of personality, 174–175
support systems, for counselors, 117
Survivor Tree, 88
symbols, in cognitive development, 10
systematic desensitization, 124, 132–133
systemically informed youth counseling, 35–56

T

tactical defenses, 175–177
tangibility, behavior assessment, 129
target behaviors, 123
targeted skills training, 274–275
teacher role-play activity, 127
teachers, school climate and, 48–49
teaching, in reality therapy, 164
technology
    community counseling, 54
    counseling and, 80–81

temperament, early childhood, 10
termination
    complexities of, 84
    counseling activities, 87–89
    defined, 81–82
    experiential play therapy, 239–240
    natural termination, 82–89
    premature, 82, 90–93
    process, 85–86
    referral and, 92–93
    signs of readiness for, 83–84
    theraplay, 244
termination of counseling, 81–93
termination (relapse) stage of change, 77–80
test anxiety, 329–330
testing stage, experiential play therapy, 239
Test of Variables of Attention (T.O.V.A.), 353
therapeutic alliance
    behavior therapy, 126
    family therapy, 214–216
    reality therapy, 165
    self-psychology, 180
therapeutic core conditions, 203
therapeutic growth stage, experiential play
        therapy, 239
therapeutic support services, 274–275
theraplay, 241, 243–244
third-party payer sources, treatment plans
        and, 257
thought records, 473–474
thought testing, 150
three *Cs* of treatment, 314–315
time management problems, counseling
        for, 325–328
toilet education and training, 523–524
token economy systems, 130–131
total behavior, reality therapy, 162–163
transference
    free association and, 188
    psychodynamic therapy, 182, 185
    self-psychology and, 180
transgender youth, 339
transmuting internalization, 180
transparency in counseling, 116–117
trauma
    abuse, 401–404
    age-related responses and reactions, 400

assessment of, 410–413
complex trauma, 410
counseling interventions, 413–423
countertransference, 261
disorders from, 408–429
disruptive behavior and, 382
family violence, 405–406
maltreatment, 401
mass violence, terror or disaster, 406–407
neglect, 404–405
type 1 and 2 events, 398
vicarious, 407
youth development and, 398–400
Trauma-Focused Cognitive Behavioral Therapy
        (TF-CBT), 159, 416, 423–425
    intimate partner violence, 345
Trauma-Focused Integrated Play Therapy (TFIPT),
        416, 426–427
trauma-informed counseling, 413–423
trauma narrative, 416–419
Trauma Symptom Checklist, 411–412
traumatic incident reduction (TIR), 416
treatment plan
    case conceptualization and, 253–254
    contextual framework for, 271–272
    dynamics of, 258
    Golden Thread approach, 257
    triad, 213
trichotillomania, 463
truancy, 330–331
trust vs. mistrust, early childhood, 11
twelve-step facilitation, 449
Twelve-Step programs, 448–449
twinship transference, 180
type 1 diabetes, 526

U

unconditional positive regard, 204, 238–239
unconscious, in psychodynamic theory, 175
undersensitivity, 362

V

vacation destination exercise, 156
Valley and Mountain, 417
values, acceptance and commitment therapy, 145
Venn diagram, mindfulness assessment, 153

verbal tracking, 236
vicarious trauma, 407
victimization
    peers, 402
    revictimization and trauma, 400
violence
    community violence and crime, 53–54
    in home, 45–47, 405–406
    homicide, 292–296
    late adolescence, 32
    mass violence, terror, or disaster, 406–407
    in school system, 50–51

W

wants, WDEP system, 166
way of being, 202–203
WDEP system, 164–166
Wechsler Intelligence Scales, 368
What My Body Gives Me, 512
When You Get Sad exercise, 319
Wide Range Achievement Test (WRAT 4), 371
wise mind, 144, 153–155
Wish Upon a Star, 89
withdrawal, substance abuse, 432, 444–445
Woodcock Reading Mastery Tests, 371
work, play as, 233
working alliance, 58–59
    challenges for, 69–70
    construction of, 68–69
working stage of counseling, 71–81
    communication skills, 71–75
writing therapy, 248, 250–252

Y

youngest children, individual psychology, 198
youth development
    depressive and bipolar disorders in, 482–483
    disruptive behavior, 376–384
    divorce/parental separation impact on, 301–305
    family transitions and, 300
    grief, loss, and bereavement, 315–321
    maltreatment and, 401
    substance abuse and, 433–436, 443–444
Youth Mania Rating Scale (YMRS), 492